Presented
by the

Fae Henick

Memorial
Fund

AMERICAN CIVIL WAR

AMERICAN CIVIL WAR

The Definitive Encyclopedia and Document Collection

VOLUME IV: O–S

Dr. Spencer C. Tucker
Editor

James Arnold and Roberta Wiener
Documents Editors

Dr. Paul G. Pierpaoli Jr.
Associate Editor

Dr. David Coffey
Assistant Editor

ABC-CLIO

Santa Barbara, California Denver, Colorado Oxford, England

Library of Congress Cataloging-in-Publication Data

American Civil War : the definitive encyclopedia and document collection / Spencer C. Tucker, Editor.
    pages cm
  Includes bibliographical references and index.
  ISBN 978-1-85109-677-0 (hardcover : alk. paper) — ISBN 978-1-85109-682-4 (ebook)
  1. United States—History—Civil War, 1861–1865—Encyclopedias.   2. United States—History—Civil War, 1861–1865—Sources.
I. Tucker, Spencer, 1937– editor.
  E468.A5329   2013
  973.703—dc23   2013016414

ISBN: 978-1-85109-677-0
EISBN: 978-1-85109-682-4

17 16 15 14   2 3 4 5

This book is also available on the World Wide Web as an eBook.
Visit www.abc-clio.com for details.

ABC-CLIO, LLC
130 Cremona Drive, P.O. Box 1911
Santa Barbara, California 93116-1911

This book is printed on acid-free paper ∞
Manufactured in the United States of America

To my good friend
G. Malcolm Louden

About the Editors

Spencer C. Tucker, PhD, has been senior fellow in military history at ABC-CLIO since 2003. He is the author or editor of 43 books and encyclopedias, many of which have won prestigious awards. Tucker's last academic position before his retirement from teaching was the John Biggs Chair in Military History at the Virginia Military Institute, Lexington, VA. He has been a Fulbright scholar, a visiting research associate at the Smithsonian Institution, and, as a U. S. Army captain, an intelligence analyst in the Pentagon. His recently published works include *The Encyclopedia of the Mexican-American War: A Political, Social, and Military History*; *The Encyclopedia of the War of 1812: A Political, Social, and Military History*; and *Almanac of American Military History*, all published by ABC-CLIO.

James R. Arnold is the author of more than 20 military history books and has contributed to numerous others. His published works include *Jeff Davis's Own: Cavalry, Comanches, and the Battle for the Texas Frontier* and *Napoleon Conquers Austria: The 1809 Campaign for Vienna,* which won the International Napoleonic Society's Literary Award in 1995. His two newest titles are *The Moro War: How America Battled a Muslim Insurgency in the Philippine Jungle, 1902–1903* and *Napoleon's Triumph: The Friedland Campaign, 1807.*

Roberta Wiener is managing editor for the *Journal of Military History.* She has written *The American West: Living the Frontier Dream* and coauthored numerous history books for the school library market, including the 10-volume *The Revolutionary War* (2002) and the 13-volume *13 Colonies* (2005).

Contents

Volume V: T–Z

Volume VI: Documents

List of Entries

Barton, Seth Maxwell
Bartow, Francis Stebbins
Bate, William Brimage
Bates, Edward
Baton Rouge, Battle of
Battle, Cullen Andrews
"Battle Hymn of the Republic"
Battles and Leaders of the Civil War
Baxter Springs, Battle of
Bayard, George Dashiell
Baylor, John Robert
Baylor's Buffalo Hunt
Bayonet
Bayou Bourbeux, Battle of
Bayou Lafourche, Battle of
Beale, Richard Lee Turberville
Beall, Lloyd James
Beall, William Nelson Rector
Bean's Station, Battle of
Beatty, Samuel
Beauregard, Pierre Gustav Toutant
Bedini, Gaetano
Bee, Barnard Elliott
Bee, Hamilton Prioleau
Beecher, Henry Ward
Belknap, William Worth
Bell, John
Bell, Tyree Harris
Belle Isle Prison, Virginia
Belmont, Battle of
Benham, Henry Washington
Benjamin, Judah Philip
Bennett, James Gordon
Bennett House
Benning, Henry Lewis
Benton, Samuel
Benton, USS
Bentonville, Battle of
Berdan, Hiram
Berdan's Sharpshooters
Bermuda
Bermuda Hundred Campaign
Berry, Hiram Gregory
Berryville, Battle of
Bibb, Henry
Bickerdyke, Mary Ann Ball
Bickley, George Washington Lafayette
Bierce, Ambrose Gwinnett

Big Bethel, Battle of
Big Black River, First Battle of
Big Black River, Second Battle of
Bigelow, John
Bird Creek, Indian Territory, Engagement at
Birdsong Ferry, Mississippi, Engagement at
Birney, David Bell
Birney, William
Bissell, William Henry
Black Codes
Black Republicans
Blackwell, Elizabeth
Blaine, James Gillespie
Blair, Austin
Blair, Francis Preston, Jr.
Blair, Francis Preston, Sr.
Blair, Montgomery
Blair's Landing, Battle of
Blakely Gun
Blanchard, Albert Gallatin
Blazer's Scouts
Bleeding Kansas
Blenker, Louis
Blockade of the Confederacy, Union
Blockade-Runners
Blountville, Tennessee, Engagement at
Blue Springs, Battle of
Blunt, James Gillpatrick
Bocock, Thomas Stanhope
Boggs, William Robertson
Bonham, Milledge Luke
"The Bonnie Blue Flag"
Boomer, George Boardman
Booneville, Battle of
Boonville, Battle of
Booth, John Wilkes
Borden, Gail, Jr.
Border States
Boreman, Arthur Inghram
Bormann Fuse
Botts, John Minor
Boudinot, Elias Cornelius
Bounty System
Boutwell, George Sewall
Bowen, John Stevens
Boyce, William Waters
Boyd, Maria Isabelle
Boydton Plank Road, Battle of

List of Tables

List of Maps

O

Oak Grove, Battle of
Event Date: June 25, 1862

Initial battle of the Seven Days' Campaign (June 25–July 1, 1862) during the Peninsula Campaign (March–July 1862). The Battle of Oak Grove, also known as the Battle of French's Field and the Battle of King's School House, occurred in Henrico County, Virginia, east of the Confederate capital of Richmond, the target of Union major general George B. McClellan's Peninsula Campaign.

Following the Battle of Seven Pines (May 31–June 1, 1862), the overly cautious McClellan, whose Army of the Potomac enjoyed an overwhelming numerical advantage over Confederate general Robert E. Lee's Army of Northern Virginia, remained quiescent for three and a half weeks. This respite allowed Lee, who had taken command of the Army of Northern Virginia from the wounded General Joseph E. Johnston, time to reorganize. Warned by intelligence reports that Confederate troops under Major General Thomas J. "Stonewall" Jackson would soon be moving from the Shenandoah Valley to reinforce Lee, McClellan finally took action. Seeking to resume the offensive before Jackson's men could arrive, McClellan tried to advance his lines westward about one and a half miles in order to control high ground on Nine Mile Road around Old Tavern, bringing Richmond within range of his heavy siege guns.

The attack would be mounted by two divisions of Major General Samuel P. Heintzelman's III Corps, those commanded by Brigadier Generals Joseph Hooker and Philip Kearny. Two brigades drawn from II and IV Corps would be held in reserve. The attack would be mounted against the three Confederate brigades of Major General Benjamin Huger's division and occurred along an east-west axis centered on the Williamsburg Road. The battle was named for a stand of tall oak trees between the two armies, known locally as Oak Grove, which had been the site of Confederate major general Daniel H. Hill's attack during the Battle of Seven Pines and had since seen numerous clashes between the pickets of both sides.

At 8:30 a.m. on June 25, Hooker ordered forward brigades commanded by Brigadier Generals Daniel E. Sickles (on the Union right) and Cuvier Grover (Union center). On the Union left, Kearny advanced only a single brigade under Brigadier General John C. Robinson. Although the Union left and center made good progress, the soldiers on the Union right had difficulty with their own abatis and swampy terrain. They then encountered stiff Confederate resistance and fell behind. Huger took advantage of the Union disorganization to mount a counterattack with Brigadier General Ambrose R. Wright's brigade against Grover's brigade in the Union center. Meanwhile, Confederate brigadier general Robert Ransom's brigade broke up a delayed attack by Sickles's men.

Heintzelman then ordered reinforcements forward and notified McClellan, who was attempting to direct the battle by telegraph three miles to the rear. In a mistaken decision, an alarmed McClellan now ordered the attack suspended and the Union troops to return to their entrenchments until he could arrive. Two and a half hours later at 1:00 p.m., McClellan, now aware of the true situation, ordered the troops forward again to retake the ground yielded earlier. Fighting continued until nightfall.

McClellan's halfhearted Union effort gained some 600 yards and failed to derail Lee's plans to take the offensive. Lee struck in force the next day at Beaver Dam Creek, north of the Chickahominy River near Mechanicsville, in what must be judged as the real beginning of the Seven Days' Campaign. Union casualties in the Battle of Oak Grove totaled 626 (68 killed, 503 wounded, and 55 missing); Confederate losses were 441 (66 killed, 362 wounded, and 13 missing).

SPENCER C. TUCKER

See also

Grover, Cuvier; Heintzelman, Samuel Peter; Hill, Daniel Harvey; Hooker, Joseph; Huger, Benjamin; Jackson, Thomas Jonathan; Johnston, Joseph Eggleston; Kearny, Philip; Lee, Robert Edward; McClellan, George Brinton; Mechanicsville, Battle of; Robinson, John Cleveland; Seven Pines, Battle of; Sickles, Daniel Edgar; Wright, Ambrose Ransom

Further Reading

Gallagher, Gary, ed. *The Richmond Campaign of 1862: The Peninsula and the Seven Days.* Chapel Hill: University of North Carolina Press, 2000.

Martin, David G. *The Peninsula Campaign, March–July 1862.* Conshohocken, PA: Combined Books, 1992.

Sears, Stephen W. *To the Gates of Richmond: The Peninsula Campaign.* New York: Ticknor and Fields, 1992.

Webb, Alexander S. *The Peninsula: McClellan's Campaign of 1862.* Secaucus, NJ: Castle Books, 2002.

Oak Hills, Battle of

See Wilson's Creek, Battle of

Ocean Pond, Battle of

See Olustee, Battle of

Odell, Moses Fowler

Birth Date: February 24, 1818
Death Date: June 13, 1866

U.S. congressman. Moses Fowler Odell was born on February 24, 1818, in Tarrytown, New York. He embarked on a career in business and then became involved in local Democratic

Party politics. In 1845 he took a patronage position as a clerk in the New York Customs House. He then worked as a public appraiser before being elected to the U.S. House of Representatives in 1860. Upon taking office in 1861, he became chairman of the Committee on Expenditures. As a War Democrat and one of the few Democrats left in the Congress, he accepted an appointment to the Joint Committee on the Conduct of the War on December 10, 1861.

The majority of this important committee was made up of Radical Republicans, so Odell was the main voice of Democratic opinion during its deliberations. He steadfastly pushed for investigations into both military affairs and personnel, which was not always well received by his fellow committee members.

In 1864, Odell did not stand for reelection and left the House in March 1865, when President Andrew Johnson appointed him as a naval agent for the port of New York. Odell held that post until he died of cancer on June 13, 1866, in Brooklyn, New York.

PAUL G. PIERPAOLI JR.

See also

Joint Committee on the Conduct of the War

Further Reading

Trefousse, Hans L. "The Joint Committee on the Conduct of the War: A Reappraisal." *Civil War History* 10 (1964): 5–19.

Offensive-Defensive Strategy

Term employed by Confederate president Jefferson Davis to characterize the South's military strategy during the Civil War. The offensive-defensive strategy was intended to reap the benefits of the defensive—which experts generally considered a stronger form of warfare than the offensive—while conducting sufficient offensive operations to keep Union forces off balance.

When hopes that a single decisive battle would end the war faded following the First Battle of Bull Run (July 21, 1861), both sides devised strategies for a protracted war. Southern leaders well understood the implications of the facts that the North was considerably more populous and had 10 times the industrial capacity of the South. Despite these great disadvantages, Southern leaders believed that the Confederacy could win the war.

Because the South's strategic objective of independence did not require conquering the North, the primary strategy could be defensive. The South would deploy its troops and fight its campaigns in order to keep Union armies out of Southern territory. The Confederates had the advantage of fighting on interior lines. Over time, Southern leaders expected Northern public opinion to tire of the war, forcing Union leaders to sue for peace.

However, a totally defensive strategy, one that passively awaits attack, surrenders certain advantages to an enemy. The major advantage it yields is the initiative—the enemy can pick the time and place of attack and pace the action as he pleases. Additionally, the Confederacy could not adopt a strictly defensive posture for political reasons. Southerners believed that their armies could defeat any Union army and demanded offensive action. An offensive component to the strategy was thus desirable and indeed necessary.

Confederate leaders therefore elected to include occasional large-scale offensive actions to supplement their overall defensive posture. The Confederates designed their attacks to disrupt Union offensive preparations, secure supplies, and influence Northern and Southern as well as foreign opinion. The ultimate intent was still defensive—the Confederates did not design their offensives to capture enemy territory, except perhaps during the Antietam Campaign (September 4–20, 1862) and the Gettysburg Campaign (June–July 1863). Instead, they hoped to create more favorable defensive or political opportunities.

The offensive-defensive strategy is essentially an attrition strategy. That is, it seeks victory by gradually wearing down enemy military forces and political will. In time, the price paid for any advance outstrips the political benefit to be gained, and a rational opponent sues for peace. The major modern criticism of the strategy as executed by the Confederacy was that it overemphasized the offensive element. Maneuvers intended to disrupt Union forces resulted in significant battles that eroded Confederate manpower as much or more than they did the Union ranks in terms of percentage of force. Confederate offensive tactics were thus unnecessarily wasteful. Critics generally believe that the Confederacy should have fought almost exclusively on the defensive, even to the point of adopting widespread guerrilla warfare, and contend that the Union could not have sustained a longer war and would have eventually conceded to Southern demands. Proponents of the offensive-defensive strategy point out how well the Confederates did and how difficult and unpopular a purely defensive strategy would have been.

J. BOONE BARTHOLOMEES

See also

Antietam Campaign; Davis, Jefferson Finis; Gettysburg Campaign; Home Front, Confederate; Home Front, Union; Strategy, CSA; Strategy, U.S.

Further Reading

Connelly, Thomas L. *The Politics of Command: Factions and Ideas in Confederate Strategy.* Baton Rouge: Louisiana State University Press, 1973.

Harsh, Joseph L. *Taken at the Flood: Robert E. Lee and Confederate Strategy in the Maryland Campaign of 1862.* Kent, OH: Kent State University Press, 1999.

Tanner, Robert G. *Retreat to Victory: Confederate Strategy Reconsidered.* Wilmington, DE: Scholarly Resources, 2002.

Oglesby, Richard James
Birth Date: July 25, 1824
Death Date: April 24, 1899

Union officer, three-time governor of Illinois, and U.S. senator. Richard James Oglesby was born on July 25, 1824, in Floydsburg, Kentucky. Orphaned as a child, he was raised by an uncle in Decatur, Illinois. After working as a farmer and tradesman, Oblesby studied law and was admitted to the bar in 1845. During the Mexican-American War (1846–1848), he served as a first lieutenant of Illinois volunteers. In 1849, lured by the California Gold Rush, he went west to seek his fortune. By 1851 he was back in Illinois practicing law, having found no significant amounts of gold. In 1860 he was elected to the Illinois Senate, where he was a strong supporter of Abraham Lincoln.

After the Civil War began in 1861, Oglesby resigned his senate seat and was appointed colonel of the 8th Illinois Infantry Regiment. He served in southern Illinois and eastern Missouri during the spring and summer of 1861 and commanded the 1st Brigade, 1st Division, under Brigadier General Ulysses S. Grant in early 1862, participating in the Battles of Fort Henry (February 6, 1862) and Fort Donelson (February 13–16). On March 21, Oglesby was promoted to brigadier general of volunteers. He received a severe wound at the Battle of Corinth (October 3–4, 1862), which sidelined him until the following spring. On November 29, he was promoted to major general.

Oglesby rejoined Grant during the Second Vicksburg Campaign (April 1–July 4, 1863) and commanded a division in the Army of the Tennessee. After Vicksburg fell, Oglesby took a medical leave of absence to completely recover from his injury. On May 26, 1864, he formally resigned his commission, hoping to be elected governor of Illinois.

Oglesby waged a successful campaign, during which he took every opportunity to laud the Lincoln administration's war policies. Taking office in early 1865, Oglesby supported

Lincoln's Reconstruction plans and sought to accommodate the administration as much as possible. After Lincoln was assassinated, Oglesby became a vociferous opponent of President Andrew Johnson's postwar policies. Oglesby proved to be a progressive governor, championing internal improvements and modernizing care for the mentally ill and the indigent.

In 1872, state Republican operatives convinced a reluctant Oglesby to run for another term as governor. The former governor struck a deal whereby if he was elected, he would promptly resign, allowing the lieutenant governor to appoint him to the U.S. Senate. Oglesby prevailed, took office on January 13, resigned on January 23, and was soon appointed to the Senate, where he served from March 1873 until March 1879. He ran successfully for a third term as governor, serving from 1885 until 1889. After running unsuccessfully for another term in the U.S. Senate, Oglesby retired to his estate in Elkhart, Illinois, where he died on April 24, 1899.

PAUL G. PIERPAOLI JR.

See also

Corinth, Battle of; Fort Donelson, Battle of; Fort Henry, Battle of; Illinois; Vicksburg Campaign, Second

Further Reading

Plummer, Mark A. *Lincoln's Rail Splitter: Governor Richard J. Oglesby.* Urbana: University of Illinois Press, 2001.
Warner, Ezra J. *Generals in Blue: Lives of the Union Commanders.* Baton Rouge: Louisiana State University Press, 2006.

Ohio

Important midwestern Union state. Ohio encompasses 41,330 square miles and is bordered by Indiana to the west, Pennsylvania and West Virginia to the east, Michigan and Lake Erie to the north, and Kentucky and West Virginia to the south. With 2,339,511 people in 1860, Ohio was the third most populous state in the Union, behind only Pennsylvania and New York. Ohio's large and diverse industrial base, impressive agricultural output, and long border along the pivotal Ohio River made it critical to the Union war effort. In some ways Ohio had certain characteristics of a border state, due in part to its proximity to Kentucky and Virginia and pockets of pro-Southern sympathizers, mainly in the southern parts of the state. Ohio's economy was also tied closely with that of the South.

By the 1860s, Ohio had developed an impressive array of industries, was home to numerous mines, and boasted a widespread network of rail lines that served almost every

corner of the state. Most of Ohio's industry was concentrated in the north along Lake Erie, from Toledo in the northwest to Cleveland in the northeast. Columbus, located in the middle of the state, and Cincinnati, on the Ohio River in the southwestern corner of the state, were also important manufacturing and rail centers. In spite of the large number of urban and industrialized areas in the state, Ohio was also a major agricultural producer, which helped feed the Union armies.

Although there were small pockets of strong pro-Confederate sympathizers and a fairly large number of Ohioans who did not support the war, the Republican Party controlled most aspects of state politics. There were some exceptions to this, however, including several Democrats in Congress. In 1863, Ohio Democrats fought valiantly to get Democrat Clement Vallandigham elected governor, going so far as to back his candidacy even after he had sought refuge in Canada for having bitterly denounced the draft. In the southern portions of the state, the so-called Peace Democrats, who did not technically support the Confederacy, nevertheless denounced the war and President Abraham Lincoln's policies. As the war continued, however, support for Lincoln solidified in the state, particularly in 1864.

In 1861, Ohioans responded with enthusiasm to Lincoln's call for soldiers, and the state quickly mustered 23 volunteer infantry regiments for three-month terms of service, 10 more than the state's quota. Later the enlistment time would be lengthened to three years of service. Recruitment fell after the initial enlistments, and during 1862–1863, draft resistance became a problem, especially in Holmes and Noble Counties. By 1864, however, recruitment enjoyed a resurgence. Over the course of the war, Ohio supported 230 infantry and cavalry regiments, 26 light artillery regiments, and 5 companies of sharpshooters. A total of 365,000 Ohioans served, making Ohio first in the nation for the percentage of men aged 18–45 serving in the war. At its peak, the percentage was 60 percent of the adult male population. Among those who served were 5,000 free blacks. Some 25,000 Ohioans died in the war.

Perhaps more than any other state, Ohio provided many military and political leaders. Among those who were born in Ohio or resided there were William T. Sherman, Ulysses S. Grant, Philip H. Sheridan, Irvin McDowell, George B. McClellan, Salmon P. Chase, and Edwin M. Stanton. Ohio politicians who would later run on their Civil war records included Presidents Rutherford B. Hayes, James A. Garfield, and William McKinley.

Ohio was relatively untouched by fighting during the war. In 1862, Confederate moves into northern Kentucky caused Cincinnati residents to take up defensive positions, but no attack on the city occurred. Most famously, during July 2–26, 1863, Confederate brigadier general John Hunt Morgan's cavalry dashed through the southern part of the state but was ultimately stopped and captured after a short battle at Salineville, Ohio.

PAUL G. PIERPAOLI JR.

See also

Morgan's Ohio Raid; Vallandigham, Clement Laird

Further Reading

Dee, Christine, ed. *Ohio's War: The Civil War in Documents.* Columbus: Ohio State University Press, 2007.

Hall, Susan. *Appalachian Ohio and the Civil War.* Jefferson, NC: McFarland, 2000.

Knepper, George W. *Ohio and Its People.* Kent, OH: Kent State University Press, 2003.

Ohio, Union Army of the

Name applied to two entirely different Union armies during the Civil War. Both were created within the Department of the Ohio, which consisted primarily of the states of Ohio, Indiana, Michigan, and Kentucky east of the Cumberland River. The first army, under the command of Major General Don Carlos Buell, was in existence from the autumn of 1861 until its name was changed to the Army of the Cumberland on October 24, 1862. The second army, led first by Major General Ambrose E. Burnside and then by Major General John M. Schofield, was created in the spring of 1863 and formally disbanded on August 1, 1865.

Buell was appointed to the command of the first Army of the Ohio in November 1861, and in February 1862 he led his army into Tennessee, occupying Nashville on February 25 and extending Union control over much of central Tennessee. One of Buell's divisions also advanced into northern Alabama, occupying Huntsville on April 11, 1862.

Buell then moved the larger part of his army on to Pittsburg Landing on the Tennessee River, where his arrival on the battlefield at Shiloh late on April 6 tipped the balance in favor of Major General Ulysses S. Grant's troops, which counterattacked the next day and pushed the enemy off the field. Most of Buell's troops moved as part of Major General Henry W. Halleck's force to Corinth, Mississippi, in May. When Confederate troops led by General Braxton Bragg invaded Kentucky, Buell moved to counter the invasion, fighting the Battle of Perryville (October 8). Less than a month after that battle, the Army of the Ohio ceased to exist when it was renamed the Army of the Cumberland.

The second Army of the Ohio was formed in the spring of 1863 after Major General Ambrose Burnside, the former commander of the Army of the Potomac, took command of the Department of the Ohio. Burnside's old command, IX Corps, followed the general to his new department. XXIII Corps was organized on April 27, 1863, from other troops in the department, and this field force became the new Army of the Ohio. After the reorganization, Burnside's troops advanced into eastern Tennessee, capturing Knoxville on September 2.

Following the Battle of Chickamauga (September 19–20, 1863), General Bragg sent Lieutenant General James Longstreet with 17,000 troops to recapture Knoxville. Burnside withdrew into the heavily defended city and withstood a siege that lasted from November 17 to December 2, 1863. When Union reinforcements approached, Longstreet withdrew into southwestern Virginia after several minor skirmishes in early December.

After Burnside was transferred to the eastern theater, Major General John M. Schofield took command of the Army of the Ohio on February 9, 1864. Schofield and part of his army then joined Major General William T. Sherman's force gathering in northern Georgia. Schofield's field troops consisted of three divisions of XXIII Corps and a Cavalry division led by Major General George Stoneman. The 12,800-man Army of the Ohio was the smallest of Sherman's three combined armies.

During the ensuing Atlanta Campaign (May 5–September 2, 1864), Schofield's force performed well, fighting in the Battles of Resaca (May 13–15), Kennesaw Mountain (June 27), and Utoy Creek (August 5–6) as well as numerous smaller skirmishes. Stoneman's cavalry division participated in a major raid designed to destroy railroads linking Atlanta to Confederate supply sources. The raid failed, however, with Stoneman and 700 of his men being taken prisoner near Macon, Georgia, on July 29.

Following the Atlanta Campaign, Schofield's corps moved back into Tennessee as the Confederate Army of Tennessee invaded its namesake state, fighting at Franklin (November 30) and Nashville (December 15–16). Schofield and most of XXIII Corps were then transferred by rail to Washington, D.C., and then by sea to North Carolina, where Schofield was placed in command of his own corps plus a newly reorganized X Corps. This force captured Wilmington, North Carolina, on February 22, 1865, and then advanced inland to link up with Sherman's troops marching north through the interior of the state. After joining Sherman on March 23, Schofield's two corps, operating as the Army of the Ohio,

Well-Known Union Armies during the Civil War

Name	Chief Area of Operation	Famous Commanders
Army of the Cumberland	Tennessee, Georgia	William S. Rosecrans George Henry Thomas
Army of Georgia	Georgia, North Carolina, South Carolina	Henry W. Slocum
Army of the Gulf	Louisiana, Alabama	Benjamin Butler Nathaniel P. Banks Edward Canby
Army of the James	Virginia	Benjamin Butler Edward Ord
Army of the Mississippi	Mississippi River region	John Pope William S. Rosecrans John A. McClernand
Army of the Ohio	Kentucky, Tennessee, Georgia	Don Carlos Buell Ambrose E. Burnside John G. Foster John M. Schofield
Army of the Potomac	Virginia, West Virginia, Maryland, Pennsylvania, North Carolina	George B. McClellan Ambrose E. Burnside Joseph Hooker George G. Meade
Army of the Shenandoah	Virginia, West Virginia	David Hunter Philip Sheridan Horatio G. Wright
Army of the Tennessee	Kentucky, Tennessee, Mississippi, Georgia, North Carolina, South Carolina	Ulysses S. Grant William T. Sherman James B. McPherson Oliver O. Howard
Army of Virginia	Virginia	John Pope

remained with Sherman's army until the war was over. The troops performed garrison duty in North Carolina until the army was officially disbanded on August 1, 1865.

RICHARD A. SAUERS

See also

Atlanta Campaign; Bragg, Braxton; Buell, Don Carlos; Burnside, Ambrose Everett; Chickamauga, Battle of; Franklin, Battle of; Franklin and Nashville Campaign; Halleck, Henry Wager; Kennesaw Mountain, Battle of; Knoxville Campaign; Longstreet, James; Ohio, Union Department of the; Perryville, Battle of; Resaca, Battle of; Schofield, John McAllister; Sherman, William Tecumseh; Shiloh, Battle of; Stoneman, George, Jr.; Wilmington, North Carolina, Engagements at

Further Reading

Castel, Albert M. *Decision in the West: The Atlanta Campaign of 1864.* Lawrence: University Press of Kansas, 1992.
Cox, Jacob D. *Atlanta.* 1882; reprint, New York: Da Capo, 1994.
Cox, Jacob D. *The March to the Sea: Franklin and Nashville.* 1882; reprint, New York: Da Capo, 1994.
Schofield, John M. *Forty Six Years in the Army.* New York: Century, 1897.

Ohio, Union Department of the

Federal military administrative unit first established on May 3, 1861, and initially commanded by Major General George B. McClellan. The Union Department of the Ohio encompassed Ohio, Indiana, and Illinois. The department was expanded by General Order No. 19 on May 9, 1861, to include portions of western Virginia, Pennsylvania, and

Maryland. McClellan was replaced by Brigadier General William Rosecrans on July 23, 1861, who commanded until September 21. Brigadier General Ormsby Mitchel assumed command that same day.

On November 9 the Department of the Cumberland merged with the Department of the Ohio, and Major General Don Carlos Buell took command of the enlarged, consolidated unit on November 15. The new department encompassed Ohio, Indiana, Michigan, and the part of Kentucky east of the Cumberland River.

On March 11, 1862, Buell's command was temporarily subsumed by the newly created Department of the Mississippi. On August 19, 1862, the Department of the Ohio was resurrected under the command of Major General Horatio Wright. The new incarnation included Ohio, Indiana, Michigan, Illinois, Wisconsin, and all of Kentucky east of the Tennessee River, including the Cumberland Gap. Major General Ambrose P. Burnside assumed command on March 25, 1863, and held the post until December 9, at which time Major General John G. Foster took command. Foster was relieved on February 9, 1864, by Major General John M. Schofield, who held command until November 17, 1864, when he was replaced by Major General George Stoneman. On January 17, 1865, the department was reorganized out of existence and was appended to the Department of the Cumberland.

PAUL G. PIERPAOLI JR.

See also

Buell, Don Carlos; Burnside, Ambrose Everett; Cumberland, Union Army of the; Foster, John Gray; McClellan, George Brinton; Mitchel, Ormsby MacKnight; Rosecrans, William Starke; Schofield, John McAllister; Stoneman, George, Jr.; Wright, Horatio Gouverneur

Further Reading

Warner, Ezra J. *Generals in Blue: Lives of the Union Commanders.* Baton Rouge: Louisiana State University Press, 2006.

Ohio Penitentiary

State prison built in Columbus, Ohio, in 1834 and used to house select Confederate prisoners of war (POWs) from early August 1863 until March 1864. The Ohio Penitentiary was located adjacent to present-day downtown Columbus and was in operation from 1834 until 1983. The last of the buildings were torn down in 1998 to make way for modern edifices. The prison was notorious for its dangerous inmates, occasional riots, and executions. It became the only site of state executions in 1897 and remained so until 1963, at which time the State of Ohio banned the death penalty. A total of 315 prisoners were executed at the penitentiary, including several women.

The prison compound was a foreboding-looking place—it covered numerous acres and featured prison buildings and cell blocks that were four stories high. There were heavy iron bars on all the windows. Discipline was harsh in the mid-19th century, and the death rate among inmates was high, owing to fights, abuse by guards, and especially illness and infectious disease. Inmates caught breaking the rules were often thrown into a dungeon-like facility in the prison's basement and fed only bread and water. At its peak in 1955, the prison's population was 5,235. The population during the Civil War is not known for certain, but it was probably around 3,000.

After Confederate raider Brigadier General John Hunt Morgan and 30 of his troopers (most of them officers) were captured on July 26, 1863, in southern Ohio, they were sent to the Ohio Penitentiary. Ohio governor David Tod believed that Camp Chase, a POW camp just outside Columbus, was not equipped to handle such high-profile detainees. He thus ordered the penitentiary's warden, Nathaniel Merion, to make room for Hunt and his men. After that, perhaps another 30–40 Confederate POWs were housed in the prison at any one time, but most were there only temporarily. At first they were housed among the general population and were subjected to the standard rules and regulations. After Morgan complained to Governor Tod that he and his men were not being accorded the standard treatment due POWs, Tod ordered Merion to ease up on the Confederate prisoners. They were then allowed to receive packages from friends and family and were permitted to buy certain items using their own money.

Morgan and six of his men launched a daring, successful escape from the penitentiary on November 26, 1863, after tunneling for 23 days through the floor of a ground-level cell, scaling the 25-foot-high walls using sheets as ropes, and eluding guards on the periphery. Three of the men were caught a few days later, but Morgan and the others made it safely to Tennessee on December 23.

After Morgan's escape, POWs were kept away from the general population and housed in cells on the top floor. They were also forbidden from taking meals in the communal dining facility. Secretary of War Edwin M. Stanton ordered all POWs at the Ohio Penitentiary to be moved to Fort Delaware on March 18, 1864. From then on, the prison housed no Confederate prisoners.

PAUL G. PIERPAOLI JR.

See also
Camp Chase, Ohio; Morgan, John Hunt; Ohio; Tod, David

Further Reading
Hesseltine, William B., ed. *Civil War Prisons.* Kent, OH: Kent State University Press, 1972.
Ramage, James A. *Rebel Raider: The Life of General John Hunt Morgan.* Lexington: University Press of Kentucky, 1986.

Okolona, Battle of
Event Date: February 22, 1864

Engagement during Major General William T. Sherman's Meridian Campaign (February 3–26, 1864). On February 1, 1864, to divert attention from his own operation to destroy the Confederate rail and supply center of Meridian, Mississippi, Sherman ordered Brigadier General William S. Smith to depart Collierville near Memphis, Tennessee, with 7,000 cavalry and raid from Pontotoc, Mississippi, through Okolona along the Memphis & Ohio Railroad, destroying track and food stocks and occupying Confederate cavalry under Major General Nathan B. Forrest, engaging and, Sherman hoped, defeating that force. Smith was then to join Sherman at Meridian on February 10.

Smith delayed his departure to await reinforcements, which Sherman subsequently considered a violation of orders. Smith did not depart until February 11, far behind schedule, with 11,000 men and 20 guns.

Proceeding through Confederate territory, Smith's men inflicted considerable damage while meeting almost no opposition. Soon some 1,000 freed slaves had joined them. On February 20, however, Sherman withdrew from Meridian after virtually destroying it. On that date Smith was nearing West Point, some 90 miles to the north. At both Prairie Station and Aberdeen, Smith's men skirmished with some of Forrest's 2,500 cavalrymen. Daunted by Forrest's reputation, uncertain as to how many men he was facing, and concerned about the safety of the many freed slaves now accompanying him, Smith planned to withdraw.

Smith ordered his men to concentrate at Prairie Station, but shortly after dawn on February 21, the Federals encountered and engaged one of Forrest's brigades, led by Colonel Jeffrey Forrest, General Forrest's youngest brother, who managed to draw Smith into a swampy area west of the Tombigbee River. Believing that this was a trap and that he was outnumbered, Smith ordered a withdrawal, leaving a rear guard to cover it. The Union rear guard held off the

Confederates for about two hours and then itself withdrew in good order. General Forrest then arrived on the scene and ordered a pursuit, with a running fight occurring during most of the day.

At dawn on February 22, Forrest attacked Smith about 4 miles south of Okolona. Another running fight occurred over a distance of some 11 miles, with both sides attacking and counterattacking. Colonel Forrest was killed in one Confederate charge. On the brink of victory, Smith broke off the fight and headed for Ponotoc. Knowing that his men were almost out of ammunition and being overwhelmed with grief at the death of his brother, General Forrest did not pursue, although Mississippi militiamen harassed the Union column all the way to the Tennessee border. In the fighting of February 20–22, the Confederates suffered 144 casualties (27 killed, 97 wounded, and 20 missing); Union losses were 388 (54 killed, 179 wounded, and 155 missing). Smith arrived back at Collierville on February 26.

SPENCER C. TUCKER

See also
Forrest, Nathan Bedford; Meridian Campaign; Sherman, William Tecumseh; Smith, William Sooy

Further Reading
Bearss, Margie. *Sherman's Forgotten Campaign: The Meridian Expedition.* Baltimore: Gateway, 1987.
Hurst, Jack. *Nathan Bedford Forrest: A Biography.* New York: Vintage Books, 1994.
Sherman, William T. *Memoirs of William T. Sherman.* New York: Library of America, 1990.
Wyeth, John Allan. *That Devil Forrest: Life of General Nathan Bedford Forrest.* Baton Rouge: Louisiana State University Press, 1987.

Old Abe

Union mascot. One of the most famous military symbols of the Civil War, Old Abe was the large bald eagle mascot of the 8th Wisconsin Infantry Regiment from 1861 until 1864. Named after President Abraham Lincoln, Old Abe was discovered as a hatchling by Chippewa Native Americans in rural northern Wisconsin in the winter of 1861. Sometime thereafter, the Indians traded the eagle for corn, and the young bird briefly became a pet of the Dan McCann family.

Soon after they acquired the bird, the McCanns presented it to the members of the 8th Wisconsin, which was raising recruits in Eau Claire. As the 8th Wisconsin mustered in, the men of the regiment, particularly those in Company C, officially swore Old Abe in as their mascot and constructed

Old Abe, the live bald eagle mascot of the 8th Wisconsin Infantry Regiment during the Civil War. (Library of Congress)

a wooden perch, where the bird would be poised regally in times of battle and during down time as well. By early 1862, the 8th Wisconsin had become known as the Eagle Regiment.

Old Abe was present for some 40 military engagements, and frequently during battle he would soar over the field, screeching and diving toward the enemy. The Confederates who encountered Old Abe derided him as the "Yankee Buzzard." There were numerous Confederate attempts to capture or kill the bird, but all ended in failure.

On September 28, 1864, Old Abe was retired and presented to the State of Wisconsin. He was then displayed in the state capitol in a cage. In February 1881 the capitol caught fire, and Old Abe suffered from smoke inhalation; he died on March 28. The eagle was then stuffed and placed back on display in the capitol, but its carcass was lost to another fire in 1904. A replica of Old Abe now stands watch in the Wisconsin capitol building.

PAUL G. PIERPAOLI JR.

See also
Wisconsin

Further Reading
Nesbit, Robert C. *Wisconsin: A History*. Revised ed. Madison: University of Wisconsin Press, 1989.
Rosholt, Malcolm, and Margaret Rosholt. *The Story of Old Abe: Wisconsin's Civil War Hero*. Rosholt, WI: Rosholt House, 1987.

Old Capitol Prison

Union prison located in Washington, D.C., that was used to house Confederate prisoners of war (POWs), spies, smugglers, political prisoners, and Union prisoners who had been convicted of various crimes. Situated on 1st Street, approximately where the U.S. Supreme Court building now stands, the main prison building had been used as a meeting place for Congress after the Capitol was torched by British forces during the War of 1812. When the Capitol had been repaired, the building became known as "Old Capitol." Thereafter it saw varied uses, mainly as a boardinghouse.

The Old Capitol building had fallen into disrepair by 1861, but it was nevertheless retrofitted as a prison and pressed into service in August 1861. It was designed to hold 500 prisoners, while a newly built annex, Carroll Prison, was to hold 1,000 inmates. Within months, however, the population had swelled to capacity, and by early 1863 as many as 2,760 prisoners were housed in the complex. Between 1861 and 1865, 5,781 prisoners were processed through the Old Capitol Prison; these included a number of Confederate generals and women who had been suspected or convicted of spying, including Belle Boyd, Virginia Lomax, and Rose O'Neal Greenhow.

Living conditions were extraordinarily difficult in the prison. Bathing facilities and waste-disposal measures were crude at best, heating in the winter was spotty, food was poor, and the prison was rife with vermin of all sorts, including rats, mice, lice, and cockroaches. The women's quarters were better on average than were the men's, but not extraordinarily so. Because of its location, William P. Wood, the prison superintendent, insisted on strict discipline. Any convict seen touching the bars that covered the windows was liable to be shot dead by guards.

Prisoners who had access to cash were allowed to purchase supplemental food and other items but at exorbitant prices. A few prisoners, especially the women, were permitted to receive small gift packages from family or friends. Despite the conditions and overcrowding, the death rate among inmates was not astronomical; it is believed that 457 detainees died between 1861 and 1865. Indeed, conditions at the Old Capitol Prison were substantially better than at other POW sites. By the autumn of 1865, U.S. officials began dismantling the prison, and within a decade both the main prison and the annex had been demolished.

PAUL G. PIERPAOLI JR.

See also

Boyd, Maria Isabelle; Prisoners of War; Prisons, Confederate; Prisons, U.S.

Further Reading

Hesseltine, William B., ed. *Civil War Prisons.* Kent, OH: Kent State University Press, 1972.

Speer, Lonnie. *Portals to Hell: Military Prisons of the Civil War.* Mechanicsburg, PA: Stackpole, 1997.

Olden, Charles Smith
Birth Date: February 19, 1799
Death Date: April 7, 1876

Governor of New Jersey (1860–1863). Charles Smith Olden was born on February 19, 1799, in Princeton, New Jersey, to a Quaker family. Until 1823, he worked in his father's store. Olden then became a chief clerk in a Philadelphia commercial enterprise. In 1826 he established his own business in New Orleans, which was a considerable success. By 1834, he had sold the business and amassed sufficient funds to return to Princeton in semiretirement. In 1845 he was elected to the New Jersey Senate, where he remained until 1851. He later joined the newly established Republican Party and sat on the board of a bank in Trenton, New Jersey.

In 1859 Olden received the Republican nomination for governor and went on to win a close election in the autumn of that year. Taking office on January 17, 1860, he did not allow his Quaker beliefs to interfere with his actions during the secession crisis and the ensuing Civil War. In the early spring of 1860, he received authorization from the state legislature to increase the size of New Jersey's militia. Although he preferred continued compromise to war, when war did come in April 1861, he steadfastly supported the Abraham Lincoln administration's war program.

In 1861 Olden helped raise some $500,000 from New Jersey banks to provide adequate war funds, and he responded promptly to the federal government's request for troops. Although he supported the Lincoln White House in most

instances, Olden decried the suspension of habeas corpus, fearing that it might be expanded to include New Jersey, and he directed state officials to prevent Union authorities from making arbitrary arrests in his state.

Olden left office on January 20, 1863, because the New Jersey Constitution barred him from serving consecutive terms. Thereafter he was a judge on the New Jersey Court of Errors and Appeals and on the Court of Pardons. In 1872 he was a presidential elector. Olden died on April 7, 1876, in Princeton, New Jersey.

PAUL G. PIERPAOLI JR.

See also

New Jersey

Further Reading

Siegel, Alan A. *Beneath the Starry Flag: New Jersey's Civil War Experience.* New Brunswick, NJ: Rutgers University Press, 2001.

Siegel, Alan A. *For the Glory of the Union: Myth, Reality and the Media in Civil War New Jersey.* Rutherford, NJ: Fairleigh Dickinson University Press, 1984.

Olmsted, Frederick Law
Birth Date: April 26, 1822
Death Date: August 28, 1903

Noted landscape architect, urban planner, and general secretary of the U.S. Sanitary Commission (1861–1863). Frederick Law Olmsted was born on April 26, 1822, in Hartford, Connecticut. His schooling was erratic, and he lost the opportunity to attend college because of illness. As a result, Olmsted explored many potential careers before a tour of England sparked his interest in landscape gardening. He envisioned so-called People's Parks in America, like the publicly owned Birkenhead Park outside Liverpool. The trip resulted in his first successful book, *Walks and Talks of an American Farmer in England* (1852).

Olmsted became involved with writing during the 1850s as a *New York Times* roving correspondent throughout the South. His keen management skills and his imaginative improvements of appearance and convenience at his Staten Island farm contributed to his appointment as superintendent for the development of Central Park in New York City in 1857. Olmsted produced the winning design for the park in collaboration with English architect Calvert Vaux. During the next 20 years, Olmsted worked intermittently on Central

Park, one of the first large parks designed specifically for public use.

With the onset of the Civil War, in 1861 Olmsted began serving as general secretary of the U.S. Sanitary Commission. Marshaling his organizational prowess, he insisted on efficiency. He streamlined the organization, centralized management, and supervised its branch offices. His insistence on these measures earned him the sobriquet "Old Boss Devil" among Sanitary Commission workers and managers. Not surprisingly, Olmsted's management style caused friction with the commission's branches, which chafed under his regimentation. He also worked to limit the influence of competing philanthropic organizations, at which he was less than successful. Olmsted resigned in September 1863, angry that the organization's executive committee would not completely support his hierarchical management style. Nevertheless, the Sanitary Commission was well run and coordinated during his tenure.

From 1863 to 1865, Olmsted was the development manager for Mariposa Estates in California; he then returned to New York, where he resumed work on Central Park. Olmsted designed other parks, including ones in Brooklyn, New York; suburban Chicago; and Boston. He also worked on the landscaping for the U.S. Capitol. Among Olmsted's many landscape designs for private estates, the most prominent was George Washington Vanderbilt's massive Biltmore estate near Asheville, North Carolina (1888), which encompassed more than 2,000 acres of mountain and river valley terrain.

Olmsted's last major design was for the World's Columbian Exposition in Chicago (1893). The design meshed with his plan for a waterfront park (Jackson Park) to be created there as part of his earlier design for a Chicago park system (1871).

Olmsted retired in 1895, but his son and stepson carried on his work. Olmsted died on August 28, 1903, in Belmont, Massachusetts, leaving a legacy of 20 parks, 7 park systems, 21 college campuses, 175 estates, and other projects in which designed landscape elements were used to enhance the scenery.

JUSTIN HARMON

See also
Sanitary Commission, U.S.

Further Reading
Hall, Lee. *Olmsted's America: An "Unpractical" Man and His Vision of Civilization.* Boston: Bullfinch, 1995.
Martin, Justin. *Genius of Place: The Life of Frederick Law Olmsted.* New York: Da Capo, 2011.

Olustee, Battle of
Event Date: February 20, 1864

Engagement during an abortive attempt to establish Union control in northern Florida. Fought about 50 miles southwest of Jacksonville in Baker County on February 20, 1864, the Battle of Olustee was the largest engagement in Florida during the war.

The campaign in northern Florida was the brainchild of Secretary of the Treasury Salmon P. Chase, who would seek the Republican nomination for president in 1864. He believed that a successful campaign in Florida, assisted by Unionists there, could bring Florida back into the Union, greatly aiding his political aspirations. President Abraham Lincoln endorsed the idea, with his own political future in mind. In December 1863, Major General Quincy A. Gillmore, commander of the Department of the South that included Florida, embraced the plan.

The War Department approved the plan on February 7, 1864. Union troops were to move inland from Jacksonville, securing Unionist strongholds and destroying Confederate supplies and rail lines. Gillmore dispatched Brigadier General Truman Seymour and a division of 5,500 men, which arrived at Jacksonville by water in mid-February. They then began moving west, with the goal of capturing the rail depot at Olustee on the Florida, Atlantic & Gulf Railroad. Seymour encountered almost no Confederate opposition. Union troops seized towns, torched Confederate camps and supply centers, and freed slaves as they marched west.

On February 20 as the Union troops approached the Olustee Depot, Seymour encountered Confederate brigadier general Joseph Finegan and a largely infantry force of some 5,000 men, supported by 12 guns. Finegan sent forward an infantry brigade under Brigadier General Alfred Colquitt to engage the Union troops, and Seymour ordered his leading brigade to seize Colquitt's artillery. The Union troops were quickly cut down. Indeed, many were so unnerved by the enfilading Confederate fire that they fled to the rear, and the pursuing Confederates seized 2 Union guns.

Heavy fighting lasted for several hours. Seymour ordered another frontal assault, which was beaten back and resulted in the loss of three additional Union guns. Late in the day Finegan committed his reserves, breaking the Union line. In late afternoon, Seymour ordered a general retreat eastward.

Union casualties in the battle were 1,861 dead or wounded, a 34 percent casualty rate, while the Confederates suffered only 946 casualties, or about 19 percent. Finnegan botched the pursuit, however, and Seymour's force reached Jacksonville without further loss and was soon back in South Carolina.

PAUL G. PIERPAOLI JR.

See also

Chase, Salmon Portland; Colquitt, Alfred Holt; Finegan, Joseph; Florida; Gillmore, Quincy Adams; Jacksonville, Florida; Seymour, Truman

Further Reading

Broadwater, Robert P. *The Battle of Olustee, 1864: The Final Union Attempt to Seize Florida.* Jefferson, NC: McFarland, 2006.
Nulty, William H. *Confederate Florida: The Road to Olustee.* Tuscaloosa: University of Alabama Press, 1990.

O'Neal, Edward Asbury
Birth Date: September 20, 1818
Death Date: November 7, 1890

Confederate officer. Edward Asbury O'Neal was born in Madison City, Alabama Territory, on September 20, 1818. O'Neal was just four years old when his father died and received his secondary education at Huntsville Green Academy. He graduated from LaGrange College in 1836. O'Neal later studied law and was admitted to the bar in 1840. He began his law practice in Florence, Alabama, and the following year was appointed to the office of solicitor for the Fourth Circuit. He unsuccessfully ran for Congress in 1848.

With the outbreak of the Civil War, on June 26, 1861, O'Neal joined the 9th Alabama Infantry Regiment, predominately drawn from northern counties along the Tennessee River. O'Neal was elected major in June 1861 and promoted to lieutenant colonel in October. In the spring of 1862 he became the colonel of the 26th Alabama Infantry. He fought with this regiment into 1863 and participated in various campaigns with the Army of Northern Virginia. O'Neal was wounded during the Battle of Seven Pines (May 31–June 1, 1862), again during the Maryland Campaign (September 1862), and a third time while temporarily leading a brigade in the Battle of Chancellorsville (May 1–4, 1863). In June 1863 O'Neal received promotion to brigadier general and command of the brigade, when Brigadier General Robert E. Rodes was promoted to division commander. However, General Robert E. Lee withdrew the promotion because of O'Neal's poor performance during the first day of fighting at the Battle of Gettysburg (July 1–3, 1863), and O'Neal reverted to his regimental command.

Early in 1864, O'Neal was sent back to Alabama to recruit and reorganize the 26th Alabama, returning to Virginia later in the spring. O'Neal and the 26th Alabama were then transferred to the Army of Tennessee at Dalton, Georgia. In June 1864 during the Atlanta Campaign (May 5–September 2, 1864), O'Neal assumed command of a brigade at Marietta but was relieved of command following the Battle of Peachtree Creek (July 20, 1864). He served the remainder of the war on detached duty with the Conscription Bureau in Alabama, arresting deserters from the Army of Tennessee.

Following the war, O'Neal returned to Florence, Alabama, and resumed his law practice. In 1875 he was elected as a delegate to the 1875 Constitutional Convention, serving as chairman of the Committee on Education. Beginning in 1882, O'Neal served two terms as governor of Alabama. He focused his administration on tax reduction, prison reform, and increased aid to education, with the Alabama legislature granting more than 46,000 acres to found the University of Alabama. At the end of his second term in 1886, O'Neal returned to public life in Florence, where he died on November 7, 1890.

R. RAY ORTENSIE

See also

Atlanta Campaign; Chancellorsville, Battle of; Gettysburg, Battle of; Lee, Robert Edward; Peachtree Creek, Battle of; Rodes, Robert Emmett; Seven Pines, Battle of

Further Reading

Carter, John C. *Welcome the Hour of Conflict: William Cowan McClellan and the 9th Alabama.* Tuscaloosa: University of Alabama Press, 2007.
Castel, Albert E. *Decision in the West: The Atlanta Campaign of 1864.* Lawrence: University Press of Kansas, 1995.
O'Neal, Edward Asbury. *The Reminiscences of Edward A. O'Neal.* New York: Columbia University, Oral History Research Office, 1972.

Opdycke, Samuel Emerson
Birth Date: January 7, 1830
Death Date: April 25, 1884

Union officer. Samuel Emerson Opdycke was born in Trumbull County, Ohio, on January 7, 1830, into a family whose members had served in the American Revolutionary War and the War of 1812. Educated in local schools, he moved to California in a futile attempt to strike it rich in the Gold Rush before returning to Ohio and settling in Warren, where he became a merchant.

An abolitionist, Opdycke enlisted in the 41st Ohio Infantry Regiment, commanded by Colonel William B. Hazen, following the First Battle of Bull Run (July 21, 1861). Opdycke was commissioned a first lieutenant on August 26, 1861. Promoted to captain in January 1862, he early on proved his fitness for high command. He won notice for his role in the Battle of Shiloh (April 6–7), when he grabbed the colors from the fallen standard-bearer and carried them at the front in an assault on April 7.

In September 1862 Opdycke resigned his commission and returned to Ohio to help recruit a new regiment—the 125th Ohio. He became its lieutenant colonel on October 1 and its colonel on January 1, 1863. Known as Opdycke's Tigers, the regiment was ordered to Kentucky and took part in the Tullahoma Campaign (June 23–July 3, 1863). Opdycke's Tigers also played an important role during the Union stand at Horseshoe Ridge in the Battle of Chickamauga (September 19–20). In the Chattanooga Campaign (October–November 1863), Opdycke's men were some of the first Union troops to gain the summit of Missionary Ridge (November 25).

Opdycke took command of a brigade in the spring of 1864, leading it during the Atlanta Campaign (May 5–September 2, 1864). Although badly wounded in the Battle of Resaca (May 13–15, 1864), Opdycke returned to action in time to lead a brigade of IV Corps in the Battle of Kennesaw Mountain (June 27, 1864).

In August 1864, Opdycke took command of a brigade in Brigadier General George D. Wagner's division of the Army of the Cumberland, serving in it for the rest of the war. Opdycke then took part in the Franklin and Nashville Campaign (November 29–December 27, 1864). In the Battle of Franklin (November 30, 1864), Wagner ordered his three brigades to take up a vulnerable position in advance of the main Union line. Opdycke argued with Wagner and marched his brigade into a reserve position behind the Union line. The Confederates broke through Wagner's advanced position, but Odpycke immediately moved his men forward and led a furious counterattack that sealed the breakthrough and captured a number of Confederates and 10 battle flags. For his role in the Union victory, Opdycke was brevetted major general of volunteers. He was promoted to full-grade brigadier general on July 26, 1865, and resigned his volunteer commission in January 1866.

Postbellum, Opdycke moved to New York City, where he became a dry goods merchant, wrote articles on the war, and was active in veterans' affairs. On April 22, 1884, in New York City, Opdycke accidentally shot himself while cleaning his pistol; he died three days later.

SPENCER C. TUCKER

See also

Atlanta Campaign; Bull Run, First Battle of; Chickamauga, Battle of; Franklin, Battle of; Franklin and Nashville Campaign; Hazen, William Babcock; Kennesaw Mountain, Battle of; Missionary Ridge, Battle of; Resaca, Battle of; Shiloh, Battle of; Tullahoma Campaign; Wagner, George Day

Further Reading

Eicher, John H., and David J. Eicher. *Civil War High Commands.* Stanford, CA: Stanford University Press, 2001.

Jacobson, Eric A., and Richard A. Rupp. *For Cause & for Country: A Study of the Affair at Spring Hill and the Battle of Franklin.* Franklin, TN: O'More, 2007.

Warner, Ezra J. *Generals in Blue: Lives of the Union Commanders.* Baton Rouge: Louisiana State University Press, 2006.

Opequon Creek, Battle of

See Winchester, Third Battle of

Orange & Alexandria Railroad

Strategic rail line tying northern Virginia with south-central Virginia. Covering some 170 miles, the Orange & Alexandria Railroad linked Alexandria in the north with Lynchburg, via Gordonsville, in the south. At Gordonsville, the line intersected with the Virginia Central Railroad, which connected Staunton in the Shenandoah Valley with Richmond. At the Orange & Alexandria's terminus in Lynchburg, the rail line converged with the Southside Railroad and the Virginia & Tennessee Railroad. The Orange & Alexandria Railroad, chartered in 1848, was a single-track system with a gauge of 4'8.5". The first phase of the line, between Alexandria and Orange County (Gordonsville), was completed in 1854; the remainder of the line was finished in 1860.

The railroad was one of the most strategic of all lines during the Civil War because of its location, and both Union and Confederate forces utilized it between 1861 and 1865. During the First Battle of Bull Run (July 21, 1861) and the Second Battle of Bull Run (August 29–30, 1862), fighting occurred all along the line in northern Virginia. The railroad was critically important to the Army of Northern Virginia, which transported thousands of soldiers on it. In the autumn of 1862, in 1863, and in the winter of 1864, numerous Union armies utilized the line to station troops along the Rappahannock River. Union officials estimated that the single line could supply a 200,000-man army if necessary.

Locomotive on the Orange & Alexandria Railroad during the Second Battle of Bull Run in August 1862. The Orange & Alexandria was a major Virginia rail line running from Alexandria south to Lynchburg. (Library of Congress)

The Confederates, however, had a hard time harnessing the railroad to full effect. The line's management was inept at best, and by early 1862 its operations were plagued by shortages of ties, rails, rolling stock, and other items. By mid-1862, a single run from Manassas Junction to Gordonsville—just 51 miles—took nearly 36 hours to complete. Nevertheless, the rail line remained opened until war's end, and in 1864 the Confederates employed it to stave off the capture of Lynchburg. After the war ended, the railroad was financially strapped, and it became a somewhat marginal line. In 1873 it came under the control of the powerful Baltimore & Ohio Railroad. Today, parts of the original line are still in use by the Norfolk Southern line and Amtrak.

PAUL G. PIERPAOLI JR.

See also

Bull Run, First Battle of; Bull Run, Second Battle of; Railroads, CSA; Railroads, U.S.

Further Reading

Angevine, Robert G. *The Railroad and the State: War, Politics, and Technology in Nineteenth Century America.* Stanford, CA: Stanford University Press, 2004.
Gabel, Christopher R. *Rails to Oblivion: The Battle of Confederate Railroads in the Civil War.* Fort Leavenworth, KS: Army Command and General Staff College, Combat Studies Institute, 2002.

Orchard Knob, Battle of
Event Date: November 23, 1863

Engagement during the Chattanooga Campaign (October–November 1863). On November 23, 1863, Major General Ulysses S. Grant, commander of the Military Division of the Mississippi, ordered Major General George H. Thomas, commanding the Army of the Cumberland, to undertake a reconnaissance in force against Orchard Knob, a prominent mound between the city of Chattanooga and Missionary Ridge, to determine if information Grant had received that Confederate general Braxton Bragg might be withdrawing his army from Missionary Ridge was correct. Grant's plans to drive the Confederates from Chattanooga were completed, but he feared that Bragg might escape before he launched his offensive.

Orchard Knob was located on a ridge between the Confederate main line, at the base of Missionary Ridge, and the Union breastworks that defended Chattanooga. Confederate brigadier general Arthur Manigault held the ridge with fewer than 700 men. Union brigadier general T. J. Wood, who commanded 5,000 troops from the Army of the Cumberland, was charged with probing the Southern position.

At 12:30 p.m., Wood marched his men out of their works and formed their ranks in the open plain between the opposing lines. The Union troops formed with such precision that the Confederate pickets believed that they were preparing for a review. Indeed, many of Manigault's men left their rifle pits to get a better look at the show.

At 1:30 p.m., a cannon at Fort Wood fired the signal for the Union line to advance, and Wood's division surged forward toward the stunned Confederates. Union artillery bombarded Orchard Knob as Manigault's men scampered to get back to their rifle pits. Wood's men easily threw the Confederate pickets back on their line along the ridge. Then, in a sharp but short engagement, the Federals drove Manigault's men from that position back on the main Confederate line at the base of Missionary Ridge. Wood's men then planted the U.S. flag on the crest of Orchard Knob, proclaiming their possession of the ground.

The Confederates had been pushed back so quickly and the engagement had been of such short duration that casualties on both sides were light, totaling fewer than 200 on each side. Generals Grant and Thomas had only intended for Wood's force to make a reconnaissance of the ground, but now that it was captured, Thomas sent word to Wood to hold Orchard Knob. Union forces then moved forward to come on line with the position at Orchard Knob, only a mile from Missionary Ridge. The following day, Grant launched his offensive against Bragg's army on Lookout Mountain and Missionary Ridge.

ROBERT P. BROADWATER

See also

Chattanooga Campaign; Manigault, Arthur Middleton; Thomas, George Henry; Wood, Thomas John

Further Reading

Cozzens, Peter, and Robert I. Girardi. *The New Annals of the Civil War.* Mechanicsburg, PA: Stackpole, 2004.

Korn, Jerry. *The Fight for Chattanooga: Chickamauga to Missionary Ridge.* Alexandria, VA: Time Life Books, 1985.

Ord, Edward Otho Cresap

Birth Date: October 18, 1818
Death Date: July 22, 1883

Union officer. Born on October 18, 1818, in Cumberland, Maryland, Edward Otho Cresap Ord moved to Washington, D.C., with his family as a young boy. Educated both locally and at home, he secured an appointment to the U.S. Military Academy, West Point, and graduated with the class of 1839. Commissioned an artillery officer, he was sent to Florida,

Union major general Edward Ord saw extensive combat during the Civil War and was severely wounded twice. Near the end of the war, he commanded the Army of the James. (Library of Congress)

where he fought in the Second Seminole War (1835–1842). Following that service, Ord distinguished himself at various western frontier posts, earning promotion to first lieutenant in 1841 and to captain in 1850. While assigned to the artillery school at Fort Monroe, Virginia, in 1859, Ord participated in the operation that captured John Brown at Harpers Ferry. Returning to the West Coast in 1860, Ord was serving in the 3rd U.S. Artillery Regiment stationed at San Francisco upon the beginning of the Civil War.

On September 14, 1861, Ord was appointed a brigadier general of volunteers and transferred to Washington, D.C. He took command of a brigade in the Army of the Potomac on October 3. Ord led a successful assault against Confederate brigadier general J. E. B. Stuart at Dranesville, Virginia, on December 20, 1861. Ord went on to command a division in Major General Irvin McDowell's corps during the early stages of the Peninsula Campaign (March–July 1862).

Promoted to major general of volunteers on May 2, 1862, Ord was then assigned to the Army of the Tennessee in the western theater. He arrived in time to witness the Confederate evacuation of Corinth, Mississippi, and took command of that city on June 22.

Ord subsequently participated in the Battles of Iuka (September 12, 1862) and Corinth (October 3–4, 1862) and was severely wounded at Hatchie River near Pocahontas, Tennessee, while pursuing Confederate major general Earl Van Dorn's forces retreating from Corinth. In June 1863 Ord returned to duty, replacing Major General John A. McClernand as commander of XIII Corps during the July siege of Jackson, Mississippi.

In August 1863, Ord was transferred to the Department of the Gulf and fought in Louisiana. The following spring, he was ordered east and served in the Department of West Virginia but remained there less than a month after being relieved of command at his own request in April 1864. In July he assumed command of XVIII Corps, Army of the James, then engaged in the Petersburg Campaign (June 15, 1864–April 3, 1865). While in command of XVIII Corps, Ord was seriously wounded again on September 29 during the attack on the Confederate positions at Fort Harrison near Richmond, for which he received the regular army brevet to major general. Upon recovery from his wounds and after returning to the field on January 8, 1865, Ord commanded the Army of the James. He remained in this position until the end of the war and was present during General Robert E. Lee's surrender at Appomattox on April 9, 1865.

Ord remained with the army after the war and, following the army reorganization of 1866, was appointed a brigadier general in the regular army and held a number of important departmental commands. He was retired in 1880 and the following year was promoted to major general on the retired list. Ord died in Havana, Cuba, on July 22, 1883, from yellow fever, which he had contracted while visiting Veracruz.

R. Ray Ortensie

See also

Corinth, Mississippi; Corinth, Mississippi, Siege of; Crater, Battle of the; Dranesville, Battle of; Iuka, Battle of; Jackson, Mississippi, Siege of; McClernand, John Alexander; McDowell, Irvin; Peninsula Campaign; Petersburg Campaign; Van Dorn, Earl

Further Reading

Cresap, Bernard. *Appomattox Commander: The Story of E.O.C. Ord.* London: Tantivy, 1981.

Eicher, John H., and David J. Eicher. *Civil War High Commands.* Stanford, CA: Stanford University Press, 2001.

Horn, John. *The Petersburg Campaign, June 1864–April 1865.* Conshohocken, PA: Combined Publishing, 1999.

Order of American Knights

Organization in the North that opposed the Union war effort. Following the issuance of the Emancipation Proclamation (January 1, 1863), an enterprising Democrat named Phineas C. Wright created an organization that he hoped would counter Republican Union Leagues by protecting civil liberties and promoting conservative policies. On February 22, 1863, Wright officially proclaimed in St. Louis the Order of American Knights. He took the name from a filibustering organization based near New Orleans. Wright attempted to establish other Order of American Knights chapters in Illinois, Indiana, and New York but generated only a handful of supporters there. The Order of American Knights opposed both the war and the draft.

Harrison H. Dodd became a leader of the Order of American Knights in Indianapolis. He devised a plan to liberate Confederate prisoners at Camp Morton in Indianapolis, seize the city's arsenal, and foment a local insurrection. Dodd, however, detailed this plan to an agent of Indiana governor Oliver P. Morton, whom Dodd trusted as a close confidant. This revelation led to Dodd's arrest and the end of the Camp Morton plot several weeks before its planned execution in August 1863. There were reports of other plans to free Confederate prisoners of war at other Northern camps and to create a Confederate army operating within the North.

Union colonel John P. Sanderson in St. Louis provided much of the information regarding the Order of American Knights. Through a network of sources both reliable and dubious, he erroneously proclaimed Clement Vallandigham as the organization's leader, cited Confederate major general Sterling Price as its designated military commander, and accused the group of treasonous activities. Government officials estimated the size of the organization at between 80,000 and 110,000 members, but these figures appear to be gross exaggerations.

On February 22, 1864, members of the Order of American Knights met to endorse George B. McClellan as the eventual Democratic presidential nominee. At this meeting, and without the presence of Wright, the leadership abandoned the secret rituals and oaths of the organization and renamed their group the Sons of Liberty, effectively ending the Order of American Knights. Regardless of their actual threat, Republicans used the Order of American Knights and other such groups' alleged activities cited in Sanderson's report as a scare tactic during the 1864 elections, in effect aiding President Abraham Lincoln's reelection that autumn.

Keith Altavilla

See also
Camp Morton, Indiana; Morton, Oliver Hazard Perry Throck; Price, Sterling; Union League of America; Vallandigham, Clement Laird

Further Reading
Klement, Frank L. *Dark Lanterns: Secret Political Societies, Conspiracies, and Treason Trials in the Civil War.* Baton Rouge: Louisiana State University Press, 1984.
Weber, Jennifer L. *Copperheads: The Rise and Fall of Lincoln's Opponents in the North.* New York: Oxford University Press, 2006.

Oregon

State located in the Pacific Northwest with an 1860 population of 52,465. Admitted to the Union on February 14, 1859, and encompassing 97,073 square miles, Oregon is bordered by the Pacific Ocean to the west, Idaho to the east, California and Nevada to the south, and the state of Washington to the north. Because Oregon was far removed from the active theaters, the state saw no combat during the Civil War, and its citizens were only indirectly affected by it.

When Oregonians voted for statehood in 1857, they also voiced their opposition to slavery. At the same time, however, they voted against the admittance of free blacks into their state. The Democrats enjoyed a majority within state politics, but they were mainly supporters of Illinois senator Stephen Douglas and were not generally secessionist-minded Democrats.

Oregon's first governor, John Whiteaker, who served from 1858 to 1862, was a proslavery Democrat whose political viewpoint was at odds with the majority of the electorate. Not surprisingly, he was succeeded by Republican A. C. Gibbs, who served from 1862 until 1866. Gibbs insisted on raising a cavalry and an infantry regiment, over the objections of many voters, although these units saw no action in the Civil War. In 1860 Edward D. Baker, an ardent Republican and a friend of Abraham Lincoln, was elected U.S. senator from Oregon. Baker enjoyed a high-profile although short stint in the Senate before he was killed in action in October 1861 while leading a Union volunteer regiment.

When the Civil War began in April 1861, most of the regular U.S. Army troops who were garrisoned in the West were withdrawn to the East, and Oregon was no exception. Thus, a number of Oregonians volunteered for military duty, which included protecting the local population from Indian raids, guarding travel routes and surveying parties, escorting wagon trains, and manning coastal fortifications.

Governor Gibbs activated the 1st Oregon Cavalry Regiment in 1862, which was disbanded in 1865, and in 1864 he permitted the establishment of the 1st Oregon Infantry Regiment, which saw service until 1867.

Paul G. Pierpaoli Jr.

See also
Baker, Edward Dickinson; Douglas, Stephen Arnold; Lincoln, Abraham

Further Reading
Edwards, Glenn Thomas. "Oregon Regiments in the Civil War Years: Duty on the Indian Frontier." Unpublished MA thesis, University of Oregon, June 1960.
Robbins, William G. *Oregon: This Storied Land.* Portland: Oregon Historical Society Press, 2005.

Orme, William Ward
Birth Date: February 17, 1832
Death Date: September 13, 1866

Union officer. William Ward Orme was born on February 17, 1832, in Washington, D.C. After graduating from Mount St. Mary's College in Emmettsburg, Maryland, he moved to Illinois, passed the bar, and began a successful legal practice in Bloomington, where he became a close of colleague of Abraham Lincoln.

Orme enlisted with the 94th Illinois Infantry Regiment on August 20, 1862, becoming its colonel. He led a brigade effectively in the Battle of Prairie Grove (December 7, 1862) in Arkansas and was rewarded with a promotion to brigadier general of volunteers later that same month, to date from November 9.

Orme next joined Major General Ulysses S. Grant's Second Vicksburg Campaign (April 1–July 4, 1863) and commanded a brigade in XIII Corps, Army of the Tennessee, but contracted tuberculosis in late June and was forced to suspend his field command. Orme then became an inspector of Union prisoner-of-war facilities, and by December 1863 he had begun serving as the supervisor of Camp Douglas in Chicago. Four months later, however, his declining health compelled him to resign from the army. Orme then became a special agent for the Treasury Department, an appointment arranged by President Lincoln. In November 1865 Orme's poor health forced him to resign that post as well, and he spent the remaining months of his life in Bloomington, Illinois, where he died on September 13, 1866.

Paul G. Pierpaoli Jr.

See also
Prairie Grove, Battle of; Vicksburg Campaign, Second

Further Reading
Eicher, John H., and David J. Eicher. *Civil War High Commands.* Stanford, CA: Stanford University Press, 2001.

Orphan Brigade

Nickname given to the Confederate 1st Kentucky Brigade. Because Kentucky did not secede from the Union, its Confederate-allied forces were never acknowledged by the state government. Because of this, the 1st Kentucky Brigade was forced to muster in and undergo training in neighboring Tennessee, which was part of the Confederacy. These activities occurred during the summer and autumn of 1861. In February 1862 when the Confederate army was expelled from Kentucky, the 1st Brigade followed it to Mississippi.

The Orphan Brigade was renowned for its esprit de corps and tenacious fighting. The brigade was commanded first by Brigadier General Simon B. Buckner, who was succeeded by Brigadier General John C. Breckinridge, who left his post in October 1862. The Kentucky Brigade was then led by Brigadier General Roger W. Hanson, who was killed at the Battle of Stones River (December 31, 1862–January 2, 1863); Brigadier General Ben Hardin Helm, who was killed at the Battle of Chickamauga (September 19–20, 1863); and finally Brigadier General Joseph H. Lewis. Several commanding generals declared the Orphan Brigade the best such outfit in the Confederate ranks.

The Orphan Brigade fought in numerous battles, including among others Shiloh (April 6–7, 1862), Baton Rouge (August 5, 1862), Stones River (December 31, 1862–January 2, 1863), Jackson (May 14, 1863), and Chickamauga (September 19–20, 1863). The brigade saw action during the entire Atlanta Campaign (May 5–September 2, 1864) and took part in the attempt to thwart Sherman's March to the Sea (November 15–December 21, 1864).

The 1st Kentucky Brigade fought with the Confederate Army of Tennessee, but because the brigade could not draw upon reserves from its home state, its numbers dwindled steadily throughout the war. Beginning the conflict with some 4,000 men, the Orphan Brigade finished with just 500. Often assigned to conduct rearguard actions after a battle, an extraordinarily risky venture, the brigade suffered a high fatality rate. Nevertheless, the desertion rate for the outfit was among the lowest of any Confederate brigade.

In the closing months of the war, the 1st Kentucky served as a cavalry unit under the command of Brigadier General Joseph H. Lewis. In early May 1865 in Washington, Georgia, Lewis was one of the last Confederate commanders in the eastern theater to surrender to Union forces. In spite of its orphan status and greatly diminished numbers as the war dragged on, the 1st Kentucky Brigade has been celebrated as one of the most effective and distinctive fighting forces of the Civil War.

Paul G. Pierpaoli Jr.

See also
Atlanta Campaign; Baton Rouge, Battle of; Breckinridge, John Cabell; Buckner, Simon Bolivar; Chickamauga, Battle of; Hanson, Roger Weightman; Helm, Benjamin Hardin; Jackson, Mississippi, Siege of; Kentucky; Lewis, Joseph Horace; Sherman's March to the Sea; Shiloh, Battle of; Stones River, Battle of; Tennessee, Confederate Army of

Further Reading
Davis, William C. *The Orphan Brigade: The Kentucky Confederates Who Couldn't Go Home.* Baton Rouge: Louisiana State University Press, 1983.
Horn, Stanley F. *The Army of Tennessee.* Norman: University of Oklahoma Press, 1993.

Orr, James Lawrence
Birth Date: May 12, 1822
Death Date: May 5, 1873

Confederate politician. James Lawrence Orr was born on May 12, 1822, in Craytonville, South Carolina. After studying law at the University of Virginia, he was admitted to the bar in 1842. He edited a newspaper in Anderson, South Carolina, for two years before being elected to the South Carolina House of Representatives, where he served from 1844 to 1847. In 1848 Orr, a Democrat, won election to the first of five successive terms in the U.S. House of Representatives, serving as Speaker from 1857 until 1859. He resumed his legal practice upon his return to South Carolina.

At first a supporter of fellow Democrat Stephen A. Douglas and a pro-Unionist, Orr changed his position and became a champion of secession when Abraham Lincoln was elected president in 1860. Indeed, Orr served as president of the South Carolina Secession Convention.

After organizing a Confederate regiment (Orr's Regiment of Rifles) and very briefly serving in the military, in December 1861 Orr was elected to the Confederate Senate and remained there throughout the Civil War. A frequent critic of Jefferson Davis, Orr accepted the fact that the South was destined to lose the war before most of his colleagues would and as early as 1864 advised seeking a negotiated settlement.

An advocate of postbellum accommodation, Orr was elected governor of South Carolina as a Republican in 1865, serving until 1868. He initially was a supporter of President Andrew Johnson's Reconstruction plans, but once again Orr shifted his political position to match political reality and quickly joined the Radical Republicans with the collapse of Johnson's popularity. While this ensured Orr's position in the short run, it cost him the support of his white constituents. In 1868 Orr was elected to a two-year term on the 8th Judicial Circuit.

At the Republican National Convention in 1872, Orr supported President Ulysses S. Grant's anti–Ku Klux Klan policy. Later that year Orr was appointed minister to Russia. Orr died of pneumonia in St. Petersburg on May 5, 1873, just a few months after his arrival.

STEVEN G. O'BRIEN

See also

Congress, CSA; Davis, Jefferson Finis; Johnson, Andrew; Radical Republicans; Reconstruction; South Carolina

Further Reading

Edgar, Walter B. *South Carolina: A History.* Columbia: University of South Carolina Press, 1998.

Leemhuis, Roger P. *James L. Orr and the Sectional Conflict.* Washington, DC: University Press of America, 1979.

Osage, Battle of the

See Marais des Cygnes River, Battle of the; Mine Creek, Battle of

---

Ostend Manifesto

A secret document advocating the U.S. acquisition of Cuba from Spain, written in Ostend, Belgium, in 1854 by U.S. diplomats James Buchanan, U.S. minister to Great Britain; John M. Mason, U.S. minister to France; and Pierre Soulé, U.S. minister to Spain. Cuba, often referred to as the "Pearl of the Antilles," with its lucrative slave-based sugarcane production, balmy climate, and proximity to the United States, had drawn the attention of leaders in the early republic, including Thomas Jefferson and John Quincy Adams. In

1848 President James K. Polk, whose policies of Manifest Destiny wrested 1 million square miles of land from Mexico, instructed the American minister to Spain, Romulus M. Saunders, to sound out Spain about selling Cuba to the United States. The Spanish government asserted that under no circumstances would it relinquish control over Cuba.

When these diplomatic overtures were thwarted, some Southerners, who perceived Cuba as a highly desirable slave territory, engaged in filibustering expeditions to seize the island by force. Two such expeditions in the early 1850s were repulsed by Spanish authorities, and the leaders of these invasions were executed, outraging many Southerners.

Relations between the United States and Spain became further strained when in March 1854 Spanish authorities in Cuba seized the American steamer *Black Warrior.* President Franklin Pierce, who supported the expansion of slave territory into Latin America, was prepared to respond forcefully to the Spanish provocation. Thus, he directed Secretary of State William Marcy, an expansionist who favored annexation of Cuba, to explore whether Spain could be persuaded to sell Cuba without interference from the English and the French. To implement this policy, Buchanan, Mason, and Soulé gathered in Ostend, Belgium, to strategize. Soulé was an exiled Frenchman who had settled in Louisiana and advocated that the United States acquire Cuba by military action if necessary. His appointment and undiplomatic actions, such as allegedly leading an anti-Spanish riot in New Orleans, exacerbated the deteriorating relations between Spain and the United States.

The three ministers met in Ostend during the summer of 1854 and issued their report to Marcy on October 18, 1854. The Ostend Manifesto suggested an offer of $120 million for the purchase of Cuba but then concluded that if Spain proved unwilling to enter negotiations, the United States would then be justified in employing military action to seize the island by force. The bellicose nature of the document was attributed mainly to the influence of Soulé.

Before the Pierce administration could act upon the recommendations made at Ostend, word of the Ostend Manifesto was leaked to the American and European press. Reaction in England and France was opposed to the manifesto, while there was a veritable uproar among Northern newspapers in the United States. Passage of the Fugitive Slave Act (1850) as part of the Compromise of 1850 along with introduction of the Kansas-Nebraska Act in Congress (passed in 1854) convinced many Northerners that Southern slave interests were intent upon expanding slavery and disrupting the sectional balance of power. Because of the political upheaval in the North and opposition from abroad, the Pierce administration disavowed the Ostend Manifesto. Nevertheless, the manifesto encouraged sectional divisions and contributed to the rise of the Republican Party.

RON BRILEY

See also

Abolitionism and the Civil War; Buchanan, James; Pierce, Franklin; Slavery

Further Reading

Ettinger, Amos Aschbach. *The Mission to Spain of Pierre Soulé, 1853–1855: A Study in the Cuban Diplomacy of the United States.* New Haven, CT: Yale University Press, 1932.

Gara, Larry. *The Presidency of Franklin Pierce.* Lawrence: University Press of Kansas, 1991.

Potter, David M. *The Impending Crisis, 1848–1861.* New York: Harper and Row, 1967.

Osterhaus, Peter Joseph
Birth Date: January 4, 1823
Death Date: January 2, 1917

Union officer. Peter Joseph Osterhaus was born on January 4, 1823, in Coblenz, Prussia. After studying at a military school in Berlin, he served as a volunteer in the Prussian Army but was compelled to leave Prussia during the unrest associated with the 1848 revolutions then sweeping Europe. Arriving in the United States in the spring of 1849, he eventually settled in Illinois, where he engaged in business pursuits in Belleville and then Lebanon. He later made his way to St. Louis, where he was involved in commercial ventures.

In the winter of 1861, Osterhaus helped recruit the 12th Missouri Infantry Regiment, but he was soon transferred to the 2nd Missouri, taking a captain's commission. He was promoted to major on April 27, 1861. After service at the Battle of Wilson's Creek (August 10, 1861), he became colonel of the 12th Missouri in December 1861 and led that regiment ably during the Battle of Pea Ridge (March 7–8, 1862). Advanced to brigadier general of volunteers on June 9, he took command of a brigade in the Army of the Southwest. In the spring of 1863, he assumed command of a division in Major General Ulysses S. Grant's command during the Second Vicksburg Campaign (April 1–July 4, 1863). Osterhaus saw action at the Battle of Champion Hill (May 16, 1863), but he was wounded the next day in the First Battle of Big Black River.

After recuperation, Osterhaus led a division of XV Corps, Army of the Tennessee, during fighting in Tennessee, and he performed well at the Battle of Missionary Ridge (November 25, 1863). He was then attached to Major General William T. Sherman's command for the Atlanta Campaign (May 5–September 2, 1864) but was away from the army during the major battles of July. On July 23, 1864, Osterhaus was advanced to major general of volunteers over the objections of General Sherman, who believed that Osterhaus had lobbied for the rank to the detriment of his command. Nevertheless, Osterhaus remained with Sherman into early 1865, commanding XV Corps during the March to the Sea (November 15–December 21, 1864) and serving as Major General E. R. S. Canby's chief of staff during the final operations against Mobile. After holding several district and department commands in the West, Osterhaus mustered out in January 1866.

Osterhaus was a merchant in St. Louis and held two diplomatic appointments, at Lyons, France (1866–1868), and Mannheim, Germany (1898–1900). Following the latter, he remained in Germany until his death on January 2, 1917, in Duisburg.

PAUL G. PIERPAOLI JR.

See also

Atlanta Campaign; Big Black River, First Battle of; Champion Hill, Battle of; Missionary Ridge, Battle of; Pea Ridge, Battle of; Sherman, William Tecumseh; Vicksburg Campaign, Second; Wilson's Creek, Battle of

Further Reading

Eicher, John H., and David J. Eicher. *Civil War High Commands.* Stanford, CA: Stanford University Press, 2001.

Warner, Ezra J. *Generals in Blue: Lives of the Union Commanders.* Baton Rouge: Louisiana State University Press, 2006.

O'Sullivan, Timothy
Birth Date: ca. 1840
Death Date: January 14, 1882

One of the most daring and respected Civil War and western frontier photographers of the 19th century. Timothy O'Sullivan was born circa 1840; some sources give his birthplace as Ireland, while others claim New York City. He began his career while only a teenager as an apprentice to famed Civil War photographers Mathew Brady and Alexander Gardner.

In the spring of 1861, O'Sullivan was commissioned a first lieutenant in the U.S. Army and saw action in South Carolina and Georgia. Honorably discharged the following spring, he joined Brady to photograph the Civil War.

With Brady's team, O'Sullivan recorded the aftermath of the Battle of Antietam (September 17, 1862), the Battle of Gettysburg (July 1–3, 1863), and the Appomattox Campaign (April 2–9, 1865), among other engagements. His images of the war, including *Harvest of Death*, which portrayed felled Union soldiers at Gettysburg, allowed Americans to experience the grim realities of the war.

O'Sullivan worked with the photographic process known as wet collodion. This required him to transport bulky equipment and supplies as well as a portable darkroom over rough battlefields and later the harsh terrain of the jungles of Panama and the deserts and mountains of the American West.

From 1867 to 1869, O'Sullivan worked with geologist Clarence King on a U.S. government–sponsored survey of the 40th Parallel, photographing mines and geologic sites in the West. In 1870 O'Sullivan joined the Darién Expedition, during which he photographed the proposed route of the Panama Canal. In May 1871 he accompanied Lieutenant George M. Wheeler on his survey of the 100th Meridian and alternated working for him and King until 1874.

In 1880 O'Sullivan was appointed chief photographer for the Department of the Treasury, but he left the position after only a few months because of poor health caused by tuberculosis. O'Sullivan ultimately died from the disease on January 14, 1882, in Staten Island, New York.

MOLLY BOMPANE

See also

Antietam, Battle of; Appomattox Campaign; Brady, Mathew; Gardner, Alexander; Gettysburg, Battle of; Photography and the Civil War

Further Reading

Horan, James D. *Timothy O'Sullivan: America's Forgotten Photographer.* New York: Bonanza Books, 1966.

Kelsey, Robin E. "Viewing the Archive: Timothy O'Sullivan's Photographs for the Wheeler Survey, 1871–74." *Art Bulletin* 85(4) (2003): 702–723.

1861 to March 1862, he was assistant secretary of war. In July 1862 he was named head of the Bureau of the Exchange of Prisoners and given the largely honorific rank of colonel.

Ould's duties included frequent meetings with Union counterparts to arrange for prisoner-of-war exchanges, making provisions for the shipping of goods and money sent by family and friends to Union prisoners being held in Confederate prisons, and processing grievances submitted by federal officials concerning the treatment of Union prisoners. He was also in charge of lodging complaints with the U.S. government concerning the treatment of Confederate prisoners. In the spring and summer of 1862 after the Union capture of New Orleans, Ould was also responsible for lodging grievances with the U.S. government over the alleged mistreatment of civilians there. When the prisoner exchange system broke down in late 1863, Ould also began working for the Confederate Secret Service, although he retained his role in prisoner exchanges and relations.

Ould was in Richmond when the city fell in April 1865, and he was promptly arrested and charged with misappropriating money that was supposed to have gone to Union prisoners during the war. He steadfastly maintained his innocence, and after nearly eight weeks of investigations, a board of U.S. officers found him not guilty. He was released in June 1865 and remained in Richmond, where he practiced law. Ould died there on December 15, 1882.

PAUL G. PIERPAOLI JR.

See also

Prisoners of War; Prisons, Confederate; Prisons, U.S.

Further Reading

Bar Association, City of Richmond. *Proceedings in Memoriam of R. C. L. Moncure and Robert Ould.* Richmond, VA: Dalton and Guthrie, 1883.

Sanders, Charles W. *While in the Hands of the Enemy: Military Prisons of the Civil War.* Baton Rouge: Louisiana State University Press, 2005.

Ould, Robert

Birth Date: January 31, 1820
Death Date: December 15, 1882

Confederate government official. Robert Ould was born on January 31, 1820, in Washington, D.C. He attended the College of William and Mary. Ould later studied law, was admitted to the bar, and commenced a legal practice in Washington. When the Confederacy was formed in 1861, he volunteered to work for the new government. From April

Overland Campaign

Start Date: May 4, 1864
End Date: June 12, 1864

Major Union offensive. New Union Army general in chief Lieutenant General Ulysses S. Grant planned his spring 1864 campaign to take advantage of superior Union numbers in a massive multipronged simultaneous effort to prevent the Confederates from shifting their dwindling resources to counter any one Union thrust. In the western theater, Major

Overland Campaign (May 4–June 12, 1864)

	Union	Confederacy
Force strength, approximate	120,000	60,000
Casualties	55,000	32,600

General William T. Sherman was to move against the Confederate Army of Tennessee in northern Georgia and drive on the vital railroad and manufacturing center of Atlanta. Meanwhile, Major General Nathaniel P. Banks would advance on Mobile. In the eastern theater, Major General George Gordon Meade's Army of the Potomac, the major Union field force of some 120,000 men, would drive south from Culpeper, Virginia, against General Robert E. Lee's Army of Northern Virginia to capture Richmond in what became known as the Overland Campaign. Grant planned to accompany Meade's army in the field. At the same time, Major General Benjamin F. Butler's 39,000-man Army of the James was to proceed up the south bank of the James River and cut Lee off from the lower South. Finally, Brigadier Generals George Crook and William W. Averell would move against the Shenandoah Valley from the west, while Major General Franz Sigel moved south to clear the Shenandoah Valley and seize the railheads of Staunton and Lynchburg. To meet Grant, Lee had 60,000 men, supported by another 30,000 men under General Pierre G. T. Beauregard in the vicinity of Richmond and Petersburg.

The Overland Campaign began on May 4, 1864, when the Army of the Potomac crossed the Rapidan River in an effort to turn the right flank of the Army of Northern Virginia. The next day the two armies fought in the densely wooded area known as the Wilderness. Lee attacked Grant's left flank, using the woods and terrain to partially nullify the Union numerical advantage. The ensuing fighting was intense, and many wounded burned to death as brush fires engulfed parts of the battlefield. In the end, however, Lee outmaneuvered his opponent, inflicting 17,500 Union casualties for Confederate casualties estimated to number some 7,500. Lee, however, had failed to stop Grant, for unlike previous rebuffs by Lee, this time the Army of the Potomac continued south, slipping around Lee's flank in an effort to get between Richmond and the Army of Northern Virginia.

Meanwhile, on May 5 during the Bermuda Hundred Campaign (May 5–20, 1864), Butler's Army of the James landed at Bermuda Hundred, a neck of land north of City Point at the confluence of the James and Appomattox Rivers and only 15 miles south of Richmond. The way to the capital appeared open. Richmond and Petersburg were then virtually undefended, their garrisons then being only about 5,000 men. The inept Butler fumbled away this golden opportunity, however. That same day Beauregard, commanding the Confederate Department of North Carolina and Southern Virginia with 18,000 men, assumed direction of Confederate defenses at Petersburg and ordered Major General George E. Pickett to contain Butler. Pickett rushed men to Bermuda Hundred, and with Butler slow to move, the Confederates bottled up the Union troops there.

Following the Battle of the Wilderness, the Army of the Potomac continued its southeast movement toward Richmond. Grant again tried to outflank Lee's Army of Northern Virginia at the crossroads village of Spotsylvania Court House. Lee anticipated the move and got there first, his men quickly throwing up entrenchments. Bloody trench warfare occurred during the next two weeks (May 7–21). On May 10, Grant hurled three corps against the Confederate lines. That evening on a very narrow front known as the Mule Shoe salient in the center of the line, Colonel Emory Upton massed 12 regiments and, following an intense, concentrated artillery bombardment, broke through at this point but was unable to exploit the situation.

Upton's limited success persuaded Grant to try the same tactic with an entire corps—Major General Winfield Scott Hancock's II Corps—at the tip of the salient. Grant's inactivity while preparing for the attack led Lee to believe that Grant was preparing to withdraw, and Lee shifted artillery from the area of the Mule Shoe, where Hancock struck with his 20,000-man corps in a predawn assault on May 12. The Union troops enjoyed initial success, taking 4,000 prisoners and shattering Major General Edward Johnson's division of Lieutenant General Richard S. Ewell's II Corps, with Johnson being among the prisoners. A furious counterattack by Major General John B. Gordon's division of Ewell's corps sealed the gap and staved off disaster. With no reserves readily available to exploit the situation, however, the Union attack ran out of steam. Subsequent Union attacks were not coordinated, and Lee was able to restore his line.

Meanwhile, on May 11, Union major general Philip H. Sheridan's 10,000-man cavalry corps raided south. At Yellow Tavern, about six miles above Richmond, Sheridan encountered 4,500 Confederate cavalry led by Major General J. E. B. Stuart. Sheridan drove the Confederates from the field, and Stuart was mortally wounded, a major loss for the Confederacy. Union casualties totaled 625, while the Confederates lost about 1,000, including 300 prisoners.

OVERLAND CAMPAIGN, MAY – JUNE, 1864

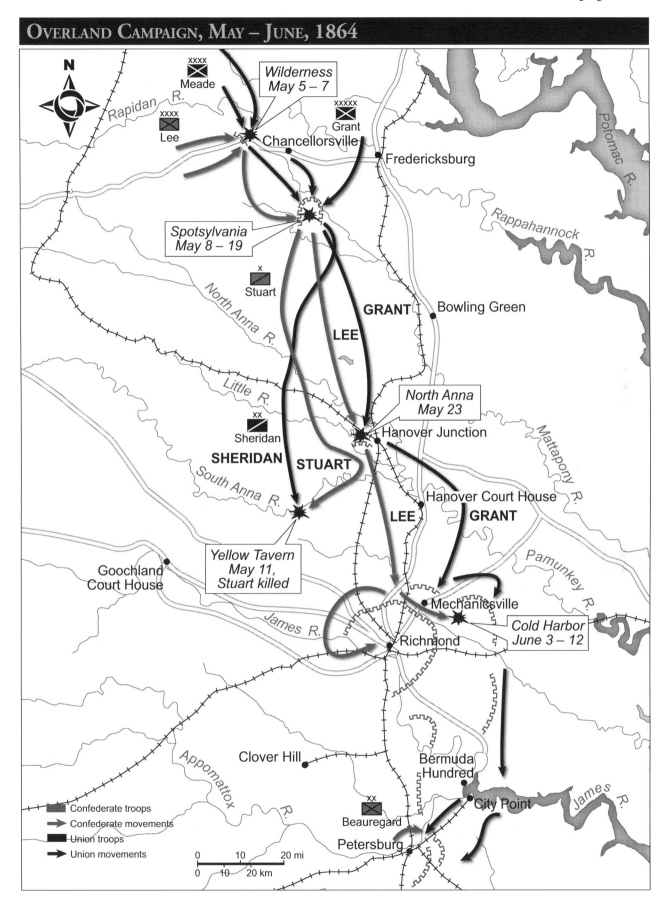

N

Rapidan R.

xxxx
Meade

xxxx
Grant

xxxx
Lee

Wilderness
May 5 – 7

Chancellorsville

Fredericksburg

Rappahannock R.

Potomac R.

Spotsylvania
May 8 – 19

x
Stuart

North Anna R.

GRANT

LEE

Bowling Green

Little R.

xx
Sheridan

North Anna
May 23

Hanover Junction

Mattapony R.

SHERIDAN   STUART

South Anna R.

Yellow Tavern
May 11,
Stuart killed

LEE   GRANT

Hanover Court House

Goochland
Court House

James R.

Mechanicsville

Pamunkey R.

Richmond

Cold Harbor
June 3 – 12

Appomattox R.

Clover Hill

Bermuda
Hundred

City Point

James R.

xx
Beauregard

Petersburg

■ Confederate troops
→ Confederate movements
■ Union troops
→ Union movements

0   10   20 mi
0   10   20 km

At Spotsylvania Court House, Lee withdrew to a newly prepared line, which Grant assaulted six days later on May 18, only to be repulsed. On May 21 following additional heavy fighting, Grant decamped, again attempting to outflank Lee's right, cutting it off from Richmond. In the Spotsylvania fighting, Union casualties totaled 14,267 men, while Lee lost more than 10,000.

Again, Lee anticipated Grant's move and established strong positions on the North Anna River on May 22, the day before Grant arrived. The ensuing Battle of the North Anna (May 23–26) was a series of small engagements, with Grant suffering 1,973 casualties and Lee perhaps 2,017.

On May 27, Grant again put the Army of the Potomac in motion, moving eastward. A delay during Grant's crossing of the Pamunkey River provided Lee with time to again place his Army of Northern Virginia between Richmond and the Union Army of the Potomac. On May 28, Union and Confederate cavalrymen again clashed in the Battle of Haw's Shop, with each side suffering about 300 casualties. While the Union army crossed the Pamunkey River without incident, Lee again moved faster than Grant expected, establishing a strong defensive position along Totopotomoy Creek. On May 29, Union forces dug in on the opposite bank of the Totopotomoy. Following cavalry engagements and minor infantry skirmishes during May 28–29, Grant ordered a general advance on May 30. Hancock's II Corps captured some entrenchments in the center of the Confederate lines but was unable to advance farther. Lee ordered Major General Jubal A. Early on the Confederate right to strike at Major General Gouverneur Warren's V corps probing the Confederate flank, but Major General Richard Anderson, ordered to assist Early, failed to arrive in time, and Early's attack was repulsed. The Battle of Totopotomoy Creek resulted in 731 Union casualties; the Confederates lost 1,159.

Once again, Grant ordered another flanking maneuver south, toward the town of Cold Harbor. Grant now had some 108,000 men; Lee, having been reinforced by 14,000 men drawn from the Shenandoah Valley and operations along the James River, now commanded 59,000. Lee was able to fortify and entrench at Cold Harbor, while Grant impatiently flung his army at the formidable Confederate position. The result was a stinging rebuff to Grant in one of the bloodiest battles of the war.

On June 3, Grant hurled three corps in a frontal assault against Lee. Within minutes, the Federals sustained some 7,000 casualties. Grant admitted that it was a major mistake. Casualty estimates for the entire Battle of Cold Harbor (May 31–June 12) vary greatly but are probably on the order of some 13,000 Union troops to only 4,600 Confederates.

Now preparing to send the Army of the Potomac across the James River, Grant next ordered Sheridan and two divisions of his Cavalry Corps westward into Louisa County to cut the Virginia Central Railroad and join with Union forces in the Shenandoah Valley, now commanded by Major General David Hunter, who had replaced Sigel. Grant planned for their combined forces to take the key Confederate rail center of Lynchburg, then join him at Richmond. Lee countered by sending his own cavalry commander, Major General Wade Hampton, and two cavalry divisions after Sheridan. Lee also dispatched Early's corps to Lynchburg to check Hunter.

During June 11–12, Sheridan and Hampton clashed in a confused battle at Trevilian Station. Sheridan enjoyed success on the first day, but the tables were turned on June 12 when the dismounted Confederate cavalrymen turned back several determined dismounted Union attacks. Sheridan withdrew after destroying about six miles of the Virginia Central Railroad. He never linked up with Hunter, who, although outnumbering Early, withdrew from Lynchburg.

Now, in a bold move that caught Lee by surprise, on the night of June 12–13 the Army of the Potomac secretly decamped from its trenches at Cold Harbor and, screened by cavalry, crossed the James River on a pontoon bridge more than 2,100 feet in length and moved against the lightly defended city of Petersburg, a vital transportation and supply center for Richmond. On June 15, Major General William F. Smith, commanding XVIII Corps of the Army of the James, failed to seize the initiative and let an incredible opportunity to take Petersburg slip away. Meanwhile, Beauregard's outnumbered forces bought Lee valuable time, repulsing a series of Union attacks on June 16–17. On June 18, Lee's army moved into prepared works at Petersburg, and Grant reluctantly opted for a siege. This long siege from June 13, 1864, until April 3, 1865, continued to sap Confederate strength.

The Overland Campaign was necessary in order for the Union to win the war. Despite reverses, most notably that of Cold Harbor, the nearly six-week-long campaign was a Union strategic success, with Grant now besieging Petersburg. The Overland Campaign was, however, the bloodiest in American history. The Union side suffered some 55,000 casualties (7,600 killed), while Confederate losses totaled some 32,600 (4,200 killed). Grant had been attacking, however, and Lee's losses were in fact higher in terms of forces engaged (more than 50 percent) than those for Grant (some 45 percent). And while Grant could make good his losses,

Lee simply could not. The Army of Northern Virginia never quite recovered from the hammering it had received.

SPENCER C. TUCKER

See also

Anderson, Richard Heron; Averell, William Woods; Banks, Nathaniel Prentice; Beauregard, Pierre Gustav Toutant; Bermuda Hundred Campaign; Butler, Benjamin Franklin; Cold Harbor, Battle of; Crook, George; Grant, Ulysses Simpson; Hampton, Wade; Hancock, Winfield Scott; Haw's Shop, Battle of; Hunter, David; Johnson, Edward; Lee, Robert Edward; Meade, George Gordon; North Anna River, Battle of the; Petersburg Campaign; Pickett, George Edward; Sheridan, Philip Henry; Sherman, William Tecumseh; Sigel, Franz; Spotsylvania Court House, Battle of; Stuart, James Ewell Brown; Totopotomoy Creek, Battle of; Trevilian Station, Battle of; Upton, Emory; Warren, Gouverneur Kemble; Wilderness, Battle of the; Yellow Tavern, Battle of

Further Reading

Grimsley, Mark. *And Keep Moving On: The Virginia Campaign, May–June 1864*. Lincoln: University of Nebraska Press, 2005.

Hess, Earl J. *Trench Warfare under Grant and Lee: Field Fortifications in the Overland Campaign*. Chapel Hill: University of North Carolina Press, 2007.

Overland Vicksburg Campaign

See Vicksburg Campaign, First

Ox Hill, Battle of

See Chantilly, Battle of

P

Pacific, Union Department of the

Federal military administrative department formed on January 1, 1861, and dissolved on June 27, 1865. The Union Department of the Pacific was headquartered at Los Angeles and encompassed the former Departments of Oregon and California. This area covered all of California, western New Mexico Territory (Arizona), Oregon, Washington, and Idaho. Commanders of the department included Brigadier General Albert S. Johnston (January–April 1861), Brigadier General Edwin V. Sumner (April–October 1861), Brigadier General George Wright (October 1861–July 1864), and Major General Irvin McDowell (July 1864–June 1865).

On July 27, 1862, the department was expanded when Utah and all of Nevada except for its southern tip came under its jurisdiction. On January 20, 1865, the newly formed Arizona Territory, which had formerly been part of the New Mexico Territory, came under the department's purview. The Department of the Pacific was replaced by the Military Division of the Pacific on June 27, 1865; it encompassed much but not all of the former department.

PAUL G. PIERPAOLI JR.

See also
Johnston, Albert Sidney; McDowell, Irvin; Sibley's New Mexico Campaign; Sumner, Edwin Vose; Wright, George

Further Reading
Eicher, John H., and David J. Eicher. *Civil War High Commands.* Stanford, CA: Stanford University Press, 2001.

Paducah, Battle of
Event Date: March 25, 1864

Engagement during Major General Nathan Bedford Forrest's 1864 raid of western Tennessee and Kentucky. In late March 1864, Forrest, on a third raid through western Tennessee, advanced with 2,800 men on Paducah, Kentucky, an important federal logistics center on the Ohio River. Accompanying him was Brigadier General Abraham Buford with his 2nd Division. Forrest hoped to be able to seize the Union depot's supplies and keep the Union forces in the area on the defensive. He also wanted to secure additional recruits, flush out guerrilla bands, and recover any deserters in the area. Forrest's men arrived at Paducah in the early afternoon on March 25, having covered nearly 100 miles in just 50 hours.

Colonel Stephen G. Hicks commanded the 665-man Union garrison at Paducah, consisting of elements of the 16th Kentucky Cavalry, the 1st Kentucky Heavy Artillery (Colored), and the 127th Illinois Infantry. Also at his disposal were the Union gunboats *Peosta* and *Paw Paw*. Around noon, Hicks's scouts along the Mayfield Road encountered Forrest's advance guard and immediately withdrew, with the Confederates close behind. Hicks now abandoned Paducah and moved the bulk of his men into Fort Anderson, a strong earthwork at the western end of the town. By 2:00 p.m., Forrest had the fort surrounded except for the side protected by the river. For an hour a heated exchange took place, during which time Colonel Albert P. Thompson, a native of Paducah, led the Confederate 3rd and 7th Kentucky Regiments in an unauthorized and ill-fated attack against the fort. Thompson was killed in the attack. Struck by a shell from one of the Union gunboats, he died within sight of his own house.

When Hicks refused Forrest's demand that he surrender Fort Anderson, Forrest advanced into Paducah and proceeded to pillage the town. The Confederates collected large amounts of clothing and 400 horses and mules as well as saddles, medicines, and other supplies. They also burned the steamer *Dacotah* at the dock, all the cotton bales on the landing, the quartermaster depot, and the railroad depot. In addition, Forrest left Paducah with 50 prisoners.

While Forrest plundered Paducah, his sharpshooters took possession of the nearby houses and exchanged shots with the Federals in Fort Anderson. This skirmishing lasted until 11:30 p.m., when the guns of the fort and the gunboats *Peosta* and *Paw Paw* bombarded the town. Hicks had warned the townspeople that Paducah might be attacked should the Confederates ever take possession. After holding Paducah for almost 10 hours, Forrest withdrew. The Confederate sharpshooters kept the Federals pinned within Fort Anderson until the bulk of the command had withdrawn south toward Mayfield.

Casualties on both sides were light. Hicks reported 14 killed and 46 wounded. Forrest reported 10 killed and 40 wounded. Newspaper reports that Forrest had missed 140 army horses hidden in a foundry caused Buford to return to Paducah on April 14. Again Hicks withdrew to Fort Anderson. After securing the horses and their equipment, Buford then withdrew to join Forrest.

JOSHUA ADAM CAMPER

See also
Buford, Abraham; Forrest, Nathan Bedford; Kentucky; Tennessee

Further Reading
Brown, Kent Masterson. *The Civil War in Kentucky: Battle for the Bluegrass*. Mason City, IA: Savas, 2000.
Harrison, Lowell H. *The Civil War in Kentucky*. Lexington: University Press of Kentucky, 1975.
Maness, Lonnie. *An Untutored Genius: The Military Career of General Nathan Bedford Forrest*. Mississippi: Guild Bindery, 1990.

Page, Charles Anderson
Birth Date: 1838
Death Date: 1873

Noted Civil War correspondent. Charles Anderson Page was born in 1838 in Lee County, Illinois. A graduate of Cornell College (Iowa) and a staunch Republican, Page worked for newspapers in Iowa and in Mount Vernon, Illinois, before going to Washington, D.C., in March 1861 to witness the inauguration of President Abraham Lincoln. Once there, Page obtained a clerk's position in the Auditor's Office of the Department of the Treasury. Mesmerized by the fighting that began in April 1861, he convinced Adams Sherman Hill, the assistant bureau chief for the *New York Tribune* in Washington, to hire him as a war correspondent.

Granted a leave of absence from his government job, Page first reported on the Battle of Gaines' Mill (June 27, 1862). He was a natural as a wartime journalist and soon came to the attention of Horace Greeley, the *Tribune*'s publisher. Pleased with Page's work, Greeley insisted that his stories carry a byline, which was a rare honor.

Page subsequently covered the other battles of the Seven Days' Campaign (June 25–July 1, 1862) as well as the closing weeks of the Peninsula Campaign (March–July 1862). He next traveled with Major General John Pope's army during the Second Bull Run Campaign (August 26–September 1, 1862). When Pope banned journalists from accompanying him, he made sure that Page was given a temporary assignment as a hospital attendant so he could report on the fighting. After the Second Battle of Bull Run (August 29–30, 1862), Page hastily traveled to the *Tribune*'s New York office, writing the coverage of the battle en route. Page's story was the first to run in any major newspaper.

Page shadowed the Army of the Potomac for the remainder of the war while continuing to perform his duties for the Treasury Department. He covered the Battle of the Wilderness (May 5–7, 1864) as well as the protracted Petersburg Campaign (June 15, 1864–April 3, 1865).

Because of Page's staunch defense of the Lincoln administration, in the late spring of 1865 President Andrew Johnson appointed Page U.S. consul to Switzerland. After he resigned that appointment, Page founded the Anglo-Swiss Company, which initially manufactured condensed milk. That enterprise survives to the present day as the Nestlé Company. Page died in 1873 in London while on a business trip.

PAUL G. PIERPAOLI JR.

See also
Greeley, Horace; Journalism; *New York Tribune;* War Correspondents

Further Reading
Tuchinsky, Adam. *Horace Greeley's* New York Tribune: *Civil War Era Socialism and the Crisis of Free Labor*. Ithaca, NY: Cornell University Press, 2009.
Williams, Robert C. *Horace Greeley: Champion of American Freedom*. New York: New York University Press, 2006.

Page, Richard Lucian

Birth Date: December 20, 1807
Death Date: August 9, 1901

Confederate officer. Born in Clarke City, Virginia, on December 20, 1807, Richard Lucian Page was a first cousin of Confederate general Robert E. Lee, whom Page greatly resembled in appearance, and of Confederate Navy captain Sidney S. Lee. Page received a midshipman's warrant in the U.S. Navy on March 1, 1824. Promoted to passed midshipman on February 20, 1830, he was advanced to lieutenant on March 26, 1834, and to commander on September 14, 1855.

On the secession of Virginia, Page had charge of naval recruitment at Norfolk. He attempted to resign his commission but was instead dismissed by the Abraham Lincoln administration on April 18, 1861. Appointed first to the Provisional Navy of Virginia as naval aide to the governor, Page supervised construction of naval defenses on the James and Nansemond Rivers.

Page was commissioned a commander in the Confederate Navy on June 10, 1861, with date of rank subsequently backdated to March 26, 1861. Assigned first to the Norfolk (Gosport) Navy Yard as an ordnance officer, Page subsequently commanded the Savannah Naval Station (1861–1862), participating in the Battle of Port Royal Sound (November 5–7, 1861) in South Carolina. He was then inspector of ordnance at the Norfolk Navy Yard during 1862. Secondary sources indicate that Page was promoted to captain sometime in 1862, but there is no indication of this in official records.

Page was assigned to a Confederate Navy ordnance facility at Charlotte, North Carolina (1862–1863). During April and May 1863, he commanded Confederate forces in the Savannah River. He then commanded the Charlotte Naval Station (1863–1864) in North Carolina.

Because of his artillery training and with the Confederate Navy having too many officers for available assignments at this point in the war, Page was detailed to the army. Commissioned a brigadier general in the Provisional Army of the Confederate States on March 1, 1864, he assumed command of the outer defenses of Mobile Bay, centered on Fort Morgan, and supervised the construction or reinforcement of forts to cover the channel into the bay and the approaches to Mobile itself. Following the defeat of Confederate naval forces in the Battle of Mobile Bay (August 5, 1864), despite being cut off and bombarded by superior Union forces, Page rejected calls from his old friend and commander of the West Gulf Blockading Squadron Rear Admiral David G. Farragut to surrender Fort Morgan unconditionally in order to spare lives. Page replied, "I am prepared to sacrifice life, and will only surrender when I have no means of defense." Page kept that pledge. Only after two weeks of incessant Union bombardment did he write to Farragut on August 23, stating that "The further sacrifice of life being unnecessary, my sick and wounded suffering and exposed, humanity demands that I ask for terms of capitulation." Controversy surrounds the surrender, as some military stores in the fort were reportedly destroyed by the Confederates after the surrender, and Page refused to hand over his sword, claiming that he had none. Page was held prisoner at Fort Delaware until July 24, 1865.

Granted parole, Page settled in Richmond, Virginia. From 1875 to 1883, he was the city's superintendent of schools. Page died in Blue Ridge Summit, Pennsylvania, on August 9, 1901.

SPENCER C. TUCKER

See also

Carter, Samuel Powhatan; Farragut, David Glasgow; Fort Delaware Prison, Delaware; Lincoln, Abraham; Lockwood, Henry Hayes; Mobile Bay, Battle of; Port Royal Sound, Battle of; West Gulf Blockading Squadron

Further Reading

Callahan, Edward W., ed. *List of Officers of the Navy of the United States and of the Marine Corps from 1775 to 1900.* 1901; reprint, New York: Haskell House Publishers, 1969.

Friend, Jack. *West Wind, Flood Tide: The Battle of Mobile Bay.* Annapolis, MD: Naval Institute Press, 2004.

Register of Officers of the Confederate States Navy, 1861–1865: As Compiled and Revised by the Office of Naval Records and Library, United States Navy Department 1931, from All Available Data. With a new introduction by John M. Carroll. Mattituck, NY: J. M. Carroll, 1981. [Originally published by the Naval Record and Library, U.S. Navy Department, in 1898 and revised in 1931.]

Thompson, Kenneth E. *Civil War Commodores and Admirals: A Biographical Directory of All Eighty-Eight Union and Confederate Navy Officers Who Attained Commissioned Flag Rank during the War.* Portland, ME: Thompson Group, 2001.

U.S. Navy Department. *Official Records of the Union and Confederate Navies in the War of the Rebellion,* Series 1, Vol. 21. Washington, DC: U.S. Government Printing Office, 1906.

Paine, Charles Jackson

Birth Date: August 26, 1833
Death Date: August 12, 1916

Union officer. Charles Jackson Paine was born in Boston, Massachusetts, on August 26, 1833, to an influential and wealthy family. He graduated from Harvard University in 1853, studied law, was admitted to the bar in 1856, and practiced law in Boston until 1861. During the early autumn of 1861, he recruited a company for the 22nd Massachusetts Infantry Regiment, which was dispatched to Washington, D.C., during the winter of 1861–1862 to help man the capital's defenses. He initially served as a captain and was promoted to major, 30th Massachusetts, on January 16, 1862. In March 1862 Paine was sent south. He was promoted to colonel on October 23, 1862, and given command of the 2nd Louisiana Volunteer Infantry.

Paine saw action during the Siege of Port Hudson (March 14–July 8, 1863), and on November 7, 1863, he was selected to command a brigade but resigned that appointment to become a staff officer for Major General Benjamin F. Butler. Paine was advanced to brigadier general of volunteers on July 4, 1864. He saw action with the Army of the James at the Second Battle of Drewry's Bluff (May 16, 1864) and the Battle of New Market Heights (September 24, 1864) and in the Fort Fisher Campaign (December 13, 1864–January 15, 1865). Paine finished the war leading an African American division under Major General Alfred Terry's X Corps in North Carolina. Brevetted major general of volunteers on January 15, 1865, Paine mustered out on January 15, 1866.

After the war, Paine became a railroad executive. He was also a skilled yachtsman and participated in numerous America's Cup competitions. Paine died on August 12, 1916, in Weston, Massachusetts.

PAUL G. PIERPAOLI JR.

See also

Butler, Benjamin Franklin; Drewry's Bluff, Second Battle of; Fort Fisher Campaign; New Market Heights, Battle of; Port Hudson, Louisiana, Siege of

Further Reading

Butler, Benjamin F. *Autobiography and Personal Reminiscences of Major-General Benj. F. Butler: A Review of His Legal, Political, and Military Career.* Boston: A. M. Thayer, 1892.

Warner, Ezra J. *Generals in Blue: Lives of the Union Commanders.* Baton Rouge: Louisiana State University Press, 2006.

Paine, Halbert Eleazer
Birth Date: February 3, 1826
Death Date: April 14, 1905

Union officer. Halbert Eleazer Paine was born on February 3, 1826, in Chardon, Ohio. He graduated from Western Reserve College in 1845 and subsequently studied law and commenced a practice in Cleveland in 1848. In 1857 he

relocated to Milwaukee, where he practiced law until the outbreak of the Civil War.

On July 2, 1861, Paine became colonel of the 4th Wisconsin Cavalry Regiment. Until February 1862, the outfit was tasked with protecting the railroads in Maryland. Paine's regiment was then sent to join the Union operations against New Orleans that resulted in its capture. Paine also saw action at the Battle of Baton Rouge (August 5, 1862), after which he refused a direct order to burn the city.

Paine took command of the 2nd Brigade, 3rd Division, XIX Corps, on January 3, 1863. On April 9 he was advanced to brigadier general and saw action during the Siege of Port Hudson (May 21–July 9, 1863). During an assault on the Port Hudson works, he was severely wounded and lost a leg to amputation. After months of convalescence, he took part in the defense of Washington, D.C., during Lieutenant Jubal A. Early's raid on the capital (June 28–July 21, 1864). Later that summer, Paine was given command of the District of Illinois; on March 13, 1865, he was brevetted major general.

After the war, Paine served in the U.S. House of Representatives as a moderate Radical Republican (1865–1871). He returned to the practice of law in Washington, D.C., in 1871 and from 1878 to 1880 served as the U.S. commissioner of patents. Paine died on April 14, 1905, in Washington, D.C.

PAUL G. PIERPAOLI JR.

See also

Baton Rouge, Battle of; Early's Raid on Washington, D.C.; New Orleans Campaign; Port Hudson, Louisiana, Siege of

Further Reading

Paine, Halbert Eleazer. *A Wisconsin Yankee in Confederate Bayou Country: The Civil War Reminiscences of a Union General.* Edited by Samuel C. Hyde Jr. Baton Rouge: Louisiana State University Press, 2009.

Warner, Ezra J. *Generals in Blue: Lives of the Union Commanders.* Baton Rouge: Louisiana State University Press, 2006.

Paine, Lewis
See Powell, Lewis Thornton

Palmer, Innis Newton
Birth Date: March 30, 1824
Death Date: September 10, 1900

Union officer. Innis Newton Palmer was born on March 30, 1824, in Buffalo, New York. He graduated from the U.S.

Military Academy, West Point, in the class of 1846 and was assigned to the Mounted Rifles, going directly from West Point to Mexico to participate in the Mexican-American War (1846–1848).

During that conflict, Palmer saw action during the Siege of Veracruz and the Battles of Cerro Gordo, Contreras, Churubusco, and Chapultepec as well as the capture of Mexico City. He was brevetted first lieutenant for Contreras and Churubusco and captain for Chapultepec, where he was severely wounded. Promoted to first lieutenant in 1853, he was appointed a captain in the new elite 2nd Cavalry Regiment in March 1855. Palmer served in various frontier posts in Texas until that state seceded in 1861.

When the Civil War began, Palmer was promoted to major in April 1861. He commanded a battalion of regular U.S. Army cavalry at the First Battle of Bull Run (July 21, 1861). Brevetted lieutenant colonel in the regular army, Palmer was appointed a brigadier general, U.S. Volunteers, on September 23, 1861. During the Peninsula Campaign (March–July 1862), he commanded a brigade in IV Corps, Army of the Potomac, at the Siege of Yorktown (April 5–May 3, 1862) and in the Battles of Williamsburg (May 5, 1862), Seven Pines (May 31–June 1, 1862), White Oak Swamp (June 30, 1862), and Malvern Hill (July 1, 1862).

Following the Peninsula Campaign, Palmer supervised the formation and initial training of regiments of volunteers from New Jersey and Delaware at a camp in Philadelphia. From December 1862 until the end of the war, he headed various commands in North Carolina, including 1st Division, XVIII Corps; the District of Pamlico; and the New Bern defenses. He was brevetted brigadier general in the regular service and major general of volunteers in March 1865. Palmer was instrumental in maintaining the flow of supplies during the Carolinas Campaign when his division defeated a Confederate offensive near Kinston, North Carolina.

Palmer remained in the army after the war as a lieutenant colonel. He was promoted to colonel and commander of the 2nd U.S. Cavalry in 1868 and spent the remainder of his career in various frontier posts in Nebraska and the Wyoming territory. He retired in March 1879 and died on September 10, 1900, in Chevy Chase, Maryland.

JASON N. PALMER

See also
Bull Run, First Battle of; Casey, Silas; Malvern Hill, Battle of; Peninsula Campaign; Seven Pines, Battle of; Sherman's March through the Carolinas; White Oak Swamp, Battle of; Williamsburg, Battle of; Yorktown, Virginia, Siege of

Further Reading
Eicher, John H., and David J. Eicher. *Civil War High Commands.* Stanford, CA: Stanford University Press, 2001.
Sears, Stephen W. *To the Gates of Richmond: The Peninsula Campaign.* New York: Ticknor and Fields, 1992.

Palmer, James Shedden
Birth Date: October 13, 1810
Death Date: December 7, 1867

Union naval officer. Born in Elizabethtown, New Jersey, on October 13, 1810, James Shedden Palmer secured a midshipman's warrant on January 1, 1825. He received promotion to passed midshipman on June 4, 1831, and to lieutenant on December 17, 1836. Following the findings of the Naval Efficiency Board established to cull deadwood from serving officers in the navy, on September 13, 1855, Palmer was placed on the reserve list. Following an appeal, Palmer was restored to the active list in 1857, with promotion to commander backdated to September 14, 1855.

When the Civil War began, Palmer was commanding the screw sloop *Iroquois* in the Mediterranean Squadron. Ordered home, on September 1, 1861, he was assigned the mission of tracking down and destroying the Confederate commerce raider *Sumter,* which had escaped from New Orleans and was preying on Northern merchant shipping. Palmer located the *Sumter* at St. Pierre, Martinique, but on the night of November 23 the raider escaped the 15-mile-wide harbor without detection. Palmer was much criticized in the Northern press for this, and Secretary of the Navy Gideon Welles ordered him relieved of command on December 14. Following exoneration by a court of inquiry, Palmer resumed command of the *Iroquois* on May 3.

With the *Iroquois* having previously been assigned to the West Gulf Blockading Squadron, Palmer continued in that squadron for the remainder of the war. On May 7, squadron commander Flag Officer David G. Farragut ordered Commander Palmer to secure both Baton Rouge, Louisiana, and Natchez, Mississippi. Arriving in his ship off the Louisiana state capital that same evening, Palmer took the surrender of Baton Rouge the next day and that of Natchez on May 13. He then took part in operations against Vicksburg.

Promoted to captain on July 16, 1862, and to commodore on February 7, 1863, Palmer assumed command of the remainder of the squadron off the mouth of the Mississippi when Farragut initiated operations to secure Mobile Bay.

When Farragut requested to be relieved of command of the squadron, Palmer commanded it from November 17, 1864, to February 23, 1865, when he was relieved by Acting Rear Admiral Henry K. Thatcher. Palmer remained with the West Gulf Blockading Squadron until May 1865, when he was transferred to Washington, D.C.

Palmer served on various boards until November 1865 and was promoted to rear admiral on July 25, 1865. In November 1867 he was named commander of the reconstituted West Indies Squadron, which became the North Atlantic Squadron that same year. He was holding that command when he died of yellow fever at St. Thomas in the Danish West Indies (now the U.S. Virgin Islands) on December 7, 1867.

SPENCER C. TUCKER

See also
Farragut, David Glasgow; *Sumter*, CSS; Thatcher, Henry Knox; Welles, Gideon; West Gulf Blockading Squadron

Further Reading
Callahan, Edward W., ed. *List of Officers of the Navy of the United States and of the Marine Corps from 1775 to 1900.* 1901; reprint, New York: Haskell House Publishers, 1969.
Thompson, Kenneth E. *Civil War Commodores and Admirals: A Biographical Directory of All Eighty-Eight Union and Confederate Navy Officers Who Attained Commissioned Flag Rank during the War.* Portland, ME: Thompson Group, 2001.
Tucker, Spencer C. *Blue and Gray Navies: The Civil War Afloat.* Annapolis, MD: Naval Institute Press, 2006.
U.S. Navy Department. *Official Records of the Union and Confederate Navies in the War of the Rebellion,* Series 1, Vol. 1. Washington, DC: U.S. Government Printing Office, 1896.

Palmer, John McAuley
Birth Date: September 13, 1817
Death Date: September 25, 1900

Union officer. Born in Eagle Creek, Kentucky, on September 13, 1817, John McAuley Palmer was raised in Illinois, where he later became an attorney. He was elected to the Illinois Senate in 1847. An ardent antislavery Unionist, Palmer served as a Republican presidential elector in 1860, and in 1861 he attended the Washington Peace Conference.

In May 1861, Palmer was commissioned colonel of the 14th Illinois Infantry Regiment. Promoted to brigadier general of volunteers on December 20, 1861, he commanded a division in the Battle of Island No. 10 (April 7, 1862). Then ordered to Mississippi, on May 8 he held a Union position near Farmington against a Confederate attack. After Union forces captured Corinth on May 30, 1862, Palmer returned to Illinois on medical leave, and there he organized the 122nd Illinois Infantry Regiment.

On August 1, Palmer returned to duty as commander of a division in the Army of the Mississippi. During the autumn of 1862, he took command of a division in the Army of the Cumberland and fought effectively in Tennessee at the Battle of Stones River (December 31, 1862–January 2, 1863), earning promotion to major general of volunteers on January 9, 1863. Palmer then participated in the Battle of Chickamauga (September 19–20, 1863). In October he took command of XIV Corps, which he led during the Chattanooga Campaign (October–November 1863) and the Atlanta Campaign (May 5–September 2, 1864). During the siege of Atlanta, Major General William T. Sherman placed Palmer temporarily under the authority of Major General John M. Schofield, nominally a junior officer. Believing that he had been slighted, Palmer asked for a transfer, and on August 7, 1864, he was reassigned to command the Department of Kentucky. He resigned from military service on September 1, 1866.

Palmer practiced law until 1869, when he became governor of Illinois. He served until 1873. Palmer switched to the Democratic Party in 1888 but failed to win another term as governor. In 1891 he was elected to the U.S. Senate, serving until 1897. Palmer died on September 25, 1900, in Springfield, Illinois.

JIM PIECUCH AND JASON LUTZ

See also
Atlanta Campaign; Chattanooga Campaign; Chickamauga, Battle of; Island No. 10, Battle of; Stones River, Battle of; Washington Peace Conference

Further Reading
Fitch, John. *Annals of the Army of the Cumberland: 1864 Edition.* Mechanicsburg, PA: Stackpole, 2003.
Warner, Ezra J. *Generals in Blue: Lives of the Union Commanders.* Baton Rouge: Louisiana State University Press, 2006.

Palmer, Joseph Benjamin
Birth Date: November 1, 1825
Death Date: November 4, 1890

Confederate officer. Born on November 1, 1825, in Rutherford County, Tennessee, Joseph Benjamin Palmer was educated at Union University and was admitted to the state bar in 1848. He practiced law in Murfreesboro and served in the Tennessee General Assembly (1849–1853). From 1855 until 1859, he was mayor of Murfreesboro.

When the Civil War began, Palmer organized a company for service in the 18th Tennessee Infantry Regiment and was elected regimental colonel. After service in central Kentucky, Palmer's regiment was eventually detailed to help defend Fort Donelson. When Fort Donelson fell to Union forces on February 16, 1862, Palmer and most of his men were taken prisoner; he was exchanged on August 15, 1862. In December 1862, Palmer assumed temporary command of a brigade. At the Battle of Stones River (December 31, 1862–January 2, 1863), he commanded the 2nd Brigade under Major General John C. Breckinridge and was severely wounded.

Following an extended convalescence, in the late summer of 1863 Palmer again held regimental command and saw action at the Battle of Chickamauga (September 19–20, 1863), where he was again seriously wounded. He did not return to the battlefield until the spring of 1864, when he commanded a brigade during the Atlanta Campaign (May 5–September 2, 1864). He was wounded a third time in the Battle of Jonesboro (August 31–September 1, 1864). On November 14, 1864, Palmer was advanced to brigadier general.

Palmer then commanded a brigade during General John B. Hood's invasion of Tennessee. Although Palmer's command was detached and missed the fighting at Franklin (November 30) and Nashville (December 15–16), it saw action around Murfreesboro in December 1864 before fighting a rearguard action as the Confederates withdrew into Alabama. Palmer's brigade next fought in North Carolina as part of the badly depleted Army of Tennessee and fought in the Battle of Bentonville (March 19–21, 1865). Palmer surrendered with General Joseph Johnston's forces at Greensboro in April.

After the war, Palmer resumed his law practice and played a key role in the Southern Historical Society. He died in Murfreesboro on November 4, 1890.

PAUL G. PIERPAOLI JR.

See also

Atlanta Campaign; Bentonville, Battle of; Chickamauga, Battle of; Fort Donelson, Battle of; Jonesboro, Battle of; Stones River, Battle of

Further Reading

Eicher, John H., and David J. Eicher. *Civil War High Commands.* Stanford, CA: Stanford University Press, 2001.

Warner, Ezra J. *Generals in Gray: Lives of the Confederate Commanders.* Baton Rouge: Louisiana State University Press, 2006.

Palmer, William Jackson
Birth Date: September 17, 1836
Death Date: March 13, 1909

Union officer. William Jackson Palmer was born on September 17, 1836, in Kent County, Delaware. In 1841 the family moved to Philadelphia, Pennsylvania, where Palmer thrived through connections in its Quaker community. In 1857 J. Edgar Thomson, president of the Pennsylvania Railroad, hired Palmer as an assistant. Palmer also organized an abolitionist lecture series during 1859 and became a Republican in 1860. At the Civil War's outset, he assisted the federal government in coordinating rail traffic between Washington, D.C., and Annapolis, Maryland. In September 1861 Palmer, commissioned a captain, recruited and led the elite Anderson Cavalry Company, or Anderson Troop, in the Department of the Ohio. Ten months later Palmer organized the 15th Pennsylvania Cavalry Regiment for the Army of the Potomac, becoming its colonel. At the Battle of Antietam (September 17, 1862), Palmer was captured behind enemy lines leading a reconnaissance detachment. He was exchanged in January 1863.

In February 1863 Palmer returned to his regiment, now with the Army of the Cumberland, to a command in disarray after 500 of his troopers had mutinied during the Battle of Stones River (December 31, 1862–January 2, 1863). He promptly cashiered incompetent officers while winning back the men's trust to lead the regiment to an impressive record. Palmer and four others won the Medal of Honor for routing a much larger force on New Year's Day 1865 at the Battle of Red Hill in Alabama. Palmer was brevetted brigadier general (volunteers) in March 1865 prior to receiving a brigade command under Major General George F. Stoneman.

After the war Palmer returned to railroading, amassing a sizable fortune. He developed the Denver & Rio Grande Railroad and founded the city of Colorado Springs, Colorado, where he retired. Palmer was paralyzed in a horse riding accident in 1906 and died at his home on March 13, 1909.

THADDEUS M. ROMANSKY

See also

Antietam, Battle of; Stoneman, George, Jr.; Stones River, Battle of

Further Reading

Sears, Stephen W. *Landscape Turned Red: The Battle of Antietam.* New York: Oxford University Press, 1992.

Storey, Brit A. "William Jackson Palmer: A Biography." Unpublished PhD dissertation, University of Kentucky, 1968.

Meyer, Jack Allen. *William Glaze and the Palmetto Armory.* Columbia: South Carolina State Museum, 1982.

Palmerston, Lord

See Temple, Henry John

Palmetto Armory

Military manufacturing facility founded in April 1851 in Columbia, South Carolina. The genesis of the Palmetto Armory can be traced to the Palmetto Iron Works, which in April 1851 received a state contract to produce 2,000 pistols, 1,000 rifles, 6,000 muskets, and 2,000 swords. The contract was the result of a defense appropriations act that had allotted the sum of $300,000 to equip South Carolina's 15,000 militiamen with modern arms and munitions. When the ironworks received the lucrative contract, one of its owners, William Glaze, transformed it into an armory that manufactured only military items.

It took Glaze and his business partners nearly a year to complete the conversion to the Palmetto Armory, a task they accomplished by purchasing the necessary manufacturing equipment from Northern foundries and arms makers. For two years they produced nothing but small arms, modeled on U.S. Army designs. The company's biggest production item was the .69-caliber musket, of which it produced at least 5,000.

The Palmetto Armory gave South Carolina an important early edge in arms manufacturing as the United States moved toward civil war in the late 1850s. Once the Civil War began in 1861, the Palmetto Armory produced bullets, shells, cannon, and equipment used to make gunpowder; it made few firearms during the war years. Its cannon were deemed unsatisfactory for military use, but the company did repair small arms, which became a lucrative concern for the armory. In the winter of 1865 during Major William T. Sherman's March through the Carolinas (February–April 1865), Union troops laid waste to the armory. It reopened after the war and operated for many years thereafter.

PAUL G. PIERPAOLI JR.

See also

Sherman's March through the Carolinas; South Carolina

Further Reading

Edgar, Walter B. *South Carolina: A History.* Columbia: University of South Carolina Press, 1998.

Palmito Ranch, Battle of

Start Date: May 12, 1865
End Date: May 13, 1865

Last recorded battle of the Civil War. Texans were aware of General Robert E. Lee's April 9, 1865, surrender and President Abraham Lincoln's assassination on April 15, and there was a general understanding on both sides that nothing was to be gained from further fighting.

In early May 1865, Colonel Theodore H. Barrett, who was without combat experience and was the new commander of Union forces at Brazos Santiago on Brazos Island in the Gulf of Mexico, ordered his forces to attack Confederate forces at Palmito Ranch, near Fort Brown outside of Brownsville. Although the reasons for the attack remain obscure, speculation has it that Barrett sought a measure of military glory.

Pursuant to Barrett's orders, during a storm on the night of May 11, 1863, Lieutenant Colonel David Branson led 250 men of the 62nd U.S. Colored Infantry and 50 men of the 2nd Texas (U.S.) Cavalry (dismounted) from the island to the mainland toward Palmito Ranch. Although the Union troops crossed successfully, they failed to achieve surprise.

In the late afternoon of May 12, Captain William N. Robinson arrived and, with fewer than 100 Confederates, forced the Union troops back to White's Ranch. Here the fighting ended for the night as both sides called for reinforcements. Barrett sent 200 men of the 34th Indiana Infantry to strengthen the Union side, which on the morning of May 13 began advancing toward Palmito Ranch. Confederate colonel John S. "Rip" Ford arrived with additional cavalry and artillery, bringing Confederate strength up to some 300 men and six guns.

Ford attacked Barrett's force about 4:00 p.m. and, using his artillery to good effect, drove them back in some disorder toward the coast. Union forces reached Brazos Island at dusk covered by fire from a Union warship. Union losses in the battle were 4 killed, 12 wounded, and 101 captured; Confederate losses were fewer than 10 wounded. A few days later Union officers met with Confederates in Brownsville, who agreed to a truce. On May 26 at New Orleans, Lieutenant General Simon B. Buckner, acting on the orders of General E. Kirby Smith, officially surrendered all Confederate forces in the Trans-Mississippi theater.

TIMOTHY J. DEMY AND SPENCER C. TUCKER

See also
Brownsville, Texas; Texas

Further Reading
Oates, Stephen B., ed. *Rip Ford's Texas.* Austin: University of Texas Press, 1987.
Tucker, Philip T. *Palmito Ranch: The Last Battle of the Civil War.* Mechanicsburg, PA: Stackpole, 2001.

Parke, John Grubb
Birth Date: September 22, 1827
Death Date: December 16, 1900

Union officer. John Grubb Parke was born on September 22, 1827, in Chester County, Pennsylvania, but resided in Philadelphia by 1835. After a year at the University of Pennsylvania, he was accepted to the U.S. Military Academy, West Point. Graduating in 1849, Parke spent his pre–Civil War career surveying state boundaries, routes for the transcontinental railroad, and the northwestern U.S.-Canadian border, where, as a first lieutenant since 1856, he was stationed in 1861. On September 9 he became a captain of engineers, joining Union forces in the East in October.

Appointed brigadier general of volunteers on November 23, 1861, Parke commanded a brigade during Major General Ambrose E. Burnside's North Carolina Expedition (February–June 1862). Advanced to major general of volunteers on July 18, 1862, Parke became Burnside's chief of staff and participated in the Battle of South Mountain (September 14, 1862), the Battle of Antietam (September 17, 1862), and the First Battle of Fredericksburg (December 13, 1862). Parke followed IX Corps westward in 1863, taking command when it reinforced Major General Ulysses S. Grant in his Second Vicksburg Campaign (April 1–July 4, 1863), and served in the Siege of Jackson, Mississippi (July 10–16, 1863). Parke returned IX Corps to Burnside in time to defend Knoxville, Tennessee (November–December 1863) against a Confederate siege. IX Corps moved back east for Grant's Overland (Richmond) Campaign (May 4–June 12, 1864), with Parke assuming permanent command when Burnside was relieved after the Battle of the Crater (July 30, 1864).

Parke was acting commander of the Army of the Potomac in the absence of Major General George G. Meade during the Battle of Fort Stedman (March 25, 1865), where Parke defeated the last Confederate offensive in the East. Brevetted through major general in the regular service, he held the substantive grade of major. On January 15, 1866, he

mustered out of volunteer service and went to the Northwest to take up surveying duties.

Parke moved between command duties and surveying. He published two studies of public works projects in 1877 and 1882. He was promoted to colonel in 1884 and was named West Point superintendent in 1887, a post he held until his retirement in 1889. Parke died in Washington, D.C., on December 16, 1900.

RUSSELL S. PERKINS

See also
Antietam, Battle of; Antietam Campaign; Burnside, Ambrose Everett; Crater, Battle of the; Fort Stedman, Battle of; Fredericksburg, First Battle of; Jackson, Mississippi, Siege of; Knoxville Campaign; Meade, George Gordon; Overland Campaign; South Mountain, Battle of; Vicksburg Campaign, Second

Further Reading
Catton, Bruce. *The Army of the Potomac: A Stillness at Appomattox.* New York: Doubleday, 1953.
Warner, Ezra J. *Generals in Blue: Lives of the Union Commanders.* Baton Rouge: Louisiana State University Press, 2006.

Parker, Ely Samuel
Birth Date: 1828
Death Date: August 30, 1895

Union officer. Ely Samuel Parker, whose Seneca name was Do-ne-ho-ga-wa (Keeper of the Western Door), was born sometime in 1828 on the Tonawanda Reservation near Indian Falls, New York. At about age 10, he enrolled in a Baptist mission school on the reservation. He later attended Cayuga Academy.

After completing his studies in 1845, Parker traveled to Washington, D.C., with a delegation of Seneca leaders to defend their land claims. Upon his return he studied law, but he was denied admission to the New York bar because the state prohibited nonwhites from practicing. Parker then studied civil engineering at Rensselaer Polytechnic Institute, graduated in 1851, and worked as an engineer.

In 1855 the U.S. government hired Parker to be chief engineer of the Chesapeake and Albemarle Canal in Virginia. Two years later he was appointed to supervise a project in Galena, Illinois, where he befriended a tanner named Ulysses S. Grant.

At the start of the Civil War, Parker volunteered to raise an Iroquois regiment for New York, but the governor refused to allow Native Americans to serve. Parker next offered his services to the federal government and was

Seneca Native American Ely S. Parker, also known as Hasanoanda, served as military secretary to Union Army commander Lieutenant General Ulysses S. Grant and attained the rank of lieutenant colonel and a brevet rank of brigadier general. He continued to serve as Grant's aide after the war with the staff rank of colonel. When Grant became president in 1869, he appointed Parker as the first Native American commissioner of Indian Affairs. (National Archives)

again rejected. However, in May 1863 his friend Grant, now a Union major general, arranged for him to be commissioned a captain of volunteers. Parker served with Grant for the remainder of the war, eventually joining the general's staff as his military secretary and attaining the rank of lieutenant colonel. Parker was awarded brevets through brigadier general of volunteers (and later in the regular army as well). Joining the regular army, he continued to serve as Grant's aide after the war with the staff rank of colonel. When Grant became president in 1869, he appointed Parker commissioner of Indian affairs. Parker immediately set out to reform the agency.

Parker's efforts to protect the Plains tribes and to reform the Bureau of Indian Affairs aroused the anger of the so-called Indian Ring, a politically connected group that had profited from the agency's corruption and sought further gains from the opening of western lands. Eventually Parker's enemies accused him of corruption. The House

Appropriations Committee launched an inquiry that exonerated Parker of all charges; however, the ordeal and continual attacks from the press caused him to resign in August 1871.

Parker moved to New York City, where he became a successful businessman. He died on August 30, 1895, in Fairfield, Connecticut.

JIM PIECUCH

See also

Grant, Ulysses Simpson; Native Americans in the Civil War

Further Reading

Armstrong, William H. *Warrior in Two Camps: Ely S. Parker, Union General and Seneca Chief.* Syracuse, NY: Syracuse University Press, 1978.

Brown, Dee. *Bury My Heart at Wounded Knee: An Indian History of the American West.* New York: Holt, Rinehart and Winston, 1970.

Parker, Foxhall Alexander, Jr.
Birth Date: August 5, 1821
Death Date: June 10, 1879

Union naval officer. Born on August 5, 1821, in New York City, Foxhall Alexander Parker Jr. was the son of U.S. Navy captain Foxhall A. Parker Sr. and the brother of Confederate Navy officer William Harwar Parker. Parker Jr. received an appointment as a midshipman on March 11, 1837. He served under his father in the frigates *Constitution* and *Brandywine* and was advanced to passed midshipman on June 29, 1843. He was promoted to acting master on November 17, 1847, and to lieutenant on September 21, 1850.

With the beginning of the Civil War, Parker helped defend Alexandria, Virginia, following the First Battle of Bull Run (July 21, 1861). He was promoted to commander on July 16, 1862. He saw service with the South Atlantic Blockading Squadron off Alexandria, Virginia; commanded a naval battery ashore in the bombardment of Fort Sumter; and then commanded the Potomac Flotilla from December 31, 1863, to July 31, 1865.

Parker was promoted to captain on July 25, 1866, and to commodore on November 25, 1872. In 1872 while he was the chief of staff of the North Atlantic Fleet, Commodore Parker devised a signals code for the fleet. Appointed superintendent of the U.S. Naval Academy, Annapolis, in 1878, he was one of the founders of the U.S. Naval Institute, created to promote naval professionalism. Parker died at Annapolis on June 10, 1879. He wrote several books, including *The*

Battle of Mobile Bay, The Naval Howitzer Afloat, and *Fleet Tactics under Steam.*

SPENCER C. TUCKER

See also

Parker, William Harwar; South Atlantic Blockading Squadron

Further Reading

Parker, Foxhall A. *The Battle of Mobile Bay and the Capture of Forts Powell, Gaines and Morgan, by the Combined Sea and Land Forces of the U.S. under the Command of Rear-Admiral Farragut and Major-General Granger.* Boston: A. Williams, 1878.

U.S. Navy Department. *Official Records of the Union and Confederate Navies in the War of the Rebellion,* Series 1, Vol. 5. Washington, DC: U.S. Government Printing Office, 1897.

Parker, Joel
Birth Date: November 24, 1816
Death Date: January 2, 1888

Governor of New Jersey. Joel Parker was born on November 24, 1816, in Freehold, New Jersey. He graduated from the College of New Jersey (Princeton) in 1839 and was admitted to the bar in 1842. Parker began a successful legal practice in Freehold and soon became involved in state Democratic politics. Elected to the state legislature in 1847, he also served as a prosecuting attorney. At the same time he was active in the state militia, rising to the rank of major general by 1861. He somewhat hesitantly backed Senator Stephen A. Douglas for his party's presidential nomination in 1860 and was concerned when Republican Abraham Lincoln won the contest that autumn, believing that his inauguration would ultimately bring disunion.

Despite his general antipathy toward Lincoln's policies, Parker supported the president once war began in April 1861. Parker was a dark-horse candidate for the New Jersey governorship, winning his party's nomination in September 1862 on the fourth ballot. On the campaign trail, Parker lambasted what he alleged were the Lincoln administration's blatant violations of civil liberties. Parker went on to win the election and took office in January 1863. In his inaugural address, he excoriated Lincoln for the Emancipation Proclamation, which he believed was unconstitutional and would only promote more discord, and berated Lincoln for the suspension of habeas corpus.

While Parker was clearly at odds with many national policies, he was nevertheless a committed Unionist and disavowed the workings of the Copperheads (War Democrats), who by 1863 controlled the New Jersey legislature. He frequently spoke out on the need to continue the war until the Confederates had been defeated and launched several successful military recruiting drives. And when Confederate forces invaded neighboring Pennsylvania in the early summer of 1863, he promptly sent the New Jersey Militia to its aid. Parker lost his reelection bid in 1865 and left office in January 1866.

Parker thereafter remained vitally engaged in Democratic politics, practiced law, and enjoyed a second term as governor during 1872–1875. In 1875 he served as state attorney general. Five years later he became a state supreme court justice, a post he held until his death on January 2, 1888, in Philadelphia.

PAUL G. PIERPAOLI JR.

See also

Copperheads; Democratic Party; Emancipation Proclamation; Habeas Corpus, Writ of, U.S.; New Jersey

Further Reading

Siegel, Alan A. *Beneath the Starry Flag: New Jersey's Civil War Experience.* New Brunswick, NJ: Rutgers University Press, 2001.

Sobel, Robert, and John Raimo, eds. *Biographical Directory of the Governors of the United States, 1789–1978,* Vol. 3. Westport, CT: Meckler Books, 1978.

Parker, Theodore
Birth Date: August 24, 1810
Death Date: May 10, 1860

Noted Unitarian clergyman and representative of almost every antebellum social reform movement in the United States. Theodore Parker was born into a New England farming family in Lexington, Massachusetts, on August 24, 1810. In 1830 he was accepted at Harvard College and completed all requirements for the bachelor of arts degree, although the degree was not conferred because he was unable to pay the required graduation fee. Nevertheless, in 1834 he was accepted to the Harvard Divinity School, from which he graduated in 1836.

Parker's first pulpit was at the Spring Street Church in the Boston suburb of West Roxbury. By 1837, he emerged as one of Boston's most famous and controversial Unitarian ministers. Inspired by thinkers such as Ralph Waldo Emerson and George Ripley, Parker incorporated transcendentalism and radical German philosophy into his Unitarian beliefs. In attacking traditional tenets from his pulpit, Parker preached that the essential truths of religion and morality were based on instinct and intuition, not external law such as the Bible or the institutional authority of church. His beliefs became so controversial that in 1845 a number of Boston gentlemen secured sufficient funds to establish the Twenty-eight Congregational Society. It became his home until 1859, a year before his death.

During the Age of Reform in American history, Parker commented on and immersed himself in seemingly every reform movement possible. He founded and edited the *Massachusetts Quarterly Review* (1847), crusaded against capital punishment, and supported prison reform, women's rights, and temperance. He also joined fellow Bostonian Dorothea Dix in her efforts to improve conditions for the mentally challenged. Parker was a devoted disciple of Brook Farm and the transcendentalists. His most notable contribution was the leadership role he assumed in the New England anti-slavery movement.

Parker's strong opposition to slavery led to his outspoken criticisms of the Mexican-American War (1846–1848). Although he was not a pacifist or Garrisonian nonresistant, he signed the Peace Pledge of Elihu Burritt, founder of the League of Universal Brotherhood and creator of the Olive Leaf Mission.

At the conclusion of the Mexican-American War, Parker expressed his regret that slavery would continue its westward path. By the 1850s, his commitment to nonviolence and his militant opposition to slavery proved incompatible. He eventually gave money to John Brown and was involved in the conspiracy that resulted in the raid on Harpers Ferry in 1859. A staunch abolitionist, Parker believed that ending slavery took precedence over his peace principles. Parker died in Florence, Italy, on May 10, 1860, while touring Europe, despite a prolonged illness.

CHARLES F. HOWLETT

See also
Abolitionism and the Civil War; Brown, John; Emerson, Ralph Waldo; Garrison, William Lloyd; Harpers Ferry, Virginia, John Brown's Raid on; Slavery; Thoreau, Henry David

Further Reading
Albrecht, Robert. *Theodore Parker.* New York: Twayne, 1971.
Commager, Henry Steele. *Theodore Parker.* Boston: Little, Brown, 1936.
Cook, Blanche, Charles Chatfield, and Sandi Cooper, eds. *Sermons on War by Theodore Parker.* New York: Garland, 1971.
Grodzins, Dean. *America's Heretic: Theodore Parker and Transcendentalism.* Chapel Hill: University of North Carolina Press, 2002.
Wright, Conrad, ed. *Three Prophets of Religious Liberalism: Channing, Emerson, Parker.* Boston: Unitarian Universalist Association, 1986.

Parker, William Harwar
Birth Date: October 8, 1826
Death Date: December 30, 1896

Confederate naval officer. Born in New York City on October 8, 1826, the son of U.S. Navy captain Foxhall A. Parker Sr., William Harwar Parker received a midshipman's warrant in the U.S. Navy on October 19, 1841. During 1842–1845 he saw service in the Mediterranean, the South Atlantic, the West Indies, and the Gulf of Mexico. During the Mexican-American War (1846–1848), Parker took part in the landing at Veracruz and in the expedition against Tabasco. After the war he was briefly at the U.S. Naval Academy, Annapolis, where he passed his examinations and was declared a passed midshipman in July 1848.

Returning to sea, from 1848 to 1850 Parker was in the sloop *Yorktown* on antislavery patrol off the west coast of Africa. During 1851 he was assigned to the U.S. Coast Survey. Following service in the screw sloop *Princeton* and in the sloop *Cyane* in the West Indies and then off the coast of New England, from 1853 to 1857 he was an instructor of navigation and astronomy at the Naval Academy. He was promoted to lieutenant on September 14, 1855. Parker then served aboard the screw frigate *Merrimack* in the South Atlantic and the Pacific. During this voyage Parker wrote a gunnery manual, *Naval Light Artillery.*

With the start of the Civil War, his brother Foxhall A. Parker Jr., another U.S. Navy officer, remained loyal to the Union, but William Parker espoused the Confederate cause and resigned his commission on April 20, 1861. He joined first the Provisional Navy of Virginia and then in June the Confederate Navy. Assigned command of the gunboat *Beaufort,* Lieutenant Parker took part in the battles at Roanoke Island and Elizabeth City, North Carolina, in February 1862 and, with his ship serving as tender to CSS *Virginia,* in the Battles of Hampton Roads (March 8–9, 1862). In May 1862, Parker served in the Confederate shore batteries during the First Battle of Drewry's Bluff on the James River below Richmond.

Following several months ashore, Parker was assigned to Charleston, South Carolina, where he became the executive officer of the Confederate ironclad *Palmetto State* and took part in the attack on the Union blockading warships on January 31, 1863. In October he became the commandant of the Confederate Naval Academy on the *Patrick Henry* at Drewry's Bluff. During May and June 1864, he also commanded the ironclad *Richmond*. In April 1865 with the destruction of the Confederate James River Squadron during the evacuation of Richmond, Parker took charge of the midshipmen guarding the removal of the Confederate gold reserves.

Following the war, Parker joined fellow former Confederate Navy officer James I. Waddell as a captain of a Pacific Mail Steamship Company ship and then was the president of Maryland Agricultural College (later the University of Maryland at College Park) until his efforts to create a cadet corps there led to his resignation at the end of 1882. Appointed minister to Korea in June 1886, Parker was removed less than a year later because of alcoholism. He retired to Washington, D.C., where he wrote his memoirs and died on December 30, 1896.

SPENCER C. TUCKER

See also

Blockade-Runners; Charleston, South Carolina, Confederate Attack on Union Blockaders; Drewry's Bluff, First Battle of; Elizabeth City, Battle of; Hampton Roads, Battles of; Ironclads, Confederate; Naval Academy, Confederate; Roanoke Island, Battle of; *Virginia*, CSS; Waddell, James Iredell

Further Reading

Conrad, James Lee. *Rebel Reefers: The Organization and Midshipmen of the Confederate States Naval Academy.* Cambridge, MA: Da Capo, 2003.

Coski, John M. *Capital Navy: The Men, Ships and Operations of the James River Squadron.* Campbell, CA: Savas, 1996.

Parker, William H. *Recollections of a Naval Officer, 1841–1865.* Edited by Craig Symonds. Annapolis, MD: Naval Institute Press, 1985.

Parker's Cross Roads, Battle of
Event Date: December 31, 1862

Engagement during Confederate brigadier general Nathan Bedford Forrest's second cavalry raid into western Tennessee (December 11, 1862–January 3, 1863). As the raid neared its end, Union brigadier general Jeremiah C. Sullivan with two brigades commanded by Colonels Cyrus L. Dunham and John W. Fuller, totaling some 3,000 men, attempted to cut off Forrest's force of about 1,800 men before the

Confederates could withdraw across the Tennessee River. Beginning at about 9:00 a.m. on December 31, Dunham and Forrest met at Parker's Cross Roads in Henderson County, some 30 miles east of Jackson, Tennessee. Confederate artillery secured an early advantage, and Dunham withdrew about a half mile and redeployed, repelling frontal feints until attacked on both flanks and the rear.

Dunham rejected Forrest's demand for unconditional surrender, and Forrest was preparing a renewed assault when Fuller's brigade arrived and surprised the Confederates with an attack on their rear. The Confederates briefly reversed their front, repelled Fuller, and then rushed past Dunham's men south to Lexington and then across the Tennessee River at Clifton. Both sides claimed victory. Union casualties totaled 27 killed and 149 wounded; the Confederates claimed to have suffered only 60 killed or wounded. Each side lost about 300 men taken prisoner.

SPENCER C. TUCKER

See also

Forrest, Nathan Bedford; Forrest's Second Tennessee Raid; Sullivan, Jeremiah Cutler

Further Reading

Hurst, Jack. *Nathan Bedford Forrest: A Biography.* New York: Vintage Books, 1994.

Lytle, Andrew Nelson. *Bedford Forrest and His Critter Company.* Nashville: J. S. Saunders, 1993.

Wyeth, John Allan. *That Devil Forrest.* Baton Rouge: Louisiana State University Press, 1987.

Paroles, Prisoner

System by which both Confederate and Union authorities handled the vast number of prisoners of war taken during the first half of the Civil War. Because the United States and the Confederate States of America believed that the war would not last long and because neither side had procedures or adequate prisons in place to handle thousands of prisoners, they made use of a parole system, which had been used by European powers for years as a relatively simple means to handle captured enemy officers. During the Civil War, however, parole was employed for both enlisted men and officers, although far more officers than enlisted men were given the opportunity to be paroled after their capture.

Parole was granted on a personal honor basis in which the captured prisoner would pledge not to take up arms until he could be formally exchanged, usually for an enemy prisoner of war of equal rank. Parole was usually granted within 10 days of an individual's capture. In many cases, the sheer volume of prisoners dictated that parole be offered within two or three days of capture. Parolees sometimes were allowed to return to their homes if they were close enough to do so. Others often stayed near their outfits and waited for the paperwork and the exchange to be finalized. Some parolees were held in temporary detention camps. Military courts at the time dictated that parolees could not be forced to take on duties that would free enemy soldiers for combat.

As the war dragged on, the number of parolees skyrocketed, as did abuses of the parole system. For example, some soldiers would purposely allow themselves to be taken prisoner so they could return to their homes while on parole. A fair number who did this never returned to duty. Many parolees held in detention camps resented their treatment, while others actively resisted being used as guards or being dispatched to the West to guard against Indian attacks. Those in detention camps often suffered from hunger, disease, bad sanitation, and abuse from guards. By 1862, Union officials began refusing to grant parole to blockade-runners, guerrillas, and irregular forces; the Confederacy was compelled to follow suit.

By 1863, the ever-increasing number of prisoners, combined with the realization that the conflict was being protracted by continually returning men to the ranks, led federal officials to end virtually all paroles and prisoner exchanges on May 25, 1863. By then, paroles and exchanges had become the Confederacy's primary means by which to replenish its armies. The Confederates were forced to retaliate in kind, and for the last two years of the war, most prisoners of war were held in perpetuity in military prisons. During the war, 463,000 Confederate soldiers and sailors became prisoners; of that number, 248,000 were paroled, most during the final surrenders. Some 212,000 Union soldiers and sailors were captured during the war, of whom approximately 17,000 were paroled.

PAUL G. PIERPAOLI JR.

See also
Prisoners of War; Prisons, Confederate; Prisons, U.S.

Further Reading
Hesseltine, William Best. *Civil War Prisons.* Kent, OH: Kent State University Press, 1972.
McPherson, James. *Battle Cry of Freedom.* New York: Oxford University Press, 1988.
Speer, Lonnie R. *Portals to Hell: Military Prisons of the Civil War.* Lincoln: University of Nebraska Press, 2005.

Parrott, Robert Parker
Birth Date: October 5, 1804
Death Date: December 24, 1877

Union officer and ordnance expert. Born on October 5, 1804, at Lee, New Hampshire, Robert Parker Parrott graduated from the U.S. Military Academy, West Point, in 1824 and remained there as an instructor until 1829. He then served as a second lieutenant in the 3rd U.S. Artillery Regiment during operations against the Creeks in the Southeast and later as assistant to the chief of the Ordnance Bureau. Promoted to captain, Parrott served as ordnance inspector at the privately owned West Point Foundry at Cold Spring, New York. In October 1836 Parrott resigned his commission to become superintendent of the foundry, a primary ordnance supplier to the army.

Parrott is best known for his development of the Parrott muzzle-loading rifled cannon, which he patented in 1861; it was one of the primary types of artillery used during the Civil War. His chief innovation in cannon design lay in heat-shrinking a wrought-iron reinforcing band around the weapon's breech, the point of greatest strain. Parrott thus economically produced a stronger, more reliable weapon.

The West Point Foundry manufactured the Model 1861 and the more simplified 1863 Parrott designs in a wide variety of calibers. The original 2.9-inch (10-pounder) field gun was quickly replaced by a 3-inch version, a move deemed necessary so that its ammunition would be interchangeable with the other primary field gun, the 3-inch Ordnance rifle. The West Point Foundry also produced the heavier 3.67-inch (20-pounder) and 4.2-inch (30-pounder) guns as well as huge 10-inch (300-pounder) siege and naval pieces. Although popular with gunners for their superior range and accuracy in all calibers, the larger Parrott guns became notorious for exploding during service. Despite such drawbacks, the Parrott gun remained popular among field gunners. Southern foundries copied it extensively for Confederate service.

Parrott also designed advanced cylindro-conical projectiles for his rifled guns. From 1856 to 1859, he collaborated with Dr. John Brahan Reed of Tuscaloosa, Alabama, in a number of government experiments, and their first projectiles were manufactured at the Washington Navy Yard. The partnership between Parrott and Reed eventually ended at the onset of the Civil War, as Reed's loyalty was with his home state. Parrott purchased an interest in Reed's patents upon Reed's return to the South in 1859. Parrott later focused primarily on perfecting his projectiles' sabots and fuses; he also developed sighting instruments for his various guns.

During a time of rampant war profiteering, Parrott's West Point Foundry supplied the federal government with weapons at the cost of their manufacture. He remained superintendent of the West Point Foundry until his retirement in 1867. Parrott died at Cold Spring on December 24, 1877.

JEFF KINARD

See also
Naval Ordnance; Parrott Gun

Further Reading
Dickey, Thomas S., and Peter C. George. *Field Artillery Projectiles of the American Civil War.* Mechanicsville, VA: Arsenal Publications II, 1993.
Hazlett, James C., Edwin Olmstead, and M. Hume Parks. *Field Artillery Weapons of the Civil War.* Newark: University of Delaware Press, 1983.
Melton, Jack W., Jr., and Lawrence E. Paul. *Introduction to Field Artillery Ordnance, 1861–1865.* Kennesaw, GA: Kennesaw Mountain Press, 1994.
Olmstead, Edwin, Wayne E. Stark, and Spencer C. Tucker. *The Big Guns: Civil War Siege, Seacoast, and Naval Cannon.* Alexandria Bay, NY: Museum Restoration Service, 1997.

Parrott Gun

The most widely used rifled gun of the Civil War. Designed by Robert P. Parrott, superintendent of the West Point Foundry, Parrott guns were easy to operate and were reliable, accurate, and relatively inexpensive to manufacture. Both sides produced them during the war. The Parrott gun was essentially a cast-iron rifled gun with a wrought-iron band shrunk over the breech, the point of greatest strain. The band was equal in thickness to half the diameter of the bore.

Parrott's first rifled gun was a 2.9-inch (land diameter) 10-pounder. Prior to the Civil War, Parrott also produced a 3.67-inch (20-pounder) and a 4.2-inch (30-pounder). Neither the army nor the navy adopted the Parrott guns until after the start of the Civil War. During the war, Parrotts were produced in bore diameters of 2.9-inch, 3-inch, 3.3-inch, 3.67-inch, 4.2-inch, 5.3-inch (60-pounder), 6.4-inch (100-pounder army, 80-pounder navy), 8-inch (200-pounder army, 150-pounder navy), and 10-inch (300-pounder army, 250-pounder navy). The guns had spiraled rifling, with three grooves and lands on the 2.9-inch to 15 grooves and lands on the 10-inch.

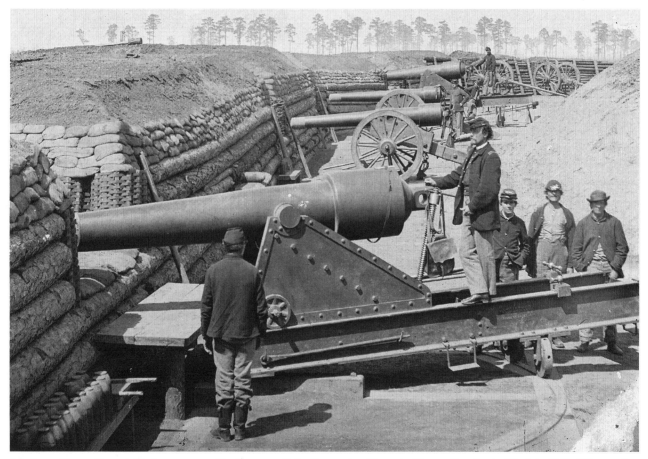

A battery of heavy Parrott rifled guns manned by Company C, 1st Connecticut Heavy Artillery, at Fort Brady, Virginia, 1864. (Library of Congress)

The smallest U.S. Navy Parrott was the 3.67-inch. The larger guns were better suited to naval service, in which weight was also not as much a factor as in field artillery on land. The 6.4-inch Parrott, for example, weighed some 9,800 pounds. With a powder charge of 10 pounds and at 35 degrees of elevation, it could fire its projectile more than five miles. The U.S. Navy employed the 8-inch Parrott in the turrets of some of its monitors, alongside a smoothbore Dahlgren.

The Parrott gun fired an elongated projectile some 3 calibers in length. Cylindro-conical in shape, it had a bronze ring at a contraction in the base. On ignition of the powder charge, the gas expanded the bronze ring into the grooves of the bore, thus imparting a spin to the projectile. Parrott projectiles were fitted with both time and percussion fuses, and there were also variations, with hardened noses to pierce armor.

Both sides during the war experienced problems with Parrott guns bursting, most notably in operations against Charleston and Fort Fisher. Parrott blamed these on premature shell explosions rather than defects in the bore, but clearly these early rifled guns experienced greater problems than did the smoothbores, especially from grit and sand in the bores. Fewer navy guns burst, which was probably attributable to an order that all rifled projectiles be thoroughly greased before they were loaded. The navy did subsequently remove its heaviest Parrotts from service, however.

From the beginning of the war through April 1864, nearly 2,000 Parrotts were manufactured for the U.S. Army and the U.S. Navy, representing about one-fifth of Union guns on land and sea. The Confederates produced their own Parrotts at the Tredegar Iron Works in Richmond in 2.9-inch, 3-inch, 3.67-inch, and 4.2-inch sizes.

SPENCER C. TUCKER

See also

Artillery, Land, CSA; Artillery, Land, U.S.; Artillery Projectiles, Sea

Further Reading

Hazlett, James C., Edwin Olmstead, and M. Hume Parks. *Field Artillery Weapons of the Civil War*. Newark: Delaware University Press, 1983.

Olmstead, Edwin, Wayne Stark, and Spencer C. Tucker. *The Big Guns: Civil War Siege, Seacoast, and Naval Cannon*. Alexandria Bay, NY: Museum Restoration Service, 1997.

Tucker, Spencer C. *Arming the Fleet: U.S. Naval Ordnance in the Muzzle-Loading Era*. Annapolis, MD: Naval Institute Press, 1989.

Parsons, Emily Elizabeth
Birth Date: March 8, 1824
Death Date: May 19, 1880

Union nurse and member of the Western Sanitary Commission. Born in Taunton, Massachusetts, on March 8, 1824, and educated in Boston, Emily Elizabeth Parsons lived with her family in Cambridge. After suffering from a bout of scarlet fever as a youth, she refused to let resulting vision and hearing impairments limit her ambitions or activities. When the Civil War began in 1861, Parsons trained as a nurse at Boston's Massachusetts General Hospital, and in October 1862 she offered her services to the U.S. military.

Parsons was sent to Fort Schuyler's MacDougall Hospital on Long Island, but her father's concern about the health risks led her to resign. She moved to New York City to seek a new appointment but failed to obtain a position. Soon she became acquainted with Jessie Benton Frémont, the wife of Union major general John C. Frémont. In January 1863 Jessie Frémont used her connections in the Western Sanitary Commission to secure Parsons an assignment at the Lawson Hospital in St. Louis, Missouri. After less than a month, Parsons received the prestigious assignment as head nurse on the steamboat *City of Alton*. In this capacity, she accompanied medical stores to Vicksburg.

During the voyage on the Mississippi River, Parsons contracted malaria. After recuperating, she became superintendent of female nurses at St. Louis's Benton Barracks Hospital, the area's largest hospital. Here Parsons nursed both white and black soldiers as well as a large number of escaped slaves. Within six months, she suffered another malarial attack and went home to Cambridge to recuperate. Ill health forced her to resign in August 1864.

Parsons nevertheless remained active during the remaining months of the war, working from her home where she collected and sent supplies to the Western Sanitary Commission in St. Louis. She also supported Chicago's Northwestern Sanitary Fair in May 1865.

Parsons maintained her commitment to hospital work during the postwar years. In 1867 she established a charity hospital for Cambridge's poor women and children, which eventually became Cambridge Hospital in 1871. Parsons, who never married, spent the remainder of her life supporting the hospital and advocating for the poor. She died on May 19, 1880, in Cambridge, Massachusetts.

KELLY D. SELBY

See also

Frémont, John Charles; Nurses; Western Sanitary Commission; Women

Further Reading

Parsons, Theophilus. *Memoir of Emily Elizabeth Parsons.* Boston: Little, Brown, 1880.

Schultz, Jane E. "The Inhospitable Hospital: Gender and Professionalism in Civil War Medicine." *Signs* 17(2) (1992): 363–392.

Parsons, Lewis Baldwin

Birth Date: April 5, 1818

Death Date: March 16, 1907

Union officer. Lewis Baldwin Parsons was born on April 5, 1818, in Perry, New York. He graduated from Yale College in 1840 and from Harvard Law School in 1844, at which time he moved to Alton, Illinois, and commenced what became a prosperous legal practice. From 1846 to 1849 Parsons was a city attorney, and from 1854 to 1860 he was chief counsel for and then president of the Ohio & Mississippi Railroad.

In October 1861, Parsons received a captain's commission upon the intercession of Major General George B. McClellan, a close friend. Because of Parsons's extensive knowledge of the railroad industry, he was assigned to the Quartermaster Department, although he would have preferred a field command.

By December 1861 Parsons was in St. Louis, where he was placed in charge of all rail and river traffic for the Department of the Mississippi. He performed his work well, and in February 1862 he was advanced to colonel, at which time he became an aide to Major General Henry W. Halleck, commander of the Department of the Missouri, with responsibility for all transport in the West. In August 1864 Parsons was dispatched to Washington, D.C., where he assumed the position of chief of transportation for all Union armies.

It is hard to overemphasize the importance of Parsons's work and his organizational prowess. Indeed, he had to essentially create a modern transport system from scratch, as the Civil War was the first major conflict that extensively employed railroads to move men and matériel. His efforts at controlling river and inland waterway transport were equally effective. In January 1865 Parsons orchestrated an achievement of great logistical complexity when he supervised the movement of Major General John Schofield's XXIII Corps from Tennessee to the vicinity of Washington, D.C., in only 17 days, after which the corps was shipped to North Carolina. On May 11, 1865, Parsons was advanced to brigadier general of volunteers.

Parsons remained in the army until he mustered out on April 30, 1866, with the brevet rank of major general. After a two-year hiatus in Europe, he settled in St. Louis, where he became a bank president. In 1875 he purchased a 3,000-acre farm in Flora, Illinois, where he died on March 16, 1907.

Paul G. Pierpaoli Jr.

See also

Mississippi, Union Department of the; Railroads, U.S.

Further Reading

Eicher, John H., and David J. Eicher. *Civil War High Commands.* Stanford, CA: Stanford University Press, 2001.

Gibson, Charles Dana, with E. Kay Gibson. *Assault and Logistics: Union Army Coastal and River Operations.* Camden, ME: Ensign, 1995.

Parsons, Mosby Monroe

Birth Date: May 21, 1822

Death Date: ca. August 15, 1865

Confederate officer. Mosby Monroe Parsons was born on May 21, 1822, in Charlottesville, Virginia. He eventually relocated to Missouri, studied law, and passed the Missouri bar. He fought in the Mexican-American War (1846–1848), serving as a captain in a volunteer cavalry unit. After that conflict, he returned to his law practice and became involved in Missouri politics. From 1853 to 1857 he was the attorney general of Missouri and was then elected to the Missouri Senate.

Parsons had strong Confederate leanings, and so it came as no surprise when he advocated secession for Missouri and backed Governor Claiborne F. Jackson's plans to take Missouri out of the Union. From early 1861 until November 1862, Parsons commanded the Missouri State Guard's 6th Division and saw action at Carthage (July 5, 1861), Wilson's Creek (August 10, 1861), and in the Siege of Corinth (May 3–30). On November 5, 1862, he formally entered Confederate service in Arkansas as a brigadier general. He commanded a brigade in the Battle of Prairie

Grove (December 7, 1862) and the Battle of Helena (July 4, 1863).

Assigned to the District of West Louisiana commanded by Major General Richard Taylor, Parsons commanded a small division and saw action at the Battle of Pleasant Hill (April 9, 1864) during the Red River Campaign (March 10–May 22, 1864). Returning to Arkansas, Parsons's men engaged Union brigadier general Frederick Steele's forces during the Camden Expedition (March 23–May 3, 1864). Thereafter, most of Parsons's service was in garrison duty in Arkansas and Louisiana.

Although Parsons had been advanced to major general at the end of April 1864 by order of General E. Kirby Smith, President Jefferson Davis never confirmed the appointment. At the end of the war, Parsons was briefly detained by Union officials and then paroled at the rank of major general. For reasons unknown, Parsons left the United States soon thereafter. He ended up in Mexico and participated in the fighting between the imperialist supporters of Emperor Maximilian, the French-installed puppet emperor, and Republican insurgents. Apparently having sided with the imperialists, Parson was killed in combat probably on August 15, 1865, in Nuevo León.

PAUL G. PIERPAOLI JR.

See also

Camden Expedition; Carthage, Battle of; Corinth, Mississippi, Siege of; Jackson, Claiborne Fox; Missouri; Pea Ridge, Battle of; Price's Missouri Raid; Red River Campaign; Steele, Frederick; Taylor, Richard; Wilson's Creek, Battle of

Further Reading

Phillips, Christopher. *Missouri's Confederate: Claiborne Fox Jackson and the Creation of Southern Identity in the Border West.* Columbia: University of Missouri Press, 2000.

Warner, Ezra J. *Generals in Gray: Lives of the Confederate Commanders.* Baton Rouge: Louisiana State University Press, 2006.

Partisan Rangers

Irregular fighting units, officially sanctioned by the Confederate government in April 1862, that were engaged in guerrilla warfare against Union forces and sometimes against civilian populations. Guerrilla warfare in the Southern states had its origins in the American Revolutionary War. In 1780 following the surrender of Continental Army and militia forces that had been besieged at Charleston, South Carolina, partisan units, commanded by officers such as Francis Marion, proved highly effective against British forces in the South. Southern memory of the successful employment of irregular forces during the Revolutionary War certainly contributed to the decision to utilize guerrilla units against Union forces.

To aid in the recruitment of irregular forces, on April 21, 1862, the Congress of the Confederate States of America passed the Partisan Rangers Act, which authorized the commissioning of officers to form bands of Partisan Rangers, to consist of cavalry and infantry units ranging in size from companies to regiments. The rangers were to be subject to the same regulations as Confederate Army personnel and were entitled to the same pay, rations, and quarters.

As the war progressed, Confederate military leaders grew uncomfortable with the methods employed by often uncontrolled irregular forces, particularly in the face of Union threats to execute hostages in response to guerrilla attacks. The most infamous Partisan Ranger operation occurred during the struggle against Union regulars and guerrillas in Kansas and Missouri. On August 21, 1863, "Colonel" William Quantrill led a force of 450 irregulars on a raid into the pro-Union town of Lawrence, Kansas, in retaliation for brutal Union behavior and the deaths of imprisoned female relatives of members of the Partisan Rangers. During the raid the town was pillaged, the bank was robbed, and many buildings were burned. The majority of the town's male population, at least 150 men and boys, were killed. In response, Union forces conducted a scorched-earth operation in several Missouri counties to deprive Quantrill of logistical support.

The Partisan Rangers Act was repealed on February 17, 1864, after General Robert E. Lee and other officers complained that the rangers were causing more problems than they were solving. Most Partisan Ranger units operating in the East were then consolidated into larger regular cavalry units of the Army of Northern Virginia. Only the ranger units of Lieutenant Colonel John S. Mosby and Captain John Hanson McNeill, which operated in a highly disciplined manner in western Virginia and West Virginia, were officially permitted to continue partisan operations. Nevertheless, some Partisan Ranger forces, such as the troops led by Quantrill, continued to conduct unauthorized guerrilla operations until the end of the Civil War.

GLENN E. HELM

See also

Guerrilla Warfare; Lawrence, Kansas, Raid on; McNeill's Rangers; Mosby's Rangers; Quantrill, William Clarke

Further Reading

Goodrich, Thomas. *Black Flag: Guerrilla Warfare on the Western Border, 1861–1865.* Bloomington: Indiana University Press, 1995.

Mackey, Robert R. *The Uncivil War: Irregular Warfare in the Upper South, 1861–1865.* Norman: University of Oklahoma Press, 2004.

Patrick, Marsena Rudolph
Birth Date: March 11, 1811
Death Date: July 27, 1888

Union officer. Marsena Rudolph Patrick was born on March 11, 1811, in Jefferson County, New York. He graduated from the U.S. Military Academy, West Point, in 1835. Patrick rose steadily through the ranks, saw combat in the Mexican-American War (1846–1848), and was a brevet major by 1850, when he resigned his commission and returned to New York, where he took up farming. In 1859 Patrick became president of the New York State Agricultural College, a post he held until 1861.

In the spring of 1861, Patrick became inspector general of New York volunteers. On March 20, 1862, he received a brigadier general's commission in the volunteer army and command of a brigade and was then dispatched to Virginia. There he skirmished with the Confederates in the Shenandoah Valley before being named military governor of Fredericksburg. He was then attached to the Army of the Potomac, in which he would serve until war's end. He led a brigade during the Battles of South Mountain (September 14, 1862) and Antietam (September 17, 1862) before becoming provost marshal for the Army of the Potomac on October 6, 1862.

By all accounts, Patrick performed his duties efficiently and expeditiously. His responsibilities were many, including intelligence gathering, protection of civilian populations, regulating trade and commerce, dealing with deserters, guarding and housing thousands of prisoners of war, and maintaining troop morale and discipline. Patrick was known for his fair but firm policies and for tight discipline combined with discretion. In the winter of 1864 he became provost marshal for all Union armies then operating against Richmond.

Brevetted major general, Patrick left the army on June 12, 1865. After a failed bid to become New York's treasurer, from 1867 to 1868 he served as president of the state agricultural society. He subsequently served as a state agricultural commissioner and was a frequent lecturer on agricultural topics. Patrick's last position was as governor of the Soldiers' Home in Dayton Ohio, where he died on July 27, 1888. A diary published in 1964 showcased Patrick's frequent annoyance with various Union commanders and his shock at the level of graft and corruption he encountered in the course of his duties.

PAUL G. PIERPAOLI JR.

See also

Antietam, Battle of; Potomac, Union Army of the; South Mountain, Battle of

Further Reading

Sparks, David S. "General Patrick's Progress: Intelligence and Security in the Army of the Potomac." *Civil War History* 10 (December 1964): 371–384.

Sparks, David S., ed. *Inside Lincoln's Army: The Diary of Marsena Rudolph Patrick, Provost Marshall General, Army of the Potomac.* New York: Thomas Yoseloff, 1964.

Patterson, Robert
Birth Date: January 12, 1792
Death Date: August 7, 1881

Union officer. Born in Cappagh, County Tyrone, Ireland, on January 12, 1792, Robert Patterson immigrated with his family to the United States in 1799 following his father's involvement in a plot against British rule in Ireland. The family settled in Pennsylvania, and the young Patterson eventually went into the banking business, where he served as a clerk in a Philadelphia countinghouse.

Patterson first saw military service during the War of 1812, when he was commissioned a first lieutenant in the 2nd Pennsylvania Militia. He went on to serve as a militia lieutenant colonel and a colonel before being commissioned a first lieutenant in the U.S. Army on April 5, 1813. Promoted to captain, Patterson served briefly on the staff of Brigadier General Joseph Bloomfield and was an assistant quartermaster general until leaving the service at the end of the war in 1815.

Following the war, Patterson returned to his commercial pursuits, engaging in manufacturing and establishing several mills. Along with his success in the business world, he became influential in Pennsylvania politics. A Jacksonian Democrat, Patterson was president of Pennsylvania's electoral college that cast its vote for Martin Van Buren in 1836. Maintaining his position as a state militia officer, Patterson also helped quell local rioting in 1838 and 1844.

Major General Robert Patterson received command of the Army of the Shenandoah shortly after the start of the Civil War. His lack of aggressiveness, however, allowed Confederate reinforcements to take part in the First Battle of Bull Run in July 1861, and shortly thereafter he was separated from the service. (Library of Congress)

On the outbreak of the Mexican-American War in 1846, Patterson was commissioned a major general of volunteers and given command of the volunteer 2nd Division of the Army of Occupation. Along with service on Major General Winfield Scott's staff, Patterson saw action during the Siege of Veracruz and was wounded during the advance on Mexico City in the Battle of Cerro Gordo (April 18, 1847). Prior to this important battle, some American commanders had planned an aggressive frontal assault on entrenched Mexican positions. However, Patterson interceded and cancelled this potentially suicidal attack. His decision played a key role in the American victory.

Following the war, Patterson took command of the Pennsylvania Militia and returned to his business interests, which continued to thrive. His acquisition of 30 cotton mills made him a wealthy man, and he continued to play an influential role in Pennsylvania politics.

National events eventually brought Patterson back to full-time military service for a third time. On the beginning of the Civil War, he received an appointment as major general of Pennsylvania volunteers in April 1861. Shortly thereafter, he received command of the Department of Pennsylvania and the Army of the Shenandoah. Ordered to retake the Harpers Ferry Arsenal from Confederate forces, Patterson moved slowly, allowing Confederate forces time to secure most of what they had captured at the arsenal. In the early summer of 1861, with Confederate forces assembling around Manassas, Virginia, Patterson was ordered to prevent Brigadier General Joseph E. Johnston's forces near Harpers Ferry from joining this larger army. However, Patterson's lack of aggressiveness allowed Johnston to outmaneuver the Union force at the Battle of Hoke's Run (July 2, 1861) and then to reinforce Confederate forces at Manassas Junction in time for the Southern victory in the First Battle of Bull Run (July 21, 1861).

Patterson was widely criticized for his failures, and his commission was not renewed. He was separated from the army under honorable conditions on July 27, 1861, at the expiration of his three-month commission.

Patterson then resumed his business interests in Philadelphia. He soon became one of the largest mill owners in the United States and also developed interests in sugar refining and cotton plantations. He also wrote a book about his Civil War service titled *A Narrative of the Campaign in the Valley of the Shenandoah in 1861* (1865), in which he claimed that Union general in chief Brevet Lieutenant General Winfield Scott had ordered him to hold his position and await further orders. From 1867 to 1881, Patterson served as president of the Aztec Club, a military society of Mexican-American War veterans. In his later years, he was a popular speaker and served on the board of trustees of Lafayette College. Patterson died on August 7, 1881, in Philadelphia.

SEAN M. HEUVEL AND ADAM P. WILSON

See also

Bull Run, First Battle of; Johnston, Joseph Eggleston; Scott, Winfield

Further Reading

Ballard, Ted. *Battle of First Bull Run*. Washington, DC: U.S. Army Center of Military History, 2004.

Eicher, John H., and David J. Eicher. *Civil War High Commands*. Stanford, CA: Stanford University Press, 2001.

Patterson, Robert. *A Narrative of the Campaign in the Valley of the Shenandoah, in 1861*. 1865; reprint. Bedford, PA: Applewood Books, 2009.

Pattersonville, Louisiana, Engagement at
Event Date: March 28, 1863

Engagement during Union major general Nathaniel Banks's 1863 Bayou Teche Campaign. On March 28, 1863, Brigadier

General Godfrey Weitzel, commanding the 2nd Brigade, 1st Division, XIX Corps, requested Union Navy acting master Thomas L. Peterson to carry out a reconnaissance in the gunboat *Diana* of Grand Lake via Bayou Teche. The *Diana,* built in 1858, was a 239-ton side-wheel steamer mounting five guns. Weitzel sent along a company each from the 12th Connecticut and 160th New York Infantry Regiments, along with his aide, Lieutenant Pickering D. Allen.

After conducting the reconnaissance, the *Diana* left Grand Lake and entered a narrow channel of the Atchafalaya River that passed below Pattersonville. There a Confederate force of perhaps 500 men, consisting of the Val Verde (Texas) Battery, a cavalry escort of Brigadier General Henry H. Sibley's Texas Brigade, and a detachment of the 28th Louisiana Infantry, ambushed the *Diana* from a concealed position on the bank. In a three-hour engagement, the *Diana* was crippled, suffering damage to its propulsion system and steering. Upon hearing the gunfire, Union reinforcements were rushed to the scene, but the *Calhoun* ran aground en route, and the *Estrella* was unable to arrive before the *Diana* had drifted ashore and the crew was forced to surrender. In the engagement, the Federals suffered 4 dead (including Peterson), 14 wounded (including Allen), and more than 100 men captured. Confederate losses are unknown.

The Confederates repaired the *Diana* and added it to their small flotilla on Bayou Teche. On April 13, 1863, while shelling Union forces in the engagement of Irish Bend and Fort Bisland (April 12–14), the *Diana* was seriously damaged by a round from a 4.2-inch (30-pounder) Parrott rifle that struck the engine room and exploded. The gunboat was able to withdraw and effect repairs and then the next morning was ordered to proceed to Irish Bend, where it helped protect the Confederate retreat from the battle there (April 13–14). On April 18, the crippled steamer was set afire by the Confederates, destroying it. Even with captured Union gunboats, Confederate land and naval forces were unable to stop Banks's campaign up the Teche and Atchafalaya Rivers, and in May Union forces reached the Mississippi above Port Hudson, isolating that garrison from Vicksburg. On July 9 after learning of Vicksburg's surrender five days earlier, Port Hudson capitulated, removing the final Confederate obstacle to Union shipping on the Mississippi.

CHRISTOPHER M. REIN

See also

Banks, Nathaniel Prentice; Irish Bend and Fort Bisland, Louisiana, Engagements at; Port Hudson, Louisiana, Action at; Vicksburg Campaign, Second; Weitzel, Godfrey

Further Reading

Irwin, Richard B. *History of the Nineteenth Army Corps.* 1892; reprint, Baton Rouge: Elliott's Book Shop Press, 1985.

Winters, John D. *The Civil War in Louisiana.* Baton Rouge: Louisiana State University Press, 1963.

Paul, Gabriel René
Birth Date: March 22, 1813
Death Date: May 5, 1886

Union officer. Gabriel René Paul was born on March 22, 1813, in St. Louis, Missouri. He graduated from the U.S. Military Academy, West Point, in 1834. Paul saw service in various posts in the West and also served in the Second Seminole War (1835–1842) and the Mexican-American War (1846–1848), rising to captain in 1846 and being brevetted for the Battle of Chapultepec. When the Civil War began in 1861, Paul was stationed in New Mexico and on April 22 was promoted to major, 8th Infantry. He was also acting inspector general of the Department of New Mexico. Paul was preoccupied with protecting his department from Confederate incursions; he also had to cope with Texas Confederates' efforts to convince Union soldiers in the territory to defect to the Confederate side.

By December 1861, Paul entered the volunteer service as colonel of the 4th New Mexico Infantry Regiment, which he headquartered at Fort Union, a post located to the northeast of Santa Fe. His immediate focus was on Confederate brigadier general Henry H. Sibley's New Mexico Campaign (November 1861–May 1862), which sought to secure the Southwest for the Confederacy. Paul helped blunt the Confederate offensive before being sent to the East. Advanced to brigadier general of volunteers in September 1862, Paul was given charge of a brigade in I Corps, Army of the Potomac, and led it at the First Battle of Fredericksburg (December 13, 1862) and the Battle of Chancellorsville (May 1–4, 1863), where it saw limited action.

During the Battle of Gettysburg (July 1–3, 1863), Paul's brigade took part in the desperate defense of Seminary Ridge on the first day of fighting. That afternoon Paul was struck in his right temple by a bullet that exited through his left eye. Miraculously he survived, but he was left blind and almost deaf. He served out much of the remainder of the war on administrative duties and retired in February 1865, having been promoted to colonel and brevetted brigadier general in the regular army. In 1866 he was placed on the retired list as a brigadier general. Paul lived in Washington, D.C., where he died on May 5, 1886.

PAUL G. PIERPAOLI JR.

See also

Chancellorsville, Battle of; Gettysburg, Battle of; New Mexico Territory; Sibley's New Mexico Campaign

Further Reading

Eicher, John H., and David J. Eicher. *Civil War High Commands.* Stanford, CA: Stanford University Press, 2001.

Warner, Ezra J. *Generals in Blue: Lives of the Union Commanders.* Baton Rouge: Louisiana State University Press, 2006.

Paulding, Hiram
Birth Date: December 11, 1799
Death Date: October 20, 1878

Union naval officer. Born in Cortlandt, New York, on December 11, 1799, Hiram Paulding received a midshipman's warrant on September 1, 1811, and saw duty during the War of 1812. He was promoted to lieutenant on April 27, 1816; to master commandant on February 9, 1837; and to captain on February 29, 1844. From 1855 to 1858, Paulding commanded the Home Squadron as commodore and then as flag officer.

From March to September 1861, Paulding was assigned as chief of the Office of Detail in the Navy Department in Washington, D.C., and was charged with selecting officers for assignments. On April 18, Secretary of the Navy Gideon Welles, furious at the refusal of the commandant of the Norfolk (Gosport) Navy Yard, Captain Charles S. McCauley, to permit the steam frigate *Merrimack* to depart that place, dispatched Paulding to replace him. The yard was then threatened with takeover by the State of Virginia. Paulding arrived at Norfolk late on April 20 following a quick trip to Washington, only to find that McCauley, believing that the yard was about to be attacked, had ordered the scuttling of all its ships. Paulding then had no choice but to continue the work already begun. He was able to get off only two ships, the screw sloop *Pawnee* towing the sailing sloop *Cumberland*, early on April 21. Once they had departed, Paulding gave the signal to torch the yard and destroy its facilities. The work of destruction on April 21 was at best only haphazard, but the result was a considerable loss not only in ships, including the *Merrimack* (which would be rebuilt by the Confederates into the ironclad *Virginia*), but also in ordnance and supplies. The Confederates' haul included 1,198 guns, including

U.S. Navy Rear Admiral Hiram Paulding joined the navy as a midshipman in 1811 and served through the Civil War. In command of the Norfolk (Gosport) Navy Yard at the start of the war, he largely botched the job of its destruction on the secession of Virginia, a great advantage to the Confederacy. (National Archives)

52 IX-inch Dahlgrens. Both Paulding and McCauley came under considerable criticism in the Northern press for their handling of the situation.

In October 1861, Paulding assumed command of the New York (Brooklyn) Navy Yard. Although he was placed on the retired list on December 21, he continued in this command. Promoted to rear admiral on the retired list on July 16, 1862, Paulding remained in command of the yard until May 1865. From 1866 to 1869, he was governor of the Philadelphia Naval Asylum and then was port admiral of Boston, Massachusetts, until October 1870. Paulding died in Huntington, New York, on October 20, 1878.

SPENCER C. TUCKER

See also

Norfolk Navy Yard; Welles, Gideon

Further Reading

Callahan, Edward W., ed. *List of Officers of the Navy of the United States and of the Marine Corps from 1775 to 1900.* 1901; reprint, New York: Haskell House Publishers, 1969.

Thompson, Kenneth E. *Civil War Commodores and Admirals: A Biographical Directory of All Eighty-Eight Union and Confederate Navy Officers Who Attained Commissioned Flag Rank during the War.* Portland, ME: Thompson Group, 2001.

Tucker, Spencer C. *Blue and Gray Navies: The Civil War Afloat.* Annapolis, MD: Naval Institute Press, 2006.

Paxton, Elisha Franklin

Birth Date: March 4, 1828
Death Date: May 3, 1863

Confederate officer. Elisha Franklin Paxton was born on March 4, 1828, in Rockbridge County, Virginia. After attending both Washington College (Washington and Lee University) and Yale University, Paxton graduated from the University of Virginia Law School. He worked as a lawyer in both Ohio and Virginia until he began to experience vision problems, which forced him to abandon his legal practice in 1859.

Paxton joined the Confederate Army on April 18, 1861, as a first lieutenant in the Rockbridge Rifles, a volunteer company from Lexington. He fought in several engagements under Brigadier General Thomas J. Jackson, including the First Battle of Bull Run (July 21, 1861). Elected major of the 27th Virginia Infantry of the famed Stonewall Brigade in October 1861, Paxton served during Jackson's Shenandoah Valley Campaign (May–June 1862) but was not well liked by his men and failed to win reelection in the spring of 1862.

Jackson, however, thought highly of Paxton and appointed him assistant adjutant with the rank of major. On November 1, 1862, Paxton was advanced to brigadier general on Jackson's recommendation and was assigned command of the Stonewall Brigade. Paxton's appointment over more senior officers rankled many, but Jackson stood by his decision.

The Stonewall Brigade was held in reserve at the First Battle of Fredericksburg (December 13, 1862) and thus saw virtually no combat. Paxton's next major engagement was at the Battle of Chancellorsville (May 1–4, 1863). Here too the Stonewall Brigade was mainly in a support role during the first two days of fighting. On the third day of combat, May 3, while Paxton was preparing his brigade for assault in the early morning hours, he was struck and killed by a minié ball.

JENNIFER HARRISON AND PAUL G. PIERPAOLI JR.

See also

Bull Run, First Battle of; Chancellorsville, Battle of; Fredericksburg, First Battle of; Jackson, Thomas Jonathan; Stonewall Brigade

Further Reading

Paxton, Frank. *The Civil War Letters of General Frank "Bull" Paxton, CSA.* Edited by John Gallatin Paxton. Hillsboro, TX: Hill Junior College Press, 1978.

Warner, Ezra J. *Generals in Gray: Lives of the Confederate Commanders.* Baton Rouge: Louisiana State University Press, 2006.

Pay, Confederate Army and Navy

In the initial months of the secession crisis, a naive optimism prevailed in the South—fueled by secessionist ardor, patriotism, and the threat of Union military action—with regard to how the troops who were volunteering or hastily being called up would be paid and supplied. In March 1861, the Confederate Congress enacted an army pay scale as follows: private, $11 per month, and corporal through sergeant major, from $13 to $21 (paid bimonthly). Officers' monthly pay ranged from $90 for first lieutenant to $150 for major and $195 for colonel, with generals at $301. The entire scale, except pay for generals, was roughly about 85 percent of the comparable U.S. Army pay scale. The Union's generals were paid far higher salaries than their Confederate counterparts, although commanding generals in charge of Confederate armies did have their base salaries handsomely supplemented with special allowances.

As in the U.S. Navy, Confederate Navy enlisted personnel were not paid in cash on a regular basis. Instead, their monthly earnings were noted in their ship's pay book and disbursed upon discharge. This placed many at a great disadvantage, as inflation made their earnings worth far less over time. The pay scale for enlisted men was ordinary seamen, $12 per month; seamen, $14 per month; able seamen, $18 per month; third-class petty officer, $20 per month; and senior petty officer, $25 per month.

Naval officers, who like their U.S. counterparts were paid only once a year, were remunerated based on the length of service and on the particular responsibilities performed. An admiral received $6,000 per year, while a captain's pay, when commanding a squadron, was $5,000 per year. On any other duty at sea, a captain earned $4,200 per year. On other duty the pay was $3,600 per year, while on leave or awaiting orders the pay was $3,000 per year. The pay of other officers was to be regulated by length of service, but as the first increase in pay was to come after five years of service, none of the officers benefited by it. The yearly pay of a commander on duty at sea was $2,825 and on other duty was $2,662. Commanders on leave or awaiting orders received $2,250 per year. First lieutenants commanding at sea received $2,550 per year, and first lieutenants on duty at sea received $1,500 per year and the same when on other duty. When on leave or awaiting orders, they received only $1,200 per year. Second lieutenants while on duty at sea were paid $1,200 per year, but when on leave or on other duty they received just $1,000 per year. Surgeons on duty at sea received $2,200 per year; when on other duty, they were paid $2,000 per year.

As the credit standing of the Confederate government eroded during the war, inflation devastated soldiers' and sailors' real earnings, and the Confederate Congress in February 1864 adjusted pay scales. Pay for privates, the great majority of Confederate soldiers, was reset at $18 per month in a revalued new issue of currency. Enlisted naval men received a similar pay adjustment.

From the very start of the fighting, Confederate soldiers could hardly depend on either regular pay or the small amounts allocated additionally for supplies. Some went months without pay, and in extreme instances, the periods in which they received no pay approached a year. Pay operations were hampered, of course, by episodes of rapid military advance or retreat, major battles, and severe weather. More enduring problems, however, made Confederate pay operations a source of intense discontent in the ranks. One problem was organizational: army paymasters were placed under control of the Treasury Department rather than (as in the U.S. Army) the Paymaster General. And the Treasury Department officers rigidly enforced policies that adversely affected morale. Most grievously, troops would be paid only from the day they themselves could document when they had formally entered Confederate service; hence, pay was denied or delayed even for soldiers (including the wounded) who had a record of battlefield service but who could not produce the necessary documentation. Thus, the men who had stepped forward in the storied wave of individual volunteering or state call-ups at the start of the conflict were left to the mercy of the governors and state legislatures for back pay that seldom materialized. Moreover, Treasury drafts sent to army paymasters often required the latter to travel to distant bank locations to obtain the currency required for distribution of pay.

By mid-1863, severe shortfalls in Confederate revenues and breakdowns in pay administration were having devastating effects on the troops. At the same time, compounding the obvious morale problems, Confederate supply officers were authorized to impress food and equipment from civilians, who were compensated with manifestly worthless promissory notes or badly depreciated currency. The consequent suffering prompted innumerable Confederate soldiers to desert and return home to help their families in distress.

Thus, the disastrous situation in pay operations became part of a vicious cycle that badly demoralized the troops. Aware that rising desertion rates were decimating his army, General Robert E. Lee singled out "insufficiency of food and nonpayment of the troops" as the major causes of Confederate desertion.

The Confederate Congress made several adjustments in policy during the war years, including provision for pay of those discharged for disabling wounds, bounties for various special services, and modest upward adjustments of officers' pay scales. By late 1863, however, such measures had become virtually irrelevant. The more fundamental problems of the Confederacy, which ultimately led to defeat, were the collapsing economy, debilitating tensions between state governors and the Jefferson Davis administration, disappearing public revenues, and finally the defeats suffered on the battlefield.

HARRY N. SCHEIBER

See also
Armies of the Confederate States, Overview; Congress, CSA; Desertion; Pay, U.S. Army and Navy

Further Reading
Nofi, Albert A. *A Civil War Treasury.* New York: Da Capo, 1995.
Scheiber, Harry N. "The Pay of Confederate Troops and the Problems of Demoralization: A Case of Administrative Failure." In *Battles Won and Lost: Essays from Civil War History,* edited by John T. Hubbell, 132–156. Westport, CT: Greenwood, 1975.
Wiley, Bell Irvin. *The Life of Johnny Reb: The Common Soldier of the Confederacy.* Revised ed. Baton Rouge: Louisiana State University Press, 2008.

Pay, U.S. Army and Navy

U.S. Army and U.S. Volunteers pay for noncommissioned personnel, usually disbursed in cash every other month, was as follows: privates, $13 per month; corporals, $14 per month; sergeants, $17 per month; first sergeants, $20 per month; and sergeant majors, $21 per month. Each enlisted man was also given a clothing and supply allowance of $3 per month. On average, nonofficer pay for U.S. soldiers and naval personnel was 15–20 percent higher than Confederate pay for the same personnel.

On June 22, 1864, in response to rising inflation, Congress approved a new pay scale, which amounted to about a 22.5 percent across-the-board increase, with privates now earning $16 per month. African Americans (U.S. Colored Troops), however, were paid less and were not given a clothing allowance. Until June 1864, African American troops received just $10 per month, compared to $13 per month for white privates. Congress authorized equal pay for black soldiers in June 1864 but retroactively only to January 1, 1864. Because an African American soldier had to show proof that he had been a free man prior to 1861 in order to receive the raise, however, virtually no black troops received the pay increase.

U.S. Army officers, who were generally paid on a monthly rather than a bimonthly schedule, were paid as follows: second lieutenants, $45 per month; first lieutenants, $50 per month; captains, $65 per month; majors, $70 per month; lieutenant colonels, $80 per month; and colonels, $90 per month. General officers' pay was brigadier generals, $124 per month; major generals, $220 per month; and lieutenant general, $270 per month. Engineering, ordnance, and other specialty officers typically earned a bit more. All officers also received additional remuneration for uniforms, equipment, and expenses incurred while in camp.

Pay and pay policies in the U.S. Navy differed considerably. Because the navy had a larger number of differentiated personnel and more ranks, the system could get quite complicated. Those under the age of 18 serving aboard ship earned $8 per month. Landsmen—untrained recruits older than 18—earned $12 per month. The regularized enlisted men's pay was as follows: ordinary seamen, $14 per month; seamen, $18 per month; coal heavers, $18 per month; second-class firemen, $25 per month; and first-class firemen, $30 per month. Enlisted men with more specialized skills earned $20–$24 per month. Naval personnel were not paid in cash on a regular basis; instead, their earnings were noted in the ship's pay book and paid upon discharge. African Americans serving in the navy received equal pay.

Officers in the navy were paid on a yearly basis. Their pay scale was as follows: ensigns, $1,200 per year; lieutenants, $1,875 per year; lieutenant commanders, $2,343 per year; commanders, $2,800 per year; captains, $3,500 per year; commodores, $4,000 per year; and rear admirals, $5,000 per year. Officers with special training, such as surgeons, earned $3,000 per year. Paymasters received $3,100 per year, while engineers earned $2,600 per year. Assistant engineers were paid $1,250 per year, while clerks received $1,500 per year. Unlike army officers, whose pay was constant, naval officers' salaries were reduced by about half when on shore duty. Naval officers and enlisted men could earn additional money if their ship happened to seize a Confederate warship or a blockade-runner, the prizes from which were typically divided among the crew after adjudication by a prize court.

Unlike the Confederate War Department, the U.S. War Department was able to pay its soldiers and sailors on a fairly regular schedule and with currency that was not being constantly devalued. Inflation, while a problem in the United States, never reached the ruinous proportions that crippled the Confederacy. Thus, Union military morale, especially as the war dragged on, tended to be higher than in the Confederate armed forces.

PAUL G. PIERPAOLI JR.

See also
Navy, U.S.; Pay, Confederate Army and Navy

Further Reading
Lord, Francis A. *They Fought for the Union.* New York: Random House, 1988.
Wiley, Bell Irvin. *The Life of Billy Yank: The Common Soldier in the Union Army.* Baton Rouge: Louisiana State University Press, 1979.

Payne, Lewis
See Powell, Lewis Thornton

Payne, William Henry Fitzhugh
Birth Date: January 27, 1830
Death Date: March 29, 1904

Confederate officer. William Henry Fitzhugh Payne was born on January 27, 1830, in Fauquier County, Virginia. He attended the Virginia Military Institute and the University of Virginia before setting up a law practice in Warrenton in 1851. He served as a commonwealth attorney until 1861, when he enlisted in the Virginia Militia as a private.

On April 26, 1861, Payne became a captain in the Black Horse Cavalry Company, which became part of the 4th Virginia Cavalry, with Payne appointed major. He saw action during the Peninsula Campaign (March–July 1862) and was wounded and captured at the Battle of Williamsburg (May 5, 1862). Exchanged several months later, he returned to active duty in September with promotion to lieutenant colonel. Payne now took temporary charge of the 2nd North

Carolina Cavalry but was soon sidelined by his lingering battle wound.

After briefly leading the 4th Virginia Cavalry, Payne again received command of the 2nd North Carolina, which he led at the Battle of Chancellorsville (May 1–4, 1863). On June 20, 1863, at the Battle of Hanover, Pennsylvania, Payne was again wounded and taken prisoner. This time he spent nearly a year in the prison camp on Johnson's Island, Ohio. Exchanged in May 1864, he was promoted to colonel of the 4th Virginia but soon took command of a cavalry brigade. Payne next saw combat in Union major general Philip H. Sheridan's Shenandoah Valley Campaign (August 7, 1864–March 2, 1865), during which Payne was finally advanced to brigadier general on November 1, 1864. Ordered to the Richmond area in the spring of 1865, he was wounded a third time at the Battle of Five Forks (April 1, 1865). Payne managed to make it to his home in Warrenton but was captured there by Union forces on April 14. He was released on May 29.

After the war, Payne returned to his Warrenton legal practice. During 1879 and 1880, he served in the Virginia legislature. He also served for a number of years as general counsel for the Southern Railway in Washington, D.C., where he died on March 29, 1904.

PAUL G. PIERPAOLI JR.

See also

Chancellorsville, Battle of; Five Forks, Battle of; Hanover, Battle of; Peninsula Campaign; Sheridan's Shenandoah Valley Campaign; Williamsburg, Battle of

Further Reading

Eicher, John H., and David J. Eicher. *Civil War High Commands.* Stanford, CA: Stanford University Press, 2001.

Warner, Ezra J. *Generals in Gray: Lives of the Confederate Commanders.* Baton Rouge: Louisiana State University Press, 2006.

Peabody, George

Birth Date: February 18, 1795
Death Date: November 4, 1869

American businessman and philanthropist. George Peabody was born on February 18, 1795, in South Danvers, Massachusetts, of old Massachusetts stock but humble means. Despite a lack of educational opportunities, Peabody attained great wealth as a merchant banker in Baltimore and later as an investment banker and importer in London.

Although Peabody remained an American patriot, after 1837 England became his commercial center and permanent home. From there, he agonized over the American Civil War, seeing it as disastrous for the nation's economy and international prestige. He believed that the conflict could have been avoided by the sort of honest mediation that had served him well in business. The British followed the war with intense interest, with the aristocracy favoring the Confederacy and the working classes favoring the Union. Peabody tried to be a positive American influence in London, maintaining friendships on both sides of the divide as a sort of informal diplomat. Still, abhorring slavery, his sympathies were with the Union, and he refused requests by Confederate agents to assist in negotiating a British loan. Because of his moderation, he was sometimes criticized by both Union and Confederate partisans.

Peabody's philosophy combined a secular form of the Puritan doctrine of stewardship with Enlightenment values. Queen Victoria herself gratefully acknowledged his Donation Fund, supplying quality housing for the British "deserving poor." After the war, Peabody routinely addressed Reconstruction in the American South through education, which he called "the debt due from the present to future generations." Keenly acknowledging his own lack of formal schooling, he concluded that education was the surest path out of poverty for both Americans and Europeans. Among his many endowments to his native land, aimed at repairing the devastations of the war, was the Peabody Education Fund, which led to the establishment in 1875 of the George Peabody College for Teachers in Nashville, Tennessee. For many decades, the college remained an independent institution dedicated to providing quality educators for the South and developing nations of the world before becoming part of Vanderbilt University. Peabody died on November 4, 1869, in London.

ALLENE S. PHY-OLSEN

See also

Diplomacy, U.S.; Great Britain; Reconstruction

Further Reading

Dabney, Charles W. *Universal Education in the South.* 2 vols. Chapel Hill: University of North Carolina Press, 1936.

Parker, Franklin. *George Peabody: A Biography.* Nashville: Vanderbilt University Press, 1995.

Peace Democrats

See Copperheads

Peace Movements

Peace or antiwar movements in both the Union and Confederacy were generally limited in scope and confined to certain geographic areas. Much of the opposition to the war on both sides was based on the dislike of conscription and the desire for reunification of the nation rather than steadfast pacifism per se. The Civil War largely silenced what had been a rather active peace movement during the antebellum years.

When war began in April 1861, the American Peace Society and its affiliates broke pacifist ranks, maintaining that the conflict was an unlawful rebellion against authority and demanding that the South return to the Union. The only steadfast opponents of the war were pacifists from the historic peace churches—the Society of Friends (Quakers), the Mennonites, and the Church of the Brethren—who opposed military conscription on religious grounds.

Both warring governments provided limited exemption from military service for religious objectors. The 1862 Pennsylvania Supreme Court case *Kneedler v. Lane,* involving a conscientious objector's challenge to the federal conscription act, was upheld, thus paving the way for objectors to be jailed for refusing to serve or to obey military orders when inducted into federal service. In the Confederacy, similar actions took place but with more authority, given President Jefferson Davis's lack of sympathy for pacifists. On both sides, religious pacifists who refused to pay war taxes witnessed seizure of their property in lieu of payment to support the war.

In the North, opposition to the draft led to the infamous riots of July 1863 in New York City. Angry over the ability of the rich to purchase exemptions, mobs sacked shops, burned numerous buildings, and fought with Union soldiers. In the rioting, several hundred lives were lost. Additional outbreaks protesting conscription took place on a lesser scale in neighboring states and in the Midwest.

In addition, Northern Peace Democrats, or Copperheads, called for a negotiated peace. Strongest in Ohio, Indiana, and Illinois and led by Clement L. Vallandigham until his arrest and conviction in May 1863, the Copperheads denounced military arrests, conscription, and other wartime enactments. Other leaders included Fernando Wood of New York and Alexander Long of Cincinnati. Their main objective was restoration of the Union, not emancipation. The Copperheads also worked with secret societies such as the Knights of the Golden Circle, later renamed the Sons of Liberty in 1864, who called for an immediate truce.

In the Confederacy, opposition to the war led to some instances of food riots and draft evasion. Yeoman farmers and laboring classes sought to avoid both the draft and paying taxes. The desire for peace was strongest in regions populated by nonplanters—much of the upper South and areas in the Appalachian Mountains. The most powerful peace demonstration occurred in North Carolina, where Governor Zebulon Vance actively campaigned against conscription. After the fall of Vicksburg and the Southern defeat at Gettysburg in July 1863, nearly 100 peace meetings were held in North Carolina. Subsequently, in many Southern states some 100,000 people joined two secret orders, the Heroes of America and the Peace Society, that sought to end the conflict by opposing the Confederacy through such tactics as driving away recruiting officers, encouraging desertion, and challenging troop morale.

Criticism of the war on both sides was based primarily on class, economic circumstances, dislike of conscription, and desire for reunion.

CHARLES F. HOWLETT

See also

Commutation; Conscientious Objectors; Copperheads; Draft Dodgers; Knights of the Golden Circle; New York City Draft Riots; Vallandigham, Clement Laird; Vance, Zebulon Baird

Further Reading

Curran, Thomas F. *Soldiers of Peace: Civil War Pacifism and the Postwar Radical Peace Movement.* New York: Fordham University Press, 2003.

Howlett, Charles F., and Robbie Lieberman. *A History of the American Peace Movement from Colonial Times to the Present.* Lewiston, NY: Edwin Mellen, 2008.

Peachtree Creek, Battle of
Event Date: July 20, 1864

Major battle of the Atlanta Campaign (May 5–September 2, 1864). Since launching his campaign to destroy the Confederate Army of Tennessee in May 1864, Union major general William T. Sherman had pushed his three armies some 100 miles into Georgia and by mid-July stood poised to take Atlanta. On July 17, Confederate president Jefferson Davis ordered the removal of General Joseph E. Johnston, commanding the Army of Tennessee, who appeared willing to yield the vital railroad and supply hub without a fight. Johnston's replacement, General John Bell Hood, had little time to address the crisis he inherited, as Sherman's massive

View of battlefield, Peachtree Creek, Georgia. Fought on July 20, 1864, this inconclusive major engagement was part of the May–September 1864 Atlanta Campaign. (Library of Congress)

force was preparing to cross the final significant natural impediment between Hood's army and Atlanta. Sherman's approach, however, presented an opportunity: Major General George Thomas's huge Army of the Cumberland, itself larger than Hood's entire force, was separated by several miles from Sherman's other two field armies. Hood understood that he was expected to fight, and he was determined to strike Thomas's isolated command just after it crossed Peachtree Creek north of the city.

On July 19, Hood issued orders for an elaborate flanking movement by Lieutenant General William J. Hardee's corps against Thomas's exposed left flank, followed by an assault by Lieutenant General Alexander P. Stewart's corps on Thomas's main line. It was a solid plan. For his part, Thomas was not expecting an attack as he began to cross Peachtree Creek and cautiously form up his forces south of that stream. The crossing was completed early on July 20.

Hood's attack was supposed to begin at 1:00 p.m., but the approach of Sherman's remaining forces to the east necessitated a clumsy, swift redeployment that delayed the advance for some two hours. When Hardee finally attacked, he still managed to achieve surprise, but the disjointed and ineffectual effort of his corps gave the Federals time to rally, and the flank held.

Stewart then unleashed his men on Thomas's center, which was manned by Major General Joseph Hooker's XX Corps. The undermanned divisions of Major Generals William W. Loring and Edward C. Walthall attacked furiously and even threatened to pierce the Union line but lacked the weight to drive home the effort. Hooker's men held strong and, aided by the well-served Union artillery, were able to restore their line. Stewart hoped to renew the attack and sought reinforcements for that purpose, but the Union threat to the east—the rapid approach of Major General

James B. McPherson's Army of the Tennessee—compelled Hood to pull the troops whom Stewart needed. By 6:00 p.m. the battle had played out, although sporadic fighting lasted into the night.

For most of the day, Sherman was unaware of Thomas's fight or that his subordinate faced the bulk of Hood's force. Sherman therefore missed an opportunity to overrun the thin lines east of the city. Hood came closer to delivering a stunning blow than Sherman would admit, but in the process the Confederates suffered some 2,500 casualties, the majority in Stewart's corps. The Army of the Cumberland lost roughly 1,700 killed or wounded. The Battle of Peachtree Creek was the first of three major fights around Atlanta during an eight-day period.

DAVID COFFEY

See also

Atlanta, Battle of; Atlanta Campaign; Hardee, William Joseph; Hood, John Bell; Hooker, Joseph; Johnston, Joseph Eggleston; Loring, William Wing; McPherson, James Birdseye; Sherman, William Tecumseh; Stewart, Alexander Peter; Thomas, George Henry; Walthall, Edward Cary

Further Reading

Castel, Albert. *Decision in the West: The Atlanta Campaign of 1864.* Lawrence: University Press of Kansas, 1992.

Coffey, David. *John Bell Hood and the Struggle for Atlanta.* Abilene, TX: McWhiney Foundation Press, 1998.

Pea Ridge, Battle of
Start Date: March 7, 1862
End Date: March 8, 1862

Engagement during the struggle to control Missouri. The Battle of Pea Ridge, also known as the Battle of Elkhorn Tavern, was fought in Benton County, Arkansas, during March 7–8, 1862. On February 10, U.S. major general Samuel R. Curtis had begun a campaign designed to clear Missouri of Confederate forces. Curtis commanded the Army of the Southwest numbering some 11,000 men, while Confederate brigadier general Sterling Price had only 8,000 men. Price offered little effective resistance, and Curtis drove the Confederates from Missouri into northwestern Arkansas.

Once in Arkansas, Price joined his forces to those of Brigadier General Ben McCulloch, and the two then withdrew to north of Fayetteville. There the Confederates reorganized under the aggressive Major General Earl Van Dorn, who had been appointed to command the Trans-Mississippi District, largely to end the quarreling that had been occurring

between Price and McCulloch. Van Dorn formed the Army of the West on March 2 and set it in motion toward the Union forces with the expectation of routing them and then invading Missouri.

Van Dorn ordered Price, McCulloch, and their men north, while Brigadier General Albert Pike was also to advance with his command, consisting primarily of three regiments of Cherokees, totaling some 800 men. In his three forces, Van Dorn commanded some 17,000 men. The ensuing battle is noteworthy as one of the few times in the war when the Confederates outnumbered their Union counterparts.

The Confederate advance began on March 4. The weather turned cold and snowy, slowing the march. To increase speed, Van Dorn left his supply wagons behind, a decision that he would later regret.

Learning of the Confederate advance, Curtis concentrated his four infantry divisions and entrenched in a strong position on Pea Ridge some 10 miles northeast of Bentonville. Some fighting occurred on March 6, when Union brigadier general Franz Sigel was slow to evacuate Bentonville and he and his men were surprised by the Confederates' advance units. But they managed to fight their way through them to the Pea Ridge line.

Van Dorn, who was ill, formulated the battle plan from an ambulance on March 6. He ordered McCulloch and Pike to feint against the Union right and center, respectively, while Price assaulted and turned the Union left near Elkhorn Tavern. To get in position for an attack the next morning, March 7, Price was obliged to march his men all night. Although skirmishing occurred between 6:00 and 7:00 a.m., Price was slow to attack. His assault did not begin until 10:30, and the Federals were thus able to prepare. Troops here under Colonel Eugene A. Carr turned back two Confederate assaults, but a third assault drove the Federals from their position. On the other end of the Union line, the Cherokees, commanded by Colonel Stand Watie, drove back one Union division, but the Federals counterattacked and retook the lost ground. McCulloch was shot and killed by a Union sharpshooter, and his men lost heart. Meanwhile, a fourth assault by Price's men drove Carr's Union troops farther west of Elkhorn Tavern, although Union reserves stabilized the line there by nightfall.

Combat resumed the next day. Curtis, guessing correctly that the Confederates were running out of ammunition (Van Dorn's supply train was a six-hour march distant), sent two of his divisions under Sigel against Price. The massed Union artillery, combined with infantry attacks, forced the Confederates to retreat. On the Union right, the other Union

Kurz & Allison print of the Battle of Pea Ridge, also known as the Battle of Elkhorn Tavern, which was fought in Benton County, Arkansas, on March 7–8, 1862. The first major Union victory in the Trans-Mississippi Theater, it brought Union control of Missouri for more than two years. (Library of Congress)

divisions attacked and smashed the Confederate left. Van Dorn had no recourse but to order a retreat.

Sigel took two divisions and marched toward Keetsville, Missouri, in the mistaken belief that the Confederates had withdrawn in that direction. By the time he had returned, any chance of effective Union pursuit had been lost. Nonetheless, Curtis had won a decisive victory against superior numbers. Union losses were 1,384 (203 killed, 980 wounded, and 201 missing) against as many as 4,600 Confederate losses, including 300 captured. The Battle of Pea Ridge was the first major Union victory in the Trans-Mississippi theater and ensured Union control of Missouri for more than two years.

SPENCER C. TUCKER

See also

Carr, Eugene Asa; Cherokees; McCulloch, Ben; Pike, Albert; Price, Sterling; Sigel, Franz; Southwest, Union Army of the; Van Dorn, Earl; Watie, Stand

Further Reading

Cunningham, Frank. *General Stand Watie's Confederate Indians.* Norman: University of Oklahoma Press, 1998.

Shea, William, and Earl Hess. *Pea Ridge: Civil War Campaign in the West.* Chapel Hill: University of North Carolina Press, 1992.

Pearson, Richmond Mumford
Birth Date: 1805
Death Date: January 5, 1878

North Carolina politician and jurist. Richmond Mumford Pearson was born in 1805 in Rowan County, North Carolina. Educated at the University of North Carolina, he studied law and established a legal practice in Salisbury, North Carolina. A pro-Union Whig, Pearson served in the North Carolina legislature before becoming a superior court judge in 1836. In 1848 he was named an associate justice of the North Carolina Supreme Court. Meanwhile, he also established a law school in the state that garnered an excellent reputation.

In 1858 Pearson was appointed chief justice of the North Carolina Supreme Court. Almost immediately, he made known his belief that secession was fundamentally unconstitutional. Despite his misgivings, however, he remained on the high court once the Civil War began, but he soon ran afoul of the Jefferson Davis administration.

After the Confederate Congress enacted a conscription law in 1862, Pearson pointedly ruled it unconstitutional and issued writs of habeas corpus to free those who had been apprehended as deserters in North Carolina. This outraged the Davis administration, which devised ways to skirt Pearson's actions, including raising the state's volunteer quotas.

In the winter of 1864 after the Confederate government had outlawed the use of substitutes as stand-ins for compulsory military service, Pearson issued a ruling that declared the move unconstitutional. Confederate officials in Richmond, tired of Pearson's conduct, simply ordered North Carolina officials to ignore the judge's rulings. Others demanded that he be impeached.

The iconoclastic Pearson remained chief justice until his death in Winston, North Carolina, on January 5, 1878, having survived various postwar crises, including a serious bid to impeach him in 1870. His embrace of the Republican Party in the late 1860s also did nothing to endear him to most North Carolinians.

PAUL G. PIERPAOLI JR.

See also

Conscription, CSA; Davis, Jefferson Finis; North Carolina

Further Reading

Hutchens, James A. "The Chief-Justiceship and Public Career of Richmond M. Pearson, 1861–1871." MA thesis, University of North Carolina, 1960.

Peck, John James
Birth Date: January 4, 1821
Death Date: April 21, 1878

Union officer. John James Peck was born on January 4, 1821, in Manlius, New York. Peck graduated from the U.S. Military Academy, West Point, in 1843. Commissioned in the artillery, he was stationed in New York. In 1846 he was assigned to Brigadier General Zachary Taylor's Army of Occupation in Texas. In the Mexican-American War (1846–1848), Peck saw combat at the Battles of Palo Alto, Resaca de la Palma, and Monterrey, earning promotion to first lieutenant in 1847. Transferred to Major General Winfield Scott's army,

Peck took part in the landing at Veracruz and fought in the battles of Scott's Mexico City Campaign through the fall of the Mexican capital. Peck was brevetted captain for the Battles of Contreras and Churubusco and to major for his role in the Battle of Molino del Rey.

Peck then served in the Quartermasters Department and in the West and saw action against the Apaches. He resigned his commission on March 1, 1853, and became associated with a New York railroad. He was a delegate to the 1856 and 1860 National Democratic Conventions, and in 1856 he ran for Congress as a Democrat but failed to win election. Peck also was one of the founders of a bank in Syracuse and was president of the Syracuse Board of Education.

On August 9, 1861, Peck received a brigadier general's commission in the Union volunteer army. Initially assigned to the defenses of Washington, D.C., he soon joined Major George B. McClellan's Army of the Potomac in the Peninsula Campaign (March–July 1862), commanding a brigade in IV Corps. Peck saw action in the Siege of Yorktown (April 5–May 3, 1862) and distinguished himself in the Battles of Williamsburg (May 5, 1862) and Fair Oaks/Seven Pines (May 31–June 1, 1862) and again during the Seven Days' Campaign (June 25–July 1, 1862), when he commanded the 2nd Division of IV Corps. For his role in the Battle of Malvern Hill (July 1, 1862), on July 25 he was advanced to major general of volunteers to date from July 4.

Following McClellan's evacuation of the Virginia Peninsula, Peck commanded the Union garrison at Yorktown. In September he assumed command of Union troops in Virginia south of the James River. Learning in advance of Confederate lieutenant general James Longstreet's plan to take Suffolk, Peck was able to take appropriate countermeasures. During the ensuing Siege of Suffolk (April 11–May 4), Peck eventually commanded three divisions. Although Longstreet's men cut the Union supply route, Peck's counteroffensive recovered the lost ground, and the Union forces were victorious at Norfleet House (April 14–15). The Confederates then lifted the siege and withdrew.

In the summer of 1863, Peck assumed command of the District of North Carolina but saw little action. Poor health forced him to take sick leave, but he returned to duty to command the Department of the East along the Canadian frontier from July 1864 until he mustered out of the service on August 25, 1865.

Postbellum, Peck returned to Syracuse, New York, where he organized and became president of the New York State Life Insurance Company. His health deteriorated, and he died in Syracuse on April 21, 1878.

SPENCER C. TUCKER

See also

Couch, Darius Nash; Longstreet, James; Malvern Hill, Battle of; McClellan, George Brinton; Norfleet House, Virginia, Engagements at; Peninsula Campaign; Scott, Winfield; Seven Days' Campaign; Seven Pines, Battle of; Suffolk, Virginia, Siege of; Williamsburg, Battle of; Yorktown, Virginia, Siege of

Further Reading

Cormier, Steven A. *The Siege of Suffolk: The Forgotten Campaign, April 11–May 4, 1863.* Lynchburg, VA: H. E. Howard, 1989.

Eicher, John H., and David J. Eicher. *Civil War High Commands.* Stanford, CA: Stanford University Press, 2001.

Warner, Ezra J. *Generals in Blue: Lives of the Union Commanders.* Baton Rouge: Louisiana State University Press, 2006.

Peck, William Raine
Birth Date: January 13, 1818
Death Date: January 22, 1871

Confederate officer. William Raines Peck was born on January 13, 1818, in Jefferson County, Tennessee. In the 1840s he migrated to Louisiana, where he purchased a large plantation along the Mississippi River. In the spring of 1861, Peck enlisted in Confederate service as a private in the 9th Louisiana Infantry Regiment but was quickly appointed a captain. He saw much action with the 9th Louisiana, mostly in II Corps, Army of Northern Virginia, while advancing steadily in rank. He participated in the Seven Days' Campaign (June 25–July 1, 1862) and the Battles of Antietam (September 17, 1862) and Gettysburg (July 1–3, 1863), among numerous other engagements.

Peck was promoted to colonel on October 8, 1863, and given charge of the 9th Louisiana, which he led ably in several engagements in Virginia during May and June 1864. On several occasions he took temporary brigade command, most notably at the Battle of Monocacy (July 9, 1864) in Maryland, where his performance earned him glowing reports from his superiors. Peck was promoted to brigadier general on February 15, 1865, but did not participate in any other major engagements.

Paroled in Vicksburg on June 6, 1865, Peck returned to his plantation, where he lived quietly but prosperously and died on January 22, 1871.

PAUL G. PIERPAOLI JR.

See also

Antietam, Battle of; Gettysburg, Battle of; Monocacy, Battle of; Seven Days' Campaign

Further Reading

Eicher, John H., and David J. Eicher. *Civil War High Commands.* Stanford, CA: Stanford University Press, 2001.

Warner, Ezra J. *Generals in Gray: Lives of the Confederate Commanders.* Baton Rouge: Louisiana State University Press, 2006.

Peebles' Farm, Battle of
Start Date: September 30, 1864
End Date: October 2, 1864

Engagement during the Petersburg Campaign (June 15, 1864–April 3, 1865). The Battle of Peebles' Farm (also known as the Battle of Poplar Springs Church) was part of Lieutenant General Ulysses S. Grant's continuing effort to probe Confederate lines at Petersburg and Richmond. By so doing, he hoped to perhaps locate a weak spot and break through it. Coupled with the Battle of New Market Heights (September 29, 1864), this engagement has been termed Grant's Fifth Offensive.

Grant ordered Major General George G. Meade, commanding the Army of the Potomac, to attack the Confederate defenses of Petersburg to keep Southern reinforcements from moving north of the James River. He was also ordered to seize the Southside Railroad, a vital link in General Robert E. Lee's tenuous supply lines.

On September 29, 1864, Meade sent about 20,000 men from Major General Gouverneur K. Warren's V Corps and Major General John G. Parke's IX Corps, screened by a cavalry division, west from the Union earthworks along the Weldon Railroad to assault a Confederate line that paralleled the Squirrel Level Road, five miles southwest of Petersburg. In midmorning, Union forces assaulted Peebles' Farm, in the process taking a Confederate fort, a nearby trench line, and 100 Confederate prisoners.

That afternoon, Brigadier General Robert B. Potter's 2nd Division of IX Corps moved left of Peebles' Farm, advancing toward the Pegram House. There it came under attack by Confederate infantry under Major Generals Cadmus Wilcox and Henry Heth. Realizing that support would not be forthcoming, Potter ordered his men, who had become disoriented, to disengage and take up a position at Peebles' Farm. Heth and Wilcox again attacked, but this time Union brigadier general Charles Griffin's men helped repel them.

On September 30 while Union forces solidified their positions at Peebles' Farm, Confederate and Union forces continued to exchange fire. Early on October 2, Union brigadier general David Gregg's cavalry repelled Confederate attacks along the Vaughan Road. Men of the Union V and IX Corps, meanwhile, pressed the Confederates, and portions of IX Corps swept past the Pegram House and came within sight of Lee's new defensive works. II Corps, led by Brigadier General Gershom Mott and now temporarily attached to IX Corps, probed the works briefly before withdrawing. This ended the three-day engagement, which cost the Federals more than 3,000 casualties. Lee's lower flank was still intact. Confederate casualties are unknown.

RICHARD A. SAUERS AND PAUL G. PIERPAOLI JR.

See also

Grant, Ulysses Simpson; Gregg, David McMurtrie; Griffin, Charles; Heth, Henry; Lee, Robert Edward; Mott, Gershom; New Market Heights, Battle of; Parke, John Grubb; Potter, Robert Brown; Warren, Gouverneur Kemble; Wilcox, Cadmus Marcellus

Further Reading

Sommers, Richard J. "The Battle No One Wanted." *Civil War Times Illustrated* 14(5) (August 1975): 10–18.

Sommers, Richard J. *Richmond Redeemed: The Siege at Petersburg.* Garden City, NY: Doubleday, 1981.

Pegg, Thomas
Birth Date: 1806
Death Date: April 22, 1866

Cherokee political leader and acting principal chief of the Cherokee Nation. Born in 1806, Thomas Pegg was from 1853 to 1855 a member of the Senate of the Cherokee Nation and a supporter of Chief John Ross. By 1861, Pegg was president of the Cherokee National Council, when he supported Ross's neutrality policy. In August 1861, however, pressure from slaveholding Cherokees, led by Stand Watie, forced Ross into opening negotiations with the Confederacy, leading to a formal treaty in November.

Union forces invaded Indian Territory in the summer of 1862. Tribal unity collapsed, and the Cherokee Nation was torn apart in the war. Ross was taken to Washington, D.C., where he faced the impossible task of convincing federal authorities that most Cherokees remained loyal to the Union, while Stand Watie had set up a rival government controlling most of Cherokee territory.

Pegg, meanwhile, received a commission as a major in John Drew's 1st Cherokee Mounted Rifles, a regiment loyal to Chief Ross. When Union forces invaded, Pegg and more than 600 of Drew's men joined the Union Army, with Pegg

being commissioned a captain in the 3rd Indian Home Guard Regiment.

On February 17–18, 1863, the Cherokee National Council met at Cowskin Prairie (northeast of present-day Grove in Delaware County, Oklahoma). Consisting primarily of soldiers serving in the Union Indian Home Guard regiments, the council elected Pegg as acting principal chief during Ross's exile in Washington. The council formally abrogated the treaty with the Confederacy, with Pegg taking the position that the treaty had been forced on the Cherokees, who remained loyal to the Union. The council also formally abolished slavery in the Cherokee Nation but also declared that freed slaves had no right to citizenship and were to leave the nation immediately. The council also asserted its right to govern the Cherokee Nation.

After the war Pegg traveled to Washington, D.C., as a member of a delegation to negotiate with the federal government, but he died there on April 22, 1866, before a new treaty could be finalized.

SPENCER C. TUCKER

See also

Cherokees; Native Americans in the Civil War; Watie, Stand

Further Reading

Gaines, W. Craig. *The Confederate Cherokees: John Drew's Regiment of Mounted Rifles.* Baton Rouge: Louisiana State University Press, 1989.

McLoughlin, William G. *After the Trail of Tears: The Cherokees' Struggle for Sovereignty, 1839–1880.* Chapel Hill: University of North Carolina Press, 1993.

Wardell, Morris L. *A Political History of the Cherokee Nation, 1838–1907.* Norman: University of Oklahoma Press, 1938.

Pegram, John
Birth Date: January 24, 1832
Death Date: February 6, 1865

Confederate officer. Born in Petersburg, Virginia, on January 24, 1832, John Pegram came from an old aristocratic Virginia family. Graduating from the U.S. Military Academy, West Point, in 1854, he was commissioned a second lieutenant in the 2nd Dragoon Regiment. After several assignments at western outposts, in 1857 he was promoted to first lieutenant and returned to West Point to teach cavalry tactics. During 1859, he was in Europe observing the Austro-Sardinian War. Following his return in 1860, he was posted to the New Mexico Territory.

In May 1861 following the secession of his home state, Pegram resigned his commission and joined the 20th Virginia Infantry as lieutenant colonel. He saw action at the Battle of Rich Mountain (July 11, 1861), where he was taken prisoner. Paroled in Baltimore in January 1862, Pegram went to Richmond to await assignment. Promoted to colonel, he was assigned to General P. G. T. Beauregard's staff as chief engineer and then held the same post for General Braxton Bragg. By the autumn, Pegram was serving as chief of staff for Major General Edmund Kirby Smith and participated in the Kentucky Campaign (August 14–October 26, 1862).

On November 7, 1862, Pegram was advanced to brigadier general, with command of a cavalry brigade in the Army of Tennessee. He saw combat at the Battle of Stones River (December 31, 1862–January 2, 1863) and at the Battle of Chickamauga (September 19–20, 1863), where he ably commanded a division. In October 1863 he was sent east to serve in the Army of Northern Virginia. At the Battle of the Wilderness (May 5–7, 1864), where he led an infantry brigade, he was wounded in the leg. Recuperated by the autumn, Pegram was sent to the Shenandoah Valley, where he assumed command of a division in II Corps during Sheridan's Shenandoah Valley Campaign (August 7, 1864–March 2, 1865). Returning east once more, Pegram saw action around Petersburg but was killed on February 6, 1865, at the Battle of Hatcher's Run, southwest of Petersburg, just three weeks after he had married. Pegram's brother, highly regarded Confederate artillerist Colonel William J. "Willie" Pegram, was killed less than two months later in the Battle of Five Forks (April 1, 1865).

PAUL G. PIERPAOLI JR.

See also

Beauregard, Pierre Gustav Toutant; Bragg, Braxton; Chickamauga, Battle of; Hatcher's Run, Battle of; Rich Mountain, Battle of; Sheridan's Shenandoah Valley Campaign; Smith, Edmund Kirby; Stones River, Battle of; Wilderness, Battle of the

Further Reading

Warner, Ezra J. *Generals in Gray: Lives of the Confederate Commanders.* Baton Rouge: Louisiana State University Press, 2006.

Pelham, John
Birth Date: September 14, 1838
Death Date: March 17, 1863

Confederate officer. John Pelham was born in Benton City, Alabama, on September 14, 1838. He entered the

Confederate major John Pelham was a brilliant young artillery officer who perfected the practice of the "flying battery," rapidly moving about his guns and seeming to be always in the right place at the right time. Pelham was mortally wounded in fighting at Kelly Ford, Virginia, on March 17, 1863. (Library of Congress)

U.S. Military Academy, West Point, in July 1856 and there excelled in artillery studies under Major Henry J. Hunt. Pelham resigned from West Point after the firing on Fort Sumter, returning to his home state in April 1861, only weeks before his anticipated graduation.

Commissioned a lieutenant in the Confederate Army, Pelham was assigned to Lynchburg, Virginia, as an ordnance officer. He fought in the First Battle of Bull Run (July 21, 1861), where he handled his guns quite effectively on Henry Hill. On the recommendation of General Joseph E. Johnston, Pelham was advanced to captain. In November 1861 he was assigned to command an eight-gun battery of horse artillery in Brigadier General J. E. B. Stuart's cavalry. Pelham gained renown during the battles of the Peninsula Campaign (March–July 1862). Advanced to major in August 1862, he again distinguished himself in the Battle of Antietam (September 17, 1862). With only two guns, which he moved rapidly about, he convinced Union officers that they faced two batteries and thereby held up the Union advance by two hours. Although Pelham fought in some 60 engagements in his brief career, probably his most famous was the First Battle of Fredericksburg (December 13, 1862). Stationed on the Confederate right wing, with a constantly shifting lone gun while under attack from some 20 Union guns, he delayed the Union advance for 45 minutes and forced 5,000 Union troops to be shifted from the main attack on Marye's Heights. In his report of the battle, General Robert E. Lee, commander of the Army of Northern Virginia, described Pelham as "the gallant Pelham."

A brilliant artillerist, Pelham perfected the concept of the flying battery, with his guns always seeming to be in the right place at the right time. He worked to train his men in the efficient management and movement of the guns, greatly improving both the speed with which the men could fire and their accuracy. His horse artillery was able to keep pace with Stuart's cavalry and provided highly effective supporting fire in countless engagements. Certainly Pelham was well liked by his men.

On March 17, 1863, at Kelly Ford, Virginia, Pelham impetuously joined in a charge by the 3rd Virginia Cavalry, only to be mortally wounded in the neck by Union shrapnel. He died at Culpeper, Virginia, that same day. Pelham was much admired for his skills and for his youthful, handsome appearance. His loss was deeply felt throughout the Confederacy, and a contemporary wrote a popular poem, "The Dead Cannoneer," in his honor. Pelham was posthumously advanced to the rank of lieutenant colonel, and General Stuart insisted that his body lie in state in Richmond. After the war, Pelham became celebrated as one of the heroes of the Lost Cause.

ROBERT H. CLEMM AND SPENCER C. TUCKER

See also

Antietam, Battle of; Artillery, Land, CSA; Bull Run, First Battle of; Fredericksburg, First Battle of; Lost Cause; Peninsula Campaign; Stuart, James Ewell Brown

Further Reading

Hassler, William Woods. *Colonel John Pelham: Lee's Boy Artillerist.* Chapel Hill: University of North Carolina Press, 1960.
Mercer, Philip. *The Gallant Pelham.* Kennesaw, GA: Continental Book Company, 1958.
Milham, Charles G. *Gallant Pelham: American Extraordinary.* Washington, DC: PublicAffairs, 1959.

Pember, Phoebe Yates Levy
Birth Date: August 18, 1823
Death Date: March 4, 1913

Confederate nurse, matron, and writer. Phoebe Yates Levy was born into privilege on August 18, 1823, in Charleston, South Carolina. There is no record of her education, but her book, surviving letters, and stories suggest that it was excellent. Around 1850, the Levy family moved to Savannah. Phoebe married Thomas Pember of Boston, who died

of tuberculosis shortly after the Civil War began. She then returned to Savannah. In 1862 the family left the city and settled in Marietta, Georgia. Through the influence of the wife of Confederate secretary of war George W. Randolph, Phoebe Pember was offered a salaried appointment as the first matron (chief nurse) at Chimborazo Military Hospital Number Two in Richmond.

Pember reported for work at the hospital in December 1862 with energetic determination. No provision had been made to house women, so she converted an outbuilding into her quarters and slept on a straw mattress. She was responsible for the 600 men in the hospital.

Confederate hospitals faced chronic shortages of food, personnel, and medical supplies, but Pember did an admirable job scrambling to secure limited resources. She had once been accused of taking up hospital work to find romance, so she was careful not to fraternize with the staff. In 1863 she moved to rooms in the city, and evenings spent with Richmond's elite raised her spirits. Pember remained devoted to her work and her patients. Making rounds twice a day, she wrote letters for patients and learned recipes to tempt homesick convalescents. When Richmond fell in 1865, Union officers took charge of the hospital and began bringing in their own wounded. Pember stayed on to care for her patients until the last had left. By early June, she rejoined her family in Georgia.

A serialized version of Pember's hospital journal was published in the *Cosmopolite* in 1866. Revised, it was issued as *A Southern Woman's Story* in 1879. Pember wrote and traveled widely before dying in Pittsburgh on March 4, 1913.

NANCY GRAY SCHOONMAKER

See also

Hospitals, Military; Nurses; Women

Further Reading

Green, Carol C. *Chimborazo: The Confederacy's Largest Hospital.* Knoxville: University of Tennessee Press, 2004.
Pember, Phoebe Yates Levy. *A Southern Woman's Story.* Columbia: University of South Carolina Press, 2002.

Pemberton, John Clifford
Birth Date: August 10, 1814
Death Date: July 13, 1881

Confederate officer. Born in Philadelphia on August 10, 1814, John Clifford Pemberton graduated from the U.S. Military Academy at West Point in 1837. Commissioned in the artillery, he served in a variety of posts, earning promotion to first lieutenant in 1842. Pemberton served in the Mexican-American War (1846–1848) and was brevetted twice for gallantry. Afterward he continued in the regular army, rising to captain in 1850.

At the beginning of the Civil War, Pemberton, at the urging of his Virginia-born wife, opted to support the Confederacy, resigning his commission in the U.S. Army and accepting a lieutenant colonelcy in the Virginia state forces. Entering the Confederate Army as a major of artillery, he was quickly appointed a brigadier general. His first major assignment was to command the coastal defenses of Charleston, South Carolina. He was advanced to major general in January 1862 and thereafter held a variety of administrative commands.

In October 1862, President Jefferson Davis appointed Pemberton lieutenant general and assigned him to command in Mississippi. The main Union target within the state was the Mississippi river town of Vicksburg. Perched on high rugged bluffs overlooking a bend in the river, Vicksburg stood as the chief barrier to Union control of the Mississippi. Although it was supported by several subsidiary outposts farther south, the most significant of which was Port Hudson, Louisiana, Vicksburg was the key to the Confederacy's hold on the Mississippi, protecting the flow of supplies from the Trans-Mississippi states of Arkansas, Louisiana, and Texas to the Southern states east of the river.

Pemberton's first test came very soon after he assumed command. A Union army commanded by Major General Ulysses S. Grant advanced into Mississippi from the north, following the tracks of the Mississippi Central Railroad. Pemberton's army retreated steadily in front of Grant, who advanced through Holly Springs and Abbeville to Oxford, 50 miles into the state. Believing his force inadequate to meet that of Grant, Pemberton called on Davis for reinforcements and meanwhile dispatched Major General Earl Van Dorn to lead a cavalry raid aimed at Grant's supply lines. Both efforts were successful. Van Dorn destroyed Grant's supply depot at Holly Springs on December 20, 1862, forcing a Union withdrawal from the state. Davis, overriding the objections of western theater commander General Joseph E. Johnston, detached 10,000 men from General Braxton Bragg's Army of Tennessee and sent them to Pemberton.

Before the reinforcements could arrive, Pemberton had successfully dealt with yet another threat. On Grant's orders, Major General William T. Sherman had led a second Union column down the Mississippi to attack Vicksburg directly from the north, hoping that Pemberton would be distracted

Confederate lieutenant general John Clifford Pemberton commanded Confederate forces in Mississippi. He did battle with Union troops under Major General Ulyssses S. Grant but was then bottled up at Vicksburg and forced to surrender following a siege, on July 4, 1863. (Library of Congress)

dealing with Grant's force in the interior. With Grant in retreat, however, Pemberton was free to turn his full attention to Sherman. The most significant factor in Confederate success was the terrain north of Vicksburg, which funneled the Union attack into a few easily defended corridors. The result was a lopsided Confederate victory at the Battle of Chickasaw Bluffs (December 26–29, 1862).

In April 1863, Grant launched a new campaign, sending his gunboats and transports past Vicksburg, then crossing his army into Mississippi below the town and marching for Jackson, squarely in Vicksburg's rear. Despite his advantage in overall numbers within the state of Mississippi, Pemberton was distracted by diversions that Grant planned and was unprepared for the speed and boldness of Grant's campaign. Pemberton's response was confused and hesitant. Ordered by Johnston to pull all his troops out of fortresses and combine them for an open-field battle against Grant in the interior of the state, Pemberton started to do so. Then he received a cryptic telegram from Davis that Pemberton interpreted to mean he was not to leave Vicksburg or Port Hudson ungarrisoned at any time. Returning the garrisons, he set out to meet Grant with a reduced field force.

Grant met and defeated Pemberton at the Battle of Champion Hill (May 16, 1863) and defeated him again the next day at Big Black River Bridge. What was left of Pemberton's field army fled back into the Vicksburg fortifications. Grant followed and laid siege. On July 4, 1863, with food running low and Grant's approach trenches only a few feet outside his breastworks, Pemberton surrendered. He was subsequently paroled and exchanged.

With no suitable command available at his rank, Pemberton resigned his lieutenant general's commission and became a lieutenant colonel in the artillery. After the war, he retired near Warrenton, Virginia, and then returned to Pennsylvania, where he died in the village of Penllyn on July 31, 1881.

STEVEN E. WOODWORTH

See also
Big Black River, First Battle of; Champion Hill, Battle of; Chickasaw Bluffs, Battle of; Grant, Ulysses Simpson; Holly Springs, Mississippi, Raid on; Johnston, Joseph Eggleston; Sherman, William Tecumseh; Van Dorn, Earl; Vicksburg Campaign, First; Vicksburg Campaign, Second

Further Reading
Ballard, Michael B. *Pemberton: A Biography.* Jackson: University Press of Mississippi, 1991.

Bearss, Edwin Cole. *The Campaign for Vicksburg.* 3 vols. Dayton, OH: Morningside, 1985–1986.

Shea, William L., and Terrence J. Winschel. *Vicksburg Is the Key: The Struggle for the Mississippi River.* Lincoln: University of Nebraska Press, 2003.

Pender, William Dorsey
Birth Date: February 6, 1834
Death Date: July 18, 1863

Confederate officer. William Dorsey Pender was born in Edgecombe County, North Carolina, on February 6, 1834. He graduated from the U.S. Military Academy, West Point, in 1854 and was assigned to service in the West, primarily with the 1st U.S. Dragoons.

Pender resigned his commission as a first lieutenant on March 21, 1861, prior to North Carolina's secession and was commissioned a captain of artillery in the regular Confederate Army. Upon his home state's secession, he became colonel of the 3rd (later 13th) North Carolina Infantry Regiment before transferring to the 6th North Carolina. Pender soon

established a reputation as a rough and tumble commander. He performed brilliantly at the Battle of Seven Pines (May 31–June 1, 1862) and in the subsequent Seven Days' Campaign (June 25–July 1, 1862), earning promotion to brigadier general to date from June 3, 1862.

Pender then assumed command of a brigade in Lieutenant General Ambrose P. Hill's Light Division. Pender saw action at the Battle of Cedar Mountain (August 9, 1862), the Battle of Harpers Ferry (September 12–15, 1862), the Battle of Antietam (September 17, 1862), the First Battle of Fredericksburg (December 13, 1862), and the Battle of Chancellorsville (May 1–4, 1863). He was the kind of commander who led from the front and, as a result, was wounded three times. Pender was advanced to major general on May 27, 1863, and assumed command of a division in Lieutenant General A. P. Hill's III Corps.

Pender's next major engagement was the Battle of Gettysburg (July 1–3, 1863). He was conspicuous on the first day of fighting. On the second day of the battle, however, he was wounded in the thigh from a shell fragment. With its new commander incapacitated, on the battle's fateful third day Pender's division participated in the ill-fated Pickett's Charge under Major General Isaac Trimble.

Pender returned to the Old Dominion with the defeated Army of Northern Virginia. By then, however, his wound had become infected. Army surgeons amputated his leg, but Pender did not long survive. He died in Staunton, Virginia, on July 18, 1863.

ALAN K. LAMM

See also
Antietam, Battle of; Cedar Mountain, Battle of; Chancellorsville, Battle of; Fredericksburg, First Battle of; Gettysburg, Battle of; Harpers Ferry, Battle of; Peninsula Campaign; Seven Pines, Battle of

Further Reading
Hassler, William E., ed. *One of Lee's Best Men: The Civil War Letters of General William Dorsey Pender.* Chapel Hill: University of North Carolina Press, 1999.

Longacre, Edward. *General William Dorsey Pender: A Military Biography.* Conshohocken, PA: Combined Publishing, 2001.

Pendleton, Alexander Swift
Birth Date: September 28, 1840
Death Date: September 23, 1864

Confederate officer. Born on September 28, 1840, near Alexandria, Virginia, Alexander Swift "Sandie" Pendleton attended Washington College (today Washington and Lee University) beginning at age 13. He taught at Washington College for 2 years following his graduation, then entered the University of Virginia in 1859 to earn a master's degree.

On May 17, 1861, Pendleton secured a commission as a second lieutenant of engineers in the Provisional Army of Virginia. A week later he reported for duty at Harpers Ferry, Virginia, where Confederate forces were organizing into the Army of the Shenandoah. However, on Pendleton's arrival, Brigadier General Thomas J. Jackson asked him to join his staff as ordnance officer.

Pendleton saw action at the First Battle of Bull Run (July 21, 1861). With his commission in the Provisional Army soon expiring, he applied for a commission in the Confederate Army and for three months served without rank.

During the First Battle of Kernstown (March 23, 1862), Pendleton was commended for his gallantry. However, three weeks after the Battle of Cedar Mountain (August 9, 1862), Pendleton was forced to leave his unit to recover in Lexington, Virginia, from what he called "Chickahominy Fever." He returned to action in time to witness the surrender of the Union garrison at Harpers Ferry on September 15, 1862, and two days later was in the midst of the Battle of Antietam (September 17). Two months after Jackson's promotion to lieutenant general in October 1862, Pendleton was promoted to major and permanently assigned as the assistant adjutant general for II Corps, Army of Northern Virginia.

Following the death of Jackson on May 10, 1863, and the reorganization of the army, General Richard Ewell assumed command of II Corps and retained Pendleton on his staff. Ewell recommended Pendleton for a lieutenant colonelcy, which he received in August 1863. During the Battle of the Wilderness (May 5–7, 1864) and the Battle of Spotsylvania Court House (May 8–21), Pendleton had two horses shot from under him but escaped unscathed.

During the summer of 1864, II Corps, now under Lieutenant General Jubal Early, was sent to the Shenandoah Valley, where during the Battle at Fisher's Hill (September 22, 1864) Pendleton was reported everywhere on the battlefield. He escaped unharmed until the battle was almost over. At dusk while trying to establish a line at Toms Brook, he received a mortal gunshot wound in the abdomen and died the following evening. Temporarily buried in Woodstock, Virginia, his body was removed and buried in Lexington on October 25, 1864, not far from Jackson's own grave.

R. RAY ORTENSIE

See also

Antietam, Battle of; Bull Run, First Battle of; Cedar Mountain, Battle of; Early, Jubal Anderson; Ewell, Richard Stoddart; Fisher's Hill, Battle of; Harpers Ferry, Virginia; Hill, Ambrose Powell; Jackson, Thomas Jonathan; Kernstown, First Battle of; Shenandoah, Confederate Army of the; Spotsylvania Court House, Battle of; Wilderness, Battle of the

Further Reading

Bean, William G. *Stonewall's Man: Sandie Pendleton.* Chapel Hill: University of North Carolina Press, 2000.

Bowers, John. *Stonewall Jackson: Portrait of a Soldier.* New York: William Morrow, 1989.

Robertson, James I., Jr. *Stonewall Jackson: The Man, the Soldier, the Legend.* New York: Macmillan, 1997.

Pendleton, George Hunt
Birth Date: July 19, 1825
Death Date: November 24, 1889

Democratic candidate for vice president in 1864. George Hunt Pendleton was born on July 19, 1825, in Cincinnati, Ohio. He attended schools in Cincinnati and received private tutoring at home. Pendleton was admitted to the Ohio bar in 1847 and began a career in law and politics. In 1853 he was elected to the Ohio Senate, and in 1856 he won a seat in the U.S. House of Representatives, where he served until March 1865.

Pendleton was a follower of Democratic senator Stephen A. Douglas in the debates on slavery and opposed extremists on both sides. When Abraham Lincoln was elected president in 1860, Pendleton worked for a compromise to prevent the South's secession. During the war, he opposed vigorous military attacks on the Confederacy. Pendleton also became an outspoken critic of the suspension of habeas corpus and the trial of civilians in military courts.

When the Democratic Party divided into factions, Pendleton became a Copperhead, or Peace Democrat. He was also close friends with fellow Ohio congressman Clement L. Vallandigham. During the winter of 1862, the two gave a series of speeches throughout the North attacking emancipation and accusing Lincoln of conspiring all along to destroy slavery.

To assuage the peace wing of the party, in 1864 Pendleton was selected as former Union general in chief George B. McClellan's running mate. McClellan and Pendleton went down to defeat in the autumn election.

When the war's end became imminent, Pendleton's attention turned to other matters. He opposed the Thirteenth Amendment, terming it unconstitutional. He also became the spokesman for the Pendleton Plan, which urged that all bonds issued by the federal government to finance the war be redeemable for greenbacks instead of hard currency. In 1869 Pendleton lost a bid for the Ohio governorship. For the next 10 years, he served as president of the Kentucky Central Railroad.

In 1878 Pendleton was elected to the U.S. Senate. There he championed civil service reform. This proved unpopular, however, and he was not reelected in 1884. He was appointed minister to Germany in 1885. Pendleton died on November 24, 1889, in Brussels, Belgium.

TIM J. WATTS

See also

Congress, U.S.; Copperheads; Democratic Party; Douglas, Stephen Arnold; Election of 1864, U.S.; McClellan, George Brinton; Slavery; Thirteenth Amendment; Vallandigham, Clement Laird

Further Reading

Mach, Thomas S. "Family Ties, Party Realities, and Political Ideology: George Hunt Pendleton and Partisanship in Antebellum Cincinnati." *Ohio Valley History* 3(2) (2003): 17–30.

Mach, Thomas S. *"Gentleman George" Hunt Pendleton: Party Politics and Ideological Identity in Nineteenth-Century America.* Kent, OH: Kent State University Press, 2007.

Pendleton, William Nelson
Birth Date: December 26, 1809
Death Date: January 15, 1883

Confederate officer. Born in Richmond, Virginia, on December 26, 1809, William Nelson Pendleton graduated from the U.S. Military Academy, West Point, in 1830 and was commissioned a second lieutenant in the 2nd Artillery Regiment. His regiment was posted to the defense of Charleston Harbor, but Pendleton contracted malaria and was assigned to the federal arsenal at Augusta, Georgia, to recover.

Ordered to West Point to teach mathematics in 1831, the next year Pendleton was assigned to the 4th Artillery. He resigned his commission in 1833 and joined the faculty of Bristol College in Pennsylvania to teach mathematics. In 1837 he joined the faculty of Newark College in Delaware in the same capacity. In 1837 Pendleton was ordained an Episcopal minister, and in 1840 he assumed a teaching position at the Episcopal Boys' High School in Wilmington, Delaware. In 1847 Pendleton gave up teaching to become the minister of All Saints' Church in Baltimore, Maryland. In 1857 he relocated to Lexington, Virginia, as pastor of Grace Episcopal Church (now R. E. Memorial Episcopal Church).

With the beginning of the Civil War, Pendleton joined the Confederate Army as a captain on March 16. On May 1 he took command of the Rockbridge Artillery battery of four guns, which he named Matthew, Mark, Luke, and John after the writers of the Gospels. On July 2, Pendleton's battery took part in the minor Battle of Falling Waters. Promoted to colonel on July 13, Pendleton served as chief of artillery for Brigadier General Joseph E. Johnston during the First Battle of Bull Run (July 21, 1861) and was slightly wounded.

Pendleton then commanded the artillery of the Confederate Army of the Potomac, which became the Army of Northern Virginia in the spring of 1862. Promoted to brigadier general on March 26, he was injured in early July when he was kicked by a mule. Given charge by General Robert E. Lee of Confederate rearguard infantry during the Battle of Shepherdstown (September 19–20) at the close of the Antietam Campaign (September 4–20), Pendleton panicked and lost four of his guns.

Pendleton continued to serve with the Army of Northern Virginia for the remainder of the war but in administrative positions, with his only active command being that of the artillery reserve. Surrendering with the rest of the army at Appomattox Court House on April 9, 1865, he was paroled and returned to Lexington.

Following the war, Pendleton resumed his position at Grace Church, which he held the remainder of his life. He played a major role in convincing Lee to move to Lexington and take up the presidency of Washington College (Washington and Lee University). Lee became a parishioner at Grace Church, with his last official act attending a vestry meeting.

Pendleton died in Lexington on January 15, 1883. His only son, Alexander Swift "Sandie" Pendleton, also served in the Confederate Army and was killed in the Battle of Fisher's Hill (September 23, 1864).

SPENCER C. TUCKER

See also

Antietam Campaign; Bull Run, First Battle of; Falling Waters, Battle of; Johnston, Joseph Eggleston; Lee, Robert Edward; Lexington, Virginia; Pendleton, Alexander Swift; Shepherdstown, Virginia, Engagement at

Further Reading

Lee, Susan P. *Memoirs of William Nelson Pendleton*. Penn Laird, VA: Sprinkle, 1991.

Warner, Ezra J. *Generals in Gray: Lives of the Confederate Commanders*. Baton Rouge: Louisiana State University Press, 2006.

Peninsula, Confederate Army of the

Armed component of the Confederate Department of the Peninsula that played an important role in the opening phase of the Peninsula Campaign (March–July 1862). The Army of the Peninsula was formally established on June 12, 1861, under the command of Colonel John B. Magruder, who was advanced to brigadier general on June 17, 1861. The army had already repelled a Union offensive at the Battle of Big Bethel (June 10, 1861). During the remainder of the summer and into the autumn, Magruder waged numerous skirmishes and arranged three defensive lines east of Richmond and onto the Virginia Peninsula—one near Hampton, another one along the Warwick River, and a third at Williamsburg. He hoped to protect the capital in Richmond and blunt a Union assault from the east.

Meanwhile, Union major general George B. McClellan was planning a full-scale assault on Richmond via an amphibious operation from Alexandria, Virginia, to Fort Monroe at the tip of the Virginia Peninsula. McClellan began his operation on March 17. By April, Magruder's force numbered about 17,000 men, situated along an eight-mile front. His force seemed ill-suited to oppose the advancing Union army of some 60,000 men. Despite being greatly outnumbered, on April 16 Magruder's men successfully resisted the Federals along the Warwick River at Lee's Mill. Magruder's stout defense helped the Confederates build up their works at Richmond and convinced McClellan that he would have to lay siege to Yorktown. On April 26, General Joseph E. Johnston took command of Magruder's men and absorbed them into his force, at which time the Army of the Peninsula ceased to exist as a separate command.

PAUL G. PIERPAOLI JR.

See also

Big Bethel, Battle of; Johnston, Joseph Eggleston; Magruder, John Bankhead; McClellan, George Brinton; Peninsula, Confederate Department of the; Peninsula Campaign

Further Reading

Eicher, John H., and David J. Eicher. *Civil War High Commands*. Stanford, CA: Stanford University Press, 2001.

Peninsula, Confederate Department of the

Confederate military administrative unit established on May 26, 1861. Colonel John B. Magruder, who was later advanced to major general, commanded the Confederate Department of the Peninsula, which was headquartered at Yorktown. The department initially encompassed part of the lower Virginia Peninsula, that region between the James and York Rivers stretching from Hampton to the east toward Jamestown and Williamsburg to the west. The area offered land and river approaches to Richmond, the Confederate capital, so the Confederates were determined to protect it from a Union offensive. On August 26, 1861, the department was expanded to include Middlesex, Matthews, and Gloucester Counties. On September 18, 1861, the department was further expanded with the addition of King and Queen, King William, Prince George, and Surry Counties, encompassing much of the peninsula.

Magruder immediately set about building and strengthening fortifications and raising troops. By December 1861, he had some 13,000 troops under his command. Magruder's defensive preparations and bluffing tactics helped stall the Union's massive Peninsula Campaign (March–July 1862), which ended in a frustrating defeat. On April 12, 1862, the department was merged with the Department of Northern Virginia, commanded by General Joseph E. Johnston.

PAUL G. PIERPAOLI JR.

See also

Johnston, Joseph Eggleston; Magruder, John Bankhead; Peninsula Campaign

Further Reading

Eicher, John H., and David J. Eicher. *Civil War High Commands*. Stanford, CA: Stanford University Press, 2001.

Peninsula Campaign

Start Date: March 1862
End Date: July 1862

First large-scale Union offensive in the eastern theater. In July 1861, President Abraham Lincoln had called to Washington Major General George B. McClellan, commander of the Department of the Ohio and recent victor over Confederate forces in western Virginia. Lincoln gave McClellan command of the Division of the Potomac, and the general had immediately formed what would be the largest field force of the war, the Army of the Potomac, and commenced its training.

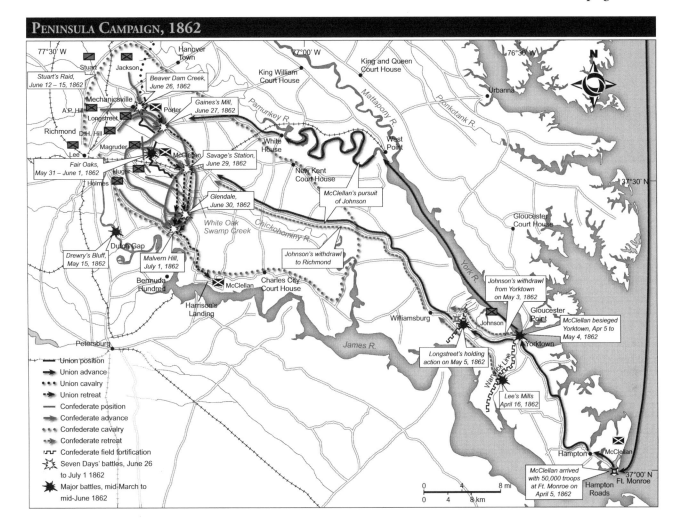

PENINSULA CAMPAIGN, 1862

On November 1 on the retirement of Brevet Lieutenant General Winfield Scott, McClellan assumed the post of general in chief, and Lincoln charged him with undertaking major offensive action against the Confederacy. Lincoln's preference was for a direct drive south from Washington, but McClellan preferred a flanking movement. Utilizing Union naval predominance, he planned to move the Army of the Potomac by water to Urbanna on the Rappahannock River, then advance overland on Richmond, 50 miles to the west.

Before McClellan could carry out his plan, however, Confederate general Joseph E. Johnston withdrew his Army of the Potomac (soon renamed the Army of Northern Virginia) south from the area of Manassas Junction near Washington to new positions south of the Rappahannock. This move forced McClellan to recast his strategy. He would instead disembark his troops at Union-held Fort Monroe at the end of the Virginia Peninsula, between the James and York Rivers, and then, supported by flanking Union naval forces, advance up the peninsula toward Richmond.

A complicating factor in McClellan's plan arose in the form of the Confederate ironclad ram *Virginia*. It sortied from Norfolk on March 8 to attack the Union naval buildup off Fort Monroe and that day sank the U.S. Navy sailing sloop *Cumberland* and the frigate *Congress* in Hampton Roads. Although the U.S. Navy ironclad *Monitor* arrived on the scene that evening and the next day fought the *Virginia* to a draw, which ensured the protection of McClellan's debarkation at Fort Monroe, the *Virginia* controlled access to the James, and Confederate shore batteries at Yorktown and Gloucester Point blocked Union access to the York.

On March 11, 1862, Lincoln, frustrated by McClellan's continued inactivity despite his own frequent orders and pleas, removed the general from the supreme command, leaving him with the Army of the Potomac, supposedly so he could concentrate on the operation against Richmond. McClellan professed to see in this an effort on the part of the president to bring about the failure of his peninsula plan.

Fearful of a Confederate descent on Washington from Confederate forces in the Shenandoah Valley while

McClellan was driving up the peninsula, Lincoln had agreed with McClellan's critics and decided to withhold Major General Irvin McDowell's large corps of some 40,000 men in order to protect the federal capital. As soon as Union forces had eliminated Confederate forces in the valley under Major General Thomas J. Jackson, McDowell would be released to move south and join McClellan against Richmond.

After a number of delays, on March 17, 1862, McClellan began embarking his forces from Alexandria, Virginia, with the U.S. Navy moving a total of some 121,500 men to Fort Monroe. McClellan then commenced what would be a glacial advance, earning him the unflattering nickname "the Virginia Creeper," after the vine of that name.

On April 4 McClellan began his advance with about 90,000 men, only to come up against the Confederate Warwick Line across the peninsula. Confederate major general John Magruder, a master of theatrics with only some 20,000 men, employed various devices, including moving his troops about in view of Union observers and building Quaker guns to convince McClellan that he had many more men than was actually the case. Indeed, McClellan asserted that Magruder commanded 100,000 men.

McClellan called for heavy siege guns and commenced a protracted siege of Yorktown. The ensuing monthlong delay gave General Johnston ample time to reinforce Magruder and also move the bulk of his forces from Culpeper into the peninsula to confront McClellan. Still, Johnston was outnumbered 2 to 1. McClellan would have available some 112,000 men, while the Confederates had only some 56,000, eventually under Johnston's direct command.

General Robert E. Lee, military adviser to President Jefferson Davis, recommended that Jackson, reinforced to some 18,000 men, demonstrate in the Shenandoah Valley in order to draw the largest number of possible Union reinforcements from McClellan. Union major general Nathaniel P. Banks was supposed to clear the valley as part of McClellan's drive on Richmond, after which he would cover Washington, permitting McDowell's corps to advance south from Fredericksburg and join McClellan at Richmond. During March 23–June 9, Jackson carried out a brilliant campaign, tying down more than 64,000 Union troops and defeating forces under Banks, Major General John C. Frémont, and Brigadier General James Shields. Jackson's intelligence and communications were excellent, and his infantry marched 646 miles during a span of 48 days, moving so quickly that they became known as "foot cavalry." In a series of battles, Jackson defeated the Union forces in detail, causing them to withdraw across the Potomac. Union losses were

approximately 8,000 men; the Confederates lost fewer than 2,500. Although this was beyond his means, there was great fear in Washington that Jackson might then strike for the capital. Lincoln detached some 20,000 men from McDowell's command and rushed them to the valley. Meanwhile, Jackson slipped away for Richmond and the critical battles there.

At Yorktown, with McClellan at last preparing to launch a major assault on the Confederate lines, Magruder slipped away on the night of May 3. Discovering the Confederate departure the next morning, the Union forces pursued. A stubborn rearguard action at Williamsburg on May 5 conducted by Major General James Longstreet prevented McClellan from coming into contact with the main portion of Johnston's army. The battle resulted in 2,239 Union and 1,703 Confederate casualties. Each side claimed victory.

In the Battle of Eltham's Landing (May 7), McClellan dispatched Brigadier General William B. Franklin's 1st Division up the York in an amphibious turning movement. In the ensuing inconclusive action, Franklin failed to intercept Johnston's supply trains withdrawing up the peninsula toward Richmond.

On May 6, Lincoln had arrived at Fort Monroe with Secretary of War Edwin Stanton. Believing that Norfolk was vulnerable and with McClellan absent, Lincoln used his powers as commander in chief to order Union warships to shell forts in the vicinity on May 8. Two days later, Union troops occupied Norfolk. This action doomed the *Virginia*. Unable to proceed up the James because of that river's shallow water, it was burned the next day to keep it from falling into Union hands.

With the only real obstacle preventing passage up the James being Confederate Fort Darling and river obstacles at Drewry's Bluff only seven miles from the Confederate capital, Lincoln urged an ascent of the river in an attempt to seize Richmond by coup de main. On May 15 in the First Battle of Drewry's Bluff, the Confederates turned back the small Union naval force.

Johnston, meanwhile, had withdrawn into the Richmond defenses, and by May 14 the Army of the Potomac had reached its base of operations at White House Landing on the Pamunkey River 20 miles from Richmond. Despite overwhelming strength, McClellan now halted to await reinforcement by McDowell's corps at Fredericksburg. By the end of May, engineers with the Army of the Potomac had constructed bridges across the Chickahominy River. About two-thirds of the army was north of the river, and one-third of the army was south of it.

A bridge on the Chickahominy River, Virginia, built May 27–28, 1862, during the Peninsula Campaign by the 5th New Hampshire Infantry Regiment. (Library of Congress)

McClellan's army was now extended in a great "V" shape, the upper arm of which stretched out to meet McDowell and the lower portion reaching out to within five miles of Richmond, just beyond Fair Oaks Station. The Union dispositions on both sides of the Chickahominy played an important role in the Battle of Seven Pines (May 31–June 1, 1862). On May 31, Johnston ordered an attack on two Union corps on the south bank of the Chickahominy, now isolated by the flooded river from the main part of McClellan's army when swollen river waters washed away the footbridges. Only the timely arrival of another corps that managed to cross the river staved off a disastrous Union defeat. In the Battle of Seven Pines, Johnston sustained heavy losses. Union casualties were under 6,000; Confederate casualties were almost 8,000, including Johnston, who was severely wounded. On June 1, Davis replaced Johnston with Lee. From June 12 to June 15, Lee's cavalry commander, Brigadier General James E. B. Stuart with a force of 1,200 men, rode entirely around McClellan's army, destroying Union supplies and rattling the Union commander, now firmly convinced that he was outnumbered.

Lee, determined to drive McClellan off the peninsula, now put together some 97,000 men (the largest force he would ever command) and hurled them against McClellan in what became known as the Seven Days' Campaign (June 25–July 1, 1862). General Jackson had just arrived from the Shenandoah Valley, and Lee planned to send Jackson and his corps in a flanking attack against Major General Fitz John Porter's corps on the north side of the Chickahominy. With most of his army concentrated just west of Mechanicsville, Lee would move against McClellan's center.

The offensive was poorly handled. Jackson, physically spent by the just-concluded Shenandoah Valley Campaign, failed to exercise effective command and displayed uncharacteristic lethargy. His men never got into the fight in the Battle of Mechanicsville on June 26. Porter managed to turn back uncoordinated Confederate assaults and, learning of Jackson's approach, retired to Gaines' Mill.

Lee again attacked Porter on June 27 in the Battle of Gaines' Mill. Jackson was again late arriving and failed to get in behind Porter's right flank, as Lee had planned. Lee managed to penetrate Porter's left, however. In danger of a double envelopment with the approach of Jackson, Porter managed to withdraw in good order, thanks to the timely arrival of Union reinforcements.

That night on McClellan's order, Porter withdrew to the south bank of the Chickahominy. Ignoring appeals from Brigadier General Philip Kearny and Major General Joseph E. Hooker that Richmond was his for the taking if he would only order offensive action, McClellan withdrew to the James River and the protection of Union gunboats. During June 29–30, Lee pursued, suffering sharp rebuffs at the hands of Union forces in battles at Savage's Station, White Oak Swamp, and Glendale-Frayser's Farm. Jackson again failed to envelop the Union right flank.

In the Battle of Malvern Hill (July 1, 1862), in the absence of McClellan, Porter exercised command, and the Army of the Potomac, supported by the heavy guns in the Union river squadron, turned back Lee's desperate attacks, during which the Army of Northern Virginia suffered more than 5,000 casualties in the span of a few hours. Although he won a clear victory, an unnerved McClellan ordered an immediate retreat to Harrison's Landing. The next day, the Confederates withdrew toward Richmond. In the Seven Days' Campaign, the Union suffered nearly 16,000 casualties, but Confederate losses were more than 20,000.

McClellan had fumbled away victory. He informed Washington during the campaign that he was outnumbered two to one, when the reverse was true. With a little more energy, the war might have been ended or drastically shortened. McClellan's contribution to the Union war effort lay in training the Army of the Potomac, not in leading it in battle.

Recognizing McClellan's failings, President Lincoln ordered Major General Henry W. Halleck from the western theater to Washington to assume the position of general in chief (July 11). Lincoln also ordered McClellan to return with his army to Washington.

SPENCER C. TUCKER

See also

Banks, Nathaniel Prentice; Davis, Jefferson Finis; Drewry's Bluff, First Battle of; Eltham's Landing, Battle of; Frémont, John Charles; Gaines' Mill, Battle of; Hampton Roads, Battles of; Hooker, Joseph; Jackson, Thomas Jonathan; Jackson's Shenandoah Valley Campaign; Johnston, Joseph Eggleston; Kearny, Philip; Lee, Robert Edward; Lincoln, Abraham; Longstreet, James; Magruder, John Bankhead; Malvern Hill, Battle of; McClellan, George Brinton; McDowell, Irvin; Mechanicsville, Battle of; Oak Grove, Battle of; Pope, John; Porter, Fitz John; Rodgers, John, Jr.; Savage's Station, Battle of; Seven Days' Campaign; Seven Pines, Battle of; Shields, James; Stuart, James Ewell Brown; Stuart's Ride around McClellan; *Virginia,*

CSS; White Oak Swamp, Battle of; Williamsburg, Battle of; Yorktown, Virginia, Siege of

Further Reading

Adams, Michael C. *Our Masters the Rebels: Speculations on Union Military Failure in the East, 1861–1865.* Cambridge, MA: Harvard University Press, 1978.

Gallagher, Gary, ed. *The Richmond Campaign of 1862: The Peninsula and the Seven Days.* Chapel Hill: University of North Carolina Press, 2000.

Martin, David G. *The Peninsula Campaign, March–July 1862.* Conshohocken, PA: Combined Books, 1992.

Mewton, Steven H. *Joseph E. Johnston and the Defense of Richmond.* Lawrence: University Press of Kansas, 1998.

Sears, Stephen W. *To the Gates of Richmond: The Peninsula Campaign.* New York: Ticknor and Fields, 1992.

Webb, Alexander S. *The Peninsula: McClellan's Campaign of 1862.* Secaucus, NJ: Castle Books, 2002.

Wheeler, Richard. *Sword over Richmond: An Eyewitness History of McClellan's Peninsula Campaign.* New York: Harper and Row, 1986.

Pennington, William
Birth Date: May 4, 1796
Death Date: February 16, 1862

New Jersey politician and Speaker of the U.S. House of Representatives. William Pennington was born on May 4, 1796, in Newark, New Jersey, into a prominent family. He graduated from the College of New Jersey (Princeton University) in 1813 and completed his legal studies in 1817. For the next nine years while his father was a district judge, Pennington was clerk of the district and circuit courts.

In 1828 Pennington was elected to the New Jersey legislature, and in 1837, running as a member of the Whig Party, he was elected governor and chancellor of the state. His one controversial decision while governor concerned the manner in which he resolved the disputed congressional election results of 1838. The Democrats claimed to have won five out of the six congressional district election races, but the county clerks certified that all six seats had been won by Whig candidates. Pennington claimed that he did not have the authority as governor to challenge the results and certified the Whig candidates as the legal winners. The battle was continued in the U.S. House of Representatives. The Whig Party and the Democratic Party were so evenly balanced in the House that whichever group was seated would determine the voting majority. Finally, three months after Congress had assembled, it decided to overturn Pennington's decision and seated the Democratic candidates.

Pennington failed to win reelection as governor in 1843 but remained active in politics. In 1858 he was elected to Congress as a Republican and served there until March 1861. On February 1, 1860, Pennington was chosen as a compromise candidate for Speaker of the House. His brief term was considered by most to be a dismal failure. His committee assignments greatly favored the Republicans, which alienated the Democrats and torpedoed any serious attempt to avert civil war. Worse, he packed the Committee of Thirty-Three, tasked with arriving at a compromise short of disunion and war, with Radical Republicans, which doomed its mission from the start. Pennington seemed to lack political savvy and was largely unable to exert control over the various factions in the House. Defeated in his 1860 reelection bid, Pennington left Congress in March 1861 and was replaced as Speaker by Galusha Grow. Pennington died on February 16, 1862, in Newark, New Jersey.

STEVEN G. O'BRIEN AND PAUL G. PIERPAOLI JR.

See also

Committee of Thirty-Three; Congress, U.S.; Grow, Galusha Aaron; Republican Party

Further Reading

Ambrosious, Lloyd E. *A Crisis of Republicanism: American Politics during the Civil War Era.* Lincoln: University of Nebraska Press, 1990.

Ilisevich, Robert D. *Galusha A. Grow: The People's Candidate.* Pittsburgh, PA: University of Pittsburgh Press, 1988.

Pennsylvania

Union state located in the Mid-Atlantic region and bordered by New Jersey to the east; Delaware, Maryland, and West Virginia to the south; West Virginia and Ohio to the west; and New York and Lake Erie to the north. Pennsylvania's abundant natural resources included anthracite and bituminous coal, petroleum, and fertile farmlands for agricultural products.

Encompassing 45,308 square miles, Pennsylvania was a key state in the Union, boasting access to Lake Erie in the northwest and deepwater oceangoing access to the Atlantic Ocean via Philadelphia in the southeast. Besides being one of the Union's largest and most important cities, Philadelphia was also home to a large seaport and significant shipbuilding facilities. Pennsylvania has widely varying terrain and climates, ranging from flat to rolling hills in the east with a fairly temperate climate to rugged mountainous areas in the west with a harsh winter climate.

A key Northern state during the Civil War, Pennsylvania lived up to its nickname the "Keystone State" by wholeheartedly supporting President Abraham Lincoln's administration with men, money, and matériel. Republican governor Andrew Gregg Curtin was inaugurated in 1861 and served throughout the war. He earned his nickname "the soldier's friend" by taking an active interest in the welfare of Pennsylvania's soldiers.

Several other Pennsylvania civilians played prominent roles in the war. Simon Cameron was Lincoln's first secretary of war, but Cameron's lackluster leadership led to his dismissal in early 1862. Democratic congressman Galusha Grow was elected Speaker of the U.S. House of Representatives in 1861; a year later he pushed the Homestead Act through Congress. Radical Republican congressman Thaddeus Stevens championed the rights of African Americans by promoting their service as soldiers, working to ensure passage of the Thirteenth Amendment to the U.S. Constitution, and supporting postwar civil rights legislation. Finally, Pennsylvania financier Jay Cooke raised more than $1.5 billion for the war effort by selling government bonds.

Pennsylvania's industrial might came into full play during the war. Indeed, the number of businesses in Pennsylvania alone totaled more than all the businesses in the entire Confederate States of America. The federal government's chief clothing supply depot was located in Philadelphia, which also contained a large navy yard, a government arsenal, the country's largest locomotive manufacturer, and dozens of textile factories that supplied wool for uniforms. The Fort Pitt Works in Pittsburgh, in western Pennsylvania, manufactured more than 1,100 cannon, while coalfields across the state, from Allentown in the east to Pittsburgh in the west, contributed significantly to the war effort. Home to the Union's largest coal deposits, Pennsylvania kept the Union's railways operating at peak capacity, fueled steam-driven naval and merchant ships, and powered innumerable factories.

The state sent roughly 360,000 white soldiers and 8,600 African American soldiers off to war. Camp Curtin, located just north of Harrisburg, the state capital, became the North's largest training camp for soldiers. Governor Curtin was instrumental in raising and equipping the Pennsylvania Reserves, a full division of 15,000 men who fought in most of the major battles in the eastern theater of the war, including the Peninsula Campaign (March–July 1862) and the Battle of Gettysburg (July 1–3, 1863).

Confederate troops entered the state on three occasions. In October 1862, Confederate cavalry raided into the state, while General Robert E. Lee's invasion in June and July 1863 was repelled at the Battle of Gettysburg. Finally, in July 1864, two brigades of Confederate cavalrymen briefly occupied Chambersburg, burning the city when its leaders rejected demands for payment of a large ransom.

Notable generals from Pennsylvania included Major General George B. McClellan, who trained and then led the Army of the Potomac, and Major General George G. Meade, who commanded the same army from the Battle of Gettysburg through the end of the war. Pennsylvania-born corps commanders included Major Generals John F. Reynolds (I Corps), Winfield S. Hancock and Andrew A. Humphreys (II Corps), Samuel P. Heintzelman (III Corps), William B. Franklin (VI and XIX Corps), John G. Parke (IX Corps), Andrew J. Smith (XVI Corps), and John Gibbon (XXIV Corps).

Some of the more notable military outfits associated with Pennsylvania include the Pennsylvania Reserves, an infantry division mobilized, trained, and supplied entirely by the state, beyond the federal quota; the Philadelphia Brigade, which took heavy losses at Gettysburg; and the 48th Regiment, made up of coal miners who dug the mine at Petersburg.

RICHARD A. SAUERS

See also

Cameron, Simon; Cooke, Jay; Curtin, Andrew Gregg; Gettysburg, Battle of; Grow, Galusha Aaron; Homestead Act; Peninsula Campaign; Stevens, Thaddeus; Thirteenth Amendment

Further Reading

Bates, Samuel P. *History of Pennsylvania Volunteers, 1861–1865.* 10 vols. 1868–1871; reprint, Wilmington, NC: Broadfoot, 1994.
Miller, William J. *The Training of an Army: Camp Curtin and the North's Civil War.* Shippensburg, PA: White Mane, 1990.
Sauers, Richard A. *Advance the Colors! Pennsylvania Civil War Battleflags.* 2 vols. Lebanon, PA: Sowers Printing Company for the Pennsylvania Capitol Preservation Committee, 1987–1991.

Pennsylvania, Prigg v.

See *Prigg v. Pennsylvania*

Pennsylvania, Union Department of

Federal military administrative unit formed on April 27, 1861, and dissolved on August 24, 1861. Headquartered in Philadelphia, the Union Department of Pennsylvania encompassed all of the states of Pennsylvania and Delaware

and the portions of Maryland not under other jurisdictions (i.e., the Departments of Annapolis and Washington). The latter essentially encompassed most of central and western Maryland. Pennsylvania Militia major general Robert Patterson was assigned command of the department and was charged with supporting pro-Unionist sentiments in western Virginia and moving into western Maryland, where his army was to advance on Harpers Ferry, Virginia, which was then controlled by Confederate forces.

To accomplish this, Patterson had to cobble together a military force known as the Army of Pennsylvania. By mid-June 1861, he had assembled a force of some 13,000 soldiers, with 16 infantry regiments and 5 cavalry companies. On July 2, Patterson's army crossed the Potomac River, where it almost immediately—and unsuccessfully—engaged a small army under Confederate general Joseph E. Johnston. Patterson could not keep Johnston's force contained to the Shenandoah Valley, enabling the Confederates to join the forces at Manassas Junction. Johnston's command then moved east and fought at the First Battle of Bull Run (July 21, 1861), a Union defeat. Patterson's campaign ended in abject failure, and by July 23 he had been relieved of command. The Department of Pennsylvania ceased to exist as of August 24, when it was absorbed by the Department of the Potomac.

PAUL G. PIERPAOLI JR.

See also

Annapolis, Union Department of; Bull Run, First Battle of; Johnston, Joseph Eggleston; Patterson, Robert; Washington, Union Department of

Further Reading

Miller, William J. *The Training of an Army: Camp Curtin and the North's Civil War.* Shippensburg, PA: White Mane, 1990.
Warner, Ezra J. *Generals in Blue: Lives of the Union Commanders.* Baton Rouge: Louisiana State University Press, 2006.

Pennsylvania Bucktails

The best-known volunteer unit recruited in Pennsylvania during the Civil War. The Pennsylvania Bucktails were known as the 13th Pennsylvania Reserves, the 42nd Pennsylvania Volunteer Infantry, the 1st Pennsylvania Rifles, and the Kane Rifle Regiment (for one of its founders, Thomas L. Kane). Seven of the regiment's 10 companies were recruited in the state's rural and mountainous counties. Some of the men floated on rafts down the West Branch of the Susquehanna River to enlist. Several wore a bucktail in their caps

The last fight of the 13th Pennsylvania Reserves, known as the "Pennsylvania Bucktails," during the Overland Campaign. The best-known Pennsylvania volunteer regiment of the war, its three-year term of service expired on June 11, 1864. (Library of Congress)

as a mark of their marksmanship, a symbol later adopted by the regiment. Commanders of the regiment included colonels Charles J. Biddle, Hugh W. McNeil, Charles F. Taylor, and W. T. Hartshorn.

The Pennsylvania Bucktails were mustered into service for three years in June 1861 as part of the division of troops known as the Pennsylvania Reserves. The regiment briefly served in western Virginia and then took part in the Battle of Dranesville (December 20, 1861). The Bucktails also took part in the Peninsula Campaign (March–July 1862) and saw action at the Second Battle of Bull Run (August 29–30, 1862).

After that, the Bucktails served with the Army of the Potomac at the Battle of South Mountain (September 14, 1862), the Battle of Antietam (September 17), and the First Battle of Fredericksburg (December 13) before being sent to the defenses of Washington, D.C., to rest and recruit new members. The regiment rejoined the army in time to fight at the Battle of Gettysburg (July 1–3, 1863). After taking

part in the Battle of the Wilderness (May 5–7, 1864), the Battle of Spotsylvania (May 8–21), and several other lesser engagements, the survivors mustered out of service on June 11 when the regiment's enlistment term expired. During its three years of service, the regiment suffered 162 men killed or mortally wounded; 90 others died from illness.

RICHARD A. SAUERS

See also

Antietam, Battle of; Bull Run, Second Battle of; Dranesville, Battle of; Fredericksburg, First Battle of; Gettysburg, Battle of; South Mountain, Battle of; Spotsylvania Court House, Battle of; Wilderness, Battle of the

Further Reading

Palm, Ronn, and Patrick Schroeder. *The Pennsylvania Bucktails: A Photographic Album of the 42nd, 149th, and 150th Pennsylvania.* Roanoke, VA: Schroeder, 2001.

Thomson, Osmund R. H., and William H. Rauch. *History of the "Bucktails": Kane Rifle Regiment of the Pennsylvania Reserve Corps (13th Pennsylvania Reserves 42nd of the Line).* Dayton, OH: Morningside House, 1988.

Pennypacker, Galusha
Birth Date: June 1, 1844
Death Date: October 1, 1916

Union officer. Galusha Pennypacker was born on June 1, 1844, in Valley Forge, Pennsylvania. Effectively orphaned at an early age by his mother's death and his father's departure to seek his fortune in the West, Pennypacker was left in the care of his paternal grandmother. He worked as a printer, studied law, and was deciding whether to accept an appointment to the U.S. Military Academy, West Point, when the Civil War began in 1861.

In April 1861 at age 16, Pennypacker entered Union service as a private in the 9th Pennsylvania but soon became quartermaster sergeant. Mustering out of his 90-day unit, he helped raise Company A of the 97th Pennsylvania Volunteer Regiment and was elected its captain on August 22, 1861. He was promoted to major in October. From 1862 through early 1864, Pennypacker ably led his men in various engagements as part of the Union X Corps in the Department of the South. In April 1864 he was promoted to lieutenant colonel as the regiment prepared to support the Army of the James. Pennypacker led part of the regiment in several engagements during the Overland Campaign (May 4–June 12, 1864). He was severely wounded on May 20 while leading an assault to retake lost ground at Bermuda Hundred. Upon recuperation he returned to the regiment in August, when he was promoted to colonel of the 97th Pennsylvania. In September he was elevated to command of the 2nd Brigade, 2nd Division, of X Corps.

In December 1864 Pennypacker's brigade was deployed to North Carolina with XXIV Corps for the campaign to capture Fort Fisher, near Wilmington. On January 15 Pennypacker led his force on an intrepid charge across a traverse under heavy fire. After planting the colors of one of his regiments, he was gravely wounded.

Pennypacker was promoted to brigadier general of volunteers effective January 15, 1865, becoming at age 20 the youngest general officer in the Union Army. This was followed on March 13 by a brevet to major general. Following multiple surgeries and at only age 22, Pennypacker joined the regular army as colonel of the 34th Infantry in 1866, at which point he received the regular army brevets to major general. In 1869 he became commander of the 16th Infantry Regiment.

Pennypacker retired on July 3, 1883, and returned home to Philadelphia. On August 17, 1891, he was awarded the Medal of Honor for his actions at Fort Fisher. In 1904 he was promoted to brigadier general on the retired list. Pennypacker died on October 1, 1916, in Philadelphia.

ALLAN S. BOYCE

See also
Bermuda Hundred Campaign; Fort Fisher Campaign; Overland Campaign

Further Reading
Gragg, Rod. *Confederate Goliath: The Battle of Fort Fisher.* New York: HarperCollins, 1991.
Warner, Ezra J. *Generals in Blue: Lives of the Union Commanders.* Baton Rouge: Louisiana State University Press, 2006.

Penny Press
Inexpensive sensationalistic newspapers that began circulating in the 1830s and were the precursors to the yellow journalism of the 1880s and 1890s. Much like modern tabloid newspapers, the penny press papers also laid the foundations of modern journalism with their emphasis on on-the-scene reporting, particularly in wartime. Unlike the partisan newspapers of the pre–Civil War period, the penny press papers (that is, newspapers that sold for a penny), such as James Gordon Bennett's *New York Herald,* emphasized sensationalistic crime stories that appealed to a large working-class reading audience. During the Civil War, the *New York Herald* and other similar newspapers sent reporters directly into the field. Because of the demands of the reading public about facts in the Civil War and the word economy that had been imposed by the telegraph, the penny press changed journalism from partisan publications to fact-based reporting.

Prior to the 1830s, newspapers were often called broadsides and were not cheap to produce. Improvements in printing technology, especially the steam-powered cylinder press (rotary press), led to great reductions in the cost of newspapers so that they could be sold for a penny, as opposed to the papers produced by the flat-plate process that commonly sold for six cents a copy. Two of the leaders in the penny press, Benjamin Day's *New York Sun* and Bennett's *New York Herald,* were aggressively hawked on the streets by paid salesmen. This led to a remarkable rise in their circulations. The *Herald* reached a circulation of more than 75,000 before the Civil War, even though the price had increased to two cents a copy. These tabloid-style papers also differed from the Jacksonian-era partisan papers, which had as their sole goal the election of candidates from specific parties and often were founded and operated by party operatives. The Jacksonian-era presses also benefited greatly from the franking privilege in Congress whereby elected officials could send for free any mail to constituents, bombarding voters with a legislator's most recent speeches or commentary.

Bennett and Day, however, emphasized stories that would appeal to buyers, especially crime and particularly the most sensationalistic and lurid stories that could be found. Relying heavily on police reports, the *Herald* and the *Sun* were really the forerunners of today's *National Enquirer,* and while penny presses failed at higher rates, before long every city had one: Philadelphia had the *Daily Transcript,* and Boston had the *Daily Ledger.* These papers appealed to immigrants, and the motto of the *Sun*—"It Shines for All"—reflected the alleged democratic effects that they had on mass publishing. Certainly the penny press made publishers such as Bennett quite wealthy.

The penny press changed reporting, which, after all, had merely meant repeating verbatim politicians' speeches in many of the Jacksonian-era papers. Bennett's reporters fought a number of legal battles to report directly from courtrooms without being held in contempt, and Bennett personally investigated the murder of a young prostitute in 1836. The *Herald* sent a reporter to cover the Mexican-American War and had more than 60 reporters covering the Civil War. By that time a revolution in journalism had taken place partly due to the telegraph, which placed a premium on word economy. Flowery and verbose stories were replaced by tightly written fact-based reporting that got to the point quickly.

Some journalism historians argue that the so-called inverted pyramid—in which the most important facts were presented first, followed by facts of lesser importance—appeared at this time. The demand for facts during the Civil War combined with the appearance of professional publishing managers killed the old partisan papers.

LARRY SCHWEIKART

See also

Newspaper, Soldiers'; Telegraph

Further Reading

Gallman, J. Matthew, et al., eds. *The Civil War Chronicle.* New York: Gramercy Books, 2003.

Harris, Brayton. *Blue and Gray in Black and White: Newspapers in the Civil War.* Herndon, VA: Brassey's, 2000.

Nord, David Paul. *Communities of Journalism: A History of American Newspapers and Their Readers.* Champaign: University of Illinois Press, 2006.

Penrose, William Henry
Birth Date: March 10, 1832
Death Date: August 29, 1903

Union officer. The son of an army officer, William Henry Penrose was born at Madison Barracks in Sackets Harbor, New York, on March 10, 1832. Penrose attended Dickinson College and worked as an engineer in Michigan before securing a commission as second lieutenant in the 3rd U.S. Infantry in April 1861. He was promoted to first lieutenant in May.

Penrose fought with his regular regiment in the Army of the Potomac during the Peninsula Campaign (March–July 1862), the Seven Days' Campaign (June 25–July 1, 1862), the Second Battle of Bull Run (August 29–30), and the First Battle of Fredericksburg (December 13, 1862). In April 1863 he entered the volunteer service as colonel of the 15th New Jersey Infantry. He led his new regiment, and temporarily a brigade, the next month during the Battle of Chancellorsville (May 1–4, 1863), for which he earned a regular army brevet. He won another brevet for his role in the Battle of Gettysburg (July 1–3, 1863). Promoted to captain in the regular army, he participated in the autumn campaigns in northern Virginia.

Penrose won another brevet for his actions during the Battle of the Wilderness (May 5–7, 1864) and took charge of his brigade in the 1st Division, VI Corps, during the Battle of Spotsylvania Court House (May 8–21). In July, VI Corps was rushed to Washington to confront the emergency occasioned by Confederate lieutenant general Jubal Early's Washington Raid (June 28–July 21) and was then attached to Major General Philip Sheridan's Army of the Shenandoah. Penrose led his brigade in the Third Battle of Winchester (September 19) and the Battle of Fisher's Hill (September 22). At Cedar Creek on October 19, he was conspicuously engaged in rallying the army after the initial surprise of the Confederate attack. Wounded in the fighting, he was brevetted brigadier general of volunteers and colonel in the regular army.

Returning to the Army of the Potomac at Petersburg, Penrose and his brigade were active in the final attack that collapsed the Confederate defenses on April 2, 1865, during which he was again wounded. Brevetted brigadier general in the regular army, he received a long-overdue promotion to full rank brigadier general of volunteers in June 1865 and mustered out of the volunteer army in January 1866.

Penrose remained in the regular army but did not see the kind of advancement enjoyed by other Civil War generals. He reverted to his substantive rank of captain, in the 3rd

Infantry, and remained as such until 1883, when he became a major in the 12th Infantry. Promoted to lieutenant colonel, 16th Infantry, in 1888 and to colonel, 20th Infantry, in 1893, he retired as colonel of the 16th Infantry in 1896. Penrose died at Salt Lake City, Utah, on August 29, 1903.

DAVID COFFEY

See also

Bull Run, Second Battle of; Cedar Creek, Battle of; Chancellorsville, Battle of; Early's Raid on Washington, D.C.; Fisher's Hill, Battle of; Fredericksburg, First Battle of; Gettysburg, Battle of; Peninsula Campaign; Petersburg Campaign; Seven Days' Campaign; Spotsylvania Court House, Battle of; Wilderness, Battle of the; Winchester, Third Battle of

Further Reading

Eicher, John H., and David J. Eicher. *Civil War High Commands.* Stanford, CA: Stanford University Press, 2001.

Warner, Ezra J. *Generals in Blue: Lives of the Union Commanders.* Baton Rouge: Louisiana State University Press, 2006.

Pensacola, Florida, Union Occupation of
Event Date: May 10, 1862

Uncontested Union recapture of the vital Florida harbor city. When Florida seceded from the Union on January 10, 1861, Lieutenant Adam J. Slemmer commanded the U.S. Army garrison of 51 men at Fort Barrancas in Pensacola. After a mob of local citizens attempted to seize the federal arsenal at the fort, on January 9, 1861, Slemmer destroyed the stocks of military supplies there and withdrew his garrison, along with 30 sailors from the nearby shipyard, across the bay to Fort Pickens on the western end of Santa Rosa Island. The next day, some 1,000 Florida and Alabama militiamen peacefully occupied Pensacola. The new Confederate government of Florida asked Slemmer to surrender Fort Pickens, but he refused.

At the time, state forces refrained from attacking the post. Later in 1861, Confederate artillery batteries on the mainland sporadically shelled Fort Pickens but did not present a serious threat to the garrison. On October 9, 1861, a Confederate force of more than 1,000 men attacked the fort's outworks but failed to take it. As the war progressed, the Confederates abandoned their quasi siege of Fort Pickens.

The Union invasion of Tennessee in early 1862 and need to shift forces to meet that threat compelled the Confederate government to evacuate Pensacola. On May 9, 1862, Confederate forces set fire to the shipyard and other military installations and withdrew. The next day, Union forces under Brigadier General Lewis G. Arnold officially occupied the city. Pensacola remained in Union hands for the rest of the war. The Federal West Gulf Blockading Squadron used the shipyard as its base of operations, and the Union Army launched numerous raids and expeditions from Fort Barrancas into Alabama and western Florida.

ROBERT B. KANE

See also

Florida; Fort Pickens, Florida

Further Reading

Driscoll, John K. *The Civil War on Pensacola Bay, 1861–1862.* Jefferson City, NC: McFarland, 2007.

Pearce, George, F. *Pensacola during the Civil War: A Thorn in the Side of the Confederacy.* Gainesville: University Press of Florida, 2000.

Pensions

Payments to veterans (or their survivors) for military service during the Civil War. Pensions were also employed to encourage Union military enlistments. Payments to veterans and their survivors, generous in 1862, evolved into something far larger. Of the 2.7 million men who served the Union, 2.4 million (87 percent) survived the war. The conflict produced record numbers of disabled veterans, however, in addition to widows and other dependents who also claimed pensions. In subsequent decades, the U.S. Congress repeatedly awarded greater amounts of money to a wider selection of Union Army veterans. Indeed, between 1880 and 1910, the federal government devoted more than a quarter of its total expenditures to pensions. About 28 percent of all American men aged 65 or older—some 500,000—received federal benefits averaging $189 per year. In addition, more than 300,000 widows, orphans, and assorted dependents also received pension checks.

The Civil War's first general pension legislation replaced various temporary enactments on July 14, 1862. The new law rapidly became the fundamental vehicle for all claims arising from military disabilities. The statute, creating the so-called general law pension system, embraced army and navy personnel as well as marines, including regulars, volunteers, and the various militias, and its application extended forward to include all future wars. This was an epochal enactment, as it marked the first time the nation had aided mothers and orphaned sisters. The legislation also increased existing payments to widows and disabled seamen. It provided pensions from $30 per month down to

Disability Pensions Issued to Union Soldiers, 1862–1888

Cause (as Listed by Pension Board)	Number
Gunshot and shell wounds	117,947
Chronic diarrhea	55,125
Incised and contused wounds	41,049
Rheumatism	40,790
Disease of heart	25,994
Disease of lungs	23,471
Disease of eyes	15,251
Single hernia	15,043
Amputations	9,159
Other	62,873
Total	406,702

$8, according to rank. For partial disabilities, it offered proportional pensions.

The general law of 1862 was the only pension system applied to the Civil War until 1890. All benefits addressed disabilities incurred directly from military service or, after the close of combat, from causes that could be tied to injuries received (or diseases contracted) while the claimant performed military service.

In the decades after 1865, additions to the law were made. Lobbying by veterans' organizations, the coupling of expanded pension benefits to hikes in protective tariffs, and competition between the major political parties for the veterans' vote all led to fundamental changes. The Arrears Act of 1879 calculated benefit awards to the newly disabled from the date of military discharge. The Disability Act of 1890 provided benefits for honorably discharged veterans who had served 90 days or more, even if their disabilities were not service related. Pensions were awarded to widows and children of former Civil War soldiers without regard to the cause of death. By the early 20th century, the pensions became de facto old-age survivors' benefits. Thus, through Civil War pensions, the U.S. government became the source of generous social provisioning for a major portion of the American citizenry long before the New Deal of the 1930s.

The U.S. government provided no pension benefits to Confederate veterans or their survivors. Beginning in the late 1880s, several Southern states enacted modest pension systems; by the mid-1890s, the 11 former Confederate states had done so. The benefits differed considerably from those offered to Union veterans. First, each state enacted a direct tax to fund its pension systems, whereas U.S. pensions were funded by indirect taxes such as tariffs. Second, the amount of money offered to veterans was calculated differently and was usually considerably less than federal pensions. Third, Confederate widows were given lower payments than their Union counterparts. Fourth, payments were not based on military rank; instead, they were based chiefly on the degree of disability. Finally, state-sponsored Confederate pensions were calculated on income and other assets; unlike the federal system, pensions were not paid to all who rendered military service. Although state pensions for Confederate veterans and their survivors did become gradually more generous over time, they never approached the size and scope of federal pensions, largely because state governments had far fewer resources at their disposal compared to the U.S. government.

JAMES G. RYAN AND PAUL G. PIERPAOLI JR.

See also

Veterans' Organizations

Further Reading

Glasson, William H. *Federal Military Pensions in the United States*. New York: Oxford University Press, 1918.

Skocpol, Theda. *Protecting Soldiers and Mothers: The Political Origins of Social Policy in the United States*. Cambridge, MA: Belknap, 1992.

Perrin, Abner Moore
Birth Date: February 2, 1827
Death Date: May 12, 1864

Confederate officer. Abner Moore Perrin was born on February 2, 1827, in the Edgefield District of South Carolina. He served as a lieutenant in the regular infantry during the Mexican-American War (1846–1848), returned to South Carolina, studied law, and was admitted to the bar in 1854. He established a law practice in Columbia that same year and worked as an attorney until 1861.

Perrin joined the 14th South Carolina Infantry Regiment as a captain in the summer of 1861 and was ordered to Port Royal, South Carolina, in January 1862. In the early spring, his regiment was sent north to Virginia to defend Richmond during the Peninsula Campaign (March–July 1862). Perrin performed ably during the Seven Days' Campaign (June 25–July 1, 1862), the Battle of Cedar Mountain (August 9, 1862), the Second Battle of Bull Run (August 29–30, 1862), the Battle of Antietam (September 17, 1862), and the First Battle of Fredericksburg (December 13, 1862), after which he was promoted to colonel. Perrin assumed command of a brigade in the spring of 1863 and led it during the Battle of Gettysburg (July 1–3, 1863). He was advanced to brigadier general on September 10, 1863.

Perrin led his brigade with distinction at the Battle of the Wilderness (May 5–7, 1864) but was killed in action on May 12, 1864, during the Battle of Spotsylvania Court House (May 8–21) in Virginia.

PAUL G. PIERPAOLI JR.

See also

Antietam, Battle of; Bull Run, Second Battle of; Cedar Mountain, Battle of; Fredericksburg, First Battle of; Gettysburg, Battle of; Peninsula Campaign; Seven Days' Campaign; Spotsylvania Court House, Battle of; Wilderness, Battle of the

Further Reading

Grimsley, Mark. *And Keep Moving On: The Virginia Campaign, May–June 1864.* Lincoln: University of Nebraska Press, 2002.

Warner, Ezra J. *Generals in Gray: Lives of the Confederate Commanders.* Baton Rouge: Louisiana State University Press, 2006.

Perry, Edward Aylesworth
Birth Date: March 15, 1831
Death Date: October 15, 1889

Confederate officer. Edward Aylesworth Perry was born in Richmond, Massachusetts, on March 15, 1831. He attended Yale but withdrew in 1851 to move to Alabama, where he taught school and studied law. In 1857 he moved to Florida, gaining admittance to that state's bar in 1858.

In January 1861 Perry joined the Pensacola Rifle Rangers and became its captain. He and his militia company participated in the Battle of Santa Rosa Island (Fort Pickens) (October 9, 1861) in Florida. Shortly afterward, the Pensacola Rifle Rangers entered Confederate service as Company A of the 2nd Florida Infantry Regiment, which was ordered to Virginia. After the death of his commanding officer on May 10, 1862, Perry became the regiment's colonel.

Perry was badly wounded at the Battle of White Oak Swamp (June 30, 1862). He recovered and received a promotion to brigadier general on August 28, 1862. Perry then led a Florida brigade through the First Battle of Fredericksburg (December 13, 1862) and the Battle of Chancellorsville (May 1–4, 1863), where he contracted typhoid fever. The illness kept him out of action during the Battle of Gettysburg (July 1–3, 1863), but his brigade, led by Colonel David Lang, took part in Pickett's Charge on July 3 and sustained heavy

losses. Wounded a second time on May 6 at the Battle of the Wilderness (May 5–7, 1864), Perry became unfit for further field service. From September 28, 1864, until war's end, he remained in Alabama in the reserves.

After the war, Perry resumed his law practice and joined the Democratic Party. From 1885 to 1889, he served as governor of Florida. Perry helped write the 1885 state constitution that replaced Florida's 1868 so-called carpetbag constitution, and he also signed a law giving Florida Confederate veterans a small state pension. After leaving office, he returned to Pensacola. Perry died on October 15, 1889, in Kerrville, Texas.

JIM PIECUCH AND ANGELA D. TOOLEY

See also

Chancellorsville, Battle of; Fort Pickens, Florida; Fredericksburg, First Battle of; White Oak Swamp, Battle of; Wilderness, Battle of the

Further Reading

Prince, Sigsbee C., Jr. "Edward A. Perry, Yankee General of the Florida Brigade." *Florida Historical Quarterly* 29 (1951): 197–225.

Warner, Ezra J. *Generals in Gray: Lives of the Confederate Commanders.* Baton Rouge: Louisiana State University Press, 2006.

Perry, Madison Starke
Birth Date: 1814
Death Date: March 1865

Governor of Florida (1857–1861) and Confederate officer. Madison Starke Perry was born in Lancaster District, South Carolina, sometime in 1814. Moving to Florida in the mid-1840s, he purchased farmland in Alachua County and became a planter. In 1848 Perry, a Democrat, was elected to the Florida legislature, and in 1850 he gained a seat in the Florida Senate. Campaigning on a strong states' rights platform, he was elected governor of Florida in 1856.

Alarmed by the results of the 1860 presidential election, Perry orchestrated Florida's exit from the Union. His November 26 message to the General Assembly inspired the passage of a measure for a state secession convention and the appropriation of funds for arms. Perry traveled to South Carolina to purchase rifled muskets for Florida's troops. On January 10, 1861, under Perry's leadership, Florida officially seceded from the Union.

On January 4, 1861, Perry ordered U.S. troops to leave the state and directed the Florida Militia to seize federal posts.

Accordingly, on January 6 the militia took the Chattahoochee Arsenal, and on January 7 Fort Marion in St. Augustine fell. In Pensacola on January 12, the Warrington Navy Yard surrendered to Florida Militia units, and the federal government abandoned Forts McRee and Barrancas.

In February 1861 Perry reorganized the state militia, but in March the newly created Confederate War Department took control of Florida's volunteer army. After Perry had furnished 5,000 Florida soldiers, the Confederate government transferred them outside the state, leaving Florida largely undefended.

In October 1861, Perry passed this precarious situation to his successor, Governor John Milton, and joined the army himself. On April 26, 1862, Perry became colonel of the 7th Florida Infantry Regiment. His command was then ordered to eastern Tennessee, a predominantly Unionist area, to support General Braxton Bragg by performing picket duty around Knoxville.

In June 1863, Perry fell ill and resigned his commission. He died on his plantation near Rochelle, Florida, in March 1865.

JIM PIECUCH AND ANGELA D. TOOLEY

See also

Bragg, Braxton; Florida; Milton, John

Further Reading

Fairbanks, George R. *Florida: Its History and Its Romance.* Jacksonville, FL: H. and W. B. Drew, 1904.
Yearns, W. Buck. *The Confederate Governors.* Athens: University of Georgia Press, 1985.

Perry, William Flank
Birth Date: March 12, 1823
Death Date: December 18, 1901

Confederate officer. William Flank Perry was born on March 12, 1823, in Jackson County, Georgia, and moved with his family to Chambers County, Alabama, in 1833. Although he had little formal education, Perry began teaching in Talladega County, Alabama, in 1848. He also studied law and was admitted to the bar in 1854, although he never established his own practice. That same year, he began serving as the state superintendent of education, a post he held until 1858. He devoted his tenure to improving public education in Alabama, creating the foundation for free public schooling in the state. He became the president of the East Alabama Female College in Tuskegee, Alabama, in 1858.

In the spring of 1862, Perry enlisted with the 44th Alabama Infantry Regiment as a private, but in less than two weeks he was promoted to major. After his strong showing at the Second Battle of Bull Run (August 29–30, 1862), he was advanced to lieutenant colonel; following the Battle of Antietam (September 17, 1862), he was promoted to colonel.

For the Battle of Gettysburg (July 1–3, 1863), Perry served under Brigadier General Evander M. Law and ably led the 44th Infantry Regiment in the attack on Little Round Top. At the Battle of Chickamauga (September 19–20, 1863), Perry was cited for gallantry; he subsequently saw action during the Battle of the Wilderness (May 5–7, 1864) and the Battle of Spotsylvania Court House (May 8–21, 1864). At the Battle of Cold Harbor (May 31–June 12, 1864), he assumed command of Law's brigade and retained the command until the war ended in April 1865. Perry was not advanced to brigadier general, however, until February 21, 1865.

After the war Perry returned to Alabama, where he farmed for a time. In 1867 he returned to his calling as an educator and was named professor of philosophy and English at Ogden College in Bowling Green, Kentucky. Perry died there on December 18, 1901.

PAUL G. PIERPAOLI JR.

See also

Antietam, Battle of; Bull Run, Second Battle of; Chickamauga, Battle of; Cold Harbor, Battle of; Gettysburg, Battle of; Law, Evander McIvor; Spotsylvania Court House, Battle of; Wilderness, Battle of the

Further Reading

Rogers, William Warren, et al. *Alabama: The History of a Deep South State.* Tuscaloosa: University of Alabama Press, 1994.
Warner, Ezra J. *Generals in Gray: Lives of the Confederate Commanders.* Baton Rouge: Louisiana State University Press, 2006.

Perryville, Battle of
Event Date: October 8, 1862

Major engagement of the Confederate Kentucky Campaign (August 14–October 26, 1862). The Battle of Perryville, also known as the Battle of Chaplin Hills, involved some 16,000 Confederates and 22,000 Union troops and was the largest Civil War battle in Kentucky. The Confederates hoped to convince Kentuckians to join their state to the Confederacy. Timed to coincide with General Robert E. Lee's invasion of the North that would culminate in the Battle of Antietam (September 17, 1862), Bragg departed Chattanooga with his Army of Mississippi of 30,000 men on August 28.

BATTLE OF PERRYVILLE, OCTOBER 8, 1862

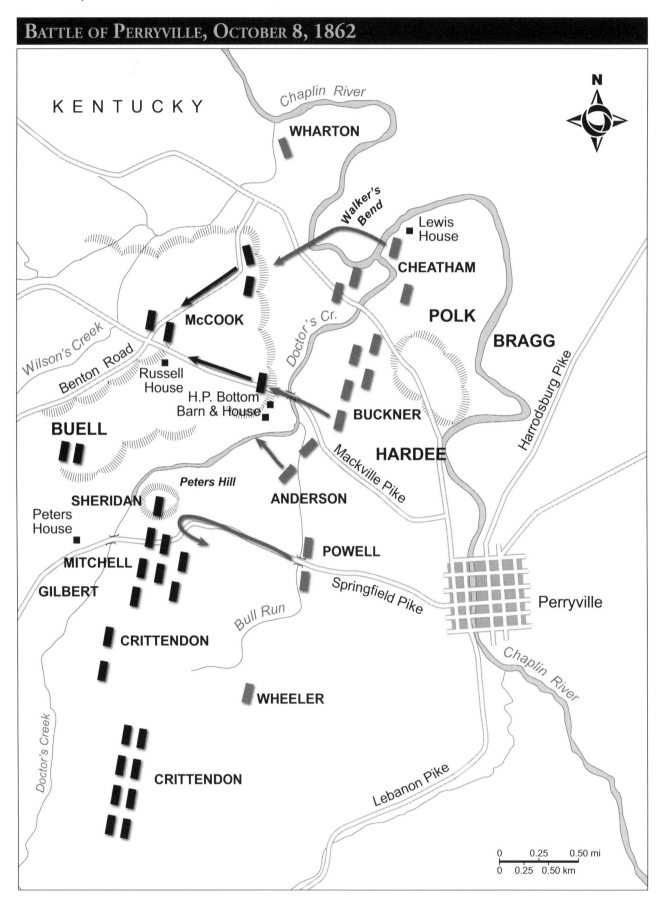

Meanwhile, Major General E. Kirby Smith pushed into Kentucky from eastern Tennessee and defeated a Union force at Richmond on August 30. After the Siege of Munfordville (September 13–17), Bragg secured most of the state and then organized at Frankfort a new Confederate government. The Confederates then had some 50,000 troops in Kentucky.

Union major general Don Carlos Buell detached some 20,000 men of his Army of the Ohio to deal with Smith and prevent the two Confederate forces from uniting, then advanced to secure Louisville. Buell moved about distractedly, however, entering Louisville only on September 25. Bragg's preoccupation with establishing a new Kentucky government allowed Buell time to reorganize his forces. Substantially reinforced and threatened with removal of command if he failed to act, on October 1 in the midst of one of the worst droughts in years, Buell departed Louisville with some 55,000 men, many of them untrained, to seek battle with Bragg.

Buell's army now converged via three separate roads on the small crossroads town of Perryville. Fighting began on October 7 with skirmishes between the two sides in the Chaplin Hulls west of Perryville. Both armies were desperately seeking to locate a source of water. Buell was slow to bring up his men, and he set the attack for October 9. Injured in a fall from his horse late on October 7, he remained miles to the rear and played no real role in the ensuing fight. As a consequence, there was little coordination among the three Union corps.

Fighting became general at dawn on October 8 as both sides tried to secure control of Doctor's Creek. Buell ordered Brigadier General Philip H. Sheridan's division to take Peters Hill, which it did, driving off Confederates there and continuing on to take Doctor's Creek. Major General Alexander M. McCook's I Corps was on the Union left, Major General Charles Gilbert's III Corps held the center, and Major General Thomas L. Crittenden's II Corps was far to the south on the Union right.

Bragg's army was in two wings. The left was commanded by Major General William J. Hardee and the right by Major General Leonidas Polk. Bragg ordered an attack en echelon by Polk's men against the Union left at Peters Hill, held by McCook. Buell, miles to the rear, did not realize that a major battle was in progress because of the effects of an acoustic shadow and was slow to reinforce. The first attack, led by Brigadier General Daniel S. Donelson, failed. A second attack, led by Brigadier General George E. Maney, was successful. The Union troops were driven back to another ridge, where they were halted by a Union brigade protected by a stone wall and led by Colonel John Starkweather.

Bragg then ordered an attack on Gilbert's men in the Union center on Springfield Pike. This assault at 2:45 p.m. was repulsed. A final Confederate attack came against McCook's center near Dixville Crossroads. It was halted by the arrival of reinforcements sent by Buell, who had finally learned of the battle at about 4:00 p.m. With the arrival of the additional Union troops and with Crittenden's corps threatening an attack, Bragg rejected appeals from his subordinates to continue the fight and withdrew his army that night. Buell failed to pursue, and Bragg continued the retreat through Cumberland Gap into eastern Tennessee, taking up a position near Murfreesboro. Union casualties in the Perryville fight totaled 4,276 (894 killed, 2,911 wounded, and 471 captured or missing); Confederate losses were 3,401 (532 killed, 2,641 wounded, and 228 captured or missing).

Although tactically a draw, the Battle of Perryville was a strategic Union victory. It was now clear that Kentuckians would not rise en masse in support of the Confederacy. For this reason, the battle is sometimes known as the Battle for Kentucky.

SPENCER C. TUCKER

See also
Acoustic Shadow; Bragg, Braxton; Buell, Don Carlos; Crittenden, Thomas Leonidas; Gilbert, Charles Champion; Hardee, William Joseph; Kentucky; Maney, George Earl; McCook, Alexander McDowell; Polk, Leonidas; Sheridan, Philip Henry

Further Reading
Brown, Kent Masterson. *The Civil War in Kentucky: Battle for the Bluegrass State.* Campbell, CA: Savas, 2000.
Cameron, Robert S. *Staff Ride Handbook for the Battle of Perryville, 8 October 1862.* Fort Leavenworth, KS: Combat Studies Institute, 2005.
Noe, Kenneth W. *Perryville: The Grand Havoc of Battle.* Lexington: University Press of Kentucky, 2001.

Personal Liberty Laws

Statutes that provided some legal protection for alleged fugitive slaves. Between 1826 and 1858 in response to the Fugitive Slave Acts of 1793 and 1850, Northern states enacted personal liberty laws to provide legal protections for alleged fugitives. In the absence of any federal procedural remedies, these state laws granted the accused the rights of habeas corpus, testimony, and jury trials. In addition, the kidnapping of suspects by slave catchers was prohibited by law.

In *Prigg v. Commonwealth of Pennsylvania* (1842), U.S. Supreme Court justice Joseph Story held that state statutes interfering with recaptures under the 1793 act were unconstitutional. In an obiter dictum, however, Story declared that states need not cooperate in the enforcement of the Fugitive Slave Act. Abolitionists quickly capitalized on this legal opportunity to initiate a new series of personal liberty laws (nine between 1842 and 1850) that prohibited the use of state officials and facilities, such as jails, in support of the federal statute.

The Compromise of 1850 included a tougher Fugitive Slave Act, demanded by Southerners who regarded the personal liberty laws of the North as an insult to Southern honor. At the same time, however, the new statute seemed to mock Northern concepts of due process with its rejection of habeas corpus, the right to testify, and the right to a jury trial. More onerous were the provisions to force citizen participation in captures, criminal penalties for assisting fugitives, and the notorious fee schedule paid to federal commissioners based on verdicts of guilt or innocence.

In response to the Fugitive Slave Act of 1850, state after state in the North passed new personal liberty laws going far beyond the earlier statutes that merely took advantage of Story's suggestions in *Prigg*. States increasingly defied the new federal statute by reaffirming rights to habeas corpus and jury trial and by prohibiting state officials from participating in captures.

In 1854 the Wisconsin Supreme Court declared the 1850 federal statute unconstitutional. In 1859 the U.S. Supreme Court heard the appeal as *Ableman v. Booth* and in a unanimous decision upheld the constitutionality of the Fugitive Slave Act and reaffirmed the supremacy of the federal judicial system over the state judiciaries. By 1859, however, the widely evaded statute had become a dead letter in much of Northern opinion, if not law, while Southerners continued to denounce personal liberty laws as outrages to property rights and honor.

ERROL MACGREGOR CLAUSS

See also

Abolitionism and the Civil War; Compromise of 1850; Contrabands; Fugitive Slave Act of 1850; *Prigg v. Pennsylvania*; Slavery; Supreme Court, U.S.

Further Reading

Campbell, Stanley W. *The Slave Catchers: Enforcement of the Fugitive Slave Law, 1850–1860.* Chapel Hill: University of North Carolina Press, 1970.

Morris, Thomas D. *Free Men All: The Personal Liberty Laws of the North, 1780–1861.* Baltimore: Johns Hopkins University Press, 1974.

Petersburg, Third Battle of
Event Date: April 2, 1865

Union victory marking the end of the long Petersburg Campaign (June 15, 1864–April 3, 1865), leading to the capture of Petersburg and Richmond. Confederate general in chief General Robert E. Lee knew that Union major general Philip Sheridan, having defeated the Confederates in the Shenandoah Valley, would soon join his 10,000 cavalry of the Army of the Shenandoah with the Army of the Potomac and the Army of the James, then deployed against the Army of Northern Virginia at Richmond and Petersburg. Lee therefore decided on a desperate surprise attack against the besiegers. Although initially successful, this attack of March 25, 1865, against the Union strong point of Fort Stedman was rebuffed, and the Union line was restored, at a cost of some 4,000 Confederate casualties to only 1,044 for the Union. Lee's final offensive of the war had been a failure. The next day Sheridan arrived at Petersburg, bringing Grant's strength up to 122,000 men, more than double that of Lee, and Lee's hold on Petersburg and Richmond could now be reckoned in days.

On April 1, Union cavalry and infantry routed the Confederates in the Battle of Five Forks at a crossroads to the west of the Confederate defenses. With much of the fighting occurring to the west, Confederate defenses to the east were weakened, and that same day Major General John C. Parke's IX Corps attacked the Confederate line held by troops under Major General John B. Gordon and anchored by Fort Mahone. The Union assault captured both the fortress and the Confederate trenches around the Jerusalem Plank Road. With Gordon already planning a counterattack to take back the lost ground, Parke requested reinforcements from Army of the Potomac commander Major General George Gordon Meade. Late that afternoon, Gordon launched his attack and nearly dislodged the Federals, but Parke managed to hold as Meade's reinforcements arrived.

Meanwhile, Grant was preparing to launch his carefully planned great offensive against the Confederate Boydton Plank Road line. It began at 4:40 a.m. on April 2, when Major General Horatio G. Wright's VI Corps assaulted the Boydton Plank Road line held by Lieutenant General A. P. Hill's Confederates. Within 20 minutes, the Union troops had punched a hole in the Confederate line. Wright's VI Corps then turned left, to the south, as Major General John Gibbon's XXIV Corps exploited the breakthrough. Crossing Boydton Plank Road, XXIV Corps turned north and headed toward Petersburg. Some stragglers from the initial breakthrough continued straight ahead, and that morning when Hill rode out with an aide to inspect the situation, he was shot and killed by two of them.

Informed of the Union breakthrough, Lee ordered Lieutenant James Longstreet to rush reinforcements down from Richmond. To purchase the time necessary for these men to arrive and take up position, Brigadier General Nathaniel H. Harris's brigade made a desperate stand at Forts Gregg and Whitworth. Gibbon attacked Fort Gregg first, with Brigadier General Robert S. Foster's division spearheading the attack. The Confederate garrison of only 300 men at Fort Gregg lacked the numbers to turn back an assault by some 5,000 Federals but were aided by heavy artillery fire from nearby Fort Whitworth. Twice the Confederates drove back Gibbon's men, but the attackers finally gained the fort's parapet. Fighting here was fierce and hand to hand, but the outcome was never in doubt. After taking Fort Gregg, the Union troops quickly overran Fort Whitworth. Longstreet's corps, however, was now arriving from Richmond, and Lee was able to temporarily stabilize and hold his last (inner) line, then evacuate Petersburg and Richmond that night. The Union attack claimed 3,500 Union casualties, while the Confederates lost some 4,250.

SPENCER C. TUCKER

See also

Early, Jubal Anderson; Five Forks, Battle of; Fort Gregg, Battle of; Foster, Robert Sanford; Gordon, John Brown; Grant, Ulysses Simpson; Harris, Nathaniel Harrison; Hill, Ambrose Powell; Lee, Robert Edward; Meade, George Gordon; Parke, John Grubb; Petersburg Campaign; Sheridan, Philip Henry; Wright, Horatio Gouverneur

Further Reading

Greene, A. Wilson. *The Final Battles of the Petersburg Campaign: Breaking the Backbone of the Rebellion.* Knoxville: University of Tennessee Press, 2008.

Horn, John. *The Petersburg Campaign, June 1864–April 1865.* Conshohocken, PA: Combined Publishing, 1999.

Trudeau, Noah Andre. *The Last Citadel: Petersburg, Virginia, June 1864–April 1865.* Baton Rouge: Louisiana State University Press, 1991.

Petersburg Campaign

Start Date: June 15, 1864
End Date: April 3, 1865

Ten-month-long struggle to capture the Confederate capital of Richmond. The Petersburg Campaign saw the longest siege in American military history. It was not a siege in the strict definition of the term in which supply lines were completely cut, nor was the campaign strictly limited to Petersburg, for the Union goal was the capture of the Confederate capital of Richmond, and there was considerable fighting over a wide area. The campaign might best be called the longest sustained operation of the war. The Petersburg Campaign also saw the largest concentration of African American troops during the conflict.

Lieutenant General Ulysses S. Grant, who assumed the position of general in chief of the Union Army in March 1864, immediately began planning a general spring offensive that would apply pressure on Confederate forces on all fronts. Major General William T. Sherman was to take Atlanta, while Major General Nathaniel P. Banks would try to take Mobile. In Virginia, Major General George Gordon Meade's Army of the Potomac of more than 100,000 men would drive south from Culpeper on Richmond, while Major General Benjamin F. Butler's 36,000-man Army of the James would move up the south bank of the James and cut General Robert E. Lee's Confederate Army of Northern Virginia off from the lower South. Brigadier generals George Crook and William W. Averell would move against the Shenandoah Valley from the west, while Major General Franz Sigel was to move south in the Shenandoah Valley and seize the railheads of Staunton and Lynchburg. To confront Grant, Lee had some 60,000 men and was supported by General P. G. T. Beauregard with 30,000 men in the Richmond-Petersburg area.

In the Overland (Richmond) Campaign (May 4–June 12, 1864), Grant hoped to bring Lee into decisive battle, destroy the Army of Northern Virginia, and capture the Confederate capital. The Overland Campaign commenced on May 4, when the Army of the Potomac crossed the Rapidan River and moved against Lee. Its associated Virginia campaigns had mixed results, however. Sigel met defeat in the Battle of New Market on May 15 and was shortly thereafter replaced by Major General David Hunter, but Crook and Averell were able to cut the rail line from Tennessee to Virginia.

**Petersburg Campaign
(June 15, 1864–April 3, 1865)**

	Union	Confederacy
Force strength, maximum, approximate	136,000	90,000
Killed, wounded, or captured	42,000	28,000

Soldiers in the trenches before battle, Petersburg, Virginia. The Union siege of Petersburg lasted from June 15, 1864, to April 3, 1865. It was the longest such effort of the war and presaged the trench warfare of World War I. (National Archives)

In the Overland Campaign itself, there were a series of sanguinary battles, commencing with the Battle of the Wilderness (May 5–7) and extending through the Battle of Cold Harbor (May 31–June 12), during which Grant repeatedly tried but failed to turn Lee's flank. The fighting was extremely costly, claiming through June 12 nearly 60,000 Union casualties—a figure equal to Lee's total strength—against Confederate losses of only 25,000–30,000, but Lee's army never quite recovered from the punishment it received.

In the Bermuda Hundred Campaign (May 5–20, 1864), meanwhile, the inept Butler fumbled away a chance to take Richmond, then held by relatively few Confederate troops under Beauregard. Reinforced, Beauregard then bottled up Butler in the Bermuda Hundred Peninsula. On June 9, Butler, aware that Lee had shifted resources north to meet Grant at Cold Harbor and that Petersburg was only lightly held, tried again. In what is known as the First Battle of Petersburg, a Union force of 4,500 men met defeat at the hands of 2,500 Confederates under Brigadier General Henry A. Wise along the so-called Dimmock Line east of the city.

At Cold Harbor, Grant was determined to keep the offensive going and decided to shift his forces south of the James to concentrate on Petersburg. Located 20 miles to the south of Richmond, this city of 18,000 people was the key rail

supply point for the Confederate capital. If Grant could take Petersburg, this would force the evacuation of Richmond.

On the night of June 12–13, the Army of the Potomac secretly decamped from its trenches at Cold Harbor and, screened by cavalry, crossed the James on a pontoon bridge more than 2,100 feet in length. On June 15, Grant, with some 15,000 men, attacked Petersburg, then held by only about 5,400 Confederates under Beauregard. Grant hurled Major General William F. Smith's XVIII Corps, Army of the James, and Major General Winfield S. Hancock's II Corps, Army of the Potomac, against the vastly outnumbered defenders. Grant's two commanders cost him a victory and the chance to end the war in 1864. Smith failed to press the assault with sufficient vigor, while Hancock, without definite orders, failed to lend Smith adequate support. During the course of the next three days, Beauregard gambled boldly by stripping his forces containing Butler at Bermuda Hundred to reinforce against Grant and turning back successive but poorly coordinated Union attacks. By the morning of June 16, Beauregard had some 14,000 men, facing 50,000 Federals. Beauregard undoubtedly rendered his greatest service to the Confederacy in the war in the skillful shifting of his meager resources early in the Petersburg fighting, defeating Grant's attacks. Lee, at first unaware of the magnitude of Grant's relocation, finally answered Beauregard's pleas for reinforcements. Both sides continued to reinforce, and by June 18 some 67,000 Union troops faced 20,000 Confederates.

Within a week there was stalemate, and both sides dug in. Field fortifications ultimately became elaborate siege lines presaging those of World War I and extending some 30 miles from the eastern outskirts of Richmond and Petersburg around to the south and then the southwest of Petersburg itself.

During the ensuing prolonged trench warfare, soldiers on both sides of the line endured periodic enemy shelling that included on the Union side fire from mammoth 13-inch siege mortars. Both sides labored to improve their defensive works, all the while contending with alternating heat and cold in addition to rain, thick mud, and choking dust. Letters to Confederate soldiers that described the desperate conditions now facing many families on the home front and in many cases ended with an appeal for the soldier to return home, combined with the difficult conditions in the trenches, led to growing Confederate desertions, especially during the winter of 1864–1865. Suffering was particularly intense that winter, with scores of Confederates crossing the lines nightly to surrender. The residents of Petersburg suffered along with the troops. The city was ill-prepared for a long siege, and conditions worsened, as Petersburg was within range of Union guns. During the long siege, more than 500 residential and commercial buildings were destroyed or damaged, and food was often in short supply.

The fighting took on a regular pattern early on. The key for the Confederates was continued control of the roads and railroads from the south and the west that supplied Richmond and Petersburg. Grant was well aware of this, and beginning as early as June 21, 1864, Union forces attempted to extend their lines westward and secure control of the Confederate rail lines: the Richmond & Petersburg Railroad; the Southside Railroad, which ran west to Lynchburg; and the Weldon Railroad (the Weldon & Petersburg Railroad), which ran north from Weldon, North Carolina, to Petersburg.

In the Battle of Jerusalem Plank Road (June 21–23), Union forces pushed west, fighting an inconclusive battle with the Confederates, who retained control of the Weldon Railroad. At the same time, General Meade ordered Brigadier Generals James H. Wilson and August Kautz to raid with their cavalry divisions and destroy Confederate track, bridges, and rail stations to the south and southwest. The Wilson-Kautz Raid (June 22–July 1, 1864) destroyed 60 miles of track but had no lasting effect. Within several weeks, the lines were back

in operation. The raid had also cost 1,445 Union casualties, about a quarter of the force involved. Wilson trumpeted a success, but Grant termed the raid a "disaster."

In the First Battle of Deep Bottom (July 27–29), Grant sought to draw Lee's men elsewhere in preparation for what became known as the Battle of the Crater (July 30, 1864). He ordered Hancock to fix the Confederates at Chaffin's Bluff, while Major General Philip H. Sheridan led two cavalry divisions across the James southeast of Richmond in an effort to take the capital or at the least ride around the city from the east and north and cut the Virginia Central Railroad from the Shenandoah Valley.

On July 30, Union forces detonated a huge mine that Pennsylvania miners in the Union army had placed in a tunnel under one of the major Confederate forts. Inept Union planning for the attack following the blast, a late change in plans, and poor Union leadership coupled with an effective Confederate reaction turned the Battle of the Crater into a Union fiasco, with nearly 3,800 Union casualties compared to only 1,500 Confederate casualties, and led to the relief of Major General Ambrose E. Burnside from command.

In the Second Battle of Deep Bottom (August 13–20), Grant attempted another thrust against Richmond, this time led by Hancock. The attack was designed in part to prevent Lee from dispatching reinforcements to aid Lieutenant General Jubal A. Early's operations in the Shenandoah Valley, and in this at least, the attack was successful.

Grant then sent Major General Gouverneur K. Warren's V Corps to attack the Weldon Railroad. The Federals ended up fighting on the defensive at the Battle at Globe Tavern (August 18–21), but the Union troops had succeeded in tearing up a considerable quantity of track along this key Confederate railroad. Grant then sent Hancock's II Corps against the Weldon Railroad, and although the Confederates won a clear victory in the ensuing Second Battle of Reams Station (August 25, 1864), they permanently lost an important portion of the Weldon line, forcing them to send supplies by wagon from the Stony Creek Depot through Dinwiddie Court House and then along the Boydton Plank Road into Petersburg.

Most of the subsequent fighting occurred to the west as Grant endeavored to secure the Southside Railroad, connecting Petersburg to Lynchburg, and also Boydton Plank Road. Then, during September 16 in the Hampton-Rosser Cattle Raid (Beefsteak Raid), the Confederates sent 4,000 men to near City Point, where they seized nearly 2,500 beef cattle.

In the Battle of Chaffin's Farm (September 29–30), Butler's Army of the James crossed the James to attack the

PETERSBURG CAMPAIGN, JUNE 15, 1864 – APRIL 3, 1865

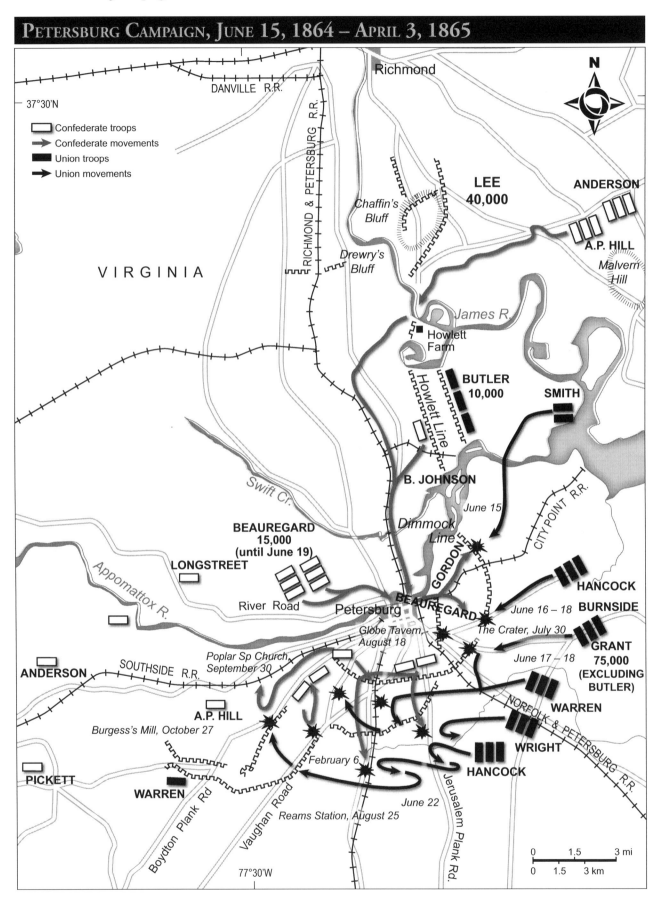

Richmond

DANVILLE R.R.

37°30'N

☐ Confederate troops
→ Confederate movements
■ Union troops
➡ Union movements

VIRGINIA

RICHMOND & PETERSBURG R.R.

Chaffin's Bluff

Drewry's Bluff

LEE 40,000

ANDERSON

A.P. HILL

Malvern Hill

James R.

Howlett Farm

BUTLER 10,000

SMITH

Howlett Line

B. JOHNSON

Swift Cr.

Dimmock Line

June 15

GORDON

CITY POINT R.R.

BEAUREGARD 15,000 (until June 19)

LONGSTREET

River Road

Appomattox R.

BEAUREGARD

Petersburg

HANCOCK

June 16 – 18

BURNSIDE

The Crater, July 30

GRANT 75,000 (EXCLUDING BUTLER)

June 17 – 18

Globe Tavern, August 18

ANDERSON

SOUTHSIDE R.R.

Poplar Sp Church, September 30

NORFOLK & PETERSBURG R.R.

WARREN

A.P. HILL

Burgess's Mill, October 27

WRIGHT

February 6

HANCOCK

Boydton Plank Rd

PICKETT

WARREN

Vaughan Road

Reams Station, August 25

June 22

Jerusalem Plank Rd.

77°30'W

| 0 | 1.5 | 3 mi |
| 0 | 1.5 | 3 km |

N

Richmond defenses north of that river. Although the Federals enjoyed initial success, the Confederates contained the attack. Lee reinforced and counterattacked unsuccessfully. He then erected a new line of works.

Grant knew that to meet Butler's attack, Lee had necessarily weakened his line elsewhere. Grant sought to take advantage by attempting to extend his left flank and cut the Confederate lines of communication southwest of Petersburg. Grant committed four infantry divisions and one cavalry division to the attack. As a consequence of the ensuing Battle of Peebles' Farm (September 30–October 2), the Federals extended their left flank to Peebles' and Pegram's farms.

Lee, worried about the heightened Federal threat to Richmond from the east, attacked the Union right flank on Darbytown Road on October 7. The Confederates routed the Union cavalry there but were halted at the main Union line on New Market Road. On October 13, Union forces assaulted the Confederates north of Darbytown Road. Repulsed, they then retired to their entrenchments along New Market Road. Butler attacked the Confederates again during October 27–28, only to be repulsed in the Battle of Fair Oaks and Darbytown Road.

Taking advantage of his superior numbers, at the same time that the Battle of Fair Oaks and Darbytown Road unfolded, Grant sent more than 30,000 Union troops under Hancock west to operate against the Boydton Plank Road. In the major Battle of Boydton Plank Road (October 27–28), the Federals gained the road, only to be driven back. The Confederates continued to control this key supply route throughout the winter.

In early February 1865, Union troops again advanced against the Boydton Plank Road. In the Battle of Hatcher's Run (February 5–7), Lee sustained heavy casualties but pushed the Federals back from this important supply line. The Federals, however, had extended their left flank to the Vaughan Road crossing of Hatcher's Run.

The last major battle of the Petersburg Campaign was the Confederate attack against Fort Stedman on March 25, 1865. Lee was well aware of growing Union strength against him. Grant now had some 125,000 men, while Lee had only some 50,000. Lee also knew that General Sheridan had rejoined Grant from the Shenandoah Valley with an additional 10,000 cavalry. To disrupt an anticipated major Union attack (which Grant actually planned to launch on March 29), Lee planned a major attack against Union Fort Stedman on March 25.

Launched with half of Lee's infantry under Major General John B. Gordon, the attack was initially successful, and

the Confederates occupied the fort. The Federals counterattacked, however, restoring the line. This was Lee's last attempt to breach the Union defenses and regain the initiative.

On April 1, Sheridan at the head of four Union cavalry divisions and V Corps of infantry crushed a Confederate force in the Battle of Five Forks; Five Forks was a major road intersection 10 miles west-southwest of Petersburg and about 5 miles west of where Lee's lines ended. The next day, Grant flung his troops in a massive assault on the thinly held Confederate lines, which now collapsed. Only a valiant stand at Fort Gregg saved the retreating Confederates from immediate and total defeat, but the Federals were in Petersburg by nightfall.

Lee now evacuated Richmond and headed west, hoping to link up with General Joseph E. Johnston in North Carolina. Grant pursued, and Lee, cut off by Union cavalry, surrendered his remaining troops to Grant at Appomattox Court House on April 9, 1865.

SPENCER C. TUCKER

See also

Appomattox Campaign; Averell, William Woods; Beauregard, Pierre Gustav Toutant; Bermuda Hundred Campaign; Boydton Plank Road, Battle of; Burnside, Ambrose Everett; Butler, Benjamin Franklin; Chaffin's Farm, Battle of; Cold Harbor, Battle of; Crater, Battle of the; Crook, George; Deep Bottom, First Battle of; Deep Bottom, Second Battle of; Early, Jubal Anderson; Fair Oaks and Darbytown Road, Battle of; Five Forks, Battle of; Fort Gregg, Battle of; Fort Stedman, Battle of; Globe Tavern, Battle of; Grant, Ulysses Simpson; Hampton-Rosser Cattle Raid; Hancock, Winfield Scott; Hatcher's Run, Battle of; Hunter, David; Lee, Robert Edward; Meade, George Gordon; Overland Campaign; Peebles' Farm, Battle of; Petersburg, Third Battle of; Reams Station, Second Battle of; Sigel, Franz; Smith, William Farrar; Sutherland's Station, Battle of; Warren, Gouverneur Kemble; Weldon & Petersburg Railroad; Wilson-Kautz Raid; Wise, Henry Alexander

Further Reading

Greene, A. Wilson. *The Final Battles of the Petersburg Campaign: Breaking the Backbone of the Rebellion.* Knoxville: University of Tennessee Press, 2008.

Horn, John. *The Petersburg Campaign, June 1864–April 1865.* Conshohocken, PA: Combined Books, 1993.

Sommers, Richard J. *Richmond Redeemed: The Siege at Petersburg.* Garden City, NY: Doubleday, 1981.

Trudeau, Noah Andre. *The Last Citadel: Petersburg, Virginia, June 1864–April 1865.* Baton Rouge: Louisiana State University Press, 1991.

Petersburg Mine, Battle of the

See Crater, Battle of the

Petigru, James Louis
Birth Date: May 10, 1789
Death Date: March 9, 1863

Pro-Union South Carolina attorney and politician. James Louis Petigru was born on May 10, 1789, outside of Abbeville, South Carolina, to a family of humble means. Nevertheless, he graduated from South Carolina College in 1809, studied law, and was admitted to the bar in 1812. Petrigru established a legal practice in Coosawatchie, South Carolina, before becoming the solicitor of the Beaufort District in 1816. Three years later he joined a well-established practice in Charleston. By 1822, he was head of the firm and had been elected attorney general of South Carolina, a post he would hold until 1830. Meanwhile, as his law practice prospered, he bought a large rice plantation along the Savannah River, where he would own as many as 120 slaves.

During the Nullification Crisis of 1828, in which numerous South Carolina politicians attempted to declare the Tariff of 1828 passed by the U.S. Congress null and void, Petrigru deplored the move, arguing forcefully that a state could not challenge a federal law in such a fashion. In 1830 Petigru was elected to the state legislature, where he led the fight against nullification.

In 1834 Petigru took on another test of states' rights when he defended a South Carolina Militia officer who refused to take a mandatory oath of loyalty to South Carolina. Petigru and other Unionists asserted that such a law was unconstitutional and placed state allegiance above allegiance to the United States. In 1838 Petigru left the legislature after being defeated for reelection. Clearly, his controversial pro-Union philosophy had all but ended his political career.

After leaving public life, Petigru plunged into several disastrous business endeavors that resulted in the loss of his Savannah River plantation. However, he continued to forge his own independent political course, backing Whig economic and internal improvement programs in his home state and defending the supremacy of the U.S. Constitution and individual civil rights. He was asked to codify all of South Carolina law in 1859, a task that took him nearly three years. It was finally adopted, with amendments, in 1872.

Although Petrigru was no abolitionist and continued to own slaves at his Charleston residence in the 1850s and early 1860s, he refused to support secession, predicting that it would ultimately lead to a cataclysm. When South Carolina became the first state to secede in December 1860, he famously remarked that "South Carolina is too small for a Republic and too large for an insane asylum." Petrigru nevertheless remained in the state after the Civil War began. Petigru's home was consumed by a fire that swept through Charleston in December 1861. His health had been precarious for some time, and Petigru died in Charleston on March 9, 1863.

PAUL G. PIERPAOLI JR.

See also

Nullification; Secession; South Carolina; Southern Unionists

Further Reading

Ford, Lacy K., Jr. *Origin of Southern Radicalism: The South Carolina Upcountry, 1800 to 1860.* New York: Oxford University Press, 1991.

Pease, William H., and Jane H. Pease. *James Louis Petigru: Southern Conservative, Southern Dissenter.* Columbia: University of South Carolina Press, 2002.

Pettigrew, James Johnston
Birth Date: July 4, 1828
Death Date: July 17, 1863

Confederate officer. Born into a wealthy planter family in Tyrrell County, North Carolina, on July 4, 1828, James Johnston Pettigrew entered the University of North Carolina and graduated as valedictorian in 1847. President James K. Polk appointed Pettigrew an assistant professor at the U.S. Naval Observatory. Pettigrew held that position for only six months and then spent 1850–1852 in Europe, during which time he briefly studied law at the University of Berlin. A linguist, Pettigrew was fluent in a half dozen languages before joining a law firm in Charleston, South Carolina.

In 1856 Pettigrew was elected to the South Carolina legislature, but his outspoken opposition to laws that sought to reopen the slave trade ensured his defeat in the next election. Pettigrew again traveled to Europe and volunteered for service in the Italian forces in the war that pitted Sardinia and France against Austria in 1859, but he saw no action. He then traveled widely in Spain, later publishing an account of his travels as *Notes on Spain and Spaniards in the Summer of 1859, with a Glance at Sardinia.*

On the secession of South Carolina from the Union on December 20, 1860, Pettigrew was appointed aide to Governor Francis Pickens and served as colonel of the 1st South Carolina Rifles. Pettigrew took an active role in efforts to secure the withdrawal of Union forces under Major Robert Anderson at Fort Sumter and then enlisted as a private in the Hampton Legion. In July 1861, Pettigrew was appointed colonel of the 12th (later redesignated the 22nd) North Carolina Infantry. On February 26, 1862, he was promoted to brigadier general and took command of a brigade in the Army of Northern Virginia, which he led until he was severely wounded in the Battle of Seven Pines (May 31–June 1, 1862) and taken prisoner. He was exchanged two months later. He then served at Petersburg, Virginia, and in North Carolina.

Returning to the Army of Northern Virginia in May 1863 in time for the Gettysburg Campaign, Pettigrew commanded a brigade consisting of the 11th, 26th, 47th, and 52nd North Carolina Infantry Regiments in Major General Henry Heth's division of Lieutenant General A. P. Hill's III Corps. Pettigrew and his men were in the thick of the fight at the Battle of Gettysburg (July 1–3, 1863) and suffered heavy casualties on the first day of fighting. When Heth was wounded, Pettigrew took command of the division and participated in Pickett's Charge on the last day of the battle, during which he was wounded in the hand but refused to leave the field until the end of the assault. He then resumed brigade command in the retreat. Eleven days later, Pettigrew was shot and mortally wounded in a skirmish at Falling Waters, Maryland. He died on July 17, 1863, at Bunker Hill, West Virginia.

SPENCER C. TUCKER AND JIM PIECUCH

See also

Anderson, Robert; Falling Waters, Battle of; Fort Sumter, South Carolina, U.S. Efforts to Relieve; Gettysburg, Battle of; Heth, Henry; Hill, Ambrose Powell; Pickens, Francis Wilkinson; Seven Pines, Battle of

Further Reading

Gragg, Rod. *Covered with Glory: The 26th North Carolina Infantry at Gettysburg.* New York: HarperCollins, 2000.

Hess, Earl J. *Lee's Tar Heels: The Pettigrew-Kirkland-MacRae Brigade.* Chapel Hill: University of North Carolina Press, 2002.

Wilson, Clyde N. *Carolina Cavalier: The Life and Mind of James Johnston Pettigrew.* Athens: University of Georgia Press, 1990.

Pettus, Edmund Winston
Birth Date: July 6, 1821
Death Date: July 27, 1907

Confederate officer. Edmund Winston Pettus was born on July 6, 1821, in Limestone County, Alabama. He attended Clinton College (Tennessee), studied law, and was admitted to the bar in 1842. Pettus opened a legal practice in Gainesville, Alabama, and became solicitor for the Seventh Circuit Court in 1844. He saw service during the Mexican-American War (1846–1848) and spent time in California before settling down in Cahaba, Alabama.

In early 1861, Pettus traveled to Mississippi to discern that state's plans for secession. At the time, his brother, John J. Pettus, was governor of Mississippi. Edmund Pettus then helped recruit the 20th Arkansas Infantry Regiment and was elected major. On October 8, 1861, he was promoted to lieutenant colonel.

After service in eastern Tennessee, Pettus saw action in the defense of Port Gibson, Mississippi, and was taken prisoner during the battle there on May 1, 1863. Escaping, he then participated in the Second Vicksburg Campaign (April 1–July 4, 1863), during which he was promoted to colonel. When Vicksburg fell on July 4, he was again taken prisoner. On his exchange in September, he was advanced to brigadier general and given command of an Alabama brigade in the Army of Tennessee.

Pettus saw action in the Battles of Lookout Mountain (November 23, 1863) and Missionary Ridge (November 25, 1863). During 1864, he was involved in all of the campaigns waged by the Army of Tennessee, including the Atlanta Campaign (May 5–September 2, 1864). Early the next year he was in North Carolina, where he saw action at the Second Battle of Kinston (March 7–10, 1865) and the Battle of Bentonville (March 19–21). Wounded in the latter battle, Pettus surrendered at Durham Station.

After the war Pettus commenced a law practice in Selma, Alabama. Elected to the U.S. Senate as a Democrat, he served from 1897 until 1907. He died in Hot Springs, North Carolina, on July 27, 1907.

PAUL G. PIERPAOLI JR.

See also

Atlanta Campaign; Bentonville, Battle of; Kinston, Second Battle of; Lookout Mountain, Battle of; Missionary Ridge, Battle of; Port Gibson, Battle of; Tennessee, Confederate Army of; Vicksburg Campaign, Second

Further Reading

Watson, Elbert L. "Edmund Winston Pettus." In *Alabama United States Senators*, 91–94. Huntsville, AL: Strode, 1982.

Wright, Marcus J. *General Officers of the Confederate Army.* Mattituck, NY: J. M. Carroll, 1983.

Pettus, John Jones
Birth Date: October 9, 1813
Death Date: January 28, 1867

Mississippi governor. Born on October 9, 1813, in Wilson County, Tennessee, John Jones Pettus moved to Kemper County, Mississippi, as a child. A self-made man, he began his political career representing Kemper County in the state legislature and later served as the president of the Mississippi Senate. In that capacity, he was briefly elevated under the Mississippi Constitution to serve as the state's governor in January 1854 after the sitting governor resigned from office five days before his elected successor was sworn in. Afterward Pettus remained in the legislature, where he loudly and dramatically defended states' rights and slavery as sectional tensions increased. In 1859 he ran for governor representing the radical wing of the state's Democratic Party, campaigning on a platform that included heavily arming the state to defend the institution of slavery should a Republican win the presidency. Pettus handily defeated his opponent, which represented a significant victory for secessionists around the state. In response to Republican Abraham Lincoln winning the presidency in November 1860, Pettus helped lead the effort to take Mississippi out of the Union.

Although Pettus promoted secession, he found the task of being a wartime governor difficult. The state's fragile military infrastructure created major logistical problems related to the distribution of military supplies and the mobilization of the state's troops. After a two-year term, Pettus won reelection in 1861, but the problems related to Mississippi's war effort only grew worse. During his second administration the state capital at Jackson fell to Union forces, as did the important port city of Vicksburg on the Mississippi River. Constitutionally restricted from seeking a third term, Pettus left office in November 1863, by which time many of his once-enthusiastic supporters were blaming him for Mississippi's setbacks.

When the state that he had led out of the Union in 1861 officially surrendered in 1865, Pettus signed a loyalty oath to the United States and, his health failing, moved to Arkansas. He died in Jefferson County, Arkansas, on January 28, 1867.

BEN WYNNE

See also

Mississippi; Pettus, Edmund Winston

Further Reading

Dubay, Robert W. *John Jones Pettus, Mississippi Fire-Eater: His Life and Times.* Jackson: University Press of Mississippi, 1975.

Wynne, Ben. *Mississippi's Civil War: A Narrative History.* Macon, GA: Mercer University Press, 2006.

toward journalism, editing two newspapers and becoming Alabama's state printer for a time. Phelan then studied law, was admitted to the bar in 1846, and commenced a law practice in Huntsville. Three years later he moved to Aberdeen, Mississippi, where he established a lucrative legal practice. A staunch proponent of the Southern cause and a close friend of Jefferson Davis, Phelan was elected to the Mississippi Senate in 1860.

As the Confederacy formed and civil war loomed, Phelan acted as the eyes and ears for Davis in Mississippi, sending him numerous reports on the state's morale and military readiness. Elected to the Confederate Senate in the autumn of 1861, Phelan was sworn into office early the following year. In the Senate, he continued to keep President Davis abreast of affairs in Mississippi and the Deep South and was frequently called upon to offer him political advice. Phelan was a strong supporter of a robust Confederate government, endowed with expansive powers to prosecute the war. Although his stance was welcomed at the Confederative executive mansion, it did not sit particularly well with many of his constituents, who were more concerned with states' rights.

Phelan dug his own political grave during 1863 when he sponsored a bill that called for the confiscation of all cotton, to be paid for in bonds, that would in turn be used to help finance a badly needed loan to prosecute and win the war. Although the bill passed the House, it died in the Senate, along with Phelan's political fortunes. Burned in effigy by cotton planters, Phelan lost his reelection bid, leaving office in 1864. During 1864 and 1865, he was a judge advocate in the Confederate Army with the rank of colonel and traveled the Confederacy presiding over various military court cases.

Postbellum, Phelan eventually settled in Memphis, where he practiced law. He died there on May 17, 1873.

PAUL G. PIERPAOLI JR.

See also

Congress, CSA; Davis, Jefferson Finis

Further Reading

Davis, William C. *Look Away! A History of the Confederate States of America.* New York: Free Press, 2002.

Thomas, Emory M. *The Confederate Nation, 1861–1865.* New York: Harper and Row, 1979.

Phelan, James

Birth Date: October 11, 1821
Death Date: May 17, 1873

Confederate senator. James Phelan was born on October 11, 1821, in Huntsville, Alabama. As a young man, he gravitated

Phelps, John Smith

Birth Date: December 22, 1814
Death Date: November 20, 1886

Union officer. John Smith Phelps was born on December 22, 1814, in Simsbury, Connecticut. He was educated at

Washington (Trinity) College, graduating in 1832. He then studied law, was admitted to the bar in 1835, and in 1837 moved to Springfield, Missouri, where he established a thriving legal practice. In 1840 he held a seat in the Missouri legislature as a Democrat, and from 1844 to 1863 he served in the U.S. House of Representatives.

In the spring of 1861, Phelps enlisted as a private in a six-month Missouri infantry regiment. He ultimately rose to the rank of colonel on December 19, 1861. Phelps saw action at the Battle of Pea Ridge (March 7–8, 1862) but mustered out of service on May 13, 1862, and returned to Washington, D.C.

On July 19, 1862, President Abraham Lincoln appointed Phelps brigadier general of volunteers and military governor of Arkansas. Phelps's commission expired in March 1863 for lack of confirmation. In poor health, Phelps resigned his post later in 1863 and by 1864 was practicing law in Springfield, Missouri.

Phelps waged an unsuccessful bid for the Missouri governorship in 1868 but was successful on his second try in 1876. Still a Democrat, he served from 1877 to 1881, at which time he resumed his legal practice. Phelps died on November 20, 1886, in St. Louis.

PAUL G. PIERPAOLI JR.

See also

Arkansas; Missouri; Pea Ridge, Battle of

Further Reading

Eicher, John H., and David J. Eicher. *Civil War High Commands*. Stanford, CA: Stanford University Press, 2001.
Warner, Ezra J. *Generals in Gray: Lives of the Confederate Commanders*. Baton Rouge: Louisiana State University Press, 2006.

Phelps, John Wolcott

Birth Date: November 13, 1813
Death Date: February 2, 1885

Union officer. John Wolcott Phelps was born on November 13, 1813, in Guilford, Vermont. After attending local schools, he graduated from the U.S. Military Academy, West Point, on July 1, 1836, and was commissioned a brevet second lieutenant. Soon after his first assignment with the 4th U.S. Artillery Regiment, he was promoted to second lieutenant on July 28, 1836. He served in the Second Seminole War (1835–1842) and was promoted to first lieutenant on July 7, 1838. The next several years were spent on garrison duty in the South and along the Canadian border before participating in the Mexican-American War (1846–1848).

Although brevetted captain for his services during the war, for unknown reasons Phelps declined to accept the nominal promotion. He received his regular promotion to captain on March 31, 1850. After service on the western frontier, Phelps resigned his commission on November 2, 1859. He returned to his home in Brattleboro, Vermont, where he campaigned against slavery and the Masonic order.

With the start of the Civil War, on May 2, 1861, Phelps was named colonel of the 1st Vermont Volunteer Regiment. Sent to Fort Monroe in Virginia, he commanded the troops who secured the nearby town of Newport News. Following promotion to brigadier general on May 17, 1861, he was transferred to the Department of the Gulf under Major General Benjamin F. Butler. In November 1861 Phelps commanded the troops who seized Ship Island, Mississippi. His regiment participated in the battles for Forts Jackson and St. Philip on the Mississippi River in April 1862 as well as in the capture of New Orleans on May 1, 1862.

While stationed near New Orleans, Phelps embarked on the first recruitment of black soldiers. Camp conditions were unhealthy, and his men were dying at the rate of two or three per day. The numbers of black fugitives, however, continued to increase. Deciding to make use of this resource, Phelps formed three regiments of African Americans and requested arms from Butler to outfit them for the defense of the camp. Butler denied his request. Instead, he ordered Phelps to use the African Americans as laborers and to cease organizing them as troops. Unwilling to become what he viewed as a slave driver, Phelps resigned his commission on August 21, 1862. The Confederate government's response to Phelps's recruitment attempt was to declare him an outlaw. Months later, President Abraham Lincoln adopted the policy of enlisting blacks and apparently offered Phelps a commission as a major general. Phelps declined the offer when the president refused to backdate the new commission to the time of his resignation.

Phelps remained in Brattleboro, where he was active in community groups and contributed to various literary and scientific journals. Resuming his campaign against the Masons, he unsuccessfully ran for president in 1880 as the American Party (Anti-Mason) candidate. In 1883 Phelps moved to Guilford, Vermont, where he remained until his death on February 2, 1885.

DONNA SMITH

See also

Abolitionism and the Civil War; Butler, Benjamin Franklin; Fort Monroe, Virginia; New Orleans Campaign

Further Reading
Howard, Cecil Hampden Cutts. *Life and Public Service of Gen. John Wolcott Phelps.* Brattleboro, VT: F. E. Housh, 1887.
Waite, Otis F. R. *Vermont in the Great Rebellion.* Claremont, NH: Tracy, Chase, 1869.

Phelps, Seth Ledyard
Birth Date: January 13, 1824
Death Date: June 24, 1885

Union naval officer. Born on January 13, 1824, in Chardon, Ohio, Seth Ledyard Phelps entered naval service as a midshipman on October 19, 1841. He was advanced to passed midshipman on August 10, 1847. Phelps first served in the Mediterranean and Brazil Squadrons and later off Africa. He also saw service in the Mexican-American War (1846–1848), following which he was stationed at the Naval Observatory and participated in the laying of the transatlantic cable. Phelps made master on June 30, 1855, and lieutenant on September 15 of the same year.

Soon after the Civil War began, Phelps was one of the first naval officers sent west to help build the Western Gunboat Flotilla. He assisted Commander John Rodgers in the conversion of the timberclads *Tyler, Lexington,* and *Conestoga.* As commander of the *Conestoga,* Phelps helped develop the tactics used with success by the U.S. Navy on the western rivers. He commanded the division of timberclads in the attack on Fort Henry, Tennessee, on February 6, 1862. On the direction of Flag Officer Andrew H. Foote, immediately following the fort's capitulation Phelps led a raid up the Tennessee River (February 6–10), reaching as far as Muscle Shoals, Alabama. He was promoted to lieutenant commander on July 16.

Following the Union capture of Island No. 10, Phelps became the flag officer and chief assistant to new commander Captain Charles H. Davis. Phelps had hoped to replace Davis on the latter's departure but lost out to Rear Admiral David D. Porter. Phelps then took command of the *Eastport,* the largest ironclad in the Mississippi Squadron.

During the Red River Campaign (March 10–May 22, 1864), Phelps directed the naval attack on Fort DeRussy, and his ships secured Alexandria, Louisiana. He then joined in the drive on Shreveport. During the subsequent withdrawal down the Red River, the *Eastport* struck a torpedo (naval mine) about eight miles below Grand Ecore, Louisiana, and sank in shallow water. Although the ship was refloated, bringing it out under tow proved to be impossible, and it had to be scuttled. Porter unfairly blamed Phelps, who resigned on October 29, 1864.

A pen and ink sketch by Carl Becker during the Civil War of Union naval officer and gunboat commander Seth L. Phelps. In February 1862, Lieutenant Phelps led an important Union raid up the Tennesseee River that reached into Alabama. (Library of Congress)

After the war, Phelps served on the District of Columbia Board of Commissioners and as minister to Peru. He died on June 24, 1885, in Lima while serving in that capacity.

GARY D. JOINER AND SPENCER C. TUCKER

See also
Davis, Charles Henry; Foote, Andrew Hull; Fort Henry, Battle of; Island No. 10, Battle of; Mississippi Squadron, U.S. Navy; Phelps's Raid up the Tennessee River; Porter, David Dixon; Red River Campaign; Riverine Warfare; Rodgers, John, Jr.; Timberclads; Torpedoes

Further Reading
Joiner, Gary. *Mr. Lincoln's Brown Water Navy: The Mississippi Squadron.* Lanham, MD: Rowman and Littlefield, 2007.
Joiner, Gary D. *One Damn Blunder from Beginning to End: The Red River Campaign of 1864.* Wilmington, DE: Scholarly Resources, 2003.
Slagle, Jay. *Ironclad Captain: Seth Ledyard Phelps & the U.S. Navy, 1841–1864.* Kent, OH: Kent State University Press, 1996.

Phelps's Raid up the Tennessee River
Start Date: February 6, 1862
End Date: February 10, 1862

Union naval raid. So confident was Flag Officer Andrew H. Foote of victory in the coming Union assault on Fort Henry on the Tennessee River that on February 2, 1862, four days before the attack and on his own initiative, he issued special orders to Lieutenant Seth Ledyard Phelps that on the fall of Fort Henry, Phelps was to move his three timberclad gunboats—the *Conestoga* (flagship), *Lexington,* and *Tyler*—up the Tennessee River. Foote ordered Phelps to disable the key 1,200-foot Memphis, Louisville & Clarksville Railroad drawbridge at Danville, 25 miles above Fort Henry, and then raid into Confederate territory as far upriver as the depth of water would allow.

Following the Union capture of Fort Henry on February 6, Phelps set out. A fast Confederate steamer, the *Dunbar,* spread the alarm in advance of Phelps's ships. En route to Danville, Phelps discovered the camp of the 48th and 51st Tennessee Regiments along the shore and stopped to shell it. At Danville, meanwhile, the Confederates loaded military supplies aboard four transports and sent them upriver, then disabled the drawbridge.

The Union ships arrived at the bridge that evening, opening fire on the *Dunbar,* which had remained in the vicinity, and forcing it upriver. Phelps then landed men, and in about an hour they succeeded in opening the drawbridge. He then left behind Lieutenant William Gwin and the *Tyler,* the slowest of his gunboats, so that its crew might destroy track and telegraph line, while Phelps proceeded with the *Conestoga* and the *Lexington.* His mission accomplished, Gwin hurried the *Tyler* upriver. The raiders did not destroy the railroad bridge as Foote had ordered, judging that this could be accomplished on their return.

Phelps's *Conestoga,* meanwhile, pressed ahead of the slower *Lexington* and gained on the heavily laden Confederate transports. The captain of one of these, the *Samuel Orr,* fired his vessel rather than see it and its contents fall into Union hands. Farther upriver, the captains of the *Appleton Belle* and the *Lynn Boyd,* realizing that they too would soon be overhauled, ran their ships ashore and fired them in turn. A tremendous explosion ripped apart the *Appleton Belle,* which had been loaded with ordnance supplies and 3,000 pounds of powder. The explosion shattered the *Lynn Boyd* and inflicted some minor damage to the *Conestoga,* 1,000 yards distant.

At 11:00 a.m. on February 7, all three gunboats arrived at Perry's Landing, Tennessee, where they discovered strong pro-Union sentiment. At 7:00 p.m. the Union gunboats reached Cerro Gordo, Tennessee. Small arms fire on the *Conestoga* produced retaliatory shelling from it and the *Tyler.* There Phelps took possession of the large 570-ton steamer *Eastport,* which had been undergoing conversion into an ironclad ram, as well as a quantity of materials intended for it, including lumber and iron plating. Although the *Eastport* had been partially scuttled, the Union sailors were able to stop the leaks and pump out the water.

Again leaving the *Tyler* behind, this time to guard his prize, Phelps pressed on with the *Conestoga* and the *Lexington.* On February 8 in Mississippi, Phelps took two small steamers, the *Muscle* and *Sally Wood,* at Waterloo Landing, the latter filled with iron destined for the Tredegar Iron Works in Richmond. A Union prize crew boarded the *Muscle* and used it to tow the *Sallie Wood* back to Cerro Gordo.

Phelps's gunboats got as far south as Florence, Alabama, on the afternoon of February 8. Here the raid ended, stopped by Muscle Shoals. The crews of the *Dunbar* and another steamer, the *Alfred Robb,* managed to prevent their capture by hiding them in a stream. The Confederates fired three other steamers, the *Julius Smith, Sam Kirkman,* and *Time.* The *Julius Smith* was cut loose with paddle wheels turning in reverse in the hopes that it would run into and destroy one or more of the raiders, but the Union gunboats easily avoided its mad passage downstream. The other two steamers were fired at the landing, but seamen from the *Conestoga* managed to save a quantity of stores from them.

A delegation of Florence citizens pleaded with Phelps not to destroy their city or the prized 15-pier railroad bridge over the river. Phelps reasoned that because Muscle Shoals impeded him from further passage upriver and because the bridge had little military value, he would leave it alone. He also assured the delegation that the Union seamen would not destroy private property. After going through warehouses and seizing a quantity of official Confederate property, Phelps ordered private property seized aboard the steamers offloaded and returned to its owners.

That same evening, the two gunboats departed Florence. Later that night they reached Cerro Gordo, where Gwin and his men had been busy loading captured supplies and readying the *Eastport* for its trip downriver. Phelps then decided to assault a Confederate camp near Savannah, Tennessee, reportedly containing some 600 men. Leaving the *Lexington* behind to guard the *Eastport,* the *Conestoga* and the *Tyler* set out. At Savannah, 130 sailors and marines went ashore with a Dahlgren boat howitzer, only to find that the camp had been hastily evacuated. The landing party removed some stores and fired others, along with the camp buildings. On the night of February 9, the *Lexington* and the *Tyler* took the *Eastport* in tow, while the *Conestoga* towed the *Sallie Wood* and the *Muscle.* But the *Muscle* sprung a leak and had to be abandoned, along with its cargo.

On February 10, Phelps's little flotilla returned to Fort Henry. The expedition had been a considerable success. It had taken three Confederate steamers and led to the destruction of six others. The large *Eastport* was a particularly valuable capture and became a Union ironclad of the same name. The expedition also secured a considerable quantity of lumber, iron plate, and other stores as well as small arms.

SPENCER C. TUCKER

See also

Foote, Andrew Hull; Fort Henry, Battle of

Further Reading

Slagle, Jay. *Ironclad Captain: Seth Ledyard Phelps and the U.S. Navy, 1841–1864.* Kent, OH: Kent State University Press, 1996.

"S. L. Phelps to Flag Officer Foote, 10 February 1862, in U.S. Navy Department." In *Official Records of the Union and Confederate Navies in the War of the Rebellion.* Series 1, Vol. 22, pp. 571–574. Washington, DC: U.S. Government Printing Office, 1908 and 1910.

Tucker, Spencer C. *Andrew Hull Foote: Civil War Admiral on Western Waters.* Annapolis, MD: Naval Institute Press, 1999.

Philadelphia Brigade

Union infantry brigade that served in the Army of the Potomac. The brigade was composed of four regiments, the 69th, 71st, 72nd, and 106th Pennsylvania Infantry, which had been recruited almost exclusively from the city of Philadelphia. Initially, the regiments were labeled the 1st, 2nd, 3rd, and 5th California Infantry to provide California with a military role in the war. The regiments were formed into the California Brigade under Colonel Edward D. Baker, a sitting U.S. senator from Oregon. After the Battle of Ball's Bluff (October 21, 1861), during which the brigade was heavily engaged and Baker was killed, the regiments were renumbered as Pennsylvania units.

Next commanded by Brigadier General William W. Burns, the brigade served in the Peninsula Campaign (March–July 1862) as the Second Division of II Corps. The brigade's next combat was at the Battle of Antietam (September 17, 1862). Commanded by Brigadier General Oliver O. Howard, the brigade encountered heavy fighting and was counterattacked in the flank and routed, suffering almost 550 casualties. Next led by Brigadier General Joshua T. Owen, the brigade participated in the Union attacks on Marye's Heights at the First Battle of Fredericksburg (December 13, 1862), where it again suffered heavy casualties.

After being in reserve at the Battle of Chancellorsville (May 1–4, 1863), the brigade was engaged at the Battle of Gettysburg (July 1–3, 1863). Under Brigadier General Alexander S. Webb, elements of the brigade helped defeat a Confederate attack on the evening of July 2. During Pickett's Charge, the brigade was positioned near the Angle and was driven back in heavy fighting before the Confederate assault was repulsed. Losses for the brigade in the battle totaled 495 men.

During the Overland Campaign (May 4–June 12, 1864), the brigade was involved at the Battle of the Wilderness (May 5–7) and the Battle of Spotsylvania Court House (May 8–21). Shortly thereafter, the brigade was disbanded. Soldiers with time left on their enlistments were consolidated into the 69th Regiment. The 106th Regiment was reduced in size to a battalion, and veterans in the other regiments were mustered out in July and August 1864.

JOSHUA MICHAEL

See also

Antietam, Battle of; Baker, Edward Dickinson; Ball's Bluff, Battle of; Burns, William Wallace; Fredericksburg, First Battle of; Gettysburg, Battle of; Howard, Oliver Otis; Overland Campaign; Peninsula Campaign; Spotsylvania Court House, Battle of; Webb, Alexander Stewart; Wilderness, Battle of the

Further Reading

Banes, Charles H. *History of the Philadelphia Brigade.* Philadelphia: Lippincott, 1876.

Gottfried, Bradley. *Stopping Pickett: The History of the Philadelphia Brigade.* Shippensburg, PA: White Mane, 1999.

Philippi, Battle of
Event Date: June 3, 1861

Early war engagement in western Virginia (present-day West Virginia). The Battle of Philippi was the first land engagement of the Civil War. With the beginning of the war in April 1861, leaders in both the North and the South recognized the strategic significance of western Virginia. The area had the ability to provide thousands of recruits to the respective armies, was rich in mineral resources, and could be used as a staging ground for launching raids into the heartland of the opponent. Most importantly, the key communications link of the Baltimore & Ohio Railroad traversed much of the region, running east-west from Martinsburg to Wheeling on the Ohio River.

Almost immediately, Confederate colonel George Porterfield occupied the rail terminus at Grafton and ordered his troops to destroy bridges northwest of Fairmont. Union major general George B. McClellan responded quickly to Porterfield's possession of the Grafton rail center. McClellan ordered Colonel Benjamin F. Kelley and the 1st (West) Virginia Volunteer Infantry to proceed cautiously from

Wheeling to Fairmont, repairing the railroad bridges between the two points. As news of Kelley's advance reached Porterfield, he requested reinforcements from Colonel Thomas J. Jackson at Harpers Ferry. Porterfield, however, was unable to secure the additional troops, so he evacuated Grafton, regrouping 15 miles to the south at Philippi.

Union forces now converged on Philippi. One column of 1,600 men under Kelley moved from Grafton, while another column of 1,400 men under Brigadier General Ebenezer Dumont moved on Philippi from Webster to the west. The two Union columns arrived at Philippi before dawn on June 3.

Fighting commenced on June 3, 1861. Kelley, augmented by regiments from Ohio and Indiana, attacked Porterfield's 800 Confederate troops, forcing them from the town. As the raw, untested recruits struggled amid the confusion of battle, Confederate forces retreated so quickly from the town that the battle became known in the North as the Philippi Races. The Union victory resulted in 15 Confederate casualties. Union forces suffered 2 men wounded, including Kelley. Porterfield was pleased that so many of his men had been able to escape, largely the result of the absence of Union cavalry. Following the hasty retreat, Union troops secured munitions, baggage, and personal effects belonging to the Confederates.

The Union victory at Philippi had profound implications for western Virginia. The region was later formed into the state of West Virginia and was admitted to the Union in 1863. Also, for the time being at least, the Union had secured control of the vital Baltimore & Ohio Railroad.

JEFFERY B. COOK

See also
Baltimore & Ohio Railroad; Kelley, Benjamin Franklin; McClellan, George Brinton; West Virginia

Further Reading
Rice, Ottis. *West Virginia: A History*. Lexington: University Press of Kentucky, 1985.
Williams, John A. *West Virginia: A History*. New York: Norton, 1984.

Philippoteaux, Paul Dominique
Birth Date: January 27, 1846
Death Date: June 28, 1923

French artist. Paul Dominique Philippoteaux was born in Paris, France, on January 27, 1846. His father Felix Philippoteaux was also a professional artist. The younger Philippoteaux was professionally trained as an artist in France at the Collège Henri IV and at the École des Beaux Arts in Paris. He became best known for cyclorama paintings, which were very large 360-degree canvas oil paintings. Viewers stood on a platform in the center of the room, with the painting on the walls around them. This method of display gave spectators the sensation of being in the midst of a scene or historical event. Philippoteaux assisted his father in the painting of his first cyclorama, *The Defense of the Fort d'Issy,* which premiered in Paris in 1871 and depicted a scene from the Franco-Prussian War.

In the United States, Philippoteaux is best known for his painting *The Battle of Gettysburg,* which portrays Pickett's Charge on July 3, 1863. The painting premiered in 1883. The French painter arrived in America in 1879 after being commissioned by private investors in Chicago to paint a cyclorama of the battle for public display.

Philippoteaux went to the battlefield in April 1882 and began research for the painting. He observed the terrain, hired a photographer to produce a series of photographs, interviewed veterans who had participated in the assault, and made scores of sketches of the landscape.

Philippoteaux then returned to France to paint the cyclorama. The original dimensions of the painting were 42 feet high and 377 feet in circumference. To create a three-dimensional viewing experience, the foreground of the painting included a display of fence posts, rifles, cartridge boxes, and mannequins. *The Cyclorama of the Battle of Gettysburg* premiered in Chicago in December 1883. Philippoteaux's painting was so well received that he painted three additional Gettysburg cycloramas, which premiered in Boston (December 1884), Philadelphia (February 1886), and New York City (October 1886). One of the artist's cycloramas has recently been restored and can be viewed at the Gettysburg National Battlefield Park. Philippoteaux died in Paris on June 28, 1923.

JENNIFER M. MURRAY

See also
Art in the Civil War; Cyclorama; Gettysburg, Battle of

Further Reading
Boardman, Sue, and Kathryn Porch. *The Battle of Gettysburg Cyclorama: A History and Guide*. Gettysburg, PA: Thomas Publications, 2008.
Thomas, Dean S. *The Gettysburg Cyclorama: A Portrayal of the High Tide of the Confederacy*. Gettysburg, PA: Thomas Publications, 1989.

Phillips, Eugenia Levy
Birth Date: 1820
Death Date: 1902

Southern partisan and Confederate spy. The sister of Phoebe Yates Pember, matron at Richmond's Chimborazo Military Hospital, Eugenia Levy was born in Charleston, South Carolina, in 1820 to a prosperous Jewish family. She was married on September 7, 1836, to Philip Phillips, who had established a successful legal practice in Mobile, Alabama. The couple lived in Mobile for 18 years.

When Philip Phillips was elected to the U.S. Congress in 1853, the family moved to Washington, D.C. Beautiful and witty, Eugenia Phillips enjoyed Washington's social life. After one term in Congress, her husband decided to practice law in Washington, and when the Civil War began, the Phillips family remained in the city.

On August 24, 1861, Eugenia, daughters Caroline and Fanny, and sister Martha were placed under house arrest

Eugenia Levy Phillips, born in the South but a resident of Washington, D.C., served the Confederate cause as a spy. (Virginia Clay-Clopton, *A Belle of the Fifties: Memoirs of Mrs. Clay, of Alabama, Covering Social and Political Washington and the South, 1853–1866,* 1905)

by Union detectives and later moved to the home of Rose O'Neal Greenhow, another suspected Confederate spy. Through appeals to influential friends, Mr. Phillips managed to secure his family's release on September 18. According to her daughter's memoir, Eugenia gave Confederate officials a coded message from Greenhow, smuggled out in a ball of yarn. The family then resettled in New Orleans, which was occupied by Union forces the following spring.

Eugenia Phillips again ran afoul of Union authorities. Major General Benjamin Butler, the Union commander in New Orleans known for his infamous Woman Order, had her arrested for laughing as a Union soldier's funeral procession passed below her balcony. Butler ordered her imprisoned on Ship Island in Mississippi Sound but allowed her to take her maid. Months of inadequate rations, heat, insects, and close confinement led to illness for both women. Mr. Phillips secured their release, and the family left New Orleans, eventually settling in Georgia. For the rest of her life, Eugenia fancied herself a Confederate heroine while leading a relatively quiet and obscure existence. She died in LaGrange, Georgia, in 1902.

NANCY GRAY SCHOONMAKER

See also
Espionage in the Civil War; Greenhow, Rose O'Neal; New Orleans, Louisiana

Further Reading
Jacobs, Joanna. "Eugenia Levy Phillips vs. The United States of America." *Alabama Heritage* 50 (1988): 22–29.
Saxon, Elizabeth Lyle. *A Southern Woman's War Time Reminiscences, by Elizabeth Lyle Saxon, for the Benefit of the Shiloh Monument Fund.* Memphis, TN: Press of the Pilcher Printing Co., 1905.

Phillips, Wendell
Birth Date: November 29, 1811
Death Date: February 2, 1884

Fierce abolitionist and social reformer. Wendell Phillips was born on November 29, 1811, in Boston, Massachusetts, into a wealthy family. He graduated in 1831 from Harvard College, where he demonstrated a flair for oratory. In 1834 he received his law degree from Harvard but soon was converted to the abolitionist cause by Ann Terry Greene, whom he married in 1837. That same year Phillips made his debut as an abolitionist orator with a speech at Faneuil Hall in Boston. This established Phillips as one of the leaders of the abolitionist movement. In 1840 Phillips attended the World Anti-Slavery Convention in London, where he joined with William Lloyd Garrison in protesting the barring of women delegates from the floor.

Throughout the 1840s, Phillips worked with Garrison, serving on the executive committee and as recording secretary of the American Anti-Slavery Society. Phillips was a frequent contributor to the *The Liberator*. He differed with Garrison's doctrine of nonresistance, however, arguing that laws such as the 1850 Fugitive Slave Act ought to be forcibly resisted.

During the turbulent 1850s, Phillips became increasingly militant. By then he had won a national reputation as a lecturer, and he used the platform to fire public sentiment against slavery. He also helped organize a vigilance committee in Boston to ensure the safe passage of fugitive slaves to Canada. Although impressed with radical abolitionist John Brown, Phillips stopped short of aiding Brown's Harpers Ferry raid in October 1859. Phillips did, however, organize the legal defense of those who had helped Brown and provided legal counsel for Brown. Phillips later delivered the eulogy at Brown's funeral.

With the beginning of the Civil War, Phillips insisted that it was more important to free the slaves than to save the Union, and he criticized President Abraham Lincoln for failing to make emancipation his primary war aim. Phillips welcomed both the Emancipation Proclamation in 1863 and the passage of the Thirteenth Amendment abolishing slavery in 1865. When Garrison called for the disbanding of the American Anti-Slavery Society, however, Phillips strongly objected.

Arguing that with emancipation the society's real work had just begun, Phillips replaced Garrison as president of the American Anti-Slavery Society. Phillips now pushed for the passage of the Fourteenth and Fifteenth Amendments. With the passage of the latter in 1870, Phillips urged that a system of free public education be established in the South so that all children, black and white, would receive an equal education. And when most Americans, including some of Phillips's former colleagues in the abolitionist movement, lost interest in the plight of the freed slaves, Phillips kept up the cry for social justice.

A supporter of other reform efforts, including women's suffrage, prison reform, and the rights of Native Americans, Phillips also took up the cause of labor in the years after the Civil War. Phillips died in Boston on February 2, 1884.

WILLIAM MCGUIRE AND LESLIE WHEELER

Brilliant orator Wendell Phillips was one of the chief figures in the pre–Civil War abolitionist movement in the United States. With the beginning of the Civil War, he insisted that it was more important to free the slaves than to save the Union, and he criticized President Abraham Lincoln for not making emancipation the primary war aim. (Library of Congress)

See also

Abolitionism and the Civil War; American Anti-Slavery Society; Brown, John; Garrison, William Lloyd

Further Reading

Stewart, James B. "Heroes, Villains, Liberty, and License: The Abolitionist Vision of Wendell Phillips." In *Antislavery Reconsidered: New Perspectives on the Abolitionists,* edited by Michael Fellman, 168–191. Baton Rouge: Louisiana State University Press, 1979.

Stewart, James Brewer. *Wendell Phillips: Liberty's Hero.* Baton Rouge: Louisiana State University Press, 1986.

Phillips, William Addison
Birth Date: January 14, 1824
Death Date: November 30, 1893

Journalist, lawyer, U.S. Army officer, and U.S. congressman. Born in Paisley, Scotland, on January 14, 1824, William Addison Phillips was educated in his hometown and immigrated with his parents to the United States in 1839. The family settled in Randolph County, Illinois, and farmed. Phillips soon took up a career in journalism, however, as editor of the *Chester Herald* from 1852 to 1855. He also studied law.

Admitted to the bar in 1855, Phillips began a practice in Lawrence, Kansas. At the same time, however, he agreed to be a special correspondent for Horace Greeley's *New York Tribune* reporting on developments in the Kansas Territory, then in turmoil over whether it would come into the Union as a slave state or a free state. Phillips's passionate articles against slavery and violence perpetrated by the proslavery faction in Kansas did much to gather public support in the North for the antislavery movement in Kansas. In 1856 Phillips played a key role with a special committee from the U.S. Congress sent to Kansas to investigate accusations of violence and election fraud.

While remaining active in the free-soil movement, in the spring of 1858 Phillips and four others founded the town of Salina and then also established the Salina Road at a time when there were no railroads west of the Missouri. In late April that same year, Phillips was elected one of three judges on the Kansas Supreme Court.

With the beginning of the Civil War, Phillips raised some of the first troops from Kansas. Commissioned as a major in the 1st Indian Home Guards, he was elected colonel and the commander of the 3rd Indian Home Guards and for a short time of the 1st Indian Brigade in Brigadier General John M. Schofield's Army of the Frontier. Later in a semi-independent role, commanding at times thousands of men, Phillips took part in most of the actions in Kansas and in Indian Territory. He was wounded three times in battle and had four horses shot from beneath him.

Elected to the Kansas House of Representatives in 1865, Phillips was then for a time an attorney in Washington, D.C., for the Cherokees. Elected as a Republican, he served three terms in the U.S. House of Representatives (March 1873–March 1879). He failed in his fourth bid and again in 1890. Phillips died on November 30, 1893, in Fort Gibson, Oklahoma.

SPENCER C. TUCKER

See also

Cherokees; Greeley, Horace; Kansas; Native Americans in the Civil War; *New York Tribune;* Schofield, John McAllister

Further Reading

Blackmar, Frank W. *Kansas: A Cyclopedia of State History.* Chicago: Standard Publishing, 1912.
"Col. William A Phillips." *Transactions of the Kansas State Historical Society, 1889–96* 5 (1896): 100–113.
"Phillips, William Addison." In *Kansas: A Cyclopedia of State History, Embracing Events, Institutions, Industries, Counties,* *Cities, Towns, Prominent Persons, Etc. . . . ,* Vol. 2, 471–472; 4 vols. in 3. Chicago: Standard Publishing, 1912.

Phillips' Legion

Confederate military organization. In the spring of 1861, William Phillips, a wealthy citizen of Marietta, Georgia, organized an army unit of three battalions: one each of infantry, cavalry, and artillery. The formation was conceived as a combined-arms unit. As originally organized in 1861, the legion included six infantry companies and four cavalry companies.

As with almost all Civil War legions, the unit was broken up early. The artillery battalion was divided into individual batteries, which were then dispersed among Confederate Army formations for the remainder of the war. Phillips, commissioned a colonel, commanded the remainder of the legion until the winter of 1862, when he suffered a severe bout of typhoid fever. The infantry and cavalry battalions were separated in July 1862.

After undergoing training, Phillips' Legion was mustered into Confederate service at Lynchburg, Virginia, on August 9. The unit was then dispatched to western Virginia (present-day West Virginia) for service in the Army of the Kanawha. In December 16, 1861, the legion was ordered to South Carolina. Expanded with the addition of three new infantry companies in the spring of 1862, the legion returned to Virginia, assigned to the Army of Northern Virginia. The legion's infantry and cavalry units were separated, but each took part in the First Battle of Fredericksburg (December 13, 1862) and the Battle of Chancellorsville (May 1–4, 1863). In the late summer of 1863, the legion's infantry was ordered to return to Georgia. The infantry served in Lieutenant General James Longstreet's corps in the early stages of the Chattanooga Campaign (October–November 1863) and the Knoxville Campaign (November–December 1863). The legion's infantry returned to the Army of Northern Virginia in April 1864. From August to November 1864, the legion's infantry served in the Shenandoah Valley before returning to the Army of Northern Virginia for the remainder of the war. The Phillips' Legion Infantry Battalion took part in more than 50 engagements in the course of the war. When the unit surrendered at Appomattox Court House on April 9, 1865, it numbered only slightly more than 90 officers and men.

The Phillips' Legion Cavalry Battalion was organized in 1861 with four companies. It was expanded during the spring of 1862 with the addition of two new companies. In May 1864, the four-company 4th Alabama Cavalry Battalion was attached to the legion cavalry until that November, when a company from the Cobb's Legion Cavalry was transferred to the Phillips' Legion.

Upon being mustered into Confederate service, the Phillips' Legion Cavalry Battalion was assigned to duty in the Department of Georgia. In September 1861 the unit was transferred to Virginia and assigned to the Cavalry Corps of the Army of Northern Virginia. The Phillips' Legion Cavalry Battalion served in that army until January 1865, when it was ordered south into North Carolina. The unit ended its service attached to the Army of Tennessee. The cavalry of Phillips' Legion participated in more than 100 engagements during the war and at least fared better than the Phillips' Legion Infantry Battalion. On April 26, 1865, 254 officers and men of the cavalry battalion surrendered near Greensboro, North Carolina.

SPENCER C. TUCKER

See also

Appomattox Court House and Lee's Surrender; Chancellorsville, Battle of; Chattanooga Campaign; Cobb's Legion; Fredericksburg, First Battle of; Knoxville Campaign

Further Reading

Coffman, Richard M. *Going Back the Way They Came: The Georgia Phillips Legion Cavalry Battalion.* Macon, GA: Mercer University Press, 2011.

Coffman, Richard M., and Kurt D. Graham. *To Honor These Men: A History of Phillips Georgia Legion Infantry Battalion.* Macon, GA: Mercer University Press, 2007.

The Photographic History of the Civil War

Ten-volume photographic history of the Civil War edited by Francis Trevelyan Miller and containing 3,629 photographs, first published during 1911–1912 to commemorate the 50th anniversary of the start of the war. An American writer and filmmaker, Miller also authored books on exploration, travel, and photography. Mathew Brady, perhaps the best known of the Civil War photographers, and his assistants produced more than 7,000 Civil War photographs. Over time, many had been damaged or lost. Eventually the remaining photographs passed to Edward Bailey Eaton, and he worked to have them published in a collection, which became Miller's *The Photographic History of the Civil War.*

The photographs in Miller's work cover every aspect of the war: battlefields, common soldiers, officers, forts, camp scenes, army movements, weapons, and war matériel. The volumes also include short articles that identify people, places, and/or situations in the photos and provide a wealth of information about the war itself. Each volume is dedicated to a specific subject and has a place and surname index. The collection also includes a chronological summary and record of historical events and of important land and naval engagements.

Miller's work remains a significant source of Civil War photographs and is the greatest single collection of Brady's photographs. Miller and his staff relied heavily on veterans' recollections to identify particular scenes and people in the photographs, and as a result some of the photo captions contain errors. The entire work was republished as a five-volume set in 1957 that included an introduction by noted historian Henry Steele Commager.

ROBERT B. KANE

See also

Ambrotype; Brady, Mathew; Photography and the Civil War

Further Reading

Miller, Francis Trevelyan, ed. *The Photographic History of the Civil War.* New York: Review of Reviews Company, 1911.

Panzer, Mary. *Mathew Brady and the Image of History.* Washington, DC: Smithsonian Institution Press for the National Portrait Gallery, 1997.

Photography and the Civil War

Photography came of age as an instrument of documentary record during the American Civil War. The French pioneers in the new technology had already captured the panorama of Paris, the City of Light, and had even made stereo views with a binocular lens camera. Portrait photography was also established in cartes de visite, studio photographs in which subjects were forced to pose awkwardly and at length. But war photography was relatively new in 1861. Some photos had indeed been made of English and French troops in the Crimea in the 1850s, but these had chiefly been stilted shots of groups or officers posed in uniform. A few pictures of American troops on review in Mexico had been made in the late 1840s. But the idea of preserving for history the images of an entire war on photographic plates was relatively new. Oliver Wendell Holmes pronounced the endeavor "the mirror with a memory."

The most important figure in American photography in the second half of the 19th century was decidedly Mathew B. Brady. Trained under the brilliant inventor of the telegraph, Samuel F. B. Morse, Brady opened his daguerreotype studio in New York City in 1844. The daguerreotype, named for its French developer, Louis Daguerre, was a process using a silver-coated copper sheet, exposed in a camera and developed by mercury vapors. Each picture was individual. The subject had to sit in a stationary pose for about 20 minutes. But under Brady's artistry, especially after he developed a method of hand coloring the images, the results could be extraordinary.

With his many photographs of the notables of his age—including writers Nathaniel Hawthorne and Mark Twain, the entertainment impresario P. T. Barnum, the actor John Wilkes Booth, and the singer Adelina Patti—Brady proved that the skilled photographer could reveal personality and character just as effectively as the portrait painter. Capturing the craggy face of President Andrew Jackson, Brady helped establish the popular image of "Old Hickory." Brady would also accommodate young soldiers in their uniforms, often the finest clothes they had ever owned, who wanted cartes de visite for the folks back home.

It is to Brady's artistry that we owe our revered images of President Abraham Lincoln, which captured the pensiveness of the man and the melancholy so reminiscent of an Old Testament prophet. Lincoln sat for Brady on several occasions, first before Lincoln's election as president at the time of his famous February 1860 address at Cooper Union in New York City, during which he argued for the government's right to limit slavery in the territories. He later said, half seriously, "Brady and the Cooper Union speech made me president."

Eventually Brady opened a gallery in Washington, D.C., as well as two additional studios in New York. When the Civil War started in April 1861, he was ready to embark on his most ambitious project—to provide a photographic record of the war. By now Brady was working with wet photographic plates, an advance that made possible his move from studio to field. Still, the process was cumbersome. It was necessary to train photographic teams and equip wagons that would carry the essential equipment, including a developing dark room and chemicals, onto battlefields. Brady assigned his trainees to cover different zones of combat, covering as much territory as possible with approximately 30 bases, photographing both Union and Confederate forces. Soon the wagons, those darkrooms on wheels, were visible on battlefields and were called "Whatsits" by the soldiers. Because

the wagons made highly visible targets, photographers as well as soldiers risked their lives.

Although Brady himself was frequently present at important battles, three of his trainees—Timothy O'Sullivan, George N. Barnard, and Alexander Gardner—also made names for themselves. Gardner, who later broke with Brady, establishing himself as a rival, would always claim that the recording of battle was his idea.

In addition to Brady's crew, other photographers got into the action. John E. Stanchak, a historian of photography, has estimated that as many as 2,000 photographers eventually participated in the war, producing some 1 million photographs. Other active firms included Levy and Cohen of Philadelphia and Haas and Peale, who operated chiefly among Union troops in the Carolinas. Although photographic equipment was not as readily available in the Confederacy, Jay D. Edwards was an important photographer who worked in the rebel states. Photographers were also used by cartographers during the war. Additionally, they were sometimes brought in to photograph sensitive documents and were even used in espionage and reconnaissance missions.

Although these men were on the battlefield with their wagons, it was still impossible to produce vivid action shots through the collodion wet-plate process. When this was attempted, backgrounds became hopelessly blurred. Nevertheless, a powerful record of less active moments resulted: Lincoln, in stovepipe hat, towering above his officers on a visit to the Antietam campaign; hospital scenes; fortifications; training camps; and landscapes, where the beauty of autumn nature made a stark contrast to the dead bodies and battle wreckage on the ground. Young soldiers, black and white, were photographed as they apprehensively awaited battle. After the war was over, Brady would exhibit in his New York gallery a poignant collection he called *Death at Antietam.* He had also planned an album, *Incidents of War,* with scenes of wartime Washington, but that project was never completed.

The end of hostilities in 1865 did not mark the conclusion of Brady's work. Among his most successful photographs would continue to be his portraits of generals. Upon the surrender Brady made haste to Appomattox, but General Robert E. Lee, his task already accomplished, had left for his home in Richmond. Brady followed him there and persuaded the defeated general to pose in uniform. The resulting photograph, which captured the grace and dignity of Lee even in defeat, helped establish the Confederate commander as a national hero. Brady would also photograph in his Washington studio General Ulysses S. Grant.

Ultimately Brady would photograph every president from Martin Van Buren to James A. Garfield, leaving a valuable archive of American leadership during a pivotal period in history. Americans were deeply moved by the vividness of the battlefield scenes and even the grimness of his photographs of the execution of the Lincoln assassination conspirators. Brady and his colleagues, with their cameras, brought the horrors of war and its aftermath to Americans on the home front, much as television imagery would do in subsequent wars in the next century.

ALLENE S. PHY-OLSEN

See also

Art in the Civil War; Brady, Mathew

Further Reading

Kagan, Neil, and Stephen G. Hyslop. *Eyewitness to the Civil War: The Complete History from Secession to Reconstruction.* Washington, DC: National Geographic, 2006.

Meredith, Roy. *Mathew Brady's Portrait of an Era.* New York: Norton, 1982.

Sandler, Martin W. *The Story of American Photography: An Illustrated History.* Boston: Little, Brown, 1979.

Pickens, Francis Wilkinson
Birth Date: April 7, 1805
Death Date: January 25, 1869

Governor of South Carolina. Francis Wilkinson Pickens was born on April 7, 1805, in St. Paul's Parish, South Carolina, into a prominent and wealthy family. Educated at Franklin College (University of Georgia) and South Carolina College, he studied law and was admitted to the bar in 1829. He was a member of the U.S. House of Representatives as a Democrat (1834–1843), earning a reputation as a fierce defender of states' rights. From 1844 to 1846, Pickens was a state senator. In 1858 he became U.S. minister to Russia, a post he held until 1860.

At first reluctant to fully support secession, Pickens finally embraced the concept but still harbored thoughts of averting war through compromise. He became governor on December 16, 1860. On December 20, South Carolina became the first state to pass a secession ordinance. Pickens immediately moved to occupy Castle Pinckney in Charleston. At about the same time, Union forces under Major Robert Anderson occupied the strategic Fort Sumter in Charleston Harbor. During the next several months, Pickens made numerous attempts to remove Union forces from the Charleston fortifications. Indeed, he sent commissioners to Washington to persuade the Union to sell Fort Sumter to the state. When that failed, he made numerous threats and even sent state forces to plead with Anderson directly. In January 1861, Pickens authorized the firing on a Union ship bringing supplies to Fort Sumter.

By early April, the standoff had made Governor Pickens look weak and indecisive. Finally, by the end of the first week in April, he supported the Confederate government's plan to bombard Fort Sumter, which occurred on April 12, beginning the Civil War. Anderson surrendered on April 14.

Thereafter, Pickens busied himself with raising troops for Confederate service. He also worked closely with Confederate military commanders to ensure adequate protection of coastal areas. When Port Royal and Hilton Head Island fell to Union forces on November 7, 1861, Pickens came under fire for the losses, although there was little he could have done to avert this. The loss prompted the state legislature to convene an executive council ostensibly to help Pickens protect the state, but in reality the council did nothing but obfuscate decision making.

In December 1862, Pickens gladly vacated the governor's chair when his term ended and returned to his plantation. The war wiped him out financially, however, and he died deep in debt on January 25, 1869, in Edgefield, South Carolina.

PAUL G. PIERPAOLI JR.

See also

Port Royal Sound, Battle of; South Carolina

Further Reading

Edgar, Walter B. *South Carolina: A History.* Columbia: University of South Carolina Press, 1998.

Edmunds, John B., Jr. *Francis W. Pickens and the Politics of Destruction.* Chapel Hill: University of North Carolina Press, 1986.

Picket

A guard formation or advance scouting team of infantry. Picket lines were used to guard encampments or bivouacs and to serve as an advance detachment that would be sent ahead of a larger force. Typically, picket guards consisted of 40 privates, 4 corporals, 2 sergeants, and 1 lieutenant. For large formations, one regiment provided one complete picket guard. Picket duty was then rotated among all of the regiments.

Pickets controlled movement into and out of a camp, usually requiring identification and authorization for individuals coming and going. Pickets were also trained to be alert for enemy activity in the vicinity of a camp and were supposed to provide warning of such, usually by way of warning shots or whistles. Advance picket guards had the most dangerous job, as their forward positions well in front of the main force made them susceptible to enemy snipers and vulnerable to capture.

PAUL G. PIERPAOLI JR.

See also

Armies of the Confederate States, Overview; Armies of the United States, Overview

Further Reading

Robertson, James. *Tenting Tonight: The Soldier's Life.* New York: Time Life, 1999.

Pickett, George Edward
Birth Date: January 25, 1825
Death Date: July 30, 1875

Confederate officer. George Edward Pickett was born on January 25, 1825, in Richmond, Virginia. His father was a successful planter and businessman who greatly indulged his son. Pickett entered the U.S. Military Academy, West Point, in 1842, graduating last in the class of 1846.

Pickett served with distinction during the Mexican-American War (1846–1848). He participated in Major General Winfield Scott's assault against Veracruz and distinguished himself at the Battle of Churubusco in August 1847, being brevetted first lieutenant. At the Battle of Chapultepec, Pickett replaced the Mexican flag with that of the 8th Infantry, earning a brevet promotion to captain. Promoted to first lieutenant in 1849 and to captain in 1855, he spent most of the prewar period in the West.

With the onset of the Civil War, Pickett cast his lot with his home state of Virginia and the Confederacy, resigning his U.S. Army commission on June 25, 1861, and taking a commission as a colonel in the Confederate Army. In January 14, 1862, Pickett was appointed a brigadier general and assigned to command a brigade under Major General James Longstreet. Pickett earned high praise from Longstreet for his bravery at the Battle of Williamsburg (May 5, 1862). On June 1, 1862, Pickett's brigade suffered some 350 casualties in the heavy fighting of the Battle of Seven Pines (May 31–June 1, 1862). Later that month, Pickett was wounded at the Battle of Gaines' Mill (June 27, 1862) and was out of action for three months.

Confederate major general George E. Pickett was a capable divisional commander who led the most famous infantry charge in U.S. history. His defeat at Gettysburg marked the high tide of Confederate fortunes. Pickett blamed General Robert E. Lee for the mistaken decision to attack the center, and strength, of the Union line. (Library of Congress)

On October 10, 1862, Pickett was advanced to major general and given command of a division in the Army of Northern Virginia. He saw only minimal action at the First Battle of Fredericksburg (December 13, 1862) but was destined to play a major role at the Battle of Gettysburg in 1863.

Pickett and his division arrived at Gettysburg, Pennsylvania, on the evening of July 2. The next morning Army of Northern Virginia commander General Robert E. Lee, over the objections of Longstreet, ordered Pickett to attack the center of the Union line holding the high ground along Cemetery Ridge. On July 3, Pickett's men and those of three other divisions bravely charged the Union line, but the advance quickly withered under punishing fire. Within 30 minutes, more than half of the approximately 12,500 men who made the charge were casualties.

While some criticized Pickett for not exercising better leadership, Pickett blamed Lee for the defeat at Gettysburg. Considered somewhat of a dandy, Pickett was never the same after that fateful day at Gettysburg. Indeed, his military reputation saw a steady decline. He saw some additional action in North Carolina and Virginia. His division was routed at Five Forks on April 1, 1865, precipitating the fall of Richmond and Petersburg. Lee relieved Pickett of his command just days before the war ended.

Following the war, Pickett engaged in several business ventures, including insurance, that were only marginally successful. He died of a liver ailment in Norfolk, Virginia, on July 30, 1875.

RON BRILEY

See also

Fredericksburg, First Battle of; Gaines' Mill, Battle of; Gettysburg, Battle of; Lee, Robert Edward; Longstreet, James; Seven Pines, Battle of; Williamsburg, Battle of

Further Reading

Gordon. Lesley J. *General George E. Pickett in Life & Legend.* Chapel Hill: University of North Carolina Press, 1998.

Hollingsworth, Alan M. *The Third Day at Gettysburg: Pickett's Charge.* New York: Holt, 1959.

McPherson, James M. *Battle Cry of Freedom: The Civil War Era.* New York: Oxford University Press, 1988.

Pickett Papers

Term used to describe the official diplomatic records of the Confederate States of America, named for John T. Pickett, the attorney who handled the transfer of the records to the U.S. government. As Union forces were closing in on the Confederate capital of Richmond, Confederate secretary of state Judah P. Benjamin charged William J. Brownwell, a State Department clerk, with taking possession of all state papers and removing them to a safe location in Charlotte, North Carolina. On March 28 Brownwell left Richmond with the records, but he never made it to Charlotte. After the Confederate surrender just days later, the clerk decided to keep the papers, hiding them in a barn outside Washington, D.C.

Realizing that the papers he now held were very valuable, Brownwell hired Washington, D.C., attorney Pickett to open negotiations with the federal government so that they might be purchased. Pickett engaged federal officials in several negotiations but did not arrive at an agreement until 1871. That year, the U.S. Congress agreed to appropriate $75,000 for the Confederacy's state papers. The payment would go through only after the authenticity of the papers had been established. Pickett took the documents to Ontario, Canada, where they were independently evaluated and authenticated.

On July 3, 1872, the so-called Pickett Papers were turned over to federal authorities; it is presumed that Pickett received a percentage of the sale price, perhaps as much as 30 percent. Pickett had advised his client to remain anonymous until the transfer and payments were received; hence, the documents came to be called the Pickett Papers. Many former Confederates were outraged with Brownwell's actions, believing that he had personally profited—quite handsomely—off of something that had never belonged to him. For that reason, Brownwell fled the United States in 1873. He died in Great Britain two years later.

Securing the Pickett Papers was of immediate importance in determining war claims and reparations. Long term, of course, the price of the papers was incalculable, as they provided a detailed historical record of the workings of the Confederate government.

PAUL G. PIERPAOLI JR.

See also

Benjamin, Judah Philip

Further Reading

Rubin, Sarah Anne. *A Shattered Nation: The Rise & Fall of the Confederacy, 1861–1868.* Chapel Hill: University of North Carolina Press, 2005.

William C. Davis. *Look Away! A History of the Confederate States of America.* New York: Free Press, 2003.

Piedmont, Battle of
Event Date: June 5, 1864

Engagement fought in Augusta County, Virginia, at the onset of Major General David Hunter's Lynchburg Campaign (May 26–June 29, 1864), also known as Hunter's Raid. As part of his multifaceted offensive to keep Confederate forces under General Robert E. Lee off balance and prevent Lee's Army of Northern Virginia from receiving reinforcements, Union general in chief Lieutenant General Ulysses S. Grant ordered an advance south in the Shenandoah Valley. However, Major General Franz Sigel met defeat in the Battle of New Market (May 15, 1864), and on May 21 Grant replaced him with Major General David Hunter as commander of the Department of West Virginia.

On May 26, Hunter again put Union forces in motion south. His immediate goal was the Confederate railroad and logistics center of Staunton, with his ultimate goal being Lynchburg. Determined to live off the rich Shenandoah Valley farms as much as possible, his forces proceeded to destroy much of what they themselves could not use.

This rapid Union response following the defeat at New Market caught the Confederates by surprise, with most of their forces in the valley having recently been moved east to join the hard-pressed Army of Northern Virginia before Richmond. Only a small cavalry brigade under Brigadier General John D. Imboden and reserves remained to confront Hunter, and they could do little except impose delay.

General Lee called on Brigadier General William E. "Grumble" Jones, commanding the Department of Southwest Virginia and East Tennessee, to move immediately to defend the valley. Jones soon arrived at Mount Crawford with reinforcements. In all, Jones had at his disposal a maximum of 5,600 men.

On June 5, Hunter proceeded south from Port Republic with some 8,500 men toward Mount Meridian. Early that morning at Mount Meridian, his cavalry drove in Imboden's far weaker force, and the Confederates fell back on the village of Piedmont. Imboden, an area native, had urged Jones to establish his defenses at Mowry's Hill in more favorable terrain and was therefore surprised to find Jones at Piedmont. Jones, the senior officer, won the argument, and the Confederates made their stand at Piedmont instead.

In the ensuing battle, superior numbers of massed Union guns systematically neutralized most of the Confederate guns. Infantry on the Union right then attacked. When Jones attempted a concentration of troops for a counterattack on his left, a gap opened in the Confederate line. At this point in the battle Jones was killed, and the Confederate line broke up under a Union attack by Colonel Joseph Thoburn's 2nd Brigade of three regiments. Inexplicably, Confederate cavalry under Brigadier General John C. Vaughn witnessed the Union attack but failed to take advantage by advancing against the now weakened Union left.

The Confederates' line disintegrated, with most of their losses occurring in the wild retreat. A successful Confederate rearguard action at New Hope allowed the bulk of the Confederates to escape. In all, the Confederates sustained perhaps 1,600 casualties (some 100 killed, 500 killed, and nearly 1,000 taken prisoner). The Confederates also lost some 1,000 small arms, although none of their guns were taken. The Union suffered 863 casualties (killed, wounded, or missing).

The Battle of Piedmont opened the way for Hunter to take the lower part of the valley. His army camped for the night and then the next day, June 6, entered its immediate objective of Staunton, the first Union troops to do so during the war. Reinforced there by Brigadier General George Crook's command from West Virginia, Hunter destroyed a good

bit of Staunton and then proceeded south to Lexington and then on to Lynchburg.

SPENCER C. TUCKER

See also

Crook, George; Grant, Ulysses Simpson; Hunter, David; Hunter's Raid; Imboden, John Daniel; Jones, William Edmondson; Lee, Robert Edward; Lexington, Virginia; Lynchburg, Battle of; New Market, Battle of; Sigel, Franz; Vaughn, John Crawford

Further Reading

Duncan, Richard R. *Lee's Endangered Left: The Civil War in Western Virginia, Spring of 1864.* Baton Rouge: Louisiana State University Press, 1998.

Patchan, Scott C. *The Battle of Piedmont and Hunter's Raid on Staunton.* Charleston, SC: History Press, 2011.

Tucker, Spencer C. *Brigadier General John D. Imboden: Confederate Commander in the Shenandoah.* Lexington: University Press of Kentucky, 2003.

Pierce, Franklin
Birth Date: November 23, 1804
Death Date: October 8, 1869

President of the United States. Franklin Pierce was born on November 23, 1804, in Hillsborough, New Hampshire. He attended academies in Hancock and Francestown, New Hampshire, then entered preparatory school at Phillips Exeter Academy. He entered Bowdoin College in 1820 and graduated third in his class in 1824. While he aspired to follow his father and serve in the military upon graduation, Pierce chose instead to pursue a career in trial law.

Admitted to the New Hampshire bar, Pierce established a successful practice in Hillsborough in 1827. Elected to the New Hampshire legislature in 1829, he served as Speaker of that body during 1832 and 1833. In 1832 at age 27, Pierce was elected to the U.S. House of Representatives as a Democrat, the youngest elected at the time. In 1837 he became the youngest elected member of the U.S. Senate. He resigned in 1842 and resumed the practice of law.

While serving as a New Hampshire district attorney from 1842 to 1847, Pierce declined the position of U.S. attorney general offered to him by President James K. Polk. In March 1847 during the Mexican-American War (1846–1848), Pierce received a commission as a brigadier general. He commanded the 1st Brigade of the 3rd Division and took part in Major General Winfield Scott's Mexico City Campaign. During the Battle of Contreras (August 19,

1847), Pierce damaged his left knee when he fell from his faltering horse.

Recognized by national party leaders as a reputable politician and a war hero, Pierce secured the Democratic presidential nomination and became the youngest president elected to date in 1852, soundly defeating the Whig Party opponent and his old commanding officer, Winfield Scott. Pierce confronted constant turmoil during his single term in the White House. He was regarded as a Northerner with Southern sympathies, and critics claimed that he sought to expand slavery into the western territories acquired from Mexico. During the Pierce administration, the United States obtained Arizona and New Mexico for $10 million through the 1853 Gadsden Purchase. This too raised suspicions in anti-Democratic circles that Pierce was intent on expanding slavery, as did the Ostend Manifesto, which revealed U.S. designs on Cuba and which Pierce was forced to disavow.

Pierce received his most visceral condemnation for supporting passage of the Kansas-Nebraska Act in 1854, which repealed the Missouri Compromise of 1820 by asserting that the doctrine of popular sovereignty would decide the issue of slavery in new territories. The ultimate result was prolonged open warfare in Kansas that came to be known as Bleeding Kansas. To make matters worse, Pierce supported the government established by proslavery forces in Kansas, even after Congress declared it to be illegitimate. Support for the controversial bill and the renegade Kansas government cost Pierce dearly politically, and he lost the Democratic nomination to James Buchanan in 1856.

Pierce did not escape public criticism when he retired to New Hampshire in 1857, however. Later he charged that the Abraham Lincoln administration had forced the nation into war and that by 1860 Northern actions had left the South no choice but to secede. Pierce won few friends in the North for his views. Suffering from acute alcoholism in his later years, Pierce died from cirrhosis of the liver in Concord, New Hampshire, on October 8, 1869.

JASON GODIN

See also

Bleeding Kansas; Buchanan, James; Democratic Party; Kansas-Nebraska Act; Lincoln, Abraham; Missouri Compromise; Popular Sovereignty

Further Reading

Gara, Larry. *The Presidency of Franklin Pierce.* Lawrence: University Press of Kansas, 1991.
Hawthorne, Nathaniel. *The Life of Franklin Pierce.* Reprint ed. New York: Garrett, 1970.
Wallner, Peter A. *Franklin Pierce: New Hampshire's Favorite Son.* Concord, NH: Plaidswede, 2004.

Pierpont, Francis Harrison
Birth Date: January 25, 1814
Death Date: March 24, 1899

Ardent opponent of Virginia's secession and governor of the Restored Government of Virginia. Francis Harrison Pierpont was born near Morgantown in western Virginia (present-day West Virginia) on January 25, 1814, but was raised in Fairmont. After graduating from Allegheny College, he taught school, studied law, and established a practice at Fairmont in 1842. His legal work for the Baltimore & Ohio Railroad proved to be highly lucrative, and in 1854 he established a coal mine near Fairmont, which made him a very wealthy man. First a Whig and then a Republican, Pierpont strongly opposed Virginia's secession in April 1861 and was determined to organize a rump government of pro-Unionists in Virginia's 27 northwestern counties.

The next month at a convention of antisecessionists in Wheeling, Pierpont led the charge for the establishment of a separate Virginia regime that would remain loyal to the Union. The delegates drafted a constitution, named their territory West Virginia, and unanimously elected Pierpont governor of the Restored Government of Virginia. Pierpont successfully raised funds to support the rump regime, mobilized and trained volunteers to defend the territory, and gained official recognition from the federal government. He lobbied Washington to admit West Virginia to the Union as a state, which was realized on June 20, 1863. A new governor was elected, however, and so Pierpont now presided over only areas in Virginia that Union forces controlled: Fairfax County, Loudon County, the town of Alexandria, the Eastern Shore region, and the area around Norfolk.

After the war, Pierpont served as governor of all Virginia until 1868, at which time he was replaced by a military governor. He returned to his law practice in Fairmont, West Virginia, and then served a term in the state legislature beginning in 1870. During 1881, he served briefly as a U.S. internal revenue collector and then helped organize the West Virginia Historical Society. Known as the "Father of West Virginia," Pierpont died in Pittsburgh, Pennsylvania, on March 24, 1899.

PAUL G. PIERPAOLI JR.

See also
Virginia; West Virginia

Further Reading
Downing, David C. *A South Divided: Portraits of Dissent in the Confederacy.* Nashville: Cumberland House, 2007.
Williams, John A. *West Virginia: A History.* Morgantown: West Virginia University Press, 2003.

See also
Espionage in the Civil War; Women

Further Reading
Ballenger, Seale. *Hell's Belles: A Tribute to the Spitfires, Bad Seeds and Steel Magnolias of the New and Old South.* Boston: Conari, 1997.
Kent, Scotti. *More Than Petticoats: Remarkable North Carolina Women.* Helena, MT: Two Dot, 2000.

Pigott, Emmeline Jamison
Birth Date: December 15, 1836
Death Date: May 26, 1919

Confederate spy. Emmeline (Emeline) Jamison Pigott (Piggot, Piggott) was born on December 15, 1836, on a coastal plantation near Morehead City, North Carolina. From 1861 to 1863, she was a nurse for Confederate troops. Her boyfriend, Stokes McRae, died as a result of wounds received during the Battle of Gettysburg (July 1–3, 1863), and after his death Pigott dedicated herself to aiding the Confederate Army by delivering mail, food, clothing, and medicine to the troops. She also offered food and medicine to Union troops in order to secure access to Union-occupied areas, thereby gathering information on Union troop movements, which she then conveyed to Confederate commanders.

In early 1864 while attempting to deliver mail, clothing, and information to Confederate troops near New Bern, North Carolina, Pigott was captured, questioned, and searched by Union Army officials, who were convinced that she was a spy. Pigott was held in a New Bern jail until her case could be tried. While in prison, Pigott, who listened to the conversations of Union troops, realized that the plans with which she had been caught that she had received from two Union Army informants were false. Irritated at her informants, she invited them to visit her in prison. There she threatened to expose them to Union officials. To prevent being charged with treason, the informants subsequently arranged for Pigott to be released from prison after 33 days of incarceration.

Although never again detained by Union troops, Pigott continued to spy for the Confederacy and deliver mail and other necessities to Confederate troops. She never married and spent the rest of her life on her family's plantation. Pigott was honorary president of the Morehead City chapter of the United Daughters of the Confederacy until her death in Morehead City on May 26, 1919.

CHARLENE T. OVERTURF

Pike, Albert
Birth Date: December 29, 1809
Death Date: April 2, 1891

Confederate officer. Born on December 29, 1809, in Boston, Massachusetts, Albert Pike spent much of his youth in Newburyport, Massachusetts. He was largely self-educated after his grammar school days, as he could not afford to attend Harvard College. From 1824 to 1831, he taught in several different Massachusetts schools. In 1832 he set out for the west.

In 1833 Pike settled in Arkansas and began teaching school in Pope County. He later became a well-regarded attorney, poet, planter, and newspaper publisher. His military service began in 1836, when he assumed command of an artillery company in the Arkansas Militia.

Pike served during the Mexican-American War (1846–1848) beginning in 1846 and saw action at the Battle of Buena Vista as a captain of a volunteer Arkansas cavalry company. On July 29, 1847, he engaged in a duel with Colonel John S. Roane of the Arkansas volunteers near Fort Smith, Arkansas. The dispute had arisen over critical comments made by Pike about the Arkansas regiment's performance and leadership at the Battle of Buena Vista and Roane's rebuttal that Pike's men had not participated in the battle. Neither man was wounded in the duel.

Although Pike initially believed that secession would be unwise, he eventually sided with secessionists in Arkansas and served as Confederate commissioner to Indian Territory before joining the Confederate Army as a brigadier general on August 15, 1861. He commanded the Department of Indian Territory chiefly because he had previously negotiated Confederate treaties with Native Americans. He raised and trained three Native American regiments for Confederate service, leading them to northern Arkansas in February 1862. His Civil War service culminated with the Battle of Pea Ridge (March 7–8, 1862), during which his Native

American regiments were routed. Following the battle, there were reports that the troops under Pike's command had scalped dead or wounded Union soldiers on the battlefield. The stories caused much embarrassment for Pike and received great attention in the Northern press. A few months later Major General Thomas C. Hindman, commander of the Trans-Mississippi District, accused Pike of having mishandled funds and war material. Pike vehemently denied the charges, and the two men engaged in a quite public war of words. Hindman eventually ordered Pike arrested, but Pike fled and took refuge in the Arkansas hill country. His resignation was accepted on November 11, 1862, but he was never court-martialed.

Following the Civil War, Pike resumed his involvement in the legal profession and practiced law in Arkansas and Washington, D.C. He also became a major figure in American Freemasonry. Pike died on April 2, 1891, in Washington, D.C.

NICHOLAS A. KREHBIEL

See also
Hindman, Thomas Carmichael; Native Americans in the Civil War; Pea Ridge, Battle of; Van Dorn, Earl

Further Reading
Brown, Walter Lee. *A Life of Albert Pike*. Fayetteville: University of Arkansas Press, 1997.

Duncan, Robert Lipscomb. *Reluctant General: The Life and Times of Albert Pike*. New York: Dutton, 1961.

Tresner, James T. *Albert Pike: The Man beyond the Monument*. New York: M. Evans, 1995.

Pillow, Gideon Johnson
Birth Date: June 8, 1806
Death Date: October 8, 1878

Confederate officer who, as one of the least successful of Confederate military leaders, came to epitomize the political general in the worst sense of the term. Born on June 8, 1806, in Williamson County, Tennessee, Gideon Johnson Pillow graduated from the University of Nashville in 1827 and practiced law in Columbia, Tennessee. There he became friends with James K. Polk. In 1846, Pillow's Democratic Party connections won him an appointment from President Polk as brigadier general of volunteers during the Mexican-American War (1846–1848). In 1847 Pillow joined U.S. forces in the drive from Veracruz to Mexico City. His performance was distinguished by industry, braggadocio, and military

Confederate brigadier general Gideon J. Pillow of Tennessee proved himself a singularly inept military commander during both the Mexican-American War and the Civil War. (Dictionary of American Portraits)

incompetence. Communicating frequently with Polk and quarreling incessantly with his commanding officer, Major General Winfield Scott, Pillow was court-martialed but officially cleared and confirmed as a major general.

Following Abraham Lincoln's election as president, Pillow called for a convention of slave states although he said that he opposed outright secession. When Tennessee joined the Confederacy, Pillow, a major general in the Tennessee Militia, was appointed a brigadier general in the Confederate Army, the only Confederate general officer awarded a lesser rank than he had held in the Mexican-American War.

During the summer of 1861, Pillow became an architect of the Confederate heartland defenses. Mesmerized by the importance of the Mississippi River, he neglected the vital Cumberland and Tennessee Rivers. In late July, Pillow led a poorly conceived and wretchedly executed invasion of Missouri. Then in early September, on the orders of Major General Leonidas Polk, Pillow crossed the Mississippi and violated Kentucky's neutrality in one of the salient Confederate blunders of the war. In Missouri, Pillow led a division against Brigadier General Ulysses S. Grant's Federals in the Battle of Belmont (November 7, 1861).

Ordered in early February 1862 to Fort Donelson on the Cumberland River, Pillow played an important role in the Confederate surrender. As second-in-command to Brigadier General John B. Floyd, Pillow commanded the Confederate left and abandoned a breakout attempt on February 14 that in all probability would have been successful. When Confederate leaders resolved to surrender Fort Donelson, Floyd relinquished command to Pillow, who in turn passed it to Brigadier General Simon Bolivar Buckner. Pillow then abandoned his men and fled across the Cumberland River to safety.

Pillow's lamentable performance at Fort Donelson cost him and the Confederacy dearly. Southerners widely denounced Pillow. On March 16, 1862, Jefferson Davis ordered him relieved of command. Pillow tried over the next six months to clear his name and appealed for another combat assignment. These efforts finally succeeded when President Davis posted him to the Army of Tennessee. Pillow reached Major General Braxton Bragg's headquarters at Murfreesboro on the morning of January 2, 1863, in the midst of the Battle of Stones River (December 31, 1862–January 2, 1863). Hastily given command of the only available brigade, Pillow appeared for the first time before his soldiers as they were preparing to attack the Union positions. Although the Tennesseans performed heroically, losing in their forlorn charge one-fourth of their number, Pillow's leadership was once again questioned. Bragg soon found a more congenial place for Pillow by naming him head of the army's newly created Volunteer and Conscript Bureau. Pillow's last command with the Confederacy was the thankless task of commissary general of prisoners in early 1865.

Pardoned by President Andrew Johnson after the war, Pillow was hounded by creditors and, bankrupt, died of yellow fever on October 8, 1878, in Helena, Arkansas.

MALCOLM MUIR JR.

See also
Belmont, Battle of; Bragg, Braxton; Breckinridge, John Cabell; Floyd, John Buchanan; Fort Donelson, Battle of; Grant, Ulysses Simpson; Stones River, Battle of; Tennessee, Confederate Army of

Further Reading
Connelly, Thomas L. *Army of the Heartland: The Army of Tennessee, 1861–1862.* Baton Rouge: Louisiana State University Press, 1967.
Hughes, Nathaniel C., and Roy P. Stonesifer Jr. *The Life and Wars of Gideon J. Pillow.* Chapel Hill: University of North Carolina Press, 1993.

Pilot Knob, Battle of
Event Date: September 27, 1864

The opening engagement of Confederate major general Sterling Price's Missouri Raid (September 19–October 28, 1864). Price had entered Missouri from Arkansas on September 19, 1864, with some 12,000 men, only a third of whom had firearms. Headed for St. Louis, he soon learned of a Union garrison at Pilot Knob, a railroad terminal in the iron-smelting and coal-mining region in the Missouri Ozarks 86 miles south of St. Louis and the site of Fort Davidson. Deciding that he could not afford such a threat in his rear, on September 26 Price sent cavalry under Brigadier General Joseph Shelby to prevent Union reinforcement from Major General Andrew J. Smith's 8,000 Union troops near St. Louis, while Price moved against Pilot Knob.

On September 24 the commander of the Union Department of the Missouri, Major General William Rosecrans, dispatched St. Louis District commander Brigadier General Thomas Ewing and 900 men from the 14th Iowa on a reconnaissance to Pilot Knob. After a clash with Price's troops on September 26, Ewing took up position at Fort Davidson. He had only some 1,000 men, while Price had some 9,000.

Price planned to take the fort with artillery on September 27 but refrained upon learning of civilian hostages there. Instead, he called for a Union surrender. Ewing, with artillery of his own and an excellent field of fire, refused. Price's three poorly coordinated direct assaults on the fort that day were turned back with horrific losses; the Confederates suffered as many as 1,200 casualties to only some 100 for the Union force. Price planned another attack at dawn, but Ewing, who was short of ammunition and would not have been able to withstand another assault, had evacuated during the night, passing between two Confederate camps. Price sent Brigadier General John S. Marmaduke after Ewing, but the Confederates soon halted the pursuit.

Price's delay at Pilot Knob enabled Union forces to reinforce St. Louis and ended any possibility of Price taking it. On September 29 Price left Pilot Knob, hoping to take the Missouri capital of Jefferson City, but it was too heavily fortified to assault.

DEBRA J. SHEFFER

See also
Ewing, Thomas, Jr.; Marmaduke, John Sappington; Price, Sterling; Price's Missouri Raid; Shelby, Joseph Orville

Further Reading
Castel, Albert. *General Sterling Price and the Civil War in the West.* Baton Rouge: Louisiana State University Press, 1968.

Steele, Phillip W., and Steve Cottrell. *Civil War in the Ozarks.* Gretna, LA: Pelican, 1994.

Pinkerton, Allan
Birth Date: August 25, 1819
Death Date: July 1, 1884

Allan Pinkerton at Antietam, Maryland, in September 1862. Head of a detective agency before the war, Pinkerton offered his services to the Union and provided intelligence to Major General George B. McClellan. Pinkerton's incorrect assessments of Confederate strength in the Peninsula Campaign only reinforced that general's innate caution. (Library of Congress)

Detective and unsuccessful Union spy during the Civil War. Allan Pinkerton was born in Glasgow, Scotland, on August 25, 1819, and immigrated to the United States in 1842. He settled in Dundee, Illinois, and worked for a time as a barrel maker. While gathering wood one day, he discovered a counterfeiting operation and took it upon himself to arrange a citizens' arrest, taking numerous men into custody with the help of neighbors. This began Pinkerton's career in law enforcement and detective work.

In 1846 Pinkerton became deputy sheriff of Kane County, Illinois, and soon held the same post in Cook County. He was designated Chicago's first official detective in 1850, and the same year he established his own private detective and security company, the Pinkerton National Detective Agency. Pinkerton had a knack for detective work, but he was also brash, pretentious, and sometimes histrionic, which did not endear him to many people.

Pinkerton provided services to numerous national firms, including several railroads, so by the eve of the Civil War, he had staked out a national reputation. Early in 1861, he discovered an assassination plot against President-elect Abraham Lincoln and provided a security detail for him as the new president traveled to Washington in March 1861. This work provided the genesis for the Federal Secret Service Agency, which Pinkerton helped organize for a short time. Lincoln would not, however, allow Pinkerton's firm to perform secret service work for him, so Pinkerton offered his services to Union major general George B. McClellan. McClellan charged Pinkerton with gauging public opinion and performing intelligence work, including estimations of Confederate troop strength and movements. It soon became evident, however, that neither Pinkerton nor his men could be relied upon for accurate intelligence.

During McClellan's Peninsula Campaign (March–July 1862), Pinkerton's shortcomings were manifest. Instead of utilizing firsthand observations of enemy positions, Pinkerton and his men tended to rely more on the observations of rattled civilians and desperate runaway slaves, which provided for much misinformation. During much of the campaign, Pinkerton's reports to McClellan consistently overestimated Confederate troop strength—sometimes by as much as a third or a half. This only reinforced McClellan's overly cautious tendencies. The Peninsula Campaign ended in abject failure, and Pinkerton's faulty intelligence certainly played a role in that failure. When Lincoln relieved McClellan from command after the Battle of Antietam (September 17, 1862), Pinkerton lost his major patron, and his reputation as a spy had been hopelessly compromised. He performed no additional work for the military and returned to Chicago.

Nevertheless, Pinkerton's company thrived, and he expanded it with offices throughout the East. He remained the nation's most celebrated detective and penned several books about his exploits, which were quite popular when they were published. As the century progressed, Pinkerton's agency became famous—or perhaps infamous—for its work in breaking labor strikes and intimidating unions. Pinkerton died in Chicago on July 1, 1884.

PAUL G. PIERPAOLI JR.

See also

Espionage in the Civil War; Lincoln, Abraham; McClellan, George Brinton; Peninsula Campaign

Further Reading

Fishel, Edwin C. *The Secret War for the Union: The Untold Story of Military Intelligence in the Civil War.* Boston: Houghton Mifflin, 1996.

MacKay, James. *Allan Pinkerton: The First Private Eye.* New York: Wiley, 1997.

Pioneers

Advanced guard infantrymen responsible for facilitating the movement of Civil War armies. Sporting crossed-axes insignia on their sleeves, pioneers paved the way for line infantry. Although they were provided weapons, pioneers relied mostly on spades, axes, mattocks, saws, billhooks, and pickaxes in order to build roads and construct bridges or breastworks along an army's marching route. During sieges, pioneers erected fieldworks, dug approaches, and constructed parallels designed to protect work parties. In addition, they built gabions, fascines, and sap rollers intended to shield friendly forces. Meanwhile, they constructed obstacles such as chevaux-de-frise and wire entanglements.

Pioneer duty often proved dangerous. Pioneers frequently spearheaded assaults and were among the first to enter the fray of combat. For example, on June 25, 1863, during the Second Vicksburg Campaign (April 1–July 4, 1863), Union captains Andrew Hickenlooper and Stewart Tresilian led a 10-man pioneer force into a crater that had resulted from the mine detonated under the 3rd Louisiana Redan. While Union soldiers waited in the cover of the approach trench, Hickenlooper, Tresilian, and the pioneers rushed forward after the explosion in order to remove any debris that might impede the infantrymen's advance. Nevertheless, the attacking infantry became trapped in the crater, forcing the pioneers to respond. They temporarily retreated to the rear and seized prefabricated head logs with loopholes that might provide those trapped in the depression with additional cover. Unfortunately, Confederate artillery fire destroyed the logs, showering the ensnared soldiers with splinters. Although the Union troops failed to breach the Confederate defenses, the pioneers displayed unsurpassed courage and ingenuity.

Throughout the war, pioneers were few in number. For example, in the Union armies, the pioneer corps at the divisional level consisted of only 100 to 150 men. As a result, commanders often forced line infantrymen to work alongside the pioneers, assisting them in the accomplishment of their assignments.

JUSTIN S. SOLONICK

See also

Vicksburg Campaign, Second

Further Reading

Thienel, Phillip M. *Mr. Lincoln's Bridge Builders: The Right Hand of an American Genius.* Shippensburg, PA: White Mane, 2000.

Woodworth, Steven E. *Nothing but Victory: The Army of the Tennessee, 1861–1865.* New York: Knopf, 2005.

Pittsburg Landing, Battle of

See Shiloh, Battle of

Pleasant Hill, Battle of
Event Date: April 9, 1864

Last significant engagement of Union major general Nathaniel P. Banks's Red River Campaign (March 10–May 22, 1864). Pleasant Hill is located in Sabine Parish in northwestern Louisiana, not far from the Texas border. On April 8, 1864, Confederate major general Richard Taylor confronted and defeated Union forces under Banks at the Battle of Mansfield (Sabine Cross Roads) in Louisiana. That night Banks withdrew roughly 15 miles south to the village of Pleasant Hill. Taylor followed and attacked Banks's force on the morning of April 9.

Taylor had his men in place on the afternoon of April 9, and at 5:00 p.m. he sent forward Major General Thomas J. Churchill's division on the Confederate right. It smashed and drove back the Union left flank brigade under Colonel Lewis Benedict. Benedict was killed in the encounter, and the Union flank was all but destroyed. Churchill's men then began pushing back Banks's center, inflicting heavy casualties. Union reserves then came forward and assaulted Churchill's right flank, throwing it back in turn.

Meanwhile, on the Union right, Colonel William M. Dwight's brigade held fast against attacking Confederate divisions under Major General John George Walker and Brigadier General Hamilton P. Bee. In these attacks the Confederates suffered heavy casualties, particularly in Walker's Texas Division.

Churchill's brigades under Colonel Mosby M. Parsons and Brigadier General James C. Tappan threatened the center of Banks's line until Colonel James W. McMillan's Union brigade launched a savage counterattack that enveloped Parsons's brigade and sent it reeling back. Taylor then ordered Brigadier General Camille Polignac's reserve brigade forward, but it did not arrive in time, and Taylor opted to withdraw. Polignac's men covered the Confederate retreat, which ended the battle. What began as a seeming Confederate victory ended in a severe setback for the Confederates.

That evening, Banks continued his retreat toward Grand Ecore near Natchitoches, Louisiana, where all of the Union forces concentrated and entrenched. Meanwhile, Taylor left a cavalry screen and marched north with his infantry toward Arkansas. Casualties in the Battle of Pleasant Hill numbered 1,369 Union soldiers killed, wounded, or captured out of 12,247 men engaged, while the Confederates lost 1,500 out of 14,300 men engaged. Pleasant Hill was one of the most important engagements in the Trans-Mississippi theater because it helped blunt the Red River Campaign and preserve western Louisiana and Texas for the Confederacy. At the same time, this Confederate tactical defeat prevented Taylor from completely crushing Banks's force.

JOHN R. LUNDBERG

See also

Banks, Nathaniel Prentice; Bee, Hamilton Prioleau; Churchill, Thomas James; Mansfield, Battle of; Parsons, Mosby Monroe; Polignac, Camille Armand Jules Marie, Prince de; Red River Campaign; Tappan, James Camp; Taylor, Richard; Walker, John George

Further Reading

Brown, Norman D., ed. *Journey to Pleasant Hill: The Civil War Letters of Captain Elijah P. Petty Walker's Texas Division C.S.A.* San Antonio: Institute of Texan Cultures, 1982.

Lowe, Richard. *Walker's Texas Division C.S.A.: Greyhounds of the Trans Mississippi.* Baton Rouge: Louisiana State University Press, 2004.

Parrish, T. Michael. *Richard Taylor: Soldier Prince of Dixie.* Chapel Hill: University of North Carolina Press, 1992.

Pleasants, Henry
Birth Date: February 17, 1833
Death Date: April 1, 1880

Union officer. The son of a wealthy Philadelphia merchant, Henry Pleasants was born in Buenos Aires, Argentina, on February 17, 1833. After his father's death in 1846, Pleasants was sent to Philadelphia to be raised by his uncle. Graduating from Central High School in 1851, Pleasants worked as an engineer for the Pennsylvania Railroad until he moved to Pottsville, Pennsylvania, where he became a successful deep-mining engineer in the Schuylkill County coalfields.

After serving in the three-month 6th Pennsylvania Volunteer Infantry in 1861, Pleasants became a captain in the 48th Pennsylvania Volunteer Infantry. After service on the North Carolina coast, the regiment was attached to IX Corps for the rest of the Civil War. Pleasants took part in the Second Battle of Bull Run (August 29–30, 1862), the Battle of Chantilly (September 1), the Battle of South Mountain (September 14), and the Battle of Antietam (September 17). On September 20, 1862, he was promoted to lieutenant colonel of the 48th Pennsylvania. Pleasants participated in the Knoxville Campaign (November–December 1863) and then in several battles in Virginia in 1864.

During the Petersburg Campaign (June 15, 1864–April 3, 1865), Pleasants, on the suggestion of some of his coal miner soldiers, suggested and received permission to dig a tunnel under the Confederate lines and explode a mine. Once completed, the 511-foot-long tunnel was packed with four tons of black powder. The mine was triggered on July 30, 1864, and blew a hole in the trenches, but IX Corps' attack during the Battle of the Crater was badly managed and was defeated. Although Pleasants's men had no role in the actual attack, a bitter Pleasants blamed army headquarters for not sufficiently supporting his men during the mine's construction. Angry over the fiasco, Pleasants asked to be discharged, which took place on December 21, 1864. He was brevetted brigadier general on March 13, 1865.

After the war, Pleasants was chief engineer of the Philadelphia & Reading Coal and Iron Company. He died in Pottsville, Pennsylvania, on April 1, 1880.

RICHARD A. SAUERS

See also

Antietam, Battle of; Bull Run, Second Battle of; Chantilly, Battle of; Crater, Battle of the; Knoxville Campaign; Petersburg Campaign; South Mountain, Battle of

Further Reading

Hess, Earl J. *Into the Crater: The Mine Attack at Petersburg.* Columbia: University of South Carolina Press, 2010.

Trudeau, Noah Andre. *The Last Citadel: Petersburg, Virginia, June 1864–April 1865.* Baton Rouge: Louisiana State University Press, 1991.

Pleasonton, Alfred
Birth Date: July 7, 1824
Death Date: February 17, 1897

Union officer. Alfred Pleasonton was born on July 7, 1824, in Washington, D.C. After attending local schools, he received an appointment to the U.S. Military Academy, West Point, from which he graduated in 1844. He served in the Mexican-American War (1846–1848) as a second lieutenant, earning a brevet. Promoted to first lieutenant in 1849 and to captain in 1855, Pleasonton campaigned with the 2nd U.S. Dragoons (later the 2nd Cavalry) in Florida against the Seminoles as well as in Kansas, the Dakota Territory, and Utah.

When the Civil War began, the 2nd Cavalry moved east to Washington, D.C., where Pleasonton was promoted to major in February 1862. He served with the Army of the Potomac in the Peninsula Campaign (March–July 1862) and was appointed brigadier general of volunteers on July 18. Pleasonton commanded the Cavalry Division of the Army of the Potomac during the Maryland Campaign, which culminated in the Battle of Antietam (September 17). When Major General J. E. B. Stuart's Confederate cavalry raided into Pennsylvania in October 1862, Pleasonton was unsuccessful in blocking its return across the Potomac River into Virginia.

Union Army major general Alfred Pleasonton commanded the Cavalry Corps of the Army of the Potomac during 1863–1864. He is shown here in Warrenton, Virginia, in September 1863. (Library of Congress)

Pleasonton continued to lead a cavalry division and saw action in the Battle of Chancellorsville (May 1–4, 1863). On June 7, 1863, commander of the Army of the Potomac Major General Joseph Hooker placed Pleasonton in command of the Cavalry Corps, with promotion to major general on June 22. On Pleasonton's watch, the Union cavalry finally gained the upper hand on Stuart. Pleasonton led the corps in the cavalry engagement at Brandy Station (June 9, 1863) and supervised his widely scattered divisions during the Battle of Gettysburg (July 1–3, 1863). His men then fought in the Second Battle of Bristoe Station (October 14, 1863) and in the Mine Run Campaign (November 26– December 2, 1863).

In early March 1864, Pleasonton testified against Major General George G. Meade during congressional hearings concerning the Battle of Gettysburg. As a result, when Union Army general in chief Lieutenant General Ulysses S. Grant suggested placing Major General Philip Sheridan in command of the Cavalry Corps, Meade did not object, and Pleasonton was relieved from corps command on March 25.

Transferred to the Department of the Missouri, Pleasonton commanded the District of Central Missouri. When Major General Sterling Price's Confederate army invaded Missouri that autumn, Pleasonton successfully defended the state capital at Jefferson City. He then organized a cavalry division and led his troops aggressively at the Battle of Westport (October 23, 1864) and during the pursuit at Mine Creek, Kansas, on October 25. Pleasonton remained in Missouri until war's end.

In July 1865, Pleasonton was sent to command the Department of Wisconsin. He remained in the regular army after the war but, unhappy over reverting to the regular army rank of cavalry major, resigned in 1868. He spent the remainder of his life in a variety of jobs, including that of internal revenue collector. In 1888 he was retroactively placed on the army retirement list as a major. Pleasonton died in Washington, D.C., on February 17, 1897.

RICHARD A. SAUERS

See also
Antietam, Battle of; Brandy Station, Battle of; Bristoe Station, Second Battle of; Chancellorsville, Battle of; Gettysburg, Battle of; Meade, George Gordon; Mine Creek, Battle of; Mine Run Campaign; Peninsula Campaign; Price, Sterling; Westport, Battle of

Further Reading
Longacre, Edward G. "Alfred Pleasonton: 'The Knight of Romance.'" *Civil War Times Illustrated* 13(8) (December 1974): 10–23.
Longacre, Edward G. *Lincoln's Cavalrymen: A History of the Mounted Forces of the Army of the Potomac.* Mechanicsburg, PA: Stackpole, 2000.

Plum Point Bend, Battle of
Event Date: May 10, 1862

Naval engagement on the Mississippi. The Battle of Plum Point Bend above Fort Pillow was the war's first real engagement between naval squadrons. Commodore Charles H. Davis, the Union commander in the battle who had taken command only the day before, characterized it as "a smart affair."

In May 1862 the Union flotilla lay above Fort Pillow, unable to pass by that place and employing long-range mortar fire to try to shell the fort into submission. An attempt to take Fort Pillow had been stymied when commander of the Department of the Missouri Major General Henry Halleck decided to remove the great bulk of Union army troops for his own campaign against Corinth. Confederate deserters had warned that the River Defense Fleet would attempt to engage the Union squadron upriver, and a Confederate sortie on the May 8 should have served as confirmation of this.

Since mid-April, the Union flotilla had followed the same routine. Daily a gunboat would tow one or more mortar boats to just above Craigshead Point, then guard the mortar boats as they lobbed 13-inch shells across the point toward Fort Pillow. On May 20 at 6:00 a.m., Union mortar boat *No. 16* with a crew of 14 men commanded by Second Master Thomas B. Gregory was in position along with its covering gunboat, Lieutenant Rodger Stembel's *Cincinnati*, the crew of which was nonchalantly going through their usual morning routine.

The Union mortar boat had just fired its fifth shell when shortly after 7:00 a.m., eight Confederate gunboats suddenly appeared around Craigshead Point. These were the *Little Rebel* (flagship), *General Bragg, General Sterling Price, General Van Dorn, General Sumter, General Thompson, General Beauregard,* and *Colonel Lovell.* Confederate senior captain James Montgomery hoped to cut out or destroy the mortar boat and/or its covering gunboat, separated from the remainder of the Union flotilla.

The Confederate steamers made straight for the *Cincinnati* as its crew desperately struggled to get under way. Although the *General Bragg* took a broadside at only 50 yards from the *Cincinnati*, it continued on and crashed into the Union gunboat. Stembel swung the bow so that the impact was at an angle, but it still tore a large hole in the *Cincinnati*'s starboard quarter, flooding its magazine. As the *General Bragg* wrenched free, another Union broadside tore into the Confederate ship, putting it hors de combat. The *General Bragg* then drifted downstream out of action.

Both the *General Sterling Price* and the *General Sumter* also then rammed the *Cincinnati,* which soon was sinking rapidly as Confederate sharpshooters began to pick off members of its crew, among them Commander Stembel, who had recklessly exposed himself on deck and now fell badly wounded. Nonetheless, the crew of the *Cincinnati* managed, with the aid of two Union tugs that appeared, to get the gunboat to the shore, where it sank in 12 feet of water. The crew then watched the rest of the action from its upper deck.

The rest of the Union ships finally got up steam and proceeded downriver. The *Mound City* and the *Carondelet* were in the lead, followed by the *Benton* and the *Pittsburg.* The other Union gunboats did not arrive in time to take part in the battle.

As the Confederate ram *Van Dorn* moved to engage the *Mound City,* it sent two 32-pounder shots as well as several volleys of musket fire into mortar boat *No. 16.* The larger shot passed completely through the unarmored mortar boat, and it was a miracle that no one aboard was injured. The crewmen had lowered the mortar's elevation and, by firing with reduced charges and dangerously short fuses, managed to burst shells over the Confederate warships. Even after *No. 16* was hit, Gregory's men continued to fire. They expended 52 shells that day, including those fired before the battle.

The *Van Dorn* rammed the *Mound City,* tearing away part of the Union gunboat's bow and causing it to rapidly take on water. Commander Augustus H. Kilty managed to get off a punishing broadside before he grounded the *Mound City* to prevent it from sinking. It had only one man wounded.

The arrival of the more powerful Union ships now tipped the balance decidedly in favor of the Union, and Montgomery soon signaled a retirement. As the Confederate vessels fled downriver, a shell from the *Carondelet* smashed into the *General Sumter*'s boilers, releasing a great cloud of steam. Rifled rounds from the Union flagship *Benton* also shattered the boilers of first the *Colonel Levell* and then the *Van Dorn,* disabling both.

During the hour-long battle, the Union side suffered only 4 wounded, 1 mortally; deserters later reported up to 108 Confederate dead. But apart from the heavy personnel losses, the South had achieved a tactical victory. Its small flotilla had temporarily disabled two of the much more powerful Union ironclads. Refloated, they were moved to Mound City for repairs.

SPENCER C. TUCKER

See also

Beauregard, Pierre Gustav Toutant; Davis, Charles Henry; Foote, Andrew Hull; Fort Pillow, Tennessee, Capture of; Halleck, Henry Wager; Montgomery, James; Welles, Gideon

Further Reading

Milligan, John D. *Gunboats down the Mississippi.* Annapolis, MD: Naval Institute Press, 1965.

Porter, David Dixon. *Naval History of the Civil War.* New York: Sherman, 1886.

Slagle, Jay. *Ironclad Captain: Seth Ledyard Phelps and the U.S. Navy, 1841–1864.* Kent, OH: Kent State University Press, 1996.

Tucker, Spencer C. *Blue and Gray Navies: The Civil War Afloat.* Annapolis, MD: Naval Institute Press, 2006.

Plymouth, Battle of
Start Date: April 17, 1864
End Date: April 20, 1864

Confederate operation to protect vital supply and communication lines. Plymouth, North Carolina, located on the south bank of the Roanoke River near its mouth, had been an important supply depot for Union forces in eastern North Carolina since its capture from the Confederates in 1862. Union brigadier general Henry W. Wessells commanded the Plymouth garrison of nearly 3,000 men. The defenders had erected a series of strong points and forts that controlled the land approaches. Plymouth was most vulnerable from the east, but several fortifications also defended it from this direction, and the area's low marshy terrain would render a ground attack here difficult. U.S. Navy lieutenant commander Charles W. Flusser had charge of the river defenses. He had four warships and a transport, the two strongest being the gunboats *Miami* and *Smithfield.* Concerned about the possible appearance of the Confederate ironclad *Albemarle,* Flusser had ordered the wooden-hulled *Miami* and *Smithfield* lashed together for combined firepower.

Plymouth provided a jumping-off position for Union assaults against the key Wilmington & Weldon Railroad, vital in supplying Richmond. In early 1864, Confederate general in chief General Robert E. Lee dispatched Brigadier General Robert F. Hoke from Virginia to capture the Union positions along the North Carolina coast. Hoke had a rigid timetable, as Union forces were preparing to invade Virginia, and the 7,000 Confederates in the operation would soon be required to move northward. Despite his sizable numerical advantage, Hoke believed that victory would depend on naval support. In response to his appeals, Confederate authorities authorized naval support in the form of the ironclad *Albemarle,* then nearing completion up the Roanoke.

Assured of support from the *Albemarle,* Hoke invested Plymouth from the land side at 4:00 p.m. on April 17, 1864, and opened artillery fire against Union Fort Gray, followed by an unsuccessful infantry assault the next morning. Fighting continued throughout April 18, with the Confederates meeting stiff resistance from the heavily outnumbered but well-entrenched defenders and also taking a heavy pounding from the heavy guns of the Union gunboats. The attackers did capture Fort Wessells, which provided an excellent position for Confederate artillery, and Confederate fire caused the transport *Bombshell* to sink at the wharf. Still, Hoke knew that success in the battle rested on the arrival of the *Albemarle.*

Mechanical problems had delayed the passage of the Confederate ironclad. Captained by Commander James W. Cooke, the *Albemarle* finally issued from the Roanoke River at 3:30 a.m. on April 19. In the ensuing Battle of Albemarle Sound, the *Albemarle* rammed and was able to sink the *Smithfield.* Flusser was the sole Union fatality in the naval engagement, although 11 other Union personnel were wounded, and 8 were captured. Only 1 Confederate was killed. The three other Union warships escaped.

Most of the land fighting on April 19 consisted of artillery fire, but with the *Albemarle* now controlling the water approaches to Plymouth and with it and an accompanying steamer, the *Cotton Plant,* shelling the Union troops ashore, Wessells surrendered at 10:00 a.m. on April 20. The Confederates took as many as 2,800 prisoners, 28 pieces of artillery, 500 horses, and considerable quantities of small arms and supplies. Confederate losses were 163 killed and 534 wounded. The threat to the Wilmington & Weldon Railroad had been removed, and Plymouth could now serve as a base from which the *Albemarle* might drive Union warships from Albemarle and Pimlico Sounds.

The fall of Plymouth led the Federals to abandon Washington, North Carolina, on August 27, although not before they had thoroughly sacked it.

SPENCER C. TUCKER

See also

Albemarle, CSS; Albemarle Sound; Albemarle Sound, Battle of; Hoke, Robert Frederick

Further Reading

Barrett, John G. *The Civil War in North Carolina.* Chapel Hill: University of North Carolina Press, 1963.

Elliott, Robert G. *Ironclad of the Roanoke: Gilbert Elliott's Albemarle.* Shippensburg, PA: White Mane, 1999.

Moss, Juanita P. *Battle of Plymouth, North Carolina (April 17–20, 1864): The Last Confederate Victory.* Westminster, MD: Heritage Books, 2003.

Tucker, Spencer C. *Blue and Gray Navies: The Civil War Afloat.* Annapolis, MD: Naval Institute Press, 2006.

Poe, Orlando Metcalfe
Birth Date: March 7, 1832
Death Date: October 2, 1895

Union officer. Orlando Metcalfe Poe was born on March 7, 1832, in Navarre, Ohio. He graduated from the U.S. Military Academy, West Point, in 1856 and was commissioned in the topographical engineers, whereupon he engaged in coastal surveys of the Great Lakes, earning promotion to first lieutenant in 1860.

When the Civil War began, Poe helped organize Ohio volunteer units and served as chief topographical engineer for the Department of Ohio. He then joined the staff of Department of the Ohio commander Major General George B. McClellan and participated in the Battle of Rich Mountain (July 11, 1861). Poe then worked on the defenses of Washington, D.C.

In September 1861, Poe was appointed colonel of the 2nd Michigan Infantry. He participated in the Peninsula Campaign (March–July 1862). Given charge of a brigade in III Corps, he saw action at the Second Battle of Bull Run (August 29–30, 1862) in the Antietam Campaign (September 4–20). Poe was promoted to brigadier general of volunteers in November 1862, but the appointment expired for lack of confirmation in March 1863. He had charge of a brigade in IX Corps during the debacle at the First Battle of Fredericksburg (December 13, 1862). When his volunteer commission expired, Poe reverted to his regular army grade of captain.

Poe was then appointed chief engineer of XXIII Corps and brevetted major for building effective defensive works at Knoxville, Tennessee. In December 1863 he was assigned duty with the Military Division of the Mississippi, becoming chief engineer in April 1864. His close association with Major General William T. Sherman was demonstrated throughout the Atlanta Campaign (May 5–September 2), during which

Poe provided invaluable assistance to the commander. Poe also served effectively during Sherman's March to the Sea (November–December) and March through the Carolinas (January–April 1865). Among Poe's responsibilities were supervising the destruction of industrial facilities, wrecking railroad lines, coordinating pontoon bridge units, and producing topographic maps. Sherman recognized Poe's talents with brevet promotions through brigadier general in the regular army in March 1865.

With the end of the war Poe returned to army engineering programs, with promotion to major in 1867, and in 1870 he became engineer for lighthouses on the Great Lakes. In January 1873 he was appointed aide to General Sherman, with the staff rank of colonel, a position Poe held until Sherman's retirement. From 1884 Poe served as superintending engineer for the construction of the shipping locks between Lakes Superior and Huron at Sault Ste. Marie, Michigan. During construction of the locks he injured his leg and subsequently died from an infection on October 2, 1895, in Detroit.

STEVEN J. RAUCH

See also

Antietam Campaign; Atlanta Campaign; Bull Run, Second Battle of; Fredericksburg, First Battle of; Rich Mountain, Battle of; Sherman's March through the Carolinas; Sherman's March to the Sea

Further Reading

Taylor, Paul. *Orlando M. Poe: Civil War General and Great Lakes Engineer.* Kent, OH: Kent State University Press, 2009.

Trudeau, Noah Andre. *Southern Storm: Sherman's March to the Sea.* New York: HarperCollins, 2008.

Point Lookout Prison, Maryland

Union prison facility. Point Lookout, located where the Potomac flows into Chesapeake Bay, featured a high fence enclosing a cluster of tents. This greatly reduced construction costs. Designed to hold 10,000 men, Point Lookout Prison (officially named Camp Hoffman) became the most populated Union prison during its 22-month existence because of its close proximity to the eastern battlefields, especially after the collapse of the prisoner exchange cartel in 1863, when prisoner-of-war numbers rose dramatically. The prison opened in August 1863 with 1,700 detainees; that number increased to 9,000 by December, 15,500 by the middle of 1864, and some 22,000 by April 1865. All the prisoners were released by June 1865.

The prison was both the largest and in some ways the worst Union camp. Located on a 40-acre sandy, barren peninsula, it was just five feet above sea level. There were chronic freshwater shortages and frequent flooding. Food rations were meager and of abysmal quality.

Point Lookout Prison was divided into two sections—30 acres for troops and 10 acres for officers, all enclosed by a 15-foot fence with a sentry gallery along the top. The officers' area contained one 160- by 20-foot building, with a kitchen at one end as a cookhouse. The soldiers' area contained eight similar buildings. Each mess had four long tables down the center and cauldrons for cooking. The living quarters consisted of tents of various size and quality, which provided only minimal shelter. Many prisoners suffered from the cold during the winter months.

The winter of 1863–1864 was especially bitter and brought hardship for the prisoners, who had insufficient clothing, little or no heat in their tents, and only one blanket for several men. Between November 1863 and February 1864, 540 prisoners died from exposure, lack of food, chronic diarrhea, scurvy, typhoid, or smallpox. A total of 3,584 men died at Point Lookout of the 52,264 prisoners held there.

DEBRA J. SHEFFER

See also

Prisoners of War; Prisons, U.S.

Further Reading

Hesseltine, William B., ed. *Civil War Prisons.* Kent, OH: Kent State University Press, 1962.

Speer, Lonnie R. *Portals to Hell: Military Prisons of the Civil War.* Mechanicsburg, PA: Stackpole, 1997.

Poison Spring, Battle of
Event Date: April 18, 1864

Engagement in Arkansas that occurred during the Camden Expedition (March 23–May 3, 1864), part of the larger Red River Campaign (March 10–May 22). On March 23 Union major general Frederick Steele departed Little Rock, Arkansas, with 8,500 men, headed to Camden to resupply and then on to Shreveport, Louisiana, where he was expected to join forces with Major General Nathaniel P. Banks and Rear Admiral David D. Porter in taking that city and then proceed into Texas. Skirmishes along the way with Confederate forces badly weakened Steele's forces and depleted his supplies. He reached Camden on April 15 but found few supplies there.

On April 17 Steele dispatched Colonel James M. Williams with a foraging party of 695 men, 438 of whom were from the 1st Kansas Colored Regiment, recruited from fugitive slaves from Arkansas and Missouri who had fled to Kansas in 1861 and 1862, along with two field guns and 198 wagons. They traveled approximately 20 miles to a place called Lee's Plantation, where they loaded corn that the Confederates had stored there, then headed back to Camden. On the morning of April 18 some four miles from the main Union encampment, Williams's force was reinforced by some 500 men and two guns, bringing his total manpower to about 1,200. Shortly thereafter at around 10:45 a.m., a Confederate force of 3,335 men under Brigadier General John S. Marmaduke and Major General Samuel B. Maxey ambushed the Union force. The Confederates caught the train in a cross fire of artillery and charged it from the front. Williams's men stood firm for nearly 45 minutes while they tried to protect his supply wagons, but the Union troops eventually broke and fled toward Camden. Union losses included four artillery pieces, all the wagons and supplies, and 301 dead or wounded. Of the dead, 117 came from the ranks of the 1st Kansas Colored Regiment. Williams later accused the Confederates of murdering wounded black soldiers and charged pro-Southern Choctaws with scalping Union dead. The Confederates vigorously denied the charges. Confederate losses were 114 dead, wounded, or missing.

DEBRA J. SHEFFER

See also

Camden Expedition; Marmaduke, John Sappington; Maxey, Samuel Bell; Red River Campaign; Steele, Frederick

Further Reading

Castel, Albert. *General Sterling Price and the Civil War in the West.* Baton Rouge: Louisiana State University Press, 1968.

Hattaway, Herman, and Archer Jones. *How the North Won: A Military History of the Civil War.* Urbana: University of Illinois Press, 1991.

Josephy, Alvin M. Jr. *The Civil War in the American West.* New York: Vintage Books, 1991.

Polignac, Camille Armand Jules Marie, Prince de

Birth Date: February 16, 1832
Death Date: November 15, 1913

Confederate officer. Camille Armand Jules Marie, Prince de Polignac, was born in Millemont in the department of Seine-et-Oise, France, into a prominent noble family on February 16, 1832. His father, Jules, Prince de Polignac, had served as premier for King Charles X of France. His mother, Mary Charlotte Parkyns, was an English aristocrat. The younger Polignac was educated at St. Stanislaus College, where he graduated with honors in mathematics in 1852. In 1853 he enlisted as a private in the French Army, having failed the entrance exam for admission to the military academy, the École Spéciale Militaire de Saint Cyr.

Polignac earned distinction during fighting in the Crimean War (1853–1856) and was promoted to second lieutenant shortly thereafter. Polignac found peacetime duty tiresome, however, and was discharged upon his request in 1859. He then left France for Nicaragua and Costa Rica, where he studied natural history and political economy while also engaging himself as a military engineer.

From Central America, Polignac made his way to New York. While in New York City he met a number of prominent Southerners including P. G. T. Beauregard, with whom Polignac sympathized as the U.S. sectional crisis deepened. Polignac returned to Central America but offered his services to the Confederacy on the beginning of the Civil War.

Polignac received a Confederate Army commission as a lieutenant colonel of infantry. He served on the staff of General Beauregard and was present with him at the Battle of Shiloh (April 6–7, 1862) and the Union advance on and siege of Corinth (May 3–30). When Confederate president Jefferson Davis replaced Beauregard with General Braxton Bragg, Polignac was one of the few staff officers whom Bragg saw fit to retain. Under Bragg, Polignac took part in the Confederate offensive into Tennessee and Kentucky and began to receive battlefield commands.

In 1863 Polignac was advanced to brigadier general and transferred to the Trans-Mississippi Department under the command of Lieutenant General Edmund Kirby Smith. Polignac led a Texas brigade under the overall command of Major General Richard Taylor in the Battle of Mansfield (April 8, 1864) in De Soto Parish, Louisiana. The battle was the first major confrontation of the Red River Campaign (March 10–May 22, 1864) and ended in a Confederate victory. During the fight, Polignac assumed command of a division after the death of Brigadier General Alfred Mouton and was advanced to major general on June 14, 1864.

As the Confederacy teetered on the verge of collapse in March 1865, Polignac was dispatched to France to request aid from Emperor Napoleon III. By the time Polignac arrived in France, the war had already ended. Rather than return to the United States, he decided to stay in France and manage his family's estates while advancing his interests in Central America. He also wrote a number of articles about the Civil War. Polignac returned to the French Army as a général de division (major general) during the Franco-Prussian War (1870–1871).

Polignac died in Paris on November 15, 1913. He held the distinction of being the last Confederate major general to die.

MICHAEL K. BEAUCHAMP

See also

Beauregard, Pierre Gustav Toutant; Bragg, Braxton; Corinth, Mississippi, Siege of; Mansfield, Battle of; Red River Campaign; Shiloh, Battle of; Smith, Edmund Kirby; Taylor, Richard

Further Reading

Barr, Alwyn. *Polignac's Texas Brigade.* Houston: Texas Gulf Coast Historical Association, 1964.
Kinard, Jeff. *Lafayette of the South: Prince Camille de Polignac and the American Civil War.* College Station: Texas A&M University Press, 2001.

Political Cartoons

Common form of political propaganda during the Civil War era. Opinion makers from across the political spectrum utilized cartoons as a way to reach the public in ways beyond written editorials and other media. Belying the serious nature of their topics, cartoons often relied heavily on caricatures of famous people and puns to provide pointed, and occasionally witty, commentary. Commonly depicted individuals during the war included U.S. president Abraham Lincoln, Confederate president Jefferson Davis, and various Union and Confederate military leaders. The cartoonists' rendition usually exaggerated well-known aspects of their subjects' physical features, backgrounds, and personalities. Also popular were national figureheads such as Columbia and Uncle Sam depicting the U.S. government and John Bull depicting Great Britain.

Although relatively widespread, the lithographic techniques used to produce most cartoons of the period limited the number of available publishers. Magazines and other illustrated weeklies, especially New York–based publications such as *Frank Leslie's Illustrated Newspaper* and *Harper's Weekly,* produced most of the more famous cartoons. When the war broke out in 1861 and circulation of Northern journals ceased in the seceded Southern states,

As this 1863 political cartoon from *Harper's Weekly* illustrates, the Civil War divided more than North and South. Northern "Peace Democrats," called Copperheads by their opponents, displayed a more sympathetic attitude toward the South after secession than did the Republicans. (Library of Congress)

crude imitators such as *Southern Punch* and the *Southern Illustrated News* attempted to fill the void. A relative lack of material resources and appropriate supplies and technology contributed to the relative inferiority of Southern cartooning.

Some of the more notable cartoonists during the Civil War were Nathaniel Currier and James Ives, Henry Stephens, Frank Beard, Matt Morgan, and Arthur Lumley. The famous Gilded Age cartoonist Thomas Nast also rose to prominence during the war, joining *Harper's Weekly* in 1862. While most cartoons regarding the Civil War came from Northern and Southern papers, foreign cartoons, particularly from British publications such as the *London Punch,* with its well-known artist Sir John Tenniel, were also widely circulated.

KEITH ALTAVILLA

See also

Currier & Ives; *Harper's Weekly;* Nast, Thomas; *Southern Illustrated News*

Further Reading

Hess, Stephen, and Milton Kaplan. *The Ungentlemanly Art: A History of American Political Cartoons.* New York: Macmillan, 1968.
Lewin, J. G., and P. J. Huff. *Lines of Contention: Political Cartoons of the Civil War.* New York: HarperCollins, 2007.
Smith, Kristen M., ed. *The Lines Are Drawn: Political Cartoons of the Civil War.* Athens, GA: Hill Street, 1999.

Polk, Leonidas
Birth Date: April 10, 1806
Death Date: June 14, 1864

Confederate officer. Leonidas Polk was born on April 10, 1806, in Raleigh, North Carolina, into a socially, politically, and militarily prestigious family. Polk's third cousin, James K. Polk, was president of the United States. Leonidas Polk attended the U.S. Military Academy, West Point. His roommate was Albert Sidney Johnston, and Polk also knew cadets Jefferson Davis and Robert E. Lee. Six months following his graduation in 1827, Polk resigned his commission as a second lieutenant to enter the Virginia Theological Seminary.

Following his ordination and because of his social position and family name, Polk rose quickly in the Episcopal Church, becoming missionary bishop to the Southwest in 1837. In 1841 he was named bishop of Louisiana. Polk played a key role in the establishment of the Episcopal University of the South in Sewanee, Tennessee. With the

An Episcopal bishop and Confederate lieutenant general, Leonidas Polk was an incompetent senior commander in the Western Theater. His seizure of Columbus, Kentucky, in 1861, was a disaster for the South because it opened the way to Union control of that proclaimed neutral state. (Library of Congress)

secession of the Deep South, Polk was instrumental in the Louisiana Convention leaving the Episcopal Church of the United States. In June 1861 Polk secured from President Jefferson Davis a major general's commission, despite the fact that Polk had never held a command and had been out of the army for more than 30 years. Polk proved to be an extraordinarily poor choice.

Many Northern newspapers ran stories expressing outrage that a man of the cloth would be engaging in active warfare, but Polk never had any difficulty combining his religious beliefs with a willingness to fight. Indeed, he relished his title "the Fighting Bishop."

Davis assigned Polk command of Department No. 2, charged with defense of the upper Mississippi River. In one of the worst decisions of the war, in September 1861 Polk led Confederate forces into the state of Kentucky, seizing Columbus on the Mississippi River, which he fortified. President Abraham Lincoln had promised that the Union would honor Kentucky's neutrality if it remained peaceful, but this move gave Brigadier General Ulysses S. Grant the excuse to take Paducah. Polk had rendered much more difficult the Confederate defense of Tennessee.

In September 1861 Polk's former West Point roommate, General Albert Sidney Johnston, took over command of the department. Polk continued as his subordinate. Polk's forces battled those led by Grant at Belmont, Missouri, on November 7, 1861. Polk commanded a corps in the Battle of Shiloh (April 6–7, 1862). He also led a corps under General Braxton Bragg in the Battle of Perryville (October 8, 1862). Polk was promoted to lieutenant general shortly thereafter, with date of rank from October 10, 1862.

Numerous accounts attest to Polk's personal courage, but having been used to almost complete autonomy as a bishop, he found it difficult to take orders. This characteristic became more pronounced when Polk was placed under the authority of the tempestuous and imperious Bragg. Indeed, Polk became a key figure in a campaign imploring President Davis to replace Bragg as commander of the Army of Tennessee. This internecine warfare proved devastating to the morale of the army. Relations between Polk and Bragg, strained in the Kentucky fighting, became worse as a consequence of the Battle of Stones River (December 31, 1862–January 2, 1863) in Tennessee and then exploded following the Battle of Chickamauga (September 19–20, 1863) in Georgia, when Bragg sought to bring Polk before a court-martial for his failure to attack when ordered.

Davis intervened, transferring Polk to command the Department of Alabama, Mississippi, and East Louisiana. There Polk failed to halt Major General William T. Sherman's advance from Vicksburg to Meridian, Mississippi. In May 1864 Polk and his Army of Mississippi, now designated a corps, reinforced General Joseph E. Johnston's Army of Tennessee at the start of the Atlanta Campaign (May 5–September 2, 1864). On June 14 at Pine Mountain, Georgia, not far from Marietta, Polk was reconnoitering Union lines when he was hit by a cannon ball and instantly killed.

DAVID SLOAN AND SPENCER C. TUCKER

See also

Belmont, Battle of; Bragg, Braxton; Chickamauga, Battle of; Davis, Jefferson Finis; Perryville, Battle of; Shiloh, Battle of; Stones River, Battle of

Further Reading

Bonds, Russell S. "Pawn Takes Bishop." *Civil War Times* 45(3) (May 2006): 52–58.

Parks, Joseph Howard. *General Leonidas Polk, C.S.A.: The Fighting Bishop.* Baton Rouge: Louisiana State University Press, 1962.

Robins, Glenn M. "Leonidas Polk and Episcopal Identity: An Evangelical Experiment in the Mid-Nineteenth Century South." PhD dissertation, University of Southern Mississippi, 1999.

Polk, Lucius Eugene
Birth Date: July 10, 1833
Death Date: December 1, 1892

Confederate officer. Lucius Eugene Polk was born on July 10, 1833, in Salisbury, North Carolina, to a well-to-do family and was the nephew of future Confederate general Leonidas Polk. Lucius Polk moved at age two with his family to Columbia, Tennessee. He attended the University of Virginia during 1850–1851 but soon thereafter relocated to Arkansas, where he purchased a plantation near Helena.

In 1861 Polk enlisted as a private in an infantry company known as the Yell Rifles, commanded by future Confederate general Patrick E. Cleburne. The unit was attached to the 15th Arkansas Infantry Regiment, in which Polk soon was a second lieutenant. The 15th Arkansas was still under Cleburne's command and saw action at the Battle of Shiloh (April 6–7, 1862), where Polk was wounded. Upon his return to duty some weeks later, he was promoted to colonel and given command of the 15th Arkansas.

Polk performed well, leading his men at the Battles of Richmond (August 29–30, 1862) and Perryville (October 8, 1862) in Kentucky. On December 13, 1862, Polk was advanced to brigadier general and given command of a brigade in Major General Carter L. Stevenson's division. Polk saw much action throughout late 1862 and during 1863. He performed admirably at the Battle of Stones River (December 31, 1862–January 2, 1863), and at the Battle of Chickamauga (September 19–20, 1863) he led an unsupported charge against stout Union breastworks. Polk was also present for the Battle of Missionary Ridge (November 25, 1863), where his brigade repulsed numerous Union advances, and performed effectively during the significant rearguard action at the Battle of Ringgold Gap (November 27, 1863).

Polk next led a brigade under Cleburne during the Atlanta Campaign (May 5–September 2, 1864) but was grievously wounded at the Battle of Kennesaw Mountain (June 27, 1864). Unable to retain his command, he returned to his family's plantation in Tennessee, where he remained until war's end. He oversaw the plantation thereafter and served a term in the Tennessee Senate, beginning in 1887. Polk died in Columbia, Tennessee, on December 1, 1892.

PAUL G. PIERPAOLI JR.

See also

Atlanta Campaign; Chickamauga, Battle of; Cleburne, Patrick Ronayne; Kennesaw Mountain, Battle of; Missionary Ridge, Battle of; Perryville, Battle of; Richmond, Battle of; Shiloh, Battle of; Stones River, Battle of

Further Reading
Eicher, John H., and David J. Eicher. *Civil War High Commands.* Stanford, CA: Stanford University Press, 2001.
Warner, Ezra J. *Generals in Gray: Lives of the Confederate Commanders.* Baton Rouge: Louisiana State University Press, 2006.

Pollard, Edward Alfred
Birth Date: February 27, 1832
Death Date: December 16, 1872

Writer, journalist, and historian. Edward Alfred Pollard was born on February 27, 1832, in Nelson County, Virginia. He graduated from Hampden-Sydney College in 1846 and subsequently studied law but gravitated toward journalism. By the early 1850s, he was engaged as a newspaperman in the gold mining regions of California. He went to Asia for two years (1856–1858) and wrote about his travel experiences. Pollard returned to Virginia in 1858, where he rigorously defended slavery and supported Southern secession.

In the spring of 1861 as the Civil War began, Pollard was hired as an editor for the *Richmond Examiner.* Although he championed the Southern cause in his reporting, he developed a visceral dislike of President Jefferson Davis and took every opportunity to lambast him and his policies, which Pollard believed were hampering the Confederate war effort. In the meantime, he began writing a massive four-volume work, published from 1862 to 1866 and titled *The Southern History of the War,* that was a contemporary account of the Civil War from a decidedly Southern point of view.

In May 1864 Pollard left for Great Britain, where he hoped to promote his book. The ship in which he sailed, the blockade-runner *Greyhound,* was captured by Union naval vessels, and Pollard was taken prisoner. He was imprisoned first at Fort Monroe and then at Fort Warren. Paroled and exchanged in January 1865, Pollard made his way back to Richmond and continued as a principal editor of the *Examiner.*

After the war Pollard continued to write and publish books, the best known of which was *The Lost Cause* (1866). Indeed, it was Pollard who first introduced the term "Lost Cause," which described a highly romanticized notion of the South's quixotic attempt to seek a peaceful disunion and its subsequent heroic military effort to attain independence and preserve its heritage by way of war. He wrote numerous other books, many of them dealing in some way with the heroics of the Southern cause. He remained a staunch of

critic of Davis, however, excoriating him in *The Life of Jefferson Davis* (1869). That book essentially portrayed the former Confederate president as an effete snob whose obduracy and political bumbling had sealed the South's fate by 1865.

Pollard went on to edit two other newspapers after 1867 and moved to New York City in the early 1870s, by which time he had become a nationalistic unionist. He died in Lynchburg, Virginia, on December 16, 1872.

PAUL G. PIERPAOLI JR.

See also
Davis, Jefferson Finis; Journalism; Lost Cause; *Richmond Examiner*

Further Reading
Maddex, Jack P. *The Reconstruction of Edward A. Pollard: A Rebel's Conversion to Postbellum Unionism.* Chapel Hill: University of North Carolina Press, 1974.
Pollard, E. A. *The Lost Cause.* New York: Gramercy, 1989.

Pomeroy, Samuel Clarke
Birth Date: January 3, 1816
Death Date: August 29, 1891

Antislavery advocate and Republican U.S. senator. Samuel Clarke Pomeroy was born on January 3, 1816, in Southampton, Massachusetts. He studied at Amherst College during 1836–1838 and then went to New York State, where he taught school. Four years later he returned to Southampton and was engaged in local politics. During 1852–1853, he held a seat in the Massachusetts legislature. In 1854 he became the chief financial agent for the New England Emigrant Aid Company.

Also in 1854, Pomeroy led a group of like-minded antislavery activists to Kansas, settling in the Lawrence area. Their presence helped precipitate the violence that became known as Bleeding Kansas. In 1858 when antislavery forces had begun to attain the upper hand in the struggle, Pomeroy moved to Atchison, where he engaged in lucrative business and real estate ventures. In 1859 he was a delegate to Kansas's Free State Convention.

In April 1861 after Kansas had attained statehood, Pomeroy took a seat in the U.S. Senate as a Republican. In the Senate, the highly ambitious Pomeroy pushed strongly for projects that would aid Kansas, including the construction of railroads. Pomeroy's most spectacular bid to achieve lasting power was his sponsorship of a round-robin letter (known as the Pomeroy Circular) published in Washington,

D.C., newspapers in February 1864 in which he asserted that President Abraham Lincoln was practically unelectable in November 1864 and that only Secretary of the Treasury Salmon P. Chase could win the presidency on the Republican ticket. Chase, embarrassed by the letter, of which he had no prior knowledge, disavowed Pomeroy's circular, and the controversy abated relatively quickly. Ironically, the circular may have actually helped Lincoln's reelection bid, as numerous Republican leaders came to the president's defense.

Pompous, self-righteous, and vain, Pomeroy resorted to frequent bribery to stay in office and to enlarge his base of patronage for Kansas. During Pomeroy's 1872 reelection bid, one Kansas legislator announced that Pomeroy had given him $7,000, with the promise of an additional $1,000, to vote for him. When the news got out, Pomeroy's Senate career was destroyed, and he left the chamber at the end of his term in March 1873. He eventually moved to Boston, where he was an advocate for prohibition and women's suffrage. Pomeroy died in Worcester County, Massachusetts, on August 29, 1891. The famed writer Mark Twain in the 1873 novel *The Gilded Age,* coauthored with Charles Dudley Warner, allegedly used Pomeroy as the model for the self-righteous, hypocritical, and bombastic Senator Dilworthy.

PAUL G. PIERPAOLI JR.

See also

Bleeding Kansas; Chase, Salmon Portland; Congress, U.S.; Kansas; Lincoln, Abraham; Pomeroy Circular; Republican Party

Further Reading

Donald, David Herbert. *Lincoln.* New York: Simon and Schuster, 1995.
Kitzhaber, Albert. "Götterdämmerüng in Topeka: The Downfall of Senator Pomeroy." *Kansas Historical Quarterly* 18 (August 1950): 243–278.

Pomeroy Circular

Round-robin–style letter sponsored and circulated by Republican U.S. senator from Kansas Samuel C. Pomeroy that criticized President Abraham Lincoln and promoted the presidential aspirations of Secretary of the Treasury Salmon P. Chase. The Pomeroy Circular made the rounds in Congress and among Republican leaders and was published in Washington, D.C., newspapers on February 22, 1864.

In the letter, Pomeroy maintained that Lincoln was virtually unelectable in 1864, hinted that the president's leadership had been lacking, and maintained that the administration had not done enough to end slavery and defeat the Confederacy. The letter claimed that only Chase could win the 1864 presidential contest. Although Chase indeed harbored presidential aspirations and had gone so far as to assemble an informal campaign, he was nevertheless deeply embarrassed when the Pomeroy Circular became public.

Chase made it clear to Lincoln that he had not been involved in the drafting or circulation of the letter and promptly offered his resignation. Lincoln believed Chase and would not accept his resignation. Ironically, the circular may have actually helped Lincoln's reelection bid, as numerous Republican leaders clamored to the president's defense. Lincoln went on to win reelection in November 1864.

PAUL G. PIERPAOLI JR.

See also

Chase, Salmon Portland; Election of 1864, U.S.; Lincoln, Abraham; Pomeroy, Samuel Clarke

Further Reading

Donald, David Herbert. *Lincoln.* New York: Simon and Schuster, 1995.
Niven, John. *Salmon P. Chase: A Biography.* New York: Oxford University Press, 1995.

Pon Pon River, Battle of the

See Willstown Bluff, Battle of

Pontoon Bridge

A floating bridge or causeway spanning a body of water and used during the Civil War to carry soldiers and war material from one shore to another. Pontoon bridges were also sometimes used as floating wharves, docks, and even makeshift railroad bridges. Compared to boats or ferries, pontoon bridges were quickly built and provided a much faster—and usually safer—way to transport troops and supplies across waterways. The U.S. Army Corps of Engineers was responsible for building most of the pontoon bridges utilized during the Civil War, while the Pioneers largely carried out such construction for the Confederacy.

The critical element in a pontoon bridge is a flat-bottom boat, known as a pontoon. Both wooden and canvas boats (canvas over wooden frames) were employed during the war, and both had their advantages and disadvantages. Wooden pontoons, at 31 feet in length, were more durable than canvas pontoons but were awkward to maneuver and required a larger construction team. Only 21 feet in length,

A pontoon bridge at Bull Run, Virginia, in 1862. (National Archives)

canvas pontoons were more easily handled and transported, but they had a very finite life span. The U.S. Army employed specially designed wagons on which the pontoons and other component parts were carried to the site of construction in pontoon trains.

Building a pontoon bridge is really quite simple. The first boat (pontoon) is securely anchored parallel to the shoreline and facing the current. A second pontoon is anchored and aligned next to the first, and so on, until the span of water has been covered. As the additional pontoons are added, each one is fastened to the others by interlocking the balks (crossties) with the gunwales. After this process is complete, the chess (flooring) is laid atop the pontoons. During the war, engineers usually covered the wooden flooring with dirt to protect it and to dampen the sounds of men, horses, and wagons crossing over it.

There were numerous pontoon bridges built during the Civil War, including those at Fredericksburg in December 1862, which allowed the Federals to cross the Rappahannock

and attack the Confederates on the heights beyond the city. Delay in materials reaching the site, however, allowed the Confederates time to reinforce. On June 14, 1864, Union engineers constructed a pontoon bridge 2,100 feet in length over the James River in a mere eight hours. As Union forces closed in on Savannah, Georgia, the Confederates erected a hastily built pontoon bridge over the Savannah River in the overnight hours of December 20, 1864. The bridge allowed Confederate forces to escape into South Carolina, and Major General William T. Sherman's army occupied the city essentially unchallenged.

PAUL G. PIERPAOLI JR.

See also

Engineers; Pioneers

Further Reading

Coggins, Jack. *Arms and Equipment of the Civil War.* New York: Doubleday, 1982.
Thienel, Phillip M. *Mr. Lincoln's Bridge Builders: The Right Hand of an American Genius.* Shippensburg, PA: White Mane, 2000.

Pook Turtles

See Cairo-Class River Ironclads, U.S. Navy

Pope, John

Birth Date: March 16, 1822
Death Date: September 23, 1892

Union officer. John Pope was born in Louisville, Kentucky, on March 16, 1822, but grew up in Kaskaskia, Illinois. He graduated from the U.S. Military Academy at West Point in 1842 and then served as a topographical engineer. During the Mexican-American War (1846–1848), he distinguished himself at the Battles of Monterrey and Buena Vista, earning brevets for each.

After the war, Pope carried out surveys in Minnesota and the American Southwest, winning promotion to first lieutenant in 1855. In 1856 he was promoted to captain. By the late 1850s, Pope was known as an expert horseman and an intrepid soldier. He was also known for his impetuosity and caustic personality.

When the Civil War began, Pope was commissioned a brigadier general of volunteers in June 1861. He held various district and field commands until February 1862, when he was assigned to command the Union Army of the Mississippi as a major general of volunteers.

Pope's army captured two key Confederate positions on the Mississippi River: New Madrid, Missouri, in mid-March 1862, and, with the assistance of the navy, Island No. 10 and its 5,000 defenders in early April. These successes earned him promotion to brigadier general in the regular army and a summons to Washington, D.C., to command the new Army of Virginia.

Pope led his troops in the Bull Run Campaign and in the Second Battle of Bull Run (August 29–30, 1862) but was convincingly defeated by Confederate forces led by General Robert E. Lee. Pope blamed the loss on his "unsoldierly" officers, who he claimed were more loyal to Major General George B. McClellan than to him. Nevertheless, he had conducted an orderly retreat to Washington, D.C. President Abraham Lincoln apparently agreed with his commander's assessment, writing that "Pope did well" but had been handicapped by a lack of loyalty among his subordinates. Despite this, Pope was removed from command the following month and assigned to head the Department of the Northwest, where the army had just defeated an uprising

Union major general John Pope won fame in the Western Theater. Called east to command the new Army of Virginia, his shortcomings as a commander were revealed in the Union defeat in the Second Battle of Bull Run on August 29–30, 1862. (National Archives)

by the Santee Sioux in Minnesota. A military tribunal had sentenced 303 Santees to death for their participation in the fighting. Responsibility for reviewing the sentences and carrying out the executions now fell to Pope. Although he favored executing the condemned Santees, he referred the matter to President Lincoln, who reduced the number of death sentences to 39.

Impressed by Pope's leadership, Lieutenant General Ulysses S. Grant created the Division of Missouri in 1864 that extended Pope's command westward to the Rocky Mountains. During the next three years, Pope vigorously prosecuted efforts to contain Native Americans in the West. He subsequently held a Reconstruction command in the South.

In 1870, Pope returned to the Department of Missouri and played a significant role in the Indian Wars on the Great Plains and in Texas. Promoted to major general in 1882, he assumed command of the Division of the Pacific. In 1886 he retired from the army. Pope died in Sandusky, Ohio, on September 23, 1892.

JIM PIECUCH

See also

Bull Run, Second Battle of; Connor, Patrick Edward; Island No. 10, Battle of; Jackson, Thomas Jonathan; Longstreet, James; McClellan, George Brinton; Sand Creek Massacre

Further Reading

Cozzens, Peter. *General John Pope: A Life for the Nation.* Urbana: University of Illinois Press, 2000.

Utley, Robert M. *Frontier Regulars: The United States Army and the Indian, 1866–1890.* New York: Macmillan, 1973.

Warner, Ezra J. *Generals in Blue: Lives of the Union Commanders.* Baton Rouge: Louisiana State University Press, 2006.

Pope's Run, Battle of

See Head of Passes, Battle of

Poplar Springs Church, Battle of

See Peebles' Farm, Battle of

Popular Sovereignty

Political doctrine that holds that the government derives its authority or right to govern from the people and that the people are the source of all political power. This doctrine is clearly reflected in the Declaration of Independence (1776). In the decades prior to the Civil War, popular sovereignty also came to be associated with the idea that the people of a particular federal territory should be able to decide for themselves whether or not slavery would be allowed there. This, of course, proved to be a major causative factor of the Civil War.

The U.S. Constitution of 1787 had left the issue and the future of slavery ambiguous, and it was unclear what the status of slavery would be during the process of admitting new territories and states to the Union. The 1820 Missouri Compromise established that slavery would be prohibited in the former Louisiana Territory north of the southern boundary of Missouri (36 degrees, 30 minutes) except in Missouri itself, where it already existed.

In 1854, Illinois Democratic senator Stephen Douglas sought to modify the Missouri Compromise to secure Southern support for a bill creating the Kansas and Nebraska Territories in the area west of Iowa and Missouri. To secure Southern support for a bill that was of little benefit or interest

to the South, Douglas proposed repealing the Missouri Compromise and including a popular sovereignty clause allowing the people of the new territories to decide for themselves if they would allow slavery, creating the prospect that more slave states might join the Union. Douglas's bill, however, reopened the divisive issue of slavery, which had already caused the Whig Party to collapse and, owing to strong Northern opposition and outrage over the bill, provoked the creation of the antislavery Republican Party in 1854, which was committed to restoring the Missouri Compromise.

In any case, in addition to strong Southern Democratic support in the House (57 votes in favor out of 59), enough Northern Democrats (44 out of 86 in the House) supported the Kansas-Nebraska Act that it passed the House of Representatives by a vote of 113 to 100 and the Senate by a vote of 37 to 14. President Franklin Pierce signed the bill into law on May 30, 1854. The Kansas-Nebraska Act, however, led to violence in the territory of Kansas (so-called Bleeding Kansas) between proslavery and antislavery forces, resulting in the deaths of more than 200 people by the end of 1856. The legacy of the Kansas-Nebraska Act is that it badly divided the nation, pushing the United States ever closer to civil war, and also fueled the rise of Abraham Lincoln as a major political figure, owing to his opposition to the act. Indeed, he unsuccessfully challenged Douglas for his Senate seat in 1858, and the resulting seven debates between the men catapulted Lincoln to prominence and prestige among Republicans in the North, which led to his election to the presidency in 1860.

STEFAN M. BROOKS

See also

Bleeding Kansas; Douglas, Stephen Arnold; Kansas; Kansas-Nebraska Act; Lincoln, Abraham; Missouri Compromise; Nebraska Territory; Republican Party; Slavery

Further Reading

Etcheson, Nicole. *Bleeding Kansas: Contested Liberty in the Civil War Era.* Lawrence: University Press of Kansas, 2004.

Johnson, Paul. *Civil War America, 1850–1870.* New York: Harper Perennial, 2011.

Porter, David Dixon
Birth Date: June 8, 1813
Death Date: February 13, 1891

Union naval officer. Born in Chester, Pennsylvania, on June 8, 1813, David Dixon Porter was the 3rd of 10 children of Commodore David Porter, who had distinguished himself in the War of 1812. David Dixon Porter's adopted brother was David G. Farragut. Porter first went to sea with his father at age 10. After brief service as a midshipman in the Mexican Navy serving under his father, during which he was wounded and was briefly a prisoner of war of the Spanish, Porter joined the U.S. Navy as a midshipman in February 1829. He became a passed midshipman in July 1835 and made lieutenant in February 1841. Routine assignments included service in the Mediterranean.

Porter distinguished himself during the Mexican-American War (1846–1848), especially in operations against Tabasco. Frustrated by the slow rate of advancement in the U.S. Navy, he took leave of absence to captain merchant vessels.

Returning to duty with the navy in 1855, Porter received command of the steamer *Supply* and then served ashore at the Portsmouth Navy Yard (1857–1860). He was on the verge of a second leave of absence when the secession crisis occurred.

On April 1, 1861, Porter received command of the powerful side-wheel frigate *Powhatan*. He circumvented both Secretary of the Navy Gideon Welles and commander of the Brooklyn Navy Yard Captain Andrew H. Foote in carrying out Secretary of War William H. Seward's plan to relieve Fort Pickens in Florida. Despite having disobeyed orders, Porter received promotion to commander on April 22.

The *Powhatan* then conducted operations in the Gulf of Mexico. Early in 1862, Porter convinced Welles and Assistant Secretary of the Navy Gustavus V. Fox that bombardment of the two Confederate forts on the lower Mississippi by a flotilla of mortar boats would be essential to the capture of the port of New Orleans.

Receiving command of the mortar flotilla under the overall command of his adopted brother and commander of the West Gulf Blockading Squadron Flag Officer Farragut, Porter carried out a six-day bombardment of Forts Jackson and St. Philip, which failed to reduce the forts. Farragut then ran past the forts with the ships of his squadron, while Porter supplied gunfire support. With the two forts then cut off by the Union ships and troops, Porter took their surrender on April 28.

On October 15, 1862, Porter, now an acting rear admiral, assumed command of the Mississippi Squadron. Naval activity then sharply increased with the initiation of joint operations against Vicksburg. In January 1863 Porter helped secure Arkansas Post. He worked closely and effectively with Major General Ulysses S. Grant and Major General William T. Sherman and was rewarded for his role in the surrender

Rear Admiral David D. Porter was one of the most important naval leaders of the Civil War. Opinionated, outspoken, and egotistical, Porter commanded the Mississippi Squadron and then the North Atlantic Blockading Squadron. He worked effectively with generals Ulysses S. Grant and William T. Sherman in operations against Vicksburg and with Brigadier General Alfred Terry against Fort Fisher. (National Archives)

of Vicksburg with advancement to permanent rear admiral over many other more senior officers, with date of rank of July 4, 1863.

In the spring of 1864, Porter commanded the naval component of the Red River Campaign, supporting army troops ashore under Major General Nathaniel P. Banks in an effort to capture Shreveport. Banks and Porter did not get along, and low water levels in the Red plagued Porter's operations. Despite myriad problems, Porter succeeded in extricating his ships and was not blamed for the fiasco, one of the great military blunders of the war.

In September 1864 Porter assumed command of the North Atlantic Blockading Squadron, and that December he assembled the most powerful naval force to that point in U.S. history: 61 warships, including 5 ironclads, mounting a total of 635 guns for an attack on Fort Fisher in an effort to close off the port of Wilmington to Confederate blockade-runners. The initial assault went poorly, thanks to ineffective cooperation on the part of the commander of the Union Army contingent, Major General Benjamin Butler. Union general in chief Ulysses S. Grant then sacked Butler and appointed Brigadier General Alfred H. Terry, who established an excellent working relationship with Porter. In a textbook amphibious operation, Fort Fisher fell to Union army and navy contingents in January 1865. In April 1865 Porter operated on the James River, forcing the Confederate commander to scuttle his squadron there and conducting President Abraham Lincoln on a tour of Richmond.

Following the war, Porter assumed the superintendency of the Naval Academy, where he remained until 1869 and introduced extensive reforms. Promoted to vice admiral in July 1866, he was advanced to admiral in August 1870. He then served as head of the Board of Inspection until his death in Washington, D.C., on February 13, 1891.

SPENCER C. TUCKER

See also

Butler, Benjamin Franklin; Farragut, David Glasgow; Foote, Andrew Hull; Fort Fisher Campaign; Fort Hindman, Battle of; Fort Pickens, Florida; Fox, Gustavus Vasa; Grant, Ulysses Simpson; New Orleans Campaign; Red River Campaign; Seward, William Henry, Sr.; Sherman, William Tecumseh; Terry, Alfred Howe; Vicksburg Campaign, First; Vicksburg Campaign, Second; Welles, Gideon

Further Reading

Hearn, Chester. *David Dixon Porter: The Civil War Years.* Annapolis: Naval Institute Press, 1996.

Melia, Tamara M. "David Dixon Porter: Fighting Sailor." In *Captains of the Old Steam Navy,* edited by James C. Bradford, 227–249. Annapolis, MD: Naval Institute Press, 1986.

Robinson, Charles M. *Hurricane of Fire: The Union Assault on Fort Fisher.* Annapolis, MD: Naval Institute Press, 1998.

Porter, Fitz John

Birth Date: August 31, 1822
Death Date: May 21, 1901

Union officer. Fitz John Porter was born in Portsmouth, New Hampshire, on August 31, 1822. His uncle, David Porter, was a noted War of 1812 hero, while his cousin, David D. Porter, was a leading Civil War admiral. Fitz John Porter graduated from the U.S. Military Academy, West Point, in 1845 and was commissioned in the artillery. He saw service during the Mexican-American War (1846–1848), winning promotion to first lieutenant and two brevets and sustaining

a wound at Chapultepec. He then returned to West Point to teach cavalry and artillery tactics and serve as adjutant to Superintendent Robert E. Lee. Porter then transferred to the Adjutant General's Office with the staff rank of captain and in 1857 served as adjutant during the Mormon disturbances in Utah. In early 1861 when the secession crisis exploded, Porter was entrusted with a mission to remove federal troops and matériel from Texas and acquitted himself well. Although his substantive rank was still first lieutenant, in May 1861 he was appointed colonel of the new regular 15th Infantry. Porter was appointed brigadier general of volunteers in August 1861, to date from May 17.

Porter performed useful service as chief of staff in the Department of Pennsylvania. After a brief stint commanding troops in the Shenandoah Valley, he trained troops in the Washington, D.C., area. His competence brought him to the attention of Major General George B. McClellan, who made him a division commander in the Army of the Potomac.

Major General Fitz John Porter, one of the most talented Corps commanders in the Union Army, performed magnificently during the Peninsula Campaign of 1862. However competent, he was brash and outspoken to the point of arrogance. Porter's unswerving loyalty to one disgraced superior, and utter contempt for another, led to a controversial trial and dismissal from the military he had served so well. (Library of Congress)

During the Peninsula Campaign (March–July 1862), Porter participated in the successful siege of Yorktown (April 5– May 3, 1862), whereupon McClellan appointed him commander of V Corps.

On June 26, 1862, at Mechanicsville, Porter masterfully deployed his men on defensive terrain and repulsed the Confederates. The next day Porter made another determined stand at Gaines' Mill until an all-out Confederate assault finally breached his line. By July 1, 1862, however, Porter had established another strong position around Malvern Hill, which dashed Lee's hopes of a victory here. McClellan's subsequent withdrawal was left unmolested, and for Porter's sterling performance he was brevetted brigadier general in the regular army and advanced to major general of volunteers on July 4, 1862.

Within weeks, McClellan was shelved in favor of Major General John Pope. Porter, a McClellan partisan, was outspoken in his criticism of President Abraham Lincoln and utterly contemptuous of Pope. This disrespect cost Porter dearly. V Corps, although still part of the Army of the Potomac, was nevertheless ordered to support Pope's Army of Virginia. Porter fought in the most controversial engagement of his brief career, the Second Battle of Bull Run (August 29–30, 1862), which turned out to be a disaster for Pope. Ordered to attack based on a faulty understanding of Confederate dispositions, Porter, who had a much better grasp of the situation than did Pope, chose to hold his ground.

Angered by what he saw as the machinations of officers still loyal to McClellan, Pope immediately sought a scapegoat of his thrashing at Bull Run and relieved Porter on September 5, 1862, charging him with disobedience, disloyalty, and misconduct. Porter gained a brief respite when McClellan, reinstalled by Lincoln as head of the army, restored him to command. Porter was present at the Battle of Antietam (September 17, 1862) but saw no combat.

In November 1862 following McClellan's second dismissal, Porter was arrested and formally relieved of command. His court-martial, considered a mockery, took place on January 21, 1863. Porter was found guilty and dismissed from the army.

Porter spent the rest of his life trying to redeem his military reputation. Finally in 1878, a board of inquiry headed by Major General John M. Schofield not only vindicated Porter but also portrayed his refusal to advance as having saved the army from destruction. Porter's actual pardon did not occur until August 5, 1886, when President Grover Cleveland restored Porter to active duty as colonel, to rank from

May 1861. Porter was retired two days later. Throughout this struggle for vindication, Porter supported himself by holding down a variety of civilian positions, including mining surveyor in Colorado, police and public works commissioner in New York City, and receiver of the New Jersey Railroad. Porter died in Morristown, New Jersey, on May 21, 1901.

JOHN C. FREDRIKSEN

See also

Bull Run, Second Battle of; Gaines' Mill, Battle of; Malvern Hill, Battle of; McClellan, George Brinton; Mechanicsville, Battle of; Peninsula Campaign; Pope, John; Yorktown, Virginia, Siege of

Further Reading

Jermann, Donald R. *Fitz-John Porter: Scapegoat of Second Manassas.* Jefferson, NC: McFarland, 2008.
Sears, Stephen W. *To the Gates of Richmond: The Peninsula Campaign.* New York: Houghton Mifflin Harcourt, 1992.

Porter, John Luke
Birth Date: September 19, 1813
Death Date: December 14, 1893

Confederate naval constructor. Born in Portsmouth, Virginia, on September 19, 1813, John Luke Porter began studying ship design at an early age in the numerous shipyards of eastern Virginia. Following his father's death in 1831, he supported his family by working as a carpenter in local yards.

In the early 1840s, Porter moved to Pittsburgh, Pennsylvania, where he designed and built ships for the U.S. Navy. During his time at Pittsburgh, Porter produced plans for an ironclad warship, although the navy was uninterested in his proposal. In 1847 Porter failed to pass the examination for naval constructors, although he remained active in maritime construction. By 1857, he had passed the exam and received an appointment as a U.S. naval constructor.

Porter opposed secession, believing that the Confederacy could not achieve independence in the teeth of Union opposition. Despite these sentiments, he resigned his position with the U.S. Navy when his native Virginia joined the Confederacy. Shortly thereafter Porter became naval constructor at the Gosport (Norfolk) Navy Yard, which Virginia had recently seized from the U.S. Navy. Although holding this post, Porter did not receive formal appointment as the South's naval constructor until January 1864. He and his two assistants reported directly to Confederate secretary of the navy Stephen R. Mallory.

A strong believer in ironclad warships, Mallory hoped that they might be able to defeat the Union naval blockade and even carry out operations against Northern ports. In early June 1861 he directed Lieutenant John M. Brooke to design an ironclad, and Brooke soon came up with a plan for a casemated vessel with inclined sides. On June 23, Brooke, Mallory, Porter, and Chief Engineer William P. Williamson from the Gosport Navy Yard met and approved the concept. But with no engines of the size required available in the Confederacy, Williamson suggested that they employ the hull, engines, and boilers on the former U.S. steam frigate *Merrimack*. Brooke and Porter agreed, and on July 11 Mallory ordered work to go forward on rebuilding the *Merrimack* as an ironclad. The rebuilt ship was commissioned the *Virginia* on February, 17, 1862. Later Brooke and Porter quarreled over who deserved credit for this most famous of all Confederate ironclads.

Porter also designed gunboats. These, while small, rendered effective service but were employed mostly as auxiliaries. Porter is chiefly known for his ironclad designs, however. Problems abounded in Southern ironclad construction, including a lack of iron plate and an absence of reliable steam engines. Partly as a result of these problems, Mallory and Porter eventually settled on smaller shallow-draft ironclads to defend Confederate harbors and rivers. The first of these were the Porter-designed six-ship Richmond-class ironclad rams: the *Chicora, North Carolina, Palmetto State, Raleigh, Richmond,* and *Savannah.* Porter also designed the two-ship Columbia class of the *Columbia* and *Texas.* The *Tennessee,* one of the most celebrated Confederate ironclads of the war, was a modified *Columbia.* Porter also designed the *Nashville,* a side-wheeler to take advantage of available river boat machinery, and twin-screw shallow-draft ironclads. Patterned after the Richmond-class ships, these included the *Wilmington* and the Milledgeville class of four ships. Only the *Milledgeville* was ever launched, and none of the ships were ever commissioned. Other shallow-draft Porter-designed Confederate ironclads were the Albemarle class of the *Albemarle, Neuse,* and another unnamed ship never commissioned. Porter also designed a lengthened four-gun version of the Albemarle class, the *Fredericksburg,* that served in the James River flotilla. Only one ship, the *Missouri,* was completed of a Porter-designed center-wheel class of ironclads.

With opportunities for former Confederates limited after the war, Porter accepted a succession of short-term jobs until 1878, when the Norfolk Navy Yard accepted his bid for employment. By 1883, he had been made superintendent of the Norfolk County Ferries, a position that allowed him to rebuild his family's finances. Porter retired from the position in 1888 and died in Portsmouth, Virginia, on December 14, 1893.

CHARLES H. WILLIAMS AND SPENCER C. TUCKER

See also

Albemarle, CSS; Brooke, John Mercer; Hampton Roads, Battles of; Ironclads, Confederate; Mallory, Stephen Russell; Navy, Confederate; Norfolk Navy Yard; *Tennessee,* CSS; *Virginia,* CSS

Further Reading

Flanders, Alan B. *John L. Porter: Naval Constructor of Destiny.* White Stone, VA: Brandyland Publishers, 2000.
Still, William N., Jr. *Iron Afloat: The Story of the Confederate Armorclads.* Columbia: University of South Carolina Press, 1985.
Still, William N., Jr., ed. *The Confederate Navy: The Ships, Men and Organization, 1861–65.* Annapolis, MD: Naval Institute Press, 1997.

Porter, William David

Birth Date: March 10, 1809
Death Date: May 1, 1864

Union naval officer. William David Porter was born in New Orleans, Louisiana, on March 10, 1809, and raised in Chester, Pennsylvania. He was the son of the War of 1812 hero Commodore David Porter, the elder brother of future admiral David Dixon Porter, and the adoptive brother of future admiral David Glasgow Farragut. William Porter went to sea at age 12 and was appointed a midshipman on January 1, 1823. He was promoted to passed midshipman on March 29, 1829; to lieutenant on December 31, 1833; and to commander on September 14, 1855.

When the Civil War began, Porter was commanding the sloop *St. Mary's.* Ordered to St. Louis, Missouri, he served in the Western Gunboat Flotilla. Given command of the ironclad *New Era,* he renamed his ship the *Essex,* after his father's command in the War of 1812. Porter participated in the attack on Fort Henry, Tennessee, on February 6, 1862, during which the *Essex* took 15 hits from the Confederate shore battery, 1 of which penetrated the middle boiler, killing or wounding 32 men. The escaping steam scalded and nearly blinded Porter.

Porter recovered and supervised the rebuilding of his ship. He then commanded the *Essex* in an attempt to destroy the Confederate ironclad *Arkansas* at Vicksburg on July 22, 1862. The *Essex* attacked the same ship above Baton Rouge on August 6, 1862, and Porter took credit for the destruction of the *Arkansas,* although the Confederate ironclad's engines had broken down and it was scuttled by its crew.

Promoted to commodore on July 16, 1862, Porter was detached from the *Essex* and held no further commands afloat. He died of heart disease in New York City on May 1, 1864.

GARY D. JOINER

See also
Arkansas, CSS; Baton Rouge, Battle of; Farragut, David Glasgow; Fort Henry, Battle of; Mississippi River; Mississippi Squadron, U.S. Navy; Porter, David Dixon; Vicksburg Campaign, Second

Further Reading
Joiner, Gary. *Mr. Lincoln's Brown Water Navy: The Mississippi Squadron.* Lanham, MD: Rowman and Littlefield, 2007.
Shea, William L., and Terrence J. Winschel. *Vicksburg Is the Key: The Struggle for the Mississippi River.* Lincoln: University of Nebraska Press, 2003.
West, Richard S., Jr. *The Second Admiral: A Life of David Dixon Porter.* New York: Coward-McCann, 1937.

Port Gibson, Battle of
Event Date: May 1, 1863

Engagement during the Second Vicksburg Campaign (April 1–July 4, 1863). The Battle of Port Gibson helped to preserve the crucial beachhead of Union troops south of Vicksburg and marked the beginning of an epic march that would ultimately secure Union control of the Mississippi River and split the Confederacy in two.

After failing to capture the important Confederate stronghold of Vicksburg through various operations, in March 1863 Union major general Ulysses S. Grant transported his Army of the Tennessee into Louisiana in an attempt to attack the city from the south. On April 30, 1863, the 24,000 men of Major General John A. McClernand's XIII Corps and Major General James B. McPherson's XVII Corps of Grant's army crossed the Mississippi River by an amphibious landing at Bruinsburg, Mississippi.

Union skirmishing with Confederate outposts near the vital crossroads of Port Gibson, located only 22 miles southwest of Vicksburg and 10 miles east of the Mississippi River, began after midnight on the morning of May 1. At 5:30 a.m., advance Union elements moved toward the town and encountered a small Confederate force commanded by Brigadier General John S. Bowen, who deployed

Brigadier General Martin E. Green's brigade to defend the Rodney Road and Brigadier General Edward Tracy's brigade to protect the Bruinsburg Road. The dense undergrowth and deep ravines outside the town were of great advantage to the defending Confederates and helped offset their severe numerical disadvantage. McClernand divided his XIII Corps along the two separate roads, with Brigadier General Peter J. Osterhaus's division advancing along the Bruinsburg Road as a diversion while the remaining three divisions under Brigadier Generals Eugene A. Carr, Alvin P. Hovey, and Andrew J. Smith attacked along the Rodney Road.

General Tracy's Confederate brigade delayed Osterhaus's division in fierce fighting along the Bruinsburg Road until midmorning, when Tracy was killed and replaced by Colonel Isham Garrott and the outnumbered Confederates were forced to fall back. Simultaneously along the Rodney Road, overwhelming Union numbers slowly drove Green's brigade back until two Confederate brigades under Brigadier General William E. Baldwin and Colonel Francis M. Cockrell arrived at around 10:00 a.m. Green's re-formed brigade redeployed to aid Tracy's brigade along the Bruinsburg Road, while Cockrell's Missouri Brigade unleashed a vicious counterattack that temporarily drove the Federals back along the Rodney Road.

Union superior numbers told, however. Reinforced by Major General John A. Logan's division of McPherson's XVII Corps, the Federals repulsed the assault and finally drove Bowen's exhausted command from the field at around 5:30 p.m. The Battle of Port Gibson cost the Confederates 60 killed, 340 wounded, and 387 missing of 8,000 men engaged as well as four cannon from the Botetourt Artillery in Virginia. Grant reported his own losses as 131 killed, 719 wounded, and 25 missing out of 23,000 men engaged. Although limited in scale, the Battle of Port Gibson enabled Grant to press his invasion into the heart of Mississippi, which would lead to four other battles in the next two months, all Union victories, and the eventual surrender of Vicksburg on July 4, 1863.

STEVEN NATHANIEL DOSSMAN

See also
Bowen, John Stevens; Grant, Ulysses Simpson; McClernand, John Alexander; McPherson, James Birdseye; Vicksburg Campaign, Second

Further Reading
Arnold, James R. *Grant Wins the War: Decision at Vicksburg.* New York: Wiley, 1997.

Ballard, Michael B. *Vicksburg: The Campaign That Opened the Mississippi.* Chapel Hill: University of North Carolina Press, 2004.

Grabau, Warren E. *Ninety-Eight Days: A Geographer's View of the Vicksburg Campaign.* Knoxville: University of Tennessee Press, 2000.

Port Hudson, Louisiana, Action at
Event Date: March 14, 1863

Engagement during the Union effort to control the Mississippi River. Following the Union capture of New Orleans in April 1862, Vicksburg, Mississippi, and Port Hudson were the only remaining Confederate Mississippi River strongholds. Securing both of these was critical to the Union strategy of controlling the Mississippi and dividing the Confederacy. Situated on the river some 25 miles above Baton Rouge, Louisiana, Port Hudson was a formidable bastion. Like Vicksburg, some 110 miles north on the river, Port Hudson was situated on high bluffs overlooking a sharp 150-degree bend of the river and was surrounded by bayous.

Following the loss of New Orleans, the Confederates strengthened Port Hudson, placing 15 heavy guns on the river bluffs at the bend and south of the city on the east bank. Major General Franklin Gardner commanded some 16,000 defenders.

In early March 1863, Union major general Nathaniel P. Banks and West Gulf Blockading Squadron commander Rear Admiral David G. Farragut agreed to mount a joint attack on Port Hudson, with Banks providing 25,000 troops from Baton Rouge. Banks departed on March 7. At Prophet's Island, five miles south of Port Hudson, Farragut assembled a powerful force, including the side-wheeler frigate *Mississippi;* the steam sloops *Hartford, Richmond,* and *Monongahela;* and the gunboats *Albatross, Genessee,* and *Kineo.* Farragut planned to bring the shore batteries under fire from mortar boats and the ironclad *Essex* at Prophet's Island as the Union ships ran past them.

Farragut coupled each of his larger ships with a lighter gunboat lashed on the port aft quarter. He reasoned that because the Confederate shore batteries were on the east bank, the larger ships would protect the smaller ones, and should one of the two ships become disabled, the other could assist it. The exception was the side-wheeler *Mississippi,* which brought up the rear alone. To provide additional firepower, Farragut ordered boat howitzers mounted on the rigging platforms of the mizzenmasts of the sloops.

The Union ships made their run on the night of March 14 but discovered an unwelcome surprise in the form of a series of locomotive headlights that the Confederates had placed along the eastern bank. Lighted, these silhouetted the ships and allowed the shore gunners to deliver an accurate fire. Although the first two Union ships, the lashed-together *Hartford* and *Albatross,* made it past safely, the next two—the *Richmond* and *Genessee*—did not fare as well. A Confederate shot struck the *Richmond,* piercing its steam drum and causing it to drift back out of the battle. In the third pair of ships, the *Kineo,* secured to the port side of the *Monongahela,* took a shot that lodged between its rudderpost and sternpost. The *Monongahela* also had its rudder damaged, and the two ships then went aground. Both ships got free but then drifted back downriver out of the battle. The last ship in line, the *Mississippi,* commanded by Captain Melancton Smith, ran aground while approaching Thomas Point. Unable to free his ship, which then came under heavy Confederate fire, Smith ordered the crew to abandon ship. The men first spiked the guns, destroyed the engines, and then set the ship on fire. It finally drifted downstream completely ablaze before blowing up. Out of its 297 crewmen, 25 were killed and 39 were reported missing. Only the *Hartford* and *Albatross* reached Waterloo, Louisiana, above Port Hudson.

Much of the responsibility for the failure of this enterprise rested with the dilatory Banks. Although his forces probed the Confederate defenses, they failed to mount an attack in sufficient force and timed to occupy the Confederate gunners. Learning of Farragut's failure, Banks then called off his own attack. The failed operation clearly showed the necessity of more effective army-navy cooperation.

SPENCER C. TUCKER

See also

Banks, Nathaniel Prentice; Farragut, David Glasgow; Gardner, Franklin; Port Hudson, Louisiana, Siege of

Further Reading

Hewitt, Lawrence L. *Port Hudson: Confederate Bastion on the Mississippi.* Baton Rouge: Louisiana State University Press, 1994.

Tucker, Spencer C. *Blue and Gray Navies: The Civil War Afloat.* Annapolis, MD: Naval Institute Press, 2006.

U.S. Navy Department. *Official Records of the Union and Confederate Navies in the War of the Rebellion,* Series 1, Vols. 19 and 20. Washington, DC: U.S. Government Printing Office, 1896–1905.

Union captain Edmund C. Bainbridge's artillery battery at Port Hudson, Louisiana, during the Union siege, May 21–July 9, 1863. The Confederates surrendered Port Hudson on the Mississippi River after the Union victory at Vicksburg. The Confederacy was then split in two. (National Archives)

Port Hudson, Louisiana, Siege of
Start Date: May 21, 1863
End Date: July 9, 1863

Engagement during the Union effort to control the Mississippi River. Taking the Confederate strongholds of Vicksburg and Port Hudson on the Mississippi and splitting the Confederacy along that river continued to be a major Union war aim. Some 25 miles above Baton Rouge, Louisiana, Port Hudson was situated on high bluffs overlooking a sharp 150-degree bend of the river and was surrounded by bayous. In May, Major General Franklin Gardner commanded some 7,500 men manning defensive works that included some 15 heavy guns controlling the river approaches and an equal number on the land side.

Following an abortive effort in March 1863 that saw the destruction of the U.S. Navy side-wheeler frigate *Mississippi*

during Rear Admiral David G. Farragut's passage of Port Hudson, unsupported by Union troops under Major General Nathaniel P. Banks, Union forces tried again in May. As a preliminary to a ground assault by Banks's 30,000-man Army of the Gulf, U.S. Navy ships in the river shelled Port Hudson (May 8–10). Banks then closed off Port Hudson from the land side on May 21.

Banks planned a ground attack supported by the large guns aboard the Union ships in the river, but the inept Union general mounted a series of uncoordinated attacks that did not make full use of his available manpower. The Union assault opened at dawn on May 27 with an attack on the Confederate left, above Port Hudson. The assault included two regiments of African American troops from Louisiana in the first employment of such troops by the Union in the war. The attack failed. At about 2:15 p.m., the Union left attacked. It and a still later advance by the Union center were rebuffed. The attackers sustained nearly 2,000 casualties, to only 250–275 for the defenders.

Claiming insufficient resources, Banks then settled for a siege, during the course of which he received some 10,000 reinforcements. He was determined to try again. On the morning of June 13, Union troops and ships in the river opened a furious bombardment of the Confederate works, firing shells at the rate of about one per second. After an hour the firing ceased, and Banks sent a note to Gardner demanding his surrender. Although his men were low on ammunition and short of supplies, Gardner refused. Banks ordered the shelling resumed and planned an assault for the next day in the form of a probe of the Confederate right, with the main attack on the center.

Early the next morning, a Union division assaulted the large fort in the Confederate center known as the Priest Cap. Although some of the Union troops breached the Confederate lines, they lacked sufficient strength to exploit the situation. Repeated follow-on attacks also failed, with the Union suffering as many as 1,805 casualties. With his subordinate commanders objecting to a continuation, Banks agreed to a halt.

Meanwhile, the Union forces employed zigzag trenches to snake closer to the Confederate positions. They also tried mining the Confederate lines, but the defenders sank a countermine and used explosives to collapse the Union shaft. The distances were sufficiently short for both sides to employ hand grenades.

Banks planned a third attack for July 7, but bad weather caused it to be postponed. News was then received of the surrender of Vicksburg to Union forces on July 4. This event rendered Port Hudson untenable, and Gardner opened negotiations on July 8 and formally surrendered the next day. The siege had lasted 48 days. Although some Confederates escaped through Union lines on the night of July 8–9, about 6,400 surrendered. The Confederates had suffered 146 killed and 447 wounded. Operations at Port Hudson claimed Union losses of more than 708 dead, 3,336 wounded, and 319 missing. Another 4,000 to 5,000 were incapacitated by heatstroke or sickness. Throughout the siege, Union ships and mortar boats had provided effective gunfire support.

The entire Mississippi was now under Union control, and the Confederacy was split. A week later, a steamer from St. Louis arrived at New Orleans with a cargo of midwestern products. President Abraham Lincoln summed up the long effort to gain control of the river: "The Father of Waters again goes unvexed to the sea."

SPENCER C. TUCKER

See also

Banks, Nathaniel Prentice; Farragut, David Glasgow; Gardner, Franklin; Port Hudson, Louisiana, Action at; Vicksburg Campaign, Second

Further Reading

Hewitt, Lawrence L. *Port Hudson: Confederate Bastion on the Mississippi.* Baton Rogue: Louisiana State University Press, 1994.

Milligan, John D. *Gunboats down the Mississippi.* New York: Arno, 1980.

Tucker, Spencer C. *Blue and Gray Navies: The Civil War Afloat.* Annapolis, MD: Naval Institute Press, 2006.

Port Republic, Battle of
Event Date: June 9, 1862

Sixth and final battle of Major General Thomas J. "Stonewall" Jackson's Shenandoah Valley Campaign (May–June 1862). At the same time that Major General John C. Frémont's troops moved from the northwest toward Port Republic via Cross Keys, Brigadier General James Shields's division of Major General Irwin McDowell's command was crossing the Blue Ridge Mountains from the east. The two Union generals hoped to trap Jackson's force between them.

While Major General Richard S. Ewell positioned his men near Cross Keys to block Frémont's advance, on June 7, 1862, Jackson placed his own troops on high ground just north of Port Republic and the confluence of the South Fork of the Shenandoah with the South River. From Conrad's Store, Shields sent two brigades to probe Jackson's defenses at Port Republic. Shields also appealed to Frémont for cooperation.

The next morning, Sunday, June 8, Union troops reached the Confederate lines, and Jackson soon learned that Union troops had forded the South River and were in the town. Jackson and his staff rode hard for the North River Bridge. He got across it just in time; two officers who brought up the rear were captured. With a little more vigor on the part of the Federals, Jackson might have been taken as well.

Jackson now ordered his artillery to fire into the Federals while Confederate infantry moved forward to clear them from Port Republic. As Jackson's men accomplished this, they could hear distant artillery fire from the Battle of Cross Keys in which Ewell was beating back Frémont.

That night Jackson ordered Ewell to leave only the brigades of Brigadier General Isaac R. Trimble and Colonel John M. Patton at Cross Keys and move the rest of his men to Port Republic. This would give Jackson four brigades to attack Shields's force. Jackson hoped to defeat Shields quickly and that same morning turn and complete the destruction of Frémont. Ewell set his men in motion to join Jackson very early on June 9.

Also early on June 9, Jackson moved his main body from high ground north of Port Republic, across the North River Bridge, and through the town. At 7:00 a.m., Jackson ordered an attack. While he was not certain of Union strength, he was reassured by the fact that Ewell was marching to join him. Jackson also believed that he had to dispatch Shields's troops before Frémont learned of the weak Confederate front at Cross Keys.

As Brigadier General Charles S. Winder's Stonewall Brigade advanced through wheat fields toward the Union lines, it came under heavy Union fire. Opposing the Confederates were only 3,000 well-positioned troops under Brigadier General E. B. Tyler, who had positioned 6 of his 16 guns on high ground to the Union left. Their fire exacted a heavy toll on the Confederates.

A bottleneck had developed at the temporary bridge built by the Confederates across the South River. Because of this, the Stonewall Brigade now found itself virtually alone. With all chance of a dual victory lost and his situation now desperate, Jackson tried to hurry units forward. He also sent orders to Ewell to make haste and directed Trimble at Cross Keys to come up through Port Republic and burn the North River Bridge behind him so that Frémont could not join the action.

Shelled to a halt, the Stonewall Brigade was just managing to hold on when Brigadier General Richard Taylor's brigade arrived. Taylor's lead regiment joined the Stonewall Brigade in the wheat fields. Taylor then attacked the battery on the Union left that was exacting such a toll. Meanwhile, out of ammunition, the brigade broke, and many of its men streamed to the rear. At this critical juncture, Ewell arrived with a brigade and blocked the Union advance, although at some cost. At the same time, Taylor's men struck the Union left flank. As the Union troops attempted to wheel to engage Taylor, three more of Ewell's regiments arrived and went into action. Now outnumbered three to one, Shields's troops were soon in full retreat.

It was then 11:00 a.m. Jackson's hopes of pursuit were dashed by the fact that Tyler's men had retreated in good order, and Frémont was to his rear. Indeed, Frémont had finally come up and ordered his artillery to shell the field, although he did not attempt an attack.

Union casualties in the Battle of Port Republic totaled 1,108 men, most of them in the retreat, including 558 prisoners. Jackson's losses were also heavy at more than 800, the most he had suffered in battle thus far.

That afternoon, Jackson put his army in motion toward Brown's Gap by a path beyond the range of Frémont's guns. At the same time, President Abraham Lincoln ordered Shields and Frémont to withdraw. Soon Jackson slipped his men out of the Shenandoah Valley in trains to Richmond in order to assist General Robert E. Lee in the Peninsula Campaign (March–July 1862).

SPENCER C. TUCKER

See also

Ashby, Turner; Cross Keys, Battle of; Davis, Jefferson Finis; Ewell, Richard Stoddart; Frémont, John Charles; Jackson, Thomas Jonathan; Lee, Robert Edward; Lincoln, Abraham; McClellan, George Brinton; McDowell, Irvin; Shields, James; Taylor, Richard; Trimble, Isaac Ridgeway; Winder, Charles Sidney

Further Reading

Collins, Darrell L. *Jackson's Valley Campaign: The Battles of Cross Keys and Port Republic, June 8–9, 1862.* Lynchburg, VA: H. E. Howard, 1993.

Tanner, Robert G. *Stonewall in the Valley: Thomas J. "Stonewall" Jackson's Shenandoah Valley Campaign, Spring 1862.* Garden City, NY: Doubleday, 1976.

Port Royal Sound, Battle of
Start Date: November 5, 1861
End Date: November 7, 1861

Union naval attack on the South Carolina coast. Following their capture of Hatteras Island, Union forces, now under Captain Samuel F. Du Pont, prepared to assault Port Royal, South Carolina. Reflecting the strength of the Confederate defenses, the force assembled for the attack on Port Royal was considerably larger than that employed against Hatteras. On October 29, 1861, Du Pont, flying his flag in the screw frigate *Wabash* (44 guns), departed Hampton Roads with 50 ships, the largest task force under single command to that point in U.S. history. The day before, he had sent on ahead to Tybee Bar off Savannah 25 sloops converted into coal ships for the squadron, escorted by the sailing sloop *Vandalia*. Du Pont's task force transported 16,000 troops commanded by Brigadier General Thomas W. Sherman. The Northern press reported the assembly of the expeditionary force, and Southern authorities had a good idea of its intended target.

On November 1, the Union expeditionary force was struck by a severe storm as it approached Port Royal. Near hurricane-force winds scattered the ships, and the mission appeared in jeopardy. But the wind soon died, and the ships gradually rendezvoused off Port Royal. Two transports had been lost, but all aboard except seven marines were saved.

On the morning of November 4, the *Wabash* and 25 other ships arrived off the bar, 10 miles east of Port Royal. Other ships soon came up, and Du Pont decided to proceed. The Confederates had removed the navigation buoys, but Union crews quickly located the channel and replaced the buoys. Du Pont then ordered in his lighter gunboats and transports. The gunboats drove off three small Confederate gunboats under Flag Officer Josiah Tattnall, escorted the transports into the roadstead beyond range of fire from the Confederate forts, and then anchored for the night.

Two Confederate earthworks, Fort Beauregard on the southern tip of Phillips Island at Bay Point and Fort Walker on the northern end of Hilton Head Island, guarded the harbor entrance. Together they mounted 43 guns. Unfortunately for the Confederates, the 2.2-mile width of the entrance of the inlet precluded effective artillery coverage.

The next morning under the supervision of Commander John Rodgers, four of the Union gunboats conducted a reconnaissance in force, drawing fire from the forts to ascertain their strength. Then, with pilots having determined that there was sufficient water for the *Wabash* to cross the bar, Du Pont ordered in the flagship, followed by the side-wheeler frigate *Susquehanna,* the steam warships *Atlantic* and *Vanderbilt,* and the transports.

The original plan had been for a joint army-navy attack, but with significant army equipment lost in the storm, Du Pont decided on a naval effort alone. Because of this and the estimate that it would take at least several days to reduce the forts from long range, despite the risk of grounding, the Union warships would engage the forts at close range.

Because the distance between Forts Beauregard and Walker precluded engaging both simultaneously, Du Pont decided to attack one at a time. Fort Walker, regarded as the more powerful, was the first. It mounted 23 guns, but only 13 of these were on the sea face. Fort Beauregard contained 20 guns; 13 commanded the water approaches, but only 7 faced the channel.

At about 9:00 a.m., Tattnall steamed out with his small flotilla to exchange long-range fire with the Union ships. He then retired, followed by some Union ships, which also dueled with the Confederate shore batteries for about 45 minutes, with little consequence for either side. Then at 3:30 p.m., Du Pont ordered a signal hoisted for the ships to get under way for the attack. As the ships stood in, both the *Wabash* and the *Susquehanna* grounded on Fishing Rip Shoals. It took two hours to get the big ships free, forcing Du Pont to call off the attack. The following day was too windy, leading to another postponement.

At 8:30 a.m. on November 7, the Union ships again got under way, and an hour later Du Pont in the *Wabash* led nine warships into Port Royal Sound. The ships kept in mid-channel and exchanged long-range fire with both forts until they were well past them. The ships then turned south and reversed course, heading southeast close by Fort Walker on its northern face. This circular plan of attack was similar to that employed by Union forces in the successful action at Hatteras. Meanwhile, five Union gunboats interposed themselves northwest of the circling larger Union ships to keep at bay Tattnall's flotilla of seven small Confederate gunboats in the upper harbor.

The action began at 9:26 a.m. Passing through the channel, the ships turned in succession according to plan, passing 800 yards from Fort Walker. They then circled and turned to midchannel, again following it in while engaging both forts at long range before turning south. The second Union pass occurred at only 600 yards from Fort Walker. Meanwhile, the inexperienced Confederate gunners found it difficult to hit the moving Union ships. Fire from Fort Walker steadily diminished, and by the time the *Wabash* was in position to commence fire for a third time with its starboard guns against the fort, return fire had entirely ceased, and the engagement was over.

At 11:15 a.m., it was clear that the Confederates had abandoned the works. Du Pont then sent Commander John Rodgers ashore under a flag of truce, and at 2:20 p.m. Rodgers raised a Union flag over the deserted Confederate works. Du Pont then ordered signals hoisted to bring up the transports and sent Commander C. R. P. Rodgers ashore with marines and seamen. By nightfall a brigade was ashore, and Fort Walker was in Union hands.

During the engagement, all but three of Fort Walker's guns on the water side had been dismounted or otherwise put out of action. Du Pont had proven that the best defense against an enemy battery was an accurate and high volume of fire; the *Wabash* alone had fired 880 rounds, including grapeshot. Although the Union ships had been hit, the Confederate gunners tended to fire high, and most of the damage was aloft and not of consequence. Aboard the ships, 8 men

ATTACK ON PORT ROYAL, NOVEMBER 7, 1861

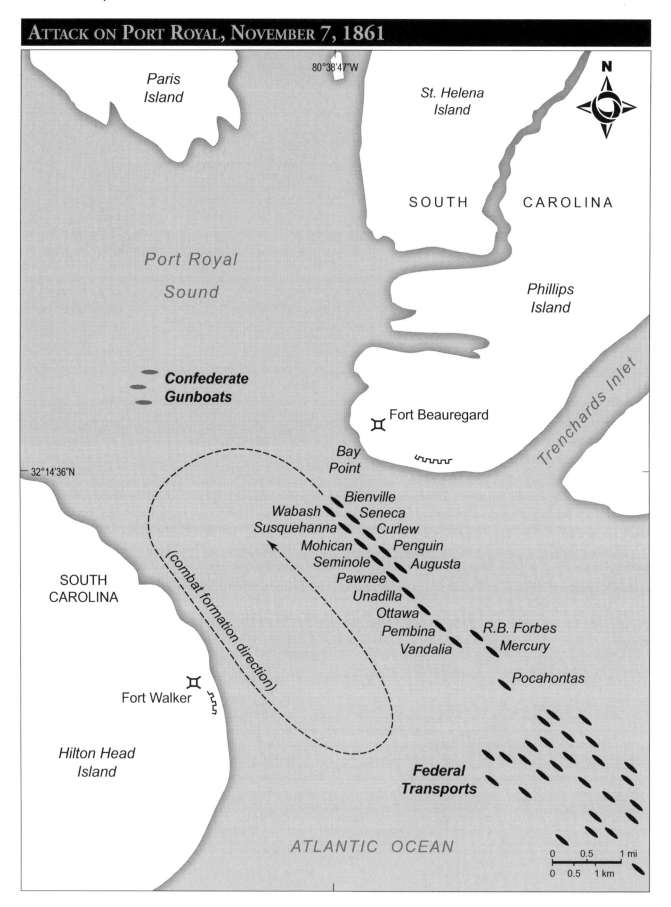

Paris
Island

80°38'47"W

St. Helena
Island

N

SOUTH   CAROLINA

Port Royal
Sound

Phillips
Island

Trenchards Inlet

Confederate
Gunboats

Fort Beauregard

Bay
Point

32°14'36"N

Bienville
Wabash   Seneca
Susquehanna   Curlew
Mohican   Penguin
Seminole   Augusta
Pawnee
Unadilla
Ottawa
Pembina   R.B. Forbes
Vandalia   Mercury

Pocahontas

(combat formation direction)

SOUTH
CAROLINA

Fort Walker

Hilton Head
Island

Federal
Transports

ATLANTIC OCEAN

0   0.5   1 mi
0   0.5   1 km

had been killed. Another 23 were wounded, 6 of these seriously. Confederate losses were 11 killed and 48 wounded. Tattnall's gunboats had been unable to intervene, although they did rescue some of the fleeing defenders from Hilton Head Island and ferry them to the mainland.

Immediately after the situation at Fort Walker had been decided, Du Pont ordered some of his ships to reconnoiter Fort Beauregard and prevent the Confederates from ferrying men and equipment from that place. Near sunset, lookouts reported that the Confederate flag had been hauled down, and Fort Beauregard was deserted. Early the next morning, a Union landing party hoisted the U.S. flag there as well. Du Pont then turned over both forts to Sherman. Fort Walker was renamed Fort Welles, while Fort Beauregard became Fort Seward.

The triumph at Port Royal was an important event, preceding any major battlefield victory for the Union Army and coming immediately on the heels of another land defeat, at Ball's Bluff on October 21. Port Royal's deep harbor provided an ideal base for extended South Atlantic Blockading Squadron operations and was soon a major naval station and supply depot. Many in the North now came to believe that steam warships could defeat all forts. This mistaken belief became an important element of future Union naval strategy. At the same time, General Robert E. Lee, given charge of reorganizing the Confederacy's South Atlantic defenses, within weeks ordered the abandonment of a number of scattered Confederate coastal positions and the withdrawal of their defenders beyond the range of Union naval guns, except at Charleston and Savannah, the defenses of which were strengthened. The Confederates thus shifted from a perimeter defense to mobile defense based on interior lines and relying on the railroads to concentrate against any major Union amphibious operation.

SPENCER C. TUCKER

See also
Ball's Bluff, Battle of; Du Pont, Samuel Francis; Lee, Robert Edward; Rodgers, John, Jr.; Sherman, Thomas West; Tattnall, Josiah

Further Reading
Browning, Robert M., Jr. *Success Is All That Was Expected: The South Atlantic Blockading Squadron during the Civil War.* Dulles, VA: Brassey's, 2002.
Tucker, Spencer C. *Blue and Gray Navies: The Civil War Afloat.* Annapolis, MD: Naval Institute Press, 2006.
U.S. Navy Department. *Official Records of the Union and Confederate Navies in the War of the Rebellion*, Series 1, Vol. 12. Washington, DC: U.S. Government Printing Office, 1901.

Posey, Carnot
Birth Date: August 5, 1818
Death Date: November 13, 1863

Confederate officer. Carnot Posey was born on August 5, 1818, in Wilkinson County, Mississippi. He earned a law degree from the University of Virginia. Upon his return to his family's plantation, Posey began a legal practice in Woodville, Mississippi. In 1846 at the start of the Mexican-American War, he became a first lieutenant in Colonel Jefferson Davis's 1st Mississippi Rifles. An intrepid soldier, Posey sustained a wound at the Battle of Buena Vista (February 23, 1847). After his return to Mississippi, he supervised his plantation and practiced law. From 1857 to 1861, he served as the U.S. district attorney for southern Mississippi.

After the start of the Civil War, Posey was commissioned a captain on May 21 but quickly was made colonel of the 16th Mississippi Infantry. Sent to Virginia, he led this regiment capably in the First Battle of Bull Run (July 21, 1861); the Battle of Ball's Bluff (October 21); the Battle of Cross Keys (June 8, 1862), when he was wounded in the chest and right arm; the Second Battle of Bull Run (August 29–30, 1862); the Battle of Harpers Ferry (September 12–15, 1862); and the Battle of Antietam (September 17, 1862). On November 1, 1862, Posey was advanced to brigadier general and given charge of a brigade in Major General Richard H. Anderson's division in the Army of Northern Virginia. Posey fought at the Battle of Chancellorsville (May 1–4, 1863) and the Battle of Gettysburg (July 1–3, 1863).

During the Second Battle of Bristoe Station (October 14, 1863), Posey sustained a nonlethal wound to the left thigh from a shell fragment. He was first taken to Culpeper, but infection set in, and he became gravely ill. Sent to Charlottesville, Posey died there on November 13, 1863.

PAUL G. PIERPAOLI JR.

See also
Anderson, Richard Heron; Antietam, Battle of; Ball's Bluff, Battle of; Bristoe Station, Second Battle of; Bull Run, First Battle of; Bull Run, Second Battle of; Chancellorsville, Battle of; Cross Keys, Battle of

Further Reading
Eicher, John H., and David J. Eicher. *Civil War High Commands.* Stanford, CA: Stanford University Press, 2001.
Warner, Ezra J. *Generals in Gray: Lives of the Confederate Commanders.* Baton Rouge: Louisiana State University Press, 2006.

Potomac, Union Army of the

Preeminent Union military force in the eastern theater. On July 25, 1861, the core of the Army of the Potomac was formed when the Departments of Northeastern Virginia and Washington were merged to create the Division of the Potomac. On August 17 the division was expanded to create the Department of the Potomac, the major field force in what would be the Army of the Potomac. Major General George B. McClellan became the department and the army's first commander and remained commander until November 1862. Thereafter, the army's commanders included Major Generals Ambrose Burnside (November 1862–January 1863), Joseph Hooker (January–June 1863), and George Meade (June 1863–June 1865). Major General John G. Parke commanded on occasion during Meade's absences. The army initially consisted of 22 brigades, but in October 1861 McClellan reorganized it into 18 divisions. Eventually McClellan divided the army into corps. Burnside employed an organization based on Grand Divisions. Myriad other organizational changes were carried out between March 1862 and June 1865. Some were instigated by Washington, while others were effected by the commanders themselves.

The principal missions of the Army of the Potomac included the defense of Washington, D.C., and areas north of Virginia; the seizure of the Confederate capital at Richmond; and the destruction of the Confederate Army of Northern Virginia.

The Army of the Potomac—at times numbering more than 100,000 men—typically required approximately 668 tons of supplies each day and normally carried with it 4,204 tons of supplies in 3,503 wagons. Wagons usually ran continuously to meet supply demands.

The Army of the Potomac fought many battles and waged numerous campaigns beginning with the Peninsula Campaign (March–July 1862), which concluded in failure, and ending with the Appomattox Campaign (April 2–9, 1865), which brought about the defeat of Confederate forces. Prior to 1864, most of the army's engagements ended inconclusively or in defeat; indeed, until then only the Battle of Gettysburg (July 1–3, 1863) was an unqualified tactical and strategic success.

At war's end, the Army of the Potomac marched in the Grand Review of the Armies in May and was formally disbanded on June 28, 1865.

DEBRA J. SHEFFER AND PAUL G. PIERPAOLI JR.

Scouts and guides of the Union Army of the Potomac at Berlin, Maryland, October 1862. (National Archives/Alexander Gardner)

See also

Burnside, Ambrose Everett; Hooker, Joseph; McClellan, George Brinton; Meade, George Gordon; Northern Virginia, Confederate Army of

Further Reading

McPherson, James M. *Battle Cry of Freedom: The Civil War Era.* Oxford: Oxford University Press, 1988.

Potomac, Union Department of the

Federal military administrative unit created on August 15, 1861. The Union Department of the Potomac was created from the existing Military Division of the Potomac and was first commanded by Major General George B. McClellan, whose army was named the Army of the Potomac. Perhaps the single most important command during the Civil War, the primary tasks of the department were to defend the federal capital at Washington, D.C., and to defeat the Confederate Army of Northern Virginia.

McClellan remained in command until President Abraham Lincoln removed him. Major General Ambrose P. Burnside took command on November 9, 1862, and remained in command until January 26, 1863, at which point he was succeeded by Major General Joseph Hooker, who commanded until June 28, 1863. Major General George G. Meade commanded from June 28, 1863, until December 30, 1864, when he was temporarily succeeded by Major General John G. Parke, who commanded until January 11, 1865, when Meade resumed command.

PAUL G. PIERPAOLI JR.

See also

Burnside, Ambrose Everett; Hooker, Joseph; McClellan, George Brinton; Meade, George Gordon; Parke, John Grubb

Further Reading

Eicher, John H., and David J. Eicher. *Civil War High Commands.* Stanford, CA: Stanford University Press, 2001.

Potomac, Union Military Division of the

Federal military administrative unit created on July 25, 1861, four days after the Union debacle at the First Battle of Bull Run (July 21, 1861). The Union Military Division of the Potomac was formed by the merging and consolidation of the existing Department of Northeastern Virginia and the Department of Washington. Major General George B. McClellan was named commander of the new division on July 27. The Division of the Potomac was organized out of existence on August 15,

1861, with the creation of the Department of the Potomac. McClellan retained command of the new entity and served as commander of the Army of the Potomac.

PAUL G. PIERPAOLI JR.

See also

Bull Run, First Battle of; McClellan, George Brinton

Further Reading

Eicher, John H., and David J. Eicher. *Civil War High Commands.* Stanford, CA: Stanford University Press, 2001.

Potter, Robert Brown
Birth Date: July 16, 1829
Death Date: February 19, 1887

Union officer. Robert Brown Potter was born on July 16, 1829, in Schenectady, New York, the son of an Episcopal bishop. Potter was privately schooled, studied law, and eventually established a prosperous practice in New York City. In the spring of 1861, he enlisted in a New York Militia unit as a private and was quickly advanced to lieutenant. Potter received a major's commission in the 51st New York Infantry on October 14, 1861, and by November he was its lieutenant colonel.

Potter saw action at the Battle of Roanoke Island (February 7–8, 1862) and then at the Battle of New Bern (March 14, 1862), where he was wounded. His next major action was the Battle of Cedar Mountain (August 9, 1862), after which he was advanced to colonel on September 10. Potter was conspicuous at the Battle of Antietam (September 17, 1862) and also saw combat at the First Battle of Fredericksburg (December 13, 1862).

After serving on garrison duty in Ohio, Potter was promoted to brigadier general on March 13, 1863, and went on to participate with IX Corps in the Second Vicksburg Campaign (April 1–July 4, 1863). From August 25, 1863, to January 17, 1864, Potter was acting commander of IX Corps, which was stationed in eastern Tennessee. From May 1, 1864, to April 2, 1865, Potter had charge of the 2nd Division, IX Corps, in Virginia. He led the division during the Battle of the Wilderness (May 5–7, 1864), the Battle of Spotsylvania Court House (May 8–21), and much of the Petersburg Campaign (June 15, 1864–April 3, 1865). A detachment of his division was also involved in the Battle of the Crater (July 30, 1864). Brevetted major general on August 1, 1864, Potter was seriously wounded during the final assault at Petersburg on April 2, 1865.

Potter never completely recovered from his injury but was promoted to full major general on September 29, 1865. He left the service on January 15, 1866, and worked for the Atlantic & Great Western Railroad for several years before traveling abroad. In 1873 Potter retired to his Newport, Rhode Island, estate, where he died on February 19, 1887.

PAUL G. PIERPAOLI JR.

See also

Antietam, Battle of; Cedar Mountain, Battle of; Crater, Battle of the; Fredericksburg, First Battle of; New Bern, Battle of; Petersburg Campaign; Roanoke Island, Battle of; Spotsylvania Court House, Battle of; Vicksburg Campaign, Second; Wilderness, Battle of the

Further Reading

Eicher, John H., and David J. Eicher. *Civil War High Commands.* Stanford, CA: Stanford University Press, 2001.

Warner, Ezra J. *Generals in Gray: Lives of the Confederate Commanders.* Baton Rouge: Louisiana State University Press, 2006.

Powell, Lewis Thornton
Birth Date: April 22, 1844
Death Date: July 7, 1865

Confederate soldier and Lincoln assassination coconspirator. Lewis Paine and Lewis Payne were among the many aliases of Lewis Thornton Powell, born in Alabama on April 22, 1844. When the Civil War broke out in 1861, Powell and his family were living in Live Oak, Florida. He volunteered for Confederate service in the spring of 1861 and on May 30 was enlisted in the Hamilton Blues, later a company of the 2nd Florida Infantry. While undergoing training in Richmond, he first met future presidential assassin John Wilkes Booth.

Powell saw action in Virginia through 1862 and was wounded and captured at the Battle of Gettysburg (July 1–3, 1863). While at the U.S. Army hospital in Baltimore, he escaped, made his way across Union lines, and rejoined Confederate forces. In early 1865 Powell deserted and took the oath of allegiance to the United States. He then went to Baltimore.

While living in Baltimore under the name Lewis Payne, Powell again met Booth, who recruited the physically powerful young veteran into the plot to kidnap Abraham Lincoln and other Union political leaders. As with other members of the conspiracy, Powell stayed at the Surratt boardinghouse. After the failure of the kidnapping attempt on March

16, 1865, the plot evolved into an assassination conspiracy. On the night of April 14, the same night President Lincoln was shot, Powell was assigned to murder Secretary of State William H. Seward. Powell obtained entry into the Seward house on the pretense of a medical errand. There he pistol-whipped Seward's son Frederick and stabbed Seward, his other son Augustus, and State Department messenger Emerick Hansell. None of the wounds proved fatal.

Powell then hid in a small wooded area but was captured on the night of April 17 as he returned to the Surratt boardinghouse in hopes of securing food. Along with other captured conspirators, Powell was tried by a military commission. He was convicted on July 6, 1865, and executed by hanging the following day in Washington, D.C.

WILLIAM E. BURNS

See also

Booth, John Wilkes; Lincoln Assassination; Seward, William Henry, Sr.

Further Reading

Prior, Leon O. "Lewis Payne, Pawn of John Wilkes Booth." *Florida Historical Quarterly* 43(1) (July 1964): 1–20.

Swanson, James L. *Manhunt: The 12-Day Chase for Lincoln's Killer.* New York: William Morrow, 2006.

Powell, William Henry
Birth Date: May 10, 1825
Death Date: December 26, 1904

Union officer. Born at Pontypool, Wales, on May 10, 1825, William Henry Powell immigrated with his family to the United States in 1830, settling in Tennessee. Leter establishing himself in Ohio, Powell became an engineer, mostly associated with iron manufacturing. With the onset of the Civil War, he recruited a mounted company that entered federal service as part of the 2nd West Virginia Cavalry, with Powell as its captain, in November 1861.

Powell and his troopers spent most of the next two years fighting small actions in western Virginia (West Virginia). He was promoted to major in June 1862, to lieutenant colonel that October, and to colonel in May 1863. As regimental commander, he was wounded and captured in an engagement at Wytheville, Virginia, on July 18, 1863.

Exchanged in February 1864, Powell assumed command of a brigade in the Cavalry Division, Department of West Virginia, in June. That August the division, commanded by Brigadier General William W. Averell, joined Major General

Philip Sheridan's Army of the Shenandoah and was hotly engaged during the Third Battle of Winchester (September 19, 1864). Shortly thereafter, Powell succeeded Averell as division commander. Although Powell did not play a major role in the decisive Battle of Cedar Creek (October 19), he was promoted to brigadier general of volunteers to rank from the date of the battle. Powell's summary execution of Confederate partisan John S. Mosby's rangers that autumn ignited controversy and may have contributed to Powell's abrupt resignation in January 1865.

After the war, Powell was engaged in nail manufacturing and moved around quite a bit before settling in Belleville, Illinois. In 1890 he was awarded the Medal of Honor for his capture of a Confederate camp in Sinking Creek Valley, Virginia, in November 1862. Powell died at Belleville on December 26, 1904.

DAVID COFFEY

See also
Cedar Creek, Battle of; Mosby's Rangers; Winchester, Third
    Battle of

Further Reading
Coffey, David. *Sheridan's Lieutenants: Phil Sheridan, His Generals, and the Final Year of the Civil War.* Lanham, MD: Rowman and Littlefield, 2005.
Wert, Jeffry D. *From Winchester to Cedar Creek: The Shenandoah Valley Campaign of 1864.* Mechanicsburg, PA: Stackpole, 1997.

Prairie Grove, Battle of
Event Date: December 7, 1862

Engagement for control of northwestern Arkansas. Union major general John M. Schofield had divided his Army of the Frontier into two widely separated parts: Brigadier General Francis J. Herron was located near Springfield, Missouri, while Brigadier General James G. Blunt, who had been ordered to advance into northwestern Arkansas, was near Fayetteville. Schofield then fell ill, and command of the army passed to Blunt.

Aware of their dispositions and hoping to defeat the Union forces in detail, Confederate major general Thomas C. Hindman gathered a force of his own at Fort Smith, Arkansas. Meanwhile, he dispatched 2,000 cavalrymen under Brigadier General John S. Marmaduke to screen his main body and harass Blunt. Blunt, however, moved forward with 5,000 men and 30 guns to meet Marmaduke, leading to the Battle of Cane Hill on November 28. Blunt

drove Marmaduke back, but he was now further separated from the rest of his army.

On December 3, 1862, Hindman set out with his main body of 11,000 men and 22 guns to attack Blunt. Blunt did not withdraw and instead took up position at Cane Hill and telegraphed Herron, 110 miles distant, for assistance. Herron immediately set out from Springfield with 6,000 reinforcements on a forced march to join Blunt. Hindman learned of Herron's movement on December 6 and hoped to be able to get between the two Union forces and defeat them in detail, striking Herron first.

Leaving a small force to occupy Blunt, on December 7 Hindman moved with Marmaduke's cavalry against Herron, then near Prairie Grove. Herron's superior artillery gradually took out the Confederate guns, forcing the Confederate infantrymen to seek safety on the rear slope of low hills. Herron then ordered an advance, which was met and blunted by a savage attack on three sides by troops under Marmaduke and Brigadier General Francis A. Shoup. Half of the attacking Federals were casualties in a matter of minutes. Hindman then ordered his own forces to advance and break the Union lines, but Herron's artillery turned them back. Herron then ordered another charge with a view toward protecting his guns, but this was defeated in turn. The Confederates then advanced a second time but were again beaten back.

Hindman was at the point of ordering a third charge when Blunt, who had ordered his men to march to the sound of the guns, came on the field, surprising the Confederates. Fighting continued until dark, when the Confederates, short of food and ammunition and with much of their artillery out of action, withdrew to Van Buren. Union losses in the battle were 1,251 of some 9,200 men engaged; the Confederates lost 1,317 men of 11,000 engaged.

Blunt then pursued Hindman and at the end of the month captured Van Buren, securing both northwestern Arkansas and western Missouri for the Union.

SPENCER C. TUCKER

See also
Blunt, James Gillpatrick; Herron, Francis Jay; Hindman, Thomas
    Carmichael; Marmaduke, John Sappington; Shoup, Francis
    Asbury

Further Reading
Cozzens, Peter. "Hindman's Grand Delusion." *Civil War Times Illustrated* 39 (October 2000): 28–35, 66–69.
Jones, Samuel. *The Battle of Prairie Grove, December 7, 1862.* Charleston, SC: Nabu, 2010.
Shea, William L. *Fields of Blood: The Prairie Grove Campaign.* Chapel Hill: University of North Carolina Press, 2009.

"The Prayer of the Twenty Millions"

Public letter to President Abraham Lincoln from Horace Greeley written on August 20, 1862. Greeley, the influential Republican editor of the *New York Tribune,* published his open editorial letter titled "The Prayer of Twenty Millions" to compel the president to abolish slavery and strictly enforce the Confiscation Acts of 1861 and 1862. The letter was so titled because Greeley claimed to speak on behalf of 20 million concerned Northerners. In his editorial, Greeley, a dedicated abolitionist, complained that the Lincoln administration was being "unduly influenced" by the border states, that the Confiscation Acts were "habitually disregarded" by Union generals, and that the inevitable defeat of the Confederacy required the destruction of slavery.

Although sections of the Confiscation Acts forbade the arrest of any Confederate fugitive slave on pain of dismissal from the service, Union major generals Don Carlos Buell and Joseph Hooker had nevertheless allowed slave owners to reclaim fugitives from within Union lines, and Major General Henry W. Halleck had denied fugitive slaves sanctuary and ordered those found in his camp evicted.

Greeley's letter reached not only the roughly 300,000 readers of the *New York Tribune* but was also picked up and subsequently printed by many smaller papers as well. Despite Lincoln's intent to issue the Preliminary Emancipation Proclamation, which he did a month later on September 22, 1862, following the Union victory at the Battle of Antietam (September 17, 1862), he did not approve of Greeley's demands. "My paramount object in this struggle," the president replied in an August 22, 1862, editorial of the *Washington Chronicle,* "is to save the Union, and is not either to save or to destroy slavery." Clearly, Lincoln's chief concern was to preserve the Union and defeat the Confederate rebellion; the abolition of slavery was of secondary importance. While Greeley's letter did not compel Lincoln to issue the Emancipation Proclamation, it certainly aroused and moved many readers. In the end, Lincoln's shrewd political strategy was to save the proclamation until it could be used with maximum impact against the South and at a time in the war that was most propitious for the North.

Jason N. Palmer

See also

Abolitionism and the Civil War; Antietam, Battle of; Buell, Don Carlos; Confiscation Acts of 1861 and 1862; Emancipation Proclamation; Greeley, Horace; Halleck, Henry Wager; Hooker, Joseph; Lincoln, Abraham

Further Reading

Benton, Joel, ed. *Greeley on Lincoln: With Mr. Greeley's Letters to Charles A. Dana and a Lady Friend, to Which Are Added Reminiscences of Horace Greeley.* Whitefish, MT: Kessinger, 2006.

Donald, David H. *Lincoln.* New York: Simon and Schuster, 1996.

Guelzo, Allen C. *Lincoln's Emancipation Proclamation: The End of Slavery in America.* New York: Simon and Schuster, 2004.

Preble, George Henry
Birth Date: February 25, 1816
Death Date: March 1, 1885

Union naval officer. George Henry Preble, born in Portland, Maine, on February 25, 1816, was the nephew of Commodore Edward Preble, who gained fame during the Barbary Wars. Preble secured a midshipman's warrant on October 10, 1835, and subsequently served in the frigate *United States* in the Mediterranean until 1838. He was promoted to passed midshipman on June 22, 1837. Preble circumnavigated the globe as acting lieutenant aboard the sloop *St. Louis* (1843–1845) and during its visit to China commanded a party of marines and sailors that quelled a riot in Guangzhou (Canton). Preble also took part in the Mexican-American War (1846–1848), participating in the captures of Alvarado, Veracruz, and Tuxpan. He was promoted to lieutenant on February 5, 1848. Preble took part in Commodore Matthew Perry's 1853 expedition to Japan, where Preble had charge of a surveying expedition.

At the beginning of the Civil War, Lieutenant Preble commanded the screw gunboat *Katahdin* in the West Gulf Blockading Squadron and took part in the passage up the Mississippi River and the capture of New Orleans in April 1862. Promoted to commander on July 16, 1862, he took command of the screw sloop *Onieda,* charged with blockading Mobile Bay, but was unable to prevent the entrance there on September 4, 1862, of the Confederate raider *Florida.* Captain John N. Maffitt of the *Florida,* whose ship resembled a British vessel, had flown British colors; Preble, fearing a repeat of the *Trent* Affair, had been slow to react and then had first fired three warning shots instead of losing a broadside. As the senior officer on station, Preble was dismissed from the navy on September 20 by Secretary of the Navy Gideon Welles for the failure, but subsequent testimony as to the Confederate ship's superior speed and considerable pressure on his behalf by friends led to Preble's reinstatement. Ironically, Preble and Maffitt had been close friends before the war.

In a second embarrassing encounter with the *Florida,* now commanded by Lieutenant Charles N. Morris, Preble

U.S. Navy commander George Henry Preble commanded the blockade of Mobile Bay but was unable to prevent the entrance there of the Confederate commerce raider *Florida* on September 4, 1862. Dismissed from the navy as a result, Preble was subsequently reinstated. (Archive Photos/Getty Images)

was in command of the sailing sloop *St. Louis* in the Mediterranean and caught up the *Florida* at Madeira. On February 28, 1863, the *Florida* outran the far slower Union ship to escape the Portuguese port of Funchal.

After the war, Preble, now commanding the steamer *State of Georgia,* rescued 600 passengers from the wrecked American steamship *Golden Rule* off Panama. Commanding the Boston Navy Yard (1866–1868), he was promoted to captain on January 29, 1867. He then commanded the screw sloop *Pensacola* until 1870 and was promoted to commodore on November 2, 1871. From 1873 to 1875, he commanded the Philadelphia Navy Yard. He was promoted to rear admiral on September 30, 1876, and commanded the South Pacific Station, after which duty he retired on February 25, 1878.

During his retirement, Preble became an avid writer and a collector of naval documents. He donated his large collection of nautical papers and books to the Navy Department

Library before his death in Boston, Massachusetts, on March 1, 1885.

WESLEY MOODY AND SPENCER C. TUCKER

See also

Florida, CSS; Maffitt, John Newland; Mobile Bay; New Orleans Campaign; *Trent* Affair; Welles, Gideon; West Gulf Blockading Squadron

Further Reading

Owsley, Frank L., Jr. *The C.S.S.* Florida: *Her Building and Operations.* Tuscaloosa: University of Alabama Press, 1965.

Paine, Nathaniel. *Biographical Notice of Rear-Admiral George H. Preble: Prepared for the Report of the Council of the American Antiquarian Society.* Worcester, MA: Press of Charles Hamilton, 1885.

Prentiss, Benjamin Mayberry
Birth Date: November 23, 1819
Death Date: February 8, 1901

Union officer. Benjamin Mayberry Prentiss was born on November 23, 1819, in Belleville, Virginia (West Virginia). In 1836 his family moved to Missouri and then in 1841 to Quincy, Illinois. There Prentiss joined the Illinois Militia and participated in the Mormon Expulsion (1844–1845). During the Mexican-American War (1846–1848), Prentiss raised a company of volunteers, was elected its captain, and fought in the Battle of Buena Vista. After the war, Prentiss was a rope manufacturer, a prominent lawyer, and a colonel in the Illinois Militia, and in 1860 he made an unsuccessful bid for election as a Republican to the U.S. House of Representatives.

With the outbreak of the Civil War, Prentiss was commissioned a colonel of the 10th Illinois Infantry Regiment in southern Illinois before being promoted on August 9, 1861, to brigadier general of volunteers, with command in northeastern Missouri. In April 1862 he was selected to command the 6th Division, Army of the Tennessee, under Major General Ulysses S. Grant. Prentiss fought in the Battle of Shiloh (April 6–7, 1862), during which he and his men held off repeated Confederate assaults on the so-called Hornet's Nest, buying valuable time for Grant, before being overrun and captured. After Prentiss was exchanged, he served on the court-martial of Major General Fitz John Porter.

In January 1863, Prentiss assumed command of the District of East Arkansas. He was promoted to major general on March 13, 1863. Prentiss defeated a Confederate attack on Helena, Arkansas (July 4, 1863), giving the Union a third victory to celebrate on Independence Day, along with the surrender of Vicksburg, Mississippi, on July 4, 1863, and the Battle of Gettysburg (July 1–3, 1863). On October 28, 1863, Prentiss resigned to resume his law practice in Quincy, Illinois.

Parlaying his military success, especially at Shiloh where he has often been credited with saving the Army of the Tennessee, and his personal acquaintances with Republican presidents Ulysses S. Grant and James A. Garfield, Prentiss held several federal appointments before becoming postmaster of Bethany, Missouri, a position he held until his death there on February 8, 1901.

RUSSELL S. PERKINS

See also

Gettysburg, Battle of; Helena, Battle of; Porter, Fitz John; Shiloh, Battle of; Tennessee, Union Army of the; Vicksburg Campaign, Second

Further Reading

Warner, Ezra J. *Generals in Blue: Lives of the Union Commanders.* Baton Rouge: Louisiana State University Press, 2006.
Woodworth, Steven E. *Nothing but Victory: The Army of the Tennessee, 1861–1865.* New York: Knopf, 2005.

President's General War Order No. 1

Order issued by President Abraham Lincoln on January 27, 1862, and coauthored by Secretary of War Edwin M. Stanton. Lincoln's primary motive in issuing the order was to motivate Major General George B. McClellan to action. In July 1861, Lincoln had appointed McClellan the principal Union commander in the eastern theater. McClellan had drilled and trained the Army of the Potomac, but as 1861 drew to a close, Lincoln had become flummoxed by McClellan's failure to mount a major offensive against Confederate forces. And although McClellan had become the Union Army's general in chief in November 1861, he refused to share his military plans with the Lincoln administration. McClellan distrusted most figures in the Lincoln administration and had come to believe that Lincoln himself could not be trusted with war planning and that his administration could not maintain secrecy. McClellan contracted typhoid fever in the late autumn, which precluded him from meeting with the president at all.

Annoyed by McClellan's secrecy and inaction, Lincoln called for strategy meetings in Washington in early January 1862, to include some of McClellan's immediate subordinates. Upon learning of this, McClellan, who was still ill, dragged himself to the meetings, beginning on January 12. Still, he refused to fully divulge his plans and made only vague promises of an advance in Kentucky. After more than two weeks had lapsed with no Union movement, Lincoln had had enough and threw down the gauntlet in the form of his General War Order No. 1 on January 27, 1862.

Lincoln ordered that by February 22, 1862, Union forces were to engage the enemy in northern Virginia, troops would be landed at Fort Monroe in eastern Virginia, and Union forces would go on the offensive in western Virginia, in southern Kentucky, and along the lower Mississippi River. In addition, flotillas located on the Mississippi River and in the Gulf of Mexico were to be in readiness to move into action when so ordered. Four days later on January 31, Lincoln's issued his Special War Order No. 1. In it he directed McClellan to personally lead the Army of the Potomac in an offensive against Confederate forces at Manassas Junction, Virginia.

McClellan received this order that same day and immediately went to the president to protest. At his request, McClellan was permitted to write out his objections. Lincoln hoped that this might finally get McClellan to put forth a war plan. On February 3, 1862, McClellan submitted a 22-page report to Stanton that first reviewed the events of the previous six months of the war. McClellan then detailed his objections to Lincoln's plan, which McClellan argued would allow large numbers of Confederates to escape.

As a substitute, McClellan put forth his so-called Urbanna Plan. It called for an advance by water up the Rappahannock River and then a land advance on Richmond from Urbanna. This would provide the shortest path to the seat of the Confederate government. McClellan believed that once Richmond fell, the Confederacy would collapse.

Although few of Lincoln's objectives in the orders were in fact achieved, he had at least motivated McClellan to action. In the future, McClellan also cooperated more closely with the administration.

THERESA STOREY HEFNER-BABB AND PAUL G. PIERPAOLI JR.

See also

Lincoln, Abraham; McClellan, George Brinton; Stanton, Edwin McMasters; Urbanna Plan

Further Reading

Perret, Geoffrey. *Lincoln's War.* New York: Random House, 2004.
Rowland, Thomas J. *George B. McClellan and Civil War History.* Kent, OH: Kent State University Press, 1998.

Sears, Stephen W. *George B. McClellan: The Young Napoleon.* New York: Ticknor and Fields, 1998.

Williams, T. Harry. *Lincoln and His Generals.* New York: Knopf, 1952.

Preston, John Smith
Birth Date: April 20, 1809
Death Date: May 1, 1881

Confederate officer. John Smith Preston was born on April 20, 1809, on an expansive estate in Abingdon, Virginia. He graduated from Hampden-Sydney College in 1824 and then attended law school at the University of Virginia and Harvard. He began a legal practice in Abingdon, but by 1840 he had moved to Columbia, South Carolina. After a brief stint there, he went to Louisiana, where he purchased a sprawling sugar plantation and secured his fortune. A gifted administrator with an obstreperous personality, Preston returned to South Carolina in 1848 and secured a seat in the South Carolina Senate, where he was an avid proponent of states' rights. He served in the Senate until 1856. By 1860, he was an avid secessionist and was a delegate to the South Carolina Secession Convention.

In February 1861, South Carolina leaders tasked Preston with traveling north to Virginia in an effort to persuade that state to secede. In April 1861 when the war began, he was a volunteer civilian aide-de-camp to Brigadier General P. G. T. Beauregard. On August 13, Confederate president Jefferson Davis, who deeply admired Preston, appointed him assistant adjutant general at the rank of lieutenant colonel. That October, Preston was dispatched to Charleston, South Carolina, to help muster in troops, an assignment he performed well.

In January 1862, Preston took command of a prison camp in Columbia, South Carolina, and also helped construct a conscription camp nearby the following spring. Although his administrative abilities were unquestioned, he alienated many Confederate officers and was retained largely because of Davis's support. On April 23, 1863, Preston was advanced to colonel, and in July he became superintendent of the Confederate Conscription Bureau.

Preston ran the bureau effectively and enforced the conscription law dutifully, even though some of his methods were deemed draconian. He was advanced to brigadier general on June 10, 1864, and remained superintendent until the bureau was disbanded in March 1865.

Dejected in the aftermath of the war, from 1865 to 1868 Preston lived in Britain, where he remained an unreconstructed Confederate. He eventually made his way back to Columbia, where he died on May 1, 1881.

PAUL G. PIERPAOLI JR.

See also
Beauregard, Pierre Gustav Toutant; Conscription, CSA; Davis, Jefferson Finis

Further Reading
Moore, Albert B., ed. *Conscription and Conflict in the Confederacy.* Reprint ed. Columbia: University of South Carolina Press, 1996.

Warner, Ezra J. *Generals in Gray: Lives of the Confederate Commanders.* Baton Rouge: Louisiana State University Press, 2006.

Preston, William
Birth Date: October 16, 1816
Death Date: September 21, 1887

Confederate officer. William Preston was born on October 16, 1816, in Louisville, Kentucky. He received a law degree from Harvard in 1838. Preston then began a legal practice in Louisville. He participated in the Mexican-American War (1846–1848) as a lieutenant colonel of Kentucky volunteers.

Preston served in the Kentucky House of Representatives in 1850 and then in the Kentucky Senate. During 1852–1855 he sat in the U.S. House of Representatives as a Whig. Preston later became a staunch Democrat and served as U.S. minister to Spain (1858–1861).

When the Civil War began, Preston became a colonel and an aide to his brother-in-law, General Albert S. Johnston. Following Johnston's death in the Battle of Shiloh (April 6–7, 1862), Preston was granted a brigadier general's commission on April 14, 1862, and he assumed command of the 3rd Brigade in a division commanded by Major General John C. Breckinridge. Preston saw action in the Siege of Corinth (May 3–30) and the Battle of Stones River (December 31, 1862–January 2, 1863), and he commanded a division at the Battle of Chickamauga (September 19–20, 1863).

In early January 1864, President Jefferson Davis appointed Preston Confederate envoy extraordinary and minister plenipotentiary to Austrian archduke Ferdinand Maximilian von of Habsburg, who had agreed to become emperor of Mexico. Davis charged Preston with the task of securing a treaty of mutual assistance and commerce between the Confederacy and Mexico. Preston traveled to Europe by way of Cuba but was unable to establish contacts with Maximilian and returned to southern Texas by way of Matamoros, Mexico, where he served under General E. Kirby Smith until war's end.

After the war Preston spent time in Mexico, Europe, and Canada before returning to Kentucky and resuming his legal practice. He again served in the commonwealth legislature during 1868–1869. Preston died on September 21, 1887, in Lexington, Kentucky.

PAUL G. PIERPAOLI JR.

See also

Chickamauga, Battle of; Corinth, Battle of; Diplomacy, Confederate; Johnston, Albert Sidney; Maximilian von Habsburg, Ferdinand; Mexico; Smith, Edmund Kirby; Stones River, Battle of

Further Reading

Sehlinger, Peter J. *Kentucky's Last Cavalier: General William Preston, 1816–1887.* Lexington: University Press of Kentucky, 2004.

Warner, Ezra J. *Generals in Gray: Lives of the Confederate Commanders.* Baton Rouge: Louisiana State University Press, 2006.

Price, Sterling
Birth Date: September 11, 1809
Death Date: September 29, 1867

Confederate officer. Sterling Price was born in Prince Edward County, Virginia, on September 11, 1809. He attended Hampden-Sydney College (1826–1827), studying under famed Virginia jurist Creed Taylor. Price then traveled to Chariton County, Missouri, where he eventually settled with his wife and children, purchasing several dozen slaves to grow tobacco. He was elected as a colonel of the Chariton County Militia and soon after entered state politics.

Price was elected to the Missouri legislature as a Democrat in 1838 and served three consecutive terms, the last two (1840–1844) as Speaker. In 1844 he was elected to the U.S. House of Representatives. He resigned from Congress following the outbreak of the Mexican-American War in 1846 and was commissioned a colonel of the 2nd Regiment of the Missouri Volunteers. Price did have some prewar combat experience in 1838, when he participated in driving Mormon elements from western Missouri.

Price arrived with his men in Santa Fe, New Mexico, in late September 1846 and assumed command of occupation forces. He suppressed an uprising in 1847 and the following

Confederate major general Sterling Price of Missouri, who had enjoyed victories as a brigadier general in the Mexican-American War, suffered defeats in the Civil War battles of Pea Ridge (March 6, 1862) and Westport (October 23, 1864). (Library of Congress)

year invaded Chihuahua, capturing the capital city, for which he received promotion to brigadier general of volunteers.

Price returned to Missouri and reentered politics, aligning himself with the Missouri proslavery Democratic faction. This resulted in his election to governor in 1853, a post he held until 1857. As governor, he supported the 1854 Kansas-Nebraska Act, opening the door for the violent struggle between proslavery and antislavery elements vying for control of Kansas. He remained largely inactive regarding the efforts of proslavery Missouri Border Ruffians in Kansas. In March 1861 he presided over the state convention and openly opposed secession. Nonetheless, he remained a proslavery proponent.

In May 1861, Missouri governor Claiborne Jackson appointed Price commander of the Missouri State Guard with the state rank of major general. On August 10, 1861, at the Battle of Wilson Creek (Oak Hill), Price helped defeat the Union army. On September 2, 1861, he routed Union forces at Dry Wood Creek, Missouri, and eventually captured nearby Fort Scott. Price then moved on to capture Lexington, Missouri, along with 3,000 men of its Union garrison. On March 7, 1862, Price and his unit, now under the command of Major General Earl Van Dorn, attacked Union forces at Pea Ridge (Elkhorn) but were ultimately repulsed. After Pea Ridge, Price was commissioned a major general in the Confederate Army.

Price saw action at the Battle of Iuka (September 19, 1862), the Battle of Corinth (October 6–7, 1862), and the Battle of Helena (July 4, 1863) but enjoyed no victories. He then participated in turning back the Camden Expedition (March 23–May 3, 1864), part of the Red River Campaign (March 12–May 20, 1864). In September 1864 he led his forces into Missouri (Price's Missouri Raid) in an effort to divert Union attention from the Union army's march through Georgia. Although his forces were successful early on, they were ultimately defeated at Westport, Missouri, on October 23, 1864, and driven from the state in a series of engagements along the Kansas border.

In April 1865, Price left the United States for Mexico. However, he returned to Missouri in January 1867 and died of cholera on September 29, 1867, in St. Louis.

CHARLES P. NEIMEYER AND JACOB C. DAMM

See also

Camden Expedition; Corinth, Battle of; Helena, Battle of; Iuka, Battle of; Jackson, Claiborne Fox; Kansas-Nebraska Act; Lexington, Missouri, Battle of; Missouri; Pea Ridge, Battle of; Price's Missouri Raid; Van Dorn, Earl; Westport, Battle of; Wilson's Creek, Battle of

Further Reading

Castel, Albert. *General Sterling Price and the Civil War in the West.* Baton Rouge: Louisiana State University Press, 1996.

Muench, James F. *Five Stars: Missouri's Most Famous Generals.* Columbia: University of Missouri Press, 2006.

Shalhope, Robert E. *Portrait of a Southerner.* Columbia: University of Missouri Press, 1971.

Price's Missouri Raid
Start Date: September 19, 1864
End Date: October 28, 1864

Confederate expedition into Missouri led by Major General Sterling Price. Ordered by the commander of the Confederate Trans-Mississippi Department General Edmund Kirby Smith, Price's Missouri Raid, also known as Price's Expedition and Price's Raid, was the last major effort by the Confederates to try to bring that state into the Confederacy or at least secure a large number of recruits for the Confederate cause. The Confederates also hoped to impact the upcoming U.S. presidential election, denying Abraham Lincoln a second term. Finally, Smith hoped to divert resources from Union

efforts elsewhere. Price's ambitious goals included the capture of St. Louis, with its stocks of war supplies, and an attack across the Mississippi River into Illinois. He also expected to secure war matériel for Confederate forces. While the operation had its successes, it ended in a major failure.

Departing Camden, Arkansas, on August 28, 1864, and proceeding north, Price added additional units on August 29 and September 13. His combined force entered Missouri on September 19. Price's Army of Missouri numbered approximately 12,000 men and 14 guns. It was essentially a cavalry force but was indifferently armed, clothed, and equipped. Many of his men were former deserters. The army consisted of three divisions, under Major General James F. Fagan and Brigadier Generals John S. Marmaduke and Joseph O. "Jo" Shelby. Price moved quickly into southeastern Missouri, with St. Louis as his first and primary objective.

Although there was skirmishing almost every day throughout the expedition, the first significant clash did not occur until September 27 in the Battle of Pilot Knob, also known as the Battle of Fort Davidson, when a much smaller Union force of approximately 1,500 troops under Brigadier General Thomas Ewing Jr. held off more than 8,500 of Price's men and then escaped with the garrison that night. Union losses totaled 213, while the Confederates suffered 800–1,000 casualties. The battle also slowed Price's advance to St. Louis, giving Union forces time to concentrate and reinforce there.

With St. Louis now too strong to take, Price turned his army westward, hoping to take the state capital of Jefferson City, the capture of which would be a major psychological blow for the Union. Strong Union defenses there made this untenable as well, so Price again changed his objective and continued north and west through Boonville to Glasgow, where a detachment of his men forced the surrender of a small Union force on October 15.

Meanwhile, the Union commander of the Department of Missouri, Major General William S. Rosecrans, and the commander of the Department of Kansas, Major General Samuel R. Curtis, had responded in force to the Confederate raid. Forces under Major General James Blunt, who was sent forward by Curtis, slowed but could not stop Price in the Second Battle of Lexington (October 19) and the Battle of the Little Blue River (October 21). Price enjoyed moderate success in an engagement at Bryan's Ford on the Big Blue River (October 22), forcing the Federals back to Westport (today part of Kansas City).

These relatively small clashes led to the Battle of Westport, the largest military engagement west of the Mississippi.

Sometimes known as "the Gettysburg of the West," it saw as many as 30,000 men engaged. Fought on October 23 between Price's Confederate Army of the Missouri and Curtis's Union Army of the Border along with Union major general Alfred Pleasonton's Provisional Cavalry Division of the Department of the Missouri, it saw repeated Confederate charges on the Union lines during a four-hour span, with the attackers rebuffed. Each side suffered about 1,500 casualties, but with Pleasonton having crossed the Big Blue River at Bryan's Ford, Price had no option but to withdraw. With Price now outnumbered some 40,000–45,000 to only 9,000 and with the Union forces closing in from different directions, Price was forced into a long retreat south along the Missouri-Kansas border area, bringing along the wagons filled with captured supplies desperately needed by Confederate forces.

Pleasonton pursued, hoping to catch Price before he could reach safety in Confederate territory in Arkansas. A series of engagements followed, including three battles on one day alone, October 25, across the state line in Kansas: the Battle of the Marais de Cygnes River, the Battle of Mine Creek, and the Battle of the Little Osage River. Price, meanwhile, defended river crossings by the wagon train. As a result of these engagements, Price lost perhaps half his wagons, a number of his guns, and hundreds of men captured.

Veering slightly east back into Missouri, Price continued his southern movement. Price's campaign effectively ended in fighting at Newtonia, Missouri, on October 28 with what was a tactical draw, after which Price reached Confederate territory. In slightly more than a month, Price had covered some 1,435 miles in what was arguably the longest raid of the war. He had engaged Union forces on 43 separate occasions, but the small quantity of supplies secured was no compensation for the loss of nearly half his command. The outcome of the expedition strengthened Lincoln's hand in the November presidential election, solidified Union control of Missouri, and marked the end of major Confederate campaigns west of the Mississippi River, although sporadic guerrilla engagements continued until the end of the war in 1865.

DONALD E. HEIDENREICH JR. AND SPENCER C. TUCKER

See also

Blunt, James Gillpatrick; Curtis, Samuel Ryan; Ewing, Thomas, Jr.; Fagan, James Fleming; Glasgow, Battle of; Lexington, Missouri, Battle of; Little Osage River, Kansas, Skirmish at; Marais des Cygnes River, Battle of the; Marmaduke, John Sappington; Mine Creek, Battle of; Missouri; Newtonia, Second Battle of; Pilot Knob, Battle of; Price, Sterling; Rosecrans, William Starke; Shelby, Joseph Orville; Westport, Battle of

Further Reading

Castel, Albert. *General Sterling Price and the Civil War in the West.* Baton Rouge: Louisiana State University Press, 1968.
Gifford, Douglas. *The Battle of Pilot Knob: Staff Ride and Battlefield Tour Guide.* Winfield, MO: Douglas Gifford, 2003.
Lee, Fred L., ed. *The Battle of Westport, October 21–23, 1864.* Kansas City, MO: Westport Historical Society, 1976.

Prigg v. Pennsylvania

U.S. Supreme Court case decided in 1842 that was the first to address the fugitive slave clause in Article 4 of the U.S. Constitution. *Prigg v. Pennsylvania* (41 U.S. 539, 1842) affirmed the constitutional right of slaveholders under the clause to recapture fugitive slaves who had escaped to another state. In *Prigg*, the Court accordingly ruled that an 1826 Pennsylvania statute was an abrogation of this unfettered right and thus was unconstitutional because it required the issuance of a state certificate prior to the removal of fugitive slaves from Pennsylvania.

In 1837 a slave catcher, Edward Prigg, seized an alleged fugitive slave, Margaret Morgan, and her children in Pennsylvania and returned them to Maryland without first obtaining a state certificate pursuant to the 1826 Pennsylvania law. Prigg was subsequently found guilty of kidnapping and failure to comply with the state law. He then appealed to the U.S. Supreme Court. Justice Joseph Story delivered the opinion of the Court. Although an antislavery advocate, Story also fervently believed in a stable and strong union. In his *Commentaries on the Constitution of the United States,* published in 1833 in the midst of the Nullification Crisis in the South, Story had attempted to restitch the then-fraying remnants of the union tapestry and mollify southern passions by asserting the North's recognition of the South's interest in slavery through its gift of the fugitive slave clause in the Constitution. *Prigg* provided the New Englander an opportunity a decade later to more vigorously stress the need for a strong union, albeit at the expense of his antislavery sentiment.

Justice Story first set the stage in *Prigg* by shifting his earlier argument in the *Commentaries* from the idea of the fugitive slave clause as a goodwill gift to one of necessity for adoption of the Constitution. This shift from gift to a mandate essential for the Constitution's approval provided him cover to assert in *Prigg* the constitutionality of the fugitive slave clause. According to Story, the intent of the framers brokered no other result, leaving the Court little wiggle room. Although the other justices wrote separate opinions, the majority of the Court concluded that a slaveholder had a constitutional right to remove his runaway slaves from another state as long as no breach of the peace occurred. Furthermore, the Court ruled that Congress possessed exclusive jurisdiction in regulating slave recapture procedures through the Fugitive Slave Act of 1793. Story also asserted that although state magistrates should enforce the provisions of this act, they were not required to do so because the states, not the federal government, paid their salaries. Thus, the Pennsylvania statute was ruled unconstitutional, and Prigg's conviction in the lower court was reversed.

Northern states would later seize on the short portion of Story's opinion relating to the states' obligations under the Fugitive Slave Act of 1793 to justify legislation prohibiting state officials from enforcing its provisions. This compilation of state legislation, coupled with the failure of the Court in *Prigg* to address the constitutionality of the act itself and the lingering question of what to do with the capture and removal of free African Americans from another state by slaveholders, further muddied the legal and political waters over the issue of slavery in antebellum America and eventually led to the act's replacement with the Fugitive Slave Act of 1850.

MARK F. LEEP

See also
Slavery; Supreme Court, U.S.

Further Reading
Finkelman, Paul. "Joseph Story and the Problem of Slavery: A New Englander's Nationalist Dilemma." *Massachusetts Legal History* 8 (2002): 65–84.
Finkelman, Paul. "The Taney Court (1836–1864): The Jurisprudence of Slavery and the Crisis of the Union." In *The United States Supreme Court: The Pursuit of Justice,* edited by Christopher Tomlins, 75–99. New York: Houghton Mifflin, 2005.

Prince, Henry
Birth Date: June 19, 1811
Death Date: August 19, 1892

Union officer. Henry Prince was born on June 19, 1811, in Eastport, Maine. He graduated from the U.S. Military Academy, West Point, in 1835 and was commissioned a second lieutenant and was assigned to the 4th U.S. Infantry Regiment. The following year, he was severely wounded in Florida during the Second Seminole War (1835–1842). After duty in the West, he participated in the Mexican-American War (1846–1848), during which he was brevetted captain for the

Battles of Contreras and Churubusco. At the Battle of Molino del Rey (September 8, 1847), Prince was again seriously wounded and was granted a three-year furlough to recover. Beginning in 1850, he saw duty along the western frontier, was a paymaster, and served in several staff capacities, rising steadily to major in 1855. Prince had suffered permanent injuries, however, and was in almost constant pain.

On April 28, 1862, Prince was appointed brigadier general of volunteers. On July 16, he was given charge of the 2nd Brigade, 2nd Division, II Corps, Army of Virginia, which saw action at the Battle of Cedar Mountain (August 9, 1862). Prince was taken prisoner there but was released in December 1862. He then served for several months in North Carolina. In early July 1863 in the aftermath of the Battle of Gettysburg (July 1–3, 1863), Prince assumed command of the 2nd Division, III Corps, Army of the Potomac. He commanded the 2nd Division during the Bristoe Campaign (October 9–20, 1863) and the Mine Run Campaign (November 26–December 2, 1863), but his poor performance during the latter led to his loss of a field command at year's end.

Prince then held a series of garrison commands. On March 13, 1865, he was brevetted brigadier general of regulars in recognition of his long service to the army. Prince mustered out of the volunteers on April 30, 1866, to resume duties as paymaster. On March 3, 1877, he was promoted to lieutenant colonel. He retired on December 31, 1879. Depressed over his steadily failing health, Prince committed suicide in a hotel room in London, England, on August 19, 1892.

PAUL G. PIERPAOLI JR.

See also
Bristoe Campaign; Cedar Mountain, Battle of; Mine Run Campaign

Further Reading
Graham, Martin F., and George Skoch. *Mine Run: A Campaign of Lost Opportunities, October 21, 1863–May 1, 1864.* Lynchburg, VA: H. E. Howard, 1987.
Warner, Ezra J. *Generals in Blue: Lives of the Union Commanders.* Baton Rouge: Louisiana State University Press, 2006.

Prisoner Exchanges
Process by which prisoners were returned to their respective military establishments. During the Civil War, more than 674,000 men were taken prisoner by both sides. Of that number, approximately 264,000 were paroled and released on the battlefield, with the balance spending time in a prisoner-of-war compound. Both sides sought the release

of their captives through exchanges, and the system functioned relatively well for the first two years of the war but collapsed when each side violated both the spirit and letter of the agreements. This breakdown forced tens of thousands of detainees to remain in prison, and more than 56,000 of them did not survive the war.

Previous American conflicts had all involved at least some prison and exchange operations. In the Revolutionary War, Americans completed a series of major exchanges with the British and devised a rank equivalency table to allow different ranks to be achieved through composition. During the War of 1812, an exchange cartel for prisoners, with a better equivalency table, allowed for continual exchanges during the conflict. In the Mexican-American War there were fewer captives, but a series of small exchange agreements had freed captured U.S. personnel.

During the second half of 1861 as the Civil War expanded and intensified, both sides had reasons to pursue prisoner exchanges. Confederate leaders, including President Jefferson Davis, believed—wrongly as it turned out—that formal recognition of the Confederacy would be implied through negotiations with the Union over prisoner exchanges. Also, the badly outnumbered Confederates needed the veteran troops who had been captured, and the Confederacy had almost no excess supplies to feed enemy detainees held in captivity. On the other hand, Union leaders hoped to regain their captured men and expected to secure more from a general exchange, because the Confederacy typically held more prisoners during the first two years of the war. However, some Union officials held that Confederate forces were guilty of treason, and this stance retarded progress toward a general exchange.

In February 1862, Union major general John E. Wool and Confederate brigadier general Howell Cobb met to discuss prisoner exchanges. The negotiations were quick, the agreement was simple, and in theory all prisoners were soon headed home. Cobb returned to Norfolk and reported his success, and the Confederacy immediately began forwarding detainees for exchange. However, that same month Union troops under Brigadier General Ulysses S. Grant captured Fort Donelson, Tennessee, and its 15,000 defenders. For the first time the Union held a surplus of prisoners, and Secretary of State Edwin M. Stanton dreaded returning able veterans to the enemy in time for the spring campaigning. He thus ordered Wool to inform Cobb that the Union would retain surplus prisoners, who might otherwise fill noncombat roles in the South and free other soldiers for frontline service.

In June 1862 negotiators met again, hoping to create an ongoing cartel. The Union dispatched Major General John A. Dix to meet Confederate representative Major General D. H. Hill. On July 22, 1862, the Dix-Hill Cartel formally commenced a new exchange system. The agreement possessed six simple articles that ensured that all prisoners could be exchanged, rank for rank or through equivalency. All captives were to be paroled within 10 days of capture and promptly delivered to a predetermined exchange point. Parolees would thus return to their own lines to await exchange, a process that might require several weeks of communications. These parolees were not to serve any military function while on parole, eliminating the fear that a surplus of parolees would alter the battlefield balance.

The Dix-Hill Cartel functioned relatively well for almost a year, allowing tens of thousands of parolees to return home. In mid-1863 a new issue arose, however, that involved how Confederate authorities would treat African American prisoners. The enlistment of black Union regiments had horrified Southern leaders, who threatened to try and execute white officers of black units. Because President Abraham Lincoln demanded equal treatment of all Union troops, the exchanges halted temporarily. The balance of captives permanently shifted on July 4, 1863, with the surrender of Vicksburg's 30,000 defenders.

Major General Grant paroled the Vicksburg captives, but even if every Union parolee in the North were exchanged, the Confederacy would still owe the equivalent of 33,600 privates. The Confederate armies desperately needed troops, and Confederate exchange commissioner Robert Ould argued that the Union had dismissed paroled troops to avoid exchanging them. To rectify this imbalance, Ould declared the Vicksburg troops exchanged. Union major general Benjamin Butler, Ould's counterpart, now declared the cartel entirely annulled. By the autumn of 1863, the Union had largely decided against further exchanges. Grant believed that such swaps sent healthy Confederates back to the field in exchange for half-starved Union troops incapable of service. While individual prisoners were still exchanged and field commanders occasionally chose to parole surrendering enemies rather than undertake the burden of holding them, exchanges virtually ceased for the last 20 months of the war.

PAUL J. SPRINGER

See also
Butler, Benjamin Franklin; Cobb, Howell; Dix, John Adams; Hill, Daniel Harvey; Ould, Robert; Prisoners of War; Prisons, Confederate; Prisons, U.S.; Wool, John Ellis

Further Reading

Sanders, Charles W. *While in the Hands of the Enemy: Military Prisons of the Civil War.* Baton Rouge: Louisiana State University Press, 2005.

Speer, Lonnie R. *Portals to Hell: Military Prisons of the Civil War.* Mechanicsburg, PA: Stackpole, 1997.

Springer, Paul J. *America's Captives: Treatment of POWs from the Revolutionary War to the War on Terror.* Lawrence: University Press of Kansas, 2010.

Prisoners of War

During the Civil War, more than 674,000 prisoners of war (POWs) were captured by both sides. More than 400,000 of them spent time in a prison enclosure, and 56,000 did not survive captivity to return home. The mortality rate, nearly 15 percent for all POWs held captive, was higher than the battlefield mortality rate of the war, demonstrating that in some fashion surrender was a more dangerous option than fighting. The high death rates were due chiefly to overcrowding, disease, poor food, substandard sanitation, and a lack of supplies.

When the war commenced in 1861, neither side expected to face a protracted conflict involving millions of soldiers. As such, neither side entered the war with plans to hold, feed, clothe, and sustain tens of thousands of POWs. Previous American experience with POW affairs was relatively scant, and little institutional memory of detainment operations remained in the U.S. Army. Although Brevet Lieutenant General Winfield Scott, the Union Army general in chief, had spent time as a POW during the War of 1812, he devoted little attention to the subject before relinquishing his post in November 1861.

As the war quickly expanded, so did the number and needs of POWs, particularly in the eastern theater. Union detainees taken by the Confederates were sent to Richmond, quickly filling the local jail there. The provost marshal of Richmond, Brigadier General John H. Winder, quickly ordered the conversion of tobacco warehouses and factories into rudimentary holding facilities. More permanent camps soon appeared on Belle Isle in the James River, where it was assumed that the prisoners could be more easily isolated from the populace. Confederates captured by the Union reported to existing federal fortifications along the East Coast, most commonly Fort Delaware, Fort McHenry, and Point Lookout, Maryland. Colonel William C. Hoffman, himself a POW on parole and awaiting exchange, assumed the role of commissary general of prisoners.

Estimated Prisoners of War during the Civil War

	Union	*Confederacy*
Total prisoners	211,411	462,634
Paroled	16,668	247,769
Died in captivity	30,218	25,976
Mortality rate	15.5%	12.1%

Even as the number of prisoners grew, both sides expected to resolve the problem through prisoner exchanges. The Confederacy held a surplus of prisoners in 1861 and believed that an exchange agreement would convey legitimacy to their cause by recognizing their right to negotiate as an equal power. President Abraham Lincoln was loath to provide such recognition, but he understood the need to redeem Union captives. In February 1862 negotiators agreed to a general exchange, using a rank equivalency table from 1813 allowing detainees of different ranks to be exchanged.

In June 1862 exchanges formally commenced, allowing each side to reduce the overcrowded facilities. The system allowed POWs to be exchanged from all branches of service, including privateers. All captives were to be paroled and forwarded to their own lines within 10 days of capture. Surplus prisoners were then held out of service by their own forces to await exchange. Although the system was imperfect, it functioned fairly well, and by the end of the year the prison compounds had virtually emptied.

At the end of 1862, the Union commenced enlistment of African American soldiers. Confederate president Jefferson Davis, fearing the possibility of a slave revolt, announced that white officers commanding black troops could be tried for inciting a servile insurrection. Lincoln threatened retaliation against Confederate prisoners for the mistreatment of any Union soldiers. The exchange cartel soon collapsed, and the number of detainees rapidly rose.

The Confederate advantage in prisoners captured ended in 1863. When Vicksburg surrendered in July 1863, Major General Ulysses S. Grant paroled its 30,000 defenders and sent them home to await exchange. The South did not possess sufficient captives for exchange but claimed that the Union had already received a surplus of parolees. After substantial debate, Confederate exchange commissioner Robert Ould unilaterally declared the Vicksburg captives exchanged. His Union counterpart, Major General Benjamin Butler, declared the cartel annulled, ensuring that the remaining and subsequent captives would languish in captivity for the rest of the war.

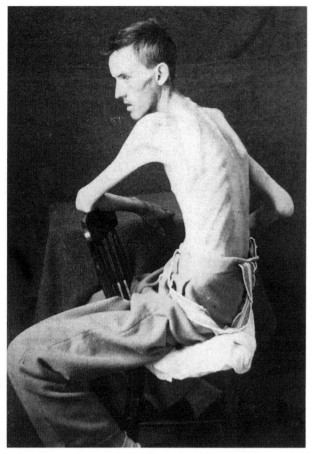

Prisoners of war, Union as well as Confederate, often had to undergo terrible conditions. Union private Jackson O. Broshears, shown here on his release in May 1864, went from 185 to only 109 pounds in little more than three months in Confederate hands. (Library of Congress)

The horrors of captivity associated with Civil War prison camps did not become manifest until 1864, when prison compounds became dangerously overcrowded and exchanges ceased. New facilities could not be completed before detainees began arriving, and supplies of food, clothing, and medicine were inadequate. On both sides, the detainment camps became disease-ridden and filthy, with some of the locations, such as Camp Sumter (Andersonville), Georgia, and Elmira, New York, suffering mortality rates of more than 30 percent. The largest contributor to POWs' misery was not a deliberate policy of mistreatment but rather a military and political system overwhelmed by the demands of the conflict. Detainees remained a low priority for each government, with both struggling to keep field armies supplied and functional. The needs of prisoners simply faded in the face of more pressing concerns. By the time the plight of captives had become well known, the war had nearly ended.

PAUL J. SPRINGER

See also

Butler, Benjamin Franklin; Elmira Prison, New York; Hoffman, William; Prisoner Exchanges; Prisons, Confederate; Prisons, U.S.; Winder, John Henry

Further Reading

Sanders, Charles W. *While in the Hands of the Enemy: Military Prisons of the Civil War.* Baton Rouge: Louisiana State University Press, 2005.

Speer, Lonnie R. *Portals to Hell: Military Prisons of the Civil War.* Mechanicsburg, PA: Stackpole, 1997.

Springer, Paul J. *America's Captives: Treatment of POWs from the Revolutionary War to the War on Terror.* Lawrence: University Press of Kansas, 2010.

Prisons, Confederate

During the Civil War, Confederate troops captured more than 211,000 Union prisoners of war. Fewer than 17,000 were paroled on the battlefield, leaving nearly 195,000 in captivity. More than 30,000 perished in Confederate prison facilities, for a mortality rate of more than 15.5 percent, compared to the Union mortality rate for Confederate prisoners of 12 percent.

Confederate leaders believed that the rebellion would require only a few skirmishes to demonstrate the seriousness of secession, and thus they did not foresee the capture and custody of so many enemy troops. The need to create a government from scratch and recruit, train, and supply an army, in addition to preparing to defend an enormous geographic region, soon overwhelmed the fledgling Confederacy. It is thus unsurprising that the need to prepare for captives remained a low priority at the outset of the conflict.

Although the first battles created an influx of prisoners, they were easily housed in the vicinity of the capital at Richmond. The Confederate provost marshal of Richmond, Brigadier General John H. Winder, became the de facto commissary general of prisoners, although he was not formally appointed to the post until late 1864. Winder initially ordered tobacco warehouses converted to prison compounds in the belief that the Union troops would soon be exchanged. However, exchange negotiations took longer than expected, and Winder began ordering detainees sent into captivity in other locations throughout the Southern states. Even when the prisoner exchange system began to function in 1862, Union prisoners sent for exchange were all routed through Richmond, ensuring that the city's detention facilities would remain almost constantly at or above capacity.

Castle Thunder, a former tobacco warehouse turned Confederate prison, in Richmond, Virginia, in 1865. Castle Thunder housed civilian prisoners, including Union spies and those charged with treason against the Confederacy. It had a well-deserved reputation for brutality. (Library of Congress)

In 1863 the exchange system effectively collapsed, largely due to accusations by each side that the other was attempting to cheat the system. Richmond's prison compounds, already too full, could not hold all of the incoming prisoners, and so Winder sought permission to construct new facilities well behind the front lines. He believed that the supply situation for prisons would be mitigated if prisoners lived near supplies of food. Construction of compounds commenced slowly, allowing Winder to relieve some of the pressure on the Richmond facilities.

Many of the new sites were poor locations, however, distant from rail lines and away from useful resources, including potable water. Many of the camps were opened before shelters could be constructed; thus, prisoners often were placed into empty stockades with poor water supplies and no construction materials. Department commanders began forwarding thousands of prisoners to these makeshift facilities, packing the stockades with new detainees. Disease and malnutrition soon spread throughout the camps. The most

notorious Confederate facility, Andersonville Prison (Camp Sumter), opened in February 1864 in west-central Georgia. Its compound, designed for up to 10,000 detainees, soon held more than 30,000. More than 100 prisoners died daily in the torrid summer months, resulting in nearly 13,000 dead at the camp in less than 11 months of operation.

After the war, contemporary politicians and later historians alleged that Confederate authorities had deliberately mistreated their captives. The commandant of Andersonville, Major Heinrich (Henry) Wirz, was tried, convicted, and executed for the deaths of prisoners in his charge in what is regarded as the first modern war crimes trial. In reality, the Confederate system, as awful as it was, reflected the general inability of the political and military leaders to create a supply system capable of maintaining their own forces, much less Union captives. The unfortunate Union prisoners were more victims of circumstance than a planned policy of torment.

Paul J. Springer

See also
Andersonville Prison, Georgia; Prisoner Exchanges; Prisoners of War; Winder, John Henry; Wirz, Heinrich Hartmann

Further Reading
Hesseltine, William B. *Civil War Prisons: A Study in War Psychology.* New York: F. Ungar, 1964.
Sanders, Charles W. *While in the Hands of the Enemy: Military Prisons of the Civil War.* Baton Rouge: Louisiana State University Press, 2005.
Speer, Lonnie R. *Portals to Hell: Military Prisons of the Civil War.* Mechanicsburg, PA: Stackpole, 1997.

Prisons, U.S.

During the Civil War, Union forces captured more than 460,000 Confederate military prisoners. More than half were paroled on the battlefield, but approximately 215,000 were sent into captivity in various Union compounds. Nearly 26,000 Confederate soldiers died in captivity, an overall mortality rate of approximately 12 percent.

Union officials initially expected the war to be a relatively short conflict. Therefore, they made inadequate preparations for the confinement and maintenance of enemy captives. Those who had expected large numbers of detainees believed that an exchange or parole system would be devised, obviating the need for an extensive prison system. Thus, the early Union prisons were primarily in the eastern theater, and many were converted state civil prison facilities ill-suited for holding military captives.

Colonel William C. Hoffman served as the Union commissary general of prisoners. His relatively low rank belied

The Old Capitol Prison in Washington, D.C. Many of those arrested following the assassination of President Abraham Lincoln were held here. The building was subsequently sold and razed, and the Supreme Court building now occupies the site. (National Archives)

the enormity of his task and greatly hampered his efforts to obtain assistance from higher-ranking field and department commanders. Even when he conveyed the urgent need for space, shelter, and sustenance of his charges, his pleas went largely unheeded. His problems were greatly compounded in 1863 when the crude but functional prisoner exchange system collapsed. That same year, major offensives by Union forces increased the number of enemy prisoners by thousands per month.

Hoffman resorted to improvisation, converting recruitment and training camps into prison compounds, which soon became massively overcrowded. The dense prisoner populations soon triggered disease outbreaks, a situation exacerbated by poorly functioning supply systems and a lack of proper hygiene among the captives. By 1864, reports of even worse conditions in Confederate prisons eroded what little compassion remained toward enemy prisoners. Hoffman ordered retaliatory reductions in the rations and medical supplies sent to each camp, allowing the mortality rate to quickly climb.

Both contemporary observers and historians have accused Union officials of deliberately mistreating their captives. Occasional recruitment of Confederate prisoners, offering them the opportunity to escape the camps in exchange for frontier service in the West, provides one possible explanation for the poor treatment of Confederate detainees. Approximately 6,000 Confederates (so-called Galvanized Yankees) chose to take the oath of allegiance and don a Union uniform, and most remained on frontier duty for the rest of the war.

In reality, it is unlikely that Union political and military leaders sought to mistreat the prisoners. They were simply overwhelmed by the demands of coordinating the largest war in the nation's history and spared little time or effort worrying about the welfare of an enemy whom many considered treasonous American citizens. While the mortality rate in the Union camps was high, it was not considered scandalous at the time and only became so in the decades after the war ended. In short, there is little evidence of intentional mistreatment of Confederate prisoners; rather, they were largely victims of bureaucratic inefficiency, strained logistics, and an inability to predict the future course of the conflict.

PAUL J. SPRINGER

See also
Hoffman, William; Prisoner Exchanges; Prisoners of War; Prisons, Confederate

Further Reading
Hesseltine, William B. *Civil War Prisons: A Study in War Psychology.* New York: F. Ungar, 1964.

Sanders, Charles W. *While in the Hands of the Enemy: Military Prisons of the Civil War.* Baton Rouge: Louisiana State University Press, 2005.

Speer, Lonnie R. *Portals to Hell: Military Prisons of the Civil War.* Mechanicsburg, PA: Stackpole, 1997.

Privateers

Privately owned vessels sailing under special commissions issued by their governments in time of war that authorized them to capture ships of an enemy power, be they warships or merchant vessels. Privateering was not new to the United States. A great many privateers had taken to the seas during both the Revolutionary War and the War of 1812.

On April 17, 1861, two days after President Abraham Lincoln called for 75,000 volunteers in the wake of the attack on Fort Sumter, Confederate president Jefferson Davis and Secretary of State Robert Toombs issued a statement accusing Lincoln of planning to invade the Confederacy. They invited applications from Confederate citizens for letters of marque and reprisal. The Confederate Congress then passed a bill recognizing a state of war with the United States and establishing regulations for "letters of marque, prizes, and prize goods" similar to those employed by the United States during the War of 1812. Davis signed the bill into law on May 6.

Davis and other Southern leaders believed that privateering was legally justified, because alone among major powers, the United States and Spain had failed to ratify the 1856 Declaration of Paris, the signatories of which foreswore the employment of privateers. Privateering seemed a natural recourse for a nation without a navy and thus dependent upon private assistance. In retaliation, on April 19 Lincoln proclaimed a blockade of the Confederate coasts and warned that privateers would be subject to the U.S. laws against piracy.

Confederate secretary of the navy Stephen R. Mallory had little confidence in privateers, but even modest success would force up insurance rates in the North and adversely affect the business sector. Also, even a few such vessels would oblige the U.S. Navy to shift warships from the blockade to hunt privateers. Mallory was strongly in favor of commerce raiding, but he wanted national cruisers, which were not available at the start of the conflict.

Lincoln's threat did not deter applications for letters of marque, with the first coming on the day after Davis's invitation. On May 10, the same day that the regulations were published, the government granted the first commission, to the 30-ton schooner *Triton* of Brunswick, Georgia. One of the smallest privateers, it was armed with a single 6-pounder and had a crew of 20 men. The largest of the Confederate privateers, the 1,644-ton steamer *Phenix,* was fitted out in Wilmington, North Carolina, at the end of May. It mounted seven guns and had a crew of 243. Although by midsummer letters of marque and reprisal had been issued to ships in most of the major Confederate ports, the chief venues remained Charleston and New Orleans. In all, the Confederacy issued letters of marque for 52 privateers.

The few Confederate privateers that made it to sea in May found easy hunting. The first success came on May 16, when the 509-ton *Calhoun* of New Orleans with five guns captured the 290-ton Union merchant bark *Ocean Eagle* from Maine off the mouth of the Mississippi. During the next two weeks, the *Calhoun* took five other Union ships, three of them whalers. Two other New Orleans privateers, the steamers *Music* and *V. H. Ivy,* captured four Union ships.

The arrival off the Mississippi of the powerful U.S. Navy screw sloop *Brooklyn* at the end of May soon put an end to privateering from the Crescent City. Although such activity at New Orleans was short-lived, privateering was just reaching its heyday along the Atlantic coast. Typical of the Atlantic coast privateers was the fast schooner *Savannah* of 53 tons with a crew of 20 men and armed with a single short 18-pounder of War of 1812 vintage turned into a rifled gun, as well as an array of muskets, pistols, and cutlasses. On June 3, the *Savannah* captured the merchant brig *Joseph* of Philadelphia, the first prize taken by a Charleston privateer. Toward evening that same day, the crew spotted another sail and ran to it, but the vessel in question turned out to be the U.S. Navy brig *Perry,* mounting six 32-pounders. Hopelessly outclassed, the *Savannah* struck after a 20-minute fight. Sailed to New York, it was there condemned and sold.

The crew of the *Savannah* became something of a cause célèbre. Branded as "pirates" by the Northern press and the U.S. government, the men were brought to trial and, under public pressure, were threatened with the death penalty. President Davis then issued a statement to the effect that if they were executed, he would hang Union officers on a one-for-one basis. For whatever reason, the U.S. government soon backed down. In February 1862, Washington decided that captured privateersmen would be treated as prisoners of war and moved from jails to military prisons.

Union warships soon ran down the remaining Confederate privateers. Some were taken at sea, while others succumbed to cutting-out operations in which Union forces went into a harbor and seized the ship by storm. Still others fell

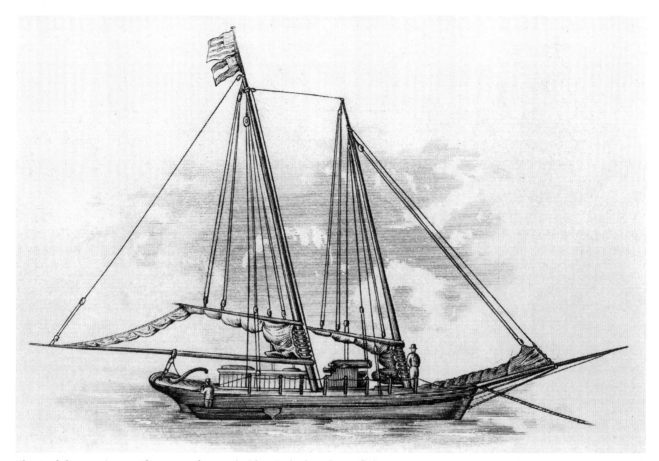

The Confederate privateer *The Savannah*. Armed with a single shot, short rifled gun, on June 3, 1861, it made the first privateer capture of the war but was that same evening taken by a Union warship. (Library of Congress)

prey to natural causes. Privateers were in fact not much used in the war. The decision of the British government, copied by the other maritime powers, to ban privateer prizes from British ports dealt a death blow to Confederate privateering. The increasing effectiveness of the Union blockade rendered it more difficult to send prizes to the South, and more and more of the prizes were recaptured. Subsequently, many privateer vessels were simply converted into blockade-runners. Two of the most unusual Confederate privateers were at New Orleans: the ironclad ram *Manassas* and the submarine *Pioneer*. The Confederate war against Union commerce was nonetheless carried on with considerable effectiveness by Mallory's regularly commissioned naval warships.

SPENCER C. TUCKER

See also

Davis, Jefferson Finis; Great Britain; Lincoln, Abraham; Mallory, Stephen Russell; Navy, Confederate; Toombs, Robert Augustus

Further Reading

Robinson, William Morrison, Jr. *The Confederate Privateers.* 1928; reprint, Columbia: University of South Carolina Press, 1990.

Tucker, Spencer C. *A Naval History of the Civil War.* Annapolis, MD: Naval Institute Press, 2006.

Prize Cases

U.S. Supreme Court case decided on March 10, 1863, upholding President Abraham Lincoln's proclamation of blockade against Confederate ports shortly after the outbreak of the Civil War in 1861. The case involved two Confederate merchant ships, one Mexican vessel, and one British ship. They were captured separately by Union warships at different ports and brought in for adjudication in a federal prize court. All four ships were condemned, with their cargoes, under the proclamation of blockade. The vessels and cargoes were sold at public auction, and the proceeds of the sales were held in the registry of the courts for the benefit of the Union government and the crews of the captors, as provided by law.

All of the owners contested the validity of the blockade proclamation and appealed to the U.S. Supreme Court.

Because the issues were identical, the four cases were consolidated for argument in a single proceeding generally known as the *Prize Cases.*

Upholding the blockade—the principal purpose of which was to prevent the exchange of Southern cotton for foreign weapons and other supplies much needed by the Confederacy—was of enormous importance to the Union. A secondary but critical issue was the delicate matter of the Court's perception of the status of the Confederacy.

Blockade is an act of war, and the Lincoln administration needed the Court to recognize that war actually existed without implying the independent sovereignty of the Confederacy. A different conclusion might have justified the British and French, both of whom badly needed Southern cotton for their textile mills, in recognizing and dealing with the Confederacy as an independent nation. This would have placed Lincoln under great pressure to consider proposals for a negotiated peace.

Although Southern-born justices led the Supreme Court, it decided the *Prize Cases* in Lincoln's favor on both issues by a vote of 5 to 4. Most historians attribute this narrow victory to the persuasive gifts of Richard Henry Dana Jr., U.S. attorney for the District of Massachusetts (and author of *Two Years before the Mast*), who was the principal advocate for the captors.

Officially, the cases are known by the names of the four ships: the *Amy Warwick, Crenshaw, Hiawatha* and *Brilliante.*

DONALD A. PETRIE

See also
Blockade of the Confederacy, Union; Dana, Richard Henry, Jr.; Supreme Court, U.S.

Further Reading
Petrie, Donald A. *The Prize Game: Lawful Looting on the High Seas in the Days of Fighting Sail.* Annapolis, MD: Naval Institute Press, 1999.
U.S. Supreme Court. "Opinion of the United States Supreme Court in the Brig Amy Warwick; The Schooner Crenshaw; The Barque Hiawatha; The Schooner Brilliante." 67 U.S. 635. Washington, DC: U.S. Government Printing Office, 1863.

Protectionism

The use of high tariffs (taxes on imported goods) to protect domestic industries from foreign competition. Treasury Secretary Alexander Hamilton instituted America's first protectionist trade policy in the 1790s to prevent cheaper English imports from smothering infant American industries. Hamilton spoke for northern manufacturing interests

who believed that the nation's economic future depended on industrial development. Southern planters, however, generally opposed burdensome tariffs as a tax on one class—consumers—for the benefit of another.

Tariff rates decreased under President Thomas Jefferson but increased again after the War of 1812. The balance tipped against protectionism during the Democrat ascendency of the Jacksonian era. Although the protariff Whigs remained politically competitive, they could not reinstate the protectionist policies called for in Henry Clay's American System. In contrast to protectionism, the Walker Tariff of 1846 reduced rates, establishing a tariff for revenue purposes only. Additional cuts in 1857 reduced import duties even further.

In 1860 the Republican Party campaigned on increasing tariff rates, and their presidential candidate, Abraham Lincoln, was a devout adherent to Henry Clay's economic nationalist and protectionist philosophy. The Republican stance on the tariff issue further alienated Southerners, who opposed protectionism and helped ensure that the Republican ticket would fare poorly in the South during the November 1860 elections. Republicans implemented a moderate tariff rate increase in March 1861 to offset the growing federal debt caused by the financial panic of 1857. The U.S. government enacted additional rate increases in August and December 1861 in response to wartime revenue needs.

In 1862 Congress passed the Morrill rates, which further increased the tariff rates on imports. With virtually no Southerners to represent the agrarian opposition in Congress and with Northern Democrats scrambling to protect industries in their own districts, the rate increase passed handily. Although considered a war measure, the new tariff contributed little to paying the massive cost of the war. Combined with the Homestead Act and Transcontinental Railroad subsidies, the Morrill Act marked the fulfillment of a Whig-inspired Republican economic agenda promised in the 1860 party platform. Further demands for revenue led to another increase in 1864, effectively doubling the 1857 rates.

In successfully tying protectionism to patriotism and fiscal solvency, the Civil War Morrill Acts ushered in a period of high rates on imports that lasted for decades.

GREGORY J. DEHLER

See also
Democratic Party; Election of 1860, U.S.; Industry; Morrill Land-Grant Colleges Act; Republican Party; Tariffs

Further Reading
Ratmer, Sidney. *The Tariff in American History.* New York: D. Van Nostrand, 1972.

Richardson, Heather Cox. *The Greatest Nation on Earth: Republican Economic Policy during the Civil War.* Cambridge, MA: Harvard University Press, 1997.

Protestant Revivals

Religious renewal movements that frequently took hold among soldiers during the Civil War. In the years between 1800 and 1861, Protestant revivalism had been branded the Second Great Awakening, and it became a distinct social as well as religious ritual. Flowing from and coupled with these revivals was a strong commitment to social reform addressing many subjects, among them slavery and abolition. Religious sentiments and impulses continued into the war years on the home fronts and in the armies. Religious motivations and convictions were strong among Union and Confederate troops, as they provided a source of meaning and comfort for understanding the hardships and tragedies of the war. A yearning for religious symbolism as well as divine assistance and favor was routinely invoked by chaplains and commanders during the war.

As soldiers from both sides went into winter camps and experienced a slower operational pace, religious revivals among Protestant soldiers erupted during the winters of 1862–1863 and 1864–1865. While there was certainly strong religious commitment by Jewish and Roman Catholic soldiers, the revivals were distinctly Protestant. Evening meetings of prayer, preaching, and singing led by chaplains, visiting clergy, and soldiers within the ranks provided spiritual renewal and alternatives to the vices and hardships of camp life and military service. When cold weather prohibited outdoor services, log chapels were often built to provide physical and spiritual refuge.

The revival spirit encompassed both enlisted men and officers, including Confederate general Robert E. Lee and Lieutenant General Thomas J. "Stonewall" Jackson. Revivals were more prominent among Confederates and were especially strong in the Army of Northern Virginia and the Army of Tennessee. In the North, the United States Christian Commission was especially prominent in providing religious, social, and recreational services to troops, often coordinating efforts with the medical services of the U.S. Sanitary Commission.

One significant outcome of the revivals in the South was the strengthening of the resolve to continue the war. By providing religious justification for participation in the war effort and bolstering the morale of the individual soldier, the revivals prolonged the will to fight.

TIMOTHY J. DEMY

See also

Chaplains

Further Reading

Miller, Randall M., Harry S. Stout, and Charles Reagan Wilson, ed. *Religion and the American Civil War.* New York: Oxford University Press, 1998.

Rable, George C. *God's Almost Chosen Peoples: A Religious History of the American Civil War.* Chapel Hill: University of North Carolina Press, 2010.

Woodworth, Stephen E. *While God Is Marching On: The Religious World of the Civil War Soldiers.* Lawrence: University of Kansas Press, 2001.

Provisional Army of the Confederate States

Confederate military organization consisting chiefly of militia units and volunteers and designed to be a temporary force that would be dissolved at the end of hostilities. The Provisional Confederate Congress authorized the Provisional Army of the Confederate States on February 28, 1861, which began organizing on April 27, 1861. The Provisional Army was designed as a separate entity from the Army of the Confederate States (regular army), which was authorized at a maximum strength of 15,000 men, although that number was never achieved during the Civil War. The regular army was designed to be controlled solely by the central government and would become the Confederacy's only army once hostilities ceased. Almost all of the Confederacy's highest-ranking officers belonged to the regular army, mainly to avoid being outranked by militia officers or volunteers.

The vast majority of Confederate militiamen and volunteers joined the Provisional Army, in which officers could normally attain a higher rank in a shorter period of time. The Provisional Army was a clear nod to states' rights, as the individual states were supposed to have control over its recruitment, organization, supply, and maintenance as well as the appointment of officers. When it was first formed, the Provisional Army included militiamen who enlisted for 12-month terms; as the war went on, however, it included hundreds of thousands of volunteers from every Confederate state as well as loyal slave states such as Kentucky, Maryland, and Missouri.

In May 1861, the Confederate government was empowered to incorporate volunteer units into the Provisional Army without states' consent, appoint field officers, and organize men into units at the brigade level and higher. Richmond gradually asserted more control over the Provisional Army, and it became largely responsible for recruitment and organization. This increased centralization and the small size of the regular army ensured that the Provisional Army became the Confederacy's principal combat force, much as the U.S. Volunteers did for the Union.

PAUL G. PIERPAOLI JR.

See also

Armies of the Confederate States, Overview; Army Organization, CSA; Congress, CSA

Further Reading

Connelly, Thomas Lawrence, and Archer Jones. *The Politics of Command: Factions and Ideas in Confederate Strategy.* Baton Rouge: Louisiana State University Press, 1973.

Eicher, John H., and David J. Eicher. *Civil War High Commands.* Stanford, CA: Stanford University Press, 2001.

Pryor, Roger Atkinson
Birth Date: July 19, 1828
Death Date: March 14, 1919

Confederate officer. Roger Atkinson Pryor was born on July 19, 1828, near Petersburg, Virginia. He graduated from Hampden-Sydney College in 1845 and studied law at the University of Virginia before being admitted to the Virginia bar in 1849. After briefly practicing law, he became involved in journalism, serving on the editorial staffs of the *Washington Union* and the *Richmond Enquirer.* In 1854 Pryor was appointed special U.S. envoy to Greece. Returning to America soon thereafter, he established the *South,* a secessionist daily newspaper, and wrote for another paper, the *States.* In 1859 he was elected to the U.S. House of Representatives, in which he backed secession and served until 1861.

Following President Lincoln's inauguration, Pryor went to Charleston, where he served as a volunteer on Brigadier General P. G. T. Beauregard's staff and was present during the bombardment of Fort Sumter. Pryor was elected to the Confederate Provisional Congress but declined in favor of entering the military. Commissioned a colonel, he assumed command of the 3rd Virginia Infantry. Elected to the First Confederate Congress, he briefly retained his seat while still serving in the field. Pryor was promoted to brigadier general on April 16, 1862, and led a brigade in the Army of Northern Virginia during the Peninsula Campaign (March–July 1862), the Second Battle of Bull Run (July 29–30, 1862), and the Battle of Antietam (September 17, 1862).

Although Pryor seems to have performed well, his brigade was broken up, and he was assigned a lackluster command in southern Virginia, from which he was ousted in March 1863. Clearly unwanted and without a field command, Pryor resigned his commission on August 18, 1863. That same month, he volunteered as a private to scout for Major General Fitzhugh Lee's cavalry. Pryor was captured while performing scouting duty on November 27, 1864, and was confined at Fort Lafayette until the spring of 1865.

Following the war, Pryor moved to New York, where he wrote for the *Daily News* until 1866. He then established a law practice in the city. In 1890 Pryor was appointed to the New York Court of Common Pleas, and in 1896 he was appointed to the New York Supreme Court, a post he held until his mandatory retirement in 1899. In 1912 he was appointed referee for the appellate division of the New York Supreme Court. Pryor died in New York on March 14, 1919.

ROBERT P. BROADWATER

See also

Antietam, Battle of; Bull Run, Second Battle of; Lee, Fitzhugh; Peninsula Campaign

Further Reading

Holzman, Robert S. *Adapt, or Perish: Life of General Roger A. Pryor.* Lancaster, UK: Gazelle Book Services, 1976.

Waugh, John C. *Surviving the Confederacy: Rebellion, Ruin, and Recovery; Roger and Sarah Pryor during the Civil War.* Boston: Harcourt, 2002.

Q

Quaker Guns

False artillery. Quaker guns were a deception, usually a log or other material shaped and painted to appear as an artillery piece from a distance. Most often employed by the Confederates, Quaker guns were used to deceive opposing forces regarding the number of artillery pieces actually possessed and to convince enemy forces that one's own side was defending a particular position when this was not actually the case. The term "Quaker gun" is a reference to the Society of Friends, the pacifist religious denomination often called Quakers. Quaker guns played a small but significant role in the American Civil War.

One early example of Quaker guns occurred on September 28, 1861, when Confederate forces evacuated Munson's Hill, Virginia, leaving their earthworks to an advancing Union force. When the Union soldiers reached the Confederate lines, they discovered two logs and one stovepipe guarding a shallow ditch rather than the three Parrott guns reported by Union scouts.

During Major General George B. McClellan's Peninsula Campaign (March–July 1862), Confederate defenders attempting to delay the Army of the Potomac again resorted to deception. In early 1862 McClellan, never an aggressive commander, refused President Abraham Lincoln's repeated request that he advance south from Washington to Richmond, choosing to believe reports that he faced almost 100,000 Confederate troops at Manassas Junction, supported by more than 300 artillery pieces. In reality, his front was opposed by only 40,000 soldiers and a wide assortment of Quaker guns. McClellan's hesitation combined with the gullibility of Union scouts led to a delay of weeks, which allowed Confederate general Joseph E. Johnston to organize the defenses of the Confederate capital.

When Johnston ordered the evacuation of the Manassas-Centreville line, newspaper reporters quickly noticed that he had left a significant quantity of desperately needed artillery. To McClellan's humiliation, after closer inspection it was determined that the "artillery" were logs painted black. In the Siege of Yorktown (April 5–May 3, 1862), Confederate major general John B. Magruder also made extensive use of Quaker guns. The Union side also employed Quaker guns in the Peninsula Campaign (March–July 1862).

PAUL J. SPRINGER

See also
Johnston, Joseph Eggleston; McClellan, George Brinton; Parrott Gun; Peninsula Campaign; Potomac, Union Army of the

Further Reading
Cullen, Joseph P. *The Peninsula Campaign, 1862: McClellan and Lee Struggle for Richmond.* Harrisburg, PA: Stackpole, 1973.
Gallagher, Gary. *The Richmond Campaign of 1862: The Peninsula and the Seven Days.* Chapel Hill: University of North Carolina Press, 2000.

Confederate "Quaker" guns, logs mounted so as to deceive Union forces, in the fortifications at Centreville, Virginia, March 1862. (National Archives)

Quakers

A Protestant religious movement founded in England in the mid-17th century. Officially known as the Society of Friends, the Quakers were founded by George Fox in England in the 1650s. Although raised an Anglican, Fox began to preach in 1647 after a spiritual vision inspired him to minister. He called for a profound spiritual renewal within England, supported the prohibition of alcohol, and preached against holidays, sports, and all other activities that diverted attention from the spirit.

The group that arose around Fox professed the belief that Christ provided individuals with an inner light so that believers could experience personal illumination from God in their daily lives. Followers of Fox became known as Quakers because they reportedly shook when filled with the Holy Spirit. As part of what was considered a radical fringe, the Quakers attracted much persecution in England and the New World. They especially stood apart with their distinctive code of dress and manners and their refusal to observe status distinctions, swear oaths, or pay tithes to the established church.

Rhode Island was an early refuge for Quakers in North America and sheltered William Penn during the 1660s. When Penn inherited the large tract of land that became

Pennsylvania, it provided Quakers with plenty of land in which to practice religious freedom and from which to gain a comfortable living. Other colonies were not so tolerant, however, and many persecuted them openly.

Quakers were among the earliest abolitionists in the New World. In England, Quakers were prominent in the antislavery and prison reform campaigns. Quakers did not believe in violence of any sort, so their members usually refused to take up arms even if the cause was a just one. Before the Civil War, breaking the laws of the land to keep the laws of their creed, Quakers smuggled many runaway slaves north on the Underground Railroad.

As the 1850s progressed, Quakers, including Lucretia Mott who founded both the Female Anti-Slavery Society and the Philadelphia Anti-Slavery Society, increased their antislavery activities. In Mott's case, she linked abolitionism with the newly emergent woman's movement. In the 1850s, Levi Coffin, also a Quaker, became a leading figure in the Underground Railroad, which appealed to a broad range of Quakers because they could circumvent what they considered to be unjust laws in a nonviolent fashion.

When war began in 1861, many Quakers were torn. While their religion precluded them from participating in the war, they also believed that the Union's cause was a just one. Quakers refused to pay commutation fees or hire a substitute to fight for them because doing so was de facto support of violence. Nevertheless, a number of Quakers quietly served in the Union Army. Most were not ostracized for their religion, which was a powerful example of the moral ambivalence that many Quakers had toward the Civil War. During the war and in the postbellum Reconstruction period, Quakers were at the forefront of private efforts to educate and support newly free African Americans.

TIM J. WATTS AND PAUL G. PIERPAOLI JR.

See also
Abolitionism and the Civil War; Churches; Mott, Lucretia Coffin

Further Reading
Bacon, Margaret Hope. *The Quiet Rebels: The Story of the Quakers in America.* Philadelphia: New Society Publishers, 1985.
Loukes, Harold. *The Discovery of Quakerism.* London: George B. Harrap, 1960.

Quantrill, William Clarke
Birth Date: July 21, 1837
Death Date: June 6, 1865

Confederate guerrilla. William Clarke Quantrill was born on July 21, 1837, in Canal Dover, Ohio. At age 16 he went west, eventually settling in Kansas, where he taught school briefly and then became a farmer. Concurrently, he became a notorious gambler and bandit. A rough-hewn and bloodthirsty individual, Quantrill soon became involved in the border fighting that erupted in Kansas and Missouri after the Civil War began in April 1861. Using the chaos to further his own agenda, he engaged in sacking pro-Union communities.

At the Battle of Wilson's Creek (August 10, 1861), Quantrill fought alongside Confederate forces, although he held no appointment in the military at that time. The following year he commenced a guerrilla campaign in Missouri, sacking Independence in August 1862. During the course of the war, his bands included the likes of George Todd, William "Bloody Bill" Anderson, Cole and Jim Younger, Frank James, and, late in the war, young Jesse James. In the early autumn of 1862, Quantrill finally received a commission as a captain in the Confederate Army, although he was never officially attached to a regular unit. His superior officers reported that he had effective leadership skills, but his decided lack of ethics proved to be a continual problem. In early November 1862, Quantrill and his company of guerrillas ambushed a

wagon train. All 12 unarmed teamsters were shot through the head. Quantrill's most despicable exploit came on August 21, 1863, when he led a band of 400 guerrillas and outlaws on a raid of Lawrence, Kansas. During the resulting melee, 150 men and boys were systematically executed. When the killing was done, Quantrill pillaged and then torched the town. News of the Lawrence massacre shocked Northerners and Southerners alike, although Confederate authorities did not revoke Quantrill's commission or discipline him in any way. In fact, he could not be controlled, and his guerrilla tactics persisted.

On October 6, 1863, Quantrill and his men attacked and looted a Union stronghold at Baxter Springs, Kansas. Later that same day, they happened upon a Union military wagon train and ambushed it; 89 Union soldiers, including 17 unarmed musicians, were murdered. After retreating to Texas, Quantrill recruited a new band with which he moved to Kentucky. He was severely wounded during a raid in Kentucky on May 10, 1865. Quantrill was subsequently captured by Union troops and died in a Louisville prison hospital on June 6, 1865.

PAUL G. PIERPAOLI JR.

See also
Baxter Springs, Battle of; Guerrilla Warfare; Lawrence, Kansas, Raid on; Wilson's Creek, Battle of

Further Reading
Leslie, Edward E. *The Devil Knows How to Ride: The True Story of William Clarke Quantrill and His Confederate Raiders.* New York: Da Capo, 1996.
Peterson, Paul R. *Quantrill of Missouri: The Making of a Guerrilla Warrior—The Man, the Myth, the Soldier.* Nashville: Cumberland House, 2003.

Quarles, William Andrew
Birth Date: July 4, 1825
Death Date: December 28, 1893

Confederate officer. William Andrew Quarles was born on July 4, 1825, in James City County, Virginia, and moved to Kentucky as a youth. He attended the University of Virginia, passed the bar in 1848, and opened a legal practice in Clarksville, Tennessee. He then served as a circuit court judge, a bank supervisor, and president of the Memphis, Clarksville & Louisville Railroad. When the Civil War began, Quarles was elected colonel of the 42nd Tennessee Infantry Regiment, serving under General Albert Sidney Johnston. In early February 1862, Quarles's regiment reported to Brigadier

General Gideon J. Pillow at Fort Donelson. Quarles saw action during the Battle of Fort Donelson (February 13–16, 1862) but was taken prisoner following the post's surrender. Exchanged late that summer, he served in Mississippi during the Second Vicksburg Campaign (April 1–July 4, 1863) and was promoted to brigadier general on August 25, 1863. Quarles then assumed command of a brigade at Mobile that was dispatched to Chattanooga in the autumn of 1863, but he arrived too late to see action at the Battle of Missionary Ridge (November 25, 1863).

After returning to Mobile, Quarles's brigade was then ordered to Georgia to take part in the Atlanta Campaign (May 5–September 2, 1864). The brigade moved north into Tennessee in the autumn of 1864, and Quarles saw action at the Battle of Franklin (November 30, 1864), where he was seriously wounded and taken prisoner. Quarles was not released until May 25, 1865. He subsequently returned to his law practice in Clarksville and sat in the Tennessee Senate (1875–1877 and 1887–1889). Quarles died in Todd County, Kentucky, on December 28, 1893.

PAUL G. PIERPAOLI JR.

See also

Atlanta Campaign; Fort Donelson, Battle of; Franklin, Battle of; Johnston, Albert Sidney; Pillow, Gideon Johnson

Further Reading

Tucker, Spencer C. *"Unconditional Surrender": The Capture of Forts Henry and Donelson, February 1862*. Abilene, TX: McWhiney Foundation Press, 2001.

Warner, Ezra J. *Generals in Gray: Lives of the Confederate Commanders*. Baton Rouge: Louisiana State University Press, 2006.

Quinby, Isaac Ferdinand
Birth Date: January 29, 1821
Death Date: September 18, 1891

Union officer. Isaac Ferdinand Quinby was born on January 29, 1821, near Morristown, New Jersey. After graduating from the U.S. Military Academy, West Point, in 1843, he was commissioned as a second lieutenant in the 2nd Artillery Regiment. He subsequently saw service during the Mexican-American War (1846–1848) and was promoted to first lieutenant in 1847. Quinby resigned his commission in 1852 and took a position as a mathematics and philosophy professor at Rochester University in New York.

With the outbreak of the Civil War in April 1861, Quinby entered the volunteer army and became colonel of the 13th New York Infantry Regiment. He led his regiment during the First Battle of Bull Run (July 21, 1861). The next month, he resigned his commission to return to teaching; however, on March 17, 1862, he once again reentered the army, this time as a brigadier general of volunteers. Ordered west, he briefly commanded the Sub-District of Columbus, Kentucky. Subsequent to that, he became the commander of the District of Mississippi.

Quinby held several other district commands before assuming command of the 7th Division, XIII Corps, in October 1862. In January 1863 Quinby's division became part of XVII Corps, commanded by Major General James McPherson. After the Yazoo Pass Expedition (February–April 1863) had begun, Quinby's division was dispatched as reinforcements. On March 20, Quinby conferred with Rear Admiral David Dixon Porter and Brigadier General Leonard F. Ross, who were leading the expedition, and it was decided that another attempt would be made to forge through the pass. When that failed, the expedition was cancelled on April 4. Quinby fell ill, however, during the operations. Although still too ill to lead his men, he was present at the Battle of Champion Hill (May 16, 1863).

On May 22, 1863, Quinby had recovered sufficiently enough to command his division during an assault on Vicksburg, Mississippi, but by June 3 illness again forced him from the field. He never again held a field command. He later commanded a draft depot in Elmira, New York, before resigning his commission on December 31, 1863.

Quinby took up his professorship, which he held until 1884. He concurrently served as a U.S. marshal from 1869 to 1877. Quinby died on September 18, 1891, in Rochester, New York.

PAUL G. PIERPAOLI JR.

See also

Bull Run, First Battle of; Champion Hill, Battle of; Vicksburg Campaign, Second; Yazoo Pass Expedition

Further Reading

Ballard, Michael. *Vicksburg: The Campaign That Opened the Mississippi*. Chapel Hill: University of North Carolina Press, 2004.

Eicher, John H., and David J. Eicher. *Civil War High Commands*. Stanford, CA: Stanford University Press, 2001.

R

Racism and Racial Prejudice

Racism and racial prejudice were endemic during the Civil War in both the North and the South. Racial prejudice was widespread among all socioeconomic groups. Those with much education were just as likely to harbor racism as were those with little or no education. Indeed, racism was quite open, disregarded by most, institutionalized, and seen as a normal way of life. Even those individuals who championed freedom and civil rights for African Americans and other racial or ethnic minorities tended to harbor certain prejudices, especially viewed from the modern perspective. However, racism was not confined to civilian life; it was prominent within the ranks of the military in both the Union and the Confederacy.

Black Americans suffered a multitude of racial injustices inflicted upon them by white society before, during, and after the war. In the landmark U.S. Supreme Court case *Dred Scott v. Sanford* (1857), a slave (Scott) was refused his freedom in spite of residing on free soil. The high court determined that slaves were not U.S. citizens and were therefore not afforded the rights of citizenship. Scott did not have the right to sue for his freedom in a court of law because he was not a citizen and thus was returned to his master. With the Court ruling in favor of slave owners, any compromise on the issue of slavery—let alone equal rights—was nearly impossible. This only bolstered the institution of slavery and promoted racial segregation.

Even though the Northern states were considered free soil and slavery was not permitted in many states, feelings of prejudice and superiority harbored by white citizens in the North were in many cases no less rigid than those of their Southern brethren. In some cities—such as Boston, Massachusetts; Philadelphia, Pennsylvania; Cincinnati, Ohio; and Providence, Rhode Island—free blacks were allowed to live alongside whites. Despite this, many services and basic constitutional rights, including education, the right to vote, and work that paid a living wage, were not available to these individuals. Indeed, most blacks in the North held menial low-paying positions such as house servants, store clerks, manual laborers, and mariners.

In the South, free black communities were virtually nonexistent, despite the fact there were 58,042 free blacks in the state of Virginia and an additional 83,942 residing in the border state of Maryland. These two states alone accounted for approximately 44 percent of the free black population in the South during the Civil War. Free blacks were not permitted to live in large enclaves, and they were usually barred from living in close proximity to whites. In South Carolina between 1859 and 1860, four pieces of legislation were proposed that would have either removed or enslaved free blacks in that state. In the South, many blacks worked menial jobs, such as laborers and house servants. Although free blacks worked in many of the same fields as their Northern counterparts, they were subjected to even harsher treatment and prejudice.

Prior to the Civil War, the U.S. Navy counted only a handful of black seamen, but the majority of their responsibilities were menial at best, and enlistments were on a quota system. The U.S. Army officially did not allow black soldiers until well into the war, with the issuance of the Emancipation Proclamation. The U.S. Marine Corps did not allow the enlistment of blacks under any circumstances; indeed, this remained so until after World War II. Militaries typically are a reflection of the larger society they serve, and so the U.S. military during the Civil War was no different.

Denying blacks the right to serve and fight was justified by several specious arguments that held that whites were superior and that blacks had lower intelligence and questionable morals and would perform poorly under the stress of combat. This mind-set of pervasive racism and bigotry could well have divided the Union Army itself without the help of Confederate secession. On several occasions during the spring of 1861 after President Abraham Lincoln's call for troops, free blacks who wished to organize and drill in Providence were broken up by police, who declared them "disorderly gatherings." Another episode, in April 1861, saw whites in Baltimore stoning a black man who had tried to join a Pennsylvania unit headed for the defense of Washington, D.C. On April 23, 1861, Union brigadier general Benjamin Butler offered to provide the Maryland governor with troops to put down a suspected slave revolt, which was in reality a small gathering of free blacks who hoped to enlist in the Union Army. For the most part, Union soldiers did not want to fight for or with blacks.

Large numbers of blacks joined the U.S. Navy during the war, making up perhaps 15–16 percent of its strength. They served aboard ships and lived alongside whites. Blacks were also ultimately permitted to serve in the Union Army but in segregated infantry and artillery units commanded by white officers; however, these units typically were not extensively utilized in combat roles. One such example included the free blacks who enlisted in Tennessee but were utilized as labor to build forts, railroads, and telegraph lines and work as teamsters. Although all-black units were usually not engaged in combat, there were instances when they truly distinguished themselves. These included engagements at Port Hudson (March 14–July 3, 1863), Milliken's Bend (June 7, 1863), and Fort Wagner (July 18, 1863). The latter of these is probably the best known. Here, the 54th Massachusetts Infantry, an all-black regiment commanded by Colonel Robert Gould Shaw, particularly distinguished itself.

The effects of racism and racial prejudice affected black soldiers not only in their everyday routines but also especially if they were captured by Confederate troops, who typically subjected them to much harsher treatment than white captive soldiers received. Many black soldiers were returned to slavery. Others were simply killed. Perhaps the most infamous instance of such prejudice occurred at the Battle of Fort Pillow (April 12, 1864), where black troops who had surrendered were slaughtered by Confederate troops.

Eric V. Reynolds

See also
African Americans; African American Sailors; African American Soldiers, CSA; African American Soldiers, U.S.; *Dred Scott Case*; 54th Massachusetts Regiment of Infantry; Fort Pillow, Battle of; Fort Wagner, South Carolina, Siege of; Freedmen; Milliken's Bend, Battle of; Port Hudson, Louisiana, Action at; Slavery

Further Reading
Astor, Gerald. *The Right to Fight: A History of African Americans in the Military*. Cambridge, MA: Da Capo, 1998.
Lovett, Bobby L. "The Negro's Civil War in Tennessee, 1861–1865." *Journal of Negro History* 61(1) (January 1976): 36–50.

Radford, William
Birth Date: September 9, 1809
Death Date: January 8, 1890

Union naval officer. William Radford was born in Fincastle, Virginia, on September 9, 1809, but moved to Kentucky as a boy. He entered the U.S. Navy on a midshipman's warrant on March 1, 1825. Radford was promoted to passed midshipman on June 4, 1831, and to lieutenant on February 9, 1837. Sea service included cruises with the West Indies, Mediterranean, and Pacific Squadrons. During the Mexican-American War (1846–1848), Radford commanded the landing party from the sloop *Warren* that captured the Mexican brig *Malek Adhel* at Mazatlán on September 7, 1846. He also took part in other Pacific coast operations during the war. Radford was promoted to commander on September 14, 1855.

When the Civil War began, Radford was commanding the steam sloop *Dacotah* in the Far East and led the first U.S. Navy expedition up the Chang Jiang (Yangtze River) to Hankou (Hankow). Because Radford was from Virginia, U.S. secretary of the navy Gideon Welles doubted his loyalty and relieved him of command, ordering him to return to the United States. Radford served as a lighthouse inspector until Welles was assured of his patriotism and gave him command of the sailing sloop *Cumberland* in the North

Atlantic Blockading Squadron in early 1862. Radford was away from his ship, on board the frigate *Roanoke* as a member of a court of inquiry, when the *Cumberland* came under attack and was sunk by the Confederate ironclad *Virginia* in Hampton Roads on March 8, 1862.

Promoted to captain on July 16, 1862, and to commodore on April 24, 1863, Radford was assigned to the New York Navy Yard. From June to August 1864, the ironclad *New Ironsides* was undergoing repairs at the Philadelphia Navy Yard, and Radford took command of that ship on its recommissioning on August 22. The *New Ironsides* was assigned to the North Atlantic Blockading Squadron, and Radford commanded it and the ironclad division during the Union attacks on Fort Fisher, North Carolina, in December 1864 and January 1865.

On January 27, 1865, Radford assumed command of the James River Squadron, supporting Lieutenant General Ulysses S. Grant's forces at City Point, Virginia. On April 28, Radford was assigned command of the North Atlantic Blockading Squadron as acting rear admiral. In June, the North Atlantic Blockading Squadron and the South Atlantic Blockading Squadron were combined into the Atlantic Squadron, and Radford assumed command of the new squadron at Port Royal, South Carolina, on July 26.

Radford commanded the Atlantic Squadron until October 1865, when he assumed command of the Washington Navy Yard and reverted to his permanent rank of commodore. He held that command until January 1869. Radford was promoted to rear admiral on July 25, 1866, and commanded the European Squadron from February 1869 to August 1870. He retired on March 1, 1870, but served on various boards until 1872. Radford died in Washington, D.C., on January 8, 1890.

SPENCER C. TUCKER

See also

City Point, Virginia; Fort Fisher Campaign; Hampton Roads, Battles of; *New Ironsides*, USS; Welles, Gideon

Further Reading

Callahan, Edward W., ed. *List of Officers of the Navy of the United States and of the Marine Corps from 1775 to 1900.* 1901; reprint, New York: Haskell House Publishers, 1969.

Roberts, William H. *New Ironsides in the Civil War.* Annapolis, MD: Naval Institute Press, 1999.

Robinson, Charles M., III. *Hurricane of Fire: The Union Assault on Fort Fisher.* Annapolis, MD: Naval Institute Press, 1998.

Thompson, Kenneth E. *Civil War Commodores and Admirals: A Biographical Directory of All Eighty-Eight Union and Confederate Navy Officers Who Attained Commissioned Flag Rank during the War.* Portland, ME: Thompson Group, 2001.

Radical Republicans

Faction of the Republican Party that tended to dominate the Northern political discourse during and after the Civil War. In general, the Radical Republicans embraced immediate emancipation, a vigorous prosecution of the war, the enlistment of African American soldiers in the army, and rigid postwar Reconstruction policies. Although the group was not a majority of the Republican Party in terms of numbers, it nevertheless held the most sway politically because many Radical Republicans held important congressional committee appointments. President Abraham Lincoln's cabinet included two prominent Radical Republicans: Secretary of War Edwin Stanton and Secretary of the Treasury Salmon P. Chase. By 1861, the Republican Party had subdivided itself into three factions—conservative, moderate, and radical. Conservatives advocated gradual emancipation and some accommodation with the Confederates, while moderates, including Lincoln, fell in politically between the conservatives and the radicals.

Many Radical Republicans tended to favor aggressive political tactics to advance their agenda. They were helped in this way by powerful senators, including Charles Sumner, Benjamin F. Wade, and Zachariah Chandler. Wade and Chandler were both on the Joint Committee on the Conduct of the War, which proved to be the bane of Lincoln's existence during the war. Prominent Radical Republicans in the House included Speaker Galusha Grow, Thaddeus Stevens (chair of the influential Ways and Means Committee), Owen Lovejoy, and Joshua Giddings. Not surprisingly, the epicenter of Radical Republican power was located in the New England states.

Lincoln had to walk something of a political tightrope to bring the three factions of his party in line on important issues. He had the most trouble with the Radical Republicans, who pushed for the controversial Confiscation Acts, an early emancipation proclamation, and the Thirteenth Amendment. Radical Republicans also dominated the Committee on the Conduct of the War, which provoked numerous controversies, including vituperative opposition to Lincoln's appointment of Major General George B. McClellan to lead the Army of the Potomac. McClellan was a Democrat.

To Lincoln's great credit, he kept the more outrageous prescriptions by the Radical Republicans at bay while co-opting some of their better ideas, most notably emancipation. He did so even after a sizable number of Radical Republicans opposed his 1864 renomination. After Lincoln's assassination in April 1865, however, Radical Republican power only grew stronger, as the moderate and savvy Lincoln was no longer available to act as a countervailing force. President Andrew Johnson, a Democrat, also strengthened the Radicals Republicans' hands, at least until 1866. He then fought them doggedly, and it was the Radical Republicans who helped spearhead Johnson's impeachment during 1867 and 1868.

Many Radical Republicans favored Southern land reform, black suffrage, and federal military-style governments for the former Confederate states; they were quite successful in implementing the latter two. The Radical Republicans also sought to punish the South if it balked at Reconstruction initiatives, going so far as to reduce congressional representation for Southern states that refused to implement black suffrage. With Johnson a political red herring and with no significant political opposition, the Radical Republicans dominated Reconstruction, putting in place a far harsher peace than Lincoln had envisioned. The Radical Republicans remained a potent political force until the mid-1870s.

PAUL G. PIERPAOLI JR.

See also

Chandler, Zachariah; Chase, Salmon Portland; Confiscation Acts of 1861 and 1862; Congress, U.S.; Emancipation Proclamation; Grow, Galusha Aaron; Joint Committee on the Conduct of the War; Johnson, Andrew; Lincoln, Abraham; Reconstruction; Republican Party; Stanton, Edwin McMasters; Stevens, Thaddeus; Sumner, Charles; Thirteenth Amendment; Wade, Benjamin Franklin

Further Reading

Goodwin, Doris Kearns. *Team of Rivals: The Political Genius of Abraham Lincoln.* New York: Simon and Schuster, 2005.

Richardson, Heather Cox. *West from Appomattox: The Reconstruction of America after the Civil War.* New Haven, CT: Yale University Press, 2007.

Railroads, CSA

From the very beginning of the Civil War, the Confederacy was at a considerable disadvantage when it came to railroads. In 1860, the South had 8,783 miles of track, while the North had nearly three times that, with 22,385 miles of track. The Confederacy had 112 railroad companies, many of which were poorly managed and equipped. Furthermore, it had only 35 interstate rail lines; the vast remainder were short feeder lines designed to take cotton and other crops to distant depots or market. Many key Southern cities were not linked with other cities because of this. To make matters worse, bridges and roadbeds tended to be badly constructed, gauge widths varied considerably, and rolling stock was often in short supply.

Railroads played a vital role in the Civil War. They were employed to move troops, supplies, and ordnance; transport agricultural products and manufactured goods from farms and plants; and during campaigns and battles served as the main supply and communications artery for armies on the move. Indeed, because many telegraph lines paralleled railroad tracks' rights-of-way, whoever controlled the rail lines controlled not only supply and troop movements but also communications.

In the early days of the war, the Confederate government was slow to organize the railroads and employ them

Total Railroad Mileage in Use by Region, 1830–1880

States/Territories	1840	1850	1860	1870	1880
Maine, New Hampshire, Vermont, Massachusetts, Rhode Island, Connecticut	513	2,596	3,644	4,327	5,888
New York, Pennsylvania, Ohio, Michigan, Indiana, Maryland, Delaware, New Jersey, Washington DC	1,484	3,740	11,927	18,292	28,155
Virginia, West Virginia, Kentucky, Tennessee, Mississippi, Alabama, Georgia, Florida, North Carolina, South Carolina	737	2,082	7,908	10,610	14,458
Illinois, Iowa, Wisconsin, Missouri, Minnesota	0	46	4,951	11,031	22,213
Louisiana, Arkansas, Oklahoma	21	107	250	331	1,621
North Dakota, South Dakota, New Mexico, Wyoming, Montana, Idaho, Utah, Arizona, Washington, Nebraska, Kansas, Texas, Colorado, California, Nevada, Oregon	0	0	239	4,578	15,466
Total	2,755	8,571	28,919	49,169	87,801

efficiently. At the same time, chaotic schedules and sky-rocketing rates made worse by rampant inflation further hampered rail efficiency. Also, the government provided little incentive to spur more efficiency among the railroads because it set limits on their profits and often expropriated railcars and locomotives with little or no remuneration. The Confederates constructed no new rail lines during the war and indeed were hard-pressed to repair lines that had been damaged or destroyed by Union troops, let alone the steam locomotives and rolling stock. Usually, Confederates repaired or replaced damaged lines by cannibalizing existing lines that were seldom used.

As the war progressed, the Union placed more and more pressure on Confederate railroads, usually by seizing or destroying the lines themselves. During and after the Atlanta Campaign (May 5–September 2, 1864), Major General William T. Sherman's scorched-earth tactics included instructions to irreparably damage Confederate rail lines. A favored tactic was to place rail ties in huge piles and torch them. Another tactic was to heat iron rails and then wrap them around trees; the results were known as "Sherman neckties."

Rail lines themselves became the focus of numerous battles and campaigns, including the Second Vicksburg Campaign (April 1–July 4, 1863), the Chattanooga Campaign (October–November 1863), and the Atlanta Campaign (May 5–September 2, 1864). In northern Virginia, Union and Confederate forces fought bitterly over control of the Manassas Gap Railroad and the Orange & Alexandria Railroad, and Union forces laid siege to Petersburg during June 15, 1864–April 3, 1865, principally because it was a critical railroad hub in central Virginia.

PAUL G. PIERPAOLI JR.

See also
Atlanta Campaign; Chattanooga Campaign; Manassas Gap Railroad; Orange & Alexandria Railroad; Petersburg Campaign; Railroads, U.S.; Sherman, William Tecumseh; Vicksburg Campaign, Second

Further Reading
Angevine, Robert G. *The Railroad and the State: War, Politics, and Technology in Nineteenth Century America.* Stanford, CA: Stanford University Press, 2004.
Black, Robert C., III. *The Railroads of the Confederacy.* Chapel Hill: University of North Carolina Press, 1998.

Railroads, U.S.
On the eve of the Civil War, there were more than 200 railroads in the United States, most of which were located in the states remaining loyal to the Union. In 1860 the United States had 30,626 miles of track, and almost two-thirds of this was in the North. Many of these lines served to connect the essentially agricultural midwestern states with the East, helping to cement the former economically and politically with the Union cause.

Most northern railroads were interconnected and had converted to a standard rail gauge (4'8.5" in width), enabling trains from different companies to use the same tracks. In the South, gauges varied widely from one railroad company to another, impeding long-distance transport of goods and people. All of this meant that the Union could transport many more troops and supplies to more places and with far fewer transfers than could the Confederacy.

Railroads proved to be of great strategic importance during the Civil War in the supply of the large field armies. Trains traveled at least five times faster than mule- or horse-drawn wagons, which meant that men or supplies moving by train usually arrived at the front in timely fashion as well as in good condition. Also, trains were far less affected by poor weather and were rarely waylaid by rain or snow. By contrast, wagons mired down on unpaved roads if the weather was wet, and the mules that pulled the wagons were themselves consumers of the fodder that was one of the chief items needed to supply a Civil War army. Beyond a certain distance, wagons became useless as supply vehicles since their teams in effect would have eaten their entire payload. Railroads suffered from none of these drawbacks.

Railroads expanded the geographical range of military operations and allowed warfare on a near-continental scale. Now armies could conduct campaigns that would have not have been possible with wagon train logistics. With increased ease of resupply, field forces could also grow in size.

Leaders on both sides in the war realized the importance of the railroads to their own operations and to those of the enemy. The First Battle of Bull Run (July 21, 1861) was precipitated by the Union desire to control the important Southern rail center at Manassas Junction, Virginia, as a first step in an advance on the Confederate capital of Richmond. Confederate brigadier general Joseph E. Johnston was able to bring 10,000 men to Manassas from the Shenandoah Valley in a movement that was largely carried out with rail transport. It was the first such rail-borne troop movement in U.S. history. Johnston's troops joined Beauregard the day before the battle and played a decisive role in its outcome.

At the beginning of the war, Northern railroads were not efficiently organized to support the war effort, and many railroad executives worried more about profits than how they

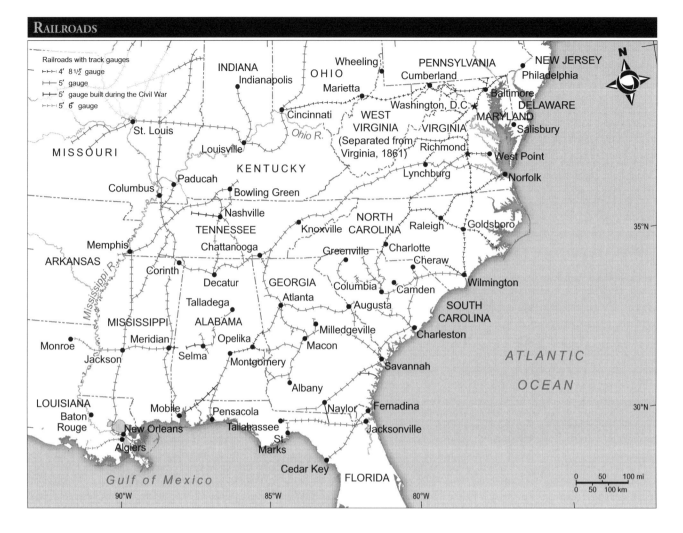

RAILROADS

Railroads with track gauges
- 4′ 8½′ gauge
- 5′ gauge
- 5′ gauge built during the Civil War
- 5′ 6″ gauge

might help win the war. Simon Cameron, Union secretary of war at the beginning of the conflict, had invested heavily in railroads, and he manipulated the rates that the War Department paid for transporting its soldiers and matériel. When Cameron's actions became public knowledge, President Abraham Lincoln demanded that he resign in January 1862. Corruption in the rail industry prompted Congress to pass the Railways and Telegraph Act of January 1862, which gave Lincoln the power to appropriate the railroads and administer them with government troops and employees to preserve public safely and enable the War Department to utilize the railways effectively in the war effort.

Faced with this get-tough legislation, most Northern railroad executives hastened to rally to the Union cause. The few lines that the government appropriated were consolidated into the United States Military Railroad. Profiteering and corruption thereafter declined, and train service became more efficient. The U.S. government did seize some Northern railroads for a short time when Confederate general

Robert E. Lee and the Army of Northern Virginia invaded Pennsylvania in June–July 1863.

The Confederates early recognized the importance of the railroads to the Union war effort, especially the Baltimore & Ohio (B&O) Railroad, and they regularly sent raiders to destroy track, bridges, and rolling stock. The Confederates continued this practice throughout the war. The North soon established military garrisons to guard rail depots and bridges. To minimize the effects of Confederate raids, Union brigadier general Herman Haupt, the War Department's innovative U.S. railroad superintendent from September 1862 to September 1863, instituted the stockpiling of essential railroad construction materials, including prefabricated bridges of wood, that could then be rushed by rail to make quick and efficient repairs where needed.

In December 1862, Confederate brigadier general Nathan Bedford Forrest successfully attacked the Mississippi & Tennessee Railroad south of Memphis. This raid, along with other Confederate operations, forced Major General Ulysses

Rail depot at the Union military supply base of City Point, Virginia, in 1864 during the Siege of Petersburg. The engine "President" in the right foreground. (National Archives)

S. Grant to abandon his first attempt to capture Vicksburg. When Grant attacked Vicksburg again in 1863, his men destroyed the five railroads that served Jackson and Vicksburg, Mississippi, imposing serious restraints on Confederate resupply and reinforcement efforts.

Confederates further signaled their recognition of the vital importance of railroad for the Union war effort during Lee's Gettysburg Campaign (June–July 1863). Railroads were among the chief targets that Lee's men marked out for destruction, burning tracks, bridges, depots, and other railroad facilities whenever possible during their march through Maryland and Pennsylvania.

When the Confederates besieged Union troops in Chattanooga after the Battle of Chickamauga (September 19–20, 1863), Lincoln and Secretary of War Edwin M. Stanton launched the largest strategic rail movement up to that point in military history. Trains carried XI and XII Corps of the Army of the Potomac, some 15,000 men, from Virginia westward across the Appalachians and then south via Nashville to join the large army that Grant was assembling in the Chattanooga area. The movement contributed directly to

the Union victory in the Battle of Chattanooga (November 23–25, 1863).

Since the war's outset, railroads had played an especially important role in the Union's central axis of advance from Louisville through Nashville and Murfreesboro to Chattanooga, since no water route allowed consistent steamboat access to the area. The rail lines hauled the supplies that kept Grant's army eating at Chattanooga, and over the months that followed the continued vigorous use of railroads built up the supply depots that allowed Sherman to begin his momentous campaign against Atlanta.

Promoted to command of all Union armies in the spring of 1864, Grant moved to Virginia to provide personal supervision to Union operations there. When he advanced the Army of the Potomac against Richmond that spring, he relied in part on waterborne transport on Chesapeake Bay and the adjoining estuaries to bring up his supplies, but it was railroads that moved the supplies from the landing places to Grant's hard-fighting army. During the siege of Richmond and Petersburg (June 15, 1864–April 3, 1865), Grant set up an enormous rail depot at City Point, Virginia, from which trains hauled supplies along the far-stretched lines to keep the army in hardtack through the weary months of trench warfare. Here as elsewhere, railroads continued to be critical in Union offensive operations.

Meanwhile, in the war's decisive western theater, Sherman launched a simultaneous campaign moving toward Atlanta that was aimed at destroying its defending Confederate army. Before he departed Chattanooga in May 1864, Sherman created a railroad battle plan. Knowing that the Confederates would attack his supply lines, he trained some 10,000 troops in railroad repair. He had abundant spare parts for railroads stored along his supply line, and he fortified key bridges, trestles, and the like with blockhouses sufficient to turn aside raiding cavalry as long as enemy artillery was not present. Throughout the campaign, Sherman's troops proved to be so adept at repairing tracks that damaged or destroyed lines were quickly put back into service.

Railroads were beyond doubt an invaluable strategic resource that helped to secure the Northern victory in the war. Without them, the war would have lasted longer and been even more costly in terms of lives lost.

KATHLEEN WARNES

See also

Atlanta Campaign; Baltimore & Ohio Railroad; Beauregard, Pierre Gustav Toutant; Bull Run, First Battle of; Cameron, Simon; Chickamauga, Battle of; Forrest, Nathan Bedford; Grant, Ulysses Simpson; Haupt, Herman; Lee, Robert Edward; Lincoln, Abraham; Railroads, CSA; Vicksburg Campaign, First

Further Reading

Angevine, Robert G. *The Railroad and the State: War, Politics, and Technology in Nineteenth Century America*. Stanford, CA: Stanford University Press, 2004.

Pickenpaugh, Roger. *Rescue by Rail: Troop Transfer and the Civil War in the West, 1863*. Lincoln: University of Nebraska Press, 1998.

Turner, George Edgar. *Victory Rode the Rails: The Strategic Place of the Railroads in the Civil War*. Indianapolis: Bobbs-Merrill, 1953.

Weber, Thomas. *The Northern Railroads in the Civil War, 1861–1865*. Bloomington: Indiana University Press, 1999.

Railways and Telegraph Act

Legislation passed by the U.S. Congress on January 31, 1862, that gave the executive branch the ability to coordinate all railroads and telegraph lines for military use. At the time, the majority of telegraph lines ran along railway rights-of-way, so these two strategic means of communication and transportation were symbiotic. Notably, the legislation included all railroads—those in the Confederacy as well as the North. That portion of the bill was critical because it permitted the U.S. government to appropriate for military use railroads in the South that were in areas captured and controlled by Union forces.

Specifically, the Railways and Telegraph Act empowered the president to appropriate for military use any rail line, rail equipment, or telegraph equipment; arrange for the maintenance and security of said lines and equipment; and subject any railway or telegraph owner or employee to military authority. On February 11, 1862, President Abraham Lincoln, using the power vested in him via the Railways and Telegraph Act, created within the War Department the U.S. Military Railroads (USMRR), headed by Daniel C. McCallum, a longtime railroad executive. The purview of the USMRR was principally privately owned railroads in occupied Confederate territory. Notably, the USMRR constructed a rail line from Washington, D.C., to Alexandria, Virginia (the latter having been secured by Union forces early in the war), which helped transport troops during the Petersburg Campaign (June 15, 1864–April 3, 1865).

To a significant extent, the railroad companies themselves precipitated the Railways and Telegraph Act. They had often not been entirely cooperative with government officials during the early stages of the war, and many railways owners seemed more interested in profits than in aiding the war effort. Furthermore, the railroads were slow to repair the numerous rail lines that had been damaged or destroyed by Confederate forces. An even greater issue was the railroads' manipulation of rates, which forced the War Department to expend more money than it should have for the transportation of troops and matériel. Once the legislation was in place, however, most railways in the North toed the line, and few were taken over by the War Department. The Railways and Telegraph Act raised some eyebrows, as it seemed to give the government virtually unlimited powers and appeared to threaten private ownership. Nevertheless, in a conflict as large as the Civil War, the legislation was essential to the Union war effort. During World War I, similar legislation was passed that was modeled after the 1862 act.

PAUL G. PIERPAOLI JR.

See also

Railroads, CSA; Railroads, U.S.

Further Reading

Angevine, Robert G. *The Railroad and the State: War, Politics, and Technology in Nineteenth Century America*. Stanford, CA: Stanford University Press, 2004.

Weber, Thomas. *The Northern Railroads in the Civil War, 1861–1865.* Bloomington: Indiana University Press, 1999.

Rains, Gabriel James
Birth Date: June 4, 1803
Death Date: August 6, 1881

Confederate officer. Gabriel James Rains was born on June 4, 1803, in Craven County, North Carolina. He graduated from the U.S. Military Academy, West Point, in 1827. Rains served during the Second Seminole War (1835–1842) as well as the Mexican-American War (1846–1848) and had risen to the rank of lieutenant colonel by 1860. Rains resigned his commission on July 31, 1861, and accepted a brigadier general's commission in the Confederate Army on September 23.

Rains eventually took charge of a brigade in Major General Daniel H. Hill's division and saw action during the Peninsula Campaign (March–July 1862). During operations on the Virginia Peninsula, Rains devised makeshift land mines using 8- and 10-inch artillery shells that he ordered buried just below the surface of the earth and that exploded under pressure. Rains's improvised mines were frowned upon at the time as controversial and beyond the bounds of civilized warfare, but as the war increased in destructiveness, such prohibitions were ignored. Criticized for his performance in the Battle of Seven Pines (May 31–June 1, 1862), Rains held no further field commands after the Peninsula Campaign. Thereafter he worked on mining the James and Appomattox Rivers and held a district command in North Carolina.

During December 1862–May 1863, Rains was the superintendent of the Volunteer and Conscript Bureau. Meanwhile, he continued his work on land and sea mines and other explosives technology. In June 1864 he was named chief of the Torpedo Bureau, a post he held until war's end, assisting in the placement of underwater mines (then known as torpedoes) in the James River and in the approaches to Charleston and Mobile.

After the war Rains lived in Atlanta before moving to Charleston, where he was a clerk in the U.S. Quartermaster Department (1877–1880). Rains died on August 6, 1881, in Aiken, South Carolina.

PAUL G. PIERPAOLI JR.

See also
Hill, Daniel Harvey; Peninsula Campaign; Seven Pines, Battle of; Torpedoes

Further Reading
Eicher, John H., and David J. Eicher. *Civil War High Commands.* Stanford, CA: Stanford University Press, 2001.
Warner, Ezra J. *Generals in Gray: Lives of the Confederate Commanders.* Baton Rouge: Louisiana State University Press, 2006.

Rains, George Washington
Birth Date: 1817
Death Date: March 21, 1898

Confederate officer. The brother of future Confederate general Gabriel James Rains, George Washington Rains was born in 1817 in Craven County, North Carolina. He graduated from the U.S. Military Academy, West Point, in 1842 and eventually became an artillery officer. Rains saw action during the Mexican-American War (1846–1848), for which he was brevetted twice before resigning as a captain in October 1856 to take over management of the Washington Iron Works located in Newburgh, New York. When the Civil War began in 1861, he went south, received a commission as a major in the Confederate Army, and was assigned to the fledgling Ordnance Bureau.

Rains soon became the Confederacy's chief expert on the procurement and processing of gunpowder. In the autumn of 1861, he selected Augusta, Georgia, as the site of the Augusta Powder Works, the principal Confederate powder manufacturer during the war. The plant became operational in May 1862. Until the autumn of 1864, Rains had charge of all munitions operations in Augusta and also commanded the city's troops. In June 1863 Rains took charge of the new Niter and Mining Bureau to increase the production of niter, a key ingredient of gunpowder. At the same time, he worked tirelessly to improve the quality and speed of gunpowder production. He was advanced to lieutenant colonel on May 22, 1862, and to colonel on July 12, 1863. By war's end, the facilities that he supervised had produced some 2.75 million pounds of gunpowder.

Rains stayed in Augusta for a time after the war, teaching chemistry at the Medical College of Georgia. He became the college's dean in 1867. He also published a booklet in 1882, *The History of the Confederate Powder Works,* that provided much useful information on the history of gunpowder manufacturing in the Confederacy. Rains later retired to Newburgh, New York, where he died on March 21, 1898.

PAUL G. PIERPAOLI JR.

See also
Augusta Arsenal; Augusta Powder Works

Further Reading
Bragg, C. L., Charles D. Ross, Gordon A. Blaker, Stephanie A. T. Jacobe, and Theodore P. Savas. *Never for Want of Powder: The Confederate Powder Works in Augusta, Georgia.* Columbia: University of South Carolina Press, 2007.
Corley, Florence F. *Confederate City: Augusta, Georgia, 1860–1865.* 2nd ed. Columbia: University of South Carolina Press, 1974.

Rains, James Edward
Birth Date: April 10, 1833
Death Date: December 31, 1862

Confederate officer. James Edward Rains was born on April 10, 1833, in Nashville, Tennessee. He received a law degree from Yale University in 1854. Returning to Nashville, he opened a legal practice and went on to serve as a city prosecutor and, later, as a district attorney for Davidson, Sumner, and Williamson Counties. In the late 1850s he was named associate editor of the *Republican Banner,* working for his friend and political ally Felix Zollicoffer.

In May 1861, Rains entered Confederate military service as a private in the 11th Tennessee Infantry Regiment. Soon elected its colonel, he saw action in the vicinity of the Cumberland Gap. Instructed to hold the gap in November 1861, he managed to occupy the area until June 1862, when Union forces launched an offensive there. Rains now returned to middle Tennessee, but in July he returned to the Cumberland Gap with reinforcements. He commanded a brigade in the Kentucky Campaign (August 14–October 26, 1862), after which he was advanced to brigadier general on November 4, 1862.

Rains next saw action at the Battle of Stones River (December 31, 1862–January 2, 1863). On the first day of fighting, Rains conducted a sweeping movement aimed at the Union right flank. While leading his men, he was hit and killed by enemy fire.

PAUL G. PIERPAOLI JR.

See also
Kentucky Campaign; Stevenson, Carter Littlepage; Stones River, Battle of; Zollicoffer, Felix Kirk

Further Reading
Eicher, John H., and David J. Eicher. *Civil War High Commands.* Stanford, CA: Stanford University Press, 2001.
Warner, Ezra J. *Generals in Gray: Lives of the Confederate Commanders.* Baton Rouge: Louisiana State University Press, 2006.

Raleigh, North Carolina, Occupation of
Event Date: April 13, 1865

Union operation during Sherman's March through the Carolinas (January–April 1865). As the Civil War was drawing to an end in March 1865, three Union forces were closing in on Raleigh, the capital of North Carolina, from separate directions: Major General William T. Sherman's 60,000-man army group from the south, Major General John M. Schofield's 30,000-man force from the east, and Major General George Stoneman's 4,000-man cavalry force from the west. Confederate forces initially put up fierce opposition but were unable to arrest the Union advances.

On April 12, however, Sherman learned that Confederate general Robert E. Lee had surrendered the Army of Northern Virginia at Appomattox Court House, Virginia, on April 9. That same day, peace delegates from North Carolina governor Zebulon Vance's office met with Sherman to discuss ending the war in their state. The next day, April 13, Raleigh's mayor, William H. Harrison, and an aide, Kenneth Rayner, surrendered the city to Union brigadier general Judson Kilpatrick, whose division then occupied the city. Sherman's capitulation conditions had been generous, and he promised that neither the city nor its citizens would be harmed so long as Union troops were not fired upon.

Sherman set up his headquarters at the now-abandoned Governor's Palace. The flagpole was chopped down, and the flag of the United States was raised over the North Carolina statehouse dome. The occupation was remarkably peaceful except for one incident in which a drunken Confederate straggler from Major General Joseph Wheeler's command fired on the Federals during the early morning of April 13. Kilpatrick had the man hanged on the spot, rejecting his request for a five-minute delay to write to his wife, but Kilpatrick took no reprisal on the city.

When Union troops learned of President Abraham Lincoln's assassination, however, many wanted to destroy Raleigh. On April 15, the night of Lincoln's death, Sherman posted extra security to prevent any violence or looting. Indeed, Sherman himself spent much of the night visiting with his men and calming them down. Within days, Union troops had begun to distribute humanitarian assistance to the city's residents. While isolated incidents of theft occurred outside Raleigh, they were not from a lack of effort on the part of Sherman and his commanders to avoid them. Raleigh thus escaped completely the destruction that had been visited on other Confederate capitals.

ALAN K. LAMM

See also

Kilpatrick, Hugh Judson; North Carolina; Sherman, William
    Tecumseh; Vance, Zebulon Baird

Further Reading

Barrett, John G. *The Civil War in North Carolina.* Chapel Hill:
    University of North Carolina Press, 1963.
Bradley, Mark L. *Bluecoats and Tar Heels: Soldiers and Civilians
    in Reconstruction North Carolina.* Louisville: University of
    Kentucky Press, 2009.

Ram Fleet, U.S.

Flotilla created in early 1862 to assist Union forces in securing control of the Mississippi River. The leading figure in the development of the Ram Fleet was civil engineer Charles Ellet Jr. As early as 1855, Ellet had been recommending the construction of ironclad rams. His suggestions had been ignored. Following the ramming and sinking of the U.S. Navy sailing sloop *Cumberland* on March 8, 1862, in the Battles of Hampton Roads by the Confederate ironclad *Virginia* (ironically constructed to Ellet's specifications), however, U.S. secretary of war Edwin Stanton embraced the notion of steam rams. Stanton authorized Ellet to oversee the procurement of nine speedy and well-built steamboats and their conversion into rams. The work was carried out at Cincinnati, Ohio; Pittsburgh, Pennsylvania; and New Albany, Indiana. Following their conversions, Ellet, now commissioned a colonel in the army, assumed command of what became known as the Ram Fleet. Ellet held that a ram's horsepower had to be in correct ratio to its deadweight tonnage. Cannon would cut speed, and Ellet therefore believed that the rams should not be armed.

Ellet plunged into the work. By mid-March 1862, the *Switzerland, Lancaster,* and *Queen of the West* were nearing readiness, and a fourth steamer, the *Monarch,* was on the stocks. The *T. D. Horner, Mingo, Lioness,* and *Dick Fulton* had been purchased and were awaiting conversion. The *Samson* served as a floating machine shop. The vessels were both side- and stern-wheel steamers. Transforming them into rams included reinforcing their hulls with additional timbers and filling their bows with timber, all to enable them to withstand the shock of ramming. The rams were under army command but for the most part operated under navy orders, an arrangement that pleased neither party.

In April the War Department learned that the Confederates were putting together a ram fleet of their own and would

The Union ram *Queen of the West* shown here attacking and damaging the Confederate gunboat *City of Vicksburg* off Vicksburg, Mississippi, on February 2, 1863. (MPI/Getty Images)

soon be heading north to aid in the defense of Fort Pillow. Stanton ordered Ellet to proceed with his four completed rams and join the Western Flotilla, then a few miles upriver from Fort Pillow. Stanton further ordered Ellet to cooperate with Western Flotilla commander Flag Officer Charles H. Davis, but Ellet, who preferred to act independently, took this directive lightly.

A few days before the arrival of the Ellet rams, Davis's gunboats were attacked by rams of the Confederate Mississippi River Defense Service in the Battle of Plum Point Bend (May 10, 1862), and two Union gunboats were put out of action. Ellet wanted an immediate attack on Fort Pillow, but Davis demurred. On June 4, however, the Confederates abandoned Fort Pillow, and the next day Davis's flotilla and Ellet's rams moved south to attack the Confederate River Defense Fleet at Memphis.

On June 6, 1862, Ellet's rams charged ahead of Davis's flotilla and engaged the Confederate steamers at Memphis. In the ensuing battle, the Confederates lost all of their rams except one that escaped downriver. Two of Ellet's rams suffered repairable damage. Ellet himself was the only Union casualty; wounded by a pistol ball, he died three weeks later from blood poisoning. His place was taken by his younger brother, Lieutenant Colonel Alfred W. Ellet, who had command of the *Monarch*. Alfred Ellet was promoted to brigadier general in November, and the unit was made part of a new amphibious command, the Mississippi Marine Brigade.

The Mississippi Marine Brigade was to act as an amphibious strike force and was assigned 10 army companies—6 of infantry and 4 of cavalry—in addition to a battery of artillery. These units were transported by 10 armed steamboat transports and 6 auxiliary steamers. At full strength, the brigade included more than 1,000 officers and men and 500 civilians.

Rear Admiral David D. Porter, who succeeded Davis in command of what now was named the Mississippi Squadron, initially welcomed the creation of the brigade, but he soon became disillusioned with Ellet's near total disregard of orders and tendency to act independently. There were also numerous complaints about the brigade's undisciplined behavior when acting ashore. The brigade subsequently took part in numerous small actions in Arkansas and Louisiana. Porter finally secured transfer of its ships to his command, but the brigade was disbanded in August 1864 and its ships transferred to other duties.

Of the original ships in the Ram Fleet, the *Lioness, Monarch, Samson, Switzerland, T. D. Horner,* and *Dick*

Fulton survived the war. The *Mingo* sank accidently at Cape Girardeau, Missouri, in November 1862. The *Queen of the West* was captured by the Confederates at Fort DeRussy, Louisiana, on February 14, 1863. The *Lancaster* was sunk by Confederate batteries as it attempted to pass Vicksburg on March 25, 1863. The *Monarch* was sunk by ice below St. Louis in December 1864.

CHARLES DANA GIBSON

See also

Davis, Charles Henry; Ellet, Alfred Washington; Ellet, Charles, Jr.; Fort Pillow, Tennessee, Capture of; Hampton Roads, Battles of; Memphis, Battle of; Mississippi Marine Brigade; Mississippi River; Mississippi Squadron, U.S. Navy; Plum Point Bend, Battle of; Porter, David Dixon; River Defense Fleet; Riverine Warfare; *Virginia,* CSS

Further Reading

Crandall, Warren D., and Isaac D. Newel. *History of the Ram Fleet and the Mississippi Marine Brigade in the War for the Union on the Mississippi and Its Tributaries: The Story of the Ellets and Their Men.* St. Louis, MO: Buschart Bros., 1907.

Gibson, Charles Dana, and E. Kay Gibson. *Assault and Logistics: Union Army Coastal and River Operations, 1861–1866.* Camden, ME: Ensign, 1995.

Hearn, Chester G. *Ellet's Brigade: The Strangest Outfit of All.* Baton Rouge: Louisiana State University Press, 2000.

Tucker, Spencer C. *Andrew Hull Foote: Civil War Admiral on Western Waters.* Annapolis, MD: Naval Institute Press, 2000.

Ramsay, George Douglas
Birth Date: February 21, 1802
Death Date: May 23, 1882

Union officer. George Douglas Ramsay was born on February 21, 1802, in Dumfries, Virginia. As a boy he moved with his family to the District of Columbia and enrolled at the U.S. Military Academy, West Point, when he was only 14 years old. After graduating near the bottom of his class in 1820, Ramsay was commissioned a second lieutenant and assigned to the artillery. Over the next several years, he held staff appointments and also served as a regimental adjutant. In the late 1820s and early 1830s, Ramsay was assigned to garrison duties in Virginia and then several posts in New England. In 1835 he became a captain in the Ordnance Department, where he would spend the rest of his career.

Ramsay subsequently supervised several arsenals on the East Coast. During the Mexican-American War

(1846–1848), he served during the Monterrey Campaign under Major General Zachary Taylor, performed admirably, and was brevetted major. From June 1847 to May 1848, Ramsay served as Taylor's chief of ordnance. When that war ended, Ramsay headed arsenals in Pennsylvania, Virginia, and Missouri.

When the Civil War began in April 1861, Ramsay was finally promoted to major and charged with commanding the strategically important Washington Arsenal in Washington, D.C. Promoted to lieutenant colonel in August 1861 and to colonel in June 1863, on September 1, 1863, he was advanced to brigadier general and at the same time was named chief of ordnance for the Union Army. The unassuming Ramsay executed his mission with considerable skill and efficiency. Among other accomplishments, he actively promoted the breech-loading rifle, a firearm that his predecessor, Brigadier General James W. Ripley, had stubbornly rejected out of hand. Ramsay also championed other new weapons that held potential while voiding those that were of questionable value or were too costly.

Ramsay's tenure as chief of ordnance was not a happy one, however. Troubles began when Secretary of War Edwin M. Stanton named as Ramsay's assistant a scheming and overly ambitious young officer who undermined Ramsay at every turn. Ramsay complained loud and often about this, and before long he was locked in a bitter clash with Stanton. The war of words ended when Stanton relieved him of his position and forced him from active service. Stanton used Ramsay's age as a cover for his action—Ramsay was 62 years old—but other officers served well beyond that age, especially during the war. As a consolation prize, Ramsay was brevetted major general on March 13, 1865.

Ramsay served as an inspector of several arsenals from 1864 to 1866 and oversaw the Washington Arsenal from 1866 to 1870, essentially as a civilian employee. That same year, Ramsay retired from public life and settled in Washington, D.C., where he died on May 23, 1882. Ramsay's son, Francis Munroe Ramsay, became a U.S. Navy rear admiral.

PAUL G. PIERPAOLI JR.

See also

Ripley, James Wolfe; Stanton, Edwin McMasters

Further Reading

Gorham, George C. *Life and Public Services of Edwin M. Stanton.* 2 vols. Whitefish, MT: Kessinger, 2006.

Peterson, Harold L. *Notes on Ordnance of the Civil War, 1861–1865.* Washington, DC: American Ordnance Association, 1959.

Ramseur, Stephen Dodson
Birth Date: May 31, 1837
Death Date: October 20, 1864

Confederate officer. Stephen Dodson Ramseur was born in Lincolnton, North Carolina, on May 31, 1837. He graduated from the U.S. Military Academy, West Point, in 1860 but resigned his U.S. commission in April 1861 to join the Confederate Army as a first lieutenant of artillery. He soon joined North Carolina State Troops as captain of the Ellis Light Artillery.

Thrown from his horse, Ramseur broke his collarbone and was out of action until the next spring. At the start of the Peninsula Campaign (March–July 1862), Ramsur commanded the artillery under Brigadier General John B. Magruder. But in April 1862 Ramseur became the colonel of the 49th North Carolina Infantry Regiment. During the Seven Days' Campaign (June 25–July 1, 1862), he was severely wounded at the Battle of Malvern Hill (July 1, 1862).

Promoted to brigadier general on November 1, 1862, Ramseur became one of the youngest generals in the Confederate Army. Given command of a brigade in Lieutenant General Thomas J. "Stonewall" Jackson's corps, Army of Northern Virginia, Ramseur nonetheless missed the First Battle of Fredericksburg (December 13, 1862). On May 3, 1863, Ramseur's brigade played a major role in the costly fighting that united the divided wings of General Robert E. Lee's army in the Battle of Chancellorsville (May 1–4). Although Ramseur was wounded in the leg, his unit was able to punch through Union lines. He took part in the Battle of Gettysburg (July 1–3, 1863) and later that year fought at the Second Battle of Bristoe Station (October 14, 1863) and in the Mine Run Campaign (November 26–December 2, 1863). He again performed conspicuously in the Battle of the Wilderness (May 5–7, 1864).

At the Battle of Spotsylvania Court House (May 8–21, 1864), Ramseur had three horses shot out from under him and was wounded in his right arm. Nevertheless, he and his unit were able to stop a major Union assault, which won him the personal thanks of General Lee. Promoted to major general on June 1, 1864, Ramseur took command of a division assigned to Lieutenant General Jubal Early's command and saw action at Cold Harbor (May 31–June 12) before moving with Early to the Shenandoah Valley.

Time and again Ramseur proved that he was a master at handling troops, excelling at the Third Battle of Winchester (September 19, 1864), the Battle of Fisher's Hill (September

22, 1864), and the Battle of Cedar Creek (October 19, 1864). Mortally wounded and captured in the latter battle, Ramseur died on October 20, 1864.

ALAN K. LAMM

See also

Bristoe Station, Second Battle of; Cedar Creek, Battle of; Chancellorsville, Battle of; Fisher's Hill, Battle of; Fredericksburg, First Battle of; Gettysburg, Battle of; Magruder, John Bankhead; Malvern Hill, Battle of; Mine Run Campaign; Seven Days' Campaign; Sheridan's Shenandoah Valley Campaign; Spotsylvania Court House, Battle of; Winchester, Third Battle of

Further Reading

Gallagher, Gary. *Stephen Dobson Ramseur: Lee's Gallant General.* Chapel Hill: University of North Carolina Press, 1985.

Kundahl, George G., ed. *The Bravest of the Brave: The Correspondence of Stephen Dodson Ramseur.* Chapel Hill: University of North Carolina Press, 2010.

Ramsey, Alexander
Birth Date: September 8, 1815
Death Date: April 22, 1903

Governor of Minnesota. Alexander Ramsey was born on September 8, 1815, near Harrisburg, Pennsylvania. Orphaned at age 10, he then lived with a maternal granduncle and worked as a clerk in his uncle's store. Ramsey enrolled for a time in Lafayette College but left to study law with a local attorney. Ramsey was admitted to the Pennsylvania bar in 1839.

A strong advocate for the Whig Party in Pennsylvania, Ramsey served in the U.S. House of Representatives (1843–1847). He next served as chair of the Whig Party's Central Committee in Pennsylvania for Zachary Taylor's presidential bid in 1848. After securing the presidency, Taylor appointed Ramsey the first territorial governor of Minnesota.

When Ramsey was confirmed on April 2, 1849, he assumed authority over a large territory with no infrastructure and few white settlers. Most of the territory was controlled by Indians. One of the first things Ramsey did was to establish judicial and legislative districts. He also had a census taken and arranged for the election of a territorial legislature. Ramsey was a pragmatic politician who recognized that internal improvements would further his own career. In this aspect, he was quite successful. The most outstanding achievement of Ramsey's term as governor was the negotiation of treaties with the Sioux in 1851, opening a large portion of southern Minnesota to white settlement. Ramsey left office in May 1853.

Ramsey remained in St. Paul, where he amassed a fortune in real estate. In 1855 he was elected mayor of St. Paul. In 1859 he was elected Minnesota's second state governor and was reelected in 1861. Ramsey reduced state expenditures, simplified administration in the various counties, and strengthened the state's school system. His job was made more difficult by the Civil War. Nevertheless, he was the first governor to offer troops to President Abraham Lincoln. During the 1862 Minnesota Sioux Uprising, Ramsey oversaw the organization and provisioning of troops for that brief conflict.

In 1863 Ramsey was elected to the U.S. Senate, serving from 1863 to 1875. There he joined the Radical Republicans in calling for a vigorous prosecution of the war and the military Reconstruction of the South. Ramsey voted to convict President Andrew Johnson during the president's impeachment trial.

Ramsey resumed private life in 1875. In 1879 President Rutherford B. Hayes appointed Ramsey secretary of war; he served until March 4, 1881. Among his accomplishments in the post, Ramsey convinced Congress to authorize an assistant secretary of war.

In 1882 Ramsey was appointed to the Edmunds Commission, which investigated polygamy among the Mormons in Utah. The commission found thousands of polygamists and recommended their disenfranchisement. Ramsey resigned from the commission in 1886 and returned to St. Paul, where he died on April 22, 1903.

TIM J. WATTS

See also

Congress, U.S.; Minnesota; Radical Republicans; Sioux Uprising

Further Reading

Haughland, John C. "Alexander Ramsey and the Republican Party, 1855–1875." PhD dissertation, University of Nebraska, 1976.

Swanholm, Marx. *Alexander Ramsay and the Politics of Survival.* St. Paul: Minnesota Historical Society, 1977.

Randolph, George Wythe
Birth Date: March 10, 1818
Death Date: April 3, 1867

Confederate officer and secretary of war (1862). A grandson of Thomas Jefferson, George Wythe Randolph was born at Monticello, Virginia, on March 10, 1818. He served for six years as a midshipman in the U.S. Navy and later attended the University of Virginia. Thereafter, he established a law practice in Richmond, Virginia, and formed a volunteer militia battery, the Richmond Howitzers, of which he was captain. After the 1860 election of Abraham Lincoln, Randolph became an ardent secessionist.

With the outbreak of the Civil War, Randolph received authorization to recruit the Richmond Howitzers up to battalion strength, and he received the rank of major commanding. In that capacity, he took part in the Battle of Big Bethel (June 10, 1861). Little more than a militarily insignificant skirmish east of Richmond, Big Bethel was much celebrated in the South as the first Confederate victory on Virginia soil. Randolph performed gallantly and received high praise from his commanding officers, leading to his promotion to colonel of the 1st Virginia Artillery.

Stationed near Richmond, Randolph was able to continue his activities in the Virginia Secession Convention. In the autumn of 1861 he took the lead in introducing legislation, which was passed, that established compulsory military service for male Virginians along the lines of the major European states.

On February 12, 1862, Randolph was promoted to brigadier general. However, poor health and the rigors of camp life began to dull his ardor for field service. Belatedly he jumped into the race for a seat in the Confederate Congress and lost.

Meanwhile, by March 1862, President Jefferson Davis was experiencing one of the Confederacy's several cabinet crises. Under heavy pressure to sack Secretary of War Judah P. Benjamin, Davis chose instead to shift him to the position of secretary of state and to select Randolph as the new secretary of war.

Randolph took office on March 17, 1862. He immediately pressed Davis with the necessity of instituting national conscription. Against Davis's inclinations, Randolph persuaded the president that such legislation must include a provision to indefinitely retain in service troops who were nearing the end of their one-year enlistments. Later that same month, Davis requested the first conscription legislation in American history. Randolph politicked actively for the passage of the bill, and after heated debate, it was adopted.

Randolph worked diligently at the heavy administrative demands of his position and took an active role in advising Davis on military operations. In the crisis later that spring caused by the landing of Union major general George B. McClellan's army at the lower end of the Virginia Peninsula between the York and James Rivers, Randolph played an important role in Confederate policy making. In crucial councils of war in the Confederate capital, Randolph sided

Confederate brigadier general George Wythe Randolph became secretary of war in March 1862. An able administrator and the Confederacy's most capable secretary of war, he had to deal with constant interference by President Jefferson Davis and resigned in November that same year. (Library of Congress)

with Davis and with Robert E. Lee in arguing that Richmond must be held and that its defense should be made as far down the peninsula as possible.

Later that year, Randolph hoped to orchestrate a Confederate counterattack aimed at retaking New Orleans, although nothing ever came of this. In November 1862, Randolph wrote to Trans-Mississippi commander Lieutenant General Theophilus Holmes suggesting that he take part of his force to the east bank of the river to cooperate with Confederate forces there. This was consistent with suggestions that Davis had previously made to Holmes, but in this case the president apparently had his pride wounded by the act of initiative from his secretary of war and took umbrage at Randolph's action. Davis demanded that the secretary retract his message to Holmes. Deeply offended, Randolph resigned on November 15.

Randolph was the Confederacy's most capable secretary of war but, as his final conflict with Davis proved, did not always work smoothly with the Confederate president. After resigning, Randolph moved to Europe for a time but soon returned. He died at Monticello on April 3, 1867.

STEVEN E. WOODWORTH

See also

Benjamin, Judah Philip; Big Bethel, Battle of; Davis, Jefferson
   Finis; Holmes, Theophilus Hunter; Lee, Robert Edward

Further Reading

Patrick, Rembert W. *Jefferson Davis and His Cabinet.* Baton
   Rouge: Louisiana State University Press, 1944.

Woodworth, Steven E. *Davis and Lee at War.* Lawrence: University Press of Kansas, 1995.

Woodworth, Steven E. *Jefferson Davis and His Generals: The Failure of Confederate Command in the West.* Lawrence: University Press of Kansas, 1990.

Ransom, Matt Whitaker

Birth Date: October 8, 1826
Death Date: October 8, 1904

Confederate officer. Born in Warren County, North Carolina, on October 8, 1826, Matt Whitaker Ransom graduated from the University of North Carolina in 1847 and, having studied law his senior year, was admitted to the bar. He then commenced practice in Warrenton. Ransom was a presidential elector on the Whig ticket in 1852. He served as attorney general of North Carolina (1852–1855) and as a member of the North Carolina House of Commons (1858–1861). He was one of three North Carolina peace commissioners to the Provisional Confederate Congress at Montgomery, Alabama, in 1861.

With the beginning of the Civil War, Ransom enlisted as a private in the North Carolina Militia in May 1861 and was commissioned lieutenant colonel of the 1st North Carolina Infantry on May 16. In April 1862, he became colonel of the 35th North Carolina Infantry, which was part of his brother Brigadier General Robert Ransom's brigade. Matt Ransom took part in the Peninsula Campaign (March–July 1862), seeing action in the Battle of Seven Pines (May 31–June 1, 1862) and the Seven Days' Campaign (June 25–July 1, 1862). He was wounded in the Battle of Malvern Hill (July 1, 1862). Ransom fought in the Battle of Antietam (September 17, 1862) but, still suffering from his wounds, missed the First Battle of Fredericksburg (December 13, 1862).

Promoted to brigadier general on June 13, 1863, Ransom succeeded his brother in command of the brigade. Ordered to North Carolina, he took part in the recapture of Plymouth on April 17, 1864; the Siege of Suffolk (April 11–May 4); and the Second Battle of Drewry's Bluff (May 16, 1864), where he was wounded in the left arm. During the Petersburg Campaign (June 15, 1864–April 3, 1865), he fought in the Battle of Fort Stedman (March 25, 1865) and saw his brigade wrecked at the Battle of Five Forks (April 1, 1865). He then took part in the Appomattox Campaign (April 2–9, 1865). Ransom was paroled at Appomattox on April 9, 1865, and pardoned on December 13, 1866.

After the war, Ransom resumed his law practice and also farmed Verona, his wife's plantation on the Roanoke River near Weldon, North Carolina. He was elected as a Democrat to the U.S. Senate in 1872 and served until 1895. From 1895 to 1897, he was U.S. minister to Mexico. He then returned to his plantation. Ransom died near Garysburg, Northampton County, North Carolina, on October 8, 1904.

SPENCER C. TUCKER

See also

Antietam, Battle of; Appomattox Campaign; Five Forks, Battle
   of; Fort Stedman, Battle of; Fredericksburg, First Battle of;
   Malvern Hill, Battle of; Peninsula Campaign; Petersburg Campaign; Plymouth, Battle of; Ransom, Robert, Jr.; Seven Days'
   Campaign; Seven Pines, Battle of; Suffolk, Virginia, Siege of

Further Reading

Eicher, John H., and David J. Eicher. *Civil War High Commands.*
   Stanford, CA: Stanford University Press, 2001.

Warner, Ezra J. *Generals in Gray: Lives of the Confederate Commanders.* Baton Rouge: Louisiana State University Press,
   2006.

Ransom, Robert, Jr.

Birth Date: February 12, 1828
Death Date: January 14, 1892

Confederate officer. Robert Ransom Jr., brother of future Confederate brigadier general Matt W. Ransom, was born on February 12, 1828, in Warren County, North Carolina. After graduating from the U.S. Military Academy, West Point, in 1850, Robert Ransom was commissioned in the dragoons and served on the frontier, earning promotion to first lieutenant in 1855 and to captain in 1861. With the onset of the Civil War, he resigned his commission. Ransom accepted a captain's commission in the Confederate Army, and in October 1861 he became colonel of the 1st North Carolina Cavalry Regiment. Plagued by poor health, Ransom sometimes alienated his men with his rigid discipline.

Advanced to brigadier general on March 1, 1862, Ransom commanded an infantry brigade in North Carolina before being transferred to the Army of Northern Virginia during the Peninsula Campaign (March–July 1862). He performed brilliantly at the Battle of Malvern Hill (July 1, 1862). He next saw action during the Antietam Campaign (September 4–20, 1862) before taking charge of a division in December, when he helped hold the Confederate center at the First Battle of Fredericksburg (December 13, 1862).

On May 26, 1863, Ransom was advanced to major general. He then commanded the District of Southeastern Virginia before taking several months' sick leave. During October and November 1863, he commanded a cavalry division in eastern Tennessee under Lieutenant General James Longstreet.

In May 1864 Ransom assumed command of a division in the Richmond-Petersburg defenses. During the Second Battle of Drewry's Bluff (May 16, 1864), Ransom's division ruptured the right flank of the Union Army of the James. Nevertheless, General P. G. T. Beauregard, Ransom's superior, faulted him for moving too tentatively and costing the Confederates a decisive victory.

Ransom led a cavalry division in the early stages of the Shenandoah Valley Campaign (August 7, 1864–March 2, 1865) but later in August was forced to take another leave of absence owing to continuing poor health. He saw no further active duty.

After the war Ransom moved to Wilmington, North Carolina, where he was employed as an express agent and a city marshal. He later became a farmer and then chief engineer of harbor and river facilities at New Bern, North Carolina, where he died on January 14, 1892.

PAUL G. PIERPAOLI JR.

See also

Antietam Campaign; Drewry's Bluff, Second Battle of; Fredericksburg, First Battle of; Malvern Hill, Battle of; Sheridan's Shenandoah Valley Campaign

Further Reading

Eicher, John H., and David J. Eicher. *Civil War High Commands.* Stanford, CA: Stanford University Press, 2001.

Warner, Ezra J. *Generals in Gray: Lives of the Confederate Commanders.* Baton Rouge: Louisiana State University Press, 2006.

Ransom, Thomas Edward Greenfield

Birth Date: November 29, 1834
Death Date: October 29, 1864

Union officer. Thomas Edward Greenfield Ransom was born on November 29, 1834, in Norwich, Vermont. He entered Norwich University in 1848, where he studied surveying and engineering for three years. He then moved to Illinois, where he worked as a civil engineer and real estate speculator. Upon the beginning of the Civil War, Ransom raised Company E of the 11th Illinois Infantry, of which he became captain on April 6, 1861. He won quick promotion to major and lieutenant colonel and suffered his first wound in an engagement at Charleston, Missouri, in August 1861. Wounded again during the Battle of Fort Donelson (February 13–16, 1862), he was advanced to colonel the following month.

Ransom was badly wounded at the Battle of Shiloh (April 6–7, 1862); upon his recovery, he served as chief of staff for Major General John McClernand. Ransom commanded a brigade in the Army of the Tennessee and was advanced to brigadier general on April 15, 1863, serving during much of the Second Vicksburg Campaign (April 1–July 4, 1863). He then transferred to the Department of the Gulf and served along the Texas coast before taking command of XIII Corps during the Red River Campaign (March 10–May 22, 1864). He was again wounded at the Battle of Mansfield (April 8, 1864). Not completely recovered, he joined Major General William T. Sherman's army as commander of the 4th Division, XVI Corps, during the Atlanta Campaign (May 5–September 2, 1864). On September 22, Ransom assumed command of XVII Corps.

As Ransom pursued Confederate troops west into Alabama, on October 21 he fell ill with typhoid and the lingering effects of his unhealed wounds. He died near Rome, Georgia, on October 29, 1864, his troops having carried him for miles on a stretcher.

ERIC V. REYNOLDS AND PAUL G. PIERPAOLI JR.

See also

Atlanta Campaign; Fort Donelson, Battle of; Mansfield, Battle of; Red River Campaign; Shiloh, Battle of; Vicksburg Campaign, Second

Further Reading

Eicher, John H., and David J. Eicher. *Civil War High Commands.* Stanford, CA: Stanford University Press, 2001.

Warner, Ezra J. *Generals in Gray: Lives of the Confederate Commanders.* Baton Rouge: Louisiana State University Press, 2006.

Rappahannock, Union Department of the

Short-lived federal military administrative command created on April 4, 1862, and dissolved on June 26, 1862. The Department of the Rappahannock was formed when President Abraham Lincoln, concerned that Washington, D.C., was inadequately protected, ordered I Corps detached from

Major General George B. McClellan's command. On April 4, 1862, I Corps of some 40,000 men became the military arm of the newly created department, which was headed by Major General Irvin McDowell. The department encompassed all of Virginia east of the Blue Ridge Mountains and south and west of the Potomac River. Also included in its jurisdiction was the area served by the strategic Fredericksburg & Richmond Railroad (including Washington, D.C.) and the area between the Potomac and Patuxent Rivers.

During the early months of McClellan's unsuccessful Peninsula Campaign (March–July 1862), the general repeatedly asked that McDowell's force be released to strike Confederate defenses north of the Confederate capital of Richmond. Lincoln and Secretary of War Edwin M. Stanton demurred, however, preferring to keep McDowell in place at his headquarters in Fredericksburg.

As it turned out, this decision was the right one, because the Confederates scored a major victory on May 25, 1862, in the First Battle of Winchester and commenced an occupation of some of the Shenandoah Valley. After that, McDowell led a large detachment of his command toward the valley in hopes of crushing the Confederates. Confederate major general Thomas J. "Stonewall" Jackson managed to outmaneuver Union forces, however.

On June 26, the Department of the Rappahannock was discontinued, with its military forces becoming part of the new Army of Virginia, commanded by Major General John Pope.

PAUL G. PIERPAOLI JR.

See also

Jackson, Thomas Jonathan; Jackson's Shenandoah Valley Campaign; Lincoln, Abraham; McClellan, George Brinton; McDowell, Irvin; Peninsula Campaign; Pope, John; Stanton, Edwin McMasters; Winchester, First Battle of

Further Reading

Eicher, John H., and David J. Eicher. *Civil War High Commands.* Stanford, CA: Stanford University Press, 2001.

Rappahannock Station, Battle of
Event Date: November 7, 1863

Engagement in northern Virginia where the Orange & Alexandria Railroad crossed the Rappahannock River. After his defeat in the Battle of Gettysburg (July 1–3, 1863), Confederate general Robert E. Lee, commander of the Army of Northern Virginia, had withdrawn into Virginia, followed by

Union major general George Gordon Meade with his Army of the Potomac. After neither army was able to gain advantage during the Bristoe Campaign (October 9–20, 1863), Lee positioned his force south of the Rappahannock River, hoping to hold that position through the upcoming winter. He maintained a fortified position on the north bank of the river at Rappahannock Station to maintain a potential crossing point on the river. Meade, now under pressure from Washington, prepared to attack Lee's army by crossing at both Rappahannock Station and Kelly's Ford, several miles downstream.

The Confederate bridgehead at Rappahannock Station consisted of a brigade under Brigadier General Harry T. Hays fortified in two makeshift redoubts and trenches. Union troops from Major General John Sedgwick's VI Corps began advancing on the Confederate position on the afternoon of November 7, at which point Hays was reinforced by a brigade under Colonel Archibald C. Godwin. This brought the number of Confederate troops in the position to about 2,000.

Lee and other Confederate senior officers believed that Meade's main attack would be at Kelly's Ford and that Rappahannock Station was secure, but at dusk Brigadier General David A. Russell's division of Sedgwick's corps launched an unexpected assault on the Confederate lines at Rappahannock Station. The Union brigades of Colonels Peter Ellmaker and Emory Upton broke through the Confederate defenses and, after some close-range fighting, routed the surprised Confederates. With only a single pontoon bridge as their means of escape, many Confederates were captured. Union casualties in the engagement totaled around 400, while the Confederates lost nearly 1,700 killed, wounded, or mostly captured.

Lee was now forced to give up plans to attack Meade and retreated south behind the Rapidan River. Coming on the heels of the Confederate defeat at Bristoe Station (October 14), the loss of so many veteran soldiers further depleted and demoralized the Army of Northern Virginia.

JOSHUA MICHAEL

See also

Bristoe Campaign; Bristoe Station, Second Battle of; Lee, Robert Edward; Meade, George Gordon; Russell, David Allen; Sedgwick, John

Further Reading

Graham, Martin F., and George F. Skoch. *Mine Run: A Campaign of Lost Opportunities, October 21, 1863–May 1, 1864.* Lynchburg, VA: H. E. Howard, 1987.

Jones, Terry L. *Lee's Tigers: The Louisiana Infantry in the Army of Northern Virginia.* Baton Rouge: Louisiana State University, 1987.

Rations, CSA

Prescribed rations for the soldiers of the Confederate Army were derived from contemporary U.S. Army regulations. Officially, each soldier in the field was allocated on a daily basis 20 ounces of salt pork, bacon, or beef; 12 ounces of hard bread; and 1 ounce of desiccated vegetables (usually potatoes, beans, or peas). Additionally, a daily communal supplement for each 100 rations included 8 quarts of beans or peas, 10 pounds of rice or hominy, 8 pounds of coffee, 10 pounds of sugar, 2 quarts of salt, and 1 gallon of vinegar.

For numerous reasons, the rations listed above were not available to troops on a consistent basis. The Confederate Department of Subsistence was poorly managed and mired in inefficient bureaucracy. Below the national level, shortages of food containers and salt for preservation caused numerous disruptive bottlenecks in the supply chain. Loss of rail links, especially in the latter part of the conflict, also made moving food to support armies of tens of thousands of men extremely problematic. And finally, the often fluid nature of campaigns, with forces covering many miles in a day, placed great stress on the limited horse-powered transport available at the tactical level.

These difficulties resulted in official decreases in ration sizes several times from 1862 to 1864, with the meat ration cut by two-thirds and the flour ration by half in two notable instances. Substitutions such as lard for bacon were sometimes made. Oftentimes, the tactical situation would preclude cooking fires, resulting in the consumption of raw meat. Coarse cornmeal was often substituted for flour in making bread, and the lack of cooking implements sometimes resulted in inventive group meals such as slosh, a combination of all available foodstuffs stewed in the largest container. Perhaps the most vexing problem facing soldiers in the field was the chronic shortage of vegetables, either dried or fresh. This lack of nutritional balance had negative physiological effects on troops already confronting harsh living conditions and had a detrimental effect on soldier health.

The average soldier possessed several potential ways to supplement his daily ration. Foraging, whether command-directed by units or opportunistically by individuals, was common. It was also possible to send food packages to soldiers via post, but this service was spotty and highly dependent upon the movement and tactical situation of the individual's unit. Finally, soldiers with the means to do so could purchase staples from a sutler, a civilian who followed the army with a wagon of provisions sold for profit. This final solution produced its own set of problems, notably resentment among soldiers not able to purchase supplemental rations.

The rations prescribed for the Confederate soldier were considered the minimum to sustain an adult male engaged in grueling physical activity. Even these lowly standards were often not reached, however, requiring improvisation to remedy the shortfall.

ROBERT M. BROWN

See also
Rations, Union

Further Reading
Billings, John D. *Hardtack & Coffee*. Lincoln: University of Nebraska Press, 1993.
Stern, Philip V. D. *Soldier Life in the Union and Confederate Armies*. Bloomington: Indiana University Press, 1961.
Wiley, Bell E. *The Life of Johnny Reb*. Baton Rouge: Louisiana State University Press, 1943.

Rations, Union

U.S. Military daily rations were set by an act of Congress in 1861. They consisted of 20 ounces of meat (salt beef or salt pork), 22 ounces of flour (hardtack), 7 ounces of potatoes, 2.65 ounces of dried beans, 1.6 ounces of green coffee, and .32 ounce of gill vinegar along with salt, yeast, pepper, and sugar. Rations were issued in bulk and distributed to individual soldiers; however, portions could not be precisely divided because most unit quartermasters were not issued scales. Soldiers had to prepare their own meals in field camps.

Even under the best of circumstances, army rations were unpalatable, as food packaging was still in its infancy. Occasionally, canned meat arrived at the camp spoiled. Meat preserved with salt was dubbed "salt horse" and had to be placed in a stream overnight before it could be eaten. Hardtack quickly became damp and moldy or infested with weevils (which could be driven out by soaking in coffee). Desiccated (dehydrated) vegetables frequently contained leaves and were so tasteless that soldiers called them "desecrated" vegetables. Compounding these problems was the fact that most soldiers did not know how to properly prepare their food. Hardtack was thus a staple in army rations. It was eaten as issued or used to make a sandwich with salted meat. Skillygalee was made of hardtack broken up, soaked in water used to boil meat, and then fried in pork fat.

Soldiers favored their coffee, and any tactical pause became a time to brew a cup of coffee, usually with sugar.

Union soldiers gather around their log hut company kitchen in 1864. During the war, Union soldiers routinely received far better rations than did their Confederate counterparts. (National Archives)

Commissary officers ensured that coffee was always available, even if other food was not. The U.S. Army experimented with a concentrated "essence of coffee," which had the consistency and flavor of axle grease. Excess coffee was frequently traded with Confederate soldiers for tobacco.

What was not included in rations was as significant as what was included. Fresh vegetables were conspicuously absent because of the difficulty of shipping on railroads prior to refrigeration. Desiccated vegetables were an attempt to solve the problem, but they required five hours to prepare. Occasionally, enterprising quartermaster or subsistence officers in the field might arrange with local farmers for a shipment of fresh vegetables or fruit, but this was far from the norm. And in the winter months, such produce was not available in any case.

Although vitamins would not be discovered until decades later, physicians nevertheless knew that diet could cure or prevent certain diseases. Potatoes were known to be effective in curing scurvy (vitamin C deficiency) but only if eaten raw. During the Civil War, Union physicians diagnosed 46,000 full-blown cases of scurvy, with 771 deaths. Many soldiers suffered from symptoms of scurvy, called cachexia, which included generalized weakness and an inability to concentrate, symptoms that were often confused with malingering.

Soldiers suffered from other diseases caused by diet. Night blindness, or nyctalopia, was considered by wartime physicians as an eye condition. Although doctors noted that it frequently accompanied scurvy and could be cured by placing the soldier on furlough, the nutritional connection (vitamin A deficiency) would not be made for another 60 years. Chronic diarrhea was another condition that was associated with scurvy. Physicians frequently treated soldiers suffering from diarrhea with a diet that included fresh vegetables.

Thousands of soldiers were rendered noneffective for combat by nutritional deficiency, notably during the

Peninsula Campaign (March–July 1862) and the Atlanta Campaign (May 5–September 2, 1864). Soldiers were able to compensate to a certain extent by foraging. Marches were often halted by soldiers falling out of ranks to dig up turnips and pick blackberries, both rich in vitamin C. During Major General William T. Sherman's March to the Sea (November 15–December 21, 1864) when the Army of the Cumberland abandoned its supply lines (and rations) to live off of the land, the incidence of scurvy, diarrhea, and night blindness among the troops decreased dramatically.

ALAN J. HAWK

See also

Atlanta Campaign; Commissary of Subsistence; Foraging; Hardtack; Medicine; Peninsula Campaign; Sherman's March to the Sea; Rations, CSA

Further Reading

Bollet, Alfred. *Civil War Medicine, Challenges and Triumphs.* Tucson: Galen, 2002.

McCarley, J. Britt. "Feeding Billy Yank: Union Rations between 1861 and 1865." *Quartermaster Professional Bulletin* (December 1988): 11–15.

Moran, Barbara. "Dinner Goes to War." *American Heritage of Invention and Technology* 14(1) (Summer 1998): 10–19.

Raum, Green Berry
Birth Date: December 3, 1829
Death Date: December 18, 1909

Union officer. Born on December 3, 1829, in Golconda, Illinois, Green Berry Raum was educated in local schools, studied law, and was admitted to the Illinois bar in 1853. He spent a year in the Kansas Territory (1856–1857), then returned home and resumed his law practice. When the Civil War began, Raum entered military service as major of the 56th Illinois Infantry Regiment on September 28, 1861. He was promoted to lieutenant colonel in June 1862 and to colonel on August 31, 1862. During the Battle of Corinth (October 3–4, 1862), Raum led a charge that recaptured several Union artillery pieces. During the Second Vicksburg Campaign (April 1–July 4, 1863), he commanded a brigade in XVII Corps. Raum was badly wounded at the Battle of Missionary Ridge (November 25, 1863).

During the Atlanta Campaign (May 5–September 2, 1864), Raum's brigade protected Union supply lines from Confederate raids. He was brevetted brigadier general on September 19 and then attained permanent brigadier of

volunteers status on February 15, 1865. After the capture of Atlanta, Raum led a brigade of XV Corps during Sherman's March to the Sea (November 15–December 21, 1864). After leading a brigade in the Shenandoah Valley, Raum resigned his commission on May 6, 1865.

After the war, Raum was the builder and first president of the Cairo & Vincennes Railroad and then served in Congress (1867–1869) as a Republican. He was appointed U.S. commissioner of internal revenue (1876–1883) and then practiced law in the nation's capital during 1883–1889. He subsequently served as U.S. commissioner of pensions (1889–1893) and then returned to Illinois and practiced law in Chicago. Raum died in Chicago on December 18, 1909.

RICHARD A. SAUERS

See also

Atlanta Campaign; Corinth, Battle of; Missionary Ridge, Battle of; Sherman's March to the Sea; Vicksburg Campaign, Second

Further Reading

Barlow, William. "U.S. Commissioner of Pensions, Green B. Raum of Illinois." *Journal of the Illinois State Historical Society* 60 (Autumn 1967): 297–312.

Cozzens, Peter. *The Shipwreck of Their Hopes: The Battles for Chattanooga.* Champaign: University of Illinois Press, 1994.

Rawlins, John Aaron
Birth Date: February 13, 1831
Death Date: September 6, 1869

Union officer. John Aaron Rawlins was born on February 13, 1831, in Galena, Illinois. Although he received little formal education, he studied law and was admitted to the bar in 1854. He commenced a legal practice in Galena and became a city attorney in 1857. Rawlins soon became acquainted with Ulysses S. Grant, who also lived in Galena. When Grant received a brigadier general's commission in August 1861, he chose Rawlins as his adjutant general. Rawlins began his military career as a captain and remained with Grant until war's end.

Rawlins became a major on May 14, 1862; a lieutenant colonel on November 1, 1862; and a brigadier general of volunteers on August 11, 1863. He handled all of Grant's orders and correspondence and advised Grant on innumerable issues, reportedly even imploring him to refrain from drinking, to which Rawlins had a strong aversion. Often irreverent and dismissive of military protocol, Rawlins was without a

John Aaron Rawlins served as Lieutenant General Ulysses S. Grant's adjutant general throughout the Civil War. Rawlins, who rose to the rank of brigadier general, was the Union Army general-in-chief's closest and most influential adviser. (National Archives)

doubt Grant's closest and most influential adviser and zealously protected his chief's privacy. Some viewed Rawlins as an interloper and a busybody, but Grant's loyalty to him was virtually unshakable.

Rawlins was advanced to brigadier general in the regular army on March 3, 1865, and also became chief of staff to General in Chief Grant. On February 24, Rawlins was brevetted to major general of volunteers; he was brevetted to major general of regulars on April 9, 1865. In the last year of the war, Rawlins contracted tuberculosis. Despite his lingering illness, in early 1869 he lobbied President Grant for the position of secretary of war. Rawlins assumed the post on March 13, 1869, but died from tuberculosis six months later on September 6, 1869, in Washington, D.C.

PAUL G. PIERPAOLI JR.

See also

Grant, Ulysses Simpson

Further Reading

Grant, Ulysses S. *The Personal Memoirs of Ulysses S. Grant.* Reprint ed., with an Introduction by Brooks D. Simpson. Lincoln: University of Nebraska Press, 1996.

Perret, Geoffrey. *Ulysses S. Grant: Soldier and President.* New York: Random House, 1997.

Raymond, Battle of
Event Date: May 12, 1863

Engagement during Union major general Ulysses S. Grant's Second Vicksburg Campaign (April 1–July 4, 1863). Following its crossing of the Mississippi River and landing at Bruinsburg on the east bank below Vicksburg on April 29, Grant's Army of the Tennessee had moved inland. On May 1, the army defeated a smaller Confederate force at Port Gibson, Mississippi, forcing the Confederates to withdraw from the nearby river port of Grand Gulf, Mississippi, which Grant established as a supply point.

Grant then proceeded northeastward. He planned to secure the Southern Railroad and isolate Vicksburg from resupply from Jackson to the east, then close on Vicksburg from that direction and end the campaign. At Vicksburg, Lieutenant General John C. Pemberton, commanding the Confederate Department of Mississippi and East Louisiana, ordered Brigadier General John Gregg, who had only just arrived with a brigade at Jackson, to proceed to Raymond and attack the Union right flank. Gregg arrived at Raymond, 20 miles southwest of Jackson, late on the afternoon of May 11 with 4,100 men. He hoped to catch the Federals by surprise but was instead surprised on May 12 when his forces mistakenly met just south of Raymond not a Union raiding party, as he had surmised, but instead the head of one of Grant's three corps columns, the 12,000 men of XVII Corps commanded by Major General James B. McPherson. XVII Corps had been moving in drum and bugle silence, protected by a strong cavalry screen.

The ensuing Battle of Raymond, which saw Gregg outnumbered 3 to 1 in manpower and 7 to 1 in artillery, was never in doubt. Defeated, Gregg fell back on Jackson. In the battle, the Federals sustained 446 casualties (68 killed, 341 wounded, and 37 missing or captured); the Confederates lost 820 (100 killed, 305 wounded, and 415 taken prisoner).

The Battle of Raymond had important consequences for the campaign. The Federals were now assured of control of the Southern Railroad, cutting Vicksburg off from resupply and Confederate forces to the east under General Joseph E. Johnston; Pemberton was also prevented from further concentrating his forces. Alerted to the threat from Jackson posed by Johnston, who had hoped to catch Grant in a vice between his own men and those of Pemberton, Grant then moved against the Mississippi capital in full force, taking Jackson following a sharp but short fight on May 14. Two days later Grant defeated Pemberton, who had sortied from

Vicksburg, in the Battle of Champion Hill, driving him back into the Vicksburg defenses.

SPENCER C. TUCKER

See also

Champion Hill, Battle of; Grant, Ulysses Simpson; Gregg, John; Jackson, Battle of; Johnston, Joseph Eggleston; McPherson, James Birdseye; Pemberton, John Clifford; Vicksburg Campaign, Second

Further Reading

Ballard, Michael B. *Vicksburg: The Campaign That Opened the Mississippi.* Chapel Hill: University of North Carolina Press, 2004.

Bearss, Edwin Cole. *The Campaign for Vicksburg.* 3 vols. Dayton, OH: Morningside, 1985–1986.

Shea, William L., and Terrence J. Winschel. *Vicksburg Is the Key: The Struggle for the Mississippi River.* Lincoln: University of Nebraska Press, 2003.

Raymond, Henry Jarvis
Birth Date: January 24, 1820
Death Date: June 18, 1869

Journalist, politician, and cofounder of the *New York Times.* Henry Jarvis Raymond was born on January 24, 1820, in Lima, New York, and graduated from the University of Vermont in 1840. He soon moved to New York City and became interested in journalism, working for Horace Greeley's *New York Tribune* (1841–1843). Raymond then joined the staff of the *Morning Courier and New York Inquirer,* a Whig newspaper. He was elected to the New York legislature in 1849, serving until 1851. In the meantime, he also took editorial control of *Harper's New Monthly Magazine.* In 1851 he cofounded the *New York Daily Times,* which was renamed the *New York Times* in 1857. Raymond also served as Speaker of the New York House of Representatives in 1851.

In 1854 while still holding his editorial responsibilities, Raymond served as New York's lieutenant governor. Two years later he relinquished his duties with *Harper's* and joined the nascent Republican Party. Raymond exercised considerable control over the *Times,* insisting on fair, thorough, and unbiased reporting while reserving partisanship for the editorial pages. He also favored factual stories and reporting that was free of rhetorical embellishments and other distractions.

During the Civil War, Raymond maintained a sizable coterie of devoted war correspondents, and he personally reported on military events during his numerous trips to Virginia. Meanwhile, New York's three major newspapers, including the *Times,* engaged in a circulation war; by 1865, Raymond's paper had the city's second-largest newspaper readership. In 1862 Raymond reentered the New York House of Representatives and again served as its Speaker. By 1864, his work and stature allowed him to draft part of the Republican Party's platform. That same year, he was elected to the U.S. House of Representatives and served a single term (1865–1867). He was not a successful national legislator and was not nominated for reelection.

After leaving Congress, Raymond concentrated on his editorial responsibilities and died on June 18, 1869, in New York City. He was the author of two books: *Disunion and Slavery* (1860) and *The Life and Public Services of Abraham Lincoln* (1860).

PAUL G. PIERPAOLI JR.

See also

Greeley, Horace; Journalism; *New York Times;* War Correspondents

Further Reading

Brown, Ernest Francis. *Raymond of the Times.* Reprint ed. Westport, CT: Greenwood, 1970.

Holzer, Harold, and Craig Symonds. *The New York Times: The Complete Civil War, 1861–1865.* New York: Black Dog and Leventhal, 2010.

Read, Charles William
Birth Date: May 12, 1840
Death Date: January 25, 1890

Confederate naval officer. Charles William Read was born in Yazoo County, Mississippi, on May 12, 1840. Read was only 10 years old when his father died, after which his mother moved the family to Jackson. Wanting to go to sea, in September 1856 Read secured a warrant as an acting midshipman and an appointment to the U.S. Naval Academy, Annapolis. Graduating last in his class of 20 in June 1860, he passed most of his brief service in the U.S. Navy in the sidewheel frigate *Powhatan,* stationed in the Gulf of Mexico. On learning of the secession of Mississippi, Read resigned his commission and was released in early February 1861.

Read then made his way to New Orleans and served as sailing master of CSS *McRae,* a bark-rigged steamer. He fought in engagements with Union ships on the lower

Mississippi, including that with Flag Officer David G. Farragut's squadron in its run to New Orleans. Read next served as second lieutenant aboard the Confederate ironclad ram *Arkansas.* Following the scuttling of that ship in the Mississippi, in November 1862 Read joined the crew of the Confederate commerce raider *Florida,* commanded by Lieutenant John N. Maffitt. Among the U.S. merchant ships taken by the *Florida* was the brig *Clarence* on May 6, 1863, and 23-year-old Lieutenant Read requested and secured permission from Maffitt to sail this prize on a daring mission to Hampton Roads to cut out a Union gunboat or a steamer.

Read set out that same day with 20 men, his ship armed with a single 12-pounder howitzer, planning to sail the 3,400 miles from Brazil to Norfolk. A month later, he took and burned his first prize. Others followed, but from the crewmen taken he learned that Union security precautions would make it impossible to enter Hampton Roads. Having taken six prizes in the *Clarence,* on June 12 Read shifted operations to one of them, the *Tacony,* which was faster than the *Clarence;* he then burned the *Clarence.* Taking other prizes in the *Tacony,* Read was soon forced to release his growing number of prisoners, which meant that his presence was no longer a secret.

Continuing north, in late June Read reached the New England fishing grounds, where he took and burned a half dozen schooners and captured a large clipper ship. By now he had exhausted his ammunition, and there were some 40 U.S. warships searching for him. Read, however, took 15 prizes in the *Tacony* before he burned that ship on June 25, 1863, after transferring to yet another prize, the small fishing schooner *Archer.*

On June 26, Read boldly sailed the *Archer* into Portland, Maine, where he captured the U.S. revenue cutter *Caleb Cushing* and managed to sail it out of the harbor. Federal officials armed two steamers and set out in pursuit. Unfortunately for Read, he was unaware of the location of the cutter's ample ammunition supply, and following a brief gunfight, he scuttled the ship and surrendered. Read and his small band had taken 21 prizes, burning 15 of them and causing widespread panic along the North Atlantic seaboard.

Exchanged in 1864, Read then distinguished himself with the James River Squadron and as commander of the sidewheel steamer CSS *Webb* during the Red River Campaign (March 10–May 22, 1864). Following the war, Read served on a British merchantman and then became master of a United Fruit Company steamer. He was a Mississippi River pilot before serving as president of the Board of Harbor

Masters at New Orleans until the late 1880s. Read died in Meridian, Mississippi, on January 25, 1890.

SPENCER C. TUCKER

See also

Arkansas, CSS; *Florida,* CSS

Further Reading

Jones, Robert A. *Confederate Corsair: The Life of Lt. Charles W. "Savez" Read.* Mechanicsburg, PA: Stackpole, 2000.
Shaw, David W. *Sea Wolf of the Confederacy: The Daring Civil War Raids of Naval Lt. Charles W. Read.* New York: Free Press, 2004.

Reagan, John Henninger
Birth Date: October 8, 1818
Death Date: March 6, 1905

Confederate politician. John Henninger Reagan was born on October 8, 1818, in Sevier County, Tennessee, and moved to Texas in 1839. There he served in the Republic of Texas Army, was deputy state surveyor (1839–1843), and studied law. Admitted to the bar in 1848, Reagan served in the state legislature (1847–1849), was a district court judge (1852–1857), and served in the U.S. House of Representatives (1857–1861). He supported Texas secession in 1861 and was elected to the Provisional Confederate Congress.

In March 1861, Reagan was persuaded to take the cabinet-level position of postmaster general. He quickly ramped up operations, recruiting former federal postal workers and attempting to make the Confederate postal service a pay-as-you-go operation, which was mandated by the Confederate Constitution. This proved to be no small task, but Reagan effectively combined and eliminated routes, exacted a major cut in railroad shipping rates, and raised postal rates. He also insisted that postal employees be exempt from military service, which rankled the War Department. By the winter of 1862, Reagan threatened to resign over the criticism aimed at him by the War Department, but President Jefferson Davis, whom Reagan admired greatly, convinced him to stay on.

Reagan soon became more than a postmaster general; he would in fact become one of Davis's closest confidants. When the Confederate government fled Richmond in the spring of 1865, Reagan was the only cabinet member to remain with Davis. Captured with Davis by Union authorities, Reagan spent several months imprisoned at Fort Warren (Boston). After his release, he requested that President Andrew Johnson not seek a punitive peace against the

John Henninger Reagan of Texas proved highly effective as Confederate postmaster general. He also became a confidant of President Jefferson Davis. (Library of Congress)

South and asked that Texans reconcile themselves to the war's outcome.

After the war, Reagan practiced law and remained active in Texas politics. He was a delegate to the 1875 Texas Constitutional Convention. He also returned to the U.S. House of Representatives, serving from 1875 until 1887, at which time he took a seat in the U.S. Senate, serving a partial term (1887–1891). Upon his return to Texas, he served as chairman of the influential Texas Railroad Commission (1891–1903). Reagan died on March 6, 1905, in Palestine, Texas.

PAUL G. PIERPAOLI JR.

See also
Cabinet, CSA; Davis, Jefferson Finis; Texas

Further Reading
Procter, Ben. *Not without Honor: The Life of John H. Reagan.* Austin: University of Texas Press, 1962.

Reagan, John H. *Memoirs, with Special Reference to Secession and the Civil War.* Edited by Walter Flavius. 1906; reprint, New York: AMS, 1973.

Reams Station, First Battle of
See Wilson-Kautz Raid

Reams Station, Second Battle of
Event Date: August 25, 1864

Engagement in Dinwiddie County, Virginia, during the Petersburg Campaign (June 15, 1864–April 3, 1865). Major General George Gordon Meade's Army of the Potomac endeavored to get behind the Confederate Army of Northern Virginia under General Robert E. Lee at Petersburg in June 1864, but Lee was able to block this thrust, and the fighting degenerated into stalemate as the Union forces conducted siege operations against both Petersburg and the nearby Confederate capital of Richmond. Searching for a way to break the deadlock, Union Army general in chief Lieutenant General Ulysses S. Grant, who had accompanied the Army of the Potomac in the field, ordered attacks on Lee's lines of communication in an effort to starve the Confederates of supplies. At the same time, Grant was under pressure to deliver a Union military victory that would buttress President Abraham Lincoln's effort to win reelection in November 1864.

Grant targeted the Weldon Railroad (also known as the Weldon & Petersburg Railroad), the vital supply line linking Lee's army with Wilmington, North Carolina, which by then was the Confederacy's only major port open for blockade-runners. In the Battle of Jerusalem Plank Road (June 21–23) and the Battle of Globe Tavern (August 18–21), Union forces enjoyed short-lived success, briefly cutting the line. After both battles, however, the Confederates were able to bridge the gap with wagon trains, and in any case they soon had the rails repaired. Grant was undaunted; he now dispatched Major General Winfield Scott Hancock's II Corps, augmented by Brigadier General David M. Gregg's cavalry, to destroy the 14 miles of Weldon track from near Globe Tavern south to Rowanty Creek.

The operation began on August 22, with Gregg's cavalry in the vanguard. The Union horsemen immediately began tearing up tracks. By August 24 Hancock's main force had occupied Reams Station and by that evening had torn up three miles of track. Realizing the serious threat that this posed to his supply line and the possible avenue of retreat for his army, Lee dispatched Lieutenant General A. P. Hill's corps, along with Major General Wade Hampton's cavalry.

Grant was then ill, and Meade was in temporary command of Union operations. Meade believed that Lee was attempting to turn the Union left flank and thus began rearranging his units accordingly, taking up a defensive stance. Unfortunately for the Federals at Reams Station, Meade failed to reinforce their section of the line, assuming that the able Hancock could hold there with the forces available. Hill, also in ill health, meanwhile passed command of his forces to his subordinate, Major General Henry Heth.

The Battle of Reams Station began on August 25 when the cavalry forces under Hampton and Gregg clashed. The Confederates forced the Union troopers back toward Reams Station. When Heth's infantry arrived, he ordered an immediate assault. Aware of the Confederate approach, Hancock had recalled his men from tearing up track and had placed them behind fortifications. The Union soldiers were unable to repulse the Confederate attack, and their lines soon collapsed. Hancock was able to rally enough men to launch a brief counterattack, however. This provided sufficient time for the bulk of his corps to withdraw toward Petersburg.

Despite destroying a few more miles of track, the Second Battle of Reams Station has to be counted as a Union defeat. Union losses in the infantry and cavalry totaled 2,747, including some 2,000 captured. The Confederate total was only 814 killed, wounded, or captured. On the negative side for the Confederates, however, from this point on they would be able to send supplies by rail on the Weldon only as far as Stony Creek Depot, 16 miles south of Petersburg. There the supplies would then have to be offloaded into wagons for movement to Dinwiddie Court House and then along the Boydton Plank Road into Petersburg.

ROBERT L. GLAZE AND SPENCER C. TUCKER

See also

Burnside, Ambrose Everett; Globe Tavern, Battle of; Gregg, David McMurtrie; Hampton, Wade; Hancock, Winfield Scott; Heth, Henry; Hill, Ambrose Powell; Meade, George Gordon; Petersburg Campaign; Warren, Gouverneur Kemble; Weldon & Petersburg Railroad; Wilson-Kautz Raid

Further Reading

Horn, John. *The Petersburg Campaign, June 1864–April 1865.* Cambridge, MA: Da Capo, 1999.

Trudeau, Noah Andre. *The Last Citadel: Petersburg, Virginia, June 1864–April 1865.* Baton Rouge: Louisiana State University Press, 1991.

Rebel Yell

Distinctive battle cry unique to Confederate military units during the Civil War. The Rebel Yell had antecedents in the war cries often associated with Celtic culture and the shouts that Native Americans employed in warfare.

Like its uncertain origin, the exact sound of the Rebel Yell has been debated for years. It was generally described

as consisting of several syllables, having a distinctive high pitch, and as being expressed with tremendous volume. There is no doubt that it was distinctly recognizable from other military cheers and often over other battlefield noises. It may have been a single cry yelled all together by a unit or the sum of massed individual yells. Variation by region and circumstance no doubt also affected the sound. Recollections of those who heard it frequently noted its eerie and almost inhuman quality.

As a war cry, the Rebel Yell was most commonly associated with offensive action (such as charging an enemy line). Expressing the emotion and intensity of combat, it contributed on a psychological level to an offensive assault, although it is difficult to separate its effects from the overall picture of combat. As the war progressed, Confederate forces used the Rebel Yell more widely, both in combat and in camp. The war cry was employed principally to intimidate enemy troops, exaggerate the size of an offensive force, and bolster morale and esprit de corps.

JOSHUA MICHAEL

See also
Armies of the Confederate States, Overview

Further Reading

Commager, Henry Steele, ed. *The Blue and the Gray.* New York: Crescent, 1995.

Wiley, Bell Irvin. *The Life of Johnny Reb.* Indianapolis: Bobbs-Merrill, 1943.

Reconstruction
Start Date: 1865
End Date: 1877

The process of restoring the seceded states to the Union and of delivering the promise of freedom and citizenship to millions of emancipated slaves. The Civil War inflicted mass devastation on the South. Many cities were destroyed, illness and hunger swept the region, the Southern economy was devastated, and thousands were left jobless. Restoring the former Confederate states to the Union and to productivity would require struggles both physical and political, especially under the new reality of emancipation. Similarly, most of the 4 million emancipated slaves, known as freedmen, found themselves destitute.

Despite the obstacles, most freedmen looked eagerly to the future. They hoped to establish their own churches and schools and to legalize their marriages. African Americans also hoped to own land to support and protect their independence. Many believed that this was their due. Union major general William T. Sherman encouraged such hopes in January 1865 when he ordered South Carolinian lands to be divided into 40-acre parcels and given to freedmen. Rumors spread that the federal government would give each freedman "40 acres and a mule."

In truth, Reconstruction began when large areas of the South fell under solid federal control. Indeed, in much of Louisiana and Tennessee, the process had begun as early as 1862. Reconstructed regions were therefore not subject to Union directives aimed at the Confederacy, such as the Emancipation Proclamation of January 1863.

Presidential Reconstruction

President Abraham Lincoln wanted to bring the seceded states back into the Union quickly. Even before the war's end, he planned for Reconstruction—rebuilding the former Confederate states and reuniting the nation. To encourage Southerners to abandon the Confederacy, Lincoln issued the Proclamation of Amnesty and Reconstruction on December 8, 1863. He gave full pardons to all Southerners—except high-ranking Confederate leaders—who swore allegiance to the U.S. Constitution and accepted federal laws ending slavery. This proclamation permitted a state to rejoin the Union when 10 percent of its residents who had voted in 1860 swore loyalty to the nation.

Many members in Congress objected to Lincoln's Ten Percent Plan. They did not trust the Confederates to become loyal U.S. citizens or to protect the rights of former slaves. In July 1864, Congress created its own Reconstruction plan in the Wade-Davis Bill. It called for the Confederate states to abolish slavery and delayed Reconstruction until a majority of each state's white males took a loyalty oath. Lincoln vetoed the bill and in his second inaugural address, delivered on March 4, 1865, clarified his goal for Reconstruction: "With malice toward none, with charity for all, with firmness in the right as God gives us to see the right, let us strive on . . . to bind up the nation's wounds . . . to do all which may achieve . . . a just and lasting peace."

How Reconstruction might have developed under Lincoln will never be known. On April 14, 1865, Confederate sympathizer John Wilkes Booth shot the president as he and his wife watched a play at Ford's Theatre in Washington. Lincoln died early the following morning. The assassination increased the distrust between the North and the South, and many Northerners believed that Booth participated in a conspiracy organized by Confederate leaders.

African Americans in Office in the South, 1870–1876

State	State Legislators	U.S. Senators	U.S. Congressmen
Alabama	69	0	4
Arkansas	8	0	0
Florida	30	0	1
Georgia	41	0	1
Louisiana	87	0	1*
Mississippi	112	2	1
North Carolina	30	0	1
South Carolina	190	0	6
Tennessee	1	0	0
Texas	19	0	0
Virginia	46	0	0
Total	633	2	15

* Elected but not seated due to election challenge.

With Lincoln's death, Vice President Andrew Johnson assumed the presidency. Johnson, a Democrat, former slave owner, and senator from Tennessee, had been chosen as Lincoln's running mate in 1864 because of his pro-Union sympathies. Despite his support for the Union and his wartime experience as Tennessee's military governor, Johnson proved ill-suited for the challenges of Reconstruction. He also lacked Lincoln's political acumen and formidable stature.

Johnson favored a government controlled by whites, and he held, as did most whites, prejudices against African Americans. In May 1865, Johnson pardoned all rebels except former Confederate officers and officeholders and the richest planters. For readmission into the Union, his plan required that states nullify their acts of secession and abolish slavery. Many Southerners supported Johnson's plan because it allowed former Confederate leaders to control Reconstruction by dominating the state governments.

Quickly, in much of the South unrepentant officers and planter elites resumed positions of authority. As lawmakers, these former Confederates made sure that the new state constitutions did not grant voting rights to freedmen. When these leaders complained about the presence of African American troops in the South, President Johnson supported their removal. Furthermore, by recognizing Mississippi's new government, Johnson overlooked the state's refusal to ratify the Thirteenth Amendment, which abolished slavery.

President Johnson's actions encouraged former Confederates to adopt laws limiting the freedom of blacks. These so-called Black Codes aimed to prevent blacks from achieving social, political, and economic equality with whites in the South. African Americans could not hold meetings unless whites were present. The codes also forbade African Americans to travel without permits, own guns, attend school with whites, or serve on juries. Most importantly, the codes reestablished white control over African American labor. To force former slaves to return to the fields, some local codes prohibited blacks from living in towns unless they were servants and from renting land outside of towns or cities. Several states required freed people to sign long-term labor contracts. Those who refused could be arrested and have their labor put up for auction. The codes also allowed judges to decide whether African American parents could support their children. Children without support could be bound, or hired out against their will. Johnson's approach therefore pleased few in the North and soon found angry opposition in Congress, where many legislators now demanded a much more punitive program.

Congressional Reconstruction

In contrast, Radical Republicans, such as Representative Thaddeus Stevens of Pennsylvania, insisted that blacks be given the right to vote. Radical Republicans believed that the proper aim of Reconstruction was to create a new South where all men enjoyed equal rights. The Radicals also saw land reform as the key to changing society in the South. Representative Stevens and Senator Charles Sumner of Massachusetts agreed that the plantations must be divided among the freeman. This economic independence would ensure black freedom and destroy the political power base of the South. Despite Stevens and Sumner's efforts, government land seizure never gained wide support. Therefore, many Radicals shifted their efforts to civil equality.

In early 1866, Congress held hearings on conditions in the South. Witnesses before the Joint Committee on Reconstruction presented evidence of violence. African Americans recounted tales of murder, physical intimidation, and vandalism, and Southern Unionists told of death threats. These reports convinced moderate Republicans to join with the Radicals. One move made by the Radicals was to extend the life of the Freedmen's Bureau. Congress created the bureau in March 1865 to aid the millions of Southerners left homeless and hungry by the war. The bureau distributed food and clothing, served as an employment agency, set up hospitals, operated schools, and also played a major role in providing education for African Americans. In February 1866 Congress passed the Freedmen's Bureau Bill to extend the life of the agency. President Johnson vetoed the bill on constitutional and financial grounds.

Furious with the president, Congress passed the Civil Rights Act of 1866, the first civil rights law in the nation's history. It declared that everyone born in the United States was a citizen with full civil rights, but it did not guarantee voting rights. Johnson vetoed the bill, arguing that it centralized power in the federal government. His veto eroded his support in Congress and united moderate and Radical Republicans against him. Congress eventually overrode Johnson's veto. In June 1866, Congress also passed the Fourteenth Amendment to the Constitution. The amendment extended equal citizenship to African Americans and all people "born or naturalized in the United States"; denied states the right to deprive anyone of "life, liberty, or property without due process of law"; and promised all citizens equal protection under the law.

By the spring and summer of 1866, many Americans grew increasingly troubled by the ongoing violence against African Americans in the South. Race riots became more common throughout the region, which made Johnson's call for leniency toward the southern rebels seem absurd. During the midterm congressional election, the Radicals seized control of Congress and decided that blacks must have the right to vote. In January 1867 a bill granting African American suffrage in the District of Columbia passed, despite Johnson's veto. Congress next extended this right to the country's territories.

The Republicans also passed the Reconstruction Acts of 1867. These divided the former Confederacy, with the exception of the already reconstructed Tennessee, into five military districts, commanded by U.S. Army generals and occupied by U.S. troops, many of whom were black. The acts also disenfranchised former Confederates and those who supported secession, thus rendering most white men in the South ineligible to vote or hold office. To gain readmission into the Union, states were required to ratify the Fourteenth Amendment as well as submit to Congress new constitutions that guaranteed all men the vote. The act further required that blacks be allowed to vote for delegates to the state constitutional conventions as well as to serve as delegates.

Throughout 1867 and 1868, the Radicals and President Johnson conducted a fierce political battle. To protect their Reconstruction policies, the Radicals passed the Tenure of Office Act in 1867, which required Senate approval of a replacement before the president could remove an appointed official who had been confirmed by the Senate. In February 1867 Johnson disregarded the Tenure of Office Act in an effort to oust Secretary of War Edwin Stanton, and the House of Representatives responded by voting to impeach the president. The trial lasted eight weeks, and the final tally in the Senate fell one vote shy of the majority needed to convict and remove Johnson from the presidency.

In 1868, Americans were set to elect a new president. The Republicans nominated Union Civil War hero General Ulysses Grant to run against Democratic hopeful Horatio Seymour. Grant defeated Seymour, but the Republicans realized that black voters had given them a decided advantage. Eager to protect this power in the North and the South, the Republicans drafted the Fifteenth Amendment, which stated that "The right of citizens of the United States to vote shall not be denied or abridged by the United States or by any state on account of race, color, or previous conditions of servitude."

Reconstruction in the South

With the passage of the Reconstruction Acts, blacks became more hopeful for equal citizenship. Many registered to vote and joined political groups such as the Union League. The league spread the views of the Republican Party to freed slaves and poor whites. The Union League also built schools and churches for African Americans. As blacks became more involved in politics, they served as delegates to all the state constitutional conventions. During Reconstruction, more than 600 African Americans were elected as representatives, and hundreds of others held state and local offices.

The arrival of northern Republicans eager to participate in the state conventions increased resentment among whites in the South. These northern Republicans, called carpetbaggers because they carried everything they owned in a carpetbag, came south in search of economic opportunities. Southerners who supported the Republican Party were called scalawags. Many supporters of Reconstruction in the South formed a Republican alliance to seize economic and political control from the planters and rebuild the South to improve conditions for poor white farmers and African Americans. To fight the Republican Party's growing power and to retract the political and social rights of blacks, the Ku Klux Klan (KKK) was founded in 1866 by six former Confederates. The organization grew quickly and attracted southerners from all classes. The KKK used terrorist tactics to intimidate Republican supporters and African Americans. Other such groups followed. During the 1870s, Congress responded to the growing violence with the Enforcement Acts, which empowered the federal government to combat such terrorism with military force.

In 1873 a severe economic depression, known as the Panic of 1873, gripped the nation. Republicans came under pressure as workers threatened strikes and farmers demanded relief. The Republicans also abandoned universal voting rights as thousands of immigrants joined the Democratic Party. The Republicans soon lost much of their support, and the Democrats in 1874 gained seats in Congress. Republicans tried one last effort to enforce Reconstruction through the Civil Rights Act of 1875, which prohibited public businesses from discriminating against African Americans. However, conservative and moderate Republicans and most Democrats began to view Reconstruction as a burden.

For the presidential election of 1876, Democrats nominated Samuel J. Tilden of New York, who challenged war hero Republican Rutherford B. Hayes of Ohio. After a contested election, Hayes entered into an agreement with leading Republicans and southern Democrats, called the Compromise of 1877. In return for the Democrats' acceptance of Hayes as president, the Republicans agreed to withdraw the remaining federal troops from the South. In 1877, the last of the Reconstruction governments fell. The individuals behind the Democratic Party's return to power were known as the Redeemers. The old guard returned with a vengeance. In almost every former Confederate state, architects of secession, planter aristocrats, and former generals dominated social and political life, as if very little had changed. They rewrote state constitutions and overturned many of the Reconstruction governments' reforms.

By abandoning Reconstruction, the Republicans abandoned millions of African Americans, who now saw their hopes for equality and opportunity dashed. Throughout the South, so-called Jim Crow laws eroded the promises contained in the Fourteenth and Fifteenth Amendments. Rigid segregation became codified, and blacks were largely barred from voting. Most African Americans faced a bleak existence, one now compounded by white resentment and racial hatred that had not existed as such before the war. Although Reconstruction failed to deliver the kind of economic and educational development that its supporters envisioned, it did provide a legal foundation for such, which unfortunately for millions went largely ignored after 1877. By failing to provide the funding for meaningful programs and by refusing to give potentially useful initiatives such as the Freedmen's Bureau needed authority and resources, Reconstruction could never provide the uplifting experience that its more idealistic proponents sought. Also, the heavy-handedness of the Radical Republicans inspired resentment and backlash. Clearly, presidential Reconstruction, especially under Johnson, proved unsatisfactory on many grounds, but congressional or military Reconstruction under the Radicals, while perhaps well intentioned, also failed in most of its aims. The situation demanded a more nuanced approach, which in the postwar political climate was impossible to achieve.

JOSHUA ADAM CAMPER

See also

Black Codes; Freedmen's Bureau; Johnson, Andrew; Ku Klux Klan; Lincoln's Reconstruction Policies; Stanton, Edwin McMasters; Stevens, Thaddeus; Sumner, Charles; Wade-Davis Bill

Further Reading

Blight, David W. *Race and Reunion: The Civil War in American Memory.* Cambridge, MA: Belknap Press of Harvard University Press, 2002.

Blum, Edward J. *Reforging the White Republic, 1865–1898: Race, Religion, and American Nationalism.* Baton Rouge: Louisiana State University Press, 2007.

Fitzgerald, Michael W. *Splendid Failure: Postwar Reconstruction in the American South.* Chicago: Ivan R. Dee, 2008.

Foner, Eric. *Reconstruction: America's Unfinished Revolution, 1863–1877.* New York: Harper Perennial Modern Classics, 2002.

McPherson, James, and James Hogue. *Ordeal by Fire: The Civil War and Reconstruction.* 4th ed. New York: McGraw-Hill, 2010.

Richardson, Heather Cox. *West from Appomattox: The Reconstruction of America after the Civil War.* New Haven, CT: Yale University Press, 2008.

Recruitment of Seamen, Union and Confederate Navies

Means of filling wartime personnel demands. To serve in the U.S. Navy, a recruit had to be at least 4'8" tall and 18 years old. No inexperienced men over age 35 were accepted, but men with naval experience were accepted to age 38. By a regulation of 1863, boys could be enlisted at age 13 but only with parental consent.

Although some U.S. Navy enlisted personnel came from the U.S. Army, most notably in the case of the gunboats on the western waters, the vast majority of seamen enlisted at regular recruiting stations, known as rendezvous, and located at the naval yards and in seaport cities where recruits were likely to be found. Shortages of seamen led both sides to offer bounties for long-term enlistment. In the Union Navy, this could be as much as $300, or two years' pay, for a three-year enlistment. Bonuses were also paid for reenlistments. Early in 1862, the Confederate Navy offered a $50 bonus to any recruit enlisting for three years or for the duration of the war.

The Confederate Congress passed a conscription law in April 1862, which provided that any trained seaman in the army could apply for transfer to the navy. With the army refusing to release recruits and with the demand high for trained seamen, in May 1863 the Confederate Congress passed a bill that required the army to release any men requested by the Navy Department who desired a transfer. Still, securing transfers was difficult.

Enlistment times in both navies varied from as little as a month in critical need to as long as the duration of the war. Three years was a normal term of enlistment early in the war for the U.S. Navy. Prohibitions were in place against enlisting foreigners, the incompetent, and "idiots," but in the Civil War—as throughout history—recruiters often looked the other way.

Both navies suffered from desertions, although no figures are available on the number. This was sufficient in the U.S. Navy for the department to hire detectives to try to chase down the culprits. Among the latter were bounty jumpers, individuals who signed on, received a significant bounty payment, and then deserted at the first opportunity in order to repeat the process in another location and under a different name.

In the U.S. Navy, a recruit was considered officially enlisted after he had signed a contract, commonly referred to as a shipping article, in the presence of a commissioned officer. This included the recruit's date of enlistment; pay, with any advances and possible bounties; and rating. Following his enlistment, the recruit reported to one of a number of receiving ships to be issued clothing and equipment and perhaps receive some training prior to ship assignment.

SPENCER C. TUCKER

See also

Bounty System

Further Reading

Canney, Donald L. *Lincoln's Navy: The Ships, Men and Organization, 1861–65.* Annapolis, MD: Naval Institute Press, 1997.

Still, William N., Jr. *The Confederate Navy: The Ships, Men and Organization, 1861–65.* Annapolis, MD: Naval Institute Press, 1997.

Tucker, Spencer C. *Blue and Gray Navies: The Civil War Afloat.* Annapolis, MD: Naval Institute Press, 2006.

Recruitment of Soldiers, Confederate and Union

Means of meeting wartime personnel needs. Voluntary military enlistment in both the Union and the Confederacy proved to be fraught with problems. Before the war began and in the early months of the conflict, neither side had difficulty raising troops. Indeed, in the North, eager volunteers had to be turned away. As the conflict progressed, however, enlistments fell off sharply, prompting both sides to resort to involuntary conscription.

On April 15, 1861, the Abraham Lincoln administration issued a call for 75,000 volunteers to serve for 90 days. The call was met enthusiastically, and by late spring more than 75,000 men had enlisted for military service. There was, however, no uniformity to enlistments at that point. Many signed on for just the 90 days, while others, such as those from New York, enlisted for federal service for two years. Ninety-day enlistees from New York were expected to provide an additional two years of duty in the state.

On May 3, 1861, Lincoln called for an additional 42,000 enlistees to serve for three years in federal service. He also requested 18,000 men to enlist for service in the U.S. Navy and another 6,347 to enlist in the Regular Army. At the same time, the War Department attempted to make enlistment periods longer in duration and more uniform—three years was the expected norm. Some states, such as New York, balked. The Lincoln administration was thus compelled to reach a compromise, and New York enlistees were generally mustered in for two years of service. Also, a number of other units were mustered in on shorter terms for political expediency. By better controlling enlistment at the federal level, the War Department was attempting to avoid having Washington, D.C., swamped with too many men at one time, which would have presented logistical nightmares in terms of housing, provisioning, and training. It was also decided that having too many volunteers idle in large encampments was not a wise idea from the standpoint of discipline and sanitation.

An example of the general antipathy toward military service in the North, especially among working-class white men and immigrants, can be found in the New York City Draft Riots (July 13–17, 1863), in which anywhere from 120 to 2,000 people lost their lives and another 2,000–8,000 were injured. The immediate catalyst had been the March 1863 Enrollment Act passed by Congress, but beyond that the melee demonstrated that the lower classes believed that they were shouldering much of the burden in terms of providing military manpower, and there was fear among the Irish that African Americans would take their jobs. The Emancipation Proclamation, having significantly altered war aims, was indeed a major contributing factor in fostering lower-class resentment.

As in the North, the Jefferson Davis administration initially had few problems raising volunteer troops. The Provisional Confederate Congress issued a call-up of state militias and authorized the raising of 100,000 volunteer recruits on March 6, 1861. Until mid-April, only 6- and 12-month enlistments from the state and local levels were accepted. Davis, however, believing that the war might well last longer than a few months, pushed for longer enlistment periods, which not surprisingly fell afoul of states' rights advocates. By the end of April 1861, Congress began allowing the national government to accept enlistees directly into military service, thus bypassing local and state recruitment efforts. This latest effort also approved, for the first time, three-year enlistment periods. By June 1, the Confederate government called for 400,000 new volunteers.

State leaders balked at such a heavy-handed national policy, however, and the Davis administration acceded to shorter 6- and 12-month enlistment terms from the state level. By early 1862 with thousands of enlistments set to expire, the Confederate Congress began to contemplate a conscription law, which was enacted in April 1862. Part of the law turned all 6- and 12-month enlistments into three-year enlistments. The law irked leaders in the individual states, who nevertheless grudgingly acceded to the exigencies of the war.

In both the South and the North, women played an important role in the enrollment process. In forming their armies, the Union and the Confederacy mobilized soldiers as members of community units, and the entire community participated. Community pride was at stake, with towns competing against one another to enroll more men into the army. For both women and men in the North and the South, the patriotic zeal of the summer of 1861 eclipsed any prior lukewarm feelings regarding the need for war. The excitement of community competition and the social activities surrounding enlistment also overshadowed the harsh reality that some of the enlistees would not return home. In the initial enlistment process in 1861, Northern and Southern women played similar roles, although evidence suggests that Southern women were given more credit for enlistments than their Northern counterparts. As the war continued, the roles of women in the two regions diverged, with Southern women increasingly opposing the enlistment of their male relatives.

PAUL G. PIERPAOLI JR. AND JOHN M. SACHER

See also

Conscription, CSA; Conscription, U.S.; New York City Draft Riots; Women

Further Reading

Clinton, Catherine, and Nina Silber, eds. *Divided Houses: Gender and the Civil War.* New York: Oxford University Press, 1992.

Geary, James W. *We Need Men: The Union Draft and the Civil War.* DeKalb: Northern Illinois University Press, 1991.

Moore, Albert B., ed. *Conscription and Conflict in the Confederacy.* Reprint ed. Columbia: University of South Carolina Press, 1996.

Rector, Henry Massey

Birth Date: May 1, 1816
Death Date: August 12, 1899

Governor of Arkansas. Henry Massey Rector was born on May 1, 1816, in Louisville, Kentucky, and moved to St. Louis as a youth. In 1835 Rector relocated to Arkansas and became a farmer on land he had inherited near Collegeville. He was a U.S. marshal (1842–1843) and served in the Arkansas Senate as a Democrat (1848–1850). He subsequently studied law and was admitted to the bar in 1854. Rector then began a successful practice in Little Rock, and from 1855 until 1859 he sat in the state legislature. He sat on the Arkansas Supreme Court (1859–1860) before running for governor in 1860.

After a hard-fought campaign, Rector became governor on November 16, 1860. He soon convened a secession convention, which first met in March 1861. The delegates initially voted against secession, which angered the pro-secessionist Rector. While the convention dithered, the governor moved boldly and unilaterally, ordering state troops to occupy Fort Smith and seize the U.S. arsenal in Little Rock. He also sent a contingent of state troops to Virginia after that state seceded in April.

Arkansas finally seceded on May 6, 1861, at which time the secession convention decided to remain in session to help supervise the war effort. Rector was not happy with this decision. Meddling by the convention combined with the state's poor finances and growing resistance to the Confederate government stymied most of Rector's plans to prepare the state for war. As time went on, Rector and the convention delegates were in a constant state of feuding. In the autumn of 1862, the state's newly adopted constitution did not endorse Rector's governorship, and he was forced to leave office on November 4, only halfway through his term in office.

Thereafter Rector resumed his legal career and farming interests. He died on August 12, 1899, in Little Rock.

PAUL G. PIERPAOLI JR.

See also

Arkansas

Further Reading

DeBlack, Thomas A. *With Fire and Sword: Arkansas, 1861–1874.* Fayetteville: University of Arkansas Press, 2003.

Moneyhon, Carl H. *The Impact of the Civil War and Reconstruction on Arkansas: Persistence in the Midst of Ruin.* Baton Rouge: Louisiana State University Press, 1994.

Red River Campaign

Start Date: March 10, 1864
End Date: May 22, 1864

Failed Union offensive in Louisiana and Arkansas preparatory to an invasion of Texas. The Red River Campaign was the largest combined operation to that point in U.S. military history and in the Civil War; it was also one of the war's major military fiascos. Major General Ulysses S. Grant favored an operation against Mobile, Alabama, but before he could assume the post of general in chief, President Abraham Lincoln and Major General Henry W. Halleck set in motion an operation to capture Shreveport, Louisiana.

Located in extreme northwestern Louisiana on the west bank of the Red River, Shreveport had long been a Union military objective. This city of 12,000 people was the capital of Confederate Louisiana and the headquarters of General Edmund Kirby Smith's Trans-Mississippi Department. An important manufacturing center and supply depot, Shreveport boasted a naval yard and was a hub for war-related industries in eastern Texas and goods shipped from Mexico. Despite military reasons for proceeding against Shreveport, the chief Union motivations were economic and political. The Red River Valley was the greatest cotton-production area in the Confederacy, with some 2 million bales stored along the river and its tributaries. The shortage of cotton had idled thousands of New England textile workers, and securing that cotton would mean New England jobs and an assist to Lincoln in the November presidential election. Additionally, French emperor Napoleon III had dispatched a sizable expeditionary force to Mexico, and Washington wanted to forestall any possible French designs on Texas.

The plan called for ships of Rear Admiral David D. Porter's Mississippi Squadron to proceed up the Red River, providing transportation and furnishing gunfire support and logistical assistance to the army. Union forces enjoyed numerical advantage in every area. Although there was no overall commander—one of the plan's major failings—Major General Nathaniel P. Banks, commanding the largest contingent, fancied himself as such. Banks's political standing in New England had secured him a major generalcy of volunteers, but despite his lack of military training, he repeatedly rejected sound advice offered by his professional subordinates. Reportedly, Banks was considering a run for the presidency in 1864 on the Republican ticket. Keeping him occupied in the West would mean that he was less likely to stir up trouble for Lincoln's own effort.

With some 19,000 infantry and 3,000 cavalry from his Department of the Gulf, Banks was to march from New Orleans to Opelousas and then north to Alexandria, where he would be joined by some 2,500 men of the U.S. Colored Corps and link up with the second Union prong of 10,000 veterans of Major General William T. Sherman's Army of the Tennessee, commanded by Brigadier General Andrew Jackson Smith. This combined force, numbering 34,500 men and 90 artillery pieces, would move north against Shreveport, supported by Porter's ships. Because of the upcoming Atlanta Campaign (May 5–September 2, 1864), Smith had strict orders not to proceed beyond Shreveport, and his men were detailed for one month only, until mid-April. At the same time, 10,400 men under Major General Frederick Steele, commander of the Department of Arkansas, would close in from the north.

Success depended on all of these columns coming together at precisely the same time. Failure of any one would place the whole plan in jeopardy. Another threat to the plan's success lay in the possibility of the Confederates concentrating to defeat the Union prongs in detail.

The Red River Campaign commenced on March 10, 1864, three days behind schedule, when Smith's men loaded into steamer transports at Vicksburg. The next evening they rendezvoused with Porter's warships off the mouth of the Red. Porter had 90 ships, the most powerful assembly of naval strength on inland waters of the war, including 13 ironclads, 12 lighter-draft gunboats, and 1 ram, along with tugs, tenders, dispatch boats, supply ships, and a hospital vessel. Porter was, however, greatly concerned about the depth of the river. In normal times, the 1,300-mile Red River, which joined the Mississippi above Baton Rouge, was navigable to Shreveport without major difficulty, but exceptionally dry weather and Confederate defensive efforts by the time the operation began considerably reduced the Red River's water level.

On March 12, the Union warships and transports entered the Red. Porter sent some ships up the Ouachita to neutralize a Confederate fortification at Trinity, and the next day Smith's men disembarked at Simmesport on the Atchafalaya River to march overland against Confederate Fort DeRussy midway between the Red River's mouth and Alexandria. With eight guns and two fieldpieces, the fort was designed to defend the water approaches. Eight miles below DeRussy, the Confederates had also erected a river obstruction. Major General John G. Walker's division of 3,300 Texas troops defended the area. Walker sent word to Major General Richard Taylor, commanding the Western District of Louisiana, who hastily ordered an evacuation. This doomed DeRussy but saved the bulk of the Texans for the important battles to come.

On March 14, the men of four of Porter's ships under Lieutenant Commander Seth L. Phelps removed the water obstructions as Smith's troops moved overland. A joint Union assault on the evening of March 14 brought Fort DeRussy's surrender. Of its 300 defenders, 185 were taken prisoner. Union casualties were 38 killed or wounded. Smith's troops then rejoined the transports, and by the morning of March 16, Alexandria was in Union hands. Porter now awaited the arrival of Banks.

Both Banks and Steele were behind schedule, however. Banks was to have been at Alexandria on March 17, but his entire force did not arrive there until March 26, and Steele did not even set out until March 16. Counting Walker's Texans, Taylor had some 7,000 men. He planned delaying actions to mask his actual strength and to engage Banks in pitched battle only at a time and place of Taylor's choosing. On March 21, however, Brigadier General Albert L. Lee's cavalry caught Confederate cavalrymen in bivouac near Alexandria and captured 350.

Banks now had 32,500 men in and around Alexandria, along with 90 guns. Porter's ships mounted 210 heavy guns. With such resources, few doubted that taking Shreveport would be an easy matter. Yet despite an order from Grant urging speed, Banks delayed to supervise local elections at Alexandria on April 1.

Porter, concerned about the dropping water level in the Red, decided to proceed. Experienced river pilot Wellington Withenbury advised him to take only his light-draft vessels and warned Porter about the "falls" at Alexandria—sandstone boulders in the river that usually were well below the surface but would be treacherous in low water. Porter ignored this sound advice in the belief that the Confederates might have as many as five ironclads in the river and that he would need his heavier ships.

The falling water in the Red resulted largely from deliberate Confederate action. The Confederates sank a large steamer athwart the river near Tone's Bayou, then turned it

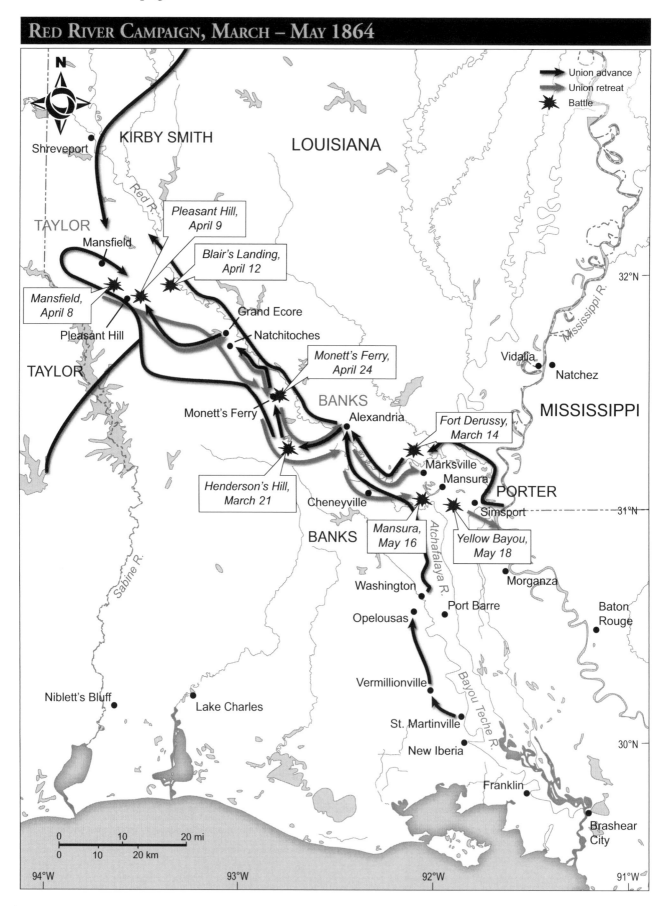

RED RIVER CAMPAIGN, MARCH – MAY 1864

into a dam, diverting the Red into old Tone's Bayou channel and thence into Bayou Pierre. Although much of the water flowed back into the Red River a few miles above Grand Ecore, a large amount remained to form a 19-mile-wide collection lake and drop the water level in the Red.

On March 29 Porter set out with a dozen ships, but it took three days just to get the large ironclad *Eastport* through the falls, and the hospital ship wrecked. Porter did get 12 warships and 30 transport steamers past Alexandria. It then took four days to cover the 100 miles to Grand Ecore. The Confederates, meanwhile, torched thousands of bales of cotton to keep them from falling into Union hands.

Lee's cavalry had departed Alexandria on March 26, and Smith's men followed the next evening. At the steamboat landing at Cotile, 22 miles north of Alexandria, Smith's troops boarded the transports. Major General William B. Franklin left Alexandria with the bulk of Banks's men on March 29. Banks left behind at Alexandria, however, an entire division of 4,000 men. Lee's cavalry took Natchitoches on March 30, and Franklin's men arrived there on April 1, covering the 60 miles from Alexandria in four days of hard marching.

Not until April 2 did Banks depart Alexandria for Grand Ecore in an army steamer. The following day, he was faced with deciding on the route to Shreveport. Smith's troops were scheduled to leave in only 12 days. Withenbury had a considerable financial investment in cotton grown near the river upstream. Knowing that it would be safe only if the army did not proceed upriver with the navy, he recommended one of two interior roads, one to the east (actually a better route but one that would take three additional days to traverse) and one far to the west. Aware of the pressing time constraints on a third of his force, Banks decided to move north along the westerly road some 20 miles inland. Banks and Porter planned to meet at a point opposite Springfield Landing, about 30 miles south of Shreveport, on April 10.

Between Grand Ecore and Shreveport, the river was narrow and winding. Afraid that the *Eastport* might ground in these conditions, Porter left it behind at Grand Ecore and proceeded with 6 ships, 3 of them ironclads. Accompanying these were 20 army transports and 2,300 of Smith's men.

Porter set out on April 7. He quickly concluded that marching along the Red would have been the best route by far for Banks. The roads were good and were flanked by wide fields, and the troops would have been able to move without the large supply train transporting 10 days of rations specified by Banks.

Banks's men resumed their march, beginning on April 6. Banks placed Lee's cavalry in front, followed by 300 supply wagons protected by the 2,500-man Corps d'Afrique, the main body of 15,000 men under Franklin, 700 wagons, and finally the bulk of Smith's force, bringing up the rear, protected by a cavalry brigade screen.

On April 7 some 3 miles north of Pleasant Hill, Lee's cavalry fought a sharp engagement with Confederate cavalry under Brigadier General Thomas Green. On April 8 the Union column reached Sabine Cross Roads, just south of Mansfield and about 40 miles south-southwest of Shreveport.

That day, with the Union column stretching over some 20 miles of road, Taylor and about 8,800 Confederates attacked its head. The Battle of Mansfield (April 8, 1864) was the decisive engagement of the campaign. Because of Banks's march arrangements, only about 12,000 Union troops actually participated. The Confederates steadily drove the Union troops back, and when the Confederates mounted a double envelopment, Union resistance collapsed. Only a stand by Brigadier General William H. Emory's division prevented complete disaster. Banks suffered 2,235 casualties and lost 20 guns, 250 wagons, nearly 1,000 draft animals, and thousands of small arms. Taylor's 1,500 casualties were actually heavier in terms of numbers of men engaged, but he had ended the Union drive on Shreveport.

Marching all night, the Union troops set up strong positions the next morning at Pleasant Hill, 14 miles south. Although still badly outnumbered, Taylor pursued and, reinforced, attacked in the late afternoon. Union counterattacks nullified initial Confederate success, and nightfall ended the fighting. Union casualties totaled 1,506; Taylor lost some 700.

Despite having achieved a tactical victory, Banks believed that his army was threatened with destruction, and he now decided to withdraw completely. The Union troops retired at night to Grand Ecore and from there to Alexandria.

Porter, meanwhile, arrived at Springfield Landing on April 10 to await Banks. Porter had dispatched ships up the Ouachita River, reaching Monroe, Louisiana, where they confiscated 3,000 bales of cotton, brought off about 800 slaves, and destroyed some property. Learning what had happened to Banks, Porter ordered his ships to descend the river, but Banks's precipitous withdrawal had freed up thousands of Confederates, who fired on the ships from the river bluffs. On April 12 at Blair's Landing, one of the Union ironclads grounded. As Union seamen worked to free it, Confederate troops attacked. The resulting engagement cost the Confederates some 300 casualties, while the squadron suffered only 7 wounded. Brigadier General Thomas Green, who had led the attack, was among the Confederate dead.

Federal transports below the falls in the Red River, April 1864, during the ill-fated Union Red River Expedition of March 10–May 22. (Library of Congress)

On April 15, Porter's ships reached Grand Ecore. That same day, however, the *Eastport* struck a torpedo (mine). Although two steam pump boats raised the badly damaged ship, the *Eastport* continued to ground, and Porter ordered it blown up on April 26.

Following the destruction of the *Eastport,* the remaining three Union warships and two pump boats got under way. They had gone about 20 miles when they reached a bend in the river and came under attack from a land force of some 1,200 men with 18 artillery pieces. The *Champion No. 3* was hit in its starboard boiler, releasing clouds of steam. Three crewmen died, but of 150–200 escaped slaves on board, only 15 survived. The pump boat was abandoned and subsequently captured. The next morning, April 27, the *Champion No. 5* was sunk. The three gunboats suffered 43 casualties but made it to Alexandria.

By April 27, Porter had 12 ships above the rapids. Banks's men were there and could provide protection, but the situation facing the squadron appeared dire. The river was rapidly falling. On April 28, Porter reported only 3.25 feet at the falls, with 7 feet required to pass his ships over. Porter was thus facing the prospect of having to destroy his ships or see them fall into the hands of the Confederates.

Engineer Lieutenant Colonel Joseph Bailey proposed constructing a dam across the river at the rapids to raise the water level. This seemed impossible, but Bailey convinced Porter, who requested and received from Banks some 3,500 men and 200–300 wagons. The soldiers razed nearby mills for materials and felled trees.

Work began on April 30, and by May 8 the project was essentially complete. One more day would have been sufficient for Porter to be able to pass his ships over the falls, but on the morning of May 9, the pressure of the water swept away part of the dam. Porter immediately ordered the shallow-draft vessels to proceed. All of these, their hatches battened down, successfully passed over the falls.

Six of the ironclads and two tugs were still stranded, but Bailey immediately went to work building three wing dams upstream at the upper falls to force the water into one channel. The earlier work had taken eight days; the new project took three days. The remaining eight ships all passed through during May 12–13.

Banks's men then also departed Alexandria. They reached Simmesport on May 16 without significant Confederate harassment. Bailey supervised construction of an improvised bridge of steamboats across the Atchafalaya, and by May 19 the entire command was over that river. Smith's troops immediately departed for Vicksburg, while most of XIX Corps proceeded east to join the Army of the Potomac. Porter's squadron reentered the Mississippi River on April 21. The campaign was over.

The Arkansas prong of the ground effort, the so-called Camden Expedition, also met defeat. When Steele learned that Confederate generals Smith and Sterling Price had joined forces against him, he ordered a retreat toward Little Rock. The Confederates retook Camden, and at Jenkins' Ferry, Arkansas, on April 29, they made contact as Steele's men waited to cross the Sabine River. The Confederates arrived in force on April 30, but Steele was able to pass the majority of his men across the river. Union casualties totaled 700 men, whereas the Confederates lost 800–1,000. In the entire effort, Union casualties were 2,750 and Confederates casualties were 2,300, but the Union losses in guns, wagons, and pack animals were far heavier. The Battle of Jenkins' Ferry also opened the way for the Confederates to invade Missouri.

Recriminations over the Red River Campaign began almost immediately. Congress investigated and subsequently placed most of the blame on Banks, who never again held a field command. Lincoln replaced him with Major General Edward R. S. Canby, and Banks subsequently left the army altogether. Aside from the destruction of considerable Confederate property, much of this self-inflicted, the Red River Campaign had been a fiasco. Sherman summed it as "One damn blunder from beginning to end."

SPENCER C. TUCKER

See also

Bailey, Joseph; Banks, Nathaniel Prentice; Blair's Landing, Battle of; Canby, Edward Richard Sprigg; Cane River Crossing, Louisiana, Engagement at; Emory, William Hemsley; Franklin, William Buel; Grant, Ulysses Simpson; Green, Thomas; Halleck, Henry Wager; Jenkins' Ferry, Battle of; Lincoln, Abraham; Mansfield, Battle of; Napoleon III; Pleasant Hill, Battle of; Porter, David Dixon; Price, Sterling; Sherman, William Tecumseh; Smith, Andrew Jackson (Union General); Smith, Edmund Kirby; Steele, Frederick; Taylor, Richard; Walker, John George

Further Reading

Joiner, Gary D. *One Damn Blunder from Beginning to End: The Red River Campaign of 1864.* Wilmington, DE: Scholarly Resources, 2003.

Sherman, William T. *Memoirs of General W. T. Sherman.* New York: Library of America, 1990.

Slagle, Jay. *Ironclad Captain: Seth Ledyard Phelps and the U.S. Navy, 1841–1864.* Kent, OH: Kent State University Press, 1996.

Tucker, Spencer C. *Blue & Gray Navies: The Civil War Afloat.* Annapolis, MD: Naval Institute Press, 2006.

U.S. Congress. *Report of the Joint Committee on the Conduct of the War, 1863–1866: The Red River Expedition.* 1865; reprint, Millwood, NY: Krauss Reprint, 1977.

Redwood, Allen Christian
Birth Date: June 19, 1844
Death Date: December 24, 1922

Confederate soldier, noted freelance writer, and artist. Allen Christian Redwood was born on June 19, 1844, at his family's plantation in Lancaster County, Virginia. As an infant, he moved with his family to Baltimore, where he was educated at a private academy. He then began studying at the Polytechnic Institute of Brooklyn (New York), but in 1861 with the beginning of the Civil War, at age 17 he returned to Virginia and enlisted as a private in the 1st Maryland Cavalry Regiment.

Redwood later transferred to the 55th Virginia Infantry Regiment and served in the Army of Northern Virginia. He saw considerable action and was taken prisoner at the Second Battle of Bull Run (August 29–30, 1862). He also participated in the Battles of Chancellorsville (May 1–4, 1863) and Gettysburg (July 1–3, 1863). For a brief period he was secretary to Brigadier General Lunsford L. Lomax before rejoining his old unit. By war's end, Redwood had been wounded on three separate occasions and had been taken prisoner for a second time, only days before the conflict ended.

Although Redwood did some sketches and drawings during the war, most of his work came in the postwar period. He was among just a handful of artists who actually served as a soldier and saw combat as a participant. His artistic renderings were hailed for their attention to detail, meticulous accuracy, and unabashed portrayals of violence and death. For many years Redwood worked on a freelance basis for such esteemed publications as *Harper's Monthly* and *Century Magazine,* and he also contributed stories that accompanied his sketches and other artwork. His art portrayed combat, prisoner-of-war camps, wartime civilian life, and accurate depictions of everyday soldiers in a variety of settings. In addition to relying upon his own observations, Redwood also used photographs—some of them iconic—to produce his renderings. Redwood's work and his status as a veteran made him quite popular with both Northern and Southern audiences. Many of Redwood's sketches that had been published in *Century Magazine* were reproduced in 1887 in the four-volume *Battles and Leaders of the Civil War.*

Redwood traveled throughout the country after the war and produced many scenes depicting the Plains Indians. In 1898, *Harper's Weekly* sent him to Cuba to cover the Spanish-American War. His works during that conflict mirrored his earlier Civil War work, which were models of the vérité style for which he was already well known. Redwood died on December 24, 1922, in Asheville, North Carolina. A large amount of Redwood's unpublished work was bequeathed to the Museum of the Confederacy in 1982.

PAUL G. PIERPAOLI JR.

See also

Art in the Civil War; *Harper's Weekly*

Further Reading

Brown, Joshua. *Beyond the Lines: Pictorial Reporting and the Crisis of Gilded Age America.* Berkeley: University of California Press, 2002.
Holzer, Harold, and Mark E. Neely Jr. *Mine Eyes Have Seen the Glory: The Civil War in Art.* New York: Orion Books, 1993.

Reeder, Andrew Horatio
Birth Date: July 12, 1807
Death Date: July 5, 1864

First governor of the Kansas Territory. Andrew Horatio Reeder was born on July 12, 1807, in Easton, Pennsylvania. After attending a private academy in Lawrenceville, New Jersey (now the Lawrenceville School), he studied law. Admitted to the bar in 1828, Reeder commenced a practice in Easton. He also soon became involved in Democratic politics at the state and local levels.

An early adherent of popular sovereignty, Reeder believed that the doctrine was the best way to handle the issue of slavery in the territories. Democratic president Franklin Pierce named Reeder as the first territorial governor on June 29, 1854, despite the fact that he never held public office. Reeder was sworn into office on July 7 but did not arrive in Kansas until October 1854. Shortly after his arrival, he embarked on a lengthy tour of the territory, which led him to believe that the issue of slavery might bring violence there. After postponing legislative elections until March 1855, which Reeder hoped would diminish proslavery and antislavery passions,

the electoral process was in large part a sham. This sparked the beginning of the violence that came to be known as Bleeding Kansas. Reeder greatly compounded the ensuing turmoil by clumsily permitting all but the most bogus votes to be counted instead of declaring the results null and void and calling for new elections.

In July 1855, the newly seated territorial legislature, which greatly favored the proslavery stance, began to enact legislation that would protect slavery in Kansas at almost any cost. Although Reeder promptly vetoed these kinds of enactments, the vetoes were just as promptly overridden. When the legislature voted to oust Reeder from office, President Pierce removed him from the governorship on August 16, 1855.

Reeder, who had become a major landholder in Kansas, remained in the territory and became a staunch antislavery advocate. When the free-staters formed their own legislature, which was not recognized by the U.S. government, Reeder was elected a U.S. congressional delegate and then a U.S. senator, but he was never seated. Under intense pressure from proslavery forces, he finally fled Kansas, at which time he went on a lecture tour informing Americans of the excesses of Kansas's slavery advocates. He also joined the Republican Party and campaigned for its 1856 presidential candidate, John C. Frémont.

By early 1857, Reeder had resumed his law practice in Easton, Pennsylvania, but would remain engaged in Republican national politics, campaigning for Abraham Lincoln in 1860. Reeder died in Easton on July 5, 1864.

PAUL G. PIERPAOLI JR.

See also

Bleeding Kansas; Kansas; Kansas-Nebraska Act; Pierce, Franklin; Popular Sovereignty

Further Reading

Etcheson, Nicole. *Bleeding Kansas: Contested Liberty in the Civil War Era.* Lawrence: University Press of Kansas, 2004.
Josephy, Alvin M. *The Civil War in the American West.* New York: Knopf, 1992.

Refugee Home Society

Organization established to create a fund and purchase land to assist fugitive slaves in Ontario, Canada. The Refugee Home Society was founded at a meeting that took place in the Detroit City Hall on May 21, 1851. The creation of the society was instigated by Michigan abolitionists. Based in Detroit, the society's main purpose was to help fugitive slaves immigrating to Canada from Michigan by purchasing blocks of land and supervising its distribution among black refugees. The society has been considered a by-product of the North American Agricultural League, the primary goal of which was to establish an agricultural union of black settlers on land purchased in Canada and the West Indies.

A year after its establishment, the Refugee Home Society merged with the Fugitive Union Society of Sandwich. David Hotchkiss, an American Missionary Association agent, along with fugitive slave Henry Bibb and his wife Mary, became its primary leaders. Unlike the other three major black settlements of Wilberforce, Dawn, and Elgin, the Refugee Home Society was not a geographically united community, as the purchased land was allocated south and east of the town of Windsor, Ontario. The society's demise was rooted in the opposing factions within the black community, and the close of the Civil War brought an end to the society's purpose.

VANJA PETRIČEVIĆ

See also

Abolitionism and the Civil War; Bibb, Henry

Further Reading

Hite, Roger W. "Voice of a Fugitive: Henry Bibb and Ante-Bellum Black Separatism." *Journal of Black Studies* 4(3) (1974): 269–284.

Landon, Fred. "Agriculture among the Negro Refugees in Upper Canada." *Journal of Negro History* 21(3) (1936): 304–312.

Ripley, Peter. *The Black Abolitionist Papers,* Vol. 2, *Canada, 1830–1865.* Chapel Hill: University of North Carolina Press, 1987.

Winks, Robin W. *The Blacks in Canada: A History.* 2nd ed. Montreal: McGill-Queen's University Press, 1997.

Reid, Hugh Thompson
Birth Date: October 18, 1811
Death Date: August 21, 1874

Union officer. Hugh Thompson Reid was born on October 18, 1811, in Union County, Indiana. He farmed for a time before attending Miami University and Indiana University. He then studied law and opened a practice. In 1839 Reid moved to Fort Madison, Iowa, where he became a successful land speculator and served a three-year term as a district attorney. In 1849 he moved to Keokuk, Iowa, and became president of the Des Moines Valley Railroad.

In late 1861, Reid began organizing what would become the 15th Iowa Infantry Regiment. On February 22, 1862, he became the outfit's colonel and was soon assigned to the Army of the Tennessee. During the first day of combat at the Battle of Shiloh (April 6–7, 1862), Reid was shot in the neck and nearly given up for dead. He survived the wound but was out of action until the autumn of 1862.

Promoted to brigadier general of volunteers in April 1863, Reid took command of the 1st Brigade, 6th Division, XVII Corps, then on duty in Louisiana. This unit was one of the few that contained African American troops. He subsequently led his men during the Second Vicksburg Campaign (April 1–July 4, 1863).

On October 3, 1863, Major General Ulysses S. Grant appointed Reid commander of the District of Cairo, headquartered at Paducah, Kentucky. The assignment was far from ideal, and Reid chafed under restrictions that included a badly understrength and poorly trained and equipped force. In April 1864 he resigned his commission, resumed the presidency of the Des Moines Valley Railroad, and practiced law. Reid died on August 21, 1874, in Keokuk, Iowa.

PAUL G. PIERPAOLI JR.

See also

Shiloh, Battle of; Vicksburg Campaign, Second

Further Reading

Eicher, John H., and David J. Eicher. *Civil War High Commands.* Stanford, CA: Stanford University Press, 2001.

Warner, Ezra J. *Generals in Blue: Lives of the Union Commanders.* Baton Rouge: Louisiana State University Press, 2006.

Reid, Whitelaw
Birth Date: October 27, 1837
Death Date: December 15, 1912

War correspondent and influential newspaper publisher. Whitelaw Reid was born on October 27, 1837, near Xenia, Ohio. He attended the Miami University of Ohio, graduating in 1856 and distinguishing himself especially in foreign languages and writing. While still in school, he had a number of articles published in newspapers as far away as Kansas.

From 1856 to 1858, Reid served as principal of a grade school in South Charleston, Ohio. Finding that work unsatisfactory, he returned to Xenia and purchased the *Xenia News,* one of two local newspapers. Politics provided most of the paper's content, and Reid soon became an ardent supporter of the Republican Party. He supported Abraham Lincoln as the best candidate for the party in the 1860 presidential election.

Poor health and lack of profits forced Reid to sell the *News* and to begin working for the *Cincinnati Gazette*. His skill at covering political events was quickly recognized, and he was soon made city editor. The outbreak of the Civil War in 1861 provided him with greater opportunities. Traveling with the Union Army as a war correspondent, Reid quickly proved himself to be a discriminating observer of military affairs. He criticized the slowness of commanders and the unpreparedness of the soldiers for combat. Reid's journalistic descriptions of the fighting at the Battle of Shiloh (April 6–7, 1862) and the Battle of Gettysburg (July 1–3, 1863) were hailed as masterpieces of comprehensiveness and clarity.

Reid was eventually banned from accompanying the army because of what was regarded as negative reporting. Prevented from taking the field, he was active in Washington, D.C., and became acquainted with Republican leaders. In 1864 he opposed Lincoln's reelection, believing him unequal to the task. Reid's connections secured him positions as librarian of the U.S. House of Representatives from 1863 to 1866 and clerk of the Military Committee. Reid was one of three newspapermen who visited Richmond immediately after its 1865 fall. His descriptions of that event and Lincoln's funeral crowned his wartime reporting.

Reid wrote the two-volume *Ohio in the War* (1868), which covered both civil and military activities. That work remains valuable today. In the autumn of 1868, Reid joined the *New York Tribune* and worked as an assistant to Horace Greeley, who became a close friend. Reid was largely responsible for the *Tribune*'s outstanding coverage of the Franco-Prussian War of 1870–1871, and he encouraged such writers as Mark Twain and Bret Harte to submit works to the paper.

In a series of Machiavellian moves following Greeley's death, Reid formed an alliance with businessman Jay Gould and obtained control over the *Tribune* from Greeley's heirs. Although never having had the flair of Greeley, Reid expanded the paper's circulation and instituted a number of innovations. He used the linotype machine, which was perfected at the paper, to set text, and he initiated the first Sunday edition in 1879. Reid hired only the best reporters, and he supported the development of wire services for distant stories. Under his control, the *New York Tribune* grew to have the largest circulation of any newspaper in the United States.

Failing health and other interests led Reid to leave most daily operations of the paper in the hands of others. He accepted an appointment as U.S. minister to France from President Benjamin Harrison in 1889 and served until 1892, during which time Reid helped to negotiate a treaty that improved commercial ties between the two nations. When Harrison ran for reelection in 1892, Vice President Levi P. Morton was passed over. Instead, Reid was selected as a compromise candidate. The campaign was listless, however, and Harrison and Reid went down to defeat.

Reid then returned to his newspaper work. President William McKinley turned down Reid's request to be appointed minister to Great Britain but did appoint him one of five peace commissioners to negotiate an end to the Spanish-American War in 1898, which resulted in the Treaty of Paris in December 1898. Following McKinley's 1901 assassination, Reid was finally named minister to Great Britain by President Theodore Roosevelt in 1905. Reid remained in that post until his death in London on December 15, 1912.

TIM J. WATTS

See also

Gettysburg, Battle of; Greeley, Horace; Lincoln, Abraham; Lincoln Assassination; Shiloh, Battle of

Further Reading

Cortissoz, Royal. *The Life of Whitelaw Reid.* New York: Scribner, 1921.

Duncan, Bingham. *Whitelaw Reid: Journalist, Politician, Diplomat.* Athens: University of Georgia Press, 1975.

Morgan, H. Wayne. *Making Peace with Spain: The Diary of Whitelaw Reid, September–December 1898.* Austin: University of Texas Press, 1965.

Reilly, James William
Birth Date: May 20, 1828
Death Date: November 6, 1905

Union officer. James William Reilly was born on May 20, 1828, in Akron, Ohio. He graduated from Mount St. Mary's College (Maryland), studied law, was admitted to the bar, and commenced a practice in Wellsville, Ohio. Reilly entered the state legislature in 1858 as a Republican and on August 30, 1862, entered federal service as colonel of the 104th Ohio Infantry Regiment. Stationed in Kentucky mostly on garrison duty for a number of months, Reilly's regiment was moved to Covington, Kentucky, in September 1862 to counter a Confederate threat on Cincinnati.

In the summer of 1863, Reilly's outfit was attached to the Army of the Ohio in eastern Tennessee and saw action in the Knoxville Campaign (November–December 1863), during which he had temporary command of a brigade. Serving under Major General William T. Sherman, Reilly was advanced to brigadier general on July 30, 1864, and took part in the Atlanta Campaign (May 5–September 2, 1864), frequently commanding a division. Reilly commanded the 3rd Division, XXIII Corps, during the Franklin and Nashville Campaign (November 29–December 27, 1864). He performed gallantly at the Battle of Franklin (November 30), where his command managed to take some 1,000 prisoners and capture 22 Confederate battle flags. Reilly continued in his divisional command during Sherman's March through the Carolinas (January–April 1865) and resigned on April 20, 1865.

Postbellum, Reilly returned to his Wellsville, Ohio, law practice and also served as president of the local bank. Reilly died on November 6, 1905, in Wellsville.

PAUL G. PIERPAOLI JR.

See also

Atlanta Campaign; Franklin, Battle of; Franklin and Nashville Campaign; Knoxville Campaign; Sherman's March through the Carolinas

Further Reading

Eicher, John H., and David J. Eicher. *Civil War High Commands.* Stanford, CA: Stanford University Press, 2001.
Warner, Ezra J. *Generals in Blue: Lives of the Union Commanders.* Baton Rouge: Louisiana State University Press, 2006.

Remington Carbine

A rifled breech-loading infantry weapon produced by the Remington Arms Company and used by the Union Army late in the Civil War. The 1863 Remington carbine was designed by Joseph Rider in 1863 (a patent was awarded on December 23, 1863); it was ordered into production by the U.S. War Department in January 1865. The Remington carbine was a split-breech firearm that weighed seven pounds and measured 33.75 inches in length. It had a two-piece walnut stock and a 20-inch barrel with an iron-blade front site and folding single-leaf rear sight graduated out to 500 yards, although the weapon was rarely employed at ranges beyond 200 yards. As a rifle, it was more accurate than smoothbore carbines and could be employed effectively against targets out to 300 yards. Although it could not be fired as rapidly as the repeating Spencer carbine, it enjoyed a higher rate of fire than its muzzle-loading counterparts and was easier to maintain and more robust than repeating carbines. It was also less costly to produce than the Spencer.

Because Remington's factories were operating during the war at maximum capacity, the company leased the manufacturing rights to the rifle to the Savage Revolving Arms Company of Middletown, Connecticut. The latter firm produced two models, in both .46 and .50 caliber. The first of the 15,000 Remington carbines to be produced (2,500 during the war) was delivered to the U.S. Army in March 1865. Production continued until May 24, 1866. The Remington was issued too late in the war to see much combat, but its light weight, simple construction, accuracy, and comparatively high rate of fire made it very popular with the troops.

CARL OTIS SCHUSTER

See also

Rifles; Spencer Repeating Rifle and Carbine

Further Reading

Davis, John C. *U.S. Army Rifle and Carbine Adoption between 1865 and 1900.* Unpublished MA thesis, Northern Illinois University, 1995.
Marcot, Roy. *The History of Remington Firearms.* Guilford, CT: Colin Gower Enterprises, 2005.

Reno, Jesse Lee
Birth Date: June 20, 1823
Death Date: September 14, 1862

Union officer. Jesse Lee Reno (originally Renault) was born in Wheeling, Virginia (West Virginia), on June 20, 1823. At age nine he moved to Venango City, Pennsylvania, with his family. He graduated from the U.S. Military Academy, West Point, in 1846 and was commissioned a second lieutenant of ordnance. In early 1847, he was dispatched to Major General Winfield Scott's army in Mexico and served throughout the Mexico City Campaign (March–September) as an artillery officer, commanding the experimental Howitzer and Rocket Company that employed so-called mountain pack howitzers and Hale rockets. Distinguished service in the Battles of Cerro Gordo and Chapultepec brought Reno brevet promotions to first lieutenant and captain.

After the war, Reno served as an instructor of mathematics at West Point during 1849 and then became assistant to the Ordnance Board at the Washington Arsenal. He also served as commanding officer of arsenals at Mount Vernon, Alabama, and Fort Leavenworth, Kansas, winning promotion to first lieutenant in 1853 and to captain in 1860. During Brevet Brigadier General Albert Sidney Johnston's campaign in Utah (1857–1858), Reno served as chief ordnance officer.

During the Civil War, in November 1861 Reno was promoted to brigadier general of volunteers. He participated in Brigadier General Ambrose Burnside's North Carolina expedition in the winter of 1861–1862 before taking command of a division in the Department of North Carolina. Promoted to major general in July 1862, Reno went north to Virginia, where he commanded a division, and temporarily IX Corps, during the Second Bull Run Campaign. During the September 1862 Maryland Campaign, Reno again led IX Corps. On September 14, 1862, near South Mountain, Reno was exhorting his men onward as they made a difficult ascent up the slope on the Union left flank to beat back the Confederates, who had seized control of Fox's Gap, when he was killed by Confederate rifle fire. Reno, Nevada, is named for him.

PAUL G. PIERPAOLI JR.

See also

Bull Run, Second Battle of; Burnside, Ambrose Everett; Jackson, Thomas Jonathan; North Carolina, Union Department of; South Mountain, Battle of

Further Reading

Eicher, John H., and David J. Eicher. *Civil War High Commands*. Stanford, CA: Stanford University Press, 2001.

Warner, Ezra J. *Generals in Blue: Lives of the Union Commanders*. Baton Rouge: Louisiana State University Press, 2006.

Republican Party

American political organization. The origins of the Republican Party, which was founded in 1854, can be traced principally to the sectional conflict stemming from the Mexican-American War (1846–1848) and the institution of slavery. The territorial acquisitions by the United States as a result of the war served to reignite debate over the expansion of slavery, undermining the precarious political balance established by the Missouri Compromise of 1820 and ultimately serving to invigorate and broaden the appeal of antislavery forces.

Debate over the status of slavery in lands acquired from Mexico began long before the 1848 Treaty of Guadalupe Hidalgo. First introduced in 1846, the Wilmot Proviso, named after Democratic congressman Davis Wilmot of Pennsylvania, had been introduced in Congress as a rider to an appropriations bill that funded expenses related to postwar treaty negotiations with Mexico. The proviso called for exclusion of slavery from any territories added to the United States as a result of treaty negotiations. The Wilmot Proviso failed to receive congressional approval, however, and the status of new territories remained in question.

The failure of the Wilmot Proviso contributed immediately to the formation of the Free Soil Party, a coalition of antislavery Democrats and the abolitionist Liberty Party.

The platform of the Free Soil Party called for the complete exclusion of slavery from all western territories, although it did not call for abolition where the institution already existed.

The Compromise of 1850 tacitly sanctioned the concept of popular sovereignty in creating the New Mexico and Utah Territories. The compromise also included tougher federal fugitive slave laws and was perceived by the antislavery camp as having a pro-Southern bias, but on the whole it appeared to defuse temporarily sectional conflict.

In 1854 President Franklin Pierce signed the Kansas-Nebraska Act, essentially abolishing the old Missouri Compromise and therefore opening most of the West to slavery on the basis of popular sovereignty. The act damaged the Democrats and all but destroyed the Whigs. In response, antislavery forces formed the Republican Party, combining the Free Soil Party with a majority of the northern Whigs.

During the antebellum period, the Republican Party was almost entirely sectional and had virtually no organization in slave states, with the limited exceptions of the border states. Nonetheless, the party successfully embraced nearly all antislavery factions, including at least the tacit support of the most ardent abolitionists. The party's platform was highly pragmatic, linking opposition to the extension of slavery with Northern economic interests. In the election of 1856, the Republicans emerged as the largest party in the North, and in 1860 the Republican Abraham Lincoln won the presidency, albeit entirely on the basis of electoral votes in the Northern states.

Most Southerners viewed the Republicans as hostile to their interests, believing—wrongly—that they sought immediate emancipation and an irrevocable end to slavery. In fact, the Republican platform in 1860 did not contain such demands. The Republicans did, however, call for internal improvements at the national level, high tariffs, and land grants, which Southerners generally opposed. As the Civil War went on, the abolitionists within the Republican Party gained prominence as Lincoln's popularity ebbed. Radical Republicans soon dominated Congress, often challenging the moderate Lincoln. In 1864 the Republican Party temporarily renamed itself the Union Party and ran a War Democrat—Andrew Johnson—along with Lincoln on the 1864 presidential ticket. After Major General William T. Sherman's triumph at Atlanta in September 1864 and a string of victories in the Shenandoah Valley by Major General Philip Sheridan, which turned the tide of the war decidedly for the North, the Lincoln-Johnson ticket easily triumphed in the November election. By now, the Republicans—including

Lincoln—had revised the war goal from one that focused exclusively on preservation of the Union to one that included complete and immediate emancipation.

Radical Republicans held sway during Reconstruction as well. They bitterly opposed the lenient terms favored by Lincoln and Johnson, demanding a punitive approach toward the former Confederate states that engendered much resentment. Heavy-handed Radical Republican Reconstruction mandated the military occupation of the South and the disenfranchisement of most white Southerners. Republican demands included acceptance of the Thirteenth, Fourteenth, and Fifteenth Amendments to the U.S. Constitution. Although former general Ulysses S. Grant served two terms in the White House as a Republican, his administration was plagued by corruption, although Grant remained quite popular. By 1876, many Republicans and most white Americans had lost enthusiasm for Reconstruction.

In the disputed 1876 presidential election, Republican Rutherford B. Hayes trailed Democrat Samuel Tilden by some 250,000 votes but split the contested electoral vote. The Compromise of 1877 that settled the question demonstrated that Republican leaders, by agreeing to abandon Reconstruction, were interested more in retaining power than in remaining devoted to their earlier principles and the millions of freed people who depended on them.

Since the end of Reconstruction, the Republican Party has remained one of the two principal political parties in the United States, along with the Democratic Party. By the early 20th century, however, the Republicans had largely abandoned their earlier concepts of an expansive federal government and had become adherents of a smaller, less activist government and laissez-faire economic policies, for which they are still known today. By the 1930s, the party also saw many of its long-devoted African American followers leave to join Democrat Franklin Roosevelt's New Deal, and the Republicans became known more for their activism on behalf of business rather than individuals or laborers.

DANIEL SKIDMORE-HESS, PAUL G. PIERPAOLI JR., AND DAVID COFFEY

See also

Abolitionism and the Civil War; Democratic Party; Free Soil Party; Johnson, Andrew; Kansas-Nebraska Act; Lincoln, Abraham; Missouri Compromise; National Union Party; Pierce, Franklin; Popular Sovereignty; Reconstruction; Slavery; War Democrats; Wilmot Proviso

Further Reading

Foner, Eric. *Free Soil, Free Labor, and Free Men: The Ideology of the Republican Party before the Civil War*. New York: Oxford University Press, 1970.

Sewell, Richard H. *Ballots for Freedom: Anti-Slavery Politics in the United States, 1837–1860*. New York: Oxford University Press, 1976.

Resaca, Battle of
Start Date: May 13, 1864
End Date: May 15, 1864

Engagement during the Atlanta Campaign (May 5–September 2, 1864). At the start of the campaign, Confederate general Joseph E. Johnston's Army of Tennessee was entrenched along Rocky Face Ridge near Dalton, Georgia. Johnston did not believe that Union troops under Major General William T. Sherman would again attack this position, because such a move had been repulsed in the First Battle of Dalton (February 22–27, 1864). Instead, Johnston assumed that Sherman would march southwest toward Rome, Georgia, through one of the gaps in the mountains of northern Georgia. Johnston believed that Mill Gap would be the most likely avenue for a Union advance, and he reinforced his line there.

Sherman, however, planned a diversionary assault on Rocky Face Ridge while moving a portion of his army closer to Atlanta. Sherman chose Major General James McPherson to lead the Army of the Tennessee through Snake Creek Gap, due south of Dalton, planning to cross the Oostanaula River near Resaca. Sherman hoped that this maneuver would sever Johnston's communication and supply lines from Atlanta and trap Johnston's force between two wings of his army group. Johnston, who kept much of the Army of Tennessee at Dalton, was caught off guard by Sherman's move. The presence of McPherson's force in Snake Creek Gap rendered the Dalton line untenable, and on the night of May 12 Johnston ordered a retreat to Resaca. Fortunately, McPherson proved timid, which allowed the Confederates time to strengthen the new Resaca position.

Only small contingents of Confederate lieutenant general Leonidas Polk's corps, which had recently arrived from Mississippi, were in position to stop the Union advance. On May 13, 1864, at Resaca, Polk's troops tried to prepare breastworks under Union artillery fire while Union skirmishers probed for weaknesses in their line. However, McPherson did not order a full assault on Polk's smaller force, a failure that Sherman had cause to regret. This gave Johnston time to order the corps under Lieutenant Generals John Bell Hood and William J. Hardee into the fray.

Heavy fighting began on the morning of May 14 and lasted until the following afternoon. Johnston's delay in recognizing the threat at Resaca did not allow the Confederate army the opportunity to properly defend that position. The Union army, using pontoons, crossed the Oostanaula. With Sherman's men threatening to sever the Confederates' rail link with Atlanta and possibly surround the Army of Tennessee, on May 15 Johnston ordered his army to retreat southward. During the battle, the Union army incurred some 5,000 casualties to only 2,800 for the Confederates.

Johnston's retreat from Resaca allowed the Federals to move one step closer to achieving their objective—the capture of Atlanta. Johnston fell back to Cassville where he planned to make a stand, abandoning more than 40 miles of northern Georgia in little more than a week as a result of the Battle of Resaca.

JASON LUTZ AND JIM PIECUCH

See also
Atlanta Campaign; Dalton, First Battle of; Hardee, William Joseph; Hood, John Bell; Johnston, Joseph Eggleston; McPherson, James Birdseye; Polk, Leonidas; Sherman, William Tecumseh

Further Reading
Bonds, Russell S. *War Like the Thunderbolt: The Battle and Burning of Atlanta.* Yardley, PA: Westholme, 2009.
Fowler, John D. *Mountaineers in Gray: The Nineteenth Tennessee Volunteer Infantry Regiment, C.S.A.* Knoxville: University of Tennessee Press, 2004.

Revolvers

Repeating firearms with revolving cylinders that have multiple chambers and at least one barrel. Alexander Forsyth's patent of mercury fulminates as priming for firearms in 1807 was a great boon in the development of handguns as well as muskets. Handguns proliferated in the 19th century.

The development of the modern revolver is credited to Samuel Colt of Hartford, Connecticut. In 1836 he formed the Patent Arms Manufacturing Company in Paterson, New Jersey. Its first product was a small five-shot .28-caliber revolver, but its most famous early design was the 1838 Colt Holster Model Paterson Revolver No. 5. Better known as the Texas Paterson, it was .36-caliber, had five cylinders, and came in 4- to 12-inch barrel lengths. This was the first revolving cylinder handgun in general use. Each chamber was separately loaded from the muzzle end and had its own nipple for the copper percussion cap. The drum chamber moved each time the hammer was cocked. Colt revolvers were adopted by both the army and the navy and saw wide service in both the Mexican-American War and the American Civil War as well as in fighting with the American Indians in the West.

At the same time, breech-loading revolvers appeared. Screw-off barrels had appeared early in the development of firearms, but in 1812 Swiss national Samuel J. Pauly, working in Paris, developed a handgun in which the barrel swiveled downward to allow it to be loaded. It utilized a self-contained cartridge of Pauly's invention, surely one of the most important developments in the history of small arms. Several methods were used to fire it.

The development of metal cartridges led to a change from muzzle-loading to breech-loading firearms. Not only were muzzle-loading rifles turned into breechloaders, but Colt revolvers were similarly transformed. Thus, in the 1870s the Colt Model 1861 navy revolver was converted to a breechloader, with the cylinder removed for reloading.

The first breech-loading revolver designed specifically for metal cartridges was the Smith and Wesson Model No. 1. Manufactured from 1857 to 1860, it had a rifled barrel and seven chambers and was hinged at the top. It utilized 22-caliber rimfire ammunition. Rifled revolvers were generally effective to a range of 50–75 yards.

The Union and the Confederacy utilized a great many types of handguns during the Civil War with, as might be expected, Southerners employing a great variety and more older types, including flintlocks. At the beginning of the war, there were at least 60 firms manufacturing handguns in the United States, most of them located in New England. During the war, the U.S. government ordered a total of 373,077 handguns.

The vast majority of Civil War soldiers did not carry handguns. The basic infantry weapon was the .58-caliber Springfield rifled musket; revolvers were not issued to infantrymen. Some soldiers who could afford handguns did purchase them privately, however. Officers and cavalrymen were routinely issued revolvers, and some artillerymen also received them.

Of principal types of revolvers employed just before and during the Civil War, Colt revolvers predominated, thanks to Colt's prewar patent on mechanically rotated cylinders. The most popular percussion handgun of its day was the Colt 1861 navy model, produced in both .36-caliber and .44-caliber models. The government purchased 17,000 of the 38,000 produced, as well as 107,000 Colt 1860 army .44-caliber revolvers. Their higher cost and the death of Colt in 1862 brought an end to government orders in 1863, however.

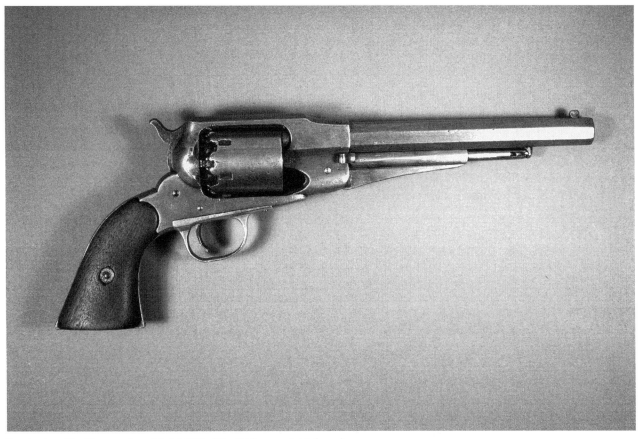

Remington .44 caliber revolver, Model 1863. (The Bridgeman Art Library)

With the expiration of the Colt patent in 1857, the firm of E. Remington and Sons took quick advantage. It produced a number of high-quality low-cost revolvers during the war, especially the .36-caliber Navy Model 1861 and the .44-caliber Army Model 1863. The government actually purchased 125,314 of the army model Remington revolvers, more than the number it bought from Colt, along with 4,901 Remington navy revolvers. The biggest advantage of the Remington was its speed of reloading. If an individual had an extra loaded cylinder, he had only to drop the loading lever, slide out the cylinder pin, replace the cylinder, slide back the pin, and shut the loading lever.

Inventor Ebenezer Townsend Starr's manufacturing firm in New York, while primarily known for its carbine, also produced an excellent .44-caliber revolver for the U.S. Army. During the war, the government purchased 47,454 Star revolvers of all types for the Union Army, making it the third most-popular handgun of the war.

Horace Smith and Daniel B. Wesson formed a partnership in 1852, known as the Smith and Wesson Company. In 1856 they developed a .22-caliber revolver employing a rim-fire cartridge. This Model 1 was immediately in demand because it utilized the easily loaded rim fire cartridge. Its small

caliber made it less effective on the battlefield, however, although it may have seen service as a boot handgun. The Model 2 Smith and Wesson .32-caliber revolver employed rim-fire ammunition. Although it was not acquired by the U.S. government during the war, many soldiers purchased the Model 2 on their own, and it saw wide service in the war and afterward on the western frontier.

The only Confederate firm of note making revolvers during the war was Griswold & Gunnison of Georgia. That firm produced for the Confederate government almost exact replicas of the Colt .36 navy revolver. Certainly the most formidable handgun of the war was that designed by New Orleans physician Jean A. F. LeMat in 1856. It had two superimposed barrels and two hammers. The top barrel fired nine .44-caliber rounds from a cylinder, while the lower .63-caliber barrel fired a load of buckshot.

With the start of the war and only limited production possible in New Orleans, LeMat returned to France to have the revolver mass-produced there for the Confederacy. When the French-produced revolvers turned out to be of poor quality, LeMat shifted production to Belgium and England. Some 3,000 LeMat revolvers were produced for the South. LeMats were manufactured in both .36-caliber and

.44-caliber models. A few so-called Baby LeMats of .32-caliber (.41-caliber shotgun barrel) may have reached the South.

SPENCER C. TUCKER

See also

Arms Manufacturing; Colt, Samuel; Rifles

Further Reading

Blair, Claude, ed. *Pollard's History of Firearms.* New York: Macmillan, 1983.

Kinard, Jeff. *Pistols: An Illustrated History of Their Impact.* Santa Barbara, CA: ABC-CLIO, 2003.

Myatt, F. *Illustrated Encyclopedia of Pistols and Revolvers.* London: Salamander Books, 1980.

Taylorson, A. *The Revolver.* 3 vols. London: Arms and Armour, 1966–1970.

Reynolds, Alexander Welch
Birth Date: April 1816
Death Date: May 26, 1876

Confederate officer. Born in Clarke County, Virginia, in April 1816, Alexander Welch Reynolds graduated from the U.S. Military Academy, West Point, in 1838 and was commissioned a second lieutenant in the infantry. After initial service in the Second Seminole War (1835–1842), Reynolds eventually became an assistant quartermaster and was assigned to duty in New Mexico. By then an army captain, he used his position to become an influential business leader in the territory. Indeed, Reynolds developed an unsavory reputation because he apparently lived far beyond his modest military salary. Financial irregularities caused him significant legal difficulties, and he was dismissed from army service in 1855 for failing to explain irregularities in his accounts. However, he was restored to service in March 1858 without loss of rank or seniority. He remained with the army until 1861.

Deciding to align himself with the Confederacy, Reynolds resigned his U.S. commission and was appointed a Confederate captain in March 1861. That July he was commissioned a colonel and given command of the 50th Virginia Infantry Regiment. He served with Brigadier General John B. Floyd in various unsuccessful operations in western Virginia before being sent to Tennessee. Reynolds was apparently not with his regiment at the Battle of Fort Donelson (February 13–16, 1862) and by April 1862 had command of a brigade in eastern Tennessee. He participated in the Kentucky Campaign (August 14–October 26, 1862) and performed well in the Second Vicksburg Campaign (April 1–July 4, 1863). Surrendered with the garrison there, he was later exchanged.

Reynolds was advanced to brigadier general on September 14, 1863, and saw much action in the Battle of Chattanooga (November 23–25, 1863). He commanded a brigade during the Atlanta Campaign (May 5–September 2, 1864) in Major General Carter L. Stevenson's division. Reynolds sustained a serious wound during the Battle of New Hope Church (May 25–27, 1864) and after his recovery commanded a district in northern Georgia. He was relieved of his command in January 1865.

Following the war, Reynolds accepted an offer, along with other Civil War veterans, to serve as a military adviser to the khedive of Egypt. On his arrival in Egypt in 1869, Reynolds was commissioned a colonel in the Egyptian Army and later fought in the Abyssinian War. Reynolds remained in Egypt for the rest of his life and died in Alexandria on May 26, 1876.

SEAN M. HEUVEL

See also

Chattanooga Campaign; Floyd, John Buchanan; New Hope Church, Battle of; Stevenson, Carter Littlepage; Vicksburg Campaign, Second

Further Reading

Jordan, Weymouth, Jr., John D. Chapla, and Shan C. Sutton. "'Notorious as the Noonday Sun': Captain Alexander Welch Reynolds and the New Mexico Territory, 1849–1859." *New Mexico Historical Review* 75 (October 2000): 457–508.

Warner, Ezra J. *Generals in Gray: Lives of the Confederate Commanders.* Baton Rouge: Louisiana State University Press, 2006.

Reynolds, Arabella Loomis Macomber
Birth Date: October 20, 1840
Death Date: July 29, 1937

Union nurse. Arabella "Belle" Loomis Macomber was born in Shelbourne Falls, Massachusetts, on October 20, 1840, to a well-connected local family. Her hometown was a stop along the Underground Railroad, and she grew up hearing many stories of the horrors of slavery and miraculous escapes from it. These experiences led her to identify strongly with abolitionism and the Union.

In April 1860 Macomber married William S. Reynolds, a druggist, and they moved to Peoria, Illinois. In 1861 William Reynolds enlisted in the 17th Illinois Infantry and was moved to the front. In August 1861 Arabella joined her husband at Bird's Point, Missouri, and followed his regiment to various stations, experiencing the same food, general living conditions, and marches as did the soldiers.

Arabella Reynolds tended wounded soldiers during the Battle of Fredericktown (October 21, 1861) in Missouri, regardless of the uniform the soldiers wore. She nursed soldiers again following the Battle at Fort Henry (February 6, 1862). At the start of the Battle of Shiloh (April 6–7, 1862), she began to dress soldiers' wounds. When the wounded were ordered to be moved to ships in the Tennessee River, where they could be better attended, she went along. On board the Union steamer *Emerald,* Reynolds worked continuously for 36 hours attending to the needs of 350 wounded men on board. Exhausted and ill, she returned to Illinois on the steamer *Blackhawk.* Her heroism at Shiloh was well known, and several prominent Illinoisans suggested that she deserved to be honored. Upon her return in May 1862, Governor Richard Yates bestowed upon her the rank of major for her service and bravery during the Battle of Shiloh. Although the title was honorific, she was regarded locally as a heroine.

Not content to remain on the sidelines for long, Reynolds returned to the front to be with her husband and saw action at Vicksburg, where she attended more wounded men. In the spring of 1864, Reynolds and her husband returned to Peoria, where she remained until her death on July 29, 1937. For the remainder of her long life, Reynolds was active in the American Red Cross and maintained a public image in an era in which women were normally not allowed such activity.

REBECCA TOLLEY-STOKES

See also

Fort Henry, Battle of; Nurses; Shiloh, Battle of; Women; Women Soldiers

Further Reading

"Major Belle Reynolds." *New York Times,* March 15, 1896.

Moore, Frank. *Women of the War: Their Heroism and Self-sacrifice: True Stories of Brave Women in the Civil War.* Alexander, NC: Blue Gray Books, 1997.

Tsui, Bonnie. *She Went to the Field: Women Soldiers of the Civil War.* Guildford, CT: TwoDot, 2003.

Reynolds, Daniel Harris
Birth Date: December 14, 1832
Death Date: March 14, 1902

Lawyer, Confederate general, and Arkansas state senator. Daniel Harris Reynolds was born on December 14, 1832, in Centerburg, Ohio. He graduated from Ohio Wesleyan University and subsequently moved to Somerville, Tennessee, where he studied law before settling in Lake Village, Arkansas. There he was admitted to the bar in 1858.

In the spring of 1861 with the onset of the Civil War, Reynolds recruited a company, which was incorporated into the 1st Arkansas Mounted Rifles, with Reynolds as captain. He saw action at the Battle of Wilson's Creek (August 10, 1861), during various skirmishes in Arkansas and Missouri, and during the Battle of Pea Ridge (March 7–8, 1862). A few weeks later his regiment was transferred east of the Mississippi.

Reynolds was promoted to major on April 14, 1862, and to lieutenant colonel on May 1. Throughout the balance of 1862, Reynolds's regiment remained in Kentucky and eastern Tennessee. Sent to Mississippi as part of the relief force commanded by General Joseph Johnston, Reynolds fought during the Siege of Jackson (July 10–16, 1863). He distinguished himself at the Battle of Chickamauga (September 19–20, 1863) and was advanced to colonel on November 17, to date from September 20.

On March 5, 1864, upon the strong recommendation of his superiors, Reynolds was appointed brigadier general and given charge of a brigade in the Army of Tennessee. He saw extensive action during the Atlanta Campaign (May 5–September 2, 1864) and the Franklin and Nashville Campaign (November 29–December 27, 1863) as well as in Sherman's March through the Carolinas (January–April 1865). Reynolds was severely wounded and lost a leg to amputation during the Battle of Bentonville (March 19–21, 1865), ending his military career.

After the war, Reynolds resumed his law practice in Arkansas and served one term in the Arkansas Senate. He died on March 14, 1902, in Lake Village, Arkansas.

PAUL G. PIERPAOLI JR.

See also

Atlanta Campaign; Bentonville, Battle of; Chickamauga, Battle of; Franklin and Nashville Campaign; Pea Ridge, Battle of; Sherman's March through the Carolinas; Wilson's Creek, Battle of

Further Reading

Eicher, John H., and David J. Eicher. *Civil War High Commands.* Stanford, CA: Stanford University Press, 2001.

Warner, Ezra J. *Generals in Blue: Lives of the Union Commanders.* Baton Rouge: Louisiana State University Press, 2006.

Reynolds, John Fulton
Birth Date: September 20, 1820
Death Date: July 1, 1863

Union officer. Born on September 20, 1820, in Lancaster, Pennsylvania, John Fulton Reynolds graduated from the U.S. Military Academy, West Point, in 1841. Reynolds first served with the artillery and spent more than five years in garrison assignments, earning promotion to first lieutenant in June 1846.

In the Mexican-American War (1846–1848), Reynolds was brevetted captain for his role in the Battle of Monterrey. During the Battle of Buena Vista in February 1847, his guns helped repulse a Mexican effort to flank the American position, for which he was brevetted major.

Following the war, Reynolds was stationed in the American West, where he fought Native Americans in Oregon's Rogue River region in 1856 and served in the Mormon Expedition (1857–1858), winning promotion to captain in 1855. Reynolds returned to West Point in September 1860 as commandant of cadets, a post he held when the Civil War began in 1861.

With the onset of the Civil War, Reynolds was promoted to lieutenant colonel of the new 14th Infantry. Appointed brigadier general of volunteers in August 1861, he helped oversee the defense of Washington, D.C., and then briefly served as military governor of Fredericksburg, Virginia. His first brigade command came with the Pennsylvania Reserves in the Army of the Potomac. While fighting in the Seven Days' Campaign (June 25–July 1, 1862), Reynolds was taken prisoner during the Battle of Gaines' Mill (June 27). He was released in a prisoner exchange on August 13. Reynolds then commanded a division at the Second Battle of Bull Run (August 29–30, 1862). During the Antietam Campaign (September 4–20, 1862), he commanded the Pennsylvania Militia, which was fully mobilized to repel Confederate general Robert E. Lee's invasion of Maryland.

On November 29, 1862, Reynolds received promotion to major general of volunteers and went on to command the Army of the Potomac's I Corps at the First Battle of Fredericksburg (December 13, 1862) and at the Battle of Chancellorsville (May 1–4, 1863). After that engagement, President Abraham Lincoln offered Reynolds command of the army, but Reynolds demurred, claiming that the president had refused to allow him to make unfettered command decisions.

Reynolds was to become one of the mythic heroes of the Battle of Gettysburg (July 1–3, 1863), where he was killed just west of the town on July 1 while leading his forces into a position in support of Brigadier General John Buford's cavalry during the opening stages of the battle. Reynolds's actions that day greatly assisted Union forces in securing the strong defensive positions that became known as the Fishhook.

NICHOLAS A. KREHBIEL

See also

Antietam Campaign; Bull Run, Second Battle of; Chancellorsville, Battle of; Fredericksburg, First Battle of; Gaines' Mill, Battle

Union major general John Fulton Reynolds became one of the heroes of the Battle of Gettysburg (July 1–3, 1863). He was killed on the first day of the battle, leading his forces in support of Brigadier General John Buford's cavalry just west of the town. His actions that day helped Union forces secure the strong defensive positions that made possible the subsequent Union victory. (National Archives)

of; Gettysburg, Battle of; Lincoln, Abraham; Seven Days' Campaign

Further Reading

Nichols, Edward J. *Toward Gettysburg: A Biography of General John F. Reynolds.* University Park: Pennsylvania State University Press, 1958.
Warner, Ezra J. *Generals in Blue: Lives of the Union Commanders.* Baton Rouge: Louisiana State University Press, 2006.

Reynolds, Joseph Jones
Birth Date: January 4, 1822
Death Date: February 25, 1899

Union officer. Born in Flemingsburg, Kentucky, on January 4, 1822, Joseph Jones Reynolds moved with his family to

Lafayette, Indiana, at age 15. He attended Wabash College at Crawfordsville for 1 year but was appointed to the U.S. Military Academy, West Point, in 1839 and graduated in 1843. Commissioned in the artillery, Reynolds served in garrison duty and then in the Army of Occupation in Texas just prior to the Mexican-American War (1846–1848), when he was assigned as an instructor at West Point, where he taught for 8 years. Reynolds was then assigned to duty in the American West until, still a second lieutenant in the 3rd Artillery, he resigned his commission in 1857. During the course of the next 4 years, Reynolds taught engineering at Washington University in St. Louis and became a wholesale grocer in Lafayette.

On the beginning of the Civil War, Reynolds was commissioned colonel of the 10th Indiana Militia on April 23, 1861, and brigadier general of the Indiana Militia on May 10. He was appointed brigadier general of U.S. Volunteers on June 14, with date of rank from May 17.

Assigned to the Department of the Ohio in charge of a brigade, Reynolds commanded at the Battle of Cheat Mountain (September 11–15, 1861). Wounded later that autumn, he resigned his commission on January 23, 1862, in order to settle the estate of his brother, with whom he was in partnership. While out of the service, Reynolds helped organize Indiana troops. Again appointed brigadier general on September 17, he was advanced to major general of volunteers on November 29.

Assigned to the Army of the Cumberland, Reynolds commanded the 4th Division of XIV Corps in the Battle of Chickamauga (September 19–20, 1863), and on October 10 during the Chattanooga Campaign (October–November 1863), he became the Army of the Cumberland's chief of staff under Major General George H. Thomas, serving until December 3. In January 1864 Reynolds took command of the defenses of New Orleans, and on July 7 he assumed command of XIX Corps and organized the campaign against Mobile. From November 1864 until April 1866, he commanded VII Corps and the Department of Arkansas.

Reynolds remained in the army after the war, becoming colonel of the 26th Infantry upon reorganization of the army in July 1866. On March 2, 1867, he was brevetted brigadier general for his role at Chickamauga and major general for the Battle of Missionary Ridge (November 25, 1863). Assigned to command the 25th Infantry in January 1870, Reynolds assumed command of the 3rd Cavalry that December, serving in the Southwest.

During the Great Sioux War of 1876–1877, Reynolds, commanding the advance forces under Brigadier General George Crook, attacked and captured Northern Cheyenne chief Lone Wolf's village on March 17, 1876. In the Battle of the Powder River, Reynolds prematurely ordered a withdrawal, leaving behind several dead and one wounded soldier, who was subsequently captured by the Indians and tortured to death. Reynolds's command decisions and his role in the battle brought his court-martial and resignation from the service on June 25, 1877. Reynolds then took up residence in Washington, D.C., where he died on February 25, 1899.

Spencer C. Tucker

See also
Cheat Mountain, Battle of; Chickamauga, Battle of; Missionary Ridge, Battle of; Mobile, Alabama, Siege of; Thomas, George Henry

Further Reading
Eicher, John H., and David J. Eicher. *Civil War High Commands.* Stanford, CA: Stanford University Press, 2001.
Warner, Ezra J. *Generals in Blue: Lives of the Union Commanders.* Baton Rouge: Louisiana State University Press, 2006.

Reynolds, Thomas Caute
Birth Date: October 11, 1821
Death Date: March 30, 1887

Confederate governor of Missouri. Thomas Caute Reynolds was born in Charleston, South Carolina, on October 11, 1821. He graduated from the University of Virginia in 1838 with a degree in law and then studied at Heidelberg University in Germany. In 1843 he settled in Virginia, and three years later he was editor of the *Petersburg Republican.* From 1846 to 1849, Reynolds was the secretary of the American Legation in Madrid, Spain. In 1849 he returned to the United States and settled in Missouri, where he practiced law and became active politically as a proslavery Democrat. On August 26, 1856, he fought a duel with B. Gratz Brown, the Republican editor of the *Missouri Democrat,* and wounded Brown in the leg. Reynolds was not injured.

In 1860 Reynolds was elected lieutenant governor of Missouri, serving with Governor Claiborne Jackson and taking office in early 1861. Reynolds and Jackson, well aware of strong free-soil sentiment in the state, had run as Unionist Democrats but privately supported the Southern Rights wing of the party. Reynolds was in fact an ardent champion of secession and helped organize secessionist militia to counter the Unionist Home Guard. He was disappointed when a state convention decided that Missouri would remain in the Union but would not actively support either side in the war. Jackson rejected President Abraham Lincoln's call for troops, and the Missouri General Assembly established the Missouri State Guard under Missouri Militia major general Sterling Price to resist attempts to force the state to comply.

After the Camp Jackson Affair of May 10, 1861, when U.S. Army captain Nathaniel Lyon arrested members of the Missouri Volunteer Militia, Price, Jackson, and Reynolds met and agreed that Reynolds should travel to Richmond, Virginia, to secure a pledge of support for the Missouri secessionists. On June 21, Reynolds met with President Jefferson Davis, who authorized assistance but declined to send troops until Missouri had actually seceded. In July, Lyon occupied the state capital of Jefferson City, and the state constitutional convention then reconvened without the pro-Southern representatives and declared the offices of Missouri governor and lieutenant governor to be vacant.

Reynolds and Jackson fled to southwestern Missouri. They convened the pro-Confederate government at Neosho, which voted to secede but was soon forced to relocate to Marshall, Texas. Reynolds, meanwhile, returned to Richmond. He was commissioned a colonel in the Confederate Army in September 1861 and served as a volunteer aide to General Albert S. Johnston but resigned the next month. In April 1862, frustrated by events, Reynolds returned to his family estate in Winnsborough, South Carolina, until December 1862, when he learned of the death of Governor Jackson.

Reynolds then assumed the governorship and returned to Richmond to work with the Missouri Confederate representatives. During the remainder of the war, he endeavored to hold the Missouri Confederate government-in-exile together and to cooperate with General Edmund Kirby Smith and the regional Confederate governors. In the hopes that he might be inaugurated in Jefferson City, Reynolds accompanied Price on his disastrous raid into Missouri (September 19–October 28, 1864), only to see the Confederate forces driven back into Arkansas.

At the end of the war Reynolds fled to Mexico City, where he served as a railroad commissioner and an unofficial adviser to Emperor Maximilian. Reynolds also began work on his memoirs, detailing his feud with Price. Returning to St. Louis in 1869, Reynolds practiced law, was elected to the state legislature in 1874, and served as a trade commissioner to South America. Reynolds, who was subject to fits of depression, committed suicide on March 30, 1887, by leaping down an elevator shaft at the customshouse in St. Louis.

SPENCER C. TUCKER

See also

Camp Jackson Affair; Jackson, Claiborne Fox; Johnston, Joseph Eggleston; Lyon, Nathaniel; Maximilian von Habsburg, Ferdinand; Missouri; Price, Sterling; Price's Missouri Raid; Smith, Edmund Kirby

Further Reading

Castel, Albert. *General Sterling Price and the Civil War in the West.* Baton Rouge: Louisiana State University Press, 1968.

Gerteis, Louis S. *Civil War St. Louis.* Lawrence: University Press of Kansas, 2001.

Reynolds, Thomas C. *General Sterling Price and the Confederacy.* Edited by Robert G. Schultz. St. Louis: Missouri History Museum, 2009.

Rhett, Robert Barnwell, Sr.
Birth Date: December 21, 1800
Death Date: September 14, 1876

South Carolina politician and ardent secessionist. Robert Barnwell Rhett Sr. was born on December 21, 1800, in Beaufort, South Carolina. As a young Charleston lawyer, then going by his birth name Robert Barnwell Smith, he won election to the South Carolina state legislature in 1826, 1828, and 1830. He served as South Carolina state attorney general in 1832. Smith changed his surname to "Rhett" in 1837 to emphasize his deep aristocratic Southern roots.

Rhett was influential in the Nullification Crisis of 1832, in which many South Carolinians, including Vice President John C. Calhoun, fought to keep a national tariff from harming their state's economy. Using the *Charleston Mercury,* Rhett influenced public opinion to favor nullification. This crisis continued until President Andrew Jackson promised military action if South Carolina did not enforce the national law.

In 1837 Rhett took a seat in the U.S. House of Representatives, where he served until 1849. He remained a loyal secessionist, or Fire-Eater, and continued calling for South Carolina to defend the rights of the South. He served in the U.S. Senate from 1850 to 1852. There Rhett made a push for a new confederacy but was disgusted by South Carolina's weakness and his slipping political influence. In 1852 he gave up his Senate seat to spearhead a private campaign for secession.

In 1858 Rhett and other Fire-Eaters met in Montgomery, Alabama, to discuss strategies for attaining secession. Disillusioned with that effort, he concluded that the only way to achieve Southern independence was to ensure a Republican victory in the 1860 election by splitting the Democratic

South Carolina congressman Robert Rhett was a staunch advocate of states' rights. Rhett was one of the principal proponents of secession in 1860 and later a harsh critic of Confederate president Jefferson Davis. (Library of Congress)

Party into Northern and Southern factions. This, of course, is exactly what happened. Considered by many to be the "father of secession," Rhett was among the first to sign a secession petition, even before South Carolina seceded from the Union in December 1860. At the 1861 Montgomery Convention, while the majority favored Jefferson Davis for president of the Confederacy, Rhett, who harbored presidential aspirations, demurred.

Rhett came to be a bitter critic of the Davis administration and, as the *Mercury* editor, published details of Confederate military strategy and troop positions to undermine the war effort. In February 1865 with Union forces having entered South Carolina, the newspaper ceased publication, and Rhett withdrew from the public spotlight. He moved to Louisiana and died in St. James Parish on September 14, 1876.

KERRY M. COHEN

See also

Calhoun, John Caldwell; *Charleston Mercury;* Davis, Jefferson Finis; Fire-Eaters; Montgomery Convention; Secession; South Carolina

Further Reading

Davis, William C. *Rhett: The Turbulent Life and Times of a Fire-Eater.* Columbia: University of South Carolina Press, 2001.

Walther, Eric H. *The Fire Eaters.* Baton Rouge: Louisiana State University Press, 1992.

Rhode Island

New England state encompassing 1,212 square miles that had an 1860 population of 174,620. Rhode Island is bordered by the Atlantic Ocean to the south, Massachusetts to the north and east, and Connecticut to the west. Abraham Lincoln carried the state easily in the 1860 presidential election, but prior to the war, political sentiments in Rhode Island were mixed—in large part because its textile industry relied heavily on cotton from the South. For many years, prominent southern families, especially from South Carolina and Georgia, had come to Newport during the summer to escape the southern heat. In the years before the war, ship owners in Rhode Island had also profited from the slave trade. However, after the commencement of the war, Rhode Island became a staunch supporter of the Union war effort.

Highly industrialized, Rhode Island had one of the largest concentrations of textile mills in the Union; thus, it was able to provide much in the way of supplies and matériel. Rhode Island industry provided the Union Army with uniforms, blankets, small arms, sabers, musket parts, cannons, iron bars, and horseshoes. Additionally, the Providence Steam Engine Company provided engines for two sloops.

Because of strong Southern sympathies in Maryland and Union fears of a Confederate invasion of that state, in April 1861 the sailing frigate *Constitution* carried midshipmen of the U.S. Naval Academy, Annapolis, to Newport, Rhode Island, where the school was relocated for the duration of the war. The academy was briefly based at Fort Adams on Narragansett Bay but was subsequently moved into the town of Newport.

Rhode Island citizens responded immediately to President Abraham Lincoln's proclamation of April 15, 1861, calling for 75,000 volunteers, and on April 16, 1861, Governor William Sprague issued an order for the organization of the 1st Rhode Island Infantry. The unit was raised in only five days and soon left for Washington, D.C. The 1st Rhode Island Infantry later participated in the First Battle of Bull Run (July 21, 1861). In total, the state provided 10 infantry regiments, 3 regiments and 1 battalion of cavalry,

3 heavy artillery regiments, 10 light artillery batteries, and 1 company of hospital guards. Among those who served were 1,837 African Americans and 1,878 sailors. Rhode Island raised some 5,000 more troops than the federal quota had stipulated, for a grand total of 23,236 men. Of that number, 1,321 died of all causes.

Batteries of the Rhode Island 1st Light Artillery were present on Cemetery Ridge opposing the Confederate advance during Pickett's Charge at Gettysburg on July 3, 1863. Prominent military leaders from Rhode Island included Major Generals Ambrose Burnside, Silas Casey, and Richard Arnold as well as Brigadier General Thomas W. Sherman and Fleet Captain (later Rear Admiral) William Rogers Taylor.

TIMOTHY J. DEMY

See also

Cotton; Naval Academy, U.S.; Sprague, William, IV; Textile Manufacturing

Further Reading

Field, Edward. *State of Rhode Island and Providence Plantations at the End of the Century: A History.* 3 vols. Boston: Mason, 1902.

Stensrud, Rockwell. *Newport: A Lively Experiment, 1639–1969.* Newport, RI: Redwood Library and Athenaeum, 2006.

Rice, Elliott Warren
Birth Date: November 16, 1835
Death Date: June 22, 1887

Union officer. Born in Allegheny City (now part of Pittsburgh), Pennsylvania, on November 16, 1835, Elliott Warren Rice was the younger brother of future Union general Samuel A. Rice. In 1836 the Rice family moved to Belmont County, Ohio. After attending Franklin College in New Athens, Ohio, in 1855 Elliott Rice relocated to Oskaloosa, Iowa, to study law with his brother. Graduating from the University of Albany School of Law in 1858, Rice returned to Osklaloosa, where he practiced law with his brother.

With the beginning of the Civil War, Rice joined the Union Army as a private in the 7th Iowa Infantry and was promoted to corporal and then to sergeant on July 24, 1861. He was commissioned major on August 30. During the Battle of Belmont (November 7, 1861), he assumed command of his regiment when the colonel was wounded and the lieutenant colonel was killed. Rice was also wounded. He fought in the Battle of Shiloh (April 6–7, 1862) and was promoted to colonel on April 7. Given command of the 1st

Brigade of the 2nd Division of XVI Corps in the Army of the Tennessee, he took part in the Battle of Corinth (October 3–4, 1862), after which he spent several months guarding railroads in Tennessee.

Appointed brigadier general of volunteers on June 20, 1864, Rice commanded the 1st Brigade, 2nd Division, XVI Corps, Army of the Tennessee, during the Atlanta Campaign (May 5–September 2, 1864), seeing action in almost all of its major battles. Briefly in July he had charge of the division itself. From October 1864 to August 1865, Rice commanded the 1st Brigade, 4th Division, XV Corps, Army of the Tennessee, taking part in Major General William T. Sherman's March to the Sea (November 15–December 21, 1864) and March through the Carolinas (January–April 1865). Rice's last engagement was the Battle of Bentonville (March 19–21, 1865). During the war, he was wounded seven times. He was brevetted major general on March 13, 1865, and mustered out of the service on August 24.

Postbellum, Rice settled in Washington, D.C., where he practiced law until 1885. Declining health prompted him to move to the home of a sister in Sioux City, Iowa, where he died on June 22, 1887.

SPENCER C. TUCKER

See also

Atlanta Campaign; Belmont, Battle of; Bentonville, Battle of; Corinth, Battle of; Fort Donelson, Battle of; Sherman's March through the Carolinas; Sherman's March to the Sea; Shiloh, Battle of

Further Reading

Eicher, John H., and David J. Eicher. *Civil War High Commands.* Stanford, CA: Stanford University Press, 2001.

Warner, Ezra J. *Generals in Blue: Lives of the Union Commanders.* Baton Rouge: Louisiana State University Press, 2006.

Rice, James Clay
Birth Date: December 27, 1829
Death Date: May 10, 1864

Union officer. Born in Worthington, Massachusetts, on December 27, 1829, James Clay Rice received little formal education but as a self-educated man entered Yale University. Following his graduation in 1854, he traveled to Natchez, Mississippi, where he taught school and directed the literary department of a local newspaper. While in Natchez, Rice studied law. In 1855 he went to New York, where he was admitted to the bar in 1856 and began his legal practice.

Rice enlisted in the 39th New York Infantry Regiment in May 1861 and by May 10 had been made a lieutenant. His regiment was originally stationed near Washington, D.C., before first seeing action during the First Battle of Bull Run (July 21, 1861). In August, Rice was promoted to captain. On September 13, he left the 39th New York to become lieutenant colonel of the 44th New York Infantry Regiment. Rice fought throughout the Peninsula Campaign (March–July 1862).

Rice, in temporary command of the regiment, performed valiantly at the Battle of Hanover Courthouse (May 27, 1862). Despite having his horse shot from under him, he rallied his men against repeated Confederate assaults. Rice performed equally well during the Seven Days' Campaign (June 25–July 1, 1862). At the Battle of Gaines' Mill (June 27, 1862), he essentially took over the regiment. On July 4 with promotion to colonel, Rice formally took command of the 44th New York.

Rice commanded the 44th New York Infantry and briefly the 3rd Brigade, 1st Division, V Corps, during the second day of the Second Battle of Bull Run (August 29–30, 1862). He then led his regiment at the Battle of Chancellorsville (May 1–4, 1863). During the second day of fighting at the Battle of Gettysburg (July 1–3, 1863), Rice performed heroically when command of the 3rd Brigade, 1st Division, V Corps, again devolved to him. In the dogged defense of Little Round Top, he rallied his men, held off repeated Confederate assaults, and ordered the successful seizure of Big Round Top. For these efforts, Rice was made a brigadier general of volunteers on August 17, 1863. He commanded the brigade until August 26, when he took command of the 2nd Brigade, 1st Division, I Corps. On March 25 he took command of the 2nd Brigade, 4th Division, V Corps, which he led during the Overland (Richmond) Campaign (May 4–June 12, 1864). On May 10, 1864, during the Battle of Spotsylvania Court House (May 8–21), a rifle ball shattered Rice's leg. He died that same day.

ADAM P. WILSON

See also

Bull Run, First Battle of; Bull Run, Second Battle of; Chancellorsville, Battle of; Gaines' Mill, Battle of; Gettysburg, Battle of; Hanover Court House, Battle of; Overland Campaign; Peninsula Campaign; Spotsylvania Court House, Battle of

Further Reading

Nash, Eugene Arus. *A History of the Forty-Fourth Regiment, New York Volunteer Infantry in the Civil War, 1861–1865.* Chicago: R. R. Donnelley and Sons, 1911.
Warner, Ezra J. *Generals in Blue: Lives of the Union Commanders.* Baton Rouge: Louisiana State University Press, 2006.

Rice, Samuel Allen
Birth Date: January 27, 1828
Death Date: July 6, 1864

Union officer. Born in Cattaraugus County, New York, on January 27, 1828, Samuel Allen Rice was the older brother of future Union general Elliott Warren Rice. The family moved when Samuel Rice was a boy, first to western Pennsylvania and then to Belmont County, Ohio. Rice attended Franklin College in New Athens, Ohio, and Union College in Schenectady, New York, where he graduated in 1849. Following a year of study at Union College Law School, Rice moved to Iowa, settling in Oskaloosa in 1851. There he established a highly successful legal practice and was elected county attorney in 1853 and Iowa attorney general in 1856 and 1858.

On August 10, 1861, Rice was commissioned colonel of the 33rd Iowa Infantry, although the regiment was not mustered into federal service until October 1, 1862. Rice's entire Civil War service occurred in the states of Missouri and Arkansas. Proceeding to Helena, Arkansas, Rice's regiment took part in the Yazoo Pass Expedition (February–April 1863). Rice then distinguished himself in the Battle of Helena (July 4, 1863).

Appointed brigadier general of volunteers on August 4, 1863, Rice commanded a brigade in the 3rd Division and for a time that division itself, VII Corps, in the Department of Arkansas. During the Camden Expedition (March 23–May 3, 1864), Rice suffered a head wound at Elkin's Ferry, Arkansas, on April 4, 1864. He was wounded again at Jenkins' Ferry, Arkansas, on April 30, shattering the bone in his right ankle. Transported home to Oskaloosa, Rice died there of his wounds on July 6, 1864.

SPENCER C. TUCKER

See also

Helena, Battle of; Jenkins' Ferry, Battle of; Yazoo Pass Expedition

Further Reading

Eicher, John H., and David J. Eicher. *Civil War High Commands.* Stanford, CA: Stanford University Press, 2001.
Warner, Ezra J. *Generals in Blue: Lives of the Union Commanders.* Baton Rouge: Louisiana State University Press, 2006.

Richardson, Albert Deane
Birth Date: October 6, 1833
Death Date: December 2, 1869

Journalist. Albert Deane Richardson was born in Franklin, Massachusetts, on October 6, 1833. At age 18 he planned to travel to the West, but he only made it as far as Pittsburgh.

There he taught school, worked on a newspaper, studied shorthand, and acted on the stage. In 1852 he went to Cincinnati, where he wrote for various newspapers. In 1857 he moved to Sumner, Kansas, but he spent much of his time at Leavenworth, Lawrence, and Topeka as a correspondent for the *Boston Journal*. Richardson also served as adjutant general of the Kansas Territory and secretary of the legislature.

In 1860 Richardson went to New Orleans as a secret correspondent for the *New York Daily Tribune* and undertook several assignments. During the Civil War, he became the chief correspondent for the *Tribune*. On May 3, 1863, while attempting, with fellow correspondents Junius Henri Browne of the *Tribune* and Richard T. Colburn of the *New York World*, to run past the Confederate batteries at Vicksburg in a tugboat, Richardson was captured; he spent the next 18 months in various Confederate prisons. On December 18, 1864, Richardson and Browne made their escape and a month later reached Union lines near Knoxville, Tennessee.

Richardson wrote two books based on his experiences. His first, *The Secret Service, the Field, the Dungeon, and the Escape* (1865), detailed his adventures in the Civil War. The second, *Beyond the Mississippi* (1866), described his earliest adventures in Kansas. Another book, his *Personal History of Ulysses S. Grant* (1868), was considered superior to the ordinary campaign biography.

In early 1869 Richardson became engaged to Abby Sage McFarland, who had recently been divorced from her husband, Daniel McFarland, who was mentally unstable. On November 25, 1869, McFarland shot Richardson at his desk in the *Tribune*'s New York City office. Richardson died a week later at the Astor House on December 2, 1869. On his deathbed, he married Abby McFarland.

MARTIN J. MANNING

See also
Journalism; *New York Tribune*

Further Reading
Cooper, George. *Lost Love: A True Story of Passion, Murder, and Justice in Old New York*. New York: Pantheon Books, 1994.
Richardson, Albert D. *The Secret Service, the Field, the Dungeon, and the Escape*. Freeport, NY: Books for Libraries, 1971.

Richardson, Israel Bush
Birth Date: December 26, 1815
Death Date: November 3, 1862

Union officer. Israel Bush Richardson was born on December 26, 1815, in Fairfax, Vermont, and graduated from the U.S. Military Academy, West Point, in 1841. He saw action during the Second Seminole War (1835–1842) and the Mexican-American War (1846–1848), during which he was brevetted twice for extraordinary service. Promoted to first lieutenant in 1846, he was advanced to captain in 1851. In 1855 Richardson resigned from the army and took up farming in Michigan. When the Civil War began in 1861, he recruited the 2nd Michigan Infantry Regiment and was elected its colonel.

During the First Battle of Bull Run (July 21, 1861), Richardson led a brigade and was advanced to brigadier general on August 9, 1861, to date from May. For the next seven months, he served in the Washington area with the Army of the Potomac. During the Peninsula Campaign (March–July 1862) and the Seven Days' Campaign (June 25–July 1, 1862), Richardson had charge of a division in II Corps. His reputation as an intrepid leader earned him the sobriquet "Fighting Dick." He was promoted to major general on July 5, 1862, and took command of a division in I Corps. Within several weeks, however, he had transferred back to II Corps.

Richardson led a division during the Second Battle of Bull Run (August 29–30, 1862) and the Battle of South Mountain (September 14, 1862). During the Battle of Antietam (September 17, 1862), Richardson led his division in multiple attacks against Confederate lines on the Bloody Lane. As he was supervising a Union artillery battery, he was hit by a Confederate shell fragment and fell gravely wounded. Richardson died from his wounds at Antietam on November 3, 1862.

PAUL G. PIERPAOLI JR.

See also
Antietam, Battle of; Bull Run, First Battle of; Bull Run, Second Battle of; Peninsula Campaign; Seven Days' Campaign; South Mountain, Battle of

Further Reading
Mason, Jack C. *Until Antietam: The Life and Letters of Major General Israel Bush Richardson, U.S. Army*. Carbondale: Southern Illinois Press, 2009.
Warner, Ezra J. *Generals in Gray: Lives of the Confederate Commanders*. Baton Rouge: Louisiana State University Press, 2006.

Richardson, Robert Vinkler
Birth Date: November 4, 1820
Death Date: January 6, 1870

Confederate officer. Born on November 4, 1820, in Granville County, North Carolina, and raised in Hardeman County,

Tennessee, Robert Vinkler Richardson studied law, passed the Tennessee bar, and opened a legal practice in Memphis. He also became involved in industrial development, investing much of his own money to increase Southern productive capacity.

Richardson entered Confederate service at the beginning of the Civil War under Brigadier General Gideon Pillow in the western theater and took part in the Battle of Shiloh (April 6–7, 1862). On September 6, 1862, the Confederate War Department authorized Richardson to organize the 1st Tennessee Partisan Ranger Regiment, and he spent the remainder of the year assembling and training that unit.

On March 16, 1863, Confederate adjutant general Samuel Cooper ordered Richardson's authority revoked after Unionists in western Tennessee accused him of depredations and operating without authority. However, before this order could be carried out, the unit was defeated by Union forces near Bolivar, Tennessee, and disbanded.

During the summer of 1863, Richardson became an agent with the Bureau of Conscription in western Tennessee. He assembled the 12th Tennessee Regiment and joined Major General Nathan Forrest's command on August 10, 1863. Richardson was appointed brigadier general to date from December 3, 1863, but President Jefferson Davis rescinded the promotion two months later after charges of malfeasance and misappropriation of funds were leveled against Richardson. Despite being relieved of command over a disciplinary dispute on July 19, 1864, on August 30 Richardson received command of the restructured 12th Tennessee and led it during the Franklin and Nashville Campaign (November 29–December 27, 1864). He was removed from command of the 12th Tennessee in January 1865.

Following the war, Richardson returned to his legal career and also became an active partner in the Selma, Marion & Memphis Railroad. During a business trip to Clarkton, Missouri, he was shot under mysterious circumstances on January 5, 1870, and died the next day.

R. RAY ORTENSIE

See also

Cooper, Samuel; Forrest, Nathan Bedford; Franklin and Nashville Campaign; Pillow, Gideon Johnson; Shiloh, Battle of

Further Reading

Johnson, Adam R., and William J. Davis. *The Partisan Rangers of the Confederate States Army: Memoirs of General Adam R. Johnson.* Abilene, TX: State House Press, 1995.

Warner, Ezra J. *Generals in Gray: Lives of the Confederate Commanders.* Baton Rouge: Louisiana State University Press, 2006.

Richmond, Battle of
Start Date: August 29, 1862
End Date: August 30, 1862

Engagement during the Confederate Kentucky Campaign (August 14–October 26, 1862). In the autumn of 1862, General Braxton Bragg led some 30,000 men of his Army of Mississippi from Chattanooga into Kentucky while Major General Edmund Kirby Smith, commander of the Confederate Department of East Tennessee, and 19,000 men entered the state at Cumberland Gap in the east. Brigadier General Patrick Cleburne's division led Smith's army, with Colonel John S. Scott's cavalry patrolling his front. On the morning of August 29 while marching north from Big Hill on the road to Richmond, Scott encountered the 55th Indiana Regiment, and a skirmish ensued.

The Indianans, supported by Colonel Leonidas Metcalfe's cavalry, pushed Scott's soldiers back into Cleburne's deployed lines and captured a mountain howitzer. As the day wore on, Union brigadier general Mahlon D. Manson advanced southward to Rogersville with reinforcements, and by evening he commanded 6,500 troops. Skirmishing and artillery fire occupied both armies for the remainder of the afternoon. That night, Manson informed his commander, Major General William Nelson, of his situation. Smith ordered Cleburne to attack in the morning and promised to reinforce him with Brigadier General Thomas J. Churchill's division.

Early on the morning of August 30, Manson moved his troops to Mount Zion Church, about five miles south of Richmond, and deployed for battle. Cleburne, advancing with 6,850 men, was wounded, and Colonel Preston Smith assumed command. Soon the Federals were routed. Manson formed a second line near Rogersville, about two miles north of his first position. Kirby Smith sent Churchill's men to attack the Union right, while Preston Smith engaged the left. Manson, unwisely countercharging into massed Confederate fire, was again routed, and Kirby Smith began a general advance.

General Nelson now assumed personal direction of the battle, forming his men in a third line just south of Richmond. Preston Smith and Churchill again charged. Nelson, wounded in the thigh, was evacuated. The Union line then collapsed in chaos. Scott's cavalry, deployed on the Union line of retreat, captured thousands, including Manson and his staff. Union casualties were 206 dead, 844 wounded, and 4,303 captured or missing. Kirby Smith lost just 78 killed, 372 wounded, and 1 missing. The way was now open for a Confederate advance on Lexington and Frankfort.

PAUL DAVID NELSON

See also
Churchill, Thomas James; Cleburne, Patrick Ronayne; Kentucky Campaign; Manson, Mahlon Dickerson; Nelson, William; Smith, Edmund Kirby; Smith, Preston

Further Reading
Lambert, D. Warren. *When the Ripe Pears Fell: The Battle of Richmond, Kentucky.* Richmond, KY: Madison County Historical Society, 1996.
McDonough, James L. *War in Kentucky: From Shiloh to Perryville.* Knoxville: University of Tennessee Press, 1994.

Richmond, Confederate Department of

Military administrative unit responsible for the defense of the Confederate capital. The Department of Richmond encompassed a small geographical area surrounding the Confederate capital of Richmond. The department's primary mission was to provide for the defense of the city. These defensive forces were known collectively as the Richmond Defenses, which included four battalions of heavy artillery (the 10th, 18th, 19th, and 20th Virginia), the Louisiana Guard Artillery, and the Confederate Engineer Company. A large local defense brigade consisting of government workers and convalescents was added to confront the threats posed by the Union offensive of 1864.

The Department of Richmond came into official existence on April 1, 1863, and was commanded by Major General Arnold Elzey. He remained in this post until April 25, 1864. During his tenure, Elzey augmented Richmond's defenses as best he could. On May 29, 1864, Elzey was succeeded in command by Lieutenant General Richard S. Ewell, who continued in command until Richmond fell to Union forces on April 3, 1865. Ewell's command only increased in importance as the war dragged on, especially during the long Petersburg Campaign (June 15, 1864–April 3, 1865).

PAUL G. PIERPAOLI JR.

See also
Elzey, Arnold; Ewell, Richard Stoddart; Longstreet, James; North Carolina and Southern Virginia, Confederate Department of; Petersburg Campaign; Richmond, Virginia

Further Reading
Eicher, John H., and David J. Eicher. *Civil War High Commands.* Stanford, CA: Stanford University Press, 2001.

Richmond, Virginia

Capital of the Confederate States of America (1861–1865), capital of the Commonwealth of Virginia, and major manufacturing center. With an 1861 population of only 38,000 people—including whites, slaves, and freedmen—Richmond ranked 25th in population among all U.S. cities but 3rd among cities south of the Mason-Dixon Line.

Richmond was founded formally in 1737, although settlers at Jamestown had explored the area as early as 1607. In 1609, a small settlement was established near the present-day site of Richmond on bluffs overlooking the James River. After its 1737 founding, Richmond developed into a commerce hub. It was tied into the transatlantic slave trade, thanks in large measure to the construction of the James River and Kanawha Canal (begun in 1785 and completed in 1851), which linked the inland western portions of Virginia with the Tidewater area. Richmond was at the epicenter of the canal system, the first such project built in the United States. When railroads eclipsed canals in the early 1850s, Richmond also became a major rail hub, which would aid the Confederate war effort.

Because of its strategic location at the fall line of the James River and its considerable manufacturing and commercial concerns, Richmond was a vital resource for the new Confederate States of America. In May 1861 following Virginia's belated secession, Confederate officials decided to move the capital from Montgomery, Alabama, to Richmond, a decision that was not without controversy. While the Confederates wanted the capital city to be close to the major theater of war, the proximity of Richmond to Washington, D.C.—just 100 miles north—meant that substantial resources would have to be expended to fortify and defend the city. This fact was all too obvious to the Union, which kept considerable pressure on the city throughout the war. The Union overland effort to capture Richmond was the chief preoccupation of the major Union field force in the eastern theater, the Army of the Potomac, throughout the course of the conflict. Thus, the area roughly between Richmond and Washington became the most contested piece of real estate during the four-year conflict, and the Confederates were often hard-pressed to defend their heartland while their men and resources were being used to defend the capital area.

Richmond was the South's leading manufacturing center, producing iron, processing tobacco, and milling flour and meal. At the start of the Civil War, Richmond also possessed the only facility capable of manufacturing rails for railroads and the heaviest cannon—the Tredegar Iron Works. The

Richmond, Virginia, 1865. (National Archives)

city boasted numerous important newspapers and publishing houses as well as one of the South's largest hospitals, which would treat thousands of wounded soldiers. Richmond was also the home to two of the largest Confederate prisoner-of-war camps: Libby Prison and Belle Isle Prison.

The Civil War radically transformed the once-sleepy Richmond, as thousands of government bureaucrats, soldiers, and civilians looking to make a fast dollar poured into the city beginning in mid-1861. This severely taxed the city's infrastructure and public services and angered many permanent and long-term Richmond residents. Not surprisingly, crime and vice skyrocketed, as saloons proliferated and prostitution and gambling became rampant. And while many Richmonders turned a tidy profit during the war years, their gains were never sufficient to offset the high inflation that had gripped the Confederacy. As the war dragged on, food and material shortages affected everyone, which in 1863 precipitated a bread riot among the city's women. By late 1864 material shortages had become critical, and a sizable number of Richmond's residents were subsisting on near-starvation rations.

To protect Richmond, Confederate forces surrounded the city with substantial earthworks and heavy guns, which were regularly augmented. During the Peninsula Campaign (March–July 1862), in which Union forces tried to attack Richmond from the south and east, jittery Richmonders demanded additional earthworks and guns. After the Kilpatrick-Dahlgren Raid (February–March 1864), the city's residents banded together and sizably augmented their local militia and defense forces. During much of the conflict, the primary task of the Army of Northern Virginia was to keep Richmond out of the Union's reach, a mandate that ultimately led to the army's collapse.

By January 1865, Union forces were closing in on the capital of the Confederacy. The Army of Northern Virginia was entrenched around Petersburg, 20 miles south of Richmond, in a valiant attempt to keep open the rail lines and protect Richmond. On April 2, 1865, Union troops breached the earthworks surrounding Petersburg, giving them a direct route into Richmond. That same day, Confederate officials and troops began fleeing the city. Ordered to destroy bridges, armories, and other facilities as they left, Confederate troops unwittingly caused a huge conflagration that incinerated a large portion of the city, including many of its important commercial establishments. Early on April 3, Union troops began entering the city and attempted to douse the fires, but by then much of Richmond lay in ruins. On April 4, President Abraham Lincoln toured the fallen city.

PAUL G. PIERPAOLI JR.

See also

Belle Isle Prison, Virginia; Kilpatrick-Dahlgren Raid; Libby Prison, Virginia; Northern Virginia, Confederate Army of; Peninsula Campaign; Tredegar Iron Works; Virginia; Washington, D.C.

Further Reading

Dabney, Virginius. *Richmond: The Story of a City.* New York: Doubleday, 1976.

Ferguson, Ernest B. *Ashes of Glory: Richmond at War.* New York: Knopf, 1996.

Lankford, Nelson D. *Richmond Burning: The Last Days of the Confederate Capital.* New York: Penguin, 2003.

Richmond, Virginia, Surrender of
Event Date: April 3, 1865

Capitulation of the Confederate capital. During early 1865, the population of the Confederate capital of Richmond, Virginia, lived under the constant threat of attack as Lieutenant General Ulysses S. Grant's Union armies laid siege to nearby Petersburg. Confederate general Robert E. Lee's Army of Northern Virginia defended Petersburg and effectively prevented the Union from capturing the Confederate capital. While many residents of Richmond manned breastworks around the capital, others also tended to the daily affairs of life in the city.

Life in Richmond changed, however, when a Union victory in the Battle of Five Forks (April 1, 1865) rendered Petersburg untenable. Lee had no choice but to abandon Richmond and Petersburg and issued orders to that effect for April 2. He also advised the Confederate government in Richmond to evacuate before the final rail lines out of the city were cut. Within hours, the news of Lee's withdrawal arrived in the capital, and the city's populace hurriedly prepared to evacuate.

Government workers gathered official documents, while workers at the Tredegar Iron Works sought to send precious stocks out of the city via rail. Private citizens descended upon banks in droves to withdraw their savings.

The government issued an official evacuation order at 4:00 p.m. on April 2, and chaos soon erupted as people tried to leave the city with as many possessions as they could gather. Confederate president Jefferson Davis and his cabinet departed by train late that evening, but many of the city's elite remained in their homes and waited for events to unfold.

Remaining Confederate soldiers destroyed paper currency, agricultural commodities, and weapons that could not be removed. By nightfall, a mob consisting of escaped prisoners and ruffians rampaged unabated through the city's streets. Fires that were set to destroy tobacco warehouses flared out of control as winds whipped the flames.

As thousands of shells from scuttled Confederate warships in the James River exploded through the night, hundreds of buildings and entire blocks of the city burned. Some citizens sought refuge in the open space of Capitol Square in front of the Virginia State House and were there when the 4th Massachusetts Cavalry Regiment of the Union Army of the James worked its way through the debris to the city center the following morning.

That same day, April 3, Union Army majors Atherton H. Stevens and Eugene E. Graves met with Richmond mayor Joseph Mayo, who gave the two officers an official note of surrender. The surrender was relayed to City Hall, where it was officially accepted by Major General Godfrey Weitzel. A somber mood prevailed in the city as Weitzel declared martial law and commanded black troops of his XXV Corps to put out the remaining fires, clear the streets, restore order, and pass out provisions. While the white population of the town resented the Union soldiers' presence, its black residents rejoiced and celebrated in the streets, warmly welcoming the Union soldiers. These same people also enthusiastically greeted U.S. president Abraham Lincoln on April 4 when he visited the city.

Lincoln characteristically ordered that Union soldiers conduct themselves responsibly, and there were few reports of untoward conduct on the part of the occupying forces. To most Americans, including Lincoln, the surrender of Richmond signaled the end of the war, and huge celebrations marked the arrival of the news in the U.S. capital.

MATTHEW J. KROGMAN

See also

Davis, Jefferson Finis; Five Forks, Battle of; Grant, Ulysses Simpson; Lee, Robert Edward; Lincoln, Abraham; Petersburg Campaign; Richmond, Virginia; Weitzel, Godfrey

Further Reading

Foote, Shelby. *The Civil War: A Narrative; Red River to Appomattox.* New York: Random House, 1974.

Weigley, Russell F. *A Great Civil War: A Military and Political History, 1861–1865.* Bloomington: Indiana University Press, 2000.

Winik, John. *April 1865: The Month That Saved America.* New York: HarperCollins, 2001.

Richmond & Petersburg Railroad

Rail line 22.5 miles in length linking Richmond and the railhead of Petersburg to the South during the Civil War. The Richmond & Petersburg Railroad, founded in 1836, was single-tracked with few sidings. This connection became critical in the winter of 1864–1865 during the Petersburg Campaign

(June 15, 1864–April 3, 1865). Because of limited trackage and equipment, the railroad could only move one brigade at a time. There was no standard gauge in the South during the Civil War, and competing rail lines typically did not meet. Five railroads served Petersburg, but none of them linked to the other. The Richmond & Petersburg Railroad was easily the most important length of track in the entire Confederacy.

Many exigencies conspired to place great pressure on the Richmond & Petersburg Railroad. First, the Confederacy had only limited metallurgical capacity and capability and produced few rails during the war. Second, the increased war usage made line maintenance even more difficult, and the Richmond & Petersburg Railroad was forced to remove rails from its Port Walthall extension to repair damaged and worn-out rails on its main line. Third, the loss of manpower in the South affected all industries, including the railroads. By 1863, losses had forced the Confederacy to begin drafting railroad workers over age 45. The Richmond & Petersburg Railroad, along with other railroads, protested the drafting of its workers and the consolidation of rail lines, however, and the government did not aggressively pursue these options. Fourth, the loss of Tennessee in 1863 forced the Confederacy to reroute all troop shipments to the Carolinas and Georgia through Richmond over the Richmond & Petersburg Railroad to Petersburg.

In early May 1864, Union major general Benjamin F. Butler's force of 39,000 men landed just east of the line at Bermuda Hundred and briefly blocked the Richmond & Petersburg Railroad. A few days later on May 9, the Confederates rallied and at Swift Creek halted Butler's advance and reopened the line. The Richmond & Petersburg Railroad continued to support General Robert E. Lee's Army of Northern Virginia in Petersburg until the city fell in early April 1865.

MICHAEL E. LYNCH

See also
Bermuda Hundred Campaign; Petersburg Campaign; Richmond, Virginia; Swift Creek, Battle of; Virginia & Tennessee Railroad

Further Reading
Sommers, Richard J. *Richmond Redeemed: The Siege at Petersburg.* New York: Doubleday, 1981.
Trudeau, Noah Andre. *The Last Citadel: Petersburg, Virginia, June 1864–April 1865.* Baton Rouge: Louisiana State University Press, 1993.

Richmond Campaign
See Overland Campaign

Richmond Enquirer

One of Virginia's oldest newspapers. The *Richmond Enquirer* was founded in 1804 by Thomas Ritchie. The paper, which steadily gained a wide readership in and out of Virginia, championed Jeffersonian democracy in its early years of operation and then came to trumpet the Democratic Party under Presidents Andrew Jackson and Martin Van Buren. The *Enquirer* was so steadfast in its support for the Democratic Party that it was given the sobriquet "The Democratic Bible." The paper came out against both secessionists and abolitionists in the 1850s; meanwhile, Ritchie died in 1854, and O. Jennings Wise took the paper's helm.

Despite its earlier opposition to secession, when Virginia seceded in April 1861, the *Enquirer* enthusiastically supported the new Confederate government. The paper's wartime editors, Richard M. Smith and Bennett M. DeWitt, championed the war policies of Confederate president Jefferson Davis, in contrast to its chief competitors, the *Whig* and *Examiner,* which seemed never to encounter a Confederate war policy they liked. Indeed, for much of the war, the *Enquirer* was seen by many as the official mouthpiece of the Davis administration.

During the war, the *Enquirer*'s circulation boomed. The paper had a reputation for its almost literary content—especially its editorials—and its extraordinary efforts to report news accurately. During the last year or so of the conflict, the *Enquirer* became somewhat critical of the Davis government under its new editor, Nathaniel Tyler, although not nearly to the extent of many other Richmond and Southern newspapers. In 1867 the *Enquirer* was bought by the *Richmond Examiner,* and publication under the *Enquirer* banner ceased.

PAUL G. PIERPAOLI JR.

See also
Davis, Jefferson Finis; Journalism; *Richmond Examiner; Richmond Whig;* Virginia

Further Reading
Andrews, J. Cutler. *The South Reports the Civil War.* Princeton, NJ: Princeton University Press, 1970.
Furgurson, Ernest B. *Ashes of Glory: Richmond at War.* New York: Knopf, 1996.

Richmond Examiner

Prosecession, antiabolition newspaper based in Richmond, Virginia, that was highly critical of the Confederate government. The *Richmond Examiner* began publication in 1847 as a rival to both the *Richmond Enquirer,* a Democratic Party mouthpiece, and the *Richmond Whig.* From the beginning, the *Examiner* took the more extremist, prosecession, Southern rights positions that its editor, John Moncure Daniel, had declared were those of Virginia's planter gentlemen. The paper was also relentlessly hostile toward Northern culture and politics.

During the 1860–1861 secession crisis, the *Examiner* called for an immediate break with the Union and castigated Virginia's leaders for their timid deliberations. At the same time, the paper kept up a steady drumbeat against President-elect Abraham Lincoln. When Virginia's secession was finally accomplished, the *Examiner* greeted the news with optimistic predictions of speedy Southern military victory and independence.

With regard to the war, the *Examiner* praised the spirit and conduct of Confederate troops but took a critical position vis-à-vis the conduct of the war by the Jefferson Davis administration. Daniel's editorials argued that Davis and indeed the entire Confederate government were too weak and pusillanimous to undertake the measures necessary to secure Southern independence. Scornful, sarcastic attacks on Davis's leadership and alleged mismanagement and impotence became the hallmark of the *Examiner.* The paper became one of the most widely read throughout the Confederacy, even as it was widely denounced for its divisive character.

During the war, Daniel and his coeditor, Edward A. Pollard, initially were unimpressed with the generalship of Robert E. Lee, but they quickly became supporters while continuing to censure Davis's failures of political leadership. On matters of military policy, the *Examiner* approved of the use of substitutes by conscripts who could afford them. The paper also early on opposed suggestions of using black troops but came around after Lee gave his assent to such plans late in the war. In addition, the *Examiner* took stands on home front issues, including drunkenness and the hardships created by monetary inflation.

At the end of March 1865, Daniel died of tuberculosis just days before Richmond was taken by Union forces. The fire that consumed much of Richmond upon the Confederate evacuation also destroyed the offices of the *Examiner.* The paper briefly resumed publication later in 1865 but closed for good in 1867.

DAVID J. KIRACOFE

See also

Davis, Jefferson Finis; Journalism; Lee, Robert Edward; Pollard, Edward Alfred; *Richmond Whig;* Secession

Further Reading

Bridges, Peter. *Pen of Fire: John Moncure Daniel.* Kent, OH: Kent State University Press, 2002.

Osthaus, Carl R. "A Study of Wartime Journalism: John M. Daniel and the Confederacy." In *Partisans of the Southern Press: Editorial Spokesmen of the Nineteenth Century,* edited by Carl Osthaus, 95–117. Lexington: University of Kentucky Press, 1994.

Richmond Light Infantry Blues

Virginia militia unit first formed on May 10, 1789. Named for its distinctive blue and white uniforms, the Richmond Light Infantry Blues became part of the 19th Regiment of Virginia Militia in 1792 and part of the 1st Virginia Regiment on May 1, 1851. Prior to the start of the Civil War in April 1861, the company volunteered for service whenever and wherever a crisis arose. The first time it saw active service was during Gabriel's Rebellion in August 1800. The next time occurred during the War of 1812. The unit was also involved in the suppression of Nat Turner's Rebellion in 1831 and was one of the units tasked with guarding John Brown after his capture at Harpers Ferry in 1859.

The Richmond Blues was activated on April 21, 1861, and mustered into Confederate service on June 30 with Colonel Richard T. W. Duke commanding. It was soon detached from the 1st Virginia Regiment (William's Rifles) and redesignated as Company A, 46th Virginia Volunteer Infantry Regiment (also referred to as the 1st or 2nd Regiment, or Wise's Legion). According to the 1861 muster rolls, 15 of the 99 soldiers of Company A were Jewish immigrants of German extraction or children of Jewish immigrants.

Company A was ordered to Roanoke Island, North Carolina, in the autumn of 1861 and placed in a brigade commanded by former Virginia governor Henry A. Wise. Wise's son, O. Jennings Wise, served as captain of the company. Part of the unit was captured and paroled at Roanoke Island, North Carolina, on February 8, 1862; Jennings Wise was mortally wounded the same day.

The men were subsequently exchanged, and Company A was assembled in Virginia on May 24, 1862, with 401 soldiers. The unit saw action in the Seven Days' Campaign (June 25–July 1, 1862) and then was transferred to the Department of South Carolina, Georgia, and Florida in the autumn of 1863. Company A took part in the defense of Charleston until it was ordered back to the Army of Northern Virginia on May 3, 1864, when it participated in the defense of Richmond.

The Light Infantry Blues was subsequently reassigned to Petersburg and participated in Petersburg Campaign (June 15, 1864–April 3, 1865). After the Battle of Sayler's Creek (April 6, 1865), the Blues and the other units of Wise's Legion won praise from General Robert E. Lee for being one of the few commands to stay relatively intact during and after the battle when so many other commands had been shattered. The unit surrendered at Appomattox Court House on April 9, 1865, with 15 officers and 116 men.

ROBERT A. LYNN

See also

Brown, John; Petersburg Campaign; Roanoke Island, Battle of; Sayler's Creek, Battle of; Seven Days' Campaign; Wise, Henry Alexander

Further Reading

Cutchins, Colonel John A. *A Famous Command: The Richmond Light Infantry Blues.* Richmond, VA: Garret and Massie, 1934.
Sifakis, Stewart. *Compendium of the Confederate Armies: Virginia.* Westminster, MD: Heritage Books, 2006.

Richmond Whig

One of three major Richmond papers during the war. The *Richmond Whig* began publication in 1824 under the editorship of John Hampden Pleasants in opposition to the influential *Richmond Enquirer,* which was largely a Democratic Party mouthpiece. By the 1830s, the *Whig* was a leading voice for the Whig Party, which was often at loggerheads with Jacksonian Democrats. In 1846, Pleasants was killed in a duel with Thomas Ritchie Jr., editor of the *Enquirer.*

During the 1860–1861 secession crisis, the *Whig* opposed Virginia's exit from the Union but was highly critical of the centralizing tendencies of the incoming Republican administration of Abraham Lincoln. Virginia voted in support of secession in April 1861 following Lincoln's call for the military suppression of the rebellion, a move that the *Whig* also denounced. Antisecession editor Robert Ridgway resigned, however, and Alexander Moseley assumed the editorship, a position he held for almost the duration of the war along with his coeditor, James McDonald.

During the war, the *Whig* became known as a leading critic of the Jefferson Davis administration, frequently heaping scorn on Davis for the same sort of executive abuses for which it had criticized Lincoln's administration. The *Whig* opposed conscription, again citing the expansion of executive powers by the commander in chief. The paper instead favored state control of military forces. *Whig* editors

were also critical of Davis's conduct of military affairs and demanded accountability for military defeats and setbacks.

At the same time, the paper supported the Confederate war effort and continued to attack the Union and Lincoln's "aggressive" war. The *Whig*'s tone could often be shrill in highlighting the brutality of Northern troops, especially against civilians. The 1863 Emancipation Proclamation likewise drew a sharp rejoinder in the *Whig*'s pages.

The *Richmond Whig* also continued to play a role in Virginia state politics as an opposition paper. Editorials attacked the leadership of Governor John Letcher, and in 1864 the paper endorsed the candidacy of William Munford against the Democrat and eventual winner, William Smith.

After the fall of Richmond in April 1865, the *Whig* became the first paper in the city to resume publication. It remained in operation until 1888.

DAVID J. KIRACOFE

See also

Davis, Jefferson Finis; Letcher, John; *Richmond Enquirer;* Secession; Smith, William; Virginia

Further Reading

Andrews, J. Cutler. *The South Reports the Civil War.* Princeton, NJ: Princeton University Press, 1970.
Furgurson, Ernest B. *Ashes of Glory: Richmond at War.* New York: Knopf, 1996.

Rich Mountain, Battle of
Event Date: July 11, 1861

Important early engagement in western Virginia (West Virginia). After the Union victory at the Battle of Philippi (June 3, 1861) and with Unionists' efforts to break western Virginia from the eastern part of the state, thereby making it a Union stronghold, Major General George McClellan moved into the region with some 20,000 Union troops. It was his assignment to support the pro-Union western counties and defend them from Confederate attack. In turn, the Confederate government dispatched Brigadier General Robert Garnett with 4,500 men to Beverly, Virginia, a crucial crossroads along the Staunton and Parkersburg Turnpike, situated about 50 miles west of the Shenandoah Valley.

Although Garnett requested reinforcements, none were forthcoming, so he instead staged a series of guerrilla raids against Union supply lines. Realizing that McClellan would likely move against his force, Garnett positioned his men on Rich Mountain, west of Beverly, and on Laurel Mountain, to

Lithograph depicting the Union victory in the Battle of Rich Mountain in western Virginia (now West Virginia), July 11, 1861. (Library of Congress)

the north. Both positions commanded unobstructed views of Beverly and the turnpike running through it.

Garnett concluded that McClellan would assault the weaker Confederate position at Laurel Hill. Preparing for McClellan's strike, Garnett moved the bulk of his forces to Laurel Hill, leaving Colonel John Pegram and 1,300 Confederates to defend Rich Mountain.

McClellan did not attack Laurel Hill as Garnett had predicted. Instead, McClellan and Brigadier General William S. Rosecrans prepared to encircle Pegram's troops at Rich Mountain. A coordinated attack was planned, with Rosecrans assailing Pegram's rear while McClellan's main force attacked from the front. On July 11 in a pouring rain, Rosecrans performed his part of the plan. He moved along an isolated route, cutting through briars and timber and reaching Rich Mountain, where he fell upon Pegram's men. Rosecrans easily swept away Confederate resistance, killing or capturing about 170 men and driving the remnants of the Confederate force into Beverly, where 550 men surrendered.

Now unable to hold the Staunton and Parkersburg Turnpike, Garnett and Pegram's remaining force withdrew,

moving eastward with Union troops in pursuit. On July 13 the Union forces caught up with Garnett at Carrick's Ford, where the general was shot and killed, the first general officer to die in the Civil War. Carrick's Ford was another Confederate defeat.

For the North, the results of the Battle of Rich Mountain were consequential. The Union victory completely dashed Confederate hopes of controlling the Baltimore & Ohio Railroad as well as the Staunton and Parkersburg Turnpike. On the political front, having eliminated the Confederate threat from western Virginia, delegates to the Second Wheeling Convention could now form the new state of West Virginia. They did so on July 20, leading two years later to the admission of that state to the Union. The victory also made McClellan an instant hero and helped elevate him to the position of Union Army general in chief.

JEFFERY B. COOK AND PAUL G. PIERPAOLI JR.

See also

Baltimore & Ohio Railroad; Carrick's Ford, Battle of; Garnett, Robert Selden; McClellan, George Brinton; Philippi, Battle of; Rosecrans, William Starke; West Virginia

Further Reading

Rice, Otis. *West Virginia: A History*. Lexington: University Press of Kentucky, 1985.

Sears, Stephen. *George McClellan: The Young Napoleon*. New York: Ticknor and Fields, 1988.

Ricketts, James Brewerton

Birth Date: June 21, 1817

Death Date: September 22, 1887

Union officer. James Brewerton Ricketts was born on June 21, 1817, in New York City and graduated from the U.S. Military Academy, West Point, in 1839. He received a commission as an artillery officer and served in the Mexican-American War (1846–1848). A captain by 1861, Ricketts fought in the First Battle of Bull Run (July 21, 1861), during which he commanded an artillery battery. Severely wounded and captured, he was held as a prisoner in Richmond until exchanged in January 1862.

Promoted to brigadier general of volunteers on April 30, 1862, to date from July 1861, Ricketts received command of an infantry division in the Army of Virginia on June 10. He led his men at the Battle of Cedar Mountain (August 9, 1862) and the Second Battle of Bull Run (August 29–30, 1862) and, in the Army of the Potomac, at the Battle of Antietam (September 17, 1862), where he was badly injured when his wounded horse fell on him.

Ricketts did not return to a field command until late March 1864, leading a division in VI Corps during the Overland (Richmond) Campaign (May 4–June 12, 1864). In July 1864 Ricketts's command, numbering 3,500 men, was ordered to Washington, D.C., to help repulse Lieutenant General Jubal Early's raid. On July 9, 1864, Ricketts reinforced Major General Lew Wallace's forces at the Battle of Monocacy in Maryland, where his division sustained the heaviest losses of all Union forces engaged. Ricketts's command took part in Major General Philip Sheridan's Shenandoah Valley Campaign (August 7, 1864–March 2, 1865). At the Battle of Cedar Creek (October 19, 1864), Ricketts temporarily commanded VI Corps and was wounded for the third time, hit in the chest by a bullet. He returned to command his division in April 1865, shortly after the surrender at Appomattox. Having been brevetted through major general in both the regular army and the volunteers, he mustered out of the volunteers in April 1866. He briefly resumed his regular army career, but his many wounds left him unfit

for duty, and he was retired on January 3, 1867, at the grade of major general. Ricketts died in Washington, D.C., on September 22, 1887.

JENNIFER M. MURRAY

See also

Antietam, Battle of; Bull Run, First Battle of; Bull Run, Second Battle of; Cedar Creek, Battle of; Cedar Mountain, Battle of; Early's Raid on Washington, D.C.; Monocacy, Battle of; Overland Campaign; Sheridan's Shenandoah Valley Campaign

Further Reading

Eicher, John H., and David J. Eicher. *Civil War High Commands*. Stanford, CA: Stanford University Press, 2001.

Warner, Ezra J. *Generals in Gray: Lives of the Confederate Commanders*. Baton Rouge: Louisiana State University Press, 2006.

Rifles

Shoulder-fired small arms in which barrels have a helical groove or grooves in the walls of the bore designed to impart greater range and accuracy to the projectile.

Advances in gun making and technology in the early 19th century significantly improved the accuracy and range of rifles that appeared on the world's battlefields by midcentury. These advances belatedly led to changes in battlefield tactics.

The basic infantry weapon until the early 19th century was the smoothbore flintlock musket. These weapons began to appear in European armies in the 1680s and remained in widespread use until the mid-19th century. Two of the best known were the English Brown Bess and the French Charleville. The Brown Bess fired a .69-caliber ball, and the Charleville fired a .65-caliber ball.

The principal drawback to the flintlock was its inaccuracy. It was a smoothbore weapon, and the musket ball did not gain the advantage of stability in flight provided to a projectile exiting from a rifled barrel. Also, black powder caused extensive fouling in the barrel after the first several shots; as a result, musket balls had to be cast in a diameter considerably smaller than the bore of the musket. The resultant gap, known as windage, which allowed an escape of the force of the ignited propellant, also caused the ball to bound down the bore in what was known as balloting. The ball might exit the muzzle at an angle, and thus 80–100 yards was the maximum effective range of the flintlock musket. The smoothbore musket had a theoretical rate of fire of three times a minute. The rifle, while it had an effective range of up to 200–300 yards, was much slower in rate of fire because the ball had to fit snugly in the bore to grip the rifling and thus was difficult to force down the barrel. Its rate of fire was approximately one shot per minute. As a result, it was considered unsuited for the tactics of the day. Armies retained special units of riflemen but as skirmishers and sharpshooters rather than as regular infantry.

Although large numbers of flintlock muskets, both smoothbore and rifled, continued in use during the Civil War, especially among militia and local defense forces, this system had been largely replaced by the new percussion cap system developed early in the 19th century by Scotsman Alexander Forsyth. The percussion cap employed fulminate of mercury and detonated when struck a blow. It was a far more reliable system of ignition than the flintlock, and one source has estimated that it reduced musket misfires from 400 to 4.5 per 1,000. This, of course, produced a tremendous increase in firepower. Muzzle-loading percussion cap muskets were in general service in armies by 1850.

The other major development was the lead cylindro-conoidal minié bullet, known simply as the minié ball. The problem with the rifle had always been that it was difficult and time-consuming to load, as the bullet had to be almost the exact size of the bore in order to grip the rifling. The minié ball, developed in the late 1840s by French Army officer Claude-Étienne Minié, had an iron plug at its base and later simply a hollowed-out area that had the same effect of expanding the soft lead of the bullet on ignition of the powder charge. This caused the bullet to grip the lands and grooves of the rifling. The new minié ball could be loaded and fired as rapidly as the old smoothbore musket but had the longer effective range of the rifle. These two developments—the percussion cap and the minié ball—led to the appalling battlefield casualties of the Civil War, because tactics tend to lag behind technology, and the generals were slow to develop new tactics to meet the new technology.

In 1855 U.S. secretary of war Jefferson Davis, subsequently president of the Confederacy, first approved the minié ball rifled musket for the U.S. Army. The most widely used rifle of the Civil War was the .58-caliber muzzleloader produced by the Springfield Arsenal in Massachusetts. By the end of 1863, most Union infantrymen were armed with the Springfield Model 1861. Some 1.5 million Model 1861 and Model 1863 Springfields were produced during the course of the war.

It took time for industry to change over to wartime production, and in any case demand for the new rifles far exceeded supply, particularly in the early months of the war. Many muskets were imported, especially by the Confederacy

early in the war. Indeed, the second most widely used infantry weapon of the Civil War was the British 1853 Pattern Enfield rifle-musket in .577 caliber. Some 900,000 of these were shipped to America during the war. A number of new Enfields fell into Union hands on the surrender of Vicksburg, Mississippi, in July 1863.

Repeating rifles and breach-loading rifles also saw use in the war. Among the dozens of types of carbines used during the war were the Sharps, Burnside, and Smith. The Spencer repeating carbine became a favorite of the Union cavalry, with the Henry lever-action repeater being the first truly rapid-fire rifle used during the conflict. However, logistics also lagged behind technology. Breach-loading carbines and repeaters fired new cartridge ammunition that was less available and considerably more expensive. In nearly every major battle, the few units armed with a repeater quickly ran out of ammunition.

James Brian McNabb and Spencer C. Tucker

See also

Arms Manufacturing; Cavalry Tactics; Infantry Tactics; Minié, Claude-Étienne; Spencer Repeating Rifle and Carbine; Springfield Model 1861 Rifle Musket

Further Reading

Bilby, Joseph. *Civil War Firearms: Their Historical Background and Tactical Use.* New York: Da Capo, 2005.
Coates, Earl, and Dean S. Thomas. *An Introduction to Civil War Small Arms.* Gettysburg, PA: Thomas Productions, 1996.
Edwards, William B. *Civil War Guns.* Gettysburg, PA: Thomas Publications, 1997.

Ringgold, Cadwalader
Birth Date: August 20, 1802
Death Date: April 29, 1867

Union naval officer. Born in Washington County, Maryland, on August 20, 1802, Cadwalader Ringgold received a midshipman's warrant on March 4, 1819. He was promoted to lieutenant on May 17, 1828, and to commander on July 16, 1849. Ringgold was on the reserve list for reason of disability in September 1855. Restored to the active list in 1857, he was promoted to captain that same year with rank backdated to April 2, 1856. At the beginning of 1861, Ringgold had been in the navy for 41 years: 18 years in assignments afloat, 9 in shore duty, and 14 waiting orders in a navy that had too many officers for available assignments.

At the start of the Civil War, Captain Ringgold was serving on special duty in Washington, D.C. In September 1861 he assumed command of the sailing frigate *Sabine,* which was undergoing repairs at the Portsmouth Navy Yard. Assigned to the Atlantic Blockading Squadron, he took up station off Georgetown, South Carolina. On November 2, 1861, his ship rescued the marines aboard the sinking steamer *Governor,* which had succumbed to a severe storm and was part of Flag Officer Samuel F. Du Pont's expeditionary force headed for Port Royal, South Carolina.

Ringgold then took his ship to New York for repairs. Sent out to search for the storeship *Vermont,* on March 29 his ship located and rescued the crew of the drifting vessel off Bermuda. Promoted to commodore on July 16, 1862, he was ordered to search for Confederate commerce raiders, especially the *Alabama,* and took his ship to Africa. Unsuccessful in this effort, he returned to New York. In June 1863 he was ordered out to search for the Confederate raider *Tacony* off New England but failed to locate it. Ringgold and his crew received the Thanks of Congress in March 1864 for their earlier rescues of the marines and the recovery of the *Vermont.*

Ringgold was on waiting orders status when he was assigned to special duty in New York City in April 1864. Placed on the retired list on August 20, 1864, he nonetheless continued in his New York City assignment until his death. He was promoted to rear admiral on the retired list in early 1867 with rank backdated to July 25, 1866. Ringgold died in New York City on April 29, 1867.

SPENCER C. TUCKER

See also

Alabama, CSS; Atlantic Blockading Squadron; Du Pont, Samuel Francis; Port Royal Sound, Battle of

Further Reading

Callahan, Edward W., ed. *List of Officers of the Navy of the United States and of the Marine Corps from 1775 to 1900.* 1901; reprint, New York: Haskell House Publishers, 1969.
Thompson, Kenneth E. *Civil War Commodores and Admirals: A Biographical Directory of All Eighty-Eight Union and Confederate Navy Officers Who Attained Commissioned Flag Rank during the War.* Portland, ME: Thompson Group, 2001.

Ringgold Gap, Battle of
Event Date: November 27, 1863

Closing battle of the Chattanooga Campaign (October–November 1863), fought in Catoosa County, Georgia. With the opening of a secure supply line (the Cracker Line) and reinforcements for the beleaguered Union forces at Chattanooga, Union commander Major General Ulysses S. Grant

began planning a breakout. The Battle of Chattanooga (November 23–25) began when some 14,000 Federals under Brigadier General Thomas J. Wood routed 600 Confederates and seized control of Orchard Knob just outside of Chattanooga. The next day, Major General Joseph Hooker, with two corps of the Army of the Potomac sent to reinforce Grant, attacked Confederate positions on Lookout Mountain and forced a retreat there, and on November 25 Grant ordered an advance on Missionary Ridge, which turned into an all-out assault. Major General George H. Thomas's Army of the Cumberland routed the center of the Confederate line, forcing Confederate commander General Braxton Bragg to order a general withdrawal of his Army of Tennessee southward into Georgia.

Bragg ordered his forces to reassemble at Dalton, Georgia, some 30 miles to the south. To accomplish this, however, he had to sufficiently delay Hooker, leading the Union pursuit, in order to extract his artillery and supply trains.

Major General Patrick R. Cleburne's division, perhaps the best such unit in the Army of Tennessee, was the Confederate rear guard. Near midnight on November 26, Bragg ordered Cleburne to deploy his division of only 4,100 men and two guns at a narrow railroad cut in the mountains where the Western & Atlantic Railroad passed through Taylor's Ridge near the town of Ringgold, Georgia, north of Dalton. Bragg instructed Cleburne "to hold this position at all hazards, and keep back the enemy until the artillery and transportation of the army are secure."

Early on November 27, the resourceful Cleburne carefully positioned his men. Centering his defense on the Ringgold Depot as an anchor, he concealed his men. Aware that he would be heavily outnumbered, Cleburne also ordered his troops to withhold their fire until the Union soldiers were almost upon them. At about 7:00 a.m. when the leading elements of Hooker's force approached and were just about to enter the gap, a withering Confederate volley drove them back. Unable to utilize his larger numbers to advantage in the narrow gap, Hooker attempted to outflank the defenders, but Cleburne had anticipated this and quickly moved men to throw back Union attacks on both flanks.

Around noon, having held the pursuing Federals at bay for more than five hours and having been informed that Bragg's supply trains had safely reached Dalton, Cleburne abandoned Ringgold Gap. Hooker's men occupied the gap by 2:00 p.m. Hooker reported casualties of 432 men, compared with Confederate losses of 480, although the Union losses were probably much higher than reported. Indeed, Grant noted the discrepancy in his official report. Grant now

The Battle of Ringgold Gap, fought in Georgia on November 27, 1863. The closing battle of the Chattanooga Campaign, it saw Confederate forces under Major General Patrick R. Cleburne turn back pursuing Union troops under Major General Joseph Hooker, allowing General Braxton Bragg's Confederate Army of Tennessee to escape. (National Archives)

terminated the pursuit, and both armies went into winter quarters. The Chattanooga Campaign was over.

In Richmond, Virginia, on February 6, 1864, the Confederate Congress voted the Thanks of Congress to Cleburne and his men: "For the victory obtained by them over superior forces of the enemy at Ringgold Gap . . . by which the advance of the enemy was impeded, our wagon train and most of our artillery saved, and a large number of the enemy killed and wounded." Indeed, it was for his actions here that Cleburne became known as the "Stonewall of the West," in reference to Brigadier General Thomas J. Jackson's defiant stand at the First Battle of Bull Run (July 21, 1861).

SPENCER C. TUCKER

See also

Bragg, Braxton; Bull Run, First Battle of; Chattanooga Campaign; Cleburne, Patrick Ronayne; Cracker Line Operation; Grant, Ulysses Simpson; Hooker, Joseph; Jackson, Thomas Jonathan; Lookout Mountain, Battle of; Missionary Ridge, Battle of; Orchard Knob, Battle of; Thanks of Congress, U.S. and CSA; Thomas, George Henry; Wood, Thomas John

Further Reading

Cozzens, Peter. *The Shipwreck of Their Hopes: The Battles for Chattanooga*. Urbana: University of Illinois Press, 1994.
Woodworth, Steven. *Six Armies in Tennessee: The Chickamauga and Chattanooga Campaigns*. New York: Bison Books, 1998.

Rio Grande Campaign

Start Date: November 2, 1863
End Date: June 29, 1864

Union military campaign aimed at occupying key points along the Rio Grande and the Texas coast of the Gulf of Mexico. Texas shared a long border with the officially neutral nation of Mexico. Although Mexican president Benito Juárez favored the Union and sought to maintain neutrality, political opponents in northern Mexico, particularly Santiago Vidaurri, governor of Tampaulipas, favored the Confederacy and encouraged trade with Texas across the Rio Grande. The French intervention in Mexico, which began in December 1861 and by 1863 had driven Juárez from power, fostered a decidedly friendlier environment for Confederate interests. This provided a much-needed outlet for Texas cotton traded with Mexico and also sent from there to Europe in exchange for foreign-manufactured goods, including weapons and other military material.

Unable to blockade Mexico, the Lincoln administration ordered Major General Nathaniel P. Banks, commander of the Department of the Gulf, to interdict trade between Texas and Mexico. Also of concern to the Union was the fear that France might enter the war in support of the Confederacy.

On November 2, 1863, 6,000 men of the Union XIII Corps commanded by Major General Napoleon Dana arrived at the Texas barrier island of Brazos Santiago near the mouth of the Rio Grande. Later that month, Union forces occupied Brownsville, some 20 miles upriver, and by January 1864 they had pushed up the Gulf Coast to Corpus Christi, Matagorda Island, Indianola, and Port Lavaca. In addition to interdicting trade with Mexico, Banks saw these moves as a precursor to the invasion of the Texas interior. A provisional Union government was established in Brownsville under Brigadier General Andrew J. Hamilton, and Confederate deserters and other pro-Union citizens were recruited into the 1st and 2nd Texas Cavalry Regiments (Union). Meanwhile, Dana was replaced by Major General Francis Herron in command of U.S. forces in the region. The occupation forces soon became restive, however, and Texans, especially cotton growers and brokers, began to demand that Confederate authorities push U.S. forces out of the region so that illicit trade could resume.

In early June 1864, Confederate colonel John S. "Rip" Ford led a motley group of about 1,300 men against Union forces in and around Brownsville. By this time, Banks had withdrawn more than half of the Union troops in southern Texas in preparation for the Red River Campaign (March 10–May 22, 1864). Unable to stop Confederate advances against Brownsville, Union troops vacated that city on June 29. By the end of September, only about 950 Union troops remained at Brazos Santiago. Although a militarily dubious Union effort, the Rio Grande Campaign nevertheless disrupted the cotton trade with Mexico for a time.

TIMOTHY J. DEMY

See also

Banks, Nathaniel Prentice; Cotton; Cotton Diplomacy; Dana, Napoleon Jackson Tecumseh; Hamilton, Andrew Jackson; Herron, Francis Jay; Red River Campaign; Texas

Further Reading

Daddysman, James W. *The Matamoros Trade: Confederate Commerce, Diplomacy, and Intrigue.* Newark: University of Delaware Press, 1984.

Townsend, Stephen A. *The Yankee Invasion of Texas.* College Station: Texas A&M University Press, 2006.

Riots, CSA

Civil unrest occurred with some frequency in the Confederacy and came mostly from Southern women because of severe shortages of and inflated prices for everyday necessities of life. Beginning in mid-1862, the civilian population of the South, particularly those living in cities and towns, began to suffer from food and clothing shortages because of rampant speculation and governmental impressment. At the same time, the Confederate Congress enacted a conscription law that allowed exemptions and substitutions for wealthier people, particularly the planter class, while poor men were drafted in large numbers.

Many families of draftees were left to fend for themselves in a political and economic system that was weighted heavily against them. Wives and mothers began writing letters to congressmen and state legislators in a vain attempt to redress these difficulties. Soon many families faced destitution and starvation, while plantation owners and merchants continued to live well and made money by speculating on the prices of bacon, flour, corn, and yarn.

As early as July 1861, women in New Orleans rioted over food shortages; a year later, the same types of disturbances occurred in Bartow County, Georgia, particularly in the town of Cartersville. The number of riots increased in 1863, with demonstrations in Richmond and Petersburg, Virginia, and High Point, Salisbury, Raleigh, and Boone, North Carolina. In Salisbury, 50 women with axes and hatchets attacked the shops of speculators and confiscated 13 barrels of flour, 1 barrel of molasses, 2 sacks of salt, and $20 in cash. In the Richmond Bread Riot on April 2, the biggest riot of the war in the South, women and men rampaged through the business district, destroying 20 stores. Virginia governor John Letcher called out the Public Guard, a state security force, and had 45 women and 10 men arrested. Twelve women and 6 men were ultimately convicted of public disorder. Some were fined, while others were sentenced to prison.

Rioting continued into 1864, with women marching through Savannah, Georgia, in April, seizing bacon, sugar, flour, rice, and salt. Three of the women were arrested, but they were subsequently released when no one would press charges against them. Two merchants demanded that the city council compensate them for $450 worth of stolen bacon, but their demand went unmet. Riots also occurred in Alabama, North Carolina, Virginia, and Texas. In February 1865, 50 soldiers' wives in Miller County, Georgia, stormed the county seat of Colquitt and stole 50 sacks of government-owned corn. The war ended with many women and children destitute and hungry, not because of Union army depredations but because of their own government's frequent impressments and indifference to the massive speculation in foodstuffs by merchants and planters.

PAUL DAVID NELSON

See also

Civil Liberties, CSA; Class Conflict, North and South; Commutation; Conscription, CSA; Home Front, Confederate; Tax-in-Kind

Further Reading

Bynum, Victoria E. *Unruly Women: The Politics of Social and Sexual Control in the Old South.* Chapel Hill: University of North Carolina Press, 1992.

Chesson, Michael B. "Harlots or Heroines? A New Look at the Richmond Bread Riot." *Virginia Magazine of History and Biography* 92 (1984): 131–175.

McPherson, James M. *Battle Cry of Freedom: The Civil War Era.* New York: Oxford University Press, 1988.

Riots, U.S.

During 1862 and 1863, civil unrest, largely from federal attempts to impose conscription, precipitated numerous outbreaks of violence in the United States. Other factors such as war weariness, economic inequalities, and racism also contributed to citizens' anger. The first acts of violence were in response to Congress's passage of the Militia Act of July 17, 1862, which enrolled men between the ages of 18 and 45 in state militias and allowed the president to call militias to federal service for a period of nine months. Mobs in several states rioted against state militia drafts, with the most serious occurring in Port Washington, Wisconsin, on October 10, 1862. There a mob attacked the courthouse, destroying draft records. They also demolished the homes of government officials. Some 600 soldiers were called out to restore order.

Much more serious rioting resulted in 1863 after Congress on March 3 enacted a national conscription law. On March 6 in Detroit, a civil disturbance occurred that resulted in many deaths and $20,000 in property damage. The worst riots occurred in New York City, where during July 13–17 as many as 2,000 people may have been killed while another 2,000–8,000 were injured. The city also sustained $2 million in property damage. Troops from Pennsylvania and West Point had to be called in to suppress the rioting. In Boston on July 14, 1863, 3 people were killed when a mob attacked the federal armory. Other disturbances took place in Wooster, Ohio; Green Bay, Wisconsin; Portsmouth, New Hampshire; Hartford, Connecticut; and Troy, New York.

Attempts to impose a draft had come at a time when Union armies had suffered a series of serious defeats coupled with mounting casualties. The fact that volunteers no longer filled the ranks was evidence of waning support for the war effort. Also, the draft law exempted anyone who could pay a $300 commutation fee or provide a substitute. Poor farmers, urban laborers, and newly arrived immigrants, already suffering from inflated prices and low wages, denounced the law as a flagrant example of class bias. Moreover, corrupt recruiting officials often cooperated with employers to keep workers from joining unions. Racial issues aggravated all of these factors. Many Northerners despised the 1863 Emancipation Proclamation, believing it to be the Republicans' first step toward black equality. Draft riots, especially in Detroit and New York, quickly became pillaging expeditions against African American neighborhoods that resulted in numerous murders and much property damage.

Despite Confederate hopes that the riots would bring the Union war effort to its knees, the Union soldiered on. Many Northern cities began paying commutation fees for its poor citizens, and in March 1864 Congress finally ended the practice altogether. At the end of the war Northern morale was unshaken, and the Union Army numbered more than 1 million men.

PAUL DAVID NELSON

See also

Civil Liberties, U.S.; Class Conflict, North and South; Commutation; Conscription, U.S.; Emancipation Proclamation; New York City Draft Riots

Further Reading

Gallman, J. Matthew. *The North Fights the Civil War: The Home Front.* Chicago: I. R. Dee, 1994.

Geary, James W. *We Need Men: The Union Draft in the Civil War.* DeKalb: Northern Illinois University Press, 1991.

McPherson, James M. *Battle Cry of Freedom: The Civil War Era.* New York: Oxford University Press, 1988.

Ripley, James Wolfe

Birth Date: December 10, 1794
Death Date: March 16, 1870

Union officer. James Wolfe Ripley was born in Windham County, Connecticut, on December 10, 1794, and graduated from the U.S. Military Academy, West Point, in 1814. Commissioned a second lieutenant of artillery, he was assigned to the defense of Sackets Harbor, New York, during the War of 1812. Ripley took part in Major General Andrew Jackson's invasion of Florida and actions of the First Seminole War (1817–1818). Promoted to captain in 1832, he was transferred to the new Ordnance Department. During 1832–1833, Ripley commanded Union forces at Fort Sumter in Charleston Harbor during the South Carolina Nullification Crisis.

Promoted to major in 1838, Ripley was assigned command of the Springfield (Massachusetts) Arsenal in 1841. He served in Mexico during the Mexican-American War (1846–1848) and was brevetted lieutenant colonel in 1848. Returning to the Springfield Arsenal afterward, in 1854 he took command of the Watertown (Massachusetts) Arsenal.

With the beginning of the Civil War, Ripley was promoted to colonel on April 23, 1861, and named chief of ordnance. He was brevetted brigadier general in the regular army on July 2 and promoted to that rank on August 3. Ripley performed effectively in the chaotic early days of the war, reorganizing his department administratively and ordering the conversion of a number of smoothbore guns to rifled pieces as well as purchasing new Parrott rifled guns from the West Point Foundry.

Ripley was, however, much criticized at the time and by historians since for his refusal to purchase rifled muskets for the infantry. He based this decision on the large number of smoothbore weapons in the federal arsenals and his belief that these could be converted to rifled pieces, which turned out to be incorrect. He also steadfastly refused to authorize the purchase of new breech-loading and repeating rifles. His resistance to change earned him the nickname "Ripley van Winkle." Ripley held that the greater firepower of the breech-loading repeaters would lead to poor fire discipline and wastage of ammunition. Individual Union units subsequently raised their own funds and purchased repeating rifles privately, although problems did develop over adequate ammunition stocks.

After frequent clashes with President Abraham Lincoln and Secretary of War Edwin M. Stanton, Ripley was replaced as head of ordnance by Colonel George D. Ramsay on September 1, 1863, and was named inspector of New England coastal fortifications. In 1865 Ripley was brevetted a regular army major general. He subsequently served as inspector of government armaments. Ripley died in Hartford, Connecticut, on March 16, 1870.

SPENCER C. TUCKER

See also

Lincoln, Abraham; Parrott Gun; Ramsay, George Douglas; Spencer Repeating Rifle and Carbine; Stanton, Edwin McMasters

Further Reading

Ripley, Warren. *Artillery and Ammunition of the American Civil War*. New York: Van Nostrand Reinhold, 1970.

Tate, Thomas K. *General James Wolfe Ripley, Chief of Ordnance: Answers to His Critics*. Charleston, SC: BookSurge, 2008.

Ripley, Roswell Sabine
Birth Date: March 14, 1823
Death Date: March 29, 1887

Confederate officer. Born in Worthington, Ohio, on March 14, 1823, Roswell Sabine Ripley was the nephew of future Union general James W. Ripley. Roswell Ripley graduated from the U.S. Military Academy, West Point, in 1843 and was assigned to the artillery. Promoted to first lieutenant on March 3, 1847, he was twice brevetted for service during the Mexican-American War (1846–1848): to captain for the Battle of Cerro Gordo and to major for the Battle of Chapultepec. Ripley published a two-volume history, *The War with Mexico,* in 1849. Marrying into a prominent Charleston, South Carolina, family in 1852, he resigned his commission on March 2, 1853, and settled in Charleston, where he became a businessman. During 1860–1861, Ripley was a major in the state militia.

Promoted to lieutenant colonel of artillery in the South Carolina Militia on January 28, 1861, Ripley had charge of artillery batteries first at Fort Moultrie, following its evacuation by Union forces, and then on Sullivan's Island. He participated in the bombardment of Fort Sumter and later commanded the post. In May 1861 Ripley received a commission as a lieutenant colonel of artillery in the Confederate Army, and on August 15 he was promoted to brigadier general and commanded at Charleston until the arrival of Major General John C. Pemberton in 1862. Thereafter Ripley headed a succession of districts in South Carolina.

Although regarded as a competent officer, Ripley reportedly constantly feuded with his superiors and subordinates, and Pemberton had him transferred to the Army of Northern Virginia. In July 1862 Ripley assumed command of the 5th Brigade in Daniel H. Hill's division during the Peninsula Campaign (March–July 1862) and fought in the Seven Days' Campaign (June 25–July 1, 1862). During the Battle of Antietam (September 17, 1862), Ripley was severely wounded in the neck. Again assigned to duty in South Carolina on his recovery, Ripley successfully directed the defenses of Charleston but again tangled with superiors and subordinates. In February 1865 he was ordered to join General Joseph E. Johnston's Army of Tennessee in North Carolina to command a division in I Corps, arriving in time to take part in the Battle of Bentonville (March 19–21).

After the war Ripley traveled to Britain, where he engaged in a manufacturing enterprise that failed, and then to France. Relocating to Charleston in 1868, he spent considerable time in New York City, where he died on March 29, 1887.

SPENCER C. TUCKER

See also
Antietam, Battle of; Bentonville, Battle of; Hill, Daniel Harvey; Johnston, Joseph Eggleston; Pemberton, John Clifford; Peninsula Campaign; Ripley, James Wolfe; Seven Days' Campaign

Further Reading
Eicher, John H., and David J. Eicher. *Civil War High Commands.* Stanford, CA: Stanford University Press, 2001.
Warner, Ezra J. *Generals in Gray: Lives of the Confederate Commanders.* Baton Rouge: Louisiana State University Press, 2006.
Wise, Stephen R. *Gate of Hell.* Columbia: University of South Carolina Press, 1994.

River Defense Fleet

Two separate lightly armed and poorly armored gunboat squadrons on the Mississippi River. The first River Defense Fleet consisted of six small converted river tugs mounting a total of seven guns and fitted with iron-reinforced prows for ramming, all under the command of Confederate Navy captain John A. Stephenson. The gunboats were the *Defense, General Breckinridge, General Lovell, Resolute, Stonewall Jackson,* and *Warrior.* All six were lost in the defeat of Confederate forces below New Orleans on April 24, 1862, and during the subsequent Union capture of the Crescent City.

The second River Defense Fleet consisted of eight gunboats constructed with double pine bulkheads bolted together and stuffed with compressed cotton. The so-called cottonclad gunboats of the River Defense Fleet mounted only one or two guns each but were somewhat faster and more agile than their Union counterparts. A number also had reinforced bows of oak and iron, enabling them to act as rams. Former riverboat captains James E. Montgomery and J. H. Townsend commanded the River Defense Fleet. The crews came from civilian steamboats and fought on the condition that they would not be subject to the orders of Confederate Navy officers.

Five gunboats of the River Defense Fleet attacked the Union flotilla commanded by Flag Officer Andrew H. Foote above Fort Pillow on the morning of April 14, 1862, but soon withdrew to the protection of Fort Pillow's batteries. On May 8, three of the rams, the *General Sumter, General Bragg,* and *General Earl Van Dorn,* made for the area where Union

mortar boats shelling Fort Pillow were usually positioned, but these had been moved shortly before and were now protected by the Union ironclads *Cairo, Cincinnati,* and *Mound City.* Again the Confederate gunboats were soon in precipitous retreat, pursued for a time by the Union ships.

On the morning of May 10, however, Montgomery led an attack by his eight gunboats against the Union flotilla, now commanded by Flag Officer Charles H. Davis. The Confederates hoped to capture or destroy the single mortar boat shelling Fort Pillow and its covering Union gunboat. This attack caught the Union squadron by surprise, and in the ensuing Battle of Plum Point Bend, the Confederate gunboats rammed and holed the ironclad *Cincinnati,* which sank along the shore in shallow water. The other Union gunboats, their steam at last up, then came up. The *Mound City* was also rammed, but its captain was able to ground his vessel to prevent it from sinking. The arrival of the more powerful Union ships, however, caused Montgomery to signal a retirement. Union rifled rounds shattered the boilers of the *General Sumter,* the *Colonel Lovell,* and the *General Earl Van Dorn,* which all suffered heavy casualties but managed to escape. Apart from the heavy personnel losses, the Southerners had won a tactical victory, temporarily disabling two much more powerful Union gunboats, which were subsequently refloated and taken back to Mound City for repairs.

With the evacuation of Fort Pillow on June 4, the River Defense Fleet withdrew to Memphis, where it was attacked on June 6 by Davis's flotilla as well as the newly arrived Union Ellet rams. Of the eight Confederate gunboats in the battle (the *General Bragg, General Sterling Price, General Earl Van Dorn, General Sumter, General Thompson, General Beauregard, Colonel Lovell,* and *Little Rebel*), only the *General Earl Van Dorn* managed to escape to Vicksburg.

SPENCER C. TUCKER

See also
Cairo, USS; Davis, Charles Henry; Foote, Andrew Hull; Fort Pillow, Tennessee, Capture of; Laird Rams; Memphis, Battle of; Montgomery, James; New Orleans Campaign; Plum Point Bend, Battle of

Further Reading
Milligan, John D. *Gunboats down the Mississippi.* Annapolis, MD: Naval Institute Press, 1965.
Slagle, Jay. *Ironclad Captain: Seth Ledyard Phelps and the U.S. Navy, 1841–1864.* Kent, OH: Kent State University Press, 1996.
Tucker, Spencer C. *Blue and Gray Navies: The Civil War Afloat.* Annapolis, MD: Naval Institute Press, 2006.

Riverine Warfare

Operations conducted on rivers and associated waterways. Prior to the Civil War, the U.S. Navy concentrated on fighting a European foe on the high seas, with no thought of the need to operate on the country's myriad inland rivers and smaller streams. With the beginning of the Civil War, however, Union naval strategy rapidly evolved into a twofold action of blockading Southern commercial ports and working in conjunction with the army on inland waters. At the start of the war, however, none of the navy's warships in home waters could operate easily in nontidal rivers. Innovation was required.

Secretary of the Navy Gideon Welles at first concentrated on building the blockading fleet and all but ignored the pressing issue of a huge internal boundary that stretched along the Ohio River to the Mississippi River and potentially to beyond St. Louis, Missouri. The Union Army initially had responsibility for handling inland riverine, or brown-water, issues.

The solution to prosecuting the naval war, even before vessels could be obtained, was contained in a course of action outlined by Union general in chief Brevet Lieutenant General Winfield Scott. What came to be known as the Anaconda Plan called for a naval blockade to starve the South from outside assistance. At the same time, the internal waterways that bisected the South would be secured and then used as an invasion path for large trained Union ground forces. The problem was that not enough ships existed for the first part, and there were none for the second; it took time to secure these.

Subjugation of inland or brown-water streams was a difficult task. Because the navy had little presence on inland waters except the Great Lakes, it was expected that the new warships would be under army control. New types of ships were also required. They had to be capable of mounting large guns but have shallow drafts and be sufficiently narrow to navigate twisting streams. The first warships were paid for and built by the army, with naval officers sent west to supervise their construction. These vessels did not fully pass to navy control until October 1862.

Gideon Welles assigned Commander John Rodgers to assist the army in this effort; like the other officers of the navy he had no experience in riverine warfare. His brief command in 1861 saw the purchase and conversion of 3 so-called timberclads, designed to protect against small arms fire only. These were the *Tyler, Lexington,* and *Conestoga.* At the same time, James Buchanan Eads built 7 innovative ironclads of the City class (Cairo class) at St. Louis, Missouri, and Mound City, Illinois. These 10 warships formed the initial nucleus of the brown-water navy. They were grouped into the Western Gunboat Flotilla. Rodgers did not get on well with imperious commander of the army's Western Department Major General John C. Frémont, and on Frémont's insistence Rodgers was recalled, replaced by Flag Officer Andrew Hull Foote. Soon Foote's warships were patrolling the larger rivers of the upper South, bombarding shore installations, and operating in conjunction with army forces.

The first action involving the squadron occurred in Missouri at the Battle of Belmont (November 7, 1861), when the *Tyler* and *Lexington* supported a landing by Brigadier General Ulysses S. Grant. Although the battle had little overall consequence, it clearly demonstrated the important role that the ships could play in supporting operations ashore. Indeed, the ship guns held the reinforcing Confederates at bay long enough for Grant's men to be brought off. Gunboats also proved important in carrying out reconnaissance deep into Confederate territory. One of the forays by the timberclad *Conestoga* under Lieutenant Seth Ledyard Phelps up the Tennessee and Cumberland Rivers discovered two large Confederate forts guarding the approaches. Fort Henry on the Tennessee River and Fort Donelson on the Cumberland River became major targets for Union forces. In the campaign to take these forts, Grant and Foote worked closely together.

The first Union target was Fort Henry. Finally securing the approval of Frémont's successor, commander of the newly formed Department of the Missouri Major General Henry W. Halleck, Grant and Foote moved in early February 1862 up the Tennessee to within striking distance of Fort Henry. There the troops debarked. With the arrival of the troops by land delayed by the poor state of the roads caused by recent heavy rains, Foote proceeded alone, attacking on February 6 and taking the poorly sited Fort Henry with four ironclads and two timberclads.

Following the capture of Fort Henry, Grant's forces moved overland to Fort Donelson, while Foote traveled there by water. Fort Donelson was situated on much higher ground. As Grant worked to contain the Confederates from the land side, Foote sought to replicate his success at Fort Henry. On February 14 Foote attacked in the same formation of four ironclads followed by two timberclads. But Fort Donelson's upper battery was 120 feet above the river, and shots from its guns struck the ironclads' sloping sides at right angles. Three of the four ironclads were disabled and drifted downstream, the flotilla sustaining 11 men killed and 43 wounded, including Foote. Despite this setback, the combination of Union naval forces and increasing land forces proved irresistible, and Fort Donelson surrendered on February 16. The capture of Forts Henry and Donelson represented the first significant Union victory in the western theater and was widely celebrated in the North. The success was also a strong impetus for additional riverine naval construction.

The timberclads *Tyler* and *Lexington* provided invaluable assistance to Grant in the Battle of Shiloh (April 6–7, 1862). At Pittsburg Landing, they provided vital close-in gunfire support to Grant's hard-pressed forces. Meanwhile, Foote was back in action with most of his ships on the upper Mississippi. The Confederates had fortified Columbus, Kentucky, and Island No. 10. The loss of Forts Henry and Donelson compromised Columbus, and the Confederates concentrated on Island No. 10, near New Madrid, Missouri.

Foote moved against the island fort in March 1862, bringing there 9 gunboats and 10 mortar boats. This time Foote worked with Brigadier General John Pope's Army of the Mississippi, which had moved overland to New Madrid downstream from Island No. 10. After ineffective long-range shelling of Island No. 10 and on Pope's urging, Foote ran 2 gunboats past the fortress at night. These ships were able to control the river and allow Pope's men to pass over to the other side of the Mississippi, cutting off Island No. 10 and forcing its surrender on April 7, 1862.

The next target was Fort Pillow. Captain Charles H. Davis replaced the ailing Foote. Meanwhile, the bulk of Pope's forces were withdrawn for service elsewhere. The day after Davis took command, the Confederates struck in the first engagement of the war between naval squadrons. Eight gunboats of the Confederate River Defense Fleet attempted to cut out a Union mortar boat and its protecting ironclad. In the Battle of Plum Point Bend (May 10, 1862), two Union ironclads, the *Cincinnati* and *Mound City,* were rammed and rendered hors de combat, while several Confederate gunboats were badly damaged.

When the Confederates were forced to abandon Fort Pillow, Davis moved downriver against Memphis. Aided by the arrival of the ships of Colonel Charles Ellet's army Ram Fleet, the Union victory was complete. In the Battle of Memphis (June 6, 1862), of the eight Confederate warships involved, all were sunk or captured except one that escaped to Vicksburg.

In October 1862 Rear Admiral David D. Porter took command of the flotilla, now renamed the Mississippi Squadron. Under Porter, the squadron considerably expanded in size, with new ships added in the form of lightly armored tinclads and river monitor ironclads. Porter worked well with both Grant and Major General William T. Sherman. This cooperation was essential in Union operations that led to the surrender of Vicksburg in July 1863.

At the same time, Flag Officer David G. Farragut, commander of the navy's West Gulf Blockading Squadron, enjoyed success on the lower Mississippi. In April 1862 he forced his way past Forts Jackson and St. Philip guarding the southern river approach to New Orleans and took the surrender of the Crescent City in another heavy blow to the South.

The western theater also saw the creation of the Mississippi Marine Brigade, organized in 1863 to combat Confederate guerrilla operations along the Mississippi River and its tributaries. In one of the U.S. military's first experiments in combined-arms operations, the brigade utilized the ships of the U.S. Army's Ram Fleet, supplemented by transports to carry infantry, cavalry, and even artillery. Ineffective and insubordinate leadership and a poor record of service ashore led to the unit's disbandment in August 1864.

The largest riverine operation of the war, the Red River Campaign (March 10–May 22, 1864) conducted by Porter and Major General Nathaniel P. Banks, involved a combined land and naval assault up Louisiana's Red River that was designed to secure Shreveport and penetrate eastern Texas. The expedition proved to be an abject failure, thanks to poor army-navy cooperation, Banks's ineptitude, and effective Confederate leadership. Stopping short of Shreveport, Banks withdrew. Meanwhile, rapidly falling water levels in the Red threatened to strand numerous Union warships above the Alexandria rapids. Ultimately they were gotten free, thanks to the construction of a coffer dam. Still, the campaign was nothing short of a fiasco.

There were also numerous but less publicized Union riverine operations in the eastern theater, where Union ships assisted Major General George B. McClellan's ill-fated Peninsula Campaign (March–July 1862) in Virginia. Union Navy control of much of the James River below Richmond was also of great importance to Grant during the Petersburg Campaign (June 15, 1864–April 3, 1865) and the Appomattox Campaign (April 2–9, 1865). Clearly, Union riverine operations played a key role in the Northern victory.

GARY D. JOINER AND SPENCER C. TUCKER

See also

Capture of; Grant, Ulysses Simpson; Ironclads, Union; Island No. 10, Battle of; Memphis, Battle of; Mississippi Marine Brigade; Mississippi River; Mississippi Squadron, U.S. Navy; Mortar Boats; New Orleans Campaign; Phelps, Seth Ledyard; Phelps's Raid up the Tennessee River; Plum Point Bend, Battle of; Pope, John; Porter, David Dixon; Ram Fleet, U.S.; Red River Campaign; River Defense Fleet; Rodgers, John, Jr.; Shiloh, Battle of; Timberclads; Tinclads; Vicksburg Campaign, Second; Welles, Gideon

Further Reading

Johnson, Robert Erwin. *Rear Admiral John Rodgers, 1812–1882.* Annapolis, MD: U.S. Naval Institute, 1967.

Joiner, Gary. *Mr. Lincoln's Brown Water Navy: The Mississippi Squadron.* Lanham, MD: Rowman and Littlefield, 2007.

Reed, Rowena. *Combined Operations in the Civil War.* Annapolis, MD: Naval Institute Press, 1978.

Shea, William L., and Terrence J. Winschel. *Vicksburg Is the Key: The Struggle for the Mississippi River.* Lincoln: University of Nebraska Press, 2003.

Simson, Jay W. *Naval Strategies of the Civil War: Confederate Innovations and Federal Opportunism.* Nashville: Cumberland House, 2001.

Symonds, Craig L., ed. *Union Combined Operations in the Civil War.* New York: Fordham University Press, 2010.

Tucker, Spencer C. *Andrew Foote: Civil War Admiral on Western Waters.* Annapolis, MD: Naval Institute Press, 2000.

Tucker, Spencer C. *Blue & Gray Navies: The Civil War Afloat.* Annapolis, MD: Naval Institute Press, 2006.

West, Richard S., Jr. *The Second Admiral: A Life of David Dixon Porter.* New York: Coward-McCann, 1937.

oversaw the construction of numerous earthworks and field fortifications on the Virginia Peninsula. Beginning in mid-1862, he was for a time acting chief engineer for the Confederacy. In October 1862, he was advanced to major and named assistant to the chief engineer. Promoted to lieutenant colonel in the summer of 1863, Rives frequently served as acting chief engineer in the absence of his superior, Major General Jeremy Francis Gilmer. Rives was advanced to colonel in the spring of 1864 and supervised the construction of numerous permanent and temporary bridges in Virginia before the Civil War ended in April 1865.

Postbellum, Rives worked as an engineer or executive for a number of railroads in the South. In the 1890s he consulted with the government of Colombia to erect a transisthmian railroad and a canal in Panama that would link the Pacific and Atlantic Oceans. Rives died on February 27, 1903, at his family's estate—Castle Hill—near Charlottesville, Virginia.

PAUL G. PIERPAOLI JR.

See also

Engineers; Gilmer, Jeremy Francis

Further Reading

Jackson, Harry L. *First Regiment, Engineer Troops, P.A.C.S.: Robert E. Lee's Combat Engineers.* Louisa, VA: R. A. E. Design and Publications, 1998.

Martin, First Lieutenant Shaun. "Confederate Engineers in the American Civil War." *Engineer: The Professional Bulletin for Army Engineers* 30 (2000): 42–46.

Rives, Alfred Landon

Birth Date: March 25, 1830
Death Date: February 27, 1903

Confederate officer. Alfred Landon Rives was born on March 25, 1830, in Paris, France, while his father was U.S. minister to France. Rives attended the Virginia Military Institute for two years and then the University of Virginia but did not graduate from either school. He then studied mathematics at the École des Ponts et Chausées in France, graduating in 1854. Upon his return to the United States, Rives worked for the Virginia Midland Railway. He later joined the U.S. Corps of Engineers as a civilian and was assistant engineer of the U.S. Capitol and Post Office buildings. In the late 1850s, he supervised the construction of the Cabin John Bridge over the Potomac River.

In April 1861, Rives was commissioned a captain in the Confederate Engineering Bureau. Based in Williamsburg, he

Rives, William Cabell

Birth Date: May 4, 1793
Death Date: April 25, 1868

Confederate congressman. William Cabell Rives was born on May 4, 1793, in Amherst County, Virginia. He attended Hamden-Sydney College before graduating from the College of William and Mary in 1809. He subsequently studied law under Thomas Jefferson and was admitted to the bar in 1814. After serving in the Virginia House of Delegates (1817–1820, 1822–1823), Rives gained national prominence as a member of the U.S. House of Representatives (1823–1829), minister to France (1829–1832, 1849–1853), and U.S. senator (1832–1834, 1836–1839, 1841–1845).

Although Rives owned 104 slaves, he was a staunch Unionist. Two factors shaped his Unionism: the influence of James Madison and the political turmoil that Rives witnessed firsthand during the French Revolution of 1848. In the 1860 presidential election, Rives supported the Constitutional Union Party, believing that adherence to the U.S. Constitution and enforcement of federal laws would prevent secession. Throughout the winter of 1860–1861, he sought protection for Southern rights within the Union. In January 1861 Rives, convinced that a national conference could stop the spread of secession to the border states, persuaded the Virginia legislature to propose the Washington Peace Conference to resolve the growing crisis. At that meeting, Rives offered no solutions but implored Northern Republicans to accept the conference's final report, which consisted of resolutions similar to the Crittenden Compromise proposals. Congress refused to consider it.

Rives then served as a delegate at the Virginia Secession Convention. There he insisted that the Constitution offered adequate protection of Southern rights but publicly warned that Virginia would leave the Union if the federal government resorted to coercion against the seceded states. He blocked acceptance of an ordinance of secession until the bombardment of Fort Sumter in April 1861. President Abraham Lincoln's subsequent call for troops ended all hope of keeping Virginia in the Union.

Rives served in the Provisional Confederate Congress and the first regular Confederate Congress until poor health forced him to resign in 1862. He died at his plantation, Castle Hill, near Charlottesville, on April 25, 1868.

DEAN FAFOUTIS

See also

Constitutional Union Party; Crittenden Compromise; Secession; Virginia; Washington Peace Conference

Further Reading

McCoy, Drew R. "Legacy: The Strange Career of William Cabell Rives." *The Last of the Fathers: James Madison and the Republican Legacy*, 323–369. New York: Cambridge University Press, 1989.
Sowle, Patrick. "The Trials of a Virginia Unionist: William Cabell Rives and the Secession Crisis, 1860–1861." *Virginia Magazine of History and Biography* 80 (January 1972): 3–20.

Roane, John Seldon

Birth Date: January 8, 1817
Death Date: April 8, 1867

Confederate officer. John Seldon Roane was born in Lebanon, Tennessee, on January 8, 1817, into a politically prominent family; his uncle, Archibald Roane, was governor of Tennessee from 1801 to 1803. After education in a local school, John Roane attended Cumberland College in Princeton, Kentucky. He moved to Pine Bluff, Arkansas, in 1837 and studied law under his older brother, Samuel Calhoun Roane. In 1842 John Roane was elected to the Arkansas General Assembly. Reelected in 1844, he was then chosen its Speaker.

With the beginning of the Mexican-American War (1846–1848), Roane raised a company of mounted infantry from Van Buren. The company became part of the 1st Arkansas Mounted Rifles, of which Roane was elected lieutenant colonel. Roane fought with the regiment in the Battle of Buena Vista in February 1847. The unit's poor performance became a matter of some controversy, leading that summer to a duel between Roane and one of the regiment's captains (and a future Confederate general), Albert Pike, although neither man was hurt.

Roane returned to Pine Bluff after the war, busying himself with his law practice and overseeing a newly acquired plantation, which by 1860 had 56 slaves. Elected governor of Arkansas as a Democrat in March 1849, Roane served until November 1852. As governor, he supported internal improvements, the establishment of a state college, and the recruitment of immigrants to the state. At loggerheads with the legislature over the means to deal with a serious state financial crisis occasioned by bank failures, he refused to stand for reelection.

Although a staunch supporter of the institution of slavery and states' rights, Roane opposed secession and, despite the beginning of the Civil War, did not enter Confederate service for almost a year. Commissioned a brigadier general on March 20, 1862, he was the de facto commander of all Confederate forces in Arkansas until the arrival there early that summer of Major General Thomas C. Hindman. Roane commanded a brigade in the Battle of Prairie Grove (December 7, 1862) and then served in garrison and detached duties in Arkansas, Louisiana, and Texas until the end of the war. Apparently he had little aptitude for military service and was not well liked by either his superiors or his men. Paroled at Shreveport on June 11, 1865, Roane returned to Pine Bluff, where he died on April 8, 1867.

SPENCER C. TUCKER

See also

Arkansas; Hindman, Thomas Carmichael; Pike, Albert; Prairie Grove, Battle of

Further Reading

DeBlack, Thomas A. *With Fire and Sword: Arkansas, 1861–1874.* Fayetteville: University of Arkansas Press, 2003.
Donovan, Timothy P., Willard B. Gatewood Jr., and Jeannie M. Whayne, eds. *The Governors of Arkansas: Essays in Political Biography.* 2nd ed. Fayetteville: University of Arkansas Press, 1995.

Roanoke Island, Battle of

Start Date: February 7, 1862
End Date: February 8, 1862

Successful Union amphibious operation. Union possession of the Hatteras Island forts offered a base for further amphibious operations against eastern North Carolina. West of the Outer Banks were six sounds, the two largest being Pamlico and Albemarle. The Confederacy had no effective means of preventing Union ships from operating on these sounds or against a number of major cities in the region.

Roanoke Island lies at the northern end of Pamlico Sound. The island controlled passage between Pamlico Sound to the south and Albemarle Sound to the north and west. Roanoke Island also dominated access to the southern termini of the Dismal Swamp Canal and the Albemarle and Chesapeake Canal, both of which reached to Norfolk, Virginia. Union forces already controlled Pamlico Sound, and securing Roanoke Island would give them access to Albemarle Sound, with its rivers leading into interior North Carolina over which railroads ran north on bridges to Norfolk. In Union hands, troops might strike from Roanoke Island against Norfolk, while shallow-draft Union warships could use the sound as an anchorage.

Flag Officer Louis M. Goldsborough, commanding the North Atlantic Blockading Squadron, and Army brigadier general Ambrose Burnside commanded the Roanoke Island operation. Sometimes known as the Burnside Expedition, it departed Hampton Roads in mid-January. Because of the shallow water in which they would have to operate, Goldsborough's 20 ships were all converted tugs, river steamers, and ferry boats. Most were lightly armed. Goldsborough's ships provided protection for some 70 transports carrying Burnside's 12,000 troops and their supplies. Once all of the ships were in position, the navy was to shell the shore installations and engage any hostile warships as well as provide fire support once the troops were ashore.

After several delays, on the morning of February 7 the flotilla got under way. With the warships leading, the flotilla proceeded through the narrow channel west of the southern tip of Roanoke Island and entered Croatan Sound, which in the best of conditions was only 7.5 feet deep.

Although they were well aware of the Union preparations, Confederate authorities had few warships, guns, or troops available. Former Virginia governor and now Confederate brigadier general Henry A. Wise commanded Roanoke Island with two North Carolina regiments totaling 1,435 men. Another 800 Confederates were at Nags Head.

Roanoke Island contained five forts with a total of 30 guns. The largest, Fort Huger on Weir's Point, mounted 12 guns but was at the narrowest northern part of Croatan Sound between the island and the mainland and thus was beyond the range of the proposed Union landing site. The chief concern to the Federals was Fort Bartow, with 9 guns, located at Pork Point. Another fort, Fort Forrest, with 8 guns, lay directly across the sound from Pork Point. Wise had ordered a double line of piles placed in the two miles of water between these two forts, and on the Union approach, the Confederates sank a number of small vessels to strengthen this barrier. Behind it, Flag Officer William D. Lynch had seven small steamers with a total of only 8 guns.

On the morning of February 7, the Union ships moved slowly up Croatan Sound, and the Union transports prepared to disembark their troops at Ashby's Harbor, several miles south of the main Confederate defenses. Goldsborough ordered his 19 gunboats forward to shell the Confederate forts and ships. By noon, the firing became general. The Confederate forts north of the obstructions were too distant to participate, and only four of Bartow's guns could engage the Union gunboats. At 1:30 p.m., Union shells set the barracks behind Fort Bartow on fire.

The Union gunboats mounted a total of 57 guns, many of which were larger and of greater range than the Confederate guns. Lynch reported that whenever his ships approached the barrier, they drew Union fire. Although only six Confederates were wounded, three seriously, damage to the Southern ships was extensive. The Union warships escaped serious injury.

The Confederate ships kept up an intermittent fire but were soon short of ammunition, and in late afternoon Lynch retired up Albemarle Sound to resupply. He was en route back to Roanoke Island when he learned of the Confederate surrender.

The earthen works of Fort Bartow on Pork Point were hard hit by the Union bombardment. But at about 5:00 p.m. with darkness coming on, Goldsborough ordered his ships to cease fire.

Meanwhile, beginning at 3:00 p.m. on February 7, Union troops began going ashore on Roanoke Island. They soon came under fire from a Confederate field gun, but the steamer *Delaware* moved in to clear their way, firing shrapnel from its IX-inch Dahlgren. Six Dahlgren howitzers on field mounts were landed in launches and then positioned

Union forces capture Roanoke Island, North Carolina, on February 7–8, 1862, giving the North one of its first significant victories of the war. (Library of Congress)

to provide security. By midnight, some 10,000 Union troops were on the island.

The next day, February 8, the Union soldiers got under way at first light, and by 9:00 a.m. the fighting was general. The Union ships again took the forts under fire, but the Union soldiers had little difficulty with the outnumbered Confederates. By 4:00 p.m., the American flag was flying over Pork Point.

Meanwhile, Union gunboat crews cleared a path through the obstructions across the sound, and by 4:00 p.m. the ships had passed into Albemarle Sound. Unable to do more than offer token long-range resistance, Lynch withdrew his gunboats up the Pasquotank River.

The Battle of Roanoke Island was a major Union victory at surprisingly little cost. The Union troops sustained little more than 250 casualties, with 47 of them killed; Union naval losses were only 6 men killed, 17 wounded, and 2 missing. Nearly 2,000 Confederates were taken prisoner, including 500 reinforcements arriving just in time to surrender.

SPENCER C. TUCKER

See also

Albemarle Sound; Burnside, Ambrose Everett; Goldsborough, Louis Malesherbes; Wise, Henry Alexander

Further Reading

Browning, Robert M., Jr. *From Cape Charles to Cape Fear: The North Atlantic Blockading Squadron during the Civil War.* Tuscaloosa: University of Alabama Press, 1993.

Tucker, Spencer C. *Blue and Gray Navies: The Civil War Afloat.* Annapolis, MD: Naval Institute Press, 2006.

U.S. Navy Department. *Official Records of the Union and Confederate Navies in the War of the Rebellion,* Series 1, Vol. 6. Washington, DC: U.S. Government Printing Office, 1897.

Robert Garrett & Sons, Inc.

Finance and transportation business founded by Robert Garrett in Baltimore, Maryland. With the help of his wealthy father-in-law, Robert Garrett formed Robert Garrett & Company in 1819 as a wholesale grocery business that sold produce, various dry goods, and manufactured products to retailers in Pennsylvania and western Maryland. The business became enormously profitable, and in 1840 Garrett allowed his two sons—Henry and John—to enter a business partnership with him; at that time, the name of the business was changed to Robert Garrett & Sons.

Before long, the Garretts branched out into other businesses, including finance and investment. During the Mexican-American War (1846–1848), the company brokered U.S. Treasury bonds to help pay for the conflict, charging a tidy commission for each transaction. The Garretts also sold food to the U.S. government for American troops serving in the war. The company meanwhile continued to deal in state-issued and commercially issued bonds. During the 1850s, Robert Garrett & Sons became a major player in the lucrative railroad financing business.

Robert Garrett died in 1857, leaving the company's operations to his son John, who that same year also became president of the Baltimore & Ohio Railroad. During the Civil War, the Baltimore & Ohio Railroad garnered numerous military-related contracts, and in 1863 it transported an unprecedented 20,000 Union troops from the Potomac River to Chattanooga in a matter of a few days.

Meanwhile, Garrett & Sons helped finance the war effort by engaging in foreign exchange transactions for George Peabody & Company, which was engaged in bond sales abroad. Opening a New York City office, Garrett & Sons also financed flour and corn exports to Europe. John Garrett cultivated close relationships with key federal officials, including Secretary of War Edwin L. Stanton and Secretary of the Treasury Salmon P. Chase.

The war divided the company's partners, however, as Henry Garrett chose to support the Confederacy. He was arrested in September 1861 in Baltimore and briefly detained for suspected treason. After that episode his health deteriorated rapidly, and he died in 1867.

John Garrett continued to run the business until his death in 1884. He also strengthened the Baltimore & Ohio Railroad, which by the late 1860s had become akin to a subsidiary of Garrett & Sons. The company remained in operation for many decades after John Garrett's death.

PAUL G. PIERPAOLI JR.

See also

Financing, U.S.; Peabody, George; Railroads, U.S.

Further Reading

Parker, Franklin. *George Peabody: A Biography*. Revised ed. Nashville: Vanderbilt University Press, 1995.

Williams, Harold A. *Robert Garrett & Sons Incorporated, 1840–1965*. Baltimore: Press of Schneidereith and Sons, 1965.

Roberts, Benjamin Stone
Birth Date: November 18, 1810
Death Date: January 29, 1875

Union officer. Benjamin Stone Roberts was born on November 18, 1810, in Manchester, Vermont, and graduated from the U.S. Military Academy, West Point, in 1835. He served in the 1st Dragoons on the frontier but resigned his commission in 1839 to become chief engineer of a railroad in upstate New York. His antebellum career was indeed varied. In 1841 Roberts became chief geologist for New York State, and the next year he went to Russia to assist in the construction of a railroad between Moscow and St. Petersburg. Returning to the United States in 1843, he opened a law practice in Iowa and was also a lieutenant colonel of militia. Roberts served as a first lieutenant in the Mounted Rifles during the Mexican-American War (1846–1848). Promoted to captain, he received brevets to major and lieutenant colonel for gallantry in action in the Battles of Chapultepec, Matamoros, and Galajara Pass. Roberts remained in the army after the war.

When the Civil War began, Roberts was stationed in New Mexico Territory. He was promoted to major in the 3rd U.S. Cavalry on May 13, 1861. On December 9, he entered the volunteer army as colonel of the 5th New Mexico Infantry. Roberts saw combat in a number of battles in New Mexico, including Val Verde (February 21, 1862), for which he was brevetted colonel in the regular army. Commissioned a brigadier general of volunteers on June 16, 1862, he served briefly as chief of cavalry and then as assistant inspector general for Major General John Pope's Army of Virginia. Roberts was wounded in the Battle of Cedar Mountain (August 9, 1862), for which action he was brevetted brigadier general in the U.S. Army. In his capacity as inspector general, Roberts subsequently prepared the charges against Major General Fitz John Porter for his role in the Union defeat in the Second Battle of Bull Run (August 29–30, 1862), leading to Porter's infamous court-martial.

Ordered to Minnesota, Roberts continued as Pope's inspector general, leading an operation against Native Americans. In March 1863 Roberts returned east to command first a brigade and then briefly a division in the Middle Department. In April he unsuccessfully opposed the raid into western Virginia (West Virginia) by Confederate forces under Brigadier Generals William E. "Grumble" Jones and John D. Imboden.

Ordered west in 1864, Roberts commanded the District of Iowa and then held a number of commands in XIX Corps,

Department of the Gulf. He finished the war commanding cavalry in the District of West Tennessee. He was brevetted major general of volunteers on March 15, 1865.

Discharged from the volunteers in January 1866, Roberts remained in the regular army and was promoted to lieutenant colonel on July 28, 1866, serving with the 3rd Cavalry Regiment in the West. He became a professor of military science at Yale University in 1868. Retiring from the army on December 15, 1870, he practiced law in Washington, D.C. He also supervised the manufacturing and sale of small arms of his invention. Roberts died in Washington, on January 29, 1875.

SPENCER C. TUCKER

See also

Bull Run, Second Battle of; Cedar Mountain, Battle of; Imboden, John Daniel; Jones, William Edmondson; Jones and Imboden Raid into West Virginia; Native Americans in the Civil War; New Mexico Territory; Pope, John; Porter, Fitz John; Val Verde, Battle of

Further Reading

Eicher, John H., and David J. Eicher. *Civil War High Commands.* Stanford, CA: Stanford University Press, 2001.

Warner, Ezra J. *Generals in Blue: Lives of the Union Commanders.* Baton Rouge: Louisiana State University Press, 2006.

Roberts, William Paul
Birth Date: July 11, 1841
Death Date: March 28, 1910

Confederate officer. William Paul Roberts was born in Gates County, North Carolina, on July 11, 1841. He was a teacher when the Civil War began. Roberts joined a local militia company as a private in June 1861 and was quickly promoted to sergeant. His company entered Confederate service as part of the 2nd North Carolina Cavalry. Roberts was commissioned a second lieutenant on August 30 and was promoted to first lieutenant on September 13, 1862; to captain on November 19, 1863; and to major on February 18, 1864.

Roberts served in his native state into the autumn of 1862, when his regiment was ordered to Virginia. He fought in the First Battle of Fredericksburg (December 13, 1862), the Siege of Suffolk (April 11–May 4, 1863), and the Battle of Brandy Station (June 9, 1863) and in numerous cavalry actions thereafter. He sustained a head wound at Haw's Shop on June 3, 1864. Promoted to colonel on June 23, 1864, he commanded his regiment in W. H. F. "Rooney" Lee's division of the Cavalry Corps, Army of Northern Virginia,

during the Petersburg Campaign (June 15, 1864–April 3, 1865). In the Second Battle of Reams Station (August 25, 1864), Roberts led a successful dismounted charge against Union breastworks that took a number of prisoners. Roberts was officially appointed brigadier general on February 23, 1865, to date from February 21, making him the youngest Confederate general.

Roberts continued in command of a brigade. He took part in the Battle of Five Forks (April 1, 1865) and was active in the Appomattox Campaign (April 2–9, 1865) before being surrendered at Appomattox Court House on April 9. He then returned to North Carolina.

In 1875 Roberts represented Gates County at the state constitutional convention, and he served in the state legislature in 1876 and 1877. In 1880 and 1884 he was elected auditor of the state. Roberts died on March 28, 1910, in Norfolk, Virginia.

SPENCER C. TUCKER

See also

Appomattox Court House and Lee's Surrender; Brandy Station, Battle of; Five Forks, Battle of; Fredericksburg, First Battle of; Lee, William Henry Fitzhugh; Petersburg Campaign; Reams Station, Second Battle of; Suffolk, Virginia, Siege of

Further Reading

Eicher, John H., and David J. Eicher. *Civil War High Commands.* Stanford, CA: Stanford University Press, 2001.

Warner, Ezra J. *Generals in Gray: Lives of the Confederate Commanders.* Baton Rouge: Louisiana State University Press, 2006.

Robertson, Beverly Holcombe
Birth Date: June 5, 1827
Death Date: November 12, 1910

Confederate officer. Beverly Holcombe Robertson was born on June 5, 1827, in Amelia County, Virginia. He graduated from the U.S. Military Academy, West Point, in 1849. From 1849 to 1861, he served in the 2nd Dragoons Regiment, mostly in the West, and was regimental adjutant (1860–1861). Promoted to first lieutenant in 1855, he was advanced to captain in March 1861. After he received a commission as a captain in the Confederate Army's Adjutant General's Department, Robertson was dismissed from the U.S. Army for disloyalty.

In the late autumn of 1861, Robertson took command of the 4th Virginia Cavalry Regiment as colonel. A stickler for discipline and a thorough taskmaster, he was nevertheless dogged by controversy and charges of incompetence. A competent commander in times of peace, he seemed just the opposite in combat. He was also far from agreeable when dealing with equals or even superior officers. The first officer under whom he served, Brigadier General J. E. B. Stuart, later remarked that Robertson was the most difficult man with whom he had ever dealt.

Robertson's prickly personality and less than stellar performance notwithstanding, he was promoted to brigadier general on June 9, 1862. Commanding the late Brigadier General Turner Ashby's cavalry brigade, Robertson participated in Major General Thomas J. "Stonewall" Jackson's Shenandoah Valley Campaign (May–June 1862). Robertson's overly cautious performance led Jackson to request Robertson's transfer. By September 1862, Robertson had been assigned to North Carolina, where he performed reasonably well in skirmishes near Kinston, Goldsborough, and New Bern. Still, his superiors complained about his poor leadership.

In May 1863, Robertson returned to Virginia. Given command of two regiments, he again served under Stuart but performed poorly in the Battle of Brandy Station (June 9, 1863), failing to guard the Confederate flank from Union cavalry attacks. During the Gettysburg Campaign (June–July 1863) and the Battle of Gettysburg (July 1–3, 1863), he remained in Virginia and was ordered to maintain contact with General Robert E. Lee's army and to keep open the pass at South Mountain. Robertson failed to fulfill either task and in October 1863 was transferred to South Carolina to command the Second Military District. He remained in the Carolinas until the end of the war.

Robertson aided in the defense of Charleston, and he also helped cover Lieutenant General William J. Hardee's forces as they evacuated the city in February 1865. Robertson surrendered to Union forces along with General Joseph E. Johnston. After the war Robertson moved to Washington, D.C., where he undertook a business career and began an insurance brokerage service. He died in Washington, D.C., on November 12, 1910.

PAUL G. PIERPAOLI JR.

See also

Ashby, Turner; Brandy Station, Battle of; Charleston, South Carolina, Evacuation of; Gettysburg, Battle of; Gettysburg Campaign; Hardee, William Joseph; Lee, Robert Edward; Jackson, Thomas Jonathan; Jackson's Shenandoah Valley Campaign; Stuart, James Ewell Brown

Further Reading

Davis, William. *The Generals of the Civil War*. New York: Quadrillion Media, 2003.

Hansen, Harry. *The Civil War: A History*. New York: Signet Classics, 2002.

Robertson, Felix Huston
Birth Date: March 9, 1839
Death Date: April 20, 1928

Confederate officer. Felix Huston Robertson was born on March 9, 1839, at Washington-on-the-Brazos, Texas. His father, Jerome Bonaparte Robertson, became a Confederate general. Felix Robertson attended Baylor University. Appointed to the U.S. Military Academy, West Point, in 1857, he resigned shortly before he would have graduated to offer his services to the Confederacy.

Commissioned a second lieutenant of artillery on March 9, 1861, Robertson participated in the shelling of Fort Sumter. He then joined the staff of Brigadier General Adley H. Gladden at Pensacola, Florida. Given command of an Alabama artillery battery, Robertson distinguished himself in the Battle of Shiloh (April 6–7, 1862). At the Battle of Stones River (December 31, 1862–January 2, 1863), his cool performance under fire was noticed by commander of the Army of Tennessee General Braxton Bragg, who secured Robertson's promotion to major and command of the artillery reserves. Robertson commanded a battalion in the Battle of Chickamauga (September 19–20, 1863). Promoted to lieutenant colonel, he assumed charge of the artillery in Major General Joseph Wheeler's Cavalry Corps and served in this capacity during the Atlanta Campaign (May 5–September 2, 1864).

On July 26, 1864, Robertson was appointed brigadier general, becoming the only Confederate general born in Texas. After serving as Wheeler's chief of staff, Robertson commanded first a brigade in Wheeler's command. Detached from Wheeler's command, Robertson participated in the October 2 defense of Saltville, Virginia, after which soldiers under his command murdered more than 100 wounded Union soldiers, including dozens of black troops, before Major General John C. Breckinridge intervened. Robertson was severely wounded in a skirmish at Buck Head Creek near Augusta, Georgia, on November 28, 1864, effectively ending his active field service.

While brave and effective in battle, Robertson was nonetheless a controversial figure and certainly a man of dubious character. His absolute loyalty to Bragg caused friction with some other officers. The harsh discipline that Robertson imposed on his men and his dark Indian-like features earned him the sobriquet "Comanche Robertson." Certainly his role in the Saltville Massacre was controversial. Breckinridge called for a court of inquiry, which Robertson successfully avoided. He was never charged with any crime for the affair. For reasons that are unclear but perhaps influenced by Breckinridge or General Robert E. Lee, who condemned the actions at Saltville, the Confederate Senate did not confirm any of Robertson's promotions from major to brigadier general. Although his substantive rank was thus captain, he was paroled as a brigadier general at Macon, Georgia.

After the war, Robertson returned to Texas and made his permanent residence in Waco. There he studied law, passed the bar, and established a thriving practice. He also invested in railroads and real estate. The last surviving Confederate general, Robertson died in Waco on April 20, 1928.

SPENCER C. TUCKER

See also

Atlanta Campaign; Bragg, Braxton; Buck Head Creek, Georgia, Engagement at; Chickamauga, Battle of; Gladden, Adley Hogan; Saltville, First and Second Battles of; Shiloh, Battle of; Stones River, Battle of

Further Reading

Mays, Thomas D. *The Saltville Massacre.* Buffalo Gap, TX: State House Press, 1998.

Warner, Ezra J. *Generals in Gray: Lives of the Confederate Commanders.* Baton Rouge: Louisiana State University Press, 2006.

Wright, Marcus J., comp., and Harold B. Simpson, ed. *Texas in the War, 1861–1865.* Hillsboro, TX: Hill Junior College Press, 1965.

Robertson, Jerome Bonaparte

Birth Date: March 14, 1815
Death Date: January 7, 1891

Confederate officer. Born in Woodford County, Kentucky, on March 14, 1815, Jerome Bonaparte Robertson was left in poverty at an early age by the death of his father. Apprenticed to a hatter, Robertson was later able to study medicine. He graduated from Transylvania College in 1835 and moved to Texas that same year. He served as a captain in the Texas Revolution (1835–1836) and then settled in Washington County, where he practiced medicine and became known as an Indian fighter.

Robertson also served in the Texas legislature and was a delegate to the state secession convention in 1861. On August 3, 1861, he was commissioned a captain in the 5th

Texas Infantry and was promoted to lieutenant colonel on October 12. He took part in the Peninsula Campaign (March–July 1862) and was wounded in the shoulder during the Seven Days' Campaign (June 25–July 1, 1862) in the Battle of Gaines' Mill (June 27). He was wounded in the groin on the second day of the Second Battle of Bull Run (August 29–30) and then was promoted to colonel on September 26 and to brigadier general on November 1.

Robertson commanded the Texas Brigade in Major General John B. Hood's Division of I Corps, Army of Northern Virginia, during the Gettysburg Campaign (June–July 1863) and was again wounded, this time in the right thigh, on July 2 during the Battle of Gettysburg (July 1–3, 1863). Transferred west with Lieutenant General James Longstreet, Robertson fought in the Battle of Chickamauga (September 19–20, 1863) and in the Knoxville Campaign (November–December 1863). Relieved of command by Longstreet for insubordination on January 16, 1864, Robertson was to be court-martialed. However, the charges were dropped, and he was ordered to assume command of the Reserve Corps in Texas.

After the war, Robertson resumed his medical practice. In 1874 he became chairman of the Texas Board of Education, and in 1879 he moved to Waco, where he became interested in railroad construction in western Texas. Robertson died in Waco on January 7, 1891. He was the father of controversial Confederate general Felix Huston Robertson.

SPENCER C. TUCKER

See also

Bull Run, Second Battle of; Chickamauga, Battle of; Gaines' Mill, Battle of; Gettysburg, Battle of; Gettysburg Campaign; Hood, John Bell; Hood's Texas Brigade; Knoxville Campaign; Longstreet, James; Peninsula Campaign; Seven Days' Campaign

Further Reading

Eicher, John H., and David J. Eicher. *Civil War High Commands.* Stanford, CA: Stanford University Press, 2001.

Warner, Ezra J. *Generals in Gray: Lives of the Confederate Commanders.* Baton Rouge: Louisiana State University Press, 2006.

Robinson, Charles

Birth Date: July 21, 1818
Death Date: August 17, 1894

Governor of Kansas (1861–1863). Charles Robinson was born on July 21, 1818, in Hardwick, Massachusetts, and attended Amherst College and the Berkshire Medical School, from which he received a medical degree in 1843. He began a practice in Fitchburg, Massachusetts, where he later established a hospital.

In 1849 Robinson was drawn west to California, where he hoped to make his fortune in the Gold Rush. This did not materialize, however, so he operated a Sacramento restaurant and became an editor of the *Settlers' and Miners' Tribune.* Robinson frequently used the publication to draw attention to the abuses of land speculators in central California. By this time, he had become an avowed free-soiler and served in the California legislature (1850–1851). When his term expired, he returned to Massachusetts to practice medicine.

In 1854 Robinson became a Kansas agent for the New England Emigrant Aid Company, which helped settlers in their moves from the East to the western frontier. At the same time, he began working to bring together the disparate antislavery forces in Kansas. In late 1855 when proslavery forces threatened violence against Wakarusa, he was appointed commander of the territory's free-soilers.

In 1856 Robinson was elected territorial governor under the illegal Topeka Constitution. His involvement in this rump regime resulted in his detention for several months during the spring and summer of 1856. Three years later he was again elected governor, this time legally under the Wyandotte Constitution, and was sworn into office on February 9, 1861. Not surprisingly, his strong antislavery position did not make him popular with all Kansans. Nevertheless, within weeks of taking office, he attempted to gird his state for war. Before long he ran into stiff headwinds, courtesy of his political adversaries, most notably the politically powerful James H. Lane, who did not support Robinson's ideology.

Lane soon launched a concerted effort to remove Robinson from office, ultimately resulting in impeachment proceedings. Robinson was cleared of any wrongdoing, but Lane's tenacious campaign against him had derailed his political career. Robinson was defeated in his 1862 reelection bid and left office on January 12, 1863.

Upon leaving office, Robinson took up residence at his home outside Lawrence, Kansas. Later he joined the liberal faction of the Republican Party and served in the Kansas Senate in 1874 and again in 1876. He ran unsuccessfully for governor twice more. Robinson died on August 17, 1894, in Lawrence, Kansas.

PAUL G. PIERPAOLI JR.

See also

Bleeding Kansas; Kansas; Lane, James Henry (Union Officer)

Further Reading

Josephy, Alvin M. *The Civil War in the American West.* New York: Knopf, 1992.

Wilson, Don W. *Governor Charles Robinson of Kansas.* Lawrence: University Press of Kansas, 1975.

Robinson, James Fisher
Birth Date: October 4, 1800
Death Date: October 31, 1882

Pro-Union governor of Kentucky (1862–1863). James Fisher Robinson was born on October 4, 1800, in Scott County, Kentucky. Educated by a private tutor as a youth, Robinson graduated from Transylvania University in 1818 and studied law. He then commenced a practice in Georgetown, Kentucky, and also farmed.

In 1851 Robinson entered electoral politics as a Whig when he was elected to the Kentucky Senate. He did not seek reelection, however, and returned to his law practice. In the meantime, he changed political affiliations and joined the Democratic Party. In 1861 he was again elected to the Kentucky Senate and was selected its Speaker on September 2, 1861. Robinson resigned the post, however, within a week.

As the position of Governor Beriah Magoffin—a Confederate sympathizer—became more tenuous during the summer of 1862, he hatched a face-saving deal with his Democratic colleagues in the Kentucky Senate. He would agree to resign his post if Robinson was again elected Speaker, which would make Robinson next in line for the governorship. The Senate complied. On August 18 Magoffin resigned, and Robinson was sworn in as governor.

Although Robinson was strongly pro-Union, he nevertheless sharply disagreed with the January 1, 1863, Emancipation Proclamation and strongly objected to the federal declaration of martial law in Kentucky and the suspension of the writ of habeas corpus for state citizens. In an attempt to better control events in his state, Robinson increased taxes to pay for a revived state militia force. The move elicited much protest among Kentucky voters. Unlike his predecessor, Robinson did a more than credible job supplying state troops for federal service.

Realizing that he was a caretaker governor, Robinson left office on September 1, 1863, when his term expired and did not seek reelection. Instead, he retired to his farm in Scott County and largely withdrew from politics. He subsequently served on the board of trustees of Georgetown College and was also president of Georgetown's Farmers' Bank. Robinson died at his home in Scott County on October 31, 1882.

PAUL G. PIERPAOLI JR.

See also
Kentucky; Magoffin, Beriah

Further Reading
Clark, Thomas D. *A History of Kentucky.* Ashland, KY: Jesse Stuart Foundation, 1992.
Harrison, Lowell H. *Kentucky's Governors.* Lexington: University Press of Kentucky, 2004.

Robinson, John Cleveland
Birth Date: April 10, 1817
Death Date: February 18, 1897

Union officer. Born in Binghamton, New York, on April 10, 1817, John Cleveland Robinson was the brother of future U.S. Army general Henry L. Robinson. John Robinson entered the U.S. Military Academy, West Point, in 1835 but was dismissed for insubordination on March 14, 1838. Commissioned directly into the army as a second lieutenant in the 5th Infantry on October 27, 1839, he served in the Mexican-American War (1846–1848) and was promoted to first lieutenant on June 18, 1846, and to captain on August 12, 1850. During the course of the next decade, he served in Florida, Texas, and Utah.

On the outbreak of the Civil War, Robinson was commanding Fort McHenry at Baltimore, Maryland. He succeeded in discouraging secession-minded Marylanders from disturbing the fort during the Baltimore Riot of April 19, 1861. He then was assigned recruiting duties in Ohio and Michigan.

On October 1, 1861, Robinson entered the volunteer army as colonel of the 1st Michigan Infantry. He was appointed brigadier general of volunteers to date from April 28. During the Peninsula Campaign (March–July 1862), he commanded a brigade in III Corps, Army of the Potomac. Wounded by a shell at Broad Run, Virginia, on August 27, he nonetheless led his brigade in the Second Battle of Bull Run (August 29–30, 1862) and the First Battle of Fredericksburg (December 13, 1862), after which he took command of a division in Major General John F. Reynolds's I Corps.

Robinson's division saw only limited action in the Battle of Chancellorsville (May 1–4, 1863) but was heavily engaged on the first day of the Battle of Gettysburg (July 1–3, 1863). The division sustained 1,685 casualties out of some 2,500

Union major general John Cleveland Robinson was known as one of the North's bravest officers and most capable divisional commanders. He was severely wounded in fighting at Spotsylvania Court House, Virginia, on May 8, 1864, forcing amputation of his left leg, which removed him from field command for the remainder of the war. (Library of Congress)

men engaged that day, when Reynolds was also killed. Robinson brought the survivors out in good order and in the subsequent reorganization was assigned command of a division in V Corps.

Robinson took part in the Overland Campaign (May 4–June 12, 1864) and was brevetted colonel in the regular army, effective May 5, for his role in the Battle of the Wilderness (May 5–7, 1864). His division was the first to reach Spotsylvania Court House early on May 8. Robinson placed himself at the head of his leading brigade and led the attack on the Confederate entrenchments. The assault failed, and Robinson was shot in the left leg, which required amputation and led to his removal from field duty. He was brevetted major general of volunteers for his actions.

On his return to active duty, Robinson commanded military districts in New York until the end of the war, when he took charge of the Freedman's Bureau in North Carolina (June–December 1866). Known during the war as one of the bravest Union Army officers and one of its most capable division commanders, Robinson was brevetted through major general in the regular army on March 13, 1865.

Remaining in the army, Robinson commanded the Department of the South (1866–1867) and the Department of the Lakes (1867–1869). Retired on May 6, 1869, as a major general because of his wartime wounds, Robinson was lieutenant governor of New York during 1872–1874 and thereafter involved himself in veterans' affairs, serving as both commander in chief of the Grand Army of the Republic and president of the Society of the Potomac. On March 28, 1894, he was awarded the Medal of Honor for his role in the Battle of Spotsylvania Court House. Blind in the last years of his life, Robinson retired to Binghamton, where he died on February 18, 1897.

SPENCER C. TUCKER

See also
Baltimore Riot; Bull Run, Second Battle of; Chancellorsville, Battle of; Fredericksburg, First Battle of; Freedmen's Bureau; Overland Campaign; Peninsula Campaign; Reynolds, John Fulton; Spotsylvania Court House, Battle of; Wilderness, Battle of the

Further Reading
Eicher, John H., and David J. Eicher. *Civil War High Commands.* Stanford, CA: Stanford University Press, 2001.
Matter, William D. *If It Takes All Summer: The Battle of Spotsylvania.* Chapel Hill: University of North Carolina Press, 1988.
Warner, Ezra J. *Generals in Blue: Lives of the Union Commanders.* Baton Rouge: Louisiana State University Press, 2006.

Rock Island Prison, Mississippi River

Union prison facility in the Mississippi River between Davenport, Iowa, and Rock Island, Illinois. On July 14, 1863, Quartermaster General M. C. Meigs ordered Captain Charles A. Reynolds of the Quartermaster Department to construct a prisoner-of-war camp at Rock Island. Construction spanned four months, from August to December 1863. The island upon which the prison was built is three miles long and about a half-mile wide. Much of it was swampy and poorly drained.

Each of the 84 barracks was 82 feet long, 22 feet wide, and 12 feet high, all facing eastward, with 12 windows, 2 doors, and 2 roof ventilators. Each building was divided between a kitchen at the west end and living and sleeping quarters at the east end, containing 60 double bunks and housing 120 prisoners. The compound contained six rows of 14 barracks 30 feet apart facing onto streets 100 feet wide except for the fourth row, which opened onto an avenue 130 feet wide—one of two avenues bisecting the prison. The stockade fence enclosed an area 1,300 feet long, 900 feet wide, and 12 feet high, with an outside boardwalk 4 feet from the top and sentry boxes every 100 feet. A guardhouse was located at each of two gates.

Rock Island had a planned capacity of 10,080 men but eventually held 12,409. The first 5,592 prisoners arrived in December 1863. The day they arrived, the temperature was 32 degrees below zero, and the barracks were inadequately heated. A smallpox epidemic broke out shortly after their arrival. Although the prison staff administered vaccine, the death toll was 94 in December, 231 in January, and 364 in February. During the 20 months that prisoners were confined at Rock Island, 1,960 prisoners and 171 Union guards died of various causes. Of the remaining prisoners, 730 were transferred to other stations, 3,876 were exchanged, 41 escaped, 5,581 were paroled, and approximately 4,000 took advantage of Abraham Lincoln's December 1863 Amnesty Proclamation and enlisted in Union units slated for western duty. Rock Island also held 213 civilians, 197 from Missouri. The facility was emptied of prisoners by July 11, 1865.

DEBRA J. SHEFFER

See also
Prisoners of War; Prisons, U.S.

Further Reading
Hesseltine, William B., ed. *Civil War Prisons.* Kent, OH: Kent State University Press, 1962.
Speer, Lonnie R. *Portals to Hell: Military Prisons of the Civil War.* Mechanicsburg, PA: Stackpole, 1997.

Rockville Expedition
Start Date: June 10, 1861
End Date: July 7, 1861

Union operation to secure Maryland. At the beginning of the Civil War, there was strong secessionist sentiment in the border state of Maryland. To help secure the state, on June 8, 1861, Union general in chief Brevet Lieutenant General Winfield Scott ordered Colonel Charles P. Stone, commander of the 14th U.S. Infantry Regiment, to proceed from Washington to the upper Potomac region. His instructions were to protect the area from Confederate inroads; cut the flow of supplies from Baltimore to Virginia; reopen the obstructed Chesapeake and Ohio Canal near Leesburg, Virginia; and reassure Maryland Unionists. If possible, Stone was also to link up with Union troops led by Major General Robert Patterson, who were about to leave Pennsylvania for operations in western Virginia.

Stone left the Washington area on June 10, moving up the Maryland side of the Potomac. He commanded some 2,500 men in three regiments and four battalions of infantry, two mounted companies, and two guns. Stone established his headquarters at Rockville, which the Union troops occupied on June 11. Detachments then took control of area towns, many of which were pro-Confederate in sentiment. Indeed, a skirmish occurred with local Confederates at Seneca Mills on June 14. Stone's men also reopened the Chesapeake and Ohio Canal almost to Edwards' Ferry, and they protected the property of many Unionists.

On June 16 as Union troops approached the strategic town of Leesburg, they spotted an unknown number of Confederate troops proceeding against them. A skirmish occurred the next day, which took the form primarily of an artillery duel. When the Confederates attempted to cross at Edwards' Ferry, Stone drove them back with artillery fire. Uncertain as to the strength of the Confederate forces, he was reluctant to proceed against Leesburg and so moved to Poolesville between Edwards' Ferry and Conrad's Ferry.

Stone's men remained in the vicinity for the next two weeks, but on June 30 Scott ordered Stone to join Patterson at Martinsburg, Virginia, northwest of Harpers Ferry. Leaving some men to protect the canal and ferries as long as possible, Stone moved upriver. On July 4, a long-range artillery duel occurred at Harpers Ferry between Stone's men and the rear guard of Confederate brigadier general Joseph E. Johnston's forces, who had just evacuated that place. Upon reaching Martinsburg on July 7, the operation came to an end. Stone assumed command of a brigade in Patterson's army.

SPENCER C. TUCKER

See also

Bull Run, First Battle of; Johnston, Joseph Eggleston; Maryland; Patterson, Robert; Scott, Winfield; Stone, Charles Pomeroy

Further Reading

Cotton, Robert I., and Mary Ellen Hayward. *Maryland and the Civil War: A House Divided.* Baltimore: Johns Hopkins University Press, 1994.
Walsh, Richard, and William Lloyd Fox. *Maryland: A History.* Baltimore: Maryland Historical Society, 1974.

Rocky Face Ridge, Battle of
Start Date: May 7, 1864
End Date: May 10, 1864

First major engagement of the Atlanta Campaign (May 5–September 2, 1864). The Battle of Rocky Face Ridge was fought in Whitfield County, Georgia, during May 7–10.

Confederate commander of the Army of Tennessee General Joseph E. Johnston had entrenched his forces on long, steep Rocky Face Ridge and eastward across Crow Valley. This terrain and the Confederate defensive positions presented Major General William T. Sherman, commanding the Military Division of the Mississippi, with his first major test of the Atlanta Campaign. Sherman commanded some 110,000 men with 254 guns; Johnston had just under 45,000 men with 138 guns. Johnston also had some 19,000 men and 50 guns in Alabama under Lieutenant General Leonidas Polk who were en route to join him.

Rocky Face Ridge is a formidable geographic barrier, running nearly north-south and to the west of Dalton, Georgia, for about 20 miles. Steep cliffs give way to a high gorge formed by Mill Creek Gap, known to locals as Buzzards Roost. Confederate engineers had dammed the creek, producing a large artificial lake across the rear of the gap. Once Sherman saw it, he called the gorge "the terrible door of death." Several miles to the south lay Dug Gap, an equally imposing fracture in the mountain.

Sherman knew that Johnston had been afforded ample time to prepare defenses and that the Confederate position here was strongly held. Major General George H. Thomas suggested to Sherman that while James B. McPherson's Army of the Tennessee and Major General John M. Schofield's Army of the Ohio fixed the defenders in place, Thomas would proceed with his four-corps-strong Army of the Cumberland down the west side of the ridge and then move eastward through unguarded Snake Gap and seize the Western & Atlantic Railroad in the Confederate rear near Resaca. This would at best allow Sherman to trap the Confederates and at worst pry them out of their strongly held defensive positions at Dalton and expose their forces to attack in the open by superior Union numbers.

Sherman rejected Thomas's proposal because the Army of the Cumberland consisted of some 70,000 men, or two-thirds of the Union strength, and because its large size would no doubt result in secrecy being lost. Sherman believed that without secrecy, there was danger in dividing his army. Sherman, however, kept the plan, deciding to send McPherson's army instead. The Army of the Tennessee numbered three corps, totaling almost 25,000 men. Not yet in line, it could march south from Chattanooga under cover of Taylor's Ridge and then move through Snake Creek Gap to Resaca. Meanwhile, Thomas would demonstrate against Johnston's line to hold him in place, as would Schofield with his 13,000 men, moving south from Red Clay, Georgia, against Johnston's right flank.

On May 6, McPherson and Schofield worked their forces into position. On May 7, Thomas and his Army of the Cumberland attacked and captured Tunnel Hill (the Chetoogeta Mountain Tunnel constructed in 1849–1850) to the northwest of Buzzards Roost, discovering that it and the rail line were undamaged. The next day, Thomas ordered his men to attack Dug Gap to the south. Here the well-entrenched defenders employed large boulders to advantage, repelling the far more numerous Federals. Thomas then decided to probe the line to the north, near Buzzards Roost.

At the same time, McPherson was proceeding south. Schofield, meanwhile, was harassed by Confederate cavalry under Major General Joseph Wheeler. Schofield dispatched a unit to deal with Wheeler on May 9, only to see it cut off and defeated at Prater's Mill with the loss of 150 men in the first Union defeat of the campaign.

That same day, Confederates under Major General Carter L. Stevenson turned back five full-scale attacks by the Army of the Cumberland against Rocky Face Ridge at Mill Creek Gap. After two days of fighting, Sherman had nothing to show but casualties. That evening, however, he received a message from McPherson that the Army of the Tennessee had met no significant opposition and was moving on Resaca. Sherman now decided to move his troops south in support of McPherson, reasoning that he must by then be in Resaca.

On May 10, leaving Thomas in place to demonstrate in front of the Confederates at Rocky Face Ridge, Sherman moved the rest of his army south. At the same time, General Polk arrived at Dalton with his forces, bringing the Confederate Army of Tennessee up to full strength. On the morning of May 11, the Confederates along Rocky Face Ridge awoke to silence in front of their lines. Stevenson informed Johnston, who ordered Wheeler on a scouting mission. The Confederate cavalry commander confirmed that the entire Union army had withdrawn and was apparently moving south along the west side of Taylor's Ridge, which paralleled Rocky Face Ridge but to the west. Johnston now had no choice but to withdraw south to Resaca, retiring there on May 12.

SPENCER C. TUCKER

See also

Atlanta Campaign; Johnston, Joseph Eggleston; McPherson, James Birdseye; Polk, Leonidas; Schofield, John McAllister; Sherman, William Tecumseh; Stevenson, Carter Littlepage; Thomas, George Henry; Wheeler, Joseph

Further Reading

Castel, Albert. *Decision in the West: The Atlanta Campaign of 1864.* Lawrence: University Press of Kansas, 1992.

Foote, Shelby. *The Civil War: A Narrative,* Vol. 3, *Red River to Appomattox.* New York: Random House, 1974.

Johnston, Joseph E. *Narrative of Military Operations, Directed, during the Late War between the States.* New York: D. Appleton, 1874.

Sherman, William T. *Memoirs of General W. T. Sherman.* New York: Library of America, 1990.

Rocky Gap, West Virginia, Engagement at

Start Date: August 26, 1863
End Date: August 27, 1863

Battle during Union brigadier general William W. Averell's August 1863 West Virginia raid. On August 5, Averell departed Winchester, Virginia, with a mixed force of some 2,000 cavalry, mounted infantry, and artillery. He marched through Moorefield and Petersburg, West Virginia, and south to Monterey, Virginia, skirmishing with Confederate forces at various points along the way. On August 22 he battled Confederate colonel William L. Jackson's men at Huntersville, outflanking them and forcing them to retreat toward Warm Springs. Averell trailed Jackson on August 24, pushing the Confederates eastward and occupying Warm Springs. The next day, the Federals marched to Callaghan's Station, destroying a saltpeter works on the Jackson River.

At 4:00 a.m. on August 26, Averell marched westward toward White Sulphur Springs in Greenbrier Country in West Virginia. At Rocky Gap in the Allegheny Mountains two miles from his destination, he encountered four regiments of deployed Virginia infantry numbering 1,900 men and commanded by Colonel George S. Patton. The Confederates had been sent by Major General Samuel Jones, commanding the Department of Western Virginia to intercept the Union troops.

Averell quickly dismounted his men, deployed them in the heavily wooded terrain, and charged Patton's waiting troops. The hard-fought battle occurred between 9:00 a.m. and 7:00 p.m. on August 26 and continued into the morning of August 27. The Confederates fought off charge after charge. Expecting reinforcements from Confederate brigadier general John D. Imboden at Monterey, Patton stubbornly continued the battle until nightfall halted the action. Both sides retained their positions that night, and in the morning Averell resumed the battle with two additional charges. At noon on August 27, with the Confederates having been reinforced and his own men running low on ammunition, Averell broke off contact and withdrew to Callaghan's Station and then on to Beverly, arriving there on August 31. Confederate casualties totaled some 168, including 30 prisoners. Union losses were more than 200. One Union rifled gun that had burst in the battle was also abandoned.

The Confederates pursued, but Averell withdrew his men in good order. Imboden sought to block Averell at Monterey but arrived too late. Commander of the Army of Northern Virginia General Robert E. Lee was not pleased that Imboden had been unable to reinforce Jones in time and that Averell had not been "more seriously punished."

PAUL DAVID NELSON AND SPENCER C. TUCKER

See also
Averell, William Woods; Averell's Raids; Imboden, John Daniel; Jones, Samuel

Further Reading
Averell, William Woods. *Ten Years in the Saddle: The Memoir of William Woods Averell.* Edited by Edward K. Eckert and Nicholas J. Amato. San Rafael, CA: Presidio, 1978.
Longacre, Edward G. *Lincoln's Cavalrymen: A History of the Mounted Forces of the Army of the Potomac, 1861–1865.* Mechanicsburg, PA: Stackpole, 2000.
Tucker, Spencer C. *Brigadier General John D. Imboden: Confederate Commander in the Shenandoah.* Lexington: University Press of Kentucky, 2002.

Roddey, Philip Dale
Birth Date: April 2, 1826
Death Date: July 20, 1897

Confederate officer. Philip Dale Roddey was born in Moulton, Alabama, on April 2, 1826. He had little or no formal education and worked as a tailor in Moulton. He then served three years as sheriff before becoming a steamboat deckhand.

With the beginning of the Civil War, in the spring of 1861 Roddey organized an independent cavalry company, the Tishomingo Rangers, also known as Roddey's Alabama Cavalry Company, that operated as scouts in northern Mississippi and Alabama. Roddey soon came to the attention of Confederate general Braxton Bragg, and Roddey and his company served as Bragg's escort during the Battle of Shiloh (April 6–7, 1862).

Roddey took part in the retreat to and siege of Corinth, Mississippi (May 3–30, 1862). Promoted to colonel in October 1862, he took command of the 4th Alabama Cavalry

Regiment. By April 1863, Roddey was commanding a cavalry brigade of some 1,400 men in the Department of Mississippi and East Louisiana. That same month, his brigade protected Brigadier General Nathan Bedford Forrest's rear and then participated in the pursuit of Colonel Abel D. Streight's cavalry raiders across Alabama. Roddey also served as commander of the District of Northern Alabama, Department of Tennessee, but was still primarily an active cavalry commander.

In August 1863 Roddey was promoted to brigadier general, commanding a brigade in the cavalry corps of Major General Joseph Wheeler in Bragg's Army of Tennessee, but often operated independently in northern Alabama. Although serving under Wheeler in the Chattanooga Campaign (October–November 1863), Roddey's brigade played no major role. Beginning in April 1864, Roddey served mostly under Forrest and participated in the Battle of Tupelo (July 14–15, 1864).

In September, Roddey resumed command of the District of Northern Alabama and in this role supported General John Bell Hood's unsuccessful November–December 1864 campaign into Tennessee. In March 1865 Roddey joined Forrest in the failed attempt to stop the advance of Brigadier General James H. Wilson's cavalry corps into Alabama and the capture of Selma.

Paroled on May 17, 1865, Roddey later became a successful businessman in New York. He died on a business trip to London on July 20, 1897.

PHILIP L. BOLTÉ

See also
Bragg, Braxton; Chattanooga Campaign; Corinth, Mississippi, Siege of; Forrest, Nathan Bedford; Sherman's March to the Sea; Shiloh, Battle of; Wheeler, Joseph

Further Reading
Longacre, Edward G. *Mounted Raids of the Civil War.* Cranbury, NJ: A. S. Barnes, 1975.
Sifakis, Stewart. *Who Was Who in the Civil War.* New York: Facts on File, 1988.

Rodes, Robert Emmett
Birth Date: March 29, 1829
Death Date: September 19, 1864

Confederate officer. Born on March 29, 1829, in Lynchburg, Virginia, Robert Emmett Rodes attended local schools and graduated from the Virginia Military Institute in 1848, where he remained as an engineering instructor until 1851, when he resigned to work as a civil engineer for the Southside Railroad and other operations, including an Alabama railroad, beginning his association with that state. In 1861 he was set to return to the Virginia Military Institute as a professor, but when the Civil War began he entered the Confederate Army.

Commissioned colonel of the 5th Alabama Infantry Regiment, Rodes fought at the First Battle of Bull Run (July 21, 1861). He was promoted to brigadier general on October 21, 1861. The following year, he suffered a severe arm wound at the Battle of Seven Pines (May 31–June 1, 1862). Rodes soon resumed his command and participated in the Battle of Gaines' Mill (June 27, 1862), but his premature return to action resulted in a three-month illness.

Upon recovery, Rodes served in the Confederate invasion of Maryland, fighting at the Battle of South Mountain (September 14, 1862) and the Battle of Antietam (September 17). He also participated in the First Battle of Fredericksburg (December 13, 1862). His outstanding performance in the Antietam Campaign led General Robert E. Lee to assign him to command of a division in January 1863. Rodes's division headed Lieutenant General Thomas J. "Stonewall" Jackson's flanking march on May 2 during the Battle of Chancellorsville (May 1–4, 1863), where Rodes's skilled leadership earned him promotion to major general.

During Lee's subsequent invasion of Pennsylvania, Rodes was part of the widely scattered Confederate vanguard. He hurried his division toward Gettysburg when Lee had learned that the Union army was nearby. Approaching from north of the town on July 1, Rodes immediately joined the Confederate attack. His division suffered heavy losses and took no significant part in the remainder of the Battle of Gettysburg (July 1–3, 1863).

Rodes fought in some small engagements during the autumn of 1863 before playing a key role in checking a Union attack at the Battle of the Wilderness (May 5–7, 1864). After fighting at the Battle of Spotsylvania Court House (May 8–21, 1864), he and his division were transferred with Lieutenant General Jubal Early's II Corps to the Shenandoah Valley in June. Rodes participated in Early's July raid on Washington, D.C. On September 19, 1864, during the Third Battle of Winchester, Rodes suffered a fatal head wound from a shell fragment and died on the field of battle.

JIM PIECUCH

See also

Antietam, Battle of; Bull Run, First Battle of; Chancellorsville, Battle of; Fredericksburg, First Battle of; Gaines' Mill, Battle of; Gettysburg, Battle of; Seven Pines, Battle of; South Mountain, Battle of; Spotsylvania Court House, Battle of; Wilderness, Battle of the; Winchester, Third Battle of

Further Reading

Collins, Darrell L. *Major General Robert E. Rodes of the Army of Northern Virginia: A Biography.* El Dorado Hills, CA: Savas Beatie, 2008.
Swisher, James K. *Warrior in Gray: General Robert Rodes of Lee's Army.* Shippensburg, PA: White Mane, 2001.

Rodgers, John, Jr.
Birth Date: August 8, 1812
Death Date: May 5, 1882

Union naval officer. Born in Havre de Grace, Maryland, on August 8, 1812, John Rodgers Jr. was the son of Commodore John Rodgers Sr., who won renown during the Barbary Wars and the War of 1812. Rodgers Jr. joined the navy as a midshipman on April 18, 1828, and served in the Mediterranean in the frigate *Constellation* and the sloop *Concord.* He was promoted to passed midshipman on June 14, 1834. Rodgers attended the University of Virginia for a year before returning to sea. He then served in the Brazil Squadron and participated in the Second Seminole War (1835–1842) before completing additional tours at sea in the Mediterranean and off Africa. He was promoted to lieutenant on January 28, 1840.

In 1852 Lieutenant Rodgers assumed command of the North Pacific Exploring Expedition that surveyed the northern Bering Sea. He was promoted to commander on September 14, 1855. Rodgers was in Washington, D.C., compiling and editing the reports of these endeavors when the Civil War began in April 1861.

Rodgers participated in the botched destruction of the Norfolk Navy Yard in Virginia in April 1861 but was taken prisoner with others by the Virginia forces. As Virginia had not yet joined the Confederacy, the legislature in Richmond decided to free Rodgers and his fellows. On May 15, Secretary of the Navy Gideon Welles ordered Rodgers to Cincinnati, Ohio, to supervise the conversion into gunboats of civilian vessels purchased by the army. These were the timberclads, the first units of the Mississippi Flotilla. In the course of these endeavors, Rodgers clashed with Major General James C. Frémont, commander of the Western Department, who caused his recall.

Assigned to the South Atlantic Blockading Squadron, Rodgers commanded the screw combatant *Flag* in

U.S. Navy captain John Rodgers Jr. came from a distinguished naval family and provided highly effective service during the Civil War both in the construction of "Timberclads" in the West and in naval operations along the Atlantic seaboard. (Library of Congress)

Commodore Samuel F. Du Pont's expedition against Port Royal, South Carolina, in November 1862 and took an active role in the surrender of Confederate Forts Walker and Beauregard. On May 15, 1862, Rodgers led a squadron up the James River and, in the ironclad *Galena,* engaged Confederate shore batteries in the four-hour First Battle of Drewry's Bluff, in which the *Galena* was badly damaged and the attempt to reach Richmond was rebuffed. He was promoted to captain on July 16, 1862.

Rodgers rejoined Du Pont's squadron and, in command of the monitor *Weehawken,* led the failed attack on Fort Sumter on April 7, 1863, in which the monitor absorbed a number of hits and was badly damaged. On June 17 in Wassaw Sound, however, Rodgers's repaired *Weehawken* defeated the Confederate ironclad *Atlanta.* Rodgers received promotion to commodore on June 17, 1863, and took command of the monitors *Canonicus* and *Dictator,* both of which were troubled with developmental problems. Rodgers saw no further fighting in the war.

After the war, Rodgers commanded the squadron off Chile and then had charge of the Boston Navy Yard. He was promoted to rear admiral on December 31, 1869. He commanded the Asiatic Squadron on a diplomatic mission to investigate the imprisonment and murder of American seamen aboard the merchantman *General Sherman.* The U.S. government also wanted a treaty to guarantee proper treatment for shipwrecked sailors and wanted diplomatic ties and trade relations with Korea. A diplomatic impasse, however, quickly turned into armed conflict. On June 10, 1871, as Rodgers ascended the Taedong River with his ships, a Korean fort opened fire. Rodgers demanded an apology and, with none forthcoming, sent sailors and marines ashore. They stormed three Korean forts and killed several hundred Koreans. This action failed to sway the Koreans to open diplomatic relations, and the Americans soon withdrew. Rodgers returned to the United States in 1872. He subsequently served on various naval boards and also commanded the Naval Observatory. Rodgers died in Washington, D.C., on May 5, 1882.

SPENCER C. TUCKER

See also

Drewry's Bluff, First Battle of; Du Pont, Samuel Francis; Fort Sumter, South Carolina, Du Pont's Attack on; *Galena,* USS; Port Royal Sound, Battle of; Timberclads; Wassaw Sound, Battle of; Welles, Gideon

Further Reading

Johnson, Robert E. "John Rodgers: The Quintessential Nineteenth Century Naval Officer." In *Captains of the Old Steam Navy,* edited by James C. Bradford, 253–274. Annapolis, MD: Naval Institute Press, 1986.
Johnson, Robert E. *Rear Admiral John Rodgers, 1812–1882.* Annapolis, MD: Naval Institute Press, 1967.

Rodman, Thomas Jackson
Birth Date: July 31, 1816
Death Date: June 7, 1871

Union officer. Thomas Jackson Rodman was born on July 31, 1816, near Salem, Indiana. He graduated from the U.S. Military Academy, West Point, in 1841, and on July 1, 1841, he was appointed a brevet second lieutenant and assigned to the U.S. Army Ordnance Department. He was promoted to first lieutenant in 1847 and to captain in 1855.

In 1844 Rodman began conducting experiments to improve the durability of heavy guns, especially the large columbiads. At the time, all cannon were cast solid of iron and then cooled from the outside to the inside, resulting in uneven cooling that weakened the integrity of the gun around the bore, which was drilled out. Rodman developed a method that employed circulating water or air to cool the casting from the inside out, producing stronger cannon that were less apt to crack or explode upon firing. The process came to bear his name. Rodman secured a patent that ultimately provided a half cent per pound for all finished guns and other castings employing his method.

Rodman also designed heavy guns that bore his name. These concentrated the weight of metal at the breech end and somewhat resembled the heavy navy smoothbore guns designed by Commander John Dahlgren (the two argued about which one had influenced the other). Rodman's guns incorporated a slight mushroom knob at the breech end with ratchets to take the elevating mechanism.

During the Civil War, Rodman served as the commander and superintendent of the Watertown Arsenal (Massachusetts) and was a member of the U.S. Army's Fortification Board, earning promotion to major in 1863. He remained at Watertown until August 3, 1865. On March 13, 1865, Rodman was brevetted brigadier general.

After the war, Rodman remained in the army at his permanent rank, and in August 1865 he was assigned to Rock Island, Illinois, to supervise the construction of a new arsenal and armory. He was advanced to lieutenant colonel on March 7, 1867. Rodman became ill, attributed to overwork, and died at Rock Island on June 7, 1871.

ROBERT B. KANE

See also
Artillery, Land, U.S.; Dahlgren, John Adolph Bernard; Rodman Guns

Further Reading
Eicher, John H., and David J. Eicher. *Civil War High Commands.* Stanford, CA: Stanford University Press, 2001.
Olmstead, Edwin, Wayne E. Stark, and Spencer C. Tucker. *The Big Guns: Civil War Siege, Seacoast, and Naval Cannon.* Alexandria Bay, NY: Museum Restoration Service, 1997.
Ripley, Warren. *Artillery and Ammunition of the Civil War.* New York: Promontory, 1970.

Rodman Guns

Series of smoothbore muzzle-loading columbiad heavy guns designed by artilleryman Captain Thomas Jackson Rodman in the late 1840s. Traditionally, foundries cast cannon as one solid metal piece and then bored out the center. Because the gun cooled from the outside inward,

the casting shrank as it cooled. As each succeeding layer cooled, it contracted, pulling away from the previously cooled metal, creating voids and tension cracks that often weakened the cannon.

Rodman developed and patented a casting method by which the gun casting cooled from the inside out by pumping water or air into a pipe inserted into the casting core. As the casting cooled, it created compression rather than tension, producing a much stronger gun. After cooling, the casting was then bored out to the required diameter. For an 8-inch bore gun, the core was 7.38 inches. Under an agreement of August 1847, Rodman was to receive a royalty of a half cent per pound on all finished guns and other castings using this method.

Rodman guns had a curved soda-bottle shape and large flat, unobtrusive mushroom cascabels with ratchets (or sockets) for the elevating mechanism. Rodman guns appeared in 8-inch, 10-inch, 13-inch, 15-inch, and 20-inch smoothbores. They fired both spherical shot and shell. Seven experimental Rodman rifled guns of 8-inch, 10-inch, and 12-inch sizes did not prove satisfactory. In all, the U.S. government secured 1,840 Rodman guns, mainly for coastal fortifications, although few saw combat.

Rodman guns were mounted on three types of carriages—a front-pintle barbette carriage, a center-pintle barbette carriage, and a casemate carriage made of wrought iron. All three carriages were similar, with an upper carriage placed on a two-rail chassis. The gun and upper carriage recoiled along the chassis, and the chassis would pivot to train the gun left or right.

Robert Parker Parrot of the West Point Foundry also employed the Rodman water core method for his large-bore rifled guns for the army and navy. The Tredegar Iron Works in Richmond, the only foundry in the South capable of producing the heaviest guns in 1861, failed to adopt the Rodman method of casting prior to the Civil War, and the Confederacy thus did not place into service any guns with the Rodman method (two were produced late in the war but were not completed in time to see service). The Tredegar Iron Works did produce large 8-inch and 10-inch solid-cast columbiads that resembled the Rodmans in external appearance.

In the 1870s and 1880s, the U.S. government converted a number of existing Rodman guns into rifled guns by reaming out a number of 10-inch guns to about 13.5 inches in bore and then inserting wrought-iron and steel rifled sleeves to produce 8-inch rifled guns.

ROBERT B. KANE

A powerful Union 15-inch Rodman gun in Battery Rodgers, Alexandria, Virginia. (National Archives)

See also

Parrott Gun; Rodman, Thomas Jackson; Seacoast Guns; Tredegar Iron Works

Further Reading

Olmstead, Edwin, Wayne E. Stark, and Spencer C. Tucker. *The Big Guns: Civil War Siege, Seacoast, and Naval Cannon*. Alexandria Bay, NY: Museum Restoration Service, 1997.

Ripley, Warren. *Artillery and Ammunition of the Civil War*. New York: Promontory Press, 1970.

Webster, Donald B., Jr. "Rodman's Great Guns." *Ordnance* 47(253) (July–August 1962): 60–62.

Roebuck, John Arthur

Birth Date: December 28, 1802

Death Date: November 30, 1879

Radical British politician and fervent supporter of the Confederate cause during the Civil War. John Arthur Roebuck

was born on December 28, 1802, in Madras, India, the son of a midlevel foreign service employee. Educated mostly in Canada, Roebuck was admitted to the bar in January 1831 and pursued a legal career. He also began to immerse himself in radical thought and politics. First elected to the House of Commons in 1832, he served four nonconsecutive terms as a member of Parliament (1832–1837, 1841–1847, 1849–1868, and 1874–1879). Much to the chagrin of his parliamentary colleagues, Roebuck supported radical internal reform but frequently lambasted both the Left and the Right. He was ambitious and often caustic, and his incendiary speeches and outrageous conduct led numerous British politicians to challenge him to duels, which he wisely never accepted.

Despite his radical liberal tendencies, Roebuck became a slavish supporter of a robust and far-reaching foreign policy that above all else protected Great Britain's vital interests. It was perhaps this mind-set that led him to favor the Confederacy over the Union when the Civil War began in April

1861. Fearing, quite correctly as it turned out, that the United States would one day challenge Great Britain's supremacy in world affairs, Roebuck believed from the very beginning of the conflict that the British government should recognize and aid the Confederacy, thereby ensuring a Confederate victory and a divided United States.

After the Confederate triumph at the Battle of Chancellorsville (May 1–4, 1863), Roebuck and William S. Lindsay readied a motion to be introduced in Parliament that would formally request that the prime minister recognize the Confederacy. Palmerston, meanwhile, hoping to quash the movement, claimed that the French no longer supported intervention and that England would not go it alone. This was not entirely true, however, and so Roebuck and Lindsay traveled to France and met with Napoleon III in June 1863, receiving assurances that France would intervene in the Civil War but only if France received British aid and support.

Roebuck introduced his motion in the House of Commons to great fanfare on June 30, 1863. His fiery speech focused on the Union blockade of the Confederacy, which he claimed had starved his nation of cotton imports, ruined the British textile industry, idled thousands of workers, and threatened to plunge the entire economy into chaos. He also revealed for the first time the results of his meeting with Napoleon. The motion and speech precipitated bitterly raucous debate, and the Palmerston government claimed that it had no word from the French on their attitudes toward recognition or intervention. Roebuck badly mishandled the motion, which was soon a dead letter. Less than two weeks after introducing the motion, Roebuck had to withdraw it.

As time went on, Roebuck became more conservative in his outlook and politics, which was evidenced by his appointment as a privy councilor by the Conservatives in 1874. Roebuck died on November 30, 1879, in London.

PAUL G. PIERPAOLI JR.

See also

Blockade of the Confederacy, Union; Chancellorsville, Battle of; Diplomacy, Confederate; Diplomacy, U.S.; France; Great Britain; Lindsay, William Schaw; Napoleon III; Temple, Henry John

Further Reading

Foreman, Amanda. *A World on Fire: Britain's Crucial Role in the American Civil War.* New York: Random House, 2011.

Jones, Howard. *Union in Peril: The Crisis over British Intervention in the Civil War.* Chapel Hill: University of North Carolina Press, 1992.

Root, George Frederick
Birth Date: August 30, 1820
Death Date: August 6, 1895

Noted songwriter and composer. George Frederick Root was born on August 30, 1820, in Sheffield, Massachusetts. At age 18, Root left his small farming town and went to Boston, where he was determined to become a musician. Already a fine flutist, he also played the organ in several Boston churches and began to teach music as well. He traveled to Europe, where in the 1840s he solidified his reputation as an outstanding teacher. In 1860 Root moved to Chicago; by that time, he was already a well-known composer. There he became a partner in a music company managed by his brother.

The Civil War inspired Root to write some of his most celebrated songs, including "The First Gun Is Fired! May God Protect the Right!" as well as "Tramp, Tramp, Tramp, the Boys Are Marching" and "The Vacant Chair." His most famous war song by far was "The Battle Cry of Freedom," which came out in August 1862. It became an immediate smash hit. Bands all across the Union played the song, and sales of sheet music were brisk. By 1864, Root's music company reported sales of 350,000 pieces of sheet music. On April 14, 1865, "The Battle Cry of Freedom" was played while the American flag was hoisted over the now-recaptured Fort Sumter. The song had also been quite popular in the Confederacy, albeit with different lyrics.

Root continued to compose and teach music for the remainder of his life, and in 1891 he wrote a well-received autobiography, *The Story of a Musical Life.* He died on Bailey Island, Maine, on August 6, 1895.

PAUL G. PIERPAOLI JR.

See also

Music

Further Reading

Branham, Robert J. *Sweet Freedom's Song: "My Country, 'Tis of Thee" and Democracy in America.* New York: Oxford University Press, 2002.

Rosecrans, William Starke
Birth Date: September 6, 1819
Death Date: March 11, 1898

Union officer. Born in Delaware County, Ohio, on September 6, 1819, William Starke Rosecrans graduated from the

Union major general William S. Rosecrans, commanding the Army of the Cumberland in the Western Theater, blundered into a trap set by the Confederates that led to the Battle of Chickamauga on September 19–20, 1863. This Union near disaster brought his removal from command. (National Archives)

U.S. Military Academy at West Point in 1842. He entered the Corps of Engineers and was promoted to first lieutenant in 1853, but in 1854 he left the army to pursue a career in business and engineering.

With the beginning of the Civil War in 1861, Rosecrans returned to uniform, joining the staff of Major General George B. McClellan. Rosecrans was appointed a brigadier general in the regular army in May 1861 and, as McClellan's chief subordinate, was the real author of most of the success in the autumn 1861 campaign in western Virginia, although McClellan appropriated all of the credit. An embittered Rosecrans sought transfer to the western theater rather than continue service under McClellan.

Assigned to the Army of the Mississippi, Rosecrans participated in the slow advance toward and siege of Corinth, Mississippi. After the capture of Corinth on May 30, 1862,

Rosecrans rose to command the Army of the Mississippi, which remained in northern Mississippi under the overall command of Major General Ulysses S. Grant. Late that summer a small Confederate army under the command of Major General Sterling Price advanced toward Iuka. Grant prepared a counterstroke against Price, but Rosecrans talked him into making the attack a two-pronged affair aimed at trapping the Confederates. Grant agreed, but Rosecrans could not get his force into position to attack on time. When he finally did so on September 19, the Confederates held Rosecrans off while their force escaped. Grant's force, prevented from hearing the sounds of Rosecrans's battle, did not get into the fight.

Two and a half weeks later, Price's army, combined with one of similar size under Major General Earl Van Dorn, moved under Van Dorn's command to attempt to recapture Corinth, which Rosecrans defended. The Confederates attacked on October 3 and 4, 1862. Rosecrans handled his troops poorly and showed definite signs of panic. Nevertheless, the stubbornness of his troops secured victory. Rosecrans made no attempt to pursue and trap the defeated Confederates until it was too late. Grant never forgave Rosecrans for this second lapse within the space of a month.

What was visible from the perspective of Washington, however, was not Rosecrans's serious shortcomings but rather the fact that Corinth had been a Union victory. As a result, President Abraham Lincoln tapped Rosecrans, appointed major general of volunteers, to take over the army that Major General Don Carlos Buell had mismanaged during the just-concluded Kentucky Campaign. On October 27, 1862, Rosecrans assumed command of that army, which was in Nashville, and christened it the Army of the Cumberland.

Rosecrans knew that Lincoln wanted aggressive action. A few weeks later when Rosecrans learned from a Chattanooga newspaper that the Confederate army under General Braxton Bragg had been weakened by the transfer of one-fourth of its infantry to Mississippi, he decided to attack. Rosecrans met Bragg's army just outside Murfreesboro, Tennessee, along the banks of Stones River on December 31, 1862, and again on January 2, prevailing in one of the fiercest and bloodiest battles of war. The Confederates retreated about 40 miles to Tullahoma.

The victory, coming in the midst of a season of Union defeats, was a political godsend for Lincoln, but the president's gratitude wore thin as Rosecrans kept his army idle for the next six months. At last in late June, Rosecrans advanced again and in a nine-day campaign of maneuver forced Bragg to fall back another 80 miles to Chattanooga.

After another six-week pause, Rosecrans again advanced and again succeeded in turning Bragg and forcing him to retreat to LaFayette, Georgia. Rosecrans, however, thought that Bragg was falling back all the way to Atlanta and pursued aggressively with his corps widely spread. In fact, Rosecrans's earlier delays had allowed Richmond to reinforce Bragg, who now outnumbered the Army of the Cumberland. The Confederate counterstroke fell at the Battle of Chickamauga (September 19–20, 1863). On the final day of the battle, Rosecrans gave an ill-conceived order that created a gap in his line just as the Confederates were launching a major assault. His army was routed except for a large contingent under Major General George Thomas, which held its ground until, close to nightfall, Rosecrans ordered it to retreat.

After Chickamauga, Rosecrans was a broken man. He pulled his troops back into Chattanooga and allowed Bragg to place him under virtual siege there. Lincoln observed that Rosecrans was acting "confused and stunned, like a duck hit on the head." The president assigned Major General Ulysses S. Grant to command of all Union armies west of the Appalachians with authority to retain Rosecrans in command of the Army of the Cumberland or to dismiss him. Grant made the obvious choice. Later in the war, Rosecrans held a minor command in Missouri. He resigned from the army in 1867.

Rosecrans next served as minister to Mexico (1868–1869). He returned to his California ranch before serving in the U.S. House of Representative (1881–1885). He then held a position in the Treasury Department until 1893. Rosecrans died at home in Redondo Beach, California, on March 11, 1898.

STEVEN E. WOODWORTH

See also

Bragg, Braxton; Buell, Don Carlos; Chickamauga, Battle of; Corinth, Battle of; Corinth, Mississippi, Siege of; Cumberland, Union Army of the; Grant, Ulysses Simpson; Iuka, Battle of; McClellan, George Brinton; Price, Sterling; Stones River, Battle of; Thomas, George Henry; Van Dorn, Earl

Further Reading

Lamers, William M. *The Edge of Glory: A Biography of General William S. Rosecrans, U.S.A.* New York: Harcourt, Brace, 1961.

McDonough, James Lee. *Stones River: Bloody Winter in Tennessee.* Knoxville: University of Tennessee Press, 1980.

Woodworth, Steven E. *Nothing but Victory: The Army of the Tennessee, 1861–1865.* New York: Knopf, 2005.

Woodworth, Steven E. *Six Armies in Tennessee: The Chickamauga and Chattanooga Campaigns.* Lincoln: University of Nebraska Press, 1998.

Ross, John
Birth Date: October 3, 1790
Death Date: August 1, 1866

Cherokee leader. John Ross was born on October 3, 1790, at Turkey Town (present-day Center, Georgia). His father was a Scotsman of loyalist sympathies; his mother was also from Scottish stock but had one-fourth Cherokee blood. Ross, whose Indian name was Kooweskowe, was educated at home by a private tutor. Around 1805, Ross's father sent him to an academy at Kingston, Tennessee. Ross learned merchandising and served as a clerk in a trading firm but maintained his connections with the Cherokees. During the War of 1812, he served as adjutant of a Cherokee regiment under Major General Andrew Jackson. Ross later established Ross's Landing (now Chattanooga) and ran a ferry and a warehouse operation there.

Ross inherited a large residence in Georgia. As his wealth and influence grew, he became more interested in the political life of the Cherokees, and the nation's chiefs selected

Chief John Ross, the greatest leader of the Cherokee Nation during the 19th century, reluctantly agreed during the Civil War to an alliance with the Confederacy. (Library of Congress)

him as their clerk in 1816. In 1817 he became a member of the National Council. He served as president of the council (1819–1826) and was elected principal chief of the Eastern Cherokees in 1828.

During the 1830s, the Cherokee Nation faced its greatest crisis as the State of Georgia sought to take over its lands. Ross tried unsuccessfully to prevent this by means of the federal courts. A minority of Cherokees who accepted removal to Indian Territory (Oklahoma) signed a fraudulent removal treaty in 1835, but Ross resisted peacefully until the very day he was forced to leave his ancestral home. Ross's own wife became a victim of the Trail of Tears, dying during the trek to Indian Territory in 1839.

When the Eastern Cherokees settled in Indian Territory, they came into conflict with the "old settlers," Western Cherokees who had moved there years before. This led to a civil war that lasted until 1846, when a new treaty with the federal government settled outstanding disputes and reconciled the factions.

Ross built a new home near Tahlequah, the capital of the Cherokee Nation. During the later 1840s and the 1850s, the Cherokees prospered economically, socially, and politically under Ross's leadership. This golden age came to an end in 1861 with the outbreak of the Civil War.

Although Ross was a slaveholder, he favored the Union. He urged neutrality, but by August 1861 he reluctantly acceded to an alliance with the Confederates, under pressure from his chief adversary Stand Watie and Confederate Indian agent Albert Pike. By the summer of 1862, the Cherokees were again involved in their own civil war, with Watie's forces fighting Cherokees loyal to Ross. After Union forces moved into Indian Territory, Ross and his family were taken prisoner but were then allowed to go to Washington, D.C., where they remained until war's end. There he attempted to convince Union officials that he and his followers had been loyal to the Union all along.

In 1866 Ross signed a treaty with the U.S. government that guaranteed the Cherokees' land rights and ensured that the Cherokee Nation would remain intact. Ross died shortly thereafter in Washington on August 1, 1866.

TIM J. WATTS

See also
Cherokees; Native Americans in the Civil War; Watie, Stand

Further Reading
Moulton, Gary E. *John Ross, Cherokee Chief.* Athens: University of Georgia Press, 1978.
Ross, John. *The Papers of Chief John Ross.* Norman: University of Oklahoma Press, 1985.

Ross, Lawrence Sullivan
Birth Date: September 27, 1838
Death Date: January 3, 1898

Confederate officer. Born in Bentonsport, Iowa Territory, on September 27, 1838, Lawrence Sullivan "Sul" Ross moved with his family to Texas in 1839. He attended Baylor University before graduating from Wesleyan University (Alabama) in 1859. In 1858 while visiting home, Ross distinguished himself and was severely wounded as a civilian scout in an army operation against Comanches in Indian Territory.

Following graduation, Ross joined the Texas Rangers, rising to the rank of captain. During a skirmish on the Pease River in December 1860, Ross recovered the white captive Cynthia Ann Parker, mother of future Comanche leader Quanah Parker, gaining much notoriety. Following the secession of Texas, Ross enlisted in a mounted company that became part of the 6th Texas Cavalry and was elected major of the regiment in September 1861.

Ross saw action at the Battle of Pea Ridge (March 7–8, 1862), earning promotion to colonel on May 14. Following the Battle of Corinth (October 3–4, 1862), his regiment covered the Confederate retreat. Ross spent most of 1863 contesting Union advances in Tennessee and Mississippi.

Promoted to brigadier general to date from December 21, 1863, Ross commanded a brigade of Texas cavalry in Brigadier General William "Red" Jackson's division, Army of Mississippi, in numerous engagements associated with the Meridian Campaign (February 3–26, 1864). In almost constant action during the Atlanta Campaign (May 5–September 2, 1864), Ross and his men rendered excellent service, helping to thwart several major Union cavalry raids. During General John Bell Hood's invasion of Tennessee (November–December 1864), the regiment covered the army's retreat from Tennessee after its collapse at Nashville. Ross's brigade spent the rest of the war on duty in Mississippi and surrendered in May 1865 while Ross was on furlough in Texas.

After the war Ross farmed near Waco, Texas; served as sheriff of McLennan County; and participated in the state constitutional convention of 1875. Elected to the Texas Senate in 1880 and as governor of Texas in 1886, in 1891 he became president of the Agricultural and Mechanical College of Texas (Texas A&M University). Ross died at his home in College Station, Texas, on January 3, 1898. Sul Ross State University in Alpine, Texas, is named in his honor.

DAVID COFFEY

See also

Atlanta Campaign; Corinth, Battle of; Jackson, William Hicks; Meridian Campaign; Pea Ridge, Battle of

Further Reading

Benner, Judith Ann. *Sul Ross: Soldier, Statesman, Educator.* College Station: Texas A&M University Press, 1983.

Castel, Albert. *Decision in the West: The Atlanta Campaign of 1864.* Lawrence: University Press of Kansas, 1992.

Rosser, Thomas Lafayette

Birth Date: October 15, 1836
Death Date: March 29, 1910

Confederate officer. Thomas Lafayette Rosser was born on October 15, 1836, in Campbell County, Virginia. In 1849 the family moved to Panola County, Texas. Rosser entered the U.S. Military Academy, West Point, in 1856, but the course of study was then five years, and he resigned on April 22, 1861, following the secession of Texas from the Union.

Joining Confederate service, Rosser was then assigned as a first lieutenant in the famed Washington Artillery of New Orleans, commanding a battery at the First Battle of Bull Run (July 21, 1861). He also led his battery during the Peninsula Campaign (March–July 1862) and was advanced to lieutenant colonel in the artillery in June. A few days later he was named colonel of the 5th Virginia Cavalry. Rosser was seriously wounded at the Battle of Mechanicsville (June 26, 1862).

In the Battle of South Mountain (September 14, 1862), Rosser's cavalry delayed the advance of Union major general William B. Franklin's VI Corps at Crampton's Gap. Rosser also played a conspicuous role at the Battle of Antietam (September 17, 1862) and then at the Battle of Kelly's Ford (March 17, 1863), where he was again seriously wounded. During the Gettysburg Campaign (June–July 1863), his regiment fought at the Battle of Hanover (June 30) and the Battle of Gettysburg (July 1–3). On September 28, 1863, Rosser was promoted to brigadier general and assumed command of the Laurel Brigade. In November of that year, he captured a large wagon train of ammunition intended for the Army of the Potomac.

Rosser's brigade took part in the Overland (Richmond) Campaign (May 4–June 12, 1864) and the Battle of Trevilian Station (June 11) and served in the Shenandoah Valley, where his brigade was crushed in the Third Battle of Winchester (September 19) and the Battle of Tom's Brook (October 9). In October of that year Rosser assumed command of Lieutenant General Jubal Early's cavalry in the Shenandoah Valley and suffered another bitter defeat at the Battle of Cedar Creek (October 19). Rosser was advanced to major general from November 1, 1864. In November 1864 and again in January 1865, he led raids into Union-held West Virginia. In the spring of 1865, Rosser took part in the Battle of Five Forks (April 1) and the Appomattox Campaign (April 2–9). He refused to surrender at Appomattox, cutting his way through Union lines in the hope of joining forces under General Joseph E. Johnston in North Carolina, but Rosser was captured in Staunton, Virginia, on May 4 and paroled shortly thereafter.

After the war, Rosser served as chief engineer of first the Northern Pacific and then the Canadian Pacific railroads. In June 1898 during the Spanish-American War, President William McKinley appointed him a brigadier general of volunteers. Rosser was honorably discharged in October 1898. He died in Charlottesville, Virginia on March 29, 1910.

ROBERT P. BROADWATER

See also

Antietam, Battle of; Appomattox Campaign; Bull Run, First Battle of; Five Forks, Battle of; Gettysburg, Battle of; Gettysburg Campaign; Hanover Court House, Battle of; Kelly's Ford, Battle of; Mechanicsville, Battle of; Overland Campaign; Peninsula Campaign; Rosser's Beverly, West Virginia, Raid; Rosser's Moorefield, West Virginia, Raid; Rosser's New Creek, West Virginia, Raid; South Mountain, Battle of

Further Reading

Bushong, Millard Kessler, and Dean McKoin Bushong. *Fightin' Tom Rosser, C.S.A.* Shippensburg, PA: Beidel Printing House, 1983.

Rosser, Thomas Lafayette, and S. Roger Keller. *Riding with Rosser.* Shippensburg, PA: Burd Street, 1997.

Rosser's Beverly, West Virginia, Raid

Start Date: January 8, 1865
End Date: January 11, 1865

Confederate foraging expedition. Brigadier General Thomas L. Rosser's attack on Beverly, West Virginia, on January 11, 1865, was easily the most successful of his three raids into Union-held West Virginia between January 1864 and January 1865. By early 1865, Confederate forces in the once-rich Shenandoah Valley were desperately short of supplies. Union troops had ravaged the valley, and the situation was so dire that some Confederate units had temporarily been disbanded, their men sent home for want of food and forage. Only a small number of infantry under Lieutenant General Jubal A. Early and cavalry under Rosser remained operational.

At the beginning of January 1865, Rosser learned of substantial Union supplies at Beverly, some 75 miles from his base at Staunton in the Shenandoah Valley. Snow and cold weather were major obstacles, as was the fact that the supplies were guarded by some 1,000 troops. Rosser was determined to make the attempt, however. Securing approval, he collected 300 volunteers, including some former residents of the Beverly area, and organized them into two detachments of 150 each under Colonels Alphonso F. Cook and William A. Morgan.

Departing on January 8, Rosser's men moved west on the Staunton and Parkersburg Turnpike via Monterey. Struggling through deep snow and rain, they forded the Greenbrier River and passed over Cheat Mountain. On the night of January 10, they camped north of Beverly. Early the next morning before sunup, the Confederates, many of them on foot, stormed into the camps of the 34th Ohio Infantry and the 8th Ohio Cavalry under overall command of Colonel Thomas Youart of the 8th Ohio. A single sentinel was taken without firing a shot, and the Federals, asleep in their log hut winter quarters, were taken completely by surprise. Most scattered or quickly surrendered. There was some fighting as some of the Union soldiers fell back through the streets of Beverly and across a bridge on the road to Buckhannon, but the actual fighting lasted only about half an hour.

In the raid, the Confederates suffered 1 killed and several wounded, including Colonel Cook. The Union troops suffered 6 killed, 32 wounded, and 580 captured (some 800 were taken, but many escaped, including Colonel Youart, before reaching Staunton). The Confederates also secured 100 horses, some 600 rifles, and 10,000 rations. After burning much of the Union encampment, Rosser and his men returned to the Shenandoah Valley with their prisoners and the supplies.

SPENCER C. TUCKER

See also
Rosser, Thomas Lafayette

Further Reading

Boyd D. *West Virginia in the Civil War.* 1963; reprint, Charleston: West Virginia Historical Education Foundation, 1994.

Bushong, Millard Kessler, and Dean McKoin Bushong. *Fightin' Tom Rosser, C.S.A.* Shippensburg, PA: Beidel Printing House, 1983.

Lang, Theodore F. *Loyal West Virginia 1861–1865.* 1895; reprint, Huntington, WV: Blue Acorn, 1998.

Rosser, Thomas Lafayette, and S. Roger Keller. *Riding with Rosser.* Shippensburg, PA: Burd Street, 1997.

Rosser's Moorefield, West Virginia, Raid
Event Date: January 29, 1864

Confederate foraging expedition. On January 28, 1864, a Confederate force consisting of Brigadier General Thomas L. Rosser's cavalry brigade, Brigadier General Edward L. Thomas's infantry brigade, and a battery of artillery quit their camps at New Market, Virginia, in the Shenandoah Valley on a raid into West Virginia. Major General Jubal A. Early, commanding the Confederate Valley District, accompanied the expedition, the goal of which was to secure supplies and cattle.

Rosser's brigade led the march and entered Union-held Moorefield, West Virginia, on January 29. Learning that a Union wagon train was moving south toward Petersburg, West Virginia, Early ordered Rosser to cross Branch Mountain with his horsemen and intercept it. Departing Moorefield on the morning of January 30 with 400 men, Rosser encountered a Union infantry regiment on the road across the mountain but charged and routed it. The Union troops fell back on Medley, where the Confederates discovered the wagon train, protected by four Union regiments and some cavalry.

Rosser sent some of his men around the Union flank while he dismounted the rest of his force and sent them against the Union front. A first frontal assault failed, but a second effort, supported by a cannon and coupled with a flanking attack, was successful. The Union soldiers fled, abandoning 95 wagons filled with supplies.

On January 31, Rosser and Thomas marched to Petersburg and there discovered stores of ammunition and additional supplies. Thomas remained at Petersburg with his infantry, while Rosser moved northward to gather cattle and sheep. Learning of the approach of Union reinforcements, Rosser returned to Petersburg, and he and Thomas then returned to the Shenandoah Valley with the 95 wagons, 80 captured Union soldiers, 1,200 cattle, and 500 sheep. The raid claimed 25 Confederate casualties.

SPENCER C. TUCKER

See also
Early, Jubal Anderson; Rosser, Thomas Lafayette; Thomas, Edward Lloyd, Jr.

Further Reading

Boyd D. *West Virginia in the Civil War.* 1963; Charleston: West Virginia Historical Education Foundation, 1994.

Bushong, Millard Kessler, and Dean McKoin Bushong. *Fightin' Tom Rosser, C.S.A.* Shippensburg, PA: Beidel Printing House, 1983.

Lang, Theodore F. *Loyal West Virginia, 1861–1865.* 1895; reprint, Huntington, WV: Blue Acorn, 1998.

Rosser, Thomas Lafayette, and S. Roger Keller. *Riding with Rosser.* Shippensburg, PA: Burd Street, 1997.

Rosser's New Creek, West Virginia, Raid
Event Date: November 28, 1864

Confederate foraging expedition. In late 1864, thousands of Union troops garrisoned forts and towns of West Virginia, protecting the vital Baltimore & Ohio (B&O) Railroad from attacks by Confederate raiders and guerrillas. Security remained a major problem, as it was impossible for the defenders to be everywhere at once. New Creek, West Virginia, appeared to be the most secure of the Union supply depots. Located in Mineral County on a ridge at the end of New Creek Valley, its Fort Kelley was garrisoned by 800 men with five guns. On November 26, Brigadier General Thomas L. Rosser departed the Shenandoah Valley with two cavalry brigades totaling some 500–600 men on a raid against New Creek. The next morning the Confederates reached Moorefield, West Virginia, where they encountered a detachment of Union soldiers from New Creek. A firefight ensued in which the more numerous Confederates easily scattered the Union troops, who spread the alarm.

Success against Fort Kelley appeared to rest on surprise, which was now lost. Regardless, Rosser proceeded. Riding all night, by dawn on November 28 the raiders were some six miles from the fort. Here Rosser met with his officers, who agreed that they should attack. Rosser dressed about 20 of his men in Union blue overcoats and sent them on foot toward the fort. Pretending to be a returning scouting party, they easily captured several groups of Union pickets, the last only two miles from the fort. Bringing up their horses, the Confederates then charged the fort.

Fort Kelley's commander, Colonel George R. Latham, had been warned of Rosser's presence at Moorefield but amazingly had not placed his command on alert. Only a few sentinels were on duty, and most men of the garrison were

eating lunch. The attackers quickly seized the fort, capturing more than 700 Union soldiers.

The Confederates took as many stores as they could and then fired the buildings, although for some reason Rosser failed to destroy the railroad bridge or tear up track. The Confederates then departed with their prisoners. Union forces failed to catch up with the raiders, who returned to their camps on December 2.

Colonel Latham was subsequently court-martialed. Found guilty of neglect of duty, he was dismissed from the service. Several months later as a Republican congressman, Latham had the verdict revoked and was granted an honorable discharge.

SPENCER C. TUCKER

See also

Baltimore & Ohio Railroad; Rosser, Thomas Lafayette

Further Reading

Boyd D. *West Virginia in the Civil War.* 1963; reprint, Charleston: West Virginia Historical Education Foundation, 1994.

Bushong, Millard Kessler, and Dean McKoin Bushong. *Fightin' Tom Rosser, C.S.A.* Shippensburg, PA: Beidel Printing House, 1983.

Lang, Theodore F. *Loyal West Virginia, 1861–1865.* 1895; reprint, Huntington, WV: Blue Acorn, 1998.

Rosser, Thomas Lafayette, and S. Roger Keller. *Riding with Rosser.* Shippensburg, PA: Burd Street, 1997.

Rost, Pierre Adolphe
Birth Date: 1797
Death Date: September 6, 1868

Confederate diplomat. Pierre Adolphe Rost was born in the Department of Lot et Garonne, France, in 1797. He attended the École Polytechnique in Paris and supported Emperor Napoleon I's return to France in 1815. After the defeat of Napoleon and the end of the Hundred Days, a dejected Rost left France and immigrated to the United States, eventually settling in Natchez, Mississippi. He subsequently studied law and commenced a practice in Natchitoches, Louisiana. He served one term in the Louisiana Senate and moved to New Orleans in 1828.

Rost also became active in the state militia and sat on the Louisiana Supreme Court for several months. He resigned to attend to his plantation in St. Charles Parish. In 1846 he was again appointed to the Louisiana Supreme Court, a post he held until 1852.

At the start of the Civil War, Confederate president Jefferson Davis appointed Rost, along with Ambrose Dudley Mann and William L. Yancey, ambassadors to Europe. Their chief aim was to secure diplomatic recognition for the Confederacy. Rost, traveling with Yancey, arrived in London on April 29, 1861. The Confederate diplomats were unsuccessful in securing British recognition, and their request for material and financial aid was rebuffed.

Believing that his French heritage would serve him well in France, Rost soon left London for Paris. He was again rebuffed, and as it turned out most French officials viewed him with contempt, pointing out his lack of diplomatic bona fides, his unsophisticated worldview, and his peculiar accent, which was now heavily tinged with Creole French. When asked how the war effort was progressing, Rost would invariably answer "*tout va bien*" ("all is well"), even when it was plainly clear that this was not the case.

Rost was sent to Madrid in the winter of 1862, where he was equally unsuccessful in securing diplomatic recognitions or material aid for the Confederacy. To make matters worse, a number of his secret dispatches to Richmond were seized when the ship in which they were being carried was captured by Union forces. In the meantime, Rost learned that his plantation had been seized and occupied by Union troops. Upon his return to the Confederacy, he settled in New Orleans and was now landless and almost penniless. Rost died in New Orleans on September 6, 1868.

PAUL G. PIERPAOLI JR.

See also

Diplomacy, Confederate; France; Great Britain; Mann, Ambrose Dudley; Yancey, William Lowndes

Further Reading

Case, Lynn M., and Warren F. Spencer. *The United States and France: Civil War Diplomacy.* Philadelphia: University of Pennsylvania Press, 1970.

Hubbard, Charles M. *The Burden of Confederate Diplomacy.* Knoxville: University of Tennessee Press, 1998.

Rousseau, Lovell Harrison
Birth Date: August 4, 1818
Death Date: January 7, 1869

Union officer. Lovell Harrison Rousseau was born on August 4, 1818, near Stanford, Kentucky. Raised in poverty, he studied law in Louisville and in 1840 migrated to Indiana, where he practiced law and served in both houses of the state legislature as a Whig. During the Mexican-American War (1846–1848), Rousseau was cited for gallantry at the Battle of Buena Vista as a captain in the 2nd Indiana Infantry. He returned from the war in 1848 to practice law in Louisville. In the period before the Civil War, he opposed secession as a Kentucky state senator.

In September 1861, Rousseau was appointed colonel of the 3rd Kentucky Infantry Regiment. Advanced to brigadier general of volunteers on October 1, he commanded a brigade and then a division in the Army of the Ohio during October 1861–October 1862. Rousseau proved himself an able combat commander at the Battle of Shiloh (April 6–7, 1862) and won promotion to major general of volunteers in October 1862 for his actions at the Battle of Perryville (October 8, 1862). He commanded a division in the redesignated Army of the Cumberland during the Battle of Stones River (December 31, 1862–January 2, 1863) and the Tullahoma Campaign (June 23–July 3, 1863). In November 1863 he assumed command of the District of Nashville; in May 1864 his command was designated the District of Tennessee.

Rousseau is best remembered for leading a daring 400-mile cavalry raid into Alabama to support Major General William T. Sherman's Atlanta Campaign (May 5–September 2, 1864). During July 10–22, 1864, Rousseau and his troopers rode through northern and central Alabama destroying Confederate supplies and severing the Montgomery & West Point Railroad before joining Sherman's army near Atlanta. Rousseau ended the war as commander of the District of Middle Tennessee.

In November 1865, Rousseau was elected to the U.S. House of Representatives from Kentucky. In Congress, he supported President Andrew Johnson but challenged radical Reconstruction policies. He quickly resigned from the House after beating an Iowa colleague with his cane but regained his seat in a special election. In 1867 Johnson appointed Rousseau a brigadier general in the regular army and placed him in charge of the delegation that took possession of Alaska from Russia. In 1868 Rousseau was brevetted major general and given command of the Department of Louisiana, where his light touch as an occupation commander endeared him to local Democrats. Rousseau died in New Orleans on January 7, 1869.

JOHN R. REESE

See also

Perryville, Battle of; Rousseau's Alabama Raid; Shiloh, Battle of; Stones River, Battle of; Tullahoma Campaign

Further Reading
Dawson, Joseph G., III. *Army Generals and Reconstruction: Louisiana, 1862–1877.* Baton Rouge and London: Louisiana State University Press, 1982.
Evans, David. *Sherman's Horsemen: Union Cavalry Operations in the Atlanta Campaign.* Bloomington: Indiana University Press, 1996.

Rousseau's Alabama Raid
Start Date: July 10, 1864
End Date: July 22, 1864

Union cavalry raid. To support his Atlanta Campaign (May 5–September 2, 1864), Major General William T. Sherman ordered Major General Lovell H. Rousseau, commander of the District of Tennessee, to assemble 2,500 cavalry at Decatur, Alabama, and then cut the Montgomery & West Point Railroad, the only open rail link between Atlanta and the western Confederacy. The raid was also designed to destroy track, equipment, and buildings between Tuskegee and Opelika.

Assembled from five cavalry regiments, Rousseau's 2,700-man force left Decatur on July 10 and pushed south into the rugged hill country of east-central Alabama. Confederate guerrillas harassed the column, but the expedition met its only serious opposition as it reached the Coosa River on July 13. As the raiders forded the river at Ten Islands the following day, they engaged in a sharp fight with elements of two Alabama cavalry regiments numbering only some 200 men under Brigadier General James H. Clanton. The Union cavalrymen then moved on to Talladega, where on July 15 they captured or destroyed a considerable quantity of Confederate rations and put the torch to two gun factories, several railroad cars, and the railroad depot.

Around sunset on July 17, Rousseau's raiders reached the Montgomery & West Point rail line at Loachapoka. The Union troopers spent the next 36 hours executing their mission in, as Rousseau reported to Sherman, "a most thorough manner." Rousseau's troopers destroyed some 30 miles of track, burned a depot, and almost set fire to the village of Loachapoka; they destroyed machine shops, a roundhouse, and a depot at Opelika as well. They also skirmished with a trainload of University of Alabama cadets and home guardsmen sent from Montgomery to stop them, an event remembered as the Battle of Chehaw.

Their mission accomplished, Rousseau and his raiders pressed on into Georgia. They completed their 400-mile march on July 22, 1864, joining Sherman's army north of Atlanta. The raid was an astounding success, one of the most productive Union cavalry operations of the war. Rousseau's raiders suffered light casualties of 12 killed and 30 wounded. The daring foray shocked Alabamians, who now realized that they were no longer safe from Union depredations.

JOHN R. REESE

See also
Atlanta Campaign; Rousseau, Lovell Harrison

Further Reading
Evans, David. *Sherman's Horsemen: Union Cavalry Operations in the Atlanta Campaign.* Bloomington: Indiana University Press, 1996.
McMillan, Malcolm C., ed. *The Alabama Confederate Reader.* Tuscaloosa: University of Alabama Press, 1963.

Rowan, Stephen Clegg
Birth Date: December 25, 1808
Death Date: March 31, 1890

Union naval officer. Born near Dublin, Ireland, on December 25, 1808, Stephen Clegg Rowan immigrated to the United States as a child. He received a midshipman's warrant on February 1, 1826, and was promoted to passed midshipman on April 28, 1832; to lieutenant on March 3, 1837; and to commander on September 14, 1855.

At the beginning of the Civil War, Rowan commanded the steam sloop *Pawnee* at Washington, D.C. Ordered to assist the effort to relieve Fort Sumter, he arrived at Charleston too late. He then participated in the evacuation of the Norfolk (Gosport) Navy Yard, after which he served in the Potomac Flotilla. On May 24, 1861, Rowan and the *Pawnee* helped take Alexandria, Virginia, for the Union, and he took part in Commander James H. Ward's engagement with Confederate shore batteries at Aquia Creek on June 1 and at Mathias Creek on June 27, when Ward was killed.

Assigned to the Atlantic Blockading Squadron, Rowan participated in the operation to secure Hatteras Inlet, North Carolina, under Flag Officer Silas H. Stringham on August 29. Given command of the converted side-wheel steamer *Delaware* in October 1861, Rowan was assigned to the new North Atlantic Blockading Squadron and had charge of the fighting ships in Flag Officer Louis M. Goldsborough's expedition to Roanoke Island and took part in the battle there on February 7–8, 1862, capturing Elizabeth City and

U.S. Navy commander Stephen C. Rowan, commanding the steam sloop *Pawnee* at Washington, D.C., secured Alexandria, Virginia, for the Union in May 1861. Later he commanded the Union's most powerful ship, the ironclad *New Ironsides,* off Charleston. (National Archives)

Edenton. Rowan commanded the Union ships in Albemarle and Pamlico Sounds with Goldsborough's absence following the Battles of Hampton Roads (March 8–9, 1862). Rowan then assisted Union land forces in the capture of New Bern, North Carolina, on March 14 and Fort Macon on April 25, actions for which he subsequently received the Thanks of Congress.

Promoted to captain on July 16, 1862, Rowan in late 1862 was assigned command of the screw frigate *Roanoke,* undergoing conversion at New York into a turreted ironclad. When the ship was found unsuitable for anything other than coast defense, Rowan in June 1863 was assigned command of the ironclad *New Ironsides* in the South Atlantic Blockading Squadron off Charleston. On October 7, 1863, Rowan's

ship survived an attack by the semisubmersible CSS *David* armed with a spar torpedo.

In early 1864 Rowan was promoted to commodore, with his commission backdated to July 16, 1862. He commanded the South Atlantic Blockading Squadron during Rear Admiral John A. Dahlgren's absence from late February to early May 1864. After the *New Ironsides* was ordered to undergo repairs at the Philadelphia Navy Yard in June 1864, Rowan was on waiting orders. On September 1, 1864, Secretary of the Navy Gideon Welles ordered Rowan to assume command of Union forces in the North Carolina Sounds. Perhaps for reasons of health, Rowan requested relief from this assignment and remained on waiting orders status with no more active service during the war.

Promoted to rear admiral on July 1, 1866, Rowan commanded the Norfolk (Gosport) Navy Yard (1866–1867) and then the Asiatic Squadron (1867–1870). Promoted to vice admiral on August 15, 1870, he was the last U.S. Navy officer to hold that rank until World War I. After 1870, Rowan held a number of different posts, including commandant of the New York Navy Yard and port admiral of New York City (1872–1876) and chairman of the Light-House Board (1883–1889). Placed on the retired list at age 80 on February 28, 1889, Rowan died in Washington, D.C., on March 31, 1890.

SPENCER C. TUCKER

See also

Atlantic Blockading Squadron; Dahlgren, John Adolph Bernard; David-Class Torpedo Boats; Goldsborough, Louis Malesherbes; Hampton Roads, Battles of; Hatteras Inlet, North Carolina, Union Assault on; New Bern, Battle of; *New Ironsides,* USS; North Atlantic Blockading Squadron; Roanoke Island, Battle of; Stringham, Silas Horton; Ward, James Harmon; Welles, Gideon

Further Reading

Callahan, Edward W., ed. *List of Officers of the Navy of the United States and of the Marine Corps from 1775 to 1900.* 1901; reprint, New York: Haskell House Publishers, 1969.

Roberts, William H. *New Ironsides in the Civil War.* Annapolis, MD: Naval Institute Press, 1999.

Thompson, Kenneth E. *Civil War Commodores and Admirals: A Biographical Directory of All Eighty-Eight Union and Confederate Navy Officers Who Attained Commissioned Flag Rank during the War.* Portland, ME: Thompson Group, 2001.

Rowanty Creek, Battle of

See Hatcher's Run, Battle of

Rowlett's Station, Battle of
Event Date: December 17, 1861

Inconclusive engagement in south-central Kentucky. The Battle of Rowlett's Station is also known as the Battle of Woodsonville and the Battle of Green River. After assuming command at Cincinnati of the Army of the Ohio in November 1861, Brigadier General Don Carlos Buell sought to establish Union control over the region and toward that end in December sent troops of Brigadier General Alexander M. McCook's 2nd Division into central Kentucky.

General Albert S. Johnston, commanding the Confederate Western Department, had established a position along the Green River, a tributary of the Ohio, near Munfordville, Kentucky. When McCook moved toward the Confederate lines, on December 10 Confederate brigadier general Thomas C. Hindman ordered the destruction of the southern portion of the Louisville & Nashville Railroad bridge over the Green River. Union colonel August Willich, commanding the 32nd Indiana Infantry, then ordered two of his companies across the river to secure a beachhead, while the remainder of his men began construction of a pontoon bridge. The 32nd Indiana completed the bridge on December 17, and four more companies then crossed the river.

Hindman ordered the Union bridge destroyed and dispatched a mixed force of Texas cavalry, Arkansas infantry, and Mississippi artillery. The principal unit involved was the 8th Texas Cavalry (subsequently named Terry's Texas Rangers), commanded by Colonel Benjamin Franklin Terry. In the ensuing fighting south of Woodsonville, Terry's cavalrymen assisted by infantry (some 1,300 men in all) repeatedly charged some 500 Union infantrymen, commanded by Lieutenant Colonel Henry von Trebra, drawn up in a hollow square formation. Terry was mortally wounded in the fighting, and the Confederates were finally forced to withdraw. Willich, who had been absent during the fighting, arrived on the scene and ordered a withdrawal to a stronger position. The Confederates, fearing that the Union side would reinforce, also withdrew.

The fighting claimed Union casualties of 10 killed and 22 wounded; the Confederates lost 33 dead and some 50 wounded. Both sides claimed victory, but the Union troops remained in place and were thus able to ensure the continued movement of Union men and supplies on the Louisville & Nashville Railroad. The battle was soon overshadowed by the Union victory at the Battle of Mill Springs (January 19, 1862).

SPENCER C. TUCKER

See also
Buell, Don Carlos; Hindman, Thomas Carmichael; McCook, Alexander McDowell; Mill Springs, Battle of; Terry's Texas Rangers; Willich, Johann August Ernst von

Further Reading
Brown, Kent Masterson. *The Civil War in Kentucky: Battle for the Bluegrass.* Mason City, IA: Savas, 2000.
Harrision, Lowell Hayes. *The Civil War in Kentucky.* Lexington: University Press of Kentucky, 1987.

Ruffin, Edmund
Birth Date: January 5, 1794
Death Date: June 17, 1865

Noted agricultural reformer, politician, and Southern nationalist. Born on January 5, 1794, in Prince George County, Virginia, Edmund Ruffin was educated at home except for a brief period at the College of William and Mary. During the War of 1812 he served as a private, returning after his father's death to take charge of the family lands at Coggin's Point on the James River.

Here Ruffin, with little practical or theoretical knowledge, began his experiments in scientific agriculture. His aim was to restore the fertility of soil worn out by years of poor methods used for single-crop farming. He discovered that the soil could be greatly improved by treating it with lime-rich elements and then rotating crops and employing proper drainage and good methods of planting. In this way, Ruffin was able to increase wheat and corn yields by 40 percent.

In 1832 Ruffin published the results of his experiments in *An Essay on Calcareous Manures* that was revised and went through many editions. Ruffin was appointed agricultural surveyor of South Carolina in 1842. His *Report of the Commencement and Progress of the Agricultural Survey of South Carolina* (1843) marked the beginning of a new era in agriculture in that state. In 1845 Ruffin was elected president of the newly formed Virginia Agricultural Society. During this period, he wrote and spoke frequently on scientific agriculture.

Also interested in politics, Ruffin served in the Virginia Senate from 1823 to 1826 and during the next 30 years earned a reputation as a champion of slavery and states' rights. By the late 1850s, he was Virginia's leading secession advocate. In 1860 he published *Anticipations of the Future,* a book that made the case for secession by depicting the

Edmund Ruffin, an indefatigable champion of the Southern cause, as a Confederate private fired the first shot of the Civil War, against Fort Sumter in Charleston Harbor on April 12, 1861. (National Archives)

advantages of an independent South. In early 1861 Ruffin moved to Charleston, South Carolina, and as an honorary member of the Palmetto Guard he won Southern acclaim by firing the first shot at Fort Sumter on April 12, 1861. He went back to Virginia later that year and was an indefatigable proponent of the Confederate cause. Financially ruined and in despair over the collapse of the Confederacy, he took his own life on June 17, 1865, in Amelia County, Virginia.

WILLIAM MCGUIRE AND LESLIE WHEELER

See also

Fort Sumter, South Carolina, Confederate Bombardment of; Virginia

Further Reading

Detzer, David R. *Allegiance: Fort Sumter, Charleston and the Beginning of the Civil War*. New York: Harcourt, 2001.
Mitchell, Betty L. *Edmund Ruffin: A Biography*. Bloomington: Indiana University Press, 1981.

Ruger, Thomas Howard
Birth Date: April 2, 1833
Death Date: June 3, 1907

Union officer. Born in Lima, New York, on April 2, 1833, Thomas Howard Ruger moved at age 13 with his family to Janesville, Wisconsin. He graduated third in his class from the U.S. Military Academy, West Point, in 1854. Commissioned in the engineers, Ruger served in that capacity at New Orleans but resigned his commission on April 1, 1855, and opened a law practice in Janesville. With the onset of the Civil War, he returned to military service.

On June 29, 1861, Ruger was commissioned lieutenant colonel of the 3rd Wisconsin and became its colonel on September 1. He led this unit as a part of Major General Nathaniel P. Banks's command in the Shenandoah Valley and in northern Virginia in the campaigns of the spring and summer of 1862 against Confederate forces commanded by Major General Thomas J. "Stonewall" Jackson. Ruger distinguished himself in the Battle of Cedar Mountain (August 9, 1862) and also participated in the Second Battle of Bull Run (August 29–30, 1862). During the Antietam Campaign (September 4–20, 1862), the 3rd Wisconsin formed part of the 3rd Brigade, 1st Division, XII Corps. Assuming command of the 3rd Brigade during the Battle of Antietam (September 17, 1862) when Brigadier General George H. Gordon took over the division, Ruger sustained a head wound in fighting near the West Woods.

Ruger was appointed brigadier general of volunteers to date from November 29, 1862. He again distinguished himself when, during the Battle of Chancellorsville (May 1–4, 1863), his 3rd Brigade helped stem Jackson's flanking attack on May 2. During the Battle of Gettysburg (July 1–3, 1863), Ruger's leadership and military acumen so impressed his commanding officer, Brigadier General Alpheus S. Williams, that Williams appointed Ruger over other more senior officers to take command of the 1st Division when Williams assumed corps command. Ruger's troop emplacements on Culp's Hill on July 2 helped ensure defeat of the Confederate attack there on July 3.

Following the Battle of Gettysburg, Ruger was dispatched to New York City to help quell the draft riots there. Ordered to the western theater, he commanded a brigade and then a division during Major General William T. Sherman's Atlanta Campaign (May 5–September 2, 1864). Ruger then commanded the 2nd Division, XXII Corps, Army of the Ohio, and fought with distinction in the Battle of Franklin (November 30) and the Battle of Nashville (December

15–16). He was brevetted major general of volunteers to date from November 30 for his role at Franklin. Ruger then moved with his division to North Carolina, where he served under Major General John M. Schofield, seeing action at the Second Battle of Kinston (March 7–10, 1865) and then occupying Wilmington.

From June 1865 to June 1866, Ruger had command of forces in North Carolina. He mustered out of volunteer service on June 20, 1866. Accepting a commission as colonel in the regular army on July 13, 1866, he commanded the 33rd Infantry. Brevetted brigadier general on March 2, 1867, for his role in the Battle of Gettysburg, Ruger was military governor of Georgia in the first half of 1868. In March 1869 he took command of the 18th Infantry. Ruger was superintendent of West Point during September 1871–September 1876 and then held commands in the West. He was promoted to brigadier general on May 19, 1886, and to major general on February 8, 1895. Ruger retired from the army on April 2, 1897, and died at Stamford, Connecticut, on June 3, 1907.

SPENCER C. TUCKER

See also

Antietam, Battle of; Atlanta Campaign; Banks, Nathaniel Prentice; Bull Run, Second Battle of; Cedar Mountain, Battle of; Chancellorsville, Battle of; Franklin, Battle of; Gordon, George Henry; Jackson, Thomas Jonathan; Jackson's Shenandoah Valley Campaign; Kinston, Second Battle of; Nashville, Battle of; New York City Draft Riots; Schofield, John McAllister; Sherman, William Tecumseh; Williams, Alpheus Starkey

Further Reading

Eicher, John H., and David J. Eicher. *Civil War High Commands.* Stanford, CA: Stanford University Press, 2001.

Heitman, Francis. *Historical Register and Dictionary of the United States Army, 1789–1903.* Washington, DC: U.S. Government Printing Office, 1903.

Warner, Ezra J. *Generals in Blue: Lives of the Union Commanders.* Baton Rouge: Louisiana State University Press, 2006.

Ruggles, Daniel

Birth Date: January 31, 1810
Death Date: June 1, 1897

Confederate officer. Daniel Ruggles was born on January 31, 1810, in Barre, Massachusetts. An 1833 graduate of the U.S. Military Academy, West Point, he married a wealthy Virginian and considered himself a Southerner. Promoted to first lieutenant in 1838 and captain in 1846, Ruggles served in the Second Seminole War (1835–1842) and the Mexican-American War (1846–1848), during which he was brevetted

major and lieutenant colonel. He spent the next dozen years in routine service, mostly in the West.

In March 1861 Ruggles resigned his U.S. Army commission to become a brigadier general of Virginia state forces. Commissioned a brigadier general in the Confederate Army on August 9, he commanded a brigade at Pensacola and New Orleans before he took command of the 1st Division, II Corps, Army of Mississippi, at Corinth.

In the lead-up to the Battle of Shiloh (April 6–7, 1862), Ruggles proved dilatory in his preparations, citing bad roads and weather and contradictory orders. His commander, General Albert Sidney Johnson, was highly annoyed with Ruggles's behavior but allowed him to retain his command. On the morning of April 6, Ruggles's men were among the first to assault the Union positions, and that afternoon Ruggles led an intrepid offensive against the Hornet's Nest. Ruggles's brutal assault steamrolled the position there, taking some 2,200 Union prisoners. On April 7, Ruggles repelled several Union attacks against exhausted Confederate forces.

The following month, Ruggles was tasked with handling Confederate logistics. In June he became commander of eastern Louisiana but held that position only until late November. In August 1863 he became a staff officer for Major General Joseph E. Johnston. More administrative posts followed until Ruggles was named chief of Confederate prisons in early 1865.

After the war Ruggles returned to his home near Fredericksburg, Virginia, where he farmed and was involved in real estate speculation. In 1884 he was named a member of the board of visitors of West Point. Ruggles died on June 1, 1897, in Fredericksburg.

PAUL G. PIERPAOLI JR.

See also

Johnston, Albert Sidney; Johnston, Joseph Eggleston; Shiloh, Battle of

Further Reading

Smith, Timothy B. *The Untold Story of Shiloh: The Battle and the Battlefield.* Knoxville: University of Tennessee Press, 2006.

Warner, Ezra J. *Generals in Gray: Lives of the Confederate Commanders.* Baton Rouge: Louisiana State University Press, 2006.

Rush's Lancers

Elite Union cavalry unit. Rush's Lancers was the name commonly used for the 6th Pennsylvania Cavalry. In August 1861, Richard H. Rush of Philadelphia received authorization to raise a regiment of cavalry in Philadelphia and Berks Counties. On October 5 the regiment was complete, and the men, most of whom were from the upper strata of Philadelphia society, were mustered into Union service. Rush was commissioned regimental colonel.

At the suggestion of Major General George B. McClellan, the unit was armed with 9-foot-long lances tipped with an 11-inch triple-edged steel blade and weighing some 8 pounds. Each lance was adorned with a pennant. Assigned to the cavalry of the Army of the Potomac, the regiment saw minor action in the Peninsula Campaign (March–July 1862), the Battle of Antietam (September 17, 1862), and the First Battle of Fredericksburg (December 13, 1862).

In May 1863, Rush's Lancers abandoned the weapon for which they were known when they were rearmed with Sharps carbines. The 6th Pennsylvania was then assigned to the Reserve Brigade of Brigadier General John Buford's 1st Cavalry Division. The regiment played a key role in the Union victory at the Battle of Brandy Station (June 9, 1863) but also suffered the highest casualties of any Northern unit on the field. The regiment also played a conspicuous role in the Gettysburg Campaign (June–July 1863), the Bristoe Campaign (October 9–20, 1863), and the Mine Run Campaign (November 26–December 2, 1863) and was almost constantly engaged during the Overland Campaign (May 4–June 12, 1864). In August 1864, the unit was detached for service in Major General Philip H. Sheridan's Shenandoah Valley Campaign (August 7, 1864–March 2, 1865).

In September 1864, enlistment terms for most of the men in the regiment expired, and the unit was reorganized for three more years. It continued to serve in the Shenandoah Valley until the spring of 1865, when it returned to the Army of the Potomac in time to take part in the Appomattox Campaign (April 2–9, 1865). Mustered out of service in August 1865, the unit suffered during the war a total of 498 men and 24 officers killed, wounded, or missing.

ROBERT P. BROADWATER

See also

Antietam, Battle of; Appomattox Campaign; Brandy Station, Battle of; Bristoe Campaign; Fredericksburg, First Battle of; Gettysburg Campaign; Mine Run Campaign; Overland Campaign; Peninsula Campaign; Sheridan's Shenandoah Valley Campaign

Further Reading

Bates, Samuel P. *History of the Pennsylvania Volunteers, 1861–1865*. 4 vols. Harrisburg, PA: B. Singerly, 1869.

Gracey, Samuel L. *Annals of the Sixth Pennsylvania Cavalry*. Lancaster, OH: Vanberg, 1996.

Russell, David Allen

Birth Date: December 10, 1820
Death Date: September 19, 1864

Union officer. Born in Salem, New York, on December 10, 1820, David Allen Russell graduated from the U.S. Military Academy, West Point, in 1845. He fought in the Mexican-American War (1846–1848), earning a brevet, and was promoted to first lieutenant on January 1, 1848, and to captain on June 22, 1854. At the start of the Civil War, he was stationed at Fort Yamhill, Oregon.

Russell served with his regular unit in the Washington defenses until he entered the volunteer army as colonel of the 7th Massachusetts Infantry on February 18, 1862. He fought with his unit in Major General George B. McClellan's Peninsula Campaign (March–July 1862) and was brevetted lieutenant colonel in the Union Army on July 1, 1862. Russell then led his regiment in the Battle of Antietam (September 17, 1862). Appointed brigadier general of volunteers on November 29, 1862, he assumed command of the 3rd Brigade, 1st Division, VI Corps, Army of the Potomac. Russell's brigade was lightly engaged in the First Battle of Fredericksburg (December 13, 1862) but took heavy casualties in the assault on Marye's Heights at Fredericksburg as part of the Battle of Chancellorsville (May 1–4, 1863). He was brevetted colonel in the Union Army for his role in the Battle of Gettysburg (July 1–3, 1863).

During the Battle of Rappahannock Station (November 7, 1863), Russell had temporary command of the 1st Division, personally leading it in an attack on the Confederate bridgehead and capturing a large number of Confederates and their equipment. Rewarded with permanent command of the 1st Division, he saw action in the Overland Campaign (May 4–June 12, 1864). His division was conspicuously engaged in the Battle of Spotsylvania Court House (May 8–21, 1864).

Russell was wounded in the arm on June 1 during the Battle of Cold Harbor (May 31–June 12, 1864). He then took part in the Petersburg Campaign (June 15, 1864–April 3, 1865), but his 1st Division was transferred with the rest of VI Corps to counter Confederate lieutenant general Jubal A. Early's Washington Raid (June 28–July 21, 1864). During Major General Philip Sheridan's subsequent Shenandoah Valley Campaign (August 7, 1864–March 2, 1865), Russell was hit in the chest by a shell fragment and killed on September 19, 1864, in the Third Battle of Winchester. He was posthumously brevetted major general in both the regulars and volunteers, with date of rank to September 19.

SPENCER C. TUCKER

See also

Chancellorsville, Battle of; Cold Harbor, Battle of; Early's Raid on Washington, D.C.; Fredericksburg, First Battle of; Gettysburg, Battle of; McClellan, George Brinton; Overland Campaign; Peninsula Campaign; Petersburg Campaign; Rappahannock Station, Battle of; Winchester, Third Battle of

Further Reading

Eicher, John H., and David J. Eicher. *Civil War High Commands.* Stanford, CA: Stanford University Press, 2001.
Warner, Ezra J. *Generals in Blue: Lives of the Union Commanders.* Baton Rouge: Louisiana State University Press, 2006.

Russell, Lord John
Birth Date: August 18, 1792
Death Date: May 28, 1878

British foreign secretary (1859–1865). Born on August 18, 1792, John Russell was the third son of the 6th Duke of Bedford, an aristocrat with liberal tendencies. Russell was educated primarily by tutors until he entered the University of Edinburgh in 1809, where he became immersed in Scottish philosophy. He left Edinburgh in 1812, however, without a degree. In 1813 Russell was elected to the British House of Commons from his home district of Tavistock. He would remain in the Commons for nearly 50 years.

As a member of the Whig Party, Russell quickly proved himself active in the cause of parliamentary and political reform. In 1830 the Whigs came to power, and throughout the 1830s Russell held a number of government positions, most notably home secretary (1835–1839) and colonial secretary (1839–1841). As a member of the opposition (1841–1846), he led the Whigs in supporting free trade and helped convince Prime Minister Sir Robert Peel to repeal the Corn Laws.

After Peel's government fell in 1846, Russell became prime minister. With high hopes for his administration, he embarked on a series of reform efforts. His progress was slowed and in some cases halted, however, by poor judgment, lackadaisical administrative practices, divisions within his own party, opposition from the Tories, and the Irish Potato Famine. Even for many Whigs, Russell's politics seemed too liberal.

Russell's government fell in 1852, but he immediately reentered the cabinet as foreign secretary under Prime

Minister Lord Aberdeen, a position that Russell held for about a year. Also, he served as leader of the House of Commons (1852–1855). He again served as foreign minister briefly under Prime Minister Viscount Palmerston's administration. As foreign minister, Russell did not prove to be a popular success. Many believed that his inept diplomacy had helped precipitate the Crimean War and that he had botched the negotiations that eventually settled the conflict.

After leaving Palmerston's government in 1855, Russell retired from politics for four years. Although he and Palmerston had often disagreed in the past, Russell agreed to serve as Palmerston's foreign secretary in 1859. Against all expectations, the two men worked together harmoniously in diplomatic matters, with Palmerston usually taking the lead. As foreign secretary, Russell faced a series of crises that occupied most of his attention.

Immediately upon assuming office, Russell was confronted with the issue of Italian unification, which he supported, thus siding against the Austro-Hungarian Empire. He also struggled to keep Britain neutral in the American Civil War, an issue over which the cabinet was fiercely divided. He did little, however, to stop the construction in a British yard of a ship that became the Confederate commerce raider *Alabama,* prompting loud protests from the United States and embroiling Britain in a difficult diplomatic situation. In October 1862 Russell suggested a joint British-French-Russian mediation effort to end the Civil War by negotiation. His proposal ultimately did not reach fruition, largely because of intransigence among British cabinet members.

Despite his controversial career as foreign secretary, when Palmerston died in October 1865, Russell became prime minister once again. His second tenure in this office proved to be brief and personally humiliating, however. With Palmerston no longer obstructing reform, Russell introduced a reform bill that would further reduce the property qualification for voting and thus extend suffrage. Dissent within his own party destroyed any hopes he had of passing the legislation, and by June 1866 his government had collapsed. Never again did Russell play a major role in any administration, but with his elevation to the peerage as an earl in 1861, he took his seat in the British House of Lords. When the Tories passed a more radical reform bill in 1867 than the one he had proposed two years earlier, Russell felt disgraced for failing where more conservative leaders had succeeded. Russell died at his home, Pembroke Lodge, on May 28, 1878.

HUBERT DUBRULLE

See also
Alabama, CSS; *Alabama* Claims; Diplomacy, Confederate; Diplomacy, U.S.; Great Britain; *Saxon* Affair

Further Reading
Prest, John M. *Lord John Russell*. Columbia: University of South Carolina Press, 1972.
Walpole, Spencer. *The Life of Lord John Russell*. 2 vols. New York: Greenwood, 1968.

Russell, William Howard
Birth Date: March 28, 1820
Death Date: February 10, 1907

Controversial British journalist whose writing infuriated Americans, North and South. William Howard Russell was born on March 28, 1820, in County Dublin, Ireland, to a prominent family. He attended but did not receive a degree from Trinity College, Dublin, and soon embarked on a career in journalism. By the mid-1850s, he had become a special correspondent for the *London Times* and was well known for his vivid writing style and keen sense of observation. War reporting became his specialty, and he covered the Crimean War as well as fighting in India and Denmark. By 1860, Russell, a close friend of the Prince of Wales, had been knighted for his journalistic exploits.

Anxious to cover the growing crisis in the United States, Russell arrived in New York City in March 1861 and immediately embarked on a two-month tour of the Confederacy, during which he outraged and alienated many Southerners with his undisguised contempt for slavery. He returned to the Union in June and was on hand to witness the First Battle of Bull Run (July 21, 1861). His report on the battle was largely a scathing indictment of the Union army's incompetence, which outraged many Northerners. Indeed, Russell was pilloried in the New York City press and even received death threats from disgruntled readers. The First Battle of Bull Run was the only battle that Russell witnessed directly. By April 1862, his unpopularity was so great that U.S. secretary of war Edwin Stanton revoked his press credentials. Russell left the United States, never to return.

Back home, Russell continued in his role as Britain's premier battlefield correspondent, covering such conflicts as the Austro-Prussian War, the Franco-Prussian War, and the Zulu War, among others. In the twilight years of his career, he edited the *Army and Navy Gazette*. He also produced two books on his Civil War experiences: *The Civil War in America* (1861) and *My Diary North and South* (1863). Russell died in London on February 10, 1907.

PAUL G. PIERPAOLI JR.

See also
Bull Run, First Battle of; Journalism

Further Reading
Crawford, Martin, ed. *William Howard Russell's Civil War: Private Diaries and Letters, 1861–1862*. Athens: University of Georgia Press, 2008.
Hankinson, Alan. *Man of War: William Howard Russell of the Times*. Farnham, Surrey, UK: Ashgate, 1982.

Russian-U.S. Relations

The democratic United States and czarist, monarchial Russia, a seemingly unlikely match, enjoyed generally amicable relations before, during, and immediately after the Civil War. At this point in history, both the United States and Russia opposed intervention in the internal affairs of another country.

In April 1861, Russian foreign minister Prince Alexander Gorchakov signaled that his nation would only recognize the U.S. government; he also stated on numerous occasions that he sympathized with the Union's predicament and deplored the war. The Civil War years saw emancipation in both nations—in February 1861 Russia liberated the serfs from control by the aristocratic landlords, and in January 1863 America freed black slaves in the still rebellious states and moved the nation one step closer toward granting complete freedom to all slaves. Each nation publicly approved the action taken by the other. With the beginning of the Civil War, St. Petersburg instructed Russian minister to the United States Eduard de Stoeckl to offer Russian mediation in an effort to bring about an end to the fighting.

In late 1862 the French, in a proposed coalition with Great Britain and Russia, pushed for intervention in the Civil War in the form of mediation and possible recognition of the Confederacy, but a firm Russian refusal killed the initiative. The United States returned the favor in 1863, when Great Britain and France asked for the Union's backing in protesting Russian actions against its Polish subjects who had risen up in rebellion. The possibility of an Anglo-French conflict with Russia, coupled with the likelihood of hostilities between the German states and Denmark, diverted the attention of the European powers, at least momentarily, from the war in America.

In 1863 the Russian Baltic fleet arrived at New York City, and its Pacific contingent sailed into San Francisco Bay. Russian naval officers were keen to view operations of the Union ironclads. Units of the Russian Navy were now in position to carry out commerce raiding in the event of war with Great Britain and France over Poland. Many in the North saw the Russian fleet's presence as a sign of support in the face of British and French treachery, while some in Europe believed that the Russian ships would join the U.S. Navy in the event of conflict between the Americans on the one hand and the British and French on the other. A rumor to that effect was widely circulating in America in the months after the South surrendered in April 1865. Certainly the presence of the Russian fleet in Northern ports raised Union morale while simultaneously lowering that of the South.

Amicable U.S.-Russian relations during the Civil War also laid the foundation for the United States to purchase Alaska in 1867 for $7.2 million.

W. Terry Lindley

See also

Diplomacy, U.S.; France; Great Britain

Further Reading

Saul, Norman E. *Distant Friends: The United States and Russia, 1763–1867*. Lawrence: University Press of Kansas, 1991.

Woldman, Albert A. *Lincoln and the Russians*. New York: World Publishing, 1952.

Rust, Albert
Birth Date: 1818
Death Date: April 3, 1870

Confederate officer. Born in Fauquier County, Virginia, in 1818, Albert Rust moved to Union City, Arkansas, in 1837. There he studied law, passed the bar, and became a lawyer and a planter. From 1842 to 1848 and again from 1852 to 1854, he was a member of the Arkansas legislature. Elected to the U.S. House of Representatives, he served there from March 1855 to March 1857. Defeated for reelection, he was again elected in November 1858 and served from March 1859 to March 1861.

Rust was a member of the Provisional Confederate Congress from March 1861 to February 1862. He entered Confederate military service on July 5, 1861, as colonel of the 3rd Arkansas Infantry, which he had recruited. His unit was ordered to western Virginia (West Virginia), and Rust served under General Robert E. Lee in the Battle of Cheat Mountain (September 11–15, 1861). Rust remained in Virginia through the winter of 1861–1862, seeing minor action.

Appointed brigadier general on March 4, 1862, Rust was ordered to the western theater, where he commanded a brigade and took part in the Battle of Corinth (October 3–4, 1862). In the spring of 1863, Rust was assigned to the Trans-Mississippi Department, where he served out the remainder of the war in Arkansas, Louisiana, and Texas. He was paroled at Austin, Texas, on July 27, 1865.

Ruined financially by the war, Rust settled on a farm on the Arkansas River near Little Rock. He died at his home on April 3, 1870.

Spencer C. Tucker

See also

Cheat Mountain, Battle of; Corinth, Battle of; Lee, Robert Edward

Further Reading

Eicher, John H., and David J. Eicher. *Civil War High Commands*. Stanford, CA: Stanford University Press, 2001.

Warner, Ezra J. *Generals in Gray: Lives of the Confederate Commanders*. Baton Rouge: Louisiana State University Press, 2006.

Ryan, Abram Joseph
Birth Date: February 5, 1838
Death Date: April 22, 1886

Poet, Roman Catholic priest, and volunteer Confederate chaplain during the Civil War. Born in Hagerstown, Maryland, on February 5, 1838, Abram Joseph Ryan was one of the most important literary figures associated with the Lost Cause, which was pervasive in Southern literature, history, and politics well into the 20th century. Ryan was raised and educated in Missouri, studying for the Roman Catholic priesthood at a seminary in Perryville, Missouri. He was ordained in September 1860, after which he served briefly on the faculty of Niagara University and in a parish in Illinois.

After the outbreak of the war, Ryan took several leaves of absence from his assigned duties and served as an unofficial chaplain and priest to units of Louisiana troops. He never enlisted or was commissioned in the Confederate Army, but in late 1863 or early 1864 he began full-time ministry as a volunteer chaplain and participated in several battles in Tennessee during 1863 and 1864.

Ryan wrote several poems during the war, most notably "In Memoriam" and "In Memory of My Brother," which remembered the brother he lost in 1863. On June 24, 1865,

Ryan's most famous poem, "The Conquered Banner," was published in the *New York Freeman's Journal* under the pen name "Moina." The poem reflected the sentimentality, religious overtones, and sense of loss felt by many in the South and became extremely popular.

After the war, Ryan served as a priest in Tennessee, Alabama, Louisiana, and Georgia. In Georgia he founded a weekly religious and political publication, the *Banner of the South*. In it he printed many of his poems as well as the work of others, including Sidney Lanier, James Ryder Randall, and Mark Twain.

Ryan continued to write and publish poetry about the Confederacy and what he considered the heroic martyrdom of its fallen troops until his death in a monastery on April 22, 1886, in Louisville, Kentucky. Among his more popular poems were "C.S.A.," "The Sword of Robert E. Lee," and "The South." In 1879 Ryan published a collection of his poetry titled *Father Ryan's Poems* (reissued in 1880 as *Poems: Patriotic, Religious, Miscellaneous*), and the collection sold well for the next 50 years, undergoing more than 40 reprints and editions.

TIMOTHY J. DEMY

See also

Literature; Lost Cause

Further Reading

Beagle, Donald R., and Bryan A. Giemza. *Poet of the Lost Cause: A Life of Father Ryan*. Knoxville: University of Tennessee Press, 2008.

Negri, Paul. *Civil War Poetry: An Anthology*. Mineola, NY: Dover, 1997.

S

Saber

Edged weapon. A saber is a backsword with a curved single-edged blade and a large hand guard that covers both the knuckles of the hand and the thumb and forefinger. Sabers were used for slashing. Those employed by heavy cavalry, however, usually had straight, often doubled-edged, blades for thrusting. Length and size of sabers varied widely. The term "saber" is drawn from the French word *sabre,* which in turn comes from the Hungarian verb *szablya* ("to cut").

Sabers were widely employed by cavalry dating from the Middle Ages but were in widespread use especially during the Napoleonic Wars of the early 19th century, when French heavy cavalry employed them in highly effective charges. The saber declined in use by the mid-19th century, with the increasing accuracy and range of rifles having rendered cavalry charges against infantry largely obsolete and with the increasing employment by the cavalrymen themselves of firearms.

During the Civil War, sabers were employed infrequently, being largely replaced with revolvers and carbines. Sabers did see sizable use in cavalry-on-cavalry engagements such as the Battle of Brandy Station (June 9, 1863) and the Battle of Gettysburg (July 1–3, 1863). Sabers remained standard equipment for U.S. Army cavalry units in the American West but were rarely carried. During World War I (1914–1918), sabers were relegated to ceremonial status.

The U.S. Army Model 1840 Cavalry Saber, which saw use in the Civil War, particularly the early years, was based on an 1822 French hussar's saber. It had a ridge around its quillon, a leather grip wrapped in wire, and a flat, slotted throat. It was 44 inches in length with a 35-inch by 1-inch blade and weighed roughly 2.5 pounds. It saw widespread service in the Mexican-American War (1846–1848) and throughout the Civil War. Its replacement, the Model 1860 Light Cavalry Saber, which was employed until the end of

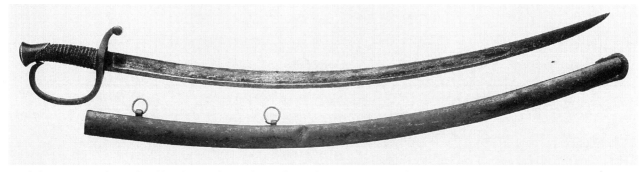

Confederate Army saber and scabbard, manufactured in Richmond, Virginia. (The Bridgeman Art Library)

the American Indian Wars, had the same curved shape and brass guard of the 1840 Model but was smaller and easier to handle. The Model 1860 was 41 inches long with a 35-inch by 1-inch blade and weighed 2 pounds, 4 ounces (3 pounds, 10 ounces, with metal scabbard). By the end of the war, more than 300,000 Model 1860 sabers had been produced.

SPENCER C. TUCKER

See also

Brandy Station, Battle of; Cavalry Tactics; Gettysburg, Battle of; Revolvers; Sharps Rifle and Carbine; Spencer Repeating Rifle and Carbine

Further Reading

Albaugh, William S., III. *Confederate Edged Weapons.* Wilmington, NC: Barefoot, 1993.
Bezdek, Richard H. *Swords of the American Civil War.* Boulder, CO: Paladin, 2007.
Thillmann, John H. *Civil War Army Swords: A Study of U.S. Army Swords from 1832 through 1865.* Lincoln, RI: Andrew Mowbray, 2008.

Sabine Cross Roads, Battle of

See Mansfield, Battle of

Sabine Pass, First Battle of
Event Date: September 25, 1862

Small naval engagement on the Texas coast. Sabine Pass, the mouth of the Sabine River, is located some 15 miles south of Port Arthur, Texas, near the Louisiana border in eastern Texas. Sabine Pass is the access point for the port of Beaumont, which gave Sabine Pass significant strategic importance.

During the Civil War, both Union and Confederate forces sought to control Sabine Pass. A railroad line from near Beaumont to Houston provided access to the interior of Texas. The Beaumont area did not export as much cotton as did Houston or New Orleans but was nevertheless a major export point as well as an entry point for arms, ammunition, and other imports from Europe. The effort to control Sabine Pass triggered two battles, one in 1862 and the other in 1863, with markedly different outcomes.

The First Battle of Sabine Pass occurred as part of the larger Union effort to capture the Texas port of Galveston. Although the Union had established a blockade of the Texas Gulf Coast soon after the war's outbreak in 1861, it had been only marginally effective. Cotton still moved overland from the rest of the Confederacy, and Texas could still export the crop through Matamoros in northeastern Mexico. Union commanders in New Orleans believed that control of Galveston and the rest of the southeastern Texas Gulf Coast was necessary to isolate Texas from the rest of the Confederacy.

The exploratory effort at Sabine Pass, which was over quickly, pitted a strong Union flotilla against a much weaker Confederate garrison. On September 25, 1862, the fourth-rate screw auxiliary *Kensington* (3 guns), the schooner *Rachel Seaman* (2 guns), and the mortar schooner *Henry James* appeared off the entrance to Sabine Pass and began shelling Fort Gibson at a distance of three miles. They hoped to draw Confederate fire so that they could determine the caliber and number of the defenders' guns. But the fort was garrisoned with only 30 infantry and artillerists and a contingent of 30 cavalrymen, whose few antiquated guns were incapable of reaching the Union ships.

When the defenders did not return fire, the Union ships sailed into the Sabine River and bombarded the fort at closer range until the Confederate defenders spiked their guns and withdrew. Following the bombardment, a Union force landed and destroyed Fort Gibson. The next day the Union sailors took the surrender of Sabine City and destroyed the railroad bridge connecting Sabine City to Taylor's Bayou. The Union force was too small to occupy the area, however, and withdrew to join the larger effort against Galveston.

The success of this first Union attack at Sabine Pass and the disruptive effects of the attack on the Confederate strategic position in Texas convinced Confederate commanders of the need to strengthen the defenses of Sabine Pass. Following the successful Confederate effort to retake Galveston in January 1863, the commanding general of Confederate forces in Texas, Major General John B. Magruder, planned stronger defenses in Sabine Pass. In consequence, a Union effort to capture the pass a year later would have radically different results.

WALTER F. BELL

See also

Galveston, Battle of; Magruder, John Bankhead; Sabine Pass, Second Battle of; Texas; Texas, Confederate Department of

Further Reading

Cotham, Edward T. *Sabine Pass: The Confederacy's Thermopylae.* Austin: University of Texas Press, 2004.
Hawkins, A. W. R., III. "The Most Extraordinary Feat of the War." *Civil War Times* 45(6) (August 2006): 36–43.

Sabine Pass, Second Battle of
Event Date: September 8, 1863

Engagement on the Texas coast. The Sabine River's mouth, known as Sabine Pass, is located some 15 miles south of Port Arthur, Texas, near the Louisiana border in eastern Texas. Sabine Pass is the access point for the port of Beaumont, which during the Civil War gave it significant strategic importance.

This second Union attempt to force open Sabine Pass grew out of the same considerations that had triggered the First Battle of Sabine Pass (September 25, 1862). Having seen his forces ejected from Galveston in January 1863, Major General Nathaniel Banks sought ways to break into the Texas interior through an operation on the Gulf Coast, and he also sought to avenge the Galveston defeat. By the autumn of 1863, Texas appeared open to invasion from several different points, and Banks believed that he saw an opportunity at Sabine Pass. He knew that a Union force had landed there successfully in September 1862 and believed that the pass would still be lightly defended.

Banks thus ordered Major General William B. Franklin to take 5,000 troops from New Orleans, seize Sabine Pass and Beaumont, and attack into the Texas interior. Franklin's force consisted of 3 infantry brigades, 10 artillery batteries, and 4 companies of the 1st Texas (Union) Cavalry. The men would be moved to Sabine Pass in seven transports, escorted by four gunboats—the *Clifton, Sachem, Granite City* and *Arizona*—under the overall command of Lieutenant Frederick Crocker.

The Union leaders were unaware that Confederate commander in Texas Major General John B. Magruder had ordered Sabine Pass's defenses to be strengthened. Confederate engineers had constructed a new fortification, Fort Griffin, just north of the one destroyed a year earlier, at the narrowest point of the pass, where attacking ships would have the greatest difficulty maneuvering. An earthwork fort with thick walls, Fort Griffin could withstand shelling from most Union guns. The fort mounted six cannon: two 24-pounders and four 32-pounders. At the time of the attack, Fort Griffin was garrisoned by 44 men of Company F of the 1st Texas Heavy Artillery Regiment, commanded by Lieutenant Richard W. Dowling. The garrison had diligently practiced its gunnery, and the gunners had carefully determined ranges and marked the aiming points with stakes to enhance accuracy. The Union force that approached Sabine Pass on September 8, 1863, thus faced much stronger defenses than had been the case a year earlier.

Poor coordination and communication further hindered the Union operation. The *Granite City* had been sent on ahead to mark the channel. Its crewmen thought that they sighted the Confederate raider *Alabama,* and the *Granite City* promptly fled. It took time for the *Granite City*'s consorts to locate that ship again, delaying the start of the attack and alerting the defenders. The Union plan called for the gunboats to enter the channel and provide covering fire for the Union troops as they went ashore.

On the morning of September 8, Crocker began the attack with his flagship, the *Clifton*. It crossed the bar and attempted to draw fire from the fort in order to determine the strength of the Confederate defenses. The *Clifton* lobbed 26 shells at the Confederates but received no return fire. Crocker then ordered the other gunboats—the *Sachem, Arizona,* and *Granite City*—and the transports over the bar.

At about 3:30 p.m., the gunboats and transports started up the pass. The Confederates withheld fire until the Union gunboats were among the aiming stakes and the gunners had the precise range. The Confederates then let loose a devastating fire. The *Sachem* was holed several times and was disabled when a 24-pounder shot went through its boiler. Another shot carried away the wheel rope of the *Clifton,* causing it to ground under the Confederate guns. Crocker fought the *Clifton* until, with 10 men killed and 9 others wounded, he believed that he had no other choice but to surrender. The *Sachem* also surrendered and was promptly taken under tow by the Confederate cottonclad *Uncle Ben.* In these circumstances, General Franklin called off the landing and ordered his transports to withdraw. Two of the transports grounded, leading Franklin to order scores of hobbled horses and mules as well as some 20,000 rations thrown overboard to lighten the load. The transports and two remaining gunboats then returned to New Orleans.

In the abortive attack, the Union lost nearly 70 men killed, wounded, or missing and another 315 captured. Confederate casualties are unknown. In this lopsided Confederate victory, considerable credit belongs to the engineers who positioned and constructed Fort Griffin, the careful preparations by its garrison, and poor planning and coordination involving Union forces, particularly Franklin's failure to land his troops and support the gunboats with an overland attack. Had the attack succeeded, the Federals would have easily taken Beaumont.

WALTER F. BELL AND SPENCER C. TUCKER

See also
Banks, Nathaniel Prentice; Galveston, Battle of; Magruder, John
    Bankhead; Sabine Pass, First Battle of; Texas, Confederate
    Department of

Further Reading
Cotham, Edward T. *Sabine Pass: The Confederacy's Thermopylae*.
    Austin: University of Texas Press, 2004.
Frazier, Donald S. *Cottonclads! The Battle of Galveston and the
    Defense of the Texas Coast*. Abilene, TX: McWhiney Founda-
    tion Press, McMurray University, 1998.

Sacramento, Battle of
Event Date: December 28, 1861

Nathan Bedford Forrest's first combat action. As Confederate and Union troops moved into Kentucky in September
1861, the Green River became the dividing line between
them. Forrest, then a lieutenant colonel and commander of
the 7th Tennessee Cavalry, conducted guerrilla and recruiting operations south of the Green River in strongly pro-
Confederate territory. Meanwhile, Union brigadier general
Thomas L. Crittenden, commander of the 5th Division of
the Army of the Ohio at Calhoun, Kentucky, contemplated
attacking Bowling Green.

On December 27, Forrest received orders to carry out a
reconnaissance toward Rumsey to ascertain Union troop
strength and intentions. The next day, Forrest marched
northward with 300 men, sending scouts ahead to reconnoiter. Just outside Greeneville, Forrest learned that a Union
cavalry force was nine miles ahead, just south of Sacramento. This was a Union scouting party of 168 men, commanded by 18-year-old Major Eli Murray, dispatched by
Crittenden the previous day to gather information. Forrest
moved quickly toward this Union force. As he neared Sacramento, he reconnoitered Murray's position from atop a
steep ridge and decided to attack the weaker Union force,
even though some of his own troopers had not yet arrived.

Forrest charged Murray's men, coming under fire at 200
yards. Soon Forrest's attack, hastily conceived and executed,
turned into a disorganized melee, and he was compelled to
fall back and await the arrival of his entire force. Meanwhile,
he deployed sharpshooters to pin down Murray's men while
sending two detachments to harass the Union flanks. Murray, believing that Forrest's withdrawal had been a retreat,
advanced his own men toward the Confederate position.
Forrest's forces, now united and reorganized, counterattacked. Within 10 minutes, the Union troops broke and fled

in a panic through Sacramento. Forrest's troopers pursued
for two miles. Forrest killed 1 Union officer and wounded
and captured 3 others but lost his mount and only narrowly
escaped death or injury himself. Finally, a remounted Forrest halted the pursuit, allowing Murray's shattered remnant to reach Calhoun. Union casualties were 11 dead and
40 captured. The Confederates lost 2 men.

PAUL DAVID NELSON

See also
Forrest, Nathan Bedford; Kentucky

Further Reading
Brown, Kent Masterson. *The Civil War in Kentucky: Battle for the
    Bluegrass*. Mason City, IA: Savas, 2000.
Jordan, Thomas, and J. P. Pryor. *The Campaigns of Lieut.-Gen. N. B.
    Forrest, and of Forrest's Cavalry*. New York: Da Capo, 1996.

Safford, Mary Jane
Birth Date: ca. December 31, 1831
Death Date: December 8, 1891

Civil War nurse. Mary Jane Safford (Stafford) was born in
Hyde Park, Vermont, on December 31 in either 1831 or 1834
(records vary). She grew up in Illinois near Joliet and subsequently worked as a governess for a German family in Canada for a short time before returning to Illinois. Here in the
summer of 1861 she met well-known Mary Ann "Mother"
Bickerdyke, the famous nurse who had gone to Cairo, Illinois, to care for Union soldiers. When an epidemic broke
out among the troops, Safford saw the need and volunteered as a nurse. She had long admired Bickerdyke and relished the opportunity to work with her. Safford could have
remained at the hospital to care for the wounded, but she
instead tended to soldiers languishing in the many camps
and soon earned the nickname "Angel of Cairo."

Traveling from camp to camp, overworked and exhausted,
Safford fashioned a truce flag from a broomstick and white
petticoat so that she would not be accidentally shot as she
moved among the tents. After service at Fort Donelson, Tennessee, she worked aboard two different transports, the *City
of Memphis* and the *Hazel Dell*. She then tended to wounded
following the Battle of Shiloh (April 6–7, 1862) and again
joined Bickerdyke in camps at Savannah. Overworked and
injured, Safford took a leave of absence to recover in Europe,
not returning until after the war.

Safford yearned to become a doctor, and in 1869 she
graduated from the Medical College for Women in New

York. She then traveled to Austria and studied at the General Hospital in Vienna before attending the University of Breslau in Germany. In Breslau, she became the first woman to perform an ovariectomy. In 1872 she opened a private practice in Chicago. She concluded her medical career as a professor at the Boston University School of Medicine and as staff doctor at the Massachusetts Homeopathic Hospital.

Safford retired to Florida, where she died in Tarpon Springs on December 8, 1891.

JAY WARNER

See also
Nurses; Women

Further Reading
Cazalet, Sylvain. *History of the New York Medical College and Hospital for Women.* New York: University of the State of New York, 1966.

Salem Church, Battle of
Start Date: May 3, 1863
End Date: May 4, 1863

Engagement near Fredericksburg, Virginia, during the Chancellorsville Campaign (April–May 1863). The Battle of Salem Church (Salem Heights) was the last significant fighting of the campaign and began when Major General John Sedgwick's VI Corps of the Union Army of the Potomac moved against the rear of the Confederate Army of Northern Virginia.

On May 3, 1863, Sedgwick advanced from his position at Fredericksburg to relieve the pressure being placed on the Union army under Major General Joseph Hooker, which had been assaulted by General Robert E. Lee's forces. VI Corps, after two failed attempts, successfully seized Marye's Heights, overlooking Fredericksburg, from Major General Jubal Early's division on the morning of May 3. This allowed Sedgwick to advance with his corps toward the rear of Lee's army at Chancellorsville, about 10 miles from Fredericksburg.

Lee responded to this threat by dispatching troops eastward from Chancellorsville to engage Sedgwick. Confederate brigadier general Cadmus Wilcox, on his own initiative, intercepted Sedgwick with his brigade, temporarily slowing VI Corp's advance. Wilcox finally made a stand at Salem Church, four miles west of Fredericksburg, on a low wooded ridge bisected by the Orange Plank Road, the main road leading from Fredericksburg to Chancellorsville. As Sedgwick's leading division deployed to attack Wilcox, Major

General Lafayette McLaws arrived with the reinforcements that Lee had sent. The previously outnumbered Confederates then repulsed the Union assault with heavy casualties and counterattacked. The advance drove the Union troops back in disorder until artillery fire finally stopped the Confederate troops.

On the morning of May 4, Early's troops reoccupied Marye's Heights, cutting Sedgwick's line of communications and trapping him between two Confederate forces, with the Rappahannock River at his back. Sedgwick arranged his corps in a U-shaped defensive position guarding Banks Ford, his only route of escape across the river. Lee attempted to coordinate an assault on Sedgwick's outnumbered troops with the three divisions that surrounded him, but the difficult terrain, exhaustion from several days of marching and fighting, and slow action by his subordinates prevented effective coordination. Only Early's division launched an attack, during which it suffered heavy casualties and was defeated. Later that night as Lee prepared to launch a nighttime assault, Sedgwick retreated across the Rappahannock to safety.

While Sedgwick missed an opportunity to fall on Lee's rear by rapid movement on May 3, Lee lost the opportunity to crush Sedgwick's exposed corps on May 4. Sedgwick's advance was successful in drawing Lee's attention from Hooker's main body, but Hooker failed to act upon this advantage. Total casualties over the two days of fighting numbered 4,700 for VI Corps and around 3,000 for the Confederates. The engagement highlighted Lee's effective use of movement to overcome his inferior numbers and the continued difficulty that the Union faced in bringing its manpower advantage to bear.

JOSHUA MICHAEL

See also
Chancellorsville, Battle of; Early, Jubal Anderson; Hooker, Joseph; Lee, Robert Edward; McLaws, Lafayette; Sedgwick, John; Wilcox, Cadmus Marcellus

Further Reading
Parsons, Philip W. *The Union Sixth Army Corps in the Chancellorsville Campaign.* Jefferson, NC: McFarland, 2006.
Sears, Stephen W. *Chancellorsville.* Boston: Houghton Mifflin, 1996.

Salineville, Battle of
Event Date: July 26, 1863

Final engagement of Confederate colonel John Hunt Morgan's Ohio Raid (July 2–26, 1863). In late June 1863, Morgan planned an ambitious raid into the North. General Braxton Bragg, commanding the Confederate Army of Tennessee, opposed the operation, but Morgan ignored his superior and set out on July 2, 1863, with 2,400 men. The raid encountered immediate difficulties. Morgan's troops suffered heavy casualties on July 4 when Union cavalry opposed their crossing of the Green River, and more men were lost the next day when Morgan captured the Union garrison at Lebanon, Kentucky. Nevertheless, Morgan persisted, crossing the Ohio River at Brandenburg into Indiana on July 8. Five days later he entered Ohio, pursued by Union cavalry under Brigadier General James M. Shackelford.

Union forces were now converged on Morgan. Union cavalry under Brigadier General Edward Hobson caught up with Morgan on July 19 at Buffington Island as his men attempted to cross the Ohio River into West Virginia. While some Confederates did make it across the river, 800 were captured. Morgan and the remaining 400 men of his command escaped but were effectively cut off from the river crossings. When another attempt to ford the river failed, Morgan headed north, eventually reaching Columbiana County and hoping to cross the Ohio River at some point and escape.

Shackelford continued the pursuit with a mixed force of some 3,000 men: cavalry, mounted infantry, artillery, and militia. On July 26, he finally managed to cut off Morgan's exhausted force, their horses worn out, at Salineville, near Lisbon. Morgan attempted to cut his way out, in the process suffering 23 dead, several wounded, and nearly 300 captured. Morgan and his few remaining men initially evaded capture but were cornered that afternoon some eight miles distant near West Point, Ohio, and were forced to surrender to Major George W. Rue of the 9th Kentucky Cavalry. The place of Morgan's surrender is considered to be the northernmost point reached by an officially organized Confederate body during the Civil War. Only some 400 of Morgan's 2,400 men made it back to Tennessee. Morgan and the rest headed to prison.

SPENCER C. TUCKER

See also

Morgan, John Hunt; Morgan's Ohio Raid; Shackelford, James Murrell

Further Reading

Duke, Basil Wilson. *A History of Morgan's Cavalry.* Cincinnati, OH: Miami Printing and Publishing, 1867.

Horwitz, Lester V. *The Longest Raid of the Civil War.* Cincinnati, OH: Farmcourt Publishing, 1999.

Ramage, James A. *Rebel Raider: The Life of General John Hunt Morgan.* Lexington: University Press of Kentucky, 1986.

Salisbury, North Carolina, Union Capture of
Event Date: April 12, 1865

Action during Union major general George Stoneman's 1865 raid into North Carolina and Virginia. On March 10, 1865, Stoneman departed from Knoxville, Tennessee, on a raid to disrupt the Virginia & Tennessee Railroad in Virginia and the North Carolina Railroad and the Danville-Greensboro line (Piedmont Railroad) in North Carolina. Stoneman commanded some 6,000 men in Brigadier General Alvan C. Gillem's division of three brigades under Colonels William J. Palmer, S. B. Brown, and John K. Miller.

After an initial foray into North Carolina, Stoneman headed north to carry out operations in southwestern Virginia. He reentered North Carolina on April 9 and at Germantown divided his force. Palmer's brigade proceeded to Salem, while the other two brigades moved against the important Confederate railway head and supply depot of Salisbury. Stoneman and the main body crossed the Yadkin River at Huntsville on April 11. East of Salisbury, Stoneman's men surprised a Confederate detachment, the men of which fled, abandoning 100 new muskets.

At Salisbury, Brigadier General William M. Gardner assembled a scratch force of 500–800 men. Among these was Colonel John C. Pemberton, now serving as an ordnance inspector. Gardner positioned these men and several guns across the Mocksville road along Grant's Creek several miles north of Salisbury, ordering his men to remove the planks from the bridge. Stoneman's men arrived early on April 12. Finding his approach to Salisbury blocked, Stoneman ordered the 12th Kentucky Cavalry Regiment to fix the defenders in place, while other cavalry detachments proceeded in both directions along the stream to locate fords, which enabled them to attack the defenders on the flanks. Meanwhile, the Union 8th and 13th Tennessee cavalrymen repaired the bridge under fire, and a spirited charge by the Union 6th Tennessee Cavalry scattered the defenders, allowing easy access to Salisbury.

Salisbury was an important prize, and Stoneman immediately posted guards to prevent looting. One of his aims was to free a large number of Union prisoners of war reportedly held at Salisbury Prison, but the men had been moved to Charlotte the month before. On April 12 and 13, Stoneman set about destroying the public buildings and military stores. First he had the contents of the Confederate supply depots thrown in the streets so that poor whites and blacks could take what they wanted. The remainder was then burned. The raiders also burned the prison, four cotton factories, some 7,000 bales of cotton, and six supply depots. Among military supplies listed by Stoneman as destroyed were 10,000 stands of arms, 1 million rounds of small arms ammunition, 10,000 artillery rounds, 6,000 pounds of powder, substantial stocks of medical supplies, and $15 million in Confederate currency. The exploding shells and flames could be heard and seen at night for miles around. Stoneman's men also destroyed railroad shops and ripped up some 15 miles of track. With only a few exceptions, the destruction was limited to public property.

On April 13, his work accomplished, Stoneman departed Salisbury with his men for eastern Tennessee.

SPENCER C. TUCKER

See also

Gardner, William Montgomery; Gillem, Alvan Cullen; Palmer, William Jackson; Pemberton, John Clifford; Salisbury Prison, North Carolina; Stoneman, George, Jr.; Stoneman's Raid into North Carolina and Virginia

Further Reading

Barrett, John G. *The Civil War in North Carolina.* Chapel Hill: University of North Carolina Press, 1963.
Hartley, Chris J. *Stoneman's Raid, 1865.* Winston-Salem, NC: John F. Blair, 2010.

Salisbury Prison, North Carolina

Confederate prison facility. On November 2, 1861, the Confederate government bought an 11-acre parcel of land, which included an old cotton mill to be converted into a prison. The prison was designed to hold Confederate soldiers convicted of crimes, suspected spies, disloyal citizens, and prisoners of war and was commanded by Commandant Major John H. Gee. The complex included a four-story brick mill and six smaller brick outbuildings. Initially, the smaller buildings were used to house detainees; some were later converted into hospital wards. Salisbury Prison was supposed to house a maximum of 2,500 prisoners.

The first detainees arrived on December 2, 1861. Until the autumn of 1864, the prison population remained below the 2,500-inmate threshold, and conditions were generally quite good. Food was abundant, cells were spacious, medical care was generally good, and the death rate was quite low. That all changed, however, in October 1864, when the prison population exploded, nearing 10,000 by year's end. The change was due chiefly to the end of the Atlanta Campaign (May 5–September 2, 1864) and the unraveling of the prisoner exchange system.

Salisbury was one of the South's most notorious prisoner-of-war camps. Water supplies became scarce and unreliable, illness and disease spread like wildfire, housing was in such short supply that many prisoners had to dig holes in the ground for shelter, and the on-site hospital lacked basic medicines and personnel. Food became scarce, and many inmates augmented their meager rations by eating acorns from nearby oak trees. Between December 1861 and October 1864, only 255 detainees died at the facility. But between November 1864 and February 1865 alone, an astounding 3,419 more died. The death rate was so high that the deceased were buried in mass graves without coffins. On November 25, 1864, a massive riot resulted in the deaths of 250 inmates.

In late 1864, Brigadier General Bradley Johnson replaced Gee as prison superintendent. Johnson directed the emptying of the facility, which was accomplished by the end of February 1865. When Union forces reached the site in April 1865, they burned the buildings to the ground. Gee was later accused of mass murder and cruelty but was acquitted of all charges in July 1866. The court reasoned that the conditions at Salisbury had not deteriorated until late 1864, when Gee was burdened with an impossibly large influx of prisoners.

PAUL G. PIERPAOLI JR.

See also

Atlanta Campaign; Johnson, Bradley Tyler; Prisoners of War; Prisons, Confederate

Further Reading

Brown, Louis A. *The Salisbury Prison: A Case Study of Confederate Military Prisons.* Wendell, NC: Broadfoot, 1992.
Speer, Lonnie. *Portals to Hell: Military Prisons of the Civil War.* Mechanicsburg, PA: Stackpole, 1997.

Salm-Salm, Agnes Elisabeth Winona Leclercq Joy
Birth Date: ca. December 25, 1844
Death Date: December 21, 1912

Socialite and wife of Union colonel Felix Salm-Salm. Agnes Elisabeth Winona Leclercq Joy was likely born on December 25, 1844, in Swanton, Vermont, although the year of her birth remains in question. Her early life is shrouded in mystery. In 1861, the strong-willed Joy went to Washington, D.C., to visit her sister. During a tour of a Union camp, she met German prince Felix Salm-Salm, and they married on August 30, 1862. Prince Felix, commissioned a colonel in the

Agnes Elisabeth Winona Leclerq Joy Salm-Salm, the American-born wife of German Prince Felix Salm-Salm, a Union Army colonel of volunteers during the Civil War. Contrary to many reports, she did not accompany her husband in the field, nor serve as a battlefield nurse. (Library of Congress)

volunteer army, was appointed commander of the 8th New York in November 1862 but saw no action before the regiment mustered out of service.

Although Agnes Salm-Salm is often depicted as a daring battlefield nurse, this almost certainly never happened during the Civil War. Indeed, she spent most of the war socializing and promoting her husband's interests in Washington, D.C., as well as in various state capitals, succeeding in securing him another regiment, the 68th New York, which protected railroads in Alabama. Felix Salm-Salm did see some action late in the war, but Agnes was not present. She was, however, instrumental in securing for him a brevet to brigadier general.

In February 1866, Prince Felix joined the Mexican Army of Emperor Maximilian von Habsburg. Princess Agnes, who had remained in the United States, soon followed. When she learned that Benito Juárez's Liberal Army had captured Maximilian and his officers in May 1867, she immediately went to the restored President Juárez to intercede on behalf of Maximilian and her husband and otherwise worked heroically to save them. Juárez granted Prince Felix his freedom

but executed the hapless emperor and two of his generals in June 1867.

In 1868, Prince Felix enlisted in the Prussian Army. During the Franco-Prussian War (1870–1871), Princess Agnes accompanied her husband in the field and served as a nurse, even after he was killed in battle on August 18, 1870. After the war she lived quietly in Germany, returning to the United States only briefly. Agnes Salm-Salm died in Karlsrule, Germany, on December 21, 1912.

MICHAEL R. HALL AND DAVID COFFEY

See also
Antietam, Battle of; Medicine

Further Reading
Coffey, David. *Soldier Princess: The Life and Legend of Agnes Salm-Salm in North America, 1861–1867*. College Station: Texas A&M University Press, 2002.
Salm-Salm, Agnes. *Ten Years of My Life*. New York: Richard Bentley and Sons, 1876.

Salm-Salm, Felix Constantin Alexander Johann Nepomuk
Birth Date: 1828
Death Date: August 18, 1870

Union officer. The younger brother of the reigning Prince Salm-Salm, who administered a small principality on the lower Rhine, Prince Felix Salm-Salm was perhaps best known for the exploits of his colorful American wife, Agnes (Joy) Salm-Salm. After receiving a military education at Berlin, Felix Salm-Salm served in the Prussian cavalry and was wounded in the 1848 Schleswig-Holstein conflict. He later joined the Austrian Army to escape creditors but soon found that situation untenable. Salm-Salm, who spoke no English, sailed for America to offer his services to Union authorities in 1861. He landed a position on Brigadier General Louis Blenker's staff and served during Jackson's Shenandoah Valley Campaign (May–June 1862), after which Blenker was relieved, costing Salm-Salm his job.

Thanks largely to his wife's efforts, Salm-Salm secured command of the 8th New York Infantry, a mostly German regiment, with which he participated in the First Battle of Fredericksburg (December 13, 1862) but in reserve. The regiment's enlistment expired in April 1863, leaving Salm-Salm without a command. Failing in his attempt to recruit a regiment, he remained unemployed for more than a year until, again with his wife's help, in June 1864 he became colonel of the 68th New York Infantry.

The regiment served mostly in rear areas, guarding the railroad at Bridgeport, Alabama, in support of Major General William T. Sherman's main effort in Georgia, but in December 1864 Salm-Salm served on Major General James Steedman's staff during the Battle of Nashville (December 15–16, 1864) and led a provisional brigade in pursuit of the scattered Confederates. On April 13, 1865, Salm-Salm was brevetted brigadier general of volunteers. Following garrison duty in Atlanta and Savannah, he mustered out of federal service in November 1865.

Months later Salm-Salm sailed for Mexico to offer his services to the beleaguered Emperor Maximilian. Salm-Salm saw some action with the emperor's troops before joining Maximilian's official staff in April 1867. Captured along with Maximilian in May, Salm-Salm was soon released, again thanks to Agnes's efforts, and thus, unlike the emperor and two of his generals, avoided execution. Salm-Salm returned to Germany, wrote a memoir of his Mexico experiences, and secured a major's commission in the Prussian Army. He was mortally wounded on August 18, 1870 in the Battle of Gravelotte (St. Privat) during the Franco-Prussian War.

DAVID COFFEY

See also

Blenker, Louis; Fredericksburg, First Battle of; Jackson's Shenandoah Valley Campaign; Maximilian von Habsburg, Ferdinand; Nashville, Battle of; Salm-Salm, Agnes Elisabeth Winona Leclercq Joy; Steedman, James Blair

Further Reading

Burton, William L. *Melting Pot Soldiers: The Union's Ethnic Regiments.* Ames: Iowa State University Press, 1988.

Coffey, David. *Soldier Princess: The Life and Legend of Agnes Salm-Salm in North America, 1861–1867.* College Station: Texas A&M University Press, 2002.

Salomon, Edward

Birth Date: August 11, 1828
Death Date: April 21, 1909

Governor of Wisconsin. Edward Saloman was born on August 11, 1828, in Strobeck, Prussia, and graduated from the University of Berlin in 1849. Later that year, he immigrated to the United States and settled in Wisconsin. After teaching school for a time, he studied law. Passing the bar in 1855, he established a successful practice. Saloman entered local politics as a Democrat, but by 1860 he had become a Republican. In 1861 he was elected lieutenant governor. He and Governor Louis P. Harvey took office in January 1862.

Harvey died on April 19 during a trip to visit Wisconsin soldiers in Tennessee, and Saloman became governor.

Saloman's coarse personality did not always ingratiate him with his constituents, but he strongly supported President Abraham Lincoln and his war policies. When Lincoln asked for more troops in June 1862, Saloman willingly obliged, but many in his state were reluctant to answer the call, especially in the immigrant communities, in which support for the war was not terribly high. During the summer of 1863, numerous Wisconsin communities witnessed draft riots, including the destructive Port Washington Draft Riot, and some draft resisters attacked the homes of Republicans and federal officials. Saloman responded with a heavy hand, ordering the arrest of hundreds of protesters and vowing to enforce the draft call by any means necessary. In the end, he raised 14 regiments but at the cost of his governorship. He did not receive his party's nomination in 1863 and left office on January 4, 1864.

Saloman campaigned for Lincoln in 1864 and ran unsuccessfully for the U.S. Senate later in the decade. By 1870, Saloman had settled in New York City, where he practiced law. He was an unsuccessful candidate for a seat on the New York Supreme Court in 1882 and later moved back to Germany. Saloman died on April 21, 1909, in Frankfurt-am-Main. His brother, Friedrich, became a brigadier general in the Union Army.

PAUL G. PIERPAOLI JR.

See also

Harvey, Louis Powell; Salomon, Friedrich C.; Wisconsin

Further Reading

Jones, Robert Huhn. *The Civil War in the Northwest: Nebraska, Wisconsin, Iowa, Minnesota, and the Dakotas.* Norman: University of Oklahoma Press, 1960.

Nesbit, Robert C. *Wisconsin: A History.* Revised ed. Madison: University of Wisconsin Press, 1989.

Salomon, Friedrich C.

Birth Date: April 7, 1826
Death Date: March 8, 1897

Union officer. Friedrich C. Saloman was born on April 7, 1826, in Strobeck, Prussia. He served briefly in the Prussian Army and then studied architecture in Berlin. Following the Revolution of 1848, he fled his homeland with his two brothers, one of whom—Edward Salomon—would later be governor of Wisconsin. Friedrich Salmon found work as a surveyor before becoming chief engineer for a Wisconsin railroad.

In 1861 Salomon joined the 5th Missouri Infantry Regiment as a captain and saw action at the Battle of Wilson's Creek (August 10, 1861). He was appointed colonel of the 9th Wisconsin Infantry on November 26, and his regiment was garrisoned at Fort Scott, Kansas, the following spring. On June 26, 1862, he was promoted to brigadier general of volunteers and given charge of the 1st Brigade of Kansas Volunteers.

In September 1862, Salomon took command of the 1st Brigade, 1st Division, Army of the Frontier. He performed competently at the Battle of Prairie Grove (December 7, 1862). In July 1863 he took charge of the 13th Division, XIII Corps, and saw action at the Battle of Helena (July 4, 1863). The next month he was given command of the District of East Arkansas. In command for less than a month, he was dispatched to Little Rock to take charge of the 3rd Division, VII Corps, Department of Arkansas.

Salomon ably led his division during the Camden Expedition (March 23–May 3, 1864) and was conspicuous at the Battle of Jenkins' Ferry (April 30, 1864), where his actions were credited with saving the Union army from disaster. After returning to Little Rock, he saw little action for the remainder of the conflict. Brevetted major general of volunteers in March 1865, he left the army on August 25, 1865.

Postbellum, Salomon served as Missouri's surveyor general before becoming surveyor general of the Utah Territory in 1877. Salomon died on March 8, 1897, in Salt Lake City, Utah.

PAUL G. PIERPAOLI JR.

See also

Camden Expedition; Helena, Battle of; Jenkins' Ferry, Battle of; Prairie Grove, Battle of

Further Reading

Eicher, John H., and David J. Eicher. *Civil War High Commands.* Stanford, CA: Stanford University Press, 2001.

Warner, Ezra J. *Generals in Blue: Lives of the Union Commanders.* Baton Rouge: Louisiana State University Press, 2006.

Saltville, First and Second Battles of
Event Dates: October 2 and
December 20–21, 1864

Engagement in southwestern Virginia that resulted in the massacre of as many as 100 Union soldiers, many of them African Americans. Saltville, located in far southwestern Virginia along the strategic Virginia & Tennessee Railroad, was so named because the area was a major producer of salt, which was crucial to the curing and preserving of meat for

army rations. In September 1864, Union brigadier general Stephen G. Burbridge was ordered to advance on Saltville and capture it, thus cutting off the Confederates' salt supply and severing the Virginia & Tennessee Railroad, then the only major link between Virginia and the military theaters in the west.

Burbridge led about 3,600 men, including some 400 African American troopers of the 5th U.S. Colored Cavalry (USCC) and part of the 6th USCC. He was delayed at Clinch Mountain and Laurel Gap by makeshift Confederate forces, however, enabling Brigadier General Alfred E. Jackson to concentrate forces near Saltville to meet the attackers. The Confederates had erected makeshift redoubts and barricades around Saltville and had some 2,800 troops with which to defend the hamlet.

In the ensuing First Battle of Saltville on the morning of October 2, the Confederates occupied the high ground. Union forces drove the Confederates back on the town of Saltville after five or six hours of fighting but ran short of ammunition, and the Confederates, who were reinforced throughout the course of the battle, managed to hold, despite a valiant assault by the 5th USCC on Chestnut Ridge. In late afternoon Burbridge withdrew, his retreat hastened by news that Confederate major general John C. Breckinridge had arrived with additional cavalry. Burbridge left behind some 350 Union dead and wounded on the battlefield.

Early the next morning under the cover of darkness, Confederate troops led by Brigadier General Felix H. Robertson and bushwhacker Champ Ferguson moved slowly toward the Union line. Finding large numbers of wounded soldiers, many of them African Americans, the Confederates began to shoot indiscriminately, although it became clear that their main targets were the wounded black soldiers. At least 100 Union wounded soldiers were slain. The massacre was shocking not only because it had violated basic rules of warfare at the time but also because it was clearly motivated by racism. It was also one of the worst atrocities of the war. Casualties during the battle and the subsequent massacre included 329 killed, wounded, or missing for the Union and 190 for the Confederates.

In December 1864 in the Second Battle of Saltville, Union troops finally took Saltville and largely leveled it in retaliation for the October massacre. After the war, Ferguson was arrested by Union authorities, charged with murder, and brought before a military commission on charges of murdering 53 people. The prosecution held that he was not, as his defense attorney claimed, a Confederate captain and hence was not subject to parole. Convicted, Ferguson was hanged on October 20, 1865. General Robertson, however, was never charged or punished for his involvement in the massacre.

PAUL G. PIERPAOLI JR.

See also

Breckinridge, John Cabell; Burbridge, Stephen Gano; Ferguson, Champ; Robertson, Felix Huston

Further Reading

Bush, Bryan S. *Butcher Burbridge: Union General Stephen Burbridge and His Reign of Terror over Kentucky.* Sikeston, MO: Acclaim, 2008.
Mays, Thomas D. *The Saltville Massacre.* Buffalo Gap, TX: State House Press, 1998.

Sand Creek Massacre
Event Date: November 29, 1864

Slaughter of peaceful Native Americans by Colorado militiamen. In the spring of 1864, some Cheyenne groups, particularly the Dog Soldiers, responded to settler encroachments on their lands in the Colorado Territory with sporadic raids. Territorial governor John Evans, hoping to use the raids as a pretext to seize mineral-rich Cheyenne and Arapaho lands, authorized Colonel John M. Chivington to attack the tribes.

Black Kettle, a Southern Cheyenne leader who favored peace, traveled to Denver for talks with Evans and Chivington in September 1864. Chivington ordered Black Kettle to take his band of 500 people to Fort Lyon, where they would be protected. When the Cheyennes arrived, the fort's commander, Major Scott Anthony, instructed them to camp 40 miles away at Sand Creek. Several hundred Arapahos accompanied the Cheyennes, but all except about 100 left Sand Creek in early November to hunt.

Chafing to strike a blow against the Native Americans, Chivington briefly considered an expedition against the Sioux. He rejected the idea as too risky, deciding instead to attack the Cheyennes and Arapahos at Sand Creek.

Chivington secretly moved 700 short-term volunteers under his command plus four howitzers of his 3rd Colorado Cavalry to Fort Lyon in late November. When Chivington announced his intention to attack the Cheyenne camp, some of his subordinate officers argued that the Native Americans were peaceful. He silenced them with the threat of a court-martial.

The troops marched throughout the night of November 28–29 and reached Sand Creek just before dawn. Some Cheyenne women spotted them, but the soldiers assured them that no harm was intended. Shortly afterward, the attack began. The Native Americans were taken by surprise, with many still asleep in their lodges. Black Kettle displayed both an American flag and a white truce flag while trying to calm his people. The troops shot down the Cheyennes clustered around the flags and charged on horseback through the camp, firing at the fleeing people. Several women were killed while attempting to surrender.

Most of Chivington's men spent the next several hours scouring the area and killing any Native Americans they found. Others engaged in a skirmish with some Cheyenne and Arapaho warriors who had taken up a defensive position outside the camp. These warriors held off the troops until nightfall and then escaped. Nine U.S. soldiers were killed and 38 wounded in the fighting. About 200 Native Americans were slaughtered, two-thirds of them women and children. Soldiers mutilated many of the corpses, even taking body parts as trophies. Some of the scalps were later displayed in a Denver theater.

The Sand Creek Massacre provoked retaliation from the Cheyennes, Arapahos, and some Sioux groups, sparking a conflict that lasted until 1869. Reports of the troops' brutality also horrified residents of the eastern states, who denounced the massacre. The congressional Committee on the Conduct of the War launched an investigation into the massacre, as did a joint committee of the U.S. House and Senate and a military commission. Although Chivington's behavior was heavily criticized, he had left the army and thus could not be punished.

JIM PIECUCH

See also

Chivington, John Milton; Colorado Territory; Evans, John

Further Reading

Brown, Dee. *Bury My Heart at Wounded Knee: An Indian History of the American West.* New York: Holt, Rinehart and Winston, 1970.
Hoig, Stan. *The Sand Creek Massacre.* Norman: University of Oklahoma Press, 1963.
Utley, Robert M. *The Indian Frontier of the American West, 1846–1890.* Albuquerque: University of New Mexico Press, 1984.

Sanders, John Caldwell Calhoun
Birth Date: April 4, 1840
Death Date: August 21, 1864

Confederate officer. John Caldwell Calhoun Sanders was born on April 4, 1840, in Tuscaloosa, Alabama, and attended the University of Alabama before enlisting in the 11th Alabama Infantry Regiment in the late winter of 1861. That spring, he was elected a company captain but saw no action until May 1862. On June 30, 1862, Sanders received a serious wound during the Seven Days' Campaign (June 25–July 1, 1862); he did not return to duty until August 11. At that time, he took command of the 11th Alabama, leading it in the Battle of Antietam (September 17, 1862), after which he was advanced to colonel. Sanders received high praise from his superiors for his performance at the First Battle of Fredericksburg (December 13, 1862).

Sanders performed well in the Battle of Chancellorsville (May 1–4, 1863) and the Battle of Gettysburg (July 1–3, 1863) but was wounded again at the latter engagement. He then served on the division's court-martial panel as he recuperated. He once again took up his old regiment's command during the spring of 1864 and led it well at the Battle of the Wilderness (May 5–7, 1864). During the Battle of Spotsylvania Court House (May 8–21, 1864), Sanders had temporary charge of his brigade. His service there brought promotion to brigadier general on May 31.

Sanders led a brigade during the early stages of the Petersburg Campaign (June 15, 1864–April 3, 1865) and orchestrated a commendable counterattack in the Battle of the Crater (July 30, 1864). Sanders was killed on August 21, 1864, as he led troops along the Weldon Railroad during the Battle of Globe Tavern.

PAUL G. PIERPAOLI JR.

See also

Antietam, Battle of; Chancellorsville, Battle of; Crater, Battle of the; Fredericksburg, First Battle of; Gettysburg, Battle of; Globe Tavern, Battle of; Petersburg Campaign; Seven Days' Campaign; Spotsylvania Court House, Battle of; Wilderness, Battle of the

Further Reading

Warner, Ezra J. *Generals in Gray: Lives of the Confederate Commanders.* Baton Rouge: Louisiana State University Press, 2006.

Eicher, John H., and David J. Eicher. *Civil War High Commands.* Stanford, CA: Stanford University Press, 2001.

Sands, Benjamin Franklin
Birth Date: February 11, 1812
Death Date: June 30, 1883

Union naval officer. Benjamin Franklin Sands was born in Baltimore, Maryland, on February 11, 1812. His family soon moved to Louisville, Kentucky, where he lived until age 16. After a year of school in Washington, D.C., he entered the U.S. Navy as a midshipman on April 1, 1828. During a career that spanned 46 years, Sands became an expert at naval surveying and hydrography. Among his inventions to facilitate survey work was a deep-sea-sounding apparatus.

Following sea duty in the Brazil Squadron and the West Indies, Sands was appointed a passed midshipman on June 14, 1834. For several years he performed coast survey work. He was promoted to lieutenant on March 16, 1840. After service in the Mediterranean, he was assigned to the Bureau of Charts and Instruments at the Naval Observatory in 1844. Sands saw action near the end of the Mexican-American War (1846–1848) and later served as a commander in the Africa Squadron. He returned to coast survey duties in 1851 and continued that work until 1858, during which time he was promoted to commander on September 14, 1855. In 1858 he became chief of the Naval Bureau of Construction and served in that capacity until 1861.

After the secession of Virginia in April 1861, Sands supervised the burning of ships and warehouses during the evacuation of Union forces and ships from the Norfolk (Gosport) Navy Yard. Probably due to navy officials' suspicions of officers from border states, Sands's next assignment to survey the Pacific coast was far from the war theaters. He was reassigned to the Atlantic coast within a year and was promoted to captain on July 26, 1862.

In October 1862 Sands became a senior officer assigned to the blockade of the Cape Fear River and Wilmington, North Carolina. To deal with the difficulty of maintaining the blockade against small, fast vessels, Sands devised a plan to use an additional outer line of blockaders. His creative formation resulted in the successful capture of more than 50 blockade-runners. The division also participated in the naval attacks on Fort Fisher, North Carolina, on December 24–25, 1864, and January 13–15, 1865. In the last months of the war, Sands commanded a division of the West Gulf Squadron that took possession of Galveston, Texas, following its surrender on June 2, 1865.

After the war Sands was promoted to commodore on July 26, 1866, and to rear admiral on April 27, 1871. From 1867 until his retirement on February 11, 1874, he headed the Naval Observatory. Sands continued to live in Washington, D.C., until his death there on June 30, 1883.

DONNA SMITH

See also

Fort Fisher Campaign; Galveston, Battle of; Galveston, Texas; Norfolk Navy Yard; West Gulf Blockading Squadron

Further Reading

Hamersly, Lewis. *The Records of Living Officers of the U.S. Navy and Marine Corps.* Philadelphia: Lippincott, 1870.

Sands, Benjamin F. *From Reefer to Rear-Admiral.* New York: Frederick A. Stokes, 1899.

Sanitary Commission, U.S.

The primary Union civilian relief organization during the Civil War. The U.S. Sanitary Commission was the outgrowth of a meeting of representatives of various relief organizations and concerned citizens in New York City in April 1861. The meeting resulted in a petition to the U.S. government to establish a sanitary commission patterned on the British example for the aid of soldiers in the field. The U.S. War Department issued and President Abraham Lincoln signed in June 1861 an official warrant establishing the U.S. Sanitary Commission, which quickly became the overarching organization that coordinated Union civilian relief efforts nationwide. Often considered a "women's organization," the commission was actually headed by men. Most prominent were its president, Reverend Henry W. Bellows, and its general secretary, Frederick Law Olmsted.

The U.S. Sanitary Commission classified its activities in three categories and organized itself along those same lines. The first category was preventive services. These entailed inspections of camps and hospitals for sanitary and health problems and the publication of pamphlets and tracts on medical and field sanitation issues. Because the civilian inspectors usually knew little about military medicine or field sanitation, the commission developed and published extensive checklists to guide inspections. Especially early in the war when officers, soldiers, and military doctors were learning their trades, such inspections produced significant results.

The second category was general relief, which the commission considered its largest function. This consisted of collecting and distributing food, clothing, blankets, medicines, and other medical supplies for sick and wounded soldiers in both field hospitals near the armies and general hospitals in major Union cities. The commission gathered and sorted supplies from more than 1,000 chapters nationwide and shipped them to agents assigned to geographical districts that corresponded roughly with the Union armies.

The third category was special relief, the term for care provided to soldiers outside the normal control of the army. This included assistance to soldiers going on or returning from leave or moving from facility to facility in the medical system. The commission operated soldiers' homes and lodges to provide these men with food and shelter as they traveled. Additionally, the commission outfitted and ran special hospital ships and railroad cars for the transportation of sick and wounded soldiers.

Initially, the U.S. Sanitary Commission collected and distributed food and materials primarily donated by individuals and families. However, as the war progressed and the need grew, the commission sought funds to purchase supplies. It instituted large and very popular fairs in major cities in the North to raise money. Direct contributions from businesses, such as free or reduced train fares and discount printing costs, made contributions go further.

The U.S. Sanitary Commission dominated relief organizations in the North and was also able to quash occasional efforts by subordinate relief groups trying to target their efforts exclusively on units from their home states. Only in the western theater, where the U.S. Christian Commission had a considerable presence, did the Sanitary Commission have significant competition. The Christian Commission eventually limited its activities in the East to matters concerning the soldiers' religious well-being.

J. BOONE BARTHOLOMEES JR.

See also

Hospitals, Military; Medicine; Nurses; Olmsted, Frederick Law; United States Christian Commission

Further Reading

Newberry, J. S. *The U.S. Sanitary Commission in the Valley of the Mississippi, during the War of the Rebellion, 1861–1866.* Cleveland, OH: Fairbanks, Benedict, 1871.

Wormeley, Katherine Prescott. *The Other Side of the War with the Army of the Potomac: Letters from the Headquarters of the United States Sanitary Commission during the Peninsular Campaign in Virginia in 1862.* Boston: Ticknor, 1889.

Sanitary Fairs

Fairs and expositions held to raise money for the U.S. Sanitary Commission (USSC). From the autumn of 1863 through the spring of 1865, cities throughout the North experienced outpourings of patriotic fervor that led to a host of sanitary fairs organized by women to supplement the diminishing finances of the USSC, charged with caring for wounded and sick soldiers.

The brainchild of Chicagoans Mary Livermore and Jane Hoge, the first fund-raising fair opened in their city on October 27, 1863, to widespread popular support. Aided by the region's various women's groups, businessmen, teachers, clergy, politicians, and farmers, the Chicago Sanitary Fair raised almost $100,000 in two weeks. Its success inspired other Northern women to organize similar events, beginning with the Western Sanitary Fair in Cincinnati, which raised triple the amount of the Chicago Sanitary Fair.

Despite the enormous success of the sanitary fair movement, USSC leaders became alarmed at some of the unintended consequences of the mania. Some female branch leaders in New York and New England, for example, became concerned that many patriotic women were devoting their spare time to planning fairs while neglecting the more critical but mundane tasks of sewing shirts, knitting socks, and preparing jams and jellies for the troops. Indeed, USSC male leaders were forced to use sanitary fair proceeds to purchase clothing and supplies to replenish diminished stocks in their central supply depots. The extravagant publicity surrounding the sanitary fairs was responsible for creating an illusion among many women that an enriched USSC had no compelling need for their continued exertions for the troops. The USSC commissioners, in an effort to exert some measure of control over the sanitary fair phenomenon, threw their support behind the 1864 male-organized Metropolitan Fair in New York City, which proved to be the most successful fundraiser of the war, netting more than $1 million.

Despite the USSC's frequent misgivings about the sanitary fairs, they marked an important watershed in the history of women's involvement in the affairs of the nation. By organizing fairs on their own, women, rather than men, made the decisions about the nature of their contribution to the war effort, moving beyond the traditional domestic realm. The sanitary fairs for which records were kept netted a total of $4,393,980, no small sum for the mid-19th century.

ERROL MACGREGOR CLAUSS

See also

Hoge, Jane Currie Blaikie; Livermore, Mary Ashton Rice; Sanitary Commission, U.S.; Western Sanitary Commission; Women

Further Reading

Attie, Jeanie. *Patriotic Toil: Northern Women and the American Civil War.* Ithaca, NY: Cornell University Press, 1998.
Giesberg, Judith. *Civil War Sisterhood: The U.S. Sanitary Commission and Women's Politics in Transition.* Boston: Northeastern University Press, 2006.

Savage's Station, Battle of
Event Date: June 29, 1862

Fourth major engagement of the Seven Days' Campaign (June 25–July 1, 1862), itself part of the Peninsula Campaign (March–July 1862). Union major general George B. McClellan's offensive up the Virginia Peninsula between the York and James Rivers against Richmond had ground to a halt in the Battle of Seven Pines (May 31–June 1, 1862), and new Confederate commander General Robert E. Lee had seized the initiative. His Army of Northern Virginia attacked McClellan's Army of the Potomac at Mechanicsville on June 26. Following the Battle of Gaines' Mill the next day, McClellan ordered excess supplies at White Horse Landing on the Chickahominy River to be burned. He detailed three corps—II Corps, commanded by Brigadier General Edwin V. Sumner; III Corps, under Brigadier General Samuel P. Heintzelman; and VI Corps under Brigadier General William B. Franklin—to form a rear guard at Savage's Station, while the remainder of the Army of the Potomac withdrew south over the Chickahominy to a new base at Harrison's Landing on the James. McClellan had a low opinion of Sumner, the senior officer of the three corps commanders, and, in a major error, failed to name a single commander of the rear guard, with the result that each of the three acted independently of the others. Savage's Station was the crossing of the Richmond & York River Railroad east of Seven Pines (present-day Sandston) along the old Williamsburg Road. Savage's Station was the site of a large Union field hospital.

Determined to drive McClellan from the peninsula, Lee put together a complicated three-pronged plan of attack. Troops under Brigadier General John B. Magruder were to attack in the center along the Williamsburg Road, with troops striking the Union right (Confederate left) under Major General Thomas J. "Stonewall" Jackson and those behind the Union left (Confederate right) under Benjamin Huger. Unfortunately for Lee, his plan called for close coordination and precise timing. However, Jackson was late, stalled north of the Chickahominy, and Huger was not where he was supposed to have been. Also, Magruder was suffering from acute indigestion and had been taking medicine that included morphine. He was in no condition to lead the attack.

At 9:00 a.m. on June 29, 14,000 Confederates under Magruder attacked the 26,000 Union troops of Sumner's II Corps, the rearmost Union corps, at Orchard Station two miles west of Savage's Station. Despite his significant numerical disadvantage, during a two-hour span Magruder succeeded in driving Sumner's men back to Savage's Station. There Sumner expected to be reinforced by Heintzelman's III Corps, only to discover that it had withdrawn south to White Oak Swamp. Informed that Jackson's men would not arrive until the next day, Magruder now proceeded cautiously, not attacking Sumner at Savage's Station until 5:00 p.m.

Photograph of Savage's Station, Virginia, on June 27, 1862, two days before the battle there. It shows the Army of the Potomac headquarters with railroad cars in the background and covered wagons in the foreground. (Library of Congress)

Confederate troops under Brigadier General Lafayette McLaws carried the brunt of the Confederate attack, striking from woods across an open field, against Brigadier General John Sedgwick's division. The Confederate right almost flanked the Union line, with fighting continuing on both sides of the Williamsburg Road until 9:00 p.m., when a driving rainstorm ended the battle and brought a Union withdrawal.

The battle claimed 919 Union casualties for only 450 for the Confederates. In their hasty retreat, Sumner's men also abandoned 2,500 of their comrades in the field hospital. Although Magruder could claim a victory, Lee held him accountable for what he regarded as a less than satisfactory outcome and failure to vigorously pursue the retreating Federals. Subsequently, Lee exiled Magruder, the hero of the Siege of Yorktown (April 5–May 3, 1862), to the Trans-Mississippi theater. Meanwhile, Lee sought to maintain the pressure on McClellan and the next day attacked him at White Oak Swamp.

SPENCER C. TUCKER

See also

Franklin, William Buel; Gaines' Mill, Battle of; Heintzelman, Samuel Peter; Johnston, Joseph Eggleston; Lee, Robert Edward; Magruder, John Bankhead; McClellan, George Brinton; McLaws, Lafayette; Mechanicsville, Battle of; Peninsula Campaign; Sedgwick, John; Seven Days' Campaign; Seven Pines, Battle of; Sumner, Edwin Vose; White Oak Swamp, Battle of; Yorktown, Virginia, Siege of

Further Reading

Burton, Brian. *Extraordinary Circumstances: The Seven Days' Battles.* Bloomington: Indiana University Press, 2001.

Gallagher, Gary W., ed. *The Richmond Campaign of 1862: The Peninsula and the Seven Days.* Chapel Hill: University of North Carolina Press, 2000.

Sears, Stephen W. *To the Gates of Richmond: The Peninsula Campaign.* New York: Ticknor and Fields, 1992.

Savannah, Georgia

Largest city in Georgia during the Civil War and one of the South's principal ports, with an 1860 population of 22,292. Savannah sits along the west bank of the Savannah River opposite South Carolina, which is on the river's east bank. Savannah is located about 15 miles from the Atlantic

Ocean and is surrounded by a vast network of expansive marshes, bayous, and swamps. The mouth of the Savannah River to the east of downtown Savannah was protected by Fort Pulaski, located on Cockspur Island, and by Fort McAllister, located to the south of Tybee Island. Fort Jackson, an old brick fort, protected the inland approaches to the city. The Union captured Fort Pulaski in April 1862 and blockaded the mouth of the Savannah River for the remainder of the war, thus strangling the city's port and trade business.

Savannah, which was founded by James Oglethorpe in 1733, was considered an affluent city in the mid-19th century. Much of the lower South's cotton passed through its port bound for foreign markets. The city also boasted considerable manufacturing for a small Southern city, especially upriver from the downtown area; this region even included an ironworks. Shipbuilding was also a lucrative concern, owing to the city's proximity to the coast and abundant supplies of pitch and turpentine, which abounded in the forests nearby. Many of southern Georgia's wealthiest citizens and planters built spectacular homes in and around Savannah, some of which stand to the present day.

The Civil War had a sizable impact on Savannah, as its economy suffered greatly from the Union blockade. The city remained physically untouched by the war until December 1864, when Major General William T. Sherman laid siege to it. Sherman's March to the Sea ended in a Union triumph when Savannah surrendered on December 21, 1864, without a shot being fired. Once order had been established, Sherman, taken by the natural and architectural beauty of Savannah, did not order his men to loot or destroy it. Instead, he sent President Abraham Lincoln a cable presenting the city to him as an early Christmas gift. After the war the city prospered, chiefly because of the Savannah Cotton Exchange, which was created in 1876 and set worldwide prices for cotton.

PAUL G. PIERPAOLI JR.

See also

Fort McAllister, Georgia, Capture of; Foster, John Gray; Hardee, William Joseph; Savannah, Georgia, Siege of; Sherman, William Tecumseh

Further Reading

Campbell, Jacqueline Glass. *When Sherman Marched North from the Sea: Resistance on the Confederate Homefront.* Chapel Hill: University of North Carolina Press, 2003.

Glatthaar, Joseph T. *The March to the Sea and Beyond: Sherman's Troops in the Savannah and Carolinas Campaigns.* New York: New York University Press, 1985.

Savannah, Georgia, Siege of
Start Date: December 9, 1864
End Date: December 21, 1864

Last military operation of Union major general William T. Sherman's March to the Sea (November 15–December 21, 1864). The siege lasted from December 9 to 21, 1864. Savannah, located about 15 miles inland along the Savannah River in southeastern Georgia, was a key blockade-running port for the Confederacy and, at the time, was Georgia's most populous city, with an 1860 population of about 23,000 people, including slaves. After capturing Atlanta on September 2, 1864, Sherman and 62,000 Union troops marched south and east through the heartland of Georgia, leaving a swath of destruction in their wake. Sherman's goal was to capture Savannah and deal a crippling blow to the already-reeling Confederacy.

Sherman's task was made somewhat easier by earlier Union victories in the vicinity of Savannah. Early in the war, the North had obtained limited success along the South Carolina and Georgia coasts. In November 1861, Union forces had captured nearby Hilton Head Island, just 20 miles north of Savannah, and took control of Port Royal Sound to the north. In April 1862 Union troops captured nearby Fort Pulaski, on Cockspur Island at the mouth of the Savannah River, which not only blocked Savannah's access to the sea but also was near enough to allow artillery to fire into the city.

These proximate Union strongholds notwithstanding, the Confederate position around Savannah was very well fortified. Early in December 1864 in anticipation of a Union assault, the Confederates raised a 10,000-man military force of regulars and militia to garrison the city. The defenders were commanded by Lieutenant General William J. Hardee. Savannah's difficult terrain, which featured vast salt marshes, swamps, bayous, and rice paddies on three sides, certainly worked in the Confederates' favor.

During December 9–10, 1863, Sherman's forces moved toward Savannah, taking positions to the city's west, south, and north. Before he could continue the operation, however, he needed supplies. On December 13, one of Sherman's divisions stormed and captured Fort McAllister, located 18 miles south of Savannah along the Ogeechee River, essentially opening the back door to Savannah. With that river now open, Union vessels moved up the Ogeechee to deliver badly needed supplies to Sherman. On December 16, ships unloaded siege guns, ammunition, food, and other supplies.

On December 17, with his men virtually surrounding the city, Sherman demanded that Hardee surrender or risk the destruction of Savannah. Hardee refused. Meanwhile, Sherman asked Major General John G. Foster, the Union commander in neighboring South Carolina, to seal off Savannah to the east, effectively trapping Hardee's forces. This, Sherman hoped, would result in a quick surrender without the need for a full attack against Savannah.

In a desperate attempt to rescue his army, Hardee decided to abandon the Savannah defenses. Toward that end, he caused a pontoon bridge to be thrown across the Savannah River in the only way out of the city. In the evening of December 20, Hardee's forces fled across the bridge, escaping into South Carolina. The following day Savannah's leaders surrendered the city, and Union forces poured into Savannah without a shot being fired.

Sherman's March to the Sea had ended in a Union triumph. Once order had been established, Sherman, taken by the natural and architectural beauty of Savannah, did not order his men to loot or destroy it. Instead, he sent President Abraham Lincoln a cable presenting the city to him as an early Christmas gift.

JENNIFER M. MURRAY AND PAUL G. PIERPAOLI JR.

See also

Fort McAllister, Georgia, Capture of; Foster, John Gray; Hardee, William Joseph; Sherman, William Tecumseh; Sherman's March to the Sea

Further Reading

Browning, Robert M., Jr. *Success Is All That Was Expected: The South Atlantic Blockading Squadron during the Civil War.* Washington, DC: Potomac Books, 2002.

Campbell, Jacqueline Glass. *When Sherman Marched North from the Sea: Resistance on the Confederate Homefront.* Chapel Hill: University of North Carolina Press, 2003.

Glatthaar, Joseph T. *The March to the Sea and Beyond: Sherman's Troops in the Savannah and Carolinas Campaigns.* New York: New York University Press, 1985.

Savannah Campaign

See Sherman's March to the Sea

Sawyer Gun and Shell

Experimental heavy rifled artillery employed on a limited basis by the U.S. Army. Sylvanus Sawyer, a Massachusetts inventor, developed the gun in the mid-1850s. He and his brothers Addison and Joseph produced cast steel rifled cannon in three bore sizes: 3.67-inch (projectile of 6 pounds),

4.62-inch (projectile of 24 pounds), and 5.8-inch (projectile of up to 53 pounds). Sawyer delivered the first of his cannon to the U.S. government in June 1861.

The key feature of Sawyer's guns was the lead covering over the projectile, which expanded into the grooves or rifling in the barrel. The rifling imparted a spin to the projectile that was supposed to give it greater accuracy at longer ranges. Unfortunately, the expansion of this lead jacket also tended to absorb the explosive shock when the black powder inside the shell detonated, which made the guns susceptible to exploding.

Although Sawyer's cannon had received favorable reports by the Ordnance Department before the war, only a few of his guns were actually purchased and used. The largest-caliber cannon were sometimes employed in coastal batteries; the smaller-caliber guns were employed only during the Peninsula Campaign (March–July 1862), and then on a very limited basis. A 5.8-inch Sawyer gun installed on the Rip Raps at the mouth of Hampton Roads in June 1861 fired on Confederate positions in the direction of Sewell's Point in one of the few successful utilizations of the weapon. It fired a charged shell weighing 48 pounds and a solid shot weighing 53 pounds. Only one Sawyer fieldpiece is known to survive.

DANA LOMBARDY

See also

Artillery, Land, U.S.; Artillery Projectiles, Land

Further Reading

Hazlett, James C., Edwin M. Olmstead, and M. Hume Parks. *Field Artillery Weapons of the Civil War.* Urbana: University of Illinois Press, 2004.

Melton, Jack W., and Lawrence E. Pawl. *Introduction to Field Artillery Ordnance, 1861–1865.* Kennesaw, GA: Kennesaw Mountain Press, 1994.

Saxon Affair
Event Date: October 30, 1863

On October 30, 1863, the British merchant bark *Saxon* had just taken on a cargo of 150 bales of wool and hides at Angra Pequeña (now Lüderitz, Namibia) on the west coast of Africa when the U.S. Navy sidewheeler steamer *Vanderbilt* (15 guns), captained by Commander Charles H. Baldwin, came in, anchored, and sent an armed boarding party in a boat. The Americans demanded the ship's papers of its master, Stephen Sheppard, and Baldwin subsequently accused the British ship's crew of having secured their cargo from the American bark *Conrad,* which had been captured by the Confederate commerce raider *Alabama* operating in the vicinity and commissioned as the Confederate raider *Tuscaloosa.*

The Americans seized the *Saxon* and ordered its crew below. In the process, Acting Master's Mate Charles Danenhower of the prize crew shot James Gray, chief mate of the *Saxon,* in the head, killing him instantly. A U.S. prize crew then sailed the *Saxon* to New York, where the fate of the ship and its cargo were to be decided by a prize court.

When word of what became known as the *Saxon* Affair was received in London, it became the subject of debate in Parliament, with numerous members demanding that the American responsible for killing Gray be put on trial in London. Prime Minister Henry John Temple, Lord Palmerston, ended the debate by stating that the British government would await the outcome of the U.S. prize court decision. Future prime minister Lord Robert Cecil angrily denounced the decision to leave resolution of the *Saxon* Affair entirely in American hands. Before Parliament went back into session, however, Foreign Secretary Lord John Russell hinted at the possibility of war, although he stated that the British would not be the ones to start it.

The American prize court ultimately determined that the seizure of the *Saxon* was unwarranted, and the ship and its cargo were restored to its British owners. Danenhower duly faced a court-martial, which found Gray's death to have been an accident. Witnesses testified that Gray had refused to obey orders from the Americans and that Danenhower had threatened him with the pistol. Danenhower claimed that he had not known the pistol was cocked and that it had accidentally discharged.

In the end, the British government took no action. The *Saxon* Affair was significant in that it revealed the changed British attitude toward the Civil War. In complete contrast to the November 1861 *Trent* Affair, the British government had opted not to strike a belligerent position toward Washington, even in the face of anger in Parliament and the press. By adopting a moderate approach, London sent a clear message that it understood the shifting tide of the war and was not going to be become entangled in the conflict.

THOMAS E. SEBRELL II

See also

Alabama, CSS; Great Britain; Russell, Lord John; Temple, Henry John; *Trent* Affair

Further Reading

U.S. Navy Department. *Official Records of the Union & Confederate Navies in the War of the Rebellion,* Series 1, Vol. 2. Washington, DC: U.S. Government Printing Office, 1894–1922.

Saxton, Rufus
Birth Date: October 19, 1824
Death Date: February 23, 1908

Union officer. Rufus Saxton was born on October 19, 1824, in Greenfield, Massachusetts. He graduated from the U.S. Military Academy, West Point, in 1849. Saxton held a variety of posts in the army thereafter, earning promotion to first lieutenant in 1855, and in the winter of 1861 he led an artillery detachment to Missouri, where he helped Brigadier General Nathaniel Lyon put down a prosecession rebellion at Fort Jackson. On May 13, Saxton was advanced to captain. He later served as quartermaster for Lyon and Major General George B. McClellan before participating in the Battle of Port Royal Sound/Hilton Head Island (November 5–7, 1861). Promoted to brigadier general of volunteers on April 15, 1862, Saxton commanded Union defenses at Harpers Ferry, Virginia, in the spring of 1862. He was later awarded the Medal of Honor for his defense of Harpers Ferry (May 26–30) during Major General Thomas J. "Stonewall" Jackson's Shenandoah Valley Campaign (May–June 1862).

In July, Saxton was again ordered south, and later that summer he was appointed military governor of the captured Sea Islands of Georgia and South Carolina, with his headquarters at Beaufort, South Carolina. Sympathetic to the plight of the newly freed slaves on the islands, he commenced a program whereby freedmen were assigned land parcels carved out of abandoned plantations, given adequate tools and seeds, and directed to become self-sufficient by planting garden plots to sustain themselves. They were also asked to produce excess agricultural products, including cotton, which the federal government would purchase from them. The program worked well and allowed many former slaves to become self-sufficient.

Meanwhile, Saxton also sought to establish a well-trained all-black military unit, which eventually became the 1st South Carolina Colored Volunteers. He mandated that recruits be treated with respect and promised the new recruits that they would be on an even par with white soldiers. This made Saxton a popular figure among blacks in his jurisdiction.

In early November 1862, Saxton allowed some of the black soldiers a chance to prove their mettle by participating in a series of raids along the lower Georgia coast. Their performance was so effective that the 1st Carolina soon became the Union Army's first official full-strength all-black regiment.

Saxton remained military governor until the fall of Savannah in December 1864, at which time he was transferred to the Freedmen's Bureau as assistant commissioner for Florida, Georgia, and South Carolina. He left that post in January 1866 and became an officer in the Quartermaster Department. In 1882 he was advanced to colonel and named assistant quartermaster general. Saxton retired in October 1888 and died on February 23, 1908, in Washington, D.C.

PAUL G. PIERPAOLI JR.

See also

African Americans; African American Soldiers, U.S.; Camp Jackson Affair; Freedmen's Bureau; Jackson's Shenandoah Valley Campaign; Port Royal Sound, Battle of

Further Reading

Eicher, John H., and David J. Eicher. *Civil War High Commands.* Stanford, CA: Stanford University Press, 2001.
Warner, Ezra J. *Generals in Blue: Lives of the Union Commanders.* Baton Rouge: Louisiana State University Press, 2006.

Sayler's Creek, Battle of
Event Date: April 6, 1865

Engagement during the Appomattox Campaign (April 2–9, 1865). The Battle of Sayler's Creek occurred on April 6 southwest of Petersburg, Virginia, not far from the towns of Farmville and Burkeville, and proved to be the fatal blow for General Robert E. Lee's Army of Northern Virginia.

Lee evacuated Petersburg and Richmond during the night of April 2, moving to the south and west. He hoped to move to Danville, Virginia, not far from the North Carolina border; resupply his army; and then link up with General Joseph Johnston's forces in North Carolina. The next morning, Union Army commander Lieutenant General Ulysses S. Grant and Major General George Gordon Meade's Army of the Potomac followed. The Federals quickly blocked the Danville Road, forcing Lee to redirect his army farther west toward Lynchburg. For almost four days, Lee's men struggled to keep ahead of Union forces as they moved fitfully westward.

On April 5 Lee decided to reorder his army, sending most of the infantry ahead while the wagon trains and rearguard divisions under Major General John B. Gordon trailed behind. On April 6 as the Confederates approached the bottomlands of Sayler's Creek, the terrain, combined with

increasing gaps in the marching columns, made the Confederates vulnerable to an attack by the pursuing Federals. The wagon trains and Gordon moved to the north to seek haven. Meanwhile, the now-isolated Confederate corps of Lieutenant Generals Richard S. Ewell and Richard H. Anderson turned and came under a blistering Union attack. Around 11:00 a.m. on April 6, Union cavalry, commanded by Major General Philip Sheridan, assailed the Confederate wagon trains. Major General George E. Pickett dispatched his men to halt the advance of the Union cavalry, while the wagon train moved to safety.

Ewell, Anderson, and Major General George Washington Custis Lee now met to discuss their best course of action. Fully aware that they were outnumbered, Ewell argued that the Confederates should break contact and retreat into the countryside, using the dense forests to blunt Union cavalry attacks. Anderson, however, prevailed upon Ewell to stay and fight it out with the Federals.

Major General Andrew Humphreys (commanding the Union II Corps) and Major General Horatio G. Wright (VI Corps), recognizing an opportunity for victory, rapidly pursued the Confederates. While Ewell and his men crossed Sayler's Creek and prepared to offer battle near the Hillsman house, the Federals rushed to attack and encircle the Confederates. Devastating artillery fire from the Union VI Corps now smashed into Ewell's haphazardly formed line. The desperate situation became even more untenable when Union cavalry began pouring out of a surrounding woodlot. Ewell hoped that he had time to move what was left of his corps into the nearby woods, but as he rode to give the retreat order, it became all too obvious that he was surrounded.

Soon, whole Confederate brigades began laying down their arms as Lee's wagon trains became trapped in the mud along Sayler's Creek. Gordon's rear guard now came under heavy attack, sustaining heavy losses. Recognizing that any further fighting would be senseless, Ewell surrendered his command. By the end of the day, approximately 8,000 Confederates had been taken prisoner, including Ewell, Custis Lee (General Lee's eldest son), Major General Joseph Kershaw, and five brigadier generals. Union forces also destroyed or captured much of Lee's wagon trains. This was the greatest number of men captured in combat during any conflict fought in North America. General Lee, clearly reeling from the defeat, lamented, "My God! Has the army dissolved?" Three days later on April 9 at Appomattox Court House, Lee himself surrendered what remained of his Army of Northern Virginia.

JENNIFER M. MURRAY AND PAUL G. PIERPAOLI JR.

See also

Anderson, Richard Heron; Appomattox Campaign; Appomattox Court House and Lee's Surrender; Ewell, Richard Stoddart; Gordon, John Brown; Grant, Ulysses Simpson; Johnston, Joseph Eggleston; Lee, Robert Edward; Lee, William Henry Fitzhugh; Northern Virginia, Confederate Army of; Pickett, George Edward; Sheridan, Philip Henry

Further Reading

Marvel, William. *A Place Called Appomattox*. Chapel Hill: University of North Carolina Press, 2000.
McPherson, James M. *Battle Cry of Freedom: The Civil War Era*. New York: Ballantine, 1988.
Smith, Derek. *Lee's Last Stand: Sailor's Creek Virginia, 1865*. Shippensburg, PA: White Mane, 2002.

Scalawags

Pejorative term used in the South after the Civil War to describe native whites who joined the Republican Party and assisted in implementing Reconstruction policies. During the Civil War, the Republican Party gained white Southern adherents in Union-occupied parts of Florida, Louisiana, and Tennessee, and this continued after the war. Perhaps two of the most prominent scalawags were former Confederate military officers Lieutenant General James Longstreet and Colonel John S. Mosby. After the imposition of congressional Reconstruction in 1867, which brought with it military occupation of the South to enforce black suffrage, and the election of Republican Ulysses S. Grant to the presidency in 1868, increasing numbers of white Southerners joined the Republican Party.

While many of these white Southerners were political opportunists, some had harbored Unionist sentiments before and during the Civil War. Native Southern white Republicans probably never exceeded 30 percent of the electorate in the Reconstruction-era South; however, along with the newly enfranchised African American voters, they helped provide the basis for Republican rule throughout most of the South during Reconstruction, which lasted until 1877. Clearly some Southern white Republicans fit the bill of the detested scalawag, some even in alliance with the hated carpetbaggers from the North. However, the majority of Southern Republicans had a genuine concern for Reconstruction, which they believed could only be accomplished by sweeping economic and political reforms no matter how unpopular they may have been.

Following the end of Reconstruction, the Democratic Party reasserted control throughout the South. After 1877, some scalawags renounced their Republican affiliations and joined the Democratic Party. Many former scalawags forsook politics altogether. However, a significant number remained active in Republican politics. For many years, scalawags continued to lead most of the state Republican Party organizations in the South. In a few Southern states, native white Republicans maintained sufficient numbers to challenge Democratic hegemony. While often maligned, the scalawags call into question the notion of a monolithic American South in unified support of slavery and secession during the Civil War.

TED BUTLER

See also

Democratic Party; Longstreet, James; Mosby, John Singleton; Radical Republicans; Reconstruction; Republican Party

Further Reading

Baggett, James Alex. *The Scalawags: Southern Dissenters in the Civil War and Reconstruction*. Baton Rouge: Louisiana State University Press, 2003.
Degler, Carl N. *The Other South: Southern Dissenters in the Nineteenth Century*. Boston: Northeastern University Press, 1982.

Scales, Alfred Moore
Birth Date: November 26, 1827
Death Date: February 8, 1892

Confederate officer. Alfred Moore Scales was born on November 26, 1827, at Reidsville, North Carolina. He attended the University of North Carolina, eventually became a lawyer, and worked as the solicitor of Rockingham County before serving four terms in the state assembly. Scales enlisted as a private in the 3rd North Carolina Infantry in 1861 and was soon elected captain. In late October he was commissioned colonel and led his regiment, now designated the 13th North Carolina, during the Siege of Yorktown (April 5–May 3, 1862) and in the Battle of Williamsburg (May 5, 1862). He also saw action during the Seven Days' Campaign (June 25–July 1, 1862). Scales performed brilliantly at the First Battle of Fredericksburg (December 13, 1862).

Scales was seriously wounded at the Battle of Chancellorsville (May 1–4, 1863). Promoted to brigadier general on June 13, 1863, and sufficiently recuperated, he saw duty at the Battle of Gettysburg (July 1–3, 1863), where his brigade sustained high casualties and where he was gravely wounded for a second time. After a lengthy convalescence in Winchester, Virginia, he took up his old command and saw considerable action in Virginia, including the Battle of the Wilderness (May 5–7, 1864), the Battle of Spotsylvania

Court House (May 8–21, 1864), and the Petersburg Campaign (June 15, 1864–April 3, 1865). Scales was on sick leave when his brigade surrendered at Appomattox on April 9, 1865.

After the war Scales settled in Greensboro, where he maintained a legal practice. During 1866–1869, he again served in the state legislature before serving as a U.S. representative during 1875–1884. He served as North Carolina governor from 1885 to 1889. During 1888–1892, Scales was president of a bank in Greensboro, where he died on February 8, 1892.

PAUL G. PIERPAOLI JR.

See also

Chancellorsville, Battle of; Fredericksburg, First Battle of; Gettysburg, Battle of; Peninsula Campaign; Seven Days' Campaign; Wilderness, Battle of the; Williamsburg, Battle of; Yorktown, Virginia, Siege of

Further Reading

Eicher, John H., and David J. Eicher. *Civil War High Commands.* Stanford, CA: Stanford University Press, 2001.

Warner, Ezra J. *Generals in Gray: Lives of the Confederate Commanders.* Baton Rouge: Louisiana State University Press, 2006.

Schenck, Robert Cumming
Birth Date: October 4, 1809
Death Date: March 23, 1890

Union officer. Robert Cumming Schenck was born on October 4, 1809, in Franklin, Ohio, and graduated from Miami University in 1827. He began a successful law practice in Dayton and was elected as a Whig to the Ohio legislature, serving from 1839 until 1843. He was then elected to the U.S. House of Representatives, serving from 1843 to 1851. From 1851 until 1853, he was U.S. minister to Brazil. Returning to his law practice, Schenck joined the Republican ranks and supported Abraham Lincoln's 1860 presidential bid.

Using his political connections, Schenck obtained a brigadier general's commission in the volunteer army on June 5, 1861, despite his lack of military experience. He commanded a brigade at the First Battle of Bull Run (July 21, 1861) and was then transferred to western Virginia. After briefly commanding forces in Cumberland, Maryland, in the spring of 1862, he was again sent to western Virginia, where he served under Major General John C. Frémont during Confederate major general Thomas J. "Stonewall" Jackson's Shenandoah Valley Campaign (May–June 1862).

When Fremont relinquished his command in June 1862, Schenck temporarily led I Corps of the Army of Virginia. During the Second Battle of Bull Run (August 29–30, 1862), Schenck commanded a division before being severely wounded. As he recovered, he was advanced to major general of volunteers, effective on August 30. He went on to head the Middle Department and VIII Corps, headquartered in Baltimore.

Elected to another term in Congress in November, Schenck resigned his commission on December 3, 1863. He served in the U.S. House of Representatives until January 1871, at which time he became minister to Great Britain. He held that post until 1876. Schenck returned to the United States that year and began practicing law in Washington, D.C., where he died on March 23, 1890.

PAUL G. PIERPAOLI JR.

See also

Bull Run, First Battle of; Bull Run, Second Battle of; Frémont, John Charles; Middle Department, Union; Jackson's Shenandoah Valley Campaign

Further Reading

Joyner, Fred B. "Robert Cumming Schenck, First Citizen and Statesman of the Miami Valley." *Ohio State Archaeological and Historical Quarterly* 58 (July 1949): 286–297.

Warner, Ezra J. *Generals in Blue: Lives of the Union Commanders.* Baton Rouge: Louisiana State University Press, 2006.

Schimmelfenning, Alexander
Birth Date: July 20, 1824
Death Date: September 5, 1865

Union officer. Alexander Schimmelfenning was born on July 20, 1824, in Lithauen, Prussia, and became an engineering officer in the Prussian Army. As a supporter of the Revolution of 1848, he was forced to flee his homeland after the army put down the rebellion. He settled in Philadelphia in 1853 and worked as a draftsman and an engineer. By 1860, he was employed by the War Department as an engineering consultant. He volunteered for service in the Union Army when the Civil War began in 1861. On September 30, 1861, he was commissioned colonel of the 74th Pennsylvania Infantry Regiment.

Having been injured when thrown from a horse and then having contracted smallpox, Schimmelfenning did not participate in any combat until the Second Battle of Bull Run (August 29–20, 1862), when he commanded a brigade under Brigadier General Carl Schurz, a fellow German expatriate. On November 29, 1862, Schimmelfenning was advanced to brigadier general and headed a brigade in XI Corps, which consisted chiefly of German Americans and German immigrants.

At the Battle of Chancellorsville (May 1–4, 1863), a Confederate force under Lieutenant General Thomas "Stonewall" Jackson inflicted heavy casualties on Schimmelfenning's brigade. During the Battle of Gettysburg (July 1–3, 1863), Schimmelfenning had temporary command of General Schurz's division, which was pummeled by the Confederates. Schimmelfenning was knocked unconscious by a recoiling gun on July 1. When he came to, he was unable to rejoin his men without the risk of being captured. Instead, he hid in a pigsty and did not emerge from hiding until after the Confederates had withdrawn on July 4.

Soon thereafter, Schimmelfenning was transferred to the Department of the South, where he contracted malaria and was on medical leave for months. Late in the war, he returned to active duty and participated in Union operations against Charleston, South Carolina. He once again became ill, this time with tuberculosis, and was given medical leave on April 8, 1865. Schimmelfenning died on September 5, 1865, in Wernersville, Pennsylvania.

PAUL G. PIERPAOLI JR.

See also

Bull Run, Second Battle of; Chancellorsville, Battle of; Gettysburg, Battle of; Schurz, Carl

Further Reading

Eicher, John H., and David J. Eicher. *Civil War High Commands.* Stanford, CA: Stanford University Press, 2001.

Warner, Ezra J. *Generals in Blue: Lives of the Union Commanders.* Baton Rouge: Louisiana State University Press, 2006.

Schofield, John McAllister
Birth Date: September 29, 1831
Death Date: March 4, 1906

Union officer. John McAllister Schofield was born in Gerry, New York, on September 29, 1831. Raised in Illinois, Schofield graduated from the U.S. Military Academy, West Point, in 1853. Commissioned a second lieutenant, he served for two years in the 1st U.S. Artillery and then returned to West Point as an instructor of physics. He was promoted to first lieutenant in 1855 but, disillusioned by the lack of promotion, secured a leave of absence in 1860 and took a position teaching physics at Washington University in St. Louis.

On the beginning of the Civil War in April 1861, Schofield was commissioned a major in the 1st Missouri Volunteers. He favorably impressed Brigadier General Nathaniel Lyon, the local Union commander, who appointed Schofield to his staff. In this capacity, Schofield accompanied Lyon in a series of small Union victories over Southern forces but advised against engaging numerically superior Confederate forces at Wilson's Creek on August 10, 1861. Lyon attacked anyway and was killed. Schofield particularly distinguished himself in the battle and in 1892 was formally awarded the Medal of Honor for his role.

On November 21, 1861, Schofield was advanced to brigadier general of volunteers. In October 1862 he took command of the Army of the Frontier and the District of Southwest Missouri. Enjoying some success driving Southern guerrillas from Missouri and Kansas, Schofield also sought a more important command. He was promoted to major general of volunteers in November 1862, but the appointment lapsed in March 1863. On May 12, 1863, he was reappointed major general of volunteers and given command of the Department of the Missouri.

Major General John M. Schofield was a highly effective Union officer during the Civil War. His troops defeated the Confederates in the Battle of Franklin on November 30, 1864. (Library of Congress)

In January 1864 Schofield assumed command of the Department and Army of the Ohio (XXIII Corps). He then participated in Major General William T. Sherman's Atlanta Campaign (May 5–September 2, 1864). When Confederate forces under General John B. Hood invaded Tennessee, Schofield eluded Hood at Spring Hill and entrenched at Franklin. In the Battle of Franklin (November 30, 1864), Schofield's men devastated the attacking Confederates. For this victory, Schofield was advanced to brigadier general in the regular army to date from the battle. He also directed his corps in the Battle of Nashville (December 15–16). Moving his forces by sea to Fort Fisher, North Carolina, Schofield occupied Wilmington on February 22, 1865, and then fought at the Second Battle of Kinston (March 7–10, 1865). Brevetted major general in the regular army, he commanded the Department of North Carolina until June.

Following the war, President Andrew Johnson appointed Schofield a confidential agent of the U.S. State Department and sent him to France, charged with negotiating with Emperor Napoleon III the withdrawal of French forces from Mexico. Schofield commanded the Department of the Potomac from August 1866 to June 1868. President Johnson then appointed him secretary of war. In March 1869 Schofield advanced to major general of regulars and took charge of the Department of the Missouri. He then commanded the Division of the Pacific and in 1873, under secret orders of Secretary of War William Belknap, traveled to Hawaii to evaluate the strategic usefulness of those islands to the United States. Upon his recommendation, the government purchased Pearl Harbor as a naval facility. In September 1876 Schofield returned to West Point as commandant, remaining there until January 1881, when he succeeded to command of the Division of the Gulf. In 1878 he also headed a board that reconsidered the court-martial of Major General Fitz John Porter and absolved him of misconduct at the Second Battle of Bull Run (August 29–30, 1862).

After successive tours with the Division of the Pacific and the Division of the Missouri, in August 1888 Schofield succeeded Lieutenant General Philip H. Sheridan as commanding general of the army. During his seven-year tenure, Schofield pressed for improvements in the life of common soldiers through better rations, higher pay, and improved standards of living. He also sought to foster professionalism among the officer corps by a system of examinations for promotion, the creation of post libraries, and strong support for service schools.

Schofield proved to be an able administrator. He clarified the military chain of command by ending a long feud with the secretary of war, subordinating the post of commanding general to the secretary's office, and agreeing to function as his senior military adviser. Schofield's final act was to advocate the adoption of a general staff on the German model to better formulate grand strategic planning. This proposal was not adopted. Schofield was promoted to lieutenant general in February 1895 and retired upon his 64th birthday that September.

Schofield strongly supported U.S. intervention in Cuba in order to end the suffering of the Cuban people. During the 1898 Spanish-American War, President William McKinley, who distrusted both commanding general Major General Nelson A. Miles and Secretary of War Russell Alger, often sought the counsel of the retired Schofield regarding military issues. Schofield also played a major role in McKinley's decision to call for an increase in the size of the regular army. In 1902 Schofield appeared before a congressional committee to support the creation of a general staff concept, contrary to the opinions of General Miles. Schofield died in St. Augustine, Florida, on March 4, 1906.

JOHN C. FREDRIKSEN AND SPENCER C. TUCKER

See also

Franklin, Battle of; Lyon, Nathaniel; Miles, Nelson Appleton; Nashville, Battle of; Ohio, Union Department of the; Sheridan, Philip Henry; Sherman, William Tecumseh; Wilmington, North Carolina, Engagements at; Wilson's Creek, Battle of

Further Reading
Connelly, Donald B. *John M. Schofield and the Politics of Generalship*. Chapel Hill: University of North Carolina Press, 2006.
McDonough, James L. *John M. Schofield: Union General in the Civil War and Reconstruction*. Tallahassee: University of Florida Press, 1972.
Schofield, John M. *Forty-Six Years in the Army*. 1897; reprint, Norman: University of Oklahoma Press, 1999.

Schurz, Carl
Birth Date: March 2, 1829
Death Date: May 14, 1906

Union officer, U.S. senator, and secretary of the interior. Carl Schurz was born on March 2, 1829, in Liblar, Prussia, near Cologne (Köln). He attended the University of Bonn but did not complete his degree. In 1852 he immigrated to the United States as a political refugee from the failed German revolutions of 1848. Schurz established himself in business in Philadelphia and then moved to Wisconsin, where he studied law and was admitted to the bar. Schurz almost

Carl Schurz immigrated to the United States from Germany in 1852 and helped rally German Americans to vote for Abraham Lincoln in 1860. Rewarded with a commission as brigadier general of volunteers and later advanced to major general, Schurz proved an inept field commander. (Library of Congress)

immediately took an active role in American politics. A supporter of the newly established Republican Party, Schurz headed the Wisconsin delegation to the Republican Convention and was appointed to the foreign department of the Republican National Committee. He rallied German American support for Abraham Lincoln's candidacy in 1860. Following Lincoln's election, Schurz received an appointment as the minister to Spain. What he had really wanted, however, was a commission in the Union Army.

Before departing for Spain in 1861, Schurz helped raise German regiments for federal service, and he returned from Spain in January 1862 to accept a commission as a brigadier general of volunteers in April 1862. Schurz served effectively in command of a division in the Army of Virginia during the Second Battle of Bull Run (August 29–30, 1862) and then assumed command of a division in the largely German XI Corps, Army of the Potomac, which was not engaged in the Battle of Antietam or the First Battle of Fredericksburg. He received promotion to major general of volunteers on March 17, 1863. Schurz nevertheless was criticized for his performance in the Battles of Chancellorsville (May 1–4, 1863) and Gettysburg (July 1–3, 1863), both of which proved

disastrous for XI Corps. This criticism continued during the Chattanooga Campaign when he arrived late for the night attack in the Battle of Wauhatchie (October 28–29, 1863). A court of inquiry later cleared him of incompetence, but Schurz never again held a field command.

Schurz stayed in the western theater until the late spring of 1864, at which point he took a leave of absence to help coordinate Lincoln's 1864 reelection bid. Schurz returned to duty to help recruit the Veteran Reserve Corps and then served as chief of staff for Major General Henry Slocum in North Carolina in the final month of the war. Schurz resigned his commission in May 1865.

After the war, Schurz worked as a journalist and represented Missouri as a Republican in the U.S. Senate (1869–1875). He then served as secretary of the interior (1877–1881) in the Rutherford B. Hayes administration. After Schurz's lengthy government service, he again pursued a career as a journalist, winning broad public approval for his principles. Schurz died in New York City on May 14, 1906.

THERESA STOREY HEFNER-BABB

See also
Bull Run, Second Battle of; Chattanooga Campaign; Gettysburg, Battle of; Wauhatchie, Battle of

Further Reading
Schurz, Carl. *The Autobiography of Carl Schurz: An Abridgement in One Volume by Wayne Andrews.* New York: Scribner, 1961.
Trefousse, Hans L. *Carl Schurz: A Biography.* Knoxville: University of Tennessee Press, 1982.

Scott, Dred
Birth Date: 1795
Death Date: September 17, 1858

African American slave who unsuccessfully sued for his freedom. Dred Scott was born a slave sometime in 1795 to the Peter Blow family in Southampton County, Virginia. In 1830 Scott moved with the Blow family to St. Louis, Missouri, and in 1832 he was sold to Dr. John Emerson, a U.S. Army surgeon, for $500. Scott then accompanied his new owner to Illinois in 1834 and two years later to Fort Snelling in the Wisconsin Territory.

In 1836 Scott received permission from his owner to marry Harriet Robinson, another slave who had also become the property of Dr. Emerson. In 1838 Scott returned to Missouri and subsequently had two children with Harriet. When Emerson died in 1843, Scott tried to purchase his freedom

Portrait of slave Dred Scott, the unsuccessful plaintiff in one of the most important court cases in U.S. history. (Library of Congress)

for $300 from Mrs. Irene Emerson, John Emerson's wife, but she refused. Scott thus decided to sue for his freedom.

In 1846, with the Blow family financing Scott's legal costs, Scott filed suit for his freedom in a St. Louis, Missouri, court. Although he lost the first trial, Scott was granted a new hearing because hearsay evidence had been inappropriately used. In 1850 a jury ruled that under the Missouri doctrine of "once free, always free," Scott's residence in both Illinois and the Wisconsin Territory—where slavery was outlawed—had made him free, and therefore his return to Missouri had not altered his status as a free man.

Mrs. Emerson appealed the verdict, and in 1852 the Missouri Supreme Court reversed the decision. When Mrs. Emerson turned the case over to her brother, John Sandford, a New York resident, the case was transferred to federal court. Scott appealed to the U.S. Supreme Court after a federal circuit court upheld the Missouri Supreme Court ruling.

On March 6, 1857, in a 7 to 2 ruling, Chief Justice Roger Taney and six associate justices ruled against Scott, while Justices John McLean and Benjamin Curtis dissented. Taney declared that Scott was not, according to the U.S. Constitution, a citizen and therefore could not sue in federal court. Scott was instead, Taney wrote, a member of a "subordinate and inferior class of beings . . . altogether unfit to associate with the white race . . . and so far inferior that they had no

right to which the white man was bound to respect." Taney also rejected Scott's claim that by traveling to Illinois and Wisconsin Territory, he was free.

After the ruling, Scott was returned to Mrs. Emerson as her property, but the sons of Scott's first owner, Peter Blow, purchased Scott and his wife, Harriet, and promptly set them free. Scott died from tuberculosis in St. Louis on September 17, 1858.

STEFAN M. BROOKS

See also

Dred Scott Case; Slavery

Further Reading

Fehrenbacher, Don E. *The Dred Scott Case: Its Significance in American Law and Politics.* Oxford: Oxford University Press, 1978.

Herda, D. J. *The Dred Scott Case.* Berkeley Heights, CA: Enslow, 1994.

Wallance, Gregory J. *Two Men before the Storm.* Austin, TX: Greenleaf Book Group, 2005.

Scott, Thomas Moore
Birth Date: 1829
Death Date: April 21, 1876

Confederate officer. Thomas Moore Scott was born in Athens, Georgia, in 1829 to a farming family. Little is known of his youth, as most of the family records were destroyed in a house fire. He traveled to New Orleans regularly as a young man for business purposes and took up residence in Louisiana in the early 1850s. Scott farmed land in Claiborne Parish, Louisiana, prior to the war, and in 1861 he recruited the 12th Louisiana Infantry Regiment. He was commissioned its colonel on August 13, 1861, when the outfit was accepted into Confederate service, and the brigade was first sent to Kentucky. The 12th Louisiana was present for but did not actively participate in the Battle of Belmont (November 7, 1861) in Missouri. Thereafter, Scott and his men helped garrison Island No. 10 and Fort Pillow.

During the winter of 1862–1863, Scott saw service around Port Hudson, Louisiana, and then participated in the Battle of Champion Hill (May 16, 1863) in Mississippi. He remained in Mississippi after the fall of Vicksburg on July 4, 1863, and served under General Joseph E. Johnston. Scott next saw duty during the Atlanta Campaign (May 5–September 2, 1864) and was advanced to brigadier general on May 24, 1864, to date from May 10. He won particular recognition for a furious attack by his brigade during the Battle of Peachtree Creek

(July 20, 1864). Seriously wounded by an exploding shell during the Battle of Franklin (November 30, 1864), Scott remained on sick leave for the rest of the war.

After the war Scott took up farming outside Homer, Louisiana, and also operated a sugar plantation along the Gulf Coast. Scott died in New Orleans on April 21, 1876.

PAUL G. PIERPAOLI JR.

See also

Atlanta Campaign; Belmont, Battle of; Champion Hill, Battle of; Johnston, Joseph Eggleston; Nashville, Battle of

Further Reading

Sword, Wiley. *The Confederacy's Last Hoorah: Spring Hill, Franklin, & Nashville.* New York: HarperCollins for the University of Kansas Press, 1992.

Warner, Ezra J. *Generals in Gray: Lives of the Confederate Commanders.* Baton Rouge: Louisiana State University Press, 2006.

Scott, William Campbell
Birth Date: November 12, 1809
Death Date: April 9, 1865

Confederate officer. Born on November 12, 1809, in Powhatan County, Virginia, William Campbell Scott graduated from Hampden-Sydney College in 1827 and received a law degree from the University of Virginia in 1829. He commenced a legal practice in his home county and subsequently served two terms in the Virginia House of Delegates. He was also a member of the Virginia Militia, rising to the rank of brigadier general. An ex-Whig and a Unionist representing two strongly Democratic and secessionist counties in the 1861 Virginia Secession Convention, he joined many others in shifting his vote for secession in the wake of the bombardment of Fort Sumter and President Abraham Lincoln's call for troops.

Scott then secured appointment as colonel of the 44th Virginia Volunteer Infantry Regiment. Shortly after the 44th was accepted into Confederate service, it was ordered to Beverly in western Virginia (now West Virginia) to reinforce Confederates under Brigadier General Robert Garnett defending against a Union incursion. The collapse of the Confederate position at Rich Mountain on July 11, 1861, left Scott in command at Beverly. His decision to abandon Beverly and retreat beyond Cheat Mountain, together with Garnett's retreat from Laurel Hill and subsequent death, left much of western Virginia open to Union occupation. Although Scott received much of the blame for this, he nevertheless continued in command.

Appointed to brigade command on May 2, 1862, Scott served in that capacity under Major General Thomas J. "Stonewall" Jackson in the Shenandoah Valley Campaign (May–June 1862), seeing action at the Battle of McDowell (May 8, 1862) and for most of the remainder of the campaign. At Port Republic (June 9, 1862) Scott's badly diminished brigade stalled the major Union thrust with a desperate charge and then regrouped to support Brigadier General Richard Taylor's final successful assault on the Lewiston Coaling. Scott received high praise for his performance.

Scott engaged in no significant military action after the Shenandoah Valley Campaign, eventually resigning his commission because of poor health. He died in Powhatan, Virginia, on April 9, 1865.

THOMAS LYNWOOD POWERS

See also

Jackson's Shenandoah Valley Campaign; McDowell, Battle of; Port Republic, Battle of; Rich Mountain, Battle of

Further Reading

Krick, Robert K. *Conquering the Valley: Stonewall Jackson at Port Republic.* New York: William Morrow, 1996.

Newell, Clayton R. *Lee vs. McClellan: The First Campaign.* New York: Regnery, 1996.

Scott, Winfield
Birth Date: June 13, 1786
Death Date: May 26, 1866

Union officer. Born at Laurel Branch near Petersburg, Virginia, on June 13, 1786, Winfield Scott briefly attended the College of William and Mary (1805) and then studied law. In the aftermath of the *Chesapeake-Leopard* Affair (June 22, 1807), Scott enlisted in a Virginia cavalry troop. In 1808 he secured a direct commission as a captain of artillery and was assigned to New Orleans. Following a letter to President Thomas Jefferson in which he sharply criticized the demonstrated incompetence of his commanding officer, Brigadier General James Wilkinson, Scott was suspended without pay for a year (1809–1810). He then returned to New Orleans (1811–1812) and was promoted to lieutenant colonel in July 1812.

Assigned to the Niagara frontier at the beginning of the War of 1812, Scott saw combat at the Battle of Queenston Heights that October and was taken prisoner. Exchanged, he was promoted to colonel in March 1813. Known as a demanding trainer who nonetheless was much concerned for the welfare of his men, in May he led the successful attack on

A brevet lieutenant general, Winfield Scott was one of the most capable officers in American history and commanded the Union Army at the beginning of the Civil War. Although old (he had been a brigadier general in the War of 1812) and not long in command, Scott developed the strategic plan that brought Union victory four long years later. (National Archives)

and capture of Fort George, Ontario, where he was wounded. Promoted to brigadier general in March 1814, Scott led a brigade in Major General Jacob Brown's invasion of Canada, distinguishing himself in July in the Battles of Chippewa and Lundy's Lane, in which he was wounded twice. His performance in these contests made him a national hero and won him the Thanks of Congress, a gold medal, and a brevet promotion to major general.

Following the war, Scott wrote the drill manual *Infantry Tactics* that became the standard on the subject in the U.S. Army for a generation. Appointed to command the Northern Department in 1815, he twice traveled to Europe to study its military establishments. In 1829 he assumed command of the Eastern Division. He helped smooth relations with South Carolina during the Nullification Crisis of 1832 and again showed great diplomatic skills in easing tensions with Britain over the U.S.-Canadian border in 1838 and 1839. He was also heavily involved in Native American affairs, negotiating the Treaty of Fort Armstrong with the Sauks and Foxes in 1832, commanding U.S. forces in 1836 during the Second

Seminole War (1835–1842), and overseeing the Cherokee removal in 1838.

Appointed commanding general of the U.S. Army with the rank of permanent major general in July 1841, during the Mexican-American War (1846–1848) Scott planned and carried out the amphibious landing at Veracruz of March 9, 1847, and the subsequent 260-mile march to Mexico City, one of the most brilliant in U.S. military history, carried out without a reverse while greatly outnumbered and deep in enemy territory. Scott's troops occupied Mexico City on September 14. He ignored President James K. Polk's orders to recommence fighting and secured peace in the Treaty of Guadalupe Hidalgo on February 2, 1848.

Scott's performance in the war brought the Thanks of Congress and the enmity of President Polk, who set out to ruin him and removed him from his post as commanding general. Scott ran for the presidency as the Whig candidate in 1852 but carried only four states.

Brevetted lieutenant general in 1855, retroactive to 1847, Scott was sent west by President Franklin Pierce to end tensions with the British over the Puget Sound area and specifically a dispute over San Juan Island. With the sectional crisis looming, in 1860 Scott urged President James Buchanan without success to make preparations for war, to include strengthening forts in the South.

In his position as general in chief and President Abraham Lincoln's closest military adviser, in April 1861 Scott urged the president to abandon Fort Sumter in South Carolina and Fort Pickens in Florida as indefensible. Some in the cabinet called Scott's loyalty into question, and Lincoln authorized expeditions to resupply both without Scott's involvement. Scott attempted without success to persuade Colonel Robert E. Lee to accept the field command of the U.S. Army in the war. Scott was also one of the few in Washington to understand that the war would be both long and difficult. Members of Congress scoffed when Scott requested 300,000 men to serve three-year enlistments rather than 90 days. The war would have proceeded quite differently had Scott's counsel been followed.

Scott developed the strategic plan to impose a naval blockade of the Confederate coasts while training a large army to then cooperate with the navy to bisect the South along its great rivers. This so-called Anaconda Plan ultimately brought victory.

After 54 years in military service and the longest tenure as a general officer in U.S. history, Scott retired from the army in November 1861, forced out and replaced by Major General George B. McClellan. Scott moved to West Point, where he wrote his memoirs and died on May 28, 1866. Known as "Old Fuss and Feathers," Scott loved display. A brilliant trainer, careful planner, consummate strategist, successful diplomat, and highly effective field commander, Scott ranks as one of the most important military leaders in U.S. military history.

SPENCER C. TUCKER

See also

Anaconda Plan; Buchanan, James; Fort Pickens, Florida; Fort Sumter, South Carolina, Confederate Bombardment of; Lee, Robert Edward; Lincoln, Abraham; McClellan, George Brinton

Further Reading

Eisenhower, John S. D. *Agent of Destiny: The Life and Times of General Winfield Scott.* Norman: University of Oklahoma Press, 1997.

Johnson, Timothy D. *Winfield Scott: The Quest for Military Glory.* Manhattan: University Press of Kansas, 1999.

Scott, Winfield. *Memoirs.* 2 vols. New York: Sheldon, 1864.

Scott v. Sandford

See Dred Scott Case

Scurry, William Read
Birth Date: February 10, 1821
Death Date: April 30, 1864

Confederate officer. William Read Scurry was born on February 10, 1821, in Gallatin, Tennessee, but moved to Texas when he was 16 years old, settling in San Augustine. During the Mexican-American War (1846–1848), he enlisted as a private in the 2nd Texas Mounted Volunteers. He performed well and mustered out in 1848 as a major. During 1859, he served as a commissioner on the Texas–New Mexico boundary commission, and in 1861 he was a delegate to his state's secession convention.

In 1861 Scurry joined the 4th Texas Cavalry as its lieutenant colonel and was a participant in Brigadier General Henry H. Sibley's failed New Mexico Campaign (November 1861–May 1862). Scurry performed well at the Battles of Val Verde (February 21, 1862) and Glorieta Pass (March 26–28, 1862) and was rewarded with a promotion to colonel in March and to brigadier general to date from September 12, 1862. In January 1863 when Major General John B. Magruder defeated Union forces at Galveston, Scurry successfully commanded a brigade there.

After commanding the Eastern Sub-District of Texas, Scurry assumed command of a brigade in Major General John G. Walker's Texas Division in Louisiana. Scurry took part in the Red River Campaign (March 10–May 22, 1864), during which he ably led his brigade at the Battles of Mansfield (April 8, 1864) and Pleasant Hill (April 9, 1864). Scurry's command was then rushed to Arkansas to oppose the Camden Expedition (March 23–May 3, 1864). On April 30 as Scurry's brigade tried to block a Union force at Jenkins' Ferry, Scurry was badly wounded but refused to abandon his men to seek medical treatment. He bled to death on the field of battle that same day.

PAUL G. PIERPAOLI JR.

See also

Glorieta Pass, Battle of; Jenkins' Ferry, Battle of; Magruder, John Bankhead; Mansfield, Battle of; Pleasant Hill, Battle of; Red River Campaign; Sibley's New Mexico Campaign; Val Verde, Battle of

Further Reading

Joiner, Gary Dillard. *One Damn Blunder from Beginning to End: The Red River Campaign of 1864.* Wilmington, DE: Scholarly Resources, 2003.

Warner, Ezra J. *Generals in Gray: Lives of the Confederate Commanders.* Baton Rouge: Louisiana State University Press, 2006.

Seacoast Guns

Artillery pieces specifically intended for coastal defense. Seacoast guns were generally the largest artillery pieces and were specifically designed to project the largest shells at long range to protect coastal areas against attacking warships. During the Civil War, however, circumstances forced both sides to employ a wide variety of lighter field and siege guns in a coastal defense role. Thus, at the very beginning of the war, the Confederates secured at the Norfolk (Gosport) Navy Yard some 1,195 cannon, including 52 IX-inch Dahlgren naval guns; many of these were soon on their way to seacoast fortifications throughout the South.

Artillery specifically intended for seacoast defense included 42-pounder guns of Model 1839, 8- and 10-inch seacoast howitzers and columbiads also of Model 1839, and the later 8-, 10-, 12-, and 15-inch Rodmans. All the aforementioned were smoothbore guns, but banded and rifled 42-pounders as well as Parrott rifled guns served in a seacoast defense role, and Union forces utilized 10-inch Parrotts against Confederate-held Fort Sumter and Charleston.

Seacoast Columbiad guns of the Confederate water battery at Warrington, Florida, February 1861. (National Archives)

Seacoast guns were usually placed on barbette platforms or swiveling casemate carriages, most of which were of iron. Although the heavy seacoast guns required block and tackle and thus took considerable time to load, this disadvantage was more than offset by their great range and hitting power.

SPENCER C. TUCKER

See also

Artillery, Land, CSA; Artillery, Land, U.S.; Dahlgren Guns; Parrott Gun; Rodman Guns

Further Reading

Lewis, Emanuel Raymond. *Seacoast Fortifications of the United States: An Introductory History.* Washington, DC: Smithsonian Institution Press, 1970.

Olmstead, Edwin, Wayne E. Stark, and Spencer C. Tucker. *The Big Guns: Civil War Siege, Seacoast, and Naval Cannon.* Alexandria Bay, NY: Museum Restoration Service, 1997.

Ripley, Warren. *Artillery and Ammunition of the American Civil War.* New York: Van Nostrand Reinhold, 1970.

Tucker, Spencer C. *Arming the Fleet: U.S. Navy Ordnance in the Muzzle-Loading Era.* Annapolis, MD: Naval Institute Press, 1990.

Sears, Claudius Wistar
Birth Date: November 8, 1817
Death Date: February 15, 1891

Confederate officer. Claudius Wistar Sears was born on November 8, 1817, in Peru, Massachusetts, and graduated from the U.S. Military Academy, West Point, in 1841. After only a year's service, he resigned from the army and became a teacher at an academy in Holly Springs, Mississippi. He also taught engineering and mathematics in New Orleans at the precursor institution to Tulane University before returning to Holly Springs.

Sympathetic to the Confederate cause, Sears enlisted in the Confederate Army with the beginning of the Civil War and soon became a captain in the 17th Mississippi Infantry Regiment. The regiment saw much action in Virginia through 1861 and 1862 before Sears returned to Mississippi. He was advanced to colonel on December 11, 1862, and assumed command of the 46th Mississippi Infantry.

Sears led his regiment ably at the Battle of Chickasaw Bluffs (December 26–29, 1862) and was on hand for much of the Second Vicksburg Campaign (April 1–July 4, 1863), during which he led a garrison detachment along the Yazoo River and performed well at the Battles of Port Gibson (May 1, 1863) and Champion Hill (May 16, 1863). Sears was taken prisoner on July 4, 1863, with the surrender of Vicksburg and was not exchanged until October.

Advanced to brigadier general to date from March 1, 1864, Sears saw action in northern Georgia with the Army of Tennessee. During the Atlanta Campaign (May 5–September 2, 1864), he was often absent due to illness and missed most of the heavy fighting. He returned to action in the Battle of Allatoona (October 5, 1864), where he was lauded for his performance.

In the autumn of 1864, Sears saw action in Tennessee, earning kudos during the Battle of Franklin (November 30, 1864), where his brigade helped to buckle the main Union line for a time. During the Battle of Nashville (December 15–16, 1864), Sears was severely wounded, losing a leg, and was taken prisoner. He was not released until June 23, 1865.

Sears eventually became chairman of the Mathematics Department at the University of Mississippi. He died on February 15, 1891, in Oxford, Mississippi.

PAUL G. PIERPAOLI JR.

See also

Allatoona, Battle of; Atlanta Campaign; Champion Hill, Battle of; Chickasaw Bluffs, Battle of; Franklin, Battle of; Nashville, Battle of; Port Gibson, Battle of; Vicksburg Campaign, Second

Further Reading

Eicher, John H., and David J. Eicher. *Civil War High Commands*. Stanford, CA: Stanford University Press, 2001.

Warner, Ezra J. *Generals in Gray: Lives of the Confederate Commanders*. Baton Rouge: Louisiana State University Press, 2006.

Secession

The withdrawal from the Union of 11 southern states. Seven states of the lower South seceded during the presidency of James Buchanan. These were South Carolina (December 20, 1860), Mississippi (January 9, 1861), Florida (January 10, 1861), Alabama (January 11, 1861), Georgia (January 19, 1861), Louisiana (January 26, 1861), and Texas (February 1, 1861).

On February 8, 1861, delegates from these states adopted the Confederate Constitution at Montgomery, Alabama, and elected Jefferson Davis president of the Confederate States of America the next day. The Virginia Secession Convention convened on February 13. Although initially rejecting secession, in the wake of the Confederate attack on Fort Sumter the convention finally approved it on April 17, two days after President Abraham Lincoln's call for 75,000 volunteers (of which Virginia would have had to supply 2,340) to suppress the insurrection.

Two states followed suit with near-unanimous convention votes in favor of secession: Arkansas (May 6, 1861) and North Carolina (May 20, 1861). A contentious popular vote for secession in Tennessee (June 8, 1861) brought the secession total to 11. The situations in Kentucky and Missouri remained ambiguous, as each claimed Union and Confederate governments. In Virginia, the Unionist western portion of the state separated from Virginia on August 20, 1862, and entered the Union on June 20, 1863, as the state of West Virginia.

Between June and September 1861, Maryland teetered on the edge of secession. On June 11, 1861, the Maryland Senate passed a resolution affirming both Maryland's allegiance to the Union and a state's right to secede and recommended recognition of the Confederacy and a halt to the war. A further meeting planned for September to consider secession was halted by the arrests of various legislators pursuant to the September 11 orders of Lincoln's secretary of war, Simon Cameron. By November 1861, the pro-Union results of the gubernatorial and legislative elections, enhanced by Union troops preventing secessionists' access to the polls, would ensure that Maryland remained in the Union.

The road to Southern secession was decades in the making, and the legitimacy of the act remains debated. Clearly relevant, against the larger backdrop of the divergence between the sections' two increasingly different civilizations, were two key issues—slavery and the Constitution—over which Unionists and secessionists came to differ. To hold that the South seceded only to preserve slavery is overly simplistic, just as it is unhistorical to argue that either side actually went to war on this issue. The best recent explanations of the sectional tension relating to slavery refer to it as a conflict of legal views over property rights (with the slaveholders demanding and the North increasingly rejecting the recognition of property in slaves, just as both recognized property in inanimate objects). Other historians term the issue "the problem of constitutional evil." The moral standards of one section evolved (although the extent and pervasiveness of this evolution should not be overestimated) beyond the compromise enshrined as positive law in the U.S. Constitution, which had implicitly recognized the existence of slavery and, as Chief Justice Roger Taney opined in the *Dred Scott* decision (1857), declined to delegate explicitly to the federal government the power to eliminate it.

State Secession by Date

State	Secession Date	Admitted to the Confederacy	Readmitted to the United States
South Carolina	December 20, 1860	February 8, 1861	July 9, 1868
Mississippi	January 9, 1861	February 8, 1861	February 23, 1870
Florida	January 10, 1861	February 8, 1861	June 25, 1868
Alabama	January 11, 1861	February 8, 1861	July 13, 1868
Georgia	January 19, 1861	February 8, 1861	July 21, 1868
Louisiana	January 26, 1861	February 8, 1861	July 9, 1868
Texas	February 1, 1861	March 2, 1861	March 30, 1870
Virginia	April 17, 1861	May 7, 1861	January 26, 1870
Arkansas	May 6, 1861	May 18, 1861	June 22, 1868
North Carolina	May 20, 1861	May 21, 1861	July 4, 1868
Tennessee	June 8, 1861	July 2, 1861	July 24, 1866
Missouri (exiled government)	October 31, 1861	November 28, 1861	Missouri remained seated in U.S. Congress
Kentucky (Russellville Convention)	November 20, 1861	December 10, 1861	Kentucky remained seated in U.S. Congress

From the seceding states' point of view, the concern was whether the North could be expected to commit indefinitely to standing by the terms of the federal compact as they envisioned them. If not, the drastic and ultimate remedy rested in an exercise of the sovereignty that they believed their states had reserved, explicitly or otherwise, while ratifying the U.S. Constitution, thus the second interpretive disconnect between the sections. Once the 1860 presidential election put into power a candidate who received all of the required electoral votes exclusively from Northern states (coupled with their fears of growing sectional disparity in population, territory, and economic power), Southern politicians came to doubt their ability to defend their sectional interests and maintain the workings of the federal compact according to their understanding of its intent. Decades of wrangling over a protective tariff for Northern manufactures, which the South saw as appropriating its wealth for support of industry in the North, created additional skepticism as to whether any protection of Southern interests was likely from a Republican administration.

The immediate effect of secession remained ambiguous during the secession winter of 1860. But once the fateful decisions were made in Charleston Harbor, a "tremendous clash," as historian Carl Degler has written, between "two national spirits" had begun. With the war under way, the proximate causes of secession faded. Instead, it became a struggle on the one hand for independence such as that of the colonies in 1776 and a struggle to preserve the "potential grandeur of the Giant of the Western World" on the other.

The result settled by force of arms the questions of secession and federal supremacy, creating in effect a new nation.

JOHN SHARPE

See also

Cameron, Simon; *Dred Scott* Case; Republican Party; Slavery; Taney, Roger Brooke

Further Reading

Adams, Charles. *When in the Course of Human Events: Arguing the Case for Southern Secession.* Lanham, MD: Rowman and Littlefield, 2000.

Graber, Mark A. *Dred Scott and the Problem of Constitutional Evil.* New York: Cambridge University Press, 2006.

Huston, James L. "Property Rights in Slavery and the Coming of the Civil War." *Journal of Southern History* 65(2) (May 1999): 249–286.

Secessionville, Battle of
Event Date: June 16, 1862

Engagement during the long Union effort against Charleston. Also known as the First Battle of James Island, the Battle of Secessionville occurred just south of Charleston, South Carolina. James Island, a swampy neck of land along the Ashley River south of Charleston, offered the most accessible Union land route to the city.

Confederate guns in a fort at Secessionville and a floating battery under Brigadier General Nathan "Shanks" Evans, commanding the 2nd Military District of South Carolina, had been shelling the camp of Union brigadier general Horatio G. Wright at Grimball's Plantation to the southwest. Early in June 1862 the commander of the Union Department of the South, Major General David Hunter, headquartered at Hilton Head Island, authorized Brigadier General Henry W. Benham, an engineer by training, to erect a battery to silence the Confederate guns. Although this new Union artillery position drove off the floating battery, it was unable to silence the guns in the Confederate fort. On June 11 before returning to Hilton Head Island, Hunter gave Benham temporary command in his own absence of the divisions under Wright and Brigadier General Isaac I. Stevens, whose men were camped to the south of Wright. Hunter ordered Benham not to precipitate a major battle.

Following a daylong bombardment from Tower Battery on June 14, however, Benham believed that he could eliminate it with the two divisions at his disposal and on June 15 ordered an attack for the next morning. The 6,600 Union troops (3,500 under Stevens and 3,100 under Wright) left their camps at 2:00 a.m. on June 16. The movement appears to have been designed to bring on a general engagement, although Benham later strongly denied that this had been his intent.

Colonel Thomas G. Lamar had actual command of the Confederate defenses at Secessionville, the strongest of which was Tower Battery, which was shaped like an "M" and stretched across the narrow neck of the peninsula, flanked by tidal marshes. Tower Battery guarded the only approach to Secessionville. Convinced by Union activity that an attack was in the offing, Lamar did what he could to strengthen the defenses, ordering his 500 defenders to dig entrenchments. Then at 2:00 a.m. on June 16, just as the Union troops were forming up in their camps, Lamar informed Evans at his Adams Run headquarters that he believed a Union attack would occur that same morning. Evans immediately assembled reinforcements to march to Lamar's assistance.

Between 3:00 and 3:30 a.m., Stevens's men captured Lamar's pickets and then, as quietly as possible, formed up for an assault. Wright's men, with Benham, were to follow. At 4:00 a.m. the Union attack began, but it was quickly halted by Confederate artillery firing first grapeshot and then canister shot. At 4:15 Evans arrived with reinforcements, bringing the defenders' strength up to 2,000 men.

Benham attempted two more assaults, both of which reached the fort's parapets but were turned back. Sometime after 9:30 that morning, Benham ordered his men to withdraw. The Battle of Secessionville claimed Confederate casualties of 52 dead, 144 wounded, and 8 missing; Union losses were 107 killed, 487 wounded, and 89 taken prisoner.

Evans renamed the Secessionville installation Fort Lamar in honor of its commander. Benham was charged with disobedience of orders. Stevens and Wright both subsequently claimed that in a council of war held the night before the attack, they had warned Benham that he was deliberately bringing on a battle in disobedience of orders. Benham sought a hearing to clear his name but did not receive one. In August, President Abraham Lincoln withdrew Benham's commission as a brigadier general, although it was later reinstated.

MICHAEL W. J. McKEOWN AND SPENCER C. TUCKER

See also

Benham, Henry Washington; Charleston, South Carolina; Hunter, David; Stevens, Isaac Ingalls; Wright, Horatio Gouverneur

Further Reading

Brennan, Patrick. *Secessionville: Assault on Charleston.* Campbell, CA: Savas, 1996.

Burton, E. Milby. *Siege of Charleston, 1861–1865.* Columbia: University of South Carolina Press, 1982.

Secret Service, CSA

Covert Confederate espionage unit. The Secret Service of the Confederate States of America served in a variety of roles, from espionage to diplomacy. Part of the Confederacy's Signal Corps, the Secret Service Bureau was a covert organization that carried out and conducted espionage and counterespionage activities principally in the North but also in occupied areas of the Confederacy. The bureau was commanded by Confederate Army major William Norris, formerly a lawyer from Baltimore who operated the service out of Richmond. Much of the bureau's activities were related to the relaying of messages to and from Confederate officials in Richmond to contacts in both Canada and Europe.

The Confederates employed an elaborate and complex method of moving messages that involved the use of postal inspectors loyal to the Confederacy through a chain of safe houses and contacts known as the Secret Line or "our government route." One of the most important tasks of the Confederate Secret Service was the collection of open-source materials such as newspapers in order to gain intelligence about Union troop movements. Much useful information was obtained through unwitting journalists who detailed troop movements in their reports from the field. Another mission of the bureau was to ensure delivery of these Northern papers to commanders in the South.

Besides utilizing journalists and Southern sympathizers who resided along the Secret Line, the Confederates also employed women who served as spies and gathered useful intelligence. One such woman, Rose Greenhow, informed the Confederates of Union troop movements just prior to the First Battle of Bull Run (July 21, 1861), which ended in a Southern victory. Belle Boyd, another notorious woman spy, supplied Major General Thomas J. "Stonewall" Jackson with regular intelligence reports. Other aspects of the Confederate Secret Service that are not well known included its involvement in the procurement of ships in Europe and in blockade-running. Numerous Southern agents were stationed at Nassau in the Bahamas, where they directed the outfitting of Southern blockade-runners.

The most audacious action conducted by the Confederate Secret Service was aimed against St. Albans, Vermont, on October 19, 1864. The intent of the raid was to disrupt the focus of Union military efforts in the South by creating the illusion that Confederate forces had far-reaching capabilities to inflict damage well behind Union lines. The force involved consisted of 21 young Confederate cavalrymen led by Lieutenant Bennett H. Young, who had been imprisoned at Camp Douglas in Illinois but escaped to Canada and enrolled as a divinity student in Toronto. Young's plan included attacks on three of the four banks located in St. Albans as well as against railhead and repair yards. In the raid, the Confederates secured $200,000 but did little damage to the town. One townsperson was killed, and another was wounded.

Eric V. Reynolds

See also

Blockade of the Confederacy, Union; Blockade-Runners; Boyd, Maria Isabelle; Bull Run, First Battle of; Espionage in the Civil War; Greenhow, Rose O'Neal; Nassau, Bahamas; Secret Service, U.S.; St. Albans, Vermont, Confederate Raid on

Further Reading

Allen, Thomas. *Intelligence in the Civil War.* Washington, DC: Central Intelligence Agency Office of Public Affairs, 1982.
Bulloch, James Dunwoody. *The Secret Service of the Confederate States in Europe,* Vol. 1. London: Richard Bentley and Sons, 1893.

Secret Service, U.S.

Union intelligence-gathering agency. During the Civil War, there was no centralized agency or department for national intelligence in the United States; rather, individual detectives or ad hoc intelligence-gathering agencies worked directly for the president or military field officers, such as Major Generals George B. McClellan and George G. Meade. Secret service work in fact encompassed a wide variety of personnel, civilian as well as military, including couriers, guides, overseas agents, cavalry patrols, army scouts, detectives, spies, Signal Corps employees, and even telegraphers.

Allan Pinkerton, head of a detective agency, provided the first significant organized secret service work beginning in July 1861. He did not work for the U.S. Army; instead, he worked directly for Army of the Potomac commander Major General McClellan, providing him with daily intelligence briefings and conducting counterintelligence work. Pinkerton's most famous work in this regard was the capture of Confederate spy Rose O'Neal Greenhow in August 1861. Pinkerton also embedded agents in the Confederate capital of Richmond, where they worked with pro-Union sympathizers.

Pinkerton remained with McClellan for some 18 months, until McClellan was relieved of command late in 1862. With his methods and assessments often questionable, Pinkerton frequently provided poor information and routinely overestimated Confederate troop strengths.

Another notable person in the history of the Secret Service was Lafayette C. Baker, who organized counterintelligence as well as security for Brevet Lieutenant General Winfield Scott, the general in chief of the U.S. Army at the commencement of the war. Because of the decentralized nature of Northern intelligence and investigative activities, both Pinkerton and Baker on occasion would shadow each other's men, creating unnecessary redundancy. In addition to espionage duties, Baker and his force of about 30 men worked on tracking down deserters, subversives, and Southerners who were accused of having committed treasonous acts against the Union. Baker's greatest recognition came with the July 1862 arrest of Maria "Belle" Boyd, who had served as a spy for Major General Thomas "Stonewall" Jackson.

After Pinkerton's exit in 1862, the U.S. Army was without an organized intelligence apparatus until the late winter of 1863, when Major General Joseph Hooker, who replaced McClellan as commander of the Army of the Potomac, created the Bureau of Military Information. It was run by Colonel George H. Sharpe, who shaped it into a major intelligence service operating chiefly in Virginia. The bureau was particularly helpful in the lead-up to the Battle of Gettysburg (July 1–3, 1863) and during the long Petersburg Campaign (June 15, 1864–April 3, 1865).

In the western theater, Major General Grenville M. Dodge cobbled together an intelligence operation in late 1862 that operated in northern Mississippi. It played an important role during the Second Vicksburg Campaign (April 1–July

4, 1863). Eventually consisting of some 120 personnel, this network also operated in eastern Tennessee and northern Georgia beginning in the midsummer of 1863.

The U.S. government also maintained agents and operatives in Europe. There the chief goal was to stymie Confederate attempts to attain official recognition from foreign governments and to prevent the Confederacy from receiving monetary and material support for its war effort. Henry S. Sanford, U.S. ambassador to Belgium, was eventually tasked with organizing these efforts in various European capitals.

President Abraham Lincoln established the Secret Service on April 14, 1865, just prior to his assassination, in an effort to thwart the growing problem of counterfeiting that was taking a heavy toll on the nation's economy. It was commissioned on July 5 as the Secret Service Division of the Department of the Treasury. The Secret Service's first chief was William Wood, who doggedly pursued and shut down more than 200 counterfeiting operations. Ironically, on the evening of April 14, 1865, John Wilkes Booth assassinated President Lincoln at Ford's Theatre in Washington, D.C. While presidential protection was not originally one of the mandates of the Secret Service, this would later define its most public mission.

ERIC V. REYNOLDS AND PAUL G. PIERPAOLI JR.

See also

Baker, Lafayette Curry; Boyd, Maria Isabelle; Dodge, Grenville Mellen; Espionage in the Civil War; Gettysburg, Battle of; Greenhow, Rose O'Neal; Hooker, Joseph; McClellan, George Brinton; Meade, George Gordon; Petersburg Campaign; Pinkerton, Allan; Secret Service, CSA; Vicksburg Campaign, Second

Further Reading

Allen, Thomas. *Intelligence in the Civil War.* Washington, DC: Central Intelligence Agency Office of Public Affairs, 1998.

Fishel, Edwin C. *The Secret War for the Union: The Untold Story of Military Intelligence in the Civil War.* New York: Houghton Mifflin, 1996.

Seddon, James Alexander
Birth Date: July 13, 1815
Death Date: August 19, 1880

Confederate secretary of war. Born near Fredericksburg, Virginia, on July 13, 1815, James Alexander Seddon graduated from the University of Virginia law school and established a successful practice in Richmond. He served two separate terms in the U.S. Congress (1845–1847 and 1849–1851), but

poor health prompted him to retire to his estate on the James River. After Virginia's secession, Seddon became a member of Virginia's provisional Confederate congressional delegation in Richmond.

In November 1862, Confederate president Jefferson Davis decided to sack his current secretary of war, George W. Randolph, because of a disagreement between them regarding the movement of troops across the Mississippi River and because Randolph tended to act independently of Davis. To fill Randolph's place, the president selected Seddon. Throughout his tenure in office—the longest of any secretary of war in the short life of the Confederacy—Seddon proved that his greatest asset was his ability to get along with Davis. Seddon was never, as some of his detractors would claim, a mere clerk running the War Department, but while exercising some independent influence, he carefully avoided any action that would seem to challenge Davis's preeminence as the mastermind of Confederate strategy.

James Alexander Seddon became Confederate secretary of war in November 1862, and held the position until February 1865. Certainly the most effective individual to hold that post, he nonetheless found it difficult to work with President Jefferson Davis who wanted to make all the important military decisions himself. (National Archives)

Seddon was initially a strong supporter of General Joseph E. Johnston and of the idea of reinforcing the Confederacy's defenses west of the Appalachians, particularly in the Mississippi Valley, at the expense of the Virginia theater of operations. In discussions with Davis and General Robert E. Lee in the spring of 1863, Seddon advocated that the divisions of Major General George E. Pickett and Major General John Bell Hood, of Lieutenant General James Longstreet's I Corps of the Army of Northern Virginia, should be transferred to Mississippi to support Lieutenant General John C. Pemberton in his efforts to defend Vicksburg.

Davis and Lee overruled Seddon, however, and the divisions remained in Lee's army to march north with him and play important roles in the Battle of Gettysburg (July 1–3, 1863). Several weeks later, with Vicksburg besieged and Johnston in central Mississippi in command of a heavily reinforced army, Davis and Seddon both strove to persuade the reluctant general to take the offensive in an attempt to raise the siege. Seddon wrote to Johnston and reminded him that as theater commander, he had authority to draw troops from General Braxton Bragg's army in Tennessee, but Johnston refused to use his discretion. When Johnston continued to balk, Seddon wrote him a personal letter urging him to attack at all costs and offering to take the responsibility himself if the result should be defeat, but nothing Seddon could say was sufficient to persuade the general to fight. Vicksburg fell on July 4, 1863, with Johnston having made no move toward the Union besiegers.

Despite Johnston's failure, Seddon continued to support the general. After Bragg's defeat at Chattanooga that autumn and subsequent removal from command by Davis, Seddon urged the president to assign Johnston to command of the Army of Tennessee, and Davis, seeing no other viable options, did so.

That summer, however, with Johnston retreating rapidly toward Atlanta, the city he was charged with protecting, Seddon's patience with the habitually retreating general finally ran out, even before the president was ready to take action. Seddon joined a number of other Confederate officials in urging Davis to sack Johnston. Finally, with the armies on the outskirts of Atlanta, Davis did so, but it was too late to save Atlanta.

Seddon was the most successful of the Confederacy's secretaries of war. However, by early 1865, the general dissatisfaction and desperation of Confederate politicians had come to encompass Seddon as well as Davis. The growing anti-Davis faction in the Confederate Congress now strove to push Davis and those around him away from the conduct of the war. In January, the Virginia legislature called for Seddon's removal as secretary of war. Humiliated by this denunciation coming from his home state, Seddon submitted his resignation on February 1.

Upon war's end, Seddon was arrested by federal authorities and briefly imprisoned at Fort Monroe. When he was released, he returned to his estate in Goochland County, Virginia, where he died on August 19, 1880.

STEVEN E. WOODWORTH

See also

Atlanta Campaign; Bragg, Braxton; Chattanooga Campaign; Davis, Jefferson Finis; Gettysburg, Battle of; Hood, John Bell; Johnston, Joseph Eggleston; Longstreet, James; Pemberton, John Clifford; Pickett, George Edward; Randolph, George Wythe; Vicksburg Campaign, Second

Further Reading

Woodworth, Steven E. *Davis and Lee at War.* Lawrence: University Press of Kansas, 1995.
Woodworth, Steven E. *Jefferson Davis and His Generals: The Failure of Confederate Command in the West.* Lawrence: University Press of Kansas, 1990.

Sedgwick, John
Birth Date: September 13, 1813
Death Date: May 9, 1864

Union officer. John Sedgwick was born on September 13, 1813, in Cornwall, Connecticut. After teaching school for two years as a young man, he enrolled at the U.S. Military Academy, West Point, graduating in 1837. As a young lieutenant, he served in several garrison assignments before being ordered to Mexico during the Mexican-American War (1846–1848), where his exemplary service was rewarded by a brevet promotion to major by war's end. He was promoted to captain in 1849. Between 1855 and 1861, he was a major in the 1st Cavalry Regiment and participated in numerous operations against Native Americans.

Promoted to lieutenant colonel and then to colonel in quick succession in early 1861, Sedgwick was appointed brigadier general of volunteers on August 31, 1861. After service in the Washington defenses, he took command of a division in the Army of the Potomac. He was wounded in heavy fighting during the Peninsula Campaign (March–July 1862). His fine performance earned him a promotion to major general of volunteers, to date from July 4, 1862. He next participated in the Battle of Antietam (September 17, 1862), in which he was seriously wounded.

Major General John Sedgwick saw wide service in the Eastern Theater battles of the Civil War and was wounded several times. He was shot and killed by a Confederate sharpshooter on May 9, 1864, during the Battle of Spotsylvania Court House in Virginia. (Library of Congress)

After a lengthy recovery, Sedgwick took command of VI Corps, which he led during the Battle of Chancellorsville (May 1–4, 1863). In that battle, he commanded the Union left in a holding action at Fredericksburg. Although he was slow to move, Sedgwick duly crossed the Rappahannock and engaged Confederate forces under Major General Jubal Early on Marye's Heights. Moving west in an effort to trap the Army of Northern Virginia between his own force and the main body of the Army of the Potomac under Major General Joseph Hooker, Sedgwick was stopped by the Confederate II Corps temporarily under Major General James E. B. Stuart and withdrew to Fredericksburg.

Sedgwick's corps did not arrive until late on the second day of the Battle of Gettysburg (July 1–3, 1863) and thus had little role in the battle. His corps saw heavy action in the Battle of the Wilderness (May 5–7, 1864), when it defended against attacks by Confederate lieutenant general Richard S. Ewell's II Corps.

On May 9, 1864, while disdaining long-range Confederate rifle fire as he supervised artillery placement at the Battle of Spotsylvania Court House (May 8–21), Sedgwick was shot in the head by a Confederate sharpshooter and died instantly.

He was widely regarded as a solid and reliable yet not particularly aggressive commander.

PAUL G. PIERPAOLI JR.

See also

Antietam, Battle of; Chancellorsville, Battle of; Early, Jubal Anderson; Ewell, Richard Stoddart; Gettysburg, Battle of; Hooker, Joseph; Peninsula Campaign; Spotsylvania Court House, Battle of; Stuart, James Ewell Brown; Wilderness, Battle of the

Further Reading

Jurgen, Robert J., and Allan Keller. *Major General John Sedgwick, U.S. Volunteers, 1813–1864.* Hartford: Connecticut Civil War Centennial Committee, 1963.

Winslow, Richard Elliott. *General John Sedgwick: The Story of a Union Corps Commander.* Novato, CA: Presidio, 1982.

Selfridge, Thomas Oliver, Jr.

Birth Date: September 6, 1836
Death Date: February 4, 1924

Union naval officer. Born in Charlestown, Massachusetts, on September 6, 1836, the son of a naval officer, Thomas Oliver Selfridge Jr. was appointed an acting midshipman on October 3, 1851. Upon his graduation at the head of his class of 1854 from the U.S. Naval Academy, Annapolis, he was promoted to midshipman. Selfridge was promoted to passed midshipman on November 22, 1856; to master on January 22, 1858; and to lieutenant on February 15, 1860.

Selfridge distinguished himself as the second lieutenant aboard the sloop *Cumberland* during the engagement with the Confederate ironclad *Virginia* in Hampton Roads on March 8, 1862. He commanded the sloop's forward battery until the ship was rammed and sunk by the *Virginia*. Selfridge was then the flag lieutenant in the North Atlantic Blockading Squadron.

Selfridge was promoted to lieutenant commander on July 16, 1862, and assigned to command the ironclad *Cairo* in the Mississippi Squadron. He gave the mistaken order that led to his ship striking two torpedoes (mines) and sinking in the Yazoo River on December 12, 1862. Selfridge escaped reprimand but was much criticized for his actions. One fellow officer noted that "Selfridge of the *Cairo* found two torpedoes and removed them by placing his vessel over them."

Selfridge next commanded one of the naval siege batteries in the Siege of Vicksburg and after that had charge of the timberclad *Conestoga,* which became the third ship in which he was an officer to be sunk when it collided below Grand Gulf, Mississippi, with the U.S. Navy river gunboat *General*

Price on March 8, 1864. He then commanded the large tin-clad *Manitou*.

Selfridge commanded the ironclad *Osage* during the Red River Campaign (March 10–May 22, 1864). On March 16, he led 150 men ashore to take possession of Alexandria, and on April 12 at Blair's Landing, his ship's guns inflicted significant casualties on Confederate troops ashore. Selfridge then commanded the ram *Vindicator* and the 5th Division of the Mississippi Squadron. Transferred to the North Atlantic Blockading Squadron, he commanded the screw gunboat *Huron* in the two attacks on Fort Fisher in December 1864 and January 1865, and he had charge of the naval landing party that contributed materially to the success of the second attack.

Promoted to commander on December 31, 1869, Selfridge commanded an expedition to explore the possibility of constructing an international canal across the Isthmus of Darien, surveying several possible routes (1870–1873). He commanded the gunboat *Enterprise* on the North Atlantic Station (1877–1880), during which time he also surveyed the Amazon River. He was advanced to captain on February 24, 1881, and headed the Torpedo Station at Newport, Rhode Island, until 1885. He then commanded the steam sloop *Omaha* in the Asiatic Squadron and was tried and acquitted by court-martial on a charge of criminal neglect that stemmed from an incident during target practice off a Japanese island when the bursting of an unexploded shell on the island caused the deaths of four Japanese. Selfridge was promoted to commodore on April 11, 1894, and to rear admiral on February 28, 1896. He retired from the navy on February 6, 1898, and died in Washington, D.C., on February 4, 1924.

SPENCER C. TUCKER

See also

Cairo, USS; Fort Fisher Campaign; Hampton Roads, Battles of; Red River Campaign; Timberclads; Tinclads

Further Reading

Tucker, Spencer C. *Blue and Gray Navies: The Civil War Afloat.* Annapolis, MD: Naval Institute Press, 2006.

U.S. Navy Department. *Official Records of the Union and Confederate Navies in the War of the Rebellion,* Series 1, Vol. 23. Washington, DC: U.S. Government Printing Office, 1910.

Seligman, Joseph
Birth Date: November 22, 1819
Death Date: April 25, 1880

Businessman and financier. Joseph Seligman was born on November 22, 1819, in Baiersdorf, Bavaria. He immigrated to the United States in 1837. Seligman initially settled in Pennsylvania, where he worked as a clerk and cashier. Two years later he started his own business with his two brothers—James and William—in Lancaster. The family business sold dry goods door to door to rural farmers. The enterprise was an immediate success, and in 1841 Seligman relocated the business to Selma, Alabama. His increasing profits allowed him to bring to America other brothers, who helped him grow the company. By the late 1840s, Seligman operated four dry goods stores in the Selma area.

Seligman went to New York City in 1848 and, along with his brothers James and William, established a clothing import enterprise, which soon became one of the city's largest businesses of its kind. Seligman soon opened branch offices in St. Louis and San Francisco. In the early months of the Civil War, he entered into a lucrative contract with the U.S. War Department to supply it with military uniforms.

In 1862 Seligman established J. and W. Seligman & Company, a banking and financial house. The bank soon had offices in Paris, London, and San Francisco. Using his financial connections, between 1862 and 1863 Seligman sold some $200 million of U.S. Treasury bonds to the various German states through a branch office he had established in Frankfurt, an immeasurable help to the Union war effort. Well after the war, in 1877 Seligman played a key role in refinancing America's war debt with the U.S. Treasury.

Seligman went on to become involved in numerous industries, including railroading, shipbuilding, steelmaking, and mining. He was a strong adherent of municipal reform and took a high-profile role in breaking the graft of the Tweed Ring in New York during the 1870s. In 1875 he was the city's rapid transit commissioner. Seligman died on April 25, 1880, during a visit to New Orleans.

PAUL G. PIERPAOLI JR.

See also

Financing, U.S.

Further Reading

Birmingham, Stephen. *Our Crowd: The Great Jewish Families of New York.* New York: Harper and Row, 1962.

Korn, Bertram. *American Jewry and the Civil War.* Philadelphia: Jewish Publication Society, 2001.

Selma, Alabama

Important manufacturing center located along the Alabama River in central Alabama. Selma was served by two strategic railroads: the Alabama & Mississippi Railroad, which helped ship finished goods to other parts of the South, and the Tennessee & Alabama Railroad, which kept the town's many industrial concerns supplied with coal and iron.

Commercial traffic on the Alabama River also connected Selma with other parts of the country, namely the port of Mobile. In 1860, Selma's population was only 1,809; an influx of workers and their families during the Civil War boosted that figure to at least 12,000 by 1865. Indeed, Selma became one of the Confederacy's most important industrial centers, second perhaps only to Richmond, Virginia.

By 1861, Selma already had a critical mass of small foundries, niter and saltpeter manufacturers, and machine shops. Selma's industrial output grew exponentially after New Orleans fell to Union forces in April 1862. That spring, Confederate officials decided to move the main Confederate arsenal at Mount Vernon, Alabama, to Selma, believing that Selma was safer and more easily defended. By the summer of 1862, the Selma Arsenal and associated naval foundry produced naval and land artillery, ammunition, and caissons. Three small Confederate ironclads were also built in the city. As a result of this wartime production, Selma's economy prospered, and the city remained physically untouched by war until the very end of the conflict.

Beginning in the winter of 1864, Confederate officials became concerned that Union military moves in Mississippi might place Selma in jeopardy. Thus, they began erecting a massive system of redoubts and fortifications, some equipped with heavy guns, along the town's perimeter. This effort, however, proved to be no match for Union forces on April 2, 1865, when they moved against Confederate lieutenant general Nathan Bedford Forrest's 5,000 defenders. Quickly overwhelmed by superior Union numbers, the withdrawing Confederates set fire to at least 35,000 bales of cotton, sparking wider fires that gutted much of the city. The damage was made much worse by Union soldiers' depredations. By April 3, much of Selma lay in ruin.

PAUL G. PIERPAOLI JR.

See also
Arms Manufacturing; Forrest, Nathan Bedford; Iron and Steel Manufacture; Selma, Battle of

Further Reading
Keenan, Jerry. "The Battle of Selma, April 1865." *North & South* 8(3) (May 2005): 60–69.
Stallworth, Clarke. *One Day in Alabama: The Civil War Years*, Vol. 3. Birmingham, AL: Seacoast Publishing, 1997.

Selma, Battle of
Event Date: April 2, 1865

One of the last significant engagements of the war. The capture of Selma, Alabama, was the chief objective of Union brevet major general James H. Wilson's cavalry raid into Alabama and Georgia in the spring of 1865. After three months of preparation and training, Wilson set out on March 22, 1865, from Gravelly Springs, Alabama, some 250 miles from Selma, in the largest cavalry raid of the war. Wilson had command of three divisions, totaling some 13,500 men. Opposing him was a much smaller Confederate cavalry force of perhaps 5,000 men led by Lieutenant General Nathan Bedford Forrest.

Although Wilson hoped to destroy Southern military facilities throughout Alabama and into Georgia, the raid's principal objective was the city of Selma. This important Confederate military manufacturing center was home to an arsenal, a facility producing heavy guns for the navy, arms factories, a powder mill, railroad shops, and military warehouses. Forrest's men were widely scattered, and Wilson allowed Forrest no time to concentrate. Wilson also divided his forces, moving them along parallel axes and confusing Forrest as to his objective.

On March 31, Wilson defeated Forrest at Montevallo, 40 miles from Selma. Wilson then directed his men toward Selma. On April 1 at Ebenezer Church, some 19 miles from Selma, Forrest attempted to halt the Union advance with 2,000 men and six guns, but the Union cavalrymen were again victorious and drove the Confederates back into the Selma defenses. The Federals also burned a strategic bridge at Centreville, preventing Forrest from being reinforced.

The Battle of Selma occurred on April 2. Forrest had deployed his men in a semicircular formation in defensive works around the city, anchored at both ends by the Alabama River. The works had been built two years earlier. Neglected thereafter, they were still formidable. The city had developed fortifications and some heavy guns. The attackers outnumbered the defenders some 9,000 men to only 4,000, with half of the Confederates largely untrained militia. The Union troopers were armed with seven-shot lever-action Spencer repeating rifles, while the Confederates for the most part had single-shot rifled muskets.

Wilson's force came up at 2:00 p.m. on April 2. By 4:00, with dispositions complete, Union brigadier general Eli Long led a dismounted assault across 600 yards of open ground against the Confederate right. Although Long's men suffered 40 killed and 260 wounded (he himself sustained a severe head wound), in some 15 minutes his 1,500 men had penetrated the Confederate defensive line. At the same time, Brigadier General Emory Upton led a picked force of 300 men in a successful Union assault to turn the Confederate left, while Wilson personally led a mounted charge by the 4th U.S. Cavalry Regiment down the Selma Road. These simultaneous Union attacks were too much for the defenders, and many of the militiamen simply broke and ran. By midevening, Wilson's men controlled Selma.

The Union soldiers took some 2,700 Confederates prisoner while suffering 318 casualties of their own. The Federals also captured 32 guns and considerable quantities of military supplies. Forrest was among the Confederate wounded, but he escaped. That night the remaining Confederates set fire to the cotton stores at Selma to keep them from falling into Union hands, but the fires spread to other parts of the city.

Wilson's men spent the next week destroying the Confederate facilities at Selma before moving on to Montgomery on April 9, taking it on April 12. The raid continued until the capture of Macon, Georgia, on April 20. The Union success at Selma, coming a week before Confederate general Robert E. Lee's surrender at Appomattox Court House, Virginia, on April 9, symbolized the collapse of the Confederate Deep South.

RICHARD A. SAUERS AND SPENCER C. TUCKER

See also
Forrest, Nathan Bedford; Upton, Emory; Wilson, James Harrison; Wilson's Raid into Alabama and Georgia

Further Reading
Jones, James Pickett. *Yankee Blitzkrieg: Wilson's Raid through Alabama and Georgia.* Athens: University of Georgia Press, 1976.

Keenan, Jerry. "The Battle of Selma, April 1865." *North & South* 8(3) (May 2005): 60–69.

Keenan, Jerry. *Wilson's Cavalry Corps: Union Campaigns in the Western Theatre, October 1864 through Spring 1865.* Jefferson, NC: McFarland, 1998.

Longacre, Edward G. *Grant's Cavalryman: The Life and Wars of General James H. Wilson.* Mechanicsburg, PA: Stackpole, 2000.

Selma Ordnance and Naval Foundry

Major Confederate foundry, shipyard, arms factory, and gunpowder works in Alabama. Established in 1861, the Selma Ordnance and Naval Foundry was second only to the Tredegar Iron Works in Richmond, Virginia, in terms of output of large seacoast defense artillery and naval artillery. Overall, the entire complex represented the Confederacy's greatest concentration of war production. Located in central Alabama but far inland from the Gulf of Mexico, Selma was the ideal location for such a manufacturing center. The Alabama River afforded direct access to Mobile Bay and was navigable to large ships. The city's two railroads meant that the Selma ordnance works was well supplied by coal and iron mines in the northern part of Alabama, while finished goods could be shipped easily to other areas of the Confederacy.

Businessman Colin J. McRae established the facility in 1861, when he was awarded a Confederate government contract to build a foundry and produce cannon in Selma. The Selma facility grew in importance as the Civil War went on, especially after the late spring of 1862, when Confederate officials decided to relocate much of the arms production of the Mount Vernon Arsenal (also located in Alabama) to Selma, which was deemed a safer site. This move had been prompted by the fall of New Orleans in April 1862. In 1863 McRae went abroad to serve as a Confederate agent in Europe and sold the foundry to the Confederate government for $450,000. At that point, Commander Catesby ap Roger Jones was placed in charge of the foundry works, which soon began producing coastal defense guns and large naval artillery. The Selma facility produced a number of large-caliber artillery pieces and was the only foundry besides the Tredegar Iron Works that produced the Brooke rifle. The most commonly produced Brooke gun at Selma was the 6.4-inch.

The Selma Ordnance and Naval Foundry continued to grow, and by 1864 it covered 50 acres and employed as many as 10,000 workers, many of whom were slaves, women, and children. Approximately 3,000 people labored in the arsenal, while the remainder worked in the foundry. The facility also included an active shipyard that produced several ironclads, including CSS *Huntsville, Tennessee,* and *Tuscaloosa.* In addition to guns and ships, the Selma works produced gun carriages, horseshoes, buttons, and other military-related equipment. It is estimated that the facility made about 50 percent of all the Confederate cannon produced between 1861 and 1865 and as much as 75 percent of the Confederacy's ammunition.

It would be difficult to overemphasize the importance of the Selma Ordnance and Naval Foundry, for it made singular contributions to the Confederate war effort. By late 1864, however, its output began to suffer because of raw material shortages and other war-related disruptions. The facility remained in Confederate hands until April 2, 1865, when Union troops under Brevet Major General James H. Wilson invaded and seized Selma. His troops proceeded to wreck the city's industry, including the arsenal and foundry facilities.

PAUL G. PIERPAOLI JR.

See also
Alabama; Iron and Steel Manufacture; Ironclads, Confederate; Jones, Catesby ap Roger; Selma, Alabama; Selma, Battle of; Wilson, James Harrison

Further Reading

Jones, James Pickett. *Yankee Blitzkrieg: Wilson's Raid through Alabama and Georgia.* Athens: University of Georgia Press, 1976.

Stephen, Walter W. "The Brooke Guns from Selma." *Alabama Historical Quarterly* 20 (Fall 1958): 462–475.

Stockham, Richard J. "Alabama Iron for the Confederacy: The Selma Works." *Alabama Review* 21 (July 1968): 163–172.

Seminoles

Native American people whose traditional territory was in Florida. Seminole means "pioneer" or "runaway," possibly from the Spanish *cimarrón* ("wild"). The Seminoles, known as such by 1775, formed in the 18th century from members of other Native American groups, mainly the Creeks. The Creeks, Choctaws, Chickasaws, Cherokees, and Seminoles were known by non–Native Americans in the 19th century as the Five Civilized Tribes.

Non-Muskogee Oconee people from southern Georgia, who moved south during the early 18th century, formed the kernel of the Seminole people. They were joined by Yamasees from South Carolina as well as by some Apalachicolas, Calusas, Hitchitis, Chiahas, and escaped black slaves.

The Seminoles considered themselves Creeks, and they supported the Creeks in war and often attended their councils. The Seminoles experienced considerable population growth after the 1814 Creek War, mainly from Muskogeans from the Upper Creek towns. Prior to the Civil War, some Seminoles owned slaves, but the slaves' obligations were minimal, and the Seminoles welcomed escaped slaves into their communities. Beginning in 1817, the Seminoles waged three brutal wars against the U.S. government in a bid to retain control over their lands (1817–1818, 1835–1842, and 1855–1858).

By 1861, the Seminoles were split. Most lived in Indian Territory (Oklahoma), while a much smaller group continued to live in the swamps and forests of Florida. The Confederates actively sought an alliance with the Seminoles, and on August 1, 1861, Chief John Jumper signed a treaty with the Confederate government, which obliged him to raise five cavalry companies that would then remain in Indian Territory and protect it from Union incursions. Other Seminole chiefs, however, deplored the alliance and counseled loyalty to the Union. Some Seminoles saw combat, most notably during the Battle of Pea Ridge (March 7–8, 1862), while others served in the Indian Cavalry Brigade commanded by Brigadier General Stand Watie.

As the Civil War progressed, more and more Seminoles chose to remain loyal to the United States, and some even enlisted in the Union Army. The Seminoles in Florida, by now few and scattered, did not involve themselves in the war, but Florida governor John Milton made certain they remained neutral. He sent agents to parley with leaders and supplied them with trade goods and even ammunition. In general, however, the Florida Seminoles remained isolated and eschewed contact with whites. Most Seminoles still in Florida relocated to reservations during the 1930s and 1940s.

BARRY M. PRITZKER AND PAUL G. PIERPAOLI JR.

See also

Florida; Indian Territory; Milton, John; Native Americans in the Civil War; Pea Ridge, Battle of; Watie, Stand

Further Reading

Debo, Angie. *A History of the Indians of the United States.* Norman: University of Oklahoma Press, 1970.

Iverson, Peter. *"We Are Still Here": American Indians in the Twentieth Century.* Arlington Heights, IL: Davidson, 1998.

Semmes, Paul Jones
Birth Date: June 4, 1815
Death Date: July 10, 1863

Confederate officer. Paul Jones Semmes was born on June 4, 1815, in Wilkes County, Georgia, the younger brother of noted Confederate naval officer Raphael Semmes. Paul Semmes attended the University of Virginia and later became a prosperous planter and banker in Columbus, Georgia. Active in the state militia, he became colonel of the 2nd Georgia Infantry Regiment in the spring of 1861, although he saw little action until 1862.

Advanced to brigadier general on March 11, 1862, Semmes saw significant combat during the Peninsula Campaign (March–July 1862). Leading a brigade under Major General Lafayette McLaws in the Army of Northern Virginia, Semmes was lauded for his performances at the Battle of Crampton's Gap (September 14, 1862), the Battle of Antietam (September 17, 1862), and the First Battle of Fredericksburg (December 13, 1862). He was conspicuous during the Battle of Chancellorsville (May 1–4, 1863) and the Battle of Gettysburg (July 1–3, 1863). At Gettysburg late on the second day of fighting, Semmes led his brigade into the Wheatfield during an assault against the Union left flank. As he charged forward, he was felled by a severe wound in the thigh. Transported to Martinsburg, West Virginia, he died of his wounds on July 10, 1863.

PAUL G. PIERPAOLI JR.

See also

Antietam, Battle of; Crampton's Gap, Battle of; Fredericksburg, First Battle of; Gettysburg, Battle of; Malvern Hill, Battle of; Peninsula Campaign; Semmes, Raphael

Further Reading

Eicher, John H., and David J. Eicher. *Civil War High Commands.* Stanford, CA: Stanford University Press, 2001.

Warner, Ezra J. *Generals in Gray: Lives of the Confederate Commanders.* Baton Rouge: Louisiana State University Press, 2006.

Semmes, Raphael
Birth Date: September 27, 1809
Death Date: August 30, 1877

Confederate naval officer. Raphael Semmes was born on September 27, 1809, in Charles County, Maryland. On April 1, 1826, Semmes secured an appointment as a midshipman in the U.S. Navy. He made passed midshipman in 1832 and lieutenant in 1837. In long leaves of absence ashore, Semmes took up the study of law and followed that profession when not at sea.

From 1837 until the Mexican-American War (1846–1848), Semmes spent most of his time on survey work along the coast of the Gulf of Mexico. In 1841 the navy ordered him to survey Mississippi Sound, and at that time he established his legal residence in Alabama. During the Mexican-American War, Semmes commanded the brig *Somers.* In December 1846 while off the eastern coast of Mexico, the ship sank in a sudden squall. Half the crew was lost, but a court-martial found Semmes blameless. In March 1847, Semmes took part in the capture of Veracruz. Later he participated in the expedition against Tuxpan and accompanied Major General Winfield Scott's forces to Mexico City as an aide to division commander Major General William J. Worth, who cited Semmes for bravery.

Following the war, Semmes again found himself in a navy with too many officers and spent much of his time on leave at the family home near Mobile, Alabama, where he practiced law for a time. In 1852 he published *Service Afloat and Ashore during the Mexican War.* Ironically, in view of later events, Semmes argued that if Mexico had employed privateers against U.S. shipping, they should have been treated as pirates. On September 14, 1855, he won promotion to

commander and in 1856 was posted to Washington, D.C., as a member of the Lighthouse Board.

Following Alabama's secession and the creation of the Confederate States of America, in February 1861 Semmes resigned his commission and traveled to Montgomery, Alabama, to enter Confederate service. President Jefferson Davis sent him into the North to purchase military and naval supplies and manufacturing equipment. Commissioned a commander in the Confederate Navy, Semmes met in mid-April with Secretary of the Navy Stephen R. Mallory. Both men favored commerce raiding as a means of hurting the North financially, weakening resolve, and forcing naval assets from blockade duties.

Mallory gave Semmes command of the steamer *Habana* at New Orleans, which was converted into the *Sumter,* the first Confederate commerce raider. Between June 1861 and January 1862, Semmes took 18 Union prizes. His ship in poor repair and blockaded by Union warships at Gibraltar, Semmes paid off the crew and abandoned the ship. In August 1862 he was advanced to captain.

Semmes next took command of a new ship contracted for the Confederates at Liverpool, England. He joined the ship at Terceira Island in the Azores. After supervising the mounting of its ordnance, Semmes in late August commissioned the ship the *Alabama.*

For nearly two years, Semmes and the *Alabama* ravaged Union shipping. Through July 1864 it took 64 prizes, and off Galveston, Texas, it sunk a Union warship, the *Hatteras.* Semmes estimated that he had burned $4,613,914 worth of shipping and cargo and bonded other ships and cargoes valued at $562,250. Another estimate places the total at nearly $6 million.

With his ship in need of repairs, Semmes finally put into Cherbourg, but on June 19, 1864, he ordered the *Alabama* out to engage the Union screw steam sloop *Kearsarge.* Perhaps it was a matter of pride, but delay would only bring more Union warships. In the ensuing engagement, the *Kearsarge* sank the *Alabama.* Semmes escaped capture, taken to Southampton on an English yacht.

Semmes finally made his way to Richmond via the West Indies, Cuba, and Mexico. Promoted to rear admiral in February 1865, he took command of the James River Squadron. When Confederate forces abandoned Richmond, Semmes was forced to destroy his ships on the night of April 2, 1865. The men of the squadron formed into a naval brigade under Semmes as a brigadier general. Semmes was the only Confederate officer to hold flag rank in both the navy and the army. After garrisoning Danville, Virginia, Semmes's unit

Captain Raphael Semmes commanded the first Confederate commerce raider, the *Sumter*, but won lasting fame as commander of the CSS *Alabama*. During a two-year span, Semmes wreaked havoc on northern shipping. With these two commerce raiders, Semmes captured 84 Union merchantmen. He also sank a U.S. Navy warship, but in June 1864, he lost a single-ship duel with the Union screw sloop *Kearsarge*. One of two Confederate rear admirals, Semmes was also an army brigadier general at the end of the war—the only Confederate to hold flag rank in both services. (Library of Congress)

joined General Joseph E. Johnston's army in North Carolina, where it surrendered.

Paroled in May 1865, Semmes returned to Mobile, where that December he was arrested and transported to Washington and held for three months. U.S. secretary of the navy Gideon Welles planned to try him before a military commission on charges that he had violated military codes by escaping from the *Alabama* after it had struck its colors. After the U.S. Supreme Court denied jurisdiction of the commissions, Semmes was released.

Semmes was briefly a probate judge of Mobile County, a professor at Louisiana State Seminary (now Louisiana State University) at Baton Rouge, and then editor of the *Memphis Daily Bulletin*. Following a profitable lecture tour, he then resumed the practice of law. In 1869 he published

Memoirs of Service Afloat: During the War between the States. Semmes died at his home in Point Clear, Alabama, on August 30, 1877.

SPENCER C. TUCKER

See also

Alabama, CSS; *Alabama* vs. *Hatteras;* Commerce Raiding, Confederate; Johnston, Joseph Eggleston; *Kearsarge*, USS; *Kearsarge* vs. Alabama; Kell, John McIntosh; Mallory, Stephen Russell; Welles, Gideon

Further Reading

Robinson, Charles M., III. *Shark of the Confederacy: The Story of the CSS Alabama.* Annapolis, MD: Naval Institute Press, 1995.

Semmes, Raphael. *Memoirs of Service Afloat, during the War between the States.* 1869; reprint, Secaucus, NJ: Blue and Gray, 1987.

Sinclair, Arthur. *Two Years on the* Alabama. Boston: Lee and Shepard, 1895.

Taylor, John M. *Confederate Raider: Raphael Semmes of the* Alabama. Washington, DC: Brassey's, 1994.

Tucker, Spencer C. *Raphael Semmes and the* Alabama. Fort Worth, TX: Ryan Place, 1996.

Seven Days' Campaign
Start Date: June 25, 1862
End Date: July 1, 1862

Series of battles fought outside of Richmond, Virginia, that were part of the larger Peninsula Campaign (March–July 1862). The Seven Days' Campaign included six major battles and numerous other smaller engagements that pitted General Robert E. Lee's Army of Northern Virginia against the numerically superior Army of the Potomac, commanded by Union major general George B. McClellan.

The Seven Days' Campaign is frequently neglected in Civil War scholarship, but it was important for many reasons. It reversed the momentum of the war, doomed McClellan's Peninsula Campaign, and saved Richmond from a Union occupation. Indeed, within a few months Lee had taken the war into the North with an invasion of Maryland. The Seven Days' Campaign also showcased the considerable abilities of Lee, who only took charge of the army on June 1, and witnessed the emergence of the Army of Northern Virginia as a formidable offensive fighting force.

In the early spring of 1862, McClellan proposed to take Richmond, not in an overland campaign as President Abraham Lincoln sought but instead by taking advantage of Union control of the sea and moving the Army of the

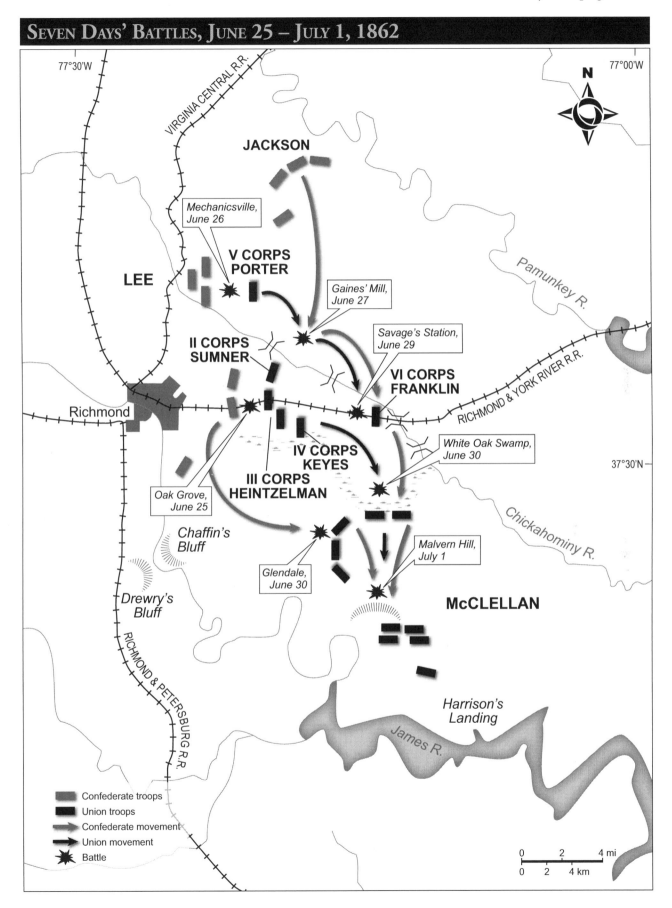

SEVEN DAYS' BATTLES, JUNE 25 – JULY 1, 1862

77°30'W

77°00'W

N

VIRGINIA CENTRAL R.R.

JACKSON

*Mechanicsville,
June 26*

**V CORPS
PORTER**

LEE

Pamunkey R.

*Gaines' Mill,
June 27*

**II CORPS
SUMNER**

*Savage's Station,
June 29*

**VI CORPS
FRANKLIN**

RICHMOND & YORK RIVER R.R.

Richmond

*White Oak Swamp,
June 30*

**IV CORPS
KEYES**

37°30'N

**III CORPS
HEINTZELMAN**

*Oak Grove,
June 25*

Chickahominy R.

*Chaffin's
Bluff*

*Malvern Hill,
July 1*

*Drewry's
Bluff*

*Glendale,
June 30*

McCLELLAN

RICHMOND & PETERSBURG R.R.

*Harrison's
Landing*

James R.

Confederate troops
Union troops
Confederate movement
Union movement
Battle

0   2   4 mi

0   2   4 km

Seven Days' Battles (June 25–July 1, 1862)

	Union	Confederacy
Force strength	104,000	97,000
Killed	1,734	3,286
Wounded	8,082	15,909
Captured or missing	6,053	946

Potomac by water to the Virginia Peninsula and then marching westward on the Confederate capital, at which time a corps under Major General Irwin McDowell, held back at the insistence of President Lincoln to protect Washington, would be released to join McClellan for the final assault. McClellan's campaign suffered from constant delays, and he became known as "The Virginia Creeper" for his glacial advance. He was hoodwinked and delayed in a siege of Yorktown (April 5–May 3), and his advance was blunted at Williamsburg (May 5), but by mid-May the Union army seemed poised to close in on Richmond.

Meanwhile, Lee, then military adviser to Confederate president Jefferson Davis, supervised construction of impressive field fortifications to protect Richmond's eastern flank. McClellan brought up heavy artillery and fortified his positions east of the city, hoping to shell Richmond and its defenders into submission. General Joseph E. Johnston, commanding Confederate forces outside of Richmond, chose to strike at one isolated section of the Union army and destroy it before reinforcements could arrive and McClellan's artillery could be put in place. The resulting engagement at Seven Pines (May 31–June 1, 1862) was a confused, poorly managed battle with no clear victor. Johnston was severely wounded, but the carnage seemed to unnerve McClellan and only reinforced his overly cautious nature. He also dithered, waiting for McDowell's corps to be released, but Lincoln held it back in light of the success of Confederate major general Thomas J. "Stonewall" Jackson's brilliant Shenandoah Valley Campaign. On June 1 Davis named Lee to take over for Johnston, and Lee decided to strike with full force with the aim of not just driving the Union army away but also destroying it. Recalling Jackson from the Shenandoah Valley, Lee prepared to move with 97,000 men against McClellan, with 103,000 men.

On June 25 McClellan advanced with Major General Joseph Hooker's division of III Corps south of the Chickahominy River in an attempt to seize a position from which to bombard Richmond. In the ensuing Battle of Oak Grove, the Confederate division of Major General Benjamin Huger gave ground grudgingly, with McClellan gaining very little in the

day's action. Lee meanwhile massed most of his army north of the river for an attack on Brigadier General Fitz John Porter's isolated V Corps.

Lee's first attack came on June 26 at Mechanicsville, or Beaver Dam Creek. The Union army was divided by the Chickahominy River and thus was vulnerable. This began a solid week of relentless combat, and neither army had experienced anything like it. Leaving only a small force to defend the direct routes to Richmond, Lee struck McClellan's army with overwhelming force. The Confederates took heavy casualties, attacking across swampy ground, but the Union defenders pulled back the next day.

The next day, June 27, an even bigger battle took place at Gaines' Mill, where Union defenders took advantage of high ground overlooking Boatswain's Swamp. Again the Confederates attacked and endured heavy losses. They finally reached the hill's crest, broke through at sunset, and won a pyrrhic victory. That night V Corps withdrew across the Chickahominy to join the rest of McClellan's army.

This sudden and relentless onslaught by Lee further unnerved McClellan, and he shifted from an offensive stance to one that would simply save his army from destruction. McClellan decided to pull his scattered army back and move to the James, where the Union Navy could supply him and provide fire support from its warships.

The next battle was fought on June 29 at Savage's Station, as Lee's army now crossed to the south side of the Chickahominy. It was another day of Confederate attacks and Union retreat that ended inconclusively, but McClellan continued his withdrawal. The best chance for Lee to defeat McClellan's army was at White Oak Swamp and Glendale, on June 30. In savage fighting there, the Confederates came close to breaking the Union lines, but the defenders held on, bringing reinforcements into the fight that lasted into the night. The engagement ended with no clear victor.

The final battle of the campaign occurred on July 1 at Malvern Hill. There Union artillery occupied the high ground, supported by several corps of infantry. Again, poor coordination doomed the Confederates as they mounted several attacks over open ground and took frightening losses, giving McClellan's forces a victory.

Following that engagement, McClellan pulled back to prepared positions at Harrison's Landing on the James River. Total losses for the Seven Days' Campaign were 15,849 for the Union (1,734 killed, 8,082 wounded, and 6,053 missing or captured) and 20,141 for the Confederates (3,286 killed, 15,909 wounded, and 946 missing or captured). During the campaign, Lee firmly established his reputation for aggressiveness and risk taking. He not only relieved Richmond but also gained the initiative in the eastern theater, although at a very high cost. He was also able to learn from his mistakes. He regrouped his divisions, bolstered his staff, and got rid of several ineffective commanders. McClellan, on the other hand, continued to cause controversy, blaming others—including the Lincoln administration—for his woes and repeatedly requesting more troops. McClellan's performance contributed to the decision to replace him.

ROBERT M. DUNKERLY

See also

Davis, Jefferson Finis; Gaines' Mill, Battle of; Jackson, Thomas Jonathan; Jackson's Shenandoah Valley Campaign; Johnston, Joseph Eggleston; Lee, Robert Edward; Lincoln, Abraham; Malvern Hill, Battle of; McDowell, Irvin; McClellan, George Brinton; Mechanicsville, Battle of; Peninsula Campaign; Savage's Station, Battle of; Seven Pines, Battle of; White Oak Swamp, Battle of

Further Reading

Burton, Brian. *Extraordinary Circumstances: The Seven Days' Battles.* Bloomington: Indiana University Press, 2001.

Sears, Stephen. *To the Gates of Richmond.* New York: Ticknor and Fields, 1992.

Wheeler, Richard. *Sword Over Richmond.* New York: Harper and Row, 1986.

Seven Pines, Battle of

Start Date: May 31, 1862
End Date: June 1, 1862

Engagement of the Peninsula Campaign (March–July 1862). The Battle of Seven Pines, also known as the Battle of Fair Oaks and the Battle of Fair Oaks Station, occurred in Henrico County east of the city of Richmond, Virginia. By May 14, U.S. major general George B. McClellan's 103,000-man Army of the Potomac had reached its advanced base on the Pamunkey River only 20 miles from the goal of Richmond. Opposing it was General Joseph E. Johnston's 60,000-man Confederate Army of the Potomac. Despite his overwhelming strength, McClellan now halted to await the arrival from Fredericksburg of Major General Irwin McDowell's 30,000-man corps, which had been recalled by President Abraham Lincoln because of the threat to Washington posed by Major General Thomas J. Jackson's Shenandoah Valley Campaign (May–June 1862).

McClellan's army was then extended in a great sideways V-shape, with the upper leg stretching out to meet McDowell

Battle of Seven Pines (Fair Oaks) (May 31–June 1, 1862)

	Union	Confederacy
Force strength, approximate	103,000	60,000
Killed	790	980
Wounded	3,594	4,749
Captured or missing	647	405

while the lower leg reached just beyond Fair Oaks Station, within five miles of Richmond. Union troops were on both sides of the Chickahominy River: three corps on the north shore to protect the Union supply line and facilitate a linkup with McDowell and two corps south of it. North of the river were V Corps, commanded by Brigadier General Fitz John Porter; VI Corps, under Brigadier General William B. Franklin; and II Corps, commanded by Brigadier General Edwin V. Sumner. South of the river were IV Corps, under Major General Erasmus D. Keyes, and III Corps, under Major General Samuel P. Heintzelman.

General Johnston, having been informed that the Union threat from the north posed by McDowell's corps had evaporated with its recall, planned to send the vast bulk of his army against the Union III and IV Corps on the south bank of the Chickahominy, now isolated from the main part of the Union army by the flooded river. Keyes's IV Corps particularly was in an exposed position close to the Confederate lines. If Johnston's men could defeat IV Corps, they would be in position to pin III Corps against the river and destroy it as well. The plan had an excellence chance of success if executed properly, but Johnston's orders were both confusing and contradictory. Major General James Longstreet, commanding the Confederate right wing, was to carry the brunt of the attack. Conditions for both sides were made worse by a heavy thunderstorm on the night of May 30 that swept away most of the Union bridges and turned the roads into quagmires.

The battle began on May 31. Although two Confederate columns came together on the Williamsburg Road, limiting the attack to a narrow front, Longstreet's men drove back IV Corps, inflicting heavy casualties. Only the timely arrival of Brigadier General John Sedgwick's division of Sumner's II Corps, which managed to get across the raging river, staved off disaster. Fighting ended at dusk. Confederate attacks resumed the next day, June 1, but the Federals had now brought up additional reinforcements, and the attackers made little progress and indeed were forced to withdraw under Union counterattacks. The Confederates then retired

The Seven Pines battlefield near Richmond, Virginia, June 1862. The Battle of Seven Pines/Fair Oaks of May 31–June 1 was one of the more significant of the war. Although a tactical Union victory, it so unnerved Union commander Major General George B. McClellan that it effectively ended his effort to take Richmond in the Peninsula Campaign. (Library of Congress)

to the Richmond defenses. McClellan did not pursue. Each side had committed about 42,000 men to the fight. Casualties were heavy. The Union sustained 5,031 casualties (790 killed, 3,594 wounded, and 647 captured or missing), while the Confederates suffered 6,134 losses (980 killed, 4,749 wounded, and 405 captured or missing).

The battle marked a significant turning point in the war. The largest battle of the eastern theater to that point, it was a tactical victory for the Union side in that the Army of the Potomac had held. But the Battle of Seven Pines unnerved the already overly cautious McClellan, always reluctant to commit his men, and saw the end of his Richmond offensive. Also, Johnston was severely wounded on the evening of May 31. He was succeeded by Major General Gustavus W. Smith, but Smith's indecisive direction of the fighting the next day led Confederate president Jefferson Davis on June 1 to name General Robert E. Lee commander of the

Confederate Army of the Potomac, which then became the Army of Northern Virginia.

SPENCER C. TUCKER

See also

Davis, Jefferson Finis; Franklin, William Buel; Heintzelman, Samuel Peter; Jackson's Shenandoah Valley Campaign; Johnston, Joseph Eggleston; Keyes, Erasmus Darwin; Lincoln, Abraham; McClellan, George Brinton; McDowell, Irvin; Peninsula Campaign; Porter, Fitz John; Sedgwick, John; Smith, Gustavus Woodson; Sumner, Edwin Vose

Further Reading

Burton, Brian K. *The Peninsula & Seven Days: A Battlefield Guide.* Lincoln: University of Nebraska Press, 2007.

Miller, William J. *The Battles for Richmond, 1862.* National Park Service Civil War Series. Fort Washington, PA: U.S. National Park Service and Eastern National, 1996.

Salmon, John S. *The Official Virginia Civil War Battlefield Guide.* Mechanicsburg, PA: Stackpole, 2001.

Sears, Stephen W. *To the Gates of Richmond: The Peninsula Campaign.* New York: Ticknor and Fields, 1992.

Seward, Frederick William
Birth Date: July 8, 1830
Death Date: April 25, 1915

Twice assistant U.S. secretary of state and the son of Secretary of State William H. Seward. Born in Auburn, New York, on July 8, 1830, Frederick William Seward graduated from Union College in 1849. He gained admittance to the New York Bar in 1851 and was associate editor of the *Albany Evening Journal* (1851–1861).

When William Seward was selected by President Abraham Lincoln as his secretary of state, he asked Frederick to serve as assistant secretary of state. In this position, the younger Seward acted as his father's chief confidant and adviser throughout the Lincoln and Andrew Johnson administrations. Because Frederick's mother usually preferred to remain at the Seward family residence in Auburn, New York, Frederick's wife Anna served as the hostess for the elder Seward's residence. Frederick Seward often served as a courier between his father and Lincoln.

In April 1865, John Wilkes Booth launched a conspiracy to assassinate President Lincoln, Vice President Andrew Johnson, and William Seward. Former Confederate soldier Lewis Powell (Lewis Paine) was assigned by the conspirators to murder Seward. On the night of April 14, 1865, the evening that Booth shot Lincoln, Powell burst into the Seward house. Secretary of State Seward had been seriously injured two weeks earlier in a carriage accident and was confined to bed with a broken jaw and arm. Powell gained access to Seward's bedroom and stabbed the secretary of state in the face and chest. When Frederick attempted to subdue the attacker, Powell clubbed him over the head with a revolver, causing a severe head injury. For several days, Frederick Seward lay unconscious and appeared to be near death. His mother nursed him, but the ordeal contributed to her fatal heart attack on June 21, 1865. Once he sufficiently recovered, Frederick resumed his duties within the State Department.

Following the Civil War, Frederick Seward assisted his father in the 1867 acquisition of Alaska and other diplomatic endeavors. After leaving government service in 1869, Seward pursued a political career in the New York State Assembly. Following his father's death in 1872, Seward spent several years collecting and organizing his father's papers and memoirs. In 1877, he reentered government service when Rutherford B. Hayes asked him again to serve in his former post under Secretary of State William Evarts. Seward served until 1879. He died in Montrose, New York, on April 25, 1915. His memoir, *Reminiscences of a War-Time Statesman and Diplomat, 1830–1915,* was published posthumously in 1916.

STEPHEN McCULLOUGH

See also
Booth, John Wilkes; Lincoln Assassination; Powell, Lewis Thornton; Seward, William Henry, Sr.

Further Reading
Seward, Frederick. *Reminiscences of a War-Time Statesman and Diplomat, 1830–1915.* New York: Putnam, 1916.
Van Deusen, Glyndon. *William Henry Seward.* New York: Oxford University Press, 1967.

Seward, William Henry, Jr.
Birth Date: June 18, 1839
Death Date: April 26, 1920

Union officer. Born in Auburn, New York, on June 18, 1839, William Henry Seward Jr. was the youngest son of William Henry Seward Sr., President Abraham Lincoln's secretary of state. The younger Seward was educated at home. From age 18 to 20, he clerked in a hardware store but in 1859 decided to follow his father, then a U.S. senator, to Washington and serve as his private secretary. In 1860 Seward returned to Auburn, where he organized a banking house, William H. Seward and Company.

During the early part of 1862, Seward engaged in the recruitment and movement of troops from New York to the front. In August 1862 he was appointed lieutenant colonel of the 138th New York Infantry Regiment, a unit that was converted to artillery and became the 9th New York Heavy Artillery in December and served in the Washington defenses. In 1863 Seward undertook a secret mission to Louisiana, carrying a confidential note from President Abraham Lincoln to Major General Nathaniel P. Banks. Although little is known about the mission, when Congress passed Bill 2161 in 1906, creating a special roll known as the "Volunteer Retired List," the *Congressional Record* refers to this mission, its successful completion, and the "danger and hardship" undertaken by Seward to complete his task.

During his time in Washington's defenses, Seward took part in the construction of several large forts on the Potomac River. Seward and the 9th New York served in the defenses of Washington until May 1864, when heavy casualties during the Overland Campaign (May 4–June 12) caused Seward's regiment and others to be pressed into service as infantry. That May, Seward and the 9th New York joined the Army of the Potomac when they became part of the 2nd Brigade, 3rd Division, VI Corps, under Brigadier General James B. Ricketts. On June 10 after valiant service during the Battle of Cold Harbor (May 31–June 12, 1864), Seward was promoted to colonel and took command of the regiment.

Seward led his regiment north to meet the threat posed by Confederate lieutenant general Jubal Early's Washington Raid (June 28–July 21, 1864). On July 9 during the Battle of Monocacy, Seward had his horse shot from under him and sustained an arm wound and a broken leg. On September 13, he was promoted to brigadier general of volunteers and, after his recovery, was assigned to command a brigade in the Department of West Virginia and briefly commanded a division.

Seward resigned his commission on June 1, 1865, and returned to Auburn, where he was involved in banking and politics until his death there on April 26, 1920.

ADAM P. WILSON

See also

Banks, Nathaniel Prentice; Cold Harbor, Battle of; Early's Raid on Washington, D.C.; Monocacy, Battle of; Overland Campaign

Further Reading

"U.S. Congress, Senate, Senator Henry M. Teller of Colorado Speaking for the Creation of a Volunteer Retired List to the Senate. S. Bill 2162. 59th Cong., 1st Sess." *Congressional Record* 489 (June 13, 1906).
Warner, Ezra J. *Generals in Blue: Lives of the Union Commanders.* Baton Rouge: Louisiana State University Press, 2006.

Seward, William Henry, Sr.
Birth Date: May 16, 1801
Death Date: October 10, 1872

U.S. politician and secretary of state (1861–1869). Born on May 16, 1801, in Florida, New York, William Henry Seward graduated from Union College in 1820 and was admitted to the New York bar in 1822. After establishing his legal practice in Auburn, New York, Seward entered politics as a strong supporter of John Quincy Adams. He also formed a close and lasting friendship with fellow politician Thurlow Weed.

As a member of New York's Anti-Mason Party, Seward was elected to the New York Senate in 1830, partly through Weed's influence. Defeated for reelection in 1833, Seward was nominated by the newly formed Whig Party for governor in 1834 but failed to win election. Running again as a Whig in 1838, he served as governor from 1839 to 1842. In that office, he became strongly identified with the growing antislavery movement when he refused to surrender three African American sailors for extradition to Virginia as runaway slaves.

As a firmly committed antislavery advocate by 1848, Seward discovered that the public mood in New York had changed enough to enable his election to the U.S. Senate on an antislavery platform. He served as a senator until March 1861. Joining the new Republican Party in 1855, he became one of the most outspoken representatives of the antislavery North. Seward saw the slavery issue as "an irrepressible conflict" between the North and the South. He believed that the issue of extending slavery into the territories was not negotiable because slavery was prohibited by "a higher law than the Constitution." He opposed the Compromise of 1850, the 1854 Kansas-Nebraska Act, and the *Dred Scott* decision of 1857.

Seward sought the Republican presidential nomination in 1860 but was deeply disappointed when the party chose

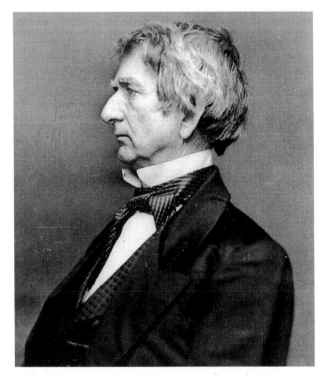

William Henry Seward was U.S. secretary of state during 1861–1869. During the Civil War, he became President Abraham Lincoln's closest cabinet adviser. (National Archives)

Abraham Lincoln as its candidate instead. Nevertheless, Seward campaigned vigorously for Lincoln and after the election accepted the appointment as secretary of state. Seward undoubtedly felt superior to Lincoln. Shortly after assuming office, Seward wrote a memo to Lincoln making it clear the secretary of state expected the president to treat him as the real leader of the administration. Seward advised Lincoln to divert attention from American disunion by precipitating a war with Spain and France and suggested that Lincoln turn over the running of the administration to him. Lincoln responded coolly.

Although it got off to a rocky start, the relationship between the two men improved quickly, with Seward emerging as Lincoln's closest adviser in the cabinet. Seward's performance as secretary of state was exemplary. Well aware of the need for public support, he conducted all diplomatic correspondence with a keen appreciation for how it might influence public opinion. He skillfully averted European intervention in the Civil War and later secured France's promise of withdrawal from Mexico.

On April 14, 1865, the night Lincoln was assassinated, Seward, who had been badly injured days earlier in a carriage accident and was confined to his bed, was also attacked by a knife-wielding coconspirator of John Wilkes Booth, Lewis Powell, who wounded Seward and four others. Seward would bear scars from the attack the rest of his life, but he eventually recovered and, instead of retiring, assumed a central role in the Andrew Johnson administration, continuing as secretary of state.

Favoring a moderate Reconstruction policy, Seward staunchly supported Johnson's conciliatory policy toward the South. Seward even traveled around the North with Johnson in 1866 and spoke on the president's behalf, at great cost to his own popularity.

In addition to playing a key role in the debate over Reconstruction, Seward also pursued efforts to expand U.S. territory after the war. During the 1850s, he had opposed the purchase of Cuba because he feared that this would only provide more land for slaveholders. After the war, however, Seward felt no such compunction about territorial expansion. In 1867 he negotiated the purchase of Alaska from Russia for $7.2 million, which many at the time dubbed "Seward's folly." Critics could not imagine what value there could be in a frozen, isolated wasteland. Seward, however, maintained that Alaska had untold natural resources of minerals, waters, furs, and fish. He also anticipated the U.S. acquisition of Hawaii, which was accomplished at the end of the century.

During the impeachment proceedings against Johnson in 1868, Seward remained fiercely loyal to the president. Retiring from public service in 1869, Seward traveled around the world in 14 months (July 1869–September 1870). He returned to his Auburn, New York, home in 1871, where paralysis gradually overcame him. Seward died there on October 10, 1872.

Steven G. O'Brien

See also
Compromise of 1850; Diplomacy, U.S.; *Dred Scott* Case; Johnson, Andrew; Kansas-Nebraska Act; Lincoln, Abraham; Mexico; Radical Republicans; Reconstruction; Republican Party

Further Reading
Donald, David Herbert. *We Are Lincoln Men: Abraham Lincoln and His Friends.* New York: Simon and Schuster, 2003.
Goodwin, Doris Kearns. *Team of Rivals: The Political Genius of Abraham Lincoln.* New York: Simon and Schuster, 2005.
Taylor, John M. *William Henry Seward: Lincoln's Right Hand.* New York: HarperCollins, 1991.

Sewing Machine

Sewing machines became an integral part of the American clothing industry during the Civil War. In 1830, Frenchman Barthelemy Thimonnier invented the first functional sewing machine. His machine, however, used the chain stitch, which proved to be problematic because it could be easily pulled apart. On September 10, 1846, Elias Howe, an American inventor, obtained a patent for a sewing machine using the stronger lock stitch, created by two interlocking threads. Utilizing the ideas of earlier inventors, Isaac Merritt Singer began mass production of the first commercially successful sewing machines in 1851. Singer's machine employed a needle that moved up and down rather than side to side. In addition, it was powered by a foot treadle rather than a hand crank. Singer went on to create an empire by capturing the lion's share of the market. Indeed, Singer sewing machines are still sold today.

In 1854 Howe, realizing that other sewing machine manufacturers were infringing on his patent, successfully sued Singer, with Singer's company being forced to pay $15 to Howe for every Singer sewing machine produced. In 1856, Singer, Howe, and two other companies pooled their patents, which meant that all other sewing machine companies had to pay a $15 royalty to the conglomerate for each sewing machine produced until the patent expired in 1877.

The Civil War greatly stimulated production and accelerated the growth of established technologies such as the sewing machine. The use of commercial sewing machines during the Civil War, especially in the production of uniforms, resulted in the development of standard-sized clothing. Prior to that time, there was no mass-produced standardized clothing, as many Americans either produced their own clothes or purchased them from local tailors or seamstresses.

The advent of the sewing machine and the Civil War that accelerated their use resulted in a virtual revolution in clothing purchases and style. Some historians speak of a "democratization of clothing," which allowed Americans of all social and economic strata to purchase clothing that was standardized and less expensive than handmade articles. In addition, the sewing machine business was at the vanguard of the coming Industrial Revolution in the United States, which made use of mass production, economies of scale, and interchangeable parts to produce technology that became cheaper and more accessible as time progressed. During the Civil War, Howe donated part of his wealth to equip a Union Army infantry regiment, and Singer donated 2,000 sewing machines to the Union Army to facilitate the mass production of uniforms.

MICHAEL R. HALL

See also

Insignia and Equipment, Union and Confederate; Uniforms, Confederate Army and Navy; Uniforms, U.S. Army and Navy

Further Reading

Carlson, Laurie. *Queen of Inventions: How the Sewing Machine Changed the World.* Minneapolis: Millbrook, 2003.
Parton, James. *History of the Sewing Machine.* Ann Arbor, MI: Scholarly Publishing Office, 2005.

Seymour, Horatio
Birth Date: May 31, 1810
Death Date: February 12, 1886

Democratic politician and New York governor. Born in Pompey Hill, New York, on May 31, 1810, Horatio Seymour was educated at Geneva Academy (now Hobart College) and at a military school in Connecticut. He also studied law at Utica, New York, and was admitted to the bar in 1832.

Seymour entered politics by serving as military secretary to New York governor William Marcy from 1833 to 1838. In 1841 Seymour was elected a state assemblyman and then became mayor of Utica the next year. In 1844 he reentered the assembly and, after pushing through important canal legislation, was elected Speaker in 1845. Following the split

in the New York Democratic Party over the slavery issue in 1848, Seymour played an important role as arbitrator between the opposing groups.

Nominated six times for governor, Seymour won the office twice, first in 1852 and again 10 years later. His first term was from 1853 to 1854, while his second endured from 1863 to 1864. Although opposed to President Abraham Lincoln's 1860 election and the January 1, 1863, Emancipation Proclamation, Seymour nevertheless supported restoration of the Union and urged loyalty to the president. As governor, he worked diligently to maintain the state's quota for Union military forces and moved swiftly to quell the New York City Draft Riots in the summer of 1863. However, he insisted that the extraconstitutional powers assumed by Lincoln's administration were the most dangerous issues to arise from the Civil War.

Aware of the difficulty in running against the popular war hero Ulysses S. Grant, Seymour was not eager to be nominated for president by the Democrats in 1868. However, when Seymour was chosen on the 22nd ballot as a compromise candidate, he reluctantly accepted. He always believed that this was the greatest political blunder of his life, as he lost the contest by more than 300,000 votes.

After his defeat, Seymour continued to play an important role in the Democratic Party, notably in his efforts to help Samuel J. Tilden reform Tammany Hall and end corrupt machine politics in New York City. Seymour died on February 12, 1886, in Ballston Spa, New York.

STEVEN G. O'BRIEN

See also

Emancipation Proclamation; New York; New York City Draft Riots

Further Reading

Bernstein, Iver. *The New York City Draft Riots: Their Significance for American Society and Politics in the Age of the Civil War.* New York: Oxford University Press, 1991.
Mitchell, Stewart. *Horatio Seymour of New York.* Cambridge, MA: Harvard University Press, 1938.

Seymour, Truman
Birth Date: September 24, 1825
Death Date: October 30, 1891

Union officer. Truman Seymour was born on September 24, 1825, in Burlington, Vermont. He graduated from the U.S. Military Academy, West Point, in 1846. Commissioned in the 1st Artillery, he saw combat during the

Mexican-American War (1846–1848), winning two brevets and promotion to first lieutenant. After the war, he taught at West Point for three years before being posted to Fort Moultrie, South Carolina, and fighting in the Third Seminole War (1855–1858).

In April 1861, Seymour was a captain serving at Fort Sumter. Brevetted major for his role during the Confederate bombardment, later in 1861 he commanded a training center at Fort Curtin, Pennsylvania, before being sent to the defenses of Washington, D.C. Seymour was appointed brigadier general of volunteers on April 28, 1862, and commanded a brigade in V Corps at the Battle of Mechanicsville (June 26, 1862) and the Battle of Gaines' Mill (June 27, 1862) and then commanding a division at the Battle of Malvern Hill (July 1, 1862). Returning to brigade command during the Second Battle of Bull Run (August 29–30, 1862), he again took charge of a division at the Battle of Antietam (September 17, 1862). Sent to the Department of the South, he commanded a number of districts along the Atlantic coast. During the Siege of Fort Wagner (July 10–September 7, 1863), he led a division of X Corps in a bloody and failed attempt to storm the Confederate position on July 18 and was seriously wounded.

Seymour became best known for his disastrous incursion into eastern Florida in the winter of 1864. He commenced his invasion at Jacksonville, debarking his troops on February 4. After conducting several raids into the interior of Florida, which encountered minimal resistance, Seymour pushed westward, believing that he would face only ineffectual Florida militia forces. Instead, he encountered a mixed force of regulars and militia at Olustee on February 20. The largest battle in Florida during the war, it ended in a rout, and Seymour hastily withdrew to the coast. Less than three months later at the Battle of the Wilderness (May 5–7, 1864), Seymour was wounded and taken prisoner.

Upon his exchange in September, Seymour led a division in VI Corps in the Shenandoah Valley, at Petersburg, and during the Appomattox Campaign (April 2–9, 1865) and was brevetted major general of volunteers and in the regular army.

Remaining in the army after the war, Seymour, promoted to major in 1866, held a variety of postings, including command of forts in Florida, Massachusetts, and Maine, until his retirement on November 1, 1876. An accomplished painter, Seymour spent the remainder of his life pursuing his artistic inclinations and lived chiefly in Florence, Italy, where he died on October 30, 1891.

PAUL G. PIERPAOLI JR.

See also
Antietam, Battle of; Appomattox Campaign; Bull Run, Second Battle of; Fort Wagner, South Carolina, Siege of; Gaines' Mill, Battle of; Malvern Hill, Battle of; Mechanicsville, Battle of; Olustee, Battle of; Wilderness, Battle of the

Further Reading
Nulty, William H. *Confederate Florida: The Road to Olustee.* Tuscaloosa: University of Alabama Press, 1990.
Warner, Ezra J. *Generals in Blue: Lives of the Union Commanders.* Baton Rouge: Louisiana State University Press, 2006.

Shackelford, James Murrell
Birth Date: July 7, 1827
Death Date: September 7, 1909

Union officer. Born in Lincoln County, Kentucky, on July 7, 1827, James Murrell Shackelford volunteered for military service in the Mexican-American War (1846–1848). He was commissioned a second lieutenant in the 4th Kentucky Infantry on October 4, 1847, and was promoted to first lieutenant in 1848.

On his return home, Shackelford became a lawyer and opened a successful practice in Louisville. Wealthy by the beginning of the Civil War, Shackelford raised the 25th Kentucky Infantry and was commissioned its colonel on January 1, 1862. The 25th Infantry participated in the Battle of Fort Donelson (February 13–16, 1862), but Shackleford resigned his commission on March 24 to return home and raise yet another regiment, the 8th Kentucky Cavalry, of which he was commissioned colonel on September 13.

Shackleford was appointed brigadier general of volunteers on January 2, 1863, and assumed command of the 1st Brigade, 2nd Division, XXIII Corps, Army of the Ohio. He won fame in the North for the capture of Confederate brigadier general John Hunt Morgan and a number of his Kentucky raiders at Salineville, Ohio, on July 26. Shackelford was wounded in the left foot at Geiger's Lake, Kentucky, on September 3. He commanded the 4th Division of XXIII Corps in Major General Ambrose E. Burnside's campaign in eastern Tennessee that autumn. Shackelford's capture of Cumberland Gap during this campaign led to him being given command of the Cavalry Corps of the Department of the Ohio in November. On December 14 at Bean's Station, Confederate forces under Lieutenant General James Longstreet turned and attacked Shackelford's command, which was shadowing the Confederates, and, after heavy fighting, forced his withdrawal.

Shackleford, now in poor health, resigned his commission on January 18, 1864. He resumed his law practice and later was appointed a judge in Indian Territory (Oklahoma). Shackleford died at Port Huron, Michigan, on September 7, 1909.

SPENCER C. TUCKER

See also

Bean's Station, Battle of; Fort Donelson, Battle of; Knoxville Campaign; Morgan's Ohio Raid; Salineville, Battle of

Further Reading

Carter, Samuel. *The Last Cavaliers: Confederate and Union Cavalry in the Civil War.* New York: St. Martin's, 1982.

Eicher, John H., and David J. Eicher. *Civil War High Commands.* Stanford, CA: Stanford University Press, 2001.

Warner, Ezra J. *Generals in Blue: Lives of the Union Commanders.* Baton Rouge: Louisiana State University Press, 2006.

Shaler, Alexander
Birth Date: March 19, 1827
Death Date: December 28, 1911

Union officer. Alexander Shaler was born on March 19, 1827, in Haddam, Connecticut, and was educated in private academies in New York City. Joining the New York Militia at age 18, he became a career militia officer, rising to the rank of major by the end of 1860. In 1861 he authored a popular manual of arms for militia personnel. In June 1861 Shaler joined the 65th New York Infantry Regiment and became its lieutenant colonel. He saw action in the Peninsula Campaign (March–July 1862), during which he became colonel of the 65th New York in July.

Shaler received command of a brigade in early 1863, and he led the 1st Brigade, 3rd Division, VI Corps, in the Battle of Chancellorsville (May 1–4, 1863). His outstanding performance on Marye's Heights earned him promotion to brigadier general on May 26, 1863, and the Medal of Honor (awarded in 1893). Leading the same unit at the Battle of Gettysburg (July 1–3, 1863), he was conspicuous on the third day of fighting when his brigade helped hold Culp's Hill.

During the winter of 1863–1864, Shaler commanded Johnson's Island Prison, a Union prisoner-of-war facility in Ohio. Soon after returning to field duty in VI Corps, Shaler was captured on the second day of combat at the Battle of the Wilderness (May 5–7, 1864) and was sent to prison camps in Georgia and South Carolina. In the autumn of 1864, he was exchanged and dispatched to the western theater. He initially commanded a brigade in XIX Corps, Department of the Gulf. From December 1864 until August 1865, Shaler commanded the 2nd Division, VII Corps, Department of Arkansas; he also commanded the White River District in Arkansas.

Shaler mustered out on August 24, 1865, as a brevet major general. After the war he was active in the New York National Guard, becoming a major general. He also served as New York City's fire commissioner and was a consultant for the Chicago Fire Department. He later served as president of a telegraph company and helped found the National Rifle Association, for which he served as president. Shaler died on December 28, 1911, in New York City.

PAUL G. PIERPAOLI JR.

See also

Chancellorsville, Battle of; Gettysburg, Battle of; Johnson's Island Prison, Ohio; Peninsula Campaign; Wilderness, Battle of the

Further Reading

Eicher, John H., and David J. Eicher. *Civil War High Commands.* Stanford, CA: Stanford University Press, 2001.

Parsons, Philip W. *The Union Sixth Corps in the Chancellorsville Campaign.* Jefferson, NC: McFarland, 2006.

Sharp, Jacob Hunter
Birth Date: February 6, 1833
Death Date: September 15, 1907

Confederate officer. Born in Pickensville, Alabama, on February 6, 1833, Jacob Hunter Sharp as an infant moved with his family to Lowndes County, Mississippi. During 1850–1851, he attended the University of Alabama. After studying law, he was admitted to the bar and then practiced law in Columbus, Mississippi.

In June 1861 Sharp enlisted in the 1st Battalion, Mississippi Infantry (later part of the 44th Mississippi Infantry), and soon was elected a captain. He fought in the Battle of Belmont (November 7, 1861), the Battle of Shiloh (April 6–7, 1862), the Kentucky Campaign (August–October 1862), and the Battle of Stones River (December 31, 1862–January 2, 1863). He was promoted to colonel in August 1863 and commanded the 44th Infantry and temporarily a brigade during the Battle of Chickamauga (September 19–20, 1863) and the Chattanooga Campaign (October–November 1863).

During the Atlanta Campaign (May 5–September 2, 1864), Sharp commanded a brigade and was conspicuous in many battles, especially the Battle of Atlanta (July 22).

Appointed temporary brigadier general on July 26, Sharp led this brigade in Major J. Patton Anderson's division of II Corps, Army of the Tennessee, and won praise for his leadership in the Battle of Franklin (November 30) during General John Bell Hood's Franklin and Nashville Campaign (November 29–December 27) and during U.S. major general William T. Sherman's Carolinas Campaign (January–April 1865). Sharp's last engagement was the Battle of Bentonville (March 19–21). He surrendered at Durham Station on April 26, although there is no record of him having been paroled.

After the war, Sharp resumed his Columbus law practice. He also purchased the local *Independent* newspaper and became president of the Mississippi Press Association. Active in the white supremacist movement, he was a member of the Mississippi legislature (1886–1890) and was for a time its Speaker. Sharp died in Columbus, Georgia, on September 15, 1907.

SPENCER C. TUCKER

See also

Anderson, James Patton; Atlanta Campaign; Bentonville, Battle of; Chattanooga Campaign; Chickamauga, Battle of; Franklin, Battle of; Franklin and Nashville Campaign; Hood, John Bell; Kentucky Campaign; Sherman's March through the Carolinas; Shiloh, Battle of; Stones River, Battle of; Tucker, William Feimster

Further Reading

Eicher, John H., and David J. Eicher. *Civil War High Commands.* Stanford, CA: Stanford University Press, 2001.

Sword, Wiley. *The Confederacy's Last Hurrah: Spring Hill, Franklin, and Nashville.* New York: HarperCollins, 1992.

Warner, Ezra J. *Generals in Gray: Lives of the Confederate Commanders.* Baton Rouge: Louisiana State University Press, 2006.

Sharpsburg, Battle of

See Antietam, Battle of

Sharpshooters

Soldiers who are highly skilled in precision shooting, mainly with rifles. Sharpshooters specialized in irregular warfare and skirmishing, and for that reason they were chiefly a psychological weapon during the Civil War. Sharpshooters and their namesake activity, sharpshooting, were not exclusive to the Civil War. Riflemen played an important role in the American Revolutionary War. In the Battle of Saratoga in 1777, for example, Continental Army sharpshooters picked off British officers. Civil War sharpshooters resembled their Revolutionary War forebears in many ways. They carried the latest rifles, specialized in skirmishing, and were sometimes formed into regiment-sized units. Conversely, they occasionally operated independently and foreshadowed snipers of the Boer War and World War I. Most sharpshooters employed Sharps and Whitworth rifles. Others used hunting rifles and privately owned, custom-built weapons.

Although Berdan's Sharpshooters, two Union regiments named after their founder, Colonel Hiram Berdan, and serving in the Army of the Potomac, were perhaps the most famous sniper units of the war, sharpshooters served on both sides and in all theaters of the conflict. While soldiers tended to loathe the sharpshooters' deadly and sneaky trade, many admired their marksmanship skills. Some sharpshooters even became celebrities. Truman Head, a 52-year-old member of Berdan's Sharpshooters, was known as "California Joe" for his home state. The Union Army of the Tennessee's Lieutenant Henry C. Foster, 23rd Indiana Infantry, earned the sobriquet "Coonskin" for his nonregulation headgear. During the Second Vicksburg Campaign (April 1–July 4, 1863), he would stuff his haversack with several days' worth of rations and occupy a shallow dugout in the area between the two armies, picking off unsuspecting Confederates. Unsatisfied with this arrangement, Foster and some members of his unit constructed a tower of railroad ties that would allow him and other marksmen to shoot at Confederates behind their earthworks. The tower became a local attraction, even warranting an inspection visit by Union Army commander Major General Ulysses S. Grant.

During the siege of Vicksburg but also the Atlanta Campaign (May 5–September 2, 1864) and the Petersburg Campaign (June 15, 1864–April 3, 1865), specialized sharpshooter regiments as well as common infantrymen engaged in sniping. Although it is impossible to ascertain the overall impact of the sharpshooting, the deadly practice did impact Civil War battlefields and helped bridge the transition to modern warfare.

JUSTIN S. SOLONICK

See also

Atlanta Campaign; Berdan's Sharpshooters; Petersburg Campaign; Rifles; Vicksburg Campaign, Second

Further Reading

Hess, Earl J. *The Rifle Musket in Civil War Combat: Reality and Myth.* Lawrence: University of Kansas Press, 2008.

Pegler, Martin. *Sniper: A History of the US Marksman.* Oxford, UK: Osprey, 2007.

Sharps Rifle and Carbine

Breech-loading firearm. The Sharps rifle was designed by Christian Sharps and patented in September 1848. It was manufactured first by A. S. Nippes at Mill Creek, Pennsylvania; then by the Robbins & Lawrence Company of Windsor, Vermont; and finally by the Sharps Rifle Manufacturing Company of Hartford, Connecticut. Sharps left the business in 1853, and chief armorer Richard S. Lawrence made a number of modifications to the rifle that ensured its success.

The Sharps featured a sliding block at the end of the barrel that allowed it to be loaded at the breech, a great advantage in combat. Nearly all prewar Sharps had a breechblock at a slight angle from perpendicular to the barrel, while those manufactured during the war featured a breechblock perpendicular to the barrel. The Sharps could be fired with either a paper cartridge or loose black powder. Its rate of fire was about 8 to 10 rounds per minute.

The rifle was 47 inches in length and weighed 9.5 pounds. The carbine was 39.5 inches in length and weighed 8 pounds. The .52-caliber Sharps fired a 475-grain bullet. Its 50-grain powder charge gave it a muzzle velocity of 1,200 feet per second.

The military Sharps employed the standard percussion cap ignition system but was also equipped with a pellet primer feed that flipped a primer over the nipple when the trigger was pulled and the hammer fell. This made the weapon far easier to fire from horseback than a rifle employing only percussion caps. An accurate weapon, the Sharps was frequently employed as a sniper rifle during the war. The shorter carbine version was a favorite of cavalrymen.

During the Civil War, the U.S. government purchased some 100,000 Sharps carbines for the cavalry and 15,000 Sharps rifles. Confederate arms factories at Richmond, Virginia, produced about 5,000 Sharps copies, usually more crudely finished. The straight-breech Sharps could be converted to fire metallic cartridges, and some 30,000 of these were modified as such after the war and employed by the army in the Indian Wars. The Sharps also saw widespread service in the West for hunting buffalo.

SPENCER C. TUCKER

See also
Rifles

Further Reading
Bilby, Joseph. *Civil War Firearms: Their Historical Background and Tactical Use.* New York: Da Capo, 2005.
Coates, Earl J., and Thomas S. Dean. *An Introduction to Civil War Small Arms.* Gettysburg, PA: Thomas, 1990.
Sellers, Frank M. *Sharps Firearms.* North Hollywood, CA: Beinfeld, 1978.
Smith, Winston O. *The Sharps Rifle: Its History, Development and Operation.* New York: W. Morrow, 1943.

Sharps carbine. The Sharps was noted for its long range and accuracy and was popular with cavalrymen of both sides during the Civil War. (Civil War Archive/The Bridgeman Art Library)

Shaw, Robert Gould
Birth Date: October 10, 1837
Death Date: July 18, 1863

Union officer. Robert Gould Shaw was born into a prominent Boston, Massachusetts, family on October 10, 1837. He enrolled at Harvard University in 1856 but dropped out in his junior year to work in his uncle's mercantile firm in New York City. When war seemed imminent in the spring of 1861, Shaw joined an elite military company as a private. Shortly after hostilities commenced, he returned home and was commissioned a second lieutenant in the 2nd Massachusetts Infantry Regiment. Promoted to captain in August 1862, he participated in the First Battle of Winchester (May 25, 1862), the Battle of Cedar Mountain (August 9), and the Battle of Antietam (September 17). Shaw was promoted to major on March 31, 1863.

Massachusetts governor John A. Andrew, a leading abolitionist, prevailed on U.S. president Abraham Lincoln to allow him to recruit an African American regiment for federal service. The 54th Massachusetts Volunteer Infantry was the first such organization raised in a free state. Andrew appointed Shaw colonel of the 54th Massachusetts on April 17, 1863. Shaw was one of the few white officers who believed that black men might make effective soldiers. He supported a boycott by his men, who received less pay than white soldiers, in which the enlisted men of the 54th Massachusetts as well as the 55th Massachusetts refused pay until Congress granted them the same rate that white soldiers received. This occurred in August 1864.

Following training, the 54th Massachusetts paraded through Boston in May 1863 and embarked for South Carolina. Following a baptism of fire on James Island on July 16, 1863, in which the 54th Massachusetts performed effectively, Major General Quincy A. Gillmore, commanding Union Army operations against Charleston, offered Shaw the opportunity to spearhead another assault on Fort Wagner, the heavily armed Confederate fortification on Morris Island. Eager to prove his men in combat and resentful over how the army had discriminated against his soldiers, Shaw readily assented.

On July 18, 1863, a Union naval bombardment lasting several hours failed to reduce the Confederate defenses at Fort Wagner, and when the Union troops attacked, they were slaughtered by the Confederate defenders. Undaunted, the 54th Massachusetts surged forward, with Shaw at its head, and gained a foothold on the parapet. Shaw stood urging his men on until struck in the heart by a bullet and killed. When

Union reinforcements failed to arrive, the surviving members of the 54th Massachusetts were forced to withdraw. Of 5,300 Union troops engaged that day, 1,515 were casualties. The 54th Massachusetts alone lost 9 killed, 147 wounded, and 100 missing and presumed dead, almost 40 percent of its strength. The defenders suffered only 175 casualties.

When a flag of truce was sent out to recover Shaw's body, Confederate garrison commander Brigadier General Johnson Hagood allowed the bodies of the other officers to be taken away but not that of Shaw. Hagood declared that he would have returned the body had Shaw been in command of white troops, but Shaw would be "buried with his niggers." This callous act, which nonetheless pleased Shaw's parents, who believed that it was what he would have wanted, helped elevate Shaw and his men to the status of martyrs in the eyes of abolitionists throughout the North. Moreover, the heroic performance of the 54th Massachusetts proved that African Americans could fight beside their white comrades in arms, and additional black units were raised. In 1882 Shaw was honored by an elaborate monument in Boston sculpted by Augustus Saint-Gaudens.

JOHN C. FREDRIKSEN

See also
Antietam, Battle of; Cedar Mountain, Battle of; 54th Massachusetts Regiment of Infantry; Fort Wagner, South Carolina, Siege of; Gillmore, Quincy Adams; Winchester, First Battle of

Further Reading
Burchard, Peter, *"We'll Stand by the Union": Robert Gould Shaw and the Black 54th Massachusetts.* New York: St. Martin's, 1993.
Duncan, Russell. *Where Death and Glory Meet: Colonel Robert Gould Shaw and the 54th Massachusetts Infantry.* Athens: University of Georgia Press, 1999.
Duncan, Russell, ed. *Blue-Eyed Child of Fortune: The Civil War Letters of Colonel Robert Gould Shaw.* Athens: University of Georgia Press, 1992.
Wise, Stephen R. *Gate of Hell: Campaign for Charleston Harbor, 1863.* Columbia: University of South Carolina Press, 1994.

Shelby, Joseph Orville
Birth Date: December 12, 1830
Death Date: February 13, 1897

Confederate officer. Joseph "Jo" Orville Shelby was born on December 12, 1830, in Lexington, Kentucky, to a wealthy and influential family. He was educated at Transylvania University and became a successful rope manufacturer before moving to Berlin, Missouri, in 1852, where he owned a hemp plantation. Shelby also became one of the largest slaveholders in the state. When violence between proslavery and antislavery factions erupted in the Kansas Territory following passage of the 1854 Kansas-Nebraska Act, Shelby led numerous cross-border raids against Kansas abolitionists, making himself a hero among proslavery Missourians.

Following the onset of the Civil War in 1861, Shelby raised a force of some 100 men for the secessionist Missouri State Guard. Subsequently, he was commissioned a cavalry captain and saw extensive service in Missouri and Kansas. In June 1862 he entered the Confederate Army and was advanced to colonel of the 5th Missouri Cavalry. Soon he was given charge of a cavalry brigade that became known as the Iron Brigade, which he largely recruited himself.

Shelby quickly gained a reputation as one of the Confederacy's best cavalry commanders in the Trans-Mississippi Department. His outfit participated in almost every major battle in the region. His raid into southern Missouri in September 1863, which was the longest cavalry raid of the war, covering 1,500 miles, is widely credited for having thwarted Union efforts to overrun Arkansas. In the process, his brigade inflicted some 1,000 Union casualties and destroyed about $2 million in property. For this exploit, Shelby was advanced to brigadier general to date from December 15, 1863.

Shelby also played a central role in Major General Sterling Price's Missouri Raid (September 19–October 28, 1864), and Shelby's actions at Westport (October 23, 1864) and Mine Creek (October 25) twice prevented the destruction of Price's force.

After the collapse of the Confederacy in April 1865, Shelby refused to surrender and took 200 men from his former command on a long march to Mexico, where he offered his services to puppet emperor Maximilian. The emperor declined the offer but granted Shelby land. Following Maximilian's demise in 1867, Shelby returned to Missouri, where he resumed his lucrative business dealings. In 1893 he was appointed a U.S. marshal for the western district of the state. Shelby died on February 13, 1897, in Adrian, Missouri.

WALTER F. BELL

See also
Kansas-Nebraska Act; Missouri; Price, Sterling; Price's Missouri Raid; Shelby's Iron Brigade; Westport, Battle of

Further Reading
Eicher, John H., and David J. Eicher. *Civil War High Commands.* Stanford, CA: Stanford University Press, 2001.
O'Flaherty, Daniel. *General Jo Shelby: Undefeated Rebel.* Chapel Hill: University of North Carolina Press, 1954.

Shelby's Iron Brigade

Highly effective Confederate cavalry brigade initially commanded by Colonel Joseph O. Shelby that operated in the Trans-Mississippi theater. Shelby's brigade, authorized by Major General Thomas C. Hindman, was organized in the spring of 1862. It was the result of recruiting efforts in Missouri undertaken by Colonels Shelby, Upton Hays, and John T. Coffee, each of whom raised one regiment. The three regiments formed a brigade, which also included an artillery battery. When organized, the force contained some 2,500 men. Shelby was placed in command, but he retained his colonel's rank. The brigade was attached to Brigadier General John S. Marmaduke's cavalry division.

Shelby's Iron Brigade became well known for its guerrilla-style tactics and other means of unconventional warfare. It was particularly skilled in raids on Union supply depots and other areas behind the lines. Shelby's force saw heavy action at Cane Hill, Arkansas, on November 28, 1862, where it protected Marmaduke's retreat into the Boston Mountains. The brigade next saw action at the Battle of Prairie Grove (December 7, 1862) and then participated in raids into Missouri during December 1862–January 1863 and April–May 1863. Shelby's raid into southern Missouri in September 1863, which was the longest cavalry raid of the war, covering 1,500 miles, is widely credited for having thwarted Union efforts to overrun Arkansas. In the process, his brigade inflicted some 1,000 Union casualties and destroyed about $2 million in property.

When Shelby was advanced to brigadier general on December 15, 1863, and given command of a division, Shelby's Iron Brigade was commanded by Colonel David Shanks. Shanks led the outfit during Price's Missouri Raid (September 19–October 28, 1864), in which he was killed in action on October 7. Shanks was succeeded in command by Colonel M. Jeff Thompson.

As the war wound down in the spring of 1865, the commanders and soldiers of Shelby's old brigade vowed to fight on, regardless of the developments in the East. When the war ended in April, Shelby himself led a contingent of men, many from his former brigade, into Mexico. There they volunteered to serve in Emperor Maximilian's army. The offer was declined, but the emperor did offer the men free land grants. Many, including Shelby, remained in Mexico until Maximilian's ouster in 1867.

PAUL G. PIERPAOLI JR.

See also
Cavalry, Confederate; Cavalry Tactics; Chattanooga Campaign; Guerrilla Warfare; Marmaduke, John Sappington; Maximilian

von Habsburg, Ferdinand; Mexico; Missouri; Price's Missouri Raid; Shelby, Joseph Orville; Trans-Mississippi Theater

Further Reading

O'Flaherty, Daniel. *General Jo Shelby: Undefeated Rebel.* Chapel Hill: University of North Carolina Press, 1954.

Sellmeyer, Deryl P. *Jo Shelby's Iron Brigade.* Gretna, LA: Pelican, 2007.

Shelley, Charles Miller

Birth Date: December 28, 1833
Death Date: January 20, 1907

Confederate officer. Charles Miller Shelley was born in Sullivan County, Tennessee, on December 28, 1833, the younger brother of Nathan George Shelley, a brigadier general of Texas state troops during the Civil War and attorney general of Texas. Charles Shelley moved with his family at an early age to Talladega, Alabama, where he became a builder.

Shelley was commissioned a first lieutenant of artillery in the Alabama Militia in February 1861 and entered Confederate service shortly thereafter. His unit was reorganized as part of the 5th Alabama Infantry, and Shelley was elected captain on May 11, 1861. He was in Virginia at the time of the First Battle of Bull Run (July 21, 1861) but did not see action there. In January 1862 he returned to Alabama to recruit the 30th Alabama Infantry and was appointed its colonel on March 21, 1862. His regiment fought in General Braxton Bragg's invasion of Kentucky (August–October) and in the Battle of Port Gibson (May 1, 1863) in Mississippi. Shelley distinguished himself in the Battle of Champion Hill (May 16, 1863) and fought at Vicksburg, where he was taken prisoner on July 4, 1863.

Following his parole on July 8, 1863, and subsequent exchange, Shelley resumed command of his regiment in the Army of Tennessee at Chattanooga and participated in the fighting there in November 1863. He took part in the major battles of the Atlanta Campaign (May 5–September 2, 1864) and on August 31 assumed command of a brigade. He was promoted to temporary brigadier general on September 17. Shelley took part in the Franklin and Nashville Campaign (November 29–December 27, 1864). During the Confederate assault on the Union positions at Franklin on November 30, his brigade suffered 432 killed or wounded of 1,100 men present. Although his horse was shot from underneath him and killed and his uniform was pierced by bullets, Shelley escaped unhurt. He continued with the Army of the Tennessee during Major General William T. Sherman's March through the Carolinas (January–April 1865). Shelley surrendered at Greensboro, where he was paroled on May 1.

After the war, Shelley spent a year in Louisiana before returning to Alabama. In 1874 he was elected sheriff of Dallas County. He served four terms in Congress as a Democrat (1877–1885) before being appointed fourth auditor of the U.S. Treasury Department. He then promoted industrial development in Birmingham, Alabama, where he died on January 20, 1907.

SPENCER C. TUCKER

See also

Atlanta Campaign; Bragg, Braxton; Champion Hill, Battle of; Franklin, Battle of; Franklin and Nashville Campaign; Kentucky Campaign; Port Gibson, Battle of; Sherman's March through the Carolinas; Vicksburg Campaign, Second

Further Reading

Eicher, John H., and David J. Eicher. *Civil War High Commands.* Stanford, CA: Stanford University Press, 2001.

Sword, Wiley. *The Confederacy's Last Hurrah: Spring Hill, Franklin, and Nashville.* New York: HarperCollins, 1992.

Warner, Ezra J. *Generals in Gray: Lives of the Confederate Commanders.* Baton Rouge: Louisiana State University Press, 2006.

Shelton Laurel Massacre

Event Date: January 18, 1863

Mass murder of Unionist North Carolinians by Confederate troops. Throughout the Civil War, there was considerable turmoil in western North Carolina's mountainous Madison County, an area of Unionist sentiment. Early in the war, the county became a haven for Confederate deserters, bushwhackers, and so-called Tories (as Union sympathizers were known). Shelton Laurel, the local name for the Laurel Valley, was the center of this activity, which prompted intervention there in early 1862 by Confederate militia. Although the locals had then professed their loyalty to the Confederacy, Unionist sympathies continued unabated, with each side preying on the other.

In January 1863, some inhabitants of Shelton Laurel raided Marshall, the county seat, to secure salt, which they claimed had been withheld from them because of their Unionist sentiments. They broke into several stores and took the salt they needed. They also ransacked the home of Colonel Lawrence M. Allen, commander of the 64th North Carolina Infantry. Informed of events, North Carolina governor Zebulon B. Vance called on Confederate brigadier general Henry Heth at Knoxville for assistance. Heth ordered to Madison County troops of the 64th Regiment, now under Lieutenant Colonel James A. Keith (Allen was ill), part of the command of Brigadier General William G. M. Davis at nearby Warm Springs (now Hot Springs). Davis subsequently reported that the 64th North Carolina had killed 12 Tories and captured 20 others but that reports of disloyalty in Madison County were exaggerated.

The true story began to come out with letters from participants. Although some details remain in dispute, such as the degree to which the 64th North Carolina had been subjected to attacks by bushwhackers, the regiment sacked some Unionist homes, beating the inhabitants (including women and children), and then rounded up 15 males aged 13 to 59. When 2 of them escaped, Keith and some of his men had those remaining taken to a gorge and there executed all 13 in cold blood, then buried the bodies in a mass grave.

This action did not, however, stop the bushwhacking, and when word of the circumstances reached Governor Vance, he demanded an investigation. Keith, who was subsequently allowed to resign on grounds of "incompetency," claimed that Heth had ordered him not to take any prisoners, although Heth vigorously denied this. After the war, Keith spent two years in jail awaiting trial for the massacre but escaped only days before a court decision that would have vindicated him.

SPENCER C. TUCKER

See also
Davis, William George Mackey; Heth, Henry; Southern Unionists; Vance, Zebulon Baird

Further Reading
Barrett, John G. *The Civil War in North Carolina.* Chapel Hill: University of North Carolina Press, 1963.
Trotter, William. *Bushwhackers! The Civil War in North Carolina; The Mountains.* Winston-Salem, NC: John F. Blair, 1991.

Shenandoah, Confederate Army of the

Established with some 2,000 volunteers, the Army of the Shenandoah was formed on April 21, 1861, under the leadership of Major Kenton Harper of the Virginia Militia at Harpers Ferry. On April 28, 1861, Brigadier General Thomas J. Jackson, also of the Virginia Militia, assumed command. On May 23, 1861, Brigadier General Joseph E. Johnston was installed as the commander.

By June 30, 1861, the original contingent of volunteers had expanded into an army of 10,654 Confederate soldiers

and troopers. By July, the Army of the Shenandoah consisted of four brigades with a total of approximately 12,000 men. Brigadier General Thomas J. Jackson commanded its 1st Brigade, while Colonel J. E. B. Stuart commanded the army's 300-man cavalry contingent, the 1st Virginia Cavalry.

In what amounted to the first invasion of the Confederacy during the Civil War, on July 1, 1861, Union major general Robert Patterson crossed the Potomac River at Williamsport with 18,000 soldiers of the Union Army of the Shenandoah and advanced into Virginia, ordered to contain Johnston in the Shenandoah Valley to prevent him from supporting Confederate forces to the east that would soon be under attack by Union brigadier general Irwin McDowell's Army of Northwestern Virginia to the east. Stuart's cavalry quickly ascertained Patterson's movements, and the Confederates soon stymied the inept Patterson's effort, allowing Johnston to transport his infantry by railroad to Manassas and arrive in time to play a key role in the Confederate victory in the First Battle of Bull Run (July 21, 1861). This was the only major engagement of the Army of the Shenandoah, which was then folded into the Army of the Potomac.

JAMES BRIAN MCNABB

See also
Bull Run, First Battle of; Jackson, Thomas Jonathan; Johnston, Joseph Eggleston; McDowell, Irvin; Patterson, Robert; Stuart, James Ewell Brown

Further Reading
Gallagher, Gary W., ed. *Struggle for Shenandoah: Essays on the 1864 Valley Campaign.* Kent, OH: Kent State University Press, 1991.
Weigley, Russell F. *A Great Civil War: A Military and Political History, 1861–1865.* Bloomington: Indiana University Press, 2004.

Shenandoah, CSS

Confederate Navy cruiser. Purchased in England in September 1864 by Confederate Agent James D. Bulloch, the *Shenandoah* was the last Confederate cruiser Bulloch managed to get to sea. The first composite auxiliary screw steamship in the world, the *Shenandoah* was originally the *Sea King* and was launched on August 17, 1863. Designed for transporting troops to India, its frames and beams were of iron, and it was planked with East Indian teak. The *Sea King* was 1,378 tons burden and 228' between perpendiculars, 38'9" in beam, and 15' in draft. Capable of nine knots under steam, the ship had one screw propeller, two boilers, and direct-acting engines.

The Confederate commerce raider *Shenandoah* undergoing repairs at Melbourne, Australia, during January–February 1865. Under able Commander James I. Waddell, the raider decimated the U.S. Arctic whaling fleet. For some time Waddell refused to believe the war was over. Not until August 1865 did he strike his guns below and sail to England. The *Shenandoah* was the only Confederate warship to circumnavigate the globe. (U.S. Naval Historical Center)

Flag Officer Samuel Barron, ranking Confederate officer in Europe, named Lieutenant Commander James I. Waddell the *Sea King*'s captain and ordered him to destroy the Union whaling fleet in the Pacific. On October 8, 1864, the *Sea King* departed the Thames estuary under a British merchant captain on what appeared to be a merchant voyage but then proceeded to Funchal on the island of Madeira to rendezvous with the supply ship *Laurel.* That ship had sailed from England the same day with Waddell and the remainder of the *Sea King*'s crew and armament. The ship's crew complement was 73 men. The armament consisted of four 8-inch and two 12-pounder smoothbore cannon and two 32-pounder rifled guns. On October 19, 1864, Waddell officially commissioned his vessel the Confederate warship *Shenandoah* and began to cruise for Union vessels.

The *Shenandoah* took six Union prizes in the Atlantic. It arrived at Melbourne, Australia, on January 25, 1865, and there underwent repairs. Except for the dry-docking and machinery repairs at Melbourne, Waddell would not have been able to undertake his subsequent mission. The *Shenandoah* sailed again on February 18, 1865, and cruised the whaling grounds in the Pacific Ocean and off Alaska. Its long stay at Melbourne allowed U.S. whaling vessels in the South Pacific to be warned and disperse, but Waddell took his ship north and decimated the Union whaling fleet.

For some time, Waddell refused to believe reports of the end of the war. Finally, after he had left northern waters, he accepted as proof a report from an English captain on August 2, 1865. Waddell then sailed the *Shenandoah* 17,000 miles, without stopping at any port, to Liverpool, England, where he arrived on November 6, 1865, and surrendered to British authorities. The trip had been made virtually under sail alone. Waddell resorted to steam only once, at night in the mid–South Atlantic to elude the U.S. Navy side-wheel frigate *Saranac*. The *Shenandoah* was the only Confederate warship to sail around the world. In all the *Shenandoah* took 38 Union vessels, of which Waddell burned 32. Damage to Union shipping was estimated at some $1.36 million.

In 1866 the *Shenandoah* was sold to the sultan of Zanzibar. Renamed the *El Majidi,* it was damaged in a hurricane off Zanzibar in April 1872. That September it sank in the Indian Ocean on the Zanzibar-Bombay route.

SPENCER C. TUCKER

See also

Bulloch, James Dunwody; Waddell, James Iredell

Further Reading

Hearn, Chester G. *Gray Raiders of the Sea: How Eight Confederate Warships Destroyed the Union's High Sea Commerce.* Camden, ME: International Marine Publishing, 1992.

Horn, Stanley F. *Gallant Rebel: The Fabulous Cruise of the C.S.S. Shenandoah.* New Brunswick, NJ: Rutgers University Press, 1947.

Morgan, Murray. *Dixie Raider: The Saga of the C.S.S. Shenandoah.* New York: Dutton, 1948.

Waddell, James T. *C.S.S. Shenandoah: The Memoirs of Lieutenant Commanding James I. Waddell.* Edited by James D. Horan. New York: Crown, 1960.

Shenandoah, Union Army of the

Union field army. Organized on August 7, 1864, as the fighting force of the Middle Military Division, the Army of the Shenandoah's tenure essentially coincided with Sheridan's Shenandoah Valley Campaign (August 7, 1864–March 2, 1865). Its principal task was to remove the threat posed by Confederate lieutenant general Jubal Early in the valley; keep Washington, D.C., safe from a Confederate advance through the valley; and ultimately destroy Early's force and anything of military or economic value in the Shenandoah Valley.

The Army of the Shenandoah, containing some 60,000 men at its peak, consisted of units from VI Corps of the Army of the Potomac, led by Major General Horatio Wright; the 1st and 2nd Divisions of XIX Corps, led by Brigadier General William Emory; the 1st and 3rd Divisions of the Cavalry Corps, Army of the Potomac, commanded by Brigadier General Alfred Torbert; and the Army of West Virginia, originally two divisions of infantry and one of cavalry, also known as VIII Corps and led by Brigadier General George Crook.

In the summer of 1864, Early's troops had conducted raids around Washington, D.C.; fought a fierce battle at Monocacy, Maryland, on July 9, 1864; and advanced as far as the suburbs of Washington. The nearby engagements had traumatized those in the federal capital, leading military planners to conclude that Early's army had to be neutralized or destroyed.

After considerable posturing and preparation, on September 19 the two valley armies collided in the savage fight of the Third Battle of Winchester. After his flank was turned, Early fell back with heavy losses. Sheridan then pressed his advantage, attacking the retreating Confederate force at Fisher's Hill on September 22. Sheridan used his cavalry to turn Early's flank once again, sending the Confederates deep into the valley. The Union troops continued their pursuit, destroying crops and barns along the way.

Sheridan reported the destruction of more than 2,000 barns filled with wheat, hay, and farming implements in addition to more than 70 mills. He had driven before the army more than 4,000 livestock and had killed and issued to the troops as meat no fewer than 3,000 sheep. Committed to a strategy of exhaustion, Sheridan emphasized his determination to destroy as many subsistence resources as possible. He was also determined to destroy Early.

When Early's army received modest reinforcements following the defeat at Fisher's Hill, scattered fighting resumed. Although still greatly outnumbered, Early decided to risk an attack in an effort to recover the valley for the Confederacy. On October 19, 1864, his troops surprised the Army of the Shenandoah at Cedar Creek near Strasburg. Catching Sheridan away conferring about the disposition of his forces, the Confederate assault achieved initial success, scattering two Union corps.

In an effort to stem the Confederate onslaught, Wright rallied the remaining troops. VI corps then stiffened, and instead of pressing the assault, the Confederates paused to gather shoes, clothing, and rations from the abandoned Union camps. Valuable time was lost, and Early, wrongly convinced that he had won a crushing victory, called a temporary halt to operations.

The tipping point at Cedar Creek came when Sheridan returned from Winchester. Sheridan's Ride became one of the epic events of the war, immortalized in art and song. By late afternoon, most of the Union units had re-formed, and the Army of the Shenandoah launched a devastating counterattack.

Early lost nearly 3,000 men, and the Battle of Cedar Creek finally broke his threadbare army. Union forces thereafter gained effective control of the valley and destroyed or expropriated practically every building, animal, and crop in the region. By the late autumn of 1864, campaigning had all but ended in the Shenandoah Valley.

On December 6, 1864, Wright's VI Corps rejoined the Army of the Potomac, and in January 1865 XIX Corps was split up, with one division sailing south to Savannah. In late February, Sheridan, with the 1st and 3rd Cavalry Divisions, marched to join Lieutenant General Ulysses S. Grant at Petersburg, leaving Torbert in command in the valley with a small force. After routing a sad remnant of Early's valley command at Waynesboro on March 2, Sheridan's all-mounted army reached the Petersburg front in late March.

In order to accommodate Sheridan as an independent commander, the 1st and 3rd Cavalry Divisions retained the designation Army of the Shenandoah through the Appomattox Campaign (April 2–9, 1865), with Brevet Major General Wesley Merritt commanding. The Army of the Shenandoah was dissolved on June 27, 1865.

DAVID M. KEITHLY AND DAVID COFFEY

See also

Cedar Creek, Battle of; Crook, George; Early, Jubal Anderson; Emory, William Hemsley; Fisher's Hill, Battle of; Merritt, Wesley; Monocacy, Battle of; Sheridan, Philip Henry; Sheridan's Shenandoah Valley Campaign; Torbert, Alfred Thomas Archimedes; Winchester, Third Battle of; Wright, Horatio Gouverneur

Further Reading

Catton, Bruce. *Never Call Retreat.* Garden City, NY: Doubleday, 1965.

Coffey, David. *Sheridan's Lieutenants: Phil Sheridan, His Generals, and the Final Year of the Civil War.* Lanham, MD: Rowman and Littlefield, 2005.

Welcher, Frank J. *The Union Army, 1862–1865: Organization and Operations,* Vol. 1, *The Eastern Theater.* Bloomington: Indiana University Press, 1989.

Shenandoah, Union Department of

Union military administrative unit. The Department of the Shenandoah existed twice between July 1861 and June 1862. The original department was activated on July 19, 1861, to include the Shenandoah Valley in western Virginia. The Maryland counties of Washington and Allegheny were added on July 25, when Major General Nathaniel P. Banks assumed command. On August 17, the department was merged into the Department of the Potomac. In April 1862 Banks assumed command of a reconstituted Department of the Shenandoah, to include Virginia west of the Blue Ridge

Mountains to the Alleghenies and the western counties of Maryland. The department was operational during Major General Thomas J. "Stonewall" Jackson's successful Shenandoah Valley Campaign (May–June 1862), during which he defeated elements of Banks's command at the Battle of Front Royal (May 23) and the First Battle of Winchester (May 25). This incarnation was dissolved in June 1862, with Banks's troops becoming II Corps, Army of Virginia.

DAVID COFFEY

See also

Banks, Nathaniel Prentice; Jackson, Thomas Jonathan; Jackson's Shenandoah Valley Campaign; Shenandoah Valley; Winchester, First Battle of

Further Reading

Eicher, John H., and David J. Eicher. *Civil War High Commands.* Stanford, CA: Stanford University Press, 2001.

Tanner, Robert G. *Stonewall in the Valley: Thomas J. "Stonewall" Jackson's Shenandoah Valley Campaign, Spring 1862.* Garden City, NY: Doubleday, 1976.

Shenandoah Valley

River valley located in western Virginia and the eastern panhandle of present-day West Virginia. The Shenandoah River consists of two forks that rise in the highlands of southern Virginia. The North Fork, about 95 miles long, and the South Fork, about 150 miles long, flow to the northeast on either side of the Masanutten Ridge. The two forks join at Fort Royal, Virginia, to form the main Shenandoah River, which flows north another 27 miles before emptying into the Potomac River at Harpers Ferry, West Virginia. Because of the northward flow of the river, proceeding down the valley meant going north, while proceeding up the valley meant to move to the south.

The Shenandoah Valley, through which the rivers flow, is one of a series of fertile valleys stretching along the eastern United States, between the Blue Ridge Mountains to the east and the Allegheny Mountains to the west. The Shenandoah Valley is bounded by the Potomac River in the north and becomes the Cumberland Valley in Pennsylvania, while to the south it is bounded by the James River and merges with the Roanoke Valley.

The Shenandoah Valley was of critical importance to the Confederacy during the Civil War. First, it was a heavily farmed region producing considerable quantities of grain; in fact, it was often called "the breadbasket of the Confederacy." Its importance was magnified by location in close proximity to one of the main areas of fighting in eastern Virginia.

The Shenandoah Valley was also strategically important as an invasion route north and south and because its northern extremity is only about 60 miles from Washington, D.C. The Blue Ridge Mountains on the eastern edge of the valley are high and sufficiently steep to mask movements north and south. Confederate general Robert E. Lee used this route for his invasion of Maryland in 1862 and of Pennsylvania in 1863.

Even more worrisome for the federal government, the vital Baltimore & Ohio Railroad crossed the Potomac River at Harpers Ferry at the northern end of the valley. The railroad was an attractive target for Confederate raids and was frequently cut and constantly threatened throughout the war.

Union forces made numerous attempts to secure the Shenandoah Valley, resulting in a number of campaigns and battles there. The most famous of these campaigns was most certainly Major General Thomas J. "Stonewall" Jackson's Shenandoah Valley Campaign (May–June 1862) in which he fought some 10 battles and skirmishes and defeated three separate Union armies. In July 1864 Confederate lieutenant general Jubal Early used the valley to launch his raid on Washington, D.C., and Major General Philip Sheridan destroyed much of the valley in his Shenandoah Valley Campaign (August 7, 1864–March 2, 1865) against Early's forces. The valley also experienced a good deal of guerrilla activity.

JOSEPH ADAMCZYK

See also
Baltimore & Ohio Railroad; Jackson's Shenandoah Valley Campaign; Sheridan's Shenandoah Valley Campaign; Virginia

Further Reading
Tanner, Robert G. *Stonewall in the Valley: Thomas J. Stonewall Jackson's Shenandoah Valley Campaign, Spring 1862.* Mechanicsburg, PA: Stackpole, 2002.
Wert, Jeffrey D. *From Winchester to Cedar Creek: The Shenandoah Campaign of 1864.* Mechanicsburg, PA: Stackpole, 1997.

Shenandoah Valley Campaigns

See Jackson's Shenandoah Valley Campaign; Sheridan's Shenandoah Valley Campaign

Shepherdstown, Virginia, Engagement at
Start Date: September 19, 1862
End Date: September 20, 1862

Last major engagement of Confederate general Robert E. Lee's Antietam Campaign (September 4–20, 1862). On September 18, 1862, one day after the Battle of Antietam, Lee and his battered army crossed the Potomac River at Boteler's Ford, a mile south of Shepherdstown in western Virginia. Knowing that if needed this ford was his army's only escape route from Maryland, Lee had ordered it protected since September 15 with two infantry brigades and 45 cannon under his chief of artillery, Brigadier General William Nelson Pendleton. Now as Lee withdrew southward, he left Pendleton's force as a rear guard to hold the ford and hinder Union major general George B. McClellan's pursuit.

On the morning of September 19, McClellan sent cavalry under Brigadier General Alfred Pleasanton to reconnoiter the ford and seize it if conditions were favorable. After assessing the Confederate defenses across the Potomac, Pleasanton wisely awaited reinforcements while shelling these positions. Late in the morning Major General Fitz John Porter arrived with his V Corps, and at nightfall he sent 2,000 infantrymen, commanded by Brigadier General Charles Griffin, across the river to assault Pendleton's defenses. Griffin's men seized four cannon before being ordered to stand down for the night. Panicked, Pendleton erroneously reported to Lee that Union troops had captured all his artillery.

On the morning of September 20, Porter sent four brigades across the Potomac to reinforce Griffin. Sweeping Pendleton's men aside, Griffin entered Shepherdstown, where he encountered Confederate major general A. P. Hill's Light Division. Believing that he was badly outnumbered, Griffin ordered his troops to fall back across the Potomac. The inexperienced 118th Pennsylvania Regiment, however, refused to retire and got pinned down by Hill's veterans. Panicked as the Confederates charged, they fled for the river. Several of them drowned as they attempted to swim across, and many others surrendered. They suffered 269 casualties out of a regiment of 737 men. For the rest of September 20, both sides held their positions, cannonading each other. Total Union casualties were 363; the Confederates suffered 291 losses.

PAUL DAVID NELSON

See also
Antietam Campaign; Griffin, Charles; Hill, Ambrose Powell; Lee, Robert Edward; Pendleton, William Nelson; Pleasonton, Alfred; Porter, Fitz John

Further Reading
McGrath, Thomas A. *Shepherdstown: Last Clash of the Antietam Campaign, September 19–20, 1862.* Lynchburg, VA: Schroeder, 2007.
Robertson, James I. *General A. P. Hill: The Story of a Confederate Warrior.* New York: Random House, 1987.

Shepley, George Foster

Birth Date: January 1, 1819
Death Date: July 20, 1878

Union officer. George Foster Shepley was born in Saco, Maine, on January 1, 1819. He studied law at Harvard University but graduated from Dartmouth College in 1837 and then was admitted to the bar in 1839. Shepley then engaged in private practice in Maine in Bangor (1839–1844) and Portland (1844–1861). He was a U.S. attorney for the District of Maine (1848–1849 and 1853–1861).

During the Civil War, Shepley was commissioned colonel of the 12th Maine Infantry on November 16, 1861. Assigned to the Department of the Gulf, he commanded a brigade in the New Orleans Campaign (April 18–May 1, 1862). He was military governor of New Orleans from May to July and then military governor of the Union-occupied parishes of Louisiana until March 1864. Shepley was appointed brigadier general of volunteers on July 18, 1862. After leaving Louisiana, he briefly headed a district in Virginia and was then chief of staff in XXV Corps, Army of the James, before serving as military governor of Richmond, Virginia, from April 3 to July 1, 1865, when he resigned his commission.

Shelby then returned to his legal profession in Portland and was a member of the Maine legislature (1866–1867). He continued in private practice until his appointment to a federal judgeship. Shepley held that post until his death in Portland, Maine, on July 20, 1878.

SPENCER C. TUCKER

See also

Louisiana; New Orleans, Louisiana; New Orleans Campaign; Richmond, Virginia; Richmond, Virginia, Surrender of

Further Reading

Eicher, John H., and David J. Eicher. *Civil War High Commands.* Stanford, CA: Stanford University Press, 2001.

Winters, John D. *The Civil War in Louisiana.* Reprint. Baton Rouge: Louisiana State University Press, 2003.

Sheridan, Philip Henry

Birth Date: ca. March 6, 1831
Death Date: August 5, 1888

Union officer. Born in Albany, New York, to Irish immigrant parents probably on March 6, 1831 (the date and place of birth are not known with certainty), Philip Henry Sheridan grew up in Somerset, Ohio. Too young to serve in the Mexican-American War (1846–1848), he attended the U.S.

Military Academy, West Point. Suspended for one year for disciplinary reasons, he graduated in 1853 and was commissioned a second lieutenant in the infantry. Sheridan then served with the 1st Infantry Regiment in Texas and with the 4th Infantry Regiment in Oregon, being promoted to first lieutenant in March 1861 on the eve of the Civil War.

Assigned to the western theater, Sheridan was promoted to captain in May 1861 and served in the 13th Infantry Regiment in southwestern Missouri and then served as quartermaster for Department of the Missouri commander Major General Henry W. Halleck during the Siege of Corinth (May 3–30, 1862). Sheridan intensely disliked staff duty and secured a transfer to the volunteer establishment as colonel of the 2nd Michigan Cavalry in May. His subsequent victory at Booneville, Mississippi, on July 1, 1862, earned him promotion to brigadier general of volunteers that September.

Sheridan commanded an infantry division and distinguished himself in the Battle of Perryville (October 8, 1862) in Kentucky and especially at the Battle of Stones River (December 31, 1862–January 2, 1863), where he perhaps saved from defeat Major General William S. Rosecrans's Army of the Cumberland. For this action, Sheridan was promoted to major general of volunteers (March 1863, with date of rank from December 31, 1862). In the Battle of Chickamauga (September 19–20, 1863), Sheridan gained laurels while in command of a division of XX Corps in the Army of the Cumberland when, after his command was caught up in the breakthrough and routed, he participated in the stand that saved the army. His men played a key role in the Union victory of the Battle of Chattanooga (November 23–25, 1853), assaulting Missionary Ridge.

When Ulysses S. Grant was promoted to lieutenant general and became the army's general in chief, he selected Sheridan to command the Army of the Potomac's Cavalry Corps of three divisions and 10,000 men. During the spring and summer of 1864, Sheridan's men won a number of victories against the weakened Confederate cavalry. Sheridan's forces took part in Grant's Overland Campaign (May 4–June 12, 1864), disrupting Confederate lines of communication, including tearing up sections of railroad track and destroying telegraph lines. Sheridan was victorious in the Battle of Yellow Tavern (May 11, 1864) in Virginia, where Confederate cavalry commander Major General James E. B. Stuart was mortally wounded. Sheridan's forces were defeated at the Battle of Trevilian Station (June 11–12, 1864), however.

In August, Grant gave Sheridan command of the Middle Military Division and its field force, the Army of the Shenandoah, and instructed him to drive the Confederates from the

Major General Philip Henry Sheridan was one of the principal Union cavalry commanders of the Civil War. In late 1864, he secured control of, and largely destroyed, the Shenandoah Valley of Virginia. Sheridan went on to become commanding general of the U.S. Army as a lieutenant general during 1885–1888. (National Archives)

Shenandoah Valley and destroy any supplies that might be of use to the Confederacy. Sheridan tangled with Confederate forces under Lieutenant General Jubal Early in the Shenandoah Valley and defeated Early in the Third Battle of Winchester (September 19, 1864) and at the Battle of Fisher's Hill (September 22, 1864). For this accomplishment, Sheridan was advanced to brigadier general in the regular army.

Sheridan was away and his army was caught off guard when Early attacked at Cedar Creek (October 18, 1864). Riding to the sound of the guns, Sheridan galloped south from Winchester (Sheridan's Ride) and helped to rally his army to victory. He then proceeded to lay waste to the Shenandoah Valley, depriving the Confederates of much-needed supplies. The extent of this destruction is seen in his boast that "A crow couldn't fly from Winchester to Staunton without taking its rations along."

Promoted to major general in the regular army (November 1864), Sheridan finished off Early in the Battle of Waynesboro (March 2, 1865) in Virginia and then marched with his cavalry to Petersburg, where he rejoined Grant. Sheridan played a major role in the final defeat of General Robert E. Lee's Army of Northern Virginia, routing the Confederates at the Battle of Five Forks (April 1) and the Battle of Sayler's Creek (April 6) near Farmville, Virginia, before trapping Lee's army near Appomattox Court House, leading to the Confederate surrender on April 9, 1865.

Sheridan was then ordered to Texas with a large force to encourage the French to quit Mexico. He remained in Texas as commander of the Military Division of the Gulf (May 1865–March 1867) and then commanded the Fifth Military District of Louisiana and Texas (March 1867), but his harsh policies soon brought his removal (September 1867).

Sheridan then took over the Department of the Missouri (September 1867) and as such was responsible for the federal effort against the hostile western Indians. When Grant became president and William T. Sherman moved up to command the army as a full general, Sheridan was promoted to lieutenant general (March 1869) and assumed command of the vast Military Division of the Missouri.

Sheridan then traveled to Europe, where he was an official observer attached to the Prussian Army during the Franco-Prussian War (1870–1871). Returning to the United States, he directed the campaign against the Sioux that resulted in the Battle of the Little Big Horn (June 25–26, 1876).

Sheridan succeeded Sherman as commanding general of the Army (1883) and was promoted to general (June 1888). Sheridan died at Nonquitt, Massachusetts, on August 5, 1888. Known as "Little Phil," Sheridan was blunt and outspoken. He was also industrious, offensive-minded, aggressive, and a superb tactical commander.

SPENCER C. TUCKER

See also

Appomattox Campaign; Appomattox Court House and Lee's Surrender; Booneville, Battle of; Chattanooga Campaign; Cedar Creek, Battle of; Chickamauga, Battle of; Corinth, Mississippi, Siege of; Early, Jubal Anderson; Fisher's Hill, Battle of; Five Forks, Battle of; Grant, Ulysses Simpson; Halleck, Henry Wager; Lee, Robert Edward; Overland Campaign; Perryville, Battle of; Rosecrans, William Starke; Sayler's Creek, Battle of; Sheridan's Richmond Raid; Sheridan's Virginia Raid; Stones River, Battle of; Stuart, James Ewell Brown; Trevilian Station, Battle of; Waynesboro, Virginia, Battle of; Winchester, Third Battle of; Yellow Tavern, Battle of

Further Reading

Hutton, Paul Andrew. *Phil Sheridan and His Army.* Lincoln: University of Nebraska Press, 1985.

Morris, Roy. *Sheridan: The Life and Wars of General Phil Sheridan.* New York: Crown, 1992.

O'Connor, Richard. *Sheridan the Inevitable.* Indianapolis: Bobbs-Merrill, 1953.

Sheridan's Richmond Raid
Start Date: May 9, 1864
End Date: May 24, 1864

Union cavalry raid by Major General Philip H. Sheridan's forces. Sheridan's Richmond Raid occurred as part of Union general in chief Lieutenant General Ulysses S. Grant's Overland (Richmond) Campaign against Confederate general Robert E. Lee's Army of Northern Virginia (May 4–June 12, 1864). Grant ordered Sheridan's force of three cavalry divisions, commanded by Brigadier Generals Wesley Merritt, David Gregg, and James Wilson, totaling 12,000 men and 32 guns, to raid Richmond, disrupt Confederate lines of communication, and defeat Confederate cavalry.

Sheridan's divisions set out from Spotsylvania Court House on May 9. Sheridan hoped to lure Confederate major general J. E. B. Stuart out of Richmond and defeat the Confederate cavalry. Stuart almost immediately learned of the raid and began a pursuit with Major General Fitzhugh Lee's division, consisting of Brigadier Generals Lunsford Lomax's and Williams Wickham's brigades along with Brigadier General James B. Gordon's independent brigade.

Sheridan's forces came in contact with the Confederates when Wickham's cavalry forces engaged Sheridan's rear guard near Jarrald's Mill; the Union troopers repulsed Wickham near Mitchell's Shop. After dusk on May 9, Sheridan's troopers reached the North Anna River. Two of the divisions made camp there, but Merritt's division continued on across the river at Anderson's Ford to Beaver Dam Station on the Virginia Central Railroad. Brigadier General George A. Custer led the attack. There Confederate guards fired the depot, but the Union cavalrymen destroyed 100 Confederate railcars and 2 locomotives and freed some 200 Union prisoners. The following day, Sheridan dispatched a brigade to Ashland, some 20 miles north of Richmond, there to destroy railroad track, supplies, and equipment.

The major confrontation with the Confederates during the raid came late on the morning of May 11, when Sheridan's advance guard made contact with dismounted Confederates at 11:00 a.m. just north of Yellow Tavern. Sheridan took time to deploy his seven brigades in the hope of destroying Stuart. In the ensuing Battle of Yellow Tavern, Sheridan's cavalrymen flanked Stuart and forced him to withdraw east. Meanwhile, Gordon attacked Sheridan's rear. Sheridan spent much of the afternoon repositioning his forces to pressure Stuart's right flank. The 1st Michigan seized a battery that was key to Confederate resistance, and

both Wickham's and Lomax's troopers withdrew, leaving the road to Richmond open. Stuart now gathered the 1st Virginia and counterattacked. As the Confederates drove the Federals back, Stuart led his men in taking up position along a fence, firing at the Federals. As Union private John Huff of the 5th Michigan Cavalry rode past, he fired at Stuart and hit him in the abdomen; Stuart died the following night. After dealing with the Confederates to his front, Sheridan then repulsed Gordon to his rear, sending the Confederates there back in disarray.

After tending to the dead and wounded, Sheridan set his men in motion toward Richmond at 3:00 a.m. on May 12. Probing the Confederate capital, Sheridan discovered that the city was well defended, and he turned toward Mechanicsville to link up with Union forces there under Major General Benjamin Butler. Sheridan's troops encountered heavy resistance near Fair Oaks from Confederate artillery stationed at Mechanicsville and breastworks thrown up by civilians along the road. Meanwhile, Gordon's cavalrymen continued to engage the Union rear, with Gordon suffering a mortal wound.

Sheridan's troopers crossed the Chickahominy River on May 12 and two days later arrived at Butler's lines at Haxall's Landing. They remained in the vicinity until May 24, at which time they rejoined the main Union army on the North Anna River.

The Richmond Raid was Sheridan's first independent cavalry action. He had ridden completely around Lee's army, destroyed supplies, disrupted communications, and defeated the Confederates in four separate engagements. The raid also had led to Stuart's death, a major loss for the Confederacy.

R. Ray Ortensie

See also

Butler, Benjamin Franklin; Custer, George Armstrong; Gordon, James Byron; Grant, Ulysses Simpson; Gregg, David McMurtrie; Lee, Fitzhugh; Lee, Robert Edward; Lomax, Lunsford Lindsay; Merritt, Wesley; Overland Campaign; Richmond, Virginia; Sheridan, Philip Henry; Stuart, James Ewell Brown; Wickham, Williams Carter; Wilson, James Harrison; Yellow Tavern, Battle of

Further Reading

Longacre, Edward G. *Lee's Cavalrymen: A History of the Mounted Forces of the Army of Northern Virginia.* Mechanicsburg, PA: Stackpole, 2002.

Longacre, Edward G. *Mounted Raids of the Civil War.* Lincoln: University of Nebraska Press, 1994.

Rhea, Gordon C. *The Battles for Spotsylvania Court House and the Road to Yellow Tavern, May 7–12, 1864.* Baton Rouge: Louisiana State University Press, 2005.

Sheridan's Shenandoah Valley Campaign
Start Date: August 7, 1864
End Date: March 2, 1865

Major Union offensive directed by Major General Philip H. Sheridan in and around Virginia's Shenandoah Valley. When Union general in chief Lieutenant General Ulysses S. Grant laid out his plans for the great offensives of 1864, including his own massive effort against General Robert E. Lee's Army of Northern Virginia, the Shenandoah Valley figured prominently. But Union forces had seen little prior success in the much contested valley, and opening clashes of 1864 brought more frustration. As Grant and Lee slugged it out in northern Virginia, on May 15 Confederate major general John C. Breckinridge's ragtag force humiliated the Union command of Major General Franz Sigel at New Market. Major General David Hunter replaced Sigel and waged a vengeful campaign of destruction, which included the burning of the Virginia Military Institute, before moving toward Lynchburg to threaten Lee's rail communications. On June 12, Lee ordered Lieutenant General Jubal A. Early and II Corps of the Army of Northern Virginia to Lynchburg, where on June 17–18 Early's forces beat back feeble probes by Hunter, who then pulled back into West Virginia, leaving the Shenandoah Valley to the Confederates and the path to the federal capital wide open.

In addition to its rich farmland, the Shenandoah Valley offered a natural corridor for invasion, as Lee had demonstrated during his advances into Maryland in 1862 and Pennsylvania in 1863. Having absorbed Breckinridges's troops into his command, Early organized his Army of the Valley into two corps, commanded by Breckinridge and Major General Robert Rodes, supported by several cavalry and artillery units. On June 28, Early's 14,000-man force marched from Staunton for a diversionary raid on Washington, hoping to relieve the pressure on Lee's army. Reaching Harpers Ferry on July 4, the Confederate raiders moved into Maryland, striking the Baltimore & Ohio (B&O) Railroad and occupying Hagerstown and Frederick, from which the Confederates collected large cash ransoms. On July 10 at Monocacy, Maryland, a hastily assembled Union force commanded by Major General Lew Wallace slowed Early's advance and bought time for Washington's defenders. After dispatching Wallace's valiant little command, Early pressed on to the outer defenses of the capital, which had been significantly reinforced. Having caused much excitement and

anxiety, Early finally turned back for the valley. He then defeated Brigadier General George Crook's West Virginia command at Kernstown on July 23 and appeared poised for another shot at Washington, once again hitting the B&O and sending his cavalry into Pennsylvania. When local leaders refused to pay an exorbitant ransom on Early's instructions, the Confederates torched Chambersburg, Pennsylvania.

Grant was determined to put an end to the menace. The situation required a unified command and an accomplished leader. On August 7, the War Department announced the establishment of the Middle Military Division, which embraced the Middle Department and the Departments of Washington, the Susquehanna, and West Virginia, with Major General Philip H. Sheridan in command. Sheridan, who had commanded the Cavalry Corps of the Army of the Potomac, was a controversial choice but had Grant's confidence. Sheridan's mission was to terminate the threat posed by Early's forces in the Shenandoah Valley and then to destroy the valley's usefulness—militarily and materially—to the Confederacy and in so doing discourage continued civilian support for the war. Sheridan was given a powerful instrument to accomplish these tasks; his Army of the Shenandoah represented a new and very lethal model.

Sheridan's force included Major General Horatio Wright's steady VI Corps from the Army of the Potomac; XIX Corps, commanded by Brigadier General William Emory, that had recently arrived in the theater after service in Louisiana; and the so-called Army of West Virginia, also known as VIII Corps, commanded by Brigadier General George Crook. What distinguished Sheridan's new command from others was the large and formidable cavalry component (a one-to-five ratio of cavalry to infantry). The Cavalry Corps, commanded by Brigadier General Alfred Torbert, included the 1st and 3rd Divisions from the Army of the Potomac and a division from the Army of West Virginia. It took many days for the various elements to arrive at Halltown and prepare for the coming offensive. In the meantime, Sheridan and Early timidly maneuvered and skirmished.

On September 19, 1864, Sheridan flung his 40,000-man army against Early's force of half that size at Winchester. The Third Battle of Winchester featured intense infantry fighting in which the outnumbered Confederates held their ground until a massive cavalry charge late in the engagement destroyed the Confederate left, while a general advance by the infantry finished the job. Early managed to withdraw what remained of his army, and a stubborn rearguard action by Major General S. Dodson Ramseur's division allowed the

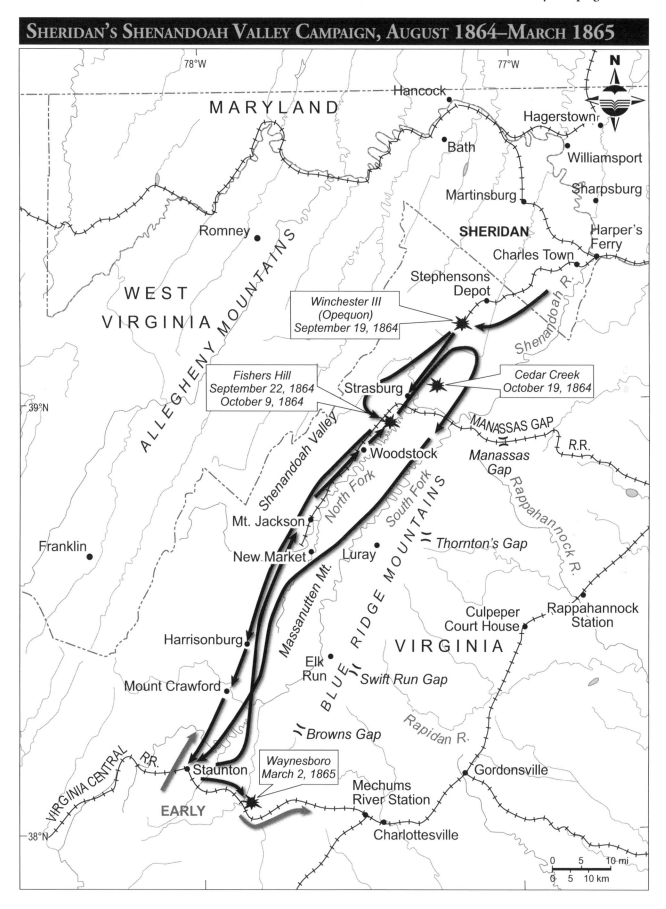

SHERIDAN'S SHENANDOAH VALLEY CAMPAIGN, AUGUST 1864–MARCH 1865

78°W

77°W

N

MARYLAND

Hancock

Hagerstown

Bath

Williamsport

Martinsburg

Sharpsburg

Romney

SHERIDAN

WEST

Charles Town

Harper's Ferry

VIRGINIA

Stephensons Depot

39°N

Winchester III (Opequon) September 19, 1864

Shenandoah R.

Fishers Hill September 22, 1864 October 9, 1864

Strasburg

Cedar Creek October 19, 1864

MANASSAS GAP

R.R.

Woodstock

Manassas Gap

Shenandoah Valley

North Fork

South Fork

Rappahannock R.

Mt. Jackson

Franklin

New Market

Luray

Thornton's Gap

BLUE RIDGE MOUNTAINS

Culpeper Court House

Rappahannock Station

VIRGINIA

Harrisonburg

Massanutten Mt.

Elk Run

Swift Run Gap

Mount Crawford

Browns Gap

Rapidan R.

VIRGINIA CENTRAL R.R.

Staunton

Waynesboro March 2, 1865

Gordonsville

Mechums River Station

EARLY

38°N

Charlottesville

0   5   10 mi

0   5   10 km

Confederates to save most of their baggage and artillery. Unfortunately for Sheridan, Brigadier General James H. Wilson's cavalry failed to cut Early's escape route, enabling the Confederates to fall back to a strong position at Fisher's Hill, some 20 miles to the south. Confederate casualties exceeded 4,000, half of which were captured or missing, including valued division commander Robert Rodes, killed in action, while Sheridan lost 5,000.

Sheridan pressed the initiative, advancing on Early's position at Fisher's Hill. On September 22, Sheridan sent VI and XIX Corps forward in a large demonstration to hold Early in place, while Crook's command, after marching overnight undetected to a concealed position on the Confederate left, crashed into the Confederate flank. As Crook's men struck, Sheridan unleashed the main line in a frontal assault up the ridge. Again the Confederate position crumbled as panicked units fled southward. This comparatively small affair resulted in only 600 Union casualties. Surprisingly, Early lost only 250 killed or wounded, but another 1,000 were captured or missing, and Early also lost 14 guns. Darkness, rain, and the inability of the cavalry to block the escape route prevented the total destruction of the Confederate force.

The cavalry had managed to take Front Royal on September 21 and dueled with Confederate horsemen the following day, but Torbert's lack of aggressiveness prevented it from sealing the deal at Fisher's Hill. On September 25, Sheridan, responding to an order from Grant, sent Wilson off to command the mounted arm of Major General William T. Sherman's force in Georgia, which facilitated the promotion of the young and aggressive Brigadier General George A. Custer to head the 3rd Cavalry Division.

Early's army meanwhile melted into the Blue Ridge Mountains awaiting reinforcement—Major General Joseph Kershaw's division and Brigadier General Thomas Rosser's brigade of cavalry from Lee's Army of Northern Virginia. The temporary disappearance of Confederate resistance allowed Sheridan to initiate the most unsavory aspect of the campaign, the utter and often wanton destruction of the valley. Although most of Sheridan's men found the work—the burning of crops, barns, and mills and the killing or driving off of livestock—distasteful in the extreme, they carried it out with incredible precision and thoroughness, occasioning in the process much suffering. After cutting a swath of devastation up the valley and seeing nothing from Early, Sheridan backtracked, trailing thousands of refugees of war. Early now sent the newly arrived Rosser to snap at the Union column. By October 8, Sheridan had had enough. The following day, Brigadier General Wesley Merritt's 1st Division

and Custer's 3rd Division routed Rosser's command at Tom's Brook. Sheridan, having believed that Early was largely finished, prepared to return VI Corps to the Army of the Potomac at Petersburg while the rest of the command moved into camps at Cedar Creek, near Middletown.

Sheridan also became involved in a disagreement with his superiors over how his army should next be employed. The debate compelled him to recall VI Corps. Secretary of War Edwin Stanton hoped to get his generals to agree by summoning Sheridan to Washington for a conference. On October 15, Sheridan traveled to the capital, leaving General Wright in command.

Early was not quite finished, however. He sent Major General John B. Gordon to examine the Union encampment. Gordon then devised a bold plan involving a daring night march followed by a surprise predawn attack on October 19. This four-division assault achieved total surprise in the Battle of Cedar Creek, routing Crook's command and XIX Corps before Wright and VI Corps managed to stabilize the situation. Sheridan, who had spent the night before in Winchester, rode to the sound of the guns, arriving on the field at about the time Early suspended the attack. Sheridan then directed an afternoon counterattack that swept the Confederates from the field. The largest battle of the campaign claimed 6,000 Union and 3,000 Confederate casualties. Sheridan assumed hero status, and victory helped cement President Abraham Lincoln's 1864 reelection.

Sheridan spent the rest of the year battling guerrilla activity and fending off Grant's attempts to get him to move against the Virginia Central Railroad. Sheridan and Early each lost significant portions of their armies during December 1864. Finally, having sent off most of his infantry, Sheridan with two divisions of cavalry marched on the Virginia Central preparatory to a reunion with Grant's army. At Waynesboro on March 2, 1865, Early made one last stand with a tiny force of 2,000, which Sheridan easily overwhelmed, taking 1,600 prisoners and all of the Rebels' baggage and artillery.

DAVID COFFEY

See also

Breckinridge, John Cabell; Cedar Creek, Battle of; Chambersburg, Pennsylvania, Burning of; Custer, George Armstrong; Early, Jubal Anderson; Early's Raid on Washington, D.C.; Fisher's Hill, Battle of; Gordon, John Brown; Grant, Ulysses Simpson; Hunter, David; Kershaw, Joseph Brevard; Merritt, Wesley; New Market, Battle of; Ramseur, Stephen Dodson; Rodes, Robert Emmett; Shenandoah Valley; Sheridan, Philip Henry; Tom's Brook, Battle of; Wallace, Lewis; Waynesboro, Virginia, Battle of; Winchester, Third Battle of; Wright, Horatio Gouverneur

Further Reading

Coffey, David. *Sheridan's Lieutenants: Phil Sheridan, His Generals, and the Final Year of the Civil War.* Lanham, MD: Rowman and Littlefield, 2005.

Gallagher, Gary W. *The Shenandoah Valley Campaign of 1864.* Chapel Hill: University of North Carolina Press, 2009.

Wert, Jeffry D. *From Winchester to Cedar Creek: The Shenandoah Campaign of 1864.* Mechanicsburg, PA: Stackpole, 1997.

Sheridan's Virginia Raid
Start Date: February 27, 1865
End Date: March 26, 1865

Union cavalry raid from the Shenandoah Valley to Petersburg. On October 19, 1864, in the northern Shenandoah Valley, Union major general Philip H. Sheridan's Army of the Shenandoah defeated Lieutenant General Jubal A. Early's Confederates in the Battle of Cedar Creek. During the rest of the autumn and that winter, Sheridan continued his destruction of crops and livestock, preventing vital stores from reaching General Robert E. Lee's Army of Northern Virginia. Most of Early's men, meanwhile, rejoined Lee at Petersburg. Military actions in the valley were limited to light skirmishing and combating partisans.

On February 20, 1865, Union general in chief Lieutenant General Ulysses S. Grant ordered Sheridan to proceed south to Lynchburg and there destroy the Confederate rail and supply center and rail lines from there in all directions as well as the adjacent James River Canal. The Virginia Central Railroad was especially important in supplying Lee's army at Petersburg. Following this, Sheridan was then to move into North Carolina to join with forces under Major General William T. Sherman.

On February 27, Sheridan departed Winchester with two cavalry divisions of 10,000 men and proceeded southward. On March 1, his men forced Early to evacuate Staunton. The next day at Waynesboro, some 12 miles east of Staunton, part of the Army of the Shenandoah under Major General George A. Custer attacked and destroyed the remnants of Early's command of some 1,700 men, the only Confederate force of any strength left in the valley. Both sides suffered fewer than 100 killed or wounded, although the Union troopers also took 1,500 prisoners, a dozen guns, and several hundred

Sketch of Union major general Philip Sheridan's Army of the Shenandoah in the Shenandoah Valley of Virginia, February or March 1864. (Library of Congress)

wagons. Early and some of his staff managed to escape, but the battle ended organized Confederate resistance in the valley and marked the end of Sheridan's Shenandoah Valley Campaign (August 7, 1864–March 2, 1865).

Sheridan then continued south. Electing not to attack heavily defended Lynchburg, he spent the next three weeks destroying farms, mills, crops, and supplies as well as tearing up track of the Virginia Central Railroad and destroying the James River Canal. Grant's orders gave Sheridan wide discretion, and Sheridan decided that instead of proceeding to North Carolina, he would rejoin the Army of the Potomac at Petersburg.

Sheridan wrote in his memoirs that "Feeling that the war was nearing its end, I desired my cavalry to be in at the death." Sheridan arrived at Petersburg on March 26, bringing Grant's strength up to 122,000 men, more than double that of Lee's force.

Sheridan played a key role in the actions to follow. On April 1, his men cut off Lee's lines of communication at Five Forks, sealing the fate of Richmond and Petersburg and forcing Lee to evacuate. In the Battle of Sayler's Creek (April 6, 1865), Sheridan effectively sealed the fate of Lee's army, capturing more than a fifth of his remaining men, and on April 9 Sheridan blocked Lee's remaining escape route at Appomattox Court House, forcing the surrender of the Army of Northern Virginia.

SPENCER C. TUCKER

See also

Appomattox Campaign; Custer, George Armstrong; Early, Jubal Anderson; Five Forks, Battle of; Grant, Ulysses Simpson; Lee, Robert Edward; Petersburg Campaign; Sayler's Creek, Battle of; Sheridan, Philip Henry; Sherman, William Tecumseh; Waynesboro, Virginia, Battle of

Further Reading

Gallagher, Gary. *The Shenandoah Valley Campaign of 1864.* Chapel Hill: University of North Carolina Press, 2006.

Mahon, Michael G. *The Shenandoah Valley, 1861–1865: The Destruction of the Granary of the Confederacy.* Mechanicsburg, PA: Stackpole, 1999.

Stackpole, Edward. *Sheridan in the Shenandoah: Jubal Early's Nemesis.* Harrisburg, PA: Stackpole, 1992.

Sherman, John
Birth Date: May 10, 1823
Death Date: October 22, 1900

Republican politician. Born on May 10, 1823, in Lancaster, Ohio, John Sherman was the younger brother of General William T. Sherman. John Sherman began the study of law at age 14. Admitted to the bar in 1844, he established a practice in Mansfield, Ohio, before moving to Cleveland in 1853. Active in politics as a member of the Whig Party and strongly opposed to slavery, Sherman helped to organize the new Republican Party in Ohio after passage of the 1854 Kansas-Nebraska Act, which he vociferously opposed. That same year, he was elected to the first of three successive terms in the U.S. House of Representatives. As chairman of the powerful Ways and Means Committee from 1859 to 1861, Sherman quickly rose to political prominence.

In 1861 Sherman won election to the U.S. Senate, where he served until 1877. As chairman of the Senate Finance Committee, he played a crucial role in formulating government financial policy during the Reconstruction era. Although he had supported the use of paper money (greenbacks) during the Civil War, he deplored the inflationary effects of relying on anything but gold as the foundation of the nation's monetary system. In 1875 he oversaw the enactment of the Specie Resumption Act.

In 1877 Sherman left the Senate to assume the post of secretary of the treasury in the Rutherford B. Hayes administration. Sherman served as treasury secretary until March 1881. Later that year, he was once more elected to the U.S. Senate to take up the seat vacated by James A. Garfield, who had been elected president. Sherman served until 1897.

Although unsuccessful in securing the Republican nomination for president in 1880, 1884, and 1888, Sherman gave his name to two important pieces of legislation passed in 1890. The first was the Sherman Antitrust Act (1890), which made it a crime for business firms to combine to prevent competition. The second was the Sherman Silver Purchase Act (1890), which dramatically increased the amount of silver purchased by the federal government. The consequences of this act proved to be disastrous for the U.S. Treasury, however, during the economic depression of 1893–1897.

President William McKinley appointed Sherman secretary of state in 1897. The move proved to be a poor choice. The combination of Sherman's advanced age, failing memory, and staunch opposition to the acquisition of overseas colonies led McKinley to request that Sherman resign from the cabinet in April 1898. Sherman died in Washington, D.C., on October 22, 1900.

PAUL G. PIERPAOLI JR.

See also

Congress, U.S.; Financing, U.S.; Greenbacks; Kansas-Nebraska Act; Reconstruction

Further Reading
Burton, Theodore. *John Sherman.* 1906; reprint, New York: AMS, 1972.
Sherman, John. *Recollections of Forty Years in the House, Senate, and Cabinet.* 2 vols. 1895; reprint, New York: Greenwood, 1968.

Sherman, Thomas West
Birth Date: March 26, 1813
Death Date: March 16, 1879

Union officer. Thomas West Sherman was born in Newport, Rhode Island, on March 26, 1813. In 1832, disappointed with his education choices, which were limited by his family's low income, he walked more than 400 miles to Washington, D.C., where he managed to secure an audience with President Andrew Jackson. Sherman had hoped to win an appointment to the U.S. Military Academy at West Point. Jackson was so impressed that he assured Sherman a spot in the class of 1836. After graduation that year, Sherman served as a second lieutenant in the 3rd Artillery Regiment during the Second Seminole War (1835–1842) and participated in the removal of the Cherokees to Indian Territory (Oklahoma). Promoted to first lieutenant in 1838 and to captain in 1846, Sherman was assigned to a variety of duties. During the Mexican-American War (1846–1848), he won a brevet promotion to major for his role in the Battle of Buena Vista.

Following the Mexican-American War, Sherman served at posts in New England, on the Minnesota frontier, and in Kansas. He commanded a small expedition to put down a Sioux rebellion in the Dakota Territory in 1859.

Following the start of the Civil War, Sherman was promoted to major in the 3rd Artillery. On May 21, 1861, he assumed command of all the light batteries in the Department of Washington, D.C., and was promoted to lieutenant colonel of the 5th Artillery. On August 6, 1861, he was appointed brigadier general of volunteers. After commanding the ground forces in the Port Royal Expedition in November, he then was dispatched to the western theater, where he commanded a division during the Siege of Corinth (May 3–30, 1862) in Mississippi.

In September 1862, Sherman was in charge of the Union position at Carrollton, Louisiana. In January 1863, he took command of a division in XIX Corps. On May 27, 1863, Sherman was wounded severely during the Port Hudson Campaign, requiring the amputation of his right leg. At the end of the war, he commanded the defenses of New Orleans. He was brevetted major general in both the regulars and volunteers.

After mustering out of the volunteer army, he served in the U.S. Army as a colonel. He subsequently commanded posts from New England to Key West, Florida, retiring in 1870 as a major general. He died in Newport, Rhode Island, on March 16, 1879.

CHARLES F. HOWLETT

See also
Banks, Nathaniel Prentice; Corinth, Mississippi, Siege of; Port Hudson, Louisiana, Action at; Thomas, George Henry; Washington, D.C., Defenses of

Further Reading
Eicher, John H., and David J. Eicher. *Civil War High Commands.* Stanford, CA: Stanford University Press, 2001.
Hewitt, Lawrence. *Port Hudson: Confederate Bastion on the Mississippi.* Baton Rouge: Louisiana State University Press, 1987.

Sherman, William Tecumseh
Birth Date: February 8, 1820
Death Date: February 14, 1891

Union officer. Born in Lancaster, Ohio, on February 8, 1820, William Tecumseh Sherman graduated 5th in his class of 42 from the U.S. Military Academy, West Point, in 1840 and was commissioned a second lieutenant of artillery. He fought in the Second Seminole War (1835–1842) in Florida and was promoted to first lieutenant (November 1841). During the Mexican-American War (1846–1848), Sherman was a staff officer under Colonel Stephen Kearny in California, winning a brevet promotion to captain. Sherman made permanent captain two years later, in June 1850.

Resigning his commission in 1853, Sherman became the agent for a St. Louis–based banking firm, but the parent bank failed in 1857. Sherman then briefly practiced law in Kansas and was superintendent of the Alexandria Military Academy (later Louisiana State University) from 1859 to 1861. Sherman had great affection for the South, but when Louisiana seceded from the Union, he resigned his position in January 1861 and moved to St. Louis.

Sherman reentered the U.S. Army as colonel of the new 13th Infantry Regiment in May 1861 and commanded a brigade in the First Battle of Bull Run (July 21, 1861). Appointed a brigadier general of volunteers that August, he was ordered to the western theater to help hold Kentucky for the Union. There his eccentric behavior prompted questions about his sanity. Temporarily relieved of his duties, he returned in Major General Henry W. Halleck's Department of the Missouri in February 1862 and assumed command

Major General William Tecumseh Sherman was one of the principal Union field commanders of the Civil War. Sherman commanded the armies that took Atlanta and then pushed to the sea and through the Carolinas. Sherman was subsequently the commanding general of the U.S. Army. (National Archives)

of the Cairo Military District, Brigadier General Ulysses S. Grant's former post.

Assuming command of a division in Grant's Army of the Tennessee, Sherman distinguished himself in the Battle of Shiloh (April 6–7, 1862), where he was slightly wounded. Promoted to major general of volunteers in May, he developed a close friendship with Grant and by that summer was Grant's principal subordinate. Sherman participated in Halleck's Corinth Campaign (May 3–30, 1862) and then the effort to take Vicksburg, where Sherman was rebuffed in fighting north of the city in the Battle of Chickasaw Bluffs (December 26–29, 1862). Sherman then led II Corps of the Army of the Mississippi and took part in the capture of Arkansas Post (January 11, 1863). His force then transferred to the Army of the Tennessee as XV Corps, and Sherman aided Grant in the capture of Vicksburg (July 4, 1863), for which Sherman was promoted to regular army brigadier general in July.

When Grant took charge in the western theater, he assigned Sherman command of the Army of the Tennessee in October 1863. Sherman then led the Union left wing in the Battle of Chattanooga (November 23–25). When Grant became Union Army general in chief, Sherman took command of the Military Division of the Mississippi in March 1864, for all practical purposes overall command of the western theater.

With his Armies of the Cumberland, the Tennessee, and the Ohio, Sherman launched a campaign against General Joseph E. Johnston's Confederate Army of Tennessee in May 1864, driving toward Atlanta, Georgia. Sherman made steady, if slow (100 miles in 74 days), progress against Johnston, who was replaced by General John Bell Hood in July. Sherman also won a series of battles against the offensive-minded Hood before resorting to a siege and ultimately occupying the major rail center of Atlanta on September 2. For this accomplishment, Sherman received the Thanks of Congress and promotion to regular army major general.

Destroying such military stocks as would not be of use to him and detaching part of his force to deal with Hood in Tennessee, Sherman began his March to the Sea on November 16, 1864. He was very much a modern general in the sense that he practiced total war, and he believed that destroying property would likely bring the war to a speedier end than would the taking of lives. Sherman encouraged his armies to forage liberally off the land, cutting a wide swath of destruction through Georgia. Reaching the coast, his forces occupied Savannah on December 21, 1864.

Turning northward, Sherman began a drive through the Carolinas on February 1, 1865, taking Columbia, South Carolina, on February 17. The city was burned, but retreating Confederate troops rather than Sherman were probably to blame. After a few last engagements, Sherman accepted the surrender of the Confederate field army under General Johnston near Durham Station, North Carolina, on April 26.

Following the war, in June 1865 Sherman took command of the Division of the Missouri. When Grant was promoted to general in July 1866, Sherman was advanced to lieutenant general, and when Grant became president in March 1869, Sherman moved up to become commanding general of the army as a full general. During his years in command, the army successfully prosecuted wars with Native Americans in the West. Here a chief concern was to protect the railroads. Sherman also practiced against the Native Americans the same sort of war as he had in 1864–1865, seeking to destroy food stocks and other resources in order to bring the fighting to a speedier conclusion. At the same time, however, he strongly opposed speculators and corrupt Indian agents who profited at Native American expense.

On June 19, 1879, Sherman delivered his "War Is Hell" speech at West Point. As commanding general, he took a deep interest in professionalism as well as in military education, establishing the School of Application for Infantry and Cavalry (today the Command and General Staff College) at Fort Leavenworth, Kansas, in 1881. He also encouraged the publication of military journals. Sherman stepped down as commanding general on November 1, 1883. He retired from the army on February 8, 1884, and lived in New York City. His two volumes of memoirs, *The Memoirs of General William T. Sherman,* are, like the man who wrote them, plain-spoken and direct. After his retirement he refused to run for president on the Republican ticket. Sherman died in New York City on February 14, 1891. An intelligent and aggressive commander who is often credited with originating modern total war, Sherman was also an able administrator and a notable military reformer.

SPENCER C. TUCKER

See also

Atlanta, Battle of; Atlanta Campaign; Bull Run, First Battle of; Chattanooga Campaign; Chickasaw Bluffs, Battle of; Corinth, Mississippi, Siege of; Fort Hindman, Battle of; Grant, Ulysses Simpson; Halleck, Henry Wager; Johnston, Joseph Eggleston; Savannah, Georgia, Siege of; Sherman's March through the Carolinas; Sherman's March to the Sea; Shiloh, Battle of; Vicksburg Campaign, First; Vicksburg Campaign, Second

Further Reading

Kenneth, Lee. *Sherman: A Soldier's Life.* New York: HarperCollins, 2001.

Marszalek, John F. *Sherman: A Soldier's Passion for Order.* New York: Free Press, 1993.

Sherman, William T. *Memoirs of General William T. Sherman.* 2 vols. Reprint ed. Bloomington: Indiana University Press, 1957.

Sherman's Land Grants

Land given to freed former slaves along the southeastern coast of the United States. As Major General William T. Sherman carried out his March to the Sea, which ended in Savannah, Georgia, in December 1864, Union forces liberated scores of slaves who had been working on the area's large plantations.

When Secretary of War Edward Stanton visited Sherman at his Savannah headquarters during the first week of January 1865, the two men discussed how best to handle the now large free black population in southeastern Georgia and southeastern South Carolina. Stanton suggested enlisting black men, who were generally eager to serve, into the

Union Army. Sherman then met with local African American leaders, who also counseled him on the subject.

After much rumination, on January 16, 1865, Sherman published his Special Field Order No. 15. The order provided for the immediate enlistment of black men into the Union ranks but also set aside a 250-mile stretch of Atlantic coastline for African American settlement. The banks of major rivers, 30 miles into the interior, were also to be set aside for such purposes. The strip of land stretched from just south of Charleston, South Carolina, and to just north of Jacksonville, Florida. Each African American family was to receive 40 acres of land within this region. Sherman's momentous order was backed by the 1862 Confiscation Act, which had held that land owned by secessionists could be subject to seizure and redistribution at the government's prerogative. The order took immediate effect, and by June 1865, some 40,000 ex-slaves had been resettled in the designated territories. Many were settled on the Sea Islands of South Carolina and Georgia, which had once been the home of huge plantations that produced rice and cotton.

Although the federal government in 1866 failed to make these land grants official by offering bona fide land titles, most blacks remained on the land for generations, gradually acquiring ownership through squatters' rights. On the Sea Islands especially, which until the late 20th century were isolated and reachable only by boat, the Gullah culture emerged and prospered, a unique blend of West African, American, and Caribbean influences. The first school for freed slaves in the South was established in June 1862 on St. Helena Island, just off the coast of Beaufort, South Carolina.

PAUL G. PIERPAOLI JR.

See also

Sherman, William Tecumseh; Sherman's March to the Sea; Stanton, Edwin McMasters

Further Reading

Hirshon, Stanley P. *The White Tecumseh: A Biography of General William T. Sherman.* New York: Wiley, 1998.

Rhyne, Nancy. *Chronicles of the South Carolina Sea Islands.* Winston-Salem, NC: John F. Blair, 1998.

Sherman's March through the Carolinas
Start Date: January 1865
End Date: April 1865

Union campaign that began in Savannah, Georgia, in mid-January 1865 and ended in Durham Station close to Raleigh,

North Carolina, on April 26, 1865. Major General William Tecumseh Sherman's march through South and North Carolina is one of the most legendary episodes and in some minds the most infamous episode of the Civil War. Although some believe it to be a watershed in the development of modern war strategy and others believe it to be the bloodiest atrocity of the war, it was in fact neither. Sherman was not the first general to live off the land, and in fact his march in many ways resembled a classic punitive expedition. What made it unique was the scale of the challenge of supplying a modern army of 60,000 men across 550 miles of enemy territory (the distance between Savannah and the original objective of Richmond) without conventional supply lines. Similarly, although the destruction of property—especially in South Carolina—was immense, there was otherwise remarkably little violence against Southern civilians.

After his March to the Sea had reached Savannah in late December 1864, Sherman received orders from Lieutenant General Ulysses S. Grant, then mired in the siege at Petersburg, to join him near Richmond, thereby setting the stage for what would become known as the Carolina Campaign. By this time, Sherman's army group had already been carefully culled down to mostly the fittest and most experienced men. The organization was, however, basically the same as it had been since leaving Atlanta. The left wing, known as the Army of Georgia, was commanded by Major General Henry W. Slocum and contained XIV and XX Corps. The right wing, the Army of the Tennessee, was led by Major General Oliver H. Howard and consisted of XV and XVII Corps. In support was a cavalry division under Brigadier General H. Judson Kilpatrick. Together with artillerymen and engineers, Sherman's command numbered roughly 60,000 men, 68 guns, 2,500 wagons, 600 ambulances, and 16,200 draft animals.

The wagons only contained forage for 7 days and provender for 20 days because Sherman, just as he had done in Georgia, intended that his men live off the land, a strategy facilitated by the skills of the ubiquitous bummers, soldiers expert at requisitioning food and other desirables. Most of the wagons therefore contained ammunition, the one commodity not freely available. As it worked out, there were few serious engagements to consume this valuable cargo.

The march began in mid-January 1865 with the movement of part of the right wing (XVII Corps and part of XV Corps) to Beaufort, South Carolina, about 35 miles to the north of Savannah; the rest of the right wing advanced overland from Savannah, securing the eastern flank for the left wing, which departed 10 days later along a route farther west. Howard's men passed through Pocotaligo and Columbia, South Carolina, and rendezvoused at Fayetteville, North Carolina, with Slocum, who moved through Blackville, Lexington, and Winnsboro.

By at least the autumn of 1864, Sherman had come to believe that Confederate civilians, especially the planter classes, must be made to directly bear the consequences of their rebellion before they would give up. In the advance across Georgia, he had encouraged his troops to engage in a sort of controlled pillaging, the target of which was usually government resources or the property of the wealthy. The wanton destruction, however, abruptly escalated as the troops crossed into South Carolina. Sherman's men, many two-year or even three-year veterans, regarded the state, the first to secede from the Union, as the center of the rebellion, and they were determined to make it pay.

The popular view that Sherman's army cut a swath of destruction 40 miles wide is not too far off the mark. The most notorious episode was the destruction of the South Carolina state capital, Columbia. In spite of the efforts of Sherman and Howard to prevent it, thousands of Union arsonists, abetted by civilian renegades, burned down one-third of the city. Union officers were often unable or unwilling to stop them. Sherman himself fretted lest efforts to discourage such behavior curb the very instincts that made his army so formidable. When the troops crossed into North Carolina, the ferocity abruptly declined, perhaps in part because North Carolina had been the last state to secede and still retained a sizable population loyal to the Union.

Armed Confederate resistance to the march generally consisted of a few small encounters with local militia and occasional clashes between the cavalry of Kilpatrick and Major General Wade Hampton. The only major engagements were on March 16, 1865, at Averasboro, North Carolina, a delaying action fought by Confederate forces under Lieutenant General William J. Hardee to create the conditions for General Joseph E. Johnston's attack three days later, resulting in the Battle of Bentonville (March 19–21).

Bentonville proved to be the largest battle of the campaign. Sherman's lines held, and on March 21 he flanked Johnston's army, forcing it back with minimum bloodshed and ammunition expenditure. Three days later Sherman rendezvoused with Major General John M. Schofield's XXIII Corps at Goldsboro, North Carolina. Raleigh fell on April 13, and with Confederate general Robert E. Lee having already surrendered on April 9 at Appomattox, Virginia, Sherman arranged a controversial peace with Johnston at Durham Station on April 26.

The cumulative damage inflicted by Sherman's army in the course of the march through Georgia and the Carolinas was immense. Vast portions of the economic infrastructure were destroyed or severely damaged, most notoriously railroads, a favorite target for Sherman's men, who had developed a remarkable talent for their destruction. Some historians maintain that the long-term impact of such ruination significantly impeded the postwar economic recovery of the South. Also destroyed were the physical manifestations of the slave-owning culture, including auction blocks and slave pens.

The strategic impact of Sherman's March through the Carolinas was undoubtedly great and arguably decisive. Initial Southern defiance gave way to the painful realization of impotence and eventually demoralization. Desertion in the Confederate ranks increased dramatically. This was an important factor in forcing Lee to abandon the siege at Petersburg, an act that led swiftly to the end at Appomattox. Yet for all its notoriety, there was an underlying humanity to Sherman's strategic vision. By destroying things, he hoped to change minds and thus obviate the need to kill people.

RAYMOND W. LEONARD

See also

Averasboro, Battle of; Bentonville, Battle of; Georgia, Union Army of; Grant, Ulysses Simpson; Hampton, Wade; Hardee, William Joseph; Hood, John Bell; Howard, Oliver Otis; Johnston, Joseph Eggleston; Kilpatrick, Hugh Judson; North Carolina; Petersburg Campaign; Schofield, John McAllister; Sherman, William Tecumseh; Slocum, Henry Warner; South Carolina; Tennessee, Union Army of the

Further Reading

Glatthaar, Joseph T. *The March to the Sea and Beyond: Sherman's Troops in the Savannah and Carolinas Campaigns.* New York: New York University Press, 1985.

Johnson, Robert Underwood, and Clarence Clough Buel, eds. *Battles and Leaders of the Civil War*, Vol. 4, *Retreat with Honor.* New York: T. Yoseloff, 1956.

Wheeler, Richard. *Sherman's March: An Eyewitness History of the Cruel Campaign That Helped End a Crueler War.* New York: HarperCollins, 1991.

Sherman's March to the Sea

Start Date: November 15, 1864
End Date: December 21, 1864

The advance by Union western theater commander Major General William T. Sherman's army group from Atlanta to Savannah, Georgia, also known as the Savannah Campaign.

Frustrated by his inability to close with and defeat General John B. Hood's Confederate Army of Tennessee, Sherman received permission from general in chief Lieutenant General Ulysses S. Grant to abandon Atlanta. Sherman sent Major General George H. Thomas and part of his Army of the Cumberland and Major John M. Schofield and his Army of the Ohio north and west to restrain Hood and defend Tennessee. Sherman then destroyed any confiscated supplies in Atlanta that might be of use to the Confederates and evacuated the city, striking east on November 15 with his army group of some 62,000 men in his March to the Sea, with the objective being the port city of Savannah.

For the march, Sherman organized his army into two wings: the right wing, the Army of the Tennessee commanded by Major General Oliver O. Howard with XV and XVII Corps totaling seven divisions, and the left wing, the Army of Georgia commanded by Major General Henry W. Slocum with XIV and XX Corps totaling six divisions. A cavalry division under Brigadier General Judson Kilpatrick operated in support of both wings. The separate wings were intended to ease supply problems but also to confuse the Confederates as to the army's actual destination.

Sherman, and Grant for that matter, believed that the quickest and ultimately least costly way to end the war was by waging total war—bringing the war home to the South by breaking the will to resist through the destruction of its economic resources. Any political constraints on such policies had been removed by President Abraham Lincoln's reelection in November. Grant hoped that the Savannah Campaign might also increase the pressure on Confederate forces besieged at Petersburg and at the least prevent Southern reinforcements from being sent there.

Sherman's men were initially supplied with 20 days of rations, but they were encouraged to forage liberally on the countryside and to destroy crops and livestock that the troops themselves could not consume. The foragers, known as bummers, were to secure the food stocks necessary while the rest of the army worked to destroy Confederate infrastructure. Sherman deliberately planned the march so as to traverse the most productive areas of the state. His Special Field Order No. 120 explicitly stated that "The Army will forage liberally on the country during the march," with the goal being to maintain at all times 10 days' worth of food stocks in the wagons and 3 days' worth of forage. In his orders, Sherman said that African Americans were permitted to join the army's route of march, but he enjoined commanders that this should be in relation to the ability to feed them and that the needs of the soldiers must always be the top priority.

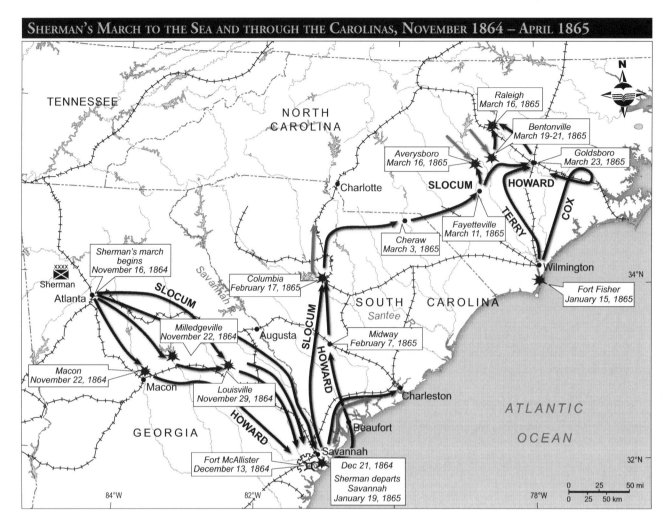

SHERMAN'S MARCH TO THE SEA AND THROUGH THE CAROLINAS, NOVEMBER 1864 – APRIL 1865

Sherman's armies cut a swath of destruction some 300 miles in length and 60 miles in width. Union troops systematically destroyed factories, some public buildings, warehouses, bridges, and rail lines. Railroad track, which the South could not replace, was torn up, and the ties were burned to heat the track, which was twisted into so-called Sherman neckties. Although Sherman gave precise orders that the destruction of mills, cotton gins, factories, and residences was vested in army commanders alone, this was not always adhered to, for there were considerable looting and wanton destruction. Sherman contended that the damage inflicted in his march, while regrettable, would serve to bring the war to a faster end and was preferable to loss in lives. Indeed, the destruction of infrastructure and industry severely impacted the ability of the South to continue the war and also had a profound psychological impact.

With never more than some 13,000 Confederate troops available to contest it, the Union advance was largely unopposed. Confederate cavalry under Major General Joseph Wheeler constituted the principal Southern military force involved. The first action of note took place at Griswoldville on November 22, when Georgia militiamen launched a series of uncoordinated attacks on Howard's right wing, only to be driven off with some 1,100 casualties (400 of them prisoners) and Union losses of only 100. Small actions occurred with Wheeler's cavalry at Ball's Ferry (November 24–25), Sandersville (November 25–26), and Buck Head Creek (November 28). On November 30, some 1,100 Georgia militiamen under Gustavus W. Smith fought a sharp engagement at Honey Hill with 5,500 Union troops under Brigadier General John P. Hatch moving from Hilton Head Island, South Carolina, to join Sherman's army group. Hatch withdrew after sustaining 134 casualties, while the Georgia militiamen suffered but 50. On December 4, Union cavalry under Kilpatrick routed the Confederates in the Battle of Waynesboro.

Soldiers of Union major general William T. Sherman's army group destroying Confederate railroad facilities and rolling stock during their March to the Sea of November–December 1864. (Library of Congress)

Union forces completed their 300-mile march when they arrived at the outskirts of Savannah on December 10. Union naval forces were waiting with supplies, and after the storming and capture of Fort McAllister on December 13, the supply ships were able to move freely up the Savannah River. The surrender of Savannah on December 21 officially brought the campaign to a close. A magnanimous Sherman spared Savannah, which became his "Christmas gift" to President Lincoln.

Sherman estimated the damage inflicted in his march at some $100 million, of which only about 20 percent was to Union advantage; the remainder was simple destruction. His forces had destroyed 300 miles of railroad track and had seized 4,000 horses, 5,000 mules, and 13,000 head of cattle as well as vast amounts of produce. The total damage was staggering and greatly hindered the ability of the South to continue the war.

SPENCER C. TUCKER

See also

Foraging; Fort McAllister, Georgia, Capture of; Honey Hill, Battle of; Hood, John Bell; Howard, Oliver Otis; Kilpatrick, Hugh Judson; Savannah, Georgia, Siege of; Schofield, John McAllister; Sherman, William Tecumseh; Slocum, Henry Warner; Smith, Gustavus Woodson; Thomas, George Henry; Waynesboro, Georgia, Battle of; Wheeler, Joseph

Further Reading

Campbell, Jacqueline Glass. *When Sherman Marched North from the Sea: Resistance on the Confederate Home Front.* Chapel Hill: University of North Carolina Press, 2003.

Glatthaar, Joseph T. *The March to the Sea and Beyond: Sherman's Troops in the Savannah and Carolinas Campaigns.* New York: New York University Press, 1985.

Kennett, Lee. *Marching through Georgia: The Story of Soldiers and Civilians during Sherman's Campaign.* New York: Harper-Collins, 1995.

Sherman, William T. *Memoirs of General W. T. Sherman.* New York: Library of America, 1990.

Trudeau, Noah Andre. *Southern Storm: Sherman's March to the Sea.* New York: HarperCollins, 2008.

Sherman's Peace Proposals

Somewhat derisive term used to describe Union major general William T. Sherman's April 1865 armistice negotiations with Confederate general Joseph E. Johnston. After the Confederates formally surrendered at Appomattox Court House on April 12, 1865, Johnston sent a messenger to Sherman's headquarters at Raleigh, North Carolina, seeking an armistice.

The two commanders met at Bennett House outside Durham Station on April 17 to hash out an agreement. During a second meeting the next day, Johnson and Sherman both signed a memo suspending hostilities and establishing postarmistice conditions. Sherman believed that he was negotiating with the blessing of the new Andrew Johnson administration, but it is clear that Sherman overstepped his authority.

The Sherman-Johnson agreement stipulated an immediate armistice, general amnesty, and the disarming of Confederate troops. It also called for the former Confederates to obey all state and federal laws, allowed state governments to be reconstituted upon presidential approval, specified the reestablishment of federal courts, and decreed that all personal and property rights of former Confederates would be protected.

President Johnson was not happy with Sherman's negotiations, which he believed were too generous and which had overstepped Sherman's authority. Secretary of War Edwin L. Stanton was reportedly apoplectic and publicly lambasted Sherman's behavior. Northern newspapers pilloried Sherman for his overreaching "peace proposals." Within days, Stanton ordered Lieutenant General Ulysses S. Grant to visit Sherman at his Raleigh headquarters.

Grant gently informed Sherman that the president and his cabinet had rejected the peace proposal. Sherman seemingly took the reversal in stride and renegotiated a new agreement with Johnston on April 26. This second round of negotiations resulted in terms that were nearly identical to those agreed to by Grant and Robert E. Lee on April 9. When Sherman read about Stanton's tirade against him in newspapers, the general was furious. Sherman continued to believe that his initial peace proposal had been entirely correct.

Paul G. Pierpaoli Jr.

See also

Appomattox Court House and Lee's Surrender; Grant, Ulysses Simpson; Johnston, Joseph Eggleston; Sherman, William Tecumseh; Stanton, Edwin McMasters; Surrender Terms

Further Reading

Glatthaar, Joseph T. "The Civil War: A New Definition of Victory." In *Between War and Peace: How America Ends Its Wars,* edited by Colonel Matthew Moten, 107–128. New York: Free Press, 2011.

Kenneth, Lee. *Sherman: A Soldier's Life.* New York: HarperCollins, 2001.

Sherwood, Isaac Ruth
Birth Date: August 13, 1835
Death Date: October 15, 1925

Union officer. Isaac Ruth Sherwood was born in Stanford, New York, on August 13, 1835. Sherwood attended the Hudson River Institute in Claverack, New York, and Antioch College in Ohio, then studied law at the Ohio Law College in Poland, Ohio. After completing his education in 1857, he purchased and became the editor of the *Williams County Gazette,* an abolitionist newspaper, in Bryan, Ohio. In October 1860, Sherwood was elected probate judge of Williams County.

With the beginning of the Civil War, Sherwood resigned his judgeship and enlisted as a private in the 14th Ohio Infantry on April 22, 1861. His unit saw action in western Virginia (present-day West Virginia) early in the war and mustered out on August 13. Sherwood then joined the 111th Ohio Infantry as a first lieutenant (September 6). He was promoted to major on February 13, 1863, and performed effectively in the Battle of Campbell's Station (November 16, 1863). Sherwood was promoted to lieutenant colonel on February 12, 1864. He took part in the Atlanta Campaign (May 5–September 2, 1864) and distinguished himself in the Battle of Resaca (May 13–15, 1864). He was brevetted brigadier general effective February 27, 1865, for his leading role in the Battle of Franklin (November 30, 1864). He then participated in the final actions of Major General William T. Sherman's March through the Carolinas (January–April 1865). He mustered out of the military on June 27, 1865.

Sherwood settled in Toledo, Ohio, where he became the editor of the *Toledo Commercial.* He also became active in the Republican Party and was elected Ohio's secretary of state in 1868 and again in 1870. In 1872 Sherwood was elected to the U.S. House of Representatives, serving one term. He then returned to Ohio and purchased the *Toledo Journal* and was its editor (1875–1884). He was elected probate judge of Lucas County in 1878 and again in 1881. Moving to Canton, in 1886 Sherwood became the editor of the *Canton News-Democrat*.

Sherwood, now a member of the Democratic Party, was again elected to the U.S. House of Representatives in 1906, serving from 1907 to 1921 and from 1923 to 1925. A pacifist, he opposed U.S. participation in World War I. Sherwood died in Toledo, Ohio, on October 15, 1925.

SPENCER C. TUCKER

See also
Franklin, Battle of; Sherman's March through the Carolinas

Further Reading
Eicher, John H., and David J. Eicher. *Civil War High Commands.* Stanford, CA: Stanford University Press, 2001.
Knight, James R. *The Battle of Franklin: When the Devil Had Full Possession of the Earth.* Charleston, SC: History Press, 2009.

Shields, James
Birth Date: May 6, 1806
Death Date: June 1, 1879

Union officer. Born in County Tyrone, Ireland, on May 6, 1806, James Shields immigrated to the United States and settled in Kaskaskia, Illinois, in 1828. He worked as a schoolteacher and studied law, being admitted to the bar in 1832. A Jackson Democrat, Shields briefly saw action in the Black Hawk War of 1832 and was elected to the Illinois legislature in 1836. He later served two terms as the state auditor of Illinois. After serving as a volunteer in the Second Seminole War (1835–1842), Shields was appointed a justice on the Illinois Supreme Court in 1843, and in 1845 President James Polk named him commissioner of the general land office.

With the outbreak of the Mexican-American War in 1846, Shields resigned his post and on July 1, 1846, was commissioned a brigadier general of volunteers, serving under Brigadier Generals Zachary Taylor and John E. Wool. Shields then joined Major General Winfield Scott's army for the Mexico City Campaign, commanding a brigade during the siege of Veracruz in March 1847.

At the Battle of Cerro Gordo (April 18, 1847), Shields was severely wounded but returned to command a brigade and saw action in the Battle of Contreras (August 20, 1847) and

later that day at the Battle of Churubusco. At the Battle of Chapultepec (September 13, 1847), he was again wounded and missed the last combat of the war. He was brevetted to major general later that year and returned home with his brigade in July 1848, at which time he was mustered out of service.

In 1848 Polk appointed Shields governor of the Oregon Territory, and in 1849 Shields was elected as a Democrat to the U.S. Senate from Illinois. He then moved to Minnesota, where he was also elected to the U.S. Senate, serving from 1858 to 1859. He subsequently settled in California.

On August 19, 1861, President Abraham Lincoln appointed Shields a brigadier general of volunteers. During Major General Thomas "Stonewall" Jackson's Shenandoah Valley Campaign (May–June 1862), Shields's division was soundly defeated at the Battle of Port Republic (June 9, 1862). He saw little action thereafter and resigned his commission on March 28, 1863. Shields settled first in California and then Missouri. He briefly returned to the U.S. Senate in 1879 for a third time when he was appointed to finish the term of a senator who had died. He served only three months and did not seek reelection. Shields died at Ottumwa, Iowa, on June 1, 1879.

BRADLEY P. TOLPPANEN

See also
Jackson, Thomas Jonathan; Jackson's Shenandoah Valley Campaign; Port Republic, Battle of

Further Reading
Condon, William H. *Life of Major-General James Shields: Hero of Three Wars and Senator from Three States.* Chicago: Press of the Blakely Printing Co., 1900.
Warner, Ezra J. *General in Blue: Lives of the Union Commanders.* Baton Rouge: Louisiana State University Press, 2006.

Shiloh, Battle of
Start Date: April 6, 1862
End Date: April 7, 1862

Arguably the first great land battle of the Civil War. The Battle of Shiloh (also known as the Battle of Pittsburg Landing) took place along the banks of the Tennessee River at Pittsburg Landing, some 23 miles north of the strategic town of Corinth, Mississippi. The battle derived its name from a small Methodist church named Shiloh (Hebrew for "place of peace").

By April 1862, Union forces had driven the Confederates from Kentucky and Tennessee; had opened the Tennessee

BATTLE OF SHILOH, APRIL 6–7, 1862

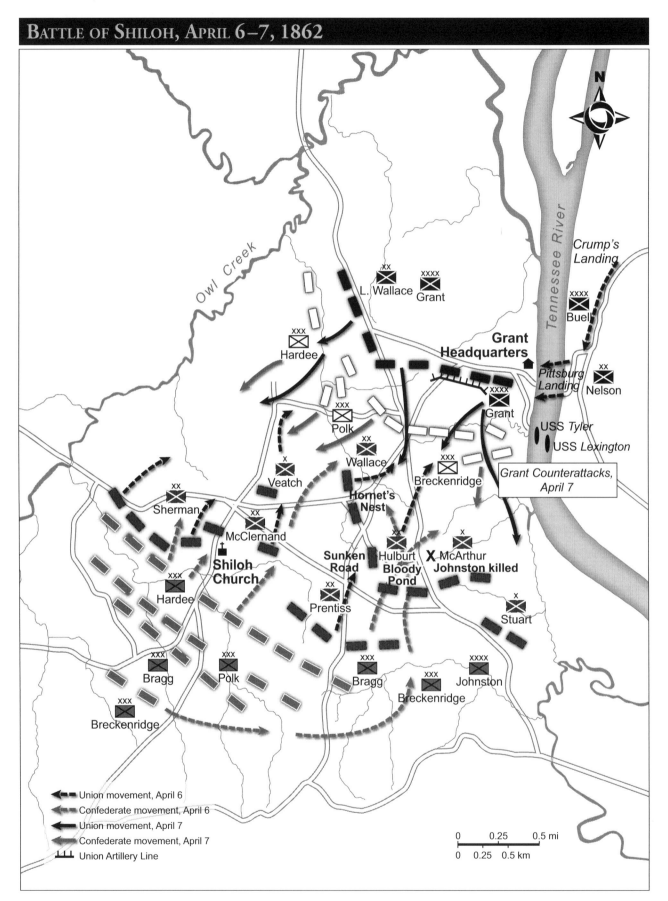

Owl Creek

Tennessee River

Crump's Landing

xx
L. Wallace

xxxx
Grant

xxxx
Buell

xxx
Hardee

Grant Headquarters

Pittsburg Landing

xx
Nelson

xxx
Polk

xxxx
Grant

USS *Tyler*

USS *Lexington*

xx
Wallace

x
Veatch

xxx
Breckenridge

Grant Counterattacks, April 7

xx
Sherman

Hornet's Nest

xx
McClernand

Shiloh Church

Sunken Road

Hulburt

xx
Hardee

xx
Prentiss

Bloody Pond

X McArthur
Johnston killed

x
Stuart

xxx
Bragg

xxx
Polk

xxx
Bragg

xxx
Breckenridge

xxxx
Johnston

xxx
Breckenridge

Union movement, April 6
Confederate movement, April 6
Union movement, April 7
Confederate movement, April 7
Union Artillery Line

| 0 | 0.25 | 0.5 mi |
| 0 | 0.25 | 0.5 km |

Fought on April 6–7, 1862 on the west bank of the Tennessee River and 23 miles north of strategic Corinth, Mississippi, the Battle of Shiloh ended in a Union victory but claimed 23,732 total casualties and was, to that date, the bloodiest battle in American history. (Library of Congress)

River to Florence, Alabama; and were preparing a conquest of the Mississippi. Stung by defeats at Fort Henry (February 6) and Fort Donelson (February 13–16) and the loss of Nashville (February 25), commander of Confederate Department No. 2 General Albert Sidney Johnston was determined to engage and defeat the Federals. He called up reinforcements and ordered a concentration at Corinth.

The strategy promulgated by Major General Henry Halleck, commander of the Union Department of the Mississippi, was to send forces down the Mississippi but also sever Confederate railroad lines across the region and take the town of Corinth, a key railhead. Halleck ordered Major General Ulysses S. Grant and his Army of West Tennessee (soon to be renamed the Army of the Tennessee) to link up with Major General Don Carlos Buell's Army of the Ohio, which was marching from Nashville. The two would then operate together in a joint offensive against Corinth. Seizing the town would cut two important Confederate railroads, the west-east Memphis & Charleston Railroad, connecting the Mississippi, Memphis, and Richmond, and also the north-south Mobile & Ohio Railroad.

Battle of Shiloh (April 6–7, 1862)

	Union	Confederacy
Force strength	75,000	44,000
Killed	1,745	1,723
Wounded	8,408	8,012
Captured or missing	2,885	959

Grant's six divisions of nearly 39,000 men arrived at Pittsburg Landing. Grant pushed his men two miles inland on the west bank of the river, where they set up camp and waited for Buell's forces, delayed in their march by heavy rains, to arrive. Grant's troops were loosely arrayed near Shiloh Church. Grant, however, had neglected to send any reconnaissance parties to ascertain Confederate strength. He was more preoccupied with his own offensive plans. As a result, defensive arrangements had been largely ignored. By early April, Grant's men were scattered throughout the area, with no attempt having been made to form any sort of battle line or even throw up rudimentary earthworks.

SHILOH CAMPAIGN, 1862

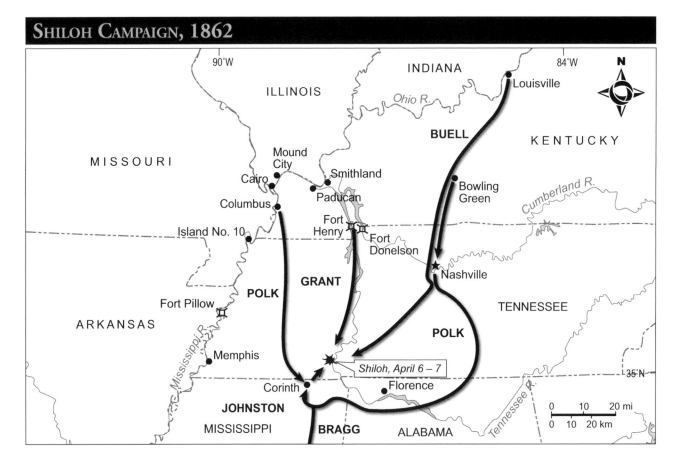

The Confederates were not quiescent, however. Johnston, who was well aware of Grant's arrival at Pittsburg Landing and probable Union intentions, was determined to strike Grant and destroy his army before Buell could arrive with his 36,000-man army. Johnston organized his army into four corps under Major Generals Leonidas Polk, Braxton Bragg, and William J. Hardee and Brigadier General John C. Breckinridge. On April 3, Johnston set out with 44,000 men from Corinth for Pittsburg Landing; however, rains turned the roads into quagmires, making progress slow and difficult. On April 5, Johnston's men were a scant four miles southwest of Shiloh, although their arrival went unnoticed by Union forces.

On April 6 at about 5:00 a.m., Johnston's men clashed with Union pickets and then struck the awakening Union army in full force, nearly overwhelming the unprepared Federals. The Confederates first hit Brigadier General William Tecumseh Sherman's division. Ill-prepared, it fell back. The Confederates then attacked the divisions commanded by Brigadier General Benjamin M. Prentiss and Major General John A. McClernand. Their troops, plus those of Sherman's re-formed division, then battled the Confederates during the

next three hours in costly fighting that slowed the Confederate assault. Superior numbers finally told, however, and the Confederates overran the Union divisions.

The Confederates were hindered not only by the stubborn Union defense but also by ill-trained troops who stopped to loot the abandoned Union camps. A faulty battle plan also contributed, as the four corps became hopelessly tangled. The offensive ground to a halt as units became disorganized. Afforded time to redeploy, Grant, who was not on the field when the attack came, rushed to the landing from nearby Savannah, Tennessee, and began to organize a defensive position around the landing. He slowly re-formed a solid defensive front centered on a sunken road held by Prentiss's men. Grant ordered it held at all costs. The Confederates described the bitter fighting there as the Hornet's Nest.

The Confederates, meanwhile, had lost their commander. At about 2:00 p.m. while directing an attack on the Union lines, Johnston was struck in the leg by a bullet that severed an artery, and he bled to death on the field. General P. G. T. Beauregard then assumed command of the Confederate forces. Fighting raged across the field. The Confederates massed 62 guns and finally blasted Prentiss into submission. He and some 2,000 defenders of the Hornet's Nest surrendered at around 5:30. By the evening of April 6, although Union forces had been driven from their camp, they had developed a strong defensive position around Pittsburg Landing, protected on their flanks by ravines and by the heavy guns of two gunboats in the river to their rear. That evening in a controversial decision, Beauregard suspended the Confederate attack, expecting to complete the destruction of the Union army in the morning.

During the night, however, lead elements of Buell's army and Major General Lew Wallace's division arrived and were immediately hurried into the line. On April 7 to Beauregard's surprise, Grant struck first. At about 7:30 a.m., Union forces began steadily pushing the Confederates back. The fighting that day was as bloody as the combat of the previous day. Late that afternoon, Beauregard pulled his battered and exhausted army back to Corinth. The Union army did not pursue.

The Battle of Shiloh was over. The first great meat-grinder battle of the war, it had cost the Union 13,038 casualties (1,745 killed, 8,408 wounded, and 2,885 captured). The Confederates lost 10,694 (1,723 killed, 8,012 wounded, and 959 missing or captured). The grisly total of 23,732 casualties from this single battle was more than the United States had suffered in all of its previous wars combined. The carnage shocked Americans, North and South.

The Union victory at Shiloh was of tremendous consequence in the war. Although criticized for his lack of preparation, Grant had survived and proven himself to be an aggressive commander. Although temporarily demoted by Halleck afterward, Grant withstood calls for his head and was sustained by President Abraham Lincoln, who famously stated, "I can't spare this man. He fights." The battle ultimately doomed the Confederate cause in the West. After a tortoise-like advance and siege directed by Halleck, the Confederates abandoned Corinth in June.

RICK DYSON

See also

Beauregard, Pierre Gustav Toutant; Bragg, Braxton; Breckinridge, John Cabell; Buell, Don Carlos; Corinth, Mississippi; Corinth, Mississippi, Siege of; Fort Donelson, Battle of; Fort Henry, Battle of; Grant, Ulysses Simpson; Halleck, Henry Wager; Hardee, William Joseph; Johnston, Albert Sidney; McClernand, John Alexander; Polk, Leonidas; Prentiss, Benjamin Mayberry

Further Reading

Daniel, Larry J. *Shiloh: The Battle That Changed the Civil War.* New York: Simon and Schuster, 1997.

Roland, Charles Pierce. *Albert Sidney Johnston: Soldier of Three Republics.* Austin: University of Texas Press, 1964.
Smith, Timothy B. *The Untold Story of Shiloh: The Battle and the Battlefield.* Knoxville: University of Tennessee Press, 2006.

Shorter, John Gill

Birth Date: April 23, 1818
Death Date: May 29, 1872

Governor of Alabama (1861–1863). John Gill Shorter was born on April 23, 1818, in Monticello, Georgia. He graduated from the University of Georgia in 1837, passed the state bar in 1838, and moved to Eufaula, Alabama, that same year. Shorter practiced law there for four years before being appointed solicitor. In 1845 he waged a successful bid for a seat in the Alabama Senate and served two terms before becoming a circuit court judge, a post he held for nine years. In early 1861 Shorter was appointed to the Alabama Secession Convention, where the avid secessionist urged immediate secession.

Later that same year, Shorter was elected to the Provisional Confederate Congress. He was an enthusiastic supporter of President Jefferson Davis's war policies and also helped craft the Confederate Constitution. Running for governor in the summer of 1861, Shorter was elected in August and took office in December.

As governor, Shorter undertook numerous measures to strengthen his state's defenses, especially around the strategic port city of Mobile, and tried to provide as many soldiers as possible to the government in the Confederate capital of Richmond. He was also lauded for the measures he took to aid families of those fighting in the war. Shorter's popularity plummeted, however, after the Union invasion of northern Alabama in the spring of 1862, which resulted in much destroyed property and general misery for those living in the region. Forced to raise taxes and institute a mandatory draft, Shorter lost his reelection bid in 1863.

After leaving office on December 1, 1863, Shorter resumed his legal practice in Eufaula but thereafter eschewed public office. He was detained and briefly imprisoned by federal authorities in 1865, but he soon returned to his law practice. Shorter died on May 29, 1872, in Eufaula, Alabama.

PAUL G. PIERPAOLI JR.

See also

Alabama; Georgia

Further Reading

Stallworth, Clarke. *One Day in Alabama*, Vol. 2, *Statehood to Civil War*. Birmingham, AL: Seacoast Publishing, 1994.

Stallworth, Clarke. *One Day in Alabama*, Vol. 3, *The Civil War Years*. Birmingham, AL: Seacoast Publishing, 1997.

Shoup, Francis Asbury
Birth Date: March 22, 1834
Death Date: September 4, 1896

Confederate officer. Francis Asbury Shoup was born on March 22, 1834, and graduated from the U.S. Military Academy, West Point, in 1855. Commissioned a second lieutenant in the 1st U.S. Artillery Regiment, he fought in the Third Seminole War (1855–1858). Resigning his commission, he studied law and opened a practice in Indiana. He also became a militia officer there. Sympathizing with the Southern cause, Shoup relocated to Florida around 1860 and began a law practice in St. Augustine.

In the spring of 1861, Shoup was named a lieutenant of a state artillery unit and then briefly led an artillery battery in Fernandina. Commissioned a major in the Confederate Army in October 1861, he was sent west and commanded a 12-gun artillery battalion in Kentucky.

Shoup was later assigned as artillery chief for Major General William J. Hardee. Shoup's expert command of massed artillery at the Battle of Shiloh (April 6–7, 1862) devastated the so-called Hornet's Nest, a Union salient. He was advanced to brigadier general on September 12, 1862, and saw action during the Battle of Prairie Grove (December 7, 1862).

In the winter of 1863, Shoup was dispatched to Mobile, Alabama, but was redirected to Mississippi. That spring, he took command of a Louisiana infantry brigade and saw considerable action during the Second Vicksburg Campaign (April 1–July 4, 1863). Taken prisoner on July 5, he was soon paroled and eventually exchanged. He then served in Mobile before joining the Army of Tennessee in northern Georgia.

Shoup then was appointed chief of artillery for General Joseph E. Johnston. Shoup saw considerable action during the Atlanta Campaign (May 5–September 2, 1864) and was lauded for the defensive works he helped erect along the Chattahoochee River. Later that year, he served as General John B. Hood's chief of staff.

When the war ended, Shoup studied for the ministry and became an Episcopal rector. He also taught mathematics, theology, and philosophy at the University of the South and the University of Mississippi. A keenly inquisitive individual, he authored several works on metaphysics and mathematics. Shoup died on September 4, 1896, in Columbia, Tennessee.

PAUL G. PIERPAOLI JR.

See also

Atlanta Campaign; Buckner, Simon Bolivar; Hardee, William Joseph; Hood, John Bell; Johnston, Joseph Eggleston; Prairie Grove, Battle of; Shiloh, Battle of; Vicksburg Campaign, Second

Further Reading

Eicher, John H., and David J. Eicher. *Civil War High Commands*. Stanford, CA: Stanford University Press, 2001.

Warner, Ezra J. *Generals in Gray: Lives of the Confederate Commanders*. Baton Rouge: Louisiana State University Press, 2006.

Shrapnel

Artillery round. Shrapnel, or spherical case shot, was invented in 1784 by Lieutenant (later lieutenant general) Henry Shrapnel (1761–1842) of the British Army. Shrapnel came up with the idea in order to extend the range of highly effective grapeshot and case (canister) shot against enemy troops.

During the Spanish siege of Gibraltar (1779–1783), the British successfully fired shells for the 5.5-inch mortar from their 24-pounder long guns, but in 1784 Shrapnel improved on this improvisation by inventing what he called "spherical case shot." Also known simply as case, the new artillery ammunition was later known simply by its designer's name. Spherical case or shrapnel consisted of a thin-walled hollow round shell filled with a small bursting charge and small iron or lead shot. A time fuse set off the charge, scattering the shot and pieces of the shell casing among opposing troops. The bursting charge was only a small one, allowing the scattered balls and burst casing to continue on the same trajectory as before the explosion (a greater charge would increase the velocity but scatter the balls more widely and reduce their effectiveness). Explosive shell had for some time been utilized in high-trajectory fire mortars but had not before been widely projected in horizontal fire by guns.

Shrapnel shells had thinner walls than other shells and had to be carefully cast. Their weight empty was about half of that for solid shot of the same caliber, but their loaded weight made them comparable to solid shot.

The British employed shrapnel during the Napoleonic Wars in 1804 in the siege of Surinam. Early shrapnel had a wooden plug and a paper fuse but in the 1850s incorporated the five-second Bormann fuse. Shrapnel was widely used in the American Civil War both on land and in naval actions, most often in the 12-pounder Napoleon and Dahlgren boat howitzers. Shrapnel soon became a staple round in the world's artillery establishments. Britain alone produced 72 million shrapnel shells during World War I.

Shrapnel was most effective against troops in the open, for its explosive force was insufficient to seriously affect troops under cover. In today's usage, the term "shrapnel" describes the fragments of a shell or bomb.

SPENCER C. TUCKER

See also

Artillery, Land, CSA; Artillery, Land, U.S.; Bormann Fuse; Dahlgren Guns; Napoleon 12-Pounder Gun

Further Reading

Ripley, Warren. *Artillery and Ammunition of the Civil War.* New York: Van Nostrand Reinhold, 1970.

Tucker, Spencer C. *Arming the Fleet: U.S. Navy Ordnance in the Muzzle-Loading Era.* Annapolis, MD: Naval Institute Press, 1989.

Sibley, Henry Hastings
Birth Date: February 29, 1811
Death Date: February 18, 1891

Union officer. Henry Hastings Sibley was born on February 29, 1811, in Detroit, Michigan. He had little formal education but became a shrewd and effective businessman. As a young man he moved to the Minnesota frontier, where he worked for the American Fur Company as a clerk and fur trapper.

Sibley proved adept at turning a profit in the fur business, and in 1835 he constructed the first private residence in all of Minnesota. In 1849 he was elected to the U.S. House of Representatives as a territorial delegate and worked hard to establish the Minnesota Territory. He served until 1853. After Minnesota was admitted to the Union, Sibley served as the state's first governor, from 1858 to 1860.

In August 1862 the Santee (Dakota) Sioux, led by Little Crow, staged an armed rebellion throughout the Minnesota River Valley. The Sioux were reacting to increased white encroachment onto their lands and had been emboldened to fight back after most Union troops serving in the region had been sent to the East to fight in the Civil War, which was then under way. The violence began on August 17, when Native Americans attacked a white settlement in Meeker County, during which 5 settlers were murdered. Similar attacks occurred in rapid succession, stunning white Minnesotans. Sibley now offered his services to the state's governor, who appointed him colonel in the state militia, with the task of putting down the Minnesota Sioux Uprising. Sibley assembled some 1,500 militiamen and went out in search of the Santee Sioux warriors.

Sibley fought several engagements, finally subduing the Native Americans at the Battle of Wood Lake (September 23, 1862). This effectively ended the uprising, which had nonetheless claimed between 500 and 800 lives among white settlers. On September 29, Sibley was given a commission as a brigadier general of U.S. Volunteers, largely because of his efforts during the uprising. The U.S. Senate failed to confirm his commission, which expired on March 4, 1863. Nevertheless, within days Sibley was reappointed, and the Senate confirmed this on March 20. Meanwhile, Little Crow and a number of his followers had managed to escape into the Dakotas.

After establishing a headquarters at St. Paul and augmenting his force with Brigadier General Alfred Sully's cavalrymen, Sibley launched an offensive into the Dakotas to ensure that the Sioux would not launch another rebellion. The resulting Sully-Sibley Campaign ended with the Battle of Stony Lake (July 28, 1863). During the campaign, Sibley's forces suffered only about a dozen casualties; the Sioux lost at least 150 men. After that, Sibley was tasked with providing security along the western frontier. In November 1865, Sibley was brevetted major general for his "efficient and meritorious" service. He mustered out of the service in April 1866.

After the war Sibley continued his business and public service career, with considerable success. He was president of a gas company, an insurance company, and a bank. He also served in the Minnesota legislature and was a member of the Board of Regents for the University of Minnesota. Sibley died in St. Paul, Minnesota on February 18, 1891.

PAUL G. PIERPAOLI JR.

See also

Dakota Sioux; Minnesota; Sioux Uprising

Further Reading

Gilman, Rhoda R. *Henry Hastings Sibley: Divided Heart.* St. Paul: Minnesota Historical Society Press, 2004.

Pedersen, Kern. *Makers of Minnesota: An Illustrated History of the Builders of Our State.* St. Paul: Minnesota Centennial Commission, 1949.

Sibley, Henry Hopkins
Birth Date: May 25, 1816
Death Date: August 23, 1886

Confederate officer. Born in Natchitoches, Louisiana, on May 25, 1816, Henry Hopkins Sibley graduated from the U.S.

Confederate brigadier general Henry Hopkins Sibley led an expedition from Texas in 1862 into New Mexico in a vain effort to secure that considerable territory for the South. (Library of Congress)

Military Academy, West Point, in 1838 and entered the 2nd U.S. Dragoons. He participated in the Second Seminole War (1835–1842) and the Mexican-American War (1846–1848), ultimately rising to captain in 1847 and earning a brevet to major. While stationed on the Texas plains (1850–1854), Sibley developed an idea for a portable military shelter replete with a stove and smoke hole and capable of housing a dozen men. He was granted a patent for his design in 1856, which came to be called the Sibley Tent.

Sibley saw service in Kansas in 1856 during the events known as Bleeding Kansas. The following year he participated in the Mormon Expedition before being dispatched to the New Mexico Territory in the army's unsuccessful bid to suppress the Navajos in 1860. Sibley was at Fort Union, New Mexico Territory, when the Civil War began and, choosing allegiance to his native Louisiana, resigned from the U.S. Army on May 13, 1861. He then accepted a commission in the Confederate Army as a brigadier general on June 17.

Aware of the tremendous economic potential for the Confederacy associated with control of southern California's seaports and the gold and silver mines of the Southwest, Sibley journeyed to Richmond and convinced Confederate president Jefferson Davis of the necessity for an invasion. Sibley assembled the Army of New Mexico at Fort Bliss, Texas, and by the end of January 1862, he was encamped with his small force of fewer than 3,000 men just north of Mesilla, the new capital of the Confederate Territory of Arizona.

Sibley's objective was to move up the Rio Grande toward Albuquerque, Santa Fe, and Fort Union, eliminating Union strongholds along the way. His plan went awry, however, on February 21, 1862, at the Battle of Val Verde, as the Army of New Mexico, although victorious in combat, lost invaluable supplies and was unable to prevent Union forces under Colonel Edward R. S. Canby at nearby Fort Craig from threatening the Confederate lifeline to Texas. A further encounter with Union forces on March 26–28 at Glorieta Pass proved to be the decisive blow to his campaign. Lacking adequate supplies and unable to live off the meager resources of New Mexico, Sibley had no choice but to fall back to Texas, with a much-reduced force of just 1,500 men.

Throughout the New Mexico Campaign, Sibley struggled with poor health and inebriation. Accusations about his drunkenness and poor generalship persisted into 1863, culminating in his court-martial after failing to obey orders from Major General Richard Taylor at the Battle of Irish Bend (April 13–14). Although acquitted of all charges on September 25, 1863, Sibley's reputation was ruined, and he remained an officer without command for the rest of the war.

In 1869 Sibley accepted a generalship in the Egyptian Army and was placed in charge of constructing coastal defenses. He soon fell victim to his old nemesis, alcohol, and was relieved of his duties in 1873. Returning to the United States, Sibley, whose service to the Confederacy had annulled any claim to royalties for his tent, spent his last years in poverty living with his daughter in Fredericksburg, Virginia, where he died on August 23, 1886.

ALAN C. DOWNS

See also

Glorieta Pass, Battle of; Irish Bend and Fort Bisland, Louisiana, Engagements at; New Mexico, Confederate Army of; New Mexico Territory; Sibley's New Mexico Campaign; Taylor, Richard; Texas, New Mexico, and Arizona, Confederate District of; Val Verde, Battle of

Further Reading

Frazier, Donald S. *Blood & Treasure: Confederate Empire in the Southwest.* College Station: Texas A&M University Press, 1995.

Thompson, Jerry. *Henry Hopkins Sibley: Confederate General of the West.* Natchitoches, LA: Northwestern State University Press, 1987.

Sibley and Grant Court-Martial

Joint court-martial of Confederate brigadier general Henry H. Sibley and Captain Alexander Grant. The court convened on September 25, 1863, to address charges leveled for events that took place during engagements with Union forces on April 12–14, 1863, at Irish Bend and Fort Bisland, Louisiana.

When Union major general Nathaniel Banks threatened Confederate positions on the Mississippi, Confederate major general Richard Taylor, with just 5,000 troops, attempted to repel the Union force of 15,000 men. At Irish Bend and Fort Bisland, the Southerners put up a valiant fight but were roundly defeated by their far more numerous opponents. Galled by the loss, Taylor sought the court-martial of his subordinate, Brigadier General Henry H. Silbey, and also brought charges against Captain Alexander Grant, who had been commanding the gunboat *Cotton* during the engagements. Because it was often difficult to assemble enough high-ranking officers for a court-martial of a general officer, the proceeding was not held until September 1863.

On September 25, 1863, the presiding judge, Major General John G. Walker, called the proceedings to order. Sibley was charged with failing to organize and execute an assault against Union forces on April 13 just below Fort Bisland; with having failed to secure a steamboat with wounded Confederates, which was subsequently captured by the Federals; and with abandoning his post in a retreat. Grant was charged with having failed to obey orders that he assist in the defense of Fort Burton and with the failure to evacuate arms and supplies from the fort.

The court-martial found both Sibley and Grant not guilty of all charges. While the court took pains to assert that Sibley's actions were less than prompt and were to that extent "censurable," it did not find him negligent due to a series of circumstances beyond his control. The court did not elaborate further. The court offered no explanation for its verdict regarding Grant. Both men resumed their pretrial commands, although the court-martial had a deleterious effect on Sibley, who subsequently suffered from poor health and alcoholism.

JOHN HEALY AND PAUL G. PIERPAOLI JR.

See also

Banks, Nathaniel Prentice; Irish Bend and Fort Bisland, Louisiana, Engagements at; Sibley, Henry Hopkins; Taylor, Richard; Walker, John George

Further Reading

Parrish, T. Michael. *Richard Taylor: Soldier Prince of Dixie.* Chapel Hill: University of North Carolina Press, 1992.

Thompson, Jerry D. *Henry Hopkins Sibley: Confederate General of the West.* College Station: Texas A&M University Press, 1996.

Sibley's New Mexico Campaign
Start Date: November 1861
End Date: May 1862

Confederate brigadier general Henry Hopkins Sibley's attempted conquest of the Southwest. In June 1861 Sibley, who had served in the regular army at many points in the West, met with Confederate president Jefferson Davis to propose an invasion and conquest of the New Mexico Territory, with hopes of extending Confederate control to California. Davis acceded to Sibley's plan, and shortly thereafter Sibley received orders to invade New Mexico.

Traveling to Texas in August, Sibley began recruiting soldiers in eastern Texas for the Confederate Army of New Mexico. By November 1861, Sibley's 3,700-man force was ready for operations and departed westward from San Antonio. The army later stopped in El Paso, where Sibley addressed the town's citizens and informed them that the Confederates were there as liberators.

When Sibley's force approached Fort Craig on February 16, 1862, Union colonel Edward R. S. Canby, the commander of that post, refused to be lured away from the fort to do battle with the Confederates. Sibley staged a makeshift siege of the Union post but withdrew when it became clear that his men would be unable to force its surrender. Sibley then advanced north along the east side of the Rio Grande. In response, a Union force from Fort Craig moved north along the west side of the river to block the Confederates from cutting the fort's supply line. The two sides waged a chaotic battle for control of the Val Verde Ford on the Rio Grande on February 21, which resulted in a costly Confederate victory. Fighting during the preceding five days had badly depleted Sibley's force of men and supplies.

The Union force then retreated to Fort Craig, where Canby decided to remain in Sibley's rear as the Confederates advanced northward and occupied Albuquerque, which they found largely bereft of needed supplies. Sibley then sent

Sibley's New Mexico Campaign

	Union	Confederacy
Fore strength	5,140	3,700
Killed, wounded, or captured	634	2,000

a detachment of 600 men to take Santa Fe, but they soon discovered that the Federals had removed or destroyed much of that town's supplies.

Meanwhile, the 1st Colorado Volunteer Infantry Regiment, commanded by Colonel John Slough, conducted a 13-day forced march from Colorado through snow and bitter cold to Fort Union, where Slough assumed command of the Union garrison. Disobeying the orders of Colonel Canby, Slough departed the fort and advanced against Sibley.

On March 26, 1862, Sibley's and Slough's forces collided in the Battle of Glorieta Pass. During the next two days, a series of engagements culminated in an apparent Confederate victory. But Sibley's success was quickly negated by a Union raiding force that destroyed the Confederate supply train. Now desperately short of supplies, Sibley slowly withdrew back to Texas, arriving in El Paso on May 4, 1862, with just 1,700 men.

GLENN E. HELM

See also

Canby, Edward Richard Sprigg; Glorieta Pass, Battle of; Sibley, Henry Hopkins; Val Verde, Battle of

Further Reading

Alberts, Don E. *The Battle of Glorieta: Union Victory in the West.* College Station: Texas A&M University Press, 1998.
Josephy, Alvin M., Jr. *The Civil War in the American West.* New York: Knopf, 1991.

Sickles, Daniel Edgar
Birth Date: October 20, 1819
Death Date: May 3, 1914

Union officer. Born in New York City on October 20, 1819, Daniel Edgar Sickles attended New York University, studied law, and was admitted to the New York State bar in 1843. A Democrat, he allied himself early with corrupt Tammany Hall politicians and served one term in the New York state assembly. In 1853 he secured an appointment as secretary to James Buchanan, then U.S. minister to Britain. Sickles served two consecutive terms in the U.S. House of Representatives from 1857 to 1861. In 1859 he gained notoriety for murdering his wife's lover, Francis Barton Key, but was acquitted on the grounds of temporary insanity, the first time this defense had been successfully argued in the United States.

Sickles supported President Abraham Lincoln's war policies. This and Sickles's work to recruit a brigade of volunteers secured him a commission as a brigadier general

of volunteers in September 1861. Sickles commanded the Excelsior Brigade and fought in the Battle of Seven Pines (May 31–June 1, 1862) and the Seven Days' Campaign (June 25–July 1). Given command of a division that September, he was advanced to major general of volunteers on November 29, 1862. During the First Battle of Fredericksburg (December 13, 1862), his division was in reserve.

During the Battle of Chancellorsville (May 1–4, 1863), Sickles commanded III Corps. His men located and struck the rear guard of Lieutenant General Thomas J. Jackson's troops carrying out the famous flanking attack. This action exposed the XI Corps flank, and the resulting gap in the Union line greatly aided Jackson's maneuver.

Sickles commanded III Corps in the Battle of Gettysburg (July 1–3, 1863). On July 2, Army of the Potomac commander Major General George Gordon Meade ordered Sickles to defend the Union left from II Corps along Cemetery Ridge to Little Round Top. Believing that the high ground to his front was better suited for defensive purposes, Sickles took the controversial decision to move forward into the now-famous Peach Orchard, not realizing that in the process he had compromised the integrity of Meade's entire

Union major general Daniel E. Sickles was brave but uneven in combat. His actions on the second day of the Battle of Gettysburg (July 1–3, 1863) remain a source of debate. (Library of Congress)

defensive position. This move occurred just as Lieutenant General James Longstreet's corps attacked and opened a gap between III and II Corps that the Confederates moved to exploit. III Corps was forced back with heavy casualties. Sickles was gravely wounded in the action and lost a leg, which some credit for preventing his court-martial. He subsequently blamed Meade for what had transpired, accusing him in the press of incompetence and claiming that his own advance had prevented Meade from withdrawing from the battlefield. Controversy over the actual consequences of Sickles's actions continued for some time thereafter.

Sickles never held another field command. Following the war, he served for a time as military governor of South Carolina. On July 28, 1866, he was appointed a colonel in the regular army and was brevetted major general on March 2, 1867. He retired from the army in 1869 at the enhanced rank of major general. President Ulysses S. Grant then appointed Sickles minister to Spain, a post he held from 1869 to 1873. Sickles again shocked polite society, this time by having an affair with deposed Queen Isabella II, earning him the sobriquet the "Yankee King of Spain." He once again served in the U.S. House of Representatives (1893–1895) and was instrumental in the establishment of the Gettysburg National Park. In 1897 he received the Medal of Honor for Gettysburg. Sickles died in New York City on May 3, 1914.

MICHAEL E. LYNCH AND SPENCER C. TUCKER

See also

Chancellorsville, Battle of; Fredericksburg, First Battle of; Gettysburg, Battle of; Hancock, Winfield Scott; Joint Committee on the Conduct of the War; Meade, George Gordon; Potomac, Union Army of the; Seven Days' Campaign; Seven Pines, Battle of

Further Reading

Keneally, Thomas. *American Scoundrel: The Life of the Notorious Civil War General Dan Sickles.* New York: Nan A. Talese/Doubleday, 2002.
Pinchon, Edgcumb. *Dan Sickles: Hero of Gettysburg and "Yankee King of Spain."* Garden City, NY: Doubleday, Doran, 1945.
Swanberg, W. A. *Sickles the Incredible.* New York: Scribner, 1956.

Sigel, Franz
Birth Date: November 18, 1824
Death Date: August 21, 1902

Union officer. Franz Sigel was born in Sinsheim in the Grand Duchy of Baden on November 18, 1824, and graduated from the Karlsruhe Military Academy in 1843. While only in his mid-20s, he led revolutionary forces in Baden during the Revolutions of 1848 and was briefly minister of war in that state's new government. Following the defeat of the revolution, he went into exile and immigrated to the United States in 1852. Establishing himself in New York, he taught a variety of subjects and became active in the militia. In 1857 he settled in St. Louis and taught school there until 1861.

A prominent member of the Republican Party in Missouri at the start of the Civil War, Sigel received an appointment as brigadier general of volunteers in August 1861, backdated to May 1861. He was active in the efforts to keep Missouri in the Union and played a tremendous role in rallying the North's German population to the Union cause. He fought with distinction in the Battle of Pea Ridge (March 7–8, 1862), earning promotion to major general of volunteers. Transferred to the eastern theater, Sigel commanded I Corps under Major General John Pope in the Second Battle of Bull Run (August 29–30, 1862) and was wounded in the hand.

Franz Sigel, a German-born Union major general, owed his high rank to political connections. Not surprisingly, he was at best a mediocre commander and suffered a serious reversal in the Battle of New Market (May 15, 1864). Sigel, however, performed useful service by rallying German Americans to the Union cause during the war. (Library of Congress)

In September 1862 Sigel assumed command of XI Corps, made up largely of German American soldiers, in the Army of the Potomac. During the First Battle of Fredericksburg (December 13, 1862), Sigel's forces were held in reserve. Sigel left the command of XI Corps in February 1863 for health reasons.

Sigel's political prominence enabled him to obtain a new command at the start of 1864 as head of the newly created Department of West Virginia. Ordered to advance south up the Shenandoah Valley, Sigel was defeated in the Battle of New Market Valley (May 15, 1864). The loss was all the more embarrassing because a charge by the young cadets of the Virginia Military Institute played a key role in the Union defeat. In July, Sigel fought briefly at Harpers Ferry but was almost immediately relieved of his command because of his poor performance. He played no further role in the war and resigned his commission in May 1865.

Following the war, Sigel worked for a time in Baltimore as a journalist before becoming a newspaper editor in New York City, where he received a number of political appointments. Sigel died in New York City on August 21, 1902.

NEIL M. HEYMAN AND PAUL G. PIERPAOLI JR.

See also

Bull Run, Second Battle of; Fredericksburg, First Battle of; New Market, Battle of; Pea Ridge, Battle of; Pope, John

Further Reading

Engle, Stephen D. *Yankee Dutchman: The Life of Franz Sigel.* Fayetteville: University of Arkansas Press, 1993.

Weigley, Russell F. *A Great Civil War: A Military and Political History, 1861–1865.* Bloomington: Indiana University Press, 2000.

Signal Communications

Visual and electrical communications. Visual communications included chiefly flags, flares, torches, rockets, and signal pistols. Many of these forms of communications had been in use for centuries. Electrical communications, which had only existed since the 1830s and were not perfected sufficiently for use until the 1840s, were embodied in the telegraph and telegraphy. The Civil War was the first major war to make widespread use of this relatively new technology.

The Confederacy made use of both forms of signal communications, but they were not centrally managed, as were Union communications, and were less well-funded and staffed. The Confederates were at a particular disadvantage when it came to telegraphy because they possessed fewer operators, much less equipment, and had far fewer miles of railroad track, next to which many telegraph wires were strung.

In the North, the two major agencies responsible for communications were the U.S. Signal Corps, created in late 1860, and the U.S. Military Telegraph Service (USMTS), established in late 1861 but not fully operational until February 1862. These two agencies often fought over missions and jurisdiction. In the early winter of 1862, the Signal Corps, under Colonel Albert J. Myer, established "flying telegraph trains" in the field to aid in battlefield communications. Using the Beardslee Telegraph apparatus, these two-wagon trains could be brought into a battlefield area and had an effective range of about five miles. They were powered by hand-cranked magnetos. Myer's attempt to usurp the mission of the Telegraph Service, however, resulted in his dismissal, and the Telegraph Service thereafter handled all electrical field communications.

By the end of 1862, there was a total of 3,571 miles of telegraph line within the USMTS system. Besides telegraphers, the service employed linemen, wagon masters, foremen, battery keepers, and others who helped the telegraphers do their jobs. As armies moved, wire had to be put up and taken down, which often resulted in casualties among the men engaged in that work. By 1864, military commanders had grown to depend upon the USMTS to help command and control their armies. By the end of the war, the USMTS consisted of about 1,200 employees who operated 15,389 miles of telegraph line and handled more than 6.5 million messages, or more than 5,000 per day. It is estimated that the USMTS cost a total of $2.655 million to operate between 1862 and 1865. The U.S. Signal Corps, which transmitted countless messages during the war, cost a total of $1.595 million to operate.

PAUL G. PIERPAOLI JR.

See also

Military Telegraph Service, U.S.; Myer, Albert James; Signal Corps, U.S. Army; Telegraph

Further Reading

Marshall, Max. *The Story of the U.S. Army Signal Corps.* New York: Franklin Watts, 1965.

Plum, William R. *The Military Telegraph during the Civil War in the United States.* Reprint ed. New York: Arno, 1974.

Raines, Rebecca R. *Getting the Message Through: A Branch History of the U.S. Army Signal Corps.* Washington, DC: Center of Military History, U.S. Army, 1999.

Scheips, Paul J. "Union Signal Communications: Innovation and Conflict." *Civil War History* 9 (December 1963): 399–421.

Signal Corps, Confederate Army

Military organization charged with communications. The Confederate Army Signal Corps suffered during the war from a paucity of manpower and equipment and, probably because it was so much smaller than its counterpart, never did achieve the separate branch status enjoyed by the U.S. Army Signal Corps. Confederate engineer captain E. Porter Alexander, who in 1859 as a U.S. Army second lieutenant had assisted future U.S. Army chief signals officer Major Albert J. Myer in testing his wigwag signaling system, served as the first signal officer in the Confederate Army. Resigning his U.S. Army commission on May 1, 1861, Alexander was commissioned a Confederate Army captain of engineers and charged with recruiting and organizing a signal corps. On June 3, Alexander became both chief ordnance officer and chief signal officer of the Confederate Army of the Potomac, soon to be the Army of Northern Virginia.

On April 19, 1862, the Confederate Congress formally authorized the establishment of the Signal Corps. This was a year before the establishment of the U.S. Army Signal Corps, but unlike the U.S. organization, the Confederate Army Signal Corps was not a separate branch; it was attached to the Adjutant and Inspector General's Department. Captain William Norris headed the corps, which was authorized for 1 major, 10 captains, 20 lieutenants, 20 sergeants, and 1,500 enlisted men. There was to be a signal officer on the staff of each corps and division.

The Confederate Signal Corps utilized equipment similar to that employed by the U.S. Army signal corps, with the notable absence of electric telegraphy as a consequence of shortages of both telegraph wire and trained operators. The Confederates employed signal flags and the Myer method of wigwag but with coded messages.

Unlike the Union Signal Corps, the Confederate Signal Corps was also charged with carrying out espionage activities to include undercover operations behind Union lines and maintenance of an information network between Washington, D.C., and Richmond. Little is known of these activities because of the deliberate destruction of its records just prior to the Confederate government's evacuation of Richmond in early April 1865 and a subsequent fire at Norris's home.

SPENCER C. TUCKER

See also

Alexander, Edward Porter; Myer, Albert James; Signal Communications; Signal Corps, U.S. Army

Further Reading

Alexander, Edward P. *Fighting for the Confederacy: The Personal Recollections of General Edward Porter Alexander.* Edited by Gary W. Gallagher. Chapel Hill: University of North Carolina Press, 1989.

Plum, William R. *The Military Telegraph during the Civil War in the United States.* Reprint ed. New York: Arno, 1974.

Raines, Rebecca R. *Getting the Message Through: A Branch History of the U.S. Army Signal Corps.* Washington, DC: Center of Military History, U.S. Army, 1999.

Signal Corps, U.S. Army

Army staff department charged with coordinating military communications. The basis of the U.S. Army Signal Corps was established on June 21, 1860, when, on the recommendation of the Secretary of War John B. Floyd, President James Buchanan signed congressional legislation appropriating $2,000 to purchase equipment for signal communications based on a system devised by Albert J. Myer. An assistant army surgeon who was interested in sign language as a means of communicating with the deaf and, later, in signaling over distances with lightweight and easily employed equipment, Myer employed a flag (a kerosene lantern at night) in what was known as wigwag signaling. In 1859 Myer and an assistant, Second Lieutenant E. Porter Alexander, were able to communicate at distances of up to 15 miles in tests at Fort Monroe, Virginia; New York Harbor; West Point, New York; and Washington, D.C.

The congressional act also authorized the appointment of a signal officer, with the rank of major, to serve on the army's staff under the secretary of war to "have charge of all signal duty and all books, papers, and apparatus connected therein." Myer had lobbied for this post and was duly appointed the first signal officer, effective June 27, 1860. Two weeks later he was ordered to the Department of New Mexico to participate in the campaign against hostile Navajos.

Recalled to Washington with the beginning of the Civil War, Myer in August 1861 submitted a proposal to Secretary of War Simon Cameron for a signal corps to consist of himself, 7 assistant signal officers, 40 warrant officers, and 40 signal artificers to build and repair signal lines. Congress took no action, but that autumn Myer also became chief signal officer for the principal Union field army in the East, the Army of the Potomac, and proceeded to set up signal training facilities in the Georgetown section of Washington and at Fort Monroe, Virginia. Meanwhile, Myer continued to lobby for legislation to establish a formal signal corps.

On March 3, 1863, President Abraham Lincoln signed into law congressional legislation establishing a separate

Signal Corps within the U.S. Army. Myer received appointment as chief signal officer with the rank of colonel. A conflict over the control of telegraphic communications soon developed, however, between Myer as chief signal officer and the superintendent of the U.S. Military Telegraph Service, a civilian bureau within the War Department that had been responsible for telegraph service and reported directly to the secretary of war, now Edwin M. Stanton. Myer was unsuccessful in this administrative battle, although he temporarily secured approval to establish signal telegraph trains (wagon trains, not railroad trains) equipped with a magnetoelectric telegraph instrument as a portable telegraph system. However, in the autumn of 1863, Myer's efforts to gain control over the electric telegraph resulted in the removal of the portable system from the jurisdiction of the Signal Corps, the transfer of the telegraph trains to the Telegraph Service, and his removal as chief signal officer on November 10.

Myer's replacement, as acting chief signal officer, was Major William J. L. Nicodemus, Myer's former assistant. By now the Signal Corps had grown to some 200 officers and 1,000 enlisted men. But Nicodemus's published 1864 report on Signal Corps activities, which revealed that Union signalers were able to read Confederate communications, angered Stanton, and Nicodemus was promptly dismissed. The last chief signal officer during the war was Colonel Benjamin F. Fisher, former chief signal officer for the Army of the Potomac, who had been taken prisoner by the Confederates during the Gettysburg Campaign and had only recently been exchanged.

With the end of the war, the Signal Corps was terminated in August 1865. At one time or another during the course of the war, some 2,900 officers and enlisted men served in the corps. Acting on the advice of U.S. Army general in chief Lieutenant General Ulysses S. Grant, Congress reestablished the Signal Corps on July 28, 1866, with Myer restored to his former post as chief signal officer. Ironically, Myer's responsibilities included control of military telegraph operations. During the next two decades, the most important military activity of the Signal Corps was the extension and operation of military telegraph lines in the American West where commercial lines were not yet available.

MARTIN J. MANNING AND SPENCER C. TUCKER

See also

Alexander, Edward Porter; Buchanan, James; Cameron, Simon; Grant, Ulysses Simpson; Lincoln, Abraham; Military Telegraph Service, U.S.; Myer, Albert James; Signal Communications; Stanton, Edwin McMasters; Telegraph

Further Reading

Brown, J. Willard. *The Signal Corps, U.S.A. in the War of the Rebellion.* New York: Arno, 1974.
Raines, Rebecca R. *Getting the Message Through: A Branch History of the U.S. Army Signal Corps.* Washington, DC: Center of Military History, U.S. Army, 1999.
Thompson, George R., and Dixie R. Harris. *The Signal Corps.* Washington, DC: Center of Military History, U.S. Army, 1966.

Sill, Joshua Woodrow
Birth Date: December 6, 1831
Death Date: December 31, 1862

Union officer. Joshua Woodrow Sill was born on December 6, 1831, in Chillicothe, Ohio, and graduated from the U.S. Military Academy, West Point, in 1853. He thereafter held numerous posts, including a stint as an instructor at West Point, earning promotion to first lieutenant in 1856. Sill left the army in January 1861 to teach in the civilian sector, but that spring he was appointed assistant adjutant general of Ohio when the Civil War began. His first combat was at the Battle of Rich Mountain (July 11, 1861) in western Virginia.

Commissioned colonel of the 33rd Ohio Infantry Regiment shortly thereafter, in November Sill was in command of a brigade in the 3rd Division, Department of the Ohio. Advanced to brigadier general of volunteers on July 16, 1862, he next took command of the 2nd Division, I Corps, Army of the Ohio, which saw action in Kentucky.

By December 1862, Sill was commanding a brigade in the 3rd Division, XIV Corps, Army of the Cumberland. On the morning of December 31, Sill's men were encamped along Stones River in Tennessee and were about to eat breakfast when the Union position came under sudden and ferocious Confederate attack. Attempting to rally his panicked troops, Sill was killed by small arms fire. After the war, Major General Philip H. Sheridan, a close friend of Sill, named Fort Sill (Oklahoma) in his memory.

PAUL G. PIERPAOLI JR.

See also

Sheridan, Philip Henry; Stones River, Battle of

Further Reading

Eicher, John H., and David J. Eicher. *Civil War High Commands.* Stanford, CA: Stanford University Press, 2001.
Warner, Ezra J. *Generals in Blue: Lives of the Union Commanders.* Baton Rouge: Louisiana State University Press, 2006.

Simms, James Phillip
Birth Date: January 16, 1837
Death Date: May 30, 1887

Confederate officer. James Phillip Simms was born on January 16, 1837, in Covington, Georgia. Very little is known of his prewar career other than the fact that he became a lawyer and practiced in Covington. He entered Confederate records on September 24, 1862, when he was named major of the 53rd Georgia Infantry Regiment. On October 8, he became its colonel.

Serving in I Corps, Army of Northern Virginia, in a division commanded by Major General Lafayette McClaws, Simms saw combat at the First Battle of Fredericksburg (December 13, 1862) and the Battle of Salem Church (May 3–4, 1863), where his regiment performed ably. He also saw action at the Battle of Gettysburg (July 1–3, 1863) and in the Chattanooga Campaign (October–November 1863) and the Knoxville Campaign (November–December 1863). Conspicuous during the latter campaign, he was also wounded.

Simms next fought at the Battle of the Wilderness (May 5–7, 1864) and the Battle of Spotsylvania Court House (May 8–21, 1864). He then saw action during Union major general Philip H. Sheridan's Shenandoah Valley Campaign (August 7, 1864–March 2, 1865). In September 1864, Simms was given a brigade command. He played a key role in the Battle of Cedar Creek (October 19, 1864). On December 8, 1864, he was advanced to brigadier general, to date from November 1. Sent to the trenches during the Petersburg Campaign (June 15, 1864–April 3, 1865), he was taken prisoner at the Battle of Sayler's Creek (April 6, 1865) during the flight to Appomattox.

Released from Fort Warren (Boston) on July 24, 1865, Simms resumed his law practice in Georgia and served in the state legislature (1865–1866 and 1877). Simms died on May 30, 1887, in Covington, Georgia.

PAUL G. PIERPAOLI JR.

See also
Cedar Creek, Battle of; Chattanooga Campaign; Fredericksburg, First Battle of; Gettysburg, Battle of; Knoxville Campaign; Petersburg Campaign; Salem Church, Battle of; Sayler's Creek, Battle of; Sheridan's Shenandoah Valley Campaign; Spotsylvania Court House, Battle of; Wilderness, Battle of the

Further Reading
Eicher, John H., and David J. Eicher. *Civil War High Commands.* Stanford, CA: Stanford University Press, 2001.

Warner, Ezra J. *Generals in Gray: Lives of the Confederate Commanders.* Baton Rouge: Louisiana State University Press, 2006.

Simms, William Gilmore
Birth Date: April 17, 1806
Death Date: June 11, 1870

South Carolina novelist, editor, and poet. William Gilmore Simms was born on April 17, 1806, in Charleston, South Carolina. A member of a Charleston-based group promoting Southern literature, in the 1830s he became one of the most popular writers in the country, with novels such as *The Yemassee* (1835) and historical romances in the tradition of Sir Walter Scott and James Fenimore Cooper set in the colonial, Revolutionary, and antebellum South. Simms became a plantation owner when he married Charleston heiress Chevilette Eliza Roach in 1836 and settled on the family's plantation, the Woodlands.

Despite his business connections and friends in the North, Simms was a devoted supporter of slavery, secession, and the Confederate cause. His works emphasized the benefits that slavery provided for loyal slaves and the unhappiness of free blacks. He also wrote *The Sword and the Distaff* (1852), better known as *Woodcraft* (1854), one of the most successful anti-Tom novels, books by Southern authors responding to the negative portrayal of slavery and plantation life in Harriet Beecher Stowe's *Uncle Tom's Cabin* (1851–1852). The hostility with which Simms's views were greeted caused him to cut short a lecture tour in the North in 1856.

The Civil War proved devastating to Simms. Chevilette died in 1863, and the Woodlands was burned twice. In addition to the damage caused to Simms's property, the war also interrupted his access to publishers and markets in the North, leading to poverty and overwork in his declining years. Simms's writings relating to the Civil War include *The Sack and Destruction of the City of Columbia, S.C.* (1865) and an edited collection titled *War Poetry of the South* (1865). Simms died in Charleston on June 11, 1870.

WILLIAM E. BURNS

See also
Literature; Slavery; Stowe, Harriet Beecher; *Uncle Tom's Cabin*

Further Reading
Guilds, John Caldwell. *Simms: A Literary Life.* Fayetteville: University of Arkansas Press, 1992.

Wimsatt, Mary Ann. *The Major Fiction of William Gilmore Simms: Cultural Tradition and Literary Form.* Baton Rouge: Louisiana State University Press, 1989.

Sims, Thomas
Birth Date: ca. 1828
Death Date: Unknown

Runaway slave. Thomas Sims was born around 1828, probably in the vicinity of Savannah, Georgia, and was owned by James Potter, a wealthy rice planter in Chatham County, Georgia. When Sims was in his teens, Potter rented him out as a laborer, and Sims soon learned the bricklaying trade. In February 1851 Sims stowed away on a ship headed to Boston, which was then at the epicenter of the growing abolitionist movement. For most of the two-week trip to Boston, Sims managed to stay hidden, but he was eventually found and locked away in a cabin before the ship arrived in Boston. When the ship docked, Sims managed to escape.

Sims survived by taking odd jobs and was sheltered by Boston's large African American population. Within several weeks, however, his presence in Boston was revealed, and on April 3, 1851, an agent for his owner, John Potter, swore out an arrest warrant against Sims. Under the newly enacted Fugitive Slave Act of 1850, authorities were duty bound to turn Sims in and ensure his return to his owner. On the evening of April 3, Boston police located Sims and jailed him in the Boston courthouse, under the watch of Union marshals.

The Millard Fillmore administration moved swiftly to extradite Sims to Georgia, but Boston's abolitionists—including the biracial Boston Vigilance Committee—moved to block Sims's extradition in court. Meanwhile, the case became one of great interest to many Bostonians. The committee hired lawyers and attempted numerous legal efforts to prevent Sims from being returned to slavery, but in the end all failed. When it became clear that Sims would indeed be extradited, hundreds of protesters choked the streets around the courthouse. On April 11 the extradition order was formally handed down, and Sims was marched to an awaiting ship on April 13 under heavy guard for the voyage south to Savannah. Some 50,000 people gathered along the route from the courthouse to the docks. Meanwhile, abolitionists and black congregations in Boston began raising $1,300 to purchase Sims's freedom.

When Sims landed in Savannah several weeks later, he was publicly beaten for his attempted escape. Less than two months later Potter sold Sims, who was then bought by a brick mason in Vicksburg, Mississippi. There Sims remained, in bondage, until the spring of 1863, when Vicksburg was under siege by Union forces. That April, Sims and his family escaped to the Union lines. He was promptly given a travel pass, and he returned to Boston. He later moved to Washington, D.C., but virtually nothing is known of his life after the late 1880s, including the date and circumstances of his death.

PAUL G. PIERPAOLI JR.

See also

Abolitionism and the Civil War; Compromise of 1850; Fugitive Slave Act of 1850; Slavery; Slaves

Further Reading

Campbell, Stanley W. *The Slave Catchers: Enforcement of the Fugitive Slave Law, 1850–1860.* Chapel Hill: University of North Carolina Press, 1970.
Lubet, Steven. *Fugitive Justice: Runaways, Rescuers, and Slavery on Trial.* Cambridge, MA: Belknap Press of Harvard University Press, 2010.

Singleton, James Washington
Birth Date: November 23, 1811
Death Date: April 4, 1892

Leading Peace Democrat during the Civil War. James Washington Singleton was born on November 23, 1811, in Frederick County, Virginia, to a distinguished family. His father, James Singleton, was a general during the Revolutionary War. In 1834, the younger Singleton moved to Mount Sterling, Illinois, where he studied medicine and briefly practiced before studying law. He was admitted to the bar in 1838 and commenced a legal practice in Mount Sterling.

Singleton joined the state militia, rising to the rank of brigadier general in 1844 and participating in the move to expel the Mormons from Illinois. From 1850 to 1854, he sat in the state legislature as a Democrat and relocated to Quincy, Illinois, in 1854. From 1860 to 1862, he again served in the Illinois legislature.

A Copperhead (or Peace Democrat) from the very beginning of the Civil War, Singleton consistently defended the institution of slavery and asserted that the Union's war effort against the Confederacy was unconstitutional. Not surprisingly, he lambasted the Republicans and decried virtually every policy of the Abraham Lincoln administration. In 1862 Singleton's extreme views cost him his seat in the state legislature. Two years later, anti-Copperhead operatives torched many of the outbuildings on his Illinois farm. That same year, he joined other hard-line Peace Democrats who refused to support George B. McClellan, the Democratic Party's presidential candidate, because McClellan refused to call for an immediate end to the war via negotiations.

In the late autumn of 1864, Singleton traveled to Canada, where he met with Cassius M. Clay, a Confederate agent there, to mull peace offers. Singleton also went to the Confederate capital at Richmond for the same purpose. The U.S. government did not underwrite Singleton's efforts, but neither did it try to stop them. In any event, Singleton's travels did nothing to end the war.

Singleton managed to polish his formerly tarnished political image and went on to serve in the U.S. House of Representatives (1879–1883). In the meantime he had served as a railroad executive, and during his time in Congress he pushed aggressively for the construction of railroads in the Midwest and especially in Illinois, which was quickly becoming the nation's rail hub. Singleton lived in Quincy until 1892, when he moved to Baltimore. He died there on April 4, 1892.

PAUL G. PIERPAOLI JR.

See also

Clay, Cassius Marcellus; Copperheads; Democratic Party; Election of 1864, U.S.; Illinois

Further Reading

Klement, Frank. *The Copperheads in the Middle West.* Chicago: University of Chicago Press, 1960.

Weber, Jennifer. *Copperheads: The Rise and Fall of Lincoln's Opponents in the North.* New York: Oxford University Press, 2006.

Sioux Uprising
Start Date: August 17, 1862
End Date: September 23, 1862

Armed clash between the Minnesota Sioux (several of the bands of Dakota people also known as the Santee Sioux) and U.S. Volunteer forces. The Sioux Uprising (also known as the Dakota War of 1862, the Minnesota Sioux Uprising, and Little Crow's War) began on August 17, 1862, along the Minnesota River in Meeker County in southwestern Minnesota and ended on September 23, 1862, with the defeat of the Sioux. One of the bloodiest Indian wars in U.S. history, the conflict claimed the lives of 500–800 settlers; Native American casualties are unknown.

In 1851 the United States and the Dakota tribes signed the Treaty of Traverse des Sioux and the Treaty of Mendota,

whereby the Dakota lands became open to white settlers. In return, the Native Americans were to receive monetary compensation as well as a stretch of land 20 miles wide and 150 miles long along the upper Minnesota River, where a reservation would be created. However, during the ratification process in the U.S. Senate, Article 3 of each treaty that guaranteed compensation to the Indians for their land was deleted. That along with rampant corruption in the Bureau of Indian Affairs ensured that the Native Americans would never receive the promised compensation.

When Minnesota entered the Union in 1858, its borders shifted from the Missouri River to the Red River. Despite appeals by Sioux chief Little Crow (Taoyateduta) to Washington, the northern half of the reservation was ceded for white settlement. Because of the failed negotiations, meanwhile, Little Crow lost much of his standing with the tribe. The Sioux were ultimately driven out of the state, and those who remained were confined to the small reservation.

White settlement in the region began to have adverse effects on Native American lifestyles. Clearing timber to make room for farmlands interrupted the natural cycle of farming, hunting, and fishing practiced by the Sioux. Also, wildlife populations of bison, elk, whitetail deer, and bear decreased steadily because of excessive hunting by the white settlers. Dwindling lands, a lack of game, and crop failures brought starvation, and the Sioux began attacking white settlers in search of food.

On August 4, 1862, representatives of the Minnesota Sioux approached the Upper Sioux Agency to plead for food. After successful negotiations, they returned on August 15 to receive their promised supplies. However, Minnesota state senator and Indian agent Thomas Galbraith refused to distribute the supplies without payment, regardless of the previous agreement. At a subsequent meeting of the Sioux, U.S. government officials, and local traders, the Native Americans pleaded with the lead trader, Andrew Myrick, for his support, to which he replied essentially that they should go away and eat grass.

This offensive and dehumanizing comment enraged the Sioux. With the U.S. Army occupied by the Civil War, the Dakota chiefs seized the opportunity for an armed uprising. The violence began on August 17, 1862. Four Sioux men, stealing food from a settlement in Meeker County, killed five white settlers. Although Chief Little Crow initially opposed a violent solution to the problem, given the uproar among the Native Americans the other chiefs were able to convince him to lead further attacks. At the council of war, the chiefs decided to attack without warning.

Myrick was one of the first to die in the subsequent attacks. He was found dead with grass stuffed into his mouth, a macabre allusion to his earlier comment. Captain John March then led a force of 44–46 men from Fort Ridgely, but the Sioux attacked the soldiers as they were attempting to cross the Minnesota River on the Redwood Ferry on August 18. Some 25 soldiers died in the ensuing Battle of Redwood Ferry. Sioux casualties are unknown.

Over the next week the Sioux, encouraged by their initial successes, attacked scores of settlements and farms, killing many white settlers in the process. They did not hesitate to attack military installations, including Forts Ridgely and Abercrombie. Fort Ridgely, now defended by about 175 men and with perhaps 300 settlers who had managed to take refuge there, came under attack by as many as 800 Sioux warriors on August 20. In two days of fighting, the defenders managed to drive off the attacking Sioux, thanks in large part to the assistance of three howitzers.

Sioux attacks also targeted the town of New Ulm. Assaults on August 19 and 23 were repulsed, although much of the town was destroyed in the second attack, and the inhabitants evacuated the settlement on August 26.

Minnesota governor Alexander Ramsey ordered Minnesota Militia colonel Henry Hastings Sibley to lead a force to relieve the settlers. Sibley was soon on the move with 1,500 men. He detached part of his force as a burial detail, and it came under attack at Birch Coulee on September 2, 1862. There 20 soldiers died and 60 more were wounded, but Sibley heard the sounds of battle, and the survivors managed to hold out until the arrival of a relief column the next day.

Sibley then went looking for the hostiles and on September 23, 1862, at the Battle of Wood Lake soundly defeated the Sioux. During the next several days, many of the Sioux defected from Little Crow and began releasing captives.

By the end of November, a military tribunal had convicted 303 Native Americans of murder and rape and sentenced them to death. At the trials the Sioux had no representation, and there was no explanation to them of the proceedings. Some trials lasted only five minutes. After a review of the records, President Abraham Lincoln differentiated between the Dakota warriors accused of crimes against the United States and those accused of rape and murder of civilians. Bishop Henry Whipple pleaded with the president for clemency for the Dakotas, and Lincoln upheld the convictions of 39 Sioux accused of rape and murder and commuted the death sentences of the others. One Sioux was later reprieved. The remaining 38 sentenced to death were hanged on December 26, 1862, at Mankato, Minnesota. It was the largest public execution in U.S. history.

In 1863, 1,300 to 1,700 Minnesota Sioux were sent to the Nebraska and Dakota Territories. Four years later, the surviving imprisoned Sioux were released. Thirty percent of them had died of disease while in prison. The remaining Sioux were sent to the Nebraska and Dakota Territories with their families in an attempt to expel the Sioux from Minnesota for good. After that, a bounty of $25 was paid for the scalp of any Sioux found within Minnesota borders. The U.S. government also abolished the reservation and voided all previous treaties with the Dakotas. Little Crow and his son, who had returned to Minnesota, were shot and killed by two farmers in the summer of 1863.

ANNA RULSKA

See also

Dakota Sioux; Lincoln, Abraham; Sibley, Henry Hastings

Further Reading

Carley, Kenneth. *The Sioux Uprising of 1862*. St. Paul: Minnesota Historical Society, 1976.

Keenan, Jerry. *The Great Sioux Uprising: Rebellion on the Plains, August–September, 1862*. Cambridge, MA: Da Capo, 2003.

Sister Nurses

Roman Catholic sisters (nuns) who served as nurses for Union and Confederate soldiers during the Civil War. Commonly referred to as "Sisters of Charity" or "Sisters of Mercy," these nonpartisan sisters responded promptly to the requests for assistance after the beginning of the war.

The sisters worked in Union military hospitals throughout the North and Midwest and in Confederate hospitals throughout the South. Many were not new to nursing, having served in civilian hospitals and asylums. However, their arrival en masse on the battlefield, in addition to many other women serving as nurses who were not associated with the Catholic Church, saw a transformation in military medical care from one that was characterized as inadequate and inconsistent to one that relied on a professionalized nursing force and significantly improved medical care.

The sisters confronted much anti-Catholic sentiment as they performed their duties. Many of the sisters were also Irish or German immigrants, which resulted in additional discrimination. One contingent, the Irish Sisters of Mercy from New York City, led by Mother Augustine MacKenna, served at Hammond General Hospital in Beaufort, North Carolina, in May 1862; the group of nine nuns helped transform the hospital from a poorly run facility to a clean, well-managed hospital providing improved care.

The various orders of nuns were well organized and thorough in the completion of their responsibilities, often providing a stark contrast between hospitals and temporary medical stations run by the various orders and those run by the Union Army and the Confederate Army. Beginning in 1861 in Fort Leavenworth, Kansas, the Union Army operated just 1 hospital, while the Catholic sisters opened and ran 20, some in unconventional venues such as barns and warehouses.

The sisters who cared for soldiers on both sides were volunteers, and as such few official government records exist regarding them or their service. It is estimated that hundreds of Catholic sisters working as nurses contracted diseases such as malaria, typhoid fever, and smallpox while caring for soldiers, and many died from these diseases. Sister Consolata Conlon, a nun working at the military hospital in Point Lookout, Maryland, was one of the few to receive a military burial after her death from typhoid fever on July 30, 1862.

JENNIFER HARRISON

See also
Catholics; Medicine; Nurses

Further Reading
Fialka, John J. *Sisters: Catholic Nuns and the Making of America.* New York: St. Martin's, 2003.
Maher, Mary Denis. *To Bind Up the Wounds: Catholic Sister Nurses in the U.S. Civil War.* New York: Greenwood, 1989.

6th Pennsylvania Cavalry
See Rush's Lancers

Slack, James Richard
Birth Date: September 28, 1818
Death Date: July 28, 1881

Union officer. James Richard Slack was born in Bucks County, Pennsylvania, on September 28, 1818. In 1837 he moved with his family to Delaware County, Indiana. Slack taught school there until 1840, when he passed the bar and relocated to Huntington, Indiana, to practice law. In 1842 he won election as county auditor. He served nine years in that position before serving seven terms as a state senator.

In October 1861 Slack helped organize the 47th Indiana Infantry, and on December 13 he received a volunteer commission as its colonel. In February 1862 Slack joined the Army of the Mississippi's campaign against first New Madrid and then Island No. 10 (February 28–April 8, 1862). During these operations, Slack commanded a brigade and established himself as an effective leader.

Throughout 1862 and early 1863, Slack saw service at numerous outposts along the Mississippi River in both Tennessee and Arkansas. During the Second Vicksburg Campaign (April 1–July 4, 1863), he led a brigade in XIII Corps. Slack saw action around the Yazoo Pass and later at Port Gibson (May 1, 1863) and Champion Hill (May 16, 1863).

Following Vicksburg, Slack received an assignment to accompany elements of XIII Corps to the Department of the Gulf in the Trans-Mississippi theater. There, he led a brigade during operations along Bayou Teche (October 1863). In 1864 Slack participated in the Red River Campaign (March 10–May 22) and afterward commanded the garrison at Thibodeaux, Louisiana. On November 10, 1864, he received a promotion to brigadier general of volunteers.

In February 1865 the War Department reorganized XIII Corps, and Slack took command of a brigade for operations against Mobile, Alabama (March–April, 1865). On March 13 Slack was brevetted major general of volunteers. His command played a vital role in the Siege of Fort Blakely (April 2–9) and the subsequent capture of Mobile.

After the war, Slack returned to Indiana and served as a circuit court judge. He died in Chicago on July 28, 1881.

JEFFERY S. PRUSHANKIN

See also
Champion Hill, Battle of; Fort Blakely, Alabama, Siege of; Island No. 10, Battle of; Mobile, Alabama, Siege of; Port Gibson, Battle of; Red River Campaign; Vicksburg Campaign, Second

Further Reading
Eicher, John H., and David J. Eicher. *Civil War High Commands.* Stanford, CA: Stanford University Press, 2001.
Warner, Ezra J. *Generals in Blue: Lives of the Union Commanders.* Baton Rouge: Louisiana State University Press, 2006.

Slack, William Yarnell
Birth Date: August 1, 1816
Death Date: March 21, 1862

Confederate officer. William Yarnell Slack was born on August 1, 1816, in Mason County, Kentucky, but moved to Boone County, Missouri, as a young boy. He studied law and established a practice in Chillicothe, Missouri. During the Mexican-American War (1846–1848), Slack served as a captain in the 2nd Missouri Volunteer Infantry Regiment. Elected to the state legislature on a proslavery ticket, he urged legislators to cast their lot with the Confederacy in 1861.

On July 4, 1861, Missouri governor Claiborne F. Jackson appointed Slack a brigadier general of the Missouri State Guard. The following day in the Battle of Carthage, Slack led the State Guard's 4th Division. He commanded that division at the Battle of Wilson's Creek (August 10, 1861), where he was seriously wounded in the hip.

After a period of recovery, Slack returned to lead his division in October. On January 23, 1862, he took command of the Guard's 2nd Brigade. During the Battle of Pea Ridge (March 7–8, 1862) in Arkansas, Slack was again seriously wounded. Carried to a nearby house, he seemed to be making a recovery. However, surgeons feared that he might be captured and insisted that he be moved to Moore's Mill, some seven miles distant. The journey proved to be too much for him, and Slack died at Moore's Mill, Arkansas, on March 21, 1862. The Confederacy granted him a posthumous promotion to brigadier general of regulars on April 17, 1862, to date from April 12.

PAUL G. PIERPAOLI JR.

See also

Carthage, Battle of; Pea Ridge, Battle of; Wilson's Creek, Battle of

Further Reading

Bridges, Hal. "A Confederate Hero: General William Y. Slack." *Arkansas Historical Quarterly* 10 (Autumn 1951): 22–36.
Warner, Ezra J. *Generals in Gray: Lives of the Confederate Commanders.* Baton Rouge: Louisiana State University Press, 2006.

Slash Church, Battle of

See Hanover Court House, Battle of

Slaughter, James Edwin

Birth Date: June 1827
Death Date: January 1, 1901

Confederate officer. James Edwin Slaughter was born in June 1827 in Culpeper County, Virginia. Although Slaughter enrolled at the Virginia Military Institute in 1845, he withdrew in 1846 to join the army and fight in the Mexican-American War (1846–1848). Rising to the rank of first lieutenant, Slaughter served in the U.S. Army until May 14, 1861, when he was dismissed for resigning his commission to join the Confederate Army as an artillery captain.

Slaughter served initially in Pensacola, Florida, on the staff of Brigadier General Braxton Bragg. Following promotion to major in November 1861, Slaughter was appointed brigadier general on March 8, 1862. He was then assigned as assistant inspector general under General Albert Sidney Johnston and served at the Battle of Shiloh (April 6–7, 1862).

Following administrative service in Kentucky, Slaughter was assigned command of troops in Mobile, Alabama. Reassigned to Galveston, Texas, in April 1863, he was chief of artillery and later chief of staff under Major General John B. Magruder. Serving in Texas until the end of the conflict, Slaughter commanded troops at the Battle of Palmito Ranch (May 12–13, 1865), a Confederate victory and widely considered to be the final battle of the Civil War. Following the war, Slaughter went abroad, spending several years in Mexico.

Returning to the United States, Slaughter pursued work as a civil engineer in Mobile, Alabama, and was also a postmaster. He later lived in New Orleans, Louisiana. Slaughter died during a visit to Mexico City on January 1, 1901.

SEAN M. HEUVEL

See also

Bragg, Braxton; Johnston, Albert Sidney; Magruder, John Bankhead; Palmito Ranch, Battle of; Shiloh, Battle of

Further Reading

Slaughter, Philip. *Genealogical and Historical Notes on Culpeper County, Virginia.* Culpeper, VA: Exponent Printing Office, 1900.
Warner, Ezra J. *Generals in Gray: Lives of the Confederate Commanders.* Baton Rouge: Louisiana State University Press, 2006.

Slavery

System of forced, uncompensated, and often lifelong labor utilized by many civilizations prior to the 20th century. Throughout history, slavery played an important part in many civilizations, providing workers in occupations as diverse as farming, mining, domestics, skilled labor, and even academics. European settlements in the New World colonies utilized slaves as a source of cheap labor to replace indentured servants. Africa served as a major source of captives, with which the American slave trade was perpetuated. By the eve of the Civil War, the great majority of slaves resided in the states of the Deep South, from the Carolinas west to Texas.

African American Population of the United States, 1840–1880

Year	Number of African Americans	% of Total U.S. Population	Slaves	% Slaves	% Nonslaves
1840	2,873,648	16.80%	2,487,355	87%	13%
1850	3,638,808	15.70%	3,204,287	88%	12%
1860	4,441,830	14.10%	3,953,731	89%	11%
1870	4,880,009	12.70%	N/A	0%	100%
1880	6,580,793	13.10%	N/A	0%	100%

Between the early 16th century and the early 19th century, some 12.8 million slaves were transported as part of the transatlantic slave trade to the New World, with approximately 10.7 million actually surviving the trip. British North America accounted for approximately 500,000 of the total, with the vast majority of those sent to the Thirteen Colonies, later to become the United States. The first Africans in the American colonies arrived on a Dutch ship that docked in Jamestown in 1619, when 20 Africans were sold to the colonists; although some were essentially indentured servants, others were indeed slaves. During the next two centuries, slavery gradually expanded throughout England's American colonies.

By the mid-1600s slavery was legal in every American colony, with slaves classified as property and having few, if any, rights. Chattel slavery became the norm in the colonies, with the children born to female slaves being classified as slaves themselves from birth. Although some slaves worked in urban environments, the vast majority were located on farms and plantations in rural regions of the Chesapeake areas of Maryland and Virginia and in the lower South. Some slaves were employed as artisans, others as domestics, and many as farm and field hands. Growing tobacco, cotton, and sugar, mostly southern crops, were labor-intensive endeavors; thus, profitable plantations required a large number of slaves to work the fields and perform manual tasks. Typical slave owners held fewer than 5 slaves; most plantations employed 10 to 20 slaves, yet the largest plantations might have had several hundred slaves. By 1860, only 25 percent of the population in the South owned slaves, while only 10,000 families owned more than 50 slaves. Most slave owners asserted that the institution of slavery was "benevolent" and benefited the African Americans under its yoke. Some slave owners even rationalized slavery on religious grounds. Whatever their rationale, slave owners fervently sought to protect the institution at virtually any cost.

After the American Revolutionary War, the new U.S. government, operating under the Articles of Confederation, passed the Northwest Ordinance of 1787, legislation that prohibited slavery in the Old Northwest Territory. Furthermore, some gradual abolition of slavery occurred in the North, with Vermont outlawing slavery in 1777 and Pennsylvania and Massachusetts either gradually abolishing slavery or prohibiting it outright. However, slavery was allowed to continue in the South. Although the word "slavery" did not appear in the U.S. Constitution of 1787 until the Thirteenth Amendment (1865), various articles and amendments offered constitutional protections to slave owners. Notable examples are clauses dealing with runaways and, most importantly, the Three-Fifths Compromise, which allowed slave states to count every five slaves as three persons in their populations for the purposes of establishing congressional representation and the distribution of taxes. The U.S. Congress banned the international slave trade in 1807, but the illegal importation of slaves continued, as did the sale of slaves within the United States.

Legally, slaves rarely had any rights and were prohibited from engaging in many activities, such as learning to read and write, leaving the plantation, or marrying without their owner's permission. Furthermore, slaves were subjected to a variety of punishments ranging from verbal and physical abuse—some of it brutal—to being executed for some offenses. At the same time, slave owners were almost never punished for killing a slave while administering discipline. The outright murder of slaves was also often overlooked by the authorities.

Slaves often resisted their condition in a variety of ways, ranging from passive forms of resistance to violence, although the latter was infrequent. Typical acts of peaceful resistance included malingering, feigning illness, slowing down work, running away, or sabotaging farm equipment. Violent forms of resistance included physical attacks against

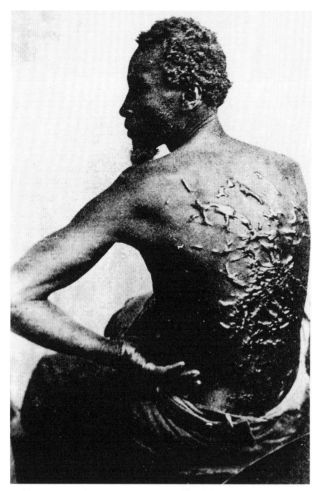

A former slave shows the scars on his back from a savage whipping he had received before his escape. He became a Union soldier during the Civil War. (Time Life Pictures/National Archives/Getty Images)

specific individuals, murder, arson, and outright revolts. The pre–Civil War era saw multiple attempted or actual slave rebellions, including Nat Turner's Revolt (1831) in Tidewater Virginia. Southern states reacted to revolts or attempted revolts by prohibiting slaves from participating in particular activities, such as gathering in large groups or traveling without passes, and also placed restrictions against free blacks and whites alike, prohibiting the latter from teaching slaves to read and write and sometimes restricting the right to manumit slaves.

America's steady territorial expansion between 1787 and 1860 resulted in continued debates about the expansion of slavery. Northern states opposed attempts to expand slavery into northern and western territories, because many individuals believed that free labor agriculture and industry could not compete against slave labor. Northerners also feared that extending slavery to new territories would

strengthen the hand of states in the South and slaveholders in general. Southerners, however, saw no reason to limit the areas where slavery could exist. As a result, various compromises and legislation were enacted to control slavery's expansion and maintain the delicate balance between free and slave states. The Missouri Compromise of 1820 allowed Missouri to enter the Union as a slave state but prohibited slavery elsewhere in the Louisiana Territory above 36 degrees 30 minutes north latitude. During the Mexican-American War (1846–1848), northern politicians offered amendments such as the Wilmot Proviso, which would have prohibited slavery in any territory acquired as a result of the war; although defeated, this demonstrated the North's growing opposition to the expansion of slavery. By the early decades of the 19th century, meanwhile, an abolitionist movement had begun to shape, and by midcentury it had grown significantly stronger and garnered much attention.

Despite congressional passage of the Fugitive Slave Act of 1850 (which was an attempt to nationalize law enforcement activities to enforce slave owners' rights regarding the return of escaped slaves), other events such as John Brown's raid against the Harpers Ferry Arsenal (October 16–18, 1859) caused great concern among slaveholders. Additionally, political parties opposed to the expansion of slavery (such as the Free Soil Party and the Republican Party) were gradually gaining strength in the North. Meanwhile, the Kansas-Nebraska Act of 1854, which ignited the idea of popular sovereignty by allowing residents of Kansas and Nebraska to decide for themselves if slavery should be permitted in their respective states, completely unraveled the Missouri Compromise and only fueled the growing rift between North and South.

Southern leaders saw Abraham Lincoln's victory in the November 1860 presidential elections as an existential threat to slavery, despite Lincoln's assurances that he would not interfere with slavery where it already existed. South Carolina seceded from the United States on December 20, 1860, and was followed later by other Southern states. By April 1861, North and South were at war.

Slaves, numbering about 4 million in 1860, were a significant labor force for the Confederacy, allowing greater numbers of whites to serve in the military. Although the majority of slaves continued working in agricultural activities, the lack of white manpower resulted in slaves being used in the industrial and mining sectors. Most slaves remained on their plantations. Some were impressed as manual laborers to work on Confederate military projects and fortifications, while others, acting as servants, accompanied their masters who had joined the Confederate Army. Slaveholders often reluctantly provided slaves to Confederate forces, recognizing that slaves working in military areas were more likely to be injured or killed and that they had greater opportunities to escape. Near the end of the war, some Confederate officials, in an attempt to supplement the badly depleted Southern forces, proposed offering slaves their freedom if they fought for the Confederacy, but this idea was never realized.

Throughout the war a number of slaves took advantage of these opportunities, fleeing to Union lines or farther north. A good number of these served as Union soldiers. Initially, no federal policy dictated how commanders were to deal with escaped slaves. Because the war was not waged principally to end slavery, many officers returned escaped slaves in order to assure Southerners that the Union was not opposing slavery. Union commanders later realized the value of slaves to the Confederate war effort, however, and began declaring them contraband of war; they were then put to work constructing fortifications and in other nonmilitary jobs. Escaped slaves also served as a source of intelligence about Confederate activities in the regions where those slaves had lived. Once Lincoln shifted part of the war's focus to eliminating slavery with the January 1863 Emancipation Proclamation, escaped slaves were not returned to the South.

Initial federal efforts to end slavery were limited at best. Lincoln's Emancipation Proclamation, for example, only authorized freeing slaves in areas in rebellion that were not under federal control, thus allowing slavery to continue to exist in loyal states and Union-occupied areas of the Confederacy, such as large portions of Louisiana and Tennessee. Congressional passage of the Thirteenth Amendment and its ratification on December 6, 1865, officially outlawed slavery in all of the United States. Freed slaves, along with other African Americans, however, continued to face many challenges in gaining full political and civil rights over the next 100 years. In many ways, black Americans in the postbellum South were subjected to a different form of slavery, not in legal terms but certainly in substance. Many labored as sharecroppers, eking out a meager existence and being beholden to their white landlords and other middle men who conspired to keep them in poverty. By the end of the 19th century, blacks in the South were actually worse off than they had been under Reconstruction, as they were subjected to legalized apartheid and institutionalized discrimination. Lynching and other acts of violence were not uncommon. In the North, African Americans tended in general to be better off than their southern counterparts, but they were still subjected to rampant discrimination and occasional violence.

WYNDHAM E. WHYNOT

See also

Abolitionism and the Civil War; African Americans; *Dred Scott Case*; Election of 1860, U.S.; Emancipation Proclamation; Free Soil Party; Kansas-Nebraska Act; Lincoln, Abraham; Missouri Compromise; Popular Sovereignty; Reconstruction; Republican Party; Thirteenth Amendment; Wilmot Proviso

Further Reading

Bonner, Robert E. *Mastering America: Southern Slaveholders and the Crisis of American Nationhood.* New York: Cambridge University Press, 2009.

Foner, Eric. *The Fiery Trial: Abraham Lincoln and American Slavery.* New York: Norton, 2010.

Horton, James Oliver, and Lois E. Horton. *Slavery and the Making of America.* New York: Oxford University Press, 2006.

Maltz, Earl M. *Slavery and the Supreme Court, 1825–1861.* Lawrence: University of Kansas Press, 2009.

Slaves

Slaves, or African-descended people in bondage, totaled nearly 4 million people in the United States in 1860. They were 13 percent of the total U.S. population and almost one-third of the South's population; about half lived on plantations in groups of 10–49 people. From Maryland to Texas, they were the property of their masters and had no rights to their bodies, property, or place. Most lived close by whites, which resulted in extensive interference from masters. Owners often tried to pacify slave families through the internal slave trade, and through sexual predation some owners destabilized slaves' lives and family lives greatly. Enslaved people, however, used the institutions of family and religion to create a world of their own from sundown to sunup.

The nuclear family exemplified slaves' ability to salvage some degree of control over their lives despite meddling masters. Slaves performed their own ceremonies and stayed married, despite separation and sale, usually to raise large families. Families often fostered religious and folk beliefs, challenging subordination. Yet slave families had no legal standing, existed at the master's whim, and never ceased to be part of the master's extended dominion. Masters regularly interfered in the slave family, most visibly through rape, concubinage, or the casual sex that some whites expected from enslaved women. The numerous children born from master-slave sexual encounters reinforced an inescapable fact—the slave family could mitigate subordination but never nullify it.

Five generations of a slave family in Beaufort, South Carolina, in 1862. (Library of Congress)

Christianity similarly played a dual role in slaves' lives. In segregated churches, white preachers taught a religion of submission to earthly powers. Slaves often adopted the same Protestant denomination as their masters but developed distinctive ceremonial content and practices. Although only some 500,000 slaves identified as Christians in 1860, many more fused the Christian message with African traditions.

The worldview and speech of all slaves generally reflected Christian presumptions. By singing spirituals, slaves rejected slavery's passivity and regimentation during spontaneous communal worship in the slave quarters. Black preachers frequently invoked Moses, the Jews' flight from

Egypt, King David, and Jesus—recast as a warrior-king—to foster joy at God's promise of personal redemption and hope in him rescuing them from bondage.

Religion and family also allowed slaves to create an enclave from subordination. At night or on Sundays within their quarters, enslaved persons found a measure of privacy, rest, and fellowship. Spirituals and folktales communicated moral values. Weddings and funerals marked important life moments. Slaves tended personal garden plots and bartered the produce with local whites at times. Dances and communal gatherings celebrated harvests and Christian feasts.

Religion, family, and communal identity helped enslaved people endure a disciplinary regime that they viewed as capricious torture. A whipping for being obstinate was often as likely as one for theft. Punishment spawned resistance, much of it subtle. Rare were large-scale slave revolts, and they never threatened the institution. What historians have labeled "silent sabotage" occurred frequently; this involved slaves working intentionally slowly, feigning sickness, or breaking tools to regulate their labor and reclaim agency against a master's authority. More common than slave revolts and more disruptive than silent sabotage were escape and personal confrontations. In both, the individual slave went beyond regulating his or her own labor to challenging the logic of the institution.

A runaway tangibly enervated the master's power to control him or her by escaping and then eluding the agents of subordination. Confrontations at the moment of discipline or resistance when a master overstepped the system's conventions (by insisting, for instance, that slaves work on a Sunday) defined the limits of the master's authority while signaling the slave's real participation in ordering the system.

The well-worn patterns of resistance bred into slavery emboldened slaves to turn the Civil War into a war of emancipation—first alone and later with the aid of the U.S. government. At the outset, some slaves endured impressment into the Confederate Army as laborers or servants. Silent sabotage and resistance increased. During 1862 and 1863, more slaves took advantage of Union advances to run away. Once within Union lines, some so-called contrabands hired themselves out as laborers to the Union Army, and more than 100,000 eventually became soldiers. During the war, countless numbers of newly liberated ex-slaves set off to find their spouses and relations, availed themselves of education provided by the Freedmen's Bureau or the U.S. Army, and established new religious communities. As they entered an era of unknowns, however, family and religion remained foundational.

THADDEUS M. ROMANSKY

See also
African Americans; African American Soldiers, CSA; African American Soldiers, U.S.; Contrabands; Freedmen's Bureau; Slavery

Further Reading
Fox-Genovese, Elizabeth. *Within the Plantation Household: Black and White Women of the Old South.* Chapel Hill: University of North Carolina Press, 1988.
Genovese, Eugene D. *Roll, Jordan, Roll: The World the Slaves Made.* New York: Vintage, 1974.
Kolchin, Peter. *American Slavery, 1619–1877.* New York: Hill and Wang, 2003.

Levine, Lawrence W. *Black Culture and Black Consciousness: Afro-American Folk Thought from Slavery to Freedom.* New York: Oxford University Press, 2007.

Slemmer, Adam Jacoby
Birth Date: January 24, 1829
Death Date: October 7, 1868

Union officer. Born in Montgomery County, Pennsylvania, on January 24, 1829, Adam Jacoby Slemmer graduated from the U.S. Military Academy, West Point, in 1850 and was assigned to the artillery. He saw service in Florida in the Third Seminole War (1855–1858) and then was stationed in southern California. Slemmer was promoted to first lieutenant on April 30, 1854. He taught at West Point from 1855 to 1859.

In January 1861 Lieutenant Slemmer was commanding Fort Barrancas on Pensacola Bay in Florida. On the secession of Florida, he moved his command to Fort Pickens on Santa Rosa Island and held the fort despite calls for its surrender and eventual bombardment—an important step in ensuring Union control of the Gulf of Mexico for the remainder of the war.

Slemmer was promoted to major in the new 16th Infantry on May 14, 1861, and that November was assigned to the Department of Western Virginia as assistant inspector general. In March 1862 he assumed the same position in the Army of the Ohio. He then took part in advance on and siege of Corinth (May 3–30) and in Major General D. C. Buell's opposition to the Confederate invasion of Kentucky that autumn. Leading a detachment of regulars, Slemmer distinguished himself in the Battle of Stones River (December 31, 1862–January 2, 1863) but was badly wounded in the left leg on the first day of fighting and taken prisoner the next day; he was released during the Confederate retreat. On April 4, 1863, Slemmer was appointed brigadier general of volunteers, to date from November 29, 1862. From July 1863 until the end of the war, he was president of a board for the examination of sick and wounded officers. He was brevetted lieutenant colonel, colonel, and brigadier general in the U.S. Army for his wartime service. Slemmer mustered out of the volunteers on August 24, 1865.

Slemmer remained in the regular army after the war and, as a lieutenant colonel, served in garrison and on boards examining officers for promotion. Assigned to command Fort Laramie in Dakota Territory (present-day Wyoming) in 1867, Slemmer died of a heart attack there on October 7, 1868.

SPENCER C. TUCKER

See also

Corinth, Mississippi, Siege of; Fort Pickens, Florida; Stones River, Battle of

Further Reading

Eicher, John H., and David J. Eicher. *Civil War High Commands*. Stanford, CA: Stanford University Press, 2001.

Warner, Ezra J. *Generals in Blue: Lives of the Union Commanders*. Baton Rouge: Louisiana State University Press, 2006.

Slidell, John
Birth Date: 1793
Death Date: July 9, 1871

Politician and Confederate commissioner to France. John Slidell was born in New York City in 1793. He graduated from Columbia College (later Columbia University) in 1810, studied law, and was admitted to the bar. He also became a prosperous businessman before the War of 1812 virtually wiped out his holdings. In 1819 he moved to New Orleans, where he practiced law. He made several failed attempts to capture a seat in the U.S. Senate but was elected to the U.S. House of Representatives, where he served from 1843 to 1845. An expansionist-minded Democrat and supporter of states' rights, Slidell was a staunch supporter of James K. Polk, who became president in 1845. Toward the end of that year, Polk tapped Slidell as U.S. minister to Mexico. His task was to convince Mexico to sell New Mexico and California to the United States and to settle the dispute surrounding the Mexico-Texas border. After arriving in Mexico City in December 1845, Slidell was angered when the Mexican government refused to meet with him. This helped set the stage for the Mexican-American War (1846–1848).

In 1853 Slidell was finally elected to the U.S. Senate, where he remained until 1861. He invariably cast his vote with the Southern bloc. Nevertheless, he remained a pro-Union moderate Democrat and backed John C. Breckinridge's 1860 presidential bid. When Republican Abraham Lincoln won the election, however, Slidell realized that he had little choice but to side with the Confederate cause. He resigned his seat in February 1861 and soon accepted an appointment as Confederate commissioner to France.

In late October 1861, Slidell and James M. Mason, who had been appointed commissioner to Great Britain, left the Confederacy, bound first for Cuba, from which they would continue to Europe aboard a British steamer. On November 8, 1861, the British mail packet *Trent,* which had left Havana the day before, was stopped by the American warship *San*

John Slidell of Louisiana was a staunch supporter of Southern rights. Appointed Confederate minister to France, Slidell and fellow Southern diplomat James Mason became the center of the November 1861 "Trent Affair" that almost brought war between the United States and Great Britain. (Library of Congress)

Jacinto. A U.S. boarding party then demanded that Mason and Slidell be remanded to American custody, a violation of British neutrality. The two men were taken aboard the *San Jacinto,* which then sailed to Boston, where Mason and Slidell were detained at Fort Warren.

The *Trent* Affair created serious problems for the Lincoln administration. Under the threat of war, London demanded that the United States release Mason and Slidell. Anxious to avoid a war with Great Britain, Secretary of State William Seward worked closely with Benjamin Disraeli and Prince Albert to end the crisis, and Mason and Slidell were allowed to continue on to Europe aboard a British warship in January 1862.

Although Sildell found considerable sympathy for the Southern cause in France, he was unable to convince the French government to officially recognize the Confederacy. Thus, the military aid that he sought, which would have included a Franco-Confederate alliance, quite eluded him. Be that as it may, numerous private French investors eagerly loaned the Confederate government money, a process in which Slidell played a central role.

When the war ended in 1865, Slidell remained in Europe, fearing retribution by federal authorities. He eventually made his way to England, where he died at Cowes, Isle of Wight, on July 9, 1871. Slidell never sought pardon from the U.S. government and never returned to the United States; he was buried in France.

PAUL G. PIERPAOLI JR.

See also

Diplomacy, Confederate; Lincoln, Abraham; Mason, James Murray; Seward, William Henry, Sr.; *Trent* Affair

Further Reading

Diket, Albert L. *Senator John Slidell and the Community He Represented in Washington, 1853–1861.* Washington, DC: University Press of America, 1982.

Mahin, Dean B. *One War at a Time: The International Dimensions of the Civil War.* Washington, DC: Brassey's, 1999.

Slocum, Henry Warner
Birth Date: September 24, 1827
Death Date: April 14, 1894

Union officer. Henry Warner Slocum was born on September 24, 1827, in Delphi, New York. He graduated from the U.S. Military Academy, West Point, in 1852. Commissioned a second lieutenant in the 1st U.S. Artillery, he fought in the Third Seminole War (1855–1858) and was promoted to first lieutenant in 1855. In 1856 Slocum resigned his commission, returned to New York, and worked as a lawyer, a state legislator, and an officer in the state militia.

On May 21, 1861, Slocum was appointed colonel of the 27th New York Infantry. He led his regiment into the First Battle of Bull Run (July 21, 1861), where he was badly wounded. Upon recovering, he was promoted to brigadier general of volunteers and given a brigade command on August 9, 1861. He led his brigade in the Army of the Potomac during the Peninsula Campaign (March–July 1862) and held a division command during the Seven Days' Campaign (June 25–July 1, 1862). On July 4, 1862, Slocum was advanced to major general of volunteers. His men saw action at the Second Battle of Bull Run (August 29–30, 1862) and the Battle of Antietam (September 17, 1862). On October 20, 1862, Slocum was chosen to command XII Corps. His men saw only limited action at the First Battle of Fredericksburg (December 13, 1862) but were heavily engaged at the Battle of Chancellorsville (May 1–4, 1863).

Henry Warner Slocum, an able career army officer, rose to the rank of major general and commander of the Union Army of Georgia during the Civil War. He later was a U.S. congressman from New York. (Library of Congress)

In the Battle of Gettysburg (July 1–3, 1863), XII Corps held the Union right flank at Culp's Hill. On July 2, one of Slocum's brigades held its position against a series of withering Confederate attacks and saved the Union line. In the autumn of 1863, XII Corps was transferred with XI Corps to the western theater under the overall command of Major General Joseph Hooker. After trying to resign rather than fight under Hooker, Slocum served only in rear areas during the Chattanooga Campaign (October–November 1863). From April to August 1864, Slocum commanded the District of Vicksburg. During the final stages of the Atlanta Campaign (May 5–September 2, 1864), he commanded XX Corps (created in April 1864 by combining the old XI and XII Corps) in the Army of the Cumberland. During Major General William T. Sherman's March to the Sea (November 15–December 21, 1864) and March through the Carolinas (January–April 1865), Slocum commanded the Army of Georgia (XIV and XX Corps).

Slocum was concerned over the losses inflicted by the army on civilians and issued orders in March 1865 that called for the correct treatment of civilian North Carolinians.

He fought at the Battle of Averasboro (March 16, 1865) but, while advancing toward Bentonville, was somewhat isolated from the rest of Sherman's army. Confederate general Joseph E. Johnston attacked, hoping to destroy Slocum's army before he could be reinforced. Although Slocum was caught by surprise, in the Battle of Bentonville (March 19–21, 1865) his men rallied and held out until Sherman arrived with reinforcements.

Slocum resigned from the military on September 28, 1865. He later became active in politics, serving in the U.S. House of Representatives as a Democrat (1869–1873, 1883–1885). Slocum died in Brooklyn, New York, on April 14, 1894.

JENNIFER M. MURRAY

See also

Antietam, Battle of; Atlanta Campaign; Bentonville, Battle of; Bull Run, First Battle of; Bull Run, Second Battle of; Chancellorsville, Battle of; Fredericksburg, First Battle of; Gettysburg, Battle of; Johnston, Joseph Eggleston; Peninsula Campaign; Seven Days' Campaign; Sherman's March to the Sea

Further Reading

Melton, Brian C. *Sherman's Forgotten General: Henry W. Slocum.* Columbia: University of Missouri Press, 2007.

Warner, Ezra J. *Generals in Blue: Lives of the Union Commanders.* Baton Rouge: Louisiana State University Press, 2006.

Slough, John Potts
Birth Date: February 1, 1829
Death Date: December 17, 1867

Union officer. John Potts Slough was born in Cincinnati, Ohio, on February 1, 1829. He attended Cincinnati Law School, became a lawyer, and was elected to the Ohio legislature at age 21. Although he pronounced his name "Slow," he was quick to anger and that same year was expelled from his seat after striking another member of the legislature with his fist during a political argument. Two years later, however, Slough became secretary of the Ohio Democratic Party. He subsequently moved to Kansas Territory but by 1860 had settled in Denver, Colorado Territory.

Slough's outspoken Democratic Party positions made his Unionist sympathies suspect, but he raised a company of the 1st Colorado Infantry and became its captain on June 24 and its colonel on August 26. In March 1862, the 1st Colorado joined Brigadier General Edward R. S. Canby's command to oppose the Confederate invasion of New Mexico led by Brigadier General Henry Hopkins Sibley. The only fighting of significance in which Slough participated occurred in the Battle of Glorieta Pass (March 26–28, 1862). Commanding a force of some 900 men, on March 28, having left the protection of Fort Union in direct violation of Canby's orders, Slough attacked some 1,100 Confederates under Colonel William Read Scurry about a half mile from Pigeon's Ranch. The fighting seesawed back and forth, but Slough eventually left the field. Scurry then drew off as well. A Confederate tactical victory, the Battle of Glorieta Pass was nonetheless a Union strategic victory, for Union forces captured Sibley's supply train, forcing the Confederates to withdraw from New Mexico.

Ordered east, Slough briefly commanded a brigade in the Army of the Shenandoah and then in the Army of Virginia. Despite having disobeyed a direct order, he managed to portray himself as having turned the tide of battle in New Mexico, and he was appointed brigadier general of volunteers to date from August 25, 1862, serving as military governor of Alexandria, Virginia. Slough also served on the court-martial that wrongfully convicted Union major general Fitz John Porter of dereliction of duty during the Second Battle of Bull Run (August 29–30, 1862).

Mustered out of the army on August 24, 1865, Slough was appointed chief justice of the New Mexico Territory. Here his intemperate manner got the best of him, and the territorial legislature passed a series of resolutions calling for his removal. On December 15, 1867, in Santa Fe, Slough got into an altercation with one of the legislators who had called for his removal and was shot and mortally wounded. Slough died two days later.

SPENCER C. TUCKER

See also

Bull Run, Second Battle of; Canby, Edward Richard Sprigg; Glorieta Pass, Battle of; New Mexico Territory; Porter, Fitz John; Scurry, William Read; Sibley, Henry Hopkins

Further Reading

Alberts, Don E. *The Battle of Glorieta: Union Victory in the West.* College Station: Texas A&M University Press, 1998.

Eicher, John H., and David J. Eicher. *Civil War High Commands.* Stanford, CA: Stanford University Press, 2001.

Warner, Ezra J. *Generals in Blue: Lives of the Union Commanders.* Baton Rouge: Louisiana State University Press, 2006.

Smalley, George Washburn
Birth Date: June 2, 1833
Death Date: April 4, 1916

U.S. journalist. George Washburn Smalley was born on June 2, 1833, in Franklin, Massachusetts, and graduated from Yale University in 1854. He subsequently studied law at Harvard and worked as an attorney in Boston (1855–1861).

In the meantime, he developed a close friendship with William Lloyd Garrison and Wendell Phillips, both noted abolitionists. Suffering from poor eyesight, Smalley was unable to serve in the Union Army. However, in the autumn of 1861, Phillips introduced Smalley to the managing editor of the *New York Tribune*, who soon hired Smalley as a war correspondent.

Smalley's first assignment, which he handled well, was to write a series of articles documenting African Americans living in Port Royal, South Carolina. He was then assigned to write about Union operations in the Shenandoah Valley in the spring of 1862. Smalley created a stir when he reported that the Union defeat at the Battle of Port Republic (June 9, 1862) had been the result of Brigadier General James Shields's ineptitude. From there, Smalley went on to report on the Antietam Campaign (September 4–20, 1862), where he shadowed Major General George B. McClellan at the Battle of South Mountain (September 14, 1862). During the Battle of Antietam (September 17, 1862), Smalley worked as a volunteer aide for Major General Joseph Hooker, which gave Smalley a unique inside view of the fighting. After the battle, Smalley rode to Frederick, Maryland, where he sent a short story on the engagement to New York via telegraph. He then boarded a train and while en route to New York penned a full account of the fight. This account was the first complete reportage published on the Battle of Antietam.

When Smalley arrived in New York, he was awarded with an editorial position, ending his field reporting. He did subsequently write a story that showcased the poor condition of the Union Army, but it was censored by the government. During the New York City Draft Riots (July 13–17, 1863), Smalley helped defend the *Tribune*'s offices from attack.

After the Civil War, Smalley covered the Austro-Prussian War during 1866 and founded a London bureau for the *Tribune* in 1867. He coordinated coverage of the Franco-Prussian War (1870–1871) and later became the U.S. correspondent for the *London Times*. He retired in 1905 in London. Smalley published several books, the most notable of which was a two-volume memoir titled *Anglo-American Memories* (1911–1912). Smalley died on April 4, 1916, in London.

PAUL G. PIERPAOLI JR.

See also

Antietam, Battle of; Antietam Campaign; New York City Draft Riots; *New York Tribune;* Port Republic, Battle of; Shields, James; South Mountain, Battle of; War Correspondents

Further Reading

Andrews, J. Cutler. *The North Reports on the Civil War.* Pittsburgh, PA: University of Pittsburgh Press, 1985.

Coopersmith, Andrew S. *Fighting Words: An Illustrated History of Newspaper Accounts of the Civil War.* New York: New Press, 2006.

Smalls, Robert
Birth Date: April 5, 1839
Death Date: February 22, 1915

A slave in the American South whose act of defiance in the Civil War made him a national hero in the North. Born into slavery on April 5, 1839, in Beaufort, South Carolina, Robert Smalls at age 12 was hired out as a laborer in nearby Charleston. There he worked a variety of jobs, including as a stevedore on the Charleston docks. The hire-out system allowed Smalls to arrange to pay an agreed-upon amount each month to his owners; earnings above this he kept for himself. At age 17 he married Hannah Jones, a hotel maid, and made a contract with her owner to purchase her and their son. Smalls also managed to join the Black Mutual Aid Society.

With the start of the Civil War, the Confederate States of America commissioned the 313-ton steamer *Planter* as

Robert Smalls was a slave in South Carolina at the beginning of the Civil War. His act of sailing a dispatch boat out to the Union blockading squadron off Charleston made him a hero in the North. After the war, he served in Congress as a Republican. (Library of Congress)

a dispatch boat and transport. This was the ship on which Smalls worked as a wheelman. Early on May 13, 1862, Smalls, his family, and a crew of slaves—17 people in all—raised the ship's anchor and escaped Charleston in the armed ship to join the Union blockading squadron. Flying a white flag, Smalls delivered his ship and its cargo to the Union cause. Appointed a pilot in the U.S. Navy, he became the captain of the *Planter* in 1863 and participated in the attack on Charleston.

After the war, in July 1868 Smalls won election as a Republican to the South Carolina state legislature, which then had a black majority. He won election in 1871 to the South Carolina Senate and in 1875 to the U.S. House of Representatives, where he served until 1879 and again from 1881 to 1887. Smalls was a staunch advocate of civil rights and opposed the imposition of segregation.

Smalls purchased his old owner's house in Beaufort and worked as a customs official during the last two decades of his life. Smalls died at Beaufort, South Carolina, on February 22, 1915.

C. ALVIN HUGHES

See also
Blockade of the Confederacy, Union

Further Reading
McPherson, James M. *The Negro's Civil War.* New York: Vintage Books, 1965.
Miller, Edward A. *Gullah Statesman: Robert Smalls from Slavery to Congress, 1839–1915.* Columbia: University of South Carolina Press, 1995.

Union major general Andrew Jackson Smith distinguished himself in the March–May 1864 Red River Campaign, at Tupelo, Mississippi in July, at Nashville (December 15–16), and in the final operations against Mobile in early 1865. (Library of Congress)

Smith, Andrew Jackson (Union General)
Birth Date: April 28, 1815
Death Date: January 30, 1897

Union officer. Born at Bucks County, Pennsylvania, on April 28, 1815, Andrew Jackson Smith graduated from the U.S. Military Academy at West Point in 1838. Commissioned a second lieutenant in the 1st Dragoons, Smith served extensively in the West and during the Mexican-American War (1846–1848), earning promotion to first lieutenant in 1845 and to captain in 1847. At the beginning of the Civil War, he commanded Fort Walla Walla in the Washington Territory and was promoted to major in May 1861. He briefly held a volunteer commission as colonel of the 2nd California Cavalry before resigning to become chief of cavalry for Major General Henry Halleck, commanding the Department of the Missouri.

Promoted to brigadier general of volunteers in March 1862, Smith participated in Halleck's slow advance on and siege of Corinth, Mississippi (May 3–30, 1862). Smith then headed an infantry division in Kentucky before assuming command of a division in Major General William T. Sherman's rebuff at the Battle of Chickasaw Bluffs (December 26–29, 1862). Smith participated in the successful operation against Fort Hindman (Arkansas Post) during January 4–12, 1863, and also participated in the Second Vicksburg Campaign (April 1–July 4, 1863). He then served in western Tennessee, assuming command of a portion of XVI Corps, Army of the Tennessee, with which he now became the Union Army's western theater troubleshooter. He was detached to support Major General N. P. Banks's Red River Campaign (March 10–May 22, 1864), playing a conspicuous role in an otherwise dismal effort, for which Smith was brevetted colonel and promoted to lieutenant colonel in the regular army. His promotion to major general of volunteers came in May. Returning to western Tennessee to deal with the threat posed to Sherman's communications during his drive on Atlanta, Smith's detachment, augmented by cavalry, went after the Confederate cavalry of Major General Nathan Bedford Forrest. Smith dealt Forrest a serious blow at the Battle of Tupelo (July 14–15, 1864), earning the brevet to brigadier general in the regular army.

Smith and his much-traveled corps then moved to Missouri in response to Major General Sterling Price's autumn raid, only to be rushed by water to Nashville in December to join the forces assembled under Major General George Thomas preparing to meet the advancing army of John Bell Hood. Smith played a significant role in the decisive defeat of Hood's mangled army at Nashville (December 15–16), for which he was brevetted major general in the regular army. Rather appropriately, Smith, given command of a reconstituted XVI Corps, was now dispatched to the Gulf Coast for the final operations against Mobile. One of the most active and important Union commanders during the final year of the war, Smith mustered out of the volunteers in January 1866. That July he was appointed colonel of the 7th Cavalry and resumed his regular army career, holding mostly administrative commands, including that of the important Department of the Missouri (1867–1868). Smith resigned in 1869 to become postmaster at St. Louis, a post he held until 1877. He later led Missouri militiamen during labor unrest. In 1889 he was placed on the army's retired list as a colonel. Smith died at St. Louis on January 30, 1897.

DAVID COFFEY

See also

Banks, Nathaniel Prentice; Chickasaw Bluffs, Battle of; Corinth, Mississippi, Siege of; Forrest, Nathan Bedford; Mobile, Alabama, Siege of; Nashville, Battle of; Price's Missouri Raid; Red River Campaign; Thomas, George Henry; Tupelo, Battle of

Further Reading

Sword, Wiley. *Embrace an Angry Wind: The Confederacy's Last Hurrah; Spring Hill, Franklin, and Nashville.* New York: HarperCollins, 1992.

Warner, Ezra J. *Generals in Blue: Lives of the Union Commanders.* Baton Rouge: Louisiana State University Press, 2006.

Smith, Andrew Jackson (Union Soldier)
Birth Date: ca. September 3, 1842
Death Date: March 4, 1932

African American Union soldier. Andrew Jackson Smith was born into slavery on or about September 3, 1842, in Kentucky. When the Civil War broke out, Andrew's father and owner, Elijah Smith, immediately enlisted in the Confederate Army. After a year's absence, he returned home on leave and indicated that he planned to take Andrew Smith back to war with him. When Andrew overheard the plans, he and another slave decided to escape. They made their way 25 miles to seek protection from a Union Army regiment, the 41st Illinois Infantry, near Smithland, Kentucky. Smith became a servant to Major John Warner.

In March 1862, Smith's regiment moved to Pittsburg Landing and participated in the Battle of Shiloh (April 6–7, 1862). During the course of the battle, Smith was struck in the head by a Confederate minié ball, which was removed, leaving only a scar. After the battle Warner, accompanied by Smith, returned to Clinton, Illinois. Smith was there when he heard that President Abraham Lincoln had authorized African American enlistment in the Union Army.

Smith left Illinois to enroll in the Massachusetts Volunteers. On May 16, 1863, he and 55 other Illinois volunteers were mustered into Company B of the 55th Massachusetts Regiment of Colored Volunteers. After the 54th Massachusetts (Colored) sister regiment of the 55th Massachusetts fought in South Carolina, it was joined by the 55th Massachusetts, and together they participated in five major engagements during the course of the next two years.

On the afternoon of November 30, 1864, the 54th and 55th Massachusetts Regiments were involved in a bloody battle at Honey Hill in South Carolina. The 55th Massachusetts regimental color sergeant was killed by an exploding shell, and Smith, now a corporal, took the state and federal flags from his hand and carried them forward through the heavy fire. Although half the officers and a third of the enlisted men in his unit were killed or wounded, Smith continued to expose himself to enemy fire by carrying the colors throughout the battle.

Smith was promoted to color sergeant soon after the battle at Honey Hill and was discharged on August 29, 1865. He eventually returned to Kentucky, where he lived out his days as a leader in Livingston County. Smith died there on March 4, 1932.

Smith was nominated for the Medal of Honor in 1916, but the U.S. Army denied the award, citing a lack of official records. Not until January 16, 2001, was Smith's valor at Honey Hill finally recognized, when President Bill Clinton presented the Medal of Honor to Smith's descendants, including his 93-year-old daughter, during a White House ceremony.

JAMES H. WILLBANKS

See also

African American Soldiers, U.S.; 54th Massachusetts Regiment of Infantry; Honey Hill, Battle of; Shiloh, Battle of

Further Reading

Gomez-Granger, Julissa. *CRS Report for Congress: Medal of Honor Recipients, 1979–2008.* Washington, DC: Congressional Research Service, RL 30011, June 4, 2008.

Reef, Catherine. *African Americans in the Military*. New York: Facts on File, 2004.

Thomas, Richard J. "Caleb Blood Smith: Whig Orator and Politician Lincoln's Secretary of Interior." Unpublished PhD dissertation, Indiana University, 1969.

Smith, Caleb Blood
Birth Date: April 16, 1808
Death Date: January 7, 1864

U.S. secretary of the interior (1861–1862). Caleb Blood Smith was born on April 16, 1808, in Boston, Massachusetts, but spent most of his youth in Ohio. After studying at Cincinnati College and Miami University of Ohio, he was admitted to the bar in 1828 and commenced a practice in Connersville, Indiana, where he also founded a Whig Party newspaper in 1832. The following year he took a seat in the Indiana legislature as a Whig, serving from 1833 to 1837 and in 1840 and 1841. In 1843 Smith was elected to the U.S. House of Representatives, where he served as a Whig until 1849. He vigorously opposed the Mexican-American War (1846–1848).

Smith returned to Ohio, where he took up a legal practice in Cincinnati and also served as a railroad executive. He then settled in Indianapolis. After becoming a member of the Republican Party in the mid-1850s, Smith was a delegate to the unsuccessful February 1861 Washington Peace Conference, which had tried to avert civil war. Because Smith had been a key player in securing Abraham Lincoln's nomination at the 1860 Republican Convention, he was offered the post of secretary of the interior. Smith took office in March 1861.

Smith's tenure proved somewhat controversial. He lavished patronage positions on supporters and even appointed his own son to a departmental post. Smith argued against relieving Fort Sumter in early 1861 lest the move provoke war, and in the summer of 1862 he wrote an unsolicited letter to President Lincoln urging him to sack Major General George B. McClellan. Smith also reportedly disagreed with the Emancipation Proclamation. In delicate health, he tendered his resignation and left office on January 1, 1863, to accept a judgeship on the U.S. District Court for the District of Indiana. Smith served in this capacity until he died in Indianapolis on January 7, 1864.

Paul G. Pierpaoli Jr.

See also
Cabinet, U.S.; Emancipation Proclamation; Lincoln, Abraham; McClellan, George Brinton; Washington Peace Conference

Further Reading
Bochin, Hal W. "Caleb B. Smith's Opposition to the Mexican War." *Indiana Magazine of History* 69 (June 1973): 95–114.

Smith, Charles Ferguson
Birth Date: April 24, 1807
Death Date: April 25, 1862

Union general. Charles Ferguson Smith was born in Philadelphia, Pennsylvania, on April 24, 1807. He graduated from the U.S. Military Academy, West Point, in 1825 and was commissioned a second lieutenant of artillery. Smith served in garrison duty at a number of posts and returned to West Point as an instructor and a commandant of cadets. Then a captain, in 1846 Smith was ordered to join Brigadier General Zachary Taylor's small Army of Observation, assigned to move into southern Texas to contest the disputed border with Mexico. Smith took command of an artillery battalion serving as infantry and fought with his unit in the Battle of Palo Alto (May 8, 1846) and at Resaca de la Palma (May 9, 1846), where he particularly distinguished himself. For his service in both battles, he was brevetted major. For his leadership in the Battle of Monterrey (September 20–24, 1846), he was brevetted lieutenant colonel.

Smith then joined Major General Winfield Scott's campaign from Veracruz to Mexico City. Smith fought in the Battle of Contreras (August 19–20, 1847) and joined in the attack on a heavily defended bridge near the fortified convent at Churubusco (August 20), winning another brevet promotion, this time to colonel. Ill, he was unable to participate in the final battles for Mexico City.

Following the war, Smith served on the frontier and took part in the Red River Expedition of 1856 and the so-called Mormon War of 1857, rising to full rank lieutenant colonel in 1855. At the start of the Civil War, Smith was in Washington, D.C., where his remarks apparently angered influential politicians. As a result, he found himself on recruiting duties in New York. Major General John C. Frémont, however, was able to secure Smith's appointment as a brigadier general of volunteers on August 30, 1861. Smith joined forces under Brigadier General Ulysses S. Grant, whom he had taught at West Point. Smith pointed out the vulnerability of Confederate Fort Henry on the Tennessee River and commanded a division in the successful attack on the fort headed by Grant and Flag Officer Andrew H. Foote on February 6, 1862.

Smith distinguished himself during the Battle of Fort Donelson (February 13–16, 1862), when he led his division into the fort. When Confederate commander Brigadier General Simon Bolivar Buckner, a former friend of Grant, asked for terms, Smith suggested to Grant that he accept nothing less than unconditional surrender, a demand that Grant adopted and that led to him becoming known as "Unconditional Surrender" Grant. Jealous of Grant's success, Union department commander Major General Henry W. Halleck urged President Abraham Lincoln to promote Smith (not Grant) to major general. Both men were advanced to that rank the next month, however. When Halleck then suspended Grant from command, he named Smith to command the Army of the Mississippi. Moving the army to Pittsburg Landing, Smith jumped into a small boat, slipped, and badly scraped himself. The wound became septic. Moved to Savannah, Tennessee, to recover, Smith died from complications of the wound on April 25, 1862. Had it not been for this accident, Smith, not Grant, would have commanded at the Battle of Shiloh (April 6–7, 1862).

SPENCER C. TUCKER

See also

Buckner, Simon Bolivar; Fort Donelson, Battle of; Fort Henry, Battle of; Frémont, John Charles; Grant, Ulysses Simpson; Halleck, Henry Wager; Shiloh, Battle of

Further Reading

Johnson, Timothy D. *A Gallant Little Army: The Mexico City Campaign.* Lawrence: University Press of Kansas, 2007.

Tucker, Spencer C. *"Unconditional Surrender": The Capture of Forts Henry and Donelson, February 1862.* Abilene, TX: McWhiney Foundation Press, 2001.

Smith, Charles Henry
Birth Date: November 1, 1827
Death Date: July 17, 1902

Union officer. Born at Hollis, Maine, on November 1, 1827, Charles Henry Smith graduated from Waterville College in 1856. He then taught school in Eastport, Maine, and studied law. With the onset of the Civil War, Smith was commissioned captain of the 1st Maine Cavalry on October 9, 1861, and was promoted to major on February 16, 1863, and then to lieutenant colonel on March 1 and to colonel on June 18. Assigned to the Army of the Potomac, Smith saw action during the campaigns in Virginia and fought at the Battle of Gettysburg (July 1–3, 1863). He was regarded as a highly effective cavalry commander during the Overland Campaign (May 4–June 12,

1864) and the Petersburg Campaign (June 15, 1864–April 3, 1865), when he commanded a brigade in Major General David M. Gregg's Division of the Cavalry Corps, Army of the Potomac. During fighting at St. Mary's (Samaria) Church, Virginia, on June 24, 1864, Smith was severely wounded in the thigh but refused to leave the field until the engagement was over. He also commanded a brigade in the Appomattox Campaign (April 2–9, 1865). During the war, Smith participated in 63 battles and engagements. He mustered out of volunteer service on August 11, 1865.

Admitted to the bar in 1864, Smith was a state senator in Maine in 1866. He was appointed colonel of the 28th U.S. Infantry on July 28, 1866. On March 1, 1867, he was brevetted both brigadier general, for his role in the Battle of Sayler's Creek (April 6, 1865), and major general, for his Civil War service.

Smith transferred to the 19th Infantry in 1869. He retired on November 1, 1891. On April 11, 1895, he was awarded the Medal of Honor for the engagement at St. Mary's (Samaria) Church. Smith died at Washington, D.C., on July 17, 1902.

SPENCER C. TUCKER

See also

Appomattox Campaign; Gettysburg, Battle of; Medal of Honor; Overland Campaign; Petersburg Campaign

Further Reading

Eicher, John H., and David J. Eicher. *Civil War High Commands.* Stanford, CA: Stanford University Press, 2001.

Warner, Ezra J. *Generals in Blue: Lives of the Union Commanders.* Baton Rouge: Louisiana State University Press, 2006.

Smith, Edmund Kirby
Birth Date: May 16, 1824
Death Date: March 28, 1893

Confederate officer. Edmund Kirby Smith was born in St. Augustine, Florida, on May 16, 1824. Smith graduated from the U.S. Military Academy, West Point, in 1845. He served in the Mexican-American War (1846–1848) and was brevetted for gallantry at the Battle of Cerro Gordo and the Battles of Contreras and Churubusco. In 1849 he returned to West Point to teach mathematics and remained there until 1852. Promoted to first lieutenant in 1851, in 1855 he became a captain in the new 2nd Cavalry Regiment, participating in numerous skirmishes with Comanches and other Native American tribes of the Southwest. He was promoted to major in January 1861.

Edmund Kirby Smith was a career officer who resigned his U.S. Army commission at the start of the Civil War. As a Confederate full general, Smith commanded the Trans-Mississippi Department, which he ran on a largely independent basis. (Library of Congress)

Smith opposed Southern secession after the election of Abraham Lincoln in November 1860, but when Smith's home state of Florida seceded from the Union, he resigned from the U.S. Army and accepted a commission as a lieutenant colonel in the Confederate Army. At the outset of the war, Smith was General Joseph E. Johnston's chief of staff and helped to prepare incoming recruits for the Army of the Shenandoah. In June 1861 Smith was promoted to brigadier general and took command of a brigade. Wounded at the First Battle of Bull Run (July 21, 1861), where he played an important role in the Confederate victory, he was promoted to major general and assigned command of the Department of East Tennessee to work in tandem with General Braxton Bragg in Tennessee in an invasion of Kentucky. Smith's forces garnered a notable victory in the Battle of Richmond (August 29–30, 1862) in Kentucky.

After a promising start, the Confederates were repelled in the Battle of Perryville (October 8, 1862). Bitterly disappointed, Smith nearly gave up his commission to enter the ministry. That same month, though, he was promoted to lieutenant general and reassigned to command the Trans-Mississippi Department. The region became known as "Kirby Smithdom" when his administrative apparatus was separated from the eastern side of the Mississippi after the Union victory at Vicksburg on July 4, 1863. Promoted to full general in February 1864, Smith operated largely on an independent basis, appointing general officers and granting promotions based on the realities of the Trans-Mississippi region. Most of these appointments and promotions could not be confirmed due to the isolated nature of his command.

Smith proved to be generally successful in defending his vast department. In 1864 his forces defeated Union efforts to take western Louisiana and invade Texas in the Red River Campaign (March 10–May 22, 1864), and they turned back the Camden Expedition (March 23–May 3, 1864), a supporting Union effort in Arkansas. But the tide of the war had turned decisively in favor of the Union, and with the surrenders of the field armies east of the Mississippi, Smith formally surrendered on May 26, 1865.

Following the war, Smith was affiliated with an insurance company and a telegraph company, both of which failed. From 1870 to 1875, he was president of the University of Nashville. He then taught mathematics at the University of the South in Sewanee, Tennessee, from 1875 until his death there on March 28, 1893.

DAVID COFFEY

See also

Bragg, Braxton; Bull Run, First Battle of; Johnston, Joseph Eggleston; Perryville, Battle of; Richmond, Battle of; Vicksburg Campaign, First

Further Reading

Parks, Joseph H. *General Edmund Kirby Smith, C.S.A.* Baton Rouge: Louisiana State University Press, 1992.

Warner, Ezra J. *Generals in Gray: Lives of the Confederate Commanders.* Baton Rouge: Louisiana State University Press, 2006.

Smith, Gerrit
Birth Date: March 6, 1797
Death Date: December 28, 1874

Noted abolitionist, philanthropist, and social reformer. Gerrit Smith was born on March 6, 1797, in Utica, New York. He graduated from Hamilton College in 1818. Smith helped his father manage a $400,000 family fortune, which the younger Smith eventually controlled. After increasing the family's wealth through shrewd investments, Smith devoted much of his time and money to good works.

Smith's involvement in philanthropy and reform began in the 1820s, when he supported the Sunday School movement and the United Domestic Missionary Society. He advocated temperance and a vegetarian diet; along with meat, he gave up spices, tea, and tobacco. Smith supported women's suffrage and, for a time, the colonization of African Americans. He was also concerned with prison reform and sought to have capital punishment abolished.

Although initially supporting the colonization of blacks to Africa, Smith took an abolitionist position in the 1830s and soon became a leading figure in the movement. He helped convert his cousin, the women's rights leader Elizabeth Cady Stanton, to this cause and also to temperance. Smith served as vice president of the American Anti-Slavery Society, and in 1836 he assumed the presidency of the New York Anti-Slavery Society.

In the 1840s, Smith tried to advance abolition through political action. In 1848 the Liberty Party nominated Smith for the presidency, but he declined to run. Meanwhile, Smith had joined the growing free-soil movement. In 1848 this antislavery coalition formed the Free Soil Party. Smith was instrumental in founding the party, which adopted his slogan "Free Men, Free Soil, and Free Trade."

Becoming increasingly militant in the 1850s, Smith joined in promoting resistance to the Fugitive Slave Act and helped runaway slaves escape to Canada. In 1852 he was elected to Congress as an independent. He served one term before he resigned. Having been recently admitted to the bar, he opened a law practice.

When the 1854 Kansas-Nebraska Act brought a rush of both proslavery and antislavery settlers into Kansas, Smith backed the antislavery faction. He gave the New England Emigrant Aid Company more than $14,000 to help eastern abolitionists settle in the West. From 1856 to 1858, Smith aided the radical abolitionist John Brown, giving him money for his 1859 raid on Harpers Ferry, Virginia. When documents implicating Smith and five other Northern abolitionists in the raid were later discovered in a Maryland farmhouse, Smith suffered a breakdown and spent several weeks in an insane asylum.

During the Civil War, Smith became a Republican, writing and speaking on behalf of the Union cause and campaigning for Abraham Lincoln's reelection in 1864. After the war, Smith's growing conservatism led him to favor a policy of moderation toward the South while advocating black suffrage. Smith died on December 28, 1874, in New York City.

WILLIAM MCGUIRE AND LESLIE WHEELER

See also

Abolitionism and the Civil War; American Anti-Slavery Society; Bleeding Kansas; Brown, John; Free Soil Party; Fugitive Slave Act of 1850; Kansas-Nebraska Act

Further Reading

Harlow, Ralph V. *Gerrit Smith, Philanthropist and Reformer.* Reprint ed. New York: Russell and Russell, 1972.
Renehan, Edward J. *The Secret Six: The True Tale of the Men Who Conspired with John Brown.* New York: Crown, 1995.

Smith, Giles Alexander
Birth Date: September 29, 1829
Death Date: November 5, 1876

Union officer. Giles Alexander Smith was born on September 29, 1829, in Jefferson County, New York. He moved to Ohio as a young man and worked in a Cincinnati dry goods store for a time before buying and operating a hotel in Bloomington, Illinois. In the summer of 1861, he joined the 8th Missouri Infantry as captain of company D and subsequently saw action at the Battles of Fort Henry (February 6, 1862), Fort Donelson (February 13–16), Shiloh (April 6–7), and Corinth (October 3–4). He was advanced to lieutenant colonel on June 12, 1862, and to colonel on June 30.

In December 1862, Smith was given charge of a brigade in the Army of the Tennessee. He saw combat at the Battle of Chickasaw Bluffs (December 26–29, 1862) and the Battle of Fort Hindman/Arkansas Post (January 9–11, 1863) and in the Second Vicksburg Campaign (April 1–July 4). That summer, he was advanced to brigadier general of volunteers. He commanded a brigade in XV Corps during the Chattanooga Campaign (October–November 1863) but was badly wounded at the Battle of Missionary Ridge (November 25, 1863). Smith next participated in the Atlanta Campaign (May 5–September 2, 1864), during which he performed conspicuously and assumed command of a division in XVII Corps. He led his division during Sherman's March to the Sea (November 15–December 21, 1864) and Sherman's March through the Carolinas (January–April 1865).

Immediately after the war, Smith commanded an African American division dispatched for occupation duties in the Southwest. Brevetted a major general of volunteers in March 1865, he was given the full rank in November 1865. He mustered out of the volunteers in February 1866. From 1869 to

1872, he served as assistant U.S. postmaster general. Smith died on November 5, 1876, in Bloomington, Illinois.

PAUL G. PIERPAOLI JR.

See also

Atlanta Campaign; Chattanooga Campaign; Chickasaw Bluffs, Battle of; Corinth, Battle of; Fort Donelson, Battle of; Fort Henry, Battle of; Fort Hindman, Battle of; Missionary Ridge, Battle of; Sherman's March through the Carolinas; Sherman's March to the Sea; Shiloh, Battle of; Vicksburg Campaign, Second

Further Reading

Eicher, John H., and David J. Eicher. *Civil War High Commands.* Stanford, CA: Stanford University Press, 2001.
Warner, Ezra J. *Generals in Blue: Lives of the Union Commanders.* Baton Rouge: Louisiana State University Press, 2006.

Smith, Green Clay
Birth Date: ca. July 4, 1826
Death Date: June 29, 1895

Union officer. Born in Richmond, Kentucky, on July 4, 1826 (some sources give July 2, 1832, as the date of birth, while his gravestone at Arlington National Cemetery lists May 1832), Green Clay Smith interrupted his studies to serve in the Mexican-American War (1846–1848) and was commissioned a second lieutenant in the 1st Kentucky Volunteer Infantry. Returning home, he graduated from Transylvania University in Lexington in 1849. After studying law, he was admitted to the bar in 1852 and went into practice with his father, John S. Smith, a prominent lawyer and member of Congress. Green Clay Smith subsequently moved to Covington, Kentucky, and opened his own practice.

Smith was a member of the Kentucky legislature at the outbreak of the Civil War. Loyal to the Union, he was commissioned colonel of the 4th Kentucky Cavalry Regiment on April 4, 1862, and advanced to brigadier general of volunteers on July 2, 1862.

On May 5, 1862, Smith's cavalry regiment took part in the defeat of Confederate raider John Hunt Morgan at Lebanon, Tennessee, but Smith was not as successful in subsequent encounters with Morgan. On March 25, 1863, General Smith's men engaged a Confederate brigade under Confederate major general Nathan Bedford Forrest that had just attacked Brentwood, Tennessee. Initially successful, Smith's men were outnumbered and driven off by the arrival of a second Confederate brigade.

Elected to Congress as an Unconditional Unionist in November 1862, Smith resigned his commission on December 1, 1863, but was brevetted major general of volunteers on March 13, 1865, for meritorious service during the war. He served in Congress from March 4, 1863, until his resignation in 1866 to accept an appointment as governor of Montana Territory. He held that post from July 1866 until his resignation in April 1869.

Ordained a Baptist minister in 1869, Smith became pastor of the Baptist church in Frankfort, Kentucky. He ran for the presidency of the United States as the candidate of the National Prohibition Party in 1876 but received fewer than 10,000 votes. Smith was pastor of the Metropolitan Baptist Church in Washington, D.C., from 1890 until his death on June 29, 1895.

SPENCER C. TUCKER

See also

Brentwood, Battle of; Morgan, John Hunt

Further Reading

Hood, James Larry. "For the Union: Kentucky's Unconditional Unionist Congressmen and the Development of the Republican Party in Kentucky, 1863–1865." *Register of the Kentucky Historical Society* 76 (July 1978): 197–215.
Warner, Ezra J. *Generals in Blue: Lives of the Union Commanders.* Baton Rouge: Louisiana State University Press, 2006.
Wyeth, John Allan. *That Devil Forrest.* Baton Rouge: Louisiana State University Press, 1987.

Smith, Gustavus Woodson
Birth Date: ca. November 30, 1821
Death Date: June 24, 1896

Confederate officer. Gustavus Woodson Smith was born in Georgetown, Kentucky, probably on November 30, 1821 (December 1, 1821, and January 1, 1822, are listed in some sources). He graduated from the U.S. Military Academy, West Point, in 1842. Detailed to the Corps of Engineers, Smith was involved in the construction of coastal fortifications. In 1844 he became assistant instructor of engineering at West Point. Smith led a company in the Mexican-American War (1846–1848) and won brevets to first lieutenant and captain. After the war Smith returned to West Point, resuming his teaching. He was promoted to first lieutenant in 1853 but resigned his commission on December 18, 1854, to pursue a career in civil engineering. He also served as street commissioner for New York City (1858–1861). Smith was in New York when the Civil War began, but apparently waiting to see what Kentucky would decide, he did not offer his services to the Confederacy until September.

On September 19, 1861, Smith was commissioned a major general in the Confederate Army and assigned to the Army of the Potomac (later the Army of Northern Virginia). As second-in-command to General Joseph Johnston, Smith led a wing of the army during the Peninsula Campaign (March–July 1862). He fought at the Battle of Seven Pines (May 31–June 1, 1862) and assumed command of the army when General Joseph E. Johnston was wounded on the first day of fighting. Succeeded in command by General Robert E. Lee, Smith became ill and took a leave of absence. In August 1862 he was assigned to command the defenses of Richmond, and in September he became commander of the Department of North Carolina and Southern Virginia.

In November 1862, Smith served briefly as interim secretary of war. Disappointed after being passed over for promotion, he resigned his commission on February 17, 1863, becoming superintendent of the Etowah Iron Works in Georgia. On June 1, 1864, he was commissioned a major general in the Georgia Militia. He commanded a division of Georgia State Troops in the Atlanta Campaign (May 5–September 2, 1864) and led the Confederate forces in the Battle of Honey Hill (November 30, 1864) in South Carolina. He was paroled at Macon, Georgia, in April 1865.

After the war Smith moved to Tennessee, where he became an iron manufacturer (1866–1870). In 1870 he moved to Kentucky, working as an insurance commissioner until 1876. He then returned to New York City and embarked on a literary career, writing numerous books and manuals. Smith died in New York City on June 24, 1896.

ROBERT P. BROADWATER

See also

Atlanta Campaign; Honey Hill, Battle of; Seven Pines, Battle of; Sherman's March to the Sea

Further Reading

Hudson, Leonne M. *The Odyssey of a Southerner: The Life and Times of Gustavus Woodson Smith*. Macon, GA: Mercer University Press, 1998.

Warner, Ezra J. *Generals in Gray: Lives of the Confederate Commanders*. Baton Rouge: Louisiana State University Press, 2006.

Smith, James Argyle
Birth Date: July 1, 1831
Death Date: December 6, 1901

Confederate officer. James Argyle Smith was born on July 1, 1831, in Maury County, Tennessee. He graduated from the U.S. Military Academy, West Point, in 1853. After serving in a variety of locales and roles, including fighting the Sioux, Smith was on leave when the Civil War began. He resigned from the army in May 1861 and took a commission as a captain in Confederate service. Advanced to major in March 1862, he served as a staff officer for Major General Leonidas Polk and soon thereafter became a lieutenant colonel of the 2nd Tennessee Infantry Regiment, which Smith helped lead at the Battle of Shiloh (April 6–7, 1862). He performed so well there that he was advanced to colonel and given charge of a consolidated unit designated the 5th Confederate (Regular) Infantry.

Smith led his regiment ably at the Battle of Perryville (October 8, 1862) as well as the Battle of Stones River (December 31, 1862–January 2, 1863). He was also commended for his effective leadership during the Battle of Chickamauga (September 19–20, 1863). Smith became a brigadier general on September 30, 1863, and took command of the Texas Brigade in Major General Patrick Cleburne's division, Army of Tennessee. The brigade performed tenaciously in the defense of Missionary Ridge (November 25, 1863), during which Smith was severely wounded. He did not return to duty until June 1864. He saw much action during the Atlanta Campaign (May 5–September 2, 1864) and was wounded again during the Battle of Atlanta (July 22, 1864). Following the Battle of Franklin (November 30, 1864), in which Cleburne was killed, Smith assumed command of the division, leading it at the Battle of Nashville (December 15–16, 1864) and during the subsequent retreat into Mississippi.

Early the next year, Smith commanded half of Major General Benjamin F. Cheatham's corps during Sherman's March through the Carolinas (January–April 1865). Smith was especially conspicuous during the Battle of Bentonville (March 19–21, 1865). Smith surrendered in Greensboro, North Carolina, and was paroled there within a few days.

After the war Smith took up residence in Mississippi, where he became a farmer. From 1877 to 1886 he served as the state superintendent of education, and from 1893 to 1897 he was an agent for the U.S. Bureau of Indian Affairs. Later still, he served as marshal of the Mississippi Supreme Court. Smith died on December 6, 1901, in Jackson, Mississippi.

PAUL G. PIERPAOLI JR.

See also

Atlanta, Battle of; Atlanta Campaign; Bentonville, Battle of; Chickamauga, Battle of; Perryville, Battle of; Sherman's March through the Carolinas; Shiloh, Battle of; Stones River, Battle of

Further Reading

Eicher, John H., and David J. Eicher. *Civil War High Commands*. Stanford, CA: Stanford University Press, 2001.

Warner, Ezra J. *Generals in Gray: Lives of the Confederate Commanders.* Baton Rouge: Louisiana State University Press, 2006.

Smith, James Youngs
Birth Date: September 15, 1809
Death Date: March 26, 1876

Governor of Rhode Island. James Youngs Smith was born on September 15, 1809, in Groton, Connecticut, and was a clerk in a general merchandise store before moving to Rhode Island as a young man. Settling in Providence, he cofounded the successful Asborn & Smith Lumber Company and then went on to establish several textile mills in both Rhode Island and Connecticut. After joining the Republican Party, Smith served as mayor of Providence from 1855 until 1857. He then served in the state legislature before launching an unsuccessful bid for governor in 1861.

Successful in his second race for governor, Smith took office in May 1863. He presided over a booming war economy but ran afoul of federal officials because he supported the state's prevailing sentiments that Rhode Islanders should not be drafted into national service. Smith instead turned to voluntary enlistments and a bounty system, which never quite satisfied federal requirements. Before leaving office in May 1866, Smith was accused of fostering corruption in the enlistment system, but he was later cleared of any wrongdoing.

Smith did not hold public office after 1866 and instead tended to his business interests as well as various charitable causes. He died on March 26, 1876, in Providence, Rhode Island.

PAUL G. PIERPAOLI JR.

See also
Rhode Island

Further Reading
Mohr, Ralph S. *Governors for Three Hundred Years (1638–1954): Rhode Island and Providence Plantations.* Providence: State of Rhode Island, Graves Registration Committee, 1954.

Smith, John Eugene
Birth Date: August 3, 1816
Death Date: January 29, 1897

Union officer. Born in Berne, Switzerland, on August 3, 1816, John Eugene Smith immigrated as a youth with his family to Philadelphia, where he became a jeweler. In 1836 he settled in Galena, Illinois. There Smith practiced his trade and became active in local politics. In 1861 he was responsible for rescuing Ulysses S. Grant from obscurity when Smith suggested to Illinois governor Richard Yates that Grant could easily raise and train an infantry regiment. Smith served briefly on Yates's staff before resigning to recruit and organize the 45th Illinois Infantry Regiment, which he commanded with the rank of colonel from July 23, 1861.

Smith took part with his regiment in the Battles of Fort Henry (February 6, 1862), Fort Donelson (February 13–16), and Shiloh (April 6–7) and the advance on and siege of Corinth (May 3–30). He was promoted to brigadier general of volunteers on November 29, 1862, and he briefly, in December 1862, commanded the 1st Brigade, 3rd Division, XIII Corps. After the reorganization and expansion of the Union forces in the western theater, Smith commanded the 8th Division, XVI Corps, Army of the Tennessee, from December 26, 1862, to April 3, 1863, followed by commands of the 1st Brigade, 3rd Division, XVII Corps, also in the Army of the Tennessee, from April 23 to June 3, 1863.

During the latter part of the Second Vicksburg Campaign (April 1–July 4, 1863), Smith commanded the 7th Division, XVII Corps, Army of the Tennessee, and then subsequently led the 2nd Division of that corps. From December 1863 until the end of the war, he commanded the 3rd Division, XV Corps, Army of the Tennessee, and participated in the Atlanta Campaign (May 5–September 2, 1864), serving in the rear; Major General William T. Sherman's March to the Sea (November 15–December 21, 1864); and Sherman's March though the Carolinas (January–April 1865). Smith commanded the District of Western Tennessee during the final months of 1865.

In April 1866 Smith, who had been brevetted major general in the volunteer army, mustered out of the volunteer service. He accepted a regular army commission as a colonel, with command of the 27th Infantry Regiment, and was brevetted brigadier and major general in the regular army for his Civil War service. Smith, who transferred to the 14th Infantry in 1870, was stationed at a succession of frontier posts until his retirement on May 19, 1881. He died in Chicago on January 29, 1897.

LOUIS BIELAKOWSKI

See also
Corinth, Mississippi, Siege of; Fort Donelson, Battle of; Fort Henry, Battle of; Sherman's March through the Carolinas;

Sherman's March to the Sea; Shiloh, Battle of; Vicksburg Campaign, Second

Further Reading

Eicher, John H., and David J. Eicher. *Civil War High Commands.* Stanford, CA: Stanford University Press, 2001.

Warner, Ezra J. *Generals in Blue: Lives of the Union Commanders.* Baton Rouge: Louisiana State University Press, 2006.

Smith, John Gregory
Birth Date: July 22, 1818
Death Date: November 6, 1891

Lawyer, railroad executive, and Republican governor of Vermont. John Gregory Smith, commonly known as J. Gregory Smith, was born on July 22, 1818, in St. Albans, Vermont. A graduate of the University of Vermont and Yale Law School, he entered a law partnership with his father in St. Albans. By the 1850s, Smith had become involved in railroad management, and in 1858 he became a trustee of the Vermont & Canada Railroad. He also served in the Vermont Senate and House of Representatives, serving as Speaker during 1862. His popularity as an astute businessman and his efficient service as Speaker of the House served him well in his election bid for governor, and he took office as a Republican in October 1863. Handily winning reelection in 1864, he served until October 1865.

Building on the work of Governor Frederick Holbrook, his immediate predecessor, Smith effectively lobbied the state assembly to appropriate money to care for wounded and ill Vermont soldiers and to expand the state's newly established military hospitals. He was also instrumental in drafting legislation that helped ensure soldiers' voting rights while they were on military duty out of state.

After leaving office, Smith continued his involvement in the railroad industry and was one of the founders of the Northern Pacific Railroad, serving as its president from 1866 until 1872. He also maintained his interest in Republican politics, chairing the Vermont delegation to the 1872, 1880, and 1884 Republican National Conventions. Smith died in St. Albans on November 6, 1891.

PAUL G. PIERPAOLI JR.

See also

Holbrook, Frederick; Vermont

Further Reading

Coffin, Howard. *Full Duty: Vermonters in the Civil War.* Woodstock, VT: Countryman, 1995.

Morrissey, Charles T. *Vermont.* New York: Norton, 1981.

Smith, Joseph Bryant
Birth Date: 1826
Death Date: March 8, 1862

Union naval officer. Joseph Bryant Smith was born in Belfast, Maine, in 1826. Appointed a midshipman on October 19, 1841, he graduated from the U.S. Naval Academy, Annapolis, in 1847. He then served aboard the side-wheel frigate *Mississippi,* with the U.S. Coast Survey, and at the Washington Navy Yard. He was promoted to master on August 22, 1855, and to lieutenant on September 14, 1855, when he was assigned to the *Merrimack.* He served in that screw frigate until 1857. In 1859 Smith was assigned to the sailing frigate *Congress* as the ship's executive officer.

On March 8, 1862, Smith was in command of the *Congress* when it came under fire from the Confederate ironclad *Virginia* (ex-*Merrimack)* during the Battles of Hampton Roads. Smith ordered the armed tug *Zouave* to tow his ship under the Union shore batteries at Newport News. This action prevented the *Virginia,* with its deep draft, from ramming the *Congress* as it had the sloop *Cumberland.* Unfortunately for Smith, the *Congress* grounded, and at about 3:30 p.m. Confederate commodore Franklin Buchanan was thus able to position the *Virginia* about 150 yards off the stern of the *Congress* and open a deadly raking fire. Only 2 of the frigate's 50 guns could be brought to bear in reply. In short order 100 men, a quarter of the Union ship's crew, were casualties. Soon both of the *Congress*'s stern guns were disabled, and Lieutenant Smith was killed, decapitated by a shell fragment at about 4:20. Still, the Union frigate took nearly an hour of punishment before it struck. On learning in Washington that the ship had surrendered, Smith's father, Commodore Joseph Smith, said simply, "Joe's dead." Lieutenant John Taylor Wood of the *Virginia* wrote that "No ship was ever fought more gallantly." Having received fire from Union troops on the shore, Buchanan took out his anger on the surrendered *Congress* and ordered the *Virginia*'s gunners to set the ship alight with hot shot; it blew up that night. In all, 120 men of the crew perished.

GERALD D. HOLLAND JR. AND SPENCER C. TUCKER

See also

Hampton Roads, Battles of; *Virginia,* CSS

Further Reading

Official Records of the Union and Confederate Navies in the War of the Rebellion, Series 1, Vol. 7. Washington, DC: U.S. Government Printing Office, 1898.

Porter, David D. *The Naval History of the Civil War.* New York: Courier Dover, 1998.

Tucker, Spencer C. *Blue and Gray Navies: The Civil War Afloat*. Annapolis, MD: Naval Institute Press, 2006.

Wood, John Taylor. "The First Fight of Iron-Clads." In *Battles and Leaders of the Civil War*, edited by Robert Underwood Johnson and Clarence Clough Buel, 692–711. Secaucus, NJ: Castle, n.d.

Smith, Martin Luther
Birth Date: September 9, 1819
Death Date: July 29, 1866

Confederate officer. Martin Luther Smith was born on September 9, 1819, in Danby, New York. He graduated from the U.S. Military Academy, West Point, in 1842. Commissioned an engineering officer, Smith served throughout the United States, and during the Mexican-American War (1846–1848) he was brevetted for his mapping work. A captain by 1856, Smith subsequently took a leave of absence and worked as chief engineer for the Fernandina & Cedar Key Railroad in Florida.

Accepting a major's commission in the Confederate Army, Smith resigned his U.S. Army commission on April 1, 1861. His long ties to the South—his wife was a Southerner—and business concerns in the South led to his decision to back the Confederacy. Sent to New Orleans in the early summer of 1861, Smith helped fortify that city's defenses before taking command of the 21st Louisiana Infantry with the rank of colonel in February 1862.

On April 11, 1862, Smith was advanced to brigadier general and given charge of the Third District in the Department of Southern Mississippi and East Louisiana. Sent to Vicksburg to help supervise the construction of defensive works, he became a major general on November 4, 1862. He remained in Vicksburg until the city fell to Union forces on July 4, 1863. Taken prisoner, Smith was finally exchanged in March 1864.

Smith subsequently became chief engineer for General Robert E. Lee before serving as chief engineer for General John B. Hood at Atlanta beginning in July 1864. Smith retained this position until October, at which time he became chief engineer for the Department of Alabama, Mississippi, and East Louisiana. In this role, he was responsible for erecting defenses around Mobile for Major General Dabney Maury. Smith was in Mobile until that port city fell to Union forces on April 12, 1865. The following month, he surrendered in Athens, Georgia.

After the war Smith operated a civil engineering business in Savannah, where he died on July 29, 1866.

PAUL G. PIERPAOLI JR.

See also

Engineers; Hood, John Bell; Maury, Dabney Herndon; Mobile, Alabama, Siege of; Vicksburg Campaign, Second

Further Reading

Eicher, John H., and David J. Eicher. *Civil War High Commands*. Stanford, CA: Stanford University Press, 2001.

Warner, Ezra J. *Generals in Gray: Lives of the Confederate Commanders*. Baton Rouge: Louisiana State University Press, 2006.

Smith, Morgan Lewis
Birth Date: March 8, 1821
Death Date: December 29, 1874

Union officer. Morgan Lewis Smith was born in Mexico, New York, on March 8, 1821. He was the elder brother of future Union general Giles A. Smith. When Morgan Smith was an infant, his family moved to Jefferson County, New York. Smith left New York at age 21, finally settling in New Albany, Indiana, around 1843, where he became a teacher. On July 19, 1845, Smith joined the U.S. Army as a private under the assumed name of Martin L. Sanford and rose to the rank of sergeant before he resigned on July 19, 1850.

Smith then moved to St. Louis, where he became a boatman on the Ohio and Mississippi Rivers. When the Civil War began, Smith recruited the 8th Missouri Regiment at St. Louis and was commissioned its colonel on July 8, 1861. He trained his regiment well, turning it into a highly effective fighting unit. Smith took part in the advance to Fort Henry and then commanded the 5th Brigade of Brigadier General Lew Wallace's Division in the Battle of Fort Donelson (February 13–16, 1862). Smith led the 1st Brigade, 3rd Division, Army of the Tennessee, in the Battle of Shiloh (April 6–7, 1862) and was appointed brigadier general of volunteers on July 16, 1862.

In November 1862, Smith assumed command of the 2nd Division of XIII Corps in the Army of the Tennessee. He was severely wounded in the hip on December 28 during the Battle of Chickasaw Bluffs (December 26–29, 1862) and was forced to leave his command to recover. Not returning to active service until October 1863, he commanded the 2nd Division, XV Corps, Army of the Tennessee, during the Chattanooga Campaign (October–November 1863) and the Atlanta Campaign (May 5–September 2, 1864) and briefly commanded XV Corps at the end of July when Major General John A. Logan assumed command of the Army of the Tennessee following the death of Major General James B. McPherson. In August, reoccurring problems with his war wounds forced Smith to give up field command. He then assumed command of the District of Vicksburg, holding this position until the end of the war. Smith resigned his commission on July 12, 1865. Strangely, he did not receive a brevet to major general.

Smith was U.S. consul general in Honolulu from 1866 to 1868. Declining the governorship of the Colorado Territory, he then moved to Washington, D.C., where he became a counsel for those with claims against the government. Smith was involved with a building association in Washington when he died suddenly on a trip to Jersey City, New Jersey, on December 29, 1874.

SPENCER C. TUCKER

See also

Atlanta Campaign; Chickasaw Bluffs, Battle of; Fort Donelson, Battle of; Fort Henry, Battle of; Logan, John Alexander; McPherson, James Birdseye; Shiloh, Battle of

Further Reading

Eicher, John H., and David J. Eicher. *Civil War High Commands.* Stanford, CA: Stanford University Press, 2001.

Warner, Ezra J. *Generals in Blue: Lives of the Union Commanders.* Baton Rouge: Louisiana State University Press, 2006.

Smith, Preston
Birth Date: December 25, 1823
Death Date: September 19, 1863

Confederate officer. Preston Smith was born in Giles County, Tennessee, on December 25, 1823. He attended Jackson College in Columbia, Tennessee, and studied law. After passing the bar, he established a legal practice in Columbia. Smith subsequently moved to Waynesboro, Tennessee, and ultimately to Memphis, where his practice flourished.

With the beginning of the Civil War, in May 1861 Smith was elected colonel of the 154th Tennessee (Senior) Regiment, a militia unit that entered Confederate service in August. He commanded a brigade during the Battle of Belmont (November 7, 1861) in Missouri. Smith led his regiment in the Battle of Shiloh (April 6–7, 1862), where he was severely wounded in the right shoulder and forced to quit the field.

Following a monthlong recuperation, Smith returned to action in the defense of Corinth, Mississippi, and participated in General Braxton Bragg's Kentucky Campaign

(August 14–October 26, 1862), commanding the 1st Brigade in Brigadier General Patrick Cleburne's 2nd Division under Major General E. Kirby Smith. When Cleburne was wounded in the Battle of Richmond (August 29–30, 1862) in Kentucky, Smith assumed temporary command of the division. In recognition of his highly effective leadership in this battle, Smith received promotion to brigadier general on October 27, 1862.

Smith was present during the last day of fighting at the Battle of Stones River (December 31, 1862–January 2, 1863) and participated in the Tullahoma Campaign (June 23–July 3, 1863). He commanded a brigade in the Battle of Chickamauga (September 19–20, 1863), when Bragg's Army of Tennessee attacked Major General William S. Rosecrans's Army of the Cumberland. During the action of September 19, Smith's forces fought the Federals in the woods, with little advantage gained on either side. That evening, Smith's men formed a part of Cleburne's attack on the Union left, but Union major general George H. Thomas had anticipated the Confederate move and established a strong defensive position so that the Confederate attack was beaten back. During this attack, Smith and his staff inadvertently rode into Union lines. They were recognized as Confederates, and Smith and two aides were felled by a Union volley. One of the aides was killed outright, and Smith was mortally wounded. Carried to the rear, he died an hour later.

SPENCER C. TUCKER

See also

Bragg, Braxton; Chattanooga Campaign; Cleburne, Patrick Ronayne; Kentucky Campaign; Richmond, Battle of; Rosecrans, William Starke; Shiloh, Battle of; Smith, Edmund Kirby; Thomas, George Henry

Further Reading

Eicher, John H., and David J. Eicher. *Civil War High Commands.* Stanford, CA: Stanford University Press, 2001.

Warner, Ezra J. *Generals in Gray: Lives of the Confederate Commanders.* Baton Rouge: Louisiana State University Press, 2006.

Woodworth, Steven. *The Chickamauga Campaign.* Carbondale: Southern Illinois University Press, 2010.

Smith, Thomas Benton
Birth Date: February 24, 1838
Death Date: May 21, 1923

Confederate officer. Thomas Benton Smith was born in Mechanicsville, Tennessee, on February 24, 1838. He was educated at the Nashville Military Institute. Smith entered the railroad industry and worked for a time with the Nashville & Decatur Railroad before enlisting in 1861 in the Confederate Army as a lieutenant in the 20th Tennessee Infantry Regiment.

Smith saw action in the Battle of Mill Springs (January 19, 1862) in Kentucky and was advanced to colonel of the regiment in May 1862. On August 5 he participated in the failed Confederate attempt to capture the Union garrison at Baton Rouge. During the engagement, Smith took temporary command of a brigade and earned praise for his performance.

During the Battle of Stones River (December 31, 1862–January 2, 1863), Smith was wounded severely. Upon recovery, he returned to duty and was again wounded at the Battle of Chickamauga (September 19–20, 1863). He recovered sufficiently to participate in the Atlanta Campaign (May 5–September 2, 1864), during which he took command of Brigadier General Robert C. Tyler's brigade.

In July 1864, Smith was advanced to brigadier general. During the campaign, he became widely known for his stoutness in combat and dogged determination to defeat Union troops. During the Franklin and Nashville Campaign (November 29–December 27, 1864), he performed brilliantly. Before the conclusion of that campaign, however, on December 16, 1864, Smith was taken prisoner by Union forces in Nashville. That same day, a colonel from an Ohio regiment spotted Smith among a group of others and singled him out for abuse. The colonel's men had apparently suffered grievously during an assault led by Smith's brigade, and the colonel sought revenge. Without warning, he savagely attacked Smith with his saber, smashing him repeatedly about the head. The wounds were so severe that a portion of Smith's brain was exposed. Miraculously, Smith recovered and eventually returned to railroad work. However, the effects of the attack—whether physical or psychological—brought about mental illness, and Smith spent the last 47 years of his life in a mental asylum. He died in Nashville on May 21, 1923.

PAUL G. PIERPAOLI JR.

See also

Atlanta Campaign; Baton Rouge, Battle of; Chickamauga, Battle of; Franklin and Nashville Campaign; Mill Springs, Battle of; Stones River, Battle of; Tyler, Robert Charles

Further Reading

Horn, Stanley F. *The Army of Tennessee.* Norman: University of Oklahoma Press, 1993.
Warner, Ezra J. *Generals in Gray: Lives of the Confederate Commanders.* Baton Rouge: Louisiana State University Press, 2006.

Smith, Thomas Kilby
Birth Date: September 23, 1820
Death Date: December 14, 1887

Union officer. Thomas Kilby Smith was born in Dorchester, Massachusetts, on September 23, 1820. While a boy, Smith moved with his parents to a farm in Hamilton County, Ohio. He graduated from Cincinnati College in 1837 and then pursued a career in law, studying under Salmon P. Chase, future U.S. secretary of the treasury and chief justice of the United States. Smith subsequently clerked in the Post Office Department in Washington, D.C., and then was a U.S. marshal for the Southern District of Ohio.

On September 9, 1861, Smith was commissioned lieutenant colonel of the 54th Ohio Infantry. He was promoted to colonel on October 31. Smith performed capably in the western theater of war in all the campaigns of the Army of the Tennessee, commencing with the Battle of Shiloh (April 6–7, 1862), when he assumed command of a brigade. During the First Vicksburg Campaign (October 16–December 29, 1862) and the Second Vicksburg Campaign (April 1–July 4, 1863), Smith served for a time on Major General Ulysses S. Grant's staff and also commanded a brigade in XV Corps. Smith was appointed a brigadier general on August 11, 1863.

Smith commanded the detached division of XVI Corps, providing protection to Rear Admiral David D. Porter's gunboats during the Red River Campaign (March 10–May 22, 1864). Smith's health having failed, he was relieved of active duty on January 17, 1865. In recognition of his effective wartime service, he was brevetted major general of volunteers on March 13, 1865. That June after the fall of Mobile, he assumed command of the District of Mobile. He mustered out of the volunteers on January 15, 1866.

After the war, Smith settled in Torresdale, part of Philadelphia, Pennsylvania. He was U.S. consul in Panama (1867–1869) and returned to Torresdale, but in 1887 he moved to New York City, where he died on December 14, 1887.

SPENCER C. TUCKER

See also

Chase, Salmon Portland; Grant, Ulysses Simpson; Porter, David Dixon; Red River Campaign; Shiloh, Battle of; Vicksburg Campaign, First; Vicksburg Campaign, Second

Further Reading

Eicher, John H., and David J. Eicher. *Civil War High Commands.* Stanford, CA: Stanford University Press, 2001.
Warner, Ezra J. *Generals in Blue: Lives of the Union Commanders.* Baton Rouge: Louisiana State University Press, 2006.

Smith, Truman
Birth Date: November 27, 1791
Death Date: May 3, 1884

U.S. congressman and senator as well as judge on the British-American Court of Arbitration, which sought to investigate and prosecute those who dealt in the international slave trade. Truman Smith was born on November 27, 1791, in Roxbury, Connecticut. After graduation from Yale College in 1815, he studied law and was admitted to the bar in 1818. Settling in Litchfield, he built a successful legal practice. He sat in the Connecticut House of Representatives (1831–1832 and 1834) as a Whig before being elected to the U.S. House of Representatives, where he served during 1845–1849 as a Whig.

Elected to the U.S. Senate in 1848, Smith served in that body from 1849 until 1854. During that time, he became chagrined at the proslavery forces who were attempting to expand slavery into the territories, an issue that had become far more divisive following the Mexican-American War (1846–1848) and the resultant land cessions in the West. When the Southern element of the Whig Party embraced the controversial Kansas-Nebraska Act of 1854, Smith resigned his seat in 1854, believing that the slavery issue would sound the death knell for his party.

Smith settled in New York City, where he established a lucrative law practice and remained keenly interested in politics. By the late 1850s, he had joined the new Republican Party. Although Smith did not champion Abraham Lincoln's 1860 presidential nomination—he favored a nominee from a border state—he did fully support Lincoln's war policies when the Civil War began in April 1861.

By 1862, Smith was convinced that slavery had to be eradicated, by the successful prosecution of the war if necessary. That same year, Lincoln named Smith to be a judge on the British-American Court of Arbitration. The result of a treaty between the two nations concluded in 1862, the tribunal was designed to render judgments in cases in which ships seized by either American or British warships were suspected of participating in the international slave trade. Smith remained on the court until 1870, when he briefly practiced law before retiring. He died on May 3, 1884, in Stamford, Connecticut.

PAUL G. PIERPAOLI JR.

See also
Kansas-Nebraska Act; Lincoln, Abraham; Republican Party; Slavery

Further Reading
Holt, Michael F. "Rethinking Nineteenth-Century American Political History." *Congress and the Presidency* 19(2) (Autumn 1992): 97–111.
Simon, John Y. "Lincoln and Truman Smith." *Lincoln Herald* 67 (Fall 1965): 124–130.

Smith, William
Birth Date: September 6, 1797
Death Date: May 18, 1887

Confederate officer and governor of Virginia. William Smith was born on September 6, 1797, in King George County, Virginia. From 1827 to 1836, he operated a successful mailcoach service from Milledgeville, Georgia, to Washington, D.C., during which time he attracted the enduring sobriquet "Extra Billy." From 1836 until 1841, Smith sat in the Virginia Senate. He then ran for a seat in the U.S. House of Representatives, where he served from 1841 to 1843 and again from 1853 to 1861.

From 1846 to 1849, Smith served as Virginia's governor. In the summer of 1861, Virginia governor John Letcher offered Smith a colonel's commission in the state militia. Smith eagerly accepted, despite his age and lack of prior military experience.

Now in Confederate service, Smith saw action at the First Battle of Bull Run (July 21, 1861), where he led the 49th Virginia Infantry Regiment and performed capably. In the autumn of 1861, Smith was elected to the Confederate Congress and served until the spring of 1862.

Smith next saw action at the Battle of Seven Pines (May 31–June 1, 1862). He also participated in the Battle of Antietam (September 17, 1862), where he was wounded and as a consequence was out of action for a number of months. Advanced to brigadier general on January 31, 1863, he received command of Brigadier General Jubal A. Early's old brigade and saw combat at the Battle of Gettysburg (July 1–3, 1863). That autumn, Smith was reelected governor after being advanced to major general on August 12, 1863.

Smith took office in January 1864 and presided over Virginia during the last months of the crumbling Confederacy. Because of a chronic shortage of funds and the nearly constant warfare in his state, Smith accomplished very little during his abbreviated tenure in office. In April 1865 he fled the capital at Richmond but surrendered several weeks later. Paroled almost immediately, he returned to his Warrenton

County estate, where he farmed until his death there on May 18, 1887.

Paul G. Pierpaoli Jr.

See also

Antietam, Battle of; Bull Run, First Battle of; Gettysburg, Battle of; Seven Pines, Battle of; Virginia

Further Reading

Fahrner, Alvin A. "The Public Career of William 'Extra Billy' Smith." PhD dissertation, University of North Carolina, 1953.

Warner, Ezra J. *Generals in Gray: Lives of the Confederate Commanders.* Baton Rouge: Louisiana State University Press, 2006.

Smith, William Duncan
Birth Date: July 28, 1825
Death Date: October 4, 1862

Confederate officer. Born in Augusta, Georgia, on July 28, 1825, William Duncan Smith graduated from the U.S. Military Academy, West Point, in 1846. Commissioned in the 2nd Dragoons, he fought in the Mexican-American War (1846–1848). He took part in the Mexico City Campaign and was seriously wounded in the Battle of Molino del Rey (September 8, 1847). On his recovery, he held garrison assignments. Smith was promoted to first lieutenant on August 18, 1851, and to captain on June 4, 1858.

With the onset of the Civil War, Smith sided with the Confederacy and resigned his U.S. Army commission on January 28, 1861. He was commissioned a major in the 1st Georgia Regular Infantry on March 16. Smith was assigned as assistant adjutant general in the defenses of Savannah on June 25. Promoted to colonel, commanding the 20th Georgia Infantry, on July 14, he was advanced to brigadier general on March 7, 1862, and the next month assumed command of the 1st Brigade, District of Georgia, in the Department of South Carolina and Georgia. In July he took command at Charleston of the First Sub-District of the District of South Carolina in the same department. Smith led one wing of Confederate forces under Brigadier General Nathan G. Evans in the Battle of Secessionville (June 16, 1862) in which the Confederates repulsed a Union attack under Brigadier General Henry W. Benham.

Smith contracted yellow fever and died in Charleston, South Carolina, on October 4, 1862.

Spencer C. Tucker

See also

Benham, Henry Washington; Evans, Nathan George; Secessionville, Battle of

Further Reading

Brennan, Patrick. *Secessionville: Assault on Charleston.* Campbell, CA: Savas, 1996.

Eicher, John H., and David J. Eicher. *Civil War High Commands.* Stanford, CA: Stanford University Press, 2001.

Warner, Ezra J. *Generals in Gray: Lives of the Confederate Commanders.* Baton Rouge: Louisiana State University Press, 2006.

Smith, William Farrar
Birth Date: February 17, 1824
Death Date: February 28, 1903

Union officer. Born in St. Albans, Vermont, on February 17, 1824, William Farrar Smith, known to his friends as "Baldy," graduated from the U.S. Military Academy, West Point, in July 1845. Commissioned in the Topographical Engineers, he was promoted to first lieutenant on March 3, 1853.

Smith conducted surveys in the Great Lakes region and in Texas, Arizona, and Florida. In Florida, Smith was stricken with malaria, which affected his health for the rest of his life. In 1856 he was assigned to the Lighthouse Service. He was also assistant professor of mathematics at West Point (1846–1848 and 1855–1856). Smith was promoted to captain on July 1, 1859.

Assigned to the staff of Brigadier General Irvin McDowell, Smith took part in the First Battle of Bull Run (July 21, 1861). He was appointed colonel of the 3rd Vermont Regiment on July 16, 1861, and after helping organize the 1st Vermont Brigade, he was appointed brigadier general of volunteers on August 13. Smith commanded a division in the Army of the Potomac during Major General George B. McClellan's Peninsula Campaign (March–July 1862) and was brevetted regular army lieutenant colonel for his role in the Battle of White Oak Swamp (June 30, 1862) during the Seven Days' Campaign (June 25–July 1, 1862). Smith was promoted to major general of volunteers on July 4, 1862.

Smith led his division with great effectiveness in the Battle of Antietam (September 17, 1862) and commanded VI Corps during the First Battle of Fredericksburg (December 13, 1862). His close friendship with the discredited McClellan and outspoken criticism of Army of the Potomac commander Major General Ambrose E. Burnside for the latter's handling of the First Battle of Fredericksburg cost Smith both his corps command and his Senate confirmation as major general. His nomination to major general expired on March 4, 1863, and he reverted to the rank of brigadier general. Smith then commanded Pennsylvania militiamen in the Department of the Susquehanna, and during the Gettysburg Campaign (June–July 1863) he retook Carlisle, Pennsylvania, which had been occupied by the Confederates.

On October 3, 1863, Smith was assigned as chief engineer of the Army of the Cumberland. In that capacity, he opened the famous Cracker Line that allowed resupply and reinforcement of Union forces at Chattanooga. This notable achievement won the thanks of Major General Ulysses S. Grant. Again nominated for major general with Grant's enthusiastic support, this time Smith was confirmed by the Senate, on March 9, 1864.

Smith commanded XVIII Corps in Major General Benjamin F. Butler's Army of the James during Grant's Overland Campaign (May 4–June 12, 1864). Smith saw action in the Bermuda Hundred Campaign (May 5–20, 1864) and the Battle of Cold Harbor (May 31–June 12, 1864). Ordered by Grant to attack the city of Petersburg on June 15, Smith, undoubtedly conscious of the Cold Harbor debacle, carried out an extensive reconnaissance and moved too deliberately, no doubt costing the Union capture of that key city and prolonging the war by many months. This might have

Major General William F. Smith commanded XVIII Corps in the Army of the James during the May–June 1864 Overland Campaign. Ordered to attack Petersburg on June 15, he was slow to move, costing the Union the early capture of that key city and prolonging the war by many months. (Library of Congress)

been forgiven, but Smith, who was often his own worst enemy, also quarreled with Butler. Relieved of command on July 19, Smith passed the remainder of the war on special duty. He was nonetheless brevetted through major general in the regular army.

Smith resigned his volunteer commission in November 1865 and resigned from the U.S. Army in 1867 and spent much of the rest of his life defending his Civil War record. From 1864 to 1873 he was president of the International Telegraph Company, and from 1875 to 1881 he was on the Board of Police Commissioners of New York, becoming its president in 1877. After 1881, he engaged in civil engineering work in Pennsylvania. Smith died in Philadelphia on February 28, 1903.

SPENCER C. TUCKER

See also

Antietam, Battle of; Bull Run, First Battle of; Burnside, Ambrose Everett; Butler, Benjamin Franklin; Carlisle, Pennsylvania; Cold Harbor, Battle of; Cracker Line Operation; Fredericksburg, First Battle of; Gettysburg Campaign; Grant, Ulysses Simpson; McClellan, George Brinton; McDowell, Irvin; Overland Campaign; Petersburg Campaign; Seven Days' Campaign; White Oak Swamp, Battle of

Further Reading

Eicher, John H., and David J. Eicher. *Civil War High Commands.* Stanford, CA: Stanford University Press, 2001.

Smith, William F. *Autobiography of Major General William F. "Baldy" Smith, 1861–1864.* Edited by Herbert M. Schiller. Dayton, OH: Morningside House, 1990.

Warner, Ezra J. *Generals in Blue: Lives of the Union Commanders.* Baton Rouge: Louisiana State University Press, 2006.

Smith, William Sooy
Birth Date: July 22, 1830
Death Date: March 4, 1916

Union officer. William Sooy Smith was born in Tarlton, Ohio, on July 22, 1830. He graduated with an engineering degree from Ohio University in 1849 and then entered the U.S. Military Academy, West Point, graduating in 1853. Smith resigned his commission on June 19, 1854, to accept a position with the Illinois Central Railroad, but he lost that post because of poor health. After two years teaching school in Buffalo, New York, in 1857 Smith established Parkinson & Smith, an engineering firm that worked on the international bridge between the United States and Canada across the Niagara River and then on the Charleston & Savannah Railroad Bridge near Savannah, Georgia.

With the beginning of the Civil War, Smith left his work in Georgia and joined the 13th Ohio Infantry Regiment. On June 26, 1861, he became its colonel. Following service with his regiment in western Virginia (present-day West Virginia), he commanded a brigade in the Army of the Ohio during the Battle of Shiloh (April 6–7, 1862), winning promotion to brigadier general of volunteers on April 15 in recognition of his performance. Smith then commanded the Army of the Ohio's 4th Division.

Smith's division was in reserve during the Battle of Perryville (October 8, 1862). He then commanded the 2nd Division, XVI Corps, Army of the Tennessee, during the Second Vicksburg Campaign (April 1–July 4, 1863). On July 20 he became chief of cavalry in the Department of the Tennessee, and in October he assumed the same position in the Military Division of the Mississippi.

In February 1864 Smith commanded a large cavalry force that proceeded south from Tennessee into Mississippi to act as a diversionary force for Major General William T. Sherman's Meridian Campaign (February 3–26, 1864). The Sooy Smith Expedition (February 11–26), as it was called, failed miserably and angered Sherman. Smith was late getting started, and although he had 11,000 men, he was turned back by numerically inferior Confederate forces under Major General Nathan Bedford Forrest at Okolona, Mississippi (October 22). Smith then performed administrative duties in Nashville until he resigned his commission for health reasons on July 15, 1864.

Smith farmed in Cook County, Illinois, until resuming his civil engineering practice in 1866. He became an internationally known figure in engineering circles for his work on pneumatic caissons in construction and on bridge design. Among his accomplishments were several Missouri River bridges, including the first all-steel bridge, the Glasgow Railroad Bridge at Glasgow, Missouri. In 1876 he was awarded the American Centennial Exposition Prize for his bridge work. Retiring to Medford, Oregon, in 1910, Smith died there on March 4, 1916.

SPENCER C. TUCKER

See also

Forrest, Nathan Bedford; Meridian Campaign; Okolona, Battle of; Perryville, Battle of; Sherman, William Tecumseh; Shiloh, Battle of; Sooy Smith Expedition

Further Reading

Eicher, John H., and David J. Eicher. *Civil War High Commands.* Stanford, CA: Stanford University Press, 2001.

Foster, Buck T. *Sherman's Mississippi Campaign.* Tuscaloosa: University of Alabama Press, 2006.

Warner, Ezra J. *Generals in Blue: Lives of the Union Commanders.* Baton Rouge: Louisiana State University Press, 2006.

Smoothbores

Firearms with unrifled barrels manufactured in both pistol and long-arm (musket) forms employed during the Civil War. Although they were technologically obsolete by 1861, smoothbore muskets were used by both sides throughout the war because equipping every soldier with the newer rifled firearms, which had both greater range and accuracy, proved to be impossible. Many of the older smoothbores used in the war had been converted from a flintlock to a percussion ignition mechanism.

As the name implies, the bore or inside diameter of the barrel of the musket or pistol was smooth, not rifled. The projectile fired from a musket was a spherical ball or round shot of .69 caliber, equivalent to a diameter of 0.69 inch, or 17.5 millimeters. Another type of smoothbore ammunition consisted of a .69-caliber buck-and-ball cartridge that consisted of a standard-sized ball and three buckshot. This increased the effective killing radius of the weapon by producing a shotgun effect.

All smoothbore muskets were muzzleloaders. This required that the ball be slightly smaller than the diameter of the barrel. Because of windage—the difference between the diameter of the barrel and that of the ball—the ball bounded down the barrel when the weapon was fired and might leave the muzzle at an angle. Smoothbores were therefore quite inaccurate at ranges of more than 50 yards but could still be effective in close-range fighting in woods and on many battlefields.

Confederate forces seized numerous federal arsenals, armories, and ordnance depots before the war began. Most of the 154,000 small arms captured were smoothbore weapons, and for the first two years of the war most Confederate infantry used smoothbores. It was not until after the Battle of Gettysburg (July 1–3, 1863) that the Confederate Army of Northern Virginia was extensively equipped with rifles.

During the war, the most common smoothbore pistols were the Model 1836 (.54 caliber) and the Model 1842 percussion pistol (.54 caliber). The most commonly used smoothbore muskets were the Models 1816 and 1840 (.69 caliber) and the Model 1842 percussion musket (.69 caliber).

The great majority of artillery pieces—land and sea— used by both sides in the Civil War were also smoothbore weapons and were referred to as such.

DANA LOMBARDY AND PAUL G. PIERPAOLI JR.

See also

Arms Manufacturing; Buck and Ball; Rifles

Further Reading

Eicher, David J. *The Longest Night: A Military History of the Civil War.* New York: Simon and Schuster, 2001.

Flayderman, Norm. *Flayderman's Guide to Antique American Firearms.* Iola, WI: Krause, 1998.

Thomas, Dean S. *Ready . . . Aim . . . Fire! Small Arms Ammunition in the Battle of Gettysburg.* Gettysburg, PA: Thomas Publications, 1993.

Smyth, Thomas Alfred

Birth Date: December 25, 1832
Death Date: April 9, 1865

Union officer. Thomas Alfred Smyth was born on December 25, 1832, in Ballyhooley, County Cork, Ireland, and immigrated to the United States in 1854. After participating in a filibustering expedition to Nicaragua led by William Walker in 1855, Smyth worked as a coach maker in Delaware. In 1861 Smyth recruited an infantry company that was part of the 24th Pennsylvania Regiment, an all-Irish outfit. After the regiment's three-month enlistment period lapsed, he became major of the 1st Delaware Infantry.

Smyth saw duty in eastern Virginia and fought in the Battle of Antietam (September 17, 1862). After fighting at the First Battle of Fredericksburg (December 13, 1862), Smyth was advanced to lieutenant colonel. On February 7, 1862, he became colonel of the 1st Delaware.

Smyth commanded his regiment at the Battle of Chancellorsville (May 1–4, 1863) and then at the Battle of Gettysburg (July 1–3, 1863), where he commanded a brigade in II Corps, Army of the Potomac, and helped turn the tide of Pickett's Charge on the third day of combat. Smith continued in a brigade command for the rest of 1863 and also took part in the Overland Campaign (May 4–June 12, 1864). He was conspicuous at the Battle of Cold Harbor (May 31–June 12, 1864) and during the Petersburg Campaign (June 15, 1864–April 3, 1865), occasionally heading a division. He was advanced to brigadier general of volunteers on October 1, 1864.

During the Appomattox Campaign (April 2–9, 1865), Smyth commanded his II Corps brigade in the pursuit of General Robert E. Lee's retreating army. Smyth was shot and mortally wounded by a Confederate sniper on April 7 near Farmville, Virginia. He died on April 9, 1865, the day of Lee's surrender. Smyth was posthumously brevetted major general of volunteers.

PAUL G. PIERPAOLI JR.

See also

Antietam, Battle of; Appomattox Campaign; Chancellorsville, Battle of; Cold Harbor, Battle of; Fredericksburg, First Battle of; Gettysburg, Battle of; Lee, Robert Edward; Overland Campaign

Further Reading

Eicher, John H., and David J. Eicher. *Civil War High Commands.* Stanford, CA: Stanford University Press, 2001.

Warner, Ezra J. *Generals in Blue: Lives of the Union Commanders.* Baton Rouge: Louisiana State University Press, 2006.

Snake Creek Gap, Georgia, Maneuvers around

Start Date: May 7, 1864
End Date: May 12, 1864

Military operations during the opening phase of the Atlanta Campaign (May 5–September 2, 1864) in northwestern Georgia. On May 7, 1864, Union major general William T. Sherman began movements to gain the Confederate rear via Snake Creek Gap to force the Army of Tennessee from its fortified positions near Dalton, Georgia. These maneuvers marked the first stage of the Union attempt to capture Atlanta, some 90 miles south of Dalton. Sherman's plan was to destroy the Western & Atlantic Railroad, the Confederate supply and communication link with Atlanta.

In February 1864, Union major general George Thomas had reconnoitered the Confederate positions around Dalton. He found the mountain range, known as Rocky Face Ridge, to be virtually impregnable but recommended that any Union movement in the area take place through one of the gaps in the range rather than along the fortified heights. Thomas chose Snake Creek Gap as the most viable option for a flanking march. It was located along Snake Creek some eight miles southwest of Dalton and is the southernmost gap in Rocky Face Ridge.

Confederate general Joseph E. Johnston, commander of the Army of Tennessee, correctly assumed that Sherman would not risk a full assault on Rocky Face Ridge. Johnston anticipated that Sherman would attempt to outflank him to the west toward Rome, Georgia, through Mill Gap but had neglected Snake Creek Gap, giving Sherman an open door to his rear. Sherman planned a diversionary assault near Rocky Face Ridge at Dug Gap, while he slipped the Army of the Tennessee through Snake Creek Gap toward the Oostanaula River and Resaca to destroy the rail link. At 4:00 p.m. on May 8, the diversionary attack at Dug Gap began. Johnston, believing that this was the expected assault, ordered Lieutenant General William J. Hardee's corps into the fray. Fighting continued into the afternoon of May 9, by which time Major General James McPherson had begun to move the Union Army of the Tennessee through Snake Creek Gap toward the rail line at Resaca. The fighting at Dug Gap blinded the

Union troops engaging the Confederates at Snake Creek Gap, Georgia, during May 7–12, 1864, early in the Atlanta Campaign. (Library of Congress)

Confederate high command to these movements. Not until May 12 would Johnston order the corps under Hardee and Lieutenant General John Bell Hood to Resaca.

Moving through Snake Creek Gap on May 9, McPherson's army was able to engage the isolated advance units of Lieutenant General Leonidas Polk's corps west of Resaca. McPherson ordered skirmishers to find weaknesses in Polk's line while Union artillery battered the mostly unprotected Confederates, but to Sherman's regret McPherson failed to order a full assault. Much of the advantage gained by the Union advance through Snake Creek Gap was lost by McPherson's hesitation. Nevertheless, McPherson's presence in Snake Creek Gap rendered the carefully prepared position at Dalton untenable and compromised his position at Resaca as well. Johnston decided to abandon Resaca and withdraw south toward Cassville. In evacuating Dalton and Resaca, Johnston had abandoned almost half of the ground between Sherman's army and Atlanta.

JASON LUTZ AND JIM PIECUCH

See also
Atlanta Campaign; Hardee, William Joseph; Johnston, Joseph Eggleston; McPherson, James Birdseye; Polk, Leonidas; Sherman, William Tecumseh; Thomas, George Henry

Further Reading
Bonds, Russell S. *War Like the Thunderbolt: The Battle and Burning of Atlanta.* Yardley, PA: Westholme, 2009.
Fowler, John D. *Mountaineers in Gray: The Nineteenth Tennessee Volunteer Infantry Regiment, C.S.A.* Knoxville: University of Tennessee Press, 2004.

Society for the Abolition of the Slave Trade

Organization founded on May 22, 1787, in London, England, that helped to inform the American abolitionist movement. Anglican minister Thomas Clarkson and his friend Granville Sharp were the principal leaders of the Society for the Abolition of the Slave Trade. Their goal in establishing the organization was the abolition of the slave trade in the British Empire, and their efforts to expose the cruelty of the slave trade had an enormous effect in turning public opinion in England against the trade and eventually against slavery itself.

While Clarkson and Sharp were Anglicans, the majority of the society's membership consisted of Quakers. In the late 18th century, England's Quakers were one of the few groups that openly denounced slavery. As a disenfranchised religious minority, the Quakers maintained a close-knit community across England, and the society relied on this network as a communication and support system.

The society's role in spreading information on the slave trade relied heavily on Thomas Clarkson's dedicated efforts. Clarkson traveled throughout England interviewing thousands of men who had been involved in the slave trade. He also gathered tools of the slave trade: chains, restraints, and implements of torture. Clarkson's research was reflected in the 1787 pamphlet *A Summary View of the Slave Trade and of the Probable Consequences of Its Abolition* and many other later publications.

The society's efforts led to a rapid change in public opinion. Towns throughout England founded their own anti–slave trade and antislavery groups, allying themselves with the society. More petitions were submitted to Parliament calling for the abolition of the slave trade than had been submitted on any single previous issue. And more than 300,000 Britons participated in a boycott of slave-grown sugar.

The society was also aided by influential members of England's upper class. Clarkson and Sharp pressured politicians, merchants, and clergymen to support the movement through presentations on the cruelty of the slave trade, often involving the display of frightening shackles and thumbscrews that Clarkson had obtained. William Wilberforce, a politician and an Anglican Evangelical, soon became the society's voice in Parliament.

Early attempts to press Parliament to abolish the slave trade were unsuccessful. However, growing evidence of the brutality of the slave trade brought new supporters to the movement. In 1807 Parliament passed the Abolition of the Slave Trade Act, which outlawed the slave trade in the British Empire. The Society for the Abolition of the Slave Trade was then disbanded, and many of its members became advocates for the abolition of slavery itself.

Most of the society's leaders had argued for the abolition of the slave trade, believing it to be a step of a gradual process in the abolition of slavery as a whole. By 1833, pressure from British abolitionists and slave revolts in the West Indies led Parliament to outlaw slavery in the British Empire. The accomplishments of the Society for the Abolition of the Slave Trade were viewed with admiration by America's fledgling abolitionist movement, which emulated many of the society's methods in its campaigns.

JEFF HALL

See also

Abolitionism and the Civil War; Slavery; Slaves

Further Reading

Hochschild, Adam. *Bury the Chains.* Boston: Houghton Mifflin, 2005.

Thomas, Hugh. *The Slave Trade.* New York: Simon and Schuster, 1997.

Society of the Army of the Potomac

Organization created in 1869 for Union veterans of the Army of the Potomac. Veterans of the X and XVIII Corps, Army of the James, were also invited to join the society. Perhaps the most famous of all Civil War armies, the Army of the Potomac was formed in August 1861 and existed for the duration of the conflict. Its chief opponent had been the Confederate Army of Northern Virginia. Between 1865 and 1870 or so, a number of former Union armies formed their own veterans' societies. The Society of the Army of the Potomac was officially founded on July 5, 1869, in New York City.

From the start, the organizers were determined to open membership to all who had served in the Army of the Potomac as well as X and XVIII Corps of the Army of the James, officers and enlisted men alike. The society was designed to promote camaraderie among veterans, help wounded veterans and their families, and perpetuate the memories of the many battles and campaigns waged between 1861 and 1865. The organization was hierarchical in structure, with an elected president and various vice presidents representing different army subcomponents, such as cavalry and artillery. A number of notable Army of the Potomac commanders served as president, including Joseph Hooker, Ambrose P. Burnside, and Philip Sheridan. Membership peaked during the late 1870s–mid-1880s but fell off as veterans died or became too infirm to remain active in the organization. By the early decades of the 20th century, the society had gradually dissolved.

PAUL G. PIERPAOLI JR.

See also

James, Union Army of the; Potomac, Union Army of the; Veterans' Organizations

Further Reading

Davies, Wallace E. *Patriotism on Parade: The Story of Veterans' and Hereditary Organizations in America, 1783–1900.* Cambridge, MA: Harvard University Press, 1955.

Marten, James. *Sing Not War: The Lives of Union and Confederate Veterans in Gilded Age America.* Chapel Hill: University of North Carolina Press, 2011.

Soldiers' Votes

Between 1861 and 1865, soldiers could cast votes in elections while in the field, a first in American history. A majority of Union states allowed their men in the field to vote, and a number of others encouraged soldiers to do so while on leave during elections. Most notably, Union soldiers participated in large numbers during the 1864 presidential election.

In the Confederacy, the states of Alabama, Georgia, Florida, North Carolina, Tennessee, and Virginia allowed their soldiers to vote but only by proxy. Although Confederate president Jefferson Davis did not face reelection during the Civil War, Southern soldiers had their own opportunities to vote, participating in elections for state offices and the Confederate Congress.

Soldiers' votes took three basic forms. Some soldiers were allowed to vote by proxy, sending their vote home to a trusted friend, who would cast the vote at an official balloting location. Other soldiers were given leave for the elections, returning home and casting their ballot in person. In some instances, official state election commissioners went to the camps, set up ballot boxes, and conducted the election in the field. These in-camp elections were usually aided by officers, who had a great influence on the process. This influence led to claims of fraud from both political parties, although these claims were fairly standard political tactics of the period and were not usually a specific concern about the military's process. Criticism of soldier voting tended to come from Democrats, partly because of the strong support given by soldiers to President Abraham Lincoln. In states such as Illinois and Indiana, Democratic-controlled legislatures refused to allow soldier voting.

In the 1864 U.S. presidential election, soldiers from 11 Union states voted, contributing more than 150,000 votes, although votes from Kansas and Minnesota troops arrived too late to be counted. Soldiers heavily supported Lincoln's reelection, voting nearly 80 percent for the president, a much higher rate than the national popular vote. This occurred in spite of the Democrats running popular former major general George B. McClellan on their ticket. It is unclear if the soldiers' vote swung any states to Lincoln's favor, but their heavy support of the president certainly solidified his strong showing nationally, demonstrating the Union's resolve to end the war through military victory.

KEITH ALTAVILLA

See also

Davis, Jefferson Finis; Democratic Party; Election of 1862, U.S.; Election of 1863, CSA; Election of 1864, U.S.; Lincoln, Abraham; McClellan, George Brinton; Republican Party

Further Reading

Frank, Joseph Allan. *With Ballot and Bayonet: The Political Socialization of American Civil War Soldiers.* Athens: University of Georgia Press, 1998.

Hyman, Harold M. "Election of 1864." In *History of American Presidential Elections, 1789–1968,* edited by Arthur M. Schlesinger Jr., 1155–1178. New York: Chelsea House Publishers, 1971.

Sons of Confederate Veterans

Confederate veterans' and Southern heritage organization. The Sons of Confederate Veterans (SCV) was formed in 1896 in Richmond, Virginia, by veterans of Confederate military service and their sons. The SCV was organized by the United Confederate Veterans (UCV) and was charged with assisting elderly members of the UCV as well as honoring the memory of the Confederacy. The SCV is the oldest hereditary organization for male descendants of Confederate military service. Membership is open to all male descendants of any veteran who served honorably in the Confederate armed forces, and the group maintains a genealogical staff to help applicants verify their ancestors' Confederate service. There are local organizations called "Camps" as well as state organizations called "Divisions," and these divisions are organized into three armies: Army of Northern Virginia, Army of Tennessee, and Army of Trans-Mississippi. The national organization, headquartered in Hattiesburg, Mississippi, since the 1950s, was moved to Columbia, Tennessee, in 1992. There were an estimated 32,000 members in the United States and abroad in 2012.

Accusations of racism have dogged the SCV throughout its history. During the 1950s and 1960s, the SCV was associated with racist organizations in opposing the Civil Rights Movement. In the 1980s the SCV modified its position and then in 1989 condemned the use of the Confederate battle flag by racist organizations. The SCV also discouraged its members from having memberships in racist organizations, and its constitution barred SCV members from political activity at SCV events. However, some members still have ties to racist organizations.

In 1994 a splinter group, the League of the South, was created to promote southern secession and became increasingly militant over the years, and some SCV members pushed for their organization to promote secession. The SCV subsequently banned all mention of secession among its ranks, and a battle soon occurred within the SCV over its direction and purpose. Conservative elements gained control in 1996 and began relaxing the ban on political activity.

Since 2000, the SCV has been accused of being more politically active and has been associated with neo-Confederate groups. The SCV constitution defines the organization as nonpolitical, nonracial, and nonsectarian, however.

The organization's official publication, the *Confederate Veteran,* is a bimonthly magazine that contains articles on the various camps of the SCV. The organization also maintains historical markers, performs Civil War reenactments, conducts research into historical controversies about the Confederacy, and promotes celebrations of the Confederacy.

At the same time, the SCV also generates controversy with its unabashed celebration of the Confederacy. Leaders of the group promote a warlike mentality not only with the militaristic structure and nomenclature of the SCV but also by portraying their cause as under attack by enemies who want to "rewrite" the history of the Civil War and portray the Confederacy in a negative light.

JIM PIECUCH AND CASEY MUSSELMAN

See also

United Confederate Veterans

Further Reading

Blight, David W. *Race and Reunion: The Civil War in American Memory.* Cambridge, MA: Harvard University Press, 2001.
Foster, Gaines M. *Ghosts of the Confederacy: Defeat, the Lost Cause, and the Emergence of the New South, 1865 to 1913.* New York: Oxford University Press, 1987.

Sons of Liberty

Secret Copperhead (Peace Democrat) society that was the successor organization of the Knights of the Golden Circle. The society attacked President Abraham Lincoln's conduct of the war and sought reunion through peaceful means. In February 1864, the newly named and revamped organization elected Peace Democrat Clement L. Vallandigham, a former Ohio congressman, as its supreme commander. Attending various Democratic conventions throughout the North, Vallandigham attempted to rekindle peace negotiations between the Union and the Confederacy by denouncing the Civil War as an unnecessary conflict. Republicans dismissed his actions and argued that the Sons of Liberty represented a Confederate conspiracy.

In the summer of 1864, Union operatives uncovered a plot in which members of the Sons of Liberty residing in the Midwest were planning an insurrection, known as the Northwest Conspiracy, designed to detach their states from the Union. Once free, the states would negotiate a separate peace with the Confederacy.

To carry out this insurrection, the Sons of Liberty collaborated with Canadian-based Confederate agents led by Thomas H. Hines, who engaged in sabotage operations against the North. They attempted to capture USS *Michigan,* the sole U.S. Navy warship on the Great Lakes, and to liberate Confederate prisoners housed at Camp Douglas in Chicago and Johnson's Island near Sandusky, Ohio. However, U.S. War Department operatives were able to infiltrate the organization's membership. The operatives arrested some of the conspirators, warned officers of the *Michigan* about the scheme, and increased the number of soldier guards stationed at the prisoner-of-war camps.

Although the initial activities of the Sons of Liberty ended in failure, federal officials warned Northern governors to remain on the lookout for other potential plots. Believing that the Sons of Liberty was a powerful organization bent on committing treasonable actions, Union authorities sent out additional agents to uncover any possible plots linked with the group.

In July 1864, members of the society planned uprisings in Chicago and New York. Prior to the scheduled rebellions, Confederate soldiers arrived in the cities to assist the Sons of Liberty. Both insurrections proved unsuccessful because federal authorities and military leaders arrested hundreds and captured a cache of arms. By the end of 1864, the Sons of Liberty's activities in the Midwest had collapsed because some members believed that they could advance their agenda through political means, chiefly by preventing Lincoln from winning reelection in the November elections. When that proved illusory, the Sons of Liberty essentially dissolved.

KEVIN M. BRADY

See also

Copperheads; Knights of the Golden Circle; Northwest Conspiracy; Vallandigham, Clement Laird

Further Reading

Klement, Frank L. *The Limits of Dissent: Clement L. Vallandigham and the Civil War.* Lexington: University Press of Kentucky, 1970.
Weber, Jennifer L. *Copperheads: The Rise and Fall of Lincoln's Opponents in the North.* New York: Oxford University Press, 2006.

Sooy Smith Expedition
Start Date: February 11, 1864
End Date: February 26, 1864

Union cavalry expedition into Mississippi led by Brigadier General William Sooy Smith that was intended to support the Meridian Campaign (February 3–26, 1864). In February 1864 Union major general William T. Sherman set out from Vicksburg, Mississippi, with the goal of capturing the important rail juncture and Confederate supply depot of Meridian. From there Sherman hoped to launch an invasion of northern Alabama. To support his operation, Sherman ordered a cavalry force commanded by Smith to push southward from Memphis, Tennessee, and link up with his force at Meridian.

Contrary to Sherman's orders, Smith decided to await reinforcements, thus delaying his expedition by 10 days. Once they left the Memphis area on February 11, Smith's 7,000 troopers with 20 artillery pieces burned crops and destroyed portions of the Memphis & Ohio Railroad. Slaves from the region, sensing an opportunity to gain their freedom, flocked to Smith's force. The Confederate cavalry commander in the region, Major General Nathan Bedford Forrest, was headquartered in Starkville, Mississippi, north of Meridian. Forrest's command was widely dispersed, and he was able to muster only about 2,500 troopers to face Smith.

After skirmishing with portions of Forrest's command, Smith decided to concentrate his forces at Prairie Station, roughly 90 miles north of Meridian. From there Smith moved to West Point, Mississippi, where he engaged part of Forrest's command under the immediate command of Colonel Jeffrey Forrest, the general's younger brother. Hoping to lure Smith deeper into the Mississippi marshland, Colonel Forrest ordered a gradual retreat. After an initial pursuit, Smith realized that he was being trapped and ordered a withdrawal. Major General Forrest then launched a pursuit of the retreating Federals. Forrest pursued and harassed Smith's force for most of the day on February 21.

On the morning of February 22, Forrest launched a major attack against Smith's command south of Okolona, Mississippi. Attacks and counterattacks continued throughout the day as Smith's column continued its withdrawal. In the meantime, Jeffrey Forrest was killed leading a failed assault. Despite this setback, Major General Forrest rallied his men and personally led a charge that succeeded in breaking the Union lines. Smith made a few more unsuccessful stands before retreating back toward Memphis. Smith reported 700 casualties, although that figure may be low, while Forrest counted 144 losses.

The Sooy Smith Expedition was a Union defeat that angered Sherman, humiliated its commander, and eventually forced Smith to resign. Forrest had successfully prevented Smith's cavalry force from linking up with Sherman's command, thus depriving that Union general of an important resource during his Meridian Campaign.

Robert L. Glaze

See also

Forrest, Nathan Bedford; Meridian Campaign; Sherman, William Tecumseh; Smith, William Sooy

Further Reading

Ballard, Michael B. *The Civil War in Mississippi: Major Campaigns and Battles.* Jackson: University Press of Mississippi, 2011.

Foster, Buck T. *Sherman's Mississippi Campaign.* Tuscaloosa: University of Alabama Press, 2006.

Wills, Brian Steel. *The Confederacy's Greatest Cavalryman: Nathan Bedford Forrest.* Lawrence: University Press of Kansas, 1992.

Sorrel, Gilbert Moxley
Birth Date: February 23, 1838
Death Date: August 10, 1901

Confederate officer. Gilbert Moxley Sorrel was born on February 23, 1838, in Savannah, Georgia. He attended Chatham Academy and was employed by the Central Railroad Bank as a clerk when the Civil War began in 1861. He received some military training in a militia unit known as the Georgia Hussars and performed two short tours of duty at Fort Pulaski and Skidaway Island, but the delay in acceptance of his unit into Confederate service led him to go to Virginia on his own. He arrived just in time for the First Battle of Bull Run (July 21, 1861), during which he served as a volunteer aide to Brigadier General James Longstreet. Rewarded with a captain's commission a few weeks later, Sorrel became Longstreet's adjutant. As Longstreet rose in rank, so too did Sorrel, from captain to major in May 1862 and to lieutenant colonel in June 1863. Sorrel was present at every engagement fought by Longstreet's I Corps and was twice wounded in action, but it was not until the Battle of the Wilderness (May 5–7, 1864) that he commanded troops in battle. There Sorrel led three brigades in a flank attack that rolled up the left of the Union II Corps. These actions garnered praise from Longstreet as well as a recommendation for promotion to brigadier general.

Promoted on October 27, 1864, Sorrel assumed command of a brigade of Georgians of Major General William Mahone's Division in III Corps. Sorrel was wounded in the leg near Petersburg and in the lung at the Battle of Hatcher's Run (February 5–7, 1865). He was returning to his command when he received news of the surrender. Sorrell returned to

Savannah after the war and was a successful businessman until his death on August 10, 1901, in Roanoke, Virginia.

WILLIAM W. KELLY JR.

See also

Bull Run, First Battle of; Hatcher's Run, Battle of; Petersburg Campaign; Wilderness, Battle of the

Further Reading

Sorrel, Gilbert Moxley. *Recollections of a Confederate Staff Officer.* Edited by Bell I. Wiley. Jackson, TN: McCowat, 1958.

Warner, Ezra J. *Generals in Gray: Lives of the Confederate Commanders.* Baton Rouge: Louisiana State University Press, 2006.

Soulé, Pierre
Birth Date: August 31, 1801
Death Date: March 26, 1870

Confederate operative. Pierre Soulé was born near Bordeaux, France, on August 31, 1801. After attending a Jesuit seminary in Toulouse and an academy in Bordeaux, he was sent into exile because of his pro-Republican activities. He then became a shepherd in the Pyrenees but was pardoned in 1818 and returned to school in Bordeaux. He subsequently studied law in Paris and practiced there. In 1825 he was arrested for writing politically subversive articles but managed to escape to England shortly thereafter. He then went to Haiti and finally to America, where he traveled extensively and mastered the English language.

Soulé eventually settled in New Orleans, where he practiced law and became involved in Democratic politics. He sat briefly in the Louisiana Senate before becoming a U.S. senator in January 1847, completing the unfinished term of a deceased senator. Soulé left office in March 1847. The next year he was elected to a full term in the U.S. Senate, serving from 1849 to 1854. There he ferociously defended states' rights.

In 1854 Soulé resigned his Senate seat to become U.S. minister to Spain. An ardent expansionist, he had already made clear his belief that the United States should acquire Cuba from Spain as quickly as possible. Not surprisingly, his tenure in Spain was a stormy one, as the Spanish government had no intention of selling or handing over its rich Cuban colony to the United States. In 1854 Soulé wrote the Ostend Manifesto, which specifically enumerated why and how the United States should acquire Mexico. By the end of the year, he had resigned his post when it became clear that his views were not universally accepted.

Soulé returned to New Orleans and the practice of law. Although he did not initially back secession, when Louisiana left the Union and the Civil War began in April 1861, he strongly supported the Confederate war effort. In the winter of 1862, city officials appointed Soulé a provost marshal in charge of mobilizing civilians to defend their city from an anticipated Union attack. When New Orleans fell in April 1862, Soulé pleaded with Confederate officials not to attempt a recapture of the city, lest it be ruined and its civilians suffer even more hardship. At about the same time, Union occupation officials arrested Soulé on charges of treason and imprisoned him at New York's Fort Lafayette.

Released in November 1862 because of alleged poor health, Soulé was supposed to remain in Boston; however, he promptly fled to the Bahamas and then made his way to Richmond, Virginia. There he lobbied Confederate officials for a military commission. He was eventually given an honorary brigadier general's commission and spent the last months of the war as an aide to General Pierre G. T. Beauregard in Charleston, South Carolina.

After the war Soulé spent time in Cuba, where he plotted an abortive scheme to form a Southern colony in Mexico. He later returned to New Orleans, where he died on March 26, 1870.

PAUL G. PIERPAOLI JR.

See also

New Orleans, Louisiana; New Orleans Campaign

Further Reading

Moore, J. Preston. "Pierre Soulé: Southern Expansionist and Promoter." *Journal of Southern History* 21(2) (May 1955): 203–223.

Winters, John D. *The Civil War in Louisiana.* Baton Rouge: Louisiana State University Press, 1963.

South, Union Department of the

Federal military administrative unit created on March 15, 1862, that initially encompassed South Carolina, Georgia, and Florida. The first commander was Major General David Hunter, whose headquarters was on Hilton Head Island. In May 1862, Hunter created a stir when he unilaterally invoked martial law and declared all slaves in the department free. President Abraham Lincoln promptly repealed the order out of fear of alienating the border states. On August 8, western Florida was removed from the command.

Hunter was succeeded on September 5, 1862, by Brigadier General John Brannan, who was replaced by Major General Ormsby Mitchell on September 17. Meanwhile, a portion of southern Georgia was transferred to another department. Brannan again commanded the department from October 27 until January 20, 1863, when Hunter resumed command. In March 1863, the Dry Tortugas and Key West became part of the Department of the Gulf, while a portion of northern Georgia was annexed by the Department of the Cumberland.

On June 12, 1863, Brigadier Quincy Gillmore took command of the Department of the South. Gillmore presided over significant military action in and around Charleston, South Carolina. On May 1, 1864, Gillmore was succeeded in command by Brigadier General John Hatch, who led the department until May 26, at which time Major General John Foster took command. Foster commanded until February 9, 1865; he was succeeded in command by Gillmore. After the capture of Fort Fisher on January 15, 1865, North Carolina was added to the department for a period of two weeks. Gillmore remained in charge until June 28, 1865, at which time the Department of the South was subdivided into smaller constituent departments. Meanwhile, on May 17, 1865, Florida had been removed from Gillmore's jurisdiction.

PAUL G. PIERPAOLI JR.

See also

Brannan, John Milton; Foster, John Gray; Gillmore, Quincy Adams; Hatch, John Porter; Hunter, David; Mitchel, Ormsby MacKnight

Further Reading

Eicher, John H., and David J. Eicher. *Civil War High Commands.* Stanford, CA: Stanford University Press, 2001.

South Atlantic Blockading Squadron

Union naval command. President Abraham Lincoln proclaimed a naval blockade of the Confederacy on April 19, 1861. In June, the U.S. Navy activated two squadrons for the purpose of enforcing the blockade: the Atlantic Blockading Squadron and the Gulf Blockading Squadron. The Blockade Board (Strategy Board) soon recommended that each of these squadrons be divided, and in September the Atlantic Squadron was split. The South Atlantic Blockading Squadron was activated on October 29, 1861, when Captain Samuel F. Du Pont assumed command. It covered the Eastern Seaboard from Cape Fear, North Carolina, to Cape Canaveral, Florida. In addition to expanding the blockade and making it more effective as more warships were made available to him, Du Pont undertook several offensive measures against the Confederate coastline. He directed the successful Union expedition against Port Royal, South Carolina

(November 5–7). On December 3, 1861, hulks and older ships loaded with rock were sunk to block access in channels to Savannah and Charleston. This Stone Fleet had little lasting effect, however.

The South Atlantic Blockading Squadron had more success in several amphibious operations. Union forces captured Fernandina Island, Florida, on March 4, 1862, and Fort Pulaski, between Tybee Island and Savannah, Georgia, on April 10. Despite these operations, blockade-runners managed to slip through the Union blockade, although this occurred with decreasing frequency as the war wore on. The largest haul for the Confederates came when the merchant steamer *Fingal* evaded capture and arrived in Savannah, Georgia, on November 12, 1861, with a substantial quantity of war matériel. Confederate officials then converted it into the ironclad *Atlanta.*

Du Pont, meanwhile, was preparing to move against Charleston. Toward that end, he demanded as many monitors as possible, and U.S. secretary of the navy Gideon Welles and Assistant Secretary of the Navy Gustavus V. Fox, long strong proponents of an operation against the "Font of the Confederacy," complied.

On January 31, 1863, the Confederates struck first when Captain Duncan N. Ingraham led the ironclads *Palmetto State* and *Chicora* in an attack on the wooden Union blockading warships off Charleston Harbor. The Confederates temporarily captured one Union warship and crippled another. Ingraham and Confederate commander in Charleston General P. G. T. Beauregard inaccurately proclaimed that the Union blockade had been broken under international law, but the U.S. Navy held that the sloop *Housatonic* had driven off the attackers. Du Pont then sent the powerful ironclad *New Ironsides* to Charleston. On June 17, 1863, the *Atlanta* sortied from Savannah and engaged the monitors *Nahant* and *Weehawken* but grounded and was captured.

Following repeated urging by Welles and Fox and less than satisfactory trials of the monitors against Fort McAllister, Georgia, Du Pont launched his long-anticipated attack on Fort Sumter in Charleston Harbor on April 7, 1863. He had seven Passaic-class monitors, the *New Ironsides,* and the experimental double-towered ironclad *Keokuk.* The ships in the squadron received worse than they gave. The *Keokuk* subsequently succumbed to damage sustained in the exchange of fire, and most of the other ships involved suffered varying amounts of damage. Du Pont's own oft-stated doubts about operations against Charleston without these being a joint army-navy enterprise led to his relief on June 4, 1863. Rear Admiral Andrew H. Foote was to replace him but died in New York City before he could take up his command. Secretary Welles reluctantly appointed Rear Admiral John A. Dahlgren, President Lincoln's choice, in his stead.

The Confederates made several efforts to break the blockade at Charleston. On the evening of October 5, 1863, the little torpedo boat *David* attacked and slightly damaged the *New Ironsides*. The Confederate submarine *H. L. Hunley* had more success. On February 17, 1864, it employed a spar torpedo to sink the screw sloop *Housatonic* but itself succumbed in the attack with the loss of its entire crew.

Dahlgren, meanwhile, was well aware of the risks involved and was reluctant to undertake any operation against Charleston that might endanger his reputation. He saw his primary mission as cooperation with the army and had approximately the same number of ironclads as had been available to Du Pont. Dahlgren worked with the army to seize Morris Island, but he continued to reject calls for an operation in Charleston Harbor by his ships alone.

Believing Fort Sumter to be partly evacuated, Dahlgren ordered a boat attack against it from Morris Island on the night of September 8–9, 1863. Alerted to the attack by a captured Union signal key, the Confederates were waiting and defeated the assault, inflicting heavy casualties on the attackers before covering Union warships could get in position. This failure ended Union offensive operations in Charleston Harbor.

During the advance of Union ground forces under Major General William T. Sherman from Savannah into South Carolina in 1865, the squadron assisted in operations on the Wando River (January 12, 1865). Charleston did not fall to the Union in February 1865. Dahlgren turned over the squadron to Rear Admiral William Radford on June 17, 1865, and then on July 25, 1865, the South Atlantic Blockading Squadron merged back with the North Atlantic Blockading Squadron to form the Atlantic Squadron.

Scholars, especially Robert Browning, have concluded that the fixation on Charleston was to the detriment of the overall blockading effort and Union military effort in the war. Failures in Union leadership thus prevented an earlier end to the war.

CHARLES J. WEXLER, WILLIAM WHYTE, AND SPENCER C. TUCKER

See also

Beauregard, Pierre Gustav Toutant; Blockade of the Confederacy, Union; Blockade-Runners; Charleston, South Carolina; Charleston, South Carolina, Confederate Attack on Union Blockaders; Dahlgren, John Adolph Bernard; David-Class Torpedo Boats; Du Pont, Samuel Francis; *Fingal,* CSS; Foote, Andrew Hull; Fort McAllister, Georgia, Union Naval Attacks on; Fort Sumter, South Carolina, Dahlgren's Attacks on; Fort Sumter, South Carolina, Du Pont's Attack on; Hatteras Inlet, North Carolina, Union Assault on; *H. L. Hunley,* CSS; *Housatonic,* USS; Ironclads, Confederate; Ironclads, Union; *New Ironsides,* USS; Port Royal Sound, Battle of; Stone Fleet; Submarines; Torpedoes; Welles, Gideon

Further Reading

Browning, Robert M., Jr. *Success Is All That Was Expected: The South Atlantic Blockading Squadron during the Civil War.* Washington, DC: Brassey's, 2002.

Hunter, Alvah Folsom. *A Year on a Monitor and the Destruction of Fort Sumter.* Columbia: University of South Carolina Press, 1987.

Wise, Stephen. *Gate of Hell: Campaign for Charleston Harbor, 1863.* Columbia: University of South Carolina Press, 1994.

Wise, Stephen. *Lifeline of the Confederacy: Blockade Running during the Civil War.* Columbia: University of South Carolina Press, 1988.

South Carolina

Deep South state and the first of the Southern states to secede from the Union. South Carolina was soon followed by six other Deep South states, which formed the Confederate States of America on February 4, 1861. The Civil War began at Charleston, South Carolina, when Confederate forces there under Brigadier General P. G. T. Beauregard bombarded the Union garrison at Fort Sumter in Charleston Harbor, forcing its surrender on April 13, 1861. This act led U.S. president Abraham Lincoln to call up 75,000 volunteers.

South Carolina encompasses 31,113 square miles of territory and is bordered by the Atlantic Ocean to the east, North Carolina to the north, and Georgia to the south and west. South Carolina is a varied state in terms of climate and topography. The state includes highlands and mountains (part of the Appalachian chain) in the northwest, predominantly clay and sandy flatlands in midstate, and low-lying sandy topography, punctuated by vast salt marshes and swamps, along the coastal plain. Extreme cold weather is uncommon throughout the state, although freezing temperatures and occasional snow and ice are not rare in the upper half of the state. Near and along the coast, especially from the city of Charleston south, the climate is subtropical, where freezing temperatures are not common and frozen precipitation is rare.

Slavery and states' rights had always been an important issue in South Carolina. Indeed, the state had considered secession in the early 1830s over the question of high tariffs. While South Carolinians remained in the Union, less than 30 years later they again flirted with secession. One of the reasons why South Carolina looked to secession and ultimately left the Union was the dominance of agriculture in the state's economy. That agricultural economy was heavily dependent upon slave labor. Because plantations and smaller-scale farming were the major means of subsistence in South Carolina, slavery was considered to be a critical linchpin in the state's prosperity. According to the 1860 census, South Carolina had a total population of 703,708 people, of whom 402,406, or 57.2 percent, were slaves. The state was also home to more than 9,000 free blacks. Whites constituted only 41 percent of the population. Most of the population was centered in the Low Country region near the coast, or in the two major cities of Columbia (the capital) and Charleston.

The major crops produced in South Carolina were cotton, rice, indigo, and sugarcane. On the Sea Islands south of Charleston, the warm, moist climate allowed for the cultivation on long-staple (or Sea Island) cotton, which was among the most expensive and sought after in the world. Most of the state's cotton was exported from Charleston to port cities in the North as well as to Europe. Great Britain, one of the world's leading textile manufacturers, received almost 75 percent of its cotton from the United States, and the majority of this came from South Carolina.

Political power in the state was held by a small minority of rich plantation owners who often lived in Charleston or Beaufort and only spent a small amount of time on their plantations. Because of the large African American population, the small planter class was able to use the fear of potential slave revolts to gain the support of poor and middle-class whites who did not own slaves themselves. Indeed, most of the state's whites did not own slaves. They often resented the planter class but nevertheless felt obliged to align themselves with upper-class whites.

Governor William H. Gist, a Democrat, led South Carolina out of the Union. Gist was known as a Fire-Eater, a term given to extremist proslavery and pro–states' rights politicians who favored leaving the Union rather than compromising their lifestyle. After receiving assurances from the governors of Florida and Mississippi that those two states would follow South Carolina's lead, Gist called for a convention that unanimously voted to make South Carolina an independent republic. While Gist called the convention, a new governor, Francis W. Pickens, was sworn into office before it could take place. Pickens's politics were similar to those of Gist, and it was under Pickens's administration that South Carolina entered the Confederacy.

Upon assuming office, Pickens called for the U.S. Army to abandon its forts within the state, including Fort Sumter in Charleston Harbor. When the commander of that fort refused, Pickens, in conjunction with Confederate president Jefferson Davis, authorized the bombardment of Fort Sumter, setting off the Civil War.

Early in the war in November 1861, Union forces took two Confederate forts in Port Royal Sound, providing an important base for subsequent Union coastal operations. Although major fighting did not come to South Carolina until 1865 during Major General William T. Sherman's Carolinas Campaign (January–April 1865), Union soldiers did occupy the Sea Islands in and around Port Royal Sound in late 1861. From these bases they harassed ships delivering supplies to South Carolina, Georgia, and Florida. The U.S. Navy instituted a blockade off Charleston and mounted a major naval assault under Rear Admiral Samuel Du Pont against Fort Sumter on April 7, 1863, which resulted in failure. Union troops tried unsuccessfully to take Battery Wagner protecting the harbor in July 1863. In mid-February 1865, Sherman's army reached Columbia, having encountered no significant opposition. The city's mayor surrendered the capital, but on February 17 a huge conflagration consumed much of the city. The cause of the fire is still unknown; some argue that retreating Confederates accidentally started it by setting goods on fire to keep them out of Union hands. Others claim that Union forces set the fire to punish the state for its role in sparking the Civil War. In any case, Charleston fell on February 21, and Union troops immediately raised the American flag over Fort Sumter for the first time since 1861.

During the war, South Carolina raised 33 infantry regiments for the Confederacy. The state also provided 7 cavalry regiments as well as 1 regiment and battalion of heavy artillery and 29 battalions of light artillery. Notable South Carolinians to serve the Confederacy included Richard Anderson, Matthew C. Butler, Nathan G. Evans, Wade Hampton, Joseph Kershaw, and Stephen D. Lee. A number of African Americans from the state fought for the North. The Union Army raised four colored regiments from South Carolina. In 1861, South Carolina had a white military-age population (ages 18–45) of 55,046, and during the war it lost more white men between the ages of 18–45 than any other Confederate state, 23 percent of its prewar white population. More than 130,000 South Carolinians served in the war. Known South Carolina dead in the war total 18,666, but the actual number who died may be as high as 23,000.

SETH A. WEITZ

See also

Charleston, South Carolina; Cotton; Fire-Eaters; Fort Sumter, South Carolina, Confederate Bombardment of; Fort Sumter, South Carolina, Du Pont's Attack on; Gist, States Rights; Pickens, Francis Wilkinson; Sherman, William Tecumseh; Sherman's March through the Carolinas

Further Reading

Edgar, Walter B. *South Carolina: A History.* Columbia: University of South Carolina Press, 1998.

Ford, Lacy K. *Origins of Southern Radicalism: The South Carolina Upcountry, 1800–1860.* New York: Oxford University Press, 1991.

Rogers, George C., Jr., and James C. Taylor. *A South Carolina Chronology, 1497–1992.* Columbia: University of South Carolina Press, 1994.

Wallace, David Duncan. *South Carolina: A Short History, 1520–1948.* Columbia: University of South Carolina Press, 1961.

South Carolina, Confederate Department of

Short-lived Confederate military administrative unit created on August 21, 1861, that encompassed all South Carolina. Commanded by Brigadier General Roswell S. Ripley and headquartered in Charleston, the Confederate Department of South Carolina included some 5,300 troops (state militia and regulars), although it was designed to operate with a contingent of 8,300 troops. During its short life span, however, the department was never able to muster that number of men.

The Confederate Department of South Carolina also contained several important defensive works, including Charleston's Sullivan Island and fortifications along the northern and southern branches of the Edisto River as well as those on the Stono River. Other important coastal defenses included those at Georgetown and along Port Royal Sound (including Fort Walker). On November 5, 1861, the department ceased to exist when it became part of the Department of South Carolina and Georgia. Two days later on November 7, 1861, Union forces assaulted and seized the area of Port Royal Sound, including Hilton Head Island and Beaufort.

PAUL G. PIERPAOLI JR.

See also

Port Royal Sound, Battle of; Ripley, Roswell Sabine; South Carolina

Further Reading

Eicher, John H., and David J. Eicher. *Civil War High Commands.* Stanford, CA: Stanford University Press, 2001.

South Carolina, Georgia, and Florida, Confederate Department of

Confederate military administrative unit established on October 7, 1862, when the Department of South Carolina and Georgia was merged with the Department of Middle and Eastern Florida. Initially, the new Confederate Department of South Carolina, Georgia, and Florida encompassed mostly the coastal regions of the three states, although it was later expanded to include territory farther west. General P. G. T. Beauregard was the first commander. When the unit was created, Beauregard was supposed to have at his disposal some 35,000 troops. Instead, he had only 15,000 troops, a number that he believed was woefully inadequate to protect Charleston (his headquarters) as well as Savannah and the long coastline of Florida. By January 1864, after receiving numerous reinforcements, his troop strength reached its zenith of 38,227.

On April 20, 1864, Beauregard was succeeded in command by Major General Samuel Jones; he commanded until October 5, 1864, when he was replaced by Lieutenant General William J. Hardee. In anticipation of the Union offensive against Savannah, Hardee moved his headquarters to Georgia. But by mid-November, Hardee had only 14,680 troops and 100 cannon to stop the Union juggernaut.

At the end of December 1864, Beauregard was placed in charge of the department west of Augusta, Georgia; Hardee retained command over the remainder of the department, mainly the coasts of Florida, Georgia, and South Carolina. On February 25, 1865, the department was organized out of existence when General Joseph E. Johnston took command of an enlarged and combined area.

PAUL G. PIERPAOLI JR.

See also

Beauregard, Pierre Gustav Toutant; Hardee, William Joseph; Johnston, Joseph Eggleston; Jones, Samuel; South Carolina and Georgia, Confederate Department of

Further Reading

Eicher, John H., and David J. Eicher. *Civil War High Commands.* Stanford, CA: Stanford University Press, 2001.

South Carolina, Union Department of

Postbellum federal administrative unit created on June 27, 1865. One of 18 such departments created at that same time, the Union Department of South Carolina encompassed the entire state of South Carolina and was intended chiefly to supervise immediate postwar occupation and early Reconstruction efforts. The department was headquartered on Hilton Head Island, just north of the Georgia–South Carolina border, and was commanded by Major General Quincy A. Gillmore, who took charge on July 18. The Department of South Carolina was part of the much larger Military Division of the Atlantic, which covered the Eastern Seaboard from Maine to South Carolina.

On November 18, 1865, Gillmore was succeeded in command by Major General Daniel E. Sickles, who relocated the department's headquarters to Charleston. On May 19, 1866, the Department of South Carolina ceased to exist as a separate entity when it was absorbed by the Department of the Carolinas. Sickles took command of the new department, with headquarters remaining in Charleston.

PAUL G. PIERPAOLI JR.

See also

Gillmore, Quincy Adams; Sickles, Daniel Edgar; South Carolina

Further Reading

Warner, Ezra J. *Generals in Blue: Lives of the Union Commanders.* Baton Rouge: Louisiana State University Press, 2006.

South Carolina and Georgia, Confederate Department of

Confederate military administrative unit established on November 5, 1861, amid the Union assault on Port Royal Sound and Hilton Head Island, South Carolina, that resulted in their capture on November 7. The Confederate Department of South Carolina and Georgia encompassed the coastal areas of South Carolina and Georgia as well as Florida's eastern coast. General Robert E. Lee was placed in command so that he could concentrate Confederate forces along the Southeast coast. With the fall of the area around Port Royal Sound and Hilton Head Island, Confederate leaders were fearful that Charleston and Savannah might meet a similar fate. The department consisted of six military districts and was headquartered in Charleston.

On March 6, 1862, Lee was succeeded in command by Major General John C. Pemberton. Most of Pemberton's forces had been massed at Charleston and Savannah. Pemberton also bolstered the seaward and landward defenses of those cities.

Pemberton was succeeded in command on August 29, 1862, by General P. G. T. Beauregard. On October 7, 1862, the department was reorganized as the Department of South Carolina, Georgia, and Florida, which included the Department of Middle and East Florida. Beauregard commanded the new department.

PAUL G. PIERPAOLI JR.

See also

Beauregard, Pierre Gustav Toutant; Lee, Robert Edward; Pemberton, John Clifford; Port Royal Sound, Battle of; South Carolina, Georgia, and Florida, Confederate Department of

Further Reading

Eicher, John H., and David J. Eicher. *Civil War High Commands.* Stanford, CA: Stanford University Press, 2001.

Southern Bivouac

Civil War veterans' magazine. In February 1879, a group of former Confederate officers created the Kentucky Chapter of the Southern Historical Society. The Southern Historical Society's chief purpose was to chronicle Southern viewpoints on historical events, primarily the Civil War. The Kentucky Chapter met monthly, sponsoring speeches from prominent members and compatriots. There was soon such an outpouring of material that it became impossible to present all of it in a meeting forum. In 1882, it was decided that the material should be published, in magazine form, so that the information could more easily be distributed to the masses.

Southern Bivouac was first published in Louisville in September 1882. The magazine published articles and poems from Civil War veterans, devoting most of its attention to people and events in the western theater of the war. Among its best features was the fact that it did not advance the sectional hatred prevalent in many other periodicals and tried to present a more conciliatory tone. In fact, many of its articles were written by Union Army veterans. Nevertheless, the magazine still did its best to praise Southern valor and uphold the correctness of the Confederate cause.

By January 1885, however, *Southern Bivouac* was in financial distress. The publisher B. F. Avery and Sons purchased the magazine in May 1885, giving operational control to Basil Duke and Richard W. Knott, editor of *Home and Farm.* Under Avery's management, *Southern Bivouac* branched out to include Southern literature in addition to Civil War history. Subscriptions increased to around 7,500 but were still far short of the number needed to make the magazine a financial success. Although subscriptions reached 15,000 in 1887, the May issue that year was the last to appear. The magazine was sold to the Century Company, and many of the articles were used in compiling the four-volume history of the war titled *Battles and Leaders of the Civil War.*

ROBERT P. BROADWATER

Woodworth, Steven, and Robin Higham, eds. *The American Civil War: A Handbook of Literature and Research.* Westport, CT: Greenwood, 1996.

Southern Illustrated News

Confederate weekly newspaper. To fill the void left by the unavailability of *Harper's Weekly* and *Frank Leslie's Illustrated Weekly* in the Confederacy during the Civil War, in September 1862 a small group of journalists and illustrators in Richmond, Virginia, established the *Southern Illustrated News.* Published weekly from September 13, 1862, to March 25, 1865, by E. W. Ayers and W. H. Wade in the office of Ayers's father's tobacco agency in Richmond, the newspaper had more than 20,000 subscribers at its peak. The *Southern Illustrated News* provided its readers with current news, literary novelties, historical legends, biographical sketches, and a few advertisements.

For more than two years, the *Southern Illustrated News* usually overcame paper and ink shortages, transportation and communication difficulties, and the lack of skilled engravers to produce an eight-page paper, modeled on *Harper's Weekly.* By 1864, however, it had become increasingly difficult to publish the newspaper. The lack of skilled engravers meant that the cover illustrations and political cartoons were crudely done. The lack of ink meant that some of the later editions were most likely printed with shoe polish. In addition, the inability to procure quality paper limited the number of copies printed. Because of these and other problems, several issues were skipped, and no copies of the newspaper from 1865 currently exist. Perhaps most problematic was the prevalence of typographical mistakes, factual errors, and erroneous news coverage. For example, the Battle of Gettysburg (July 1–3, 1863) was initially reported as a Confederate victory. Regardless, the reporting of war news by the *Southern Illustrated News* makes the newspaper a valuable source for scholars studying the Confederate press during the Civil War.

MICHAEL R. HALL

See also
Gettysburg, Battle of; *Harper's Weekly;* Newspaper, Soldiers'

Further Reading
Mott, Frank Luther. *A History of American Magazines,* Vol. 2, *1850–1865.* Cambridge, MA: Belknap, 1938.
Van Tuyll, Debra R. *The Southern Press in the Civil War: American Wars and the Media in Primary Documents.* Westport, CT: Greenwood, 2005.

See also
Battles and Leaders of the Civil War; Veterans' Organizations

Further Reading
Bercovitch, Sacvan, and Cyrus R. Patell. *The Cambridge History of English and American Literature.* Cambridge: Cambridge University Press, 1995.
Matthews, Gary. *Basil Wilson Duke, CSA.* Lexington: University Press of Kentucky, 2005.

Southern Historical Society Papers

Historical periodical. Considered by many historians to be an indispensable primary resource for the study of the Confederate States of America, the *Southern Historical Society Papers* (*SHSP*) was the official publication of the Southern Historical Society, headquartered in Richmond, Virginia. The society was founded in 1870 to preserve the memory of the Confederacy for future historians. The *SHSP* began publication in 1876 as a monthly magazine. Denied access to captured Confederate records held in Washington, D.C., and alarmed over U.S. government plans to publish the *Official Records,* the Southern Historical Society called for loans of original manuscripts to publish in its new magazine. The response was overwhelming, resulting in the publication of myriad battle reports, maps, troop rosters, official government correspondence, wartime speeches, memoirs, diaries, and other related documents. The costs of publishing the material were covered by annual membership dues to the Southern Historical Society and individual and corporate donations.

The *SHSP* was issued monthly until 1890, when it became an annual publication. By the 1920s, however, as its editors and contributors grew older, retired, or died, the *SHSP* was published irregularly. The last published volume (52) was finally released in 1959. Highlights of the *SHSP* include a thorough discussion of the reasons for the Confederate defeat at the Battle of Gettysburg (July 1–3, 1863) in the issues of the 1870s and 1880s; a roster of the men who surrendered at Appomattox on April 9, 1865 (Volume 15, 1887); and the complete journals of the Confederate Congress (Volumes 44–52, 1923–1959).

RICHARD A. SAUERS

See also
Gettysburg, Battle of

Further Reading
Robertson, James I., comp. *Southern Historical Society Papers,* Vols. 1–52, *1876–1959.* Millwood, NY: Kraus International, 1980.

Southern Literary Messenger

Civil War–era magazine published in Richmond, Virginia. First appearing in August 1834, The *Southern Literary Messenger* was considered a principal cultural voice of the South before and during the Civil War, until it ceased publication in 1864. However, its editorial tenor was often inconsistent, changing focus and tone with its numerous owners and editors.

The writer Edgar Allen Poe was an early contributor, receiving many accolades for his contributions, the first being "Bernice," a short story published in April 1835. Poe also assisted in editing the magazine while still serving as a contributor, and in December 1835 he became its third editor, remaining in the post until January 1837. He continued to contribute stories until his death in 1849.

In its early years the magazine was politically neutral, striving for a literary focus. From 1843 to 1847, the emphasis was on Southern history. From 1848 to 1860, the magazine's emphasis was restored to literary subjects, but as debates over slavery and sectionalism intensified and subscriptions decreased, threatening bankruptcy, a proslavery but otherwise Unionist position was adopted in hopes of increasing Southern readership.

After May 1860, a new editor, George W. Bagby, who favored secession, made the magazine a political voice, declaring its support for the Southern Confederacy in December 1860. His outspoken political positions and antagonistic attitudes cost the magazine most of its Northern readers and many readers in the South as well, forcing several price increases. Sold in late 1863, the *Southern Literary Messenger* ceased publication in June 1864.

TIMOTHY J. DEMY

See also

Literature

Further Reading

Minor, Benjamin B. *The Southern Literary Messenger, 1834–1864.* Columbia: University of South Carolina Press, 2007.

Mott, Frank L. A. *A History of American Magazines.* New York: D. Appleton, 1930.

Southern Manifesto

Proclamation of Southern solidarity signed by 6 U.S. senators and 23 U.S. representatives in Congress on December 14, 1860, at the beginning of the secession crisis. The Southern Manifesto was a Southern response to the election of Abraham Lincoln to the presidency the month prior. It was drafted by Senators James L. Pugh (Alabama) and Louis T. Wigfall (Texas).

The manifesto essentially put the nation on warning that an independent Southern confederacy would soon be forming because Northern leaders had failed to grant the Southern states adequate guarantees that their rights would be respected and protected. This included the right to own slaves. Once the manifesto was made public, a large number of Southern moderates came to the conclusion that further efforts to seek compromise with the North would not prevent secession. Six days later South Carolina became the first state to vote for secession, beginning the secession movement that would encompass most Southern states by the spring of 1861.

PAUL G. PIERPAOLI JR.

See also

Congress, U.S.; Lincoln, Abraham; South Carolina; Wigfall, Louis Trezevant

Further Reading

Ambrosious, Lloyd E. *A Crisis of Republicanism: American Politics during the Civil War Era.* Lincoln: University of Nebraska Press, 1990.

McPherson, James M. *Battle Cry of Freedom: The Civil War Era.* New York: Oxford University Press, 2003.

Southern Nationalism

Phenomenon that emerged in the American South early in the 19th century that embodied a strong sense among Southerners of cultural and socioeconomic distinctiveness. This mind-set often included the idea that the South was culturally and socially superior to the rest of the nation, particularly the more industrialized northeastern states. Southern nationalists began to view themselves as the true heirs of the values of the American Revolution, which they believed stood for individualism, states' rights, and limited government. This feeling of distinctiveness fueled the growing secessionist movement as the sectional schism over slavery deepened during the mid-19th century and ultimately led to the 1861 creation of the Confederate States of America, a nation based on the dominance of a white male upper-class dependency on slavery.

The sources of this sense of Southern distinctiveness were rooted in the differences in economic development between North and South and the presence of black slavery. With territorial expansion westward and the steady growth of manufacturing in the North, Southerners increasingly found themselves in the minority on issues such as tariffs and slavery. Many Southerners fell back on states' rights as a protective device to support the status quo. As sectional differences over slavery intensified, states' rights advocates, led by prominent Southern planters and professionals such as Edmund Ruffin and William Lowndes Yancey, became more strident in their nationalistic beliefs and increasingly embraced Southern nationhood and independence from the United States.

Southern nationalism rested on a belief in the South's economic and social superiority. In this ideal society, upper-class men governed benevolently. Southern nationalists viewed the industrial expansion and the growth of free labor in the North as a threat to a way of life that they held sacred. Moreover, Southerners held to an antiquated notion of honor that permitted the use of violence in case of affronts to one's personal honor or that of his family, state, or class.

At the same time, Southern nationalists viewed so-called Yankees as people out to gain power and wealth at the expense of the South. On the eve of secession, concerns over the future of slavery and the preservation of the Southern culture strengthened Southern nationalists' drive to leave the Union.

Although a minority in terms of numbers, secessionists eventually took 11 slave states out of the Union due chiefly to their determination, cohesiveness, and political and economic dominance. However, broad segments of Southern society never embraced the Southern nation. Small farmers, shopkeepers, and the like who owned no slaves simply had little in common with the planter class. The strains brought on by the Civil War generated widespread dissent and resistance, particularly among lower-class women, nonslaveholding farmers and industrial workers, and the slaves themselves. The eventual collapse of the Confederacy owed much to the failure of Southern nationalism to take root among these groups.

WALTER F. BELL

See also

Ruffin, Edmund; Secession; Slavery; Yancey, William Lowndes

Further Reading

Franklin, John Hope. *The Militant South, 1800–1861*. Cambridge, MA: Harvard University Press, 1956.

Thomas, Emory M. *The Confederate Nation, 1861–1865*. New York: Harper and Row, 1979.

Southern Unionists

Southerners who opposed secession and remained loyal to the United States. A significant portion of the Southern white population remained reluctant to answer the secessionists' clarion call after the 1860 presidential election. Far from being a secessionist monolith, Southern society in fact contained a number of considerable political, social, and economic fissures that were widened by the Civil War.

Nonslaveholding whites formed the core of Southern Unionism. They were typically small farmers and shopkeepers and those living in areas outside of the Cotton Belt, in areas such as the Appalachian regions of western Virginia and North Carolina, eastern Tennessee, and northern Alabama. Pockets of Unionism could also be found in the Pine Barrens of Georgia and the Ozark Plateau region of northwestern Arkansas.

Although their reasons for remaining loyal to the Union spanned a broad spectrum of beliefs and ideologies, Southern Unionists frequently represented citizens' vehement opposition to the Confederate government rather than enthusiastic support for the federal government. These dissenters, often derogatorily referred to as "tories" or "homemade Yankees," endured the wrath of their secessionist neighbors that devolved into widespread violence within Southern communities and lingered long after the war's end. Additionally, of course, the South's slaves eagerly supported the federal government as a means to attain freedom.

President Abraham Lincoln believed that secessionists had stifled Southern loyalists during the secession crisis, and the Unionist victories in the upper South beginning with Tennessee in February 1861 seemingly confirmed this opinion. Despite the outbreak of hostilities, Lincoln remained convinced that Southern Unionism would quickly reassert itself in the presence of Union troops and serve as a base to reestablish federal authority in occupied areas. Guerrilla attacks and the evolution of a hard-war policy in the occupied South, however, muted any Southern Unionist resurgence. Yet, Southern anti-Confederate sentiment exploded in 1862 with Richmond's new conscription and confiscation policies, resulting in widespread desertions from the army, civilian riots, and the election of many antisecession legislators to the Second Confederate Congress.

Lincoln's largely conciliatory policies concerning the South's restoration, including Tennessee's exclusion from the 1863 Emancipation Proclamation and his selection of Tennessee's Democrat and Unionist senator Andrew Johnson as his vice presidential running mate in 1864, were all calculated measures to encourage Southern Unionism and exploit the Confederacy's internal divisions.

During the war, approximately 100,000 white Southerners joined federal military units or raised Unionist regiments within their states. More than 200,000 black freedmen also flocked to Union lines and bolstered Union ranks. Their absence from the Confederate workforce further undermined the Southern war effort. Most white

Southern Unionist troops performed antiguerrilla sweeps in their communities, while black Southerners were largely relegated to garrison or rear-area operations.

DEREK W. FRISBY

See also
African Americans; Election of 1864, U.S.; Emancipation Proclamation; Lincoln, Abraham; Johnson, Andrew; Secession

Further Reading
Current, Richard N. *Lincoln's Loyalists: Union Soldiers from the Confederacy*. New York: Oxford University Press, 1992.
Freehling, William. *The South vs. The South: How Anti-Confederate Southerners Shaped the Course of the Civil War.* New York: Oxford University Press, 2002.

Southern Virginia, Confederate Department of

Confederate military administration unit formally established on April 1, 1863. On that date, three departments were created from the existing Confederate Department of North Carolina and Southern Virginia: the Department of Southern Virginia, the Department of Richmond, and the Department of North Carolina. The area was split into three parts to enable Confederate officials to better manage military affairs.

The Department of Southern Virginia encompassed an area south of the James River to the Virginia–North Carolina state line and east of Powhatan County. The first—and only—commander was Major General Samuel G. French. On May 28, 1863, the department became a part of the new Department of North Carolina and Southern Virginia, which now also incorporated Petersburg, Virginia. Major General Daniel H. Hill took command.

PAUL G. PIERPAOLI JR.

See also
French, Samuel Gibbs; Hill, Daniel Harvey

Further Reading
Eicher, John H., and David J. Eicher. *Civil War High Commands.* Stanford, CA: Stanford University Press, 2001.

South Mountain, Battle of
Event Date: September 14, 1862

Engagement during the Antietam Campaign (September 4–20, 1862). The Battle of South Mountain (September 14, 1862), known in some early Confederate accounts as the

Battle of Boonsboro Gap, was considered a rearguard action on the part of Confederate general Robert E. Lee to delay Union forces at the passes in the Blue Ridge Mountains of western Maryland while he secured his supply lines through the Shenandoah Valley and consolidated his Army of Northern Virginia to fight Major General George B. McClellan's Army of the Potomac at a place of Lee's choosing.

On September 9 Lee divided his army, sending Major General Thomas J. "Stonewall" Jackson's command to capture Harpers Ferry, Virginia, while divisions under Major Generals James Longstreet and Daniel Harvey Hill proceeded to Hagerstown, Maryland. Securing a copy of Lee's entire plan of operations, McClellan belatedly sent one corps to intercept the Harpers Ferry operation in the vicinity of Crampton's Gap, while the rest of his army marched on the National Road toward Turner's Gap.

On the evening of September 13, Confederate cavalry reported the Union advance. Hill ordered one brigade under Brigadier General Alfred Colquitt to block the pass and positioned Brigadier General Samuel Garland's brigade in support. On the morning of September 14, Hill observed from the summit the encampment of a Union corps. He repositioned Garland's brigade one mile south at Fox's Gap, called his other three brigades back to Turner's Gap, and requested support from Longstreet.

Action began at Fox's Gap at 9:00 a.m. as the Kanawha Division of Union major general Jesse Reno's IX Corps attacked Garland's position. Garland fell mortally wounded, and his troops gave way until bolstered by the remaining brigades of Hill's division and reinforcements from Longstreet. After a midday lull Reno attacked again, but he too was killed in action. Hill and Longstreet continued to reinforce the position, but by dusk IX Corps had gained the summit of Fox's Gap.

The Turner's Gap fight began in the afternoon, when Union brigadier general John Gibbon's Iron Brigade attacked Colquitt's entrenched troops. Major General Joseph Hooker's I Corps attacked north of the gap in order to flank Hill's position. One of Hill's brigade commanders, Brigadier General Robert Rodes, repositioned his men to stop Hooker's advance, while two of Longstreet's brigades moved up to assist Rodes and Colquitt. The combined Confederate forces delayed Hooker from reaching the summit of South Mountain before nightfall. Union forces suffered 1,813 casualties; the Confederates suffered 2,685.

Overnight, Hill and Longstreet withdrew their divisions from the mountain and passed west through Boonsboro, Maryland, toward Sharpsburg and the Potomac River. Given Jackson's success at Harpers Ferry and McClellan's slow

The Battle of South Mountain, Maryland, September 14, 1862, fought during the September 4–20 Antietam Campaign. (Library of Congress)

pursuit, Lee decided to make his stand on the high ground north of Sharpsburg, resulting in the Battle of Antietam on September 17.

BRIT K. ERSLEV

See also
Antietam, Battle of; Antietam Campaign; Colquitt, Alfred Holt; Crampton's Gap, Battle of; Hill, Daniel Harvey; Garland, Samuel, Jr.; Gibbon, John; Hooker, Joseph; Longstreet, James; Reno, Jesse Lee; Rodes, Robert Emmett

Further Reading
Priest, John Michael. *Before Antietam: The Battle for South Mountain.* Shippensburg, PA: White Mane, 1992.
Sears, Stephen W. *Landscape Turned Red: The Battle of Antietam.* New York: Houghton Mifflin, 1983.

Southwest, Confederate Department of the

Confederate military administrative unit created on December 23, 1863. Commanded by Lieutenant General Leonidas Polk, the Confederate Department of the Southwest encompassed the former Confederate Department of Mississippi and East Louisiana as well as the Department of Alabama and East Mississippi and was an alternate designation for the Department of Alabama, Mississippi, and East Louisiana, used during Polk's tenure. The Department of the Southwest included most of Alabama, Mississippi, and Louisiana east of the Mississippi River, including those areas already occupied by Union troops. During late 1863 and early 1864, Polk led troops against Union operations launched in Mississippi by Major General William T. Sherman.

The Department of the Southwest ceased to exist as of May 9, 1864, when it became the Department of Alabama, Mississippi, and East Louisiana. At that time, Polk and most of the troops from the department went to Georgia, where they would participate in the Atlanta Campaign (May 5–September 2, 1864).

PAUL G. PIERPAOLI JR.

See also
Mississippi and East Louisiana, Confederate Department of; Polk, Leonidas

Further Reading
Eicher, John H., and David J. Eicher. *Civil War High Commands.* Stanford, CA: Stanford University Press, 2001.

Southwest, Union Army of the

Short-lived field force. Also referred to as the Army of Southwest Missouri, the Union Army of the Southwest was a Union command operating in the Trans-Mississippi theater. The army was constituted on December 25, 1861, and was first commanded by Brigadier General Samuel R. Curtis. The Army of the Southwest operated as the primary field force of the Union Military District of Southwest Missouri for most of 1862. Curtis remained in command until August 1862. He was succeeded by Brigadier Generals Frederick Steele (August 29–October 7, 1862) and Eugene Carr (October 8–November 12, 1862).

Although designated an army, the Army of the Southwest never numbered more than 11,000 men, drawn mainly from Missouri. About half the soldiers were German immigrants from St. Louis and eastern Missouri. The army consisted of three divisions, commanded by Brigadier Generals Franz Sigel and Alexander Asboth and Colonel Jefferson C. Davis. In addition, Curtis later organized an additional division under the command of Carr.

The Army of the Southwest was actively engaged in the pursuit of Confederate forces under Major Generals Sterling Price and Earl Van Dorn. The largest engagement it fought was the Battle of Pea Ridge (March 7–8, 1862). The Union's success at Pea Ridge all but ended the Confederate threat to Missouri. After Pea Ridge, the Army of the Southwest fell victim to Union priorities in other theaters, and most of its units were sent to support the Union Army of the Tennessee. By November 1862, the Army of the Southwest was a small disorganized force existing as an army in name only.

WALTER F. BELL

See also

Arkansas; Carr, Eugene Asa; Curtis, Samuel Ryan; Missouri; Pea Ridge, Battle of; Steele, Frederick

Further Reading

Keegan, John. *The American Civil War: A Military History.* New York: Knopf, 2009.

Monaghan, Frank. *Civil War on the Western Border, 1854–1865.* Boston: Little, Brown, 1955.

Southwestern Army, Confederate

Confederate military force created on December 23, 1863. The Department of the Southwest and the Southwestern Army were under the command of Lieutenant General Leonidas Polk. Initially the army was quite small, consisting of just two infantry divisions, under Major Generals Samuel G. French and William W. Loring, and two cavalry outfits, commanded by Major Generals Nathan B. Forrest and Stephen D. Lee.

Polk's command had two principal goals: to protect Mobile, Alabama, from Union attack and to oppose and harass Union major general William T. Sherman's forces in northern Mississippi. Polk accomplished both with considerable success, significantly augmenting Mobile's defenses and inflicting considerable damage on Sherman's army.

Polk and his army, now numbering some 14,000 men, were sent to Atlanta on May 1, 1864, to aid in that city's defense. The department was renamed the Department of Alabama, Mississippi, and East Louisiana on May 9, 1865, and passed under the command of Major General Stephen D. Lee.

PAUL G. PIERPAOLI JR.

See also

Atlanta Campaign; Forrest, Nathan Bedford; French, Samuel Gibbs; Lee, Stephen Dill; Loring, William Wing; Polk, Leonidas; Sherman, William Tecumseh

Further Reading

Eicher, John H., and David J. Eicher. *Civil War High Commands.* Stanford, CA: Stanford University Press, 2001.

Southwestern Virginia, Confederate Department of

Confederate military administrative unit established on May 8, 1862. The Confederate Department of Southwestern Virginia encompassed the southwestern corner of Virginia to the Kentucky border, or as far west as combat operations permitted. The department also had several other names and configurations, including the Trans-Allegheny Department, the Department of Western Virginia, the Department of Southwestern Virginia and East Tennessee, and the Department of Western Virginia and East Tennessee. The Army of Southwest Virginia was the military arm of the department.

Major General William W. Loring commanded the department from May 8 to October 16, 1862; he was succeeded by Brigadier General John Echols (October 16–November 10). Brigadier General John S. Williams commanded during November 10–25; he was succeeded in command by Brigadier General Samuel Jones, who commanded from November 25, 1862, to February 25, 1864. Major General John C. Breckinridge succeeded Jones in command (March 5–July 22, 1864). Brigadier General John H. Morgan commanded the department from July 22 until his death on September 4, 1864. General Breckinridge now reassumed command and led the department. On February 25, 1865, the department became a subset of the Confederate Valley District.

PAUL G. PIERPAOLI JR.

See also
Breckinridge, John Cabell; Echols, John; Jones, Samuel; Loring, William Wing; Morgan, John Hunt; Williams, John Stuart

Further Reading
Eicher, John H., and David J. Eicher. *Civil War High Commands.* Stanford, CA: Stanford University Press, 2001.

Spanish Fort, Battle of
See Mobile, Alabama, Siege of

Sparrow, Edward
Birth Date: December 29, 1810
Death Date: July 4, 1882

Confederate politician. Edward Sparrow was born on December 29, 1810, in Dublin, Ireland, but immigrated with his parents to the United States when he was quite young. The family settled in Columbus, Ohio, and Sparrow attended Kenyon College before studying law. He practiced for a short time in Ohio before moving to Louisiana. There he became a very successful attorney, and by the mid-1850s he owned a sprawling plantation in Carroll Parish, Louisiana. By 1860, he had become one of the wealthiest planters in the state.

Sparrow was a delegate to the 1861 Louisiana Secession Convention, where he urged immediate secession. He was then a representative in the Provisional Confederate Congress (1861–1862), where he helped draft the Confederate Constitution and sat on the important Military Affairs Committee. In the autumn of 1861 he was elected to the Confederate Senate, where he would remain until 1865. He chaired the Military Affairs Committee and pressed for centralization of the Confederate Army. He also often stated his opinion that the Confederate Congress should play a more central role in military decision making. As the war dragged on, Sparrow became critical of some of President Jefferson Davis's selections for high military commands. On several occasions, Sparrow disparaged General Braxton Bragg's operations and sought a larger role for General P. G. T. Beauregard, a close personal friend.

As 1865 dawned and the Confederacy's chances of prevailing in the war grew ever more remote, Sparrow believed that only the harshest of measures could reverse that trend. Indeed, he believed that the central government in Richmond should consolidate all of its resources, even if this meant endowing President Davis with dictatorial powers. Sparrow also urged the Confederate government to procure supplies by any means necessary, including the confiscation of private property. By 1865, however, it was too late to implement such drastic measures.

Postbellum, Sparrow returned to his plantation and practiced law. He died on July 4, 1882, in Carroll Parish, Louisiana.

PAUL G. PIERPAOLI JR.

See also
Beauregard, Pierre Gustav Toutant; Bragg, Braxton; Congress, CSA; Davis, Jefferson Finis; Louisiana

Further Reading
Davis, William C. *Look Away! A History of the Confederate States of America.* New York: Free Press, 2002.
Thomas, Emory M. *The Confederate Nation, 1861–1865.* New York: Harper and Row, 1979.

Spar Torpedo
Explosive device placed at the end of a long pole or spar. During the Civil War, mines were known as torpedoes, for the electric ray fish that shocked its prey. The Confederacy used large numbers of torpedoes against Union warships in rivers and off its ports and also employed torpedoes offensively. Confederate general P. G. T. Beauregard, commanding at Charleston, advocated construction of small vessels mounting a spar torpedo in the bow to attack blockading warships. Such craft were designed to operate very low in the water. Encouraged by Beauregard, Confederate Army captain Francis D. Lee carried out a number of experiments and supervised construction of a torpedo boat, the *Torch*. Some 150 feet in length, it was launched in July 1863.

The Confederates regarded the *New Ironsides* as the principal threat of the Union blockaders. The *Torch* made an attempt to sink it. Shortly after midnight on August 21, 1863, a crew of 12 men sortied in the *Torch*, now armed with an unusual triple spar torpedo, with each warhead weighing 100 pounds. The *New Ironsides* was then at anchor, swinging with the tide, and this movement and the *Torch*'s poor engine prevented it from striking the Union ship broadsides.

The Confederates also built much smaller vessels, 48.5 feet long, known for the prototype as the David class. A half dozen others of this design were laid down, but only

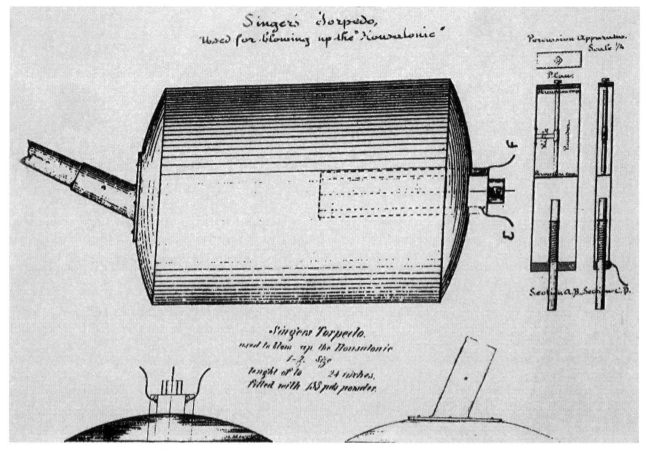

A diagram showing the design of the torpedo (naval mine) attached to the spar of the Confederate submarine *H. L. Hunley*. (AP Photo/Bruce Smith)

a few were actually completed. Operating low in the water, the David-class vessels resembled a submarine but were in fact strictly surface vessels propelled by a steam engine. The vessels took in water as ballast to run on the surface awash, but the open hatch, necessary to provide air for the steam engine, invited disaster through swamping. With a crew of four, the David-class vessels mounted a spar torpedo containing 60 pounds of powder.

On the night of October 5, 1863, the *David,* commanded by Lieutenant William T. Glassell, set out. It got to within 50 yards of the *New Ironsides* before it was discovered. The crew of the *David* managed to place their mine, which exploded. Although damaged, the *New Ironsides* was soon repaired and back in service. Although the *David* escaped, Glassell and another member of the crew were captured. The Confederates carried out other such attempts against Union ships at Charleston but without success. Union crews took precautions, including posting picket boats, antitorpedo netting, and boat howitzers kept loaded with canister.

The Union side also employed spar torpedoes. On October 18, 1864, Lieutenant William T. Cushing and 14 volunteers used a spar torpedo mounted at the bow of a small steam launch to sink the Confederate ironclad ram *Albemarle* at Plymouth, North Carolina.

SPENCER C. TUCKER

See also

Albemarle, CSS, Destruction of; Beauregard, Pierre Gustav Toutant; Cushing, William Barker; *H. L. Hunley,* CSS; *New Ironsides,* USS; Submarines; Torpedoes

Further Reading

Bradford, R. B. *History of Torpedo Warfare.* Newport, RI: U.S. Torpedo Station, 1882.

Hartman, Gregory K., with Scott C. Truver. *Weapons That Wait: Mine Warfare in the U.S. Navy.* Annapolis, MD: Naval Institute Press, 1991.

Lundeberg, Philip K. *Samuel Colt's Submarine Battery: The Secret and the Enigma.* Washington, DC: Smithsonian Institution Press, 1974.

Perry, Milton F. *Infernal Machines: The Story of Confederate Submarine and Mine Warfare.* Baton Rouge: Louisiana State University Press, 1965.

Roland, Alex. *Underwater Warfare in the Age of Sail.* Bloomington: Indiana University Press, 1978.

Spaulding, Elbridge Gerry
Birth Date: February 24, 1809
Death Date: May 5, 1897

U.S. congressman and chief proponent of the 1862 Legal Tender Act. Elbridge Gerry Spaulding was born on February 24, 1809, in Cayuga County, New York. After studying law, he was admitted to the bar in 1836 and established a practice in Buffalo, New York. He also entered the banking business and was elected mayor of Buffalo in 1847. The following year he served as a New York state assemblyman, and he was elected to the U.S. House of Representatives in 1848 as a Whig, serving from 1849 to 1851. From 1854 to 1855, Spaulding was the treasurer of New York State.

During the 1850s, Spaulding amassed a small fortune through his banking and legal ventures, and in 1858 he was elected as a Republican to the U.S. House of Representatives, where he would remain until 1863. A member of the important Ways and Means Committee, Spaulding was soon tasked with helping the U.S. government fund rapidly accelerating war spending, which was having a deleterious effect on the nation's credit and currency. In early 1862 he introduced a bill in the House that recommended making paper currency, not backed by gold or silver, legal tender, except for duties on imports and interest on the public debt. The U.S. Constitution did not specifically authorize the government to issue paper currency, but U.S. attorney general Edward Bates nevertheless approved the measure.

Spaulding's plan created a great deal of controversy in the House and even divided the Ways and Means Committee itself. After considerable debate, Congress passed the first Legal Tender Act on February 25, 1862, authorizing the printing of $150 million in unbacked treasury notes. Printed on only one side in green ink, they soon became known as greenbacks. Spaulding did not stand for reelection in 1862 and left Congress in March 1863.

Spaulding returned to Buffalo and resumed his lucrative banking and legal careers. He was also engaged in a number of charitable endeavors. Spaulding died on May 5, 1897, in Buffalo.

PAUL G. PIERPAOLI JR.

See also
Financing, U.S.

Further Reading
Murray, Robert Bruce. *Legal Cases of the Civil War*. Mechanicsville, PA: Stackpole, 2003.

Ritter, Gretchen. *Goldbugs and Greenbacks: The Antimonopoly Tradition and the Politics of Finance in America*. Cambridge: Cambridge University Press, 1999.

Speed, James
Birth Date: March 11, 1812
Death Date: June 25, 1887

U.S. attorney general. James Speed was born in Jefferson County, Kentucky, to a well-to-do family on March 11, 1812. His brother, Joshua, became one of President Abraham Lincoln's closest friends. After studying at St. Joseph's College and Transylvania University, James Speed passed the bar in 1833 and commenced a practice in Louisville. Contrary to his brother, he held a strong aversion to slavery. Speed sat for one term in the commonwealth legislature beginning in 1847, and prior to the Civil War he spoke out passionately against secession while urging Kentuckians to remain neutral if civil war came.

When the Civil War began in 1861, Speed unabashedly supported the Union war effort, casting aside his former neutrality. He took a seat in the Kentucky Senate that same year and coordinated with his brother Joshua secret arms transfers to the state's pro-Union sympathizers. James Speed heartily embraced the Emancipation Proclamation and authored a bill that authorized the confiscation of Confederate property in his state, to include slaves. When his term expired in July 1863, he became a special adviser to Lincoln on matters relating to Kentucky.

In late November 1864, Lincoln appointed Speed U.S. attorney general; he took office on December 2, 1864. Speed championed the president's policies of moderation toward the Southern states, but after Lincoln was assassinated in April 1865, Speed came to embrace the Radical Republicans' more punitive policies toward the South. He also urged the immediate extension of suffrage to African Americans. Speed resigned his post on July 17, 1866, because he had come to oppose some of President Andrew Johnson's Reconstruction policies.

Upon his return to Louisville, Speed resumed his legal practice and remained actively engaged in his state's Republican politics. He also taught law for a time at Louisville University. Speed died on June 25, 1887, in Louisville.

PAUL G. PIERPAOLI JR.

See also
Johnson, Andrew; Kentucky; Lincoln, Abraham; Radical Republicans; Speed, Joshua Fry

Further Reading

Bush, Bryan S. *Lincoln and the Speeds: The Untold Story of a Devoted and Enduring Friendship.* Morley, MO: Acclaim Press, 2008.

Donald, David Herbert. *Lincoln.* New York: Simon and Schuster, 1995.

Speed, Joshua Fry
Birth Date: November 4, 1814
Death Date: May 29, 1882

Close friend and confidant of President Abraham Lincoln. Born in Louisville, Kentucky, on November 14, 1814, Joshua Speed is regarded by many historians as Lincoln's most intimate friend. The scion of a well-to-do family, Speed grew up on a Kentucky plantation before leaving for Illinois at age 18. Settling in Springfield, he became a partner in a local general store. In April 1837, 28-year-old Abraham Lincoln arrived in Springfield with all of his possessions loaded in two saddlebags. After confessing to Speed that he did not have the $17 necessary to purchase a mattress, sheets, and a pillow, Speed offered to let Lincoln share his double bed, a common arrangement at the time, in the store's loft. Lincoln lived there for the next three years.

In 1841 Speed left Springfield to return to Kentucky to try his hand at farming. The Lincoln-Speed correspondence that began at this time has provided historians with perhaps the deepest insight into the future president's personality. A number of these letters addressed Lincoln's concerns and doubts about his relationship with Mary Todd and detailed his reasons for initially breaking off their engagement. Speed's subsequent advice encouraged Lincoln to resume the engagement and marry Todd, which he did in 1842.

Speed's return to Kentucky also initiated a gradual division in the political views between the two men. Speed, the son of slaveholders, believed firmly that the federal government had to protect slavery. In 1851 Speed moved to Louisville and became successful in the real estate business. Both Speed and his brother, James, became active in Kentucky politics. Despite remaining at odds with Lincoln regarding slavery, proclaiming that he was "much distressed" and "could not eat or sleep" after the announcement of the 1862 Preliminary Emancipation Proclamation, Speed remained an ardent Unionist during the Civil War and even aided in the smuggling of arms to Union forces in Kentucky. Lincoln used Speed and his brother as liaisons and as advisers on wartime issues relating to Kentucky. Speed died in Louisville, Kentucky, on May 29, 1882.

STEVE FLAIG

See also

Emancipation Proclamation; Lincoln, Abraham

Further Reading

Carwardine, Richard. *Lincoln: A Life of Purpose and Power.* New York: Knopf, 2003.

Donald, David Herbert. *Lincoln.* New York: Simon and Schuster, 1995.

Spencer Repeating Rifle and Carbine

Among the first widely issued repeating rifles. Designed by Christopher M. Spencer and patented by him on March 6, 1860, the Spencer repeating rifle was a manually operated lever-action repeating rifle. It had a tube magazine in the wooden stock, which held seven copper cartridges and was easily removed for loading. As with the later Winchester rifle, the trigger guard was the actuating mechanism on the Spencer rifle. Once the cartridge in the chamber had been fired, the operator pulled down on the trigger guard, which both rotated the breechblock and at the same time extracted the spent cartridge case, ejecting the latter when the trigger guard reached the terminus of its travel.

When the trigger guard was at its lowest position, the breechblock engaged with the rear of a cartridge in the magazine. The action of pulling the trigger guard back up to its original position seated the cartridge case in the breech of the rifle. The hammer needed to be cocked manually for every shot, but apart from this, all the user had to do was aim and fire.

The rifle weighed 10 pounds and was 47 inches in length with a barrel length of 22 inches. The cavalry version was shorter, with an overall length of 39 inches, and weighed 8.25 pounds. It had a 20-inch barrel. Both were of .52-caliber and used rimfire cartridges. The bullet was 285 grains, and the powder charge was 48 grains.

Conservatism in the Ordnance Department, headed by Colonel James W. Ripley ("Ripley Van Winkle" as he was known to his detractors), delayed adoption of the Spencer rifle by the military. However, Spencer was eventually able to gain an audience with President Abraham Lincoln, who subsequently invited him to demonstrate the weapon. Much impressed, Lincoln ordered that it be placed in production. The Spencer rifle was first adopted by the Union Navy and then was ordered by the Union Army. It did not reach the army in significant numbers until 1863, and it never did replace the standard-issue muzzle-loading Springfield rifle. The Spencer rifle did, however, become the favored weapon for cavalry units, who used the shorter, lighter carbine version. The Confederates occasionally captured Spencers, but with the South unable to manufacture the cartridges because of a shortage of copper, the Confederates could only make limited use of it.

The Spencer rifle proved itself in the Battle of Hoover's Gap (June 24, 1863), when Union mounted troops under Colonel John T. Wilder, who had purchased Spencers with their own funds, easily defeated a force of Confederates. Spencers also played an important role in cavalry engagements in the Battle of Gettysburg on July 1 and 3, 1863. Whereas a soldier with a rifled muzzleloader could fire only 2–3 shots a minute, one armed with the Spencer could fire as many as 20 shots a minute—more if he was able to take advantage of a cartridge box that contained as many as 14 preloaded magazines. Not only could the soldier with a Spencer put down a greater volume of fire, but these could be aimed rounds. The only disadvantage of the Spencer was the relatively small powder charge in the cartridge, which limited its range. Effective range was 200–500 yards.

The rifle cost the government $37.50 each, while the carbine sold for $25.50. The Spencer proved to be very reliable under combat conditions. In 1869, the Spencer Repeating Rifle Company was sold to the Fogerty Rifle Company and ultimately to Winchester. In all, some 200,000 rifles and carbines were manufactured. The Spencer marked the first adoption of a removable magazine-fed infantry rifle by any country. Many Spencer carbines were later sold as surplus to France and saw service in the Franco-German War (1870–1871).

SPENCER C. TUCKER

See also

Gettysburg, Battle of; Lincoln, Abraham; Rifles; Ripley, James Wolfe

Further Reading

Coates, Earl J., and Dean S. Thomas. *An Introduction to Civil War Small Arms*. Gettysburg, PA: Thomas Publications, 1996.
Marcot, Roy M. *Spencer Repeating Firearms*. Revised ed. Irvine, CA: Northwood Heritage Press, 1995.
Westwood, David. *Rifles: An Illustrated History of Their Impact*. Santa Barbara, CA: ABC-CLIO, 2005.

Spinner, Francis Elias
Birth Date: January 21, 1802
Death Date: December 31, 1890

U.S. congressman and treasurer of the United States. Francis Elias Spinner was born on January 21, 1802, in Herkimer County, New York. He apprenticed as a candy maker and a harness maker before becoming involved in the mercantile business beginning in 1824. He also enlisted in the New York Militia, eventually rising to the rank of major general. Spinner was named Herkimer County deputy sheriff in 1829 and later served as sheriff (1834–1837). Thereafter he entered the banking field, beginning as a cashier and eventually becoming president of the Mohawk Bank. Spinner held several other posts, including commissioner of schools and inspector of state turnpikes.

From 1845 to 1849, Spinner was auditor and deputy naval officer for the Port of New York City. In 1854 he successfully ran for a seat in the U.S. House of Representatives as a Democrat, taking office in March 1855. There he consistently opposed the introduction of slavery into new territories. In 1856 he ran for reelection as a Republican and won, serving until March 3, 1861. Spinner was a strong supporter of Abraham Lincoln in the 1860 election, and for his loyalty Lincoln named him U.S. treasurer. Spinner commenced his tenure on March 16, 1861.

By all accounts, Spinner performed his duties admirably, even amid the financial turmoil caused by the Civil War. Charged with overseeing the printing and distribution of paper currency (greenbacks), Spinner's office was frequently understaffed and overworked. When Congress rebuffed his requests for more help, he improvised by hiring women in large numbers to act as clerks and stenographers. This was considered revolutionary at a time in which women were relegated to the home and men usually performed clerical tasks. By 1865, there were nearly 400 women working in the treasurer's office, most of whom were terminated upon the war's conclusion.

Spinner resigned his post on July 1, 1875, when Congress challenged his authority. He retired to Jacksonville, Florida, where he died on December 31, 1890.

PAUL G. PIERPAOLI JR.

See also

Greenbacks; Legal Tender Acts; Lincoln, Abraham; Women

Further Reading

Ritter, Gretchen. *Goldbugs and Greenbacks: The Antimonopoly Tradition and the Politics of Finance in America*. Cambridge: Cambridge University Press, 1999.
Unger, Irwin. *The Greenback Era*. Princeton, NJ: Princeton University Press, 1968.

Spotsylvania Court House, Battle of
Start Date: May 8, 1864
End Date: May 21, 1864

Major engagement of the Overland (Richmond) Campaign (May 4–June 12, 1864). Union general in chief Lieutenant General Ulysses S. Grant accompanied the Army of the

BATTLE OF SPOTSYLVANIA COURT HOUSE, MAY 8 – 21, 1864

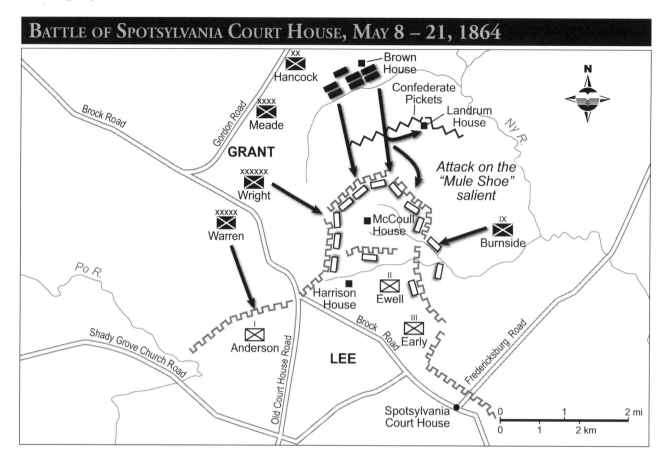

Potomac, commanded by Major General George Gordon Meade. General Robert E. Lee commanded the Confederate Army of Northern Virginia of some 52,000 men. The fighting at Spotsylvania Court House proved extremely bloody, and although Union casualties were much higher than those for the Confederates, Grant was nevertheless able to continue his larger offensive.

Following the Battle of the Wilderness (May 5–7, 1864), Grant tried to move his Union forces around Lee's right flank in order to strike at Richmond. On May 8 Major General Gouverneur K. Warren, commanding V Corps, received orders to capture Spotsylvania Court House. Anticipating this move, Lee had already ordered Major General James E. B. Stuart, commanding his cavalry, and I Corps under Major General Richard H. Anderson to Spotsylvania. The Confederates reached the town first on May 9.

Union advance troops began probing the Confederate position later that day, and during the skirmishing that ensued, Union major general John Sedgwick (VI Corps) was killed. Lee had deployed his men in a trench line stretching about four miles, with artillery placed to assist in the defense. The one major weakness in his line was a salient called the Mule Shoe, which extended about a mile beyond

the main line of trenches near the center of the Confederate line. It was at this point on May 10 that the Union army launched an attack with 12 regiments led by Colonel Emory Upton. This attack succeeded in taking the position, but the attackers were then forced back by a Confederate counterattack and thus made no significant penetration.

During the night of May 11–12, Lee began to build a new trench line to the rear of the Mule Shoe. However, this line was not yet complete when on May 12 Grant ordered an attack with an entire corps under the command of Major General Winfield S. Hancock. This assault nearly split the Confederate army in two, chiefly because much of the Confederates' artillery had been withdrawn to positions along the second line. The Confederate line held only because Major General Ambrose Burnside's supporting attacks on the right flank were poorly managed. As a result, Lee was able to weaken the line there to strengthen his center.

Lee personally led units of his II Corps forward until the men insisted that he retire for his own safety. More than 4,000 Confederates were taken prisoner in the initial attack. For the next day and most of the night, the Confederate army fought to regain the ground it had lost. The heaviest fighting took place along a section of the trenches known as the

Angle. By early morning on May 13, following the recapture of the Mule Shoe, Lee ordered his men to retreat to the newly prepared second line. There was a relative lull in the fighting until May 18, when Grant launched an attack with two of his corps, which was repulsed with heavy casualties.

Grant was now convinced that he could not take the position at Spotsylvania without unacceptable casualties and once more moved around Lee's flank to the southeast toward the North Anna River. For the entire engagement, Confederate casualties totaled just more than 13,000, while Union losses were more than 18,000. Although the Confederates claimed a victory, Lee could ill afford such losses (which were higher in percentage of total force than those of the Union), and many of his casualties had been among veteran troops. Union forces, meanwhile, still managed to edge closer to Richmond.

RALPH MARTIN BAKER

See also

Anderson, Richard Heron; Burnside, Ambrose Everett; Grant, Ulysses Simpson; Hancock, Winfield Scott; Lee, Robert Edward; Meade, George Gordon; Overland Campaign; Sedgwick, John; Stuart, James Ewell Brown; Upton, Emory; Warren, Gouverneur Kemble; Wilderness, Battle of the

Further Reading

Bonekemper, Edward H. *A Victor, Not a Butcher: Ulysses S. Grant's Overlooked Military Genius.* Washington, DC: Regnery, 2004.

Cannan, John. *The Bloody Angle: Hancock's Assault on the Mule Shoe Salient, May 12, 1864.* Cambridge, MA: Da Capo, 2002.

Matter, William D. *If It Takes All Summer: The Battle of Spotsylvania.* Chapel Hill: University of North Carolina Press, 1988.

Rhea, Gordon C. *The Battles for Spotsylvania Court House and the Road to Yellow Tavern.* Baton Rouge: Louisiana State University Press, 1994.

Sprague, John Wilson
Birth Date: April 4, 1817
Death Date: December 24, 1893

Union officer. Born in White Creek, New York, on April 4, 1817, John Wilson Sprague enrolled at Rensselaer Polytechnic Institute in Troy, New York, at age 13 but never graduated. He worked for several years in the grocery business in Troy. In 1845 he moved to Erie County, Ohio, where he became involved in the shipping and commission trade. When the Civil War began, Sprague recruited a company and served as its captain. On May 19, 1861, the company was mustered into federal service as part of the 7th Ohio Infantry.

In August 1861 Sprague received a leave of absence to return home. Shortly thereafter, he was captured by Confederate troops. As a prisoner, he was taken to Richmond, Virginia, and Charleston, South Carolina, until exchanged in January 1862. Following his release, on January 23 Sprague was appointed colonel of the 63rd Ohio Infantry. On February 10, the 63rd reported to Brigadier General William T. Sherman at Paducah, Kentucky. Sherman then ordered the regiment to report to Major General John Pope at Commerce, Missouri. Under Pope's command, Sprague led the regiment in the Battles of New Madrid (March 3–14, 1862) and Island No. 10 (April 7, 1862). He then fought in the Battle of Corinth (October 3–4, 1862), where the regiment suffered heavy casualties. Following Corinth, Sprague and the 63rd Ohio served mainly on garrison duty in northern Alabama, northern Mississippi, and western Tennessee.

In April 1864 Sprague received command of a brigade of the 4th Division, XVI Corps, Army of the Tennessee, prior to the opening of the Atlanta Campaign (May 5–September 2, 1864). On July 22 he was assigned to guard Sherman's supply trains at Decatur, Georgia. Despite his force being outnumbered, Sprague successfully defended the trains during a four-hour Confederate assault, losing only one wagon. For his courageous defense, Sprague was awarded the Medal of Honor (issued posthumously in 1894). On July 30, he was promoted to brigadier general of volunteers.

Sprague commanded his brigade, now in XVII Corps, under Sherman throughout the March to the Sea (November 15–December 21, 1864) and the March through the Carolinas (January–April 1865). On March 13, 1865, Sprague was brevetted major general of volunteers.

When the war ended, Sprague was relieved of command and assigned to the Freedmen's Bureau, in charge of the district encompassing Arkansas, Missouri, Kansas, and subsequently Indian Territory. He mustered out in September 1866. Sprague then engaged in the railroad business and helped found the city of Tacoma, Washington, where he lived until his death on December 24, 1893.

ADAM P. WILSON

See also

Atlanta Campaign; Corinth, Battle of; Island No. 10, Battle of; Sherman's March through the Carolinas; Sherman's March to the Sea

Further Reading

Smith, Charles H. *The History of Fuller's Ohio Brigade, 1861–1865.* Cleveland: Press of A. J. Watt, 1909.

Warner, Ezra J. *Generals in Blue: Lives of the Union Commanders.* Baton Rouge: Louisiana State University Press, 2006.

Sprague, Kate Chase
Birth Date: August 13, 1840
Death Date: July 31, 1899

Northern socialite and controversial daughter of Salmon P. Chase, secretary of the treasury and chief justice of the Supreme Court. Kate Chase was born in Cincinnati, Ohio, on August 13, 1840. As a member of a well-to-do and politically prominent family, she was educated at prestigious boarding schools in the East, and when her father became governor of Ohio, she served as the unofficial first lady of the state, her father having been widowed three times by the time he was elected governor. She became well known for her lavish parties and clothes. Her 1863 marriage to William Sprague, himself a wealthy man, was said to be one of the great social events of the 1860s.

Politically astute, Kate Sprague acted as her father's hostess when he moved to Washington, D.C., to assume the post of treasury secretary. Her husband's money and influence, coupled with her father's political connections, enabled Sprague to run in rarified circles, throwing fashionable parties even during the war years. Harboring a visceral dislike for President Abraham Lincoln, whom she likened to a country rube, she actively promoted her father's presidential aspirations. Indeed, there is evidence to suggest that she had a hand in the infamous Pomeroy Circular of 1864, which repudiated Lincoln's leadership and urged voters to embrace Chase for the 1864 Republican Party nomination. Chase disavowed any connection to the circular, but he nevertheless had campaigned quietly behind the scenes in an effort to unseat Lincoln.

In 1868 when Chase sought the presidential nomination of the Democratic Party, to which he had formerly belonged, Kate Sprague was one of his most vocal supporters, waging a tireless campaign that was, in the end, unsuccessful. Meanwhile, the Sprague marriage had failed, and financial setbacks in the 1870s finally forced a divorce in 1882. Sprague embarked on a grand European tour for several years before returning home in 1886, now practically bankrupt. She resided on her father's estate in Washington, D.C., but in her twilight years was so financially strapped that she resorted to selling milk and chickens door-to-door to wealthy Washingtonians, some of whom she had feted at her grand soirees when she was young. Sprague died in Washington, D.C., on July 31, 1899.

PAUL G. PIERPAOLI JR.

See also
Chase, Salmon Portland; Pomeroy Circular

Further Reading
Lamphier, Peg A. *Kate Chase and William Sprague: Politics and Gender in a Civil War Marriage.* Lincoln: University of Nebraska Press, 2003.
Niven, John. *Salmon P. Chase: A Biography.* New York: Oxford University Press, 1995.

Sprague, William, IV
Birth Date: September 12, 1830
Death Date: September 11, 1915

Governor of Rhode Island and U.S. senator. William Sprague IV was born on September 12, 1830, in Cranston, Rhode Island, the scion of a wealthy and influential family that made its fortune in textiles. He entered the family commercial empire at age 15, and by the time he was 26, he and his brothers were running the business, which continued to expand and included a railroad. Sprague was often flighty, irresponsible, and vain, but in 1859 Rhode Island's Union Party nominated him for governor over the Republicans' candidate, who was deemed too radical. Sprague accepted the nomination and won the election in 1860, although some argued that he had purchased his huge landslide by bribery. He was reelected in 1861 and immediately embraced the Union's war effort, sending one of the first state regiments, which he had helped to equip with his own funds, to Washington, D.C. Sprague personally accompanied the troops south, served as an aide to Brigadier General Ambrose E. Burnside, and was a participant at the First Battle of Bull Run (July 21, 1861). Thereafter, Sprague lobbied the War Department for a major generalship, promising in return that he would coerce the Rhode Island legislature into repealing a statute that limited volunteers' enlistments to three-month terms. President Abraham Lincoln quashed the deal, and instead Sprague was offered a brigadier general's commission, which he refused, arguing that Rhode Islanders would consider the rank a slight. In 1862 Sprague attended the governors' conference in Altoona, Pennsylvania, but played no significant role there. Elected to a third term, he resigned the governors' post in March 1863 to take a seat in the U.S. Senate, where he served until 1875. In November 1863 he wed Kate Chase, daughter of Secretary of the Treasury Salmon P. Chase, who was considered the belle of Washington. The two drifted apart, however, a development that was fueled by Sprague's drinking and his wife's alleged affair with New York senator Roscoe Conkling. They divorced in 1882.

With his fortune largely eroded by the Panic of 1873 and the resulting economic depression, Sprague became increasingly unstable. Later defeated in another bid for governor, he built a palatial mansion in Narragansett, where he served as president of the town council beginning in 1900. A fire gutted the home in 1909, at which time Sprague and his second wife moved to Paris, where he died on September 11, 1915.

PAUL G. PIERPAOLI JR.

See also

Bull Run, First Battle of; Rhode Island

Further Reading

Belden, Thomas Graham, and Marva Robins Belden. *So Fell the Angels.* Boston: Little, Brown, 1956.

Lamphier, Peg A. *Kate Chase and William Sprague: Politics and Gender in a Civil War Marriage.* Lincoln: University of Nebraska Press, 2003.

Springfield Armory

Major U.S. arms manufacturing facility in Massachusetts. The origins of the Springfield Armory date to 1777, when General George Washington and Brigadier General Henry Knox chose the site—on a hill overlooking Springfield, Massachusetts—as the location for the first U.S. arsenal. During the American Revolutionary War, the arsenal stored muskets, cannon, and other weapons but produced only paper cartridges.

The arsenal became known as the Springfield Armory in 1794, when President Washington approved on-site small arms manufacturing there. That year the U.S. government began the domestic production of muskets, eliminating dependence on foreign sources. Construction then began on several new buildings. Production of the Model 1795 flintlock musket soon followed.

Armory staff embarked on a long tradition of innovation in both manufacturing processes and the weapons themselves. In 1819 the armory designed and implemented a new lathe that produced standardized gun stocks. This standardization was a high priority for the army because it enabled the fast replacement of broken parts on the battlefield.

After the Federals abandoned the only other national armory at Harpers Ferry early in the Civil War, the Springfield Armory became the principal source of the North's rifled muskets. These new rifled muskets (known as the Model 1861 Springfield Rifle-Musket) used both the percussion-cap firing system and the armory's 1855 rifled barrel, whose spiral grooves gave greater accuracy to each round.

This standard Union rifle was extremely accurate at 500 yards and could be fired up to six times a minute. It also fired the new minié ball round, achieving lethality at greater ranges than before.

At its peak production during the war, the Springfield Armory employed 3,400 people and produced 1,000 muskets each working day. By war's end, a total of 793,434 Springfield rifles had been produced there. This was out of a total of approximately 1.7 million rifles manufactured in the North during the war by the armory and private contractors combined.

The armory continued to develop new manufacturing techniques and provide the army's basic rifle needs. Later firearms included the M1892 Krag-Jorgensen, the M1903 Springfield rifle used in World War I, and the M1 Garand employed in World War II, the Korean War, and the Vietnam War. The M14 was the last rifle developed by the Springfield Armory. The armory then served as a development and testing laboratory until it was closed in 1968.

MARTIN K. GORDON

See also

Harpers Ferry, Virginia; Rifles

Further Reading

Ball, Robert W. D. *Springfield Armory Shoulder Weapons, 1795–1968.* Dubuque, IA: Antique Trader Books, 1999.

National Park Service. *Springfield Armory National Historic Site: Massachusetts.* Washington, DC: U.S. Government Printing Office 1997.

Springfield Model 1861 Rifle Musket

The most widely used infantry weapon of the Civil War. In 1855, U.S. secretary of war Jefferson Davis, future president of the Confederacy, approved adoption by the U.S. Army of the .58-caliber muzzle-loading rifled musket. The new weapon combined the percussion cap system of ignition with the minié ball projectile. Such weapons had come into widespread use in the world's armies at midcentury. The percussion cap greatly increased reliability of fire and hence firepower, while rifling increased the effective range from some 80–100 yards to 300 yards. Thanks to the invention of the expanding cylindro-conoidal bullet known as the minié ball, the rifle could now be loaded as rapidly as the smoothbore musket. The 1861 model came to be named for the Springfield arsenal, its original production facility.

The Model 1861 Springfield was 56 inches in length with a 40-inch barrel and weighed 9.5 pounds. It had flip-up leaf sights and fired a bullet of 500 grains at a muzzle velocity of

The muzzle-loading .58 caliber Springfield Model 1861 rifled musket. (Civil War Archive/The Bridgeman Art Library)

950 feet per second and had a maximum effective range of 300 yards. The Model 1863 was essentially the same weapon but incorporated redesigned barrel bands and a new hammer. The Springfield's heavy, slow-moving lead bullet could exact frightful damage, tumbling in flight, flattening on impact, and tearing away chunks of bone, which necessitated amputations.

With its attached 18-inch bayonet, the weapon stood taller than the average soldier of the time. The Springfield Model 1861 could be loaded and fired about three times per minute. The standard issue of ammunition going into combat was 40 paper cartridges per man, which would therefore provide only about a dozen minutes of sustained rapid fire.

The Springfield Armory could not produce the requisite number required, and some 20 firms also contracted to build the weapon. During the war, approximately 1.5 million Model 1861 and Model 1863 guns were produced by a wide variety of manufacturing facilities, but Southern firms accounted for less than 1 percent of the total.

SPENCER C. TUCKER

See also

Arms Manufacturing; Infantry Tactics; Minié, Claude-Étienne; Rifles

Further Reading

Bilby, Joseph. *Civil War Firearms: Their Historical Background and Tactical Use.* New York: Da Capo, 2005.

Edwards, William B. *Civil War Guns.* Gettysburg, PA: Thomas Publications, 1997.

Graf, John F. *Standard Catalog of Civil War Firearms.* Iola, WI: Krause, 2009.

Spring Hill, Battle of
Event Date: November 29, 1864

Engagement during General John Bell Hood's Franklin and Nashville Campaign (November 29–December 27, 1964). Following the fall of Atlanta on September 2, 1864, Hood attempted to draw Union major general William T. Sherman's forces out of that city by marching into Tennessee. Instead of sending all of his men in response, however, Sherman detached Major General George Thomas with part of his Army of the Cumberland and Major General John M. Schofield's Army of the Ohio to Nashville to thwart Hood's design. Thomas in turn placed Schofield in command of roughly 20,000 men in IV and XXIII Corps in southern Tennessee to oppose Hood. Hood, marching rapidly, had his 30,000 Confederates drawn up in front of the town of Columbia, Tennessee, on the south side of the Duck River by November 27. Schofield, meanwhile, had concentrated his men on the north bank of the Duck.

Hood planned a flanking maneuver involving two of his army corps, roughly 20,000 men. They would cross the Duck upriver from Columbia and cut off the Union line of retreat at the village of Spring Hill. Hood ordered his other corps to remain in front of Columbia and fix Schofield in place. On the morning of November 29, Hood set his columns into motion, but difficulties arose because of confusion over the roads north of Columbia. This unplanned delay allowed Schofield sufficient time to move two brigades, roughly 3,500 men, into place to guard Spring Hill against what he thought would be a cavalry raid on his supply line.

When the Confederates arrived at Spring Hill, Hood ordered Major General Frank Cheatham to employ his lead division to block the Franklin and Columbia Turnpike, Schofield's only route of retreat. By 3:30 p.m. on November 29, Cheatham had his lead division, commanded by Major General Patrick Cleburne, in place and ordered it forward. Cleburne's men then charged toward Colonel Luther Bradley's lead brigade guarding the turnpike. Bradley's men broke and ran, but Union artillery arrested Cleburne's advance, and the Confederate general ordered his division back to the cover of a nearby creek bed.

Cheatham, who had orders only to block the pike, now decided to try to overrun the Union troops guarding the town of Spring Hill and the turnpike. By this time, Schofield had learned the precariousness of his situation and started his army north from Columbia. Casualties amounted to only about 200 killed, wounded, or captured on both sides. As darkness fell, both Confederate corps arrayed themselves within 100 yards of the Franklin and Columbia Turnpike but because of a series of miscommunications failed to block the thoroughfare as Schofield's entire army marched by them in the darkness. This almost inexplicable turn of events allowed the Union army to escape defeat and capture.

An infuriated Hood learned the next morning that Schofield's entire force had gotten past him and was located several miles away at Franklin. Hood's frustration manifested itself in his orders for the disastrous frontal assaults that constituted the Battle of Franklin (November 30, 1864). The engagement at Spring Hill was significant because it represented the best chance for a Confederate victory during Hood's 1864 Tennessee campaign.

JOHN R. LUNDBERG

See also

Cheatham, Benjamin Franklin; Cleburne, Patrick Ronayne; Franklin, Battle of; Hood, John Bell; Schofield, John McAllister; Sherman, William Tecumseh; Thomas, George Henry

Further Reading

Connelly, Thomas Lawrence. *Autumn of Glory: The Army of Tennessee 1862–1865.* Baton Rouge: Louisiana State University Press, 1974.

Sword, Wiley. *Embrace an Angry Wind: The Confederacy's Last Hurrah; Spring Hill, Franklin and Nashville.* Columbus, OH: General's Books, 1994.

Symonds, Craig L. *Stonewall of the West: Patrick Cleburne and the Civil War.* Lawrence: University Press of Kansas, 1997.

Stafford, Leroy Augustus
Birth Date: April 13, 1822
Death Date: May 8, 1864

Confederate officer. Leroy Augustus Stafford was born on April 13, 1822, at Greenwood Plantation near Cheneyville, Louisiana. Educated in Tennessee and Kentucky, he went on to become one of Louisiana's premier planters. In 1845 he became sheriff of Rapides Parish and then served as an enlisted man in the Mexican-American War (1846–1848). After the war Stafford became involved with the local militia, and by 1861 he was a captain of a company known informally as the Stafford Guards.

In the spring of 1861, Stafford joined the Confederate Army as the lieutenant colonel of the 9th Louisiana Infantry. That October, he was advanced to colonel of the 9th Louisiana.

Stafford led his regiment during Major General T. J. "Stonewall" Jackson's Shenandoah Valley Campaign (May–June 1862) and temporarily held a brigade command during the latter portions of the Seven Days' Campaign (June 25–July 1, 1862). Stafford also assumed brigade command during the Second Bull Run Campaign (August 9–September 1, 1862). He then resumed command of his old regiment, which he led at the Battle of Antietam (September 17, 1862), where once again he was called upon to lead the brigade. He sustained a wound there but soon recuperated. Stafford next saw combat at the First Battle of Fredericksburg (December 13, 1862).

The following year, Stafford performed competently at the Battle of Chancellorsville (May 1–4, 1863) and then at the Battle of Gettysburg (July 1–3, 1863), where he led a charge up Cemetery Hill on the second day of fighting. On October 8, 1863, Stafford was advanced to brigadier general and took command of the 2nd Louisiana Brigade, which he led during the Mine Run Campaign (November 26–December 2, 1863).

On the first day of the Battle of the Wilderness (May 5–7, 1864), Stafford was mortally wounded leading his brigade. Evacuated to Richmond, he died there on May 8, 1864.

PAUL G. PIERPAOLI JR.

See also

Antietam, Battle of; Chancellorsville, Battle of; Fredericksburg, First Battle of; Gettysburg, Battle of; Jackson's Shenandoah Valley Campaign; Mine Run Campaign; Seven Days' Campaign; Wilderness, Battle of the

Further Reading

Eicher, John H., and David J. Eicher. *Civil War High Commands.* Stanford, CA: Stanford University Press, 2001.

Warner, Ezra J. *Generals in Gray: Lives of the Confederate Commanders.* Baton Rouge: Louisiana State University Press, 2006.

Stager, Anson
Birth Date: April 20, 1825
Death Date: March 26, 1885

Union officer. Anson Stager was born on April 20, 1825, in Ontario County, New York. At age 16 he was introduced to electric telegraphy and began to work in that field. He eventually helped construct a telegraph line from Philadelphia to Harrisburg, Pennsylvania, and was placed in charge of a telegraph office in 1846. By 1856, Stager had risen to become the first general superintendent of the Western Union Company.

When the Civil War began in the spring of 1861, Ohio's governor requested that Stager help secure telegraph communications, for which he developed a simple but effective cipher key. In October 1861, the U.S. War Department sought better control of the nation's telegraph infrastructure and organized the U.S. Military Telegraph Service (USMTS), a quasi-military organization that consisted of trained civilian telegraphers. Stager was initially appointed to the USMTS as a captain and an assistant quartermaster to help manage property and disburse funds. In February 1862, the War Department took control of all telegraph lines in the United States for military use. Stager was then named superintendent of the USMTS and promoted to colonel.

Stager developed a close relationship with Secretary of War Edwin Stanton, who viewed the USMTS as critical for managing the war. President Abraham Lincoln spent hours in the War Department telegraph office sending, receiving, and reading messages from field commanders. This ability was enhanced by Stager's continuous development and improvement of encryption methods to include strict control of codebooks, access to which was denied to senior officers and even the president. As a result, the Confederacy was unable to break any Union telegraph codes.

Stager served until September 1865 and was brevetted brigadier general of volunteers for his wartime service. In 1869 he moved to Chicago, where he cofounded the Western Electric Manufacturing Company, serving as its president until his death on March 26, 1885, in Chicago.

STEVEN J. RAUCH

See also

Railways and Telegraph Act; Stanton, Edwin McMasters; Telegraph

Further Reading

Plum, William R. *The Military Telegraph during the Civil War in the United States.* Reprint ed. New York: Arno, 1974.

Romano, Kevin. "The Stager Ciphers and the U.S. Military's First Cryptographic System." *Army Communicator* 27 (Winter 2002): 56–59.

Scheips, Paul J. "Union Signal Communications: Innovation and Conflict." *Civil War History* 9 (December 1963): 399–421.

Stahel-Szamvald, Julius
Birth Date: November 5, 1825
Death Date: December 4, 1912

Union officer. Julius Stahel-Szamvald was born on November 5, 1825, in Szeged, Hungary. Of German descent, he entered the Austro-Hungarian Army in his early 20s but left the service to join the anti-Austrian revolutionary Hungarian nationalist forces of Louis Kossuth. Stahel-Szamvald fled Hungary

after Kossuth's defeat in 1849 and eventually settled in New York City, working as a journalist and teacher. At some point he dropped Szamvald from his surname. When the Civil War began, Stahel enlisted in the 8th New York Infantry, a regiment he helped raise. Serving as its lieutenant colonel, he led the regiment at the First Battle of Bull Run (July 21, 1861). He was promoted to colonel on August 11, 1861, and to brigadier general, commanding four principally German regiments, on November 12. He served in the Battle of Cross Keys (June 8, 1862) and the Second Battle of Bull Run (August 29–30, 1862), both times earning praise from his superiors. Stahel commanded a division in the largely German XI Corps, which was in reserve during the Battle of Antietam (September 17) and the First Battle of Fredericksburg (December 13). He briefly commanded the corps before assuming command of the Cavalry Division in the Washington defenses. He was advanced to major general on March 17, 1863.

Stahel was then transferred to command the cavalry in the Department of the Susquehanna. In 1864 he was sent to command the cavalry division attached to the army of friend and patron Major General Franz Sigel. At the Battle of New Market (May 15, 1864), Stahel led a disastrous charge, contributing to the Union defeat there. He was more successful in the Battle of Piedmont (June 5, 1864) under Sigel's replacement, Major General David Hunter, for which Stahel was awarded the Medal of Honor in 1893. Wounded at Piedmont, Stahel spent the rest of the war in Washington and resigned his commission on February 8, 1865.

After the war, Stahel worked as a mining engineer and served as U.S. consul in Yokohama and Shanghai. He died in New York City on December 4, 1912.

WILLIAM E. BURNS

See also

Bull Run, First Battle of; Bull Run, Second Battle of; Cross Keys, Battle of; Hunter, David; New Market, Battle of; Piedmont, Battle of; Sigel, Franz

Further Reading

Engle, Stephen D. *Yankee Dutchman: The Life of Franz Sigel.* Baton Rouge: Louisiana State University Press, 1999.

Warner, Ezra J. *Generals in Blue: Lives of the Union Commanders.* Baton Rouge: Louisiana State University Press, 2006.

St. Albans, Vermont, Confederate Raid on
Event Date: October 19, 1864

Daring Confederate raid from Canada. The raid took place at the small town of St. Albans, Vermont, not far from the

Canadian border, on October 19, 1864, and was carried out by 21 Confederate soldiers under the command of Lieutenant Bennett H. Young. The goals of the raid were to secure funds for the Confederate war effort and to draw Union troops away from the war fronts in the South. Launched from Canadian soil, the St. Albans raid was the northernmost military engagement of the Civil War.

Young had escaped to Canada from a Union prisoner-of-war camp in the spring of 1864. Once there, he received authorization from the Confederate government to attempt the release of other Confederate detainees. Two such attempts failed, but Young was allowed to lead a raid into a Union town in order to secure funds for the Confederate war effort. He entered Vermont alone, conducted a quick reconnaissance, and selected St. Albans for the operation. Other Confederates joined him, and passing themselves off as travelers, they thoroughly reconnoitered the town, located its four banks and stables, and planned their robberies and escape routes. The remaining Confederate soldiers arrived in twos and threes by different routes and trains, found rooms in a number of local hotels, and waited for the attack order.

The men assembled at 3:00 p.m. on October 19 and then entered the four St. Albans banks and the stable. Shocked residents were forced into the town square. The Confederates secured the considerable sum of $208,000, then escaped to Canada on stolen horses. The raid was well planned, and casualties were low, with one St. Albans man killed and a small number wounded. No Confederate casualties were reported.

Eventually 13 of the raiders, including Young, were apprehended in Canada. American authorities considered entering Canada to secure the men, but such action would have violated British neutrality. The U.S. government demanded their extradition, but Great Britain allowed the Canadian courts to try the raiders. Young and his men were ultimately released by the Canadians on technicalities and soon journeyed to the Confederacy with the stolen cash. Canada, however, agreed to reimburse St. Albans for the lost money and paid $50,000, a sum equal to what was found on those raiders who had been captured.

RICHARD M. MICKLE

See also
Vermont

Further Reading
Kinchen, Oscar A. *Daredevils of the Confederate Army: The Story of the St. Albans Raiders.* Boston: Christopher Publishing House, 1959.
Van Doren Stern, Philip. *Secret Missions of the Civil War.* New York: Wings Books, 1990.

Stanley, David Sloane
Birth Date: June 1, 1828
Death Date: March 13, 1902

Union officer. David Sloane Stanley was born on June 1, 1828, in Cedar Valley, Ohio. He graduated from the U.S. Military Academy, West Point, in 1852. Commissioned a second lieutenant of dragoons, he was assigned to duty in Texas and California. As a captain serving at Fort Washita (Indian Territory) in 1861, Stanley led his men to Fort Leavenworth, Kansas, when the Civil War began. He participated in the Battle of Wilson's Creek (August 10, 1861) and was appointed brigadier general of volunteers on September 28. He then commanded a division in the Battle of Island No. 10 (April 7, 1862), the advance on and siege of Corinth (May 3–30, 1862), the Battle of Iuka (September 19, 1862), and the Battle of Corinth (October 3–4, 1862). In November 1862 Stanley was named chief of cavalry for the Army of the Cumberland. He saw action at the Battle of Stones River (December 31, 1862–January 2, 1863) and in the Tullahoma Campaign (June 23–July 3, 1863). He was promoted to major general in April 1863, to date from November 29, 1862.

Stanley commanded a division and then IV Corps in the Army of the Cumberland during the Atlanta Campaign (May 5–September 2, 1864). He led his corps at the Battle of Jonesboro (August 31–September 1, 1864), where Major General William T. Sherman faulted him for allowing Lieutenant General William J. Hardee to escape entrapment.

Stanley was next sent to Tennessee, under Major General George H. Thomas, to oppose the Confederate army of General John Bell Hood. At the Battle of Franklin (November 30, 1864), Stanley displayed conspicuous gallantry in leading his men in a countercharge and received a serious wound in his neck. He was later awarded the Medal of Honor for his bravery at Franklin. Having been brevetted through major general in the regular army, he mustered out of the volunteers in February 1866.

Following the war, Stanley was appointed colonel of the 22nd U.S. Infantry and served in the Dakota Territory until 1874. His regiment was then sent to Texas to put down an Indian uprising. In 1882 he was assigned command of the District of New Mexico, and in 1884 he was promoted to brigadier general and assigned command of the Department of Texas. He retired in 1892. From 1893 to 1898, he served as governor of the Soldiers' Home in Washington, D.C. Stanley died in Washington, D.C., on March 13, 1902.

ROBERT P. BROADWATER

See also

Atlanta Campaign; Corinth, Battle of; Corinth, Mississippi, Siege of; Franklin, Battle of; Island No. 10, Battle of; Jonesboro, Battle of; Stones River, Battle of; Tullahoma Campaign; Wilson's Creek, Battle of

Further Reading

Fitch, John. *Annals of the Army of the Cumberland.* Mechanicsburg, PA: Stackpole, 2003.

Stanley, David Sloane. *An American General: The Memoirs of David Sloane Stanley.* Santa Barbara, CA: Narrative Press, 2003.

_____

Stanley, Henry Morton
Birth Date: January 28, 1841
Death Date: May 10, 1904

Confederate soldier, Union soldier and sailor, and famous international journalist, explorer, and adventurer. Henry Morton Stanley was born John Rowlands on January 28, 1841, in Denbigh, Wales. In 1859 he became a cabin boy on the *Windermere,* bound for New Orleans. On arrival in the United States, Rowlands was befriended by a local merchant, Henry Hope Stanley, whose first and last names he adopted (he added Morton later).

Henry Morton Stanley was in Arkansas in 1861 running one of his surrogate father's stores when the American Civil War began. Enlisting in the 6th Arkansas Infantry, he fought in the Battle of Shiloh (April 6–7, 1862), where he was captured and transferred to Camp Douglas, Illinois. He was released two months later only after agreeing to join the Union Army. Ill from his time in prison, Stanley was discharged after only a few weeks of service and returned to England in November 1862. The following year, he went back to the United States and enlisted in the U.S. Navy. Stanley saw action during the Fort Fisher Campaign (December 13, 1864–January 15, 1865).

Stanley became famous around the world beginning in the late 1860s. He traveled the far reaches of the globe and was a merchant marine, a special correspondent for the *New York Evening Post,* and a longtime reporter for the *New York Herald.* He led a medical missionary trip into the interior of Africa and an expedition to locate the source of the Nile River, and he explored the African Congo. Stanley published a number of best-selling books detailing his exploits, but he is perhaps best known for having located the long-missing English missionary David Livingstone in a village near Africa's Lake Tanganyika in November 1871. When Stanley spotted the missionary, he purportedly asked, "Dr. Livingstone, I presume?" The words made Stanley an instant celebrity. He was involved in a host of organizations and sat in Parliament (1895–1900).

Stanley was later much criticized for unleashing violence upon the natives in the Congo, including alleged atrocities. His exploits provided the foundation for Joseph Conrad's *Heart of Darkness.* In failing health, Stanley died in London on May 10, 1904.

MELISSA STALLINGS

See also

Fort Fisher Campaign; Journalism; Shiloh, Battle of

Further Reading

Bierman, John. *Dark Safari: The Life behind the Legend of Henry Morton Stanley.* New York: Knopf, 1990.

Hochschild, Adam. *King Leopold's Ghost: A Story of Greed, Terror, and Heroism in Colonial Africa.* New York: Houghton Mifflin, 1998.

_____

Stanly, Edward
Birth Date: January 10, 1810
Death Date: July 12, 1872

Politician and Union military governor of North Carolina (1862–1863). Born in New Bern, North Carolina, on January 10, 1810, in 1829 Edward Stanly graduated from the American Literary, Scientific, and Military Academy (which became Norwich University in 1834). He then studied law, was admitted to the state bar in 1832, and opened a law office in Washington, North Carolina. Entering politics as a member of the Whig Party, Stanly was elected to the U.S. House of Representatives in 1836, where he served from 1837 to 1843.

After his district was gerrymandered and he was defeated for reelection, Stanly represented Beaufort County in the state legislature (1844–1846), served as state attorney general (1847), and then again was a member of the state legislature (1848–1849). After another two terms in the U.S. House of Representatives (1849–1853), Stanly left North Carolina and went to California, where he established a law practice.

In April 1862, Stanly was surprised when he received notice that he was appointed military governor of North Carolina, effective May 26, 1862. U.S. secretary of war Edwin Stanton informed Stanly that he would act as governor until loyal citizens could organize a new government that conformed to the U.S. Constitution. Stanly was also to uphold existing laws and support loyalists in Union-occupied parts of eastern North Carolina.

Stanly's tenure as military governor was marked by controversy, as he tried to return escaped slaves to masters who professed loyalty to the Union and questioned schools that were educating blacks, which was still illegal in North Carolina. Confederate authorities simply ignored Stanly and sent all official communications to Union military officers. When President Abraham Lincoln announced the Emancipation Proclamation in January 1863, Stanly offered to resign. Lincoln initially refused, but Stanly was insistent and finally left office on March 2, 1863.

Stanly then returned to California and resumed his law practice. He died in San Francisco on July 12, 1872.

RICHARD A. SAUERS

See also
North Carolina

Further Reading
Brown, Norman D. *Edward Stanly: Whiggery's Tarheel "Conqueror."* Tuscaloosa: University of Alabama Press, 1974.
Harris, William C. "Lincoln and Wartime Reconstruction in North Carolina, 1861–1863." *North Carolina Historical Review* 63 (1986): 149–168.

Stannard, George Jerrison
Birth Date: October 20, 1820
Death Date: June 1, 1886

Union officer. George Jerrison Stannard was born on October 20, 1820, in Georgia, Vermont. He worked as a farmer, schoolteacher, and foundry operator law clerk. When the Civil War began in 1861, Stannard was serving as colonel of the 4th Regiment of Vermont's state militia. In June 1861 he became lieutenant colonel of the 2nd Vermont Volunteer Infantry, leading the unit at the First Battle of Bull Run (July 21, 1861) and during the Peninsula Campaign (March–July 1862).

On July 9, 1862, Stannard was appointed colonel of the 9th Vermont Volunteer Infantry. During the Antietam Campaign (September 4–20, 1862), the 9th Vermont was among approximately 12,000 Union troops occupying the federal arsenal at Harpers Ferry, Virginia. On September 15, 1862, the 9th Vermont, along with the rest of the Union force there, became prisoners when Colonel Dixon S. Miles surrendered Harpers Ferry to the Confederates. Stannard was exchanged in January 1863.

On March 11, 1863, Stannard was appointed brigadier general of volunteers and given command of the 2nd Vermont Brigade, Army of the Potomac. Stannard's brigade helped to repulse Pickett's Charge at Gettysburg on July 3, 1863. Stannard was wounded in the fighting that day but remained on the field to command his men. After he recovered, he joined the Army of the James in eastern Virginia. During an attack on Fort Harrison (September 29–30, 1864), he was wounded in his right arm, which resulted in its amputation. On October 28, 1864, Stannard was brevetted major general of volunteers. For the remainder of the war, he was assigned administrative duty in Vermont.

After the war, Stannard served with the Freedmen's Bureau before resigning from the army in June 1866. He thereafter worked as a customs official and from 1881 until his death was the doorkeeper for the U.S. House of Representatives. Stannard died in Washington, D.C., on June 1, 1886.

JENNIFER M. MURRAY

See also
Antietam Campaign; Bull Run, First Battle of; Gettysburg, Battle of; Harpers Ferry, Virginia; James, Union Army of the; Peninsula Campaign

Further Reading
Eicher, John H., and David J. Eicher. *Civil War High Commands.* Stanford, CA: Stanford University Press, 2001.
Warner, Ezra J. *Generals in Blue: Lives of the Union Commanders.* Baton Rouge: Louisiana State University Press, 2006.

Stanton, Edwin McMasters
Birth Date: December 19, 1819
Death Date: December 24, 1869

U.S. attorney general and secretary of war. Edwin McMasters Stanton was born in Steubenville, Ohio, on December 19, 1819. He attended Kenyon College for two years and then studied law on his own under the tutelage of an attorney in Columbus. Stanton was admitted to the Ohio bar in 1836.

Having practiced law successfully in both Ohio and Pennsylvania, Stanton moved to Washington, D.C. Indeed, his work as a federal government special counsel tasked with litigating bogus land claims in California caught the attention of the James Buchanan administration. In December 1860, President Buchanan appointed Stanton attorney general of the United States. When Abraham Lincoln became president in March 1861, Stanton left his post.

On January 15, 1862, Lincoln appointed Stanton secretary of war following Simon Cameron's resignation on charges of

Staunch defender of the Union, Edwin M. Stanton served in Abraham Lincoln's cabinet as secretary of war. A fine administrator, Stanton created a highly efficient War Department and as such played an important role in the Union victory. (National Archives)

mismanagement and corruption. A strong defender of the Union and an ardent patriot, Stanton eagerly accepted the offer, even though his salary went from a then-astronomical $45,000 per year to $8,000 per year as a cabinet officer.

During the Civil War, Stanton was a major force within the War Department. He reorganized the way in which it did business by establishing stringent guidelines governing the system of competition for contracts. He also established the policy for regulating the Union railroad system and placed all telegraph operations under the department's control. Not surprisingly, his drive for efficiency and honesty made him as many enemies as friends. Nevertheless, his formidable administrative skills impressed friend and foe alike.

Stanton played a key role in the appointment and removal of Union Army commanders. The most celebrated instance of this came when he requested that his former friend, Major General George McClellan, be relieved of his command for repeated failures to take the offensive. Stanton oversaw all military operations and, along with Lincoln, helped shaped Union military strategy. Stanton also pressured the

president to issue the Emancipation Proclamation and to enlist African American troops.

In 1864 Stanton left the Democratic Party and became a Republican. The assassination of Lincoln shocked Stanton, despite a rather testy relationship between the two men by that time. Stanton briefly assumed control of the government until Vice President Andrew Johnson took the oath of office on April 15, 1865.

When Reconstruction began, Stanton remained as head of the War Department and oversaw the demobilization of the Union armies. At first, he supported Johnson's more lenient Reconstruction policy until reports of violence against freedmen became known. With U.S. Army commanding general Ulysses S. Grant at his side, Stanton tried to convince Johnson to accept Congress's Reconstruction plan and even supported Johnson's veto of the Tenure of Office Act.

Johnson's ultimate refusal to change his views on Reconstruction policies forced Stanton into an alliance with congressional members, and Johnson's opposition to the First and Second Reconstruction Acts pushed him to support more radical policies. With Grant, Stanton drafted the Third Reconstruction Act, which removed the armies in the South from the president's control. When Johnson demanded that Stanton resign, the secretary of war refused. On August 11, 1867, Johnson replaced him with Grant. Congress, however, promptly ordered Stanton restored to his office under the terms of the Tenure of Office Act. Grant immediately stepped down, and Stanton resumed his duties. In February 1868, Johnson again sought to replace Stanton, causing Stanton to blockade himself in his office. Meanwhile, on February 22, 1868, the House of Representatives voted to impeach Johnson for violating the Tenure of Office Act.

Throughout the impeachment proceedings, Stanton remained in office. After the Senate acquitted Johnson, Stanton resigned on May 26, 1868, and returned to private life. When a seat on the U.S. Supreme Court became available in 1869, President Ulysses S. Grant appointed Stanton to the post in appreciation for his friendship and service. Before he could assume his place on the Supreme Court, however, Stanton died of an asthma attack on December 24, 1869, in Washington, D.C.

CHARLES F. HOWLETT

See also

Cameron, Simon; Emancipation Proclamation; Grant, Ulysses Simpson; Johnson, Andrew; Lincoln, Abraham; Lincoln's Reconstruction Policies; McClellan, George Brinton; Reconstruction

Further Reading

Goodwin, Doris K. *Team of Rivals: The Political Genius of Abraham Lincoln.* New York: Simon and Schuster, 2005.

McKitrick, Eric L. *Andrew Johnson and Reconstruction.* New York: Oxford University Press, 1988.

Thomas, Benjamin P., and Harold M. Hyman. *Stanton: The Life and Times of Lincoln's Secretary of War.* New York: Knopf, 1962.

Stanton, Elizabeth Cady
Birth Date: November 12, 1815
Death Date: October 26, 1902

Abolitionist and a leading figure in the early women's rights movement. Elizabeth Cady was born on November 12, 1815, in Johnstown, New York. Her father was a prominent attorney, and she was well educated at the Johnstown Academy until she was 16 years old, winning numerous academic awards and honors. She married Henry Brewer Stanton in 1840.

Elizabeth Cady Stanton is credited with initiating the women's rights and suffrage movement at Seneca Falls, New York, in 1848, where she presented her "Declaration

One of the more radical of the 19th-century suffragists and women's rights leaders, Elizabeth Cady Stanton sought to free women from the legal obstacles that prevented them from achieving equality with men. (Library of Congress)

of Sentiments." Stanton's activism extended well beyond suffrage; she was also concerned with various other legal protections and rights for women, including women's parental and custody rights, property rights, employment and income rights, and divorce laws. Stanton was committed to the abolition of slavery and often worked closely with her abolitionist husband and her cousin Gerrit Smith, also an ardent abolitionist.

In the aftermath of the Civil War, Stanton and Susan B. Anthony ardently expressed their commitment to women's suffrage and refused to support passage of the Fourteenth Amendment to the Constitution (adopted in 1868 and designed chiefly to grant basic rights to former slaves). They also would not support the Fifteenth Amendment (adopted in 1870 and designed to regulate voting rights for former slaves). Their stance caused a schism in the women's rights movement. Their opposition was based on the argument that while the amendments granted legal protections and suffrage to black males, the same rights were not extended to women, be they white or black.

Stanton remained a leading women's rights activist throughout her life, traveling widely, penning many influential essays, and lecturing extensively on women's rights. She died on October 26, 1902, in New York City.

ANDREW BYERS

See also

Abolitionism and the Civil War; Anthony, Susan Brownell; Fifteenth Amendment; Fourteenth Amendment; Women

Further Reading

Baker, Jean H. *Sisters: The Lives of America's Suffragists.* New York: Hill and Wang, 2005.

Stanton, Elizabeth Cady. *The Elizabeth Cady Stanton–Susan B. Anthony Reader: Correspondence, Writings, Speeches.* Boston: Northeastern University Press, 1992.

Ward, Geoffrey C. *Not for Ourselves Alone: The Story of Elizabeth Cady Stanton and Susan B. Anthony; An Illustrated History.* New York: Knopf, 1999.

Starke, Peter Burwell
Birth Date: 1815
Death Date: July 13, 1888

Confederate officer. Born in Brunswick County, Virginia, sometime in 1815, Peter Burwell Starke and his brothers operated a stage line until he moved to Bolivar County, Mississippi, in the 1840s. He served in the Mississippi House of Representatives (1846–1854) and was elected in 1856 to the Mississippi Senate, which he left in February 1862 when he was appointed colonel of the 28th Mississippi Cavalry Regiment.

In 1862 and early 1863, Starke served in the defense of Vicksburg, and he and his regiment operated mostly in northern Mississippi, skirmishing with Union forces and providing intelligence to Lieutenant General John C. Pemberton at Vicksburg. After the fall of that city on July 4, 1863, Starke participated in Confederate general Joseph E. Johnston's unsuccessful defense of Jackson, Mississippi (July 10–16, 1863). Into the spring of 1864, Starke commanded first his regiment and then a brigade in the cavalry division commanded by Brigadier General William H. Jackson in various redesignated commands in Mississippi and adjacent states.

In the summer of 1864, Jackson's division was transferred to the Army of Tennessee, and Starke fought in the Atlanta Campaign (May 5–September 2, 1864). Starke was advanced to brigadier general on November 4, 1864. He then saw action during the Franklin and Nashville Campaign (November 29–December 27, 1864). Starke also led his brigade in Alabama in the closing months of the war before surrendering on May 6, 1865.

Following the war, Starke was on the board of the Mississippi levee commission and served one term as sheriff of Bolivar County. He returned to Virginia in 1873 and died there in Lawrenceville on July 13, 1888. His brother, William Edwin Starke, also served as a Confederate brigadier general but was mortally wounded in the Battle of Antietam (September 17, 1862).

PHILIP L. BOLTÉ AND PAUL G. PIERPAOLI JR.

See also

Atlanta Campaign; Franklin and Nashville Campaign; Jackson, Mississippi, Siege of; Vicksburg Campaign, Second

Further Reading

Eicher, John H., and David J. Eicher. *Civil War High Commands.* Stanford, CA: Stanford University Press, 2001.

Warner, Ezra J. *Generals in Gray: Lives of the Confederate Commanders.* Baton Rouge: Louisiana State University Press, 2006.

Starke, William Edward
Birth Date: 1814
Death Date: September 17, 1862

Confederate officer. Born in Brunswick County, Virginia, in 1814, William Edward Starke was the elder brother of future Confederate general Peter B. Starke. After operating with his brothers a stage line between Lawrenceville and Petersburg,

Virginia, William Starke moved to Louisiana, where he became a successful cotton broker.

In June 1861, Starke secured a commission as a lieutenant colonel in the 53rd Virginia Infantry. He first served as a staff officer for Brigadier General Robert S. Garnett in western Virginia. In August, Starke was aide-de-camp to General Robert E. Lee. Starke was appointed colonel of the 60th Virginia Infantry on October 12, 1861. He was wounded in fighting at Glendale, Virginia, on June 30, 1862, during the Seven Days' Campaign (June 25–July 1). In late July 1862, Starke took command of the 2nd Louisiana Brigade in Major General Thomas J. "Stonewall" Jackson's former division of II Corps in the Army of Northern Virginia.

Promoted to brigadier general on August 6, 1862, Starke took part in the Second Battle of Bull Run (August 29–30) and assumed command of the Stonewall Division following the wounding of Brigadier General William B. Taliaferro. Starke took part in Lee's Antietam Campaign (September 4–20, 1862) and the capture of Harpers Ferry (September 12–15, 1862). During the Battle of Antietam (September 17, 1862), Starke again assumed command of the division and led it into action but that morning was struck by three bullets and died an hour later.

SPENCER C. TUCKER

See also

Antietam, Battle of; Antietam Campaign; Bull Run, Second Battle of; Harpers Ferry, Battle of; Jackson, Thomas Jonathan; Lee, Robert Edward; Taliaferro, William Booth

Further Reading

Eicher, John H., and David J. Eicher. *Civil War High Commands.* Stanford, CA: Stanford University Press, 2001.

Sears, Stephen. *Landscape Turned Red: The Battle of Antietam.* New York: Ticknor and Fields, 1983.

Warner, Ezra J. *Generals in Gray: Lives of the Confederate Commanders.* Baton Rouge: Louisiana State University Press, 2006.

Star of the West, USS

A two-deck 1,172-ton side-wheel schooner-rigged U.S. ship that entered service in 1852. Originally the *San Juan,* the ship was built by Jeremiah Simonson at Greenpoint (Brooklyn), New York, for shipping tycoon Cornelius Vanderbilt. The ship made regular runs between New York City and Nicaragua before Vanderbilt sold it in 1856 to Marshall O. Roberts of New York.

Following the secession of South Carolina on December 20, 1860, Major Robert Anderson had concentrated his small U.S. Army detachment in Charleston at Fort Sumter

Artist's depiction of the steamer *Star of the West*, approaching Fort Sumter in Charleston Harbor with reinforcements for the Union garrison there, January 9, 1861. (Library of Congress)

in Charleston Harbor. Fort Sumter was soon under siege by South Carolina and eventually by Confederate forces, who demanded its surrender. Fort Sumter was also running low on supplies. President James Buchanan finally agreed that something had to be done to supply the garrison. Plans to send the heavily armed screw sloop *Brooklyn* were rejected as too provocative, but Buchanan approved the dispatch of a merchant ship instead. Roberts chartered the *Star of the West* to the War Department for this mission.

Captained by John McGowan, the *Star of the West* sailed from New York City on January 5, 1861, with supplies and 200 reinforcements. Efforts to keep this operation secret failed when the Northern press published news of the ship's sailing and its intended mission. This information was telegraphed to Charleston.

When early on January 9 the *Star of the West* arrived off Charleston Harbor and attempted to reach Fort Sumter, cadets of the Military College of South Carolina (the Citadel), manning batteries at Fort Moultrie and Morris Island, opened fire on the ship in the first hostile shots of the Civil War. After a shot across its bow, the *Star of the West* ran up a large American flag. This failed to deter the gunners, whose fire hulled the ship twice. His ship moderately damaged, McGowan returned to New York. Buchanan refused to consider this an act of war, as no blood had been shed.

Three months later, the *Star of the West* was again chartered by the federal government to repatriate Union soldiers held by Confederate authorities near Indianola, Texas, but on April 19, 1861, the ship was captured by the Confederate steamer *General Rusk*. Renamed the *St. Philip*, it was employed by the Confederates as both a hospital ship and a receiving ship at New Orleans.

With the impending capture of New Orleans in the early spring of 1862 by Union forces, the *St. Philip* was moved upriver with Confederate specie, which it delivered to Vicksburg, Mississippi. The ship was then moved to the Yazoo

River. The Confederates scuttled the *St. Philip* in the Talla-hatchie River on March 11, 1863, to block the ships of the Mississippi Squadron, under the command of Union rear admiral David D. Porter, during the Yazoo Pass Expedition.

ROBERT A. LYNN AND SPENCER C. TUCKER

See also

Anderson, Robert; Buchanan, James; Fort Sumter, South Carolina, U.S. Efforts to Relieve; Mississippi Squadron, U.S. Navy; New Orleans Campaign; Porter, David Dixon; Yazoo Pass Expedition

Further Reading

Garrison, Webb. *Lincoln's Little War: How His Carefully Crafted Plans Went Astray.* Nashville: Rutledge Hill, 1997.

Tucker, Spencer C. *Blue and Gray Navies: The Civil War Afloat.* Annapolis, MD: Naval Institute Press, 2006.

U.S. Navy Department, Naval History Division. *Civil War Naval Chronology, 1861–1865.* Washington, DC: U.S. Government Printing Office, 1971.

Steamships

Ships powered by steam engines. Steam power applied to ship propulsion brought about revolutionary changes in naval strategy, tactics, and organization. Steam engines augmented and later replaced the masts, sails, and rigging used by mariners for centuries to harness the power of the wind. Once reliable and efficient steam propulsion systems were developed, faster and larger ships were constructed for both commercial and military purposes and were capable of carrying unprecedented cargo payloads and armaments.

Steam propulsion first proved its value on inland waterways, where winds were unreliable and human effort often had to be harnessed to move boats against strong currents. Frenchman Marquis Claude de Jouffroy d'Abbans is credited with building the first steam-powered boat. Launched in 1783, his *Pyroscaphe* could operate for only a few minutes as it struggled to overcome the current of the Sâone River near Lyons where it was tested. Improvements to the design of steam engines by Thomas Newcomen, James Watt, Oliver Evans, and Richard Trevithick were quickly applied to naval propulsion, and in 1790 American John Fitch built a steam launch that could attain a speed of eight miles per hour and reliably navigate the Delaware River between Philadelphia and Burlington, New Jersey. In 1807 Robert Fulton constructed the *Clermont*, a 150-foot-long paddlewheel ship that is widely acknowledged as the first practical and economical vessel powered by steam. The first transatlantic crossing by a ship equipped with a steam engine occurred in 1819 when

the 350-ton *Savannah*, fitted with a side-mounted paddlewheel, traveled from Georgia to St. Petersburg, Russia, in 50 days, using both steam and sails.

As increasing numbers of steam vessels were built, side- and rear-mounted paddlewheel ships (paddlers) proved to be slow, inefficient, and subject to breakdowns that were difficult to repair on the open ocean. Sailing ships thus continued their dominance until the mid-19th century.

Compound engines, first introduced in 1854, ran multiple pistons connected to a single crankshaft and, when used aboard ship, greatly increased the mechanical power output of a steam propulsion system. Coupled with advances in metallurgy applied to the design of boilers that increased the maximum safe operating pressure of the superheated water that drove the pistons to generate power, compound engines extended the cruising range and increased the maximum speed of steamships to match the performance of sailing vessels. Other engine improvements soon followed. These included condensers, which lengthened the working life of steam engines by reducing mineral deposits from the seawater supply that fed the boilers; double expansion engines, which conserved water and fuel during engine operation; and triple- and quadruple-expansion engines, which further improved the efficiency and power output of shipboard steam propulsion systems.

Despite early successes with steam propulsion, considerable time elapsed before the steam engine found favor with conservative naval authorities responsible for warship design and construction; early steam warships were consigned to harbor defense and coastal patrol duties on account of unreliable engines, small size, and minimal armament. The U.S. Navy was the first navy in the world with a steam-powered warship. Robert Fulton's *Demologus* (later the *Fulton*) of 1815 was a catamaran with a central paddlewheel located between thick twin hulls to protect it from enemy fire. It was essentially a floating battery that mounted powerful guns behind thick bulwarks. Specifically intended to defend New York Harbor, under steam power it could move about at 5.5 knots. In 1837 with other navies experimenting with steam, the U.S. Navy launched a second steam warship, the *Fulton II.*

Because early steam engines were so inefficient and relatively little fuel could be carried, steam warships retained sail rigs, a practice continued well past the Civil War, indeed to the end of the 19th century. In 1842 the U.S. Navy took a temporary lead over other navies with its side-wheelers *Mississippi* and *Missouri.* While the *Missouri* succumbed to fire in 1843, the *Mississippi* had an exceptional service record, proving the value of steam propulsion in warships during the Mexican-American War (1846–1848) and serving as the flagship of Commodore Matthew C. Perry's squadron in the opening of Japan. The *Mississippi* remained in service well into the Civil War, when it was destroyed in March 1863 by Confederate shore batteries at Port Hudson, Louisiana.

The screw propeller, credited both to Francis Petit Smith of England and John Ericsson of Sweden, helped overcome many of the objections to steam propulsion for warships. More efficient than the paddlewheel because the entire propeller remained underwater, it was also protected from enemy fire. The U.S. Navy steam sloop *Princeton* of 1843 was the world's first propeller-driven warship. It incorporated a number of other firsts, including being the first warship with its machinery below the waterline (where it would be protected from enemy shot). Ericsson designed its power plant and propeller. The *Princeton* also incorporated the change to an armament of fewer and more powerful guns capable of firing both spherical shot and explosive shell. In tests between paddlewheel- and propeller-driven ships, the latter proved superior. Despite the shortcomings of early steam propulsion, even traditionalists among the naval officers came to appreciate the ability of steam as an auxiliary power source for maneuvering in conditions of contrary wind or no wind at all.

The new warfare waged under steam power brought new demands and new hazards. The fire room on a typical large Civil War steam warship had four vertical boilers, each of which held four furnaces. To achieve a speed of five knots without sails, the four boilers would consume as much as 3,400 pounds of anthracite coal per hour. To sustain a speed of six knots, a Cairo-class river ironclad consumed 2,000 pounds of coal per hour. Regardless of training, there was no way to prepare for a boiler explosion or ruptured steam tubes. During the Battle of Plum Point Bend (May 10, 1862) on the Mississippi River, Union rifled shells smashed into the boilers of three Confederate steamers, disabling them and releasing clouds of steam that killed more than 100 Confederates.

Despite problems, the number of steam warships continued to multiply. In March 1861, the U.S. Navy had only 90 ships, 42 of which were actually in commission. Twenty-three of these were steamers; the other 19 relied entirely on the wind for their propulsion. By the end of the war, the U.S. Navy had 671 vessels of all types. It counted 113 screw steamers and 52 paddle-wheeler steamers especially constructed for naval purposes; 71 ironclads; 323 steamers, either purchased or captured, fitted for naval purposes; and

112 sailing vessels of all kinds. The vast majority of ships in the Union fleet, 559 ships, were steam-powered.

By the 1890s, highly efficient steam engines were being installed on a new generation of large warships fitted with steel armor and long-range rifled guns arranged in turrets that were turned with steam shunted from the engine boiler. These new ships were faster, more maneuverable, and more powerful than their wood and iron predecessors. Improvements continued, including the steam turbine engine and the marine diesel engine.

SHANNON ALLEN BROWN AND SPENCER C. TUCKER

See also

Cairo-Class River Ironclads, U.S. Navy; Ericsson, John; Mississippi River; Plum Point Bend, Battle of

Further Reading

Bennett, Frank M. *The Steam Navy of the United States.* Pittsburgh, PA: Press of W. T. Nicholson, 1898.
Gardiner, Robert, ed. *Steam, Steel, and Shellfire: The Steam Warship, 1815–1905.* Annapolis, MD: Naval Institute Press, 1992.
Rowland, K. T. *Steam at Sea: A History of Steam Navigation.* New York: Praeger, 1970.

Stearns, George Luther
Birth Date: January 8, 1809
Death Date: April 9, 1867

Industrialist, abolitionist, and army recruiter. George Luther Stearns was born on January 8, 1809, in Medford, Massachusetts. In 1818, his father died. Six years later, the 15-year-old Stearns abandoned his educational pursuits to help support his mother and siblings by taking a job as a dry goods store clerk. He went on to become a wealthy merchant and industrialist. Much of his wealth came from manufacturing flexible pile lead.

A religious man, Stearns was raised as a Calvinist before accepting Unitarianism. Like many Christian philanthropists, he advocated social reform, most notably temperance. In the 1840s he also embraced abolitionism and subsequently participated in the Underground Railroad, creating the Medford station. In 1848 he supported the Free Soil Movement. After implementation of the 1854 Kansas-Nebraska Act, Stearns gave liberally to the New England Emigrant Aid Company and became director of the Massachusetts Kansas Aid Company in an attempt to make Kansas a free state. He also joined five other radical reformers in a secret committee to fund John Brown's 1859 raid on Harpers Ferry, Virginia. Stearns had the distinction of being

Brown's greatest financial backer, supplying him with 200 Sharps rifles.

During the Civil War, Stearns worked tirelessly to advance his abolitionist principles. Believing that black soldiers were instrumental in advancing racial equality, Stearns played a key role in recruiting the 54th and 55th Massachusetts Colored Infantry Regiments and the 5th U.S. Colored Cavalry. In the summer of 1863, Secretary of War Edwin L. Stanton named Stearns the assistant adjutant general for the recruitment of African American troops, with the rank of major. Stearns oversaw the recruitment of more than 13,000 African American troops and helped to aid their families. After the war, he helped found the Freedmen's Bureau. Stearns died on April 9, 1867, in New York City.

KEVIN P. S. TANNER JR.

See also

Abolitionism and the Civil War; African Americans; African American Soldiers, U.S.; Brown, John; 54th Massachusetts Regiment of Infantry; Kansas-Nebraska Act

Further Reading

Heller, Charles E. *Portrait of an Abolitionist: A Biography of George Luther Stearns, 1809–1867.* Westport, CT: Greenwood, 1996.

Stearns, Frank Preston. *The Life and Public Services of George Luther Stearns.* Philadelphia: Lippincott, 1907.

Steedman, James Blair
Birth Date: July 29, 1817
Death Date: October 18, 1883

Union officer. James Blair Steedman was born in Northumberland County, Pennsylvania, on July 29, 1817. He had little formal education. Orphaned at age 15 when both his parents died, he became a printer. In 1835 he joined the Republic of Texas Army and fought in the Texas War of Independence (1835–1836). He moved to Ohio and began publishing the *Northwest Democrat* newspaper in 1838. Incredibly diversified, he then became a successful contractor involved in canal and railroad construction. Beginning in 1847, Steedman served two terms in the Ohio General Assembly. He then worked as a railroad conductor before going to California in 1849 to prospect for gold. Returning to Ohio, he served on the state board for public works (1852–1857). He was also admitted to the state bar and opened a law practice in Toledo. He became editor of the *North-Western Democrat* and the *Toledo Times* and a major general in the Ohio Militia in 1857. He also held a printing contract with the U.S. government (1856–1860). Steedman was a delegate to the 1860 Democratic National Convention, where he supported Stephen Douglas, and in 1860 Steedman ran unsuccessfully for the U.S. House of Representatives.

With the beginning of the Civil War, Steedman raised the 90-day 14th Ohio Infantry and was elected its colonel on April 27, 1861. The 14th Ohio first saw action in western Virginia (present-day West Virginia) in the Battle of Philippi (June 3, 1861). Steedman remained colonel of the 14th Ohio, which reenlisted as a three-year regiment on September 1, 1861.

Steedman's regiment was ordered to the western theater and took part in the Battle of Mill Springs (January 19, 1862) in Kentucky and in the Siege of Corinth (May 3–30, 1862) in Mississippi. Advanced to brigadier general of volunteers on July 17, 1862, Steedman assumed command of a brigade in the Army of the Ohio. He distinguished himself in the Battle of Perryville (October 8) and the Battle of Stones River (December 31, 1862–January 2, 1863) as well as during the Tullahoma Campaign (June 23–July 3, 1863).

Steedman was a hero of the Battle of Chickamauga (September 19–20, 1863). Commanding a division in the Reserve Corps of the Army of the Cumberland, he played a key role in staving off a Union disaster when his men arrived just in time to prevent Major General George H. Thomas's XIV Corps from being swept from the field. Steedman commanded the post of Chattanooga during the Chattanooga Campaign (October–November 1863) and until May 1864. Promoted to major general of volunteers in April 1864, he commanded the District of Etowah, Department of the Cumberland, from June to November 1864, in which role he supported Major General William T. Sherman's advance on Atlanta (May–September) and his March to the Sea (November–December).

Rushed to Nashville during Confederate general J. B. Hood's invasion of Tennessee, Steedman commanded 11 regiments of troops totaling some 5,200 men in the Battle of Nashville (December 15–16, 1864) and again distinguished himself. During June–December 1865, he commanded the Department of Georgia. He resigned from the army on August 18, 1866, and became collector of internal revenue at New Orleans (1866–1869). Returning to Toledo, he became editor of the *Northern Ohio Democrat,* and in 1870 he was elected to the Ohio Senate. In 1883 Steedman was appointed Toledo chief of police, holding that position until his death in Toledo on October 18, 1883.

SPENCER C. TUCKER

See also

Chattanooga Campaign; Chickamauga, Battle of; Corinth, Mississippi, Siege of; Mill Springs, Battle of; Nashville, Battle of; Perryville, Battle of; Philippi, Battle of; Stones River, Battle of; Thomas, George Henry

Further Reading
Eicher, John H., and David J. Eicher. *Civil War High Commands.* Stanford, CA: Stanford University Press, 2001.
Warner, Ezra J. *Generals in Blue: Lives of the Union Commanders.* Baton Rouge: Louisiana State University Press, 2006.
Woodworth, Steven. *The Chickamauga Campaign.* Carbondale: Southern Illinois University Press, 2010.

Steele, Frederick
Birth Date: January 14, 1819
Death Date: January 12, 1868

Union officer. Frederick Steele was born in Delhi, New York, on January 14, 1819. He graduated from the U.S. Military Academy, West Point, in 1843 in the class that included Ulysses S. Grant. Following garrison duty in New York and Michigan, Steele saw service in the Mexican-American War (1846–1848) and was brevetted first lieutenant on August 20, 1847, for his role in the Battle of Contreras and to captain on September 13 for the Battle of Chapultepec. Promoted to first lieutenant on June 6, 1848, Steele was advanced to captain on February 5, 1855, and was stationed in California, Minnesota, Nebraska, and Kansas. In 1861 he was at Fort Leavenworth.

With the beginning of the Civil War, Steele was promoted to major in the 11th Infantry on May 14, 1861, and assigned to the Army of the West. His first important action came in the Battle of Wilson's Creek (August 10, 1861) in Missouri. He was appointed colonel of the 8th Iowa Infantry on September 23 and took command of a brigade in the 5th Division of the Army of the West. Steele was promoted to brigadier general of volunteers on January 29, 1862, and assigned to the District of Southwest Missouri. In May he assumed command of the 1st Division, Army of the Southwest, and took part in the Arkansas Campaign in 1862 that saw the occupation of Helena.

Steele took command of a division in Major General William T. Sherman's XIII Corps, Army of the Tennessee, on December 13, 1862, and took part in the Battle of Chickasaw Bluffs (December 26–29, 1862) and in the capture of Fort Hindman/Arkansas Post (January 9–11, 1863). Steele was promoted to major general of volunteers on March 17, 1863, with date of rank of November 29, 1862. During the Second Vicksburg Campaign (April 1–July 4, 1863), Steele commanded the 1st Division in XV Corps.

Following the capture of Vicksburg, Steele was given charge of U.S. forces in Arkansas (VII Corps) and ordered to clear the state of Confederate forces. He captured Little Rock

on September 10, 1863. The next spring he was ordered to cooperate with Major General Nathaniel P. Banks in the Red River Campaign (March 10–May 22, 1864) by driving on Shreveport from Little Rock. Both Banks and Steele were late in setting out, and the campaign was a fiasco. Steele's force was driven back to Little Rock, but in the Battle of Jenkins' Ferry (April 30), he managed to get most of his command across the Sabine River.

On March 13, 1865, Steele was brevetted brigadier general in the U.S. Army for Little Rock and major general in the U.S. Army for Vicksburg. In the spring of 1865, he commanded a division in the Siege of Mobile (March 25–April 12). During June and July, he commanded the Western District of Texas.

Steele remained in the army after the war and was appointed colonel of the 20th Infantry on July 28, 1866. That October, he was assigned command of the Department of the Columbia. He mustered out of the Volunteers on January 1, 1867. Steele died on January 12, 1868, from injuries sustained in a horse and buggy accident while on leave in San Mateo, California.

SPENCER C. TUCKER

See also
Banks, Nathaniel Prentice; Chickasaw Bluffs, Battle of; Fort Hindman, Battle of; Grant, Ulysses Simpson; Little Rock Campaign; Mobile, Alabama, Siege of; Red River Campaign; Sherman, William Tecumseh; Wilson's Creek, Battle of

Further Reading
Eicher, John H., and David J. Eicher. *Civil War High Commands.* Stanford, CA: Stanford University Press, 2001.
Warner, Ezra J. *Generals in Blue: Lives of the Union Commanders.* Baton Rouge: Louisiana State University Press, 2006.

Steele, William
Birth Date: May 1, 1819
Death Date: January 12, 1885

Confederate officer. Born in Albany, New York, on May 1, 1819, William Steele graduated from the U.S. Military Academy, West Point, in 1840 and was assigned to the 2nd Dragoons, earning promotion to first lieutenant in 1846. He took part in the Mexican-American War (1846–1848) and was brevetted first lieutenant for his role in the Battles of Contreras and Churubusco. He was promoted to captain in 1851.

Much of Steele's pre–Civil War service was in Texas, and he married into a Texas family in 1850. With the beginning of the Civil War, Steele resigned his U.S. Army commission on May 30, 1861. He was commissioned colonel of the

7th Texas Cavalry on October 29 and took part in Brigadier General Henry Hopkins Sibley's New Mexico Campaign (November 1861–May 1862).

Appointed brigadier general with date of rank from September 12, 1862, Steele commanded Confederate forces in Indian Territory (Oklahoma) in 1863. In 1864 he took charge of the defenses of Galveston, Texas, and also participated in the Red River Campaign (March 10–May 22, 1864), fighting as a part of Major General Richard Taylor's command and winning plaudits for his role in the Battle of Pleasant Hill (April 9, 1864) in Louisiana. When Brigadier General Thomas Green was killed in the Battle of Blair's Landing (April 12, 1864), Steele assumed command of his cavalry division until a permanent replacement was named. He then led his command to Arkansas before returning to Texas. He was paroled at San Antonio, Texas, on August 4, 1865.

Steele settled in San Antonio, where he became a merchant. Moving to Austin in 1873, he was adjutant general of Texas (1874–1879), carrying out a reorganization of the Texas Rangers. Steele died in San Antonio on January 12, 1885.

SPENCER C. TUCKER

See also

Blair's Landing, Battle of; Green, Thomas; Pleasant Hill, Battle of; Red River Campaign; Sibley's New Mexico Campaign; Taylor, Richard

Further Reading

Eicher, John H., and David J. Eicher. *Civil War High Commands.* Stanford, CA: Stanford University Press, 2001.

Joiner, Gary D. *One Damn Blunder from Beginning to End: The Red River Campaign of 1864.* Wilmington, DE: Scholarly Resources, 2003.

Warner, Ezra J. *Generals in Gray: Lives of the Confederate Commanders.* Baton Rouge: Louisiana State University Press, 2006.

Webb, Walter Prescott. *The Texas Rangers.* 1935; reprint, Austin: University of Texas Press, 1982.

Steele's Bayou Expedition
Start Date: March 14, 1863
End Date: March 25, 1863

Operation during the lengthy Union effort to capture Vicksburg. The Steele's Bayou Expedition (March 14–25, 1863) was a precursor to the Second Vicksburg Campaign (April 1–July 4, 1863). U.S. Navy Mississippi River Squadron commander Rear Admiral David D. Porter hoped to be able to land Union troops above Haynes' Bluff, turning the Confederate flank. The entrance to Steele's Bayou lies six miles upriver from the mouth of the Yazoo River and seven miles north of Vicksburg by land.

With the apparent failure of the Yazoo Pass Expedition (February–April 1863), Porter discovered what he believed to be an alternative approach that would enable Union forces to assault Vicksburg from the northeast and thus avoid the necessity of engaging the city's formidable river batteries. Porter planned to proceed from the Mississippi River via the mouth of the Yazoo River north into Steele's Bayou and then on through Black Bayou, Deer Creek, and southward through the Rolling Fork and Big Sunflower Rivers back into the Yazoo River to assault Confederate defenses at Haynes' Bluff and Drumgould's Bluff.

Porter began the expedition on March 14, 1863, entering Steele's Bayou with the ironclads *Mound City, Louisville, Carondelet, Cincinnati,* and *Pittsburg,* along with four mortar schooners and four tugs. Major General William T. Sherman and 10,000 men of his XV Corps followed. Porter soon discovered, however, that the bayou channels were narrow, shallow, and overgrown, drastically slowing progress, as Union sailors had to remove numerous low-hanging branches and fallen trees. In certain spots, the ships could make only a half a mile per hour. In Black Bayou, progress was slowed by a dense forest of trees that had to be pushed aside or dragged from the water. While navigating Deer Creek, Porter's fleet encountered repeated Confederate obstructions near the Rolling Fork of the Sunflower River, which slowed the expedition further. Trees and undergrowth there again impeded progress, and Union seamen were forced to employ boat howitzers loaded with grape and canister shot to chase away Confederate sharpshooters.

As the flotilla approached the Sunflower River, a Confederate transport appeared and deposited both troops and light artillery on the levee. Porter estimated Confederate strength at about 4,000 men, and the Union transports with Sherman's men were then some distance off. The Confederates, members of Brigadier General Winfield Scott Featherston's brigade, were soon at work felling trees behind the squadron in an effort to trap the Union ships in place.

Recognizing the possibility that his fleet and men could be trapped and destroyed, Porter quickly requested aid from Sherman, sending a former slave acquainted with the area and entrusted with a note written on a tissue paper and wrapped in a tobacco leaf. While awaiting a reply, Porter prepared orders to scuttle the flotilla if necessary to prevent the ships from falling into Confederate hands.

As the Union troops struggled to reach Porter, the admiral attempted to deal with the Confederates ahead of him.

Unable to elevate his ships' guns sufficiently to engage the Confederate artillery on the top of the levee, Porter blasted away at the troops on the shore.

Sherman arrived with three of his regiments at Rolling Fork on March 22, and there was some skirmishing as they drove the Confederates from both banks. Then Porter's fleet slowly withdrew back along the same route to Hill's Plantation from whence it had started. Skirmishing occurred in Black Bayou during March 24–25. The March 14–25 expedition had covered 140 miles—70 each way—but, as with its predecessors, had ended in failure. As Porter summed up, "With the end of this expedition end all my hopes of getting Vicksburg in this direction."

Porter lost one engineer killed and four sailors wounded by sniper fire. Sherman's infantry suffered two deaths. Confederate casualties are not known. The Steele's Bayou Expedition represented perhaps the best opportunity for Confederate forces to eliminate a significant portion of the Mississippi Squadron during the campaign. Porter's squadron would play a vital role throughout the Second Vicksburg Campaign until the city's surrender on July 4, 1863.

STEVEN NATHANIEL DOSSMAN AND SPENCER C. TUCKER

See also

Featherston, Winfield Scott; Porter, David Dixon; Sherman, William Tecumseh; Vicksburg Campaign, Second; Yazoo Pass Expedition

Further Reading

Arnold, James R. *Grant Wins the War: Decision at Vicksburg.* New York: Wiley, 1997.

Ballard, Michael B. *Vicksburg: The Campaign That Opened the Mississippi.* Chapel Hill: University of North Carolina Press, 2004.

Winshel, Terrance J. *Vicksburg: Fall of the Confederate Gibraltar.* Abilene, TX: McWhiney Foundation Press, 1999.

Steel Manufacture

See Iron and Steel Manufacture

Stembel, Roger Nelson
Birth Date: December 17, 1810
Death Date: November 20, 1900

Union naval officer. Roger Nelson Stembel was born in Middletown, Maryland, on December 17, 1810. He received a midshipman's warrant on March 27, 1832, and was promoted to passed midshipman on June 23, 1838. He saw extensive service afloat in the West India, Mediterranean, Home, Brazil, China, and East India Squadrons and was promoted to lieutenant on October 26, 1843.

At the start of the Civil War, Stembel was assigned to the Western Gunboat Flotilla. There he helped oversee the conversion of three merchant steamers into so-called timberclads and took command of one of them, the *Lexington.* Promoted to commander on July 1, 1861, he saw action at Lucas' Bend (September 10, 1861), in the Battles of Belmont (November 7, 1861) and Fort Henry (February 6, 1862), and during the capture of Island No. 10 (March–April 1862). While commanding the ironclad *Cincinnati* in the bombardment of Fort Pillow beginning in April, Stembel took part in the Battle of Plum Point Bend (May 10, 1862). His ship having been rammed and in sinking condition, he was on deck directing operations when he was hit and badly wounded by a Confederate sharpshooter.

Invalided in 1863 as a consequence of his wound, Stembel served ashore at Pittsburgh, Pennsylvania, during 1864 and 1865. Promoted to captain on July 25, 1866, he commanded the screw sloop *Canandaigua* in the European Squadron (1865–1867). He was advanced to commodore on July 13, 1870, and was then stationed ashore at Boston. Stembel retired on December 27, 1872. He was promoted to rear admiral on the retired list on June 5, 1874. Stembel died in New York City on November 20, 1900.

SPENCER C. TUCKER

See also

Belmont, Battle of; Fort Henry, Battle of; Island No. 10, Battle of; Plum Point Bend, Battle of; Timberclads

Further Reading

Tucker, Spencer C. *Andrew Foote: Civil War Admiral on Western Waters.* Annapolis, MD: Naval Institute Press, 2000.

Tucker, Spencer C. *Blue and Gray Navies: The Civil War Afloat.* Annapolis, MD: Naval Institute Press, 2006.

Stephens, Alexander Hamilton
Birth Date: February 11, 1812
Death Date: March 4, 1883

Vice president of the Confederate States of America. Born in Crawfordville, Georgia, on February 11, 1812, Alexander Hamilton Stephens graduated from the Franklin College (University of Georgia) in 1832. After teaching for two years, he studied law and opened a successful practice in Crawfordville. In 1836 he was elected to the Georgia House of

Alexander Hamilton Stephens of Georgia was vice president of the Confederate States of America. A doctrinaire advocate of states' rights, Stephens headed the Confederate delegation to the unsuccessful Hampton Roads Peace Conference in February 1865. (National Archives)

Representatives, and in 1842 he moved to the Georgia Senate. That same year he was elected to the U.S. House of Representatives, and he was reelected every two years from that time through 1856. He did not seek reelection in 1858. Until his last two terms in Congress, Stephens was a Whig, but as the sectional crisis heated up, he became a more strident defender of slavery and switched his party affiliation to the Democrats.

During the secession crisis of 1860 and 1861, Stephens served as a member of the Georgia Secession Convention but advocated that the Southern states remain within the Union. Although he claimed that the Southern states had the right to secede, he argued that such a step was unnecessary because the Republicans would not have the political power in Congress to accomplish their antislavery goals, even with possession of the White House, and that the U.S. Supreme Court would long remain a reliable bulwark of slavery. When secession nevertheless occurred, Stephen was elected a member of the convention that founded the Confederacy and became its first congress. When the convention assembled in February 1861 in Montgomery, Alabama, Stephens

helped write the Confederate Constitution and then was elected vice president on February 9, 1861.

The following month in Savannah, Georgia, Stephens made his most famous speech. In the address that came to be known as the "Cornerstone Speech," he emphatically stated that slavery was the sole cause of the breakup of the Union. The Founding Fathers, he maintained, had been wrong in their fundamental belief that all human beings are created with equal rights to life, liberty, and the pursuit of happiness. "Our new government," he went on to explain, "is founded upon exactly the opposite idea; its foundations are laid, its cornerstone rests, upon the great truth that the negro is not equal to the white man; that slavery—subordination to the superior race—is his natural and normal condition." The Confederate government, he added, was "the first, in the history of the world, based upon this great physical, philosophical, and moral truth."

During the Civil War, Stephens became a perpetual thorn in the side of President Jefferson Davis's administration. Stephens was a doctrinaire advocate of states' rights, and the fact that the Confederacy, as he himself had admitted, was not about states' rights meant that Stephens was part of a small but vocal minority protesting various ways in which the Davis administration, with the support of the Confederate Congress, set aside what Stephens saw as strict observance of the Confederate Constitution and the niceties of states' rights in order to wage war more effectively. Stephens spent most of the war not in the Confederate capital at Richmond but rather at his estate, called Liberty Hall, near Crawfordville, vigorously denouncing Davis and the Confederate government, of which Stephens nevertheless remained vice president. Scholars have speculated that one reason Davis never indulged his known desire to assume field command of one or more of the Confederacy's armies was that Stephens was unavailable and could not be trusted to administer the government even temporarily in Davis's absence.

Late in the war, Stephens added his voice to those calling for some sort of negotiated peace, and he also added unwillingness to negotiate to the long catalog of sins for which he denounced Davis.

Davis astutely dealt with the rising clamor for negotiation by appointing Stephens to lead a commission to meet with Union authorities. Stephens's delegation met with Lincoln and U.S. secretary of state William H. Seward on a Union steamer in Hampton Roads on February 3, 1865. Lincoln was willing to make vast concessions, including the possibility of monetary compensation for slaves, but insisted on union and complete emancipation. As Davis had anticipated, the majority of the Confederate people were unwilling to accept such terms and rallied to support the war for the remaining 10 weeks until final collapse in April.

Union forces captured Stephens at Liberty Hall on May 11, 1865, and briefly imprisoned him at Fort Warren in Boston. After the war he wrote *A Constitutional View of the War between the States,* in which he maintained that the Confederacy had been fighting for states' rights and constitutionalism after all. For a time, he resumed his career in the U.S. House of Representatives and served as Georgia's governor for only a few months before his death in Atlanta on March 4, 1883.

STEVEN E. WOODWORTH

See also

Davis, Jefferson Finis; Hampton Roads Peace Conference; Lincoln, Abraham; Montgomery Convention; Seward, William Henry, Sr.

Further Reading

Richardson, E. Ramsay. *Little Aleck: A Life of Alexander H. Stephens, the Fighting Vice-President of the Confederacy.* Indianapolis: Bobbs-Merrill, 1932.

Schott, Thomas E. *Alexander H. Stephens of Georgia: A Biography.* Baton Rouge: Louisiana State University Press, 1988.

Von Abele, Rudolph. *Alexander H. Stephens: A Biography.* Westport, CT: Negro Universities Press, 1946.

Steuart, George Hume
Birth Date: August 24, 1828
Death Date: November 22, 1903

Confederate officer. George Hume Steuart was born in Baltimore, Maryland, on August 24, 1828. He graduated from the U.S. Military Academy, West Point, in 1848 and was commissioned in the 2nd Dragoons. Steuart was promoted to first lieutenant in the new 1st Cavalry on March 3, 1855, and to captain on December 20, 1855. Most of his service was on the western frontier.

With the beginning of the Civil War, Steuart resigned his U.S. Army commission on April 22, 1861. He was commissioned a captain of cavalry in the Confederate Army on March 16, 1861, and was appointed lieutenant colonel of the 1st Maryland Infantry on June 17. Steuart saw combat at the First Battle of Bull Run (July 21, 1861), when he commanded the regiment. He was promoted to colonel to date from July 21 and appointed brigadier general effective March 6, 1862.

Assigned to Major General Richard S. Ewell's division in the Valley District during April and May 1862, in June Steuart took command of a brigade in II Corps of the

Army of Northern Virginia and took part in Major General Thomas J. "Stonewall" Jackson's Shenandoah Valley Campaign (May–June 1862). Steuart was seriously wounded in the Battle of Cross Keys (June 8, 1862).

Following a protracted recovery, from May 1863 to May 1864 "Maryland" Steuart, as he came to be known, commanded a brigade in Major General Edward Johnson's Division, II Corps, Army of Northern Virginia. Steuart was wounded in the arm at Payne's Farm, Virginia, on November 27, 1863, during the Mine Run Campaign (November 26–December 2, 1863). Taken prisoner on May 12 at Spotsylvania, Virginia, he was exchanged on August 3.

For the remainder of the war, Steuart commanded a brigade in Major General George E. Pickett's division of I Corps. Steuart took part in the Petersburg Campaign (June 15, 1864–April 3, 1865), the Battle of Five Forks (April 1, 1865), and the Appomattox Campaign (April 2–9, 1865). He was paroled at Appomattox on April 9 and pardoned on November 26, 1865.

After the war Steuart became a farmer in Anne Arundel County, Maryland. He was also for many years commander of the Maryland division of the United Confederate Veterans. Steuart died at South River, Maryland, on November 22, 1903.

SPENCER C. TUCKER

See also

Appomattox Campaign; Bull Run, First Battle of; Cross Keys, Battle of; Ewell, Richard Stoddart; Five Forks, Battle of; Jackson's Shenandoah Valley Campaign; Johnson, Edward; Mine Run Campaign; Petersburg Campaign; Pickett, George Edward; United Confederate Veterans

Further Reading

Eicher, John H., and David J. Eicher. *Civil War High Commands.* Stanford, CA: Stanford University Press, 2001.

Warner, Ezra J. *Generals in Gray: Lives of the Confederate Commanders.* Baton Rouge: Louisiana State University Press, 2006.

Stevens, Clement Hoffman
Birth Date: August 14, 1821
Death Date: July 25, 1864

Confederate officer. Clement Hoffman Stevens was born in Norwich, Connecticut, on August 14, 1821. When Stevens was very young, his family moved to Florida and then to Pendleton, South Carolina. For several years Stevens was secretary to his relative, U.S. Navy commodore William Shubrick. In 1842 Stevens joined the Planters and Mechanics Bank at Charleston and was its cashier at the beginning of the Civil War.

First a colonel in the South Carolina Militia, Stevens developed harbor defenses at Charleston. Regarded as an ordnance expert, he designed a revolutionary battery, reinforced by railroad iron, for the defense of Morris Island. Stevens fought in the First Battle of Bull Run (July 21, 1861) and was wounded there while serving as a volunteer aide-de-camp to his brother-in-law, Brigadier General Bernard Bee, who was killed in the battle.

Elected colonel of the 24th South Carolina Infantry on April 1, 1862, Stevens commanded that regiment and was again wounded in the Battle of Secessionville (June 16, 1862). He served at various places along the Carolina coast for the next 11 months. Sent west in a brigade commanded by Brigadier General States Rights Gist, Stevens served in the so-called Army of Relief during the Second Vicksburg Campaign (April 1–July 4, 1863). He then joined the Army of Tennessee. While fighting in the Battle of Chickamauga (September 19–20, 1863), he was again badly wounded on September 20.

Praised for his bravery in battle, Stevens was known as "Rock" by his men. He was appointed brigadier general on January 20, 1864, and commanded a brigade in Major General William H. T. Walker's division of I Corps in the Army of Tennessee during the Atlanta Campaign (May 5–September 2, 1864). Stevens led his brigade with great effectiveness until wounded in the head during the Battle of Peachtree Creek (July 20, 1864). Taken to Atlanta, he died there on July 25, 1864.

SPENCER C. TUCKER

See also

Atlanta Campaign; Bee, Barnard Elliott; Bull Run, First Battle of; Chickamauga, Battle of; Peachtree Creek, Battle of; Secessionville, Battle of; Vicksburg Campaign, Second; Walker, William Henry Talbot

Further Reading

Castel, Albert. *Decision in the West: The Atlanta Campaign of 1864.* Lawrence: University Press of Kansas, 1992.

Eicher, John H., and David J. Eicher. *Civil War High Commands.* Stanford, CA: Stanford University Press, 2001.

Warner, Ezra J. *Generals in Gray: Lives of the Confederate Commanders.* Baton Rouge: Louisiana State University Press, 2006.

Stevens, Isaac Ingalls

Birth Date: March 25, 1818
Death Date: September 1, 1862

Union officer. Isaac Ingalls Stevens was born in Andover, Massachusetts, on March 25, 1818. Frail and plagued by ill health as a child, he stood barely five feet tall as an adult.

Nevertheless, his keen intellect and driven ambitions served him well. After attending Phillips Academy for a brief time, he enrolled at the U.S. Military Academy at West Point and graduated first in his class in 1839. He was commissioned a second lieutenant of engineers and served along the East Coast constructing and fortifying defensive works, earning promotion to first lieutenant in 1840. Stevens saw action during the Mexican-American War (1846–1848) in the Battles of Cerro Gordo, Churubusco, and Contreras. Brevetted captain and then major, he was seriously wounded during the drive on Mexico City in September 1847.

During a long convalescence, Stevens wrote *Campaigns of the Rio Grande and of Mexico,* which was published in 1851. In the autumn of 1849, he began serving as the chief assistant to Alexander Bache, head of the U.S. Coast Survey in the War Department. In 1852 Stevens staunchly supported Franklin Pierce's Democratic Party presidential bid. Stevens delivered a number of electrifying speeches on behalf of Pierce and also penned numerous editorials backing his candidacy. As a result, after Pierce became president in 1853, he promptly rewarded Stevens with the governorship of the Washington Territory. Stevens resigned his army commission in March 1853 to take up his new position.

Stevens's tenure as governor was steeped in controversy. Although he worked indefatigably and in accordance with policies set in Washington, his handling of Native Americans especially left much to be desired. Both whites and Native Americans accused him of extreme hubris and having dictatorial proclivities. In an attempt to reserve land for white settlement and to make room for a proposed transcontinental railway, Stevens entered into negotiations with the various Native American tribes in the region to purchase millions of acres of land and to limit tribes to prescribed reservations. The resultant Indian unrest brought a heavy-handed response. In 1856 Stevens successfully ran for the U.S. House of Representatives, representing his territory. He took office in March 1857 and was reelected in 1858. In 1860 he served as chairman of the John C. Breckinridge campaign for the presidency.

When the Civil War began in April 1861, Stevens promptly sought an army commission. In July 1861 he was commissioned colonel of the 79th New York Infantry Regiment, a unit that had been plagued by poor leadership and mutiny. Within weeks, Stevens had whipped the 79th New York into shape, taking it south to Virginia and then to South Carolina. In September 1861 Stevens was promoted to brigadier general of volunteers. He commanded the army post in Beaufort, South Carolina, and on June 16, 1862, led an infantry division in the failed assault on Secessionville, south of Charleston.

Stevens was then ordered to Virginia to assume command of a division in XI Corps, Army of the Potomac, which supported the Army of Virginia in the Second Bull Run Campaign. He saw early action in the Second Battle of Bull Run (August 26–September 1, 1862) and brought up the rear of Major General John Pope's army during the withdrawal to Washington, D.C. Stevens's force was assaulted by Confederate troops under Major General Thomas J. Jackson at the Battle of Chantilly (September 1, 1862) in Virginia. During the melee, Stevens was struck and killed instantly by a rifle ball to the head. He was posthumously promoted to major general of volunteers.

PAUL G. PIERPAOLI JR.

See also

Bull Run, Second Battle of; Chantilly, Battle of; Jackson, Thomas Jonathan; Secessionville, Battle of

Further Reading

Doty, James, ed. *Journal of Operations of Governor Isaac Ingalls Stevens of Washington Territory in 1855.* Fairfield, WA: Ye Galleon, 1978.

Miller, Christopher. *Prophetic Worlds: Indians and Whites on the Columbia Plateau.* Seattle: University of Washington Press, 2003.

Richards, Kent. *Isaac I. Stevens: Young Man in a Hurry.* Provo, UT: Brigham Young University Press, 1993.

Congressman Thaddeus Stevens of Pennsylvania chaired the House Ways and Means Committee and led the Radical Republicans in Congress. He insisted on aggressive prosecution of the war and urged harsh treatment of the South. (National Archives)

Stevens, Thaddeus
Birth Date: April 4, 1792
Death Date: August 11, 1868

Influential Pennsylvania politician who led the Radical Republicans in Congress. Born on April 4, 1792, in Danville, Vermont, Thaddeus Stevens grew up in poverty after his father abandoned the family but graduated from Dartmouth College in 1814. He then moved to Pennsylvania, was admitted to the state bar in 1816, and established a law practice in Gettysburg.

Stevens began his political career in 1833 in the state legislature, where he served until 1841, taking stands against slavery and freemasonry. He quickly established a reputation as an aggressive, fiercely uncompromising leader in Pennsylvania affairs. During this period, Stevens, a determined abolitionist, defended fugitive slaves free of charge. He once reportedly paid $300 to secure the release of a hotel servant who was about to be sold away from his family.

After eight years in the state legislature, Stevens was elected to the U.S. House of Representatives as a Whig in 1848 and served until 1853. Opposed to the Compromise of 1850, he was especially virulent and caustic in his denunciation of the Fugitive Slave Act (1850). After leaving the House in 1853 in disgust over the moderation of his colleagues on the slavery issue, Stevens joined the new Republican Party in 1856. Reelected to the House in 1858 as a Republican, he used his sarcastic wit, knowledge of parliamentary procedure, and eloquence to become the leader of the Radical Republicans. First as the chairman of the Ways and Means Committee and then as the head of the Appropriations Committee, Stevens came to command tremendous authority in the House.

Stevens's passion earned him the admiration of many of his colleagues. However, his stubbornness, harsh language, and vindictive nature, while making him a formidable adversary, prevented him from achieving greatness. As chairman of the House Ways and Means Committee during the Civil War, he urged President Abraham Lincoln to deal harshly with the "rebels" of the South. Stevens also called for the emancipation of all slaves and the confiscation of planter estates in the South to be divided into small farms for the freed African Americans. Stevens helped to secure the passage of increased protective tariffs, encouraged the construction of railroads through government subsidies, backed the issuing of paper money (greenbacks), and fought to allow African Americans to enlist in the Union Army.

After Andrew Johnson became president in April 1865, Stevens served on the Joint Committee on Reconstruction. He openly battled against the conciliatory policies of the president. Stevens succeeded in imposing military Reconstruction on the South, which he viewed as a "conquered province" with which Congress could do as it pleased. Throughout the first few years of Reconstruction, Stevens remained an ardent supporter of granting full African American civil rights and believed that the South should be severely punished for what he saw as its treachery.

It was Stevens who introduced the resolution in the House calling for the impeachment of President Johnson. However, Stevens's failing health prevented him from taking part in the trial itself. Deeply depressed by the president's acquittal in 1868, Stevens died shortly thereafter on August 11, 1868, in Washington, D.C.

STEVEN G. O'BRIEN

See also

Congress, CSA; Johnson, Andrew; Lincoln, Abraham; Radical Republicans; Reconstruction

Further Reading

Benedict, Michael Les. *A Compromise of Principle: Congressional Republicans and Reconstruction, 1863–1869.* New York: Norton, 1874.

Trefousse, Hans Louis. *Thaddeus Stevens.* Mechanicsburg, PA: Stackpole, 2001.

Stevens, Walter Husted
Birth Date: August 24, 1827
Death Date: November 12, 1867

Confederate officer. Born at Penn Yan, New York, on August 24, 1827, Walter Husted Stevens graduated from the U.S. Military Academy, West Point, in 1848 and was commissioned in the engineers. He was promoted to first lieutenant on July 1, 1855. Stevens's assignments were almost exclusively in Louisiana and Texas. This fact and his marriage to a sister of future Confederate general Louis Hébert made Stevens a Southerner in sentiment.

Stevens attempted to resign his U.S. Army commission but was refused (he was dismissed from the service on May 2, 1861). He then secured a commission as a major of engineers in the Confederate Army on March 16. He served as engineer on the staff of Brigadier General P. G. T. Beauregard in the First Battle of Bull Run (July 21, 1861) and was then chief engineer for General Joseph E. Johnston and the Army of Virginia and served in the Peninsula Campaign (March–July 1862). When General Robert E. Lee succeeded Johnston in command of the Army of Northern Virginia, Lee assigned Stevens the task of improving the defenses of Richmond, to which he devoted much time and energy.

Stevens was promoted to colonel on March 3, 1863. Named chief engineer of the Army of Northern Virginia, he was appointed brigadier general on August 28, 1864. He had charge of improving and extending the formidable Petersburg defenses during the long siege there (June 15, 1864–April 3, 1865). Supposedly the last uniformed Confederate officer to evacuate Richmond during the night of April 2, 1865, Stevens surrendered with the rest of the Army of Northern Virginia at Appomattox, Virginia, and was paroled there on April 9, 1865.

Postbellum, Stevens immigrated to Mexico and accepted the position of chief engineer of the Mexican Imperial Railroad from Emperor Maximilian, who sought to construct a rail line from Mexico City to Veracruz. Stevens died of yellow fever in Veracruz on November 12, 1867.

SPENCER C. TUCKER

See also

Beauregard, Pierre Gustav Toutant; Bull Run, First Battle of; Hébert, Louis; Johnston, Joseph Eggleston; Lee, Robert Edward; Peninsula Campaign; Petersburg Campaign

Further Reading

Eicher, John H., and David J. Eicher. *Civil War High Commands.* Stanford, CA: Stanford University Press, 2001.

Trudeau, Noah Andre. *The Last Citadel: Petersburg, Virginia, June 1864–April 1865.* Baton Rouge: Louisiana State University Press, 1991.

Warner, Ezra J. *Generals in Gray: Lives of the Confederate Commanders.* Baton Rouge: Louisiana State University Press, 2006.

Stevenson, Carter Littlepage
Birth Date: September 21, 1817
Death Date: August 15, 1888

Confederate officer. Carter Littlepage Stevenson was born near Fredericksburg, Virginia, on September 21, 1817. He graduated from the U.S. Military Academy, West Point, in 1838 and was commissioned in the 5th Infantry. He was promoted to first lieutenant on September 22, 1840, and to captain on June 30, 1847. Stevenson served on the western frontier and performed well during the Mexican-American War (1846–1848). He subsequently served in Texas and Florida and in the Utah Expedition.

With the start of the Civil War, his commanding officer failed to submit Stevenson's resignation, and Stevenson was duly dismissed from the U.S. Army on June 25, 1861. The following month he was appointed colonel of the 53rd Virginia Infantry. He served as assistant adjutant general of the Army of the Northwest from July 1861 to March 1862. Appointed a brigadier general on February 27, 1862, he assumed command of a brigade in the Army of East Tennessee in March and engaged the Federals commanded by Brigadier General George W. Morgan at Cumberland Gap on June 18.

Appointed major general on October 10, 1862, Stevenson commanded a division in the Department of Mississippi and East Louisiana. He took part in the Second Vicksburg Campaign (April 1–July 4, 1863) and was taken prisoner with the surrender of Vicksburg on July 4.

Exchanged on October 16, 1863, Stevenson commanded a division first in the Army of Tennessee, seeing combat in its major battles from the Chattanooga Campaign (October–November), during which he commanded the troops driven from Lookout Mountain on November 24, to the Battle of Bentonville (March 19–21, 1865) in North Carolina, with the exception of the Battle of Franklin (November 30, 1864). He was particularly active during the Atlanta Campaign (May 5–September 2, 1864) and during and after the Battle of Nashville (December 15–16, 1864), when his division covered the army's retreat from Tennessee. He was paroled at Greensboro, North Carolina, on May 1, 1865.

Following the war, Stevenson was employed as a civil and mining engineer. He died at Caroline County, Virginia, on August 15, 1888.

SPENCER C. TUCKER

See also

Atlanta Campaign; Bentonville, Battle of; Chattanooga Campaign; Morgan, George Washington; Nashville, Battle of; Vicksburg Campaign, Second

Further Reading

Eicher, John H., and David J. Eicher. *Civil War High Commands.* Stanford, CA: Stanford University Press, 2001.

Warner, Ezra J. *Generals in Gray: Lives of the Confederate Commanders.* Baton Rouge: Louisiana State University Press, 2006.

Stevenson, John Dunlap
Birth Date: June 8, 1821
Death Date: January 22, 1897

Union officer. John Dunlap Stevenson was born in Staunton, Virginia, on June 8, 1821. A graduate of South Carolina College, Stevenson studied law in Staunton and was admitted to the Virginia bar but then moved to Missouri, where he opened a law practice. He fought in the Mexican-American War (1846–1848) as a captain in the 1st Missouri Mounted Volunteers (June 1846–June 1847). He then moved to St. Louis and was several times elected to the Missouri state legislature.

With the beginning of the Civil War, Stevenson remained loyal to the Union and was commissioned colonel of the 7th Missouri Infantry on June 1, 1861. He fought in the Battle of Shiloh (April 6–7, 1862) and commanded a brigade in XIII Corps of the Army of the Tennessee during the Battle of Corinth (October 3–4, 1862). Appointed brigadier general of volunteers on March 13, 1863, to date from November 29, 1862, he commanded the 3rd Brigade, 3rd Division, XVII Corps, Army of the Tennessee, from December to July 1863, serving with the brigade throughout the Second Vicksburg Campaign (April 1–July 4, 1863). He briefly commanded his division before heading the District of Corinth.

In preparation for the Atlanta Campaign (May 5–September 2, 1864), Stevenson commanded 2,500 men protecting the Tennessee & Alabama Railroad. He resigned his commission on April 22, 1864. But on August 8, he was reappointed brigadier general with his original date of rank and took command of the District of Harpers Ferry, West Virginia, which he headed until April 1865. Brevetted major general on March 13, 1865, he mustered out of the Volunteers on January 15, 1866.

After the war, Stevenson was commissioned colonel of the 30th Infantry on July 28, 1866. On March 2, 1867, he was brevetted brigadier general for his role in the Battle of Champion Hill (May 16, 1863). After a period without assignment (March 1869–December 1870) during a reduction in the size of the army, Stevenson assumed command of the 25th Infantry. Discharged on his own request on December 31, 1870, Stevenson resumed his law practice in St. Louis, where he died on January 22, 1897.

SPENCER C. TUCKER

See also

Champion Hill, Battle of; Corinth, Battle of; Harpers Ferry, Virginia; Shiloh, Battle of; Vicksburg Campaign, Second

Further Reading

Eicher, John H., and David J. Eicher. *Civil War High Commands.* Stanford, CA: Stanford University Press, 2001.

Warner, Ezra J. *Generals in Blue: Lives of the Union Commanders.* Baton Rouge: Louisiana State University Press, 2006.

Stewart, Alexander Peter
Birth Date: October 2, 1821
Death Date: August 30, 1908

Confederate officer. Alexander Peter Stewart was born on October 2, 1821, in Rogersville, Tennessee. He graduated from the U.S. Military Academy, West Point, in 1842 and was commissioned a second lieutenant of artillery but resigned his commission three years later. Stewart subsequently taught at Cumberland University (Lebanon, Tennessee) as well as the University of Nashville.

Although he was a member of the Whig Party and opposed secession, when Tennessee voted to secede, Stewart cast his lot with his native state. When Tennessee's forces were mustered into the Confederate Army on August 15, 1861, Stewart held the rank of major in an artillery unit. On November 8, 1861, he was promoted to brigadier general. He went on to play a role in virtually every campaign waged by what became the Confederate Army of Tennessee, including the Battle of Shiloh (April 6–7, 1862); the Battle of Stones River (December 31, 1862–January 2, 1863), after which he became a division commander; the Battle of Chickamauga (September 19–20, 1863); the battles for Chattanooga (November 23–25, 1863); the Atlanta Campaign (May 5–September 2, 1864); and General John Bell Hood's failed invasion of Tennessee (September 18–December 27, 1864). Known as "Old Straight," Stewart proved to be a capable commander and was promoted to major general on June 2, 1863, and to lieutenant general on June 23, 1864, when he assumed command of a corps during the Atlanta Campaign. He commanded the remnant of the Army of Tennessee during the Carolina Campaign and fought well in the Battle of Bentonville (March 19–21, 1865).

After the war, Stewart resumed working at Cumberland University. After pursuing business interests in St. Louis, Missouri, he was elected chancellor of the University of Mississippi in 1874 and served in this capacity for 12 years. Stewart died on August 30, 1908, in Biloxi, Mississippi.

ROBERT L. GLAZE

See also
Atlanta Campaign; Chattanooga Campaign; Chickamauga, Battle of; Franklin and Nashville Campaign; Shiloh, Battle of; Tennessee, Confederate Army of

Further Reading
Connelly, Thomas Lawrence. *Autumn of Glory: The Army of Tennessee, 1862–1865.* Baton Rouge: Louisiana State University Press, 1971.
Elliott, Sam Davis. *Soldier of Tennessee: General Alexander P. Stewart and the Civil War in the West.* Baton Rouge: Louisiana State University Press, 2004.
Woodworth, Steven E. *Jefferson Davis and His Generals: The Failure of Confederate Command in the West.* Lawrence: University Press of Kansas, 1990.

Stilington's Hill, Battle of
See McDowell, Battle of

St. John, Isaac Munroe
Birth Date: November 19, 1827
Death Date: April 7, 1880

Confederate officer. Born in Augusta, Georgia, on November 19, 1827, but raised in New York City, Isaac Munroe St. John graduated from Yale University in 1845. Following a short period of interest in the law, he moved to Baltimore, Maryland, in 1847 and became assistant editor of the *Baltimore Patriot* newspaper. He then settled on the career for which he was most suited, civil engineering, working for the Baltimore & Ohio Railroad. In 1855 he returned to Georgia and worked on the Blue Ridge Railroad.

With the beginning of the Civil War, St. John initially joined the Confederate Army as a private in the South Carolina Militia, but when his engineering expertise became known, he was assigned as chief engineer to Major General John B. Magruder. Commissioned a captain of engineers in February 1862, St. John rendered valuable service in the construction of Confederate fortifications during the early part of Union major general George B. McClellan's Peninsula Campaign (March–July 1862).

Promoted to major in May 1862, St. John was assigned to the new Nitre Bureau in Richmond, which was responsible for the production of gunpowder, work that was absolutely essential to the war effort. His important contributions in organizing the production and distribution of gunpowder led to his promotion to lieutenant colonel on May 28, 1863, and to colonel on June 15, 1864. His operation evolved into the Bureau of Nitre and Mining. Under St. John's direction, the bureau produced an abundant supply of saltpeter for gunpowder production but proved less successful in extracting iron ore and coal as vital areas came under Union control. With the unpopular and ineffective commissary general Colonel Lucius B. Northrop in poor health, St. John assumed that post on February 16, 1865, as a brigadier general.

St. John accompanied Jefferson Davis and other Confederate officials when they evacuated Richmond on April 2, 1865. St. John surrendered in Thomasville, Georgia, on May 23. Returning to Richmond, he took the amnesty oath there on June 18.

St. John then resumed his career as a civil engineer in Kentucky, and from 1866 to 1869 he was chief engineer of the Louisville, Cincinnati & Lexington Railroad. In 1870 he became chief engineer of the City of Louisville, and in 1871 he became a consulting engineer of the Chesapeake & Ohio Railroad and chief engineer of the Lexington & Big Sandy Railroad. St. John held these posts until his death at White Sulphur Springs, West Virginia, on April 7, 1880. Like his colleague Josiah Gorgas, St. John was a largely unsung hero of the Confederate war effort.

SPENCER C. TUCKER

See also

Davis, Jefferson Finis, Capture of; Magruder, John Bankhead; McClellan, George Brinton; Nitre Bureaus; Peninsula Campaign

Further Reading

Eicher, John H., and David J. Eicher. *Civil War High Commands.* Stanford, CA: Stanford University Press, 2001.

Warner, Ezra J. *Generals in Gray: Lives of the Confederate Commanders.* Baton Rouge: Louisiana State University Press, 2006.

Stoeckl, Eduard Andreevich de

Birth Date: 1804
Death Date: 1892

Russian diplomat and minister plenipotentiary to the United States (1854–1869). Eduard Andreevich de Stoeckl was born in Constantinople (now Istanbul) in the Ottoman Empire in 1804 while his father Andreas served as Austrian minister to the Porte. Stoeckl's mother was a Russian noblewoman. As a young man, Stoeckl found work as a functionary in the Russian diplomatic corps, and in 1841 he traveled to the United States, where he was a secretary in the Russian legation. He gradually rose through the diplomatic ranks, and in 1850 he became chargé d'affaires, the number two position in the U.S. legation. In 1854 he was named Russian minister plenipotentiary to the United States. In this capacity, he wrote many letters to Prince Alexander Gorchakov, the Russian foreign minister, detailing the building sectional crisis in America and expressing his belief that the tension would ultimately result in disunion and perhaps civil war.

Stoeckl had meanwhile become an ally and admirer of New York senator William H. Seward, whom Stoeckl believed might be able to head off secession if elected to the presidency in 1860. When that failed to occur and Abraham Lincoln was elected that November, the Russian minister's letters to Gochakov provided great detail on the secession of Southern states, beginning with South Carolina in December 1860. Stoeckl also wrote of his low opinion of Lincoln and his relatively high regard for Confederate president Jefferson Davis, whom he had gotten to know during the latter's U.S. Senate career. After the war began, in the late spring of 1861 Stoeckl met with Seward and offered Russian mediation of the conflict. Seward rejected the offer, but Stoeckl was duty bound to maintain Russian neutrality.

As the war went on, Stoeckl met frequently with his British and French counterparts in Washington. And although he had doubts that the Union would triumph, he said nothing publicly that would even hint of favoritism. This strict neutrality helped convince U.S. officials that Russia was the most steadfast of friends among the major powers of Europe. In 1863 Stoeckl convinced the imperial court to send some of its naval assets on a goodwill visit to the United States. That summer, Russia's Atlantic Fleet made a call at New York Harbor, while its Pacific Fleet visited San Francisco. This further cemented the U.S.-Russian relationship.

In 1866 after the war, Stoeckl conferred with Secretary Seward about the possibility of selling Alaska to the United States. That autumn, Stoeckl visited Gorchakov in Russia, who gave him the green light to engage the Americans in negotiations. The following year, Seward signed a treaty that purchased Alaska for $7.2 million, or about 2 cents per acre. Czar Alexander II rewarded Stoeckl with a lump-sum payment of $25,000 and a pension of $6,000 per year. Believing that he had deserved more recognition and remuneration, Stoeckl asked to be relieved of his post in 1868 and left the United States in 1869. He thereafter lived mostly in Paris, where he died in 1892.

PAUL G. PIERPAOLI JR.

See also

Lincoln, Abraham; Russian-U.S. Relations; Seward, William Henry, Sr.

Further Reading

Saul, Norman E. *Distant Friends: The United States and Russia, 1763–1867.* Lawrence: University Press of Kansas, 1991.

Woldman, Albert A. *Lincoln and the Russians*. New York: World Publishing, 1952.

Stolbrand, Charles John
Birth Date: May 11, 1821
Death Date: February 3, 1894

Union officer. Charles John Stolbrand (Carlos Meuller Stohlbrand) was born near Kristianstad, Sweden, on May 11, 1821. In 1839 he entered the Swedish Army as an artillery cadet. He saw combat during the First Schleswig-Holstein War (1848), when he and some of the members of his regiment assisted the Danes in the defense of Copenhagen against the invading Prussians. In 1850 Stolbrand immigrated to the United States, where he became active in the Swedish community in Chicago.

With the beginning of the Civil War, Stolbrand organized an artillery company and was commissioned its captain on October 5, 1861. He was promoted to major on December 3. Stolbrand distinguished himself as an artillery officer in the Army of the Tennessee but was injured in a fall from his horse near Union City, Missouri, on March 31, 1862. He took part in the First Vicksburg Campaign (October 16–December 29, 1862), the Second Vicksburg Campaign (April 1–July 4, 1863), and the Chattanooga Campaign (October–November 1863).

Stolbrand was serving as chief of artillery in a division in XVI Corps in the Army of the Tennessee at the beginning of the Atlanta Campaign (May 5–September 2, 1864) and was captured near Kingston, Georgia, on May 19, 1864, while reconnoitering. Escaping from the notorious Confederate Andersonville Prison in Georgia, he rejoined the army in October, taking command of the artillery in XV Corps. His command numbered some 1,000 men and 46 guns.

Stolbrand took part in Major General William T. Sherman's March to the Sea (November 15–December 21, 1864) and March through the Carolinas (January–April 1865), but in January 1865, discouraged about his failure to win promotion, he requested to be mustered out of the service. Sherman did not want to lose a valuable officer, so he asked Stolbrand to carry important dispatches to President Abraham Lincoln. One of these was a request from Sherman for Stolbrand's advancement. Upon reading this, Lincoln appointed Stolbrand a brigadier general of volunteers on the spot, on February 18, 1865. During the last few months of the war, Stolbrand commanded the 2nd Brigade, 4th Division, XVII Corps.

Stolbrand left the army on January 15, 1866. Later that year he settled in Columbia, South Carolina, and became active politically as a Republican. A delegate to the 1868 Republican National Convention, he was a presidential elector for Ulysses S. Grant. Stolbrand also was superintendent of the South Carolina state penitentiary and then superintendent of the new federal courthouse and post office in Charleston. He died in that city on February 3, 1894.

Spencer C. Tucker

See also

Andersonville Prison, Georgia; Atlanta Campaign; Chattanooga Campaign; Lincoln, Abraham; Sherman, William Tecumseh; Sherman's March through the Carolinas; Sherman's March to the Sea; Vicksburg Campaign, First; Vicksburg Campaign, Second

Further Reading

Eicher, John H., and David J. Eicher. *Civil War High Commands*. Stanford, CA: Stanford University Press, 2001.
Warner, Ezra J. *Generals in Blue: Lives of the Union Commanders*. Baton Rouge: Louisiana State University Press, 2006.

Stone, Charles Pomeroy
Birth Date: September 30, 1824
Death Date: January 23, 1887

Union officer. Charles Pomeroy Stone was born in Greenfield, Massachusetts, on September 30, 1824. He graduated from the U.S. Military Academy, West Point, in 1845. Stone fought in the Mexican-American War (1846–1848), earning two brevets, and after the conflict spent 18 months in Europe studying the French, Prussian, and Swedish Armies. On his return, he was assigned as chief of ordnance for the Department of the Pacific in August 1851, receiving promotion to first lieutenant in 1853. Stone resigned his commission in 1856, taking a position with the Mexican government to conduct a mineral survey. In December 1860 while in Washington, he was asked to return to the army as inspector general of the city's militia.

On May 14, 1861, Stone was appointed colonel of the new 14th U.S. Infantry Regiment and was promoted to brigadier general of volunteers on August 6. He led a brigade in the Shenandoah Valley under Major General Robert Patterson before assuming command of a division on the upper Potomac River. At the Battle of Ball's Bluff (October 21, 1861), his subordinate Colonel Edward Baker, a sitting U.S. senator and friend of President Abraham Lincoln, rashly attacked Confederate forces and was soundly beaten. Baker was killed, and Stone was held responsible for the affair. The Joint Committee on the Conduct of the War ordered Stone's arrest in February 1862. He was held for more than six months at Forts Lafayette and Hamilton without being charged. On August 16, 1862, without apology or explanation, he was released and was eventually assigned to Major General Nathaniel Banks's army. Stone served as chief of staff for Banks during the Siege of Port Hudson (May 21–July 9, 1863) and the Red River Campaign (March 10–May 22, 1864). Typhoid and mental fatigue eventually forced his resignation on September 13, 1864.

After the war, Stone worked as a mining engineer in Virginia. From 1870 to 1883 he was chief of staff in the Egyptian Army, becoming a lieutenant general. Upon returning to America, he worked as an engineer for the Florida Ship Canal Company before serving as chief engineer for the construction of the Statue of Liberty's pedestal. Stone died in New York City on January 23, 1887.

ROBERT P. BROADWATER

See also

Baker, Edward Dickinson; Ball's Bluff, Battle of; Lincoln, Abraham; Port Hudson, Louisiana, Siege of; Red River Campaign

Further Reading

Holien, Kim B. *Battle at Ball's Bluff.* Orange, VA: Moss, 1996.
Winkler, H. Donald. *Civil War Goats and Scapegoats.* Nashville: Cumberland House, 2008.

Stone, Kate

See Holmes, Sarah Katherine Stone

Stone, William Milo
Birth Date: October 14, 1827
Death Date: July 8, 1893

Union officer and governor of Iowa (1864–1868). William Milo Stone was born on October 14, 1827, in Jefferson County, New York. As a youth, he moved with his family to Ohio, where he received some secondary education. After serving as a boat crew member on the Ohio River and apprenticing as a chair maker, he studied law on his own initiative and was admitted to the bar in 1851. In 1854 he relocated to Knoxville, Iowa, setting up a law practice there. He also took control of the local newspaper, the *Knoxville Journal.* By 1856, Stone had become interested in politics and had joined the fledgling Republican Party, serving as an

early party organizer. From 1857 to 1858, he held a district judgeship.

When the Civil War broke out in 1861, Stone enlisted in the Union Army as a private, rising to the rank of colonel, in the 22nd Iowa, in short order. He saw action and was wounded at the Battle of Liberty (September 17, 1861), also known as the Battle of Blue Mills, in Missouri. He was captured during the Battle of Shiloh (April 6–7, 1862). Later exchanged, he returned to command of the 22nd Iowa and then briefly commanded a brigade in the Army of Southeast Missouri before commanding a brigade in the Army of the Tennessee during the Second Vicksburg campaign (April 1–July 4, 1863). Stone resigned his commission in August 1863 and returned to Iowa.

Successfully running for Iowa governor in 1863, Stone was sworn into office in January 1864. He was elected to a second term in 1865. As governor, Stone strongly supported the Union war effort, pushed for the formation of a state agricultural college, helped establish Iowa's first organized militia, organized assistance to families with members serving in the war, revoked the ban on the immigration of free blacks to Iowa, and helped shepherd Iowa's passage of the Thirteenth Amendment to the U.S. Constitution, which banned slavery. Stone, a personal friend of Abraham Lincoln, was on the train that returned the president's body to Illinois and represented Iowa at Lincoln's funeral.

After leaving office in January 1868, Stone temporarily left public life to pursue his law practice and a business venture. In 1877 he returned to politics, serving a one-year term in the Iowa House of Representatives (1878–1879). After serving for a time as the commissioner of the Land Office in Washington, D.C., Stone died in Oklahoma City, Oklahoma Territory, on July 8, 1893.

PAUL G. PIERPAOLI JR.

See also

Republican Party; Thirteenth Amendment

Further Reading

Sage, Leland L. *A History of Iowa.* Ames: Iowa State University Press, 1974.
Wall, Joseph Frazier. *Iowa: A Bicentennial History.* New York: Norton, 1980.

Stone Fleet

Failed Union attempt to obstruct access to key Southern ports. In October and November 1861, the U.S. Navy Department purchased a number of hulks, many of them former whaling vessels, with the intention of loading them with stones and sinking them as block ships in the channels off Charleston and Savannah. The plan called for 25 to be placed off Savannah and 20 off Charleston. Secretary of the Navy Gideon Welles also promised the commander of the South Atlantic Blockading Squadron, Commodore Samuel F. Du Pont, any additional hulks required for similar operations elsewhere.

The assembly of the large number of ships at Savannah in what became known as the Stone Fleet may have led Confederate leaders to assume that a major Union amphibious operation was imminent. In any case, it helped bring the Confederacy's decision to abandon its fort on Wassaw Island, which dominated one means of access (the other being Tybee Roads) to the Savannah River.

The Stone Fleet was not a success, however. Seventeen of the hulks ultimately made it to Savannah on December 4, although a number were in sinking state, and four of these went down before they could be properly placed. Others were indeed scuttled off Tybee Island.

On December 20, Captain Charles H. Davis supervised the placement of 16 other Stone Fleet ships in the main ship channel on the bar at Charleston. While this action did block that channel for a time, blockade-runners could still access the port through the North and Maffitts Channels, and the operation had little long-range advantage for the Union blockaders. Indeed, the operation was something that Welles preferred to forget. General Robert E. Lee, then commanding the Confederate Military Department of South Carolina, Georgia, and Florida, called it an "abortive expression of the malice and revenge of a people," but he also correctly concluded that the Stone Fleet revealed that the North was not then considering an attack on Charleston and that the Confederates should therefore prepare for attacks elsewhere along the coast.

SPENCER C. TUCKER

See also

Davis, Charles Henry; Du Pont, Samuel Francis; South Atlantic Blockading Squadron; Welles, Gideon

Further Reading

Browning, Robert M., Jr. *Success Is All That Was Expected: The South Atlantic Blockading Squadron during the Civil War.* Dulles, VA: Brassey's, 2002.

Tucker, Spencer C. *Blue and Gray Navies: The Civil War Afloat.* Annapolis, MD: Naval Institute Press, 2006.

U.S. Navy Department. *Official Records of the Union and Confederate Navies in the War of the Rebellion,* Series 1, Vol. 12. Washington, DC: U.S. Government Printing Office, 1901.

Stoneman, George, Jr.
Birth Date: August 22, 1822
Death Date: September 5, 1894

Union officer. George Stoneman Jr. was born on August 22, 1822, in Busti, New York, and graduated from the U.S. Military Academy, West Point, in 1842. Initially assigned to the 1st Dragoons, he served in a variety of posts in the Southwest and in California, saw combat during the Mexican-American War (1846–1848), and took part in numerous actions against Native Americans. He was promoted to first lieutenant in 1854 and the next year became a captain in the new 2nd Cavalry Regiment. He was stationed in Texas when the Civil War began and was promoted to major in May 1861.

Stoneman was appointed a brigadier general of volunteers on August 13, 1861. He led a cavalry brigade in the Army of the Potomac before being given command of an infantry division during the Peninsula Campaign (March–July 1862). Promoted to major general, to date from November 29, 1862, Stoneman led III Corps at the First Battle of Fredericksburg (December 13, 1862). He assumed command of the Cavalry Corps, Army of the Potomac, in February 1863.

In the run-up to the Battle of Chancellorsville (May 1–4, 1863), Stoneman led the Cavalry Corps on a large raid (April 28–May 8, 1863). Major General Joseph Hooker ordered Stoneman on a wide sweep south to disrupt the Confederate Army of Northern Virginia's lines of supply and communication between Fredericksburg and Richmond, but the raid was put off by heavy rain, and when it did occur, Stoneman proceeded cautiously and failed to halt the supplies to Confederate general Robert E. Lee's Army of Northern Virginia. Hooker's decision to send Stoneman on the raid was a major mistake, as it deprived his army of critical intelligence and uncovered his right flank. Hooker blamed Stoneman in part for his defeat in the Battle of Chancellorsville and relieved him of command on May 22.

Stoneman was ordered to Washington, D.C., and from July held a desk job as chief of the Cavalry Bureau. He again received a field command in the early spring of 1864 when he took command of a cavalry division in Major General William T. Sherman's Atlanta Campaign (May 5–September 2, 1864). During Stoneman's disastrous raid with Brigadier General Edward McCook (July 26–31), Stoneman disobeyed his orders to sever Atlanta's rail communications in a forlorn effort to liberate Union prisoners at Macon and Andersonville and was captured on July 31 with some 700 of his men, giving him the distinction of being the highest-ranking Union officer

Major General General George Stoneman Jr. had a mixed record commanding Union cavalry raids. Captured along with some 700 of his men in Georgia during one of these raids, he was the highest ranking Union officer taken prisoner by the Confederates during the Civil War. (Library of Congress)

taken by the Confederates in the war. On Sherman's request, Stoneman was exchanged three months later.

In December 1864 Stoneman led another raid, this time to strike the salt and lead works in southwestern Virginia. This was by far his most successful foray; his force sustained few casualties and captured 4 towns, 19 cannon, 3,000 small arms, 25,000 rounds of artillery ammunition, and some 900 prisoners. Finally, during March 20–April 26, 1865, as Union forces were marching through North Carolina, Stoneman raided in western Virginia and western North Carolina, ripping up rail lines and destroying rail depots and Confederate ammunition stocks. By then, however, the raids had little military significance, as the war was all but won. Brevetted through major general in the regular army, Stoneman mustered out of the volunteers in September 1866.

Stoneman remained in the regular army after the war as colonel of the 21st Infantry, but he resigned in 1871 after his actions as commander of the Department of Arizona were called into question. He moved to California's San Gabriel

Valley and became involved in state politics. He was governor of California from 1883 to 1887. Stoneman died in Buffalo, New York, on September 5, 1894.

PAUL G. PIERPAOLI JR.

See also

Atlanta Campaign; Fredericksburg, First Battle of; Hooker, Joseph; Peninsula Campaign; Stoneman and McCook's Raid; Stoneman's Raid during the Chancellorsville Campaign; Stoneman's Raid in Southwestern Virginia; Stoneman's Raid into North Carolina and Virginia

Further Reading

Fordney, Ben Fuller. *George Stoneman: A Biography of the Union General.* Jefferson, NC: McFarland, 2008.
Warner, Ezra J. *Generals in Blue: Lives of the Union Commanders.* Baton Rouge: Louisiana State University Press, 2006.

Stoneman and McCook's Raid
Start Date: July 26, 1864
End Date: July 31, 1864

Union cavalry operation during the Atlanta Campaign (May 5–September 2, 1864). In July 1864, Union western theater commander Major General William T. Sherman's forces were closing in on Atlanta. Finding it too strongly fortified and too extensive to invest, Sherman decided to send cavalry both east and west of the city to destroy lines of communication between Atlanta and the remainder of the Confederacy, forcing the Confederates to abandon the city.

Sherman ordered Major General George Stoneman, with three brigades of some 6,500 men, to proceed east of Atlanta, while Brigadier General Edward M. McCook and 3,500 men moved west of the city. The two were to join forces at Lovejoy's Station, then cut the Macon & Western Railroad, the major rail link supplying Army of Tennessee commander General John B. Hood's forces at Atlanta. Sherman also authorized Stoneman, on the latter's request, to proceed farther south in an effort to release some 30,000 Union prisoners of war being held at Macon and Andersonville but on condition that the rail connection had been severed first.

Stoneman set out on July 26 but ignored Sherman's orders and headed for Macon first. On July 27, Stoneman detached Brigadier General Kenner Garrard, sending him to Flat Rock to protect his rear. Stoneman crossed the Yellow River near Covington and proceeded down its left bank toward Macon. As a consequence of Stoneman's decision, Confederate major general Joseph Wheeler was able to employ his 10,000 cavalry to defeat each of what were now three Union columns in detail. On July 28, Wheeler's men routed Garrard's division, which then returned to the Union lines.

On July 30, meanwhile, parts of Stoneman's command wrecked railway facilities at Gordon and Griswold Station, destroying several locomotives and dozens of cars as well as a long railroad bridge over the Oconee. At Macon, however, Stoneman was turned back by strongly entrenched Georgia militiamen. After briefly shelling the Confederate positions, he attempted to withdraw. Early on July 31, he was brought to bay at Sunshine Church, 19 miles northeast of Macon, by 1,300 Confederate cavalry under Brigadier General Alfred Iverson Jr. Tricked into believing that he was surrounded by a superior force, Stoneman covered the escape northward of two of his brigades, then surrendered with about 700 men to Iverson. (Stoneman thus had the distinction of being the highest-ranking Union officer taken by the Confederates in the war. He was held prisoner before being exchanged late in September on Sherman's request.)

McCook, meanwhile, had proceeded south, crossed the Chattahoochee River below Campbellton by his pontoon bridge, then marched to Lovejoy's Station. With no sign of Stoneman, he set his men to work tearing up two miles of track, burning two trains of cars, and cutting five miles of telegraph lines. He also came across a Confederate wagon train and burned 500 wagons, killed 800 mules, and captured 422 Confederates. On July 30 near Newman, however, he was surrounded by Confederate cavalry and infantry and forced to abandon his prisoners and fight his way out. McCook lost about 600 men killed or captured before he and the remainder of his command were able to return piecemeal to Turner's Ferry.

The Confederates quickly repaired the damage inflicted. Altogether Sherman's cavalrymen had failed in their mission and had lost some 2,000 men in what served as a significant boost to the morale of the Atlanta defenders. The raid also reinforced Sherman's already low opinion of cavalry.

Hood then dispatched Wheeler's cavalry on a monthlong (August 10–September 10) raid against Union supply lines. This action failed to deter Sherman, however.

SPENCER C. TUCKER

See also

Garrard, Kenner; Hood, John Bell; Sherman, William Tecumseh; Stoneman, George, Jr.; Wheeler, Joseph

Further Reading

Black, Robert, W. *Cavalry Raids of the Civil War.* Mechanicsburg, PA: Stackpole, 2004.
Carter, Samuel. *The Last Cavaliers: Confederate and Union Cavalry in the Civil War.* New York: St. Martin's, 1982.
Katcher, Philip, and Richard Hook. *Union Cavalryman, 1861–1865.* London: Reed International Books, 1995.
Sherman, William T. *Memoirs of W. T. Sherman.* New York: Library of America, 1990.

Stoneman's Raid during the Chancellorsville Campaign
Start Date: April 28, 1863
End Date: May 8, 1863

Counterproductive Union cavalry raid during the Chancellorsville Campaign. After taking command of the Union Army of the Potomac following the First Battle of Fredericksburg (December 13, 1862), Major General Joseph Hooker consolidated the army's cavalry into a single corps of nearly 10,000 men. Major General George Stoneman commanded the corps, which was organized into three divisions of two brigades each under Brigadier Generals Alfred Pleasonton, William W. Averell, and David M. Gregg; these six brigades contained 21 volunteer regiments. Brigadier General John Buford led a reserve brigade of five regiments of regulars. Hooker intended that the cavalry play a more aggressive role than it had in the past.

As he prepared to move against Confederate general Robert E. Lee's Army of Northern Virginia at Fredericksburg, Hooker ordered two of the cavalry divisions and the reserve brigade (retaining only the one division under Pleasonton) to carry out a major raid southward to disrupt Lee's supply and communication lines. Hooker instructed Stoneman to get between Lee's army and Richmond, "isolate him from his supplies," and "inflict on him every possible injury." The raid was to occur before Hooker carried out the main Union turning effort to the west of Fredericksburg, with the hope that it would starve Lee of supplies and force him to withdraw from Fredericksburg.

The raid was to commence from Falmouth on April 13, with the crossing of the Rappahannock River the next day. On April 14, the Union cavalrymen skirmished with and drove off Confederate defenders at Kelly's Ford, but a severe storm brought flooding and made fording the river impossible. It was two weeks later, on April 28, when Stoneman's cavalrymen were able to cross the Rappahannock, immediately followed by the Union infantry.

Stoneman's troopers were in two columns totaling 7,400 men and four batteries of horse artillery. Averell's division constituted the first and smaller column, while Stoneman accompanied the second column of Gregg's division and Buford's brigade. Averell's command was to ride to Gordonsville, disperse rebel cavalry said to be off to the west, destroy track of the Orange & Alexandria Railroad, and mask the movement of the second column, which had as its goal the destruction of the critical Richmond, Fredericksburg, & Potomac Railroad.

The raid was for all intents and purposes a failure. Averell passed most of his time at Rapidan Station, where the Orange & Alexandria Railroad crossed the Rapidan, confronted by two regiments of dismounted Virginia cavalry but also held in place by a false report that a large Confederate force under Major General Thomas J. "Stonewall" Jackson was lying in wait at Gordonsville. On May 4, Hooker relieved the cautious Averell and ordered his command turned over to Pleasonton.

Stoneman, meanwhile, proceeded cautiously, concerned about the location of Major General James E. B. Stuart's Confederate cavalry. The main Union column reached the south bank of the North Anna River on May 2 and commenced its work of destruction. The Union troopers captured a small Confederate wagon supply train, burned a bridge over the North Anna, and tore up some five miles of track of the Virginia Central Railroad, which, however, was not a key target. Two companies of the 1st Maine Cavalry fell in with some 1,000 Confederate cavalry under Brigadier General H. F. "Rooney" Lee, who captured two-thirds of them. Some of Stoneman's men came within 10 miles of Richmond, but on May 5, with most of his horses judged not fit to continue, Stoneman ordered his men to retrace their steps, only to discover that the Confederate engineers had already repaired the earlier work of destruction. The troopers recommenced that work before regaining Union lines on May 8.

The raid was one of Hooker's major mistakes of the Chancellorsville Campaign. The damage inflicted during it was easily repaired, and supplies had continued to flow to Lee's army without interruption. Moreover, cavalrymen remaining under Pleasonton were insufficient to provide the intelligence that Hooker needed regarding Lee's movements and to cover Hooker's right wing. The raid, which was reviewed positively by the Northern press, did serve as an important morale booster to Union cavalrymen and marked the beginning of Union offensive cavalry operations in Virginia.

Looking at Stoneman's 200 casualties, of which three-fourths were from straggling and only one-fourth from battle, Hooker with some justification believed that Stoneman had not been sufficiently aggressive. Hooker considered Stoneman partly responsible for the failure of the campaign

and removed him from command on May 22. Stoneman became chief of the Cavalry Bureau in July, while Pleasonton assumed command of the Cavalry Corps.

SPENCER C. TUCKER

See also

Averell, William Woods; Buford, John; Chancellorsville, Battle of; Fredericksburg, First Battle of; Gregg, David McMurtrie; Hooker, Joseph; Lee, Robert Edward; Lee, William Henry Fitzhugh; Pleasonton, Alfred; Stuart, James Ewell Brown

Further Reading

Black, Robert W. *Cavalry Raids of the Civil War.* Mechanicsburg, PA: Stackpole, 2004.

Katcher, Philip, and Richard Hook. *Union Cavalryman, 1861–1865.* London: Reed International Books, 1995.

Longacre, Edward G. *Lincoln's Cavalrymen: A History of the Mounted Forces of the Army of the Potomac.* Mechanicsburg, PA: Stackpole, 2000.

Sears, Stephen W. *Chancellorsville.* Boston: Houghton Mifflin, 1996.

Stoneman's Raid in Southwestern Virginia
Start Date: December 10, 1865
End Date: December 29, 1865

Successful Union cavalry raid. Destruction of the Confederate saltworks at Saltville in southwestern Virginia had long been a major Union military objective. Salt was necessary to preserve meat, and Saltville was the site of the most important saltworks in the South. Its importance can be gauged by the increase in production there from 15,000 bushels annually before the war to 4 million bushels in 1864. The destruction of the saltworks would greatly impair Confederate Army commissary activities.

Following the defeat of a Union force under Brigadier General Stephen G. Burbridge in the First Battle of Saltville (October 2, 1864), Major General George Stoneman took command of the Union cavalry in eastern Tennessee. Meanwhile, forces in Confederate major general John C. Breckinridge's Department of Western Virginia and East Tennessee had been greatly depleted by the demand for manpower elsewhere, most notably to the east in the Richmond-Petersburg area. Stoneman was aware of that fact and was determined to capitalize on it.

After consolidating cavalry led by Burbridge and Brigadier General Alvan C. Gillem, on December 10, 1864, Stoneman departed Knoxville for Bristol with some 5,700 men: 4,200 cavalry and horse artillery under Burbridge and a brigade of 1,500 Tennessee horsemen under Gillem. At Kingsport,

Tennessee, on December 13, the Union raiders encountered and defeated an understrength Confederate cavalry brigade commanded by Brigadier General Basil W. Duke, capturing its supply train and 84 men. The next day near Bristol, Stoneman defeated another Confederate cavalry unit under Brigadier General John C. Vaughan, preventing it from linking up with the rest of the Confederate forces under Breckinridge at Saltville and securing some 300 prisoners. On December 15, Stoneman first occupied Bristol and then Abington, Virginia, where he burned a number of buildings. He then bypassed Saltville to move against lead mines at Wytheville. In an effort to stop him, Breckinridge moved from Saltville to Marion, and on December 17–18 at Marion, the Confederates held their own against vastly superior Union numbers before withdrawing that evening southward toward North Carolina. Stoneman then destroyed the lead works and mines.

On December 20, Stoneman's men entered Saltville, now undefended except by local militiamen and teamsters. The Union troops easily brushed these aside, and during the next two days they destroyed much of the saltworks as well as quantities of salt. On December 22, they quit Saltville to return to Knoxville. In the course of 12 days, Stoneman's men took 900 prisoners, 19 guns, some 3,000 muskets, and perhaps 3,000 horses and mules. In addition to the saltworks and lead mines and works, he also destroyed bridges and a number of factories and did considerable damage to the Virginia & Tennessee Railroad. Stoneman's men returned to Knoxville on December 29, having ridden some 460 miles.

SPENCER C. TUCKER

See also

Burbridge, Stephen Gano; Duke, Basil Wilson; Gillem, Alvan Cullen; Saltville, First and Second Battles of; Stoneman, George, Jr.; Vaughn, John Crawford

Further Reading

Black, Robert W. *Cavalry Raids of the Civil War*. Mechanicsburg, PA: Stackpole, 2004.
Carter, Samuel. *The Last Cavaliers: Confederate and Union Cavalry in the Civil War*. New York: St. Martin's, 1982.
Katcher, Philip, and Richard Hook. *Union Cavalryman, 1861–1865*. London: Reed International Books, 1995.

Stoneman's Raid into North Carolina and Virginia
Start Date: March 20, 1865
End Date: April 26, 1865

Union cavalry raid near the end of the Civil War. On February 27, 1865, Union general in chief Lieutenant General

Ulysses S. Grant ordered Major General George H. Thomas, commanding the Army of the Cumberland, to instruct Major General George Stoneman at Knoxville, Tennessee, essentially to repeat his raid of December 1864 and disrupt the Virginia & Tennessee Railroad in Virginia and the North Carolina Railroad and the Danville-Greensboro line (Piedmont Railroad) in North Carolina and destroy other Confederate infrastructure and property. Stoneman's force consisted of Brigadier General Alvan C. Gillem's division of three brigades under Colonels William J. Palmer, S. B. Brown, and John K. Miller.

Stoneman's force of 6,000 men and four guns formed at Mossy Creek near Knoxville. The men departed on March 20, reached Morristown, and then proceeded via Bull's Gap across Iron Mountain to Boone, North Carolina, on March 26, which they took by surprise. The raiders then crossed the Blue Ridge Mountains to Wilkesboro on March 29 and from there entered southwestern Virginia on April 2. Encountering little resistance, they destroyed cotton mills and burned cotton while living off the produce of the areas through which they rode. In Virginia, they occupied the depot of Christiansburg on the Virginia & Tennessee Railroad and then proceeded to tear up track from Wytheville to within four miles of Lynchburg. Freed African American males who were fit for military service were enlisted in the 119th U.S. Colored Troops.

Stoneman then headed south again, reentering North Carolina on April 9. He then divided his force. Palmer's brigade proceeded to Salem, while the other two brigades moved against Salisbury. Palmer's men tore up track of the North Carolina Railroad north and south of Greensboro. They then moved on to High Point, where they burned the depot and 1,700 bales of cotton.

Stoneman and the main body crossed the Yadkin River at Huntsville on April 11. East of Salisbury, Stoneman's men surprised a Confederate detachment. Its men fled, abandoning 100 new muskets.

On April 12, Stoneman's men entered the important Confederate railway hub and supply depot of Salisbury. Stoneman had hoped to be able to free a large number of Union prisoners of war being held at Salisbury Prison, but the men had been moved the month before. The raiders burned the prison, four cotton factories, 7,000 bales of cotton, and substantial quantities of supplies. Stoneman's men also tore up a considerable length of railroad track.

On April 13, Stoneman headed for eastern Tennessee, proceeding by way of Statesville and Lenoir. On April 19, Major E. E. C. Moderwell and 250 men burned the 1,150-foot bridge of the Charlotte & South Carolina Railroad spanning the Catawba River. After a skirmish with Confederate cavalry, Moderwell returned to the main body with the Confederate bridge guard of 230 prisoners, 2 artillery pieces, and 200 horses. Stoneman then occupied Asheville on April 25 before reentering Tennessee on April 26.

In all, Stoneman's raid covered more than 600 miles and led to the capture of 2,000 prisoners, 23 artillery pieces taken in action and 21 that had been abandoned, and a large number of small arms. Despite the raid's tactical success, it accomplished little in a strategic sense, as the war was all but over. The raid's main effect was to slow the postwar recovery of the region.

SPENCER C. TUCKER

See also

Gillem, Alvan Cullen; Grant, Ulysses Simpson; Palmer, William Jackson; Salisbury, North Carolina, Union Capture of; Salisbury Prison, North Carolina; Stoneman, George, Jr.; Thomas, George Henry

Further Reading

Barrett, John G. *The Civil War in North Carolina.* Chapel Hill: University of North Carolina Press, 1963.
Hartley, Chris J. *Stoneman's Raid, 1865.* Winston-Salem, NC: John F. Blair, 2010.

Stones River, Battle of
Start Date: December 31, 1862
End Date: January 2, 1863

Large sanguinary engagement fought outside of Murfreesboro, Tennessee. Following the Confederate defeat at Perryville, Kentucky, on October 8, 1862, Union forces moved into central Tennessee. That same month, Major General William S. Rosecrans assumed command of the Union Army of the Cumberland, assigned to conduct operations in Tennessee.

Prodded by his superiors to act, Rosecrans waited until he believed that he had accumulated sufficient supplies, departing Nashville on December 26, 1862. His army moved in three columns southeastward in the direction of Chattanooga. Major General Alexander M. McCook commanded the right wing, Major General George H. Thomas had charge of the center, and Major General Thomas L. Crittenden commanded the left wing. Crittenden's left wing advanced astride the Nashville & Chattanooga Railroad, which crossed Stones River.

The Union force totaled approximately 47,000 men. During December 26–30 the army covered about 30 miles, almost reaching Murfreesboro, where Confederate general Braxton

Bragg and his 38,000-man Army of Tennessee awaited the Union advance on Stones River. Bragg's army was deployed on a 4-mile front, approximately 1.5 miles west and northwest of Murfreesboro. Lieutenant Generals Leonidas Polk and William Hardee commanded Bragg's two corps. Bragg's cavalry consisted of two brigades of experienced horsemen commanded by Brigadier Generals Joseph Wheeler and John Wharton. As the two armies closed, both Bragg and Rosecrans planned offensive actions. Ironically, the two commanders came up with approximately the same plan of holding with their right flank and attacking with their left.

Bragg began the battle. At 6:22 a.m. on December 31, Major General John P. McCown's division of Hardee's corps, supported by Wharton's cavalry, struck the Union right flank, where General McCook's corps was supposed to attack at 7:00 a.m. to extend the Confederate line, but the Union soldiers were then just finishing breakfast and were taken completely by surprise. Major General Patrick R. Cleburne's division moved just behind McCown. These divisions of Hardee's corps drove back McCook's corps. Meanwhile, the Confederate cavalry circled wide to harass the Union rear.

Brigadier General Philip Sheridan, commanding a division of McCook's corps, rallied his men and repelled three Confederate attacks, briefly holding up the Southern advance. But by midmorning, the entire Union flank was in retreat and being driven back into Thomas's corps.

As the Federals fell back on the Nashville Pike, Rosecrans recalled the first Union division sent across Stones River, one of two that were to have assaulted the Confederate right, held by Major General John C. Breckinridge's single division. Rosecrans then shifted two divisions into a defensive posture in front of the massed Union artillery at the Nashville Pike. The spirited Union defense of Round Forest, a wooded area around the pike and the paralleling Chattanooga & Nashville Railroad that became known as Hell's Half Acre, bought time for General Thomas to construct a new Union defensive line to meet the Confederate attack driving in the Union right. The new line ran perpendicular to the old position and parallel to the Nashville Pike. The Union lines now came to resemble a narrow "V" shape. Supported by massed artillery to their rear, the Union defenders beat back numerous Confederate attacks.

Following the initial attack, Bragg did little to influence the battle. Although he had belatedly ordered Polk's forces to join the Confederate attack by striking the Union center, Polk committed his troops piecemeal. By nightfall and the close of the first day of battle, the new Union line had held.

Having now won a tactical victory, Bragg was convinced that Rosecrans would soon withdraw. Throughout New

BATTLE OF STONES RIVER, DECEMBER 1862 – JANUARY 1863

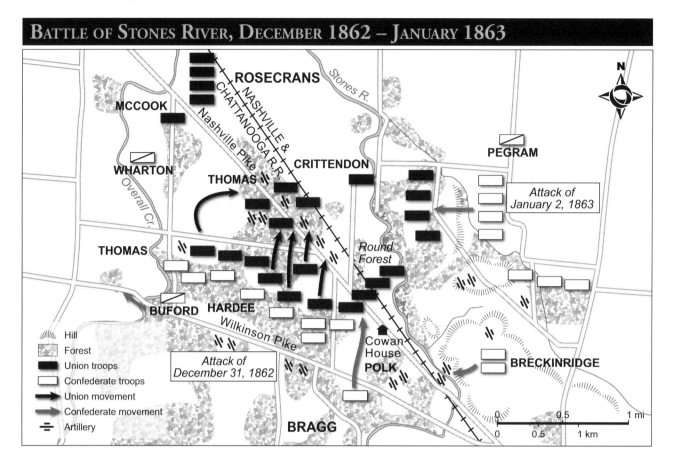

Year's Day as Bragg waited, however, Rosecrans remained in place, and both sides warily watched the other. With the Federals still holding their positions, at 4:00 p.m. on January 2 Bragg ordered Breckinridge to attack the Union left on the east side of Stones River with his 4,500 men in order to seize the high ground there. Observing the Confederates to his front massing for the attack, General Crittenden ordered his artillery commander, Major John Mendenhall, to mass his guns at the ford where the first Union division had crossed earlier. Although the attacking Confederates drove the Union forces back with impressive vigor, at 4:45 p.m. Mendenhall opened up with his 57 massed guns, tearing great holes in the Confederate ranks and driving Breckinridge back to his original position, with frightful losses.

On the night of January 2, the commanders of two Confederate divisions that had sustained heavy casualties on December 31 wrote to Bragg asking for a withdrawal. Polk seconded the suggestion. At first Bragg angrily rejected it, but on the morning of January 3, believing falsely that Rosecrans had been reinforced, Bragg ordered a withdrawal for that evening to Tullahoma, Tennessee. Rosecrans declined to pursue his adversary, contenting himself with occupying Murfreesboro.

The cost of the three-day battle was high for both sides. Union casualties numbered 1,730 dead, 7,802 wounded, and 3,717 missing. Southern losses were almost as great: 1,294 dead, 7,845 wounded, and 1,027 missing.

Although technically a Confederate victory, the Battle of Stones River opened Chattanooga to a Union advance. The battle also accelerated a growing lack of confidence in Bragg.

JAY A. MENZOFF AND SPENCER C. TUCKER

See also

Bragg, Braxton; Crittenden, Thomas Leonidas; Cumberland, Union Army of the; Hardee, William Joseph; McCook, Alexander McDowell; Nashville, Battle of; Polk, Leonidas; Rosecrans, William Starke; Sheridan, Philip Henry; Tennessee, Confederate Army of; Thomas, George Henry

Further Reading

Connelly, Thomas L. *Autumn of Glory: The Army of Tennessee, 1862–1865.* Baton Rouge: Louisiana State University Press, 1971.
Cozzens, Peter. *No Better Place to Die: The Battle of Stones River.* Champlain: University of Illinois Press, 1991.
McDonough, James Lee. *Stones River: Bloody River in Tennessee.* Knoxville: University of Tennessee Press, 1980.

Stonewall, CSS

One of two ironclad rams built at Bordeaux, France, by Lucien Arman for the Confederate government. Only the *Stonewall* reached Southern hands. Contracted for by Confederate agent James D. Bulloch and laid down in 1863 under the cover name of *Sphinx* (as supposedly being intended for the Egyptian government), the *Stonewall* was launched in June 1864. Two months earlier with the tide of war decidedly favoring the North, Paris decided that the ship would not be sold to the Confederacy and arranged for its sale to Denmark instead. Renamed the *Staerkodder,* it was intended for service in Denmark's 1864 war with Prussia and Austria. When the ship failed to reach Denmark before that country lost the war, Copenhagen refused the ship. The French builders were able to arrange its transfer to the Confederacy, and the ship was commissioned at sea in January 1865 as the *Stonewall,* although it was officially known as the *Olinde* to allay suspicion.

The *Stonewall* displaced 1,390 tons and measured 186'9" in length overall (157'6" between perpendiculars), with a maximum beam of 32'6" and a draft of 14'3". It was propelled by two direct-acting engines on two screws and was capable of 10.8 knots. Crew size was 135 men. Fitted with a pronounced submerged ram bow, the *Stonewall* mounted three rifled guns: one 11-inch 300-pounder in the bow to fire directly ahead and two 5-inch 70-pounders carried aft in a turret. The ship was protected by a 3.5" to 4.75" armor belt backed by 16" of wood, with 4.5" armor on the casemate and turrets.

Officers for the ram came from the late Confederate cruiser *Florida,* headed by Captain Thomas J. Page. The *Stonewall* underwent some repairs at Ferrol, Spain, and then steamed to Lisbon to take on coal, from which port it sailed on March 28, easily outdistancing the pursuing U.S. warships *Niagara* and *Sacramento* under the command of Captain Thomas T. Craven, who believed that his adversary was too powerful and had earlier refused battle. Page hoped to attack Port Royal, South Carolina, but contrary winds led him to steam to Nassau and then to Havana. In the latter port, Page learned that the war was over. He then turned the ship over to Cuban authorities in return for money to pay off his crew.

The French-built ironclad ram CSS *Stonewall* lying at anchor off Washington, D.C., in summer 1865. The CSS *Stonewall* was built in France for the Confederacy but was transferred to the South too late to take an active role in the war. (Library of Congress)

Handed over to the United States in July 1865, the *Stonewall* sailed to the Norfolk Navy Yard, where it was sold to the shogun of Japan. Seized by forces loyal to the emperor when it arrived at Yokohama in April 1868 and renamed the *Koketsu,* it led the assault on the shogun's stronghold at Hakodate in July 1869. Renamed the *Azuma* in 1881, it was stricken from the active list in 1888 and broken up in 1908.

The second Stonewall-class ship, built under the name *Cheops,* was also launched in June 1864. Sold by the builder to Prussia, it entered that nation's service as the *Prinze Adalbert* in October 1865. Rearmed and completed in 1866, it was broken up in 1878.

SPENCER C. TUCKER

See also

Bulloch, James Dunwody; Craven, Thomas Tingey

Further Reading

Bulloch, James Dunwody. *The Secret Service of the Confederate States in Europe, or How the Confederate Cruisers Were Equipped.* New York: Modern Library, 2001.

Navy Historical Division, Navy Department. *Civil War Naval Chronology, 1861–1865.* Washington, DC: U.S. Government Printing Office, 1971.

Silverstone, Paul. *Warships of the Civil War Navies.* Annapolis, MD: Naval Institute Press, 1989.

Stonewall Brigade

Confederate infantry brigade first commanded and molded by Brigadier General Thomas J. "Stonewall" Jackson. Composed of five regiments raised primarily in the Shenandoah Valley—the 2nd, 4th, 5th, 27th, and 33rd Virginia Infantry—the Stonewall Brigade was mustered into service under Jackson's command in May 1861. The elite Rockbridge Artillery served with the brigade until October 20, 1862.

When first organized, the unit numbered 2,611 men. That number varied greatly during the brigade's three-year existence, falling to as low as 635 men after the Second Battle of Bull Run (August 29–30, 1862). At its peak strength, the brigade numbered 3,681 men during the Battle of Chancellorsville (May 1–4, 1863), when then–Major General Jackson was shot by his own men and mortally wounded.

The brigade, along with its commander, received the nickname "Stonewall" at the First Battle of Bull Run (July 21, 1861). At the battle, the brigade played a pivotal role in holding Henry House Hill against several Union assaults. Brigadier General Barnard Bee's cry "There stands Jackson like a stone wall! Rally behind the Virginians!" became the source of the nickname for the general and the brigade in the aftermath of the battle.

Shortly after Jackson was promoted, the brigade was sent to the Shenandoah Valley, where Brigadier General Richard Garnett assumed command on December 7, 1861. The brigade served throughout Jackson's Shenandoah Valley Campaign (May–June 1862). That same spring, Brigadier General Charles Winder replaced Garnett and led the brigade for the remainder of the campaign and during the Seven Days' Campaign (June 25–July 1, 1862).

The brigade participated in all the major battles of the eastern theater. In particular, it saw heavy action at the Battles of Antietam (September 17, 1862), Chancellorsville (May 1–4, 1863), Gettysburg (July 1–3, 1863), and the Wilderness (May 5–7, 1864). At the Battle of Spotsylvania Court House (May 8–21, 1864), the Stonewall Brigade was overrun and essentially destroyed in a massive Union assault. The survivors, around 200 men, were consolidated with other depleted Virginia regiments into a single brigade.

Eight officers served as commander (permanent or temporary) of the brigade during the war, and several were killed leading it. Of the eight, only three lived to see the end of the war. Many claim that the Stonewall Brigade never completely recovered from the loss of its beloved commander at Chancellorsville. Brigadier General James Walker served as the final commander of the Stonewall Brigade when it ceased to exist as a distinct unit after Spotsylvania.

The Stonewall Brigade was certainly among the finest units in the Confederate Army early in the war and enjoyed a well-deserved reputation as a fast-marching and hard-fighting command.

JOSHUA MICHAEL AND PAUL G. PIERPAOLI JR.

See also

Antietam, Battle of; Bee, Barnard Elliott; Bull Run, First Battle of; Bull Run, Second Battle of; Chancellorsville, Battle of; Garnett, Richard Brooke; Gettysburg, Battle of; Jackson, Thomas Jonathan; Jackson's Shenandoah Valley Campaign; Seven Days' Campaign; Spotsylvania Court House, Battle of; Walker, James Alexander; Wilderness, Battle of the; Winder, Charles Sidney

Further Reading

Casler, John O. *Four Years in the Stonewall Brigade.* Columbia: University of South Carolina, 2005.

Robertson, James I. *The Stonewall Brigade.* Baton Rouge: Louisiana State University, 1963.

Wert, Jeffrey D. *A Brotherhood of Valor: The Common Soldiers of the Stonewall Brigade, C.S.A., and the Iron Brigade, U.S.A.* New York: Simon and Schuster, 1999.

Stoughton, Edwin Henry
Birth Date: June 23, 1838
Death Date: December 25, 1868

Union officer. Edwin Henry Stoughton was born on June 23, 1838, in Chester, Vermont. He graduated from the U.S. Military Academy, West Point, in 1859. Stoughton was commissioned and assigned garrison duty in New York but soon took a leave of absence. On September 25, 1861, he took command of the 4th Vermont Infantry Regiment with the rank of colonel. During the winter of 1861–1862, he was assigned to the Washington, D.C., defenses. He participated in part of the Peninsula Campaign (March–July 1862) but was on leave from July to November 1862. Upon his return on November 5, he was advanced to brigadier general of volunteers and again assigned to the defenses of Washington.

Stoughton established his headquarters in Fairfax Court House. There on March 8, 1863, he was taken by surprise by 29 Confederates raiders led by Lieutenant John S. Mosby. Allegedly, Stoughton, a heavy drinker and womanizer, was stone drunk and with one of his romantic conquests. Before the Union soldiers could fully react, Mosby and his men had escaped with Stoughton and 32 other Federals, including 2 captains, as well as 58 horses.

Stoughton was released in a prisoner exchange in May 1863, but by then he had become a laughing stock in the Union Army. To make matters even worse, the Senate failed to confirm his promotion to brigadier, which expired. Without a field command, he resigned his commission, settled in New York City, studied law, and opened a legal practice with an uncle. Stoughton died in New York City on December 25, 1868.

PAUL G. PIERPAOLI JR.

See also
Mosby, John Singleton; Mosby's Rangers; Peninsula Campaign

Further Reading
Coffin, Howard. *Full Duty: Vermonters in the Civil War.* Woodstock, VT: Countryman, 1995.
Warner, Ezra J. *Generals in Blue: Lives of the Union Commanders.* Baton Rouge: Louisiana State University Press, 2006.

Stovall, Marcellus Augustus
Birth Date: September 18, 1818
Death Date: August 4, 1895

Confederate officer. Marcellus Augustus Stovall was born in Sparta, Georgia, on September 18, 1818. After attending school in Massachusetts, at age 17 Stovall enlisted in the Richmond Blues of Augusta, Georgia, to fight in the Second Seminole War (1835–1842). In 1836 he secured an appointment to the U.S. Military Academy, West Point, but was forced to resign after only one year because of illness. After a year of travel in Europe, he settled on an estate near Rome, Georgia, and became a captain of artillery in a Georgia Militia company.

Commissioned colonel in the 2nd Georgia Militia Artillery in August 1861, Stovall entered Confederate service as lieutenant colonel of the 3rd Georgia Infantry Battalion on October 8. Stationed in eastern Tennessee, he was with Major General Edmund Kirby Smith's forces during the Confederate invasion of Kentucky (August 14–October 26, 1862). Attached to the Army of Tennessee, Stovall took part in the Battle of Stones River (December 31, 1862–January 2, 1863) and was promoted to brigadier general in April, to date from January 20. He was then sent to Mississippi as part of the relief force before returning to the Army of Tennessee. Commanding a brigade in Major General John C. Breckinridge's division of D. H. Hill's Corps, Stovall distinguished himself in the Battle of Chickamauga (September 19–20, 1863) and participated in the Chattanooga Campaign (October–November 1863).

Stovall took part in the Atlanta Campaign (May 5–September 2, 1864) and the Franklin and Nashville Campaign (November 29–December 27, 1864). He then joined the remainder of the Army of Tennessee under General Joseph E. Johnston in North Carolina, where it surrendered.

Pardoned on May 9, 1865, Stovall returned to Augusta, Georgia, where he became a cotton broker and also operated the Georgia Chemical Works, which manufactured fertilizer. Stovall died in Augusta on August 4, 1895.

SPENCER C. TUCKER

See also
Atlanta Campaign; Breckinridge, John Cabell; Chickamauga, Battle of; Franklin and Nashville Campaign; Johnston, Joseph Eggleston; Smith, Edmund Kirby; Stones River, Battle of

Further Reading
Eicher, John H., and David J. Eicher. *Civil War High Commands.* Stanford, CA: Stanford University Press, 2001.
Warner, Ezra J. *Generals in Gray: Lives of the Confederate Commanders.* Baton Rouge: Louisiana State University Press, 2006.

Stowe, Harriet Beecher
Birth Date: June 14, 1811
Death Date: July 1, 1896

Abolitionist and author of the best-selling antislavery novel *Uncle Tom's Cabin.* Harriet Beecher was born on June 14,

Abolitionist Harriet Beecher Stowe was the author of *Uncle Tom's Cabin* (1852). This highly influential book, which would be translated into many languages, depicted the evils of slavery. It fueled antislavery sentiment in the North and enraged whites in the South. (National Archives)

1811, in Litchfield, Connecticut, the daughter of well-known Congregational minister Lyman Beecher. Her younger brother, Henry Ward Beecher, became one of the most popular preachers of his day.

Harriet Beecher was educated at Miss Pierce's school in Litchfield and then at the Hartford Female Seminary. There, at age 16, she began teaching. She was greatly influenced by her father, a leader in the evangelical movement who inspired in his family a strong sense of public duty. In 1832 the family moved to Cincinnati, Ohio, where Lyman Beecher became president of Lane Theological Seminary and pastor of the Second Presbyterian Church. Harriet Beecher now began to teach at the Western Female Institute and in 1836 married Calvin Stowe. She also wrote a geography book for children and a number of sketches that were published in the *Western Monthly Magazine.*

During these years, Harriet Beecher Stowe began storing up impressions that she would later use in her antislavery masterpiece. Living in a border city, she was very much aware of and disturbed by the existence of slavery in nearby Kentucky, and in 1849 she visited a Kentucky plantation.

In 1850 Stowe and her husband returned to New England, where he joined the faculty of Bowdoin College. Caught up in the heated discussion of the 1850 Fugitive Slave Act, Stowe declared the law an abomination and vowed to do something about it. She then began work on a long tale about slavery, titled *Uncle Tom's Cabin, or Life among the Lowly.* The novel was published in book form in 1852. Although no one expected the book to be popular, more than 300,000 copies of it were sold within the first year. The book also sold well abroad.

Uncle Tom's Cabin was the first book by an American author to have as its hero an African American. In the novel, Stowe attacks the institution of slavery rather than white Southerners, who for the most part are presented as well-meaning.

Uncle Tom's Cabin appealed strongly to readers. And because the book presented the horrors of slavery in vivid human terms, it had a very powerful impact. President Abraham Lincoln only slightly exaggerated when upon meeting Stowe in 1863, he said, "So you're the little woman who wrote the book that made this big war." While fueling antislavery sentiment in the North, the book infuriated Southerners, who charged that Stowe knew nothing about plantation life and grossly misrepresented it. In response to her critics, Stowe published *A Key to Uncle Tom* (1853), a nonfiction work containing documentary evidence that supported her indictment of slavery.

Stowe's second antislavery novel was inspired by the growing conflict over the spread of slavery into Kansas and Nebraska. The hero of *Dred: A Tale of the Dismal Swamp* (1856) is an escaped slave and outlaw living in the North Carolina swamps who preaches to a band of fugitives and has a vision of a holy war. The novel reflected Stowe's new militancy, shared by her brother Henry, who was at this time sending rifles to aid the antislavery settlers in Kansas.

After *Uncle Tom's Cabin* and *Dred*, Stowe continued to write novels, producing on average almost a book a year for the next 30 years. In the settings, characters, and themes of her later novels, however, she returned to the New England of her childhood. After her husband's retirement from teaching in 1864, the Stowes moved to Hartford, Connecticut. In 1889 Stowe compiled her autobiography, *The Life and Letters of Harriet Beecher Stowe.* She died on July 1, 1896, in Hartford.

WILLIAM MCGUIRE AND LESLIE WHEELER

See also

Abolitionism and the Civil War; Beecher, Henry Ward; Fugitive Slave Act of 1850; Kansas-Nebraska Act; Literature; *Uncle Tom's Cabin;* Women

Further Reading
Hedrick, Joan D. *Harriet Beecher Stowe: A Life.* New York: Oxford University Press, 1995.
McFarland, Philip. *Loves of Harriet Beecher Stowe.* New York: Grove, 2007.

Strader v. Graham

U.S. Supreme Court case in 1851 in which the justices—without dissent—rejected the argument that a slave could become free through residence in a free state and held that the decision of state courts (in this case Kentucky) was final in determining the status of a sojourner. In 1841, Kentucky businessman Christopher Graham allowed three of his slaves who were musicians to travel to Ohio and Indiana for performances, after which they had traditionally returned to Kentucky. When the slaves later fled to Canada after initially boarding a steamboat owned by Jacob Strader, Graham sued him for the value of the lost slaves. Strader's defense argued that the slaves had become free while residing in the free states and were no longer Graham's property.

Such an argument was not uncommon. Before 1830 (1844 in Kentucky), nearly every slave state recognized either the power of a free-state constitution, the Northwest Ordinance, or the Missouri Compromise to emancipate slaves who had resided (sojourned) even briefly in a free state or territory. After 1830, however, increasing sectional tensions resulted in a general rejection of such freedom suits by Southern courts, legislatures, and public opinion and by 1860 the federal courts as well.

Kentucky's Court of Appeals ruled for Graham, holding that the slaves' brief sojourns in Ohio and Indiana had not changed their status in Kentucky. Strader then appealed to the U.S. Supreme Court in 1850, claiming that the Kentucky decision violated the Northwest Ordinance. The Supreme Court held that it lacked jurisdiction to review the Kentucky court's ruling because it was based entirely on state law and then proceeded to declare its agreement with the Kentucky court's decision that Kentucky law on the status of the slaves was paramount, despite the time spent in the free states.

In 1857 the Supreme Court, on hearing oral arguments in *Dred Scott v. Sandford,* initially favored a simple reliance on the precedent provided by *Strader* that Missouri law should prevail. For reasons still unclear, however, the Court's majority reversed itself a few days later and decided to address the momentous issues initially avoided: the citizenship of blacks and the power of Congress to legislate on slavery in the territories.

ERROL MACGREGOR CLAUSS

See also
Dred Scott Case; Missouri Compromise; Slavery; Supreme Court, U.S.; Taney, Roger Brooke

Further Reading
Fehrenback, Don E. *The Dred Scott Case: Its Significance in American Law and Politics.* New York: Oxford University Press, 1978.
Finkelman, Paul. *An Imperfect Union: Slavery, Federalism, and Comity.* Chapel Hill: University of North Carolina Press, 1981.

Strahl, Otho French
Birth Date: June 3, 1831
Death Date: November 30, 1864

Confederate officer. Otho French Strahl was born on June 3, 1831, in Morgan County, Ohio. He was a graduate of Ohio Wesleyan University and subsequently studied law. Admitted to the bar in 1858, Strahl established a thriving legal practice in Dyersburg, Tennessee.

In May 1861, Strahl entered Confederate service as a captain in the 4th Tennessee Infantry but was soon elected lieutenant colonel. He first saw combat during the Battle of Shiloh (April 6–7, 1862) and was promoted to colonel on April 24. He endured the Siege of Corinth (May 3–30) and participated in General Braxton Bragg's Kentucky Campaign (August 14–October 26, 1862), seeing heavy fighting at the Battle of Perryville (October 8, 1862). Strahl saw more fierce fighting at the Battle of Stones River (December 31, 1862–January 2, 1863). He assumed command of his brigade during the Tullahoma Campaign (June 23–July 3, 1863), being advanced to brigadier general on July 28, 1863.

Strahl ably commanded his brigade in I Corps, commanded by Major General Frank Cheatham, of the Army of Tennessee, at the Battle of Chickamauga (September 19–20, 1863), where his men launched repeated attacks on the Union center. Strahl's brigade next saw combat during the Chattanooga Campaign (October–November 1863) and was heavily engaged at the Battle of Missionary Ridge (November 25, 1863). Strahl performed well during the Atlanta Campaign (May 5–September 2, 1864) before seeing action during the Franklin and Nashville Campaign (November 29–December 27, 1864). During the Battle of Franklin (November 30, 1864), Strahl led his brigade in a frontal assault on the entrenched Union position. Amid close-in heavy fighting, Strahl was shot and killed as he was handing reloaded rifles to his men near the front lines.

PAUL G. PIERPAOLI JR.

See also

Atlanta Campaign; Chattanooga Campaign; Chickamauga, Battle of; Corinth, Mississippi, Siege of; Franklin, Battle of; Franklin and Nashville Campaign; Missionary Ridge, Battle of; Shiloh, Battle of

Further Reading

Eicher, John H., and David J. Eicher. *Civil War High Commands.* Stanford, CA: Stanford University Press, 2001.

Warner, Ezra J. *Generals in Gray: Lives of the Confederate Commanders.* Baton Rouge: Louisiana State University Press, 2006.

Strategy, CSA

Strategy refers to the larger use of military power and should not be confused with tactical (battlefield) events or with operational efforts (campaigns). At the beginning of the Civil War in April 1861, the Confederacy implemented a cordon strategy, or cordon defense, meaning that it tried to defend its entire perimeter and soon had troops scattered from Virginia to Texas. Notably, the South defaulted to this strategy rather than adopting it purposefully.

The cordon was expanded into Kentucky on September 3, 1861, when Confederate major general Leonidas K. Polk destroyed the state's self-declared neutrality by authorizing its invasion, with Confederate president Jefferson Davis's support. This disastrous act opened the South's western regions to Union penetration—particularly via the Cumberland and Tennessee Rivers. The result was that the Confederates removed an important buffer while broadening the war to an arena that the South could not adequately defend. Strategically, the defense held sway.

Union forces captured Fort Henry (February 6) and Fort Donelson (February 16) on the Tennessee and Cumberland Rivers, respectively, shattering the Confederate cordon. The South now responded with a strategy of concentration. The impetus for this in the West came from Major General Braxton Bragg. He believed that the South's forces were too dispersed and thus needed to strip the periphery, concentrate the forces, and attack.

The same month in the East, both Jefferson Davis and General Joseph E. Johnston began worrying over the exposed position of Johnston's forces in northern Virginia. When Union major general George McClellan launched his Peninsula Campaign (March–July 1862), Johnston pushed for the concentration of the Confederate forces in his department. Concentration guided the South's strategic thinking for the next two years, but this left the Confederates weak in many areas where they could not afford to be.

In the East, the Confederates had no choice but to concentrate against McClellan's forces. In the West, General Albert Sidney Johnston, with Davis's advice, eventually gathered an army at Corinth, Mississippi, to protect the Mississippi Valley. Davis urged a counteroffensive, hoping to recoup Confederate losses. Concentration was certainly the correct Confederate response, but choosing Corinth as the site was a strategic error because this left the vital center of the Confederacy unprotected. Only the Union's failure to push into central Tennessee and Georgia saved the South from an early defeat.

By July 1862, Davis's military thoughts turned to the offensive, and he had two commanders willing and eager to give life to his intentions—Generals Braxton Bragg and Robert E. Lee. In fact, they were already doing so without Davis's prompting. There seems to have arisen nearly simultaneously among the three of them the idea that the South's poor strategic situation in July 1862 could be salvaged only by offensive action. This took the form of a multipronged, multiarmy offensive that stretched from Mississippi to Maryland. Davis had clear strategic objectives for this campaign: regaining Tennessee and bringing Kentucky and Maryland into the Confederate fold. Nothing went as planned, however. The Confederates headed north, laboring under the impression that the residents of Kentucky and Maryland eagerly awaited freedom from Union bondage. This was not the case. Moreover, particularly in the western theater, the offensive was plagued by poor operational planning, an unclear command structure, and fuzzy operational (campaign) objectives. These offensives accomplished very little. This was also the only time that the Confederacy launched such a series of intertwined offensives.

Afterward Davis sought the establishment of better command and control over the western theater. Although he did not like doing so, he gave Joseph E. Johnston the command. Running this vast area effectively required a leader with vision and decisiveness. Johnston possessed neither of these and consistently proved to be unwilling to exercise his command in the face of Union pressure against many points of the South.

Johnston's most immediate problem in the spring of 1863 was trying to save Vicksburg. To do this, he believed that he needed a larger field army to attack the Union forces under Major General Ulysses S. Grant, something about which Johnston was undoubtedly correct. Johnston figured out that the Confederate army defending Vicksburg mattered more than the city itself. Vicksburg's fall would not dramatically impact the Confederacy's ability to resist, but losing the army would. Davis, however, wanted Vicksburg held, a glaring example of the Confederacy's insistence on holding key geographical points while tying up valuable military resources. On May 17, 1863, Johnston sent a note to Vicksburg's defender, Lieutenant General John C. Pemberton, telling him to abandon the city and save the army if Haines Bluff, north of the city, became untenable. Pemberton elected to stay. This cumulative failure of Confederate leadership cost the South not only the town of Vicksburg, which fell on July 4, 1863, but also Pemberton's army (although much of it would fight again).

In the summer of 1863 as Grant's forces aimed at Vicksburg, Robert E. Lee went north. Strategically, Lee believed that the only way the Confederacy could win the war was to break the Union's will, thus convincing the Northern populace to turn against the war. Lee believed that this could be done through defeating Union armies, particularly in the North, and perhaps even destroying a Union army.

But the reality was that the best chance the South had of cracking Union public opinion was to protract the war, thus raising its costs (particularly in blood) beyond what the Union was willing to pay. Protraction does not necessarily mean the pursuit of a Fabian-style strategy built upon the avoidance of battle, one mode of doing so. This offensive culminated in Lee's defeat at the Battle of Gettysburg (July 1–3, 1863).

From late 1863 to 1865, the Confederacy fought a defensive war. The South strengthened itself as best it could as its leaders looked to recoup their territorial losses, particularly in Tennessee. What emerged was an enormously convoluted and often irrational discussion over just how this should be done. None of this debate addressed the key issue: How does the South win the war? Davis never asked this most important question. Meanwhile, strategically, until May 1864, Northern leaders gave the Confederates a breather when they did not have to, and the South failed to use this to improve its strategic position.

Donald Stoker

See also

Bragg, Braxton; Davis, Jefferson Finis; Fort Donelson, Battle of; Fort Henry, Battle of; Gettysburg, Battle of; Grant, Ulysses Simpson; Johnston, Albert Sidney; Johnston, Joseph Eggleston; Lee, Robert Edward; McClellan, George Brinton; Pemberton, John Clifford; Peninsula Campaign; Polk, Leonidas; Strategy, U.S.; Vicksburg Campaign, Second

Further Reading

Stoker, Donald. *The Grand Design: Strategy and the U.S. Civil War.* Oxford: Oxford University Press, 2011.

Stoker, Donald. "There Was No Offensive-Defensive Confederate Strategy." *Journal of Military History* 73 (April 2009): 571–590, 608–610.

Strategy, U.S.

Strategy pertains to the larger use of military power and should not be confused with tactical (battlefield) events or operational efforts (campaigns). The first significant strategic suggestion that President Abraham Lincoln received came from General in Chief Winfield Scott: the Anaconda Plan. This involved blockading the Southern coast to suffocate the Confederacy while pushing a column of 80,000 trained men down the Mississippi River to cut the South in two. Lincoln instituted the blockade promptly, but he initially rejected the Mississippi push; he wanted a quick war with a quick end. This led to a two-pronged invasion of Virginia that culminated in the Union defeat at the First Battle of Bull Run (July 21, 1861).

In August 1861, Lincoln brought Major General George B. McClellan to Washington. McClellan composed a strategic plan that called for offensive action against a variety of points in the Confederacy at the same time. He hoped to end the war in one grand campaign—after proper preparations. This plan, however, and its subsequent versions were all weakened by McClellan's insistence that the army under his command deliver the biggest and thus the decisive punch. Other offensive movements were thus subservient to his advance. This meant that if McClellan did not move, strategic paralysis could grip the Union. This indeed happened, for a time.

As 1862 dawned, Lincoln, increasingly frustrated and besieged politically, pushed his commanders to advance. In a January 13, 1862, letter to Major General Don Carlos Buell, Lincoln wrote that the Union should make use of its superior manpower to press the South at many different points. Simultaneous pressure was Lincoln's strategic approach. On January 27, 1862, he issued General War Order No. 1, designating February 22, 1862, as "the day for a general movement of all the land and naval forces of the United States against the insurgent forces." Union generals sat.

Immense arm-twisting from Lincoln, along with the initiative of western theater Union leaders such as Brigadier General Ulysses S. Grant and Flag Officer Henry Foote, finally got Union forces moving. Grant and Foote seized Fort

Henry (February 6, 1862) and Fort Donelson (February 16) on the Tennessee and Cumberland Rivers, respectively, as Buell's forces marched through Kentucky into Tennessee. In March 1862, McClellan launched his ill-fated Peninsula Campaign (March–July 1862) in Virginia, one element of his larger offensive plan; other prongs moved in the West. McClellan, however, was still thinking in terms of destroying the South in a single multipronged campaign.

On March 11, 1862, after McClellan went to the peninsula, Lincoln relieved him from his post as general in chief (although he kept his Army of the Potomac command). Lincoln put no one else in the job and proceeded, with the help of Secretary of War Edwin M. Stanton, to do the job—and do it badly. For a time, Union strategy had no guiding hand.

In the autumn of 1862 and the winter of 1862–1863, the Union exerted pressure around the perimeter of the Confederacy. Major General Henry W. Halleck, who became the Union general in chief on July 11, 1862, was now doing something similar to what both McClellan and Lincoln had earlier advocated. But Union generals, particularly in the East, continued to clash with Lincoln over how to fight the war. By late 1862, Lincoln was convinced that one of the requirements of Union victory was the destruction of the Confederate Army of Northern Virginia, led by General Robert E. Lee. Lincoln's generals thus focused on taking Richmond, despite the president's urging to the contrary.

Meanwhile, the continuation of the war drove its political and military escalation. In January 1863, Lincoln made emancipation a political objective (or war aim). This was an effort to take a Confederate strength and add it to the Union column. It was also an element of the expanding Union war against Southern property. Initially, the Union and the Confederacy generally confined the violence to the enemy's armed forces. This changed in mid-1862, however, as frustrated Union politicians and soldiers began insisting that Southern civilians, as Union major general William T. Sherman later called it, begin to feel "the hard hand of war." Confederate property—civilian and governmental—became a target. Tied to this was the addition of Union raids against Confederate resources and industrial sites. This was institutionalized as an element of Union strategy by late 1863 and led to exhaustion of the enemy in terms of both will and resources. Union leaders decided to destroy any element of the South's ability to prosecute the war that the Union could not take for its own use.

After the Union victories in the Battle of Gettysburg (July 3, 1863) and the Second Vicksburg Campaign (April 1–July 4, 1863) and Major General William S. Rosecrans's relatively bloodless securing of Chattanooga, Tennessee, and its environs (September 1863), the Union gave the Confederacy the most important strategic gift it could bequeath: time. Instead of striking the body, the Union flailed at the Confederacy's edges. Two things drove this: Lincoln's desire to counter French political influence deriving from Napoleon III's Mexican intervention and Halleck's insistence upon "cleaning up" the Confederacy's peripheral regions.

All of the strands of Union strategy came together when Ulysses S. Grant became the Union general in chief in February 1864. He composed a strategic plan for ending the war by November that included simultaneous attacks against the main Confederate armies in Georgia and Virginia as well as key areas and cities. The plan was a good one that was based on a clear understanding of the political, strategic, and operational realities facing any Union offensive and included simultaneous, mutually supporting operations. Grant was also willing to destroy Confederate armies using attrition if his primary plan did not yield victory. An adjunct element was the use of raids against Confederate supply and industrial points. But there was a big flaw: the various operational prongs needed good commanders. Most of the operational prongs did not have them, and Grant's plan fell apart when he launched his offensive in May 1864.

Grant's plan and its modifications, however, nevertheless laid the groundwork for Union victory. Sherman took Atlanta on September 2, 1864, securing Lincoln's reelection and the continuance of the war. The Confederate defense of Atlanta and Virginia decimated the Army of Tennessee and crippled the Army of Northern Virginia, respectively. Sherman attacked Southern resources, armies, and will in the March to the Sea (November 15–December 21, 1864) in Georgia and his March through the Carolinas (January–April 1865). The Union attrition eventually brought victory, with Lee forced to evacuate Richmond and Petersburg and surrender to Grant on April 9, 1865. Confederate general Joseph E. Johnston surrendered to Sherman in North Carolina on April 26.

DONALD STOKER

See also

Anaconda Plan; Atlanta Campaign; Buell, Don Carlos; Bull Run, First Battle of; Foote, Henry Stuart; Fort Donelson, Battle of; Fort Henry, Battle of; Gettysburg, Battle of; Grant, Ulysses Simpson; Halleck, Henry Wager; Lee, Robert Edward; Lincoln, Abraham; McClellan, George Brinton; Scott, Winfield; Sherman, William Tecumseh; Sherman's March through the Carolinas; Sherman's March to the Sea; Stanton, Edwin McMasters; Vicksburg Campaign, Second

Further Reading

Donald Stoker. *The Grand Design: Strategy and the U.S. Civil War.* Oxford: Oxford University Press, 2011.

U.S. Congress. *The War of the Rebellion: A Compilation of the Official Records of the Union and Confederate Armies.* 128 vols. Washington, DC: U.S. Government Printing Office, 1880–1901. Available on CD-ROM: Phillip Oliver, ed., *The Civil War CD-ROM* (Carmel: Guild Press of Indiana, 1996–2000).

Strawberry Plains, Virginia

See Deep Bottom, First Battle of; Deep Bottom, Second Battle of

Streight, Abel D.

Birth Date: June 17, 1828
Death Date: May 27, 1892

Union officer. Abel D. Streight was born in Wheeler, New York, on June 17, 1828. He later moved to Cincinnati and then to Indianapolis, where he attained some prominence as a publisher, lumber dealer, and member of the Republican Party. On December 12, 1861, he was commissioned colonel of the 51st Indiana Infantry Regiment.

Streight's regiment was assigned to the Army of the Cumberland but saw little action during the first years of the war. In the spring of 1863, however, Streight devised a plan to cut the rail line supplying Confederate forces in Tennessee. He intended to strike the Western & Atlantic Railroad in the vicinity of Rome, Georgia, while Brigadier General Grenville M. Dodge made a diversionary attack on Tuscumbia, Alabama. To speed his movement, Streight decided to mount his force of 1,500–2,000 men on mules.

Streight, commanding a provisional brigade, and Dodge left Eastport, Mississippi, on April 21. They occupied Tuscumbia on April 24, and Streight then moved eastward across Alabama. On April 28, Confederate brigadier general Nathan Bedford Forrest with 1,200 cavalry set off in pursuit of Streight. At Sand Mountain on April 29, Streight repulsed Forrest's attack and launched a counterattack that captured two cannon and 40 prisoners. Streight continued his march, fighting rearguard actions to check Forrest's pursuit. Forrest caught up with Streight's exhausted soldiers on May 3. Despite being heavily outnumbered, Forrest bluffed Streight into surrendering.

Streight was sent to Libby Prison in Richmond, where he and more than 100 other Union prisoners dug a tunnel and escaped in early 1864. After reaching Union lines, Streight was assigned to command a brigade in IV Corps. He fought at the Battles of Franklin (November 30, 1864) and Nashville (December 15–16, 1864) and was brevetted brigadier general in March 1865. However, he resigned from the army that same month.

After the war, Streight resumed his business career and in 1876 was elected to the first of two terms as an Indiana state senator. He died in Indianapolis on May 27, 1892.

JIM PIECUCH

See also

Dodge, Grenville Mellen; Forrest, Nathan Bedford; Franklin, Battle of; Nashville, Battle of; Streight's Raid

Further Reading

Willett, Robert L. *The Lightning Mule Brigade: Abel Streight's 1863 Raid into Alabama.* Carmel, IL: Guild, 1999.

Wills, Bryan Steel. *A Battle from the Start: The Life of Nathan Bedford Forrest.* New York: HarperCollins, 1992.

Streight's Raid

Start Date: April 21, 1863
End Date: May 3, 1863

Unsuccessful Union foray into northern Alabama to cut the railroad supplying Confederate forces in Tennessee. In the spring of 1863, Union colonel Abel D. Streight proposed to support Union operations against Confederate general Braxton Bragg's Army of Tennessee by severing Bragg's supply line. Streight planned to strike the Western & Atlantic Railroad, which carried supplies north from Atlanta, while a second Union force under Brigadier General Grenville M. Dodge diverted Confederate attention by raiding Tuscumbia, Alabama. Streight's command, a provisional brigade numbering between 1,500 and 2,000 men, was to be mounted on mules to speed its movement.

Streight was delayed, however, because of the poor condition of the available mules and a Confederate cavalry raid on April 19, 1863, which deprived Streight of some 200 animals. Dodge and Streight finally set out from Eastport, Mississippi, on April 21. At Tuscumbia, which the Union forces occupied on April 24, Streight separated from Dodge and headed east across Alabama.

Learning of the raid, Bragg dispatched Brigadier General Nathan Bedford Forrest and his cavalry to check the Union forces, but it was not until April 28 that Forrest learned that Streight had separated from Dodge. Forrest set off in pursuit with 1,200 cavalry, pressing hard despite bad weather. That same night, Streight left Moulton, Alabama, and marched 35 miles to Sand Mountain.

Forrest caught up with Streight on April 29 while the Union troops were moving through Day's Gap. The Union forces repulsed the Confederate attack, and Streight counterattacked, capturing two cannon. Union losses were about 30 killed or wounded; Forrest lost 40 men captured and several others killed or wounded. Streight resumed his march until reaching Hog Mountain, where he used the captured artillery to hold off the Confederates. After exhausting the ammunition, the Union troops spiked and abandoned the guns.

Streight continued on to Blountsville, Gadsden, and Cedar Bluff, Alabama, near the Georgia border, holding off his pursuers in a series of rearguard actions. On May 2, Streight's exhausted soldiers again checked Forrest as they crossed Black Creek and burned the bridge, seemingly escaping the Confederates at last. However, a teenaged girl, Emma Sansom, guided Forrest to a ford. The pursuit resumed, and on May 3 Forrest reached Streight's position.

The rigorous pursuit had reduced Forrest's force to only 600 men, so he decided to bluff Streight into surrendering. During a parley with Streight, Forrest moved his men and cannon in and out of the woods, creating the illusion that his force greatly outnumbered Streight's 1,466 men. Deceived, Streight surrendered. Forrest's victory enhanced his reputation and ended the threat to Bragg's supply line.

Jim Piecuch

See also

Dodge, Grenville Mellen; Forrest, Nathan Bedford; Streight, Abel D.

Further Reading

Hurst, Jack. *Nathan Bedford Forrest: A Biography*. New York: Knopf, 1993.

Wills, Brian Steel. *A Battle from the Start: The Life of Nathan Bedford Forrest*. New York: HarperCollins, 1992.

Stribling, Cornelius Kinchiloe
Birth Date: September 22, 1796
Death Date: January 17, 1880

Union naval officer. Born in Pendleton, South Carolina, on September 22, 1796, Cornelius Kinchiloe Stribling received a midshipman's warrant on June 18, 1812. He was promoted to lieutenant on April 1, 1818; to commander on February 28, 1840; and to captain on August 1, 1853. Stribling commanded the East India Squadron from March 1859 to July 1861.

Despite having been born in South Carolina, Stribling remained loyal to the Union. Placed on the retired list on December 21, 1861, he was nonetheless assigned to board duties. He was promoted to commodore on the retired list on July 16, 1862. From November 1862 to September 1864, Stribling commanded the Philadelphia Navy Yard.

On October 12, 1864, Stribling assumed command of the East Gulf Blockading Squadron at Key West, Florida. On May 30, 1865, he applied to be relieved of his command for reasons of health, but Secretary of the Navy Gideon Welles had already decided to do away with the squadron, and on June 9 Stribling was ordered to strike his flag and turn over his command to Acting Rear Admiral Henry K. Thatcher, the West Gulf Blockading Squadron commander, who now assumed command of the combined new Gulf Squadron on July 5.

Promoted to rear admiral on the retired list on July 25, 1866, Stribling was a member of the Lighthouse Board from 1866 to 1871. He died in Martinsburg, West Virginia, on January 17, 1880. His son, Lieutenant John N. Stribling, a graduate of the Naval Academy at Annapolis, joined the Confederate Navy at the same rank at the end of 1861 and died of yellow fever aboard the *Florida* in 1862.

Spencer C. Tucker

See also

Florida, CSS; Thatcher, Henry Knox; West Gulf Blockading Squadron

Further Reading

Callahan, Edward W., ed. *List of Officers of the Navy of the United States and of the Marine Corps from 1775 to 1900*. 1901; reprint, New York: Haskell House Publishers, 1969.

Thompson, Kenneth E. *Civil War Commodores and Admirals: A Biographical Directory of All Eighty-Eight Union and Confederate Navy Officers Who Attained Commissioned Flag Rank during the War*. Portland, ME: Thompson Group, 2001.

Stringham, Silas Horton
Birth Date: November 7, 1797
Death Date: February 7, 1876

Union naval officer. Born in Middletown, New York, on November 7, 1797, Silas Horton Stringham entered the U.S. Navy on a midshipman's warrant on November 15, 1809, at barely 12 years of age. During the War of 1812, he served in the frigate *President* and was promoted to lieutenant on December 9, 1814. He saw service in the Mediterranean during the Algerine War (1816) in the brig *Spark* and then served in the anti–slave trade patrols off Africa in the sloop

Cyane and in West Indian antipiracy duties (1821–1824). He was promoted to commander on March 3, 1831, and to captain on September 8, 1841.

Stringham next commanded the New York Navy Yard (1844–1846). In the Mexican-American War (1846–1848), he commanded the ship of the line *Ohio* and took part in the bombardment of Veracruz. He then commanded the Norfolk (Gosport) Navy Yard (1848–1852). Stringham commanded the Mediterranean Squadron (1853–1856) before taking charge of the Boston Navy Yard (1856–1861).

In 1861 President James Buchanan called Stringham, then a veteran of 52 years of naval service, to Washington to advise him on naval matters. Stringham suggested that the president reinforce Fort Sumter in Charleston Harbor, but nothing was done until it was too late. On May 1, Stringham took command of the Coast Blockading Squadron, charged with blockading the entire Confederate coastline from Alexandria, Virginia, to Key West, Florida. Three weeks later it became the Atlantic Blockading Squadron. In August 1861 Stringham carried out the first combined operation of the war, during which in a textbook operation the six warships of his squadron secured Hatteras Inlet, North Carolina.

Stringham subsequently came under criticism, both from within the Navy Department and in the press, for the inadequacies of the Union blockade effort and for failing to follow up his Hatteras victory by venturing into the North Carolina sounds. Stung by these unwarranted attacks, Stringham submitted his resignation on September 16, 1861. This came at an ideal time, because the Blockade Board had concluded that the Confederate Atlantic seaboard was too long for one man to supervise. Secretary of the Navy Gideon Welles agreed. The Atlantic Blockading Squadron was split into two commands: the North Atlantic Blockading Squadron and the South Atlantic Blockading Squadron.

Stringham resigned his command on September 16, 1861, and was placed on the retired list on December 21, 1861. He soon resumed naval service as commander of the Boston Navy Yard in 1862 and served until the end of the war. He was advanced to rear admiral on the retired list on July 16, 1862, and was port admiral at New York during 1870–1872. Stringham died at Brooklyn, New York, on February 7, 1876.

SPENCER C. TUCKER

See also

Blockade of the Confederacy, Union; Hatteras Inlet, North Carolina, Union Assault on; North Atlantic Blockading Squadron; South Atlantic Blockading Squadron; Welles, Gideon

Further Reading

Browning, Robert M., Jr. *From Cape Charles to Cape Fear: The North Atlantic Blockading Squadron during the Civil War.* Tuscaloosa: University of Alabama Press, 1993.

Tucker, Spencer C. *Blue and Gray Navies: The Civil War Afloat.* Annapolis, MD: Naval Institute Press, 2006.

U.S. Navy Department. *Official Records of the Union and Confederate Navies in the War of the Rebellion,* Series 1, Vol. 6. Washington, DC: U.S. Government Printing Office, 1897.

Strong, George Crockett
Birth Date: October 16, 1832
Death Date: July 20, 1863

Union officer. George Crockett Strong was born on October 16, 1832, in Stockbridge, Vermont, and was reared in Easthampton, Massachusetts. He graduated from the U.S. Military Academy, West Point, in 1857 and became an ordnance officer. In 1859 he was appointed assistant superintendent of the Watervliet Arsenal in New York. A first lieutenant by 1861, Strong was named chief ordnance officer for the Department of Northeastern Virginia and saw action during the First Battle of Bull Run (July 21, 1861). That September, he became adjutant general for Major General Benjamin F. Butler with the volunteer rank of major.

After Butler's force was dispatched to Louisiana, Strong became the general's chief of staff in February 1862. Strong then served in a series of field commands, which included leading an expedition to Biloxi and Pass Christian, Louisiana, from Ship Island (April 3–4, 1862) and a September 13 raid on a Confederate supply depot in Ponchatoula, Louisiana. For his solid performances, he was advanced to brigadier general of volunteers on March 23, 1863, to date from November 29, 1862. Upon his promotion, he was dispatched to the coast of South Carolina.

Working under Major General Quincy A. Gillmore, commander of the Department of the South, Strong participated in the Siege of Fort Wagner (July 10–September 7, 1863). The assault that he led on the Confederate stronghold on July 11 was repulsed, and his brigade took heavy casualties. On July 18, Strong spearheaded another attack on Fort Wagner; this too was repulsed, with Strong's brigade again suffering heavy losses. During this assault, Strong was wounded in the thigh. The injury was not considered life-threatening, and he was evacuated north for treatment in New York City. On the trip, however, Strong contracted tetanus and died in New York City on July 20. The next day, unaware that Strong had expired, Congress confirmed his promotion to major general of volunteers.

PAUL G. PIERPAOLI JR.

See also

Bull Run, First Battle of; Fort Wagner, South Carolina, Siege of

Further Reading

Eicher, John H., and David J. Eicher. *Civil War High Commands.* Stanford, CA: Stanford University Press, 2001.

Warner, Ezra J. *Generals in Blue: Lives of the Union Commanders.* Baton Rouge: Louisiana State University Press, 2006.

Strong, George Templeton
Birth Date: January 26, 1820
Death Date: July 21, 1875

U.S. Sanitary Commission official and prolific diarist. George Templeton Strong was born in New York City in January 1820 to a prosperous family. After graduating from Columbia College in 1838, he joined his father's law firm and was admitted to the bar in 1844. Strong moved among New York's intellectual and moneyed elite and in 1853 became a trustee of Columbia College.

In June 1861, Strong agreed to serve as a member of the U.S. Sanitary Commission's executive committee; he also served as the organization's treasurer (1861–1865). In that capacity, he helped raise and disperse some $5 million from various companies throughout the United States. Strong also frequently visited army camps, prisons, and battlefields and met often with U.S. government officials, including President Abraham Lincoln, Secretary of War Edwin M. Stanton, and high-ranking army officers.

Strong became best known for his diary, chronicling nearly 40 years and encompassing 2,250 handwritten pages. He made his first entry in October 1835, with the last entry written a short time before his death in 1875. The diary did not become known to scholars until the 1930s. Strong's diary proved to be a treasure trove of information about and observations of a turbulent era in American life, from an eyewitness perspective. Strong had well-formed opinions and notions about myriad contemporary issues that usually reflected his well-educated upper-middle-class mindset. Among other things, one can trace the trajectory from unionism to abolitionism that occurred during the Civil War. Strong also detailed his and others' opinions about John Brown's 1859 Harpers Ferry Raid, Lincoln's leadership and noted addresses, and the 1863 New York City Draft

Riots. Among the entries were scattered but detailed portraits of the era's leaders, many of whom Strong had met personally, including Lincoln. Ken Burns's celebrated PBS documentary *The Civil War* (1990) quoted liberally from Strong's diary.

Strong's last decade was plagued by poor health and financial difficulties. He retired from legal work in 1872 but continued his philanthropic work until his death in New York City on July 21, 1875.

PAUL G. PIERPAOLI JR.

See also

Brown, John; Literature; New York City Draft Riots; Sanitary Commission, U.S.

Further Reading

Nevins, Allan, and Milton H. Thomas, eds. *The Diary of George Templeton Strong*, Vols. 1–2. New York: Macmillan, 1952, 1954.

Wormeley, Katherine Prescott. *The Other Side of the War with the Army of the Potomac: Letters from the Headquarters of the United States Sanitary Commission during the Peninsular Campaign in Virginia in 1862.* Boston: Ticknor, 1889.

Stuart, David
Birth Date: March 12, 1816
Death Date: September 12, 1868

Union officer. David Stuart was born on March 12, 1816, in Brooklyn, New York; his father, Robert Stuart, was a well-to-do merchant and was a business partner of the renowned fur trader John Jacob Astor. After graduating from Amherst College in 1838, David Stuart studied law, moved to Michigan, and was admitted to the state bar in 1842. He established a practice in Detroit and was then appointed city attorney. In 1844 he became Wayne County's prosecuting attorney. Stuart was elected as a Democrat to the U.S. House of Representatives, serving from 1853 until 1855; his reelection bid in 1854 was not successful.

Stuart subsequently relocated to Chicago, where he served as an attorney for the Illinois Central Railroad. On June 22, 1861, he entered federal service as lieutenant colonel of the 42nd Illinois Infantry. On October 31, 1861, he was appointed colonel of the 55th Illinois Infantry.

Stuart sustained a serious wound during the Battle of Shiloh (April 6–7, 1862), during which he had temporary charge of the 2nd Brigade in Major General William T. Sherman's division. On November 29, 1862, President Abraham Lincoln appointed Stuart a brigadier general of volunteers.

As such, he led a brigade at the Battle of Chickasaw Bluffs (December 26–29, 1862) and the Battle of Fort Hindman/Arkansas Post (January 9–11, 1863).

The U.S. Senate failed to confirm Stuart's promotion to brigadier general in March 1863, and on April 3 he resigned his commission and returned to Detroit, where he revived his legal practice. Stuart died on September 12, 1868, in Detroit.

PAUL G. PIERPAOLI JR.

See also

Chickasaw Bluffs, Battle of; Fort Hindman, Battle of; Sherman, William Tecumseh; Shiloh, Battle of

Further Reading

Kenneth, Lee. *Sherman: A Soldier's Life.* New York: HarperCollins, 2001.

Sherman, William T. *Memoirs of General William T. Sherman.* 2 vols. Reprint ed. Bloomington: Indiana University Press, 1957.

Stuart, James Ewell Brown
Birth Date: February 6, 1833
Death Date: May 12, 1864

Confederate officer. James Ewell Brown "Jeb" Stuart was born at the family farm of Laurel Hill in Patrick County, Virginia, on February 6, 1833. He attended Emory and Henry College (1848–1850) but left to enter the U.S. Military Academy, West Point, from which he graduated in 1854. Commissioned in the Mounted Rifles, Stuart was assigned to Fort Davis, Texas. In 1855 he transferred to the new 1st Cavalry Regiment. He spent much of the next half decade on frontier duty in Bleeding Kansas. Stuart was promoted to first lieutenant on December 20, 1855.

In November 1859, Stuart traveled to Washington, D.C., to discuss a government contract for a hook he had invented with which to attach a saber to a cavalryman's belt. While there, Colonel Robert E. Lee, who had been superintendent at West Point when Stuart was a cadet, requested and secured Stuart as his aide when he led a company of marines to Harpers Ferry to subdue the insurrection led by John Brown.

Stuart returned to Kansas and was promoted to captain on April 22, 1861, but with the secession of Virginia he resigned his U.S. Army commission in May and accepted a commission as a lieutenant colonel in the Virginia infantry. He then organized the 1st Virginia Cavalry Regiment at Harpers Ferry and was commissioned a colonel in the Confederate Army on July 16. Stuart distinguished himself in the

First Battle of Bull Run (July 21, 1861), when he led a charge that helped ensure the Confederate victory. Receiving command of a brigade, he was promoted to brigadier general on September 24.

During the Peninsula Campaign (March–July 1862), Stuart was charged with determining whether the Union right flank was vulnerable to attack. Having accomplished this mission, rather than simply return to camp, Stuart with his 1,200 men rode entirely around the Union army, covering 150 miles and taking a number of prisoners, horses, and supplies and helping to unnerve already cautious Union commander Major General George B. McClellan. The ride made Stuart famous throughout the South.

Stuart commanded the Army of Northern Virginia's cavalry during the Seven Days' Campaign (June 25–July 1, 1862) and took part in the pursuit of the withdrawing Union forces. He then fought in the Battle of Malvern Hill (July 1) but prematurely opened fire with an artillery piece that revealed his presence and may have cost the Confederate

Confederate major general James Ewell Brown (J. E. B.) Stuart commanded the cavalry of the Army of Northern Virginia. The flamboyant but highly effective Stuart was mortally wounded in the Battle of Yellow Tavern, Virginia, on May 11, 1864. (National Archives)

victory. This did not prevent Stuart from being promoted to major general on July 25, when his command was organized into the Cavalry Division, Army of Northern Virginia.

In the run-up to the Second Battle of Bull Run (August 29–30, 1862), Stuart raided Union commander Major General John Pope's headquarters at Catlett's Station on August 22–23 and covered Major General Thomas J. "Stonewall" Jackson's advance to Bristoe Station and Manassas and aided him at the Battle of Groveton (August 28). Stuart then took part in the Confederate invasion of Maryland, culminating in the Battle of Antietam (September 17). On October 10–11, Stuart led 1,800 men in a raid on Chambersburg, Pennsylvania, in an unsuccessful effort to destroy the iron bridge over Conococheague Creek but circumnavigating the Army of the Potomac for a second time. During the First Battle of Fredericksburg (December 13, 1862), Stuart had command of the artillery on the Confederate right.

That winter, Stuart's men held the Confederate line south of the Rappahannock River and provided timely intelligence to Lee on the Union crossing that culminated in the Battle of Chancellorsville (May 1–4, 1863). During that battle, his men helped protect Jackson's flanking movement. When Jackson was wounded, Stuart took temporary command of his corps. On June 9, 1863, Stuart and his men were surprised by a Union attack led by Major General Alfred Pleasanton that ended in the largest cavalry battle ever fought in North America, at Brandy Station, marking the end of Stuart's dominance in the eastern theater.

Stuart, who until this point had enjoyed Lee's full confidence and praise, played a controversial role in the Gettysburg Campaign (June–July 1863). Lee assigned Stuart the task of protecting the right flank of the Army of Northern Virginia in its movement north but gave the always reliable Stuart discretionary powers. However, a large Union concentration prevented Stuart from crossing the Potomac until June 27–28, farther east than he intended. This cut him off from Confederate forces under Lieutenant General Richard S. Ewell, but rather than trying to close with Ewell, Stuart proceeded north on his own. Stuart's reputation for reliability led Lee to mistakenly assume that the Union Army of the Potomac was still in its camps north of the Rappahannock and led to Lee being forced to fight at Gettysburg (July 1–3, 1863). Stuart arrived only on the afternoon of July 2, incurring a rebuke from Lee. Stuart's division was then bested by Union cavalry on the third day of the battle.

After Gettysburg, the flamboyant Stuart always remained in close contact with Lee. In September, Stuart's command was organized into a corps, but Stuart did not receive the customary promotion to lieutenant general. His cavalry provided invaluable information on Union movements at the start of the Overland Campaign (May 4–June 12, 1864).

Stuart was mortally wounded in the Battle of Yellow Tavern (May 11, 1864) in Virginia when his 4,500 cavalrymen attempted to halt 10,000 Union cavalry under Major General Philip H. Sheridan. Stuart died the next day. While flamboyant, Stuart was an uncommonly able cavalry commander who excelled in reconnaissance and the employment of cavalry in support of offensive infantry operations.

SPENCER C. TUCKER

See also

Antietam, Battle of; Antietam Campaign; Brandy Station, Battle of; Brown, John; Bull Run, First Battle of; Bull Run, Second Battle of; Catlett's Station, Virginia, Stuart's Raid on; Cooke, Philip St. George; Dumfries, Virginia, Stuart's Raid on; Ewell, Richard Stoddart; Fredericksburg, First Battle of; Gettysburg, Battle of; Gettysburg Campaign; Groveton, Battle of; Harpers Ferry, Virginia, John Brown's Raid on; Jackson, Thomas Jonathan; Lee, Robert Edward; Malvern Hill, Battle of; McClellan, George Brinton; Overland Campaign; Peninsula Campaign; Seven Days' Campaign; Sheridan, Philip Henry; Stuart's Chambersburg Raid; Stuart's Ride around McClellan

Further Reading

Longacre, Edward G. *The Cavalry at Gettysburg.* Lincoln: University of Nebraska Press, 1986.

Longacre, Edward G. *Lee's Cavalrymen: A History of the Mounted Forces of the Army of Northern Virginia.* Mechanicsburg, PA: Stackpole, 2002.

Wert, Jeffry D. *Cavalryman of the Lost Cause: A Biography of J. E. B. Stuart.* New York: Simon and Schuster, 2008.

Wittenberg, Eric J., and J. David Petruzzi. *Plenty of Blame to Go Around: Jeb Stuart's Controversial Ride to Gettysburg.* New York: Savas Beatie, 2006.

Stuart's Chambersburg Raid
Start Date: October 10, 1862
End Date: October 11, 1862

Confederate cavalry raid to Chambersburg, Pennsylvania. Chambersburg is located in south-central Pennsylvania some 50 miles southwest of Harrisburg and not far from the Maryland border. After the Battle of Antietam (September 17, 1862), General Robert E. Lee's Army of Northern Virginia withdrew across the Potomac River into Virginia to rest and resupply. Major General George B. McClellan's much larger Army of the Potomac remained in Maryland, encamped from Williamsport eastward to the Monocacy River. McClellan's supply base was at Hagerstown,

Maryland, where rail lines led north through the Cumberland Valley to Harrisburg and east toward Washington, D.C.

Lee was worried that McClellan would cross the river and attack before his own men were resupplied and ready to fight the larger Union army. To delay the enemy advance and gain information about McClellan's intentions, Lee conferred with his cavalry commander, Major General J. E. B. "Jeb" Stuart. Together, they developed a bold plan. Stuart would lead 1,800 of his best horsemen across the river just west of the Union camps and then circle behind them into southern Pennsylvania. The target was Chambersburg, the seat of Franklin County and a small Union supply point. Five miles north of Chambersburg was a railroad bridge over the Conococheague Creek. If this bridge could be destroyed, supplies to the Union Army would be delayed while the bridge was rebuilt. Lee also told Stuart that he was free to seize civilian horses to resupply his men and to take hostages to exchange for Southern civilians in Union prisons.

On the foggy morning of October 10, 1862, Stuart's horsemen splashed across the Potomac at McCoy's Ford, scattering Union pickets on the opposite bank. Although McClellan was soon alerted that Confederate cavalrymen had crossed the river, he did not know their destination. Union troops went on alert, and cavalry began to scout the terrain around his army's camps.

Stuart's soldiers rode rapidly northward, passing through Mercersburg by noon on October 10 and reaching the outskirts of Chambersburg shortly before nightfall. There was no resistance as his men fanned out through the city, cutting telegraph wires and paroling captured soldiers in local hospitals. However, the detachment sent north to burn the railroad bridge returned after finding that the bridge was made of iron and would not burn. Early on October 11, Stuart's men rode out of Chambersburg after setting fire to the railroad depot, several warehouses filled with military supplies, some machine shops, and several rows of railroad cars.

The Confederate horsemen next rode east to Cashtown and then filed south toward the Potomac. After successfully evading pursuing Union cavalry, Stuart's exhausted men crossed the Potomac River at White's Ford on October 12. The Chambersburg Raid had been a great success. Only two men had been wounded, but the raiders brought back with them 1,200 new horses and several civilian hostages. The destroyed military stores in Chambersburg were worth an estimated $250,000. Even though Stuart's raid had not seriously affected the Union supply situation, it gave the already cautious McClellan even more to worry about.

RICHARD A. SAUERS

See also

Antietam, Battle of; Lee, Robert Edward; Maryland; McClellan, George Brinton; Northern Virginia, Confederate Army of; Pennsylvania; Potomac, Union Army of the; Stuart, James Ewell Brown

Further Reading

Greater Chambersburg Area of Commerce. *Southern Revenge! Civil War History of Chambersburg, Pennsylvania.* Shippensburg, PA: White Mane, 1989.

Price, Channing. "Stuart's Chambersburg Raid: An Eyewitness Account." *Civil War Times Illustrated* 4 (January 1966): 8–15, 42–44.

Thomas, Emory M. *Bold Dragoon: The Life of J. E. B. Stuart.* New York: HarperCollins, 1986.

Stuart's Ride around McClellan
Start Date: June 12, 1862
End Date: June 15, 1862

Confederate cavalry raid during the Peninsula Campaign (March–July 1862). On June 10, 1862, Confederate general Robert E. Lee called his cavalry commander Brigadier General J. E. B. "Jeb" Stuart to his headquarters and asked him to gather information on the right flank of Major General George B. McClellan's 100,000-man Union Army of the Potomac, then very close to Richmond. Lee, preparing for offensive action, was particularly interested in learning the strength and disposition of the Union's V Corps and information on the terrain between the Chickahominy River and the Totopotomoy Creek.

Stuart eagerly accepted Lee's mission but proposed a more daring idea. Stuart suggested that instead of gathering the intelligence information required and immediately returning the way he came, he continue his ride around McClellan's forces, encircling the Army of the Potomac. He would thus return to Richmond from the southeast. Both Lee and Stuart recognized the inherent danger of this operation, but they believed that its unexpected nature, combined with McClellan's overly cautious tendencies, would ensure success.

Stuart's force totaled 1,200 cavalrymen from the 1st and 9th Virginia Regiments, part of the 4th Virginia Regiment, two squadrons of the Jeff Davis Mississippi Legion, and a two-gun detachment of horse artillery. On June 11 Lee issued orders to Stuart to proceed with the mission. These called on Stuart to exercise caution but left him considerable discretion, and there can be little doubt that Lee endorsed Stuart's plan.

At dawn on June 12, Stuart began his ride. That first day, Stuart and his men encountered only token resistance from the Federals. On the afternoon of June 13, Stuart's forces reached Old Church, where they engaged elements of the 5th U.S. Cavalry and burned a nearby Union encampment. By this point, Stuart had gathered the information he needed and could have returned to Lee but instead decided to undertake his plan to ride completely around McClellan's army. The extended expedition took Stuart and his men 9 miles to a crossing on the York River and then another 11 miles to Forge Bridge, where they crossed the Chickahominy River before they took a northwestward approach along the James River to return to Richmond.

Stuart was about an hour's ride beyond Old Church before his position was reported by Union troops. A force of 500 men of the Union Cavalry Reserve, commanded by Brigadier General Philip St. George Cooke, Stuart's father-in-law, prepared to challenge the intruders. Cooke, believing that infantry also accompanied Stuart, demanded that Union infantry accompany his pursuit. Consequently, the Union chase was cautious and never truly a threat to Stuart's mission.

Once he had crossed the Chickahominy, Stuart advanced toward Richmond alone, moving north, and arrived in the Confederate capital on the morning of June 15. His men arrived late that same afternoon. Stuart's expedition captured 170 Union soldiers and more than 300 horses and mules and also destroyed numerous Union supply wagons. All of this was accomplished at the cost of only 1 man killed, Captain William Latané of the 9th Virginia. Stuart's ride covered some 100 miles. Although McClellan would continue his campaign in an attempt to capture Richmond, Stuart's ride was a great propaganda victory for the Confederates and made Stuart a legendary figure.

JENNIFER M. MURRAY

See also

Cooke, Philip St. George; Lee, Robert Edward; McClellan, George Brinton; Peninsula Campaign; Stuart, James Ewell Brown

Further Reading

Sears, Stephen W. *To The Gates of Richmond: The Peninsula Campaign.* New York: Ticknor and Fields, 1992.

Thomas, Emory. *Bold Dragoon: The Life of J. E. B. Stuart.* Norman: University of Oklahoma Press, 1999.

Studebaker, Clement
Birth Date: March 21, 1831
Death Date: November 27, 1901

Blacksmith and wagon maker whose company was a major supplier of wagons for the Union war effort. Clement Studebaker was born on March 12, 1831, in Pinetown, Pennsylvania. In 1836 he moved to Ashland, Ohio, where his father

set up trade as a blacksmith and wagon maker. At age 19, Studebaker moved to South Bend, Indiana, to teach district school. In his free time he also worked as a blacksmith.

In 1852 with very little money and a few tools, Studebaker and his older brother Henry established the firm of H. & C. Studebaker. They were blacksmiths and, as their father had done, took on extra work making wagons. Soon the demand for wagons exploded, and H. & C. Studebaker eventually produced more than 750,000 wagons.

By the mid-1850s the brothers had received their first of many government contracts, and their productivity and insistence on quality earned them a good reputation in the business. Studebaker also shrewdly thought to burn the name Studebaker onto each of the government wagons, a move that greatly increased the name recognition of the product and general demand for the vehicles.

Studebaker's brother John replaced Henry in the partnership with Studebaker in 1857. During the Civil War, Studebaker's company was awarded numerous lucrative federal contracts; by the end of 1862, it had supplied in excess of 5,000 wagons to the Army of the Potomac alone. Profits from these contracts were substantial, averaging 20 percent. The typical Studebaker wagon required six mules or horses and was extremely durable. It could accommodate up to 1,400 short rations and eight days of short forage for mules or 25 containers of small arms ammunition. Soon the business became the largest maker of horse-drawn vehicles in the world.

It was John Studebaker who would catapult the company into national prominence as an automobile manufacturer after Clement Studebaker's death in 1901. The name plate endured until 1966. Clement Studebaker remained active in business, educational issues, and his other interests until his death on November 27, 1901, in South Bend, Indiana.

NEIL HAMILTON

See also

Home Front, Union

Further Reading

Bonsall, Thomas E. *More Than They Promised: The Studebaker Story.* Stanford, CA: Stanford University Press, 2000.

Carlock, Walter, *The Studebaker Family in America, 1736–1976.* South Bend, IN: Studebaker Foundation, 1976.

Sturgis, Samuel Davis
Birth Date: June 11, 1822
Death Date: September 28, 1889

Union officer. Samuel Davis Sturgis was born in Shippensburg, Pennsylvania, on June 11, 1822. He graduated from the

U.S. Military Academy, West Point, in 1846 and was assigned as a brevet second lieutenant to the 2nd Dragoons on July 1. He was commissioned second lieutenant in the 1st Dragoons on February 1, 1847. During the Mexican-American War (1846–1848), Sturgis was making a reconnaissance near Buena Vista, Mexico, when he was taken prisoner on February 20, 1847. He was exchanged on February 28. Sturgis was promoted to first lieutenant on July 15, 1853, and to captain in the new 1st Cavalry on March 3, 1855. Assigned to the West, he took part in a number of campaigns against hostile Indians.

At the start of the Civil War, Sturgis was stationed at Fort Smith, Arkansas. Refusing to surrender to the Confederates, he marched his men and moved some of their equipment to Fort Leavenworth. He was promoted to major on May 3, 1861, and in the Battle of Wilson's Creek, Missouri (August 10), he commanded Union forces after the death of Brigadier General Nathaniel Lyon. Sturgis was brevetted lieutenant colonel on August 10 for Wilson's Creek and thereafter continued to serve in the Missouri-Kansas region.

Appointed brigadier general of volunteers in March 1862 with date of rank of August 10, 1861, Sturgis was transferred east in command of a brigade assigned to the defense of Washington, D.C., and took part in the Second Battle of Bull Run (August 29–30, 1862), for which he was brevetted colonel in the regular army. He commanded the 2nd Division of IX Corps in the Battle of South Mountain (September 14, 1862); the Battle of Antietam (September 17, 1862), when one of the brigades of his division finally took what became known as Burnside's Bridge; and the First Battle of Fredericksburg (December 13, 1862).

Assigned to the Army of the Ohio in March 1863, Sturgis held a succession of relatively unimportant commands in Tennessee and Mississippi before commanding the Cavalry Corps of the Army of the Ohio. Defeated by Major General Nathan Bedford Forrest in the Battle of Brice's Crossroads (June 10, 1864), Sturgis was relieved of duty, effectively ending his active Civil War service. On March 13, 1865, Sturgis was brevetted both brigadier general in the regular army for South Mountain and major general in the regular army for Fredericksburg.

Mustered out of the volunteers on August 24, 1865, Sturgis remained in the army after the war, reverting to his regular rank of lieutenant colonel and assigned to the 6th Cavalry. Appointed colonel of the 7th Cavalry Regiment (of which George A. Custer was lieutenant colonel) on May 6, 1869, he was stationed at a number of posts in the West until he was retired for reason of age on June 11, 1886. Sturgis died in St. Paul, Minnesota, on September 28, 1889.

SPENCER C. TUCKER

See also
Brice's Crossroads, Battle of; Bull Run, Second Battle of; Fredericksburg, First Battle of; Lyon, Nathaniel; South Mountain, Battle of; Wilson's Creek, Battle of

Further Reading
Eicher, John H., and David J. Eicher. *Civil War High Commands.* Stanford, CA: Stanford University Press, 2001.
Warner, Ezra J. *Generals in Blue: Lives of the Union Commanders.* Baton Rouge: Louisiana State University Press, 2006.

Submarine Battery Service

Confederate naval organization charged with the development and use of electric mines. On June 18, 1862, Confederate Army brigadier general Gabriel J. Rains, who had employed land mines defensively early in the Peninsula Campaign, was given charge of mining the James River to protect that water route to the Confederate capital of Richmond. On September 11, 1862, Rains was ordered to turn over his command to Confederate Navy lieutenant Hunter Davidson, an associate of Confederate Navy commander Matthew Fontaine Maury, who had established the Submarine Battery Service. Rains took command of the new Torpedo Bureau.

Maury, a former U.S. Navy officer with an international scientific reputation, believed that mines, then known as torpedoes, were the best means to defend the Confederate waterways. He favored an electric mine that he called a submarine battery. It consisted of an iron tank filled with gunpowder that would be anchored in place. An operator on shore would explode the mine using a battery that sent an electrical charge through insulated wire. The Confederacy was chronically short of insulated wire and batteries, however, and the available batteries could weigh as much as 280 pounds.

The Submarine Battery Service enjoyed the full support of Confederate secretary of the navy Stephen R. Mallory but few others. Mallory often had to intervene directly so that the service could obtain the supplies it needed. The army chief of ordnance refused to even see a representative from the service, but Davidson was able to have the iron containers specially built for his mines at the Tredegar Iron Works in Richmond. The service had its own electrician, R. O. Crowley, who modified the electric batteries so that one man could carry them. Funding was initially hard to come by, but in May 1863 the Confederate Congress appropriated $20,000 for the manufacture of submarine batteries. The following year it appropriated $350,000; in the last year of the war, the total was $6 million.

By the autumn of 1862, Davidson and his men had the James River sufficiently mined so that those soldiers guarding the river against a Union crossing could be transferred to other theaters. On August 4, 1863, the U.S. Navy gunboat *Commodore Barney,* a former New York ferryboat, struck one of the Submarine Battery Service's torpedoes. Two crewmen drowned, and the ship was disabled. On May 6, 1864, the U.S. Navy gunboat *Commodore Jones,* another New York ferryboat conversion, was sunk by an electric torpedo that had been submerged for nearly two years.

All members of the service were required to take an oath of secrecy not to divulge information about their work. In view of the dangerous nature of their work, men of the Submarine Battery Service all received bonuses. Among the dangers was the threat by Union officials to hang any of its members they caught.

By July 1864, Union forces had largely cleared the James River of electric torpedoes, and the Confederacy resorted to less complicated percussion detonated mines but with little success. Throughout the war, runaway slaves informed Union leaders of the location of mines. In the last months of the war, R. O. Crowley had deserted the Confederacy and was guiding Union ships past the stationary torpedoes. Even though the Submarine Battery Service sank only one ship during the war, Confederate president Jefferson Davis credited the service with keeping the James River in Confederate hands for most of the war.

WESLEY MOODY

See also

Davidson, Hunter; Davis, Jefferson Finis; Mallory, Stephen Russell; Maury, Matthew Fontaine; Richmond, Virginia; Riverine Warfare; Spar Torpedo; Submarines; Torpedoes; Tredegar Iron Works

Further Reading

Coski, John M. *Capital Navy: The Men, Ships and Operations of the James River Squadron.* Campbell, CA: Savas, 1996.

Perry, Milton F. *Infernal Machines: The Story of Confederate Submarine and Mine Warfare.* Baton Rouge: Louisiana State University Press, 1965.

Wolters, Timothy S. "Electric Torpedoes in the Confederacy: Reconciling Conflicting Histories." *Journal of Military History* 72(3) (July 2008): 755–783.

Youngblood, Norman. *The Development of Mine Warfare: A Most Murderous and Barbarous Conduct.* Westport, CT: Greenwood, 2006.

Submarines

Watercraft capable of independent operation below the surface of the water. Submersibles have only limited underwater capability. American inventors had experimented with submarines since David Bushnell's *Turtle* of the Revolutionary War. Among other submarines proposed or built in the years before the Civil War were two by the Indiana shoemaker Lodner D. Phillips, the second of which succeeded in diving to 100 feet in 1852. Phillips offered his boat to the U.S. Navy but was rejected; he was turned down again when he offered to build another submarine at the outbreak of the Civil War in 1861.

Nevertheless, the Civil War stimulated unofficial interest in submarines in both the Union and the Confederacy. The side in war without a major surface fleet is invariably the one most interested in new technology to offset the advantage held by its opponent. It was therefore no surprise that the Confederacy experimented widely with torpedoes (naval mines) and with semisubmersibles (Davids) and submarines to deliver the torpedoes. Inventors in the Confederacy produced several submarines, the best known being James R. McClintock's series of boats, initially built as private-venture privateers. The first, the *Pioneer,* was built for Horace L. Hunley's New Orleans privateering consortium but was scuttled before becoming operational when the city fell to the Union in April 1862. McClintock then built the *Pioneer II* at Mobile. Efforts to make first an electric motor and then a steam plant functional both failed, and McClintock had to revert to a hand-cranked propeller to drive his boat. The *Pioneer II* was not a great success, and it sank while being towed to attack the Union fleet off Fort Monroe. The expanded consortium constructed a third boat, the *H. L. Hunley,* whose trials proved more successful; its transfer in July 1863 to Charleston, South Carolina, led General P. G. T. Beauregard, the local commander, to propose its use to break the Union blockade. The Confederate Navy, reluctant to trust the abilities or enthusiasm of the boat's civilian crew, seized it and manned it with naval personnel. An accident drowned five of its crew on August 30, and another accident on October 15 drowned the entire replacement crew, including Hunley himself. Nonetheless, the boat finally went into action, with a third crew, on the night of February 17, 1864, sinking the steam sloop *Housatonic* but failing to return. The novelist Clive Cussler funded an expedition that located the wreck of the *H. L. Hunley* in May 1995. It was raised in August 2000 for conservation in Charleston.

In addition to a series of semisubmersible spar torpedo boats, known as Davids, for the Confederate Navy, the South produced several other submarines. Little is known about the origins of a boat built at New Orleans in June 1861, although it is most probably the vessel that was found during dredging operations there in 1879; it is now on exhibit

The possibility of building a submarine capable of sinking a Union warship was advanced early in the Civil War. This illustration appeared in *Harper's Weekly* in 1861 and shows a Confederate submarine preparing to attack the Union screw frigate *Minnesota*. (Library of Congress)

at the Louisiana State Museum in the city. The Tredegar Iron Works at Richmond, Virginia, built at least one boat to a design by William Cheeney. After successful trials on the James River in October 1861, it was sunk while attacking a Union ship in Hampton Roads the following month. John Halligan designed a submarine, the *St. Patrick,* that was built at the Selma Navy Yard for the Confederate Navy and commissioned in January 1865. The *St. Patrick* made an abortive attack on the gunboat *Octorara* on January 27 and most probably was scuttled in April when the war came to an end.

At least three Northern projects saw fruition. The first, the *Alligator,* was the brainchild of Brutus de Villeroi, a French immigrant inventor who, in 1859, had built a submarine for a Philadelphia treasure-hunting consortium. (Before coming to the United States, de Villeroi had taught mathematics in France. His students, it seems, included Jules Verne, whose 1870 novel *Twenty Thousand Leagues under the Sea* greatly popularized the notion of submarines.) De Villeroi's earlier project still was extant in 1861 when war came, and he staged a dramatic demonstration in Philadelphia Harbor to promote his concepts.

The *Alligator* was built for the U.S. Navy by the Philadelphia Navy Yard but was never formally commissioned.

After ineffective trials in the James and Appomattox Rivers (the waters there were too shallow), the boat was refitted at Washington Navy Yard and dispatched to engage in operations off Charleston, South Carolina. While under tow to the war zone, the *Alligator* foundered in a storm off the North Carolina Outer Banks on April 2, 1863; no lives were lost. The wreck is still the object of search efforts.

Also vying for a navy contract was Julius Kroehl, a German immigrant engineer who had considerable experience working with diving bells. Kroehl built his design as a private venture after de Villeroi won the official contract, but Kroehl's boat was still incomplete at the end of the war. Kroehl succeeded, however, in selling both his *Sub Marine Explorer* and his own expertise to the Pacific Pearl Company in 1866 as a platform for exploiting the prolific pearl oyster beds off the Panamanian Pacific coast, where it operated for three years.

The third Northern boat, the *Intelligent Whale,* was built by the American Submarine Company, a group of speculators who planned to use it as a privateer. When that plan failed and the U.S. Navy declined to accept the boat, construction slowed, and it was not completed until 1866. In 1872 the navy eventually agreed to undertake trials of the *Intelligent Whale,* which failed, and the submarine was abandoned. It still survives, however, and is on exhibit at the National Guard Militia Museum of New Jersey at Sea Girt.

PAUL E. FONTENOY

See also

Alligator, U.S. Navy Submarine; David-Class Torpedo Boats; *H. L. Hunley,* CSS; *Housatonic,* USS; Spar Torpedo; Torpedoes

Further Reading

Fontenoy, Paul E. *Submarines: An Illustrated History of Their Impact.* Santa Barbara, CA: ABC-CLIO, 2007.
Ragan, Mark K. *Union and Confederate Submarine Warfare in the Civil War.* Mason City, IA: Savas, 1999.

Substitutes

Individuals hired for military service in the place of others. Usually, men seeking to hire substitutes to fulfill their conscription duty were wealthy or had occupations or jobs that were considered essential to the war effort. During the Civil War, conscription laws in both the North and the South essentially permitted legalized draft evasion by allowing an individual to hire a substitute to serve in the military in his place. The provision for substitutes was instituted to prevent skilled laborers and businessmen involved in war-related industries from being drafted; however, many abused the system, and it eventually came to be seen as a sham that promoted chicanery and profit making.

As originally established, the conscription system allowed any white adult male to hire an able-bodied substitute to replace him in wartime service. Obviously, only men with monetary means could afford to do this, as substitutes demanded several hundred dollars in payment at the beginning of the war. As the war dragged on and manpower shortages became a problem, especially in the South, the fees exacted by substitutes could be as high as several thousand dollars, virtually ensuring that only the wealthiest could afford to secure a substitute. The more demand there was for substitutes, the higher the fees.

As the profit-making motive became an important part of the system, brokers soon came to dominate the procurement of substitutes. For a set fee, or a percentage of the fee paid to the substitute whom they represented, brokers would match an individual seeking a substitute with an appropriate substitute. Not surprisingly, the system bred inequities and outright fraud. Sometimes, unscrupulous substitute brokers would take fees from men buying substitutes, provide them with phony documentation, and then leave town without providing the service they had promised. Many substitutes had disabilities so severe that they were unable to perform military duty, which was a direct violation of the statute that demanded that substitutes be able-bodied. And some men became professional substitutes; that is, they would agree to serve as a substitute, collect the payment, and then skip town, only to perpetrate the same fraud somewhere else. Some individuals became wealthy by such conduct.

Brokers also began to prey on foreigners and adolescent boys, whom they would lure into their trap and then draft as substitutes without their consent. In large port cities, particularly in the North, some brokers sponsored kidnapping rings whereby a genial con artist would get a foreigner or foreign seaman inebriated until he passed out, transport him to a military camp, and leave him there. As this practice increased, many of its victims sued for their release from military duty, which brought the practice to the public's attention. Foreign governments also intervened on behalf of their citizens who had been kidnapped. Eventually, public backlash against such schemes brought them to a virtual halt.

As the inequities and chicanery of the system became readily apparent, civilians in both the North and the South began to complain loudly about the use and procurement of substitutes. Indeed, by 1863, abuses of the system led the Confederacy to ban the use of substitutes altogether. This decision was also precipitated by a veritable manpower crisis in the Southern states by mid-1863. Besides the complaints emanating from the civilian sector, the military establishment soon began to bitterly denounce the use of substitutes. The system was a primary cause for flagging morale in the military ranks, and the rank-and-file soldier, who on average earned just $16 per month in pay, came to deeply resent the profits being made by substitutes and their brokers. Especially in the South, the system of substitutes and other means by which to avoid military conscription seemed to confirm the conclusion that the Civil War was being fought by poor men to further enrich wealthy men.

PAUL G. PIERPAOLI JR.

See also

Conscription, CSA; Conscription, U.S.

Further Reading

Geary, James W. *We Need Men: The Union Draft in the Civil War.* DeKalb: Northern Illinois University Press, 1991.
Moore, Albert Burton. *Conscription and Conflict in the Confederacy.* Columbia: University of South Carolina Press, 1996.

Suffolk, Virginia, Siege of
Start Date: April 11, 1863
End Date: May 4, 1863

Confederate military operation in southeastern Virginia. After Union major general Ambrose E. Burnside's failed Mud March in January 1863, the opposing Union and Confederate armies in Virginia went into winter quarters on opposite sides of the Rappahannock River. To prevent the massed Union force in Suffolk along the Nanesmond River southeast of Richmond from threatening the Confederate capital at Richmond or his Army of Northern Virginia, General Robert E. Lee dispatched Lieutenant General James Longstreet and two divisions to southeastern Virginia. Consequently, Longstreet was given command of the Department of Virginia and North Carolina. In addition to protecting Richmond and Lee's army, Longstreet was tasked with foraging food for the Army of Northern Virginia. If the opportunity presented itself, he was also to capture the Union garrison of some 17,000 men at Suffolk, commanded by Major General John J. Peck. The Northern commander had constructed an impressive array of fortifications that ringed the city and were supplemented with numerous artillery batteries. Longstreet initially planned to capture the city with the help of the Confederate Navy; however, this assistance was unavailable. The strength of the Union fortifications, the lack of naval support, and the threat of Union gunboats led Longstreet to opt for a siege instead of a frontal attack. He believed that an assault on the Union lines would prove fruitless. His siege consisted largely of sporadic skirmishing and artillery duels. Furthermore, adverse weather often impeded operations. The Confederates had placed artillery batteries on the Nansemond River at Norfleet House and Fort Huger/Hill's Point, both of which engaged Union gunboats. The former battery was defeated in a duel with Union artillery on April 15, and the latter was captured by Union infantry on April 19. All the while, a portion of Longstreet's command was gathering supplies to send to Lee's army.

The inconclusive nature of the siege, coupled with word from Lee that the Union Army of the Potomac—now under the command of Major General Joseph Hooker—was again on the move, led Longstreet to lift the siege on May 4 and move northward. Although he failed to take Suffolk and would not reach Lee in time to take part in the Battle of Chancellorsville (May 1–4, 1863), Longstreet's foray into southeastern Virginia did provide the Confederate army with much-needed food and forage. Total estimated casualties during the operation were 260 for Union forces and 900 for the Confederates.

ROBERT L. GLAZE

See also
Chancellorsville, Battle of; Fort Huger, Virginia; Longstreet, James; Peck, John James

Further Reading
Cormier, Steven A. *The Siege of Suffolk: The Forgotten Campaign, April 11–May 4, 1863*. Lynchburg, VA: H. E. Howard, 1989.
Hess, Earl J. *Field Armies and Fortifications in the Civil War: The Eastern Campaigns, 1861–1864*. Chapel Hill: University of North Carolina Press, 2005.
Wert, Jeffry D. *General James Longstreet: The Confederacy's Most Controversial Soldier*. New York: Touchstone, 1993.

Sullivan, Jeremiah Cutler
Birth Date: October 1, 1830
Death Date: October 11, 1890

Union officer. Jeremiah Cutler Sullivan was born in Madison, Indiana, on October 1, 1830. He entered the U.S. Navy as a midshipman on October 12, 1848, but resigned his commission on April 14, 1854, to study law. When the Civil War began, Sullivan helped recruit the 6th Indiana Infantry, becoming one of its captains on April 18, 1861, and taking part in the Battle of Philippi (June 3, 1861) in western Virginia (present-day West Virginia). On the expiration of the regiment's three-month enlistment term, Sullivan was commissioned colonel of the 13th Indiana Infantry on June 19 and fought in the Battle of Rich Mountain (July 11, 1861).

Sullivan commanded a brigade in Brigadier General James Shields's division during Major General Thomas J. "Stonewall" Jackson's Shenandoah Valley Campaign (May–June 1862) and took part in the First Battle of Kernstown (March 23, 1862). Sullivan was appointed a brigadier general of volunteers with date of rank from April 28, 1862.

Ordered to the western theater, Sullivan commanded a brigade in Major General William S. Rosecrans's Army of the Mississippi, seeing combat in the Battle of Iuka (September 19, 1862) and then in the Battle of Corinth (October 3–4, 1862), when he was wounded by a shell splinter on October 3.

From December 1862 to March 1863, Sullivan had charge of the District of Jackson, Tennessee, where he did battle with the forces of Brigadier General Nathan Bedford Forrest. Sullivan was assistant inspector general of the Army of the Tennessee during the Second Vicksburg Campaign

(April 1–July 4, 1863) and then became chief of staff of that army's XV Corps.

Sullivan returned to the eastern theater in September 1863 to serve in the Department of West Virginia under Major General Benjamin F. Kelley, his father-in-law, helping to guard a stretch of the Baltimore & Ohio Railroad. Sullivan was wounded in the head and hand in the Battle of Piedmont (June 5, 1864). He then commanded the 1st Brigade in the Kanawha District of the Department of West Virginia from August to October 1864, when he was apparently placed on awaiting orders status. He resigned on May 11, 1865.

After the war Sullivan lived in Maryland, but he moved to California in 1878. Although a lawyer, he did not practice that profession and indeed held only minor clerical positions. Sullivan died in Oakland, California, on October 11, 1890.

SPENCER C. TUCKER

See also

Corinth, Battle of; Forrest, Nathan Bedford; Iuka, Battle of; Jackson's Shenandoah Valley Campaign; Kernstown, First Battle of; Philippi, Battle of; Piedmont, Battle of; Rich Mountain, Battle of; Rosecrans, William Starke; Shields, James; Vicksburg Campaign, Second

Further Reading

Eicher, John H., and David J. Eicher. *Civil War High Commands.* Stanford, CA: Stanford University Press, 2001.
Warner, Ezra J. *Generals in Blue: Lives of the Union Commanders.* Baton Rouge: Louisiana State University Press, 2006.

Sully, Alfred
Birth Date: May 22, 1821
Death Date: April 27, 1879

Union officer. Alfred Sully was born in Philadelphia, Pennsylvania, on May 22, 1821. The son of noted painter Thomas Sully, Alfred Sully became an accomplished artist in his own right. Upon graduation from the U.S. Military Academy, West Point, in 1841, he was commissioned a second lieutenant in the 2nd Infantry and participated in the Second Seminole War (1835–1842). He later was assigned to garrison duty at Sackets Harbor, New York, until the start of the Mexican-American War (1846–1848), in which he served and won promotion to first lieutenant. Sully was promoted to captain in 1852 and assigned to the western frontier, where he engaged in expeditions against the Rogue River Indians in 1853 and the Cheyennes in 1860–1861.

When the Civil War began, Sully went east. He served in northern Missouri until November 1861 and in the defenses of Washington, D.C., until March 1862, when he entered the volunteer army as colonel of the 1st Minnesota Infantry and joined the Army of the Potomac. That month Sully was promoted to major in the regular service. He fought at Yorktown (April 5–May 3, 1862), Seven Pines (May 31–June 1), Savage's Station (June 29), White Oak Swamp (June 30), and Malvern Hill (July 1). For his performance at Seven Pines, Sully was brevetted lieutenant colonel, and for his conduct at Malvern Hill, he was brevetted colonel.

Having assumed command of a brigade in II Corps during the Seven Days' Campaign (June 25–July 1, 1862), Sully again distinguished himself at South Mountain (September 14) and Antietam (September 17), which earned him promotion to brigadier general of volunteers on September 26, 1862. Sully fought in the First Battle of Fredericksburg (December 13, 1862) and the Battle of Chancellorsville (May 1–4, 1863).

In the midst of the Minnesota Sioux Uprising (August 17–September 23, 1862), Sully, an experienced Indian fighter, was assigned to the command of the District of Dakota. He led several expeditions against the Indians, most notably at Whitestone Hill on September 3–5, 1863. He then assumed command of the District of Iowa and launched a punitive campaign against the Sioux that resulted in the Battle of Killdeer Mountain (July 28, 1864). Sully was brevetted major general of volunteers and brigadier general in the regular army before mustering out of the volunteers in April 1866.

Resuming his regular army career, Sully was promoted to lieutenant colonel and served in a number of administrative assignments. He was again ordered to the West, where he led several expeditions against the Native Americans. Promoted to colonel of the 21st Infantry in 1873, Sully died at Fort Vancouver, Washington, on April 27, 1879.

JOSHUA ADAM CAMPER

See also

Antietam, Battle of; Chancellorsville, Battle of; Fredericksburg, First Battle of; Malvern Hill, Battle of; Savage's Station, Battle of; Seven Days' Campaign; Seven Pines, Battle of; Sioux Uprising; South Mountain, Battle of; White Oak Swamp, Battle of; Yorktown, Virginia, Siege of

Further Reading

Clodfelter, Michael. *The Dakota War: The United States Army versus the Sioux, 1862–1865.* Jefferson, NC: McFarland, 1998.
The National Cyclopaedia of American Biography. New York: James T. White, 1904.

Sultana Disaster
Event Date: April 27, 1865

The worst maritime disaster of the Civil War. The sinking of the side-wheel steamer *Sultana* in the Mississippi River a few miles north of Memphis claimed some 1,700 to 1,800 lives, most of them Union soldiers recently released from Confederate prison camps at Andersonville and Cahaba.

The *Sultana* was built in Cincinnati in 1863 and displaced 1,719 tons. With a crew of 85 and a legal capacity of 376 people, the ship served as a supply and troop transport between New Orleans and St. Louis during the war. On April 24, 1865, the *Sultana* arrived at Vicksburg from New Orleans to pick up Union troops for their transfer north.

At the time, the Mississippi River was at flood stage, and the ship's boilers were leaking badly. Captain J. C. Mason ordered the boilers repaired and then began to take on the Union troops. The soldiers, eager to return home after their long ordeal, crowded into the ship. Muster rolls were not taken before the boarding, and the *Sultana* shoved off upstream with approximately 2,300 passengers.

Memphis was the first stop, and here again the boilers had to be repaired. Soon after the *Sultana* departed Memphis and while navigating through a series of islands known as the Hens and Chickens, one of the ship's boilers exploded. The explosion was seen and heard from Memphis, several miles downriver. Ships in the vicinity rushed to assist, but the steamboat had literally been blown apart; some survivors were thrown more than 100 feet.

Many of the crew and passengers were killed outright in the blast, while others drowned. A number, weak from their captivity, did not have the stamina to stay afloat in the current; others were able to grab onto floating debris. For days after the disaster, rescuers fished survivors from the river. Some 500–600 were taken to Memphis hospitals, where about one-third later died.

Because of the timing of this tragedy, it received scant attention from the press. The recent assassination of

The steamboat *Sultana*. On April 27, 1865, crowded with released Union prisoners of war, the *Sultana* exploded and sank in the Mississippi River near Memphis, Tennessee. The worst maritime disaster of the war, it claimed 1,700–1,800 lives. It has been suggested that the blast was caused by a Confederate coal torpedo. (Library of Congress)

President Abraham Lincoln on April 14, 1865, combined with the surrenders of General Robert E. Lee's army on April 9, 1865, and Joseph E. Johnston on April 26, overshadowed the incident. Investigations later concluded that both army officers and civilians were at fault, but no formal charges were ever brought. Some claimed that a Confederate coal torpedo had caused the boiler explosion, but this has never been proven.

WILLIAM WHYTE

See also

Coal Torpedo

Further Reading

Huffman, Allen. *Sultana: Surviving the Civil War, Prison, and the Worst Maritime Disaster in American History.* New York: HarperCollins, 2009.

Potter, Jerry O. *The* Sultana *Tragedy: America's Greatest Maritime Disaster.* Gretna, LA: Pelican, 1992.

Sumner, Charles

Birth Date: January 6, 1811
Death Date: March 11, 1874

U.S. senator and abolitionist. Born in Boston on January 6, 1811, Charles Sumner graduated from Harvard Law School in 1833. After a brief stint teaching law at Harvard (1835–1837), he spent three years in Europe. Returning to the United States in 1840, Sumner began the practice of law in Boston. He became an ardent abolitionist. He opposed the annexation of Texas and the Compromise of 1850, seeing the latter as an effort by Southern politicians to expand slavery into the territories acquired in the Mexican-American War (1846–1848).

Sumner was elected to the U.S. Senate in 1851 by Democrats and Free-Soilers. He opposed the Kansas-Nebraska Act in 1854, seeing it as a plot to convert free territory into a dreary region of despotism. In May 1856 he delivered a speech titled "The Crime against Kansas" in which he denounced the Kansas-Nebraska Act and criticized several members of Congress for yielding to the slaveholding interests in the country, among these South Carolina senator Andrew P. Butler, who was absent from the Senate at the time. Two days later Congressman Preston Brooks, a cousin of Butler, believing that Sumner's speech was a libel on South Carolina, viciously beat Sumner with a cane over the head some 30 times on the Senate floor.

The incident, referred to as "Bleeding Sumner," joined Bleeding Kansas as a symbol of Southern irrationality and violence in defense of slavery and strengthened Northern

Massachusetts senator Charles Sumner, a staunch abolitionist, strongly supported the war effort. As one of the leaders of the Radical Republicans, Sumner rejected any compromise with the South. (National Archives)

public opinion against slavery. Brooks, meanwhile, was celebrated as a hero in the South and was reelected almost unanimously in November 1856. Sumner, who won reelection to the Senate as a Republican in 1857, was so badly injured as a result of the attack that he was unable to resume his place in the Senate for more than three years.

When Southern states began seceding from the Union in December 1860, Sumner refused to consider any compromise to restore the Union. When the Civil War began in April 1861, Sumner urged President Abraham Lincoln to emancipate the slaves and grant equal rights to black people. During the war Sumner emerged as one of the leading Radical Republicans, opposing Lincoln's lenient plan for restoring the South to the Union. By leaving the Union, Sumner believed that Southern states had committed "state suicide," forfeiting their rights as states and turning their status to that of territories. At Sumner's urging, the readmission of Southern states to the Union after the Civil War was made contingent on their recognition of black equality and suffrage.

In May 1868 Sumner led the Radical Republicans in the impeachment proceedings against President Andrew

Johnson. But Sumner was unhappy when the Senate failed to remove Johnson from office. In 1869 Sumner was elected to his fourth term as a senator, but his health began to deteriorate in the early 1870s. On March 10, 1874, Sumner suffered a heart attack in the Senate chamber and died in Washington, D.C., the next day.

JAMES SCYTHES

See also

Abolitionism and the Civil War; Bleeding Kansas; Compromise of 1850; Johnson, Andrew; Kansas-Nebraska Act; Lincoln, Abraham; Lincoln's Reconstruction Policies; Radical Republicans; Reconstruction

Further Reading

Donald, David Herbert. *Charles Sumner.* New York: Da Capo, 1996.
Donald, David Herbert. *Charles Sumner and the Coming of the Civil War.* New York: Knopf, 1961.

Sumner, Edwin Vose
Birth Date: January 30, 1797
Death Date: March 21, 1863

Union officer. Edwin Vose Sumner was born in Boston, Massachusetts, on January 30, 1797. He was educated at the Milton Academy before enlisting in the army as a second lieutenant on March 3, 1819, and was promoted to first lieutenant in 1823. Sumner served in the Black Hawk War (1832) and on March 4, 1833, was promoted to captain and assigned to the 1st U.S. Dragoons. In 1838 he was detailed to command the cavalry instructional school at Carlisle Barracks, Pennsylvania. From 1842 to 1845, he served at Fort Atkinson, Iowa Territory. With the outbreak of the Mexican-American War (1846–1848), Sumner was promoted to major on June 30, 1846, and assigned to the 2nd U.S. Dragoons. He saw action in numerous battles and sustained a wound during the Battle of Cerro Gordo (April 18, 1847). Sumner was brevetted lieutenant colonel and colonel during the conflict.

On July 23, 1848, Sumner was promoted to lieutenant colonel. From 1851 to 1853, he served as the acting military governor of the New Mexico Territory. On March 3, 1855, he was advanced to colonel and given command of the newly formed 1st U.S. Cavalry Regiment.

On March 16, 1861, Sumner was promoted to brigadier general and given command of the Department of the Pacific. In November 1861 he was called east to assume command of a division in Major General George B. McClellan's

Union major general Edwin Vose Sumner commanded the II Corps of the Army of the Potomac in the March–July 1862 Peninsula Campaign and the Battle of Antietam (September 17) but died of a heart attack in March 1863. (Library of Congress)

Army of the Potomac. On March 8, 1862, Sumner assumed command of the newly formed II Corps, which he led during the Peninsula Campaign (March–July 1862), and was appointed major general of volunteers. On July 16, 1862, he was brevetted major general in the regular army for his services in the campaign. He led his corps at the Battle of Antietam (September 17, 1862) and commanded the Right Grand Division at the First Battle of Fredericksburg (December 13, 1862) before asking to be relieved of command. Appointed to command the Department of the Missouri, Sumner was given until the spring of 1863 to report for duty, but he died at his daughter's home in Syracuse, New York, on March 21, 1863, from a heart attack.

ROBERT P. BROADWATER

See also

Antietam, Battle of; Fredericksburg, First Battle of; Peninsula Campaign; Savage's Station, Battle of

Further Reading

Armstrong, Marion V., Jr. *Unfurl Those Colors! McClellan, Sumner, & the Second Army Corps in the Antietam Campaign.* Tuscaloosa: University of Alabama Press, 2008.
Long, William Wallace. *A Biography of Edwin Vose Sumner, U.S.A., 1797–1863.* Albuquerque: University of New Mexico Press, 1971.

Sumter, CSS

First Confederate commerce raider. Confederate secretary of the navy Stephen R. Mallory was a staunch advocate of commerce raiding, which he hoped would drive up insurance rates in the North and bring economic pressure to bear on the Abraham Lincoln administration. On April 18, 1861, Mallory appointed Commander Raphael Semmes to convert the former steamer packet *Habana,* purchased by the Confederate government at New Orleans. Launched in 1857, the ship had been employed on the New Orleans to Havana route and was renamed the *Sumter.*

Workmen stripped the *Sumter* down to what became the gun deck, which was then reinforced. The ship also received additional coal bunkers and was rerigged as a barkentine. With its retractable funnel and screw propeller, there would be no outward means to identify the ship as a steamer. The *Sumter* was 437 tons and measured 134 feet in length, 30 feet in beam, and 12 feet in draft. Armament consisted of a IX-inch Dahlgren gun in pivot mount and four 32-pounders in broadside. Semmes signed on 114 officers and men.

The ship was commissioned on June 3, 1861, and Semmes then ran his ship down to the mouth of the Mississippi River. On June 30 he set out, hoping to escape the blockading U.S. Navy side-wheeler frigate *Powhatan* and screw sloop *Brooklyn.* In one of the most exciting chases of the war, the *Sumter*

managed to outrun the *Brooklyn.* On July 3 the *Sumter* took its first prize, the merchant bark *Golden Rocket.* Semmes was, however, handicapped by the British government's May 14 neutrality proclamation, which was replicated by the other leading maritime powers. As there were thus very few places where captured vessels might be sold, Semmes and other Confederate captains routinely burned the merchant ships they captured.

Semmes cruised the Caribbean and took other Northern ships. He then sailed along the South American coast to Brazil and back to the West Indies. Convinced that he would be more successful in European waters, Semmes headed into the Atlantic. Late in November, the *Sumter* narrowly escaped an encounter with the powerful U.S. Navy screw sloop *Iroquois* but during the crossing took additional prizes.

On January 3, 1862, the *Sumter* put into Cádiz in poor repair, but Spanish authorities there would not permit an overhaul of its engine and ordered Semmes to depart. On January 18 Semmes took two final prizes, and a day later he put into Gibraltar. British authorities there were more accommodating, but U.S. Navy warships, including the powerful screw sloop *Kearsarge,* arrived. Because his ship needed repairs that could not be made at Gibraltar, Semmes bowed to the inevitable and, under authorization from Confederate commissioner James M. Mason in London, in April

The Confederate commerce raider CSS *Sumter* running the blockade off Pass à l'Outre and escaping the pursuing Union screw sloop USS *Brooklyn,* June 30, 1861. (Library of Congress)

laid up the *Sumter*, paid off most of its crew, and departed for England. In December 1862, the *Sumter* was sold to a British firm and put back into commercial service as the *Gibraltar*. In 1863 it became a blockade-runner. The *Gibraltar* was apparently lost in a storm in 1867.

Despite the *Sumter* being both too small and too slow to be an effective commerce raider, Semmes had taken 18 prizes in just six months. He had burned 7, and another 7 were seized by Cuban authorities to return to their Union owners. The cost to the Confederate government of running the *Sumter* was only $28,000, a figure less than the least valuable of its prizes.

SPENCER C. TUCKER

See also

Commerce Raiding, Confederate; Mallory, Stephen Russell; Mason, James Murray; Semmes, Raphael

Further Reading

Semmes, Raphael. *Memoirs of Service Afloat during the War between the States.* 1869; reprint, Secaucus, NJ: Blue and Gray, 1987.

Tucker, Spencer C. *Raphael Semmes and the* Alabama. Abilene, TX: McWhiney Foundation Press, 1996.

Supreme Court, Confederate

The Confederacy's highest authorized judicial body that never came into being, however. Although the Provisional Confederate Constitution (Article III), ratified on March 16, 1861, in Montgomery, Alabama, provided for the creation of a national supreme court, concerns over individual states' rights prevented the Confederate government from ever establishing or convening a high court. The court was to be modeled precisely after the U.S. Supreme Court, which at the time had nine justices who were appointed by the executive branch, confirmed by the Senate, and served lifetime appointments barring illegal or inappropriate behavior while in office. The court would have exercised judicial review over state courts as well as lower national courts.

From the start, Confederate politicians argued passionately over the creation and judicial scope of a supreme court. Many, including Senator William L. Yancey (Alabama), who led the opposition over the court's judicial review parameters, believed that it should not have authority over state courts. Citing the problems caused by the U.S. Supreme Court's rulings prior to the Civil War, which its detractors claimed had stripped away states' rights, many Confederates were loath to create a court that might follow the same pattern.

During 1862, the Confederate Congress attempted to come to terms with the establishment of a supreme court but was never able to strike a workable compromise. The Confederate Senate that year passed an amendment that would have forbade the court from making appeal rulings, but the House of Representatives refused to go along. By early 1863, the court issue was sidelined, and no supreme court was ever established. Thus, most legal cases were decided in state courts, with no judicial oversight. While this might have pleased states' rights proponents, it certainly had the possibility of creating a chaotic legal situation in which laws in one state might have been illegal in another state.

PAUL G. PIERPAOLI JR.

See also

Congress, CSA; Supreme Court, U.S.; Yancey, William Lowndes

Further Reading

Davis, William C. *Look Away! A History of the Confederate States of America.* New York: Free Press, 2003.

Robinson, William M. *Justice in Grey: A History of the Judicial System of the Confederate States of America.* Cambridge, MA: Harvard University Press, 1941.

Supreme Court, U.S.

Highest judicial body in the United States. At the beginning of the Civil War, the U.S. Supreme Court of nine justices had a decidedly pro-Southern bias. However, between 1861 and 1864, President Abraham Lincoln was able to nominate 5 justices to the high court, changing its makeup dramatically. His appointees included Salmon P. Chase as chief justice in 1864 and Noah H. Swayne, Samuel F. Miller, David Davis, and Stephen Field all as associate justices between 1861 and 1863, at which time the Court was expanded to 10 members. By then, it was also strongly pro-Union. Prior to that, Court rulings under Chief Justice Roger B. Taney reflected a pro-Southern, proslavery, and anti-Republican bias. Just prior to and during the Civil War, the Supreme Court's most important decisions were in the areas of presidential wartime powers, military matters, and civil rights.

Under Chief Justice Taney, the court in *Strader v. Graham* (1851) refused to consider a petition from Kentucky's appeals court that had declared slaves who had been carried briefly to Ohio as free, thereby upholding state jurisdiction over slavery. *Scott v. Sanford* (1857) established that slaves, not being U.S. citizens, could not sue in federal court. The decision further established that a slave's temporary residence in a free state or territory did not confer freedom and that Congress lacked the authority to prohibit slavery in

United States territories. *Ableman v. Booth* (1859) sustained the fugitive slave legislation of 1850.

Many constitutional issues facing the Supreme Court concerned military matters, with a number of decisions actually rendered after the war. The *Prize Cases* (1863) justified Lincoln's April 1861 blockade proclamation for Southern ports because a state of war had existed at the time. The minority, which included Taney, argued that an internal insurrection was not tantamount to a legal state of war. Lincoln's 1861 decree confiscating telegraph and railway properties linking Washington, D.C., and Annapolis, Maryland, was validated as constitutional in *Miller v. U.S.* (1871). In 1863 the *Peterhoff*, a British ship, was seized by a Union warship on the basis that despite the fact that it was heading for Matamoros, Mexico, it was in fact evading the Northern blockade via a continuous voyage (meaning its cargo was destined for the Confederacy by way of Mexico). The Court ruled that even though contraband in the shipment was subject to capture, the noncontraband portion could not be confiscated because it was carried from Matamoros, an unblockaded harbor, across land. Chief Justice Chase declared secession unlawful in *Texas v. White* (1869), affirming that the U.S. Constitution of 1787 formed an unbreakable federal bond.

The Supreme Court opined on other wartime questions. In *Roosevelt v. Meyer* (1863), the justices refused to rule on whether Congress had the constitutional authority to issue legal tender paper money, concluding that it had no jurisdiction over the matter. However, *Hepburn v. Griswold* (1870) voided greenback laws, a ruling reversed in the *Legal Tender Cases* (1871) in which the tribunal said that the Constitution's currency provision permitted the issuance of paper money.

The Court also resisted state hindrance of federal war functions. New York's attempt to tax the assets of a financial institution with U.S. stock and bond investments undermined the authority of the national government to raise money, the justices reasoned in *Bank of Commerce v. New York* (1863). The *Bank Tax Cases* (1865) upheld the national banking system and found capital outlays in federal securities not subject to state assessments. Wartime revenue laws were confirmed in *Pacific Insurance Company v. Soule* (1867), when the Constitution's direct tax provision was clarified in relation to domestic revenue statutes.

Resolving national and state differences, *Freeman v. Howe* (1861) held that federal tribunals were not subject to state court jurisdiction, and *Almy v. California* (1861) invalided a state stamp tax on gold shipments because the levy was on exports, a duty violating the Constitution.

The Court also tried to reconcile military necessities with individual civil liberties. In *Ex Parte Merryman* (1861), Taney rejected Lincoln's decision to suspend the writ of habeas corpus, arguing that the constitutional section governing the suspension identifies legislative power only, meaning that only Congress can suspend habeas corpus. Taney also asserted that the Constitution contains no powers to apprehend civilians by military personnel without the approval of civil tribunals, nor does it allow citizen imprisonment indeterminately without trial. *Ex Parte Vallandingham* (1863) denied a reconsideration of Clement L. Vallandingham's suit. Vallandingham, a civilian defendant and a Lincoln administration detractor, had been tried in a military court in an area of the country not engaged in fighting. The Supreme Court stated that its power, originating from the Judiciary Act of 1789 as well as the Constitution, did not cover the procedures of a military tribunal. Therefore, the Supreme Court had no say in the matter. Yet following the war, *Ex Parte Milligan* (1866) judged the military trial of a civilian unconstitutional.

In the end, the Supreme Court during the 1850s, 1860s, and 1870s rendered decisions on matters of great importance, setting precedents that would stand the test of time for generations. In all, the high court did a commendable job of defending civil liberties and establishing the limits of presidential wartime powers. During the Civil War, however, the Court was less successful in seeing that its rulings on strictly military matters were enforced.

RODNEY J. ROSS

See also

Chase, Salmon Portland; Civil Liberties, U.S.; *Dred Scott* Case; *Ex Parte Merryman; Ex Parte Milligan;* Habeas Corpus, Writ of, U.S.; Lincoln, Abraham; Matamoros, Mexico; Taney, Roger Brooke

Further Reading

Farber, Daniel. *Lincoln's Constitution.* Chicago: University of Chicago Press, 2003.
Schwartz, Bernard. *A History of the Supreme Court.* New York: Oxford University Press, 1993.

Surratt, John Harrison
Birth Date: April 13, 1844
Death Date: April 2, 1916

Innkeeper, Confederate spy, and accused coconspirator in President Abraham's Lincoln assassination. John Harrison Surratt was born on April 13, 1844, in Prince George's

County, Maryland. He attended a local Catholic seminary until September 1862. At that time, he assumed his late father's job as the local postmaster and proprietor of a tavern in present-day Clinton, Maryland. By now Surratt had become a Confederate partisan, and for that reason he was stripped of his postmaster duties in November 1863. Before then, however, he had already begun to work as a Confederate courier and spy, operating as far as New York and Canada.

Surratt met acclaimed actor and future presidential assassin John Wilkes Booth in Washington in December 1863 and almost immediately began working for him. Although Surratt's connections to Booth were not extensive, he did apparently help Booth make connections with Confederate officials and may even have traveled for him. Surratt was evidently not directly involved in Booth's failed attempted kidnapping of Lincoln on March 17, 1865, but by then Booth was staying in a Washington boardinghouse run by Surratt's mother, Mary Elizabeth Jenkins Surratt. When Lincoln was shot on April 14, 1865 (he died the following morning), Surratt was in Elmira, New York, on a courier mission.

Surratt's mother was quickly implicated in the assassination plot and was arrested, tried, and hanged on July 7, 1865. John Surratt set plans to flee North America, as he was wanted by the U.S. government. In September 1865 he left Canada aboard a steamer bound for England. Once there, he was quickly recognized, forcing him to flee to Italy, where he joined a papal military regiment under an alias and took part in the Italian War of Unification against the forces led by Italian nationalist Giuseppe Garibaldi. When Surratt's identity was discovered, he was imprisoned on the orders of Pope Pius IX and was to be extradited to the United States.

The clever Surratt managed to escape from his Italian captors and fled to Alexandria, Egypt, in November 1866. He was again arrested and was sent back to the United States. His trial for complicity in Lincoln's murder began on June 10, 1867, and lasted for 62 days. In the end, he was acquitted and set free. To this day, the extent to which Surratt was connected to Booth's schemes remains unclear.

Surratt subsequently worked as a teacher in Maryland before he settled in Baltimore, where he was employed by an oceangoing freight company until his retirement in August 1915. Surratt died on April 2, 1916, in Baltimore.

PAUL G. PIERPAOLI JR.

See also

Booth, John Wilkes; Espionage in the Civil War; Lincoln Assassination; Surratt, Mary Elizabeth Jenkins

Further Reading

Lewis, Lloyd. *The Assassination of Lincoln: Myth and Reality.* Lincoln: University of Nebraska Press, 2000.

Steers, Edward, ed. *The Trial: The Assassination of President Lincoln and the Trial of the Conspirators.* Lexington: University of Kentucky Press, 2003.

Surratt, Mary Elizabeth Jenkins
Birth Date: 1823
Death Date: July 7, 1865

Confederate sympathizer who was executed for her role in the Abraham Lincoln assassination. Mary Elizabeth Jenkins was born in Prince George's County, Maryland, in 1823. When Jenkins was 16 years old, she met John Harrison Surratt; they married in August 1840. In the early 1850s, John Surratt built an inn and tavern near present-day Clinton, Maryland. Located at the junction of two major thoroughfares just 12 miles from Washington, D.C., the tavern became an immediate success. Surratt also became the local

Mary Surratt, alleged member of the Booth conspiracy that assassinated President Abraham Lincoln. Tried and found guilty, she was hanged. Surratt is the subject of the 2011 film *The Conspirator.* (Courtesy New-York Historical Society)

postmaster. He later purchased rental property, a boarding-house on H Street in Washington, D.C.

During the Civil War, the tavern and hotel became a haven for Confederate spies, couriers, and smugglers. John Surratt unexpectedly died in January 1862, leaving many unpaid debts. Seventeen-year-old John Surratt Jr. now became postmaster, and he continued many of the covert services that his father had provided to the Confederacy. By November 1863, local Union forces became suspicious of the Surratts' sympathies, and John lost his position as post-master. He soon became a Confederate courier, drawing the Surratts deeper into treasonous activity.

In the autumn of 1864, Mary Surratt decided to lease the tavern and move her family to Washington, D.C., into the boardinghouse her husband had purchased a decade earlier. The empty house soon filled with paying boarders, some of whom were involved in the plot to kill President Lincoln and other Union leaders. Future presidential assassin John Wil-kes Booth was a frequent visitor.

After Booth's assassination of Lincoln on April 14 (the president died the following morning), Mary Surratt was almost immediately implicated in the conspiracy. Her board-inghouse was searched, and several residents were taken into custody, including Surratt, who was arrested on April 17.

Surratt's trial, held before a military tribunal rather than a civil court, lasted seven weeks. Daily newspaper reports gripped the nation. Eight of the accomplices, including Surratt, were tried and convicted. Her supporters sought to appeal the verdict to no avail. On the afternoon of July 7, 1865, Mary Surratt was hanged at the Old Capitol Prison with three other coconspirators. She thus became the first woman executed by the U.S. government. John Surratt Jr. was the only known accomplice to avoid conviction. Booth was shot and killed while hiding in a barn in southern Mary-land. Four more accomplices faced life sentences.

During and immediately following Mary Surratt's trial and execution, many Southerners maintained the illu-sion that she was an innocent victim of a vengeful North-ern court. For decades, sympathizers carried on the call for justice and retribution for Surratt's hanging, portraying her as the epitome of wronged Southern womanhood. While most historians now agree that Surratt was indeed a willing accomplice, her execution remains hotly debated.

KATE CLIFFORD LARSON

See also
Surratt, John Harrison

Further Reading
Leonard, Elizabeth D. *Lincoln's Avengers: Justice, Revenge, and Reunion after the Civil War.* New York: Norton, 2004.

Trindal, Elizabeth Steger. *Mary Surratt: An American Tragedy.* Gretna, LA: Pelican, 1996.

Surrender Terms

Agreed-upon conditions for capitulation. In the final 10 months of the war, overwhelming Union military power and resources pushed the Confederate armies to the break-ing point. Union general in chief Lieutenant General Ulysses S. Grant, accompanying Major General G. Gordon Meade's Army of the Potomac in the field, held Confederate general Robert E. Lee's Army of Northern Virginia in a vise grip, as Lee defended Richmond and Petersburg and Grant exerted intense pressure to sever the rail lines supplying those cit-ies. By April 1865, Lee could no longer defend his lines, and he fled westward in hopes of uniting with General Joseph E. Johnston's army in North Carolina.

As Lee moved west, Grant pursued. Lincoln had ordered Grant to hold no discussions with Lee unless they were about the complete capitulation of Lee's army. On April 9 after a series of skirmishes, with the way south blocked by Union cavalry under Major General Philip Sheridan, Lee, whose men were desperately short of food, was compelled to meet Grant at Appomattox Court House to discuss sur-render terms.

If Lincoln harbored concerns about Grant's negotiating ability, they soon proved to be groundless. At his meet-ing with Lee, Grant demonstrated remarkable clarity of thought and writing skill, composing surrender terms on the spot. They were generous. Taking no prisoners, Grant simply secured the paroles of officers and men, who were not to take up arms until they were properly exchanged. Officers could keep their side arms, and both officers and men, who provided their own horses, were to keep their horses and personal effects. All government equipment was to be surrendered. Grant concluded the agreement with a sentence that embodied the spirit of the capitulation, declaring that Lee and his men were to be allowed to return home and not be disturbed by U.S. authorities as long as they observed their paroles and obeyed the laws. Lee signed the agreement, and Grant forwarded it to the secretary of war. Grant also ordered rations released to feed the starving Confederates.

On April 18 when Confederate general Joseph E. John-ston, commanding the Army of Tennessee and several attached entities, surrendered in North Carolina to Major General William T. Sherman, commanding the Union army group in North Carolina, Washington rejected these as being more generous than those accorded Lee. Sherman was thus ordered to issue terms identical to those of Grant. Johnston agreed to these on April 26. On May 4 at Citronelle, Alabama, Lieutenant General Richard Taylor surrendered the forces of his Department of Alabama, Mississippi, and East Louisiana, which represented the last organized Confederate forces east of the Mississippi River, to Major General Edward R. S. Canby. The terms were identical to those granted the Confederates at Appomattox Court House.

In the Trans-Mississippi region, Lieutenant General Simon Bolivar Buckner, representing General E. Kirby Smith, surrendered that department and the Confederacy's last major field army (although it had largely dissolved) to Canby at New Orleans on May 26. Smith surrendered to Canby a week later at Galveston, Texas. Isolated Confederate commands continued the surrender process until June.

PAUL DAVID NELSON

See also
Appomattox Campaign; Canby, Edward Richard Sprigg; Grant, Ulysses Simpson; Johnston, Joseph Eggleston; Lee, Robert Edward; Lincoln, Abraham; Meade, George Gordon; Sheridan, Philip Henry; Sherman, William Tecumseh; Taylor, Richard

Further Reading
Catton, Bruce. *A Stillness at Appomattox*. Garden City, NY: Doubleday, 1953.
Glatthaar, Joseph T. "The Civil War: A New Definition of Victory." In *Between War and Peace: How America Ends Its Wars*, edited by Colonel Matthew Moten, 107–128. New York: Free Press, 2011.
Marvel, William. *A Place Called Appomattox*. Carbondale: Southern Illinois University Press, 2008.

Susquehanna, Union Department of

Federal military administrative unit established on June 10, 1863. Expecting a Confederate advance into Pennsylvania in the late spring of 1863, Secretary of War Edwin M. Stanton decided to partition Pennsylvania into two military departments. On June 10, his General Order No. 172 created the Union Department of the Susquehanna, to be commanded by Major General Darius M. Couch. Headquartered in Chambersburg, the department covered all of the state east of Johnstown and Laurel Hill. Upon assuming command the next day, Couch immediately began mobilizing volunteer soldiers and militia to defend the state.

After the Battle of Gettysburg (July 1–3, 1863), the Confederate threat eased considerably, and Couch's command was now chiefly concerned with routine administrative duties. The department was expanded on April 4, 1864, when the

Department of the Monongahela was appended to it, including western Pennsylvania and adjoining counties in Ohio and West Virginia. In August 1864 the department fell under the jurisdiction of the Middle Military Division. On December 1, 1864, with Couch still commanding, the Department of the Susquehanna was dissolved when the Department of Pennsylvania was resurrected, covering the entirety of the state.

PAUL G. PIERPAOLI JR.

See also
Couch, Darius Nash; Gettysburg, Battle of; Monongahela, Union Department of; Pennsylvania

Further Reading
Eicher, John H., and David J. Eicher. *Civil War High Commands*. Stanford, CA: Stanford University Press, 2001.

Sutherland's Station, Battle of
Event Date: April 2, 1865

Culminating battle of the nearly 10-month-long Petersburg Campaign (June 15, 1864–April 3, 1865). At 4:30 a.m. on April 2, 1865, following weeks of preparation, the Union Army of the Potomac launched a massive four-corps offensive against the now thinly held Confederate lines at Petersburg, Virginia. The Confederate Army of Northern Virginia crumbled under the assault, also known as the Third Battle of Petersburg. Major General Horatio A. Wright's VI Corps made the decisive breakthrough, with Union forces occupying the Confederate defensive works from Hatcher's Run to the Boydton Plank Road.

Confederate general in chief General Robert E. Lee understood the consequences of the Union attack and immediately began planning to evacuate Petersburg and Richmond, ordering the defenders to hold as long as they could. Some 500 Confederates at Fort Gregg purchased sufficient time for the erection of an inner line to protect the Confederate rear.

As fighting at Fort Gregg raged, to the west Union major general Andrew A. Humphreys's II Corps attacked Confederate forces under Major General Henry Heth holding the line from Hatcher's Run to White Oak Road. The attackers took possession of the Crow Salient and proceeded up Claiborne Road in the direction of Five Forks. Humphreys had wanted to continue the attack with his entire corps, but Army of the Potomac commander Major General George G. Meade had specifically ordered that all divisions turn and face toward Petersburg. Union general in chief Lieutenant General Ulysses S. Grant, however, who had orchestrated the Army of the Potomac's offensive and was closely following developments, specifically ordered Major General Nelson A. Miles's division of II Corps to continue to exploit the breakthrough westward. Miles pushed on up the Claiborne Road to Sutherland's Station, where Heth's force had redeployed in hopes of holding the Southside Railroad, the critical Confederate supply line into Petersburg.

Miles's troops arrived near Sutherland's Station at about 3:00 p.m. and immediately charged into the disorganized Confederates. Although the Confederates turned back two Union attacks, they could not defeat a third attack and broke, giving Union forces firm control of the Southside Railroad. In the fierce combat at Sutherland's Station, the Union side suffered 370 casualties, but the Confederates sustained some 600 killed or wounded as well as 1,000 taken prisoner and two guns captured.

Grant, meanwhile, delayed a final assault on Fort Gregg while he awaited word regarding the success of Miles's attack. This hesitation enabled Lee to escape to the west, commencing the Appomattox Campaign (April 2–9, 1865), with Grant soon in pursuit.

SPENCER C. TUCKER

See also

Appomattox Campaign; Fort Gregg, Battle of; Grant, Ulysses Simpson; Heth, Henry; Humphreys, Andrew Atkinson; Lee, Robert Edward; Miles, Nelson Appleton; Petersburg, Third Battle of; Petersburg Campaign; Wright, Horatio Gouverneur

Further Reading

Greene, A. Wilson. *The Final Battles of the Petersburg Campaign: Breaking the Backbone of the Rebellion.* Knoxville: University of Tennessee Press, 2008.

Horn, John. *The Petersburg Campaign, June 1864–April 1865.* Conshohocken, PA: Combined Books, 1993.

Marvel, William. *Lee's Last Retreat: The Flight to Appomattox.* Chapel Hill: University of North Carolina Press, 2002.

Trudeau, Noah Andre. *The Last Citadel: Petersburg, Virginia, June 1864–April 1865.* Baton Rouge: Louisiana State University Press, 1991.

Sutlers

Civilians attached to army units and licensed to sell goods not provided to the troops by the government. There were very few documented sutlers in the Confederate armies, generally because of a lack of goods and very high prices. Union Army regulations usually allowed each regiment its own sutler. Occasionally there were also sutlers attached to larger units, such as brigades and divisions. Sutlers were most often appointed by regimental colonels and were

Sutlers Row in Chattanooga, Tennessee, 1864. (National Archives)

present with their units when they were in camp or winter quarters. Rarely were sutlers in combat situations.

The army provided an approved list of items that a sutler could sell. This list included stamps, stationery, pens and pencils, tobacco, shoes and socks, razors, shirts, and various reading materials. More popular were the foodstuffs available for purchase, such as canned milk, eggs, syrup, molasses, candy, condiments, and baked goods. Prices were supposed to be set by boards of officers, but a perusal of contemporary letters reveals that soldiers often complained about the high prices charged by many sutlers. Sutlers could sell on credit, not to exceed one-third of a man's monthly pay. When the paymaster disbursed his funds, a sutler could be present and have his credit deducted from a soldier's pay.

When a number of men in a unit became sufficiently annoyed with a sutler, "cleaning out" the sutler frequently occurred. When a unit decided to clean out a sutler, soldiers would distract the man while others stole his goods. Rampant sutler abuses during the Civil War led the army to abolish the practice soon after the conflict.

RICHARD A. SAUERS

See also

Commissary of Subsistence; Rations, CSA; Rations, Union

Further Reading

Lord, Francis A. *Civil War Sutlers and Their Wares.* New York: Thomas Yoseloff, 1969.

Spear, Donald P. "The Sutler in the Union Army." *Civil War History* 16 (June 1970): 121–138.

Swamp Angel

An 8-inch Parrott rifled gun employed to shell Charleston, South Carolina. In early July 1863, U.S. forces landed on the southern end of Morris Island on the south side of the main entrance to Charleston Harbor. They quickly overran about two-thirds of the island but were stopped by Confederate Fort Wagner, just out of range of Charleston. On August 2, 1863, however, following an engineering study of the swamps on the island, Union major general Quincy A. Gillmore ordered the emplacement of a battery there some 4.5 miles from Charleston for artillery capable of firing across the harbor and reaching the city. Construction of the battery and parapet was a considerable undertaking and included 13,000 sandbags weighing a total of more than 800 tons; 123 timbers 15–18 inches in diameter and 45–55 feet in length; 5,000 feet of 1-inch board; 9,500 feet of 3-inch board; 1,200 pounds of spikes, nails, and iron; and 75 fathoms of rope.

Following completion of the platform, Union soldiers dragged there and mounted on August 17 while under fire from Confederate artillery on James Island a 16,700-pound

The Marsh Battery of the Union Parrot 8-inch rifled "Swamp Angel" gun on Morris Island, South Carolina. The gun had shelled Charleston beginning on August 22, 1863, but blew up the next day. (Library of Congress)

8-inch 200-pounder Parrott rifle manufactured by the West Point Foundry. The soldiers dubbed it the "Swamp Angel."

On August 21, Gillmore sent a message to the Confederate commander at Charleston, General P. G. T. Beauregard, demanding that he evacuate the Morris Island forts and Fort Sumter or the city would be shelled. Receiving no reply by the end of the four-hour limit imposed, Gillmore ordered the shelling to commence. He claimed that it was within the bounds of international law because Charleston was both a Confederate naval base and a military manufacturing center.

At 1:30 a.m. on August 22, the Swamp Angel fired its first round at Charleston, followed by 15 additional shots before dawn. Alarm bells and whistles immediately went off in Charleston. Four of the rounds were explosive shells; the other 12 were filled with an incendiary known as Greek fire.

On August 23, the gun crew fired 20 additional rounds at the city, but the last round disabled the gun, bursting the breech and blowing off the reinforcing band. No other guns were placed in the battery, and the physical damage to Charleston caused by the Swamp Angel was minimal, although its shells did set some fires and caused no small panic among the citizens. Charleston remained defiant, however.

After the war, the Swamp Angel was sold for scrap and moved to Trenton, New Jersey. Before it could be broken up, its provenance was discovered, and the gun was then turned into a monument in a city park, where it can be seen today.

SPENCER C. TUCKER

See also

Beauregard, Pierre Gustav Toutant; Charleston Harbor, Siege of; Gillmore, Quincy Adams; Parrott Gun

Further Reading

Cauthen, Charles Edward. *South Carolina Goes to War, 1860–1865*. Columbia: University of South Carolina Press, 2005.

Olmstead, Edwin, Wayne E. Stark, and Spencer C. Tucker. *The Big Guns: Civil War Siege, Seacoast, and Naval Cannon*. Alexandria Bay, NY: Museum Restoration Service, 1997.

Rosen, Robert. *A Short History of Charleston*. Columbia: University of South Carolina Press, 1997.

Sweeny, Thomas William
Birth Date: December 25, 1820
Death Date: April 10, 1892

Union officer. Born in County Cork, Ireland, on December 25, 1820, Thomas William Sweeny at age 12 followed his widowed mother to America and subsequently found a job in a law publication firm. During the Mexican-American War (1846–1848), Sweeny was commissioned a second lieutenant of the 1st New York Infantry on November 23, 1846. He was wounded in the head in the Battle of Contreras and lost his right arm in the Battle of Churubusco. He secured a commission in the regular army as a second lieutenant in the 2nd Infantry on March 3, 1848. Mustered out of volunteer service on March 16, Sweeny was promoted to first lieutenant of regulars on June 11, 1851. Assigned to the West, he was wounded in the neck by an arrow in Cocopa County, California, in May 1852. He was promoted to captain on January 19, 1861.

With the beginning of the Civil War, Sweeny served first under Brigadier General Nathaniel Lyon at St. Louis, Missouri, and then under Brigadier General Franz Sigel at Carthage. In the Battle of Wilson's Creek (August 10, 1861), in which Lyon was killed, Sweeny was badly wounded and had to be carried from the field. In January 1862, Sweeny became colonel of the 52nd Illinois Infantry and fought in the Battle of Fort Donelson (February 13–16). In the Battle of Shiloh (April 6–7), he commanded a brigade and was again wounded. He also commanded a brigade in the Battle of Corinth (October 3–4).

Appointed brigadier general of volunteers on March 16, 1863, with date of rank from November 29, 1862, Sweeny passed most of 1863 in garrison duties in Tennessee and Mississippi. He commanded a division in XVI Corps during the Atlanta Campaign (May 5–September 2, 1864), during which he was arrested and court-martialed for having engaged in a fistfight with his corps commander, Major General Grenville M. Dodge, and fellow brigade commander Brigadier General John W. Fuller on July 25, 1864. Following a lengthy trial, Sweeny was acquitted. He was mustered out of the volunteers on August 24, 1865, and dismissed from the regulars on December 29, 1865, for being absent without leave. He was reinstated as a major in the 16th Infantry, probably because of political considerations, on November 8, 1866.

Sweeny was also involved in the Fabian movement that sought the invasion and conquest of Canada. Unassigned on March 15, 1869, with the reduction in the size of the army, he was, perhaps surprisingly, retired as a brigadier general on May 11, 1870. Sweeny died at Astoria, New York, on April 10, 1892.

SPENCER C. TUCKER

See also

Corinth, Battle of; Dodge, Grenville Mellen; Fort Donelson, Battle of; Fuller, John Wallace; Lyon, Nathaniel; Shiloh, Battle of; Sigel, Franz; Wilson's Creek, Battle of

Further Reading

Eicher, John H., and David J. Eicher. *Civil War High Commands.* Stanford, CA: Stanford University Press, 2001.

Warner, Ezra J. *Generals in Blue: Lives of the Union Commanders.* Baton Rouge: Louisiana State University Press, 2006.

Swift Creek, Battle of
Event Date: May 9, 1864

Engagement in Virginia during the Bermuda Hundred Campaign (May 5–20, 1864). Also known as the Battle of Arrowhead Church, the Battle of Swift Creek took place in Chesterfield County, Virginia, near the Confederate capital of Richmond, when Union major general Benjamin F. Butler, commander of the Army of the James, attempted to cut the Confederate supply lines, particularly the Richmond & Petersburg Railroad, supporting General Robert E. Lee's Army of Northern Virginia north of Richmond.

Attacking south on the Richmond Turnpike toward Petersburg, Butler's forces were met and halted by the Confederates along a part of 50-mile-long Swift Creek, which rises west of Richmond and then flows into the Appomattox River. The Confederate line extended from Brander's Bridge in the west across the turnpike and almost to Fort Clifton in the east. The initial Union advance ran into the 11th South Carolina Infantry Regiment of Brigadier General Johnson Hagood's command. Union brigadier general Charles A. Heckman's 1st Brigade, 2nd Division, XVIII Corps, then formed up, only to meet a premature attack by the 21st South Carolina Infantry charging across the Swift Creek bridge. The Union soldiers fired a series of volleys against the Confederates, cutting down a large number of them.

At the same time as the Battle of Swift Creek was occurring, to the east five Union gunboats moved up the Appomattox River to bombard Fort Clifton, while Edward W. Hincks's division of U.S. Army Colored Troops in the Army of the James moved through marshy terrain toward the fort from the land side. The Confederates drove off the gunboats, and the land attack was abandoned.

Skirmishing continued throughout the night. The 8th Connecticut Infantry, armed with Sharps rifles, turned back a Confederate assault across the railroad bridge over Swift Creek east of the turnpike. The next morning, Butler ordered a withdrawal. The Confederates soon had the track damage repaired. Casualties in this inconclusive day of fighting totaled 990 on the two sides.

SPENCER C. TUCKER

See also

Bermuda Hundred Campaign; Butler, Benjamin Franklin; Hagood, Johnson; Heckman, Charles Adam; Hincks, Edward Winslow; Sharps Rifle and Carbine

Further Reading

Grant, Ulysses S. *Personal Memoirs.* New York: Modern Library, 1999.

Robertson, William Glenn. *Backdoor to Richmond: The Bermuda Hundred Campaign, April–June 1864.* Baton Rouge: Louisiana State University Press, 1987.

Swinton, William
Birth Date: April 23, 1833
Death Date: October 24, 1892

Newspaper correspondent. William Swinton was born on April 23, 1833, in Salton, Scotland. Immigrating with his family to New York in 1843, Swinton first studied to be a Presbyterian minister at Knox College, Toronto, as well as at Amherst College, but he did not graduate from either school before becoming a teacher. He taught languages at several schools and published his first book in 1859. That same year, he became a correspondent for the *New York Times* under the editorial direction of his brother John.

Reporting from the front during the Civil War, William Swinton was everywhere, from the Battle of Antietam (September 17, 1862) to the ongoing naval operations in Charleston Harbor. He scored a journalistic coup by reporting on fighting during the Battle of Chancellorsville (May 1–4, 1863) before his competitors. Swinton was, however, unpopular with some Union officers for his unethical reporting methods. During the Battle of the Wilderness (May 5–7, 1864), he was caught eavesdropping on a planning session between Lieutenant General Ulysses S. Grant and Major General George G. Meade. The warning he received did not prevent him from later attempting to bribe a telegraph operator for confidential information. Major General Ambrose E. Burnside sentenced Swinton to be shot, but Grant, through Meade, commuted the sentence, stripped him of his press credentials, and sent him back to New York.

Despite being kept away from the front for the last year of the conflict, Swinton strongly supported the Union war effort by writing tracts for President Abraham Lincoln's 1864 reelection and published a book attacking the wartime performance of Lincoln's opponent, former major general George B. McClellan. After the war, Swinton published two histories of the Civil War and several textbooks. In 1869 he became chair of the English program at the University of California–Berkeley. Swinton resigned in 1872 to devote himself to full-time writing in New York City, where he died on October 24, 1892.

RUSSELL S. PERKINS

See also

Antietam, Battle of; Burnside, Ambrose Everett; Chancellorsville, Battle of; Grant, Ulysses Simpson; Lincoln, Abraham; McClellan, George Brinton; Meade, George Gordon; Wilderness, Battle of the

Further Reading

Andrews, J. Cutler. *The North Reports the Civil War*. Pittsburgh, PA: University of Pittsburgh Press, 1955.

Harris, Brayton. *War News: Blue and Gray in Black and White; Newspapers in the Civil War*. Washington, DC: Brassey's, 2010.

Sykes, George
Birth Date: October 9, 1822
Death Date: February 8, 1880

Union officer. George Sykes was born on October 9, 1822, in Dover, Delaware, and graduated from the U.S. Military Academy, West Point, in 1842. Serving in the Mexican-American War (1846–1848), Sykes was promoted to first lieutenant in September 1846 and brevetted captain for his actions at the Battle of Cerro Gordo. He also served in the Third Seminole War (1855–1858) and was promoted to captain in 1855.

Promoted to major in the regular army following the outbreak of the Civil War in 1861, Sykes commanded the only regular infantry on the field in the First Battle of Bull Run (July 21, 1861), where he performed effectively. Promoted to brigadier general, U.S. Volunteers, on September 28, 1861, he commanded the 2nd Division in Major General Fitz John Porter's V Corps, Army of the Potomac, during the Peninsula Campaign (March–July 1862) and the Second Battle of Bull Run (August 29–30, 1862), the Battle of Antietam (September 17, 1862), the First Battle of Fredericksburg (December 13, 1862), and the Battle of Chancellorsville (May 1–4, 1863).

On November 29, 1862, Sykes was promoted to major general. He assumed command of V Corps, Army of the Potomac, when Major General George Meade replaced Major General Joseph Hooker as commander of the Army of the Potomac on June 28, 1863. At the Battle of Gettysburg (July 1–3, 1863), Syke's corps played a key role in the Union's stubborn defense on July 2, stopping Confederate attacks at Little Round Top, driving the remainder of Major General John B. Hood's brigades across the Valley of Death, and ending the contest at the Wheatfield.

Because of Sykes's uninspiring and overly cautious performance during the Mine Run Campaign (November 26–December 2, 1863), however, he was relieved of command when the Army of the Potomac was reorganized. Sykes commanded a district in the Department of Kansas from April 20, 1864, to June 7, 1865, and received brevets in the regular army to major general. When the war ended, he reverted to lieutenant colonel in the regular army and was assigned to the 5th Infantry Regiment. On January 12, 1868, he was promoted to colonel and given command of the 20th Infantry Regiment. Sykes died while still on active duty at Fort Brown (now Brownsville), Texas, on February 8, 1880.

JASON N. PALMER

See also

Antietam, Battle of; Bull Run, First Battle of; Bull Run, Second Battle of; Chancellorsville, Battle of; Fredericksburg, First Battle of; Gettysburg, Battle of; Mine Run Campaign; Peninsula Campaign

Further Reading

Eicher, John H., and David J. Eicher. *Civil War High Commands*. Stanford, CA: Stanford University Press, 2001.

Tagg, Larry. *The Generals of Gettysburg*. El Dorado Hills, CA: Savas, 1998.

Warner, Ezra J. *Generals in Blue: Lives of the Union Commanders*. Baton Rouge: Louisiana State University Press, 2006.